THE NATURE AND SCOPE OF SOCIAL SCIENCE

THE CENTURY PHILOSOPHY SERIES

JUSTUS BUCHLER, *Editor*

THE NATURE and SCOPE of SOCIAL SCIENCE

A CRITICAL ANTHOLOGY

edited by LEONARD I. KRIMERMAN
University of Connecticut

APPLETON-CENTURY-CROFTS
Educational Division
MEREDITH CORPORATION

New York

For information address the publisher, Appleton-Century-Crofts,
Educational Division, Meredith Corporation,
440 Park Avenue South, New York, N. Y. 10016.

619-1

Library of Congress Card Number: 69-13107

PRINTED IN THE UNITED STATES OF AMERICA

390-52678-9

for O. R.,
companion to the uncompanionable

Unannexed from the Earth, might not the Moon shine both day and night?
R. Gansblaschen

Preface

This anthology brings together 57 selections which share at least one common ambition: that of identifying the proper aims, methods, and concepts of the social sciences. The result is a collective attempt to define the nature and scope of social science, i.e., to determine first, how the scientific community can best investigate human conduct and second, how much of the latter *can* (and how much *cannot*) be understood, measured, explained, and predicted by the former. The controversy begun in Part I as to whether and in what sense a science of man is possible thus remains central throughout the text, even while its key terms — "science," "human conduct," "possible," — themselves become the focus of analysis and controversy.

All eight parts of the anthology are introduced by editorial essays; and none of these is intended to merely summarize or draw comparisons. Where a selection is discussed, this is usually done to place in sharper focus my own conception of the main issues with which it deals and the most defensible way of resolving them. Thus one should not expect these introductions to be nonpartisan, to remain uncommitted concerning the relative merits of what they introduce. In particular, the reader should prepare to be urged to accept the following theses: (*i*) that there are cogent objections and plausible alternatives to the covering law analysis of scientific explanation (introductions to Parts II and IV); (*ii*) that the methods of natural and social science are fundamentally dissimilar (Parts III, IV, VI, and VIII); (*iii*) that *verstehen* (interpretative understanding) is indispensable for acquiring knowledge in the social sciences (Parts V and VIII); (*iv*) that where human actions are performed intentionally it is impossible to explain them by reference to empirical covering laws (Part IV); (*v*) that mental concepts such as *believing*, *desiring*, *dreaming*, *imagining*, cannot be equated with or reduced to physical concepts and, in some cases at least, they are incompatible with operational definitions and measurement techniques (Parts V and VI); (*vi*) that "social laws" or uniformities, e.g., that Catholics have lower suicide rates than Protestants, that every revolution produces counter-revolutionary activity, that men increase their consumption as their income increases but not to the same extent as the increase in their income, are either disguised analytic truths (true by virtue of what their terms mean) or arise from the avoidable activities, motives, and beliefs of individual agents (Parts III, IV, and VII); (*vii*) that since social scientists cannot avoid being committed to value-judgments of a distinctive sort, objectivity must take a different form in the social as opposed to the natural sciences (Part VIII).

The plan of this book took root some four years ago, while I was attempting to organize a seminar in the philosophy of social science: something was needed, I felt then, that would bring recent work in the philosophy of history and philosophy of mind (e.g., selections 9, 28, 33, 34, and 43) together with what social scientists (and others) thought about the theories and methods they employed (see selections 3, 23, 39, 41, 51, and 55). The union, I still believe, is bound to be mutually profitable.

My original plan has been the beneficiary of invaluable assistance from many quarters: Professor Justus Buchler read all of the introductory essays, commented on them, and made suggestions as to selections that should or should not be included; Professor Herbert Heidelberger wrote the essay that appears as selection 34 especially for inclusion in this anthology; my friend and former colleague Helene Schell, drawing upon equally impressive reserves of persistence and penetration, forced me to rethink (and possibly clarify) the arguments in the introduction to Part VI; Rita Samrow ungrudgingly typed and retyped draft upon draft of the introductions; Bruce Johnson, Bruce Richter, and O. R. gave extensive and meticulous aid in compiling the bibliography; S. DeBonis and W. Kinnaman helped with proofreading; the comprehensive and finely-wrought indexes are entirely the work of Sister Grace Parker, OSH; Jack K. Burton and Marjorie Kalins of Appleton-Century-Crofts supplied editorial encouragement and advice at many crucial points. For all of this, and most of all for the scrupulous intractability of my students at LSU in New Orleans and the University of Connecticut, I am warmly appreciative.

L. I. K.

Contents

I

THE SCIENCE of MAN: THREE CONFLICTING PERSPECTIVES

The three selections which introduce this book do battle with a common issue, one which throughout various refinements and transformations remains central for all of the subsequent parts. This is the issue of whether, or to what extent, scientific inquiry can provide ways of explaining and understanding the activities of men. For Collingwood, any "science of human nature," if viewed on the model of natural science, is open to two decisive objections. The first of these arises from his analysis of human action: every act which men perform, he asserts, has both an "inside" and an "outside," an internal and external, dimension. When an athlete swings a bat, or throws a javelin, there occur of course certain physical (external) movements describable by such concepts as duration, velocity, location, and magnitude. But concepts of this sort will hardly supply a complete identification of the action performed. Was it a practice throw or one designed to win a competition? Did the batter swing in defiance of previous orders or as part of a signalled plan to protect a base runner? The internal dimension — comprised of the agent's objectives, beliefs, attitudes, and standards of conduct — also demands a hearing. Now according to Collingwood, for the events with which natural science is concerned, "this distinction between the outside and inside of an event does not arise. The events of nature are mere events, not the acts of agents whose thought the scientist endeavors to trace." Scientific method, as developed in chemistry or physics, is thus incapable of "penetrating to the inside of events and detecting the thought which they express." Any science of human nature employing this method will likewise be restricted to natural events, events which lack an internal dimension. It will thus alienate itself from what is most distinctive about human agents, and yield an understanding of their conduct which is necessarily and permanently incomplete.

Collingwood's attack against importing the methods of natural science into the study of man has a second thrust. It is perhaps the most fundamental aim of these methods to discover what Skinner calls "uniformities" and what Mill refers to as "constant laws" and "laws of unerring uniformity." But scientific uniformities or laws, like those connecting the volume, temperature, and pressure of gases, must have universal scope: they cannot hold merely for England from the reign of Elizabeth I to that of Victoria or for America during the Age of Jackson. On the contrary, to be considered as laws at all, they must hold for every time and place and for any historical period or social order. (But see here selections 9, 16, and 18 below.) It is Collingwood's claim, however, that the regularities and patterns in human life are all historically conditioned. True generalizations concerning human activities are possible, but these will merely summarize specific historical periods or cultural norms: the uniformities essential to the early Mayan culture or to mercantile capitalism during the Industrial Revolution have long since been replaced by patterns which owe their existence and nature to very different social and historical forces. It is the neglect of this historical dependency that Collingwood deemed "the fallacy inherent in the very idea of a science of human nature." Out of such neglect arises the vain hope of "establishing the permanent and unchanging laws of human nature." In brief, any study of human behavior, however wide its scope, will "never be more than a generalized description of certain phases in human history." And this means that any such study will lack a crucial feature of the natural sciences, i.e., universally applicable laws.

In different ways, both Mill and Skinner can be seen as replying to the challenge set forth by Collingwood's appraisal of "the science of human nature." The chapter from Mill's *System of Logic* reprinted below sketches a distinction between exact and inexact sciences, according to whether they can identify all or only the major portion of the (causal) factors on which their predictions depend. One *might* argue that Collingwood overlooked this distinction and thus mistakenly concluded that no science of man is possible, when he had shown, at most, that human activity cannot (as yet?) be regarded as the subject of an *exact* science. Moreover, there are inexact sciences concerned with such wholly external natural phenomena as clouds, storms, and tides. Thus, even if a science of human nature were inherently inexact, would this alone compel it to adopt methods at variance with those relied on in the physical sciences?

In *Science and Human Behavior*, B. F. Skinner issues a more elaborate reply to the Collingwood position. After presenting an account of the attitudes, objectives, and presuppositions of science, Skinner rebuffs several popular objections to a science of human behavior, e.g., that the behavior of individual subatomic particles is not at present wholly predictable and is thus incompatible with the scientific postulate that all events are "determined" or unavoidable; and that since human actions are unique and unrepeatable, they cannot be fully understood in terms of statistical regularities or universal laws.

Skinner's reply to these complaints, and, by implication, to Collingwood's attack, has two main tendencies. In the first place, he relentlessly insists that those who develop arguments against the *possibility* of a behavioral science prejudge what is essentially a "pragmatic" or experimental issue. Can the scientific method deal with all aspects of human conduct? Can the results of animal experiments provide confirmation for theories purporting to explain how men learn, perceive, and make decisions? These questions, Skinner argues, are like the questions of whether science can explain, predict and control hurricanes and the growth of cancerous tissue: only the future will tell. They cannot be resolved, as Collingwood implies, by appealing to a philosophical analysis of the concept "human action." (On this point, see also selections 22, 27, 29, and 36 and the introductions to Parts IV – VIII.) The success of a program which applies the methods of physical science to human behavior "must be evaluated in terms of its achievements rather than any *a priori* contentions."

Skinner's counterattack however is primarily grounded on the current accomplishments of behavioral psychology, a discipline, he contends, which is completely "within the bounds of a natural science." This behavioral science, we are told, has *already* been successful in locating environmental variables that have a lawful connection with, and thus permit one to predict and control, both animal and human activity. One of its findings, for example, is that "if we only occasionally reinforce a child for good behavior, the behavior survives after we discontinue reinforcement much longer than if we had reinforced every instance." Skinner thus goes beyond simply affirming that the central issue of this Part — indeed the entire book — must be resolved through controlled experiment. He does not merely deny that this issue can be settled by reflecting on the meaning and presuppositions of concepts used to identify human actions, e.g., concepts which selections 29, 33, and 34 classify as *psychological* or *intentional*. He advances the further thesis that, regardless of future results, contemporary psychologists have already accumulated enough empirical evidence to demonstrate the feasibility of "a functional analysis which specifies behavior as a dependent variable and proposes to account for it in terms of observable and manipulable physical conditions." (But does Skinner's science of behavior attempt to record evidence of types of behavior which are *not* thus accountable? Do behavioral scientists permit themselves to make use of the concepts and attitudes required to recognize instances of voluntary action or the internal aspects of human conduct? Or do they ignore or rule out — *a priori* — the possibility of forms of behavior which run counter to a Skinnerian "functional analysis"? This point is approached again in selection 29 and on pages 353 to 361 below.)

Here, then, are three radically opposed appraisals of the idea of a science of man: one which finds it inherently misconceived and unable to account for the most distinctive features of its alleged subject matter; another for which this idea proposes a desirable, but unattempted and only partially attainable program of inquiry; and a third which regards the science of human behavior as an established discipline, whose future development and scope can neither be estimated nor limited by philosophical argument. It seems plain, however, that these three perspectives, whatever their differences and despite Skinner's professed empiricism, are equally entangled in *philosophical* issues, e.g., the epistemological question of whether and to what extent, if any, social scientists can obtain knowledge of human conduct, especially if they confine themselves to the methods and concepts characteristic of physical science. And it is to such fundamental and apparently unavoidable issues that Parts II – VIII constantly return, and in ways that amplify and provide criteria for evaluating the divergent philosophical presuppositions of Collingwood, Mill, and Skinner.

The A Priori Impossibility of a Science of Man 1

from *The Idea of History*
R. G. COLLINGWOOD

Human Nature and Human History

THE SCIENCE OF HUMAN NATURE

Man, who desires to know everything, desires to know himself. Nor is he only one (even if, to himself, perhaps the most interesting) among the things he desires to know. Without some knowledge of himself, his knowledge of other things is imperfect: for to know something without knowing that one knows it is only a half-knowing, and to know that one knows is to know oneself. Self-knowledge is desirable and important to man, not only for its own sake, but as a condition without which no other knowledge can be critically justified and securely based.

Self-knowledge, here, means not knowledge of man's bodily nature, his anatomy and physiology; nor even a knowledge of his mind, so far as that consists of feeling, sensation, and emotion; but a knowledge of his knowing faculties, his thought or understanding or reason. How is such knowledge to be attained? It seems an easy matter until we think seriously about it; and then it seems so difficult that we are tempted to think it impossible. Some have even reinforced this temptation by argument, urging that the mind, whose business it is to know other things, has for that very reason no power of knowing itself. But this is open sophistry: first you say what the mind's nature is, and then you say that because it has this nature no one can know that it has it. Actually, the argument is a counsel of despair, based on recognizing that a certain attempted method of studying the mind has broken down, and on failure to envisage the possibility of any other.

It seems a fair enough proposal that, in setting out to understand the nature of our own mind, we should proceed in the same way as when we try to understand the world about us. In studying the world of nature, we begin by getting acquainted with the particular things and particular events that exist and go on there; then we proceed to understand them, by seeing how they fall into general types and how these general types are interrelated. These interrelations we call laws of nature; and it is by ascertaining such laws that we understand the things and events to which they apply. The same method, it might seem, is applicable to the problem of understanding mind. Let us begin by observing, as carefully as possible, the ways in which our own minds and those of others behave under given circumstances; then, having become acquainted with these facts of the mental world, let us try to establish the laws which govern them.

Here is a proposal for a 'science of human nature' whose principles and methods are conceived on the analogy of those used in the natural sciences. It is an old proposal, put forward especially in the seventeenth and eighteenth centuries, when the principles and methods of natural science had been lately perfected and were being triumphantly applied to the investigation of the physical world. When Locke undertook his inquiry into that faculty of understanding which 'sets Man above the rest of sensible Beings, and gives him all the Advantage and Dominion which he has over them', the novelty of his project

From *The Idea of History* by R. G. Collingwood. Oxford University Press, New York, 1946, pp. 205–231 and 315–320. Reprinted by permission.

lay not in his desire for a knowledge of the human mind, but in his attempt to gain it by methods analogous to those of natural science: the collection of observed facts and their arrangement in classificatory schemes. His own description of his method as an 'historical, plain Method' is perhaps ambiguous; but his follower Hume was at pains to make it clear that the method to be followed by the science of human nature was identical with the method of physical science as he conceived it: its 'only solid foundation', he wrote, 'must be laid on experience and observation'. Reid, in his *Inquiry into the Human Mind*, was if possible even more explicit. 'All that we know of the body, is owing to anatomical dissection and observation, and it must be by an anatomy of the mind that we can discover its powers and principles.' And from these pioneers the whole English and Scottish tradition of a 'philosophy of the human mind' was derived.

Even Kant did not take an essentially different view. He certainly claimed that his own study of the understanding was something more than empirical; it was to be a demonstrative science; but then he held the same view concerning the science of nature; for that also, according to him, has in it an *a priori* or demonstrative element, and is not based merely on experience.

It is evident that such a science of human nature, if it could attain even a tolerable approximation to the truth, could hope for results of extreme importance. As applied to the problems of moral and political life, for example, its results would certainly be no less spectacular than were the results of seventeenth-century physics when applied to the mechanical arts in the eighteenth century. This was fully realized by its promoters. Locke thought that by its means he could 'prevail with the busy Mind of Man, to be more cautious in meddling with things exceeding its Comprehension; to stop, when it is at the utmost of its Tether; and to sit down in a quiet Ignorance of those Things, which, upon Examination, are found to be beyond the reach of our Capacities'. At the same time, he was convinced that the powers of our understanding are sufficient for our needs 'in this state', and can give us all the knowledge we require for 'the comfortable provision for this life, and the way that leads to a better'. 'If [he concludes] we can find out those Measures, whereby a Rational creature, put in the state which Man is in this World, may and ought to govern his Opinions and Actions depending thereon, we need not be troubled that some other things escape our knowledge.'

Hume is even bolder. ''Tis evident', he writes, 'that all the sciences have a relation, more or less, to human nature . . . since they lie under the cognizance of men, and are judged of by their powers and faculties. 'Tis impossible to tell what changes and improvements we might make in these sciences were we thoroughly acquainted with the extent and force of human understanding.' And in sciences directly concerned with human nature, like morals and politics, his hopes of a beneficent revolution are proportionately higher. 'In pretending, therefore, to explain the principles of human nature, we in effect propose a complete system of the sciences, built on a foundation almost entirely new, and the only one upon which they can stand with any security.' Kant, for all his habitual caution, claimed no less when he said that his new science would put an end to all the debates of the philosophical schools, and make it possible to solve all the problems of metaphysics at once and for ever.

It need not imply any underestimate of what these men actually achieved if we admit that these hopes were in the main unfulfilled, and that the science of human nature, from Locke to the present day, has failed to solve the problem of understanding what understanding is, and thus giving the human mind knowledge of itself. It was not through any lack of sympathy with its objects that so judicious a critic as John Grote found himself obliged to treat the 'philosophy of the human mind' as a blind alley out of which it was the duty of thought to escape.

What was the reason for this failure? Some might say that it was because the undertaking was in principle a mistake: mind cannot know itself. This objection we have already considered. Others, notably the representatives of psychology, would say that the science of these thinkers was not sufficiently scientific: psychology was still in its infancy. But if we ask these same men to produce here and now the practical results for which those early students hoped, they excuse themselves by saying that psychology is still in its infancy. Here I think they wrong themselves and their own science. Claiming for it a sphere which it cannot effectively occupy, they belittle the work it has done and is doing in its proper field. What that field is, I shall suggest in the sequel.

There remains a third explanation: that the 'science of human nature' broke down because its method was distorted by the analogy of the natural sciences. This I believe to be the right one.

It was no doubt inevitable that in the seventeenth and eighteenth centuries, dominated as they were by the new birth of physical science, the eternal problem of self-knowledge should take shape as the problem of constructing a science of human nature. To any one reviewing the field of human research, it was evident that physics stood out as a type of inquiry which had discovered the right method of investigating its proper object, and it was right that the experiment should be made of extending this method to every kind of problem. But since then a great change has come over the intellectual atmosphere of our civilization. The dominant factor in this change has not been the development of other natural sciences like chemistry and biology, or the transformation of physics itself since more began to be known about electricity, or the progressive application of all these new ideas to manufacture and industry, important though these have been; for in principle they have done nothing that might not have been foreseen as implicit in seventeenth-century physics itself. The really new element in the thought of to-day as compared with that of three centuries ago is the rise of history. It is true that the same Cartesian spirit which did so much for physics was already laying the foundations of critical method in history before the seventeenth century was out;[1] but the modern conception of history as a study at once critical and constructive, whose field is the human past in its entirety, and whose method is the reconstruction of that past from documents written and unwritten, critically analysed and interpreted, was not established until the nineteenth, and is even yet not fully worked out in all its implications. Thus history occupies in the world of to-day a position analogous to that occupied by physics in the time of Locke: it is recognized as a special and autonomous form of thought, lately established, whose possibilities have not yet been completely explored. And just as in the seventeenth and eighteenth centuries there were materialists, who argued from the success of physics in its own sphere that all reality was physical, so among ourselves the success of history has led some people to suggest that its methods are applicable to all the problems of knowledge, in other words, that all reality is historical.

This I believe to be an error. I think that those who assert it are making a mistake of the same kind which the materialists made in the seventeenth century. But I believe, and in this essay I shall try to show, that there is at least one important element of truth in what they say. The thesis which I shall maintain is that the science of human nature was a false attempt — falsified by the analogy of natural science — to understand the mind itself, and that, whereas the right way of investigating nature is by the methods called scientific, the right way of investigating mind is by the methods of history. I shall contend that the work which was to be done by the science of human nature is actually done, and can only be done, by history: that history is what the science of human nature professed to be, and that Locke was right when he said

[1] 'Historical criticism was born in the seventeenth century from the same intellectual movement as the philosophy of Descartes.' E. Bréhier, in *Philosophy and History: Essays presented to Ernst Cassirer* (Oxford, 1936), p. 160.

(however little he understood what he was saying) that the right method for such an inquiry is the historical, plain method.

THE FIELD OF HISTORICAL THOUGHT[2]

I must begin by attempting to delimit the proper sphere of historical knowledge as against those who, maintaining the historicity of all things, would resolve all knowledge into historical knowledge. Their argument runs in some such way as this.

The methods of historical research have, no doubt, been developed in application to the history of human affairs: but is that the limit of their applicability? They have already before now undergone important extensions: for example, at one time historians had worked out their methods of critical interpretation only as applied to written sources containing narrative material, and it was a new thing when they learnt to apply them to the unwritten data provided by archaeology. Might not a similar but even more revolutionary extension sweep into the historian's net the entire world of nature? In other words, are not natural processes really historical processes, and is not the being of nature an historical being?

Since the time of Heraclitus and Plato, it has been a commonplace that things natural, no less than things human, are in constant change, and that the entire world of nature is a world of 'process' or 'becoming'. But this is not what is meant by the historicity of things; for change and history are not at all the same. According to this old-established conception, the specific forms of natural things constitute a changeless repertory of fixed types, and the process of nature is a process by which instances of these forms (or quasi-instances of them, things approximating to the embodiment of them) come into existence and pass out of it again. Now in human affairs, as historical research had clearly demonstrated by the eighteenth century, there is no such fixed repertory of specific forms. Here, the process of becoming was already by that time recognized as involving not only the instances or quasi-instances of the forms, but the forms themselves. The political philosophy of Plato and Aristotle teaches in effect that city-states come and go, but the idea of the city-state remains for ever as the one social and political form towards whose realization human intellect, so far as it is really intelligent, strives. According to modern ideas, the city-state itself is as transitory a thing as Miletus or Sybaris. It is not an eternal ideal, it was merely the political ideal of the ancient Greeks. Other civilizations have had before them other political ideals, and human history shows a change not only in the individual cases in which these ideals are realized or partially realized, but in the ideals themselves. Specific types of human organization, the city-state, the feudal system, representative government, capitalistic industry, are characteristic of certain historical ages.

At first, this transience of specific forms was imagined to be a peculiarity of human life. When Hegel said that nature has no history, he meant that whereas the specific forms of human organization change as time goes on, the forms of natural organization do not. There is, he grants, a distinction of higher and lower in the specific forms of nature, and the higher forms are a development out of the lower; but this development is only a logical one, not a temporal, and in time all the 'strata' of nature exist simultaneously.[3] But this view of nature has been overthrown by the doctrine of evolution. Biology has decided that living organisms are not divided into kinds each permanently distinct from the rest, but have developed their present specific forms through a process of evolution in time. Nor is this conception limited to the field of

[2] In the argument of this section I owe much to Mr. Alexander's admirable essay on 'The Historicity of Things', in the volume on *Philosophy and History* already quoted. If I seem to be controverting his main thesis, that is not because I disagree with his argument or any part of it, but only because I mean more than he does by the word 'historicity'. For him, to say that the world is 'a world of events' is to say that 'the world and everything in it is historical'. For me, the two things are not at all the same.

[3] *Naturphilosophie: Einleitung. System der Philosophie*, § 249, *Zusatz* (*Werke*, Glockner's edition, vol. ix, p. 59).

biology. It appeared simultaneously, the two applications being closely connected through the study of fossils, in geology. To-day even the stars are divided into kinds which can be described as older and younger; and the specific forms of matter, no longer conceived in the Daltonian manner, as elements eternally distinct like the living species of pre-Darwinian biology, are regarded as subject to a similar change, so that the chemical constitution of our present world is only a phase in a process leading from a very different past to a very different future.

This evolutionary conception of nature, whose implications have been impressively worked out by philosophers like M. Bergson, Mr. Alexander, and Mr. Whitehead, might seem at first sight to have abolished the difference between natural process and historical process, and to have resolved nature into history. And if a further step in the same resolution were needed, it might seem to be provided by Mr. Whitehead's doctrine that the very possession of its attributes by a natural thing takes time. Just as Aristotle argued that a man cannot be happy at an instant, but that the possession of happiness takes a lifetime, so Mr. Whitehead argues that to be an atom of hydrogen takes time — the time necessary for establishing the peculiar rhythm of movements which distinguishes it from other atoms — so that there is no such thing as 'nature at an instant'.

These modern views of nature do, no doubt, 'take time seriously'. But just as history is not the same thing as change, so it is not the same thing as 'timefulness', whether that means evolution or an existence which takes time. Such views have certainly narrowed the gulf between nature and history of which early nineteenth-century thinkers were so conscious; they have made it impossible to state the distinction any longer in the way in which Hegel stated it; but in order to decide whether the gulf has been really closed and the distinction annulled, we must turn to the conception of history and see whether it coincides in essentials with this modern conception of nature.

If we put this question to the ordinary historian, he will answer it in the negative. According to him, all history properly so called is the history of human affairs. His special technique, depending as it does on the interpretation of documents in which human beings of the past have expressed or betrayed their thoughts, cannot be applied just as it stands to the study of natural processes; and the more this technique is elaborated in its details, the farther it is from being so applicable. There is a certain analogy between the archaeologist's interpretation of a stratified site and the geologist's interpretation of rock-horizons with their associated fossils; but the difference is no less clear than the similarity. The archaeologist's use of his stratified relics depends on his conceiving them as artifacts serving human purposes and thus expressing a particular way in which men have thought about their own life; and from his point of view the palaeontologist, arranging his fossils in a time-series, is not working as an historian, but only as a scientist thinking in a way which can at most be described as quasi-historical.

Upholders of the doctrine under examination would say that here the historian is making an arbitrary distinction between things that are really the same, and that his conception of history is an unphilosophically narrow one, restricted by the imperfect development of his technique; very much as some historians, because their equipment was inadequate to studying the history of art or science or economic life, have mistakenly restricted the field of historical thought to the history of politics. The question must therefore be raised, why do historians habitually identify history with the history of human affairs? In order to answer this question, it is not enough to consider the characteristics of historical method as it actually exists, for the question at issue is whether, as it actually exists, it covers the whole field which properly belongs to it. We must ask what is the general nature of the problems which this method is designed to solve. When we have done so, it will appear that the special problem of the historian is one which does not arise in the case of natural science.

The historian, investigating any event in the past, makes a distinction between what may be called the outside and the inside of an event. By the outside of the event I mean everything belonging to it which can be described in terms of bodies and their movements: the passage of Caesar, accompanied by certain men, across a river called the Rubicon at one date, or the spilling of his blood on the floor of the senate-house at another. By the inside of the event I mean that in it which can only be described in terms of thought: Caesar's defiance of Republican law, or the clash of constitutional policy between himself and his assassins. The historian is never concerned with either of these to the exclusion of the other. He is investigating not mere events (where by a mere event I mean one which has only an outside and no inside) but actions, and an action is the unity of the outside and inside of an event. He is interested in the crossing of the Rubicon only in its relation to Republican law, and in the spilling of Caesar's blood only in its relation to a constitutional conflict. His work may begin by discovering the outside of an event, but it can never end there; he must always remember that the event was an action, and that his main task is to think himself into this action, to discern the thought of its agent.

In the case of nature, this distinction between the outside and the inside of an event does not arise. The events of nature are mere events, not the acts of agents whose thought the scientist endeavours to trace. It is true that the scientist, like the historian, has to go beyond the mere discovery of events; but the direction in which he moves is very different. Instead of conceiving the event as an action and attempting to rediscover the thought of its agent, penetrating from the outside of the event to its inside, the scientist goes beyond the event, observes its relation to others, and thus brings it under a general formula or law of nature. To the scientist, nature is always and merely a 'phenomenon', not in the sense of being defective in reality, but in the sense of being a spectacle presented to his intelligent observation; whereas the events of history are never mere phenomena, never mere spectacles for contemplation, but things which the historian looks, not at, but through, to discern the thought within them.

In thus penetrating to the inside of events and detecting the thought which they express, the historian is doing something which the scientist need not and cannot do. In this way the task of the historian is more complex than that of the scientist. In another way it is simpler: the historian need not and cannot (without ceasing to be an historian) emulate the scientist in searching for the causes or laws of events. For science, the event is discovered by perceiving it, and the further search for its cause is conducted by assigning it to its class and determining the relation between that class and others. For history, the object to be discovered is not the mere event, but the thought expressed in it. To discover that thought is already to understand it. After the historian has ascertained the facts, there is no further process of inquiring into their causes. When he knows what happened, he already knows why it happened.

This does not mean that words like 'cause' are necessarily out of place in reference to history; it only means that they are used there in a special sense. When a scientist asks 'Why did that piece of litmus paper turn pink?' he means 'On what kinds of occasions do pieces of litmus paper turn pink?' When an historian asks 'Why did Brutus stab Caesar?' he means 'What did Brutus think, which made him decide to stab Caesar?' The cause of the event, for him, means the thought in the mind of the person by whose agency the event came about: and this is not something other than the event, it is the inside of the event itself.

The processes of nature can therefore be properly described as sequences of mere events, but those of history cannot. They are not processes of mere events but processes of actions, which have an inner side, consisting of processes of thought; and what the historian is looking for is these processes of thought. All history is the history of thought.

But how does the historian discern the thoughts which he is trying to discover? There is only one way in which it can be done: by re-thinking them in his own mind. The historian of philosophy, reading Plato, is trying to know what Plato thought when he expressed himself in certain words. The only way in which he can do this is by thinking it for himself. This, in fact, is what we mean when we speak of 'understanding' the words. So the historian of politics or warfare, presented with an account of certain actions done by Julius Caesar, tries to understand these actions, that is, to discover what thoughts in Caesar's mind determined him to do them. This implies envisaging for himself the situation in which Caesar stood, and thinking for himself what Caesar thought about the situation and the possible ways of dealing with it. The history of thought, and therefore all history, is the re-enactment of past thought in the historian's own mind.

This re-enactment is only accomplished, in the case of Plato and Caesar respectively, so far as the historian brings to bear on the problem all the powers of his own mind and all his knowledge of philosophy and politics. It is not a passive surrender to the spell of another's mind; it is a labour of active and therefore critical thinking. The historian not only re-enacts past thought, he re-enacts it in the context of his own knowledge and therefore, in re-enacting it, criticizes it, forms his own judgement of its value, corrects whatever errors he can discern in it. This criticism of the thought whose history he traces is not something secondary to tracing the history of it. It is an indispensable condition of the historical knowledge itself. Nothing could be a completer error concerning the history of thought than to suppose that the historian as such merely ascertains 'what so-and-so thought', leaving it to some one else to decide 'whether it was true'. All thinking is critical thinking; the thought which re-enacts past thoughts, therefore, criticizes them in re-enacting them.

It is now clear why historians habitually restrict the field of historical knowledge to human affairs. A natural process is a process of events, an historical process is a process of thoughts. Man is regarded as the only subject of historical process, because man is regarded as the only animal that thinks, or thinks enough, and clearly enough, to render his actions the expressions of his thoughts. The belief that man is the only animal that thinks at all is no doubt a superstition; but the belief that man thinks more, and more continuously and effectively, than any other animal, and is the only animal whose conduct is to any great extent determined by thought instead of by mere impulse and appetite, is probably well enough founded to justify the historian's rule of thumb.

It does not follow that all human actions are subject-matter for history; and indeed historians are agreed that they are not. But when they are asked how the distinction is to be made between historical and non-historical human actions, they are somewhat at a loss how to reply. From our present point of view we can offer an answer: so far as man's conduct is determined by what may be called his animal nature, his impulses and appetites, it is non-historical; the process of those activities is a natural process. Thus, the historian is not interested in the fact that men eat and sleep and make love and thus satisfy their natural appetites; but he is interested in the social customs which they create by their thought as a framework within which these appetites find satisfaction in ways sanctioned by convention and morality.

Consequently, although the conception of evolution has revolutionized our idea of nature by substituting for the old conception of natural process as a change within the limits of a fixed system of specific forms the new conception of that process as involving a change in these forms themselves, it has by no means identified the idea of natural process with that of historical process; and the fashion, current not long ago, of using the word 'evolution' in an historical context, and talking of the evolution of parliament or the like, though natural in an age when the science of nature was regarded as the only true form of knowledge, and when other forms of knowledge, in order to justify their existence, felt bound to assimilate themselves to that model, was the result of confused thinking and a source of further confusions.

There is only one hypothesis on which natural processes could be regarded as ultimately historical in character: namely, that these processes are in reality processes of action determined by a thought which is their own inner side. This would imply that natural events are expressions of thoughts, whether the thoughts of God, or of angelic or demonic finite intelligences, or of minds somewhat like our own inhabiting the organic and inorganic bodies of nature as our minds inhabit our bodies. Setting aside mere flights of metaphysical fancy, such an hypothesis could claim our serious attention only if it led to a better understanding of the natural world. In fact, however, the scientist can reasonably say of it 'je n'ai pas eu besoin de cette hypothèse', and the theologian will recoil from any suggestion that God's action in the natural world resembles the action of a finite human mind under the conditions of historical life. This at least is certain: that, so far as our scientific and historical knowledge goes, the processes of events which constitute the world of nature are altogether different in kind from the processes of thought which constitute the world of history.

HISTORY AS KNOWLEDGE OF MIND

History, then, is not, as it has so often been mis-described, a story of successive events or an account of change. Unlike the natural scientist, the historian is not concerned with events as such at all. He is only concerned with those events which are the outward expression of thoughts, and is only concerned with these in so far as they express thoughts. At bottom, he is concerned with thoughts alone; with their outward expression in events he is concerned only by the way, in so far as these reveal to him the thoughts of which he is in search.

In a sense, these thoughts are no doubt themselves events happening in time; but since the only way in which the historian can discern them is by re-thinking them for himself, there is another sense, and one very important to the historian, in which they are not in time at all. If the discovery of Pythagoras concerning the square on the hypotenuse is a thought which we to-day can think for ourselves, a thought that constitutes a permanent addition to mathematical knowledge, the discovery of Augustus, that a monarchy could be grafted upon the Republican constitution of Rome by developing the implications of *proconsulare imperium* and *tribunicia potestas*, is equally a thought which the student of Roman history can think for himself, a permanent addition to political ideas. If Mr. Whitehead is justified in calling the right-angled triangle an eternal object, the same phrase is applicable to the Roman constitution and the Augustan modification of it. This is an eternal object because it can be apprehended by historical thought at any time; time makes no difference to it in this respect, just as it makes no difference to the triangle. The peculiarity which makes it historical is not the fact of its happening in time, but the fact of its becoming known to us by our re-thinking the same thought which created the situation we are investigating, and thus coming to understand that situation.

Historical knowledge is the knowledge of what mind has done in the past, and at the same time it is the redoing of this, the perpetuation of past acts in the present. Its object is therefore not a mere object, something outside the mind which knows it; it is an activity of thought, which can be known only in so far as the knowing mind re-enacts it and knows itself as so doing. To the historian, the activities whose history he is studying are not spectacles to be watched, but experiences to be lived through in his own mind; they are objective, or known to him, only because they are also subjective, or activities of his own.

It may thus be said that historical inquiry reveals to the historian the powers of his own mind. Since all he can know historically is thoughts that he can re-think for himself, the fact of his coming to know them shows him that his mind is able (or by the very effort of studying them has become able) to think in these ways. And conversely, whenever he finds certain historical matters unintelligible, he has discovered a limitation of his own mind; he has discovered that there are certain ways in which he is not, or no longer, or not yet, able to think. Certain historians, sometimes whole generations of historians, find in certain periods of history nothing intelligible, and call them dark ages; but such phrases tell us nothing about those ages themselves, though they tell us a great deal about the persons who use them, namely that they are unable to re-think the thoughts which were fundamental to their life. It has been said that *die Weltgeschichte ist das Weltgericht;* and it is true, but in a sense not always recognized. It is the historian himself who stands at the bar of judgement, and there reveals his own mind in its strength and weakness, its virtues and its vices.

But historical knowledge is not concerned only with a remote past. If it is by historical thinking that we re-think and so rediscover the thought of Hammurabi or Solon, it is in the same way that we discover the thought of a friend who writes us a letter, or a stranger who crosses the street. Nor is it necessary that the historian should be one person and the subject of his inquiry another. It is only by historical thinking that I can discover what I thought ten years ago, by reading what I then wrote, or what I thought five minutes ago, by reflecting on an action that I then did, which surprised me when I realized what I had done. In this sense, all knowledge of mind is historical. The only way in which I can know my own mind is by performing some mental act or other and then considering what the act is that I have performed. If I want to know what I think about a certain subject, I try to put my ideas about it in order, on paper or otherwise; and then, having thus arranged and formulated them, I can study the result as an historical document and see what my ideas were when I did that piece of thinking: if I am dissatisfied with them, I can do it over again. If I want to know what powers my mind possesses as yet unexplored, for example, whether I can write poetry, I must try to write some, and see whether it strikes me and others as being the real thing. If I want to know whether I am as good a man as I hope, or as bad as I fear, I must examine acts that I have done, and understand what they really were: or else go and do some fresh acts and then examine those. All these inquiries are historical. They proceed by studying accomplished facts, ideas that I have thought out and expressed, acts that I have done. On what I have only begun and am still doing, no judgement can as yet be passed.

The same historical method is the only one by which I can know the mind of another, or the corporate mind (whatever exactly that phrase means) of a community or an age. To study the mind of the Victorian age or the English political spirit is simply to study the history of Victorian thought or English political activity. Here we come back to Locke and his 'historical, plain Method'. Mind not only declares, but also enjoys or possesses, its nature, both as mind in general and as this particular sort of mind with these particular dispositions and faculties, by thinking and acting, doing individual actions which express individual thoughts. If historical thinking is the way in which these thoughts are detected as expressed in these actions, it would seem that Locke's phrase hits the truth, and that historical knowledge is the only knowledge that the human mind can have of itself. The so-called science of human nature or of the human mind resolves itself into history.

It will certainly be thought (if those who think in this way have had patience to follow me thus far) that in saying this I am claiming more for history than it can ever give. The false view of history as a story of successive events or a spectacle of changes has been so often and so authoritatively taught in late years, especially in this country, that the very meaning of the word has become debauched through the assimilation of historical process to natural process. Against misunderstandings arising from this source I am bound to protest, even if I protest in vain. But there is one sense in which I should agree that the resolution of a science of mind into history means renouncing part of what a science of mind commonly claims, and, I think, claims falsely. The mental scientist, believing in the universal and therefore unalterable truth of his conclusions, thinks that the account he gives of mind holds good of all future stages in mind's history: he thinks that his science shows what mind will always be, not only what it has been in the past and is now. The historian has no gift of prophecy, and knows it; the historical study of mind, therefore, can neither foretell the future developments of human thought nor legislate for them, except so far as they must proceed — though in what direction we cannot tell — from the present as their starting-point. Not the least of the errors contained in the science of human nature is its claim to establish a framework to which all future history must conform, to close the gates of the future and bind posterity within limits due not to the nature of things (limits of that kind are real, and are easily accepted) but to the supposed laws of the mind itself.

Another type of objection deserves longer consideration. It may be granted that mind is the proper and only object of historical knowledge, but it may still be contended that historical knowledge is not the only way in which mind can be known. There might be a distinction between two ways of knowing mind. Historical thought studies mind as acting in certain determinate ways in certain determinate situations. Might there not be another way of studying mind, investigating its general characteristics in abstraction from any particular situation or particular action? If so, this would be a scientific, as opposed to an historical, knowledge of mind: not history, but mental science, psychology, or the philosophy of mind.

If such a science of mind is to be distinguished from history, how is the relation between the two to be conceived? It seems to me that two alternative views of this relation are possible.

One way of conceiving it would be to distinguish between what mind is and what it does: and to entrust the study of what it does, its particular actions, to history, and reserve the study of what it is for mental science. To use a familiar distinction, its functions depend on its structure, and behind its functions or particular activities as revealed in history there lies a structure which determines these functions, and must be studied not by history but by another kind of thought.

This conception, however, is very confused. In the case of a machine, we distinguish structure from function, and think of the latter as depending on the former. But we can do this only because the machine is equally perceptible to us in motion or at rest, and we can therefore study it in either state indifferently. But any study of mind is a study of its activities; if we try to think of a mind absolutely at rest, we are compelled to admit that if it existed at all (which is more than doubtful) at least we should be quite unable to study it. Psychologists speak of mental mechanisms; but they are speaking not of structures but of functions. They do not profess ability to observe these so-called mechanisms when they are not functioning. And if we look closer at the original distinction we shall see that it does not mean quite what it seems to mean. In the case of a machine, what we call function is really only that part of the machine's total functioning which serves the purpose of its maker or user. Bicycles are made not in order that there may be bicycles, but in order that people may travel in a certain way. Relatively to that purpose, a bicycle is functioning only when some one is riding it. But a bicycle at rest in a shed is not ceasing to function: its parts are not inactive, they are holding themselves together in a particular order; and what we call possession of its structure is nothing but this function of holding itself thus together. In this sense, whatever is called structure is in reality a way of functioning. In any other sense, mind has no function at all; it has no value, to itself or to any one else, except to be a mind, to perform those activities which constitute it a mind. Hume was therefore right to maintain that there is no such thing as 'spiritual substance', nothing that a mind is, distinct from and underlying what it does.

This idea of a mental science would be, to use Comte's famous distinction, 'metaphysical', depending on the conception of an occult substance underlying the facts of historical activity; the alternative idea would be 'positive', depending on the conception of similarities or uniformities among those facts themselves. According to this idea, the task of mental science would be to detect types or patterns of activity, repeated over and over again in history itself.

That such a science is possible is beyond question. But two observations must be made about it.

First, any estimate of the value of such a science, based on the analogy of natural science, is wholly misleading. The value of generalization in natural science depends on the fact that the data of physical science are given by perception, and perceiving is not understanding. The raw material of natural science is therefore 'mere particulars', observed but not understood, and, taken in their perceived particularity, unintelligible. It is therefore a genuine advance in knowledge to discover something intelligible in the relations between general types of them. What they are in themselves, as scientists are never tired of reminding us, remains unknown: but we can at least know something about the patterns of facts into which they enter.

A science which generalizes from historical facts is in a very different position. Here the facts, in order to serve as data, must first be historically known; and historical knowledge is not perception, it is the discerning of the thought which is the inner side of the event. The historian, when he is ready to hand over such a fact to the mental scientist as a datum for generalization, has already understood it in this way from within. If he has not done so, the fact is being used as a datum for generalization before it has been properly 'ascertained'. But if he has done so, nothing of value is left for generalization to do. If, by historical thinking, we already understand how and why Napoleon established his ascendancy in revolutionary France, nothing is added to our understanding of that process by the statement (however true) that similar things have happened elsewhere. It is only when the particular fact cannot be understood by itself that such statements are of value.

Hence the idea that such a science is valuable depends on a tacit and false assumption that the 'historical data', 'phenomena of consciousness', or the like upon which it is based are merely perceived and not historically known. To think that they can be thus merely perceived is to think of them not as mind but as nature; and consequently sciences of this type tend systematically to dementalize mind and convert it into nature. Modern examples are the pseudo-history of Spengler, where the individual historical facts which he calls 'cultures' are frankly conceived as natural products, growing and perishing 'with the same superb aimlessness as the flowers of the field', and the many psychological theories now fashionable, which conceive virtues and vices, knowledge and illusion, in the same way.

Secondly, if we ask how far the generalizations of such a science hold good, we shall see that its claim to transcend the sphere of history is baseless. Types of behaviour do, no doubt, recur, so long as minds of the same kind are placed in the same kind of situations. The behaviour-patterns characteristic of a feudal baron were no doubt fairly constant so long as there were feudal barons living in a feudal society. But they will be sought in vain (except by an inquirer content with the loosest and most fanciful analogies) in a world whose social structure is of another kind. In order that behaviour-patterns may be constant, there must be in existence a social order which recurrently produces situations of a certain kind. But social orders are historical facts, and subject to inevitable changes, fast or slow. A positive science of mind will, no doubt, be able to establish uniformities and recurrences, but it can have no guarantee that the laws it establishes will hold good beyond the historical period from which its facts are drawn. Such a science (as we have lately been taught with regard to what is called classical economics) can do no more than describe in a general way certain characteristics of the historical age in which it is constructed. If it tries to overcome this limitation by drawing on a wider field, relying on ancient history, modern anthropology, and so on, for a larger basis of facts, it will still never be more than a generalized description of certain phases in human history. It will never be a non-historical science of mind.

To regard such a positive mental science as rising above the sphere of history, and establishing the permanent and unchanging laws of human nature, is therefore possible only to a person who mistakes the transient conditions of a certain historical age for the permanent conditions of human life. It was easy for men of the eighteenth century to make this mistake, because their historical perspective was so short, and their knowledge of cultures other than their own so limited, that they could cheerfully identify the intellectual habits of a western European in their own day with the intellectual faculties bestowed by God upon Adam and all his progeny. Hume, in his account of human nature, never attempted to go beyond observing that in point of fact 'we' think in certain ways, and left undiscussed the question what he meant by the word 'we'. Even Kant, in his attempt to go beyond the 'question of fact' and settle the 'question of right', only showed that we must think in these ways if we are to possess the kind of science which we actually possess. When he asks how experience is possible, he means by experience the kind of experience enjoyed by men of his own age and civilization. He was, of course, not aware of this. No one in his time had done enough work on the history of thought to know that both the science and the experience of an eighteenth-century European were highly peculiar historical facts, very different from those of other peoples and other times. Nor was it yet realized that, even apart from the evidence of history, men must have thought in very different ways when as yet they were hardly emerged from the ape. The idea of a science of human nature, as entertained in the eighteenth century, belonged to a time when it was still believed that the human species, like every other, was a special creation with unalterable characteristics.

The fallacy inherent in the very idea of a science of human nature is not removed by pointing out that human nature, like every kind of nature, must according to the principles of modern thought be conceived as subject to evolution. Indeed, such a modification of the idea only leads to worse consequences. Evolution, after all, is a natural process, a process of change; and as such it abolishes one specific form in creating another. The trilobites of the Silurian age may be the ancestors of the mammals of to-day, including ourselves; but a human being is not a kind of wood-louse. The past, in a natural process, is a past superseded and dead. Now suppose the historical process of human thought were in this sense an evolutionary process. It would follow that the ways of thinking characteristic of any given historical period are ways in which people must think then, but in which others, cast at different times in a different mental mould, cannot think at all. If that were the case, there would be no such thing as truth: according to the inference correctly drawn by Herbert Spencer, what we take for knowledge is merely the fashion of present-day thought, not true but at the most useful in our struggle for existence. The same evolutionary view of the history of thought is implied by Mr. Santayana, when he denounces history as fostering 'the learned illusion of living again the life of the dead', a subject fit only for 'minds fundamentally without loyalties and incapable or fearful of knowing themselves'; persons interested not in 'the rediscovery of an essence formerly discovered or prized', but only in 'the fact that people once entertained some such idea'.[4]

The fallacy common to these views is the confusion between a natural process, in which

[4] *The Realm of Essence*, p. 69.

the past dies in being replaced by the present, and an historical process, in which the past, so far as it is historically known, survives in the present. Oswald Spengler, vividly realizing the difference between modern mathematics and that of the Greeks, and knowing that each is a function of its own historical age, correctly argues from his false identification of historical with natural process that to us Greek mathematics must be not only strange but unintelligible. But in fact, not only do we understand Greek mathematics easily enough, it is actually the foundation of our own. It is not the dead past of a mathematical thought once entertained by persons whose names and dates we can give, it is the living past of our own present mathematical inquiries, a past which, so far as we take any interest in mathematics, we still enjoy as an actual possession. Because the historical past, unlike the natural past, is a living past, kept alive by the act of historical thinking itself, the historical change from one way of thinking to another is not the death of the first, but its survival integrated in a new context involving the development and criticism of its own ideas. Mr. Santayana, like so many others, first wrongly identifies historical process with natural process, and then blames history for being what he falsely thinks it to be. Spencer's theory of the evolution of human ideas embodies the error in its crudest form.

Man has been defined as an animal capable of profiting by the experience of others. Of his bodily life this would be wholly untrue: he is not nourished because another has eaten, or refreshed because another has slept. But as regards his mental life it is true; and the way in which this profit is realized is by historical knowledge. The body of human thought or mental activity is a corporate possession, and almost all the operations which our minds perform are operations which we learned to perform from others who have performed them already. Since mind is what it does, and human nature, if it is a name for anything real, is only a name for human activities, this acquisition of ability to perform determinate operations is the acquisition of a determinate human nature. Thus the historical process is a process in which man creates for himself this or that kind of human nature by re-creating in his own thought the past to which he is heir.

This inheritance is not transmitted by any natural process. To be possessed, it must be grasped by the mind that possesses it, and historical knowledge is the way in which we enter upon the possession of it. There is not, first, a special kind of process, the historical process, and then a special way of knowing this, namely historical thought. The historical process is itself a process of thought, and it exists only in so far as the minds which are parts of it know themselves for parts of it. By historical thinking, the mind whose self-knowledge is history not only discovers within itself those powers of which historical thought reveals the possession, but actually develops those powers from a latent to an actual state, brings them into effective existence.

It would therefore be sophistical to argue that, since the historical process is a process of thought, there must be thought already present, as its presupposition, at the beginning of it, and that an account of what thought is, originally and in itself, must be a non-historical account. History does not presuppose mind; it is the life of mind itself, which is not mind except so far as it both lives in historical process and knows itself as so living.

The idea that man, apart from his self-conscious historical life, is different from the rest of creation in being a rational animal is a mere superstition. It is only by fits and starts, in a flickering and dubious manner, that human beings are rational at all. In quality, as well as in amount, their rationality is a matter of degree: some are oftener rational than others, some rational in a more intense way. But a flickering and dubious rationality can certainly not be denied to animals other than men. Their minds may be inferior in range and power to those of the lowest savages, but by the same standards the lowest savages are inferior to civilized men, and those whom we call civilized differ among themselves hardly less. There are even among non-human animals the beginnings of historical life: for example, among cats, which do not wash by instinct but are taught by their mothers. Such rudiments of education are something not essentially different from an historic culture.

Historicity, too, is a matter of degree. The historicity of very primitive societies is not easily distinguishable from the merely instinctive life of societies in which rationality is at vanishing-point. When the occasions on which thinking is done, and the kinds of things about which it is done, become more frequent and more essential to the life of society, the historic inheritance of thought, preserved by historical knowledge of what has been thought before, becomes more considerable, and with its development the development of a specifically rational life begins.

Thought is therefore not the presupposition of an historical process which is in turn the presupposition of historical knowledge. It is only in the historical process, the process of thoughts, that thought exists at all; and it is only in so far as this process is known for a process of thoughts that it is one. The self-knowledge of reason is not an accident; it belongs to its essence. This is why historical knowledge is no luxury, or mere amusement of a mind at leisure from more pressing occupations, but a prime duty, whose discharge is essential to the maintenance, not only of any particular form or type of reason, but of reason itself.

CONCLUSIONS

It remains to draw a few conclusions from the thesis I have tried to maintain.

First, as regards history itself. The methods of modern historical inquiry have grown up under the shadow of their elder sister, the method of natural science; in some ways helped by its example, in other ways hindered. Throughout this essay it has been necessary to engage in a running fight with what may be called a positivistic conception, or rather misconception, of history, as the study of successive events lying in a dead past, events to be understood as the scientist understands natural events, by classifying them and establishing relations between the classes thus defined. This misconception is not only an endemic error in modern philosophical thought about history, it is also a constant peril to historical thought itself. So far as historians yield to it, they neglect their proper task of penetrating to the thought of the agents whose acts they are studying, and content themselves with determining the externals of these acts, the kind of things about them which can be studied statistically. Statistical research is for the historian a good servant but a bad master. It profits him nothing to make statistical generalizations, unless he can thereby detect the thought behind the facts about which he is generalizing. At the present day, historical thought is almost everywhere disentangling itself from the toils of the positivistic fallacy, and recognizing that in itself history is nothing but the re-enactment of past thought in the historian's mind; but much still needs to be done if the full fruits of this recognition are to be reaped. All kinds of historical fallacies are still current, due to confusion between historical process and natural process: not only the cruder fallacies of mistaking historical facts of culture and tradition for functions of biological facts like race and pedigree, but subtler fallacies affecting methods of research and the organization of historical inquiry, which it would take too long to enumerate here. It is not until these have been eradicated that we can see how far historical thought, attaining at last its proper shape and stature, is able to make good the claims long ago put forward on behalf of the science of human nature.

Secondly, with regard to past attempts to construct such a science.

The positive function of so-called sciences of the human mind, whether total or partial (I refer to such studies as those on the theory of knowledge, of morals, of politics, of economics, and so forth), has always tended to be misconceived. Ideally, they are designed as accounts of one unchanging subject-matter, the mind of man as it always has been and always will be. Little acquaintance with them is demanded in order to see that they are nothing of the sort, but only inventories of the wealth achieved by the human mind at a certain stage in its history. The *Republic* of Plato is an account, not of the unchanging ideal of political life, but of the Greek ideal as Plato received it and re-interpreted it. The *Ethics* of Aristotle describes not an eternal morality but the morality of the Greek gentleman. Hobbes's *Leviathan* expounds the political ideas of seventeenth-century absolutism in their English form. Kant's ethical theory expresses the moral convictions of German pietism; his *Critique of Pure Reason* analyses the conceptions and principles of Newtonian science, in their relation to the philosophical problems of the day. These limitations are often taken for defects, as if a more powerful thinker than Plato would have lifted himself clean out of the atmosphere of Greek politics, or as if Aristotle ought to have anticipated the moral conceptions of Christianity or the modern world. So far from being a defect, they are a sign of merit; they are most clearly to be seen in those works whose quality is of the best. The reason is that in those works the authors are doing best the only thing that can be done when an attempt is made to construct a science of the human mind. They are expounding the position reached by the human mind in its historical development down to their own time.

When they try to justify that position, all they can do is to exhibit it as a logical one, a coherent whole of ideas. If, realizing that any such justification is circular, they try to make the whole depend on something outside itself, they fail, as indeed they must; for since the historical present includes in itself its own past, the real ground on which the whole rests, namely the past out of which it has grown, is not outside it but is included within it.

If these systems remain valuable to posterity, that is not in spite of their strictly historical character but because of it. To us, the ideas expressed in them are ideas belonging to the past; but it is not a dead past; by understanding it historically we incorporate it into our present thought, and enable ourselves by developing and criticizing it to use that heritage for our own advancement.

But a mere inventory of our intellectual possessions at the present time can never show by what right we enjoy them. To do this there is only one way: by analysing them instead of merely describing them, and showing how they have been built up in the historical development of thought. What Kant, for example, wanted to do when he set out to justify our use of a category like causation, can in a sense be done; but it cannot be done on Kant's method, which yields a merely circular argument, proving that such a category can be used, and must be used if we are to have Newtonian science; it can be done by research into the history of scientific thought. All Kant could show was that eighteenth-century scientists did think in terms of that category; the question why they so thought can be answered by investigating the history of the idea of causation. If more than this is required; if a proof is needed that the idea is true, that people are right to think in that way; then a demand is being made which in the nature of things can never be satisfied. How can we ever satisfy ourselves that the principles on which we think are true, except by going on thinking according to those principles, and seeing whether unanswerable criticisms of them emerge as we work? To criticize the conceptions of science is the work of science itself as it proceeds; to demand that such criticism should be anticipated by the theory of knowledge is to demand that such a theory should anticipate the history of thought.

Finally, there is the question what function can be assigned to the science of psychology. At first sight its position appears equivocal. On the one hand, it claims to be a science of mind; but if so, its apparatus of scientific method is merely the fruit of a false analogy, and it must pass over into history and, as such, disappear. And this is certainly what ought to happen so far as psychology claims to deal with the functions of reason itself. To speak of the psychology of reasoning, or the psychology of the moral self (to quote the titles of two well-known books), is to misuse words and confuse issues, ascribing to a quasi-naturalistic science a subject-matter whose being and development are not natural but historical. But if psychology avoids this danger and renounces interference with what is properly the subject-matter of history, it is likely to fall back into a pure science of nature and to become a mere branch of physiology, dealing with muscular and nervous movements.

But there is a third alternative. In realizing its own rationality, mind also realizes the presence in itself of elements that are not rational. They are not body; they are mind, but not rational mind or thought. To use an old distinction, they are psyche or soul as distinct from spirit. These irrational elements are the subject-matter of psychology. They are the blind forces and activities in us which are part of human life as it consciously experiences itself, but are not parts of the historical process: sensation as distinct from thought, feelings as distinct from conceptions, appetite as distinct from will. Their importance to us consists in the fact that they form the proximate environment in which our reason lives, as our physiological organism is the proximate environment in which they live. They are the basis of our rational life, though no part of it. Our reason discovers them, but in studying them it is not studying itself. By learning to know them, it finds out how it can help them to live in health, so that they can feed and support it while it pursues its own proper task, the self-conscious creation of its own historical life . . . .

History and Freedom

We study history, I have maintained, in order to attain self-knowledge. By way of illustrating this thesis, I shall try to show how our knowledge that human activity is free has been attained only through our discovery of history.

In my historical sketch of the idea of history I have tried to show how history has at last escaped from a state of pupilage to natural science. The disappearance of historical naturalism, however, entails the further conclusion that the activity by which man builds his own constantly changing historical world is a free activity. There are no forces other than this activity which control it or modify it or compel it to behave in this way or in that, to build one kind of world rather than another.

This does not mean that a man is always free to do what he pleases. All men, at some moments in their lives, are free to do what they want: to eat, being hungry, for example, or to sleep, being tired. But this has nothing to do with the problem to which I have referred. Eating and sleeping are animal activities, pursued under the compulsion of animal appetite. With animal appetites and their gratification or frustration history is not concerned. It makes no difference to the historian, as an historian, that there should be no food in a poor man's house; though it may and must make a difference to him as a man with feelings for his fellow creatures; and though as an historian he may be intensely concerned with the shifts by which other men have contrived to bring about this state of things in order that they should be rich and the men who take wages from them poor; and equally concerned with the action to which the poor man may be led not by the fact of his children's unsatisfied hunger, the fact, the physiological fact, of empty bellies and wizened limbs, but by his thought of that fact.

Nor does it mean that a man is free to do what he chooses; that in the realm of history proper, as distinct from that of animal appetite, people are free to plan their own actions as they think fit and execute their plans, each doing what he set out to do and each assuming full responsibility for the consequences, captain of his soul and all that. Nothing could be more false. Henley's rhyme does no more than utter the fantasy of a sick child who has discovered that he can stop himself crying for the moon by making believe that he has got it. A healthy man knows that the empty space in front of him, which he proposes to fill up with activities for which he accordingly now begins making plans, will be very far from empty by the time he steps into it. It will be crowded with other people all pursuing activities of their own. Even now it is not as empty as it looks. It is filled with a saturate solution of activity, on the point of beginning to crystallize out. There will be no room left for his own activity, unless he can so design this that it will fit into the interstices of the rest.

The rational activity which historians have to study is never free from compulsion: the compulsion to face the facts of its own situation. The more rational it is, the more completely it undergoes this compulsion. To be rational is to think; and for a man who proposes to act, the thing that it is important to think about is the situation in which he stands. With regard to this situation, he is not free at all. It is what it is, and neither he nor anyone else can ever change that. For though the situation consists altogether of thoughts, his own and other people's, it cannot be changed by a change of mind on the part of himself or anyone else. If minds change, as they do, this merely means that with the lapse of time a new situation has arisen. For a man about to act, the situation is his master, his oracle, his god. Whether his action is to prove successful or not depends on whether he grasps the situation rightly or not. If he is a wise man, it is not until he has consulted his oracle, done everything in his power to find out what the situation is, that he will make even the most trivial plan. And if he neglects the situation, the situation will not neglect him. It is not one of those gods that leave an insult unpunished.

The freedom that there is in history consists in the fact that this compulsion is imposed upon the activity of human reason not by anything else, but by itself. The situation, its master, oracle, and god, is a situation it has itself created. And when I say this I do not mean that the situation in which one man finds himself exists only because other men have created it by a rational activity not different in kind from that by which their successor finds himself to be in it and acts in it according to his lights; and that, because human reason is always human reason, whatever may be the name of the human being in whom it works, the historian can ignore these personal distinctions and say that human reason has created the situation in which it finds itself. I mean something rather different from that. All history is the history of thought; and when an historian says that a man is in a certain situation this is the same as saying that he thinks he is in this situation. The hard facts of the situation, which it is so important for him to face, are the hard facts of the way in which he conceives the situation.

If the reason why it is hard for a man to cross the mountains is because he is frightened of the devils in them, it is folly for the historian, preaching at him across a gulf of centuries, to say 'This is sheer superstition. There are no devils at all. Face facts, and realize that there are no dangers in the mountains except rocks and water and snow, wolves perhaps, and bad men perhaps, but no devils.' The historian says that these are the facts because that is the way in which he has been taught to think. But the devil-fearer says that the presence of devils is a fact, because that is the way in which he has been taught to think. The historian thinks it a wrong way; but wrong ways of thinking are just as much historical facts as right ones, and, no less than they, determine the situation (always a thought-situation) in which the man who shares them is placed. The hardness of the fact consists in the man's inability to think of his situation otherwise. The compulsion which the devil-haunted mountains exercise on the man who would cross them consists in the fact that he cannot help believing in the devils. Sheer superstition, no doubt: but this superstition is a fact, and the crucial fact in the situation we are considering. The man who suffers from it when he tries to cross the mountains is not suffering merely for the sins of his fathers who taught him to believe in devils, if that is a sin; he is suffering because he has accepted the belief, because he has shared the sin. If the modern historian believes that there are no devils in the mountains, that too is only a belief he has accepted in precisely the same way.

The discovery that the men whose actions he studies are in this sense free is a discovery which every historian makes as soon as he arrives at a scientific mastery of his own subject. When that happens, the historian discovers his own freedom: that is, he discovers the autonomous character of historical thought, its power to solve its own problems for itself by its own methods. He discovers how unnecessary it is, and how impossible it is, for him, as historian, to hand these problems over for solution to natural science; he discovers that in his capacity as historian he both can and must solve them for himself. It is simultaneously with this discovery of his own freedom as historian that he discovers the freedom of man as an historical agent. Historical thought, thought about rational activity, is free from the domination of natural science, and rational activity is free from the domination of nature.

The intimacy of the connexion between these two discoveries might be expressed by saying that they are the same thing in different words. It might be said that to describe the rational activity of an historical agent as free is only a roundabout and disguised way of saying that history is an autonomous science. Or it might be said that to describe history as an autonomous science is only a disguised way of saying that it is the science which studies free activity. For myself, I should welcome either of these two statements, as providing evidence that the person who made it had seen far enough into the nature of history to have discovered (*a*) that historical thought is free from the domination of natural science, and is an autonomous science, (*b*) that rational action is free from the domination of nature and builds its own world of human affairs, *Res Gestae*, at its own bidding and in its own way, (*c*) that there is an intimate connexion between these two propositions.

But at the same time I should find in either statement evidence that the person who made it was unable (or for some ulterior purpose had decided to profess himself unable) to distinguish between what a person says and what is implied in what he says: unable, that is, to distinguish the theory of language, or aesthetics, from the theory of thought, or logic; and was therefore committed, for the time being at least, to a verbalistic logic, in which the logical connexion between two thoughts which imply each other is confused with the linguistic connexion between two sets of words which 'stand for the same thing'.

I should see, too, that his attempt to burke the problems of logic by substituting for them problems in linguistics was not based on any very just appreciation of the nature of language, because I should see that, of two synonymous verbal expressions, he was assuming that one really and properly means the thing 'for which it stands', while the other means this only for the insufficient reason that the person who uses it means that by it. All of which is very disputable. Rather than approve such errors, I should prefer to leave the matter where I have left it; to say that these two statements (the statement that history is an autonomous science and the statement that rational activity is free in the sense described) are not synonymous forms of words but express discoveries neither of which can be made without making the other. And arising out of this, I will observe that the 'free-will controversy' which was so prominent in the seventeenth century had a close connexion with the fact that the seventeenth century was the time when scissors-and-paste history in its simpler forms was beginning to dissatisfy people, and when historians were beginning to see that their own house needed setting in order or that historical studies ought to take example from the study of nature, and raise themselves to the level of a science. The desire to envisage human action as free was bound up with a desire to achieve autonomy for history as the study of human action.

But I do not leave the matter there; because I wish to point out that of the two statements I am considering, one is necessarily prior to the other. It is only by using historical methods that we can find out anything about the objects of historical study. No one will assert that he knows more than historians do about certain actions done in the past concerning which historians claim to have knowledge, and that he knows this in such a way that he can satisfy both himself and other people that that claim is groundless. It follows that we must first achieve a genuinely scientific and therefore autonomous method in historical study before we can grasp the fact that human activity is free.

This may seem contrary to facts; for surely, it will be said, many people were already aware that human activity is free, long before that revolution took place by which history raised itself to the level of a science. To this objection I will offer two answers, not mutually exclusive, but the one relatively superficial, the other, I hope, a little more profound.

(i) They were aware, perhaps, of human freedom; but did they grasp it? Was their awareness a knowledge that deserved the name of scientific? Surely not; for in that case they would not only have been convinced of it, they would have known it in a systematic way, and there would have been no room for controversy about it, because those who were convinced of it would have understood the grounds of their conviction and been able to state them convincingly.

(ii) Even if the revolution by which history has become a science is only about a half-century old, we must not be deceived by the word 'revolution'. Long before Bacon and Descartes revolutionized natural science by expounding publicly the principles on which its method was based, people here and there had been using these same methods, some more often, some more rarely. As Bacon and Descartes so justly pointed out, the effect of their own work was to put these same methods within the grasp of quite ordinary intellects. When it is said that the methods of history have been revolutionized in the last half-century, this is what is meant. It is not meant that examples of scientific history will be sought in vain before that date. It is meant that whereas, earlier, scientific history was a thing of rare occurrence, hardly to be found except in the work of outstanding men, and even in them marking moments of inspiration rather than the even tenor of study, it is now a thing within the compass of everyone; a thing which we demand of everybody who writes history at all, and which is widely enough understood, even among the unlearned, to procure a livelihood for writers of detective stories whose plot is based upon its methods. The sporadic and intermittent way in which the truth of human freedom was grasped in the seventeenth century might, to say the least of it, have been a consequence of this sporadic and intermittent grasp on the method of scientific history.

2

Man: The Subject of an Inexact Science?

from *A System of Logic*
JOHN STUART MILL

That There Is, or May Be, a Science of Man

1. It is a common notion, or at least it is implied in many common modes of speech, that the thoughts, feelings, and actions of sentient beings are not a subject of science, in the same strict sense in which this is true of the objects of outward nature. This notion seems to involve some confusion of ideas, which it is necessary to begin by clearing up.

Any facts are fitted, in themselves, to be a subject of science, which follow one another according to constant laws; although those laws may not have been discovered, nor even be discoverable by our existing resources. Take, for instance, the most familiar class of meteorological phenomena, those of rain and sunshine. Scientific inquiry has not yet succeeded in ascertaining the order of antecedence and consequence among these phenomena, so as to be able, at least in our regions of the earth, to predict them with certainty or even with any high degree of probability. Yet no one doubts that the phenomena depend on laws, and that these must be derivative laws resulting from known ultimate laws, those of heat, electricity, vaporisation, and elastic fluids. Nor can it be doubted that if we were acquainted with all the antecedent circumstances, we could, even from those more general laws, predict (saving difficulties of calculation) the state of the weather at any future time. Meteorology, therefore, not only has in itself every natural requisite for being, but actually is, a science; though, from the difficulty of observing the facts on which the phenomena depend (a difficulty inherent in the peculiar nature of those phenomena), the science is extremely imperfect; and were it perfect, might probably be of little avail in practice, since the data requisite for applying its principles to particular instances would rarely be procurable.

A case may be conceived, of an intermediate character between the perfection of science, and this its extreme imperfection. It may happen that the greater causes, those on which the principal part of the phenomena depends, are within the reach of observation and measurement; so that if no other causes intervened, a complete explanation could be given not only of the phenomena in general, but of all the variations and modification which it admits of. But inasmuch as other, perhaps many other, causes, separately insignificant in their effects, co-operate or conflict in many or in all cases with those greater causes; the effect, accordingly, presents more or less of aberration from what would be produced by the greater causes alone. Now if these minor causes are not so constantly accessible, or not accessible at all to accurate observation, the principal mass of the effect may still, as before, be accounted for, and even predicted; but there will be variations and modifications which we shall not be competent to explain thoroughly, and our predictions will not be fulfilled accurately, but only approximately.

It is thus, for example, with the theory of the tides. No one doubts that Tidology (as Dr. Whewell proposes to call it) is really a science. As much of the phenomena as depends on the attraction of the sun and moon

From *A System of Logic*, Vol. II, by John Stuart Mill, Longman's Green & Co., Ltd., London, 1876, pp. 430–435.

is completely understood, and may in any, even unknown, part of the earth's surface be foretold with certainty; and the far greater part of the phenomena depends on those causes. But circumstances of a local or casual nature, such as the configuration of the bottom of the ocean, the degree of confinement from shores, the direction of the wind, &c., influence in many or in all places the height and time of the tide; and a portion of these circumstances being either not accurately knowable, not precisely measurable, or not capable of being certainly foreseen, the tide in known places commonly varies from the calculated result of general principles by some difference that we cannot explain, and in unknown ones may vary from it by a difference that we are not able to foresee or conjecture. Nevertheless, not only is it certain that these variations depend on causes, and follow their causes by laws of unerring uniformity; not only, therefore, is tidology a science, like meteorology, but it is, what hitherto at least meteorology is not, a science largely available in practice. General laws may be laid down respecting the tides, predictions may be founded on those laws, and the result will in the main, though often not with complete accuracy, correspond to the predictions.

And this is what is or ought to be meant by those who speak of sciences which are not *exact* sciences. Astronomy was once a science, without being an exact science. It could not become exact until not only the general course of the planetary motions, but the perturbations also, were accounted for, and referred to their causes. It has become an exact science, because its phenomena have been brought under laws comprehending the whole of the causes by which the phenomena are influenced, whether in a great or only in a trifling degree, whether in all or only in some cases, and assigning to each of those causes the share of effect which really belongs to it. But in the theory of the tides, the only laws as yet accurately ascertained are those of the causes which affect the phenomenon in all cases, and in a considerable degree; while others which affect it in some cases only, or, if in all, only in a slight degree, have not been sufficiently ascertained and studied to enable us to lay down their laws, still less to deduce the completed law of the phenomenon, by compounding the effects of the greater with those of the minor causes. Tidology, therefore, is not yet an exact science; not from any inherent incapacity of being so, but from the difficulty of ascertaining with complete precision the real derivative uniformities. By combining, however, the exact laws of the greater causes, and of such of the minor ones as are sufficiently known, with such empirical laws or such approximate generalizations respecting the miscellaneous variations as can be obtained by specific observation, we can lay down general propositions which will be true in the main, and on which, with allowance for the degree of their probable inaccuracy, we may safely ground our expectations and our conduct.

2. The science of human nature is of this description. It falls far short of the standard of exactness now realized in Astronomy; but there is no reason that it should not be as much a science as Tidology is, or as Astronomy was when its calculations had only mastered the main phenomena, but not the perturbations.

The phenomena with which this science is conversant being the thoughts, feelings, and actions of human beings, it would have attained the ideal perfection of a science if it enabled us to foretell how an individual would think, feel, or act, throughout life, with the same certainty with which astronomy enables us to predict the places and the occultations of the heavenly bodies. It needs scarcely be stated that nothing approaching to this can be done. The actions of individuals could not be predicted with scientific accuracy, were it only because we cannot foresee the whole of the circumstances in which those individuals will be placed. But further, even in any given combination of (present) circumstances, no assertion, which is both precise and universally true, can be made respecting the manner in which human beings will think, feel, or act. This is not, however, because every person's modes of thinking, feeling, and acting, do not depend on causes; nor can we doubt that if, in the case of any individual, our data could be complete, we even now know enough of the ultimate laws by which mental phenomena are determined, to enable us in many cases to predict, with tolerable certainty, what, in the greater number of supposable combinations of circumstances, his conduct or sentiments would be. But the impressions and actions of human beings are not solely the result of their present circumstances, but the joint result of those circumstances and of the characters of the individuals: and the agencies which determine human character are so numerous and diversified, (nothing which has happened to the person throughout life being without its portion of influence,) that in the aggregate they are never in any two cases exactly similar. Hence, even if our science of human nature were theoretically perfect, that is, if we could calculate any character as we can calculate the orbit of any planet, *from given data*; still, as the data are never all given, nor ever precisely alike in different cases, we could neither make positive predictions, nor lay down universal propositions.

Inasmuch, however, as many of those effects which it is of most importance to render amenable to human foresight and control are determined, like the tides, in an incomparably greater degree by general causes, than by all partial causes taken together; depending in the main on those circumstances and qualities which are common to all mankind, or at least to large bodies of them, and only in a small degree on the idiosyncrasies of organization or the peculiar history of individuals; it is evidently possible with regard to all such effects, to make predictions which will *almost* always be verified, and general propositions which are almost always true. And whenever it is sufficient to know how the great majority of the human race, or of some nation or class of persons, will think, feel, and act, these propositions are equivalent to universal ones. For the purposes of political and social science this *is* sufficient. As we formerly remarked, an approximate generalization is, in social inquiries, for most practical purposes equivalent to an exact one: that which is only probable when asserted of individual human beings indiscriminately selected, being certain when affirmed of the character and collective conduct of masses.

It is no disparagement, therefore, to the science of Human Nature, that those of its general propositions which descend sufficiently into detail to serve as a foundation for predicting phenomena in the concrete, are for the most part only approximately true. But in order to give a genuinely scientific character to the study, it is indispensable that these approximate generalizations, which in themselves would amount only to the lowest kind of empirical laws, should be connected deductively with the laws of nature from which they result; should be resolved into the properties of the causes on which the phenomena depend. In other words, the science of Human Nature may be said to exist, in proportion as the approximate truths, which compose a practical knowledge of mankind, can be exhibited as corollaries from the universal laws of human nature on which they rest; whereby the proper limits of those approximate truths would be shown, and we should be enabled to deduce others for any new state of circumstances, in anticipation of specific experience.

The proposition now stated is the text on which the two succeeding chapters will furnish the comment.

The Empirical Case for a Science of Behavior 3

from *Science and Human Behavior*

B. F. SKINNER

The application of science to human behavior is not so simple as it seems. Most of those who advocate it are simply looking for "the facts." To them science is little more than careful observation. They want to evaluate human behavior as it really is rather than as it appears to be through ignorance or prejudice, and then to make effective decisions and move on rapidly to a happier world. But the way in which science has been applied in other fields shows that something more is involved. Science is not concerned just with "getting the facts," after which one may act with greater wisdom in an unscientific fashion. Science supplies its own wisdom. It leads to a new conception of a subject matter, a new way of thinking about that part of the world to which it has addressed itself. If we are to enjoy the advantages of science in the field of human affairs, we must be prepared to adopt the working model of behavior to which a science will inevitably lead. But very few of those who advocate the application of scientific method to current problems are willing to go that far.

Science is more than the mere description of events as they occur. It is an attempt to discover order, to show that certain events stand in lawful relations to other events. No practical technology can be based upon science until such relations have been discovered. But order is not only a possible end product; it is a working assumption which must be adopted at the very start. We cannot apply the methods of science to a subject matter which is assumed to move about capriciously. Science not only describes, it predicts. It deals not only with the past but with the future. Nor is prediction the last word: to the extent that relevant conditions can be altered, or otherwise controlled, the future can be controlled. If we are to use the methods of science in the field of human affairs, we must assume that behavior is lawful and determined. We must expect to discover that what a man does is the result of specifiable conditions and that once these conditions have been discovered, we can anticipate and to some extent determine his actions.

This possibility is offensive to many people. It is opposed to a tradition of long standing which regards man as a free agent, whose behavior is the product, not of specifiable antecedent conditions, but of spontaneous inner changes of course. Prevailing philosophies of human nature recognize an internal "will" which has the power of interfering with causal relationships and which makes the prediction and control of behavior impossible. To suggest that we abandon this view is to threaten many cherished beliefs — to undermine what appears to be a stimulating and productive conception of human nature. The alternative point of view insists upon recognizing coercive forces in human conduct which we may prefer to disregard. It challenges our aspirations, either worldly or otherworldly. Regardless of how much we stand to gain from supposing that human behavior is the proper subject matter of a science, no one who is a product of Western civilization can do so without a struggle. We simply do not want such a science.

Conflicts of this sort are not unknown in

the history of science. When Aesop's lion was shown a painting in which a man was depicted killing a lion, he commented contemptuously, "The artist was obviously a man." Primitive beliefs about man and his place in nature are usually flattering. It has been the unfortunate responsibility of science to paint more realistic pictures. The Copernican theory of the solar system displaced man from his pre-eminent position at the center of things. Today we accept this theory without emotion, but originally it met with enormous resistance. Darwin challenged a practice of segregation in which man set himself firmly apart from the animals, and the bitter struggle which arose is not yet ended. But though Darwin put man in his biological place, he did not deny him a possible position as master. Special faculties or a special capacity for spontaneous, creative action might have emerged in the process of evolution. When that distinction is now questioned, a new threat arises.

There are many ways of hedging on the theoretical issue. It may be insisted that a science of human behavior is impossible, that behavior has certain essential features which forever keep it beyond the pale of science. But although this argument may dissuade many people from further inquiry, it is not likely to have any effect upon those who are willing to try and see. Another objection frequently offered is that science is appropriate up to a certain point, but that there must always remain an area in which one can act only on faith or with respect to a "value judgment": science may tell us *how* to deal with human behavior, but just *what* is to be done must be decided in an essentially nonscientific way. Or it may be argued that there is another kind of science which is compatible with doctrines of personal freedom. For example, the social sciences are sometimes said to be fundamentally different from the natural sciences and not concerned with the same kinds of lawfulness. Prediction and control may be forsworn in favor of "interpretation" or some other species of understanding. But the kinds of intellectual activities exemplified by value judgments or by intuition or interpretation have never been set forth clearly . . . .

Some Important Characteristics of Science

Science is first of all a set of attitudes. It is a disposition to deal with the facts rather than with what someone has said about them. Rejection of authority was the theme of the revival of learning, when men dedicated themselves to the study of "nature, not books." Science rejects even its own authorities when they interfere with the observation of nature.

Science is a willingness to accept facts even when they are opposed to wishes. Thoughtful men have perhaps always known that we are likely to see things as we want to see them instead of as they are, but thanks to Sigmund Freud we are today much more clearly aware of "wishful thinking." The opposite of wishful thinking is intellectual honesty — an extremely important possession of the successful scientist. Scientists are by nature no more honest than other men but, as Bridgman has pointed out, the practice of science puts an exceptionally high premium on honesty. It is characteristic of science that any lack of honesty quickly brings disaster. Consider, for example, a scientist who conducts research to test a theory for which he is already well known. The result may confirm his theory, contradict it, or leave it in doubt. In spite of any inclination to the contrary, he must report a contradiction just as readily as a confirmation. If he does not, someone else will — in a matter of weeks or months or at most a few years — and this will be more damaging to his prestige than if he himself had reported it. Where right and wrong are not so easily or so quickly established, there is no similar pressure. In the long run, the issue is not so much one of personal prestige as of effective procedure. Scientists have simply found that being honest — with oneself as much as with others — is essential to progress. Experiments do not always come out as one expects, but the facts must stand and the expectations fall. The subject matter, not the scientist, knows best. The same practical consequences have created the scientific atmosphere in which statements are constantly submitted to check, where nothing is put above a precise description of the facts, and where facts are accepted no matter how distasteful their momentary consequences.

Scientists have also discovered the value of remaining without an answer until a satisfactory one can be found. This is a difficult lesson. It takes considerable training to avoid premature conclusions, to refrain from making statements on insufficient evidence, and to avoid explanations which are pure invention. Yet the history of science has demonstrated again and again the advantage of these practices.

Science is, of course, more than a set of attitudes. It is a search for order, for uniformities, for lawful relations among the events in nature. It begins, as we all begin, by observing single episodes, but it quickly passes on to the general rule, to scientific law. Something very much like the order expressed in a scientific law appears in our behavior at an early age. We learn the rough geometry of the space in which we move. We learn the "laws of motion" as we move about, or push and pull objects, or throw and catch them. If we could not find some uniformity in the world, our conduct would remain haphazard and ineffective. Science sharpens and supplements this experience by demonstrating more and more relations among events and by demonstrating them more and more precisely. As Ernst Mach showed in tracing the history of the science of mechanics, the earliest laws of science were probably the rules used by craftsmen and artisans in training apprentices. The rules saved time because the experienced craftsman could teach an apprentice a variety of details in a single formula. By learning a rule the apprentice could deal with particular cases as they arose.

In a later stage science advances from the collection of rules or laws to larger systematic arrangements. Not only does it make statements about the world, it makes statements about statements. It sets up a "model" of its subject matter, which helps to generate new rules very much as the rules themselves generate new practices in dealing with single cases. A science may not reach this stage for some time.

The scientific "system," like the law, is designed to enable us to handle a subject matter more efficiently. What we call the scientific conception of a thing is not passive knowledge. Science is not concerned with contemplation. When we have discovered the laws which govern a part of the world about us, and when we have organized these laws into a system, we are then ready to deal effectively with that part of the world. By predicting the occurrence of an event we are able to prepare for it. By arranging conditions in ways specified by the laws of a system, we not only predict, we control: we "cause" an event to occur or to assume certain characteristics.

Behavior as a Scientific Subject Matter

Behavior is not one of those subject matters which become accessible only with the invention of an instrument such as the telescope or microscope. We all know thousands of facts about behavior. Actually there is no subject matter with which we could be better acquainted, for we are always in the presence of at least one behaving organism. But this familiarity is something of a disadvantage, for it means that we have probably jumped to conclusions which will not be supported by the cautious methods of science. Even though we have observed behavior for many years, we are not necessarily able, without help, to express useful uniformities or lawful relations. We may show considerable skill in making plausible guesses about what our friends and acquaintances will do under various circumstances or what we ourselves will do. We may make plausible generalizations about the conduct of people in general. But very few of these will survive careful analysis. A great deal of unlearning generally takes place in our early contact with a science of behavior.

Behavior is a difficult subject matter, not because it is inaccessible, but because it is extremely complex. Since it is a process, rather than a thing, it cannot easily be held still for observation. It is changing, fluid, and evanescent, and for this reason it makes great technical demands upon the ingenuity and energy of the scientist. But there is nothing essentially insoluble about the problems which arise from this fact.

Several kinds of statements about behavior are commonly made. When we tell an anecdote or pass along a bit of gossip, we report a *single event* — what someone did upon such and such an occasion: "She slammed the door and walked off without a word." Our report is a small bit of history. History itself is often nothing more than similar reporting on a broad scale. The biographer often confines himself to a series of episodes in the life of his subject. The case history, which occupies an important place in several fields of psychology, is a kind of biography which is also concerned mainly with what a particular person did at particular times and places: "When she was eleven, Mary went to live with her maiden aunt in Winchester." Novels and short stories may be thought of as veiled biography or history, since the ingredients of even a highly fanciful work of fiction are somehow or other taken from life. The narrative reporting of the behavior of people at particular times and places is also part of the sciences of archeology, ethnology, sociology, and anthropology.

These accounts have their uses. They broaden the experience of those who have not had firsthand access to similar data. But they are only the beginnings of a science. No matter how accurate or quantitative it may be, the report of the single case is only a preliminary step. The next step is the discovery of some sort of *uniformity*. When we tell an anecdote to support an argument, or report a case history to exemplify a principle, we imply a general rule, no matter how vaguely it may be expressed. The historian is seldom content with mere narration. He reports his facts to support a theory — of cycles, trends, or patterns of history. In doing so he passes from the single instance to the rule. When a biographer traces the influence of an early event upon a man's later life, he transcends simple reporting and asserts, no matter how hesitantly, that one thing has caused another. Fable and allegory are more than storytelling if they imply some kind of uniformity in human behavior, as they generally do. Our preference for "consistency of character" and our rejection of implausible coincidences in literature show that we expect lawfulness. The "manners" and "customs" of the sociologist and anthropologist report the *general* behavior of groups of people.

A vague sense of order emerges from any sustained observation of human behavior. Any plausible guess about what a friend will do or say in a given circumstance is a prediction based upon some such uniformity. If a reasonable order was not discoverable, we could scarcely be effective in dealing with human affairs. The methods of science are designed to clarify these uniformities and make them explicit. The techniques of field study of the anthropologist and social psychologist, the procedures of the psychological clinic, and the controlled experimental methods of the laboratory are all directed toward this end, as are also the mathematical and logical tools of science.

Many people interested in human behavior do not feel the need for the standards of proof characteristic of an exact science; the uniformities in behavior are "obvious" without them. At the same time, they are reluctant to accept the conclusions toward which such proof inescapably points if they do not "sense" the uniformity themselves. But these idiosyncrasies are a costly luxury. We need not defend the methods of science in their application to behavior. The experimental and mathematical techniques used in discovering and expressing uniformities are the common property of science in general. Almost every discipline has contributed to this pool of resources, and all disciplines borrow from it. The advantages are well established.

Some Objections to a Science of Behavior

The report of a single event raises no theoretical problems and comes into no conflict with philosophies of human behavior. The scientific laws or systems which express uniformities are likely to conflict with theory because they claim the same territory. When a science of behavior reaches the point of dealing with lawful relationships, it meets the resistance of those who give their allegiance to prescientific or extrascientific conceptions. The resistance does not always take the form of an overt rejection of science. It may be transmuted into claims of limitations, often expressed in highly scientific terms.

It has sometimes been pointed out, for example, that physical science has been unable to maintain its philosophy of determinism, particularly at the subatomic level. The Principle of Indeterminacy states that there are circumstances under which the physicist cannot put himself in possession of all relevant information: if he chooses to observe one event, he must relinquish the possibility of observing another. In our present state of knowledge, certain events therefore appear to be unpredictable. It does not follow that these events are free or capricious. Since human behavior is enormously complex and the human organism is of limited dimensions, many acts may involve processes to which the Principle of Indeterminacy applies. It does not follow that human behavior is free, but only that it may be beyond the range of a predictive or controlling science. Most students of behavior, however, would be willing to settle for the degree of prediction and control achieved by the physical sciences in spite of this limitation. A final answer to the problem of lawfulness is to be sought, not in the limits of any hypothetical mechanism within the organism, but in our ability to demonstrate lawfulness in the behavior of the organism as a whole.

A similar objection has a logical flavor. It is contended that reason cannot comprehend itself or — in somewhat more substantial terms — that the behavior required in understanding one's own behavior must be something beyond the behavior which is understood. It is true that knowledge is limited by the limitations of the knowing organism. The number of things in the world which might be known certainly exceeds the number of possible different states in all possible knowers. But the laws and systems of science are designed to make a knowledge of particular events unimportant. It is by no means necessary that one man should understand all the facts in a given field, but only that he should understand all the *kinds* of facts. We have no reason to suppose that the human intellect is incapable of formulating or comprehending the basic principles of human behavior — certainly not until we have a clearer notion of what those principles are.

The assumption that behavior is a lawful scientific datum sometimes meets with another objection. Science is concerned with the general, but the behavior of the individual is necessarily unique. The "case history" has a richness and flavor which are in decided contrast with general principles. It is easy to convince oneself that there are two distinct worlds and that one is beyond the reach of science. This distinction is not peculiar to the study of behavior. It can always be made in the early stages of any science, when it is not clear what we may deduce from a general principle with respect to a particular case. What the science of physics has to say about the world is dull and colorless to the beginning student when compared with his daily experience, but he later discovers that it is actually a more incisive account of even the single instance. When we wish to deal effectively with the single instance, we turn to science for help. The argument will lose cogency as a science of behavior progresses and as the implications of its general laws become clear. A comparable argument against the possibility of a science of medicine has already lost its significance. In *War and Peace*, Tolstoy wrote of the illness of a favorite character as follows:

> Doctors came to see Natasha, both separately and in consultation. They said a great deal in French, in German, and in Latin. They criticised

one another, and prescribed the most diverse remedies for all the diseases they were familiar with. But it never occurred to one of them to make the simple reflection that they could not understand the disease from which Natasha was suffering, as no single disease can be fully understood in a living person; for every living person has his individual peculiarities and always has his own peculiar, new, complex complaints unknown to medicine — not a disease of the lungs, of the kidneys, of the skin, of the heart, and so on, as described in medical books, but a disease that consists of one out of the innumerable combinations of ailments of those organs.

Tolstoy was justified in calling every sickness a unique event. Every action of the individual is unique, as well as every event in physics and chemistry. But his objection to a science of medicine in terms of uniqueness was unwarranted. The argument was plausible enough at the time; no one could then contradict him by supplying the necessary general principles. But a great deal has happened in medical science since then, and today few people would care to argue that a disease cannot be described in general terms or that a single case cannot be discussed by referring to factors common to many cases. The intuitive wisdom of the old-style diagnostician has been largely replaced by the analytical procedures of the clinic, just as a scientific analysis of behavior will eventually replace the personal interpretation of unique instances.

A similar argument is leveled at the use of statistics in a science of behavior. A prediction of what the *average* individual will do is often of little or no value in dealing with a particular individual. The actuarial tables of life-insurance companies are of no value to a physician in predicting the death or survival of a particular patient. This issue is still alive in the physical sciences, where it is associated with the concepts of causality and probability. It is seldom that the science of physics deals with the behavior of individual molecules, atoms, or subatomic particles. When it is occasionally called upon to do so, all the problems of the particular event arise. In general a science is helpful in dealing with the individual only insofar as its laws refer to individuals. A science of behavior which concerns only the behavior of groups is not likely to be of help in our understanding of the particular case. But a science may also deal with the behavior of the individual, and its success in doing so must be evaluated in terms of its achievements rather than any a priori contentions.

The extraordinary complexity of behavior is sometimes held to be an added source of difficulty. Even though behavior may be lawful, it may be too complex to be dealt with in terms of law. Sir Oliver Lodge once asserted that "though an astronomer can calculate the orbit of a planet or comet or even a meteor, although a physicist can deal with the structure of atoms, and a chemist with their possible combinations, neither a biologist nor any scientific man can calculate the orbit of a common fly." This is a statement about the limitations of scientists or about their aspirations, not about the suitability of a subject matter. Even so, it is wrong. It may be said with some assurance that if no one has calculated the orbit of a fly, it is only because no one has been sufficiently interested in doing so. The tropistic movements of many insects are now fairly well understood, but the instrumentation needed to record the flight of a fly and to give an account of all the conditions affecting it would cost more than the importance of the subject justifies. There is, therefore, no reason to conclude, as the author does, that "an incalculable element of self-determination thus makes its appearance quite low down the animal scale." Self-determination does not follow from complexity. Difficulty in calculating the orbit of the fly does not prove capriciousness, though it may make it impossible to prove anything else. The problems imposed by the complexity of a subject matter must be dealt with as they arise. Apparently hopeless cases often become manageable in time. It is only recently that any sort of lawful account of the weather has been possible. We often succeed in reducing complexity to a reasonable degree by simplifying conditions in the laboratory; but where this is impossible, a statistical analysis may be used to achieve an inferior, but in many ways acceptable, prediction. Certainly no one is prepared to say now what a science of behavior can or cannot accomplish eventually. Advance estimates of the limits of science have generally proved inaccurate. The issue is in the long run pragmatic: we cannot tell until we have tried.

Still another objection to the use of scientific method in the study of human behavior is that behavior is an anomalous subject matter because a prediction made about it may alter it. If we tell a friend that he is going to buy a particular kind of car, he may react to our prediction by buying a different kind. The same effect has been used to explain the failures of public opinion polls. In the presidential election of 1948 it was confidently predicted that a majority of the voters would vote for a candidate who, as it turned out, lost the election. It has been asserted that the electorate reacted to the prediction in a contrary way and that the published prediction therefore had an effect upon the predicted event. But it is by no means necessary that a prediction of behavior be permitted to affect the behaving individual. There may have been practical reasons why the results of the poll in question could not be withheld until after the election, but this would not be the case in a purely scientific endeavor.

There are other ways in which observer and observed interact. Study distorts the thing studied. But there is no special problem here peculiar to human behavior. It is now accepted as a general principle in scientific method that it is necessary to interfere in some degree with any phenomenon in the act of observing it. A scientist may have an effect upon behavior in the act of observing or analyzing it, and he must certainly take this effect into account. But behavior may also be observed with a minimum of interaction between subject and scientist, and this is the case with which one naturally tries to begin.

A final objection deals with the practical application of a scientific analysis. Even if we assume that behavior is lawful and that the methods of science will reveal the rules which govern it, we may be unable to make any technological use of these rules unless certain conditions can be brought under control. In the laboratory many conditions are simplified and irrelevant conditions often eliminated. But of what value are laboratory studies if we must predict and control behavior where a comparable simplification is impossible? It is true that we can gain control over behavior only insofar as we can control the factors responsible for it. What a scientific study does is to enable us to make optimal use of the control we possess. The laboratory simplification reveals the relevance of factors which we might otherwise overlook.

We cannot avoid the problems raised by a science of behavior by simply denying that the necessary conditions can be controlled. In actual fact there is a considerable degree of control over many relevant conditions. In penal institutions and military organizations the control is extensive. We control the environment of the human organism in the nursery and in institutions which care for those to whom the conditions of the nursery remain necessary in later life. Fairly extensive control of conditions relevant to human behavior is maintained in industry in the form of wages and conditions of work, in schools in the form of grades and conditions of work, in commerce by anyone in possession of goods or money, by governmental agencies through the police and military, in the psychological clinic through the consent of the controllee, and so on. A degree of effective control, not so easily identified, rests in the hands of entertainers, writers, advertisers, and propagandists. These controls, which are often all too evident in their practical application, are more than sufficient to permit us to extend the results of a laboratory science to the interpretation of human behavior in daily affairs — for either theoretical or practical purposes. Since a science of behavior will continue to increase the effective use of this control, it is now more important than ever to understand the processes involved and to prepare ourselves for the problems which will certainly arise . . . .

The Variables of Which Behavior is a Function

The practice of looking inside the organism for an explanation of behavior has tended to obscure the variables which are immediately available for a scientific analysis. These variables lie outside the organism, in its immediate environment and in its environmental history. They have a physical status to which the usual techniques of science are adapted, and they make it possible to explain behavior as other subjects are explained in science. These independent variables are of many sorts and their relations to behavior are often subtle and complex, but we cannot hope to give an adequate account of behavior without analyzing them.

Consider the act of drinking a glass of water. This is not likely to be an important bit of behavior in anyone's life, but it supplies a convenient example. We may describe the topography of the behavior in such a way that a given instance may be identified quite accurately by any qualified observer. Suppose now we bring someone into a room and place a glass of water before him. Will he drink? There appear to be only two possibilities: either he will or he will not. But we speak of the *chances* that he will drink, and this notion may be refined for scientific use. What we want to evaluate is the *probability* that he will drink. This may range from virtual certainty that drinking will occur to virtual certainty that it will not. The very considerable problem of how to measure such a probability will be discussed later. For the moment, we are interested in how the probability may be increased or decreased.

Everyday experience suggests several possibilities, and laboratory and clinical observations have added others. It is decidedly not true that a horse may be led to water but cannot be made to drink. By arranging a history of severe deprivation we could be "absolutely sure" that drinking would occur. In the same way we may be sure that the glass of water in our experiment will be drunk. Although we are not likely to arrange them experimentally, deprivations of the necessary magnitude sometimes occur outside the laboratory. We may obtain an effect similar to that of deprivation by speeding up the excretion of water. For example, we may induce sweating by raising the temperature of the room or by forcing heavy exercise, or we may increase the excretion of urine by mixing salt or urea in food taken prior to the experiment. It is also well known that loss of blood, as on a battlefield, sharply increases the probability of drinking. On the other hand, we may set the probability at virtually zero by inducing or forcing our subject to drink a large quantity of water before the experiment.

If we are to predict whether or not our subject will drink, we must know as much as possible about these variables. If we are to induce him to drink, we must be able to manipulate them. In both cases, moreover, either for accurate prediction or control, we must investigate the effect of each variable quantitatively with the methods and techniques of a laboratory science.

Other variables may, of course, affect the result. Our subject may be "afraid" that something has been added to the water as a practical joke or for experimental purposes. He may even "suspect" that the water has been poisoned. He may have grown up in a culture in which water is drunk only when no one is watching. He may refuse to drink simply to prove that we cannot predict or control his behavior. These possibilities do not disprove the relations between drinking and the variables listed in the preceding paragraphs; they simply remind us that other variables may have to be taken into account. We must know the history of our subject with respect to the behavior of drinking water, and if we cannot eliminate social factors from the situation, then we must know the history of his personal relations to people resembling the experimenter. Adequate prediction in any science requires information about all relevant variables, and the control of a subject matter for practical purposes makes the same demands.

Other types of "explanation" do not permit us to dispense with these requirements or to fulfill them in any easier way. It is of no help to be told that our subject will drink provided he was born under a particular sign of the zodiac which shows a preoccupation with water or provided he is the lean and thirsty type or was, in short, "born thirsty." Explanations in terms of inner states or agents, however, may require some further comment. To what extent is it helpful to be told, "He drinks because he is thirsty"? If to be thirsty means nothing more than to have a tendency to drink, this is mere redundancy. If it means that he drinks because of a state of thirst, an inner causal event is invoked. If this state is purely inferential — if no dimensions are assigned to it which would make direct observation possible — it cannot serve as an explanation. But if it has physiological or psychic properties, what role can it play in a science of behavior?

The physiologist may point out that several ways of raising the probability of drinking have a common effect: they increase the concentration of solutions in the body. Through some mechanism not yet well understood, this may bring about a corresponding change in the nervous system which in turn makes drinking more probable. In the same way, it may be argued that all these operations make the organism "feel thirsty" or "want a drink" and that such a psychic state also acts upon the nervous system in some unexplained way to induce drinking. In each case we have a causal chain consisting of three links: (1) an operation performed upon the organism from without — for example, water deprivation; (2) an inner condition — for example, physiological or psychic thirst; and (3) a kind of behavior — for example, drinking. Independent information about the second link would obviously permit us to predict the third without recourse to the first. It would be a preferred type of variable because it would be nonhistoric; the first link may lie in the past history of the organism, but the second is a current condition. Direct information about the second link is, however, seldom, if ever, available. Sometimes we infer the second link from the third: an animal is judged to be thirsty if it drinks. In that case, the explanation is spurious. Sometimes we infer the second link from the first: an animal is said to be thirsty if it has not drunk for a long time. In that case, we obviously cannot dispense with the prior history.

The second link is useless in the *control* of behavior unless we can manipulate it. At the moment, we have no way of directly altering neural processes at appropriate moments in the life of a behaving organism, nor has any way been discovered to alter a psychic process. We usually set up the second link through the first: we make an animal thirsty, in either the physiological or the psychic sense, by depriving it of water, feeding it salt, and so on. In that case, the second link obviously does not permit us to dispense with the first. Even if some new technical discovery were to enable us to set up or change the second link directly, we should still have to deal with those enormous areas in which human behavior is controlled through manipulation of the first link. A technique of operating upon the second link would increase our control of behavior, but the techniques which have already been developed would still remain to be analyzed.

The most objectionable practice is to follow the causal sequence back only as far as a hypothetical second link. This is a serious handicap both in a theoretical science and in the practical control of behavior. It is no help to be told that to get an organism to drink we are simply to "make it thirsty" unless we are also told how this is to be done. When we have obtained the necessary prescription for thirst, the whole proposal is more complex than it need be. Similarly, when an example of maladjusted behavior is explained by saying that the individual is "suffering from anxiety," we have still to be told the cause of the anxiety. But the external conditions which are then invoked could have been directly related to the maladjusted behavior. Again, when we are told that a man stole a loaf of bread because "he was hungry," we have still to learn of the external conditions responsible for the "hunger." These conditions would have sufficed to explain the theft.

The objection to inner states is not that they do not exist, but that they are not relevant in a functional analysis. We cannot account for the behavior of any system while staying wholly inside it; eventually we must turn to forces operating upon the organism from without. Unless there is a weak spot in our causal chain so that the second link is not lawfully determined by the first, or the third by the second, then the first and third links must be lawfully related. If we must always go back beyond the second link for prediction and control, we may avoid many tiresome and exhausting digressions by examining the third link as a function of the first. Valid information about the second link may throw light upon this relationship but can in no way alter it.

A Functional Analysis

The external variables of which behavior is a function provide for what may be called a causal or functional analysis. We undertake to predict and control the behavior of the individual organism. This is our "dependent variable" — the effect for which we are to find the cause. Our "independent variables" — the causes of behavior — are the external conditions of which behavior is a function. Relations between the two — the "cause-and-effect relationships" in behavior — are the laws of a science. A synthesis of these laws expressed in quantitative terms yields a comprehensive picture of the organism as a behaving system.

This must be done within the bounds of a natural science. We cannot assume that behavior has any peculiar properties which require unique methods or special kinds of knowledge. It is often argued that an act is not so important as the "intent" which lies behind it, or that it can be described only in terms of what it "means" to the behaving individual or to others whom it may affect. If statements of this sort are useful for scientific purposes, they must be based upon observable events, and we may confine ourselves to such events exclusively in a functional analysis. We shall see later that although such terms as "meaning" and "intent" appear to refer to properties of behavior, they usually conceal references to independent variables. This is also true of "aggressive," "friendly," "disorganized," "intelligent," and other terms which appear to describe properties of behavior but in reality refer to its controlling relations.

The independent variables must also be described in physical terms. An effort is often made to avoid the labor of analyzing a physical situation by guessing what it "means" to an organism or by distinguishing between the physical world and a psychological world of "experience." This practice also reflects a confusion between dependent and independent variables. The events affecting an organism must be capable of description in the language of physical science. It is sometimes argued that certain "social forces" or the "influences" of culture or tradition are exceptions. But we cannot appeal to entities of this sort without explaining how they can affect both the scientist and the individual under observation. The physical events which must then be appealed to in such an explanation will supply us with alternative material suitable for a physical analysis.

By confining ourselves to these observable events, we gain a considerable advantage, not only in theory, but in practice. A "social force" is no more useful in manipulating behavior than an inner state of hunger, anxiety, or skepticism. Just as we must trace these inner events to the manipulable variables of which they are said to be functions before we may put them to practical use, so we must identify the physical events through which a "social force" is said to affect the organism before we can manipulate it for purposes of control. In dealing with the directly observable data we need not refer to either the inner state or the outer force.

The material to be analyzed in a science of behavior comes from many sources:

(1) Our *casual observations* are not to be dismissed entirely. They are especially important in the early stages of investigation. Generalizations based upon them, even without explicit analysis, supply useful hunches for further study.

(2) In *controlled field observation*, as exemplified by some of the methods of anthropology, the data are sampled more carefully and conclusions stated more explicitly than in casual observation. Standard instruments and practices increase the accuracy and uniformity of field observation.

(3) *Clinical observation* has supplied extensive material. Standard practices in interviewing and testing bring out behavior which may be easily measured, summarized, and compared with the behavior of others. Although it usually emphasizes the disorders which bring people to clinics, the clinical sample is often unusually interesting and of special value when the exceptional condition points up an important feature of behavior.

(4) Extensive observations of behavior have been made under more rigidly controlled conditions in *industrial, military, and other institutional research*. This work often differs from field or clinical observation in its greater use of the experimental method.

(5) *Laboratory studies of human behavior* provide especially useful material. The experimental method includes the use of instruments which improve our contact with behavior and with the variables of which it is a function. Recording devices enable us to observe behavior over long periods of time, and accurate recording and measurement make effective quantitative analysis possible. The most important feature of the laboratory method is the deliberate manipulation of variables: the importance of a given condition is determined by changing it in a controlled fashion and observing the result.

Current experimental research on human behavior is sometimes not so comprehensive as one might wish. Not all behavioral processes are easy to set up in the laboratory, and precision of measurement is sometimes obtained only at the price of unreality in conditions. Those who are primarily concerned with the everyday life of the individual are often impatient with these artificialities, but insofar as relevant relationships can be brought under experimental control, the laboratory offers the best chance of obtaining the quantitative results needed in a scientific analysis.

(6) The extensive results of *laboratory studies of the behavior of animals below the human level* are also available. The use of this material often meets with the objection that there is an essential gap between man and the other animals, and that the results of one cannot be extrapolated to the other. To insist upon this discontinuity at the beginning of a scientific investigation is to beg the question. Human behavior is distinguished by its complexity, its variety, and its greater accomplishments, but the basic processes are not therefore necessarily different. Science advances from the simple to the complex; it is constantly concerned with whether the processes and laws discovered at one stage are adequate for the next. It would be rash to assert at this point that there is no essential difference between human behavior and the behavior of lower species; but until an attempt has been made to deal with both in the same terms, it would be equally rash to assert that there is. A discussion of human embryology makes considerable use of research on the embryos of chicks, pigs, and other animals. Treatises on digestion, respiration, circulation, endocrine secretion, and other physiological processes deal with rats, hamsters, rabbits, and so on, even though the interest is primarily in human beings. The study of behavior has much to gain from the same practice.

We study the behavior of animals because it is simpler. Basic processes are revealed more easily and can be recorded over longer periods of time. Our observations are not complicated by the social relation between subject and experimenter. Conditions may be better controlled. We may arrange genetic histories to control certain variables and special life histories to control others — for example, if we are interested in how an organism learns to see, we can raise an animal in darkness until the experiment is begun. We are also able to control current circumstances to an extent not easily realized in human behavior — for example, we can vary states of deprivation over wide ranges. These are advantages which should not be dismissed on the a priori contention that human behavior is inevitably set apart as a separate field.

II

THE LOGIC of SCIENTIFIC INQUIRY: SOME BASIC ISSUES

The selections just concluded set more issues in motion than they resolve. They raise, in fact, the pivotal questions on which the remaining sections converge: Is there a fundamental dichotomy between the natural and social sciences (see especially parts III, IV, and VIII)? What types of explanations and theories are characteristically provided by social scientists (parts IV and VII)? Can language which refers to the internal dimension of human activity be legitimately replaced by language descriptive of its external aspects (parts V and VI)? There is one problem generated by part I, however, which seems to require more immediate attention than the others, i.e., what sort of enterprise is science itself? One cannot profitably consider whether human behavior is wholly or only partially accessible to scientific explanation without a detailed analysis of the presuppositions, methods, and aims involved in scientific inquiry. But no such analysis appears anywhere in part I.

The following selections should help to repair this omission. The first two are classic expositions of doctrines which have recently held a commanding position within the philosophy of science. (These doctrines, in outline, are just visible in the notion of science assumed above by Skinner: see, for example, his emphasis on prediction and manipulation as essential aims of scientific theory and his contention that if "we are to use the methods of science in the field of human affairs, we must assume that behavior is lawful and determined.") Thus, Hempel and Oppenheim agree with Popper in maintaining (1) that every science seeks to establish empirical laws which can be used to explain and predict specific events or regularities and (2) that there is an essential "unity of method" between the natural and social sciences, in that explanations of human (purposive, social, intentional) conduct must satisfy the same criteria as those advanced to account for tropistic movements or refractive phenomena. Popper sees this unity as involving the dictum (3) that the only way for *any* science to test or reason about the merits of proposed laws is through the "hypothetical-deductive method," that is, by deriving empirical consequences from suggested universal hypotheses and comparing these consequences with the results of direct observation. Hempel and Oppenheim carry their analysis much further — but in a fashion compatible with Popper's assurance that "[scientific] methods always consist in offering deductive causal explanations" — by advancing the following propositions:

(4) Empirical laws like "Water is an optically denser medium than air" and "Alcohol boils at 78.3 degrees C." are falsifiable descriptions of uniformities. They are not analytic statements like "Whatever is mammalian is warm-blooded" or "Every square contains four right angles." Given any empirical law of the form 'Every A is a B', it is always possible to consistently describe an A which is not a B; the term '. . . is a B' forms no part of the meaning assigned to '. . . is an A'. Furthermore, the sole or primary function of laws in scientific inquiry is to serve as major premisses in explanations (or predictions) which have the form described in propositions 5 and 6 below.

(5) No scientific explanation of a particular event E can be acceptable unless it manages to "subsume" E under or deduce it from empirical laws (or statistical correlations), together with statements describing conditions antecedent to E. An explanation of this "covering law" type is designed to establish that, in the stated conditions, the occurrence of E was unavoidable, that under those circumstances there was no way of preventing it. (If statements like "The chances are 3 in 4 that children born of two mongoloid parents will also be mongoloid" are used instead of universal laws, the occurrence of E is shown "to be expected with high inductive probability.") In brief, a necessary condition for the adequacy of any scientific explanation is that the explanans, the "sentences which are adduced to account for the phenomenon," contain at least one universal (or statistical) law.

(6) The only difference between a scientific explanation and a scientific prediction of E is of "a pragmatic character," that is, depends solely on whether E has already occurred at the time we happen to be concerned with it. Explanations of past events and predictions of those to come, if acceptable, have *identical logical forms:* their premisses refer to laws and antecedent conditions and their conclusions describe E and follow necessarily from the premisses (for anyone who accepts the premisses, it is inconsistent to deny that E occurred). Given this symmetry between explanation and prediction, no explanation is tenable unless the laws and conditions to which it appeals "could have served as a basis for predicting the phenomenon in question."

(7) To explain E by the covering law model is much the same as identifying the factor(s) which *caused* E to occur; given that the explanation is acceptable, we have a causal recipe for producing events similar to E, and vice versa. When Hempel and Oppenheim, for example, explain the temporary drop of mercury within a thermometer immersed in hot water by citing the uniformity with which glass tubes expand when heated, this provides us with the causal recipe: "To produce a temporary drop in a mercury column, heat the glass which contains it." Moreover, this recipe can be fruitfully employed only if there is a lawlike connection between the two sorts of events which it mentions.

(8) Proposed explanations of human behavior which do not conform to the covering law model — especially those claiming to express an "empathetic understanding" of human motives or beliefs — will be found to consist in (a) mere description or clarification of the explanandum, i.e., the phenomenon or act to be explained or (b) intuitive hunches whose adequacy, if testable at all, rests on the tacit assumption of universal laws. For example, Collingwood suggests that Caesar's passage across the Rubicon might be explained in terms of the general's "defiance of Republican law." But would such an "explanation" provide anything besides a fuller description of Caesar's act? Can it do more than reveal that the explanandum is not (simply) "Caesar's crossing the Rubicon" but "Caesar's crossing the Rubicon in defiance of Republican law?" If not, the explanandum has been clarified but not explained. However, let us assume that Collingwood's suggestion does provide a genuine explanation. Will this not result from its implicit reliance on some general law like "Military leaders anxious to gain or retain political authority will defy the commands of civilian law-makers?" In other words, either what Collingwood offers merely clarifies, and does not explain, the explanandum, or it can be fitted into the covering law model. (But see here selections 9 and 26 below.) It is a consequence worth noting of propositions 5 and 8 that an action is either voluntary or scientifically explainable, but not both. For a voluntary act is avoidable, in the sense that the agent who performed it could have done otherwise under exactly the same external circumstances.

But for Hempel and Oppenheim, to explain scientifically a piece of conduct is to subsume it under a general law; and this establishes that the act was *not* avoidable under the circumstances.

(9) Concepts referring to a person's intentions, beliefs, attitudes, and feelings (to what Collingwood spoke of as the "inside" aspect of human action), may be translated into physical terms, i.e., into terms which classify acts as similar on the basis of attributes like weight, size, duration, location, and velocity. Such definitions or reductions are legitimate because it is not possible to publicly and directly test propositions containing ordinary "mental" concepts like '. . . is angry' or '. . . prefers blondes to brunettes'. These concepts denote phenomena or states which "are not accessible by an outside observer;" hence, the need for indirect or "operationally determined" methods to decide where and when they apply.

It is these nine propositions, then, which circumscribe the "covering law" position, a position advanced or presupposed by selections 4 and 5 and roundly rejected by both Hanson and Scriven. Hanson's contributions to this attack are focused on propositions 3 and 4. The first, he claims, falsely denies that there is a form of reasoning (which he terms *retroduction*) involved in catching or discovering hypotheses, distinct from that involved in "cooking" or establishing them. Hanson's arguments against proposition 3 appear to have consequences for other portions of the covering law position. For the "conditions of adequacy" specified by Hempel and Oppenheim on page 55 below require that the premisses of acceptable scientific arguments either "deductively imply" or "lend strong inductive support" to their conclusions. But retroduction, as conceived by Peirce and analyzed by Hanson, is a form of argument that (1) provides grounds for the initial proposing, rather than final acceptance, of scientific hypotheses yet (2) is *neither deductive nor inductive.*

Against proposition 4, Hanson displays what he views as an irreducible variety of functions assigned to "laws" by practicing scientists. Fundamental among these is that of shaping new "conceptual frameworks" within which surprising or apparently unrelated data can be organized into intelligible patterns. When a precept like Newton's law of inertia is used in this capacity, it provides neither causal recipes nor a basis for prediction and control. On the contrary, Hanson alleges, it has a function prior to explanation: that of determining what phenomena we count as having actually occurred and which of these requires an explanation. As a result,

> In the ordinary mechanics of middle-sized bodies a statement of the law of inertia is practically invulnerable. It could hardly be false. Whatever proves a body's motion not to be rectilinear also proves that it is acted on by forces. Thus a form of words, 'If A then B', at first used so that what it expresses could be false, comes to express what could not be false. [See page 86 below.]

Scriven's articles offer a full-dress critique of the covering law model and its court of corollaries (in particular, propositions 5 and 8). His objections are sharpened by the introduction of a number of alternative concepts of explanation each of which, Scriven argues, is often used with success in cases where the covering law model breaks down or is inapplicable. Prominent among these is the "selection explanation," which has important connections with one of the most insistent and pivotal disputes in this book. For in Part V, Scriven is to call upon this concept of explanation to argue in favor of Collingwood's assertion, and against Skinner's denial, that a man's behavior can sometimes be adequately explained by referring solely to his beliefs, intentions, and values, i.e., to the internal dimension of his conduct.

The controversy over the covering law position is continued by the two concluding contributions to this section, both of which employ much the same dialectical strategy. Grünbaum defends proposition 6 and Hempel propositions 5 and 8. But both contend that leading objections to these propositions are aimed at doctrines that only resemble but in fact are not elements of the covering law view. Thus, Grünbaum isolates *epistemological* from *logical* symmetry and alleges that Scriven, among others, has attacked the former when he should have been attacking the latter. That is, Scriven's arguments in selection 10, according to Grünbaum, can only show that the conclusion of an adequate explanation is often *known with greater certainty* than the conclusion of a corresponding prediction (epistemological asymmetry). But this leaves intact proposition 6's claim that the *logical relation* between the premisses and conclusion of an acceptable explanation is the same as that between the premisses and conclusion of a justified prediction (logical symmetry). And Hempel insists that his early account (selection 5) was not intended to cover *all* types of explanation. He charges that Scriven objects to propositions 5 and 8 by appealing to explanations outside of science, i.e., in common sense or literary contexts. "The Logic of Explanation," however, did not attempt to clarify the sense carried by "explain" in such sentences as "He is giving an explanation of the difference between categorical and hypothetical imperatives." or "Can you explain to me once more how to avoid Memphis on our trip to St. Louis?" On the contrary, it was designed to analyze only "scientific explanations" and indeed, concentrated exclusively on the "theoretical nonpragmatic" aspects of this subclass.

These tactical moves, however, seem far from conclusive. It may be argued, for example, that if Scriven has misread Hempel, the debt has been repaid. For surely it is Scriven's explicit view that selection explanations, though they do not comply with Hempelian requirements of adequacy, are nonetheless an acceptable form of *scientific* explanation, employed by both natural and social scientists. And Scriven's account of explanations of this type (pages 108–113 and pages 122–125 below) is offered by way of throwing light on their *logical structure*, or their "theoretical nonpragmatic" aspects; that is, it deals with such questions as (1) what kinds of general statements appear in the explanans of selection explanations; (2) how does the relation between the explanans and explanandum in selection explanations differ from that in Hempelian or "derivation" explanations; and (3) what "standards of evidence," to use Scriven's phrase, are characteristically involved in appraising selection explanations. Now in order to show that selection explanations have no force against his analysis of scientific explanation, Hempel must establish that they play no (noneliminable) role in scientific reasoning or that they are never adequate (are always incomplete or inconclusive). But he does not argue for either of these claims, and thus fails to undermine the status of selection explanations as counterexamples to propositions 5 and 8 of the covering law position.[1]

[1] For more detailed discussions of the covering law position and the alternatives to it, see the bibliography for this part.

The Hypothetical-Deductive Method and the Unity of Social and Natural Science

4

from *The Poverty of Historicism*

KARL R. POPPER

The Unity of Method

I suggested in the foregoing section that the deductive methods there analyzed are widely used and important — more so than Mill, for example, ever thought. This suggestion will now be further elaborated, in order to throw some light on the dispute between naturalism and anti-naturalism. In this section I am going to propose a doctrine of the unity of method; that is to say, the view that all theoretical or generalizing sciences make use of the same method, whether they are natural sciences or social sciences. (I postpone the discussion of the historical sciences until section 31.) At the same time, some of these doctrines of historicism which I have not yet sufficiently examined will be touched upon, such as the problems of Generalization; of Essentialism; of the role played by Intuitive Understanding; of the Inexactitude of Prediction; of Complexity; and of the application of Quantitative Methods.

I do not intend to assert that there are no differences whatever between the methods of the theoretical sciences of nature and of society; such differences clearly exist, even between the various natural sciences themselves, as well as between the various social sciences. (Compare, for example, the analysis of competitive markets and of Romance languages.) But I agree with Comte and Mill — and with many others, such as C. Menger — that the methods in the two fields are fundamentally the same (though the methods I have in mind may differ from those they had in mind). The methods always consist in offering deductive causal explanations, and in testing them (by way of predictions). This has sometimes been called the hypothetical-deductive method,[1] or more often the method of hypothesis, for it does not achieve absolute certainty for any of the scientific statements which it tests; rather, these statements always retain the character of tentative hypotheses, even though their character of tentativeness may cease to be obvious after they have passed a great number of severe tests.

Because of their tentative or provisional character, hypotheses were considered, by most students of method, as *provisional in the sense that they have ultimately to be replaced by proved theories* (or at least by theories which can be proved to be 'highly probable', in the sense of some calculus of probabilities). I believe that this view is mistaken and that it leads to a host of entirely unnecessary diffi-

From *The Poverty of Historicism* by Karl R. Popper, Torchbook edition, Harper & Row, Publishers, New York, and Routledge & Kegan Paul, Ltd., London, pp. 130–143.

[1] See V. Kraft, *Die Grundformen der wissenschaftlichen Methoden* (1925).

culties. But this problem[2] is of comparatively little moment here. What is important is to realize that in science we are always concerned with explanations, predictions, and tests, and that the method of testing hypotheses is always the same (see the foregoing section). From the hypothesis to be tested — for example, a universal law — together with some other statements which for this purpose are not considered as problematic — for example, some initial conditions — we deduce some prognosis. We then confront this prognosis, whenever possible, with the results of experimental or other observations. Agreement with them is taken as corroboration of the hypothesis, though not as final proof; clear disagreement is considered as refutation or falsification.

According to this analysis, there is no great difference between explanation, prediction and testing. The difference is not one of logical structure, but rather one of emphasis; it depends on *what we consider to be our problem* and what we do not so consider. If it is not our problem to find a prognosis, while we take it to be our problem to find the initial conditions or some of the universal laws (or both) from which we may deduce a *given* 'prognosis', then we are looking for an *explanation* (and the given 'prognosis' becomes our 'explicandum'). If we consider the laws and initial conditions as given (rather than as to be found) and use them merely for deducing the prognosis, in order to get thereby some new information, then we are trying to make a *prediction*. (This is a case in which we *apply* our scientific results.) And if we consider one of the premises, i.e. either a universal law or an initial condition, as problematic, and the prognosis as something to be compared with the results of experience, then we speak of a *test* of the problematic premise.

The result of tests is the *selection* of hypotheses which have stood up to tests, or the *elimination* of those hypotheses which have not

[2] See my *Logic of Scientific Discovery*, on which the present section is based, especially the doctrine of tests by way of deduction ('deductivism') and of the redundancy of any further 'induction', since theories always retain their hypothetical character ('hypotheticism'), and the doctrine that scientific tests are genuine attempts to falsify theories ('eliminationism'); see also the discussion of testability and falsifiability.

The opposition here pointed out, between *deductivism* and *inductivism*, corresponds in some respects to the classical distinction between *rationalism* and *empiricism:* Descartes was a deductivist, since he conceived all sciences as deductive systems, while the English empiricists, from Bacon on, all conceived the sciences as collecting observations from which generalizations are obtained by induction.

But Descartes believed that the principles, the premises of the deductive systems, must be secure and self-evident — 'clear and distinct'. They are based upon the insight of reason. (They are synthetic and *a priori* valid, in Kantian language.) As opposed to this, I conceive them as tentative conjectures, or hypotheses.

These hypotheses, I contend, must be refutable in principle: it is here that I deviate from the two greatest modern deductivists, Henri Poincaré and Pierre Duhem.

Poincaré and Duhem both recognized the impossibility of conceiving the theories of physics as inductive generalizations. They realized that the observational measurements which form the alleged starting point for the generalizations are, on the contrary, *interpretations in the light of theories*. And they rejected not only inductivism, but also the rationalistic belief in synthetic *a priori* valid principles or axioms. Poincaré interpreted them as analytically true, as definitions; Duhem interpreted them as instruments (as did Cardinal Bellarmino and Bishop Berkeley), as means for the ordering of the experimental laws — the experimental laws which, he thought, were obtained by induction. Theories thus cannot contain either true or false information: they are nothing but instruments, since they can only be convenient or inconvenient, economical or uneconomical; supple and subtle, or else creaking and crude. (Thus, Duhem says, following Berkeley, there cannot be logical reasons why two or more theories which contradict one another should not all be accepted.) I fully agree with both these great authors in rejecting inductivism as well as the belief in the synthetic *a priori* validity of physical theories. But I cannot accept their view that it is impossible to submit theoretical systems to empirical tests. Some of them are testable, I think; that is, refutable in principle; and they are therefore synthetic (rather than analytic); *empirical* (rather than *a priori*); and *informative* (rather than purely instrumental). As to Duhem's famous criticism of crucial experiments, he only shows that crucial experiments can never *prove* or establish a theory; but he nowhere shows that crucial experiments cannot *refute* a theory. Admittedly, Duhem is right when he says that we can test only huge and complex theoretical systems rather than isolated hypotheses; but if we test two such systems which differ in one hypothesis only, and if we can design experiments which refute the first system while leaving the second very well corroborated, then we may be on reasonably safe ground if we attribute the failure of the first system to that hypothesis in which it differs from the other.

stood up to them, and which are therefore rejected. It is important to realize the consequences of this view. They are these: all tests can be interpreted as attempts to weed out false theories — to find the weak points of a theory in order to reject it if it is falsified by the test. This view is sometimes considered paradoxical; our aim, it is said, is to establish theories, not to eliminate false ones. But just because it is our aim to establish theories as well as we can, we must test them as severely as we can; that is, we must try to find fault with them, we must try to falsify them. Only if we cannot falsify them in spite of our best efforts can we say that they have stood up to severe tests. This is the reason why the discovery of instances which confirm a theory means very little if we have not tried, and failed, to discover refutations. For if we are uncritical we shall always find what we want: we shall look for, and find, confirmations, and we shall look away from, and not see, whatever might be dangerous to our pet theories. In this way it is only too easy to obtain what appears to be overwhelming evidence in favour of a theory which, if approached critically, would have been refuted. In order to make the method of selection by elimination work, and to ensure that only the fittest theories survive, their struggle for life must be made severe.

This, in outline, is the method of all sciences which are backed by experience. But what about the method by which we *obtain* our theories or hypotheses? What about *inductive generalizations*, and the way in which we proceed from observation to theory? To this question (and to the doctrines discussed in section 1, so far as they have not been dealt with in section 26) I shall give two answers. (*a*) I do not believe that we ever make inductive generalizations in the sense that we start with observations and try to derive our theories from them. I believe that the prejudice that we proceed in this way is a kind of optical illusion, and that at no stage of scientific development do we begin without something in the nature of a theory, such as a hypothesis, or a prejudice, or a problem — often a technological one — which in some way *guides* our observations, and helps us to select from the innumerable objects of observation those which may be of interest.[3] But if this is so, then the method of elimination — which is nothing but that of trial and error discussed in section 24 — can always be applied. However, I do not think that it is necessary for our present discussion to insist upon this point. For we can say (*b*) that it is irrelevant from the point of view of science whether we have obtained our theories by jumping to unwarranted conclusions or merely by stumbling over them (that is, by 'intuition'), or else by some inductive procedure. The question, 'How did you first *find* your theory?' relates, as it were, to an entirely private matter, as opposed to the question, 'How did you *test* your theory?' which alone is scientifically relevant. And the method of testing described here is fertile; it leads to new observations, and to a mutual give and take between theory and observation.

Now all this, I believe, is not only true for the natural but also for the social sciences. And in the social sciences it is even more obvious than in the natural sciences that we cannot see and observe our objects before we have thought about them. For most of the objects of social science, if not all of them, are abstract objects; they are *theoretical* constructions. (Even 'the war' or 'the army' are abstract concepts, strange as this may sound to some. What is concrete is the many who are killed; or the men and women in uniform, etc.) These objects, these theoretical constructions used to interpret our experience, are the result of constructing certain *models* (especially of institutions), in order to explain certain experiences — a familiar theoretical method in the natural sciences (where we construct our models of atoms, molecules, solids, liquids, etc.). It is part of the method of explanation by way of reduction, or deduc-

[3] For a surprising example of the way in which even botanical observations are guided by theory (and in which they may be even influenced by prejudice), see O. Frankel, 'Cytology and Taxonomy of Hebe, etc.', in *Nature*, vol. 147 (1941), p. 117.

tion from hypotheses. Very often we are unaware of the fact that we are operating with hypotheses or theories, and we therefore mistake our theoretical models for concrete things. This is a kind of mistake which is only too common.[4] The fact that models are often used in this way explains — and by so doing destroys — the doctrines of methodological essentialism (cp. section 10). It explains them, for the model is abstract or theoretical in character, and so we are liable to feel that we see it, either within or behind the changing observable events, as a kind of permanent ghost or essence. And it destroys them because the task of social theory is to construct and to analyse our sociological models carefully in descriptive or nominalist terms, that is to say, *in terms of individuals*, of their attitudes, expectations, relations, etc. — a postulate which may be called 'methodological individualism'.

The unity of the methods of the natural and social sciences may be illustrated and defended by an analysis of two passages from Professor Hayek's *Scientism and the Study of Society*.[5] In the first passage, Professor Hayek writes:

'The physicist who wishes to understand the problems of the social sciences with the help of an analogy from his own field would have to imagine a world in which he knew by direct observation the inside of the atoms and had neither the possibility of making experiments with lumps of matter nor the opportunity to observe more than the interactions of a comparatively few atoms during a limited period. From his knowledge of the different kinds of atoms he could build up models of all the various ways in which they could combine into larger units and make these models more and more closely reproduce all the features of the few instances in which he was able to observe more complex phenomena. But the laws of the macrocosm which he could derive from his knowledge of the microcosm would always remain "*deductive*"; they would, because of his limited knowledge of the data of the complex situation, scarcely ever enable him to predict the precise outcome of a particular situation; and he could never verify them by controlled experiment — although they might be *disproved* by the observation of events which according to his theory are impossible'.

I admit that the first sentence of this passage points to certain differences between social and physical science. But the rest of the passage, I believe, speaks for a complete *unity of method*. For if, as I do not doubt, this is a correct description of the method of social science, then it shows that it differs only from such interpretations of the method of natural science as we have already rejected. I have in mind, more especially, the 'inductivist' interpretation which holds that in the natural sciences we proceed systematically from observation to theory by some method of generalization, and that we can 'verify', or perhaps even prove, our theories by some method of induction. I have been advocating a very different view here — an interpretation of scientific method as deductive, hypothetical, selective by way of falsification, etc. And this description of the method of natural science agrees perfectly with Professor Hayek's description of the method of social science. (I have every reason to believe that my interpretation of the methods of science was not influenced by any knowledge of the methods of the social sciences; for when I developed it first, I had only the natural sciences in mind,[6] and I knew next to nothing about the social sciences.)

But even the differences alluded to in the first sentence of the quotation are not so great as may appear at first sight. It is undoubtedly true that we have a more direct knowledge of the 'inside of the human atom' than we have

[4] With this and the following paragraph, cp. F. A. von Hayek, 'Scientism and the Study of Society', parts I and II, *Economica*, vols. ix and x, where methodological collectivism is criticized and where methodological individualism is discussed in detail.

[5] For the two passages see *Economica*, vol. IX, p. 289 f. (italics mine).

[6] Cp. *Erkenntnis*, III, p. 426 f., and my *Logik der Forschung*, 1935, whose sub-title may be translated: 'On the Epistemology of the Natural Sciences'.

of physical atoms; but this knowledge is intuitive. In other words, we certainly use our knowledge of ourselves in order to frame *hypotheses* about some other people, or about all people. But these hypotheses must be tested, they must be submitted to the method of selection by elimination. (Intuition prevents some people from even imagining that anybody can possibly dislike chocolate.) The physicist, it is true, is not helped by such direct observation when he frames his hypotheses about atoms; nevertheless, he quite often uses some kind of sympathetic imagination or intuition which may easily make him feel that he is intimately acquainted with even the 'inside of the atoms' — with even their whims and prejudices. But this intuition is his private affair. Science is interested only in the hypotheses which his intuitions may have inspired, and then only if these are rich in consequences, and if they can be properly tested. (For the other difference mentioned in Professor Hayek's first sentence, i.e. the difficulty of conducting experiments, see section 24.)

These few remarks may also indicate the way in which the historicist doctrine expounded in section 8 should be criticized — that is to say, the doctrine that social science must use the method of intuitive understanding.

In the second passage, speaking of social phenomena, Professor Hayek says: '. . . our knowledge of the principle by which these phenomena are produced will rarely if ever enable us to predict the precise result of any *concrete* situation. While we can explain the principle on which certain phenomena are produced and can from this knowledge *exclude the possibility of certain results*, e.g. of certain events occurring together, our knowledge will in a sense be only negative, i.e. it will merely enable us to preclude certain results but not enable us to narrow the range of possibilities sufficiently so that only one remains'.

This passage, far from describing a situation peculiar to the social sciences, perfectly describes the character of natural laws which, indeed, can never do more than *exclude certain possibilities*. ('You cannot carry water in a sieve'; see section 20, above.) More especially the statement that we shall not, as a rule, be able 'to predict the precise result of any *concrete* situation' opens up the problem of the inexactitude of prediction (see section 5, above). I contend that precisely the same may be said of the concrete physical world. In general it is only by the use of artificial experimental isolation that we can predict physical events. (The solar system is an exceptional case — one of natural, not of artificial isolation; once its isolation is destroyed by the intrusion of a foreign body of sufficient size, all our forecasts are liable to break down.) We are very far from being able to predict, even in physics, the precise results of a *concrete* situation, such as a thunderstorm, or a fire.

A very brief remark may be added here on the problem of complexity (see section 4, above). There is no doubt that the analysis of any concrete social situation is made extremely difficult by its complexity. But the same holds for any concrete physical situation.[7] The widely held prejudice that social situations are more complex than physical ones seems to arise from two sources. One of them is that we are liable to compare what should not be compared; I mean on the one hand concrete social situations and on the other hand artificially insulated experimental physical situations. (The latter might be compared, rather, with an artificially insulated social situation — such as a prison, or an experimental community.) The other source is the old belief that the description of a social situation should involve the mental and perhaps even physical states of everybody concerned (or perhaps that it should even be reducible to them). But this belief is not justified; it is much less justified even than the impossible demand that the description of a concrete chemical reaction should involve that of the atomic and sub-atomic states of all the elementary particles involved (although chemistry may indeed be reducible to physics). The belief also shows traces of

[7] A somewhat similar argument can be found in C. Menger, *Collected Works*, vol. II (1883 and 1933), pp. 259–60.

the popular view that social entities such as institutions or associations are concrete natural entities such as crowds of men, rather than abstract models constructed to interpret certain selected abstract relations between individuals.

But in fact, there are good reasons, not only for the belief that social science is less complicated than physics, but also for the belief that concrete social situations are in general less complicated than concrete physical situations. For in most social situations, if not in all, there is an element of *rationality*. Admittedly, human beings hardly ever act quite rationally (i.e. as they would if they could make the optimal use of all available information for the attainment of whatever ends they may have), but they act, none the less, more or less rationally; and this makes it possible to construct comparatively simple models of their actions and inter-actions, and to use these models as approximations.

The last point seems to me, indeed, to indicate a considerable difference between the natural and the social sciences — perhaps *the most important difference in their methods*, since the other important differences, i.e. specific difficulties in conducting experiments (see end of section 24) and in applying quantitative methods (see below), are differences of degree rather than of kind. I refer to the possibility of adopting, in the social sciences, what may be called the method of logical or rational construction, or perhaps the 'zero method'.[8] By this I mean the method of constructing a model on the assumption of complete rationality (and perhaps also on the assumption of the possession of complete information) on the part of all the individuals concerned, and of estimating the deviation of the actual behaviour of people from the model behaviour, using the latter as a kind of zero co-ordinate.[9] An example of this method is the comparison between actual behaviour (under the influence of, say, traditional prejudice, etc.) and model behaviour to be expected on the basis of the 'pure logic of choice', as described by the equations of economics. Marschak's interesting 'Money Illusion', for example, may be interpreted in this way.[10] An attempt at applying the zero method to a different field may be found in P. Sargant Florence's comparison between the 'logic of large-scale operation' in industry and the 'illogic of actual operation'.[11]

In passing I should like to mention that neither the principle of methodological individualism, nor that of the zero method of constructing rational models, implies in my opinion the adoption of a psychological method. On the contrary, I believe that these principles can be combined with the view[12] that the social sciences are comparatively independent of psychological assumptions, and that psychology can be treated, not as the basis of all social sciences, but as one social science among others.

In concluding this section, I have to mention what I consider to be the other main difference between the methods of some of the theoretical sciences of nature and of society. I mean the specific difficulties connected with the application of quantitative methods, and especially methods of measurement.[13] Some of these difficulties can be, and have been, overcome by the application of statistical methods, for example in demand analysis. And they *have to be overcome* if, for example, some of the equations of mathematical economics are to provide a basis even of merely qualitative applications; for without such measurement we should often not

[8] See the 'null hypothesis' discussed in J. Marschak, 'Money Illusion and Demand Analysis', in *The Review of Economic Statistics*, vol. XXV, p. 40. — The method described here seems partly to coincide with what has been called by Professor Hayek, following C. Menger, the 'compositive' method.

[9] Even here it may be said, perhaps, that the use of rational or 'logical' models in the social sciences, or of the 'zero method', has some vague parallel in the natural sciences, especially in thermodynamics and in biology (the construction of mechanical models, and of physiological models of processes and of organs). (Cp. also the use of variational methods.)

[10] See J. Marschak, *op. cit.*

[11] See P. Sargant Florence, *The Logic of Industrial Organisations* (1933).

[12] This view is more fully developed in ch. 14 of my *Open Society*.

[13] These difficulties are discussed by Professor Hayek, *op. cit.*, p. 290 f.

know whether or not some counteracting influences exceeded an effect calculated in merely qualitative terms. Thus merely qualitative considerations may well be deceptive at times; just as deceptive, to quote Professor Frisch, 'as to say that when a man tries to row a boat forward, the boat will be driven backward because of the pressure exerted by his feet'.[14] But it cannot be doubted that there are some fundamental difficulties here. In physics, for example, the parameters of our equations can, in principle, be reduced to a small number of natural constants — a reduction which has been successfully carried out in many important cases. This is not so in economics; here the parameters are themselves in the most important cases quickly changing variables.[15] This clearly reduces the significance, interpretability, and testability of our measurements.

[14] See *Econometrica*, I (1933), p. 1 f.

[15] See Lionel Robbins, in Economica, vol. V, especially p. 351.

The Covering Law Analysis of Scientific Explanation 5

from *The Logic of Explanation*

CARL G. HEMPEL
and PAUL OPPENHEIM[1]

INTRODUCTION

To explain the phenomena in the world of our experience, to answer the question "why?" rather than only the question "what?", is one of the foremost objectives of all rational inquiry; and especially, scientific research in its various branches strives to go beyond a mere description of its subject matter by providing an explanation of the phenomena it investigates. While there is rather general agreement about this chief objective of science, there exists considerable difference of opinion as to the function and the essential characteristics of scientific explanation. In the present essay, an attempt will be made to shed some light on these issues by means of an elementary survey of the basic pattern of scientific explanation and a subsequent more rigorous analysis of the concept of law and of the logical structure of explanatory arguments.

The elementary survey is presented in Part I of this article; Part II contains an analysis of the concept of emergence; in Part III, an attempt is made to exhibit and to clarify in a more rigorous manner some of the peculiar and perplexing logical problems to which the familiar elementary analysis of explanation gives rise.

Elementary Survey of Scientific Explanation

SOME ILLUSTRATIONS

A mercury thermometer is rapidly immersed in hot water; there occurs a temporary drop of the mercury column, which is then followed by a swift rise. How is this phenomenon to be explained? The increase in temperature affects at first only the glass tube of the thermometer; it expands and thus provides a larger space for the mercury inside, whose surface therefore drops. As soon as by heat conduction the rise in temperature reaches the mercury, however, the latter expands, and as its coefficient of expansion is considerably larger than that of glass, a rise of the mercury level results. — This account consists of statements of two kinds. Those of the first kind indicate certain conditions which are realized prior to, or at the same time as, the phenomenon to be explained; we shall refer to them briefly as antecedent con-

From *Philosophy of Science*, 15:2 (April, 1948), pp. 135–146, 152–157, and 172–174.

[1] This paper represents the outcome of a series of discussions among the authors; their individual contributions cannot be separated in detail. The technical developments contained in Part IV, however, are due to the first author, who also put the article into its final form. [Part IV omitted in this reprinting.]

Some of the ideas presented in Part II were suggested by our common friend, Kurt Grelling, who, together with his wife, became a victim of Nazi terror during the war. Those ideas were developed by Grelling in a discussion, by correspondence with the present authors, of emergence and related concepts. By including at least some of that material, which is indicated in the text, in the present paper, we feel that we are realizing the hope expressed by Grelling that his contributions might not entirely fall into oblivion.

We wish to express our thanks to Dr. Rudolf Carnap, Dr. Herbert Feigl, Dr. Nelson Goodman, and Dr. W. V. Quine for stimulating discussions and constructive criticism.

ditions. In our illustration, the antecedent conditions include, among others, the fact that the thermometer consists of a glass tube which is partly filled with mercury, and that it is immersed into hot water. The statements of the second kind express certain general laws; in our case, these include the laws of the thermic expansion of mercury and of glass, and a statement about the small thermic conductivity of glass. The two sets of statements, if adequately and completely formulated, explain the phenomenon under consideration: They entail the consequence that the mercury will first drop, then rise. Thus, the event under discussion is explained by subsuming it under general laws, i.e., by showing that it occurred in accordance with those laws, by virtue of the realization of certain specified antecedent conditions.

Consider another illustration. To an observer in a row boat, that part of an oar which is under water appears to be bent upwards. The phenomenon is explained by means of general laws — mainly the law of refraction and the law that water is an optically denser medium than air — and by reference to certain antecedent conditions — especially the facts that part of the oar is in the water, part in the air, and that the oar is practically a straight piece of wood. — Thus, here again, the question "*Why* does the phenomenon happen?" is construed as meaning "according to what general laws, and by virtue of what antecedent conditions does the phenomenon occur?"

So far, we have considered exclusively the explanation of particular events occurring at a certain time and place. But the question "Why?" may be raised also in regard to general laws. Thus, in our last illustration, the question might be asked: Why does the propagation of light conform to the law of refraction? Classical physics answers in terms of the undulatory theory of light, i.e. by stating that the propagation of light is a wave phenomenon of a certain general type, and that all wave phenomena of that type satisfy the law of refraction. Thus, the explanation of a general regularity consists in subsuming it under another, more comprehensive regularity, under a more general law. — Similarly, the validity of Galileo's law for the free fall of bodies near the earth's surface can be explained by deducing it from a more comprehensive set of laws, namely Newton's laws of motion and his law of gravitation, together with some statements about particular facts, namely the mass and the radius of the earth.

THE BASIC PATTERN OF SCIENTIFIC EXPLANATION

From the preceding sample cases let us now abstract some general characteristics of scientific explanation. We divide an explanation into two major constituents, the explanandum and the explanans.[2] By the explanandum, we understand the sentence describing the phenomenon to be explained (not that phenomenon itself); by the explanans, the class of those sentences which are adduced to account for the phenomenon. As was noted before, the explanans falls into two subclasses; one of these contains certain sentences C_1, $C_2, \ldots, C_k$ which state specific antecedent conditions; the other is a set of sentences $L_1, L_2, \ldots L_r$ which represent general laws.

If a proposed explanation is to be sound, its constituents have to satisfy certain conditions of adequacy, which may be divided into logical and empirical conditions. For the following discussion, it will be sufficient to formulate these requirements in a slightly vague manner; in Part III, a more rigorous analysis and a more precise restatement of these criteria will be presented.

I. *Logical conditions of adequacy*

(R1) The explanandum must be a logical consequence of the explanans; in other words, the explanandum must

[2] These two expressions, derived from the Latin *explanare*, were adopted in preference to the perhaps more customary terms "explicandum" and "explicans" in order to reserve the latter for use in the context of explication of meaning, or analysis. On explication in this sense, cf. Carnap [Concepts], p. 513. — Abbreviated titles in brackets refer to the bibliography at the end of this article.

be logically deducible from the information contained in the explanans, for otherwise, the explanans would not constitute adequate grounds for the explanandum.

(R2) The explanans must contain general laws, and these must actually be required for the derivation of the explanandum. — We shall not make it a necessary condition for a sound explanation, however, that the explanans must contain at least one statement which is not a law; for, to mention just one reason, we would surely want to consider as an explanation the derivation of the general regularities governing the motion of double stars from the laws of celestial mechanics, even though all the statements in the explanans are general laws.

(R3) The explanans must have empirical content; i.e., it must be capable, at least in principle, of test by experiment or observation. — This condition is implicit in (R1); for since the explanandum is assumed to describe some empirical phenomenon, it follows from (R1) that the explanans entails at least one consequence of empirical character, and this fact confers upon it testability and empirical content. But the point deserves special mention because, as will be seen in §4, certain arguments which have been offered as explanations in the natural and in the social sciences violate this requirement.

II. *Empirical condition of adequacy*

(R4) The sentences constituting the explanans must be true.

That in a sound explanation, the statements constituting the explanans have to satisfy some condition of factual correctness is obvious. But it might seem more appropriate to stipulate that the explanans has to be highly confirmed by all the relevant evidence available rather than that it should be true. This stipulation however, leads to awkward consequences. Suppose that a certain phenomenon was explained at an earlier stage of science, by means of an explanans which was well supported by the evidence then at hand, but which had been highly disconfirmed by more recent empirical findings. In such a case, we would have to say that originally the explanatory account was a correct explanation, but that it ceased to be one later, when unfavorable evidence was discovered. This does not appear to accord with sound common usage, which directs us to say that on the basis of the limited initial evidence, the truth of the explanans, and thus the soundness of the explanation, had been quite probable, but that the ampler evidence now available made it highly probable that the explanans was not true, and hence that the account in question was not — and had never been — a correct explanation. (A similar point will be made and illustrated, with respect to the requirement of truth for laws, in the beginning of §6.)

Some of the characteristics of an explanation which have been indicated so far may be summarized in the following schema:

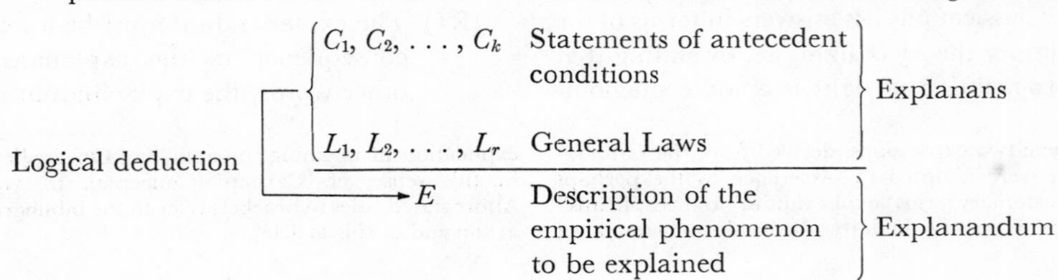

Let us note here that the same formal analysis, including the four necessary conditions, applies to scientific prediction as well as to explanation. The difference between the two is of a pragmatic character. If E is given, i.e. if we know that the phenomenon described by E has occurred, and a suitable set of statements $C_1, C_2, \ldots, C_k, L_1, L_2. \ldots, L_r$ is provided afterwards, we speak of an explanation of the phenomenon in question. If the latter statements are given and E is derived prior to the occurrence of the phenomenon it describes, we speak of a prediction. It may be said, therefore, that an explanation is not fully adequate unless its explanans, if taken account of in time, could have served as a basis for predicting the phenomenon under consideration.[3] — Consequently, whatever will be said in this article concerning the logical characteristics of explanation or prediction will be applicable to either, even if only one of them should be mentioned.

It is this potential predictive force which gives scientific explanation its importance: only to the extent that we are able to explain empirical facts can we attain the major objective of scientific research, namely not merely to record the phenomena of our experience, but to learn from them, by basing upon them theoretical generalizations which enable us to anticipate new occurrences and to control, at least to some extent, the changes in our environment.

Many explanations which are customarily offered, especially in prescientific discourse, lack this predictive character, however. Thus, it may be explained that a car turned over on the road "because" one of its tires blew out while the car was travelling at high speed. Clearly, on the basis of just this information, the accident could not have been predicted, for the explanans provides no explicit general laws by means of which the prediction might be effected, nor does it state adequately the antecedent conditions which would be needed for the prediction. — The same point may be illustrated by reference to W. S. Jevons's view that every explanation consists in pointing out a resemblance between facts, and that in some cases this process may require no reference to laws at all and "may involve nothing more than a single identity, as when we explain the appearance of shooting stars by showing that they are identical with portions of a comet".[4] But clearly, this identity does not provide an explanation of the phenomenon of shooting stars unless we presuppose the laws governing the development of heat and light as the effect of friction. The observation of similarities has explanatory value only if it involves at least tacit reference to general laws.

In some cases, incomplete explanatory arguments of the kind here illustrated suppress parts of the explanans simply as "obvious"; in other cases, they seem to involve the assumption that while the missing parts are not obvious, the incomplete explanans could at least, with appropriate effort, be so supplemented as to make a strict derivation of the explanandum possible. This assumption may be justifiable in some cases, as when we say that a lump of sugar disappeared "because" it was put into hot tea, but it is surely not satisfied in many other cases. Thus, when certain peculiarities in the work of an artist are explained as outgrowths of a specific type of neurosis, this observation may contain significant clues, but in general it does not afford a sufficient basis for a potential prediction of those peculiarities. In cases of this kind, an incomplete explanation may at best be considered as indicating some positive correlation between the antecedent conditions adduced and the type of phenomenon to be explained, and as pointing out a direction in which further research might be carried on in order to complete the explanatory account.

The type of explanation which has been considered here so far is often referred to as causal explanation. If E describes a particular event, then the antecedent circumstances de-

[3] The logical similarity of explanation and prediction, and the fact that one is directed towards past occurrences, the other towards future ones, is well expressed in the terms "postdictability" and "predictability" used by Reichenbach in [Quantum Mechanics], p. 13.

[4] [Principles], p. 533.

scribed in the sentences $C_1, C_2, \ldots, C_k$ may be said jointly to "cause" that event, in the sense that there are certain empirical regularities, expressed by the laws $L_1, L_2, \ldots, L_r$, which imply that whenever conditions of the kind indicated by $C_1, C_2, \ldots, C_k$ occur, an event of the kind described in E will take place. Statements such as $L_1, L_2, \ldots, L_r$, which assert general and unexceptional connections between specified characteristics of events, are customarily called causal, or deterministic laws. They are to be distinguished from the so-called statistical laws which assert that in the long run, an explicitly stated percentage of all cases satisfying a given set of conditions are accompanied by an event of a certain specified kind. Certain cases of scientific explanation involve "subsumption" of the explanandum under a set of laws of which at least some are statistical in character. Analysis of the peculiar logical structure of that type of subsumption involves difficult special problems. The present essay will be restricted to an examination of the causal type of explanation, which has retained its significance in large segments of contemporary science, and even in some areas where a more adequate account calls for reference to statistical laws.[5]

[5] The account given above of the general characteristics of explanation and prediction in science is by no means novel; it merely summarizes and states explicitly some fundamental points which have been recognized by many scientists and methodologists.

Thus, e.g., Mill says: "An individual fact is said to be explained by pointing out its cause, that is, by stating the law or laws of causation of which its production is an instance", and "a law of uniformity in nature is said to be explained when another law or laws are pointed out, of which that law itself is but a case, and from which it could be deduced." ([Logic], Book III, Chapter XII, section 1.) Similarly, Jevons, whose general characterization of explanation was critically discussed above, stresses that "the most important process of explanation consists in showing that an observed fact is one case of a general law or tendency." ([Principles], p. 533.) Ducasse states the same point as follows: "Explanation essentially consists in the offering of a hypothesis of fact, standing to the fact to be explained as case of antecedent to case of consequent of some already known law of connection." ([Explanation], pp. 150–51.) A lucid analysis of the fundamental structure of explanation and prediction was given by Popper in [Forschung], section 12, and, in an improved version, in his work [Society], especially in Chapter 25 and in note 7 referring to that chapter. — For a recent characterization of explanation as subsumption under general theories, cf., for example, Hull's concise discussion in [Principles], chapter I. A clear elementary examination of certain aspects of explanation is given in Hospers [Explanation], and a concise survey of many of the essentials of scientific explanation which are considered in the first two parts of the present study may be found in Feigl [Operationism], pp. 284ff.

EXPLANATION IN THE NON-PHYSICAL SCIENCES. MOTIVATIONAL AND TELEOLOGICAL APPROACHES

Our characterization of scientific explanation is so far based on a study of cases taken from the physical sciences. But the general principles thus obtained apply also outside this area.[6] Thus, various types of behavior in laboratory animals and in human subjects are explained in psychology by subsumption under laws or even general theories of learning or conditioning; and while frequently, the regularities invoked cannot be stated with the same generality and precision as in physics or chemistry, it is clear, at least, that the general character of those explanations conforms to our earlier characterization.

Let us now consider an illustration involving sociological and economic factors. In the fall of 1946, there occurred at the cotton exchanges of the United States a price drop which was so severe that the exchanges in New York, New Orleans, and Chicago had to suspend their activities temporarily. In an attempt to explain this occurrence, newspapers traced it back to a large-scale speculator in New Orleans who had feared his holdings were too large and had therefore begun to liquidate his stocks; smaller speculators had then followed his example in a panic and had thus touched off the critical decline. Without attempting to assess the merits of the argument, let us note that the explanation here suggested again involves

[6] On the subject of explanation in the social sciences, especially in history, cf. also the following publications, which may serve to supplement and amplify the brief discussion to be presented here: Hempel [Laws]; Popper [Society]; White [Explanation]; and the articles *Cause* and *Understanding* in Beard and Hook [Terminology].

statements about antecedent conditions and the assumption of general regularities. The former include the facts that the first speculator had large stocks of cotton, that there were smaller speculators with considerable holdings, that there existed the institution of the cotton exchanges with their specific mode of operation, etc. The general regularities referred to are — as often in semi-popular explanations — not explicitly mentioned; but there is obviously implied some form of the law of supply and demand to account for the drop in cotton prices in terms of the greatly increased supply under conditions of practically unchanged demand; besides, reliance is necessary on certain regularities in the behavior of individuals who are trying to preserve or improve their economic position. Such laws cannot be formulated at present with satisfactory precision and generality, and therefore, the suggested explanation is surely incomplete, but its intention is unmistakably to account for the phenomenon by integrating it into a general pattern of economic and socio-psychological regularities.

We turn to an explanatory argument taken from the field of linguistics.[7] In Northern France, there exist a large variety of words synonymous with the English "bee," whereas in Southern France, essentially only one such word is in existence. For this discrepancy, the explanation has been suggested that in the Latin epoch, the South of France used the word "apicula", the North the word "apis". The latter, because of a process of phonologic decay in Northern France, became the monosyllabic word "é"; and monosyllables tend to be eliminated, especially if they contain few consonantic elements, for they are apt to give rise to misunderstandings. Thus, to avoid confusion, other words were selected. But "apicula", which was reduced to "abelho", remained clear enough and was retained, and finally it even entered into the standard language, in the form "abbeille". While the explanation here described is incomplete in the sense characterized in the previous section, it clearly exhibits reference to specific antecedent conditions as well as to general laws.[8]

While illustrations of this kind tend to support the view that explanation in biology, psychology, and the social sciences has the same structure as in the physical sciences, the opinion is rather widely held that in many instances, the causal type of explanation is essentially inadequate in fields other than physics and chemistry, and especially in the study of purposive behavior. Let us examine briefly some of the reasons which have been adduced in support of this view.

One of the most familiar among them is the idea that events involving the activities of humans singly or in groups have a peculiar uniqueness and irrepeatability which makes them inaccessible to causal explanation because the latter, — with its reliance upon uniformities, presupposes repeatability of the phenomena under consideration. This argument which, incidentally, has also been used in support of the contention that the experimental method is inapplicable in psychology and the social sciences, involves a misunderstanding of the logical character of causal explanation. Every individual event, in the physical sciences no less than in psychology or the social sciences, is unique in the sense that it, with all its peculiar characteristics, does not repeat itself. Nevertheless, individual events may conform to, and thus be explainable by means of, general laws of the causal type. For all that a causal law asserts is that any event of a specified kind, i.e. any event having certain specified characteristics, is

[7] The illustration is taken from Bonfante [Semantics], section 3.

[8] While in each of the last two illustrations, certain regularities are unquestionably relied upon in the explanatory argument, it is not possible to argue convincingly that the intended laws, which at present cannot all be stated explicitly, are of a causal rather than a statistical character. It is quite possible that most or all of the regularities which will be discovered as sociology develops will be of a statistical type. Cf., on this point, the suggestive observations by Zilsel in [Empiricism] section 8, and [Laws]. This issue does not affect, however, the main point we wish to make here, namely that in the social no less than in the physical sciences, subsumption under general regularities is indispensable for the explanation and the theoretical understanding of any phenomenon.

accompanied by another event which in turn has certain specified characteristics; for example, that in any event involving friction, heat is developed. And all that is needed for the testability and applicability of such laws is the recurrence of events with the antecedent characteristics, i.e. the repetition of those characteristics, but not of their individual instances. Thus, the argument is inconclusive. It gives occasion, however, to emphasize an important point concerning our earlier analysis: When we spoke of the explanation of a single event, the term "event" referred to the occurrence of some more or less complex characteristic in a specific spatio-temporal location or in a certain individual object, and not to *all* characteristics of that object, or to all that goes on in that space-time region.

A second argument that should be mentioned here[9] contends that the establishment of scientific generalizations — and thus of explanatory principles — for human behavior is impossible because the reactions of an individual in a given situation depend not only upon that situation, but also upon the previous history of the individual. — But surely, there is no *a priori* reason why generalizations should not be attainable which take into account this dependence of behavior on the past history of the agent. That indeed the given argument "proves" too much, and is therefore a *non sequitur*, is made evident by the existence of certain physical phenomena, such as magnetic hysteresis and elastic fatigue, in which the magnitude of a specific physical effect depends upon the past history of the system involved, and for which nevertheless certain general regularities have been established.

A third argument insists that the explanation of any phenomenon involving purposive behavior calls for reference to motivations and thus for teleological rather than causal analysis. Thus, for example, a fuller statement of the suggested explanation for the break in the cotton prices would have to indicate the large-scale speculator's motivations as one of the factors determining the event in question. Thus, we have to refer to goals sought, and this, so the argument runs, introduces a type of explanation alien to the physical sciences. Unquestionably, many of the — frequently incomplete — explanations which are offered for human actions involve reference to goals and motives; but does this make them essentially different from the causal explanations of physics and chemistry? One difference which suggests itself lies in the circumstance that in motivated behavior, the future appears to affect the present in a manner which is not found in the causal explanations of the physical sciences. But clearly, when the action of a person is motivated, say, by the desire to reach a certain objective, then it is not the as yet unrealized future event of attaining that goal which can be said to determine his present behavior, for indeed the goal may never be actually reached; rather — to put it in crude terms — it is (a) his desire, present before the action, to attain that particular objective, and (b) his belief, likewise present before the action, that such and such a course of action is most likely to have the desired effect. The determining motives and beliefs, therefore, have to be classified among the antecedent conditions of a motivational explanation, and there is no formal difference on this account between motivational and causal explanation.

Neither does the fact that motives are not accessible to direct observation by an outside observer constitute an essential difference between the two kinds of explanation; for also the determining factors adduced in physical explanations are very frequently inaccessible to direct observation. This is the case, for instance, when opposite electric charges are adduced in explanation of the mutual attraction of two metal spheres. The presence of those charges, while eluding all direct observation, can be ascertained by various kinds of indirect test, and that is sufficient to guarantee the empirical character of the explanatory statement. Similarly, the presence of certain motivations may be ascertainable only by indirect methods, which may include reference to linguistic utterances of the subject

[9] Cf., for example, F. H. Knight's presentation of this argument in [Limitations], pp. 251–52.

in question, slips of the pen or of the tongue, etc.; but as long as these methods are "operationally determined" with reasonable clarity and precision, there is no essential difference in this respect between motivational explanation and causal explanation in physics.

A potential danger of explanation by motives lies in the fact that the method lends itself to the facile construction of ex-post-facto accounts without predictive force. It is a widespread tendency to "explain" an action by ascribing it to motives conjectured only after the action has taken place. While this procedure is not in itself objectionable, its soundness requires that (1) the motivational assumptions in question be capable of test, and (2) that suitable general laws be available to lend explanatory power to the assumed motives. Disregard of these requirements frequently deprives alleged motivational explanations of their cognitive significance.

The explanation of an action in terms of the motives of the agent is sometimes considered as a special kind of teleological explanation. As was pointed out above, motivational explanation, if adequately formulated, conforms to the conditions for causal explanation, so that the term "teleological" is a misnomer if it is meant to imply either a non-causal character of the explanation or a peculiar determination of the present by the future. If this is borne in mind, however, the term "teleological" may be viewed in this context, as referring to causal explanations in which some of the antecedent conditions are motives of the agent whose actions are to be explained.[10]

Teleological explanations of this kind have to be distinguished from a much more sweeping type, which has been claimed by certain schools of thought to be indispensable especially in biology. It consists in explaining characteristics of an organism by reference to certain ends or purposes which the characteristics are said to serve. In contradistinction to the cases examined before, the ends are not assumed here to be consciously or subconsciously pursued by the organism in question. Thus, for the phenomenon of mimicry, the explanation is sometimes offered that it serves the purpose of protecting the animals endowed with it from detection by its pursuers and thus tends to preserve the species. — Before teleological hypotheses of this kind can be appraised as to their potential explanatory power, their meaning has to be clarified. If they are intended somehow to express the idea that the purposes they refer to are inherent in the design of the universe, then clearly they are not capable of empirical test and thus violate the requirement (R3) stated in §3. In certain cases, however, assertions about the purposes of biological characteristics may be translatable into statements in non-teleological terminology which assert that those characteristics function in a specific manner which is essential to keeping the organism alive or to preserving the species.[11] An attempt to state precisely what is meant by this latter assertion — or by the similar one that without those characteristics, and other things being equal, the organism or the species would not survive — encounters considerable difficulties. But these need not be discussed here. For even if we assume that biological statements in teleological form can be adequately translated into descriptive statements about the life-preserving function of certain biological characteristics, it is clear that (1) the use of the concept of purpose is

[10] For a detailed logical analysis of the character and the function of the motivation concept in psychological theory, see Koch [Motivation]. — A stimulating discussion of teleological behavior from the standpoint of contemporary physics and biology is contained in the article [Teleology] by Rosenblueth, Wiener and Bigelow. The authors propose an interpretation of the concept of purpose which is free from metaphysical connotations, and they stress the importance of the concept thus obtained for a behavioristic analysis of machines and living organisms. While our formulations above intentionally use the crude terminology frequently applied in philosophical arguments concerning the applicability of causal explanation to purposive behavior, the analysis presented in the article referred to is couched in behavioristic terms and avoids reference to "motives" and the like.

[11] An analysis of teleological statements in biology along these lines may be found in Woodger [Principles], especially pp. 432ff.; essentially the same interpretation is advocated by Kaufmann in [Methodology], chapter 8.

not essential in these contexts, since the term "purpose" can be completely eliminated from the statements in question, and (2) teleological assumptions, while now endowed with empirical content, cannot serve as explanatory principles in the customary contexts. Thus, e.g., the fact that a given species of butterflies displays a particular kind of coloring cannot be inferred from — and therefore cannot be explained by means of — the statement that this type of coloring has the effect of protecting the butterflies from detection by pursuing birds, nor can the presence of red corpuscles in the human blood be inferred from the statement that those corpuscles have a specific function in assimilating oxygen and that this function is essential for the maintenance of life.

One of the reasons for the perseverance of teleological considerations in biology probably lies in the fruitfulness of the teleological approach as a heuristic device: Biological research which was psychologically motivated by a teleological orientation, by an interest in purposes in nature, has frequently led to important results which can be stated in non-teleological terminology and which increase our scientific knowledge of the causal connections between biological phenomena.

Another aspect that lends appeal to teleological considerations is their anthropomorphic character. A teleological explanation tends to make us feel that we really "understand" the phenomenon in question, because it is accounted for in terms of purposes, with which we are familiar from our own experience of purposive behavior. But it is important to distinguish here understanding in the psychological sense of a feeling of empathic familiarity from understanding in the theoretical, or cognitive, sense of exhibiting the phenomenon to be explained as a special case of some general regularity. The frequent insistence that explanation means the reduction of something unfamiliar to ideas or experiences already familiar to us is indeed misleading. For while some scientific explanations do have this psychological effect, it is by no means universal: The free fall of a physical body may well be said to be a more familiar phenomenon than the law of gravitation, by means of which it can be explained; and surely the basic ideas of the theory of relativity will appear to many to be far less familiar than the phenomena for which the theory accounts.

"Familiarity" of the explicans is not only not necessary for a sound explanation — as we have just tried to show — , but it is not sufficient either. This is shown by the many cases in which a proposed explicans sounds suggestively familiar, but upon closer inspection proves to be a mere metaphor, or an account lacking testability, or a set of statements which includes no general laws and therefore lacks explanatory power. A case in point is the neovitalistic attempt to explain biological phenomena by reference to an entelechy or vital force. The crucial point here is not — as it is sometimes made out to be — that entelechies cannot be seen or otherwise directly observed; for that is true also of gravitational fields, and yet, reference to such fields is essential in the explanation of various physical phenomena. The decisive difference between the two cases is that the physical explanation provides (1) methods of testing, albeit indirectly, assertions about gravitational fields, and (2) general laws concerning the stength of gravitational fields, and the behavior of objects moving in them. Explanations by entelechies satisfy the analogue of neither of these two conditions. Failure to satisfy the first condition represents a violation of (R3); it renders all statements about entelechies inaccessible to empirical test and thus devoid of empirical meaning. Failure to comply with the second condition involves a violation of (R2). It deprives the concept of entelechy of all explanatory import; for explanatory power never resides in a concept, but always in the general laws in which it functions. Therefore, notwithstanding the flavor of familiarity of the metaphor it invokes, the neovitalistic approach cannot provide theoretical understanding.

The preceding observations about familiarity and understanding can be applied, in a similar manner, to the view held by some scholars that the explanation, or the understanding, of human actions requires an empathic understanding of the personalities of the agents.[12] This understanding of another person in terms of one's own psychological functioning may prove a useful heuristic device in the search for general psychological principles which might provide a theoretical explanation; but the existence of empathy on the part of the scientist is neither a necessary nor a sufficient condition for the explanation, or the scientific understanding, of any human action. It is not necessary, for the behavior of psychotics or of people belonging to a culture very different from that of the scientist may sometimes be explainable and predictable in terms of general principles even though the scientist who establishes or applies those principles may not be able to understand his subjects empathically. And empathy is not sufficient to guarantee a sound explanation, for a strong feeling of empathy may exist even in cases where we completely misjudge a given personality. Moreover, as the late Dr. Zilsel has pointed out, empathy leads with ease to incompatible results; thus, when the population of a town has long been subjected to heavy bombing attacks, we can understand, in the empathic sense, that its morale should have broken down completely, but we can understand with the same ease also that it should have developed a defiant spirit of resistance. Arguments of this kind often appear quite convincing; but they are of an *ex post facto* character and lack cognitive significance unless they are supplemented by testable explanatory principles in the form of laws or theories.

Familiarity of the explanans, therefore, no matter whether it is achieved through the use of teleological terminology, through neovitalistic metaphors, or through other means, is no indication of the cognitive import and the predictive force of a proposed explanation. Besides, the extent to which an idea will be considered as familiar varies from person to person and from time to time, and a psychological factor of this kind certainly cannot serve as a standard in assessing the worth of a proposed explanation. The decisive requirement for every sound explanation remains that it subsume the explanandum under general laws. . . .

Logical Analysis of Law and Explanation

PROBLEMS OF THE CONCEPT OF GENERAL LAW

From our general survey of the characteristics of scientific explanation, we now turn to a closer examination of its logical structure. The explanation of a phenomenon, we noted, consists in its subsumption under laws or under a theory. But what is a law, what is a theory? While the meaning of these concepts seems intuitively clear, an attempt to construct adequate explicit definitions for them encounters considerable difficulties. In the present section, some basic problems of the concept of law will be described and analyzed; in the next section, we intend to propose, on the basis of the suggestions thus obtained, definitions of law and of explanation for a formalized model language of a simple logical structure.

The concept of law will be construed here so as to apply to true statements only. The apparently plausible alternative procedure of requiring high confirmation rather than truth of a law seems to be inadequate: It would lead to a relativized concept of law, which would be expressed by the phrase "sentence *S* is a law relatively to the evidence *E*". This does not seem to accord with the meaning customarily assigned to the concept of law in science and in methodological inquiry. Thus, for example, we would not say that Bode's general formula for the distance of the planets from the sun was a law relatively to the astronomical evidence available in the 1770s, when Bode propounded it, and that it ceased to be a law after the discovery of Neptune and the determination of its distance from the

[12] For a more detailed discussion of this view on the basis of the general principles outlined above, cf. Zilsel [Empiricism], sections 7 and 8, and Hempel [Laws], section 6.

sun; rather, we would say that the limited original evidence had given a high probability to the assumption that the formula was a law, whereas more recent additional information reduced that probability so much as to make it practically certain that Bode's formula is not generally true, and hence not a law.[13]

Apart from being true, a law will have to satisfy a number of additional conditions. These can be studied independently of the factual requirement of truth, for they refer, as it were, to all logically possible laws, no matter whether factually true or false. Adopting a convenient term proposed by Goodman,[14] we will say that a sentence is lawlike if it has all the characteristics of a general law, with the possible exception of truth. Hence, every law is a lawlike sentence, but not conversely.

Our problem of analyzing the concept of law thus reduces to that of explicating the meaning of "lawlike sentence". We shall construe the class of lawlike sentences as including analytic general statements, such as "A rose is a rose", as well as the lawlike sentences of empirical science, which have empirical content.[15] It will not be necessary to require that each law-like sentence permissible in explanatory contexts be of the second kind; rather, our definition of explanation will be so constructed as to guarantee the factual character of the totality of the laws — though not of every single one of them — which function in an explanation of an empirical fact.

What are the characteristics of lawlike sentences? First of all, lawlike sentences are statements of universal form, such as "All robins' eggs are greenish-blue", "All metals are conductors of electricity", "At constant pressure, any gas expands with increasing temperature". As these examples illustrate, a lawlike sentence usually is not only of universal, but also of conditional form; it makes an assertion to the effect that universally, if a certain set of conditions, C, is realized, then another specified set of conditions, E, is realized as well. The standard form for the symbolic expression of a lawlike sentence is therefore the universal conditional. However, since any conditional statement can be transformed into a non-conditional one, conditional form will not be considered as essential for a lawlike sentence, while universal character will be held indispensable.

But the requirement of universal form is not sufficient to characterize lawlike sentences. Suppose, for example, that a certain basket, b, contains at a certain time t a number of red apples and nothing else.[16] Then the statement

(S_1) Every apple in basket b at time t is red

is both true and of universal form. Yet the sentence does not qualify as a law; we would refuse, for example, to explain by subsumption under it the fact that a particular apple chosen at random from the basket is red. What distinguishes S_1 from a lawlike sentence? Two points suggest themselves, which will be considered in turn, namely, finite scope, and reference to a specified object.

[13] The requirement of truth for laws has the consequence that a given empirical statement S can never be definitely known to be a law; for the sentence affirming the truth of S is logically equivalent with S and is therefore capable only of acquiring a more or less high probability, or degree of confirmation, relatively to the experimental evidence available at any given time. On this point, cf. Carnap [Remarks]. — For an excellent non-technical exposition of the semantical concept of truth, which is here applied, the reader is referred to Tarski [Truth].

[14] [Counterfactuals], p. 125.

[15] This procedure was suggested by Goodman's approach in [Counterfactuals]. — Reichenbach, in a detailed examination of the concept of law, similarly construes his concept of nomological statement as including both analytic and synthetic sentences; cf. [Logic], chapter VIII.

[16] The difficulty illustrated by this example was stated concisely by Langford ([Review]), who referred to it as the problem of distinguishing between universals of fact and causal universals. For further discussion and illustration of this point, see also Chisholm [Conditional], especially pp. 301f. — A systematic analysis of the problem was given by Goodman in [Counterfactuals], especially part III. — While not concerned with the specific point under discussion, the detailed examination of counterfactual conditionals and their relation to laws of nature, in Chapter VIII of Lewis's work [Analysis], contains important observations on several of the issues raised in the present section.

First, the sentence S_1 makes, in effect, an assertion about a finite number of objects only, and this seems irreconcilable with the claim to universality which is commonly associated with the notion of law.[17] But are not Kepler's laws considered as lawlike although they refer to a finite set of planets only? And might we not even be willing to consider as lawlike a sentence such as the following?

(S_2) All the sixteen ice cubes in the freezing tray of this refrigerator have a temperature of less than 10 degrees centigrade.

This point might well be granted; but there is an essential difference between S_1 on the one hand and Kepler's laws as well as S_2 on the other: The latter, while finite in scope, are known to be consequences of more comprehensive laws whose scope is not limited, while for S_1 this is not the case.

Adopting a procedure recently suggested by Reichenbach,[18] we will therefore distinguish between fundamental and derivative laws. A statement will be called a derivative law if it is of universal character and follows from some fundamental laws. The concept of fundamental law requires further clarification; so far, we may say that fundamental laws, and similarly fundamental lawlike sentences, should satisfy a certain condition of non-limitation of scope.

It would be excessive, however, to deny the status of fundamental lawlike sentence to all statements which, in effect, make an assertion about a finite class of objects only, for that would rule out also a sentence such as "All robins' eggs are greenish-blue", since presumably the class of all robins' eggs — past, present, and future — is finite. But again, there is an essential difference between this sentence and, say, S_1. It requires empirical knowledge to establish the finiteness of the class of robins' eggs, whereas when the sentence S_1 is construed in a manner which renders it intuitively unlawlike, the terms "basket *b*" and "apple" are understood so as to imply finiteness of the class of apples in the basket at time *t*. Thus, so to speak, the meaning of its constitutive terms alone — without additional factual information — entails that S_1 has a finite scope. — Fundamental laws, then, will have to be construed so as to satisfy what we have called a condition of non-limited scope; our formulation of that condition however, which refers to what is entailed by "the meaning" of certain expressions, is too vague and will have to be revised later. Let us note in passing that the stipulation here envisaged would bar from the class of fundamental lawlike sentences also such undesirable candidates as "All uranic objects are spherical", where "uranic" means the property of being the planet Uranus; indeed, while this sentence has universal form, it fails to satisfy the condition of non-limited scope.

In our search for a general characterization of lawlike sentences, we now turn to a second clue which is provided by the sentence S_1. In addition to violating the condition of non-limited scope, this sentence has the peculiarity of making reference to a particular object, the basket *b*; and this, too, seems to violate the universal character of a law.[19] The restriction which seems indicated here, should however again be applied to fundamental lawlike sentences only; for a true general statement about the free fall of physical bodies on the moon, while referring to a particular object, would still constitute a law, albeit a derivative one.

It seems reasonable to stipulate, therefore, that a fundamental lawlike sentence must be of universal form and must contain no essential — i.e., uneliminable — occurrences of

[17] The view that laws should be construed as not being limited to a finite domain has been expressed, among others, by Popper ([Forschung], section 13) and by Reichenbach ([Logic], p. 369).

[18] [Logic], p. 361. — Our terminology as well as the definitions to be proposed later for the two types of law do not coincide with Reichenbach's, however.

[19] In physics, the idea that a law should not refer to any particular object has found its expression in the maxim that the general laws of physics should contain no reference to specific space-time points, and that spatio-temporal coordinates should occur in them only in the form of differences or differentials.

designations for particular objects. But this is not sufficient; indeed, just at this point, a particularly serious difficulty presents itself. Consider the sentence

(S_3) Everything that is either an apple in basket *b* at time *t* or a sample of ferric oxide is red.

If we use a special expression, say "*x* is ferple", as synonymous with "*x* is either an apple in *b* at *t* or a sample of ferric oxide", then the content of S_2 can be expressed in the form

(S_4) Everything that is ferple is red.

The statement thus obtained is of universal form and contains no designations of particular objects, and it also satisfies the condition of non-limited scope; yet clearly, S_4 can qualify as a fundamental lawlike sentence no more than can S_3.

As long as "ferple" is a defined term of our language, the difficulty can readily be met by stipulating that after elimination of defined terms, a fundamental lawlike sentence must not contain essential occurrences of designations for particular objects. But this way out is of no avail when "ferple", or another term of the kind illustrated by it, is a primitive predicate of the language under consideration. This reflection indicates that certain restrictions have to be imposed upon those predicates — i.e., terms for properties or relations, — which may occur in fundamental lawlike sentences.[20]

More specifially, the idea suggests itself of permitting a predicate in a fundamental lawlike sentence only if it is purely universal, or, as we shall say, purely qualitative, in character; in other words, if a statement of its meaning does not require reference to any one particular object or spatio-temporal location. Thus, the terms "soft", "green", "warmer than", "as long as", "liquid", "electrically charged", "female", "father of" are purely qualitative predicates, while "taller than the Eiffel Tower", "medieval", "lunar", "arctic", "Ming" are not.[21]

Exclusion from fundamental lawlike sentences of predicates which are not purely qualitative would at the same time ensure satisfaction of the condition of non-limited scope; for the meaning of a purely qualitative predicate does not require a finite extension; and indeed, all the sentences considered above which violate the condition of non-limited scope make explicit or implicit reference to specific objects.

The stipulation just proposed suffers, however, from the vagueness of the concept of purely qualitative predicate. The question whether indication of the meaning of a given predicate in English does or does not require reference to some one specific object does not always permit an unequivocal answer since English as a natural language does not provide explicit definitions or other clear explications of meaning for its terms. It seems therefore reasonable to attempt definition of the concept of law not with respect to English or any other natural language, but rather with respect to a formalized language — let us call

[20] The point illustrated by the sentences S_3 and S_4 above was made by Goodman, who has also emphasized the need to impose certain restrictions upon the predicates whose occurrence is to be permissible in lawlike sentences. These predicates are essentially the same as those which Goodman calls projectible. Goodman has suggested that the problems of establishing precise criteria for projectibility, of interpreting counterfactual conditionals, and of defining the concept of law are so intimately related as to be virtually aspects of a single problem. (Cf. his articles [Query] and [Counterfactuals].) One suggestion for an analysis of projectibility has recently been made by Carnap in [Application]. Goodman's note [Infirmities] contains critical observations on Carnap's proposals.

[21] That laws, in addition to being of universal form, must contain only purely universal predicates was clearly argued by Popper ([Forschung], sections 14, 15). — Our alternative expression "purely qualitative predicate" was chosen in analogy to Carnap's term "purely qualitative property" (cf. [Application]). — The above characterization of purely universal predicates seems preferable to a simpler and perhaps more customary one, to the effect that a statement of the meaning of the predicate must require no reference to particular objects. For this formulation might be too exclusive since it could be argued that stating the meaning of such purely qualitative terms as "blue" or "hot" requires illustrative reference to some particular object which has the quality in question. The essential point is that no one specific object has to be chosen; any one in the logically unlimited set of blue or of hot objects will do. In explicating the meaning of "taller than the Eiffel Tower", "being an apple in basket b at the time t", "medieval", etc., however, reference has to be made to one specific object or to some one in a limited set of objects.

it a model language, *L*, — which is governed by a well-determined system of logical rules, and in which every term either is characterized as primitive or is introduced by an explicit definition in terms of the primitives.

This reference to a well-determined system is customary in logical research and is indeed quite natural in the context of any attempt to develop precise criteria for certain logical distinctions. But it does not by itself suffice to overcome the specific difficulty under discussion. For while it is now readily possible to characterize as not purely qualitative all those among the defined predicates in *L* whose definiens contains an essential occurrence of some individual name, our problem remains open for the primitives of the language, whose meanings are not determined by definitions within the language, but rather by semantical rules of interpretation. For we want to permit the interpretation of the primitives of *L* by means of such attributes as blue, hard, solid, warmer, but not by the properties of being a descendant of Napoleon, or an arctic animal, or a Greek statue; and the difficulty is precisely that of stating rigorous criteria for the distinction between the permissible and the non-permissible interpretations. Thus the problem of setting up an adequate definition for purely qualitative attributes now arises again; namely for the concepts of the metalanguage in which the semantical interpretation of the primitives is formulated. We may postpone an encounter with the difficulty by presupposing formalization of the semantical meta-language, the meta-meta-language, and so forth; but somewhere, we will have to stop at a nonformalized meta-language, and for it a characterization of purely qualitative predicates will be needed and will present much the same problems as non-formalized English, with which we began. The characterization of a purely qualitative predicate as one whose meaning can be made explicit without reference to any one particular object points to the intended meaning but does not explicate it precisely, and the problem of an adequate definition of purely qualitative predicates remains open.

There can be little doubt, however, that there exists a large number of property and relation terms which would be rather generally recognized as purely qualitative in the sense here pointed out, and as permissible in the formulation of fundamental lawlike sentences; some examples have been given above, and the list could be readily enlarged. When we speak of purely qualitative predicates, we shall henceforth have in mind predicates of this kind. . . .

Bibliography

Throughout the article, the abbreviated titles in brackets are used for reference.

BEARD, Charles A., and HOOK, Sidney. [Terminology] Problems of terminology in historical writing. Chapter IV of Theory and practice in historical study: A report of the Committee on Historiography. Social Science Research Council, New York, 1946.

BERGMANN, Gustav. [Emergence] Holism, historicism, and emergence. *Philosophy of science*, vol. 11 (1944), pp. 209–221.

BONFANTE, G. [Semantics] Semantics, language. An article in P. L. Harriman, ed., The encyclopedia of psychology. Philosophical Library, New York, 1946.

BROAD, C. D. [Mind] The mind and its place in nature. New York, 1925.

CARNAP, Rudolf. [Semantics] Introduction to semantics. Harvard University Press, 1942.

———. [Inductive Logic] On inductive logic. *Philosophy of science*, vol. 12 (1945), pp. 72–97.

———. [Concepts] The two concepts of probability. *Philosophy and phenomenological research*, vol. 5 (1945), pp. 513–532.

———. [Remarks] Remarks on induction and truth. *Philosophy and phenomenological research*, vol. 6 (1946), pp. 590–602.

———. [Application] On the application of inductive logic. *Philosophy and phenomenological research*, vol. 8 (1947), pp. 133–147.

CHISHOLM, Roderick M. [Conditional] The contrary-to-fact conditional. *Mind*, vol. 55 (1946), pp. 289–307.

CHURCH, Alonzo. [Logic] Logic, formal. An article in Dagobert D. Runes, ed. The dictionary of philosophy. Philosophical Library, New York, 1942.

DUCASSE, C. J. [Explanation] Explanation, mechanism, and teleology. *The journal of philosophy*, vol. 22 (1925), pp. 150–155.

FEIGL, Herbert. [Operationism] Operationism and scientific method. *Psychological review*, vol. 52 (1945), pp. 250–259 and 284–288.

GOODMAN, Nelson. [Query] A query on confirmation. *The journal of philosophy*, vol. 43 (1946), pp. 383–385.

————. [Counterfactuals]. The problem of counterfactual conditionals. *The journal of philosophy*, vol. 44 (1947), pp. 113–128.

————. [Infirmities] On infirmities of confirmation theory. *Philosophy and phenomenological research*, vol. 8 (1947), pp. 149–151.

GRELLING, KURT and OPPENHEIM, Paul. [Gestaltbegriff] Der Gestaltbegriff im Lichte der neuen Logik. *Erkenntnis*, vol. 7 (1937–38), pp. 211-225 and 357–359.

GRELLING, Kurt and OPPENHEIM, Paul. [Functional Whole) Logical Analysis of "Gestalt" as "Functional whole". Preprinted for distribution at Fifth Internat. Congress for the Unity of Science, Cambridge, Mass., 1939.

HELMER, Olaf and OPPENHEIM, Paul. [Probability] A syntactical definition of probability and of degree of confirmation. *The journal of symbolic logic*, vol. 10 (1945), pp. 25–60.

HEMPEL, Carl G. [Laws] The function of general laws in history. *The journal of philosophy*, vol. 39 (1942), pp. 35–48.

————. [Studies] Studies in the logic of confirmation. *Mind*, vol. 54 (1945); Part I: pp. 1–26, Part II: pp. 97–121.

HEMPEL, Carl G. and OPPENHEIM, Paul. [Degree] A definition of "degree of confirmation". *Philosophy of science*, vol. 12 (1945), pp. 98–115.

HENLE, Paul. [Emergence] The status of emergence. *The journal of philosophy*, vol. 39 (1942), pp. 486–493.

HOSPERS, John. [Explanation] On explanation. *The journal of philosophy*, vol. 43 (1946), pp. 337–356.

HULL, Clark L. [Variables] The problem of intervening variables in molar behavior theory. *Psychological review*, vol. 50 (1943), pp. 273–291.

————. [Principles] Principles of behavior. New York, 1943.

JEVONS, W. Stanley. [Principles] The principles of science. London, 1924. (1st ed. 1874.)

KAUFMANN, Felix. [Methodology] Methodology of the social sciences. New York, 1944.

KNIGHT, Frank H. [Limitations] The limitations of scientific method in economics. In Tugwell, R., ed., The trend of economics. New York, 1924.

KOCH, Sigmund. [Motivation] The logical character of the motivation concept. *Psychological review*, vol. 48 (1941). Part I: pp. 15–38, Part II: pp. 127–154.

LANGFORD, C. H. [Review] Review in *The journal of symbolic logic*, vol. 6 (1941), pp. 67–68.

LEWIS, C. I. ([Analysis] An analysis of knowledge and valuation. La Salle, Ill., 1946.

MCKINSEY, J. C. C. [Review of HELMER and OPPENHEIM [Probability]. *Mathematical reviews*, vol. 7 (1946), p. 45.

MILL, John Stuart. [Logic] A system of logic.

MORGAN, C. Lloyd. Emergent evolution. New York, 1923.

————. The emergence of novelty. New York, 1933.

POPPER, Karl. [Forschung] Logik der Forschung. Wien, 1935.

————. [Society] The open society and its enemies. London, 1945.

REICHENBACH, Hans. [Logic] Elements of symbolic logic. New York, 1947.

————. [Quantum mechanics] Philosophic foundations of quantum mechanics. University of California Press, 1944.

ROSENBLUETH, A., WIENER, N., and BIGELOW, J. [Teleology] Behavior, Purpose, and Teleology. *Philosophy of science*, vol. 10 (1943), pp. 18–24.

STACE, W. T. [Novelty] Novelty, indeterminism and emergence. *Philosophical review*, vol. 48 (1939), pp. 296–310.

TARSKI, Alfred. [Truth] The semantical conception of truth, and the foundations of semantics. *Philosophy and phenomenological research*, vol. 4 (1944), pp. 341–376.

TOLMAN, Edward Chase. [Behavior] Purposive behavior in animals and men. New York, 1932.

WHITE, Morton G. [Explanation] Historical explanation. *Mind*, vol. 52 (1943), pp. 212–229.

WOODGER, J. H. [Principles] Biological principles, New York, 1929.

ZILSEL, Edgar. [Empiricism] Problems of empiricism. In *International encyclopedia of unified science*, vol. II, no. 8. The University of Chicago Press, 1941.

————. [Laws] Physics and the problem of historico-sociological laws. *Philosophy of science*, vol. 8 (1941), pp. 567–579.

Retroduction: Scientists Are Not Confined to the H-D Method 6

from *Patterns of Discovery*
NORWOOD R. HANSON

Was Kepler's struggle up from Tycho's data to the proposal of the elliptical orbit hypothesis really inferential at all? He wrote *De Motibus Stellae Martis* in order to set out his reasons for suggesting the ellipse. These were not deductive reasons; he was working from *explicanda* to *explicans*. But neither were they inductive — not, at least, in any form advocated by the empiricists, statisticians and probability theorists who have written on induction.[1]

Aristotle lists the types of inferences. These are deductive, inductive and one other called 'ἀπαγωγή'. This is translated as 'reduction'.[2] Peirce translates it as 'abduction' or 'retroduction'. What distinguishes this kind of argument for Aristotle is that

> the relation of the middle to the last term is uncertain, though equally or more probable than the conclusion; or again an argument in which the terms intermediate between the last term and the middle are few. For in any of these cases it turns out that we approach more nearly to knowledge . . . since we have taken a new term.[3]

After describing deduction in a familiar way, Peirce speaks of induction as the experimental testing of a finished theory.[4] Induction

> sets out with a theory and it measures the degree of concordance of that theory with fact. It never can originate any idea whatever. No more can deduction. All the ideas of science come to it by the way of Abduction. Abduction consists in studying facts and devising a theory to explain them. Its only justification is that if we are ever to understand things at all, it must be in that way. Abductive and inductive reasoning are utterly irreducible, either to the other or to Deduction, or Deduction to either of them. . . .[5]

> Deduction proves that something *must* be; Induction shows that something *actually is* operative; Abduction merely suggests that something *may be*.[6]

> . . . man has a certain Insight, not strong enough to be oftener right than wrong, but strong enough not to be overwhelmingly more often wrong than right. . . . An Insight, I call it, because it is to be referred to the same general class of operations to which Perceptive Judgments belong. . . . If you ask

From *Patterns of Discovery* by Norwood R. Hanson, Cambridge University Press, London, 1958, pp. 85–90.

[1] Preliminary to the discussion following must be an appreciation of the logical distinction between (1) reasons for accepting an hypothesis H, and (2) reasons for suggesting H in the first place. (1) is pertinent to what makes us say H is true, (2) is pertinent to what makes us say H is plausible. Both are the province of logical inquiry, although H-D theorists discuss only (1) saying that (2) is a matter for psychology or sociology — not logic. This is just an error. What leads to the initial formation of H — the 'click', intuition, hunch, insight, perception, etc. — this *is* a matter of psychology. But many hypotheses flash through the investigator's mind only to be rejected on sight. Some are proposed for serious consideration, however, and with good reasons. Kepler would have had good *reasons* for rejecting the hypothesis that Jupiter's moons cause the apparent accelerations of Mars at 90° and 270°. He also had good reasons for proposing that *all* the planets move in ellipses (after having established only that Mars does). This analogical type of hypothesis though, could not possibly *establish* that all planets move in ellipses. We are discussing the rationale behind the proposal of hypotheses as possible *explicantia*. H-D theorists never raise the problem at all.

[2] By Jenkinson; cf. *Prior Analytics* (Oxford, ed. Ross); vol. II, p. 25.

[3] *Op. cit.* vol. II, p. 25. Cf. also *Posterior Analytics*, vol. II, p. 19. Cf. 'The particular facts are not merely brought together but there is a new element added to the combination by the very act of thought by which they are combined. . . . The pearls are there, but they will not hang together till someone provides the string' (Whewell, *Novum Organum Renovatum*, pp. 72, 73).

[4] Vol. v, § 145.

[5] *Op. cit.* § 146.

[6] § 171.

an investigator why he does not try this or that wild theory, he will say 'It does not seem *reasonable*'.[7]

Peirce regards an abductive inference (such as 'The observed positions of Mars fall between a circle and an oval, so the orbit must be an ellipse') and a perceptual judgment (such as 'It is laevorotatory') as being opposite sides of the same epistemological coin. *Seeing that* is relevant here. The dawning of an aspect and the dawning of an explanation both suggest what to look for next. In both, the elements of inquiry coagulate into an intelligible pattern. The affinities between seeing the hidden man in a cluster of dots and seeing the Martian ellipse in a cluster of data are profound. 'What can our first acquaintance with an inference, when it is not yet adopted, be but a perception of the world of ideas?'[8] But '. . . abduction, although it is very little hampered by logical rules, nevertheless is logical inference, asserting its conclusion only problematically, or conjecturally, it is true, but nevertheless having a perfectly definite logical form'.[9]

Before Peirce treated retroduction as an inference[10] logicians had recognized that the reasonable proposal of an explanatory hypothesis was subject to certain conditions. The hypothesis cannot be admitted, even as a tentative conjecture, unless it would account for the phenomena posing the difficulty — or at least some of them. This is understressed in most H-D accounts of physical theory, and it is non-existent in simple inductive accounts. The form of the inference is this:

1. Some surprising phenomenon P is observed.

2. P would be explicable as a matter of course if H were true.

3. Hence there is reason to think that H is true.

H cannot be retroductively inferred until its content is present in 2. Inductive accounts expect H to emerge from repetitions of P. H-D accounts make P emerge from some unaccounted-for creation of H as a 'higher-level hypothesis'.

'Mars' positions would fall between a circle and the oviform as a matter of course if its orbit were elliptical'; 'the distance dropped by a body would be $\frac{1}{2}at^2$ as a matter of course if the acceleration of a freely falling body were constant'. The H's here did not result from any actuarial or statistical processing of increasingly large numbers of the P's. Nor were they just 'thought of', the P's being deducible from them.[11]

Perceiving the pattern in phenomena is central to their being 'explicable as a matter of course'. Thus the significance of any blob or line in earlier diagrams eludes one until the organization of the whole is grasped; then this spot, or that patch, becomes understood as a matter of course. Why does Mars appear to accelerate at 90° and 270°? — (P). Because its orbit is elliptical — (H). Grasping this plot makes the details explicable, just as the impact of a weight striking clay becomes intelligible against the laws of falling bodies. This is what philosophers and natural philosophers were groping for when they spoke of discerning the nature of a phenomenon, its essence,[12] this will always be the trigger of physical inquiry. The struggle for intelligibility (pattern, organization) in natural philosophy has never been portrayed in inductive or H-D accounts.

Consider the bird-antelope in fig. 6-1. Now it has additional lines. Were this flashed on to a screen I might say 'It has four feathers'. I may be wrong: that the number of wiggly lines on the figure is other than four

[7] §§ 173, 174.

[8] § 194.

[9] § 188.

[10] In 1867, cf. *Collected Papers*, vol. II, bk. III, ch. 2, part III.

[11] Cf. Braithwaite, *Scientific Explanation*, p. ix, ll. 7–11. Cf. Peirce: 'How was it that the man was ever led to entertain that true theory? You cannot say that it happened by chance' (*op. cit.* vol. V, § 591), and 'How few were the guesses that men of surpassing genius had to make before they rightly guessed the laws of nature' (vol. V, § 604).

[12] Cf. Goethe: 'In science all depends on what is called an *aperçu*, on a recognition of what is at the bottom of the phenomena' (*Geschichte der Farbenlehre* (*Werke*, Weimar, 1887–1918) (4, 'Galileo')), and Einstein: 'The discovery of these elemental laws . . . is helped by a feeling for the order lying behind the appearance' (preface to Planck's *Where is Science Going?* (London, 1933)).

Fig. 6–1

is a conceptual possibility. 'It has four feathers' is thus falsifiable, empirical. It is an observation statement. To determine its truth we need only put the figure on the screen again and count the lines.

The statement that the figure is of a bird, however, is not falsifiable in the same sense. Its negation does not represent the same conceptual possibility, for it concerns not an observational detail but the very pattern which makes those details intelligible. One could not even say 'It has four feathers' and be wrong about it, if it was not a feathered object. I can show you your error if you say 'four feathers'. But I cannot thus disclose your 'error' in saying of the bird-antelope that it is a bird (instead of an antelope).

Pattern statements are different from detail statements. They are not inductive summaries of detail statements. Still the statement, 'It's a bird' is truly empirical. Had birds been different, or had the bird-antelope been drawn differently, 'It's a bird' might not have been true. In some sense it is true. If the detail statements are empirical, the pattern statements which give them sense are also empirical — though not in the same way. To deny a detail statement is to do something within the pattern. To deny a pattern statement is to attack the conceptual framework itself, and this denial cannot function in the same way.

P and *H* must have further logical properties in order to figure in '*P* would be explicable as a matter of course if *H* were true'. If *H* is meant to explain *P*, then *H* cannot itself rest upon the features in *P* which required explanation. This is why the peculiar colour and odour of chlorine (*P*) are not explained by reference to atoms in a volume of chlorine, each one having the colour and odour in question (*H*). Grasping this point is essential for any understanding of the fundamental concepts of modern particle physics.[13] This feature of retroductive reasoning shows why elementary particles must be unpicturable; why all electrons must be identical; why the 'state' of a proton cannot be determined precisely; why recent attempts to rectify particle theory have necessarily forced physicists to consider matter as lacking in any direct, physically interpretable properties. These things philosophers fail to grasp, perhaps because they are inclined to regard physical theory either as an inductive compound on the one hand, or as a kind of deductive system on the other. Of all men Kepler was in the best position to say 'Mars has no unique orbit, and I can prove it'. He did not say this. Galileo could have said $s = \frac{1}{2}at^2$, and no more, but he pressed on. Newton pressed on; Einstein, Bohr, De Broglie, Schrödinger, Heisenberg and Dirac pressed on — for explanations, which no amount of statistical repetition or deductive ingenuity alone could ever supply.

The critical moment comes when the physicist perceives that one might reason about the data in such and such a way. One might explain this welter of phenomena *P*, throw it all into an intelligible pattern, by supposing *H* to obtain. But *P* controls *H*, not vice versa. The reasoning is from data to hypotheses and theories, not the reverse.

> Retroduction . . . begins always with colligation, of course, of a variety of separately observed facts. . . . How remarkable it is . . . that the entire army of logicians . . . should have left it to this mineralogist [Whewell] to point out colligation as a generally essential step in reasoning.
>
> Abduction . . . amounts . . . to observing a fact and then professing to say what . . . it was that gave rise to that fact. . . .[14]

Kepler's was a great retroduction. Galileo's discovery that gravitational acceleration is constant was another. We left him in 1604

[13] Cf. ch. VI.

[14] Peirce, *op. cit.* §§ 581 and 602.

with the wrong hypothesis about freely falling bodies. He had told Sarpi that the velocities of a falling body were proportional to the distances it had fallen. By 1609 Galileo had realized his mistake, and was arguing that the body's velocities were proportional not to the distances fallen but rather to the times of fall. This was an innovation of great importance; for the relation between a velocity parameter, $v \propto t$, is not a 'natural' one in the way that '2 gm. plus 2 gm. equals 4 gm.' is. This is already a step towards the modern situation, wherein a theoretical physicist must be expert in the theory of functions. Triumphs in contemporary physics consist in discovering that one parameter can be regarded as a function of some other one. The 'real' physical relation between them may be unobvious or non-existent. In his hypothesis of 1609 Galileo's feet are on this path: he is pursuing a prior *explicans*, one having something to do with acceleration. Galileo's thirty-four-year march towards his final explanation is punctuated with misconceptions and erroneous arguments which it would be instructive to re-examine, but the matter cannot be pursued here.[15] Suffice it to say that he always tries to explain his original data by fashioning general hypotheses and theories 'in their image'. His hypotheses are never inductive summaries of his data; nor does he actively doubt them until he can deduce new observation statements which experiments confirm. Galileo knew he had succeeded when the constant acceleration hypothesis patterned the diverse phenomena he had encountered for thirty years. His reasoned advance from insight to insight culminated in an ultimate physical *explicans*. Further deductions were merely confirmatory; he could have left them to any of his students — Viviani or Toricelli. Even had verification of these further predictions eluded seventeenth-century science, this would not have prevented Galileo from embracing the constant acceleration hypothesis, any more than Copernicus and Kepler were prevented from embracing heliocentrism by the lack of a telescope with which to observe Venus' phases. Kepler needed no new observations to realize that the ellipse covered all observed positions. Newton required no new predictions from his gravitation hypothesis to be confident that this really did explain Kepler's three laws and a variety of other given data.

Physical theories provide patterns within which data appear intelligible. They constitute a 'conceptual Gestalt'.[16] A theory is not pieced together from observed phenomena; it is rather what makes it possible to observe phenomena as being of a certain sort, and as related to other phenomena.[17] Theories put phenomena into systems. They are built up 'in reverse' — retroductively. A theory is a cluster of conclusions in search of a premiss. From the observed properties of phenomena the physicist reasons his way towards a keystone idea from which the properties are explicable as a matter of course. The physicist seeks not a set of possible objects, but a set of possible explanations.

[15] The classical studies on this subject are those of Duhem: *De l'accélération produite par une force constante*, Congrès International de Philosophie (Genève, 1905); *Etudes sur Léonard de Vinci; Les précurseurs Parisiens de Galilée* (Paris, 1913).

[16] 'When we wish to introduce ideas whose connexion is represented in a mathematical law, we cannot first introduce the ideas and then impose the law on the symbols representing the magnitudes involved, for until we have the law the ideas are not made clear and definite. The numbers of arithmetic are not *entities* on which the laws of arithmetic are imposed. . . . The description of any dynamical phenomenon is always relative to some system of reference' (Watson, *On Understanding Physics*, p. 120).

[17] 'The experimental verifications are not the basis of the theory, but its culmination' ('Physique et metaphysique', *Revue des questions scientifiques*, XXXVI (1897)).

Retroduction and the Logic of Scientific Discovery

7

from *Is There a Logic of Scientific Discovery?*

NORWOOD R. HANSON

Is there a logic of scientific discovery? The approved answer to this is "No." Thus Popper argues:[1] "The initial stage, the act of conceiving or inventing a theory, seems to me neither to call for logical analysis nor to be susceptible of it." Again, "There is no such thing as a logical method of having new ideas, or a logical reconstruction of this process." Reichenbach writes that philosophy of science "cannot be concerned with [reasons for suggesting hypotheses], but only with [reasons for accepting hypotheses]."[2] Braithwaite elaborates: "The solution of these historical problems involves the individual psychology of thinking and the sociology of thought. None of these questions are our business here."[3]

Against this negative chorus, the 'Ayes' have *not* had it. Aristotle (*Prior Analytics* II, 25) and Peirce[4] hinted that in science there may be more problems for the logician than just analyzing the arguments supporting already invented hypotheses. But contemporary philosophers are unreceptive to this. Let us try once again to discuss the distinction F. C. S. Schiller made between the 'Logic of Proof' and the 'Logic of Discovery.'[5] We may be forced, with the majority, to conclude 'Nay.' But only after giving Aristotle and Peirce a sympathetic hearing. Is there *anything* in the idea of a 'logic of discovery' which merits the attention of a tough-minded, analytic logician?

It is unclear what a logic of discovery is a logic of. Schiller intended nothing more than "a logic of inductive inference." Doubtless his colleagues were so busy sectioning syllogisms that they ignored inferences which mattered in science. All the attention philosophers now give to inductive reasoning, probability, and the principles of theory construction would have pleased Schiller. But, for Peirce, the work of Popper, Reichenbach, and Braithwaite would read less like a *Logic of Discovery* than like a *Logic of the Finished Research Report*. Contemporary logicians of science have described how one sets out reasons in support of a hypothesis once proposed. They have said nothing about the conceptual context within which such a hypothesis is initially proposed. Both Aristotle and Peirce insisted that the proposal of a hypothesis can be a reasonable affair. One can have good reasons, or bad, for suggesting one kind of hypothesis initially, rather than some other kind. These reasons may differ in type from those which lead one to accept a hypothesis once suggested. This is not to deny that one's reasons for proposing a hypothesis initially may be identical with his reasons for later accepting it.

One thing must be stressed. When Popper, Reichenbach, and Braithwaite urge that there is no logical analysis appropriate to the psychological complex which attends the conceiving of a new idea, they are saying nothing which Aristotle or Peirce would reject. The

From *Current Issues in the Philosophy of Science* by H. Feigl and G. Maxwell, copyright © 1961 by Holt, Rinehart and Winston, Inc., New York, pp. 20–35. Reprinted by permission of the publishers.

[1] Karl Popper, *The Logic of Scientific Discovery*. New York: Basic Books, 1959, pp. 31–32.

[2] Hans Reichenbach, *Experience and Prediction*. Chicago: Univ. of Chicago Press, 1938, p. 382.

[3] R. B. Braithwaite, *Scientific Explanation*. Cambridge: Cambridge Univ. Press, 1955, pp. 21–22.

[4] C. S. Peirce, *Collected Papers*. Cambridge (Mass.): Harvard Univ. Press, 1931, Vol. I, Sec. 188.

[5] F. C. S. Schiller, "Scientific Discovery and Logical Proof," Charles Singer, ed., *Studies in the History and the Methods of the Sciences*. Vol. I. Oxford: Clarendon Press, 1917.

latter did not think themselves to be writing manuals to help scientists make discoveries. There could be no such manual.[6] Apparently they felt that there is a *conceptual* inquiry, one properly called "a logic of discovery," which is *not* to be confounded with the psychology and sociology appropriate to understanding how some investigator stumbled on to an improbable idea in unusual circumstances. There are factual discussions such as these latter. Historians like Sarton and Clagett have undertaken such circumstantial inquiries. Others — for example, Hadamard and Poincaré — have dealt with the psychology of discovery. But these are not logical discussions. They do not even turn on conceptual distinctions. Aristotle and Peirce thought they were doing something other than psychology, sociology, or history of discovery; they purported to be concerned with a *logic* of discovery.

This suggests caution for those who reject wholesale any notion of a logic of discovery on the grounds that such an inquiry can *only* be psychology, sociology, or history. That Aristotle and Peirce deny just this has made no impression. Perhaps Aristotle and Peirce were wrong. Perhaps there is no room for logic between the psychological dawning of a discovery and the justification of that discovery *via* successful predictions. But this should come as the conclusion of a discussion, not as its preamble. If Peirce is correct, nothing written by Popper, Reichenbach, or Braithwaite cuts against him. Indeed, these authors do not discuss what Peirce wishes to discuss.

Let us begin this uphill argument by distinguishing

(1) reasons for accepting a hypothesis *H*, from
(2) reasons for suggesting *H* in the first place.

This distinction is in the spirit of Peirce's thesis. Despite his arguments, most philosophers deny any *logical* difference between these two. This must be faced. But let us shape the distinction before denting it with criticism.

What would be our reasons for accepting *H*? These will be those we might have for thinking *H* true. But the reasons for suggesting *H* originally, or for formulating *H* in one way rather than another, may not be those one requires before thinking *H* true. They are, rather, those reasons which make *H* a *plausible type of conjecture*. Now, no one will deny *some* differences between what is required to show *H* true, and what is required for deciding *H* constitutes a plausible kind of conjecture. The question is: Are these logical in nature, or should they more properly be called "psychological" or "sociological"?

Or one might urge, as does Professor Feigl, that the difference is just one of refinement, degree, and intensity. Feigl argues that considerations which settle whether *H* constitutes a plausible conjecture are of the *same type* as those which settle whether *H* is true. But since the initial proposal of a hypothesis is a groping affair, involving guesswork amongst sparse data, there *is* a distinction to be drawn; but this, Feigl urges, concerns two ends of a spectrum, ranging all the way from inadequate and badly selected data to that which is abundant, well diversified, and buttressed by a battery of established theories. The issue therefore remains: Is the difference between reasons for accepting *H* and reasons for suggesting it originally one of logical type, or one of degree, or of psychology, or of sociology?

Already a refinement is necessary if our original distinction is to survive. The distinction just drawn must be reset in the following, more guarded, language. Distinguish now

(1′) reasons for accepting a particular, minutely specified hypothesis *H*, from
(2′) reasons for suggesting that, whatever specific claim the successful *H* will make, it will, nonetheless, be a hypothesis of one *kind* rather than another.

Neither Aristotle, nor Peirce, nor (if you will excuse the conjunction) myself in earlier

[6] "There is no science which will enable a man to bethink himself of that which will suit his purpose," J. S. Mill, *A System of Logic*, III, Chap. I.

writings,[7] sought this distinction on these grounds. The earlier notion was that it was some particular, minutely specified *H* which was being looked at in two ways: (1) what would count for the acceptance of that *H*, and (2) what would count in favor of suggesting that same *H* initially.

This latter way of putting it is objectionable. The issue is whether, *before* having hit a hypothesis which succeeds in its predictions, one can have good reasons for anticipating that the hypothesis will be one of some particular *kind*. Could Kepler, for example, have had good reasons, *before* his elliptical-orbit hypothesis was established, for supposing that the successful hypothesis concerning Mars' orbit would be of the noncircular kind?[8] He *could* have argued that, whatever path the planet *did* describe, it would be a closed, smoothly curving, plane geometrical figure. Only this *kind* of hypothesis could entail such observation-statements as that Mars' apparent velocities at 90 degrees and at 270 degrees of eccentric anomaly were greater than any circular-type *H* could explain. Other *kinds* of hypotheses were available to Kepler: for example, that Mars' *color* is responsible for its high velocities, or that the dispositions of Jupiter's moons are responsible. But these would not have struck Kepler as capable of explaining such surprising phenomena. Indeed, he would have thought it *un*reasonable to develop such hypotheses at all, and would have argued thus. [Braithwaite counters: "But exactly which hypothesis was to be rejected was a matter for the 'hunch' of the physicists."[9] However, which *type* of hypothesis Kepler chose to reject was not just a matter of 'hunch.']

I may still be challenged. Some will continue to berate my distinction between reasons for suggesting which type of hypothesis *H* will be, and reasons for accepting *H* ultimately.[10] There may indeed be "psychological" factors, the opposition concedes, which make certain types of hypotheses 'look' as if they might explain phenomena. Ptolemy knew, as well as did Aristarchus before him and Copernicus after him, that a kind of astronomy which displaced the earth would be theoretically simpler, and easier to manage, than the hypothesis of a geocentric, geostatic universe. *But*, philosophers challenge, for psychological, sociological, or historical reasons, alternatives to geocentricism did not 'look' as if they could explain the absence of stellar parallax. This cannot be a matter of logic, since for Copernicus one such alternative *did* 'look' as if it could explain this. Insofar as scientists have *reasons* for formulating types of hypotheses (as opposed to hunches and intuitions), these are just the kinds of reasons which later show a particular *H* to be true. Thus, if the absence of stellar parallax constitutes more than a psychological reason for Ptolemy's resistance to alternatives to geocentricism, then it *is* his reason for rejecting such alternatives as *false*. Conversely, his reason for developing a geostatic type of hypothesis (again, absence of parallax) was his reason for taking some such hypothesis as *true*. And Kepler's reasons for rejecting Mars' color or Jupiter's moons as indicating the kinds of hypotheses responsible for Mars' accelerations were reasons which also served later in establishing some hypothesis of the noncircularity type.

So the objection to my distinction is: The only *logical* reason for proposing *H* will be of a certain type is that *data* incline us to think some *particular H* true. What Hanson advocates is psychological, sociological, or historical in nature; it has no logical import for the differences between proposing and establishing hypotheses.

Kepler again illustrates the objection. Every historian of science knows how the

[7] Cf. *Patterns of Discovery*. Cambridge, Mass.: Harvard Univ. Press, 1958, pp. 85–92; "The Logic of Discovery," in *Journal of Philosophy*, LV, 25, 1073–1089, 1958; More on "The Logic of Discovery," *op. cit.*, LVII, 6, 182–188, 1960.

[8] Cf. *De Motibus Stellae Martis*. Munich, pp. 250ff.

[9] *Op. cit.*, p. 20.

[10] Reichenbach writes that philosophy "cannot be concerned with the first, but only with the latter" (*op. cit.*, p. 382).

idea of uniform circular motion affected astronomers before 1600. Indeed, in 1591 Kepler abandoned a hypothesis because it entailed other-than-uniform circular orbits — something simply inconceivable for him. So psychological pressure against forming alternative types of hypotheses was great. But *logically* Kepler's reasons for entertaining a type of Martian motion other than uniformly circular were his reasons for accepting that as astronomical truth. He first encountered this type of hypothesis on perceiving that no simple adjustment of epicycle, deferent, and eccentric could square Mars' observed distances, velocities, and apsidal positions. These were also reasons which led him to assert that the planet's orbit is not the effect of circular motions, but of an elliptical path. Even after other inductive reasons confirmed the truth of the latter hypothesis, these early reasons were *still* reasons for accepting H as true. So they cannot have been reasons merely for proposing which type of hypothesis H would be, and nothing more.

This objection has been made strong. If the following cannot weaken it, then we shall have to accept it; we shall have to grant that there is *no* aspect of discovery which has to do with logical, or conceptual considerations.

When Kepler published *De Motibus Stellae Martis*, he had established that Mars' orbit was an ellipse, inclined to the ecliptic, and had the sun in one of the foci. Later (in the *Harmonices Mundi*) he generalized this for other planets. Consider the hypothesis H': *Jupiter's* orbit is of the noncircular type.

The reasons which led Kepler to formulate H' were many. But they included this: that H (the hypothesis that *Mars'* orbit is elliptical) is true. Since Eudoxos, Mars had been the typical planet. (*We* know why. Mars' retrogradations and its movement around the empty focus — all this we observe with clarity from earth because of earth's spatial relations with Mars.) Now, Mars' dynamical properties are usually found in the other planets. If its orbit is ellipsoidal, then it is reasonable to expect that, whatever the exact shape of the other orbits (for example, Jupiter's), they will all be of the noncircular type.

But such reasons would not *establish* H'. Because what makes it reasonable to anticipate that H' will be of a certain type is *analogical* in character. (Mars does x; Mars is a typical planet; so perhaps all planets do the same kind of thing as x.) Analogies cannot establish hypotheses, not even *kinds* of hypotheses. Only observations can do that. In this the hypothetico-deductive account (of Popper, Reichenbach, and Braithwaite) is correct. To establish H' requires plotting its successive positions on a smooth curve whose equations can be determined. It may then be possible to assert that Jupiter's orbit is an ellipse, an oviform, an epicycloid, or whatever. But it would not be reasonable to expect this when discussing only what type of hypothesis is likely to describe Jupiter's orbit. Nor is it right to characterize this difference between 'H-as-illustrative-of-a-type-of hypothesis' and 'H-as-empirically established' as a difference of psychology only. *Logically*, Kepler's analogical reasons for proposing that H' would be of a certain type were good reasons. But, logically, they would not then have been good reasons for asserting the truth of a specific value for H' — something which could be done only years later.

What are and are not good reasons for reaching a certain conclusion is a logical matter. No further observations are required to settle such issues, any more than we require experiments to decide, on the basis of one's bank statements, whether one is bankrupt. Similarly, whether or not Kepler's reasons for anticipating that H' will be of a certain kind are *good* reasons is a matter for logical inquiry.

Thus, the differences between reasons for expecting that some as yet-undiscovered H will be of a certain type and those that establish this H are greater than is conveyed by calling them "psychological," "sociological," or "historical."

Kepler reasoned initially by analogy. Other kinds of reasons which make it plausible to propose that an *H*, once discovered, will be of a certain type, might include, for example, the detection of a formal symmetry in sets of equations or arguments. At important junctures Clerk Maxwell and Einstein detected such structural symmetries. This allowed them to argue, before getting their final answers, that those answers would be of a clearly describable type.

In the late 1920's, before anyone had explained the "negative-energy" solutions in Dirac's electron theory, good analogical reasons could have been advanced for the claim that, whatever specific assertion the ultimately successful *H* assumed, it would be of the Lorentz-invariant type. It could have been conjectured that the as yet undiscovered *H* would be compatible with the Dirac explanation of Compton scattering and doublet atoms, and would fail to confirm Schrödinger's hunch that the phase waves within configuration space actually described observable physical phenomena. All this could have been said before Weyl, Oppenheimer, and Dirac formulated the "hole theory of the positive electron." Good analogical reasons for supposing that this *type* of *H* would succeed could have been and, as a matter of fact, were advanced. Indeed, Schrödinger's attempt to rewrite the Dirac theory so that the negative-energy solutions disappeared was *rejected* for failing to preserve Lorentz invariance.

Thus, reasoning from observations of *A*s as *B*s to the proposal "All *A*s are *B*s" is different in type from reasoning analogically from the fact that *C*s are *D*s to the proposal "The hypothesis relating *A*s and *B*s will be of the same type as that relating *C*s and *D*s." (Here it is the *way* *C*s are *D*s which seems analogous to the way *A*s are *B*s.) And both of these are typically different from reasoning involving the detection of symmetries in equations describing *A*s and *B*s.

Indeed, put this way, what *could* an objection to the foregoing consist of? Establishing a hypothesis and proposing by analogy that a hypothesis is likely to be of a particular type surely follow reasoning which is different in type. Moreover, both procedures have a fundamentally logical or conceptual interest.

An objection: "Analogical arguments. and those based on the recognition of formal symmetries, are used because of inductively established beliefs in the reliability of arguments of that type. So, the cash value of such appeals ultimately collapses into just those accounts given by *H-D* theorists."

Agreed. But we are not discussing the *genesis* of our faith in these types of arguments, only the *logic* of the arguments themselves. *Given* an analogical premise, or one based on symmetry considerations — or even on enumeration of particulars — one argues *from* these in logically different ways. Consider what further moves are necessary to convince one who doubted such arguments. A challenge to "All *A*s are *B*s" when this is based on induction by enumeration could only be a challenge to justify induction, or at least to show that the particulars are being correctly described. This is inappropriate when the arguments rest on analogies or on the recognition of formal symmetries.

Another objection: "Analogical reasons, and those based on symmetry are *still* reasons for *H* even after it is (inductively) established. They are reasons *both* for proposing that *H* will be of a certain type and for accepting *H*."

Agreed, again. But, analogical and symmetry arguments could never *by themselves* establish particular *H*s. They can only make it plausible to suggest that *H* (when discovered) will be of a certain type. However, inductive arguments can, by themselves, establish particular hypotheses. So they must differ from arguments of the analogical or symmetrical sort.

H-D philosophers have been most articulate on these matters. So, let us draw out a related issue on which Popper, Reichenbach, and Braithwaite seem to me not to have said the last word.

J. S. Mill was wrong about Kepler (*A System of Logic*, III, 2–3). It is impossible to reconcile the delicate adjustment between theory, hypothesis, and observation recorded in *De Motibus Stellae Martis* with Mill's statement that Kepler's first law is but "a compendius expression for the one set of directly observed facts." Mill did not understand Kepler (as Peirce notes [*Collected Papers*, I, p. 31]). (It is equally questionable whether Reichenbach understood him: "Kepler's laws of the elliptic motion of celestial bodies were inductive generalizations of observed fact . . . [he] observed a series of . . . positions of the planet Mars and found that they may be connected by a mathematical relation . . .")[11] Mill's *Logic* is as misleading about scientific discovery as any account proceeding *via* what Bacon calls "*inductio per enumerationem simplicem ubi non reperitur instantia contradictoria*." (Indeed Reichenbach observes: "It is the great merit of John Stuart Mill to have pointed out that all empirical inferences are reducible to the *inductio per enumerationem simplicem*. . . .")[12] The accounts of *H-D* theorists are equally misleading.

An *H-D* account of Kepler's first law would treat it as a high-level hypothesis in an *H-D* system. (This is Braithwaite's language.) It is regarded as a quasi-axiom, from whose assumption observation-statements follow. If these are true — if, for example, they imply that Uranus' orbit is an ellipse and that its apparent velocity at 90 degrees is greater than at aphelion — then the first law is confirmed. (Thus Braithwaite writes: "A scientific system consists of a set of hypotheses which form a deductive system . . . arranged in such a way that from some of the hypotheses as premises all the other hypotheses logically follow . . . the establishment of a system as a set of true propositions depends upon the establishment of its lowest level hypotheses . . .")[13]

This describes physical theory more adequately than did pre-Baconian accounts in terms of simple enumeration, or even post-Millian accounts in terms of ostensibly not-so-simple enumerations. It tells us about the logic of laws, and what they do in finished arguments and explanations. *H-D* accounts do not, however, tell us anything about the context in which laws are proposed in the first place; nor, perhaps, were they even intended to do so.

The induction-by-enumeration story *did* intend to do this. *It* sought to describe good reasons for initially proposing *H*. The *H-D* account must be silent on this point. Indeed, the two accounts are not strict alternatives. (As Braithwaite suggests they are when he remarks of a certain higher-level hypothesis that it "will not have been established by induction by simple enumeration; it will have been obtained by the hypothetico-deductive method. . . .")[14] They are thoroughly compatible. Acceptance of the second is no reason for rejecting the first. A law *might* have been inferred from just an enumeration of particulars (for example, Boyle's law in the seventeenth century, Bode's in the eighteenth, the laws of Ampere and Faraday in the nineteenth, and much of meson theory now). It could *then* be built into an *H-D* system as a higher order proposition. If there is anything wrong with the older view, *H-D* accounts do not reveal this.

There *is* something wrong. It is false. Scientists do not always discover every feature of a law by enumerating and summarizing observables. (Thus even Braithwaite[15] says: "Sophisticated generalizations (such as that about the proton-electron constitution of the hydrogen atom) . . . [were] certainly not derived by simple enumeration of instances . . .") But *this* does not strengthen the *H-D* account as against the inductive view. There is *no* *H-D* account of how "sophisticated generalizations" are *derived*. On his own principles, the *H-D* theorist's lips are sealed on this matter. But there are conceptual considerations which help us understand the *reasoning* that is sometimes successful in determining the type of an as-yet-undiscovered hypothesis.

Were the *H-D* account construed as a description of scientific practice, it would be

[11] Reichenbach, *op. cit.*, p. 371.
[12] *Ibid.*, p. 389.
[13] Braithwaite, *op. cit.*, pp. 12–13.
[14] *Ibid.*, p. 303.
[15] *Ibid.*, p. 11.

misleading. (Braithwaite's use of "derived" is thus misleading. So is his announcement [p. 11] that he is going to explain "*how we come to make* use of sophisticated generalizations.") Natural scientists do not "start from" hypotheses. They start from data. And even then not from commonplace data, but from surprising anomalies. (Thus Aristotle remarks[16] that knowledge begins in astonishment. Peirce makes perplexity the trigger of scientific inquiry.[17] And James and Dewey treat intelligence as the result of mastering problem situations.)[18]

By the time a law gets fixed into an *H-D* system, the *original* scientific thinking is over. The pedestrian process of deducing observation-statements begins only after the physicist is convinced that the proposed hypothesis is at least of the right type to explain the initially perplexing data. Kepler's assistant could work out the consequences of H' and check its validity by seeing whether Jupiter behaved as H' predicts. This was possible because of Kepler's argument that what H had done for Mars, H' might do for Jupiter. The *H-D* account is helpful here; it analyzes *the argument of a completed research report.* It helps us see how experimentalists elaborate a theoretician's hypotheses. And the *H-D* account illuminates yet another aspect of science, but its proponents have not stressed it. Scientists often dismiss explanations alternative to that which has won their provisional assent along lines that typify the *H-D* method. Examples are in Ptolemy's *Almagest*, when (on observational grounds) he rules out a moving earth, in Copernicus' *De Revolutionibus* . . . , when he rejects Ptolemy's lunar theory, in Kepler's *De Motibus Stellae Martis*, when he denies that the planes of the planetary orbits intersect in the center of the ecliptic, and in Newton's *Principia*, when he discounts the idea that the gravitational force law might be of an inverse cube nature. These mirror formal parts of Mill's *System of Logic* or Braithwaite's *Scientific Explanation.*

Still, the *H-D* analysis remains silent on reasoning which often conditions the discovery of laws — reasoning that determines which type of hypothesis is likely to be most fruitful to propose.

The induction-by-enumeration story views scientific inference as being from observations to the law, from particulars to the general. There is something true about this which the *H-D* account must ignore. Thus Newton wrote: "The main business of natural philosophy is to argue from phenomena. . . ."[19]

This inductive view, however, ignores what Newton never ignored: the inference is also from *explicanda* to an *explicans.* Why a beveled mirror shows spectra in sunlight is not explained by saying that all beveled mirrors do this. Why Mars moves more rapidly at 270 degrees and 90 degrees than could be expected of circular-uniform motions is not explained by saying that Mars (or even all planets) always move thus. On the induction view, these latter might count as laws. But only when it is explained why beveled mirrors show spectra and why planets apparently accelerate at 90 degrees will we have laws of the type suggested: Newton's laws of refraction and Kepler's first law. And even before such discoveries were made, arguments in favor of those *types* of laws were possible.

So the inductive view rightly suggests that laws are somehow related to inferences *from* data. It wrongly suggests that the resultant law is but a summary of these data, instead of being an explanation of these data. A logic of discovery, then, might consider the structure of arguments in favor of one *type* of possible explanation in a given context as opposed to other *types.*

H-D accounts all agree that laws explain data. (Thus Braithwaite says: "A hypothesis to be regarded as a natural law must be a general proposition which can be thought to explain its instances; if the reason for believing the general proposition is solely direct

[16] Aristotle, *Metaphysics* 982b, 11ff.

[17] Peirce, *op. cit.*, Vol. II, Book III, Chap. 2, Part III.

[18] Cf. John Dewey, *How We Think.* London: Heath & Co., 1909, pp. 12f.

[19] Newton, *Principia*, Preface.

knowledge of the truth of its instances, it will be felt to be a poor sort of explanation of these instances . . ." [*op. cit.*, p. 302].) *H-D* theorists, however, obscure the initial connection between thinking about data and thinking about what kind of hypothesis will most likely lead to a law. They suggest that the fundamental inference in science is from higher-order hypotheses to observation-statements. This may characterize the setting out of one's reasons for making a prediction after *H* is formulated and provisionally established. It need not be a way of setting out reasons in favor of proposing originally of what type *H* is likely to be.

Yet the original suggestion of a hypothesis type is often a reasonable affair. It is not as dependent on intuition, hunches, and other imponderables as historians and philosophers suppose when they make it the province of genius but not of logic. If the establishment of *H* through its predictions has a logic, so has the initial suggestion that *H* is likely to be of one kind rather than another. To form the first specific idea of an elliptical planetary orbit, or of constant acceleration, or of universal gravitational attraction does indeed require genius — nothing less than a Kepler, a Galileo, or a Newton. But this does not entail that reflections leading to these ideas are nonrational. Perhaps *only* Kepler, Galileo and Newton had intellects mighty enough to fashion these notions initially; but to concede this is not to concede that their reasons for first entertaining concepts of such a type surpass rational inquiry.

H-D accounts begin with the hypothesis as given, as cooking recipes begin with the trout. Recipes, however, sometimes suggest, "First catch your trout." The *H-D* account is a recipe physicists often use after catching hypotheses. However, the conceptual boldness which marks the history of physics shows more in the ways in which scientists *caught* their hypotheses than in the ways in which they elaborated these once caught.

To study only the verification of hypotheses leaves a vital part of the story untold — namely, the reasons Kepler, Galileo, and Newton had for thinking their hypotheses would be of one kind rather than another. In a letter to Fabricius, Kepler underlines this:

Prague, July 4, 1603

Dear Fabricius,

. . . You believe that I start with imagining some pleasant hypothesis and please myself in embellishing it, examining it only later by observations. In this you are very much mistaken. The truth is that after having built up an hypothesis on the ground of observations and given it proper foundations, I feel a peculiar desire to investigate whether I might discover some natural, satisfying combination between the two . . .

Had any *H-D* theorist ever sought to give an account of the way in which hypotheses in science *are discovered*, Kepler's words are for him. Doubtless *H-D* philosophers have tried to give just such an account. Thus, Braithwaite[20] writes: "Every science *proceeds* . . . by thinking of general hypotheses . . . from which particular consequences are deduced which can be tested by observation . . . ," and again, "Galileo's deductive system was . . . presented as deducible from . . . Newton's laws of motion and . . . his law of universal gravitation . . ."

How would an *H-D* theorist analyze the law of gravitation?

(1) First, the hypothesis *H*: that between any two particles in the universe exists an attracting force varying inversely as the square of the distance between them ($F = \lambda Mm/r^2$).
(2) Deduce from this (in accordance with the *Principia*).
 (a) *Kepler's* Laws, and
 (b) *Galileo's* Laws.
(3) But particular instances of (a) and (b) square with what is observed.
(4) Therefore *H* is, to this extent, confirmed.

The *H-D* account says nothing about how *H* was first puzzled out. But now consider why, here, the *H-D* account is *prima-facie* plausible.

Historians remark that Newton's reflections on this problem began in 1680 when Halley asked: "If between a planet and the sun there

[20] *Op. cit.*, pp. xv, xi, 18.

exists an attraction varying inversely as the square of their distance, what then would be the path of the planet?" Halley was astonished by the immediate answer: "An ellipse." The astonishment arose not because Newton *knew* the path of a planet, but because he had apparently deduced this from the hypothesis of universal gravitation. Halley begged for the proof; but it was lost in the chaos of Newton's room. Sir Isaac's promise to work it out anew terminated in the writing of the *Principia* itself. Thus the story unfolds as an *H-D* plot: (1) from the suggestion of a hypothesis (whose genesis is a matter of logical indifference — that is, psychology, sociology, or history) to (2) the deduction of observation statements (the laws of Kepler and Galileo), which turn out true, thus (3) establishing the hypothesis.

Indeed, the entire *Principia* unfolds as the plot requires — from propositions of high generality through those of restricted generality, terminating in observation-statements. Thus Braithwaite[21] observes: "Newton's *Principia* [was] modelled on the Euclidean analogy and professed to prove [its] later propositions — those which were confirmed by confrontation with experience — by deducing them from original first principles . . ."

Despite this, the orthodox account is suspicious. The answer Newton gave Halley is not unique. He could have said "a circle" or "a parabola," and have been equally correct. The general answer is: "A conic section." The greatest mathematician of his time is not likely to have dealt with so mathematical a question as that concerning the possibility of a formal demonstration with an answer which is but a single value of the correct answer.

Yet the reverse inference, the retroduction, *is* unique. Given that the planetary orbits are ellipses, and allowing Huygen's law of centripetal force and Kepler's rule (that the square of a planet's period of revolution is proportional to the cube of its distance from the sun), the *type* of the law of gravitation can be inferred. Thus the question, "If the planetary orbits are ellipses, what form will the gravitational force law take?" invites the unique answer, "an inverse square type of law."

Given the datum that Mars moves in an ellipse, one can (by way of Huygen's law and Kepler's third law) explain this uniquely by suggesting how it might follow from a law of the inverse square type, such as the law of universal gravitation was later discovered to be.

The rough idea behind all this is: Given an ellipsoidal eggshell, imagine a tiny pearl moving inside it along the maximum elliptical orbit. What *kind* of force must the eggshell exert on the pearl to keep the latter in this path? Huygen's weights, when whirled on strings, required a force in the string, and in Huygen's arm, of $F_{(k)} \propto r/T^2$ (where r signifies distance, T time, and k is a constant of proportionality). This restraining force kept the weights from flying away like stones from David's sling. And something like this force would be expected in the eggshell. Kepler's third law gives $T^2 \propto r^3$. Hence, $F_{(k)} \propto r/r^3 \propto 1/r^2$. The force the shell exerts on the pearl will be of a kind which varies inversely as the square of the distance of the pearl from that focus of the ellipsoidal eggshell where the force may be supposed to be centered. This is not yet the law of gravitation. But it certainly is an argument which suggests that the law is likely to be of an inverse square type. This follows by what Peirce called 'retroductive reasoning.' But what *is* this retroductive reasoning whose superiority over the *H-D* account has been so darkly hinted at?

Schematically, it can be set out thus:

(1) Some surprising, astonishing phenomena $p_1, p_2, p_3 \ldots$ are encountered.[22]

[21] *Op. cit.*, p. 352.

[22] The astonishment may consist in the fact that p is at variance with accepted *theories* — for example, the discovery of discontinuous emission of radiation by hot black bodies, or the photoelectric effect, the Compton effect, and the continuous β-ray spectrum, or the orbital aberrations of Mercury, the refrangibility of white light, and the high velocities of Mars at 90 degrees. What is important here is *that* the phenomena are encountered as anomalous, not *why* they are so regarded.

(2) But $p_1, p_2, p_3 \ldots$ would not be surprising were a hypothesis of *H*'s type to obtain. They would follow as a matter of course from something like *H* and would be explained by it.

(3) Therefore there is good reason for elaborating a hypothesis of the type of *H*; for proposing it as a possible hypothesis from whose assumption $p_1, p_2, p_3 \ldots$ might be explained.[23]

How, then, would the discovery of universal gravitation fit this account?

(1) The astonishing discovery that all planetary orbits are elliptical was made by Kepler.

(2) But such an orbit would not be surprising if, in addition to other familiar laws, a law of 'gravitation,' of the inverse square type obtained. Kepler's first law would follow as a matter of course; indeed that kind of hypothesis might even explain why (since the sun is in but one of the foci) the orbits are ellipses on which the planets travel with non-uniform velocity.

(3) Therefore there is good reason for further elaborating hypotheses of this kind.

This says something about the rational context within which a hypothesis of *H*'s type might come to be "caught" in the first place. It begins where all physics begins—with problematic phenomena requiring explanation. It suggests what might be done to particular hypotheses once proposed—namely, the *H-D* elaboration. And it points up how much philosophers have yet to learn about the kinds of reasons scientists might have for thinking that one kind of hypothesis may explain initial perplexities; why, for example, an inverse square type of hypothesis may be preferred over others, *if* it throws the initially perplexing data into patterns within which determinate modes of connection can be perceived. At least it appears that the ways in which scientists sometimes reason their way *towards* hypotheses, by eliminating those which are certifiably of the wrong type, may be as legitimate an area for conceptual inquiry as are the ways in which they reason their way *from* hypotheses.

Recently, in the Lord Portsmouth collection in the Cambridge University Library, a document was discovered which bears on our discussion. There, in "Additional manuscripts 3968, No. 41, bundle 2," is the following draft in Newton's own hand:

> And in the same year [1665, twenty years before the *Principia*] I began to think of gravity extending to ye orb of the Moon, and (having found out how to estimate the force with which a globe revolving within a sphere presses the surface of the sphere), from Kepler's rule . . . I deduced that the forces which keep the planets in their Orbs must be reciprocally as the squares of their distances from the centres about which they revolve . . .

This manuscript corroborates our argument. ("Deduce," in this passage, is used as when Newton speaks of deducing laws from phenomena—which is just what Aristotle and Peirce would call "retroduce.") Newton *knew* how to estimate the force of a small globe on the inner surface of a sphere. (To compare this with Halley's question and our pearl-within-eggshell reconstruction, note that a sphere can be regarded as a degenerate ellipsoid—that is, where the foci superimpose.) From this and from Kepler's rule, $T^2 \propto r^3$, Newton determined that, whatever the final form of the law of gravitation, it would very probably be of the inverse-square type. These were the reasons which led Newton to think further about the details of universal gravitation. The reasons for accepting one such hypothesis of this type *as a law* are powerfully set out later in the *Principia* itself; and they are much more comprehensive than anything which occurred to him at this early age. But without such preliminary

[23] This is a free development of remarks in Aristotle (*Prior Analytics*, II, 25) and Peirce (*op. cit.*). Peirce amplifies: "It must be remembered that retroduction, although it is very little hampered by logical rules, nevertheless, is logical inference, asserting its conclusion only problematically, or conjecturally, it is true, but nevertheless having a perfectly definite logical form" (*op. cit.*, Vol. I, p. 188).

reasoning Newton might have had no more grounds than Hooke or Wren for thinking the gravitation law to be of an inverse-square type.

The morals of all this for our understanding of contemporary science are clear. With such a rich profusion of data and technique as we have, the arguments necessary for *eliminating* hypotheses of the wrong type become a central research inquiry. Such arguments are not always of the *H-D* type; but if for that reason alone we refuse to scrutinize the conceptual content of the reasoning which precedes the actual proposal of definite hypotheses, we will have a poorer understanding of scientific thought in our time. For our own sakes, we must attend as much to how scientific hypotheses are caught, as to how they are cooked.

Scientific Laws Are Many-Splendored Things 8

from *Patterns of Discovery*
NORWOOD R. HANSON

Laws of classical particle physics exercise philosophers. Statements of these laws are in some sense empirical, yet they seem often to resist the idea of disconfirmation: evidence against them is sometimes impossible to conceive.

Newton stressed the empirical basis of dynamics: Broad has inherited this interest in the evidence supporting dynamical law statements; he regards them as substantive, descriptive, empirical propositions. Myriad confirmations[1] and a central place in the system of dynamical concepts — these are the only reasons why it is difficult to imagine a macrophysical world in which the laws do not obtain.

But other thinkers are impressed by the resistance of dynamical law statements to falsification. Poincaré is typical of those who regard such statements as conventions, or definitions, or procedural rules, or boundary conditions.[2] Hence, for him it is their empirical aspects that must be explained, or explained away.

Seen through classical dichotomies, classical mechanics is challenging. It springs from empirical propositions against which disconfirmation is not always conceivable. Disconfirmation would result not in conceptions which negate those in the law statements, but in no coherent conceptions at all. Apparently we must explain away either their conventional aspects or their contingent features; they are not to float betwixt and between. (Kant refused to explain away either. He was in some ways a better observer of physics than his critics; for him, being betwixt and between was the virtue of Newton's dynamics.)

So much for the celebrated question 'What is the logical status of the laws of classical particle physics?', to which Broad, Poincaré and Kant have given important, but single-valued answers. The question itself is misleading. It is like asking 'What is *the* use of rope?'. The replies to this are no fewer than the uses for rope. There are as many uses for the sentences which express dynamical law statements as there are types of context in which they can be employed. In trying to provide *the* answer to the above query, Broad, Poincaré and Kant (not to mention Mill, Whewell, Mach, Pearson, Russell, Braithwaite and Toulmin) have shown how versatile physicists really are with the sentences and formulae of dynamics. There is no such thing as *the* law of inertia, *the* law of force, *the* law of gravitation.

Let us contrast the actual scientific uses of dynamical law statements with philosophical commentaries on their status. This will raise questions about the relationship between the uses of law sentences and the logic of law statements, about the ways in which the latter can be regarded as *a priori*, and about other matters.

A

Dynamical law statements help to explain physical events. An event is explained when

From *Patterns of Discovery* by Norwood R. Hanson, Cambridge University Press, London, 1958, pp. 93–105.

[1] In the physics of molar bodies moving at moderate speeds through 'middle sized' spaces.

[2] Cf. e.g. *The Foundations of Science*, p. 28 (l. 5), pp. 97, 99, 102, 106, 125, 318, 328.

it is traced to other events which require less explanation; when it is shown to be part of an intelligible pattern of events.

On striding into my study I slide abruptly across the floor — it has just been polished. There is no more to say, no need for further explanation. This means, not that there is no further explanation, but only that it is too obvious; the effect on perambulation of polished floors is no secret. That my floor has been polished is all the explanation needed for this performance: the general reason why shoe leather slips on polish is not of immediate relevance in explaining why I slipped. Trace an event to incidents which are commonplace and we are rarely interested in tracing it further. The pattern is too clear.

When events have been explained by linking them to statements of the laws of classical particle physics, however, this cannot be because the *explicans* is commonplace. Aristotle was able to detect the commonplace, yet he would have denied at least part of the first law of motion, namely: 'All bodies remain either at rest or in uniform rectilinear motion, unless compelled by impressed forces to change their state.'[3] This is not obviously true; the Philosopher treats it as clearly false.[4]

But some Newtonians felt that this law statement explained events not because it expressed a commonplace, but because *it* needed no explanation. That the area within a circle is the maximum for any closed curve of that perimeter needs no explanation; that is what circles are. The quotation above sets out how bodies do move; what further is there to explain? Kepler's discovery left nothing further to explain about Mars' motion. Dynamical explanations derive from statements like this one above. Why expect that this statement can itself be explained dynamically?[5]

So a statement of the law of inertia describes a kind of event (inertial motion) whose explanation, while not obvious, is not as a matter of principle required. What is to be said of this comment on the law of inertia? Some events need less explaining than others. That the Earth moves needs less explaining than that it moves in an ellipsoidal orbit and rotates on its axis; these latter require all the explaining needed by the former, and more besides.

If that to which I refer when accounting for events needs more explaining than that to which you refer, then your explanation is better than mine. Kepler's astronomy needed less supplementary explanation than Tycho's, and so was better. Galileo's cosmology required less explanation than did that of his Ptolemaic adversary, Simplicius: therefore Galileo's was better.[6] Because Aristotle's account of the natural motion of bodies required more *ad hoc* explanation than the account in the first law of motion, Newton's was better.

Apparently, then, the best explanation must show how an event needing no explanation (inertial motion) is connected with observed events. But this makes it seem that the goal of physics is to explain the contingent in terms of the *a priori*; to account for events needing explanation in terms of those which need none at all. The goal seems to be to relate vulnerable statements with those which are invulnerable. This view is not absent from the history of mechanics. Latter-day Newtonians regarded dynamical law statements as needing no explanation whatever;[7] for various reasons they were treated

[3] 'Corpus omne perseverare in statu suo quiescendi vel movendi uniformiter in directum, nisi quotenus a viribus impressis cogitur statum illum mutare' (Newton, *Philosophiae Naturalis Principia Mathematica*, 'Axioms').

[4] Aristotle, *De Caelo* (trans. Ross, Oxford University Press, 1928), 276a (22ff.), 277a (14ff.), 294b (32ff.); *Physica*, 256a (5–21), esp. 11, 29 and 30, 256b, 258b (10ff.) 260a (l. 12ff.), esp. 265a (13), and ll. 28–35, 266b (25–35) and 267a.

[5] Newton, *Principia*. Cf. Cote's preface to the 2nd ed. (1713).

[6] Cf. Galileo, *Dialogues Concerning the Two Chief World Systems* (Univ. of California, 1953). The First Day, esp. pp. 45, 52; the Second Day, esp. pp. 113, 115ff., 188ff., 248, 253, 257ff.; the Third Day, esp. pp. 320ff., etc.

[7] Atwood and Whewell and Lagrange may be cited; the Royal Society of the late eighteenth and early nineteenth centuries was full of physicists of this temperament.

as prescriptive, immutable, *a priori*. Indeed, this is what such statements seemed designed to be — the ultimate shackles in chains of physical explanation.[8] Many physicists have used them thus.

Apparently a statement of the first law needs no explanation, because it could not be false; yet it tells us what happens in nature, or what would happen if certain conditions were realized. Thus the empirical grounds for asserting the first law are events like slipping on polished floors, or observing how a round rock moves across ice with but slightly diminishing velocity until it slows to a halt. When the first law statement seems not to hold, the reason can always be found: ground glass on the ice, perhaps, or the discovery that the rock is a lodestone, etc. The law encapsulates and extrapolates much information about events, yet it seems beyond disconfirmation: it could not but be true.

'But surely, after having been kicked across the smoothest ice a rock could stop abruptly. It could return to where it was kicked, or even describe circles.[9] This could happen without ground glass, magnets, or anything else. Is this not possible?'

Here some will reply 'Yes', others 'No'. As before, this is not an experimental issue; it concerns the organization of concepts. The man who says 'No' might continue:

Once in motion a rock cannot suddenly stop unless something stops it. It cannot return to the kicker's toe unless something brings it back — a magnet, or a jet of air, or invisible threads. It cannot turn circles unless guided by imperceptible grooves in the ice. It would not be a rock, not even a physical body, unless when free of impressed forces it was 'in statu suo quiescendi vel movendi uniformiter in directum'. Anything else is unthinkable.

When others would regard anomalous events as falsifying the law, this person would say 'That only shows the presence of some hidden mechanism.[10] Or else what we took for a rock is not a rock at all.' The first law is less vulnerable to experience for him than for others. He may even regard any event which apparently disconfirms the law statement as itself guaranteeing that (despite appearances) the moving body was not free of impressed forces; or did, in fact, move in a straight line; or was no ordinary physical body. We all reason this way sometimes; physicists observing rocks on ice certainly do so. In the ordinary mechanics of middle-sized bodies a statement of the law of inertia is practically invulnerable. It could hardly be false. Whatever proves a body's motion not to be rectilinear also proves that it is acted on by forces. Thus a form of words, 'If A then B', at first used so that what it

[8] Cf. esp. Helmholtz: 'The task of physical science is to reduce all phenomena of nature to forces of attraction and repulsion the intensity of which is dependent only upon the mutual distance of material bodies. Only if this problem is solved are we sure that nature is conceivable' (*Über die Erhaltung der Kraft*). Cf. Euler: 'The whole of Natural Science consists in showing in what state the bodies were when this or that change took place, and that, . . . just that change had to take place which actually occurred' (*Anleitung zur Naturlehre* (in *Opera Posthuma*, II, Leipzig and Berlin, 1911), vol. vi, § 50).

[9] Cf. Galileo, *Two Chief World Systems*, pp. 28–32.

[10] This type of reasoning led to the discovery of Neptune by V. J. Leverrier (1846), the greatest triumph of Newton's mechanics. The companion stars of Sirius and Procyon were also discovered before they were seen. (Incidentally, the philosophical examination of Leverrier's work has yet to be written. How remarkable that this man should have raised classical mechanics to its highest pinnacle by predicting the unseen Neptune as being responsible for observed aberrations in the orbit of Uranus; yet by this same argument he postulated the 'planet' Vulcan to explain Mercury's precessions at perihelion, and classical mechanics met its most telling failure. It cannot have been the fate of many physicists to have served both as the saviour and as the executioner of a physical theory.)

Cf. Hertz (*Principles of Mechanics*, Bk. II, p. 735): 'At first it might have appeared that the fundamental law was far from sufficient to embrace the whole extent of facts which nature offers us. . . . We saw, however, that we could also investigate abnormal and discontinuous systems if we regarded their abnormalities and discontinuities as only apparent; that we could also follow the motion of unfree systems if we conceived them as portions of free systems; that, finally, even systems apparently contradicting the fundamental law could be rendered conformable to it by admitting the possibility of concealed masses in them.'

expresses could be false, comes to express what could not be false.[11]

Alcohol boils at 78.3° C. Many people, even alcoholics, do not know this. But most of them know what to look for when asked 'Is that fluid alcoholic?', 'Is there alcohol in that beaker?', 'Is the liquid in the beaker boiling?' and 'What does the thermometer indicate?'. They know how to answer 'What did the thermometer indicate when the alcohol boiled?'. We learn empirically that it always reads 78.3° C;[12] and so invariant is this that it is virtually part of what we mean by 'alcohol' — at least in physics. A fluid that does not boil at 78.3° C. is not alcohol. That it should be is inconceivable. Similarly, the idea of a rock moving in a circle *proprio motu* over ice makes the physicist's imagination boggle.

In general, to say that something is A (e.g. alcohol) is to remark a characteristic cluster of properties a_1–a_n (e.g. a clear, bright liquid with a unique odour and viscosity). To say that something is B (e.g. boiling) is also to remark a cluster of features b_1–b_n (e.g. an agitated fluid whose surface is broken with bubbles and steam). Put A in circumstances C (where c_1–c_n involves being in a hot beaker containing a thermometer registering 78.3° C.). The result of a few trials of this might be summarized: 'If A is put in C it becomes B.' If shortly after these few trials we find a_1–a_n in circumstances c_1–c_n, but b_1–b_n absent, we might quickly say: 'So it is not really true that any A placed in C becomes B.' If, however, we *never* happen upon a_1–a_n in c_1–c_n where b_1–b_n are absent, then the property 'becoming B in C' may get built into the meaning of 'A'. This is not bound to happen, but it may, and often it does. When it does, the form of words 'A in C is B' becomes a formula permitting us to infer directly, and without possibility of error, from something's being an A in C to the presence of B.[13] At first 'A in C is B' simply summarized a few trials of A in C. The occasional absence of B could have been countenanced, just as we can now countenance a piano with red keys, or a Cambridge winter without rain. B's absence would only have led us to deny that every case of A in C is also B. But when 'b_1–b_n' is put into the meaning of 'A is in C', the absence of B when A is in C is inconceivable. Whatever colour its keys, a piano must be a percussive stringed instrument. A Cambridge winter must include Saint Valentine's day, whatever the humidity. And whatever else alcohol may do, it must boil at 78.3° C.

The laws of physics, of particle physics especially, are used sometimes so that disconfirmatory evidence is a conceptual possibility, and sometimes, as above, so that it is not. This is not the historical point that physical laws begin life as empirical generalizations, but (through repeated confirmations, and good service in theory and calculation) they graduate to being 'functionally *a priori*'. Lenzen and Pap mark this well; Broad concedes it, but insists that the 'cash value' of law statements always rests in their relation to observation; Poincaré demurs, on the grounds that the laws of physics must keep in touch with experience. But the possible orderings of experience are limitless; we force upon the subject-matter of physics the ordering we choose.[14]

These authors regard the shift in a law's logic (meaning, use) as primarily of genetic interest. They agree that at any one stage in

[11] Cf. A. Pap, *The A Priori in Physical Theory* (New York, 1946), pp. 1–55; V. F. Lenzen, *Physical Theory* (New York, 1931), pp. 10–15 and parts I and II.

[12] When, that is, the substance is free of impurities and when the experiment is free of abnormalities. These conditions will be assumed.

[13] Thus Hertz writes: 'We consider the problem of mechanics to be to *deduce* from the properties of a material system which are independent of the time, those phenomena which take place in time and the properties which depend on the time. For the solution of this problem we lay down the following, and only the following, fundamental law, *inferred from experience*' (*Principles of Mechanics*, vol. II, p. 308, my italics).

[14] Cf. James: 'All the magnificent achievements of mathematical and physical science . . . proceed from our indomitable desire to cast the world into a more rational shape in our minds than the shape into which it is thrown there by the crude order of our experience' (*Essays in Pragmatism* (Hafner, 1948), p. 38).

Sigwart: 'That there is more order in the world

the development of physics a law is treated in just one way, as empirical or as 'functionally *a priori*': in 1687 the law of inertia was apparently nothing but an empirical extrapolation; but in 1894 it functioned mostly in an *a priori* way. But this attitude is inadequate. It derives from the belief that a law sentence can at a given time have but one type of use. But the first law sentence can express as many things named 'The Law of Inertia' as there are different uses to which the sentence can be put. Now, as in 1894 and in 1687, law sentences are used sometimes to express contingent propositions, sometimes rules, recommendations, prescriptions, regulations, conventions, sometimes *a priori* propositions (where a falsifying instance is unthinkable or psychologically inconceivable), and sometimes formally analytic statements (whose denials are self-contradictory). Few have appreciated the variety of uses to which law sentences can be put at any one time, indeed even in one experimental report. Consequently, they have supposed that what physicists call 'The Law of Inertia' is a single discrete, isolable proposition. It is in fact a family of statements, definitions and rules, all expressible via different uses of the first law sentence. Philosophers have tendered single-valued answers to a question which

---

than appears at first sight is not discovered *till the order is looked for*' (*Handbuch zu Vorlesungen über die Logik* (Tübingen, 1835), Bd. II, S. 382).

The readings which supported Boyle's law would have supported a number of other correlations as well. We regard the readings as describing two intersecting curves, as in (*a*) below.

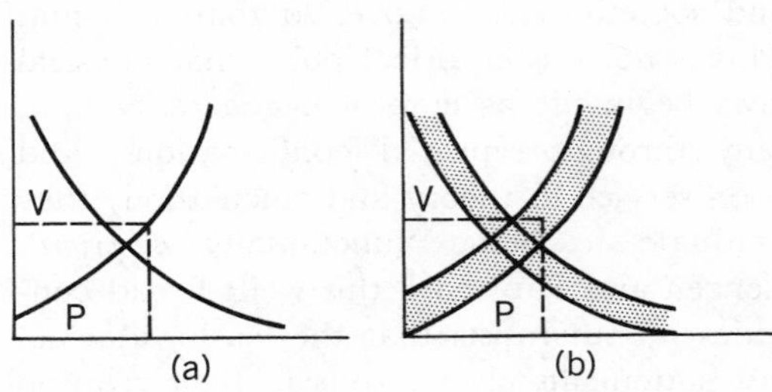

(a) (b)

This representation is possible only after the readings have been thoroughly corrected. If anything, the readings describe two 'belts' or 'ribbons' of possible data, as in (*b*) above.

How could a laboratory measurement approximate to a number, which is logically sharp? Contrast Kepler's geometrically clean ellipse with Tycho's 'fuzzy' data. You can only get within the neighbourhood of a number or of an ellipse. Volume lies between two points, covers an interval. In 'verifying' Boyle's Law one always gets 'areas' of readings, never a line. And of an infinite number of curves that can pass through that area the physicist chooses one. [Even here Boyle never made the choice. His successors drew the curve through his data. As Leibniz remarks: 'What a pity that, for all his hundreds of experiments, [Boyle] provides no new general ideas for the interpretation of nature' (*Die Philosophischen Schriften*).]

Cf. a paper by A. H. Yates in *Flight* (14 June 1957), where the above considerations are generalized:

'If values of some quantity, y, are measured for a range of values of another variable, x, we are faced with the problem of drawing a curve through a series of points, as in Fig. 8–1:

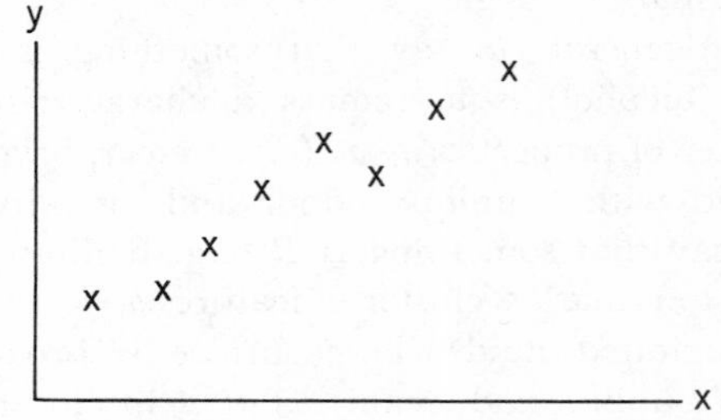

What kind of curve should be drawn? . . . Doubts often arise because the observer fails to realize that each cross is merely the centre of an area. He should constantly have in mind the accuracy of his measurement. If, for example, y is the reading of airspeed and x is the engine thrust, then there is an accuracy to be associated with each reading, such as $\pm$ 1 kt. in speed and $\pm$ 10 lb. in thrust. If these are indicated, we have:

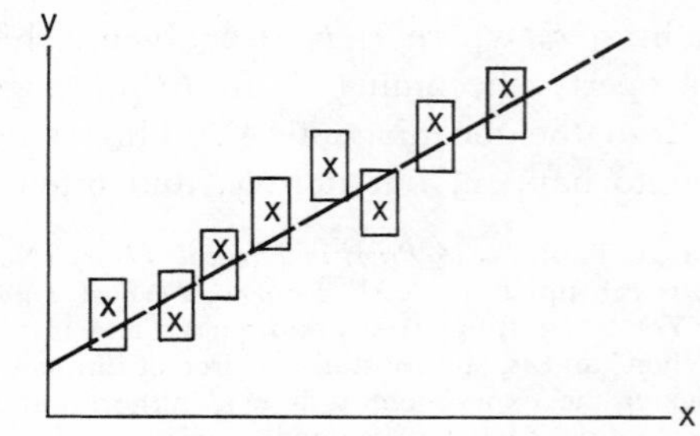

and there is little to be said for drawing anything more elaborate than a straight line' (p. 809).

Cf. also 'Accuracy and Commonsense' by the present author, in *Flight* (28 June 1957), p. 856.

differs little from "What is *the* use of rope?". Once having decided their answers, they have to deprecate other obvious and, for their points of view, awkward uses of dynamical law sentences.

B

Consider in detail the second law: 'Change of motion is proportional to the motive force impressed and acts in the right line on which the force is impressed.'[15]

Many stress the experiential root of this law statement, as they do with the first. The experience rests in the sensations accompanying muscular exertion when we pull, push and lift.[16] This effort, our experience of which is apparently direct and not further definable, we call 'force'. The direction of a moved body's acceleration is that in which we work our muscles in moving it. So, like acceleration, force is representable in vector notation.

Different amounts of force are required to produce a given acceleration in, for instance, a cannon ball and a tennis ball. Conversely, a given amount of force will produce different accelerations in these bodies. However, the direction of acceleration is constant for all bodies — cannon balls and tennis balls alike. Therefore, to each body must be assigned a certain scalar property; let us call it 'the inertial mass *m*'. The simplest equation embracing all we have so far accounted for is:

$$F = ma = m(dv/dt) = m(d^2s/dt^2).$$ [17]

Forces derive from many sources, of which muscle power is but one variety.[18] Physics in general is concerned with the nature of these; but mechanics simply takes force as given, whatever their nature. It is concerned only with computing their effects, not their genesis.[19] $F = m(d^2s/dt^2)$ allows essential computations to be made, but within mechanics questions about what 'F' represents are irrelevant.[20]

Nonetheless, '$F = m(d^2s/dt^2)$' has many distinct uses within mechanics. Consider these accounts:

1. F is *defined* as $m(d^2s/dt^2)$. In dynamics that is what 'F' means. It would be self-contradictory to treat 'F' as if it were not strictly replaceable by '$m(d^2s/dt^2)$'. (This is like our earlier examples.)

2. It is psychologically inconceivable that F should be other than $m(d^2s/dt^2)$. A world in which this did not obtain might as a matter of strict logic be possible, but it is not a world of which any consistent idea can be formed. On this equation rests all macrophysical knowledge. Were the world not truly described thus, the system, so useful in dealing with machines, tides, navigation and the heavens would crash into unthinkable chaos.

3. Perhaps, despite all appearances, $F = m(d^2s/dt^2)$ is false — unable adequately to describe physical events. Perhaps another set of conceptions could be substituted. Nonetheless this would be unsettling. $F = m(d^2s/dt^2)$ facilitates the collection and organization of a mountain of facts and theory. It patterns our ideas of physical events coherently and logically. So the second law, though empirical, cannot be falsifiable in any ordinary way, as are the statements which follow from initial conditions in accordance with this law.

4. $F = m(d^2s/dt^2)$ summarizes a large body of experience, observations, and experiments of mechanical phenomena. It is as liable to upset as any other factual statement. Disconfirmatory evidence may turn up tomorrow. Then we should simply write off $F = m(d^2s/dt^2)$ as false.

[15] 'Mutationem motus proportionalem esse vi motrici impressae, et fieri secundum lineam rectam qua via illa imprimitur' (Newton, *Principia*, 'Axioms').

[16] Cf. e.g. Broad, *Scientific Thought* (London, 1923), p. 162. Cf. Mach, *Science of Mechanics* (Open Court, 1942), pp. 244–6, and Joos, *Theoretical Physics*, p. 82, l. 4.

[17] m is assumed constant. A more cautious formulation would be $F = d/dt(mv) = du/dt$, which leaves open the question of the constancy of mass (cf. W. Kaufmann in *Göttinger Nachrichten*, 8 Nov. 1901).

[18] Newton, *Principia*, p. xvii, ll. 27–7.

[19] *Ibid.* p. 5 (last para.) and p. 192, Scholium.

[20] As Broad suggests, *Perception, Physics and Reality*, p. 349, ll. 8–10.

5. $F = m(d^2s/dt^2)$ is not a statement at all, hence not true, false, analytic, or synthetic. It asserts nothing. It is either:

(*a*) a rule, or schema, by the use of which one can infer from initial conditions; or

(*b*) a technique for measuring force, or acceleration, or mass; or

(*c*) a principle of instrument construction — to use such an instrument is to accept $F = m(d^2s/dt^2)$, and no result of an experiment in which this instrument was used could falsify the law; or

(*d*) a convention, one of many ways of construing the phenomena of statics, dynamics, ballistics and astronomy; or

(*e*) '$F = m(d^2s/dt^2)$' demarcates the notation we accept to deal with macrophysical mechanics. Our concern here, (*a*)–(*e*), is not with the truth or falsity of the second law. We are interested only in the utility of $F = m(d^2s/dt^2)$ as a tool for controlling and thinking about dynamical phenomena.

The actual uses of '$F = m(d^2s/dt^2)$' will support each of these accounts.[21] This means not just that among physicists there have been spokesmen for each of these interpretations, but that a particular physicist on a single day in the laboratory may use the sentence '$F = m(d^2s/dt^2)$' in all the ways above, from 1–5, without the slightest inconsistency. Examples of this follow.

Every physics student knows of Atwood's machine. Two unequal masses, m_1 and m_2, are fixed to the ends of a (practically) massless thread, running over a (practically) massless, frictionless pulley. Assign the following arbitrary values to m_1 and m_2:

$$m_1 = 48 \text{ gm.},$$

$$m_2 = 50 \text{ gm.}$$

Then,[22]

$$a = 980\frac{50 - 48}{50 + 48} = 980\frac{2}{98} = 20 \text{ cm./sec.}^2$$

This is predicted by the second law.

A well-known physics book follows a similar account with the query: 'Suppose we perform the above experiment and find experimentally a value for a which agrees with the predicted value . . . *Does it mean that we have proved Newton's second law?*' The author continues, '. . . this question is absurd, since Newton's second law is a definition and hence incapable of proof . . . the Atwood machine is essentially a device for measuring the acceleration of gravity g by the determination of a rather than a set-up for the verification of Newton's second law.'[23]

This exemplifies account 1. Physicists do use the second law sentence to express a definition when they need to; they have done so for three centuries. When so used, any statement potentially contradictory to what the sentence expresses may be dismissed as

[21] These accounts (1–5) are neither exclusive nor exhaustive.

[22] By the second law, the unbalanced force on m_1 is $F - m_1g = m_1a$. The unbalanced force on m_2 comprises its weight m_2g, plus the upward pull (F) of the string. This can be expressed as $m_2g - F = m_2a$.

Thus
$$F = m_2g - m_2a = m_2(g - a).$$

Substituting this in

$$F - m_1g = m_1a;$$

$$m_2(g - a) - m_1g = m_1a,$$

or
$$m_2g - m_2a - m_1g = m_1a.$$

This is the same as

$$a(m_2 + m_1) = g(m_2 - m_1),$$

and from this it follows that

$$a = g\frac{m_2 - m_1}{m_2 + m_1}.$$

[23] A. Kolin, *Physics* (McGraw-Hill, 1950), pp. 46–7. Cf. Humphreys and Beringer, *Atomic Physics* (Harper, New York, 1950), 'Newton's laws are not physical laws . . . but are definitions of the basic concepts in dynamics . . . Newton's second law provides us with a working definition of force' (pp. 38–9). 'These laws are the foundation of ordinary dynamics and simultaneously form the basic definitions, hypotheses and deductions of the theory' (*ibid.* p. 37). Clerk Maxwell, *Matter and Motion* (London, 1920), ' "Impressed" force . . . is completely defined and described in Newton's three laws of motion . . .' (111, 40, p. 27). Poincaré, *Science and Hypothesis* (London, 1905), 'This [second] law of motion . . . ceases to be regarded as an experimental law, it is now only a definition' (p. 100); and 'Les principes de la dynamique nous apparaissent d'abord comme des vérités expérimentales; mais nous avons été obligés de nous en servir comme définitions', 'Des Fondements de la Géometrie', in *Revue de Meta-Physique et de la Morale* (1899), p. 267.

absurd.[24] George Atwood himself found it useful so to use the second law sentence.[25] However, were a statement of the second law nothing but 'a definition and hence incapable of proof', Atwood would have wasted his time in writing his *Treatise*. For his famous machine was invented solely to demonstrate the empirical truth of the law. In the eighteenth century a statement of the second law was regarded universally as a "substantive statement'; a contingent, universal, descriptive proposition. Atwood remarks: 'The laws of motion . . . ought not only to be strictly consistent among themselves, but with matter of fact . . . since any single instance which could be produced of a disagreement or inconsistency would invalidate the whole theory of motion. . . .'[26]

The object of Atwood's neglected *Treatise* was to show that attacks by Bernoulli, Leibniz and Poleni on the law's validity rested on improperly constructed apparatus.[27] He wished to verify it as a substantive statement of fact.[28] With an accurate scale mounted behind m_1, a well-made pendulum, a silk thread of negligible mass and a light pulley (mounted in four friction wheels), Atwood showed[29] that when $m_1 = 48$ gm. and $m_2 =$ 50 gm. then the acceleration of m_2 is indeed 20 cm./sec.^{2}. The results were carefully recorded and generalized: they squared with the predictions of the second law. For Atwood this fully confirmed the law.

The point is, if Atwood believed his experiment to verify the statement of the second law, then it must have been thought possible for the machine to have turned up evidence against the law statement. If nothing can falsify a proposition, nothing can verify it either. It was logically possible that m_2 should have accelerated at 5 cm./sec.^{2}, or 50 cm./sec.^{2}. This exemplifies account 4; the second law sentence was used as a contingent universal statement, against which disconfirmatory evidence might weigh at any time. Doubtless this commended itself to Broad when he wrote:

> It is certain that the Second Law, as originally stated, was not intended for a definition of force but for a substantial statement about it. Unquestionably the sensational basis of the scientific concept of force is the feelings of strain that we experience when we drag a heavy body along, or throw a stone, or bend a bow.[30]

It is certain also that Newton often puts the sentence to this use.[31] So we have two distinct uses to which physicists have put '$F = m(d^2s/dt^2)$'. They have used in different ways the sentence expressing the law statement: as the result of definitions (account 1), and as an empirical generalization (account 4). Other uses must be considered as well.

[24] Cf. Newton, *Principia*, '[This] will make the system of the two bodies . . . to go forwards *in infinitum* with a motion continually accelerated; which is absurd and contrary to the first law' (p. 25). (The first law is, of course, only a special case of the second, i.e. where $\Sigma F = 0$.) Similar arguments can be found throughout the *Principia*.

[25] G. Atwood, *A Treatise on the Rectilinear Motion and Rotation of Bodies, with a Description of Original Experiments Relative to the Subject* (Cambridge, 1784). Cf. p. 4, 'The laws of motion have been esteemed not only physically but mathematically true'.

[26] *Ibid.* p. 30.

[27] *Ibid.* p. 33, 'Many experiments have been produced . . . to disprove the Newtonian measure . . . it immediately belongs to the present subject to determine whether the conclusions which have been drawn from these experiments arise from any inconsistency between the Newtonian measures of force and matter of fact' (p. 30).

[28] In this he only obeyed Newton's dicta: 'The qualities of bodies are only known to us by experiments, we are to hold for universal all such as universally agree with experiments' (Bk. III, Appendix, Rule Three). 'We are to look upon propositions inferred by general induction from phenomena as accurately or very nearly true' (Rule Four). 'Particular propositions are inferred from the phenomena, and afterwards rendered general by induction' (p. 547). 'Analysis consists in making experiments and observations and in drawing general conclusions from them by induction' (*Opticks* (1721), p. 380).

[29] Cf. *Treatise*, pp. 298ff.

[30] Broad, *Scientific Thought*, p. 162, and cf. pp. 163 (bottom), and 164 (ll. 16–18).

[31] '[In] the laws of Nature . . . there appears . . . not the least shadow of necessity. . . . These therefore we must . . . learn . . . from observations and experiments. . . . All sound and true philosophy is founded on the appearances of things' (*Principia*, Cote's preface). 'Such principles . . . are confirmed by abundance of experiments' (p. 21, Scholium). Cf. further references in the *Principia*, p. 24, ll. 28–9, pp. 325–6, p. 398, p. 294. '*The laws observed during the motion of bodies acted on by constant forces* admit of easy illustrations from matter of fact' (my italics). Also p. 308, ll, 21–3 and p. 329, para. III.

Account 2 suggested a use of the sentence which, while expressing what obtains in nature, still seemed inhospitable to any idea of evidence against the law. Indisputably, physicists do use laws in this way, now as in the eighteenth century. Thus Atwood says: '(The) Laws of Motion are assumed as Physical Axioms; . . . although the mind does not assent to them on intuition, yet as they are of the most obvious and intelligible kind . . . appear the most proper to be received as principles from which the theory of motion in general may be regularly deduced.'[32] He continues: 'These three physical propositions, having been assumed as principles of motion, reduce the science of mechanics to mathematical certainty, arising not only from the strict coherence of innumerable properties of motion deduced from them *a priori*, but from their agreement with matter of fact.' And then, 'There is no kind of motion but what may be referred to (these) three easy and obvious propositions, the truth of which it is impossible to doubt.'[33] Compare William Whewell, writing in 1834:

> The laws of motion . . . are so closely interwoven with our conceptions of the external world, that we have great difficulty in conceiving them not to exist, or to exist other than they are. . . . If we in our thoughts attempt to divest matter of its powers of resisting and moving, it ceases to be matter, according to our conceptions, and *we can no longer reason upon it with any distinctness*. And yet . . . the properties of matter . . . do not obtain by any absolute necessity . . . there is no contradiction in supposing that a body's motion should naturally diminish.[34]

Physicists often use law sentences as described in account 2. They regard them as empirically true, and yet such that evidence against them is unthinkable.

Philosophers may think these physicists are confused; but the confusion is a difficult one to resist. Certain systems of propositions are empirically true; and therefore the fundamental propositions on which such systems rest must (in some sense) be empirically true as well. However, they are often treated as axioms; they delimit and give definition to the subject-matter to which the system can apply. But nothing describable within the system could refute the laws. Disconfirmatory evidence counts against the system as a whole, not against any of its fundamental parts; it only shows that the system does not hold where it might have held. No part of classical mechanics *per se* enumerates contexts in which it will apply, so no part of the system is proved false when it is discovered not to apply in some context.[35]

Law statements, then, are empirically true, because the system in which they are set is empirically true; but counter-evidence does not disconfirm them. Only in terms of law statements can evidence relevant to the (lower-level) hypotheses of the system be appreciated as confirmatory or disconfirmatory.

Account 4 minimizes this systematic setting of the second law statement. Sometimes it is right and proper to do this. But sometimes the physicist is concerned with the *system* of dynamics, within which nothing disconfirms the laws because they determine those types of phenomena to which the system can apply.

Suppose no alternative systems of concepts were available with which to describe and explain a type of phenomenon; the scientist would then have but one way of thinking about the subject-matter. Nineteenth-century physics provides an example: aberrations in the perihelion of Mercury made Leverrier uncomfortable; but to have scrapped celestial mechanics then would have been to refuse to think about the planets at all. In this sense classical dynamics is empirically true of macrophysical phenomena. (What system could offer a 'more accurate' account of a collision between billiard balls?) Yet the system is true in such a way that the idea of evidence which would falsify its laws often cannot be formed. Account 2 would on

[32] *Treatise*, p. 2.

[33] *Treatise*, p. 279.

[34] W. Whewell, *Astronomy and General Physics* (London, 1834), pp. 211, 212 (my italics).

[35] Cf. Wittgenstein, *Tractatus*, 6. 342.

some occasions be supported by most physicists, in theory and in practice.[36]

This leaves accounts 5 and 3 to be discussed. Account 5 is familiar enough. When invoked as an 'inference pattern' a statement of the second law is not likely to be called into question by any of the conclusions it warrants. Would $(p.(p \supset q)) \supset q$ be upset by anything inferred in accordance with it? In Atwood's machine, if initial conditions are given as $m_1 = 48$ gm. and $m_2 = 50$ gm. and we wish to infer by way of the second law to the acceleration of m_2, then, if we are actually using the law, the inference pattern itself cannot come under suspicion. It is accepted as a way of reasoning from initial conditions to conclusions.[37]

Similarly, $F = m(d^2s/dt^2)$ can be a 'statement of how force is to be measured for scientific purposes'. Broad advocated this in 1913.[38] But ten years later[39] he dismissed the idea because the measurement of the rate of change of momentum is not the only way to measure force. This strengthens the suggestion that Broad's account is single-valued. Does it follow from the fact that there may be alternative ways of measuring force, that measuring the rate of change of momentum is not *a* way of measuring force? Surely '$F = m(d^2s/dt^2)$' has been used thus. Newton infers from his pendulum experiment that, since different masses have identical constant accelerations towards the earth's centre, a constant force is acting whose magnitude is proportional to the masses of the bodies concerned.[40] This use of the formula predominates in the work of engineers; it inclines some philosophers to regard the second law as *nothing but* a principle of instrument design, or of notation, or of inference.[41] The fundamental formulae of dynamics certainly have such uses, but not to the exclusion of other equally important uses. The same might be said of Broad's emphatic 'single-valued' conclusion: 'The second law, is, therefore, neither a definition nor a statement as to how force is to be measured; but is a substantial proposition, asserting a connexion between two independently measurable sets of facts in nature.'[42]

'$F = m(d^2s/dt^2)$' can sometimes be used to express a definition, sometimes a statement of how force is to be measured, sometimes a substantial proposition (often with disconfirmatory evidence easily conceivable, but sometimes not). What physicists call 'the second law' really consists in everything that can be expressed by way of different uses of this formula.

[36] The synthetic *a priori* view of the laws of mechanics, first articulated by Kant (*Kritik der Reinen Vernunft*, Leipzig, 1781), and later by Natorp (*Die Logische Grundlagen der Exakten Wissenschaften* (Berlin, 1910)), and Cassirer (*Determinismus und Indeterminismus in der Modernen Physik*, Goteborg, 1937), is not just a quaint philosopher's invention. It was an important, if misguided, attempt to do justice to actual uses of laws in physics. Physicists stilll make the attempt: thus Peierls writes: 'People sometimes argue whether Newton's second law is a definition of force or of mass, or whether it is a statement of an objective fact. *It is really a mixture of all these things*' (*The Laws of Nature* (Allen and Unwin, 1955), p. 21). Cf. Broad: 'This mixture of convention and observation is a very common feature in scientific laws' (*Scientific Thought*, p. 160). But dynamical laws are not *mixtures*. '$F = m(d^2r/dt^2)$' can be used in physics in different ways. This does not make the second law a *mixture*, whatever that may mean. Cf. Weyl: 'In its place [i.e. the clear-cut division into *a priori* and *a posteriori*] we have a rich scale of gradations of stability' (*Philosophy of Mathematics and Natural Science*, p. 154).

[37] The *Principia* abounds with this use of the second law: Cf. e.g. p. 14 (Cor. I, l. 9), p. 17 (Cor. III, l. 2), p. 20 (Cor. V, l. 5), p. 21 (Cor. VI, l. 2 and Schol. l. 3), p. 25 (ll. 31–2), p. 42 (Prop. II, ll. 1 and 6), p. 44 (ll. 1, 6, 14), p. 136 (l. 9), p. 162 (l. 6), p. 164 (l. 6), p. 166 (l. 19), p. 169 (ll. 2, 11), etc., and see esp. p. 244 (Schol. l. 8), p. 327 (Section VII, l. 11), p. 368 (l. 1), p. 410 (l. 13), p. 414 (last l.), and p. 442 (l. 11).

[38] *Perception, Physics and Reality*, p. 322, ll. 20–5.

[39] In *Scientific Thought*, p. 165.

[40] *Principia*, Section VI, pp. 303–26.

[41] Wittgenstein seems at times to suggest this: 'Newtonian Mechanics . . . brings the description of the universe to a unified form' (*Tractatus*, 6. 341). 'Mechanics determines a form of description by saying: All propositions in the description of the world must be obtained in a given way from a number of given propositions — the mechanical axioms.'

The position is adopted explicitly by Watson: 'What we have called the laws of nature are the laws of our methods of representing it' (*On Understanding Physics* (Cambridge Univ. Press, 1939), p. 52); and by Toulmin: 'Laws of Nature do not function as premises *from which* deductions to observational matters are made, but as rules of inferences *in accordance with which* empirical conclusions may be drawn from empirical premises' (*The Philosophy of Science* (Hutchinson's University Library, 1953)).

[42] *Scientific Thought*, p. 165.

The Covering Law Position: A Critique and an Alternative Analysis

9

Truisms as the Grounds for Historical Explanations[1]

MICHAEL SCRIVEN

1. *The Problem.* Some historical explanations appear to be so well supported by the evidence that we cannot reasonably doubt them. A very plausible current analysis of historical explanations leads to the conclusions that an explanation can only be beyond reasonable doubt when (*a*) we have general laws that are also beyond reasonable doubt and (*b*) we are in a position to make predictions that are beyond reasonable doubt. Yet it appears that historians are not in possession of such general laws nor in a position to make such predictions.

I here propose an alternative analysis which is consistent with the existence of good explanations and the non-existence of *comparably* good laws and predictions. But I do not thereby deny the existence of *rough* generalizations about behavior, and predictions which are *sometimes* highly probable. Let us begin by examining the analysis of explanations which produces the paradox.

2. *The Deductive Model of Explanation.* Suppose we wish to explain why William the Conqueror never invaded Scotland. The answer, as usually given, is simple enough; he had no desire for the lands of the Scottish nobles, and he secured his northern borders by defeating Malcolm, King of Scotland, in battle and exacting homage.[2] There seem to be no laws involved in this explanation. But what makes us so sure that it *is* the correct explanation? Might not someone with no desire for the lands, and with no fears about invasion, nevertheless invade? There might perhaps be word of some great treasure stored in Malcolm's castles. Unless such possibilities are ruled out, we cannot be sure that the explanation given is adequate. Furthermore, we cannot assume that what *look* like good reasons against invasion actually were the decisive factors in this case unless we have some definite information about William's reasonableness. For the explanation to be watertight, it will have to contain many such facts about the situation and the participants. And the only way in which such facts, however numerous, can guarantee the explanation is via the truth of some *general* proposition that connects such facts with such an effect — for the further particular proposition asserting temporal adjacency is no guarantee of causal efficacy. To sum up: one set of facts cannot be a watertight explanation of another fact unless we can guarantee they are adequate to produce it — and the only kind of guarantee that connects facts is a law. Failing such a law, we cannot be certain our explanation is adequate, and even if it is not inadequate it may instead be redundant or irrelevant. Having such a law, and being in possession of the explanatory facts, we are in a position to predict the exact occurrence to be explained. If we were not, if some other event is implied by these facts and laws, then we most certainly lack an explanation of what

Reprinted with permission of The Macmillan Company, New York, from *Theories of History* edited by Patrick Gardiner, pp. 443–471.

[1] I am greatly indebted to Paul Edwards for much painstaking and helpful criticism.

[2] E.g., *Shorter Cambridge Medieval History*, Vol. I, p. 585.

actually happens. Indeed it is in just such a situation, where our knowledge leads us to expect something other than the actual occurrence, that we call for an explanation.

Such, in brief, is the argument that ties together the certainty of explanations with the possession of laws and the possibility of predictions. In its most convincing form, it is due to Professor C. G. Hempel.[3] I refer to it as "the deductive model of explanation" because it proposes as a criterion for good explanations the deducibility of a statement of the facts to be explained from statements of the antecedent conditions and relevant laws. I have the greatest respect for its powers, its interest, and its adherents, but I shall argue that it is wrong, not only in detail but in conception. Whether my criticisms are persuasive or not, I hope they will have some interest in so far as they bear on the nature of historical knowledge, judgment, and understanding.

3. *Survey of Difficulties with the Deductive Model.* It will perhaps help the reader to find his way in the paper if I now adumbrate briefly my main objections to the deductive model of historical explanation, not all of which I shall deal with in any detail here. I argue (3.1) that it can be formulated only by ignoring the distinction between an explanation and its justification; (3.2) that this distinction opens the way for abandoning the need for laws (and that the logical arguments for the necessity of such laws are unsound); (3.3) that such laws are not available even in the physical sciences, and, if they were, would not provide explanations of much interest; (3.4) that history possesses in abundance the only kind of general statement required for good explanations; (3.5) that the logical argument for correlation of good predictions with good explanations is not formally sound and has a limited range of application and little practical significance even in that range; that good predictions are impossible in large areas of the natural and applied sciences where simple quantitative laws and measuring techniques are not available; but that in such areas, as in history, good explanations of the poorly predictable events are commonly available; (3.6) that more illuminating analogues for historical explanation can be found in procedures such as "explaining the way," "explaining how something works," "explaining what something means," and in notions such as "dramatic inevitability," rather than in subsumption under physical laws.

Two of these objections (3.3 and 3.5) are founded upon an examination of the physical sciences into which I shall not enter here,[4] and comparatively brief reference will be made to them. The remainder will be treated in less detail than I think is required for an adequate defense of them, but I hope at sufficient length to indicate the possibility and perhaps interest of an alternative analysis of historical explanations.

3.1. *Explanations and Their Justifications.* When scientists were asked to explain the variations in apparent brightness of the orbiting second-stage rocket that launched the first of our artificial satellites, they replied that it was due to its axial rotation and its asymmetry. This explanation, perhaps illustrated by moving a pencil through the air while turning it, was perfectly adequate even for the newsmen. Yet it contains no laws. Why then should we feel any inadequacy about an historical explanation such as the one about William (in 2 above) simply because it lacks laws? It would be said (to apply the general defense of the deductive model given above) that a "complete" or "proper" statement of the explanation must contain laws in order that the alleged consequence can be *deduced;* and that only in the scientific case just quoted can this be done, since we do not have in our possession laws adequate to complete the historical explanation. All that the latter provides, indeed, is

[3] "The Function of General Laws in History," *Journal of Philosophy,* 1942 . . . But Mill, as Bury points out, already saw the main point (*System of Logic,* Bk. VI); and before him d'Holbach, d'Alembert and Condorcet (see Isaiah Berlin, *Historical Inevitability*).

[4] . . . Vol. III of *Minnesota Studies in the Philosophy of Science* (Univ. of Minn. Press).

". . . something that might be called an *explanation sketch.* Such a sketch consists of a more or less vague indication of the laws and initial conditions considered as relevant, and it needs 'filling out' in order to turn into a full-fledged explanation. This filling-out requires further empirical research, for which the sketch suggests the direction. . . ."[5] Now I have an alternative description of what Hempel calls explanation-sketches (and which include the scientists' account of the rocket phenomenon as well as the historians' account of William's noninvasion of Scotland). I regard them as explanations as they stand, not incomplete in any sense in which they should be complete, but certainly not including the *grounds* which we should give if pressed to support them. Just as we must distinguish a statement about the population of the ancient Greek city of Poseidonis (Paestum) from our grounds for believing it, so we must distinguish the statement of an explanation from our grounds for putting it forward as such; and amongst these grounds a further distinction is useful.

It may be the case that we have insufficient grounds for the assertions actually occurring in what we normally call an explanation; and in that case we would certainly be justified in complaining that the explanation was ill-supported or — in the event of actual falsehood — *inaccurate.* Or it may be that the statements offered are well-supported and true but do not fully *explain* what they were supposed to explain; and here we might plausibly say that the explanation is incomplete or *inadequate.* And, thirdly, it may be that, through misunderstanding, the proposed explanation is not of the *kind* required; then we would describe it as inappropriate or *irrelevant.* I think we can more profitably employ this tripartite division of the deficiences of explanations than the single blanket terms "incorrect" or "incomplete" or "improper." The kinds of grounds which are required for defense against the errors of inaccuracy (which I take to include extreme dubiety), inadequacy, and irrelevance are radically different. The first comprise our evidence for the truth of the statements actually made, and I shall refer to them as *truth-justifying grounds.* These would include our evidence for supposing that William did not want the lands of Scotland, for example. The second consist in our grounds for thinking that the statements made are adequate for a certain task — the task of explaining (in *some way*) whatever it is they are supposed to explain. I shall refer to them as *role-justifying grounds;* and it is in this category that the general laws lacking from our "explanation-sketches" would go, if we had them. The third group support our interpretation of the practical requirements of the person or public to whom we address our explanation — for example, that they need an explanation of someone's behavior in terms of his intentions rather than his muscular operations, or of the rocket's variation in apparent brightness in terms of properties of the rocket rather than the mechanism of vision. The considerations which lead us to propose one rather than another type of explanation I shall call *type-justifying grounds.*

To illustrate the whole set of distinctions consider the attempt to explain why Cortes sent out a third expedition to Baja California after the failure of the first two. Characteristically, we first judge from the context that the type of explanation required is probably in terms of his reasons rather than his character, and certainly in terms of those rather than the neurophysiology of his brain processes. We might make the first of these type-judgments on the grounds that such replies as "He was just stubborn" here leave unanswered what appears to be an important part of the question, viz., Cortes' motives. But it is not entirely clear from the inadequate description of the context that such an inference is justified. It is more clear that *some* restrictions on the type of explanation can be reasonably inferred from the fact that an individual historical figure is involved, and thus a general reply in terms of the neurophysiology of decision processes is not appropriate. This is not to say that in *certain*

[5] op. cited, p. 42.

cases, a *specific* neurophysiological account may not be perfectly appropriate in a historical explanation: monarchs can have brain tumors with an effect on history not translatable into the language of reasons and instincts. It *is* to say that a general account of Cortes' brain processes, perfectly true though it might be, would be of no value just because it is both true and general, i.e., it would not tell us what it was specifically about this man at this time that led him to this decision. It is perfectly true that the apparent brightness of the rocket varies because a varying number of photons is passing into the retina of the observer; but this would also be true if the rocket were symmetrical and being illumined by a light-source of variable brightness, etc., and our interest lies in having one of these states *of the particular object* of enquiry selected out for us as the explanation, i.e., in being told whether it is the shape and motion of the rocket or the varying illumination of it that is responsible for what we see. Again, in certain contexts it might be appropriate to give an elaborate explanation involving laws and analogies, etc.; whereas in other contexts a simpler type of explanation is entirely adequate. Sometimes explanations consist simply in denying what is apparently a presupposition of the enquirer (see below), sometimes they require the provision of a great deal of new knowledge, sometimes an assertion of the relevance of old knowledge. These lead to differences in the type of explanation which we might call complexity-differences of type as opposed to category-differences of type (general physiological, particular external causal, particular intentions, characterological, etc.).

Yet in both the cases given in the last paragraph we can imagine contexts (e.g., class discussions in cybernetics or the physiology of vision) where exactly the explanation we have excluded would be the appropriate one: where the mention of Cortes' name or the rocket is intended merely to lend a little interest to the illustration. The possibility of making such an error — remote though it is — demonstrates the existence of an inference from type-justifying grounds to the conclusion that a certain type of explanation is relevant or appropriate. Not that the inference is made and applied explicitly; its conclusion is simply *expressed* by giving an answer of a certain type. The only error involved in giving the wrong type of answer is inappositeness; it does *not* explain what it is supposed to explain, but it is not inaccurate, nor incapable of explaining through inadequacy. There is no such thing as *the* explanation of something unless a decision is made about *type*.

Now it would be absurd to include considerations of the kind involved in selecting the type of explanation, as *part of the explanation itself*. Yet there is no essential difference between doing that and including role- or truth-justifying grounds in the explanation. In the present case, having made a rough decision about the type of answer to give, we might next consider what particular reasons or character traits or combination of these actually explain Cortes' behavior. Suppose we accept the view which Merriman appears to favor in *The Rise of the Spanish Empire:* that the prospect of gigantic booty, and considerable confidence that by leading the expedition himself the previous causes of failure could be overcome, were the determining factors. There are still two avenues of attack on this account; and correspondingly we may produce in defense either (i) our grounds for supposing that Cortes did *in fact* anticipate the taking of great wealth from the natives and their land, and that he did in fact believe the expedition would succeed under his guidance — the grounds might be the evidence of diaries, eyewitness reports in correspondence, etc. — or (ii) our grounds for supposing that these facts do *explain* his action; exactly what these grounds are is the disputed question, which we shall shortly examine in detail. These two kinds of grounds are, respectively, truth-justifying and role-justifying. Notice once more the peculiarity of insisting that remarks about diaries and correspondence must necessarily form part of the explanation of Cortes' decision.

They *are* properly part of the evidence for our assertion that he had certain considerations in mind. They are *not* properly part of an explanation (of one of his actions) which affirms that he *had* these considerations in mind. Similarly, the laws of inertia and optics are not part of the scientists' explanation of the rocket-phenomenon in the context described (and there is no such thing as "the [correct] explanation," independently of context), though they are required for its justification; and whatever it is we produce as grounds for supposing that Cortes' economic motives and risk-evaluation explain his decision is not part of the explanation itself.

It may appear that we are quibbling over words here, that it is of little importance to decide exactly what is included in an explanation and what in its justification. Now the only goal of the logician dealing with the concept of explanation is to provide an accurate account of the procedure of giving an explanation as compared with, say, a description or — presumably — a justification. Moreover, if one hopes to extract from one's analysis some practical consequences for the careful historian and the historiographer, as Hempel certainly does, then one must not judge in advance what is or is not going to be an important distinction. I hope that I shall succeed in showing that the distinction just made has extremely important consequences for the historiographer, and that they are diametrically opposed to those to which Hempel is led. This importance in application we shall now attempt to demonstrate.

It is clear that the procedure of justifying assertions about historical figures, whether they be causal or not, does not necessarily end at any particular point; having come to the diaries we may have to go on and defend our ascription of particular authors to them, etc. These further grounds, grounds for supposing our first-level grounds to be true, can be called *second-level grounds.* This regress connects up with and can be dealt with analogously to the old puzzle about complete explanations — how can anything ever be completely explained, when, in order to explain anything, we must appeal to something else which we have not explained? The answer to this is, of course, that an explanation is essentially a linkage of what we do not understand to what we do understand, and there can be no such linkage if we understand *nothing;* so the idea of a complete explanation (in this sense) is the idea of a linkage of two things when there is only one thing to link, and, like the sound of one hand clapping, is a logical echo, a thing of no substance whose loss is no loss. Similarly, we can never give a "complete" justification of a statement; but to say this is only to say that justifications have to begin. It is better not to use the word "complete" in such a sense, thereby abandoning any possibility of ever applying it, for we normally use it in the perfectly good sense of "providing enough evidence to make doubt unreasonable." Exactly how much this is, will depend upon the context, upon what kind of doubts are being considered and what kind of assertion is being made (singular, universal, statistical, theoretical, observational, etc.).

Apply our treatment of these puzzles to the Hempelian notion of a complete explanation. At first it seems quite different; for in this case a natural stopping-point appears. An explanation will be said to be complete when it enables the deduction of the fact to be explained from at least one law plus antecedent conditions. Notice that if mere deduction were required, any statement of fact (or law) could be deduced from a logically trivial inflation of it (e.g., its double negation) and would thereby be completely explained! Would it not be a little remarkable if by merely widening the compass of the deduction to include a law we could convert the analysis into a universal panacea for all explanation-needs? Is it not going to be likely that this kind of "complete explanation" will in some contexts provide too much and in some too little, and in others the wrong type of explanation or even no explanation at all? Indeed, is there not a possibility that in some cases we cannot give it but can nevertheless give an excellent explanation? I shall argue that the answer to all these questions is affirmative.

Now it is true that, by comparison with the sense of "complete" in the elementary puzzle of the last paragraph, Hempel's notion correctly avoids the analogous temptation of saying that an explanation is incomplete when it does not explicitly include its *second-level* grounds (and then the third-level . . .). *But* is it not the case that in requiring the explanation to include not merely the facts which are produced (e.g., about the rocket's shape or Cortes' aim) but also the *first-level* role-justifying grounds, Hempel actually takes one step of just the same persuasive but illegitimate regress? His argument for insisting on the inclusion of such grounds in any "complete" explanation is simply that without them we cannot be sure we have the correct explanation. It is also true that without evidence for the statements of fact we put forward as the explanation in the contexts described, we would not have a correct explanation; and the same applies to our judgment of explanation-type. Yet we clearly recognize the illegitimacy of claiming that for completeness' sake, our evidence for these judgments should be included in the explanation. It should be seen from the beginning that the completeness or correctness of an explanation is a notion without meaning except in a given context from which the type can be inferred and in which the required facts are known. This is greatly obscured by the supposition that in science there is always something known as *the* explanation of a particular phenomena regardless of context. On the contrary, there are many non-competing types of explanation for scientific phenomena, just as for historical. We are misled, because there is a considerable communality of context in discussions amongst scientists with similar training and interests; but there is no way of deciding whether "the" explanation of the Budde effect in chlorine (its increase in volume upon exposure to light) is the thermodynamic one or the photochemical one or both, without some context being provided as basis for a type-judgment. *Given* details of the context, we can here, as in history, produce facts and not laws as a perfectly adequate explanation and can reject the claim that *completeness* requires more, while freely conceding that *justification* will require more — perhaps role-justifying grounds, perhaps also (or instead) truth- or type-justifying grounds. For justifying, too, as we have seen, is not a procedure for which a type or amount can be specified independently of context. And a justification, no less than an explanation, is complete if it does exactly what is (properly) required in the context.

It is not merely that we can, in certain contexts, *assume* that the audience has no need to be reminded of the relevant laws — although this is important enough, and one could hardly propose an analysis of, e.g., "political joke" or "scientific discovery" accordingly to which they were essentially incomplete unless the entire background was also presented. Explanations are practical, context-bound affairs, and they are merely converted into something else when set out in full deductive array. Just as the joke becomes, when all the context is laboriously presented, a sociological explanation of a joke (and is usually no longer funny), so the explanation when dressed in its deductive robes becomes a proof or a justification of an explanation (and usually no longer explains but demonstrates). And the scientific discovery would become a chapter in a history of science.

But the situation is far more serious; for this preliminary failure to see that explanation is a valuable but workaday notion, very different from its Sunday cousin, deductive justification, leads Hempel to overlook the possibility of highly verifiable explanations for which *the general laws cannot be formulated*. The Sunday raiment is not always available, even for the hardest-working explanation.

3.2. *Explanations without Laws.* Once we remove from an explanation's back the burden of its own proof we are in a better position to see the criteria for judging both. A striking feature of the family of explanations is their diversity of types — and it appears quite possible that a different kind of justification may be required for each type of explanation. An extraordinary attempt has been made in the literature of this subject to identify explanations with the answers to Why questions. The most cursory examination of both scientific and historical writing makes it clear that there are many occasions when questions beginning What, How, Who, Which, Where and When produce explanations; and explanations are also given in response to the raising of eyebrows, and in public lectures where no-one asks or has in mind *any* question.[6] The criterion of the Why question as stimulus must be modified to require only the possibility of such a question. But if explanations are the answers to *possible* Why questions, it is readily shown they are also answers to, e.g., possible What questions, since "Why did Cortes go?" is different only in being less precise than "What caused (or convinced) Cortes to go?" I think the Why-criterion was produced because of a dim recognition that contexts determine whether a statement (or set of statements) constitutes an explanation; and I think that it fails because syntactical form is an unreliable indicator of those context differences that distinguish explanations — in the very sense intended by the authors concerned — from, e.g., descriptions. Certainly there are sets of statements which in one context would be regarded as perfect explanations and in another as mere descriptions, and in another as inappropriate responses to a request for an explanation, etc.

The question naturally arises whether we can give any enlightening short characterization of an explanation at all, or whether the concept is one of those which we only come to understand in depth via the colligation of a great variety of examples, each sharing some properties with some others but lacking any non-trivial, wholly common properties (some candidates are "thing," "state," "scientific method," "game," "vehicle," "clock," "language," "machine"). If it is any help to say that explanations must produce understanding and not simply knowledge, this can be said. We know twice two is four, the date of our birthday, the color of the carpet; but this knowledge does not in itself consist in understanding something; something further is involved in understanding how an intelligent man could buy a carpet of this color, etc. To be more specific about explanations than this is to restrict the concept; and the apparent attractions of so doing have proved to be largely illusory. The increased manageability has always been offset by corresponding limitations on the scope of any conclusions about what standards should be met by *sound* explanations, since such conclusions require proving that other types of explanation are *un*sound, not merely explanations *in another sense.*

In so far as there are different respects in which one can be said to lack understanding of an act, a condition, a tendency, a law, etc., so far there are different ways in which it can be explained. For historical explanation this *does not* have the consequence that explanations are judged by some purely subjective standard of empathetic acceptability, since to say an historical phenomenon is understood is not to say someone (or everyone) *thinks* he understands it. There are objective tests for understanding just as for knowing or inferring. They happen not to be syntactical tests as are (supposedly) those for deducing; but then explanation is not a syntactical but a pragmatic notion. If we want to know whether someone understands William's failure to invade Scotland, we know the kind of question to ask him over and above the questions which tell us whether he knows that William did in fact fail to invade Scotland. If we want to know whether someone understands the rules of succession in the Hanoverian monarchy, we produce another type

[6] It is clear in Hempel and Oppenheim's monograph "The Logic of Explanation" (see in this volume, pp. 54–68 above) that they take the Why-What difference to distinguish explanation from "mere description." But Dray discusses explanations in response to How questions in "Explanatory Narrative in History," *Philosophical Quarterly*, 1954, pp. 15–27.

of question; but again it is not just a simple question intended to elicit knowledge of some specific fact about the rules. The most obvious difference is that *more* knowledge is required before a claim of understanding can be justified. More accurately, *what* one understands is something *different* from what one knows: one understands *an action*, one knows *when an action occurs* or *who* does it, etc.; or one understands a *body of constitutional law*, whereas one knows *what the laws are*, etc. Very loosely, this difference is brought out by saying that understanding (and hence explanation) involves *knowing all about* something with respect to a certain category of questions. Thus to understand an action involves, in some contexts, knowing about the motives for it, the character of the actor and the circumstances of the action; and it is easy to see where the deductive model fits in here, offering a criterion for exactly what one has to know, viz., any law and statements of particular fact such that they entail the description of the act. To this claim we shall return immediately; but first notice the hopelessness of such an analysis of understanding the rules of Hanoverian succession. No physical laws are deductively invoked in the explanation of these; explanation here consists in exegetical clarification and examination of the relations between the rules, e.g., with respect to consistency, redundancy, function, etc.

A *second* question would concern the *origin* of the rules or their development. It has commonly been argued that only the latter question is a request for an historical explanation. But the first kind of explanation meets two possible criteria; it occurs in history books, and it is a proper answer to Why questions, e.g., Why couldn't a Hanoverian king's nephew always (legitimately) succeed? Now it is certainly not a *specifically historical* kind of explanation, since it occurs also in textbooks of law, for example. This is an objection that Hempel would scarcely bring, since he is arguing for the essential similarity of historical explanations and, in his case, scientific explanations, the difference being only the restriction of the latter to the past. And that restriction is met by the study of *Hanoverian* rather than current institutions.

In short it seems clear that historians provide some explanations which in no sense involve laws of nature; and we may add to the example given a wide range of other types, including, for example, the explanation of the symbolism of the Imperial regalia at a coronation (the relevance to other social sciences such as anthropology being evident).

The value of these examples lies not only in their downright contradiction of the too-glib assumption that only the *causal explanation of events* concerns historians (an assumption which also happens to be false for physics, and which anyhow does not save the deductive model) but in the light they throw on certain types of explanation which tend to be forced into the deductive mold in the absence of alternatives. Consider the problem of explaining the *significance* of a certain action or trend of actions — the assassination of an Archduke, or a wave of selling in steels. Naturally there is some connection between the significance of an action and its causes and effects ("its significance as a manifestation of . . . "), but does this make such explanations causal explanations? Certainly it does not; for, in the first place, to list and evaluate the important effects of an action is not to subsume *it* under a causal law, not to give a causal explanation of *it*. In explaining the significance of an event (or trend, or condition) — and there are few more common types of explanation in history — we are not trying to show why, given its antecedent conditions, it was to be expected, but rather to show that, given that it happened, it was of a certain importance. Putting it bluntly, we are discussing the event in terms of an evaluation of its effects rather than a listing of its causes. And it will not do to say that we are "really" explaining *its effects in terms of it*, since the enquirer may not have *any* idea of the event's consequences. This makes it very unsatisfactory to say he's "really" looking for an explanation of *them*.

Perhaps there still hangs over us the Damoclean sword devised by Hume to make uneasy the armchairs of philosophers who talk of causes and deny laws. But the sense in which Hume said a law is involved in a causal assertion hardly suffices to establish the deductive model of explanation *in toto*. Even if Hume was correct, it only follows that each particular causal statement is an instance of a law; it does not follow that the *explanation* of (the significance of) event E consists in a *deduction* of E from laws *plus* antecedent conditions. Furthermore, though I do not have the space to prove it here, Hume's argument can be saved only by a modification which eliminates what Hempel defines as a law.[7]

At this stage we could go on to examine further types of historical explanation which seem most appropriately analyzed without mention of laws, but to describe them convincingly we need first to examine the plausibility of Hempel's analysis for Hempel's own examples. For it is important to see that his analysis is itself most inapplicable to actual cases, and the reasons for this, before we accept it as an analysis of good (or even ideal) explanation.

The preceding section, 3.1, sought to establish the gulf between explanations and their justifications. It follows that from the form of an explanation (which *is* given) one cannot infer a *unique* form for its justification (which is *not* given); as long as the right *types* and *combination* of grounds are produced, their exact content can vary considerably. Suppose we explain Cortes' action in Merriman's way (by appeal to his cupidity and confidence), *and suppose we accept Hempel's criterion of deducibility*, then any combination of laws and antecedent conditions from the following sets would constitute a formal justification of the explanation (would "complete" the "explanation-sketch," in Hempel's terminology):

I (i) All confident wealth-seeking people undertake any venture which offers wealth.
(ii) The third voyage envisioned by Cortes offered wealth.
(iii) Cortes was confident and wealth-seeking.

II (i) All confident people seeking very great wealth undertake any venture which offers very great wealth.
(ii) The third voyage envisioned by Cortes offered very great wealth.
(iii) Cortes was confident and seeking very great wealth.

III (i) All confident people with Cortes' background of experience, seeking very great wealth, undertake any venture involving the hazards of this one, which offers very great wealth.
(ii) The third voyage envisioned by Cortes involved the hazards that it involved and offered very great wealth.
(iii) Cortes was confident and had Cortes' background of experience and was seeking very great wealth.

This series admits of both padding — by interpolating further sets between, e.g., II and III — and extending — by continuing beyond III. But as it stands it illustrates an awkward dilemma for the deductive model. Set I (where, in our terminology, (i) is a role-justifying ground, (ii) and (iii) are the explanation itself) clearly satisfies the requirement of deducibility, i.e., of entailing what is to be explained, and has a nice straightforward general law in (i) and nice straightforward antecedent conditions in (ii) and (iii). But (i) is obviously and hopelessly false. The sensible move, in order to "save the explanation" (as the deductive-model supporters would put it), is to see whether some modification of the general law cannot be found which *is* true and which *can* be applied by supplementation of the antecedent conditions from our considerable stock of other knowledge about the man and the situation. Set II is an attempt at this; again it satisfies Hempel's formal requirement of deducibility, and would

[7] The point is somewhat elaborated in another paper, "The Present Status of Determinism in Physics," *Journal of Philosophy*, 1957, pp. 727–733. See also the Appendix to the present paper.

be a good explanation if only the statements were correct. Alas, even though less hopelessly wrong than I (i), the law II (i) is clearly much too general to be true. One can be entirely clear about the correctness of the explanation of Cortes' action in terms of his greed, etc., and not in any way committed to a belief in II (i). But there looms ahead the embarrassing threat of III (i), which seems a natural result of trying to state the law more precisely. The embarrassments of III consist in the increasing triviality of the components. The "law" has become more trivial, i.e., less general, in the course of becoming more nearly correct and now appears quite possibly to have only one instance, viz., Cortes in this situation. The "antecedent conditions," instead of invoking more of our knowledge about the circumstances, actually have no new (identifiable) empirical content, though they contain an empty gesture or two in the direction of our further knowledge.

Is there not *some* way in which we can improve II without falling into the trap of III, with its law which we can regard as a mere dressing-up in general terms of exactly the "explanation-sketch" we are supposed to be "filling-out"? Just as the deductive model would be an absurdity if it allowed deduction from the double-negation of the description of whatever it is to be explained (since then any true statement would be explained by its double negation), so it would be an absurdity if it allowed deduction from laws which were obtained by pseudo-generalization of an explanation-sketch we have rejected as "incomplete." If I say cupidity and confidence explain Cortes' action and I am told this is not a satisfactory explanation, the criticism is rendered trivial if I am allowed to avoid it by muttering that I really meant: "Everyone with confidence and cupidity and otherwise just like Cortes and in just such a situation, will undertake such a venture; and Cortes had confidence and cupidity." The "law" must be applicable, and "just like" is too vague for application. Hempel says it must have the form: "In every case where an event of a specified kind C occurs at a certain place and time, an event of a specified kind E will occur at a place and time which is related in a specified manner to the place and time of the occurrence of the first event."[8] Now "specified kind" presumably does not include something as vague as "just like this." At any rate, either it does, in which case it appears any explanation-sketch is trivially completable, or it does not, in which case it appears we have never found a law of the kind required and hence have no right to the certainty with which we affirm some historical explanations.

I do not assume the second horn of this dilemma established by my treatment of one example; but a moment's thought makes clear that the actual process of filling-in between II and III (or their analogues in any other case), giving closer and closer non-trivial descriptions of the circumstances C, will do no more than make one feel it more and more *probable* that such a C will be an E, and at no stage could one, with much confidence, make the universal claim that "Every C is an E." (Weakening the universal law to a probability assertion shatters the deductive model, as we shall see.) But a much more important alternative to this case must first be considered. The very idea that we should lose faith in an explanation because we cannot formulate a role-justifying ground for it is absurd. Let us take a case where we can be sure beyond any reasonable doubt that we have a correct explanation and let us see whether we can formulate the required Hempelian laws. As you reach for the dictionary, your knee catches the edge of the table and thus turns over the ink-bottle, the contents of which proceed to run over the table's edge and ruin the carpet. If you are subsequently asked to explain how the carpet was damaged you have a complete explanation. You did it, by knocking over the ink. The certainty of this explanation is primeval. It has absolutely nothing to do with your knowledge of the relevant laws of physics; a cave-man could supply the same account and be quite as certain of it. Now it is quite true

[8] op. cited, page 35.

that the *truth* of this explanation is empirical and in this sense *it* depends on the laws of nature. But its *certainty* has nothing to do with your ability to quote the laws. You have some knowledge about what happens when you knock things over, but so does the cave-man, and this kind of knowledge is totally unlike knowledge of the laws of nature: If you were asked to produce the role-justifying grounds for your explanation, what could you do? *You could not produce any true universal hypothesis* in which the antecedent was identifiably present (i.e., which avoids such terms as "knock hard enough"), and the consequent is the effect to be explained. If you tried to find something you did know to be true, it would have to be something like: "If you knock a table hard enough it will cause an ink-bottle that is not too securely or distantly or specially situated to spill over the edge (if it has enough ink in it)." But even this needs tightening up in a dozen ways to get the table loose, and the carpet stained. The best we can do is to modify it with a "probably" before the word "cause." It then becomes a truism — who could deny it, but who would bother to say it? Moreover it does not save the deductive model. There is no universal hypothesis which will; and one looks to physics for them in vain. For the explanation has become not one whit more certain since the laws of elasticity and inertia were discovered; and psychology is just as irrelevant to the corresponding historical explanations, which are already beyond doubt. The simple fact must be faced that certain evidence is adequate to guarantee certain explanations without the benefit of deduction from laws.

Now one important point can be made about the relationship of such explanations to the laws of physics that expresses part of the deductive model's *point*. In saying that our knocking over the ink caused the damage, we *are* committing ourselves to the view that laws of nature will not be found to contradict this assertion of a connexion. One *might* put this by saying that in certain cases we are in a position to judge, not that certain specifiable laws apply, but that *some* laws must apply. But it is *very* odd to say this rather than that we can sometimes be quite sure of causal statements even when we do not know any relevant laws. This capacity for identifying causes is learnt, is better developed in some people than in others, can be tested, and is the basis for what we call *judgments*.

Let it be noted that Hempel's own and only detailed example of an explanation from the physical sciences, on which he founds his analysis, is *conceded by him* not to be sufficiently well formulated to meet his own criteria: ". . . even that much more detailed statement of determining conditions and universal hypotheses would require amplification in order to serve as a sufficient basis for the deduction of the conclusion. . . ."[9] The physicist *judges*, inductively, and from his knowledge and experience, what the explanation is; and the judgment cannot be converted into a deduction. The historian does no less and it would surely be unfair to ask him to do more.

Yet can the deductive model not be saved by the substitution of probability-statements for universal hypotheses? Indeed it cannot, for one cannot *deduce* from any law of the form "If C then probably E," combined with the antecedent condition C, that E occurs. One can only deduce that E *probably* occurs, and we are not trying to explain a probability but an event. So the criterion of deduction must be abandoned if the criterion of universal hypotheses is abandoned; and what is then left of the deductive model? We have instead an *inductive* model of explanation, where for laws we have probability truisms, and for deduction probability inference. But in what sense does such an analysis provide an improved or more complete kind of explanation, an ideal model of explanation? In none, for what is to be gained by quoting truisms rather than particular and relevant causal judgments? What is added to, or "completed" about, our explanation of the damaged carpet by production of some truism concerning the probable effect of knocking tables on which ink-bottles stand? And in history what is gained by Merriman's expla-

[9] op. cited, page 38.

nation of Cortes' action if he adds that sufficient confidence and a great desire for wealth may well lead a man to undertake a hazardous and previously unsuccessful venture?

Can we do no better than this? Indeed we can formulate universal hypotheses which become less and less obviously false, but never one that appears to be true. And, more to the point, why should we be committed to any that we can formulate? The causal judgment itself we will support; but we do it directly, not via some yet to be propounded and then dubious laws. Is it not absurd to talk of supporting a causal judgment except via a law? Well, what laws do I produce in support of my causal analysis of the damaged carpet? I tell you in particular detail what happened (my truth-justifying grounds), and if you push for role-justifying grounds, I produce the truism. A gap remains, a logical possibility of error due to the sloppiness of the truism with its terms like "hard enough," etc. But logical possibilities of error are no concern to any scientist, and in the face of the detailed description given, what *reasonable* possibility of error can be pointed out that should be excluded? There is none: what else *could possibly* have been the cause in such a case?

In the Cortes case, we know about his confidence and greed, we know the truism that makes the possession of such characteristics a possible explanation, but we also count pretty heavily on another vague proposition (though it can be incorporated into the first one) to the effect that if a man has these characteristics and does undertake a hazardous voyage and there are no other apparent causes, then it is *very* probable these were the causes. We can do something towards filling in the list of other possible causes from our stock of truisms about behavior; though of course it's not often that we are called on to do so, i.e., that we are pushed to second-level grounds. But *we recognize* such possible causes very reliably indeed, and in examining the evidential situation, any indications of the presence of one of them rings an alarm in the mind of the practiced historian. One may say that an historian's *principles of judgment* are most nearly, though inadequately, expressed in the form of truisms; and one sees immediately why historians have fought shy of producing these as "the laws on which their explanations are based." They are trivial, though not empty; and can only look like shoddy pre-scientific laws, whereas historical explanations are neither shoddy nor pre-scientific. The paradox is resolved by seeing that the sense in which good historical explanations are based on such truisms is simply that the explanations can only be denied by someone who is prepared to deny such an obviously true statement (assuming he is attacking the role-justifying dimension of support). The truism tells us nothing *new* at all; but it says *something* and it says something *true*, even if vague and dull. It ill fits into a deductive proof; but it has no need to do so, since the justification of an explanation is a context-dependent *inductive* procedure (and not necessarily a *predictively* useful procedure).

Three final and important points. There is nothing unusual to science about the use of reliable procedures of inference, even predictive inference, which cannot be stated in terms of applicable principles. The trained ear of the musician, the trained eye of the lumberman or the tracker, the professional hands of the cheese-maker — all these embody skills which undoubtedly exist, enable accurate diagnosis and/or prediction, *and cannot be expressed in terms of statements which others can objectively apply to perform the same tasks.* The great medical diagnosticians may be able to *train* their students to almost the same level of success, but they can formulate very few of the laws according to which they operate, and even when they can, it is not in a form which enables us to go and do likewise. The sophistication of physics lies in its vocabulary and the quantitative nature of its laws; that of clinical medicine in its vocabulary and the acuity of the sensory perceptions required; while history is not sophisticated in any of these ways. But the sophistications mentioned, vital though they are for predictions of some kinds, are in no way necessary for the attainment of explanatory certainty. And in history — unconcerned with predictions — we find the mother subject for explanations. There they are, simple and unadorned, logically no different from those in common-sense talk about people and physical objects (or many of those in physics and clinical medicine), no less certain for being unhampered by the superstructure of theories and instruments, algebras and unobservable entities. The discoveries of scientists may extend the range of historical explanation, but they are not required to underwrite it.

I cannot conclude this section without suggesting to the reader that an historian might view with suspicion a proffered explanation of an historical event which consisted in showing it to be an instance of a universal generalization. I have just argued that Hempelian analysis does not provide necessary conditions for an explanation; now I mention that its claims for sufficiency are equally suspect. To this point I shall return later.

Finally, it may be thought that my "explanations" are simply Hempel's "explanation-sketches," and my truisms loose forms of his laws. This would be an unsatisfactory translation. The important distinction between explanations of any kind is their certainty; and this, I have argued, is quite unconnected with the availability of universal hypotheses, which constitutes Hempel's criterion for judging "explanation-sketches." Explanatory certainty in fact depends on exactly those standards of evidence which we apply in judging explanations of things we see happening. History *always* (but reporting *often*) requires some accessory investigation of witnesses, documents, radio-carbon dating, etc.; but this can often enough be done with enough success to eliminate reasonable doubt. The "universal hypotheses" are entirely mythical; but in any event they are unnecessary. If an historical explanation were found which did involve a universal hypothesis, it would not, in the eyes of historians, be any better for that. Hempel defines his term "universal hypothesis" clearly and it is in his sense that they are mythical; but in no useful alternative sense could one regard truisms as laws which could save the deductive model, since deduction of non-probability statements from them is impossible. Then nothing remains to the model except the claim that, underlying explanations (assumed to be all causal), there are laws which (from the psychologist's point of view) it would be nice for some psychologist to locate, and which history might one day be able to use, but which are neither involved in nor necessary for good historical explanation.

3.3 *The Comparison with the Physical Sciences.* It is worth noting in passing that explanations in the physical sciences, apart from being irrelevant as a model for history since they are connected with predictions in a way historical explanations are not, are by no means examples of the deductive model. A number of the points already made carry over directly to explanations in engineering and applied physics, and we can for the moment ignore any special features of the explanation of laws, since these obviously have little relevance to historical explanation. The most striking demonstration that explanations in physics are not natural subjects for the deductive model is afforded by the failure of Hempel, on his own admission, to produce a single example that meets the conditions. Certainly he gives a perfectly good example of a physical explanation (of the cracking of a radiator in a car left out on a freezing night); but he does not succeed in formulating it in such a way that the required conclusion is entailed by it. The reason is fairly clear; the laws of physics are not truisms but informative laws which can be formulated with some precision and they enable us to explain hitherto obscure phenomena, but *they too* require judgment in their application. To explain something when the only known relevant general statements are *truisms* requires that the judgment carry most of the weight, e.g., the judgment that "enough" or "too much" or "similar," etc., are here applicable. It is usually unnecessary to mention the relevant truisms while defending an historical explanation, because these are rarely in doubt, only their application; and nothing in their formulation helps us to decide that. In physics, the situation is different. First, we are often concerned to explain rather precisely measured and quantitatively described phenomena; so quantitative relations between their properties will be required. Secondly, these laws are not commonly known (though amongst physicists, where they *are* known, they are rarely quoted in an explanation) and hence may well be exactly what is lacking in the enquirer's understanding of the situation. Thirdly, supporting the causal judgment commonly involves some *calculation* using the law(s), and so brings them in.

Now it might be the case that physical laws could be so formulated and measurements so made as to virtually eliminate the element of judgment; indeed it rarely is required to perform one of its common tasks in historical explanation, the interpretation of the truism's characteristic, vague terms "possible," "naturally," "eventually," etc. But the world is not so simple, and the laws of nature are remarkably imperfect instruments. To begin with, they are never better than approximations. We know of no important quantitative law, in optics, acoustics, thermodynamics, magnetism, gravitation, etc., which is held to be exact.[10] The deviations are not at the limits of measurement but often observable with the grossest instruments. The Gas Laws are good examples; around 6° K the divergence of helium from the value predicted by the laws is of the same order of magnitude as the value itself. The natural reply is to state the laws' *scope* with care. But the scope, i.e., the range of accuracy, varies depending on the size of the permissible error, and in most cases they have no scope at all without measured error. Consequently, *deduction* of the *exact* values to be explained from such laws is a matter of chance.

But cannot the laws be reformulated so that they are exact? Better approximations can be produced, such as Van der Waals' equation which takes account of the finite size of the molecules — an important source of error. But these in turn are inexact for other reasons. The only way an exact form can be obtained is by empirical test at each temperature for each substance under each condition: an infinite task. Speaking practically, one can in some cases take enough readings to provide a basis for a curve which gives the required degree of approximation. When the constant-volume hydrogen gas thermometer was the basis for the temperature scale, the fantastic work involved in this undertaking was done. But already the inapplicability of the findings for hydrogen to other gases was apparent, and since 1927 the idea has been abandoned. So the Gas Law is abandoned for the Van der Waals law, and this for the hydrogen graph; and already we have lost both the manageability and the range of application of the simple law. The result, fatal to Hempel's examples, is that no explanation quoting the relatively inaccurate simple forms — all that he mentions — can be regarded as satisfactory in the deductive model, since they are known not to be exactly true. And the obvious and correct reply that they are true *enough*, for explaining most gross phenomena, immediately lets in the element of judgment with respect to terms like "enough," whose absence had appeared to distinguish physical explanations. There are further stages in the dialectic of exploring the extent of this judgment, but the important and originally invisible similarity to the historical examples should now be apparent, as well as the irrelevance of the deductive model to both.

The second source of difficulty with the deductive model in physics arises over the selection of the appropriate laws to invoke. It is by no means sufficient to produce laws

[10] Certain limit-forms and other non-quantitative forms of, or deviations from, laws are held to be categorically true, e.g., the unattainability form of the Nernst Heat Theorem ("Absolute zero is unattainable"). Of course, there are corresponding "laws" in history e.g. "No one has ever conquered three continents"; but they usually lack an essential ingredient of the physical law which we shall discuss below.

which apply somehow or other to a particular phenomenon. A judgment of type is required, as in history; and this judgment must be made in a way which cannot itself be deductively justified from known and exact laws about the people who seek explanations. These two objections attack the deductive model's claim to provide necessary and sufficient conditions for explanation in physics. They are just two of many difficulties for it, but their import can be summed up by saying that in physics one can sometimes provide explanations in terms of laws (since there *are* laws) but that (*a*) other kinds of explanations are also given and are equally satisfactory and that (*b*) even the first kind does not fit the deductive model.

A more useful distinction than that between explanations in history and those in physical sciences is a distinction between what we may call *derivation-explanations* and *selection-explanations*, a distinction between kinds of explanation rather than subject matter. In physics the occasional greater relevance of the deductive model is in part due to the fact that understanding a phenomenon described in great numerical detail often requires understanding exactly how its properties can be mathematically derived from certain mathematically expressed physical laws (neither laws nor derivation being absolutely strict). Asking for an explanation may actually be asking for a demonstration of this possibly long and complex derivation; and so we encounter a novel explanation-type, the derivation-explanation. Its novelty lies, not in the *requirement* of inferribility, but in the fact that the explanation consists solely in *demonstrating* this. Lest it should be supposed that this is more correctly analyzed as simply a request for a proof, it is worth mentioning an interesting example from the history of physics. For a long time both Hooke and Pardies sought to explain the behavior of a light ray passing from one medium to another (Snell's Law), from the assumption that light was a wave phenomenon. At last the trick was turned by Huygens (*Traité de la Lumière, etc.*, Leyden, 1690), who produced the proof. This is referred to by Whittaker as "the explanation of refraction",[11] all the premises were already at hand, and only the derivation remained to be found. In this context, the explanation *is* the derivation. Now this possibility is done little justice by the deductive model, with its syllogistic form, where no student of elementary logic could fail to complete the inference, given the premise. And the deductive model also requires exact truth of the premises and exact deduction, both too strong.

By contrast, there are many cases where the derivation from laws can readily be accomplished but the scientists are, justifiably, concerned to find something more; and it is these cases which lead us to suspect that even if we had laws in history, it would by no means follow that explanation would be facilitated. We shall examine this possibility briefly in a later section. Here I wish to call attention to the extreme opposite of the derivation explanation, the case where we give an explanation which in no way depends on our possession of any exact or even quantitative laws. What we have is a range of formally possible explanations connected with an effect of the observed kind by truisms or definitions (or, perhaps, laws); and on the basis of the facts of the case, we *select* one of the antecedents as the explanation. It is the particular facts, not the general propositions or the derivation, which provides the explanation in such cases. Thus, in the Cortes case, there are several formally possible explanations within the appropriate types. Cortes may have acted under orders, to escape boredom, from stupidity, to avoid recall, etc. We are concerned with selecting from this range the appropriate explanation, and we do so directly from the evidence about his circumstances and character. The point of the explanation is to locate the

[11] *History of the Theories of the Aether and Electricity*, Vol. I, p. 24. Derivation-explanations are more common in physics because we are often there concerned with explaining laws for which they are usually appropriate.

relevant causal antecedent, not to prove it is a possible one; we are not doubting that receiving orders of the appropriate kind can constitute an explanation of a hazardous and previously unsuccessful type of venture, but are unclear (do not understand) whether it was this or something else (in *this* case) that explains the matter. In calling for a derivation-explanation we know the facts and laws but can't see *how* they explain; in the selection-explanation case we know how each possible set of circumstances could explain but we don't know *which* set applies.

In physics we give selection-explanations which depend not on truisms but on genuine laws, as in the explanation of the varying brightness of the sputnik rocket, where we select the shape and motion as the explanation rather than the varying brightness of the sun, or cyclic fatigue of the eye, etc. Do the scientists investigate the antecedents of other possible causal explanations? No; they *judge* they have the right one, just as the historian does: and the historian's judgment, like the physicist's, unformalizable, is aided by "empathy." So physics has a monopoly on derivation-explanations, but also uses selection-explanations. There is no greater virtue in the explanations in *physics* than [in] selection-explanations. For the only surplus value of the physical law over the truism lies in the field of prediction of simple quantitative phenomena and not in that of explanation, where the only requirement to be met is attainment of that level of certainty and accuracy which the context requires. And step for step, level for level, the explanations based on truisms can match those based on laws; the extra precision of the latter isn't a working part in the machinery of selection-explanations. It does not follow from anything here said that laws *cannot* be used in historical explanations. They may (obviously) be involved in accessory studies, e.g., tree-ring dating, and hence figure in the second-level grounds for explanations involving date-ascriptions. They could conceivably become more relevant to special cases of historical explanations, e.g., in cases where relative rates of learning are involved. And sloppy laws of the kind which new concepts drag along with them and in which their meaning is to be found, e.g., Freudian ideas, sometimes provide a useful type of general statement intermediate between laws and truisms. I shall say a little more about the general properties of statements that *can* serve as explanations in the next section. It is worth remembering that the kind of evidence available in history is usually *gross observable behavior descriptions*, and that precise laws about behavior usually require physiological data or other special instrument-requiring data. So truisms are often the *best* we can expect.

3.4. *The Nature of the General Statements in Explanations.* If I want a causal explanation, deduction from a non-causal although universal hypothesis is of no use at all. Sunrise follows sunrise, but I can't *explain* why a sunrise occurs today by producing the perfectly valid deduction of its occurrence from this law plus the fact that there was a sunrise yesterday. The explanation required is presumably in terms of the mechanics of the solar system, and the premise offered merely multiplies the number of instances of the unexplained phenomena. Proponents of the deductive model sometimes argue that an explanation *has* been given here, and what is *now* being asked for (or perhaps what was "really" meant by the original question) is an explanation of the *law* that sunrises follow sunrises. This is an artificial solution, since (*a*) exactly the same point arises in connection with explaining a law: deduction from a more general law, e.g., about sunrises always occurring on planets in single-star planetary systems would be — almost inevitably — non-explanatory, because it yields no understanding of the motions that lie behind any one case of the sun "rising"; and (*b*) when I ask for a causal explanation of an event, it may be that what is required will incidentally explain a generalization, but this is hardly proof that it was the generalization which I wanted explained — sometimes one doesn't know the generalization *exists*.

The most natural salvaging move here

would be to allow only *causal* laws, not all universal hypotheses, to serve as premises for explanation. This goes too far in the other direction because sometimes we are not seeking a causal explanation, e.g., when explaining the structure of the Egyptian ruling class, but it suggests a most important requirement for the underlying "generalizations." If we are interested in the explanation of a particular event, as is usual in history and common in engineering, astronomy, and applied physics, we are naturally not satisfied unless we are confident the response actually applies *to this particular event;* and the plausibility of the deductive model in part springs from this necessity for tying down the generalizations to the particular case by *unambiguous statements of antecedent conditions.* This is asking too much, for a variety of reasons that we have discussed before; but it does again suggest a *desirable* criterion for the kind of generalization used as grounds for explanations. The third way in which we can get some idea of what is required is by looking at the inadequacies of a merely statistical generalization as a role-justifying ground; remembering that exact laws are virtually unknown, it is all the more serious that a statement such as "C's cause something quite like E's" or "73% of C's are (or cause) E's" should be profoundly unsatisfactory as a ground for giving C as an explanation of this E. How can we ever be sure that C explains E if we lack exact laws? Is it that we have statistical laws with a *very high* percentage figure, say around 90%, in them? Rather clearly not, since we have almost no reliable statistical *laws* (as opposed to summaries of data at a fixed time or over a given period) outside very limited realms of physics.

The answer I wish to suggest is a radical one. I suggest there is a category of general statements, a hybrid with some universal features and some statistical features, from which alone can be selected the role-justifying grounds for good explanations of individual events. It includes the truisms I have talked about before, many natural laws, some tendency statements and probability statements, and — in other areas less relevant to explaining — rules, definitions, and certain normative statements in ethics. The crucial common property of these statements is best illustrated by examples, but can be described as norm-defining; they have a *selective immunity* to apparent counter-examples. Wishing to indicate their differences from the typical analytic and synthetic statements, as well as their central norm-defining role, I shall refer to them as "normic statements." The statement that "rhombi" means the same as "equilateral parallelograms" (N_1) is a typical normic statement. It is not analytic in the way that the statement "Rhombi are equilateral parallelograms" is analytic, because its denial is not self-contradictory.[12] It is not synthetic in the way that "Rhombi are easier for children to draw than circles" is synthetic, because understanding all the terms in it is enough to establish its truth. The relation between the facts of linguistic usage and the truth of such statements as N_1 is not a simple one. On the one hand, if *nobody ever* uses the words in an interchangeable way, we should feel the statement was clearly false. On the other hand, a few erring learners of the geometer's vocabulary can misuse these terms without *in any way* making us view the statement as dubious. Is it not then a statistical report on usage? Essentially not; or at least only in the sense of being non-universal yet non-singular and empirical. In deciding whether it is correct, we apply a very complex analysis to the apparent exceptions. We dismiss exceptions amongst those learning the language, take very little account of those among the rare users, wholly ignore cases of code usages, pay some but not much attention to puns or bad cross-word-puzzle clues, etc., etc. One might say that the word "rhombi" has a different meaning in these contexts; but N_1 is a reference to no special context, i.e., it refers to the "proper" use, and our problem is exactly

[12] But see my "Definitions, Explanations, and Theories," Vol. II, *Minnesota Studies in the Philosophy of Science.*

that of identifying what counts for and against assertions about the "proper" use. N_1 captures the facts about a certain strand of usage, a strand which we know *how* to recognize but which could not be accurately described in any manageable statement. My contention is that our descriptive language contains many complex territories inhabited by some genus of normic statement and that we know a great deal about their habits and habitat, although little of it is, and much can scarcely be, explicitly formulated. (Think of the limitations on the formulability of the skilled knowledge of the surgeon, diagnostician, helmsman, swimmer, calculating genius, etc.) In judging definitions in a dictionary or a debate, we call on our system of rating the various instances of usage with respect to the normic genus of meaning-statements, a system which we know well (as language-users) but could ill state.

Analogously, we can deal with normic statements involving the language of rules. The assertion that the penalty for a revoke, in bridge, is two tricks (N_2) is not a simple description of what people do, nor of what the rule-book says. Many players ignore it, others do not know it, others misapply it; but (*a*) it is nevertheless a correct statement, and (*b*) under suitable empirical circumstances it would be falsified, e.g., if the Contract Bridge Control Board changed the rule, *and* there was no breakaway faction formed, *and* tournament committees made no special exceptions, etc. A similar analysis can be applied in many other fields and is, in my opinion, absolutely crucial to a correct understanding of ethical judgements, contrary to the view of those who see the appropriate analogy there to be expressions of feeling or imperatives, etc.

But let us bring these brief general considerations to bear on the present subject. Normic statements about behavior can take various syntactical forms and it is easy to see how they have previously been dismissed too easily, or too readily amalgamated into standard categories. I shall try to select some that might be produced as role-justifying grounds in historical explanations. Consider "A conscientious Secretary of the Treasury would not reveal forthcoming rises in the federal discount rate to his banker acquaintances" (N_3); "Strict Orthodox Jews fast on the Day of Atonement" (N_4); "Power corrupts" (N_5); "Other things being equal a greater number of troops is an advantage in battle" (N_6); "Proportional representation tends to give minorities excessive power" (N_7); "The American bourgeoisie normally reacts with hostility to those on whom it is dependent" (N_8); "A rise in the tariff characteristically produces a decline in the value of imports" (N_9); etc. Other modifiers that indicate normic statements are "ordinarily," "typically," "usually," "properly," "naturally," "under standard conditions," "probably." But, as in N_1, N_2 and N_4, no modifier is necessary; and modifiers sometimes have other uses.

One might term the study of normic statements in this area the logic of *guarded generalizations*. None of these assertions is definitionally true (even though N_3 and N_4 might be called quasi-definitional, they are not analytic), but none can be falsified by the simple procedure involved in dealing with such generalizations as "All members of Parliament in 1700 represented less than 20,000 souls" (G_1); "Whenever the tariff rises, the value of imports falls" (G_2), etc. Nor are they at all like exact or vague statistical statements involving percentages or "most," "nearly all," etc., though some of these are important and useful as factual assertions in the grounds of explanations. The statistical statement is less informative than the normic statement in a very important way, although an exact statistical statement may be informative in a way a normic statement is not. The statistical statement does not say anything about the things to which it refers except that some do and some do not fall into a certain category. The normic statement says that *everything* falls into a certain category *except* those to which *certain special conditions* apply. And, although the normic statement itself does not explicitly list what count as exceptional conditions, it employs a vocabulary which reminds us of our knowledge of this, our trained judgment of exceptions. In the case of the meaning-statement N_1, we know how to evaluate the import of the statement, not as a universal statement about all actual usage of the terms referred to, but as a statement about specially favored kinds of usage, i.e., we know what counts as an exception; similarly with the rule-statement, the ethical statements, and finally N_3–N_9. (With N_7–N_9, we leave the truisms and become less confident about dependent explanations.) When we read the statement about the behavior of Orthodox Jews on the Day of Atonement, we do not take it to be falsified (or disconfirmed) by discovering a devout but seriously ill Orthodox Jew who is granted rabbinical dispensation to eat on such a day to save his life. Nor does this show him to be other than a strict Orthodox Jew; so the statement is not analytic. But, in the absence of knowledge that such special conditions applied, we would have a prima-facie case for reclassifying him; and this is the mark of the quasi-definitional normic statement.

Now if the exceptions were few in number and readily described, one could convert a normic statement into an exact generalization by listing them. Normic statements are useful where the system of exceptions, although perfectly comprehensible in the sense that one can learn how to judge their relevance, is exceedingly complex. We see immediately the analogy with — in fact, the normic character of — physical laws. The physicist's *training* makes him aware of the system of exceptions and inaccuracies, which, if simpler, could be put explicitly into the statement of scope. In fact, some of the grosser features are commonly incorporated in the statement of the scope of a law; interestingly enough, a study of laws reveals that occasionally an obviously normic (in fact, quasi-definitional) form is adopted, as when they are about *ideal* gases, or apply up to the *fatigue* point, or for *homogeneous* media, etc., where a large part of the procedure of telling whether a gas is ideal, a metal fatigued, etc., is to see whether the law applies. In such cases the law really amounts to a sophisticated "mnemonic device," that awful epithet with which Hempel labels the procedure of the *verstehen* and empathy theorists! The study of behavior, history, or the social sciences makes us aware of (develops our skill in recognizing) the exceptions to the truisms or, more generally, the normic statements which serve the role analogous to laws in these fields. We do not go around decrying all physical laws as false (although they are not exactly true) because they serve the crucial explanatory role of singling out a preferred value from which, it is alleged, all deviations can be explained. There is indeed a conventional element here in the sense that we have to judge between competing systems of norms by judging the simplicity, etc., of the explanations of deviations from them. But there is also a very substantial empirical element.

Essentially, a causal explanation of an individual occurrence must use normic role-justifying grounds because (*a*) there aren't any true universal hypotheses to speak of and (*b*) statistical statements are too weak — they abandon the hold on the individual case. The normic statement tells one what had to happen in *this* case, unless certain exceptional circumstances obtained; and the historical judgment is made (and open to verification) that these circumstances did not obtain. An event can rattle around inside a network of statistical laws, but is located and explained by being so located in the normic network. Not with mathematical exactitude, indeed, nor beyond all possibility of error, but often as exactly and certainly as our observations are exact and certain.

Looking back to the explanation of William's non-invasion of Scotland we can see this analysis in application.

The failure to invade takes place in a situation about which we know enough to make certain truisms relevant. Specifically, we see a man who seems to have even more reason for invading Scotland than he did for invading England (for Scotland unconquered was more of a threat to England than ever England was to William before he invaded her). It is a truism that a reasonable man with better reasons for doing something than he had when he previously did it will do it again; it is a truism that preventing attack is a good reason for invasion when victory is certain without too much fighting and moral considerations are not too highly regarded. We judge he is a man to whom such reasons were apparent, and for whom they would be weighty. Yet he does not invade. The *need* for an explanation is thrust on us by the system of normic statements; my analysis thus makes clear why we find ourselves in the odd position of explaining why something did *not* happen, one of the points of this example. Now, there are several ways in which the matter might be explained. There may be an error of fact in our understanding of the situation which removes the pressure of the truisms; there may be further facts which feed into and hence alter the expectations from the same still relevant truisms — constituting grounds for an allowable exception, or grounds for modifying our judgment of the presence of "enough" incentive, "too much" fighting, etc. In the present case, we discover further facts which refute our preliminary conclusion that the same reasons applied to the invasion of Scotland (viz., that William now had ample land for his supporters), and we also discover that he subjugated Malcolm without actually invading his land. The first makes the truism about reasonable men with *better* reasons inapplicable; the second provides a standard exception to the truism about the reasonableness of protective invasion which jointly provides the pressure for explanation. Neither truism is literally a universal truth, neither is statistical; the utility of both lies not in their form but in the possibility of learning how to apply them by training the judgment. Even this formulation is too kind; for indeed it is the judgment which precedes the formula, and the issues are not fought over the truism but over the particular explanations which it reflects but does not support.

3.5. *Predictions.* I shall here only mention what seem to me the more obvious reasons for abandoning the idea that explanations and predictions are complementary in the sense argued by Hempel. (". . . an explanation . . . is not complete unless it might as well have functioned as a prediction . . ."[13]) First, there are the non-causal explanations involving explanations of significance, symbolism, etc., from which no predictions follow at all. Second, there are the cases where we have a universal hypothesis which we can use for highly reliable prediction, e.g., that the appearance of sun-spots is followed by widespread radio disturbance; it certainly does not follow from our ability to predict here that we have an *explanation* of what we predict — sun-spots may be a complete mystery except for this regular correlation. Third, there are clearly cases where our inability to predict a future event in no way counts against the certainty with which we can explain one of its consequences in terms of it. Thus we could never have predicted the Lisbon earthquake, but it is absurd to question our explanation of the wreckage and misery in terms of the virtually simultaneous earthquake. This is, in some empty sense of "prediction," compatible with the deductive model's claims; but it brings home that some of the essential limitations on prediction of historical events need not be reflected in any limitations on their explanation. Here we could never have predicted the wreckage and misery, *until the* (simultaneous) *earthquake*, i.e., no prediction worth the name was possible; but the utility of explanations is not judged by the time-interval between their formulation and the moment to which they refer.[14]

[13] op. cited, p. 38.

[14] It is by no means only geological catastrophes that have historical consequences without being predictable. The rain that saved Washington from Howe, the conception of a child by a queen, the hard winter of the retreat from Moscow, the failure of a bomb, are other cases.

Fourth, a more important and, I think, interesting point. There is a kind of limiting case of the last consideration which constitutes a serious drawback for the complementarity view. When, and only when, a man *has* murdered his wife, we know something about him of the very greatest value and without which we could not make a reliable prediction of the murder, even if we knew him to be tremendously jealous of her relations with another man: we know he is capable of murder. It is comparatively easy to find the motive for murder, i.e., to explain it, when we are very confident there is a motive and know there has been a murder. But it is very difficult to tell from information about a man's jealousy that he is so jealous that he *will* commit murder. It is this use of the necessary condition truism "There must be a motive for a murder," plus the limited list of possible motives, plus the evidence as to what obtained, that makes the explanation easier than the prediction. Similarly we can explain a Cabinet Minister's resignation in terms of his disagreement on policy, even though our knowledge of him and of the issue could not in advance have entitled us to predict it with any reliability. The change in our information about him is our knowledge that he committed (and hence was capable of, i.e., had a certain character) the act we have to explain; hence we have more *data* for explaining than we did for predicting. Hence the former may be certain and the latter not: but not vice versa. This possibility is easily overlooked in physics because the increment of information arising from the event's occurrence is usually negligible in comparison with that on which laws are based. But it occurs there, and especially in astronomy (dealing with the explosions of stars which reveal their composition only as they die).

A much more important reason why this point has been overlooked is because it is thought to lead only to trivial "explanations" of the form, "He did it because he was capable of it." But explanations *based on truisms* are not trivial explanations, for they may be selection-explanations of the greatest value. "He drank the wine because he was thirsty" is as good an explanation, when empirically supported, as is "He drank because there was a gun in his back" or "He drank because he was nervous," etc., just because only one of these can be true and selecting one is informative because it rules the others out. "He killed her from jealousy" can most easily be supported if we have evidence that he could, for whatever reason, get to the point of murder (and this we have only after his action), plus evidence that he was motivated by jealousy (which we have before his action), plus truisms. This is a non-trivial explanation, but its ingredients preclude its conversion into a prediction of the event in question (for which it is too late) or of future ones (for which it is irrelevant, since a previous murder is not good grounds for expecting another, nor for not expecting it). There may perhaps seem to be some residual logical sense in which the explanation, once given, could serve as a prediction, but it is of no more importance than the sense in which laws are involved in particular statements. For a prediction is by definition such that it *could* be given before the event, but these predictions, requiring data from the event, logically could *not* be given before it. I believe this point accounts for a crucial advantage of history and constitutes a crucial rebuttal of the suggestion that history is incomplete until it has predictively useful laws.

3.6. *Other Models of Explanation.* Perhaps one can only break the hold of a logical model by persisting with one alternative; but I have here elected to multiply the alternatives in the hope that their diversity may open up at least one fruitful way of dealing with the difficulties which I have no doubt overlooked in each of them. In conclusion I want to mention two radically different models or analogies as a final attempt to shake loose our thought from the cast in which it is set by the interesting but, I think, unsound analysis of the deductive model.

An illuminating comparison can be found between many historical explanations and straightforward procedures such as explaining the way to a certain place (cf. explaining the northward spread of Gothic cathedral architecture or explaining how the scientific revolution developed in Europe). But the most interesting analogy of all, perhaps, is to be found between explanatory narrative in history and the development of the dramatic plot in a play or novel. Literary critics have often written of the criterion of "inevitability": it is said that a good play must develop in such a way that we are surprised at each development, i.e., cannot predict it, but then see the development as necessary, i.e., can explain it. Since I have been arguing that in history prediction is usually difficult or impossible but explanation often good and sometimes certain, it seems worth examining the comparison. We can begin by eliminating the exaggerations. First, even in good plays it is too much to require that prediction is always impossible; it is rather that frequent and/or important, interesting developments take place. Correspondingly, there are many predictions that we can make about behavior (and consequently about future history or future discoveries about past history), some of them with the greatest confidence.[15] Second, it is also too much to claim that *no* changes in the plot or character development are possible, since even large changes if made earlier (with the appropriate later changes) must be possible. After all, the early part of the play constitutes the only foundations on which one can *base* judgments of inevitability thereafter, the plot not being inevitable before the first line is written. So in history, given the data we have up to a certain point, there are a number of possible subsequent turns of fortune, none of which would seem to us inexplicable. Is it not an inadequate sense of explanation which makes it possible to explain each of several alternatives (though not "anything that happens")? No; for to say that we can and would explain several different alternatives does not mean we would give the *same* explanation for each. In so far as the act itself is required for the explanation of the act, so far inevitability is only retrospective. Explanation is retrospective; and the inevitability of determinism is explanatory rather than predictive. Hence freedom of choice, which is between future alternatives, is not incompatible with the existence of causes for every event. But this is to stray.

The *point* of the criterion of dramatic inevitability remains and is an excellent one; it is the necessity for *plausibility in depth.* The play must survive all analysis of its plausibility; there must not be an inconsistency between an earlier act by a character and a later that cannot be accounted for by the intervening development. The play must be consistent with what we know or discover of human behavior. So, too, must historical explanation be plausible in depth, must survive analysis and further discoveries. But no more than the playwright must the historian be able to give the laws of behavior in order to give a plausible account. He is vulnerable to them, but does not seek them or require them (unlike the physicist — though not so unlike the automobile mechanic). What must be given by the playwright to make the plot's unfolding seem inevitable in retrospect is not unlike what must be found and given by the historian to make his narrative explanatory. This we can do; but we would have to go beyond the bounds of historical data and interests, to abandon history, if we sought to eliminate all surprise. Our records of the past and present make it quite certain that to abandon historical explanations for this goal is to abandon the only relevant, and an entirely satisfactory ap-

[15] Scullard has a nice example in which he commits himself in some detail to an account of what would have happened if. . . . This is logically of the same nature as "what will happen if . . ." and more common in history, since the historian is only in his spare time a prophet. "This view seems to imply that Flaminus, if superseded, would not have advocated peace (and betraying the Greeks) because the glory of enforcing such a peace would fall to another. But surely if he had successfully managed the acceptance of terms, he would have spiked the guns of his political opponents since the peace would have been recognized as that of the negotiator. . . ." *Roman Politics 220–150 B.C.* (Oxford, 1951), p. 103.

proach, for a hope which is as misguided as, if no less interesting than, the hope for an aesthetic computer that will eliminate the necessity for any judgments of artistic merit.

Historical explanations are secure against the depredations of future scientific discoveries just as much as any scientific explanations are, law-based or not. The reason is that they are based on extremely reliable knowledge of behavior, despite its being usually too well known to be worth mentioning, and too complex to permit any precise formulation. It is a central error to suppose with Hempel that scientific laws are either more accurate or more useful than truisms as grounds for historical explanation. But Boswell was too modest when he said: "Great abilities are not requisite for an Historian; for in historical composition all the greatest powers of the human mind are quiescent. He has facts ready to his hand; so there is no exercise of invention. Imagination is not required in any high degree; only about as much as is used in the lower kinds of poetry. Some penetration, accuracy, and colouring will fit a man for the task, if he can give the application which is necessary" (*Life of Johnson* [Oxford], Vol. I, p. 284). To get the facts ready to one's hand, to avoid invention in reporting them, to penetrate their meaning and illuminate their presentation — it might well be said that these *are* tasks to tax the greatest powers of the human mind.

Explanation and Prediction as Non-Symmetrical 10

Explanation and Prediction in Evolutionary Theory

MICHAEL SCRIVEN

SATISFACTORY EXPLANATION OF THE PAST IS POSSIBLE EVEN WHEN PREDICTION OF THE FUTURE IS IMPOSSIBLE

The most important lesson to be learned from evolutionary theory today is a negative one: the theory shows us what scientific explanations need not do. In particular it shows us that one cannot regard explanations as unsatisfactory when they do not contain laws, or when they are not such as to enable the event in question to have been predicted. This conclusion, which is contrary to the usual view of scientific explanation[1,2] has important consequences for research in those subjects in which serious errors are known to arise in the application of the available regularities to individual cases. These subjects include a great part of biology, psychology, anthropology, history, cosmogony, engineering, economics, and quantum physics. I shall refer to such studies as "irregular subjects"; and the thesis of this article is that scientific explanation is perfectly possible in the irregular subjects even when prediction is precluded. One consequence of this view is that the impossibility of a Newtonian revolution in the social sciences, a position which I would maintain on other grounds, is not fatal to their status as sciences.[3] Another consequence is the reassessment of Darwin's own place in the history of science relative to Newton's.

Darwin's Importance

We often confuse three criteria in estimating the importance of the great figures in the history of thought. The first is the indispensability of what they wrote or said, regardless of its effect, judged as a stage in the development of our present beliefs. From this point of view, to earn a place in history, a man need only be the first to discover the material or express the idea in question. The second criterion is their effect on other thinkers, and nonthinkers, which, unlike the first, requires publication and recognition (or misinterpretation). The third criterion is the extent of their personal indispensability. To judge this, we must make some estimate of the time that would have elapsed before the same contribution would have been made by others, had the individual under assessment never existed. If we introduce an index of "lucky fame" as the ratio of a man's importance on the second criterion to his importance on the third, it seems very likely that Darwin has the highest index of lucky fame in history. In fact, what is often regarded as his key contribution was formulated by Wallace before Darwin published it. Ad-

From *Science*, Vol. 130 (August 28, 1959), pp. 477–482.

[1] See, for example, R. B. Braithwaite, *Scientific Explanation* (Cambridge Univ. Press, New York, 1953); K. R. Popper, *The Logic of Scientific Discovery* (Hutchinson, London, 1959), p. 59.

[2] C. G. Hempel and P. Oppenheim, "The logic of explanation," in H. Feigl and M. Brodbeck, Eds. *Readings in the Philosophy of Science* (Appleton-Century-Crofts, New York, 1953), pp. 319–352.

[3] The grounds are roughly that we already know of crucial variables that are not within the observational range that defines the science. (See "A possible distinction between traditional scientific disciplines and the study of human behavior," in *Minnesota Studies in the Philosophy of Science*, vol. 1, *The Foundations of Science and the Concepts of Psychology and Psychoanalysis*, H. Feigl and M. Scriven, Eds. (Univ. of Minnesota Press, Minneapolis, 1956).

mittedly, almost the same calamity befell Newton, but only with respect to his gravitational work; his optics, dynamics, and mathematics are each enough to place him in the front rank. Moreover, Darwin's formulations were seriously faulty, and he appears to have believed in what many of his disciples regard as superstition, the inheritance of acquired characteristics and the benevolence of Natural Selection. Of course, Newton believed that some orbital irregularities he could not explain were due to the interference of angels, but he did achieve a large number of mathematically precise and scientifically illuminating deductions from his theory, which is more than can be said of Darwin. Somehow, we feel that Darwin didn't quite have the *class* that Newton had. But I want to suggest that Darwin was operating in a field of a wholly different kind and that he possessed to a very high degree exactly those merits which can benefit such a field. In place of the social scientists' favorite Myth of the Second Coming (of Newton), we should recognize the Reality of the Already-Arrived (Darwin); the paradigm of the explanatory but nonpredictive scientist.

Let us proceed by examining briefly the attempts by Darwin and others to encapsulate the principles of evolution in the form of *universal* laws and base *predictions* on them; and let us contrast their lack of success in these endeavors with the tremendous efficacy of the *explanations* they produced. During this comparison we shall try to extract the formal properties of the two key types of proposition that are associated with explanations in the irregular subjects: one type of proposition is a weaker relative of predictions, and the other type is a weaker relative of laws.

Hypothetical Probability "Predictions"

The suggestion that in evolution we see the "survival of the fittest" has some well-known difficulties. In the first place, the definition of "the fittest" is difficult even when made relative to a particular environment. It is fairly obvious that no characteristics can be identified as contributing to "fitness" in all environments. Thus, strength may increase the chance of fighting so much that it decreases the chance of survival, and intelligence may be antiadaptive in anti-intellectual societies. Furthermore, maximum specialization for a particular environment is in general incompatible, morphologically and genetically, with maximum flexibility to withstand sudden environmental changes.[4] We are inclined to say that the organisms adopting the former line of development tend to be "fitter" *until* the change occurs, and the latter fitter *when* it occurs. Whatever we say, it is quite clear that we cannot predict which organisms will survive except in so far as we can predict the environmental changes. But we are very poorly equipped to do this with much precision since variations in the sun's output and even interstellar influences have substantial effects, quite apart from the local irregularities of geology and climate. However, these difficulties of prediction do not mean that the idea of fitness as a factor in survival loses all its *explanatory* power. It is not only true but obvious that animals which happen to be able to swim are better fitted for surviving a sudden and unprecedented inundation of their arid habitat, and in some such cases it is just this factor which explains their survival. Naturally we could have said in advance that *if* a flood occurred, they would be *likely* to survive; let us call this a hypothetical probability prediction. But hypothetical predictions do not have any value for actual prediction except in so far as the conditions mentioned in the hypothesis are predictable or experimentally producible: hence there will be cases where we can *explain why* certain animals and plants survived even when we could not have *predicted that* they would. And it is a feature of the irregular subjects that, unlike classical atomic physics, the irregularity-producing factors lie outside their

[4] The best advanced discussion of "fitness" with which I am acquainted is J. M. Thoday, "Components of fitness," in "Evolution," *Symposia Soc. Exptl. Biol. No. 7 (1953)* (1954).

range of observation and are not predictable by reference to any factors within this range.[5]

It should be noted that these "predictions" are not easily falsified by observation, since they only assert the *likelihood* of a certain outcome. Their cash value is thus very much like that of a promissory note which says, "*If* I ever have enough money, I will *probably* pay you $100," whereas an ordinary prediction is like a check for the sum.

A second kind of difficulty with the "survival of the fittest" principle is that many organisms are killed by factors wholly unconnected with *any* characteristics they possess — for example, they happen to be sitting where a tree or a bomb falls. Of course, this is sometimes due to a habit or property they possess; but that is not always true, since even identical twins with identical habits do not always die together. This really shows that (i) even at the limits of stretching, "the fittest" refers to characteristics of an organism, and spatiotemporal location is *not* such a characteristic (in physics, the study of the "properties of matter" covers elasticity and molecular structure but not location), and (ii), location sometimes determines survival. So it is simply false to suppose that "fitness" *universally* determines survival. Of course, one could go a step further and define "the fittest" as "those which survive"; this is not stretching but breaking the concept, and this step would be fatal to all the scientific claims of the theory. We can get by with a tendency-statement instead of an exact law, because it justifies hypothetical and hence occasionally testable predictions and also explanations, but not with a tautology.

H. Graham Cannon is thus entirely mistaken when he says: "So Darwin pointed out that in the struggle for existence it will be those most fitted to survive who do in fact survive. . . . What are the fittest? Simply those that survive".[6] Darwin's discovery was that in the world the way it is (and has been), the fitness of the organism, in a perfectly recognizable but complex sense of "fitness" was very often the *explanation* of its survival. In a world where accidents were extremely frequent and mobility was very low, Darwin could never have supported this claim: there would not be enough correlation between the possession of observably useful characteristics and survival to make it plausible. It was partly because the opposing theory of the time was supernatural that insufficient attention was paid to the difference between Darwin's account and other possible naturalistic accounts of the history of life. If good luck in the avoidance of accidents, rather than fitness, was the dominant theme of that history, Darwinism would have been unimportant. And in it there was still the unexplained existence of variations. But Darwinism, like cosmological theories of continual creation, had the added advantage that it spread the inexplicable element *thin*, thus making it scientifically more palatable than a large lump at the beginning, whether the lump be matter or numbers of species. Darwin's success lay in his empirical, case by case by case, demonstration that recognizable fitness *was* very often associated with survival, and that the small random variations *could* lead to the development of species. He did not discover *an exact universal law* but the utility of *a particular indicator* in looking for explanations.

Survival of a Species

In this Darwin was greatly assisted by a feature of the data which constitutes a third difficulty in the attempt to sum up his account under the formula "survival of the fittest," no matter how *fittest* is defined. This is, of course, the fact that our concern is with survival for thousands of generations, not

[5] In quantum physics we envisage the further possibility that there are no such factors, only the irregularity in the individual events, but we have the partial compensation of some statistical regularities. These are in some respects more informative than the nonquantitative probability and tendency statements of psychotherapy, personality theory, psephology, and so on.

[6] H. G. Cannon, *The Evolution of Living Things* (Manchester Univ. Press, Manchester, England, 1958).

with survival to adulthood for one; and certain factors enter into, or are absent from, an explanation of the form of the *ultimate descendants* of a certain population, by comparison with an explanation of the form of *the adults* in the original population. In particular, we must add the variations in reproductive efficiency (including mating efficiency, where sexual reproduction is involved) and in parental rearing efficiency, as well as genetic variability, and subtract some considerations that affect postclimacteric survival.[7] However, this transition to what Simpson calls the "differential reproduction of the best-adapted" does not eliminate the effect of the first and second points above; they apply with undiminished force. The theory in this form can deal with a different and more appropriate task; but it is still not capable of generating more than hypothetical probability predictions since both extensive and local catastrophes will play a large part in determining the survivors, regardless of their characteristics. And in the same way as with the simpler version of the principle, though more efficiently, we shall in retrospect still be able to *explain* many features of the record by reference to the characteristics of the surviving animals and the nature of the environmental changes. But we shall not be able to do this always; for there will still be the cases where a whole population, or that subset of it carrying certain characteristics, will be annihilated in a way that requires and justifies no reference to its adaptiveness, yet makes a substantial difference in the record of life on earth.

At this point one may wish to say that these explanations, too, are part of evolutionary biology. They are certainly part of the history of life on earth, and they are certainly naturalistic explanations. The problem is like that resolved by the great philosopher of history, Collingwood, when he laid it down that the history of man is the history of ideas; we feel that floods and earthquakes have some importance for history, but one can of course discuss their *effects* on man within Collingwood's definition. In our case, we can include such explanations as part of evolutionary biology if we wish, and admit that Darwin's theory and Mendel's additions are not involved or relevant. Or we may omit it and concede that evolutionary theory cannot alone explain the morphology and paleontology that is its field. Which decision we make is not important; but a recognition of the point, however described, is. For we cannot assess Darwin's contribution except by comparing the extent of the domain of his explanations with the domain in which we can and need appeal only to explanations of a kind that Linnaeus (or anyone else who thought the species separately created and by their nature unchanging) would have found perfectly acceptable.[8]

Considerations Novel to Darwin

When, today, we reach the point where we are discussing a *sequence* of generations in terms of natural selection, we find ourselves faced with a fourth difficulty in any attempt to state exact laws of evolution. It is the first of those we have discussed which involves a consideration wholly novel to Darwin — the idea of random mutations.[9] Essentially,

[7] But senile adults may have properties of evolutionary interest — for example, in a gregarious society, especially a gerontocracy. It might seem that we can then include them as environmental conditions for the prospective parents, but this is inadequate (an example is the well-known case of the worker bees). A case where senile maladaptiveness is irrelevant is that of the coiled oyster.

[8] The problem of accounting for, for example, the departure of the dinosaurs did not in fact arise until 34 years after Linnaeus' death, with Cuvier's work; but it is too commonly assumed that nonevolutionists would have *had* to assert, as they usually did with the few fossils of extinct forms recognized in the 18th century, that the animals still existed in some as-yet-unexplored part of the globe. They could also have said that a catastrophe that indiscriminately annihilated the life forms in some area was responsible — that is, one of the catastrophes discussed in the second point above. This involves no commitment to evolution.

[9] Darwin believed in unpredictable variation, of course, but the several genetic origins of this were not understood by him, nor for that matter were they clear to Mendel.

this is a feature of the theory with a logical character which is the opposite of the catastrophes because the mutations, more or less unpredictably, *add* a new element while the natural accidents unpredictably *subtract* an old one. Again, we can sometimes be sure that the new element is a mutation after it appears — for example, nonalbinism in an albino population. That is, we can explain (in a weak sense here, though with some mutations we can go into details) the phenotypic appearance of an organism by identifying it as a mutation, although we could not have predicted it. Or to be more precise, we might have predicted it, because it does sometimes happen and we might have just had a hunch it was about to crop up. But we cannot give any *rational grounds* for supposing it to be more than a remote possibility that a particular litter from an albino strain will contain a nonalbino, whereas we can be perfectly confident that, when it occurs, it is a mutant, and we can sometimes be confident of the focus of the mutated gene on the chromosome and even of the cause and *modus operandi* of the mutation.

As a fifth and final point, one which does directly contradict one of Darwin's conclusions in the first edition of *The Origin of Species*, we must mention another side of the second point, about "accidental deaths." Just as some organisms and species are exterminated regardless of their characteristics, so some survive despite the handicap of maladaptive (that is, the handicap of antiadaptive and of nonadaptive) characteristics. The "pressure of the environment" is a statistical pressure, and Fisher's proofs of the efficiency of this pressure even on small differences in adaptiveness, being statistical proofs, implicitly allow the possibility that sometimes the unlikely will occur. It is evident from the fossil record that it must have occurred many times, and dynasties have stood when an all-or-none law of selection would have felled them — have stood and have founded a genealogy that would not otherwise have existed. The notion of "random preadaptation," an important explanatory device in neo-Darwinism, relies on just this point. What is true of organisms is true of characteristics, and we have to abandon Darwin's original belief that "every detail of structure in every living creature" has either current or ancestral utility. Not only the mainly nonadaptive form of some antelope horns but some antiadaptive characteristics — either linked genetically with more useful properties, or providing a component for a highly adaptive heterozygote, or by chance alone — will survive for a greater or lesser time, with small and large effects on the course of organic development. The best we can do in the face of such difficulties is to talk of "differential reproduction of the fittest *and the fortunate*." Yet, here again, as in the case of mutations, we have explanations at hand which have no counterpart in the realm of predictions. We can explain the unlikely outcomes of partially random processes, though we cannot predict them. We are not hard put to explain that a man's death was due to his being struck by an automobile, even when we could not have predicted the event. Now this kind of case does admit of hypothetical probability prediction, but as we shall see, there are cases where not even this sickly relative of ordinary predictions is possible.

The Logic of Predictions and Explanations

It is natural enough that the logic of explanation should appear to parallel that of prediction. Sometimes, in fact, it does. There are specific occasions, particularly in classical physics, when we explain and predict by reference to the same laws. But this is an accident, not a necessity, as it turns out. Put the matter in general logical terms and the similarity still appears to hold: to predict, we need a correlation between present events and future ones — to explain, between present ones and past ones. And who would wish to insist that a difference of tense has any logical significance? As Hempel and Oppenheim say (2, pp. 322, 323), "The difference between the two is of a pragmatic character . . . whatever will be said . . . concerning the logical characteristics of explanation or prediction will be applicable to either. . . ." They suggest, plausibly enough, that if we cannot derive the event to be explained from known general laws which connect it with antecedent conditions, we are likely to be deceiving ourselves if, in retrospect, we regard it as explained by reference to those antecedent conditions. And if we can so derive it, then we are in a position to predict it.

Naturally, previous writers on this subject have not overlooked such examples as unpredictable catastrophes being used as the explanation of their consequences. But they have taken the existence of hypothetical probability predictions, which are of course possible in such cases,[10] to show that the event explained could *in principle* have been predicted. That is, a prediction of the event being explained was possible if we had known, or after we did know, the *catastrophe* was going to occur, but *before* the event. This is a somewhat unhelpful sense of "in principle," since until that day when *everything* is predictable, there remains the fact that we can often explain what we could not predict, and surely this feature should be mirrored in any analysis of these notions. Furthermore, there are good grounds for saying we *cannot even in principle* predict everything (uncertainty principle, classical unpredictability of a computer's state); hence, good grounds for saying that even in principle explanation and prediction do *not* have the same form. Finally, it is not in general possible to list all the exceptions to a claim about, for example, the fatal effects of a lava flow, so we have to leave it in probability form; this has the result of eliminating the very degree of certainty from the prediction that the explanation has, when we find the fossils in the lava. But we can go further; we can show, quite independently, a gross logical difference between the two. (There is a large area of noncausal explanation in the sciences in which the two are completely unrelated, but I confine my remarks to causal explanation.)

For when we get down to some exact cases, we do discover something asymmetrical about the two situations, prediction and explanation. What we are trying to provide when making a prediction is simply a claim that, *at a certain time*, an *event* or state of affairs will occur. In explanation we are looking for a *cause*, an event that not only occurred earlier but stands *in a special relation* to the other event. Roughly speaking, the prediction requires only a correlation, the explanation more. This difference has as one consequence the possibility of making predictions from indicators other than causes — for example, predicting a storm from a sudden drop in the barometric pressure. Clearly we could not say that the drop in pressure in our house caused the storm: it merely presaged it. So we can sometimes predict what we cannot explain. But can we ever explain what we could not have predicted, *even if we had had* the information about the antecedent conditions? That is, can we explain when even hypothetical probability prediction is impossible? This seems less likely, roughly because finding causes is harder than finding correlations. Yet it is possible, and, in some areas of knowledge, common. For sometimes the kind of correlation we need for prediction is absent, but a causal relationship can be identified. Although the point is the same, it may be helpful to take an example from a different field.

Retrospective Causal Analyses

If we discover that certain industrial chemicals, frequent abrasion, and a high level of radiation exposure sometimes cause skin cancer, we are in no way committed to the view that cancer *frequently follows* exposure to these irritants. Among the voca-

[10] For example, "If there is a volcanic eruption which produces a vast lava stream, then organisms in its path will probably be destroyed."

tions which involve such exposure, cancer may be very rare (although *substantially more frequent* than in other vocations). It is presumed that some unknown conditions such as hereditary predisposition, low perspiration production, or accidental environment factors are responsible for the difference between those who develop cancer and those who do not. Nevertheless, when a middle-aged fisherman comes in to a clinic, his face and hands black from years of ultraviolet exposure, and a growth on the back of one hand is diagnosed as a small carcinoma, the physician who can discover no evidence for the relevance of other known causal factors is in a very good position to assert that the cause *was* excessive exposure to the sun.

The form of this argument, which is so often used by the evolutionary biologist, the engineer, and the historian among others in the non-Newtonian fields, is quite complicated and is best approached by taking a very simple example first. (This corresponds to the example of the barometer which enables one to predict but not explain a storm.) Here, we can explain but not predict, whenever we have a proposition of the form "The only cause of X is A" (I) — for example, "The only cause of paresis is syphilis." Notice that this is perfectly compatible with the statement that A is often not followed by X — in fact, very few syphilitics develop paresis.[11] Hence, when A is observed, we can predict that X is *more* likely to occur than without A, but still extremely unlikely. So we must, on the evidence, still predict that it will *not* occur. But if it does, we can appeal to (I) to provide and guarantee our explanation. Naturally there are further questions we would like answered if we are research scientists, such as what the particular conditions are that, in this case, combined with A to bring about X. But the giving of causes, and of scientific explanations and descriptions in general, is not the giving of "complete" accounts; it is the giving of useful and enlightening partial accounts. In fact, even the "complete" account merely includes some extra relevant factors — it simply generates even more puzzling questions as to why the *whole* set of factors is sufficient. The search for a *really* complete account is never-ending, but the search for causes is often *entirely* successful, and someone who saw a man killed by an automobile but refused to accept the coroner's statement that this was the cause of death on the grounds that some people survive being hit by a car, does not understand the term *cause*. The coroner is perfectly correct, even though other factors are involved.

Turning to the more general form of the argument, where several causes of X are known, we see that it has the following form:

1) Conditions or events A, A', A'', . . . sometimes cause X (for example, prolonged sunburn or skin abrasion or some other factor sometimes causes skin cancer).

2) There are some unknown causes of X, but the majority of those cases of X which are preceded by A or A' or . . . are caused by that A.

3) The incidence of X in the population of A's is very small (for example, only a few people in groups receiving the same amount of sun develop skin cancer).

4) A particular individual i is known to have met the condition A, but not the conditions A', A'' . . . (for example, i has had as much sun as is needed to produce cancer in some people).

From these premises, the only prediction we can make about i is that he will not develop X. Suppose now that:

5) i develops X.

We may now deduce that the cause of this was probably (and sometimes certainly) A. Hence an event which cannot be predicted

[11] People have sometimes argued that if A *really* is the cause of X, it must *always* be followed by X. This is to confuse causes with sufficient conditions, and practically to abolish them from the applied sciences, since there are almost no absolutely reliable statements of sufficient conditions available there. Causes are not necessary conditions either; their logical nature is complex, though there is relatively little difficulty in using the term "cause" correctly — a situation which characterizes other fundamental terms in science, such as "probability," "truth," "explanation," "observation," "science," and "simplicity."

from a certain set of well-confirmed propositions can, if it occurs, be explained by appeal to them, and there is no "in principle" possibility of predicting 5 from 1 to 4. It is of course true, and trivial, that other data might enable one to predict 5. But I have only wished to argue that the kind of knowledge we do have about evolution enables us to provide well-justified and informative explanations, without predictions.

To go one step further, it is probably not possible to list all the known causes for an evolutionary event such as the extinction of a species; but we do not need to, as long as we can *recognize* them with some reliability. When they are present, we can still identify the causes of events *after* they happen, without committing the fallacy of *post hoc ergo propter hoc*, which the requirement of predictability-in-principle was designed to avoid.

Careless use of such arguments does produce *ad hoc* explanations; but it is an error to conclude that in general such arguments are vacuous, as do those who think the theory of evolution wholly empty, and thus capable of "explaining" anything. Cannon says, "forty years ago, it appeared to me that orthodox Mendelism . . . was capable of explaining *any* genetical result" (*6*, p. 83); and he regards neo-Mendelism as even more "omnipotent." But he mistakes the explanatory fertility of a theory for explanatory omnipotence — — that is, vacuity. If we find a markedly nonbinomial distribution of characteristics in each generation of descendants from a genotypically well-identified pair, we cannot explain this by merely mentioning some *possible* cause. We have to show, as in the cancer case, that (i) this cause was in fact present, (ii) *independent* evidence supports the claim that it can produce this effect, and (iii) no other such causes were present. That this can be done is the mark, and a well-earned mark, of success: in this case, of Mendelism, and in more general cases, of evolutionary theory.

Notice that we do not have to be able to give a law of the usual form of classical physics, a universal functional relationship, let alone a mathematical one. Indeed I prefer to avoid using the term "law" of propositions like 1; they are, logically speaking, particular and not universal hypotheses. However, they can usually be established only by study of a range of cases and hence in some sense might be said to "reflect" a regularity or set of regularities. The logical key to the whole affair is that one can identify a cause without knowing what the conditions are which are necessary for its causal efficacy. When someone says that the explanation of the Irish elk's extinction was the swamping of its habitat, he means that *in the circumstances* this event was sufficient to ensure its extinction, and had this event not occurred, it would have survived. But he would immediately agree that (i) he could not exhaustively specify the circumstances which are essential, although we have in mind the terrain and climate and the animal's weight, hoof size, predators, reproductive habits, and so on; and (ii) there are other possible causes (for example, an invasion of Arctic wolves) which, had *they* been present, would have led to the same effect in circumstances which were in every respect the same except for their presence and the absence of flooding. A more complex but basically similar analysis is required for other cases — for example, the explanation of man's uniqueness, among the bipedal mammals, in running rather than leaping like the kangaroo, in terms of his arboreal ancestors.[12] These cases illustrate the weakness of talking about "applying a universal law" in order to explain; if you have one, it may be helpful, but if you do not, you may still know a good deal about the possible and actual causes of the events you are studying. Without the universal law, it is not possible to make predictions. The elks might have survived that degree of flooding for all we could produce in the way of laws to the contrary; but if they did not, and nothing else changed, we can reasonably conclude that the explanation is the flooding.

It is not surprising, therefore, that when

[12] J. Maynard Smith, *The Theory of Evolution* (Penguin, Baltimore, Md., 1958), p. 245.

we turn to the attempts of Darwin and the Mendelians to formulate some laws of the traditional kind, or to make predictions, we find the results to be very unsatisfactory. As Waddington says, even the modern attempt to develop a mathematical approach to evolution has not "led to any noteworthy quantitative statements about evolution. . . . The formulae involve parameters . . . most of which are still too inaccurately known to enable quantitative predictions to be made or verified".[13] And if this is the case for the mathematical theory, the case is much worse for exact statements which do not involve the flexibility of mathematical relationships. What can be said is well expressed by Darwin in his autobiography, where he says that *when* there is a struggle for existence, "favorable variations would *tend* to be preserved, and unfavorable ones to be destroyed." Tendency statements like this are explanation-indicators; they justify no more than very weak hypothetical predictions with unspecified conditions ("*if* everything else was the same, then . . ."), for they tell us nothing about the likelihood of conditions of struggle or the strength of the tendency. Perhaps the best way to express their empirical content is to say that they suggest that certain future states of affairs are very *unlikely* — namely, equilibrium of a mixed population *when* there is competition for survival. Indeed Darwin too readily concludes from Malthus' argument that "a struggle for existence inevitably follows," or again, "there must in every case be a struggle for existence, either one individual with another of the same species, or with the individuals of distinct species, or with the physical conditions of life".[14] The legitimate conclusion must contain the qualifying terms "eventually" and "*ceteris paribus*," and a less definite basis for purposes of prediction would be hard to find.

[13] C. D. Waddington, "Epigenetics and evolution," in "Evolution," *Symposia Soc. Exptl. Biol. No. 7 (1953)* (1954).

[14] C. R. Darwin, *The Origin of Species*; these and the preceding passages are quoted by Flew in his illuminating essay "The Structure of Darwinism," in *New Biology* (Penguin, Baltimore, Md., 1959).

But when we have only such statements, we have a great deal, though we lack much. Often it will be beyond the capacity of a particular subject, such as evolutionary biology or molar psychology, to provide more than this, especially when dealing with past events. Darwin's greatness lay in the use to which he put such statements in explanation, and as he says in the last chapter of *The Origin of Species*, "It can hardly be supposed that a false theory would explain, in so satisfactory a manner as does the theory of natural selection, the several large classes of facts above specified." His work indeed showed that the theory was not *false*. I hope that this study may make clearer why it is not *trivial*, although its principles cannot be precisely formulated, and although it is not committed to any predictions about the future course of evolution, despite Darwin's hopeful voice on the last page of his great work: "We may feel certain that the ordinary succession by generation has never once been broken, and that no cataclysm has desolated the whole world. Hence we may look with some confidence to a serene future of great length." I wish that the great strength of his theory did indeed justify such a prediction. But I fear it is only committed to the view that *if* the struggle for existence continues, the forms of life will *probably* change. Its great commitment and its profound illumination are to be found in its application to the lengthening past, not the distant future: in the tasks of explanation, not in those of prediction.

Further Reading

[1] The outstanding work on the logical problems of biology, and, in my view, an extremely important book, is Morton Beckner's *The Biological Way of Thought* (Columbia Univ. Press, New York, 1959).

Explanation and Prediction Are Symmetrical 11

from *Temporally-Asymmetric Principles, Parity Between Explanation and Prediction, and Mechanism and Teleology*

ADOLF GRÜNBAUM

. . . It remains to deal in some detail with Scriven's extensive critique of Hempel's thesis. Scriven argues that (i) evolutionary explanations and explanations like that of the past occurrence of paresis due to syphilis fail to meet the symmetry requirement by not allowing corresponding predictions, (ii) predictions based on mere *indicators* (rather than causes) such as the prediction of a storm from a sudden barometric drop are not matched by corresponding explanations, since *indicators* are not explanatory though they may serve to predict or, in other cases, to retrodict. And these indicator-based predictions show that the mere inferability of an *explanandum* does *not* guarantee scientific understanding of it, so that symmetry of inferability does not assure symmetry of scientific understanding between explanation and prediction.

I shall now examine several of the paradigm cases adduced by Scriven in support of these contentions.

Evolution Theory

He cites evolutionary theory with the aim of showing that "Satisfactory explanation of the past is possible even when prediction of the future is impossible."[1]

Evolutionary theory does indeed afford valid examples of the epistemological asymmetry of assertibility. And this for the following two reasons growing out of our § 2: (1) the ubiquitous role of interactions in evolution brings the recordability asymmetry into play. And that asymmetry enters not only into the assertibility of the *explanandum*. For in cases of an H-prediction based on an *explanans* containing an *antecedent* referring to a *future* interaction, there is also an asymmetry of assertibility between H-prediction and H-explanation in regard to the *explanans*, and (2) the existence of biological properties which are *emergent* in the sense that even if all the laws were strictly *deterministic*, the occurrence of these properties could *not* have been *predicted* on the basis of any and all laws which could possibly have been discovered by humans in advance of the first known occurrence of the respective properties in question. Thus, evolutionary theory makes us familiar with past biological changes which were induced by prior *past* interactions, the latter being post-assertible on the basis of present records. And these past interactions can serve to explain the evolutionary changes in question. But the logical relation between *explanans* and *explanandum* furnishing this explanation is completely *time-symmetric*. Hence this situation makes for asymmetry only in the following innocuous sense: since corresponding future interactions cannot be rationally preasserted — there being no advance records of them — there is no corresponding preassertibility of those future evolutionary changes that will be effected by future interactions.

From *Philosophy of Science*, 29:2 (April, 1962), pp. 162–170.

[1] M. Scriven, "Explanation and Prediction in Evolutionary Theory," see page 117 in this volume.

In an endeavor to establish the existence of an asymmetry damaging to Hempel's thesis on the basis of the account of a case of non-survival given in evolutionary theory, Scriven writes:

there are . . . good grounds [of inherent unpredictability] for saying that even in principle explanation and prediction do *not* have the same form. Finally, it is not in general possible to list all the exceptions to a claim about, for example, the fatal effects of a lava flow, so we have to leave it in probability form; this has the result of eliminating the very degree of certainty from the prediction that the explanation has, when we find the fossils in the lava.[2]

But all that the lava case entitles Scriven to conclude is that the merely *probabilistic* connection between the occurrence of a lava flow and the extinction of certain organisms has the result of depriving pre-*assertibility* of the very degree of certainty possessed by post-assertions here. Scriven is not at all justified in supposing that *predictive inferability* in this case lacks even an iota of the certainty that can be ascribed to the corresponding post-explanatory inferability. For wherein does the greater degree of certainty of the post-explanation reside? I answer: only in the assertibility of the *explanandum*, *not* in the character of the logical relation between the *explanans* (the lava flow) and the *explanandum* (fatalities on the part of certain organisms). What then must be the verdict on Scriven's contention of an asymmetry in the *certainty* of prediction and post-explanation in this context? We see now that this contention is vitiated by a confusion between the following two radically *distinct* kinds of asymmetry: (i) a difference in the degree of certainty (categoricity) of our knowledge of the truth of the *explanandum* and of the claim of environmental unfitness made by the *explanans*, and (ii) a difference in the "degree of entailment," as it were, linking the *explanandum* to the *explanans*.

Very similar difficulties beset Scriven's analysis of a case of biological survival which is accounted for on the basis of environmental fitness. He says:

It is fairly obvious that no characteristics can be identified as contributing to "fitness" in all environments. . . . we cannot predict which organisms will survive except in so far as we can predict the environmental changes. But we are very poorly equipped to do this with much precision.[3] . . . However, these difficulties of prediction do not mean that the idea of fitness as a factor in survival loses all of its *explanatory* power. . . . animals which happen to be able to swim are better fitted for surviving a sudden and unprecedented inundation of their arid habitat, and in some such cases it is just this factor which explains their survival. Naturally we could have said in advance that *if* a flood occurred, they would be likely to survive; let us call this a hypothetical probability prediction. But hypothetical predictions do not have any value for actual predictions except in so far as the conditions mentioned in the hypothesis are predictable . . .: hence there will be cases where we can *explain why* certain animals and plants survived even when we could not have *predicted that* they would.[4]

There would, of course, be complete agreement with Scriven, if he had been content to point out in this context, as he does, that there are cases in which we can "*explain why*" but not "*predict that*." But he combines this correct formulation with the incorrect supposition that cases of post-explaining survival on the basis of fitness constitute grounds for an indictment of Hempel's thesis of symmetry. Let me therefore state the points of agreement and disagreement in regard to this case as follows. Once we recognize the ubiquitous

[2] *Ibid.*, p. 122.

[3] The environmental changes which Scriven goes on to cite are all of the nature of *interactions* of a potentially open system. And it is this common property of theirs which makes for their role in precluding the predictability of survival.

[4] *Ibid.*, p. 118.

In a recent paper "Cause and Effect in Biology," [*Science* 134 (1961), p. 1504], the zoologist E. Mayr overlooks the fallacy in Scriven's statement which we are about to point out and credits Scriven with having "emphasized quite correctly that one of the most important contributions to philosophy made by the evolutionary theory is that it has demonstrated the independence of explanation from prediction." And Mayr rests this conclusion among other things on the contention that "The theory of natural selection can describe and explain phenomena with considerable precision, but it cannot make reliable predictions."

role of *interactions* we can formulate the valid upshot of Scriven's observations by saying: insofar as future fitness and survival depend on future interactions which cannot be predicted from given information, whereas past fitness and survival depended on past interactions which *can be* retrodicted from that same information, there is an epistemological asymmetry between H-explanation and H-prediction in regard to the following: the assertibility both of the antecedent fitness affirmed in the *explanans* and of the *explanandum* claiming survival.

This having been granted as both true and illuminating, we must go on to say at once that the following considerations — which Scriven can grant only on pain of inconsistency with his account of asymmetry in the lava case — are no less true: the scientific inferability from a cause and hence our understanding of the *why* of survival furnished by an *explanans* which *does* contain the antecedent condition that the given animals are able to swim during a sudden, unprecedented inundation of their arid habitat is *not* one iota more probabilistic (i.e., less conclusive) in the case of a *future* inundation and survival than in the case of a *past* one. For if the logical nerve of intelligibility linking the *explanans* (fitness under specified kinds of inundational conditions) with the *explanandum* (survival) is only probabilistic in the *future* case, how could it possibly be any less probabilistic in the past case? It is evident that post-explanatory inductive inferability is entirely on a par here with predictive inferability from fitness as a cause. Why then does Scriven feel entitled to speak of "probability prediction" of *future* survival *without also* speaking of "probability explanation" of past survival? It would seem that his reason is none other than the pseudo-contrast between the *lack* of pre-assertibility of the *explanandum* (which is conveyed by the term "probability" in "probability prediction") with the obtaining of post-explanatory inductive inferability of the *explanandum*. And this pseudo-contrast derives its plausibility from the tacit appeal to the *bona fide* asymmetry between the pre-assertibility and post-assertibility of the *explanandum*, an asymmetry which cannot score against Hempel's thesis.

The Paresis Case

In a further endeavor to justify his repudiation of Hempel's thesis, Scriven says:

> we can explain but not predict whenever we have a proposition of the form "The only cause of X is A" (I) — for example, "The only cause of paresis is syphilis." Notice that this is perfectly compatible with the statement that A is often not followed by X — in fact, very few syphilitics develop paresis (II). Hence, when A is observed, we can predict that X is *more* likely to occur than without A, but still extremely unlikely. So, we must, on the evidence, still predict that it will *not* occur. But if it does, we can appeal to (I) to provide and guarantee our explanation. . . . Hence an event which cannot be predicted from a certain set of well-confirmed propositions can, if it occurs, be explained by appeal to them.[5]

In short, Scriven's argument is that although a past case of paresis can be explained by noting that syphilis was its cause, one cannot predict the future occurrence of paresis from syphilis as the cause. And he adds to this the following oral comment:

> Suppose for the moment we include the justification of an explanation or a prediction in the explanation or prediction, as Hempel does. From a general law and antecedent conditions we are then entitled to deduce that a certain event will occur in the future. This is the deduction of a prediction. From one of the propositions of the form the only possible cause of y is x and a statement that y has occurred we are able to deduce, not only that x must have occurred, but also the proposition the cause of y in this instance was x. I take this to be a perfectly sound example of deducing and explanation. Notice however, that what we have deduced is not at all a description of the event to be explained, that is we have not got an *explanandum* of the kind that Hempel and Oppenheim envisage. On the contrary, we have a specific causal claim. This is a neat way of

[5] *Ibid.*, p. 122.

making clear one of the differences between an explanation and a prediction; by showing the different kinds of proposition that they often are. When explaining Y, we do not have to be able to deduce that Y occurs, for we typically know this already. What we have to be able to deduce (if deduction is in any way appropriate) is that Y occurred *as a result of* a certain X, and of course this needs a very different kind of general law from the sort of general law that is required for prediction.

I shall now show that Scriven's treatment of such cases as post-explaining paresis on the basis of syphilis suffers from the same defect as his analysis of the evolutionary cases: *Insofar as there is an asymmetry, Scriven has failed to discern its precise locus, and having thus failed, he is led to suppose erroneously that Hempel's thesis is invalidated by such asymmetry as does obtain.*

Given a particular case of paresis as well as the proposition that the only cause of paresis is syphilis — where a "cause" is understood here with Scriven as a "contingently necessary condition" — what can be inferred? Scriven maintains correctly that what follows is that both the paretic concerned had syphilis and that in his particular case, syphilis was the cause in the specified sense of "cause". And then Scriven goes on to maintain that his case against Hempel is established by the fact that we are able to assert that syphilis *did cause* paresis while *not* also being entitled to say that syphilis *will cause* paresis. But Scriven seems to have completely overlooked that our not being able to make both of these assertions does *not* at all suffice to discredit Hempel's thesis, which concerns the time-symmetry of the *inferability* of the *explanandum* from the *explanans.* The inadequacy of Scriven's argument becomes evident the moment one becomes aware of the *reason* for not being entitled to say that syphilis "will cause" paresis though being warranted in saying that it "did cause" paresis.

The sentences containing "did cause" and "will cause" respectively *each* make *two* affirmations as follows: (i) the assertion of the *explanandum* (paresis) *per se*, and (ii) the affirmation of the obtaining of a causal *relation* (in the sense of being a contingently necessary condition) between the *explanans* (syphilis) and the *explanandum* (paresis). Thus, for our purposes, the statement "Syphilis *will cause* person Z to have paresis" should be made in the form "Person Z will have paresis *and* it will have been caused by syphilis", and the statement "Syphilis *did cause* person K to have paresis" becomes "Person K has (or had) paresis *and* it was caused by syphilis". And the decisive point is that in so far as a *past* occurrence of paresis can be inductively *inferred from* prior syphilis, so also a future occurrence of paresis can be. For the causal relation or connection between syphilis and paresis is incontestably time-symmetric: precisely in the way and to the extent that syphilis *was* a necessary condition for paresis, it also *will* be! Hence the only *bona fide* asymmetry here is the record-based but innocuous one in the *assertibility* of the *explanandum per se*, but there is no asymmetry of *inferability* of paresis from syphilis. The former innocuous asymmetry is the one that interdicts our making the predictive assertion "will cause" while allowing us to make the corresponding post-explanatory assertion "did cause". And it is this fact which destroys the basis of Scriven's indictment of Hempel's thesis. For Hempel and Oppenheim did *not* maintain that an *explanandum* which can be post-asserted can *always* also be pre-asserted; what they did maintain was only that the *explanans* never post-explains any better or more conclusively than it implies predictively, there being complete symmetry between post-explanatory *inferability* and predictive *inferability* from a given *explanans.* They and Popper were therefore fully justified in testing the adequacy of a proffered *explanans* in the social sciences on the basis of whether the post-explanatory inferability of the *explanandum* which was claimed for it was matched by a corresponding predictive inferability, either inductive or deductive as the case may be.

What is the force of the following comment by Scriven: in the post-explanation of paresis we do not need to infer the *explanandum* from the *explanans* à la Hempel and Oppenheim, because we know this already from prior records (observations) of one kind or another; what we do need to infer instead is that the *explanandum*-event occurred *as a result of* the cause (necessary condition) given by the *explanans*, an inference which does *not* allow us to *predict* (i.e. pre-assert) the *explanandum*-event? This comment of Scriven's proves only that here there is record-based post-assertibility of paresis but no corresponding pre-assertibility.

In short, Scriven's invocation of the paresis case, just like his citation of the cases from evolutionary theory, founders on the fact that he has confused an *epistemological* asymmetry with a *logical* one. To this charge, Scriven has replied irrelevantly that he has been at great pains in his writings — as for example in his discussion of the barometer case which I shall discuss below — to distinguish valid arguments based on true premisses which do qualify as scientific explanations from those which do not so qualify. This reply is irrelevant, since Scriven's *caveat* against identifying (confusing) arguments based on true premisses which are both valid *and* explanatory with those which are valid without being explanatory does not at all show that he made the following crucial distinction here at issue: the distinction between (1) a difference (asymmetry) in the assertibility of either a conclusion (*explanandum*) or a premise (*explanans*), and (2) a difference (asymmetry) in the inferability of the *explanandum* from its *explanans*. Although the distinction which Scriven does make cannot serve to mitigate the confusion with which I have charged him, his distinction merits examination in its own right.

To deal with it, I shall first consider examples given by him which involve *non*-predictive valid deductive arguments to which he denies the status of being explanatory arguments. And I shall then conclude my refutation of Scriven's critique of Hempel's thesis by discussing the following paradigm case of his: the deductively valid *predictive* inference of a storm from a sudden barometric drop, which he adduces in an endeavor to show that such a valid deductive inference could not possibly qualify as a post-*explanation* of a storm.

It would be agreed on all sides, I take it, that no *scientific understanding* is afforded by the deduction of an *explanandum* from itself even though such a deduction is a species of valid inference. Hence it can surely be granted that the class of valid deductive arguments whose conclusion is an *explanandum* referring to some event or other is wider than the class of valid deductive arguments affording scientific understanding of the *explanandum*-event. But it is a quite different matter to claim, as Scriven does, that no *scientific understanding* is provided by those valid deductive arguments which ordinary usage would not allow us to call "explanations". For example, Scriven cites the following case suggested by S. Bromberger and discussed by Hempel[6]: the height of a flagpole is deducible from the length of its shadow and a measurement of the angle of the sun taken in conjunction with the principles of geometrical optics, but the height of the flagpole could not thereby be said to have been "explained". Or take the case of a rectilinear triangle in physical space for which Euclidean geometry is presumed to hold, and let it be given that two of the angles are 37° and 59° respectively. Then it can be deductively inferred that the third angle is one of 84°, but according to Scriven, this would not constitute an explanation of the magnitude of the third angle.

Exactly what is shown by the flagpole and angle cases concerning the relation between valid deductive arguments which furnish scientific understanding and those which, according to ordinary usage, would qualify as "explanations"? I maintain that while differing in one respect from what are usually called "explanations", the aforementioned valid deductive arguments yielding the height of the flagpole and the magnitude of the third

[6] Cf. C. G. Hempel, "Deductive-Nomological vs. Statistical Explanation," *Minnesota Studies in the Philosophy of Science*, Vol. III, section IV.

angle provide scientific understanding no less than explanations do. And my reasons for this contention are the following.

In the flagpole case, for example, the *explanandum* (stating the height of the flagpole) can be deduced from two different kinds of premisses: (i) an *explanans* of the type familiar from geometrical optics and involving laws of coexistence rather than laws of succession, antecedent events playing no role in the *explanans*, and (ii) an *explanans* involving causally antecedent events and laws of succession and referring to the temporal genesis of the flagpole as an artifact. But is this difference between the kinds of premisses from which the *explanandum* is deducible a basis for claiming that the coexistence-law type of *explanans* provides less *scientific understanding* than does the law-of-succession type of *explanans*? I reply: certainly not. And I hasten to point out that the difference between *pre*-axiomatized and axiomatized geometry conveys the measure of the scientific understanding provided by the *geometrical* account given in the flagpole and angle cases on the basis of laws of coexistence. But is it not true after all that ordinary usage countenances the use of the term "explanation" only in cases employing causal antecedents and laws of succession in the *explanans*? To this I say: this *terminological* fact is as unavailing here as it is philosophically unedifying.

Finally, we turn to Scriven's citation of cases of deductively valid predictive inferences which, in his view, invalidate Hempel's thesis because they could not possibly also qualify as post-explanations.

The Barometer Case

Scriven writes:

> What we are trying to provide when making a prediction is simply a claim that, at a certain time, an event or state of affairs will occur. In explanation we are looking for a cause, an event that not only occurred earlier but stands in a special relation to the other event. Roughly speaking, the prediction requires only a correlation, the explanation more. This difference has as one consequence the possibility of making predictions from indicators other than causes — for example, predicting a storm from a sudden drop in the barometric pressure. Clearly we could not say that the drop in pressure in our house caused the storm: it merely presaged it. So we can sometimes predict what we cannot explain.[7]

Other cases of the barometer type are cases such as the presaging of mumps by its symptoms and the presaging of a weather change by rheumatic pains.

When we make a predictive inference of a storm from a sudden barometric drop, we are inferring an effect of a particular cause from another (earlier) effect of that same cause. Hence the inference to the storm is *not* from a *cause* of the storm but only from an *indicator* of it. And the law connecting sudden barometric drops to storms is therefore a law affirming only an indicator type of connection rather than a causal connection.

The crux of the issue here is whether we have no scientific understanding of phenomena on the strength of their deductive inferability from indicator laws (in conjunction with a suitable antecedent condition), scientific understanding allegedly being provided only by an *explanans* making reference to one or more casuses. If that were so, then Scriven could claim that although the mere *inferability* of particular storms from specific sudden barometric drops is admittedly time-symmetric, there is *no* time-symmetry in *positive* scientific understanding. It is clear from the discussion of the flagpole case that the *terminological* practice of restricting the term "explanation" though *not* the term "prediction" to cases in which the *explanans* makes reference to a partial or total cause rather than to a mere indicator cannot settle the questions at issue, which are: would the type of argument which yields a *prediction* of a future *explanandum*-event (storm) from an indicator-type of premiss furnish any scientific understanding, and, if so, does this type of argument provide the same positive

[7] M. Scriven, "Explanation and Prediction in Evolutionary Theory," this volume p. 122.

amount of scientific understanding of a corresponding *past* event (storm)?

These questions are, of course, *not* answered in the negative by pointing out correctly that the law connecting the cause of the storm with the storm can serve as a *reason* for the weaker indicator-law. For this fact shows only that the causal law can account for both the storm and the indicator law, but it does not show that the indicator law cannot provide any scientific understanding of the occurrence of particular storms. To get at the heart of the matter, we must ask what distinguishes a causal law from an indicator law such that one might be led to claim, as Scriven does, that subsumption under indicator laws provides no scientific understanding at all, whereas subsumption under causal laws does.

Let it be noted that a causal law which is used in an *explanans* and is not itself derived from some wider causal law is fully as *logically contingent* as a mere indicator law which is likewise not derived from a causal law but is used as a premise for the deduction of an *explanandum* (either predictively or post-dictively, i.e., H-explanatorily). Why then prefer (predictive or post-dictive) subsumption of an *explanandum* under a causal law to subsumption under a mere indicator law? The justification for this preference would seem to lie not merely in the greater generality of the causal law; it also rests on the much larger number of empirical contingencies which must be ruled out in the *ceteris paribus* clause specifying the relevant conditions under which the indicator law holds, as compared to the number of such contingencies pertaining to the corresponding causal law. But this difference in both generality and in the number of contingencies does not show that the indicator-law provides no scientific understanding of particular phenomena subsumable under it; it shows only, so far as I can see, that one might significantly speak of *degrees* of scientific understanding. And this conclusion is entirely compatible with the contention required by the symmetry thesis that the barometric indicator law furnishes the same positive amount of scientific understanding of a past storm as of a future one predicted by it.

I believe to have shown, therefore, that with respect to the symmetry thesis, *Hempel ab omni naevo vindicatus.*[8]

[8] Believing (incorrectly) to have cleansed Euclid of all blemish, G. Saccheri (1667–1733) published a book (Milan, 1733) under the title: *Euclides ab omni naevo vindicatus*.

The Covering Law Position: A Reply to Critics 12

from *Explanation and Prediction by Covering Law*

CARL G. HEMPEL

. . . Since limitations of space preclude any attempt at completeness of coverage in this study of criticisms directed against the covering-law analysis of explanation,[1] I propose to single out for consideration in this final section just one interesting and important group of those criticisms.

As I pointed out at the beginning, the covering-law models are intended to exhibit the logical structure of two basic modes of *scientific explanation*, of two logically different ways in which empirical science answers questions that can typically be put into the form 'Why is it the case that X'?, where the place of 'X' is occupied by some empirical statement. Requests for explanations in this sense are often expressed also by means of other phrasings; but the 'Why?' form, even if not uniformly the simplest or most natural one, is always adequate to indicate — pre-analytically, and hence not with the utmost precision — the sense of 'explanation' here under analysis, and to set it apart from the various other senses in which the word 'explain' and its cognates are used. To put forward the covering-law models is not, therefore, to deny that there are many other important uses of those words, and even less is it to claim that all of those other uses conform to one or other of the two models.

For example, an explanation of why every equilateral triangle is equiangular, or why an integer is divisible by 9 whenever the sum of its digits in decimal representation is so divisible requires an argument whose conclusion expresses the proposition in question, and whose premises include general geometrical or arithmetical statements, but not, of course, empirical laws; nor, for that matter, is the explanandum statement an empirical one. This sort of explaining, though rather closely related to the kind with which we are concerned, is not meant to be covered by our models.

Nor, of course, are those models intended to cover the vastly different senses of 'explain' involved when we speak of explaining the rules of a game, or the meaning of a hieroglyphic inscription or of a complex legal clause or of a passage in *Finnegan's Wake*, or when we ask someone to explain to us how to repair a leaking faucet. Giving a logical and methodological analysis of scientific explanation is not the same sort of thing as writing an entry on the word 'explain' for the *Oxford English Dictionary*. Hence to complain, as Scriven does, of the "hopelessness" of the deductive model because it does not

From the *Delaware Seminar on Philosophy of Science*, Vol. I, John Wiley & Sons, Inc., New York, 1962, pp. 125–133.

[1] The important recent discussions and new contributions with which, to my regret, I cannot deal in this paper include, for example, the precise and incisive critique by Eberle *et al* [7] of the formal definition, set forth in Sec. 7 of Hempel and Oppenheim [17], of the concept of potential explanans for languages which have the syntactic structure of the first-order functional calculus without identity. The authors prove that the proposed definition is vastly too liberal to be adequate. An ingenious modification which avoids the difficulty in question has been constructed by one of the three critics, D. Kaplan [18]. An alternative way of remedying the shortcoming in question has been proposed by J. Kim in one section of his doctoral dissertation [19]; his procedure is to be published in a separate article under the title "On the Logical Conditions of Deductive Explanation." Two other illuminating studies both of which raise certain questions about the deductive model of explanation, and which I can only mention here, are Bromberger [3] and Feyerabend [4]. Several earlier critical and constructive comments on the covering-law models are acknowledged and discussed in reference 14.

fit the case of "understanding the rules of Hanoverian succession" (ref. 22, p. 452) is simply to miss the declared intent of the model. And it is the height of irrelevance to point out that "Hempel and Oppenheim's analysis of explanation absolutely presupposes a descriptive language" (which is true), whereas "there are clearly cases where we can explain without language, e.g., when we explain to the mechanic in a Yugoslav garage what has gone wrong with the car" (ref. 24, p. 192). This is like objecting to a definition of 'proof' constructed in metamathematical proof theory on the ground that it does not fit the use of the word 'proof' in 'the proof of the pudding is in the eating,' let alone in '90 proof gin.' I therefore cheerfully concede that wordless gesticulation — however eloquent and successful — which is meant to indicate to a Yugoslav garage mechanic what has gone wrong with the car does not qualify as scientific explanation according to either of the two covering-law models; and I should think that any account of scientific explanation which did admit this case would thereby show itself to be seriously inadequate.

In support of his insistence on encompassing all those different uses of the word 'explain,' Scriven maintains, however, that they have the same "logical function," about which he says: "the request for an explanation presupposes that *something* is understood, and a complete answer is one that relates the object of inquiry to the realm of understanding in some comprehensible and appropriate way. What this way is varies from subject matter to subject matter . . . ; but the *logical function* of explanation, as of evaluation, is the same in each field. And what counts as complete will vary from context to context within a field; but the logical category of complete explanation can still be characterized in the perfectly general way just given" (ref. 24, p. 202; italics his). But while the general observation with which this passage begins may well be true of many kinds of explanation, neither it nor the rest of the statement specifies what could properly be called a *logical* function of explanation; this is reflected in the fact that such terms as 'realm of understanding' and 'comprehensible' do not belong to the vocabulary of logic, but rather to that of psychology. And indeed, the psychological characterization that Scriven offers here of explanation makes excellent sense if one construes explanation as a pragmatic concept. Before considering this construal, I want to indicate briefly why I do not think that explanation in all the different senses envisaged by Scriven can be held, in any useful and enlightening sense, to have the same "logical function."

One of the reasons is the observation that the objects of different kinds of explanation do not even have symbolic representations of the same logical character: Some explanations are meant to indicate the meaning of a word or of a linguistic or nonlinguistic symbol, which will be represented by an expression that is not a statement, but a name ('the integral sign,' 'the swastika') or a definite description ('the first pages of *Finnegan's Wake*'); while other explanations are meant to offer reasons, grounds, causes, or the like for something that is properly represented by a statement; for example, a mathematical truth, some particular empirical event, or an empirical uniformity such as that expressed by Galileo's law of free fall. Thus, first of all, the logical character of the explanandum-expression is different in these two classes of explanations.

Secondly, the task of specifying meanings and that of specifying grounds, reasons, causes, etc., surely are not of the same logical character; and still a different kind of task is involved in explaining how to make Sacher Torte or how to program a certain type of digital computer. And while any of these and other kinds of explanation may be said to be capable of enhancing our "understanding" in a very broad sense of this word, it is worth noting that the requisite sense is so inclusive as to be indifferent to the important distinction between knowing (or coming to know) that p, knowing (or coming to know) why p, knowing (or coming to know) the meaning of S, and knowing (or coming to know) how to do Z. To be sure, the application of any concept to two different cases may be said to disregard certain differences between them; but the differences in the tasks to be accomplished by different sorts of explanation reflect, as I have tried to indicate, *differences* precisely *in the logical structure* of the corresponding explanations.

As I suggested a moment ago, Scriven's observations on the essential aspects of explanation are quite appropriate when this concept is understood in a pragmatic sense. Explanation thus understood is always explanation for someone, so that the use of the word 'explain' and its cognates in this pragmatic construal requires reference to someone to whom something is explained, or for whom such and such is an explanation of so and so. One elementary sentence form for the pragmatic concept of explanation is, accordingly, the following:

Person *A* explains *X* to person *B* by means of *Y*.

Another, simpler, one is

Y is an explanation of *X* for person *B*.

Here, *Y* may be the production of certain spoken or written words, or of gestures; it may be a practical demonstration of some device; or, perhaps, in Zen fashion, a slap or an incongruous utterance.

The pragmatic aspects of explanation have been strongly emphasized by several recent writers, among them Dray[2] and, as we have seen, Scriven. Indeed, the pragmatic concept may claim psychological and genetic priority over the theoretical nonpragmatic one, which the covering-law models are intended to explicate. For the latter is an abstraction from the former, related to it in a manner quite similar to that in which metamathematical concepts of proof — which might figure in sentences of the form 'String of formulas *U* is a proof of formula *V* in system *S*' — are related to the pragmatic concept of proof, which would typically figure in phrases such as '*Y* is a proof of *X* for person *B*.' Whether, say, a given argument *Y* proves (or explains) a certain item *X* to a given person *B* will depend not only on *X* and *Y* but quite importantly on *B*: on his interests, background knowledge, general intelligence, standards of clarity and rigor, state of mental alertness, etc., at the time; and factors of this kind are, of course, amenable to scientific investigation, which might lead to a pragmatic theory of proof, explanation, and understanding. Piaget and his group, for example, have devoted a great deal of effort to the psychological study of what might be called the conception of proof in children of different ages.

But for the characterization of mathematics and logic as objective disciplines, we clearly need a concept of proof which is not subjective in the sense of being relative to, and variable with, individuals; a concept in terms of which it makes sense to say that a string *Y* of formulas is a proof of a formula *X* (in such and such a theory), without making any mention of persons who might understand or accept *Y*; and it is concepts of this nonpragmatic kind which are developed in metamathematical proof theory.

The case of scientific explanation is similar. Scientific research seeks to give an account — both descriptive and explanatory — of empirical phenomena which is objective in the sense that its implications and its evidential support do not depend essentially on the individuals who happen to apply or to test them. This ideal suggests the problem of constructing a nonpragmatic conception of scientific explanation — a conception that requires reference to puzzled individuals no more than does the concept of mathematical proof. And it is this nonpragmatic conception of explanation with which the two covering-law models are concerned.

To propound those models is therefore neither to deny the existence of pragmatic aspects of explanation, nor is it to belittle their significance. It is indeed important to

[2] See, for example, reference 6, p. 69, where the author says: "... as I shall argue further in this, and in succeeding chapters, there is an irreducible pragmatic dimension to explanation."

bear in mind that when a particular person seeks an explanation for a given phenomenon, it may suffice to bring to his attention some particular facts he was not aware of; in conjunction with his background knowledge of further relevant facts, this may provide him with all the information he requires for understanding, so that, once the "missing item" has been supplied, everything falls into place for him. In other cases, the search for an explanation may be aimed principally at discovering suitable explanatory laws or theoretical principles; this was Newton's concern, for example, when he sought to account for the refraction of sunlight in a prism. Again at other times, the questioner will be in possession of all the requisite particular data and laws, and what he needs to see is a way of inferring the explanandum from this information. Scriven's writings on explanation suggest some helpful distinctions and illustrations of various kinds of puzzlement that explanations, in this pragmatic sense, may have to resolve in different contexts. But to call attention to this diversity at the pragmatic level is not, of course, to show that nonpragmatic models of scientific explanation cannot be constructed, or that they are bound to be hopelessly inadequate — any more than an analogous argument concerning the notion of proof can establish that theoretically important and illuminating nonpragmatic concepts of proof cannot be constructed. As is well known, the contrary is the case.

On these grounds we can also dismiss the complaint that the covering-law models do not, in general, accord with the manner in which working scientists actually formulate their explanations.[3] Indeed, their formulations are usually chosen with a particular audience — and thus with certain pragmatic requirements — in mind. But so are the formulations which practicing mathematicians give to their proofs in their lectures and writings; and the metamathematical construal of the concept of proof purposely, and reasonably, leaves this aspect out of consideration.

I think it is clear then, from what has been said, that many — though by no means all — of the objections that have been raised against the covering-law models, as well as some of the alternatives to them that have been suggested, miss their aim because they apply to nonpragmatic concepts of explanation certain standards that are proper only for a pragmatic construal.

References[4]

[1] Bartley, W. W. III, "Achilles, the Tortoise, and Explanation in Science and History," *The British Journal for the Philosophy of Science*, **13**, 15–33 (1962).

[2] Brodbeck, M. "Explanation, Prediction and 'Imperfect' Knowledge," in Feigl and Maxwell, Eds., *Minnesota Studies in the Philosophy of Science*, University of Minnesota Press, 1962, pp. 231–272.

[3] Bromberger, S. "The Concept of Explanation," Ph.D. thesis, Harvard University, 1961.

[4] Carnap, R. *Logical Foundations of Probability*, University of Chicago Press, Chicago, 1950.

[5] Carnap, R. "Statistical and Inductive Probability." Reprinted, from a pamphlet published in 1955, in E. H. Madden, Ed., *The Structure of Scientific Thought*, Houghton Mifflin, Boston, 1960.

[6] Dray, W. *Laws and Explanation in History*, Oxford University Press, London, 1957.

[7] Eberle, R., Kaplan, D. and Montague, R. "Hempel and Oppenheim on Explanation," *Philosophy of Science*, **28**, 418–428 (1961).

[8] Feigl, H. and Maxwell, G., Eds., *Minnesota Studies in the Philosophy of Science*, Vol. III, University of Minnesota Press, Minneapolis, 1962.

[9] Feyerabend, P. K. "Explanation, Reduction, and Empiricism," in Feigl and Maxwell (ref. 8), 28–97.

[10] Grünbaum, A. "Temporally Asymmetric

[3] On this point, cf. also the discussion in Bartley [1], Sec. 1, which, among other things, defends Popper's presentation of the deductive model against this charge. For some comments in a similar vein, see Pitt [20], pp. 585, 586.

[4] [*Some of the works cited here by Hempel are not referred to in the segment of his essay reprinted in this volume. Editor's note.*]

Principles, Parity between Explanation and Prediction, and Mechanism Versus Teleology," *Philosophy of Science*, 29, 146–170 (1962).

[11] HEMPEL, C. G. "The Function of General Laws in History," *The Journal of Philosophy*, **39**, 35–48 (1942). Reprinted in P. Gardiner, Ed., *Theories of History*, Allen and Unwin, London, and The Free Press, Glencoe, Ill., 1959, pp. 344–356.

[12] HEMPEL, C. G. "The Theoretician's Dilemma," in H. Feigl, M. Scriven, and G. Maxwell, Eds., *Minnesota Studies in the Philosophy of Science*, Vol. II, University of Minnesota Press, Minneapolis, 1958, pp. 37–98.

[13] HEMPEL, C. G. "The Logic of Functional Analysis," in L. Gross, Ed., *Symposium on Sociological Theory*, Row, Peterson and Co., Evanston, Ill., and White Plains, N. Y., 1959, pp. 271–307.

[14] HEMPEL, C. G. "Deductive-Nomological *vs.* Statistical Explanation," in Feigl and Maxwell (ref. 8), pp. 98–169.

[15] HEMPEL, C. G. "Rational Action," *Proceedings and Addresses of the American Philosophical Association*, Vol. XXXV, The Antioch Press, Yellow Springs, Ohio, 1962, pp. 5–23.

[16] HEMPEL, C. G. "Explanation in Science and in History," in R. G. Colodny, Ed., *Frontiers of Science and Philosophy*, University of Pittsburgh Press, Pittsburgh, 1962, pp. 7–33.

[17] HEMPEL, C. G. and OPPENHEIM, P. "Studies in the Logic of Explanation," *Philosophy of Science*, **15**, 135–175 (1948). Sections 1–7 of this article are reprinted in H. Feigl and M. Brodbeck, Eds., *Readings in the Philosophy of Science*, Appleton-Century-Crofts, New York, 1953, pp. 319–352.

[18] KAPLAN, D. "Explanation Revisited," *Philosophy of Science*, **28**, 429–436 (1961).

[19] KIM, J. "Explanation, Prediction, and Retrodiction: Some Logical and Pragmatic Considerations," Ph.D. thesis, Princeton University, 1962.

[20] PITT, J. "Generalizations in Historical Explanation," *The Journal of Philosophy*, **56**, 578–586 (1959).

[21] SCHEFFLER, I. "Explanation, Prediction, and Abstraction," *British Journal for the Philosophy of Science*, **7**, 293–309 (1957).

[22] SCRIVEN, M. "Truisms as the Grounds for Historical Explanations," in P. Gardiner, Ed., *Theories of History*, Allen and Unwin, London, and The Free Press, Glencoe, Ill., 1959, pp. 443–475.

[23] SCRIVEN, M. "Explanation and Prediction in Evolutionary Theory," *Science*, **130**, 477–482 (1959).

[24] SCRIVEN, M. "Explanations, Predictions, and Laws," in Feigl and Maxwell (ref. 8), pp. 170–230.

EDITOR'S NOTE

In the preceding selection (and on page 308 below), Hempel speaks of *two* covering-law models. One of these we are familiar with from selection 4: it is the "deductive-nomological" model in which (1) the laws employed are all of unrestricted universal form and (2) the truth of the statements in the explanans makes it logically impossible for the explanandum statement to be false (i.e., it is self-contradictory to assert the former and deny the latter). The second, or "inductive-probabilistic" model also relies on laws, but some of these at least, in contrast with (1) above, "are not of strictly universal, but of statistical character." Examples of such laws would be: "Nine out of ten persons who enter graduate school in philosophy never complete their degrees," "75% of all offspring of midgets are midgets," "If one deals bridge hands from an ordinary deck, the chances are better than .99999 that no player will receive thirteen cards of the same suit."

The relation between explanans and explanandum in an inductive-probabilistic explanation, given the statistical nature of its laws, differs from that described in (2) above. On one hand, if you assert that every blue-eyed child is the product of blue-eyed parents and that Jean's parents both have blue eyes, then you cannot consistently deny that Jean has blue eyes. But in the second form of explanation, conceding the truth of every item in an explanans (e.g., that Bill is the child of Tom and Sue who are both midgets and that three-quarters of all offspring of midgets are midgets) permits one to intelligibly reject the explanandum (it remains possible that Bill is of normal stature). The explanatory premisses here do not logically or validly imply the statement identifying the event to be explained; they merely show that that event was to be expected, that its non-occurrence was unlikely, highly improbable, etc.

In brief, both types of explanations appeal to uniformities (patterns exhibited by certain classes) and — given the truth of their explanans statements — both establish that the event to be explained was predictable, that there is more evidence for saying that it did occur than for denying this. Their differences lie, in Hempel's words, "in the character of the laws invoked and, as a consequence, in the logical character of the inference that links the statement of the phenomenon in question to the explanatory information."

III

IS SOCIAL SCIENCE METHODOLOGICALLY DISTINCT from NATURAL SCIENCE?

III

The covering law position, especially propositions 2 and 3, unequivocally denies what Richard Rudner has called "the separatist view," i.e., that a sharp dichotomy exists between the methods of social science and those of natural science. And nothing in the spirited critiques of Hanson and Scriven protests against this denial: there is no good reason to restrict Hanson's concept of retroduction to physics and chemistry and Scriven explicitly advances his two main innovations, explanation by selection and the notion of normic connections, as bipartisan possessions. Thus, though separatism and the covering law position are incompatible, it is possible to reject both: by establishing that the main patterns of scientific reasoning and validation, though common resources of natural and social scientists, do not all comply with Hempel-Oppenheim criteria (or with the hypothetical-deductive model). In other words, the covering law position can be attacked in two very different ways. The first, which is exemplified by Hanson and Scriven and by selection 16 below, contends that propositions 1-9 inaccurately portray scientific inquiry in *both* the natural and social sciences. Selections 13, 22, and 27 (among others) illustrate the second line of attack. They accept, or raise no objections to, what Hempel and Popper advance, so long as it is construed as an analysis of the methods and concepts of physical science. But this analysis, they assert, misrepresents the objectives and patterns of inquiry appropriate within the social sciences; there is no nontrivial sense in which the methods of social and natural scientists can be "unified." (It would, for example, be trivial to insist simply that they were unified in "seeking truth," or "acquiring knowledge," or "providing explanations.") It is this second and separatist alternative to the covering law position which is expressed and contested in selections 13 through 16.

Yet in many ways, these four selections continue and extend the controversies introduced in parts I and II. Consider first the debate between Grünbaum and Buck over the implications of reflexive predictions — roughly, those whose truth value depends on whether and when people come to believe them — for social science. In the course of this debate, Buck sets forth views that appear to conflict with Skinner's total rejection of "explanations in terms of inner states or agents" (page 37 above). In certain cases, Buck claims, "the holding of a predictive belief must be causally relevant to the occurrence or nonoccurrence of what is predicted." An example of Robert Merton's (which Buck does not accept) involves rural whites who are taught to believe B: that local Negroes will generally be irresponsible and untrustworthy. Out of this belief, the Negroes are then treated with disrespect and distrust and prevented from exercising anything beyond minimal initiative and responsibility. One result of this discriminatory treatment is likely to be that many Negroes are in fact dehumanized to the point of not developing responsible and trustworthy dispositions. (In Merton's terms, B is "self-fulfilling.") In this case, the truth value of B, the occurrence or nonoccurrence of what it affirms, depends on the extent to which it is popularly believed. Surely one and probably the major hindrance to Negro development would be removed if the town's white population wholeheartedly rejected its belief in B. Can we not say, therefore, that the "inner state" of belief in B is at least a part of the explanation of continued discrimination and of the Negroes' limited development of certain capacities and attitudes? Would any explanation be acceptable here which ignored or bypassed the "causal efficacy" of this belief?

Buck's position on B is that it is not reflexive since racial discrimination might persist even when B was recognized as false.

> . . . it is far from clear that our typical racist discriminator could be talked out of discrimination by drawing his attention to communities in which there was no discrimination, and in which the Negroes did not manifest the undesirable traits. I can't quite see the racist abandoning discrimination because certain factual beliefs he held had been shown to be false. [See page 156 below.]

But there are those who discriminate without being irredeemable racists. And if their conviction in B is shattered, then, other factors remaining constant, they will have less reason to discriminate and tend to discriminate less. B, perhaps, is not the only source from which racial prejudice draws support. It is, however, one of them. What is difficult is not so much getting the racist to abandon "discrimination because certain factual beliefs he held had been shown to be false," but enabling him to uproot those entrenched factual beliefs, crucial among which is B.

Though Buck separates social from natural science by appealing to the notion of a reflexive prediction, he refuses to conclude that "the reflexivity of predictions creates a serious methodological problem for the social sciences." His optimism should be compared with the following view, advanced by Alan Gewirth in selection 17 below:

> In dealing with social phenomena, social science deals largely if not entirely with things which impinge directly on men's values — wealth, power, various kinds of interpersonal relations, and so on. The aim of social science may be said to be to attain knowledge of the laws of these matters — that is, of their cause-effect relations. Since, however, man as conscious voluntary agent is in large part both the knower and the subject-matter of these laws, his knowledge of their impact on his values may lead him to react on the laws reflexively in order to change them. *Consequently, the laws of the social sciences cannot have the same fixity or permanence as the laws of the natural sciences.* [emphasis added] [See page 218 below.]

Gewirth sees reflexive predictions as implying what may be termed the *voluntarist thesis.* According to this thesis, virtually all social uniformities have the following form: whenever A (intermittent reinforcement) then B (longer-surviving behavior), *so long as the agents involved do not know about or care to alter the correlation.* But no such rider attaches to physical laws: that blue-eyed parents have only blue-eyed children does not depend on what men know nor on what they desire. Self-fulfilling and self-defeating predictions can be viewed as confirming voluntarism. With this in their favor, they not only lend fresh support to the separatist's rejection of the covering law position, but may well create "methodological problems," especially for social scientists who accept propositions 1, 2, 5 and 8.[1]

Further arguments for separatism are set forth in H. A. Hodges' instructive exposition of Wilhelm Dilthey. One of these affirms a direct connection between proposition 9 and the more explanation-centered elements of the covering law position. For Dilthey refuses to allow that expressions or "objectifications" of mind (which include

[1] The voluntarist thesis is elaborated, employed, and defended in the introductions to parts VI–VIII. See in particular part VII and its discussion of methodological individualism; this view, at its best, is a form of voluntarism.

such familiar human products as flower gardens, diaries, and wills as well as "post-impressionist painting" and "empirical treatises on the characters and passions of men") can be reduced entirely to physical components. And this refusal provides one ground for his claim that "the discovery of general laws . . . is hardly possible in the human studies." The question thus emerges: "How much of the covering law position and its criteria for acceptable explanations would be uprooted by a refutation of proposition 9?"

The concentration by both Dilthey and Machlup on what the latter terms the "distance [of scientific theory] from everyday experience" may take us part of the way towards such a refutation. For if the language of social science cannot depart from that of ordinary discourse, then surely it must retain and not eliminate concepts referring to intentions, attitudes, beliefs, and emotions. This line of argument is discussed extensively in parts V and VI below. And in selection 26, Peter Winch offers a contemporary statement of Dilthey's separatist doctrine that social scientists, as opposed to natural scientists, cannot divorce themselves from the life-patterns (forms of life, language-games) they would understand. They cannot impose their own alien categories on these forms, but must seek to grasp any social process "from the point of view of the agents concerned in it." In an important passage, Winch maintains:

> Now if the position of the sociological investigator (in a broad sense) can be regarded as comparable, in its main logical outlines, with that of the natural scientist, the following must be the case. The concepts and criteria according to which the sociologist judges that, in two situations, the same thing has happened, or the same action performed, must be understood *in relation to the rules governing sociological investigation*. But here we run against a difficulty; for whereas in the case of the natural scientist we have to deal with only one set of rules, namely those governing the scientist's investigation itself, here *what the sociologist is studying*, as well as his study of it, is a human activity and is therefore carried on according to rules. And it is these rules, rather than those which govern the sociologist's investigation, which specify what is to count as 'doing the same kind of thing' in relation to that kind of activity. [See page 320 below.]

If this is so, then Dilthey's contention that sociology and political theory involve "the same kind of thinking as we use in the concerns of every day" would appear true, and there is reason to suspect proposition 9 and its advocacy of operationist and reductionist eliminations of mental concepts. (On this point see selections 22, 23, and 30 through 34 as well as the introductions to parts IV, V, and VI.)

Besides supplementing earlier discussions of the covering law position, the present part inaugurates a fresh set of issues, those concerned with "values and objectivity in the social sciences." Thus, Dilthey maintains, while Machlup denies, that the social sciences are less "objective" than the natural sciences, and Helmer and Rescher examine closely what it means for a discipline to be objective and whether objectivity can be identified with the utilization of "exact" concepts and "precise" laws and predictions.[2]

The issue of what sort of objectivity, if any, is within the reach of judgments and explanations in social science is by no means the only one on which our four selections advance conflicting views. If Dilthey had compiled a "score-card" of distinctions between the social and natural sciences, it would have scarcely resembled the one which sums up Machlup's arguments. And Helmer and Rescher are in fundamental opposition to all of the other positions set forth in this section. They deride as overly simple

[2] The notion of objectivity is considered in selections 40, 44, 53–57 and by the introductions to parts VI and VIII.

the account of scientific inquiry contained in propositions 1 through 9 and suggested by Grünbaum's view that reflexive predictions are not unique to the social sciences. For selection 16, science is no monolithic enterprise, nor does it conform to any univocal set of canons — no more than art, religion, and many other types of human activity. Some scientific disciplines (the "exact sciences") do indeed fit neatly under the covering law model: these operate with geometrically sharp concepts, formalized criteria for drawing inferences, and mathematically measurable data. But other parts of science, while still providing "explanation and prediction in a reasoned, and therefore inter-subjective, fashion," are imprecise: their laws (or "quasi-laws") are loose approximations; their terms have no sharply defined boundaries (and hence give rise to many borderline or undecidable cases); their data resist most or all of the four types of measurement discussed in selection 40 below. The methods and principles of inquiry characteristic of these inexact areas within science, Helmer and Rescher contend, cannot be accounted for by the covering law position. To take just one example, "the presence of less-than-universal principles in the inexact sciences," they assert, "creates an asymmetry between the methods of explanation and those of prediction in these fields." (But is it clear that quasi-laws — or any other element of the inexact sciences — cannot be used as well in explanations as in predictions? The "exercise of expert judgment" is required, we are told, in *predicting* future election outcomes by appealing to the limited generalization that the opposition party tends to gain in a U.S. off-year election. But why isn't such reliance on expertise just as necessary in *explaining*, say, the deviation from this quasi-law in 1934?)

Helmer and Rescher also oppose the belief common to Buck, Dilthey, and Machlup that "there exists an epistemological difference in principle between the social sciences on the one hand and the natural or physical sciences on the other." They remind us that "various departments of physics, such as the theory of turbulence phenomena" have been content to work with imprecise concepts and, as well, to rely on quasi-laws which permit of exceptions. It seems to follow from this reminder that "inexactness is not a prerogative of the social sciences." (See also section 3.3 of selection 9 above.) The moral is then drawn that a correct grasp of scientific method requires that we outgrow the task of separating social from natural science, and replace it with that of contrasting laws, predictions, explanation, experimentation, measurement, and concept-formation in the exact sciences with their analogues in the inexact sciences.

Helmer and Rescher's objections to the separatist view raise an important, albeit second-order issue: by what tests or criteria can we evaluate proposed distinctions between the physical and social sciences?

A complete answer would be far too long to attempt here, but one point warrants special notice. For it seems that there are at least two senses, which we may term the *strong* and the *weak*, of the claim that the methods of the social scientist must be kept distinct from those employed by physical scientists. To establish a strong distinction, the separatist must show that some method (of classification, explanation, experimentation, etc.) utilized by *all* of the natural (social) sciences can at *no* point be used in the social (natural) sciences. Thus, Dilthey is sometimes interpreted as holding that intuitive understanding (*verstehen*) of mental expressions is indispensable throughout the social sciences, but has no place whatever in any physical science. The test for a weak distinction is less stringent: what suffices here is that a method which *could* be employed by *every* natural (social) science is one that can be introduced only within some, and not in all, regions of social (natural) science. It is probably in this weak sense that those who focus on measurement as a basis for distinguishing the natural and social sciences should be understood. (See also Hodges on Dilthey's *limited* denial of laws in social science: page 150 below.) In any case, a separatist need not deny that measurement is *occasionally* possible within the study of man. On the contrary, he can concede this, but also argue that while physical data universally allow of measurement, not every concept applicable to human conduct denotes a property with measurable units.

The point of distinguishing these two forms of the separatist rejection of propositions 2 and 3 may be illustrated by examining the main thesis advanced by Helmer and Rescher. They argue, as we have seen, that because neither realm can boast of greater exactness or precision, "the social sciences cannot be separated from the physical on methodological grounds." This thesis can be criticized in two different ways. In the first place, it too quickly assumes that there are no methodological differences besides those bound up with the dichotomy between exact and inexact disciplines. For even if the social and natural sciences were equally exact, they might still be distinguished along other lines, e.g., if only the former advanced arguments and explanations which could not be evaluated without appealing to one or more of the following: (a) empathetic understanding (see, e.g., selections 27, 39, and 54); (b) the concept of rationality (selections 22, 24, 26, 29, 38, and 43); (c) irreducible psychological notions (selections 26, 29, 32, 33, 34, and 44); (d) normative or ethical standards (selections 53, 54, and 55); . . . . (e) a unique kind of ideal type (selections 38 and 39).

Secondly, our account of strong and weak separatism should also raise difficulties for Helmer and Rescher. They argue that there are exact and inexact areas within both social and natural science. If true, this would show only that no *strong* distinction can be drawn between the two in regard to exactness. It entirely bypasses the view that some forms of human activity, but no physical events, are incompatible with exact laws or with the sort of precision that results from employing operational definitions or techniques of quantitative measurement. This unrefuted view, however, affirms a weak distinction between the social and natural sciences: it sees exactness as a feature any concept or generalization in physics, chemistry, biology, etc., can in principle attain, but which it makes no sense or is self-contradictory to ascribe to certain descriptions of human conduct. (See here, e.g., selections 22, 27 and in particular Norman Malcolm's attack, in selection 44, on attempts to render our concept of dreaming precise by introducing criteria external to the dreamer's report.) So, granting everything which Helmer and Rescher affirm, it is still possible to draw a weak distinction, *in regard to exactness*, between the social and natural sciences. And this, coupled with their neglect of alleged methodological distinctions which do not depend on the notion of exactness, provides a second reason for regarding their arguments against separatism as inconclusive.

The Separatist Case: Basic Contrasts Between the Social and Natural Sciences 13

from *Wilhelm Dilthey, An Introduction*

H. A. HODGES

Dilthey's writings are full of comparisons between the human studies and the natural sciences, and the question is gone into from several points of view. Putting together the results of the various discussions, we obtain an account of the methods of the human studies which may be summed up in the following six points.

1. Natural science finds its evidence in the observation of physical things and processes, while the human studies find theirs in the understanding of expressions or "objectifications" of mind. There is common ground here, for of course the expressions are physical things and processes, though most physical things and processes are not expressions. But the two ways of approach are different, and lead to different kinds of discovery.

Our everyday world, the world of perception and common sense, is composed of objects related to one another in space and time, by likenesses and differences, and by cause-effect relationships, and common experience can trace the connections well enough to give us adequate guidance for ordinary purposes. Science, however, in search for greater detail and greater precision, has been compelled to write off as subjective first one and then another element in the object as perceived, until now the world of natural science is strikingly different from the world of common sense, and vexatious questions have arisen for philosophy concerning the sense in which either of the two can be called "real" or "objective". The scientist's own view is usually that the world of his theories is the real world, and that the world of perception and common sense is a world of appearance generated by the response of a perceiving subject to stimuli coming from the real world.

However this may be, the position in the human studies is very different. The basic fact here is that certain objects and processes in the world of ordinary experience are perceived not merely as existing or occurring at a given place and time, but as proceeding from a mental life whose expressions or manifestations they are. We do not infer this, we perceive it, we read the life in its expressions as we read the meaning in a printed text, and so the physical expression leads us through into a dimension of being beyond itself, an inwardness and a structural system answering to our own. It is this that the human studies explore, and they reveal it as a world within a world, *imperium in imperio*, much smaller in extent than the physical order of nature, but incomparably richer in interest for us who are part of it and understand it from within. They do not all go equally deep, or trace the web of causal connection equally far afield. Thus psychology is privileged in a peculiar degree to study the complicated processes which go on in the individual consciousness and below its threshold, the vague feelings, the half-formulated ideas, the passing impulses quickly suppressed, the false starts and recoveries of balance, the indecisions and conflicts, which are the intimate reality of the individual mind. But biography knows less of these things, and history neither cares nor

From *Wilhelm Dilthey, An Introduction* by H. A. Hodges, Routledge & Kegan Paul, Ltd., London, 1944, pp. 72–83.

is able to trace them with any confidence, and for jurisprudence they are wholly irrelevant. What matters here is something different but equally important, something not private to the individual consciousness, but public property among all the minds which have anything to do with law — a set of ideas and practices which are normative in that sphere of activity and give meaning to everything that happens there. The jurist is concerned not with what goes on privately in the minds of judge and jury, counsel and prisoner, but only with the law which they are all concerned to see administered, and which is the objectively rational content of what they do. Here are two extremes between which the human studies move, the individual-subjective and the social-objective. But at both ends and everywhere between, what we discover is mind, life, meaning. Everywhere we understand before we explain, and understand more than we explain, and the analysis which makes explanation possible is itself only possible within the framework of a continual grasp of the whole.

2. Between the world of common experience and the world of natural science is a wide gap which is not easily bridged. In common experience we take things substantially as they appear, as coloured, resonant, fragrant, continuous in space, possessing all the qualities presented to us by our senses. With objects so conceived we find it possible to work out a system of nature which gives us all the knowledge and control that we need for everyday purposes, and in ordinary life we take this view of nature for granted. For two thousand years most scientists took it for granted too, and sought by thinking harder and longer, but still on the same lines as in common sense, to build up a science of nature. The results were very poor, and the triumphant career of modern science could not begin until a revolution had been wrought in methods and assumptions, and a point of view adopted which was far from that of common sense. The new point of view dismissed as irrelevant and probably unreal everything in the object which cannot be expressed as a quantity. The so-called secondary qualities disappear, and even the primary qualities are changed; for with the advance of knowledge it has begun to appear that matter is not continuous in space, but is compounded of very many very small particles moving very quickly through a space which is not what common sense and Euclid have led us to believe. The longer scientific research continues, the further it goes from the picture of things presented by common sense. It is a striking illustration of Dilthey's point that to-day a popular writer on natural science has found it an effective literary stroke to begin with a head-on collision between the two views, and another has written a best-seller under the title of *The Mysterious Universe.* The paradoxical character of the scientific view of nature and the artificiality of its starting-point would be better realized than they are if they were not so familiar; but most educated people to-day have learned to live with the scientific world-picture as well as with that of common sense, and inhabit a universe which is a rough-and-ready conflation of the two.

In the human studies the case is different. The ideas and principles at work in our ordinary understanding of persons and events have proved themselves capable of development without fundamental alteration into the scientific study of man and society. When we read the account of current events in the newspapers, or contemplate and appreciate (say) a Matisse, and then pass from these things of the here and now to work out a sociology or a political theory, or a historical and critical study of post-impressionist painting, our thinking does not change in logical character, it does not dismiss as unreal or irrelevant things which we had been taking seriously hitherto, or take to itself new and challenging principles of method. It widens its range, it acquires a new persistence and depth and a new degree of critical caution, but it is still the same kind of thinking as we use in the concerns of every day. The continuity is perfect from daily experience to autobiography, biography, and history, and from everyday reflection on human nature to psychology and the social sciences. And as the human studies grow thus easily out of ordinary experience, they are more sensitive than the natural sciences to the effects of contemporary social conditions. Thus French society in the *grand siècle*, depending on the Court and governed more by men than by principles, could not encourage a systematic psychology or jurisprudence, economic or political theory, but could and did produce a host of memoirs and empirical treatises on the characters and passions of men; these treatises affected the poetry of the time, and through that, in turn, the philosophers and the historians. Thus the whole body of the arts and the human studies together reflect the general experience and outlook of their age. Add to this that the human studies owe much of their stimulus to practical needs; we have seen how the social sciences arose in the first instance out of such needs, and it is in fact impossible to write history, political theory, aesthetics (to name only three) without reference to current problems and movements, and the result will show evidence of this preoccupation even if it is not deliberate propaganda for one point of view. Again, whereas the object of the natural sciences, the physical world, stood complete before them from the outset, the human studies have had to watch their object grow through the centuries, and as long as history continues we shall have new possibilities of experience finding realization as new circumstances call them forth. The political theorist of Plato's day had much less experience to draw upon than we. The object has grown, and the study with it, and of course the study has also in some measure reacted upon the object; for this too is distinctive of the human studies, that they tend to make themselves true by influencing human action. Further, as the object changes and we with it, it becomes harder and harder to avoid reading our own thought and experience into the minds of earlier generations, and so the facts themselves become distorted by the psychological distance at which we stand from them.

For all these reasons the human studies are incapable of the same objectivity and precision as the natural sciences. The newcomer to these disciplines finds them, in Dilthey's words, "standing over against him as a chaos of relativities".[1] This is not to say that they have no standards of precision or objectivity at all. The scepticism which says so is cheap and ignorant. But they are inferior in this respect to the natural sciences, and this is the price they pay for their greater concreteness and nearness to the wealth and colour of common experience.

3. The units out of which natural science builds up its world are hypothetical constructions, divested of all sensuous quality, unperceived and imperceptible, and nothing is known or can be conceived of them but the relations in which they stand. In themselves they are strictly homogeneous. One atom is exactly like another atom of the same element, they react identically in identical situations, they have no known individuality at all. The laws which govern them are also hypothetical constructions, abstractly formulated with great precision and verified by experiment, but telling us nothing of the inner nature of the units or the character of the influence which they have upon one another.

In the human studies it is the other way round. The units here are individual minds, real, concrete, known to us as they are, and the only realities which are so known. We are ourselves such units, and perceive our own inner structure, and in understanding we transpose this into others, and so are able to follow the course of their inner life. By the same means we also understand how they influence and respond to one another, since in ourselves we experience what it is to exert influence and also to receive it, and we transpose these experiences also into the others whom we understand. Further, our knowledge of the structural system gives us the clue to the fundamental law of their interactions, for these also proceed according to the same pattern which obtains within a single mind. As an idea arising in one mind can arouse

[1] *G.S.*, I, 413.

feeling and desire in that same mind, so also the same idea, expressed by the one mind and understood by others, can evoke feelings and desires in them, and become a social force. Thus through the medium of communication the structural system expands until it includes the whole world of minds in a web of constant interaction, and we understand and experience in ourselves the nature of these relationships.

The expansion of the structural system is the sober truth behind the high-sounding theories which try to account for the unity of social groups by appealing to a "group mind" alleged to be distinct from the minds of individuals. It is a speculative theory, going far beyond the range of possible verification, and it is by speculative philosophers such as the post-Kantian idealists that it has most often been put forward, though psychologists have also had a hand in it. Dilthey dismisses it as methodologically unsound. But it is no sounder to recoil from the group mind theory to the opposite extreme represented by the individualism of Hobbes and Bentham, for which the relations between individual human beings are at bottom fortuitous contacts, and all social co-operation the aggregate of many individual self-centrednesses. This too is really a speculative theory, for it is derived from an excessive preoccupation with atomic physics and not from genuine empirical study of human life. Both theories offend against Dilthey's principle of "understanding life (which means human life as seen in history and society) in terms of itself".[2] The human studies must and can draw their explanatory principles neither from metaphysics nor from natural science, but from a descriptive analysis of what we actually experience. The first thing revealed by such analysis is the structural system, which operates as has been shown not only within the individual mind, but also between minds, and so constitutes the link which makes communication and association possible. On this basis groups of people live together in community with one another, and within such groups there is an increasing tendency for the individual to come to regard the interests of the group as his own, to think and feel and act for it as well as for himself, and in short to develop what is called public spirit. It is in this that group solidarity consists, and of course it can go so far as to entitle us to speak of the group as having a collective memory and will, and acting as an individual. These phrases are all right as metaphors, but not as literal truth. The truth behind them is the structural system.

The present-day reader will observe that the group mind theory in the form given to it by Durkheim after Dilthey's death does not offend against Dilthey's canon. It is not a hypostatization of the group, but a recognition of the truth that the mere fact of being together in a group in certain circumstances has a powerful effect on the consciousness of all the individuals concerned. The processes by which this result is brought about can be described in terms of Dilthey's structural system. On the other hand, the collective unconscious of Jung, which is alleged to be carried by physical inheritance, which is a biological hypothesis and very doubtful even as such, would meet with no recognition from Dilthey.

4. In early times, when the human studies were still young, this knowability of their units and relationships told in their favour, and enabled them to reach a state of what Dilthey calls "classic perfection" in some branches while the natural sciences were still in their first clumsy beginnings. During the two thousand years between the Ionian physicists and the revolution in method in the days of Galileo, the natural sciences went fumbling about and making little progress. But in history and political theory, in grammar and rhetoric and literary criticism, the ancients were able to do work which can still teach us something to-day. On the other hand, when once the revolution in natural science had been wrought, the study of nature went ahead with unprecedented rapidity and power, and the human studies have fallen behind. Not that they have failed to make progress of their

[2] *G.S.*, V, 4 et al.

own. Since the middle of the eighteenth century the writing of history has undergone a revolution which Dilthey is not alone in comparing with the earlier revolution in natural science. New studies have grown up, archaeology and prehistory, comparative philology, comparative religion and mythology, ethnology, psychology, economics, sociology, which together cover the world of mind with a completeness and a consciousness of method and purpose that is quite new. But these new studies have not been marked by that general agreement among those at work in them which is so striking a feature of natural science, their progress is slower and their impact upon everyday life immeasurably weaker. Why is this?

It is because the method of natural science, though hard to discover in the first place, is of a character which reduces doubt and error to a minimum. The technique of exact measurement and experiment can verify hypotheses of a surprising subtlety and complexity, and more than compensates for the remoteness of the hypotheses from perception and common sense. This method cannot be applied with the same success in the human studies. Minds and their states and processes are not quantities as material things and their states and processes are, and the application of measurement to them has to be indirect and incomplete. Experimentation labours under difficulties. And the individuals who are our units are really individual, i.e., heterogeneous, no two being precisely alike in any respect. The result is that the discovery of general laws, which is the greatest triumph of natural science, is hardly possible in the human studies. Experimental psychology can do it for the lower mental functions, sensation and the reflexes, economics can do it for the quantitative aspects of production and exchange, but over the greater part of our field we have only empirical generalizations, expressing tendencies which operate by and large, imprecise in form and open to exceptions, instead of the precise experimental laws of natural science.

Dilthey points out that the natural sciences themselves are not all alike in this respect. The traditional inductive logic, which almost identifies science with the discovery of laws, draws its most striking examples from the sciences of inorganic nature, but in biology a different element begins to make itself felt. Not that organic phenomena are in fact less conformable to law than inorganic, but that we find it easy and interesting to study them also by a different method, the comparative method, which is a descriptive study of types. There has always been a tendency, whose history Dilthey traces in *On Comparative Psychology*, for the comparative method to pass over from biology into the human studies, and in recent times it has been used with conspicuous success in founding new branches of enquiry, viz., philology and comparative mythology. Dilthey thinks it is indispensable throughout the human studies, though he does not define them in terms of it as Windelband and Rickert do. The defining characteristic of the human studies is understanding and the interpretation of expressions.

This is because Dilthey recognizes a further truth. The comparative method, just as much as the search for laws, is a way of generalizing, and natural science, even when using comparative methods, still cares for the type first and for the individual mainly as a case of it. But the human studies find an absorbing interest in the individual as such. It is the individual that is the immediate object of understanding (*das Verstehen*), and the human studies find their centre of interest not in generalizations based on this, but in the "loving understanding (*Verständnis*) of the personal, the reliving (*Nacherleben*) of the inexhaustible totalities"[3] which are individual persons and groups. That is not to say that we do not generalize, seeking types and even laws so far as we are able; but these discoveries are not allowed to rest in themselves, they are used to enrich and clarify our understanding of the concrete facts of history.

5. It is generally recognized that the natural sciences have no interest in judgments of value. Their *Wertfreiheit* is one of

[3] *G.S.*, V, 266.

their most treasured attributes. It is regarded as the bulwark of their objectivity and impartiality — if impartiality is the proper word for a determination to keep right outside the field of dispute. Some would have the human studies purchase objectivity at the same price, but this, says Dilthey, is contrary to their very nature. All thinking in the human studies is axiological. They select their facts and formulate their questions from the standpoint of value. This blunt statement will evoke different responses in different readers. Some will be surprised, some will be incredulous, and some will accept it as evidence that the human studies cannot claim to be really knowledge.

Let us examine what it does and does not mean.

Every human action is an attempt, deliberate or not, to achieve some end or purpose. What tends to further our ends we call good, what tends to frustrate them we call evil, and this is the basis of our standards of value. The understanding of human beings is inseparable from the understanding and even the provisional acceptance of their value-standards; for to understand a man's action involves understanding his purposes, and judging of his success or failure in carrying them out, i.e., in achieving the values which he has set before himself. It is the same when we understand a social group, a nation, a historical movement, or anything else that can come before us in historical and social study. In every case we find men acting under the guidance of their own conceptions of value, and we take note of these conceptions and compare purpose with execution. Our own value-standards play a part also, for it is they which determine our choice of subject in the first place. No one can study the whole of history or society, we have to select. No one can tell all that he knows about the thing which he has studied. He has to select and edit. In both cases we select what we consider to be important, either intrinsically or by virtue of its wider bearings; and in the last analysis our standard of importance is our standard of value. We judge a thing important if, and in proportion as, it affects the achievement or maintenance of what we consider valuable. Anything else we dismiss. Thus in two ways value lies at the basis of the human studies. The recognition and pursuit of values by historical agents is an integral part of what we study, and the direction and the manner of our study are determined by the values which we ourselves recognize.

This does not mean that we must never study anything but what we consider good. The realm of value includes evil as well as good. Failure, frustration, even deliberate refusal to recognize values are as interesting as achievement and lofty inspiration. Earthquakes and famines, plagues, wars, which afflict a people or destroy a civilization, are as important for the damage they do as economic, political, cultural or religious achievements are for their inherent value.

Nor does it follow that the student must distort the facts to fit his personal prejudices. Suppose he is studying the French Revolution. Here is an event upon which judgments have varied and still vary with no small violence. But one thing is agreed between those who approve, and those who disapprove, and those who have no decided opinion — that, good or bad, the Revolution was at any rate no mean event, but highly important and worthy of study. Now, it is clear that those who were concerned in it had decided views of their own, for and against, and these views are known and can be understood by one who is willing to examine the evidence. If we do this, and if we do not merely register the fact that *X* held this view and *Y* held that, but enter imaginatively into their views and so into the actions and sufferings which were their outcome, we shall end by reliving the Revolution from within as we do the plot of a well-written play. We shall see the events at every moment in the light of value-standards, but of value-standards native to the process itself. It will interpret and judge itself for us. To such an understanding it is not necessary for us to add a judgment of our own, framed from our personal point of view and from our own perspective in time, and if we do, our judgment will not be absolute or infallible; but it will be wiser in proportion as we have already understood the process from the point of view of the agents concerned in it.

6. Lastly, we come to what Dilthey calls the architectonic of the human studies. We saw how he had learned from Comte to see the natural sciences as a pyramid, the base consisting of mechanics (or mathematics according to Comte himself), the study of the simplest and most widely prevalent type of law in nature, and the higher levels dealing successively with more complex laws and covering a narrower range of phenomena. The laws of the higher levels are superimposed upon, but do not abrogate, those of the lower levels; and so the sciences are logically dependent upon one another, the simpler being always prior to the more complex. Comte had reduced the human studies to the single science of sociology and added this as a crowning story to the scientific pyramid. But Dilthey dissents from this.

The human studies cannot be a continuation of the hierarchy of the natural sciences, because they rest upon a different foundation: not observation of physical events, but understanding of expressions. And while the structure of the physical world is hierarchic, and this fact is reflected in the scientific hierarchy, the structure of the world of mind is not hierarchic, and the relations between the human studies must accordingly be different. They are relations of "mutual dependence", and Dilthey traces them throughout the human studies and the cognitive processes on which they rest. Inner experience and the understanding of others are mutually dependent; for we can neither understand others except by projecting ourselves into them, nor see ourselves clearly without the comparisons afforded by our understanding of others. Self-knowledge and understanding of others are together presupposed in any attempt to find general truths, and yet the general truths throw a new light upon self-knowledge and understanding, which is indispensable if these are to reach their full efficiency. Common experience is the basis of art and yet receives a new breadth and clarity from art. Art in turn coins ideas and phrases, registers insights, and in various ways stimulates the development of the human studies, which react in obvious ways upon art. Among the human studies themselves, biography and history support one another, the one giving deeper intimacy and concreteness of detail, the other pointing to the wider system of processes in which the individual is involved; individual psychology and the social sciences complement one another in much the same way; and the whole historical-biographical approach to the facts is both debtor and creditor in relation to the generalizing-systematizing approach. It should follow that there is no logical order in which the human studies must reach maturity, but that they must develop side by side. It should also follow that there is no one human study which is the *grundlegende Wissenschaft* or basis for the rest . . . .

Do Reflexive Predictions Pose Special Problems for the Social Scientist?

14

Reflexive Predictions

ROGER C. BUCK

I

The general notion of what I call a reflexive prediction is widely familiar. A prediction comes true because it comes to the attention of actors on the social scene whose actions will determine its truth-value. Or a prediction turns out false because those same actors become aware of the prediction, and its falsity issues from the actions they are thus led to initiate. I call the first kind of prediction self-fulfilling; the second self-frustrating. Social phenomena involving the reflexive operation of predictions and beliefs are well known. Presumably many cases of bank failure, back in the bad old days when the government still permitted banks to fail, involved the self-fulfilling operation of expectations of such failure, perhaps fed by rumors (predictions) of failure. Again stock market rumors and reports from investors' advisory services sometimes operate in a similar way. The function of pari-mutual machines at race tracks is to ensure that certain predictions prove self-frustrating: namely, predictions of the form "Horse A will win and will pay off well." The political ideas of an 'underdog effect' or a 'bandwaggon effect' have the notion of reflexive prediction built into them. Indeed one can construct a hypothetical case, using simplifying assumptions analogous to those of economists, in which a pollster (say Gallup) can control the outcome of a close election, but cannot produce a correct public prediction of who will win. Such cases involve a strong underdog effect. Another case, frequently offered as a paradigm in the literature, concerns an agricultural economist's forecast of a future price for wheat. Suppose he forsees an oversupply, and a consequent sharp drop in wheat prices. His prediction comes to the attention of the growers who believe it and decide to switch land to other purposes. So many of them thus switch so much land that the expected oversupply fails to materialize. Perhaps the price even rises a bit. And yet it is fully possible that our economist's prediction, falsified by self-frustrating factors, might have turned out true had it not been disseminated!

So much for a sketchy indication of the type of prediction I am concerned with. I shall address myself to three main problems concerning this category of predictions. First, I shall tackle the typical logician's problem of the precise definition of reflexivity for predictions — a problem which is more intricate than might be supposed. Second, I shall consider the suggestion that the possibility of such reflexive predictions raises special and acute methodological problems for the social sciences. My last problem will concern the explicit suggestion that "this characteristic of predictions is peculiar to human affairs" ([5], p. 129,) and the implicit suggestion that this peculiarity marks a philosophically significant difference between the social and natural sciences.[1] Here I shall consider

From *Philosophy of Science*, 30:4 (October, 1963), with "Comments" by Adolf Grünbaum and "Rejoinder" by Buck, pp. 359–374.

[1] Cf. [5], pp. 128–130 and pp. 421–436. See also 6, pp. 894–904; and 7, pp. 12–16 where Popper puts such suggestions in the mouth of his synthetic but lively "historicist" opponent.

primarily a counter-example to the unique-to-human-affairs thesis, which has been proposed by Grünbaum.

II

Our first question is: When are we to count a prediction reflexive? Clearly not all true predictions are self-fulfilling, nor are all false predictions self-frustrating. Robert Merton speaks at one point of "the social scientist [who] everlastingly faces the possibility that his prediction will enter into the situation as a *new and dynamic* factor changing the very conditions under which the prediction initially held true." ([5], p. 129). Clearly Merton's phrase "initially held true" is meant to be getting at our problem of a differentiating criterion, in the self-frustrating case. But there are problems with his formulation. Elsewhere he speaks of "the self-fulfilling prophecy . . . [which evokes] . . . a new behavior which makes the originally false conception come true." ([5], p. 423) But what is this *initial* status of predictions? Is there such a thing as the original, or basic status for predictions, from which (because of, say, publication) they may later depart? Or, if the words "initially" and "originally" are meant in a temporal sense, is there any clear meaning in the notion of a prediction, the very same prediction of the very same event, having at one time one truth-value, and at another time, the other? I think not.

Rather, the situation seems to be that we are here contrasting what actually did happen (and hence what truth-value the prediction actually takes), with what would have happened in other circumstances (and hence with the truth-value which the same prediction would, in these other circumstances have had). That the prediction is reflexive entails that its dissemination was a causal factor in the social situation which would have included the event predicted, had the prediction been true. This dissemination must have been causally relevant to the occurrence of that event in the self-fulfilling case or to its non-occurrence in the self-frustrating case. Further, at least in all the standard examples in the literature, the causal efficacy of such dissemination must be mediated by the formation of beliefs on the part of the various actors on the social scene, and by their behaving in a way which can be reasonably described as "acting on" those beliefs. Again, in all standard cases, any relevant beliefs thus formed will include the belief that the prediction in question is true.

Let me add a few further remarks about this attempt to understand precisely what a reflexive prediction is. I shall use the term "private" to describe predictions which have not been disseminated and brought to the attention of the actors involved. Similarly "public" will refer to those predictions which are disseminated. First, I want to stress that as regards the content or significance of the prediction, as regards *what is predicted*, we must assume the public and the private prediction to be identical. Otherwise, given our criterion, there is no *single* prediction to be called reflexive. Next, we may note that any claim that a prediction is reflexive involves assessing what would have been the case had its dissemination status been different. Such assessment requires knowledge of the truth of counterfactual conditionals, — of conditionals whose antecedents are false. It requires that the empirical scientist claim to know something for which by the very description of the situation he cannot directly test.

Another point worth noting is that while the dissemination status of a prediction must be *a* causal factor relative to what it predicts, we need not suppose that it is ever the only factor involved. The dissemination may be a causally necessary condition for truth (or falsity), but it need never be causally sufficient.

Next there is a curious symmetry which I wish to discuss. Consider a prediction which would be false if public and true if private — i.e., a prediction which if actually disseminated would be called self-frustrating. But now suppose it is kept private. Are we not then entitled to call it a self-fulfilling private prediction on the grounds that a certain causal factor, namely its non-dissemination, prevented it from being false. After all, it does take opposite truth-values depending on its dissemination status! Might we not generalize this result and declare that the class of reflexive predictions includes not only all those public predictions whose truth-value is other than it would have been if private, but also all those private predictions whose truth-value is other than it would have been if public. This suggestion is in some ways attractive, but it will not do.

One counter suggestion involves the claim that while dissemination is something positive, non-dissemination is merely negative; and merely negative states of affairs can have no causal efficacy. But this suggestion just is not in accordance with the customary employment of the concept of causation. An absence or a lack of, say, typhoid vaccine can just as properly be said to have caused an epidemic, as can the occurrence of severe flooding which disrupts the sewer system. And in general we deal repeatedly in terms of such negative causes. The real objection turns on another idea, namely on the notion of standard conditions, or of other-things-being-equal, which is at least tacitly involved in virtually every causal claim.

One does not pick out just any old necessary condition for an event and call it a cause. The presence of oxygen is a necessary condition for the occurrence of fire, but it could properly be called the cause of some specific fire only in rather special circumstances. (One of these might be a fire breaking out within some experimental apparatus in a situation in which the experiment would normally be conduted in an oxygen-free atmosphere.) And a variant of this point is the crucial objection to the argument from symmetry sketched above. If it is normal or usual, as it very often is, that certain kinds of social predictions not come to the attention of the actors whose doings are predicted, then it is fatuous to call a private prediction of one of these kinds reflexive on the grounds that dissemination would have changed its truth-value. And surely the vast majority of the predictions of e.g., the social sciences are not disseminated widely enough to affect any significant number of the social actors involved. There may be classes of predictions whose normal status is wide dissemination. Our wheat price forecaster may be hired by the Agriculture Department to issue public predictions. If, discouraged by repeated failure, he were one day to write down his prediction, lock it in a vault, and refuse to predict publicly; and if that prediction were to come true; we might in these *special* circumstances be tempted to call his private prediction self-fulfilling. For here his deliberate refusal to disseminate his prediction would be abnormal, would have violated the usual standard conditions. But surely such cases are rare.

We may summarize the criteria for a reflexive prediction then as follows. A prediction is reflexive if and only if:

(1) Its truth-value would have been different had its dissemination status been different,
(2) The dissemination status it actually had was causally necessary for the social actors involved to hold relevant and causally efficacious beliefs,
(3) The prediction was, or if disseminated, would have been believed and acted upon, and finally
(4) Something about the dissemination status or its causal consequences was abnormal, or at the very least unexpected by the predictor, by whoever calls it reflexive, or by those to whose attention its reflexive character is called.

In his *Social Theory and Social Structure*, Merton's interest in reflexive predictions is focused chiefly on their role as social mechanisms within his subject matter. In particular, he proposes a sociological analysis of certain problems in race relations where he holds that reflexively operating predictions and beliefs are involved. At least in general outline, Merton's argument is surely familiar. The in-group, let us call them the WASPs (white, Anglo-Saxon Protestants — the term is said to be that of Carmine De Sapio), predict and lead each other to believe that the out-group will manifest various socially undesirable traits. So the WASPs act to isolate and discriminate against the outgroup, say Negroes, in various ways. And these discriminatory actions produce the very traits predicted. Is this a clear case of reflexive prediction? I doubt it.

In the bank failure case, the expectation of failure was essential to the concerted action. But in the discrimination case I should rather have supposed that the prediction of, or the belief in the manifestation of undesirable traits, would be at most a rationalizing afterthought. One would suppose that the depositors could be talked out of their actions if they could be convinced that the bank would not fail if they refrained from withdrawing. But it is far from clear that our typical racist discriminator could be talked out of discrimination by drawing his attention to communities in which there was no discrimination, and in which the Negroes did not manifest the undesirable traits. I can't quite see the racist abandoning discrimination because certain factual beliefs he held had been shown to be false. In short, it is not clear that discrimination in race relations is ordinarily a matter of *acting on* explicit cognitive belief. MacIver, incidentally, describes the same phenomenon that Merton is interested in, using however, not the concept of self-fulfilling prediction, but rather that of a vicious circle ([3], pp. 61–68 especially). The WASPs discriminate against the Negroes, this leads as before to the development of undesirable social traits to which the WASPs react by continuing and perhaps intensifying their discrimination, and so on. Here the whole circle is a causal-behavioral one, in which no one need be supposed to be *acting on* any explicitly held beliefs. It seems to me that given the essential role of such beliefs in the paradigm cases of reflexive prediction, MacIver's conceptual scheme may fit the envisaged situation better than Merton's.

But even if we accept Merton's assimilation of the racial discrimination cases to reflexive predictions there are other problems in his treatment of it. Such discrimination instances "the mechanism of the self-fulfilling social belief, in which confident error generates its own spurious confirmation." ([5], p. 128). Here we see his unclear idea of some "initial" or "original" status for predictions leading him into a confusing blend of moral and methodological appraisal. That the so-called prediction actually was "originally false" we have seen to be logically incoherent. Even that it *would* have been false, if undisseminated, is a claim which is difficult to establish. As logical appraisal, this imputation of error is wholly arbitrary. The belief was not "in error," nor is it shown that the confirmation was "spurious." What Merton has in mind is presumably the contrast with the situation which would develop if a different "social belief" were current. If people believed that there were no important social differences, that colored people would in normal circumstances manifest the same social patterns and traits as whites, then presumably if they acted on this belief all would be well. But surely we must notice that this belief too might be self-fulfilling, that from the point of view of logical appraisal it too could, with equal logical reason, be misleadingly spoken of as "confident error generating its own spurious confirmation."

There is, indeed, error in the situation Merton describes. But it is moral error, not logical or methodological mistake. And while we can all no doubt join Merton in deploring the moral error, I think we should insist on keeping morals and methodology distinct. Parenthetically, we may note that MacIver offers much the same blend of moral and non-moral considerations with his term "vicious circle." The circularity is straightforwardly causal, but the viciousness is neither causal nor logical. The term "vicious" represents MacIver's moral appraisal of the situation. The parallel with Merton becomes clear when we note that MacIver must acknowledge also the possibility of a "beneficent circle," where race relations are good and happy. And here, too, while the circularity will be causal, the beneficence will not.

III

We may now turn to ask whether the existence of reflexive prediction poses special problems for the social scientist. *Prima facie* the answer must be "yes". The social scientist himself predicts in his official capacity as scientist. And predictions play a crucial role in the processes of science. The adequacy of theory and law is tested by deriving predictions from statements of initial conditions in conjunction with such theories and laws. If you call into question the legitimacy of confirmation following on success in prediction, or of disconfirmation following on failure in prediction, you strike at something very fundamental indeed in science.

Let us begin consideration of the social scientist's methodological problem with a new and fanciful example, this time from sociology. Suppose that an expert in the study of crime and of prisons predicts for the near future a drastic increase in the number of felonies (and of consequent convictions) unaccompanied by any increase in available detention space, and hence resulting in terrible overcrowding in our prisons. Now suppose he wonders whether his prediction may prove self-frustrating. Perhaps the would-be felons will learn of and become convinced by his prediction, and perhaps they will therefore refrain in significant numbers from the felonies they would otherwise have committed, being willing, so to speak, to run the risk of ordinary prisons but not of very crowded ones.

Suspecting that his prediction may be reflexive what should he do? Perhaps his first thought will be to draw attention to the possible consequences of the dissemination of his prediction. Can he not thereby be both scientifically honest and exhibit his sophisticated awareness of the dangers of reflexivity? But a little thought may suggest that this line of attack is problematical. For if his first prediction by itself would have been self-frustrating, then clearly this "drawing attention to the possible consequences" which is logically simply another prediction, is also very likely in its turn to be self-frustrating. If believing the first prediction restrained any would-be felons, then believing the second will likely send some of them back to their original felonious plans. Nor is a third prediction likely to fare any better than the second.

Clearly we have the following situation. Any given prediction in the series (1st, 2nd, 3rd, etc.), can in principle take account of the social consequences of the dissemination of all the earlier predictions. Hence there is no numbered prediction in the series whose reflexive consequences cannot be warned against. On the other hand no prediction in the series can possibly warn of the consequences of *its own* dissemination. A prediction which tried to do this could be shown to be logically reflexive, and such logical reflexivity can in turn be shown to involve a strictly vicious infinite regress. In certain circumstances, however, such a series may "converge," as it were. Grünberg and Modigliani have shown this for various economic situations[2]. What happens in such cases of convergence is best described by saying that a true though self-fulfilling prediction may be arrived at in an area where most or all other predictions would be self-frustrating. Their point may be illustrated graphically for the case of wheat price forecasting.

Assumptions:

(1) Expected future price is the sole determinant of actual future production. (S — S' represents future production as a function of expected price.)

(2) Actual future production is the sole determinant of actual future price — i.e., of the price our economist is now trying to predict. (D — D' represents future price as a function of future production.)

(3) Planters expect the future price to be what our economist predicts it will be, if he predicts. If he doesn't predict, they expect last year's price to obtain again.

[2] 2, pp. 465–478. For analogous considerations in the sphere of political science, see [8], pp. 245–253.

P_1 = Last year's price. Dotted lines and arrows show that the correct **private** prediction, in these circumstances, is P_2.

P_3 = The price that will actually obtain of the prediction of price P_2 is **publicized.** Solid lines and arrows show this.

P_k = The only price prediction which can be publicized and still turn out true. Dashes and double arrows show this.

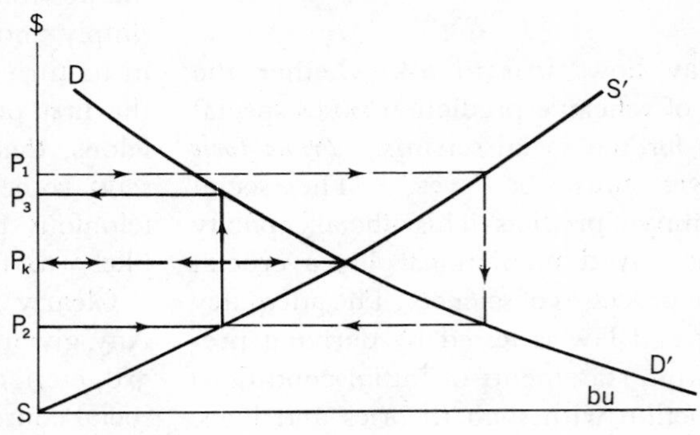

Fig. 13–1

The question might be raised as to whether there is any good reason for calling, say P_2, *the* correct prediction, as opposed to P_3; or for calling P_3, *the* correct prediction as opposed to P_2, in the absence of information about whether predictions are normally publicized.

Notice further that if P_3, in turn, is publicized, the actual price, P_4, will be slightly higher than P_2. And if P_4 in turn is publicized, the actual price, P_5, will be slightly lower than P_3. With curves such as those used here such a series of predictions will thus ultimately converge on P_k, the "equilibrium point." If lines representing all the members of the series were drawn in (thus hopelessly cluttering our diagram) the configuration of all these lines would provide us with an example of the "spider web" of equilibrium analysis in economics. (See below.) Whether or not any particular series will generate such a spider web, and thus tend towards equilibrium, depends on the slopes of the curves involved.

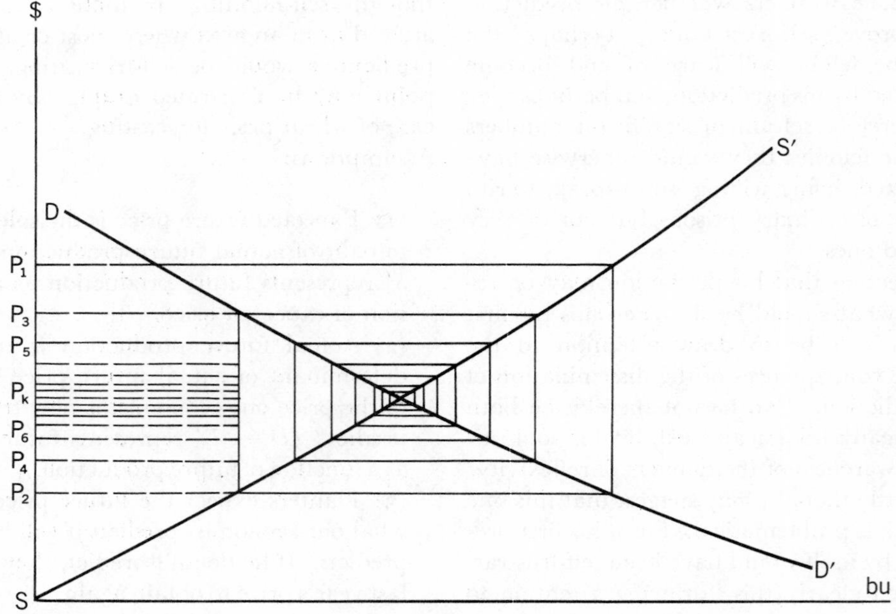

Fig. 13–2

How serious, then, is the methodological problem for the social scientist? In my view, not very! He can always investigate the question whether any specific prediction is likely to operate reflexively. Sometimes such considerations may reveal that it is not reflexive. Our sociologist may discover that his prediction of increased felonies and crowded prisons will come to the attention of only his professional colleagues. And he may conclude that *their* felonious tendencies are either too slight to issue in action, or too strong to be deterred by prospects of crowding. In this case he can dismiss his concern.

In some cases it may be deemed desirable to deliberately restrict dissemination of the prediction. In fact, such restriction has long been employed in medical experimentation with new drugs and vaccines. Members of the experimental and control groups are not told which is their status, in order to guard against the reflexive operation of beliefs which such information might induce.

And even if the reflexivity of a prediction must be merely warned against; even if that warning may in its turn prove reflexive — still something has been achieved. The possible reflexivity of that specific prediction has been noted. A possible correction of that particular scientific claim has been suggested. And is this not the typical situation in an empirical science offering corrigible claims? It may indeed be the case that all scientific propositions are corrigible, but it certainly is never the case at any one time that all have been tested for possible correction.

IV

We have next to consider whether reflexive predictions occur only when people are involved. We may note that the essential question is whether the beliefs and actions of human beings must be causally relevant to the truth-value of a reflexive prediction. It does not matter whether the actual state of affairs predicted, e.g., so many acres under wheat next July, is a human action or not. Our consideration of this issue is restricted to a counter-example proposed by Grünbaum.

Merton held in the first edition of his *Social Theory and Social Structure* that "this characteristic of predictions is peculiar to human affairs." ([4], p. 122). In support of this view he notes that a "meteorologist's prediction of continued rainfall has until now not perversely led to the occurrence of a draught" ([4], p. 122) and that "predictions of the return of Halley's comet do not influence its orbit." ([4], p. 181). Grünbaum cites these remarks and challenges Merton's view: ([2], pp. 239–240).

> "To be sure, these particular predictions of purely physical phenomena are not self-stultifying any more than those social predictions whose success is essentially independent of whether they are made public or not. But instead of confining ourselves to commonplace meteorological and astronomical phenomena, consider the goal-directed behavior of a servo-mechanism like a homing device which employs a feed-back and is subject to automatic fire control. Clearly every phase of the operation of such a device constitutes an exemplification of one or more *physical* principles. Yet the following situation is *allowed* by these very principles: a computer predicts that, in its present course, the missile will miss its target, and the communication of this information to the missile in the form of a new set of instructions induces it to alter its course and thereby to reach its target, contrary to the computer's original prediction. How does this differ, in principle, from the case where the government economist's forecase of an oversupply of wheat has the effect of instructing the wheat growers to alter their original planting intentions?"

Grünbaum's paper had come to Merton's attention before he put out his revised edition of *Social Theory and Social Structure*. The revised edition, like the first, says "this characteristic of predictions is peculiar to human affairs. It is not found among predictions about the world of nature." ([5], p. 129). At this point he adds parenthetically, in the revised edition only, "except as natural phenomena are technologically shaped by men." ([5], p. 129). Here there is a footnote quoting most of what I have quoted from Grünbaum.

We need spend little time on Merton's

parenthetical qualification. It is at best a *de facto* truth that physical systems displaying Grünbaum's analog of reflexive predictions, are to be found only when technologically shaped by man. It is logically possible that such a servo-mechanism come about naturally, without human intervention. And this is another way of saying that if Grünbaum's counter-example really is a case of reflexive prediction, then nothing can be deduced from a definition of physics which would exclude such prediction.[3] Hence Merton's parenthetical qualification concedes enough to Grünbaum to rob the original uniqueness claim of any philosophical interest.

But is Grünbaum's case really an example of *prediction* at all? The word "really" tags this question as metaphysical, and we could easily proceed from here to a lengthy and inconclusive discussion of whether machines think. The metaphysical issue emerges in another fashion if we consider that two very natural reactions to Grünbaum's example are in fact question-begging. The first and most obvious one is the simple rejection on the grounds that machines, even servo-mechanisms, cannot have beliefs, and *a fortiori* cannot act on them — only people can do this sort of thing. A diametrically opposed reaction, natural for at least some reductivist philosophers of science, might run as follows:

> The only sort of sense that science can make of talk about believing and acting on beliefs must ultimately be in terms of the input of stimuli and the subsequent behavior of the person thus stimulated. These, and regular sequences of these, are all an empirical science can possibly mean by talk of belief and action — all we can ever have empirical evidence for. But clearly Grünbaum has described a physical mechanism in which such regular sequences of inputs and subsequent behavior can be observed. So his counter-example to Merton's thesis is decisive.

I want to try to avoid both of these question-begging responses. I propose to do this by granting for purposes of argument that the behavior of machines can be in relevant ways analogous to human behavior. Then I want to suggest that even granting this, there are still inadequacies in Grünbaum's counter-example. The key lies in the difference between acting on a belief and acting on orders.

In Grünbaum's example the computer communicates "information to the missile *in the form of a set of instructions*" (my italics). He then asks how this differs in principle from the case where the "economist's forecast *has the effect of instructing the wheat growers* to alter their original planting intentions" (my italics). I think there is a straightforward answer to this rhetorical question. There certainly is *a* difference between information in the form of a set of instructions and information which has the effect of instructing. The former is, after all, a matter of instructions, directives, orders — an analog of what would appear in the imperative mood. The missile's response to these instructions might analogically be described as obedient or disobedient, but I cannot see that the missile can even analogically be described as informed or misinformed. On the other hand, no *orders* have been issued to the wheat growers. They cannot be described as disobedient if they fail to alter their planting intentions. They have received information (in the indicative mood); they may or may not have acted rationally on that information, but they have neither obeyed or disobeyed.

I think this objection is serious. After all, even our tough-minded empiricist must grant that, in observing and describing the behavior of others we do often manage to classify some items of such behavior as acting on orders, and other items as acting on belief. For many cases of such classification we can achieve considerable intersubjective agreement on how to classify the item in question. This fact of intersubjective agreement strongly supports the presumption that we are all using the same empirical data in thus classifying. It is very difficult not to suppose that our criteria for such classification are empirical, however difficult it may be to set them forth clearly.

[3] A point which Grünbaum himself stresses in anticipating a rejoinder such as Merton's parenthetical qualification. [1], p. 240.

Grünbaum himself describes the missile as receiving "information *in the form of instructions.*" This seems to me to make it clear that the missile's situation is more nearly the analog of a person obeying orders, than of a person acting on belief. So the question of the role of belief in the mechanisms of reflexive prediction becomes central. Suppose Jones is following some line of action A, and I conclude that if he continues this line of action he will fail to do something which for me, though perhaps not for Jones, is an objective, O. So I issue instructions (orders) to Jones to abandon A and follow instead the line of action B. Jones does so, and O is achieved. When I say that I am taking it for granted that the behavior of missiles can be in relevant ways analogous to human behavior, what I mean is that I am prepared to raise no questions here about whether, say, the situation of Jones just described might be precisely analogous to that of the missile described by Grünbaum.

The point of my doubts about Grünbaum's analogy can be brought out equally well by discussing Jones' situation. Let us note the divergencies from the standard case of reflexive prediction. As in the standard case *I* may be thought of as predicting something, *viz.* that A will not lead to O. But, unlike the standard case, this prediction need not come to Jones' attention. Jones is acting on instructions (orders), not on a belief. Even if the prediction does come to his attention, he need not believe it. He may well do B because he has been ordered to, while all the time doubting whether O will result, or even believing A to have been more likely to achieve O than B. But for the wheat forecast to act reflexively the growers must learn of it, believe it, and act on it.

This certainly is *a* difference. And, if it be granted that for human beings we can empirically distinguish between acting on a belief and acting on orders, it could well be a difference "in principle." That even Grünbaum finds it natural to assimilate his example to acting on orders is clear from his expression "information in the form of instructions." As his counter-example stands it does not count against Merton's thesis, and we must return a verdict of "not proved" on Grünbaum's charges.

It becomes clear that for an argument analogous to Grünbaum's to be effective we must imagine that our technicians and engineers should build yet another kind of machine — a machine whose range of "behavior" differs strikingly from that of Grünbaum's servomechanism. This new machine must be such that for at least some of its "behavior" we would find the language of "belief" and "acting on" more appropriate than that of "instructions" and "orders." Whether or not this could happen is partly, but only partly, a technological question. It is also a question about the concepts of "belief" and "acting on." And those conceptual questions would take us beyond the confines of the present paper.

Here I have been primarily concerned to explore the idea of reflexive prediction, and assess its relevance for the philosophy of science. In the context of such exploration, and relative to the standard examples given, the explicit involvement of "belief" and "acting on" is as natural as the economists' concept of the economic man. I have tried to sharpen up the concept of reflexive prediction, and to use the concept thus clarified in a criticism of one proposed sociological analysis. I have also tried to indicate the difficulties which reflexive predictions may lead to in the social sciences, and to argue that despite certain appearances, the problems thus raised are amenable to ordinary scientific treatment. I have not directly argued for Merton's uniqueness thesis, but I have supported it indirectly by urging that Grünbaum's counter-example will not do. My argument locates, in the ideas of "belief" and "acting on," those conceptual issues which I think must be faced in assessing any proposed counter-example analogous to Grünbaum's.

References

[1] GRÜNBAUM, Adolf, "Historical Determinism, Social Activism, and Predictions in the Social

Sciences." *British Journal for the Philosophy of Science*, 1956, VII.

[2] Grünberg, Emile and Modigliani, Franco, "The Predictability of Social Events." *Journal of Political Economy*, 1954, LXII.

[3] MacIver, R. M., *The More Perfect Union*, New York: Macmillan, 1948.

[4] Merton, Robert K., *Social Theory and Social Structure*, 1st edition, Glencoe, Ill.: The Free Press, 1949.

[5] Merton, Robert K., *Social Theory and Social Structure*, rev. edition, Glencoe, Ill.: The Free Press, 1957.

[6] Merton, Robert K., "The Unanticipated Consequences of Purposive Social Action." *American Sociological Review*, 1936, 1.

[7] Popper, Karl, *The Poverty of Historicism*, London: Routledge and Kegan Paul, 1957.

[8] Simon, Herbert A., "Bandwaggon and Underdog Effects and the Possibility of Election Predictions." *Public Opinion Quarterly*, 1954, XVIII.

Comments on Professor Roger Buck's Paper "Reflexive Predictions"

ADOLF GRÜNBAUM

Professor Buck has given an illuminating account of the logical status of reflexive predictions in the social sciences. He tells us that the classification of a prediction as reflexive is predicated on a tacit distinction between the "normal" and the "abnormal" or perturbed conditions under which it is made. This seems to me to be a perceptive and sound circumscription of the class of reflexive predictions as encountered in the social sciences. He goes on to show helpfully how the social scientist can cope with the pitfalls of *spurious* disconfirmation and *spurious* confirmation which are created by "self-frustrating" and "self-fulfilling" predictions respectively. And Professor Buck then offers some searching doubts concerning the adequacy of regarding self-fulfilling predictions as the pattern of racial discrimination against minority groups. Finally, he presents objections to my critique ([1], pp. 239–240) of Robert Merton's claim that self-defeating and self-fulfilling predictions are endemic to the domain of human affairs and are "not found among predictions about the world of nature." ([2], p. 181).

I find much of what Professor Buck says in the latter connection about the difference between acting on a belief and acting on orders both correct and interesting. But I believe that he has misconstrued the *range* of Merton's denial of the existence of physical analogues to reflexive social predictions. Correlatively, Professor Buck seems to me to have misunderstood the sense in which I intended to adduce cybernetic phenomena from physics as a counter-example to Merton's denial. And since this issue is the only one on which I believe Professor Buck to have erred, I shall devote my remarks to a clarification of it.

The precise sense of Merton's denial of the existence of self-stultifying predictions among predictions about the world of nature emerges from his statement of the physical examples which he uses to illustrate his denial. Thus he tells us that a "meteorologist's prediction of continued rainfall has until now not perversely led to the occurrence of a drought" and that "predictions of the return of Halley's comet do not influence its orbit." It will be noted that Merton points to the fact that the making or occurrence of physical predictions has not *led to* a stultifying outcome and has not had an altering *influence* on the phenomena to which the physical predictions pertain. I take it, therefore, that the existence in purely physical contexts of advance information or predictions which are *causally relevant* to a *contrary* outcome does constitute a counter-example to Merton's thesis. The relevant point of my paper of 1956 was merely to call attention to the fact that in physical no less than in sociological contexts, the existence of advance information or of predictions can be *causally relevant* to the occurrence of a *contrary* outcome. And my present claim is that none of the useful things that Professor Buck has said can serve to invalidate this contention. That the range of Merton's denial was indeed meant to be as broad as I took it to be is shown by his concession to me in the second edition of his book that physical phenomena involving certain kinds of artifacts are an exception to his claim.[1]

The force of my counter-example does *not* depend at all on whether one is a crude behaviorist or a traditional mind-body interactionist in one's conception of human activity which springs from the *beliefs* of the agents. I contend that my counter-example is also cogent within the philosophical framework of interactionism, and hence I am fully prepared to grant the following to the introspectionist psychologist: only sentient beings can entertain *beliefs*, and servo-mechanisms whose components are *not* bio-chemical are unable to believe anything, to suffer the

[1] Cf. p. 129n of the 1957 edition, published by the Free Press in Glencoe, Ill.

sorrows of unrequited love or to experience a loss of self-esteem during periods of unemployment. I would only wish to caution the introspectionist against being misled into supposing that the difference between human beings and servo-mechanisms in regard to consciousness can score in the slightest against my counter-example to Merton's thesis. For it is trite that social predictions refer to sentient beings *as such* whereas the predictions of physics do not. And nothing that I said in criticism of Merton requires that I ascribe to physical systems either the property of entertaining beliefs *or any analogue thereto*. In fact, nothing in my counter-example requires the computer to relay the predictive or advance information *as such* to the missile which that information concerns. It is therefore *irrelevant* for Professor Buck to note that there is indeed a difference between information in the form of a set of instructions and information which has the effect of instructing by first generating beliefs. Accordingly, my counter-example does not require, as Professor Buck would have it, that physical systems behave as if they entertained beliefs instead of acting on orders.

More fundamentally, the anti-behaviorist must guard carefully against raising the following untenable objection to my counter-example: the charge that it fails because it makes no sense to say that a non-sentient computer has advance information or makes a prediction. I say that this charge is untenable, because it rests on the confusion between (1) the status of physically-registered information as a *bona fide advance-indicator* with (2) the *epistemic use* which a sentient human makes of this indicator state when believing in a corresponding prediction. As well say that a sudden barometric drop is not an advance indicator of an impending storm, unless a human being makes epistemic use of that sudden drop. Or that a geological trace is *not* a *retrodictive* indicator, unless a human interprets it as warrant for a retrodiction.[2] It is therefore unavailing to object to me that when a human being makes a prediction, he is *thinking* of the future, whereas when a computer produces a series of marks on a tape, there is no *conscious* anticipation of anything by the computer.

I have emphasized that the missile's reception of radiation which alters the components of its motion so as to render it target-directed does not constitute the reception by the missile of the predictive information *as such*. And I made this point in my 1956 paper by speaking *metaphorically* of the communication of "a new set of instructions" to the missile (p. 240). I therefore quite agree with Professor Buck that the reception of the altering influence by the missile is much more akin to Jones' reception of an order based on a prediction by another person who does *not* bring the prediction to Jones' attention, than it is to the case of the release of an economic prediction to the wheat growers who then believe it and act on it. But this is not at all damaging to my contention. Furthermore, I prefer to forego the analogy with acting on orders along with my complete disavowal of any analogy to acting on beliefs. For logically the analogy of acting on orders is a slippery slope, since it could be maintained quite rightly that acting on orders *involves* acting on beliefs which are distinct from the orders acted upon.

I therefore agree with Professor Buck that beliefs do indeed play a causal role in the stultification of a social prediction. And I allowed for this fact *to the extent required by my critique of Merton* when I spoke of the economic forecast as having "the effect of instructing the wheat growers to alter their planting intentions" while speaking of the computer's communicating a new set of instructions to the missile.

It would seem, therefore, that Professor Buck's interesting observations do not constitute a basis for rejecting my assertion that advance information can be causally relevant

[2] For a more detailed discussion of the properties of advance indicators and of retrodictive indicators, cf. A. Grünbaum, *Philosophical Problems of Space and Time*, Alfred A. Knopf, New York, 1963, Chapter 9, Section A.

to a stultifying kind of outcome in purely physical no less than in sociological contexts. And hence I invite his assent to this proposition.

References

GRÜNBAUM, A., "Historical Determinism, Social Activism, and Predictions in the Social Sciences", *The British Journal for the Philosophy of Science* 7 (1956).

MERTON, R. K., *Social Theory and Social Structure*, Glencoe, 1949.

Rejoinder to Grünbaum

ROGER C. BUCK

Professor Grünbaum has a number of kind things to say about my analysis of reflexive predictions. All of these I much appreciate. After saying them he turns his attention, quite properly, to the issue which divides us. I shall do likewise.

Grünbaum and I appear to be engaged in a polite exercise of talking past each other. The issue between us is elusive. And it is so largely because we appear to be in disagreement as to "the precise sense of Merton's denial of the existence of self-stultifying predictions among predictions about the world of nature." (p. 370)[1] And even this formulation of Grünbaum's may further muddy the waters. For neither I nor Merton is interested in denying the existence of *such* predictions. A prediction of the quantity of next year's wheat crop may well be a prediction "*about* the world of nature." The crucial question, as I see it, is not what the prediction is *about*. A prediction is self-stultifying in a sense which qualifies it as what I call a "reflexive prediction" in virtue of the causal mechanisms which mediate between the event which is the issuance of that prediction and the non-occurrence of the event predicted. If these causal mechanisms involve that people come to believe the prediction, if their holding such beliefs is a necessary or at least a non-redundant element in the set of conditions for the prediction's failure — then it is reflexive and self-stultifying. The subject matter of the prediction, what it is "about," is irrelevant here. Indeed the subject matter could very well be the behavior of missiles. The use of the expressions "physical prediction" and "social prediction" serves to obscure this same issue. That a prediction is physical or social, in the sense of its subject matter, guarantees nothing about its capacity to qualify as reflexive.

Debate over Merton's intentions is perhaps idle. I took him to be setting forth a sensible claim, which he then erroneously abandoned in the light of Grünbaum's counter-example. In his "Comments" Grünbaum appears to take Merton's claim as one which is indefensible on the face of it. Consider an automatic sprinkling system for fire protection, equipped with Monel metal plugs which melt as soon as a fire gets started. This melting of the Monel metal plugs seems to be, in Grünbaum's sense, a "bona fide advance indicator" of approaching conflagration. Such melting could have an epistemic use, which must indeed be distinguished from its status as a mere physical indicator. If the system is working properly the melting of the plugs will be followed by an outpouring of water (or foaming chemical), and the fire will be extinguished. But here surely we have "the existence in a purely physical context of advance information or predictions [in a non-epistemic sense, of course] which are *causally relevant* to a *contrary* outcome . . ." (p. 370).[2]

It is hard to believe that Grünbaum supposed Merton's denial to entail the claim that such well-known devices as automatic sprinkling systems do not exist. Yet he now seems so to construe that denial. It is even harder to believe that Merton would wish to be so construed. In any event, I did not so understand him. In the light of Merton's examples of self-fulfilling and self-frustrating prophecies I took him to hold, as I do, that in such cases the holding of a *predictive belief* must be causally relevant to the occurrence or non-occurrence of what is predicted. Thus when he accepted Grünbaum's counter-example I supposed that he saw the missile's behavior as, in relevant respects, analogous to acting on a belief. One could hardly suppose that the Monel metal plugs melt because they believe there will otherwise be a damaging fire. But one might find it less unnatural to speak, analogically, of a complicated, electronically controlled servomechanism as believing something or other. In any event, this line of

[1] [*Page 163, this volume. Editor's note.*]

[2] [*ibid, page 163.*]

reasoning led me to my exploration of the differences between acting on a belief and acting on orders, and to my eventual rejection of Grünbaum's counter-example. It is certainly a bona fide counter-example to the thesis Grünbaum now attributes to Merton.

Grünbaum invites my assent to the proposition that "advance information [non-epistemic, of course] can be causally relevant to a stultifying kind of outcome in purely physical no less than in sociological contexts," (p. 372)[3]. I gladly assent! There are indeed, automatic sprinkling systems!

[3] [*ibid, page 165.*]

On the Alleged Inferiority of the Social Sciences 15

Are the Social Sciences Really Inferior?

FRITZ MACHLUP

If we ask whether the "social sciences" are "really inferior," let us first make sure that we understand each part of the question.

"*Inferior*" to what? Of course to the natural sciences. "Inferior" in what respect? It will be our main task to examine all the "respects," all the scores on which such inferiority has been alleged. I shall enumerate them presently.

The adverb "*really*" which qualifies the adjective "inferior" refers to allegations made by some scientists, scholars, and laymen. But it refers also to the "inferiority complex" which I have noted among many social scientists. A few years ago I wrote an essay entitled "The Inferiority Complex of the Social Sciences."[1] In that essay I said that "an inferiority complex may or may not be justified by some 'objective' standards," and I went on to discuss the consequences which "the *feeling* of inferiority" — conscious or subconscious — has for the behavior of the social scientists who are suffering from it. I did not then discuss whether the complex has an objective basis, that is, whether the social sciences are "really" inferior. This is our question to-day.

The subject noun would call for a long disquisition. What is meant by "*social sciences,*" what is included, what is not included? Are they the same as what others have referred to as the "moral sciences," the "Geisteswissenschaften," the "cultural sciences," the "behavioral sciences"? Is Geography, or the part of it that is called "Human Geography," a social science? Is History a social science — or perhaps even *the* social science *par excellence*, as some philosophers have contended? We shall not spend time on this business of defining and classifying. A few remarks may later be necessary in connection with some points of methodology, but by and large we shall not bother here with a definition of "social sciences" and with drawing boundary lines around them.

The Grounds of Comparison

The social sciences and the natural sciences are compared and contrasted on many scores, and the discussions are often quite unsystematic. If we try to review them systematically, we shall encounter a good deal of overlap and unavoidable duplication. None the less, it will help if we enumerate in advance some of the grounds of comparison most often mentioned, grounds on which the social sciences are judged to come out "second best":

1. Invariability of observations
2. Objectivity of observations and explanations
3. Verifiability of hypotheses
4. Exactness of findings
5. Measurability of phenomena
6. Constancy of numerical relationships
7. Predictability of future events
8. Distance from every-day experience
9. Standards of admission and requirements

We shall examine all these comparisons.

Invariability of Observations

The idea is that you cannot have much of a science unless things recur, unless phenomena

From *The Southern Economic Journal*, 27:3 (January, 1961), pp. 173–184.

[1] Published in *On Freedom and Free Enterprise: Essays in Honor of Ludwig von Mises*, Mary Sennholz, ed. (Princeton: Van Nostrand, 1956), pp. 161–172.

repeat themselves. In nature we find many factors and conditions "invariant." Do we in society? Are not conditions in society changing all the time, and so fast that most events are unique, each quite different from anything that has happened before? Or can one rely on the saying that "history repeats itself" with sufficient invariance to permit generalizations about social events?

There is a great deal of truth, and important truth, in this comparison. Some philosophers were so impressed with the invariance of nature and the variability of social phenomena that they used this difference as the criterion in the definitions of natural and cultural sciences. Following Windelband's distinction between generalizing ("nomothetic") and individualizing ("ideographic") propositions, the German philosopher Heinrich Rickert distinguished between the generalizing sciences of nature and the individualizing sciences of cultural phenomena; and by individualizing sciences he meant historical sciences.[2] In order to be right, he redefined both "nature" and "history" by stating that reality is "nature" if we deal with it in terms of the *general* but becomes "history" if we deal with it in terms of the *unique*. To him, geology was largely history, and economics, most similar to physics, was a natural science. This implies a rejection of the contention that all fields which are normally called social sciences suffer from a lack of invariance; indeed, economics is here considered so much a matter of immutable laws of nature that it is handed over to the natural sciences.

This is not satisfactory, nor does it dispose of the main issue that natural phenomena provide *more* invariance than social phenomena. The main difference lies probably in the number of factors that must be taken into account in explanations and predictions of natural and social events. Only a small number of reproducible facts will normally be involved in a physical explanation or prediction. A much larger number of facts, some of them probably unique historical events, will be found relevant in an explanation or prediction of economic or other social events. This is true, and methodological devices will not do away with the difference. But it is, of course, only a difference in degree.

The physicist Robert Oppenheimer once raised the question whether, if the universe is a *unique* phenomenon, we may assume that *universal* or *general* propositions can be formulated about it. Economists of the Historical School insisted on treating each "stage" or phase of economic society as a completely unique one, not permitting the formulation of universal propositions. Yet, in the physical world, phenomena are not quite so homogeneous as many have liked to think; and in the social world, phenomena are not quite so heterogeneous as many have been afraid they are. (If they were, we could not even have generalized concepts of social events and words naming them.) In any case, where reality seems to show a bewildering number of variations, we construct an ideal world of abstract models in which we create enough homogeneity to permit us to apply reason and deduce the implied consequences of assumed constellations. This artificial homogenization of types of phenomena is carried out in natural and social sciences alike.

There is thus no difference in invariance in the sequences of events in nature and in society as long as we theorize about them — because in the abstract models homogeneity is assumed. There is only a difference of degree in the variability of phenomena of nature and society if we talk about the real world — as long as heterogeneity is not reduced by means of deliberate "controls." There is a third world, between the abstract world of theory and the real unmanipulated world, namely, the artificial world of the experimental laboratory. In this world there is less variability than in the real world and more than in the model world. But this third world does not exist in most of the social sciences (nor in all natural sciences). We shall see later that the mistake is often made

[2] Heinrich Rickert. *Die Grenzen der naturwissenschaftlichen Begriffsbildung* (Tübingen: Mohr-Siebeck, 1902).

of comparing the artificial laboratory world of manipulated nature with the real world of unmanipulated society.

We conclude on this point of comparative invariance, that there is indeed a difference between natural and social sciences, and that the difference — apart from the possibility of laboratory experiments — lies chiefly in the number of relevant factors, and hence of possible combinations, to be taken into account for explaining or predicting events occurring in the real world.

Objectivity of Observations and Explanations

The idea behind a comparison between the "objectivity" of observations and explorations in the natural and social sciences may be conveyed by an imaginary quotation: "Science must be objective and not affected by value judgments; but the social sciences are inherently concerned with values and, hence, they lack the disinterested objectivity of science." True? Frightfully muddled. The trouble is that the problem of "subjective value," which is at the very root of the social sciences, is quite delicate and has in fact confused many, including some fine scholars.

To remove confusion one must separate the different meanings of "value" and the different ways in which they relate to the social sciences, particularly economics. I have distinguished eleven different kinds of value-reference in economics, but have enough sense to spare you this exhibition of my pedagogic dissecting zeal. But we cannot dispense entirely with the problem and overlook the danger of confusion. Thus, I offer you a bargain and shall reduce my distinctions from eleven to four. I am asking you to keep apart the following four meanings in which value judgment may come into our present discussion: (a) The analyst's judgment may be biased for one reason or another, perhaps because his views of the social "Good" or his personal pecuniary interests in the practical use of his findings interfere with the proper scientific detachment. (b) Some normative issues may be connected with the problem under investigation, perhaps ethical judgments which may color some of the investigator's incidental pronouncements — obiter dicta — without however causing a bias in his reported findings of his research. (c) The interest in solving the problems under investigation is surely affected by values since, after all, the investigator selects his problems because he believes that their solution would be of value. (d) The investigator in the social sciences has to explain his observations as results of human actions which can be interpreted only with reference to motives and purposes of the actors, that is, to values entertained by them.

With regard to the first of these possibilities, some authorities have held that the social sciences may more easily succumb to temptation and may show obvious biases. The philosopher Morris Cohen, for example, spoke of "the subjective difficulty of maintaining scientific detachment in the study of human affairs. Few human beings can calmly and with equal fairness consider both sides of a question such as socialism, free love, or birth-control."[3] This is quite true, but one should not forget similar difficulties in the natural sciences. Remember the difficulties which, in deference to religious values, biologists had in discussions of evolution and, going further back, the troubles of astronomers in discussions of the heliocentric theory and of geologists in discussions of the age of the earth. Let us also recall that only 25 years ago, German mathematicians and physicists rejected "Jewish" theorems and theories, including physical relativity, under the pressure of nationalistic values, and only ten years ago Russian biologists stuck to a mutation theory which was evidently affected by political values. I do not know whether one cannot detect in our own period here in the United States an association between political views and scien-

[3] Morris Cohen, *Reason and Nature: An Essay on the Meaning of Scientific Method* (New York: Harcourt, Brace, 1931), p. 348.

tific answers to the question of the genetic dangers from fallout and from other nuclear testing.

Apart from political bias, there have been cases of real cheating in science. Think of physical anthropology and its faked Piltdown Man. That the possibility of deception is not entirely beyond the pale of experimental scientists can be gathered from a splendid piece of fiction, a recent novel, *The Affair*, by C. P. Snow, the well-known Cambridge don.

Having said all this about the possibility of bias existing in the presentation of evidence and findings in the natural sciences, we should hasten to admit that not a few economists, especially when concerned with current problems and the interpretation of recent history, are given to "lying with statistics." It is hardly a coincidence if labor economists choose one base year and business economists choose another base year when they compare wage increases and price increases; or if for their computations of growth rates expert witnesses for different political parties choose different statistical series and different base years. This does not indicate that the social sciences are in this respect "superior" or "inferior" to the natural sciences. Think of physicists, chemists, medical scientists, psychiatrists, etc., appearing as expert witnesses in court litigation to testify in support of their clients' cases. In these instances the scientists are in the role of analyzing concrete individual events, of interpreting recent history. If there is a difference at all between the natural and social sciences in this respect, it may be that economists these days have more opportunities to present biased findings than their colleagues in the physical sciences. But even this may not be so. I may underestimate the opportunities of scientists and engineers to submit expert testimonies with paid-for bias.

The second way in which value judgments may affect the investigator does not involve any bias in his findings or his reports on his findings. But ethical judgments may be so closely connected with his problems that he may feel impelled to make evaluative pronouncements on the normative issues in question. For example, scientists may have strong views about vivisection, sterilization, abortion, hydrogen bombs, biological warfare, etc., and may express these views in connection with their scientific work. Likewise, social scientists may have strong views about the right to privacy, free enterprise, free markets, equality of income, old-age pensions, socialized medicine, segregation, education, etc., and they may express these views in connection with the results of their research. Let us repeat that this need not imply that their findings are biased. There is no difference on this score between the natural and the social sciences. The research and its results may be closely connected with values of all sorts, and value judgments may be espressed, and yet the objectivity of the research and of the reports on the findings need not be impaired.

The third way value judgments affect research is in the selection of the project, in the choice of the subject for investigation. This is unavoidable and the only question is what kinds of value and whose values are paramount. If research is financed by foundations or by the government, the values may be those which the chief investigator believes are held by the agencies or committees that pass on the allocation of funds. If the research is not aided by outside funds, the project may be chosen on the basis of what the investigator believes to be "social values," that is, he chooses a project that may yield solutions to problems supposed to be important for society. Society wants to know how to cure cancer, how to prevent hay fever, how to eliminate mosquitoes, how to get rid of crab grass and weeds, how to restrain juvenile delinquency, how to reduce illegitimacy and other accidents, how to increase employment, to raise real wages, to aid farmers, to avoid price inflation, and so on, and so forth. These examples suggest that the value component in the project selection is the same in the natural and in the social sciences. There are instances, thank God, in which the investigator selects his project out of sheer intellectual curiosity and does not give "two hoots" about the social importance of his findings. Still, to satisfy curiosity is a value too, and indeed a very potent one. We must not fail to mention the case of the graduate student who lacks imagination as well as intellectual curiosity and undertakes a project just because it is the only one he can think of, though neither he nor anybody else finds it interesting, let alone important. We may accept this case as the exception to the rule. Such exceptions probably are equally rare in the natural and the social sciences.

Now we come to the one real difference, the fourth of our value-references. Social phenomena are defined as results of human action, and all human action is defined as motivated action. Hence, social phenomena are explained only if they are attributed to definite types of action which are "understood" in terms of the values motivating those who decide and act. This concern with values — not values which the investigator entertains but values he understands to be effective in guiding the actions which bring about the events he studies — is the crucial difference between the social sciences and the natural sciences. To explain the motion of molecules, the fusion or fission of atoms, the paths of celestial bodies, the growth or mutation of organic matter, etc., the scientist will not ask why the molecules want to move about, why atoms decide to merge or to split, why Venus has chosen her particular orbit, why certain cells are anxious to divide. The social scientist, however, is not doing his job unless he explains changes in the circulation of money by going back to the decisions of the spenders and hoarders, explains company mergers by the goals that may have persuaded managements and boards of corporate bodies to take such actions, explains the location of industries by calculations of such things as transportation costs and wage differentials, and economic growth by propensities to save, to invest, to innovate, to procreate or prevent procreation, and so on. My social-science examples were all from economics, but I might just as well have taken examples from sociology, cultural anthropology, political science, etc., to show that explanation in the social sciences regularly requires the interpretation of phenomena in terms of idealized motivations of the idealized persons whose idealized actions bring forth the phenomena under investigation.

An example may further elucidate the difference between the explanatory principles in non-human nature and human society. A rock does not say to us: "I am a beast,"[4] nor does it say: "I came here because I did not like it up there near the glaciers, where I used to live; here I like it fine, especially this nice view of the valley." We do not inquire into value judgments of rocks. But we must not fail to take account of valuations of humans; social phenomena must be explained as the results of motivated human actions.

The greatest authorities on the methodology of the social sciences have referred to this fundamental postulate as the requirement of "subjective interpretation," and all such interpretation of "subjective meanings" implies references to values motivating actions. This has of course nothing to do with value judgments impairing the "scientific objectivity" of the investigators or affecting them in any way that would make their findings suspect. Whether the postulate of subjective interpretation which *differentiates* the social sciences from the natural sciences should be held to make them either "inferior" or "superior" is a matter of taste.

Verifiability of Hypotheses

It is said that verification is not easy to come by in the social sciences, while it is the chief business of the investigator in the natural sciences. This is true, though many do not fully understand what is involved and, consequently, are apt to exaggerate the difference.

One should distinguish between what a British philosopher has recently called "high-

[4] Hans Kelsen, *Allgamiene Staatslehre* (Berlin: Springer, 1925), p. 129. Quoted with illuminating comments in Alfred Schütz, *Der sinnhafte Aufbau der sozialen Welt* (Wien: Springer, 1932).

level hypotheses" and "low-level generalizations."[5] The former are postulated and can never be *directly* verified; a single high-level hypothesis cannot even be *indirectly* verified, because from one hypothesis standing alone nothing follows. Only a *whole system* of hypotheses can be tested by deducing from some set of general postulates and some set of specific assumptions the logical consequences, and comparing these with records of observations regarded as the approximate empirical counterparts of the specific assumptions and specific consequences.[6] This holds for both the natural and the social sciences. (There is no need for *direct* tests of the fundamental postulates in physics — such as the laws of conservation of energy, of angular momentum, of motion — or of the fundamental postulates in economics — such as the laws of maximizing utility and profits.)

While entire theoretical systems and the low-level generalizations derived from them are tested in the natural sciences, there exist at any one time many unverified hypotheses. This holds especially with regard to theories of creation and evolution in such fields as biology, geology, and cosmogony; for example (if my reading is correct), of the theory of the expanding universe, the dust-cloud hypothesis of the formation of stars and planets, of the low-temperature or high-temperature theories of the formation of the earth, of the various (conflicting) theories of granitization, etc. In other words, where the natural sciences deal with non-reproducible occurrences and with sequences for which controlled experiments cannot be devised, they have to work with hypotheses which remain untested for a long time, perhaps forever.

In the social sciences, low-level generalizations about recurring events are being tested all the time. Unfortunately, often several conflicting hypotheses are consistent with the observed facts and there are no crucial experiments to eliminate some of the hypotheses. But everyone of us could name dozens of propositions that have been disconfirmed, and this means that the verification process has done what it is supposed to do. The impossibility of controlled experiments and the relatively large number of relevant variables are the chief obstacles to more efficient verification in the social sciences. This is not an inefficiency on the part of our investigators, but it lies in the nature of things.

Exactness of Findings

Those who claim that the social sciences are "less exact" than the natural sciences often have a very incomplete knowledge of either of them, and a rather hazy idea of the meaning of "exactness." Some mean by exactness measurability. This we shall discuss under a separate heading. Others mean accuracy and success in predicting future events, which is something different. Others mean reducibility to mathematical language. The meaning of exactness best founded in intellectual history is the possibility of constructing a theoretical system of idealized models containing abstract constructs of variables and of relations between variables, from which most or all propositions concerning particular connections can be deduced. Such systems do not exist in several of the natural sciences — for example, in several areas of biology — while they do exist in at least one of the social sciences: economics.

We cannot foretell the development of any discipline. We cannot say now whether there will soon or ever be a "unified theory" of political science, or whether the piecemeal generalizations which sociology has yielded thus far can be integrated into one comprehensive theoretical system. In any case, the quality of "exactness," if this is what is meant by it, cannot be attributed to all the natural sciences nor denied to all the social sciences.

[5] Richard B. Braithwaite, *Scientific Explanation: A Study of the Function of Theory, Probability and Law in Science* (Cambridge, Mass.: Harvard University Press, 1953).

[6] Fritz Machlup, "The Problem of Verification in Economics," *Southern Economic Journal*, July 1955.

Measurability of Phenomena

If the availability of numerical data were in and of itself an advantage in scientific investigation, economics would be on the top of all sciences. Economics is the only field in which the raw data of experience are already in numerical form. In other fields the analyst must first quantify and measure before he can obtain data in numerical form. The physicist must weigh and count and must invent and build instruments from which numbers can be read, numbers standing for certain relations pertaining to essentially non-numerical observations. Information which first appears only in some such form as "relatively" large, heavy, hot, fast, is later transformed into numerical data by means of measuring devices such as rods, scales, thermometers, speedometers. The economist can begin with numbers. What he observes are prices and sums of moneys. He can start out with numerical data given to him without the use of measuring devices.

The compilation of masses of data calls for resources which only large organizations, frequently only the government, can muster. This, in my opinion, is unfortunate because it implies that the availability of numerical data is associated with the extent of government intervention in economic affairs, and there is therefore an inverse relation between economic information and individual freedom.

Numbers, moreover, are not all that is needed. To be useful, the numbers must fit the concepts used in theoretical propositions or in comprehensive theoretical systems. This is rarely the case with regard to the raw data of economics, and thus the economic analyst still has the problem of obtaining comparable figures by transforming his raw data into adjusted and corrected ones, acceptable as the operational counterparts of the abstract constructs in his theoretical models. His success in this respect has been commendable, but very far short of what is needed; it cannot compare with the success of the physicist in developing measurement techniques yielding numerical data that can serve as operational counterparts of constructs in the models of theoretical physics.

Physics, however, does not stand for all natural sciences, nor economics for all social sciences. There are several fields, in both natural and social sciences, where quantification of relevant factors has not been achieved and may never be achieved. If Lord Kelvin's phrase, "Science is Measurement," were taken seriously, science might miss some of the most important problems. There is no way of judging whether non-quantifiable factors are more prevalent in nature or in society. The common reference to the "hard" facts of nature and the "soft" facts with which the student of society has to deal seems to imply a judgment about measurability. "Hard" things can be firmly gripped and measured, "soft" things cannot. There may be something to this. The facts of nature are perceived with our "senses," the facts of society are interpreted in terms of the "sense" they make in a motivational analysis. However, this contrast is not quite to the point, because the "sensory" experience of the natural scientist refers to the *data*, while the "sense" interpretation by the social scientist of the ideal-typical inner experience of the members of society refers to basic *postulates* and intervening variables.

The conclusion, that we cannot be sure about the prevalence of non-quantifiable factors in natural and social sciences, still holds.

Constancy of Numerical Relationships

On this score there can be no doubt that some of the natural sciences have got something which none of the social sciences has got: "constants," unchanging numbers expressing unchanging relationships between measurable quantities.

The discipline with the largest number of constants is, of course, physics. Examples are the velocity of light ($c = 2.99776 \times 10^{10}$ cm/sec), Planck's constant for the smallest increment of spin or angular momentum ($h = 6.624 \times 10^{-27}$ erg. sec), the gravitation constant ($G = 6.6 \times 10^{-8}$ dyne cm^2 gram^{-2}), the Coulomb constant ($e = 4.8025 \times 10^{-10}$ units), proton mass ($M = 1.672 \times 10^{-24}$ gram), the ratio of proton mass to electron mass ($M/m = 1836.13$), the fine-structure constant ($\alpha^{-1} = 137.0371$). Some of these constants are postulated (conventional), others (the last two) are empirical, but this makes no difference for our purposes. Max Planck contended, the postulated "universal constants" were not just "invented for reasons of practical convenience, but have forced themselves upon us irresistibly because of the agreement between the results of all relevant measurements."[7]

I know of no numerical constant in any of the social sciences. In economics we have been computing certain ratios which, however, are found to vary relatively widely with time and place. The annual income-velocity of circulation of money, the marginal propensities to consume, to save, to import, the elasticities of demand for various goods, the savings ratios, capital-output ratios, growth rates — none of these has remained constant over time or is the same for different countries. They all have varied, some by several hundred per cent of the lowest value. Of course, one has found "limits" of these variations, but what does this mean in comparison with the virtually immutable physical constants? When it was noticed that the ratio between labor income and national income in some countries has varied by "only" ten per cent over some twenty years, some economists were so perplexed that they spoke of the "constancy" of the relative shares. (They hardly realized that the 10 per cent variation in that ratio was the same as about a 25 per cent variation in the ratio between labor income and non-labor income.) That the income velocity of circulation of money has rarely risen above 3 or fallen below 1 is surely interesting, but this is anything but a "constant." That the marginal propensity to consume cannot in the long run be above 1 is rather obvious, but in the short run it may vary between .7 and 1.2 or even more. That saving ratios (to national income) have never been above 15 per cent in any country regardless of the economic system (communistic or capitalistic, regulated or essentially free) is a very important fact; but saving ratios have been known to be next to zero, or even negative, and the variations from time to time and country to country are very large indeed.

Sociologists and actuaries have reported some "relatively stable" ratios — accident rates, birth rates, crime rates, etc. — but the "stability" is only relative to the extreme variability of other numerical ratios. Indeed, most of these ratios are subject to "human engineering," to governmental policies designed to change them, and hence they are not even thought of as constants.

The verdict is confirmed: while there are important numerical constants in the natural sciences, there are none in the social sciences.

Predictability of Future Events

Before we try to compare the success which natural and social sciences have had in correctly predicting future events, a few important distinctions should be made. We must distinguish hypothetical or conditional predictions from unconditional predictions or forecasts. And among the former we must distinguish those where all the stated conditions can be controlled, those where all the stated conditions can be either controlled or unambiguously ascertained before the event, and finally those where some of the stated conditions can neither be controlled nor ascertained early enough (if at all). A conditional prediction of the third kind is such an "iffy" statement that it may be of no use unless one can know with confidence that it would be highly improbable for these problematic conditions (uncontrollable and not ascertainable before the event) to interfere with the prediction. A different kind of distinction concerns the numerical definiteness of the prediction: one may predict that a certain magnitude (a) will change, (b) will

[7] Max Planck, *Scientific Autobiography and Other Papers* (New York: Philosophical Library, 1949), p. 173.

increase, (c) will increase by at least so-and-so much, (d) will increase within definite limits, or (e) will increase by a definite amount. Similarly, the prediction may be more or less definite with respect to the time within which it is supposed to come true. A prediction without any time specification is worthless.

Some people are inclined to believe that the natural sciences can beat the social sciences on any count, in unconditional predictions as well as in conditional predictions fully specified as to definite conditions, exact degree and time of fulfilment. But what they have in mind are the laboratory experiments of the natural sciences, in which predictions have proved so eminently successful; and then they look at the poor record social scientists have had in predicting future events in the social world which they observe but cannot control. This comparison is unfair and unreasonable. The artificial laboratory world in which the experimenter tries to control all conditions as best as he can is different from the real world of nature. If a comparison is made, it must be between predictions of events in the real natural world and in the real social world.

Even for the real world, we should distinguish between predictions of events which we try to bring about by design and predictions of events in which we have no part at all. The teams of physicists and engineers who have been designing and developing machines and apparatuses are not very successful in predicting their performance when the design is still new. The record of predictions of the paths of moon shots and space missiles has been rather spotty. The so-called "bugs" that have to be worked out in any new contraption are nothing but predictions gone wrong. After a while predictions become more reliable. The same is true, however, with predictions concerning the performance of organized social institutions. For example, if I take an envelope, put a certain address on it and a certain postage stamp, and deposit it in a certain box on the street, I can predict that after three or four days it will be delivered at a certain house thousands of miles away. This prediction and any number of similar predictions will prove correct with a remarkably high frequency. And you don't have to be a social scientist to make such successful predictions about an organized social machinery, just as you don't have to be a natural scientist to predict the result of your pushing the electric-light switch or of similar manipulations of a well-tried mechanical or electrical apparatus.

There are more misses and fewer hits with regard to predictions of completely unmanipulated and unorganized reality. Meteorologists have a hard time forecasting the weather for the next 24 hours or two or three days. There are too many variables involved and it is too difficult to obtain complete information about some of them. Economists are only slightly better in forecasting employment and income, exports and tax revenues for the next six months or for a year or two. Economists, moreover, have better excuses for their failures because of unpredictable "interferences" by governmental agencies or power groups which may even be influenced by the forecasts of the economists and may operate to defeat their predictions. On the other hand, some of the predictions may be self-fulfilling in that people, learning of the predictions, act in ways which bring about the predicted events. One might say that economists ought to be able to include the "psychological" effects of their communications among the variables of their models and take full account of these influences. There are, however, too many variables, personal and political, involved to make it possible to allow for all effects which anticipations, and anticipations of anticipations, may have upon the end results. To give an example of a simple self-defeating prediction from another social science: traffic experts regularly forecast the number of automobile accidents and fatalities that are going to occur over holiday weekends, and at the same time they hope that their forecasts will influence drivers to be more careful and thus to turn the forecasts into exaggerated fears.

We must not be too sanguine about the success of social scientists in making either unconditional forecasts or conditional predictions. Let us admit that we are not good in the business of prophecy and let us be modest in our claims about our ability to predict. After all, it is not our stupidity which hampers us, but chiefly our lack of information, and when one has to make do with bad guesses in lieu of information the success cannot be great. But there is a significant difference between the natural sciences and the social sciences in this respect: Experts in the natural sciences usually do not try to do what they know they cannot do; and nobody expects them to do it. They would never undertake to predict the number of fatalities in a train wreck that might happen under certain conditions during the next year. They do not even predict next year's explosions and epidemics, floods and mountain slides, earthquakes and water pollution. Social scientists, for some strange reason, are expected to foretell the future and they feel badly if they fail.

Distance from Every-Day Experience

Science is, almost by definition, what the layman cannot understand. Science is knowledge accessible only to superior minds with great effort. What everybody can know cannot be science.

A layman could not undertake to read and grasp a professional article in physics or chemistry or biophysics. He would hardly be able to pronounce many of the words and he might not have the faintest idea of what the article was all about. Needless to say, it would be out of the question for a layman to pose as an expert in a natural science. On the other hand, a layman might read articles in descriptive economics, sociology, anthropology, social psychology. Although in all these fields technical jargon is used which he could not really understand, he might *think* that he knows the sense of the words and grasps the meanings of the sentences; he might even be inclined to poke fun at some of the stuff. He believes he is — from his own experience and from his reading of newspapers and popular magazines — familiar with the subject matter of the social sciences. In consequence, he has little respect for the analyses which the social scientists present.

The fact that social scientists use less Latin and Greek words and less mathematics than their colleagues in the natural science departments and, instead, use everyday words in special, and often quite technical, meanings may have something to do with the attitude of the layman. The sentences of the sociologist, for example, make little sense if the borrowed words are understood in their non-technical, every-day meaning. But if the layman is told of the special meanings that have been bestowed upon his words, he gets angry or condescendingly amused.

But we must not exaggerate this business of language and professional jargon because the problem really lies deeper. The natural sciences talk about nuclei, isotopes, gallaxies, benzoids, drosophilas, chromosomes, dodecahedrons, Pleistocene fossils, and the layman marvels that anyone really cares. The social sciences, however, — and the layman usually finds this out — talk about — him. While he never identifies himself with a positron, a pneumococcus, a coenzyme, or a digital computer, he does identify himself with many of the ideal types presented by the social scientist, and he finds that the likeness is poor and the analysis "consequently" wrong.

The fact that the social sciences deal with man in his relations with fellow man brings them so close to man's own everyday experience that he cannot see the analysis of this experience as something above and beyond him. Hence he is suspicious of the analysts and disappointed in what he supposes to be a portrait of him.

Standards of Admission and Requirements

High-school physics is taken chiefly by the students with the highest I.Q.'s. At college the students majoring in physics, and again at graduate school the students of physics, are reported to have on the average higher I.Q.'s than those in other fields. This gives physics and physicists a special prestige in schools and universities, and this prestige carries over to all natural sciences and puts them somehow above the social sciences. This is rather odd, since the average quality of students in different departments depends chiefly on departmental policies, which may vary from institution to institution. The preeminence of physics is rather general because of the requirement of calculus. In those universities in which the economics department requires calculus, the students of economics rank as high as the students of physics in intelligence, achievement, and prestige.

The lumping of all natural sciences for comparisons of student quality and admission standards is particularly unreasonable in view of the fact that at many colleges some of the natural science departments, such as biology and geology, attract a rather poor average quality of student. (This is not so in biology at universities with many applicants for a premedical curriculum.) The lumping of all social sciences in this respect is equally wrong, since the differences in admission standards and graduation requirements among departments, say between economics, history, and sociology, may be very great. Many sociology departments have been notorious for their role as refuge for mentally underprivileged undergraduates. Given the propensity to overgeneralize, it is no wonder then that the social sciences are being regarded as the poor relations of the natural sciences and as disciplines for which students who cannot qualify for *the* sciences are still good enough.

Since I am addressing economists, and since economics departments, at least at some of the better colleges and universities, are maintaining standards as high as physics and mathematics departments, it would be unfair to level exhortations at my present audience. But perhaps we should try to convince our colleagues in all social science departments of the disservice they are doing to their fields and to the social sciences at large by admitting and keeping inferior students as majors. Even if some of us think that one can study social sciences without knowing higher mathematics, we should insist on making calculus and mathematical statistics absolute requirements — as a device for keeping away the weakest students.

Despite my protest against improper generalizations, I must admit that averages may be indicative of something or other, and that the average I.Q. of the students in the natural science departments is higher than that of the students in the social science department.[8] No field can be better than the men who work in it. On this score, therefore, the natural sciences would be superior to the social sciences.

The Score Card

We may now summarize the tallies on the nine scores.

1. With respect to the invariability or recurrence of observations, we found that the greater number of variables — of relevant factors — in the social sciences makes for more variation, for less recurrence of exactly the same sequences of events.

2. With respect to the objectivity of observations and explanations, we distinguished several ways in which references to values and value judgments enter scientific activity. Whereas the social sciences have a requirement of "subjective interpretation of value-motivated actions" which does not exist in the natural sciences, this does not affect the proper "scientific objectivity" of the social scientist.

3. With respect to the verifiability of hypotheses, we found that the impossibility of controlled experiments combined with the larger number of relevant variables does make verification in the social sciences more diffi-

[8] The average I.Q. of students receiving bachelor's degrees was, according to a 1954 study, 121 in the biological sciences, and 122 in economics, 127 in the physical sciences, and 119 in business. See Dael Wolfe, *America's Resources of Specialized Talent: The Report of the Commission on Human Resources and Advanced Training* (New York: Harpers, 1954), pp. 319–322.

cult than in most of the natural sciences.

4. With respect to the exactness of the findings, we decided to mean by it the existence of a theoretical system from which most propositions concerning particular connections can be deduced. Exactness in this sense exists in physics and in economics, but much less so in other natural and other social sciences.

5. With respect to the measurability of phenomena, we saw an important difference between the availability of an ample supply of numerical data and the availability of such numerical data as can be used as good counterparts of the constructs in theoretical models. On this score, physics is clearly ahead of all other disciplines. It is doubtful that this can be said about the natural sciences in general relative to the social sciences in general.

6. With respect to the constancy of numerical relationships, we entertained no doubt concerning the existence of constants, postulated or empirical, in physics and in other natural sciences, whereas no numerical constants can be found in the study of society.

7. With respect to the predictability of future events, we ruled out comparisons between the laboratory world of some of the natural sciences and the unmanipulated real world studied by the social sciences. Comparing only the comparable, the real worlds — and excepting the special case of astronomy — we found no essential differences in the predictability of natural and social phenomena.

8. With respect to the distance of scientific from every-day experience, we saw that in linguistic expression as well as in their main concerns the social sciences are so much closer to pre-scientific language and thought that they do not command the respect that is accorded to the natural sciences.

9. With respect to the standards of admission and requirements, we found that they are on the average lower in the social than in the natural sciences.

The last of these scores relates to the current practice of colleges and universities, not to the character of the disciplines. The point before the last, though connected with the character of the social sciences, relates only to the popular appreciation of these disciplines; it does not aid in answering the question whether the social sciences are "really" inferior. Thus the last two scores will not be considered relevant to our question. This leaves seven scores to consider. On four of the six no real differences could be established. But on the other three scores, on "Invariance," "Verifiability," and "Numerical Constants," we found the social sciences to be inferior to the natural sciences.

The Implications of Inferiority

What does it mean if one thing is called "inferior" to another with regard to a particular "quality"? If this "quality" is something that is highly valued in any object, and if the absence of this "quality" is seriously missed regardless of other qualities present, then, but only then, does the noted "inferiority" have any evaluative implications. In order to show that "inferiority" sometimes means very little, I shall present here several statements about differences in particular qualities.

"Champagne is inferior to rubbing alcohol in alcoholic content."

"Beef steak is inferior to strawberry jello in sweetness."

"A violin is inferior to a violoncello in physical weight."

"Chamber music is inferior to band music in loudness."

"Hamlet is inferior to Joe Palooka in appeal to children."

"Sandpaper is inferior to velvet in smoothness."

"Psychiatry is inferior to surgery in ability to effect quick cures."

"Biology is inferior to physics in internal consistency."

It all depends on what you want. Each member in a pair of things is inferior to the other in some respect. In some instances it may be precisely this inferiority that makes the thing desirable. (Sandpaper is wanted *because* of its inferior smoothness.) In other instances the inferiority in a particular respect may be a matter of indifference. (The violin's inferiority in physical weight neither adds to nor detracts from its relative value.) Again in other instances the particular inferiority may be regrettable, but nothing can be done about it and the thing in question may be wanted none the less. (We need psychiatry, however much we regret that in general it cannot effect quick cures; and we need biology, no matter how little internal consistency has been attained in its theoretical systems.)

We have stated that the social sciences are inferior to the natural sciences in some respects, for example, in verifiability. This is regrettable. If propositions cannot be readily tested, this calls for more judgment, more patience, more ingenuity. But does it mean much else?

The Crucial Question: "So What?"

What is the pragmatic meaning of the statement in question? If I learn, for example, that drug E is inferior to drug P as a cure for hay fever, this means that, if I want such a cure, I shall not buy drug E. If I am told Mr. A is inferior to Mr. B as an automobile mechanic, I shall avoid using Mr. A when my car needs repair. If I find textbook K inferior to textbook S in accuracy, organization, as well as exposition, I shall not adopt textbook K. In every one of these examples, the statement that one thing is inferior to another makes pragmatic sense. The point is that all these pairs are *alternatives* between which a choice is to be made.

Are the natural sciences and the social sciences alternatives between which we have to choose? If they were, a claim that the social sciences are "inferior" could have the following meanings:

1. We should not study the social sciences.
2. We should not spend money on teaching and research in the social sciences.
3. We should not permit gifted persons to study social sciences and should steer them toward superior pursuits.
4. We should not respect scholars who so imprudently chose to be social scientists.

If one realizes that none of these things could possibly be meant, that every one of these meanings would be preposterous, and that the social sciences and the natural sciences can by no means be regarded as alternatives but, instead, that both are needed and neither can be dispensed with, he can give the inferiority statement perhaps one other meaning:

5. We should do something to improve the social sciences and remedy their defects.

This last interpretation would make sense if the differences which are presented as grounds for the supposed inferiority were "defects" that can be remedied. But they are not. That there are more variety and change in social phenomena; that, because of the large number of relevant variables and the impossibility of controlled experiments, hypotheses in the social sciences cannot be easily verified; and that no numerical constants can be detected in the social world — these are not defects to be remedied but fundamental properties to be grasped, accepted, and taken into account. Because of these properties research and analysis in the social sciences hold greater complexities and difficulties. If you wish, you may take this to be a greater challenge, rather than a deterrent. To be sure, difficulty and complexity alone are not sufficient reasons for studying certain problems. But the problems presented by the social world are certainly not unimportant. If they are also difficult to tackle, they ought to attract ample resources and the best minds. Today they are getting neither. The social sciences are "really inferior" regarding the place they are accorded by society and the priorities with which financial and human resources are allocated. This inferiority is curable.

Exact vs. Inexact Sciences: A More Instructive Dichotomy?

16

On the Epistemology of the Inexact Sciences

OLAF HELMER
and NICHOLAS RESCHER

The Mythology of Exactness

It is a fiction of long standing that there are two classes of sciences, the exact and the inexact, and that the social sciences by and large are members of the second class — unless and until, like experimental psychology or some parts of economics, they mature to the point where admission to the first class may be granted.

This widely prevalent attitude seems to us fundamentally mistaken; for it finds a difference in principle where there is only one of degree, and it imputes to the so-called exact sciences a procedural rigor which is rarely present in fact. For the sake of a fuller discussion of these points, let us clarify at the very outset the terms "science", "exact science", and "inexact science", as they are intended here.

For an enterprise to be characterized as *scientific* it must have as its purpose the explanation and prediction of phenomena within its subject-matter domain and it must provide such explanation and prediction in a reasoned, and therefore intersubjective, fashion. We speak of an exact science if this reasoning process is formalized in the sense that the terms used are exactly defined and reasoning takes place by formal logico-mathematical derivation of the hypothesis (the statement of the fact to be explained or predicted) from the evidence (the body of knowledge accepted by virtue of being highly confirmed by observation). That an exact science frequently uses mathematical notation and concerns itself about attributes which lend themselves to exact measurement we regard as incidental rather than defining characteristics. The same point applies to the precision, or exactness, of the predictions of which the science may be capable. While precise predictions are indeed to be preferred to vague ones, a discipline which provides predictions of a less precise character, but makes them correctly and in a systematic and reasoned way, must be classified as a science.

In an inexact science, conversely, reasoning is informal; in particular, some of the terminology may, without actually impeding communication, exhibit some inherent vagueness; and reasoning may at least in part rely on reference to intuitively perceived facts or implications. Again, an inexact science rarely uses mathematical notation or employs attributes capable of exact measurement, and as a rule does not make its predictions with great precision and exactitude.

Using the terms as elucidated here — and we believe that this corresponds closely to accepted usage — purely descriptive surveys or summaries, such as the part of history that is mere chronology or, say, purely descriptive botany or geography, are not called *sciences*. History proper, on the other hand, which seeks to explain historical transactions and to establish historical judgments having some degree of generality, is a science; it is in fact largely coincident with political science, except that its practitioners focus their interest

From *Management Science*, 6:1 (October, 1959), pp. 25–52.

on the past while the political scientists' main concern is the present and the future.

As for *exactness*, this qualification, far from being attributable to all of the so-called natural sciences, applies only to a small section of them, in particular to certain subfields of physics, in some of which exactness has even been put to the ultimate test of formal axiomatization. In other branches of physics, such as parts of aerodynamics and of the physics of extreme temperatures, exact procedures are still intermingled with unformalized expertise. Indeed the latter becomes more dominant as we move away from the precise and usually highly abstract core of an exact discipline and towards its applications to the complexities of the real world. Both architecture and medicine are cases in point. Aside from the respective activities of building structures and healing people, both have a theoretical content, — that is, they are predictive and explanatory ("this bridge will not collapse, or has not collapsed, because . . ."; "this patient will exhibit, or has exhibited, such and such symptoms because . . ."). They must therefore properly be called sciences, but they are largely inexact since they rely heavily on informal reasoning processes.

If in addition to these examples we remember the essentially in-between status of such fields as economics and psychology, both of which show abundant evidence of exact derivations as well as reliance on intuitive judgment (exhibiting intermittent use of mathematical symbolism and of measurable attributes and an occasional ability to predict with precision) it should be obvious that there is at present no clear-cut dichotomy between exact and inexact sciences, and, in particular, that inexactness is not a prerogative of the social sciences.

However, leaving aside their present comparative status, it still might be possible to hold the view that there exists an epistemological difference in principle between the social sciences on the one hand and the natural or physical sciences on the other, in the sense that the latter, though not necessarily quite exact as yet, will gradually achieve ultimate exactness, while the former, due to the intangible nature of their subject-matter and the imperfection in principle of their observational data, must of necessity remain inexact. Such a view would be based upon false premises, viz., a wholly misguided application of the exactness vs. inexactness distinction. Indeed, the artificial discrimination between the physical sciences with their (at least in principle) precise terms, exact derivations and reliable predictions as opposed to the vague terms, intuitive insights and virtual unpredictability in the social sciences has retarded the development of the latter immeasurably.

The reason for this defeatist point of view regarding the social sciences may be traceable to a basic misunderstanding of the nature of scientific endeavor. What matters is not whether or to what extent inexactitudes in procedures and predictive capability can eventually be removed; rather it is *objectivity*, i.e., the intersubjectivity of findings independent of any one person's intuitive judgment, which distinguishes science from intuitive guesswork however brilliant. This has nothing to do with the intuitive spark which may be the origin of a new discovery; pure mathematics, whose formal exactness is beyond question, needs that as much as any science. But once a new fact or a new idea has been conjectured, no matter on how intuitive a foundation, it must be capable of objective test and confirmation by anyone. And it is this crucial standard of scientific objectivity rather than any purported criterion of exactitude to which the social sciences must conform.

In rejecting precision of form or method as well as degree of predictability as basic discriminants between the social and the physical sciences it thus remains to be seen whether there might not in fact be a fundamental epistemological difference between them with regard to their ability to live up to the same rigorous standard of objectivity. Our belief is that there is essentially no such difference, in other words, that the social sciences cannot be separated from the physical on methodological grounds. We hope to convince the reader of the validity of our position by offering, in what follows, at least some indications as to how the foundations for a uniform epistemology of all of the inexact sciences might be laid — be they social sciences or "as yet" inexact physical sciences.

Our goal is more modest than that of presenting a comprehensive epistemology of the inexact sciences. We merely wish to outline an epistemological attitude toward them that we would like to see adopted more widely. Since epistemology is concerned with the role of evidence in the attainment of scientific laws and with the scientific procedures implied by that role, we need to re-examine the status of such things as laws, evidence, confirmation, prediction and explanation, with special reference to the case of inexact sciences.

Historical Laws

Let us first take a brief look at historical science in order to obtain some illustrative examples of the form of laws in the social sciences and of the function they perform. An *historical law* may be regarded as a well-confirmed statement concerning the actions of an organized group of men under certain restrictive conditions (such group actions being intended to include those of systems composed conjointly of men and nonhuman instrumentalities under their physical control). Examples of such laws are: "A census takes place in the U. S. in every decade year", "Heretics were persecuted in 17th century Spain", "In the sea fights of sailing vessels in the period 1653–1803, large formations were too cumbersome for effectual control as single units". Such statements share two features of particular epistemological importance and interest: they are *law-like*, and *loose*. These points require elaboration.

To consider law-likeness, let us take for example the statement about the cumbersomeness of large sailing fleets in sea fights. On first view, this statement might seem to be a mere descriptive list of characteristics of certain particular engagements: a shorthand version of a long conjunction of statements about large-scale engagements during the century and a half from Texel (1653) to Trafalgar (1803). This view is incorrect, however, because the statement in question is more than an assertion regarding characteristics of certain actual engagements. Unlike mere descriptions, it can serve to explain developments in cases to which it makes no reference. Furthermore, the statement has counterfactual force. It asserts that in literally any large-scale fleet action fought under the conditions in question (sailing vessels of certain types, with particular modes of armament, and with contemporaneous communications methods) effectual control of a great battle line is hopeless. It is claimed, for example, that had Villeneuve issued from Cadiz some days earlier or later he would all the same have encountered difficulty in the management of the great allied battle fleet of over thirty sail of the line, and Nelson's stratagem of dividing his force into two virtually independent units under prearranged plans would have facilitated effective management equally well as at Trafalgar.

The statement in question is thus no mere descriptive summary of particular events; it functions on the more general plane of law-like statements, specifically, in that it can serve as a basis for explanation, and that it can exert counterfactual force. To be sure, the individual descriptive statements which are known and relevant do provide a part of the appropriate evidence for the historical generalization. But the content of the statement itself lies beyond the sphere of mere description, and in taking this wider role historical laws become marked as genuine law-like statements.

The second important characteristic of historical laws lies in their being "loose". It has been said already that historical laws are (explicitly or obliquely) conditional in their logical form. However, the nature of these conditions is such that they can often not be spelled out fully and completely. For instance, the statement· about sailing fleet tactics has (among others) an implicit or tacit condition relating to the state of naval ordnance in the 18th century. In elaborating such conditions, the historian delineates what is typical of the place and period. The full implications of such reference may be vast and inexhaustible; for instance, in our example, ordnance ramifies *via* metal-working technology into metallurgy, mining, etc. Thus the conditions which are operative in the formulation of an historical law may only be indicated in a general way and are not necessarily (indeed in most cases cannot be expected to be) exhaustively articulated. This characteristic of such laws is here designated as *looseness*.

It is this looseness of its laws which typifies history as an inexact science in the sense in which we have used the term: in a domain whose laws are not fully and precisely articulated there exists a limit to exactitude in terminology and reasoning. In such a sphere, mathematical precision must not be expected. To say this implies no pejorative intent whatever, for the looseness of historical laws is clearly recognized as being due, not to slipshod formulation of otherwise precise facts, but to the fundamental complexities inherent in the conceptual apparatus of the domain.

A consequence of the looseness of historical laws is that they are, not universal, but merely quasi-general in that they admit exceptions. Since the conditions delimiting the area of application of the law are often not exhaustively articulated, a supposed violation of the law may be explicable by showing that a legitimate (but as yet unformulated) precondition of the law's applicability is not fulfilled in the case under consideration. The laws may be taken to contain a tacit caveat of the "usually" or "other things being equal" type. An historical law is thus not strictly universal in that it must be taken as applicable to all cases falling within the scope of its explicitly formulated conditions; rather it may be thought to formulate relationships which obtain generally, or better, *as a rule*.[1]

Such a "law" we will term a *quasi-law*. In order for the law to be valid, it is not necessary that no apparent exceptions occur, it is only necessary that, if an apparent exception should occur, an adequate explanation be forthcoming, an explanation demonstrating the exceptional characteristic of the case in hand by establishing the violation of an appropriate (if hitherto unformulated) condition of the law's applicability.[2]

For example, the historical law that in the pre-revolutionary French navy only persons of noble birth were commissioned is not without apparent exceptions, since in particular the regulation was waived in the case of the great Jean Bart, son of a humble fisherman, who attained great distinction in the naval service. We may legitimately speak here of an *apparent* exception; for instead of abandoning this universal law in view of the cited counter-example, it is more expedient to maintain the law but to interpret it as being endowed with certain tacit amendments which, fully spelled out, would read somewhat as follows: "In the pre-revolutionary French navy as a rule only persons of noble birth were commissioned, that is, unless the regulation was explicitly waived or an oversight or fraud occurred or some other similarly exceptional condition obtained." While it

[1] This point has been made by various writers on historical method. Charles Frankel, for example, puts it as follows in his lucid article on "Explanation and Interpretation in History": "It is frequently misleading to take statements such as 'Power corrupts, and absolute power corrupts absolutely', when historians use them, as attempts to give an exact statement of a universal law. . . . But such remarks may be taken as statements of strategy, rules to which it is best to conform in the absence of very strong countervailing considerations." (*Philosophy of Science*, vol. 24, 1957, p. 142.)

[2] In his book *The Analysis of Matter* (London, 1927), Bertrand Russell writes "Our prescientific general beliefs are hardly ever without exceptions; in science, a law with exceptions can only be tolerated as a makeshift" (p. 191). We regard this as true only in some of the physical sciences. A far juster view was that of Alfred Marshall (*Principles of Economics*, 1892): "The laws of economics are to be compared with the law of the tides, rather than with the simple and exact law of gravitation. For the actions of men are so various and uncertain, that the best statement of tendencies, which we can make in a science of human conduct, must needs be inexact and faulty."

may be objected that such a formulation is vague — and indeed it is — it cannot be said that the law is now so loose as to be vacuous; for the intuitive intent is clear, and its looseness is far from permitting the law's retention in the face of just any counter-example.[3] Specifically, if a reliable source brings to light one counter-instance for which there is no tenable explanation whatsoever to give it exempt status, an historian may still wish to retain the law in the definite expectation that some such explanation eventually be forthcoming; but should he be confronted with a succession or series of unexplained exceptions to the law, he would no doubt soon feel compelled to abandon the law itself.

We thus have the indisputable fact that in a generally loose context, that of history being typical of the inexact sciences, it would be hopeless to try to erect a theoretical structure which is logically, perhaps even esthetically, on a plane with our idealistic image of an exact theory. Yet, if we consider the situation, not from the standpoint of the wishful dreamer of neat and tidy theory construction, but from that of the pragmatist in pursuit of a better understanding of the world through reasoned methods of explanation and prediction, then we have good reason to take heart at the sight even of quasi-laws, and we should realize that the seemingly thin line between vagueness and vacuity is solid enough to distinguish fact from fiction reasonably well in practical applications.

Quasi-Laws in the Physical Sciences

We have chosen to illustrate the nature of limited generalizations (quasi-laws) by means of the graphic example of historical laws. Use of this example from a social-science context must not, however, be construed as implying that quasi-laws do not occur in the natural, indeed even the physical sciences. In many parts of modern physics, formalized theories based wholly on universal principles are (at least presently) unavailable, and use of limited generalizations is commonplace, particularly so in applied physics and engineering.

Writers on the methodology of the physical sciences often bear in mind a somewhat antiquated and much idealized image of physics as a very complete and thoroughly exact discipline in which it is never necessary to rely upon limited generalizations or expert opinion. But physical science today is very far from meeting this ideal. Indeed some branches of the social sciences are in better shape as regards the generality of their laws than various departments of physics, such as the theory of turbulence phenomena, high-velocity aerodynamics, or the physics of extreme temperatures. Throughout applied physics in particular, when we move (say in engineering applications) from the realm of idealized abstraction ("perfect" gases, "homogeneous" media, etc.) to the complexities of the real world, reliance upon generalizations which are, in effect, quasi-laws becomes pronounced. (Engineering practice in general is based on "rules of thumb" to an extent undreamed of in current theories of scientific method.)

Thus no warrant whatever exists for using the presence of quasi-laws in the social sciences as validating a methodological separation between them on the one hand and the physical sciences on the other. A realistic assessment of physical science methods shows that quasi-laws are here operative too, and importantly so.

With this in mind, let us now turn to a closer examination of the role played by laws — or quasi-laws — in prediction and explanation.

Explanation and Prediction

A somewhat simplified characterization of scientific explanation — but one which none-

[3] Michael Scriven . . . speaks of historical generalizations as having a "selective immunity to counter-examples" [*in his paper* "Truisms as the Grounds for Historical Explanations", *reprinted as selection 9 in this volume*. Editor's note.]

the-less has a wide range of applicability, particularly in the physical sciences — is that explanation consists in the *logical derivation* of the statement to be explained from a complex of factual statements and well-established general laws. One would, for example, explain the freezing of a lake by adducing (1) the fact that the temperature fell below 32°F and (2) the law that water freezes at 32°F. These statements, taken together, yield the statement to be explained deductively.[4]

This deductive model of explanation, while adequate for many important types of explanations encountered in the sciences, cannot without at least some emendation be accepted as applying to all explanations. For one thing there are probabilistic explanations, which can be based upon statistical (rather than strictly universal) laws. ("I did not win the Irish Sweepstakes because the chances were overwhelmingly against my doing so.") And then there are what we have been referring to as quasi-laws, occurring in the inexact sciences, which because of their escape clauses cannot serve as the basis of strict *derivation*, and yet can carry explanatory force. (For example, the quasi-law quoted earlier surely explains — in the accepted sense of the word — why the French fleet which supported Washington's Yorktown campaign was commanded by a nobleman (namely, the Comte de Grasse).)

The uncertainty of conclusions based on quasi-laws is not due to the same reason as that of conclusions based on statistical laws. For a statistical law asserts the presence of some characteristic in a certain (presumably high) percentage of cases, whereas a quasi-law asserts it in all cases for which an exceptional status (in some ill-defined but clearly understood sense) cannot be claimed.

We note for the moment, however, that the schema of explanation when either type of non-universal law is involved is the same, and in fact identical with what it would be were the law universal; and an explanation is regarded as satisfactory if, while short of logically *entailing* the hypothesis, it succeeds in making the statement to be explained highly *credible* in the sense of providing convincing evidence for it. (We shall return to a discussion of the concept of evidence below.)

With regard to prediction as opposed to explanation, analyses of scientific reasoning often emphasize the similarities between the two, holding that they are identical from a logical standpoint, inasmuch as each is an instance of the use of evidence to establish an hypothesis, and the major point of difference between them is held to be that the hypothesis of a prediction or of an explanation concerns respectively the future or the past. This view, however, does not do justice to several differences between prediction and explanation which are of particular importance for our present purposes.[5]

First of all, there are such things as *unreasoned* predictions — predictions made without any articulation of justifying argument. The validation of such predictions lies not in their being supported by plausible arguments, but may, for example, reside in proving sound *ex post facto* through a record of successes on the part of the predictor or predicting mechanism.

It is clear that such predictions have no analogue in explanations; only reasoned predictions, based upon the application of established theoretical principles, are akin to explanations. However, even here there is an important point of difference.

By the very meaning of the term, an explanation must *establish* its conclusion, showing that there is a strong warrant why the fact to be explained — rather than some possible alternative — obtains. On the other hand, the conclusion of a (reasoned) prediction need not be well established in this sense; it suffices that it be rendered *more tenable than comparable alternatives*. Here then is an im-

[4] For a full discussion of this matter, see C. G. Hempel and P. Oppenheim, "Studies in the Logic of Explanation", *Philosophy of Science*, vol. 15, 1948, pp. 135–175. [*See selection 5 above.*]

[5] On the contrast between prediction and explanation see further I. Scheffler, "Explanation, Prediction, and Abstraction", *British Journal for the Philosophy of Science*, vol. 7 (1957), pp. 293–309, and N. Rescher, "On Prediction and Explanation", *ibid.*, vol. 8 (1958), pp. 281–290.

portant distinction in logical strength between explanations and predictions: An explanation, though it need not logically rule out alternatives altogether, must beyond reasonable doubt establish its hypothesis as *more credible than its negation.* Of a prediction, on the other hand, we need to require only that it establish its hypothesis simply as *more credible than any comparable alternative.* Of course predictions may, as in astronomy, be as firmly based in fact and as tightly articulated in reasoning as any explanation. But this is not a general requirement to which predictions *must* conform. A doctor's prognosis, for example, does not have astronomical certitude, yet practical considerations render it immensely useful as a guide in our conduct because it is far superior to reliance on guesswork or on pure chance alone as a decision-making device.

Generally speaking, in any field in which our ability to forecast with precision is very limited, our actions of necessity are guided by only slight differences in the probability which we attach to possible future alternative states of the world, and consequently we must permit predictions to be based upon far weaker evidence than explanations. This is especially true of a science such as history, or rather its predictive counterpart — political science. Here, in the absence of powerful theoretic delimitations which narrow down the immense variety of future possibilities to some manageable handful, the *a priori* likelihood of any particular state of affairs is minute, and we can thus tolerate considerable weakness in our predictive tools without rendering them useless. Consider, for example, the quasi-law that in a U.S. off-year election the opposition party is apt to gain. This is certainly not a general law, nor is it intended to be a summary of statistics. It has implicit qualifications of the "ceteris paribus" type, but it does claim to characterize the course of events "as a rule" and it generates an expectation of the explainability of deviations. On this basis, an historical (or political) law of this sort can provide a valid, though limited, foundation for sound predictions.

The epistemological asymmetry between explanation and prediction has not, it seems to us, been adequately recognized and taken into account in discussion of scientific method. For one thing, such recognition would lead to a better understanding of the promise of possibly unorthodox items of methodological equipment, such as quasi-laws, for the purposes of prediction in the inexact sciences. But more generally it would open the way to explicit consideration of a *specific methodology of prediction*—a matter which seems to have been neglected to date by the philosophers of science. As long as one believes that explanation and prediction are strict methodological counterparts, it is reasonable to press further with solely the explanatory problems of a discipline, in the expectation that only the tools thus forged will then be usable for predictive purposes. But once this belief is rejected, the problem of a specifically predictive method arises, and it becomes pertinent to investigate the possibilities of predictive procedures autonomous of those used for explanation.

Before discussing such possibilities in greater detail, it is imperative, in order to avoid various misunderstandings, that we give a brief clarification of the meaning of probability and of some associated concepts.

Probability

From the viewpoint of the philosophy of science the theory of probability occupies a peculiar position. To the extent that it deals with relations among propositions it is part of semantics and thus of pure logic. To the extent that it deals with credibility, rational beliefs, and personal expectations, it is part of empirical pragmatics and thus a social science. (The view, not held by us, that probability theory properly belongs entirely in the second field rather than the first is sometimes referred to as *psychologism.*)[6] Even for

[6] An incisive critique of psychologism is given in chapter II of R. Carnap's book, *Logical Foundations of Probability* (Chicago, 1950).

the logical part of the theory, the foundations are not yet established very firmly, and only with regard to applications to the simplest forms of one-place predicate languages has real progress been made to date.[7] Because of this, some vagueness must still be accepted even in discussing the purely logical aspects of probability; that is, unless we were content to confine ourselves to the aforementioned simplest case, which we are not, since the linguistic demands of the inexact sciences transcend these limits of simplicity even more frequently than do those of the exact sciences.

It is convenient to distinguish three probability concepts, namely *relative frequency*, *degree of confirmation*, and *personal* (or *subjective*) *probability*. Of these, the first is an objective, empirically ascertainable property of classes of physical objects or physical events; the second is also purely objective, namely a logical relation between sentences; the third is a measure of a person's confidence that some given statement is true, and is thus an essentially subjective matter. Let us briefly consider each of these three probability concepts.

RELATIVE FREQUENCY

Relative frequency requires the statement of a reference class (of objects or events), also called the population. If the class is finite it is simply the ratio of the number of elements having some property or trait divided by the total number of elements in the class. Thus we speak of the relative frequency of males in the present U. S. population, or of rainy days in Los Angeles in the first half of this century.[8] Sometimes the notion of relative frequency is extended to classes of either indefinite or infinite size. For example, we may speak of the relative frequency of male births in the U. S. over an extended period, without precisely specifying that period; or we may speak of the relative frequency "in the long run" of Heads in tosses with a particular coin, where the sequence of tosses is of indefinite length, and may even be idealized into an infinite sequence (in which case the "relative frequency" is the limit of the relative frequencies of the finite subsequences). In a situation like this, it is even customary to ascribe this probability, that is, the relative frequency of Heads in the long run, as a property to the coin itself (in particular, a "fair coin" is one for which this probability is $\frac{1}{2}$). But it is best to interpret such a statement merely as a paraphrase for the longer statement that in a long sequence of possible tosses with this coin (but not so long as to alter the physical characteristics of the coin) the relative frequency of Heads will be such and such.

DEGREE OF CONFIRMATION

The degree of confirmation is a logical relation between two sentences, the hypothesis H and the evidence E. The degree of confirmation of H on the basis of E is intended to be a measure of the credibility rationally imparted to the truth of H by the assumed truth of E. Precise definitions have thus far been suggested only for the one-place predicate calculus. In the simplest case, where E has the form of a statistical record of n observations, to the effect that exactly m out of n objects examined had a property P, and where the hypothesis H ascribes this property P to an as yet unexamined object, then the degree of confirmation of H on the basis of E, or $dc(H, E)$, is defined to be either the observed relative frequency m/n or else a quantity very close to it (and having the same limit as n gets large) which may differ somewhat from m/n due to technical requirements of elegance of the formalism. It is irrelevant for our present purposes which particular definition we adopt, but to fix the idea let us assume simply that in the above case $dc(H, E) = m/n$.

[7] See R. Carnap's massive study of the *Logical Foundations of Probability* (Chicago, 1950), and various studies cited by him in the extensive Bibliography, in particular those of Helmer, Hempel, and Oppenheim.

[8] It is a technical refinement into which we need not here enter that in applications it is common to use, instead of the relative frequency proper, some statistical *estimate* thereof.

If E does not have the simple form of a statistic or H does not just affirm another like instance, then some plausible extension of the definition of '*dc*' is required; this may lead to cases where no single number can reasonably be specified but where the evidence merely warrants a narrowing down of the probability of H to several possible numbers or an interval of numbers. For instance, if H is the hypothesis that a certain Irish plumber will vote Democratic in the next presidential election, and the evidence E amounts solely to saying that 70 percent of the Irish vote Democratic and 20 percent of the plumbers do; then all that one might reasonably assert is that the required probability lies somewhere between .2 and .7.

Ambiguities of this kind can, of course, be removed by *fiat* (and in fact this has been the path followed in the formalisms proposed to date by Carnap). That is to say, one can transfer the ambiguity from the object language to the metalanguage, by stating the matter as follows: There are several ways in which '*dc*' can be defined, but under each particular definition the degree of confirmation is a single-valued function.

No matter which of these two alternatives is chosen, at least the situation can still be resolved, as long as we are dealing with one-place predicates only. As soon as we move into a subject-matter where adequate discourse requires multi-place predicates or predicates of several logical levels, no formal proposals for an extended definition of '*dc*' are as yet available, and we have to rely largely on trained intuition as to how a numerical measure of the "credibility rationally imparted to H by E" should be estimated in specific cases.

Since it is not the purpose of this article to deal at length with the foundations of probability theory, while on the other hand the use of some notion of degree of confirmation in the vague sense introduced here seems to us unavoidable, we shall largely have to ignore the technical problems pointed out above. For practical purposes this means, not that we shall maintain the fiction of a well-defined formula being available which permits computation of $dc(H, E)$ for all H and E, but rather that we shall assume that, in specific cases arising in situations of interest, reasonable and knowledgeable persons, when confronted with the question of ascertaining a value of $dc(H, E)$, will find this definitely, if vaguely, meaningful and will arrive at estimates of the value that will not be too widely disparate. This leads us to the next probabilistic concept we must discuss.

PERSONAL PROBABILITY

Personal, or subjective probability is a measure of a person's confidence in, or subjective conviction of, the truth of some hypothesis. With Savage[9] it is measured behavioristically in terms of the person's betting behavior. If a person thinks that H is just about as likely as its negation $\sim H$, then if he were placed in a situation where he had to make an even bet on either H or $\sim H$, he would presumably be indifferent to this choice. Similarly, if he thought H to be twice as likely as $\sim H$, he would have no preference as to which side to take in a 1:2 bet on $H: \sim H$. Generalizing this idea, we shall say that the person attaches the personal probability p to the hypothesis H if he is found to be indifferent between the choice of receiving, say, one dollar if H turns out to be true or receiving $\frac{p}{1-p}$ dollars if H turns out to be false (his "personal expectation" in either case being p dollars).[10]

We shall call a person "rational" if (1) his preferences (especially with regard to betting options) are mutually consistent or at least,

[9] L. J. Savage, *The Foundations of Statistics*, New York, 1952.

[10] There are certain well-known difficulties connected with this behavioristic approach, which we will ignore here. We will merely mention that, in experimental situations designed to elicit personal probabilities, care must be taken that the stakes involved are in a range where the utility of money is effectively linear and the utility (or disutility) of gambling is negligible.

when inconsistencies are brought to his attention, he is willing to correct them; (2) his personal probabilities are reasonably stable over time, provided he receives no new relevant evidence; (3) his personal probabilities are affected (in the right direction) by new relevant evidence; and (4) in simple cases where the evidence E at his disposal is known, and E and H are such that $dc(H, E)$ is defined, his personal probability regarding H is in reasonable agreement with the latter; in particular, he is indifferent as to which side to take in a bet which to his knowledge is a "fair" bet.

A (predictive) "expert" in some subject-matter is a person who is *rational* in the sense discussed, who has a large background knowledge E in that field, and whose predictions (actual or implicit in his personal probabilities) with regard to hypotheses H in that field show a record of comparative successes in the long run. This is very much of a relative concept, as it depends on the predictive performance of which the average non-expert in the field would be capable. (In a temperate climate, a lay predictor can establish an excellent record by always forecasting good weather, but this would not support a claim to meteorological expertise.) We will return to a more detailed consideration of predictive expertise below.

With regard to the relationship between degree of confirmation and personal probability, it may be said that $dc(H, E)$ is intended to be a conceptual reconstruction of the personal probability which an entirely rational person would assign to H, given that his entire relevant information is E. In practice this relation can be applied in both directions: In simple cases where we have a generally acceptable definition of "dc" we may judge a person's rationality by the conformity of his personal probabilities — or of his betting behavior — with computable (or, if his information E is uncertain, estimable) dc-values. Conversely, once a person has been established as rational and possibly even an expert in a field, we may use his personal probabilities as estimates, on our part, of the degrees of confirmation which should be assigned given hypotheses.

We shall make use of these probability concepts below, primarily in connection with the use of expert judgment for predictive purposes. But we must first consider the use of evidence in prediction, beginning with some examples to illustrate the problems arising in the predictive use of probabilistic evidence.

Some Examples of the Use of Evidence in Prediction

The simplest use of evidence occurs when there is a direct reference to prior instances. Will my car start on this cold morning? Its record of successful starting on previous cold mornings is around 50 percent. I would be unduly hopeful or pessimistic in assigning as personal probability of its starting today a number significantly different from $\frac{1}{2}$. This use of a record of past instances as a basis for probability assignments with regard to future events is a common, and generally justified, inductive procedure (and of course is the basis on which a definition of degree of confirmation is constructed). However, under some circumstances it is a very poor way indeed of marshalling evidence.

Consider the case of Smith, who has been riding the bus to work for a year, the fare having been 10¢. One morning he is required to pay 15¢. Smith may wonder if his return fare that evening will be 10¢. It is highly unlikely — despite the great preponderance of 10¢ rides in Smith's sample. For Smith well knows that public transportation fares do change, and not by whim but by adoption of a new fare structure. In the light of this item of *background information*, it is unreasonable for Smith to base his personal probability directly on the cumulative record of past instances.

This illustrates the need for the use of background knowledge as indirect evidence, in the sense of furnishing other than direct instance confirmation. This need is encountered constantly in the use of evidence, and it constitutes one of the prime obstacles to a more sophisticated definition of degree of confirmation than has hitherto been achieved. Consider another example. Will my new neighbor move away again within five years? He is a carpenter (the average carpenter moves once every 10 years) and a bachelor (the average bachelor moves once every 3 years). I can assess the likelihood of my neighbor's moving within the next five years relative to either the reference class of carpenters or that of bachelors. Which one I should choose, or what weight I should give to each, must depend strongly on my background information as to the relative relevance of occupation versus marital status as a determining factor in changes of domicile.

Such reference-class problems arise even with statistical information of the simplest kind. Consider a sample of 100 objects drawn at random from a population, with the following outcome as regards possession of the properties *P* and *Q*:

	has *Q*	has not *Q*
has *P*	1	9
has not *P*	89	1

Given this information, what is the probability that another object drawn from the population, which is known to have the property *P*, will also have the property *Q*? Should we use a value around 0.1 (since only 1 of 10 observed *P*'s is a *Q*) or a value around 0.9 (since altogether 90 percent of the observed sample has the property *Q*)? Here again, an expedient use of the statistical evidence before us must rely on background information, if any, regarding the relevance of *P*-ness to *Q*-ness. If we know that most Texans are rich and most barbers poor, and are given as only item of information specifically about a man by the name of Jones that he is a Texan barber, we would do well to assign a low probability to the statement that Jones is rich, precisely because occupation is known to us to be more relevant to financial status than is location.

The Role of Expertise in Prediction

The implication of the examples we have been discussing is that a knowledge about past instances or about statistical samples — while indeed providing valuable information — is not the sole and sometimes not even the main form of evidence in support of rational assignments of probability values. In fact the evidential use of such *prima facie* evidence must be tempered by reference to background information, which frequently may be intuitive in character and have the form of a vague recognition of underlying regularities, such as analogies, correlations, or other conformities whose formal rendering would require the use of predicates of a logical level higher than the first.

The consideration of such underlying regularities is of special importance for the inexact sciences, particularly the social sciences (but not exclusively)[11] because in this sphere we are constantly faced with situations in which statistical information matters less than knowledge of regularities in the behavior of people or in the character of institutions, such as traditions and customary practices, fashions and mores, national attitudes and climates of opinion, institutional rules and regulations, group aspirations, and so on. For instance, in assessing the chances of a Republican presidential victory in 1960, a knowledge of the record of past election successes matters less than an insight into current trends and tendencies; or in answering a question as to the likelihood, say, of U. S. recognition of Communist China by 1960, it is hard to point to any relevant statistical evidence, yet there exists a host of relatively undigested but highly relevant background information.

This non-explicitness of background knowledge, which nonetheless may be significant or

[11] Use of background information, to temper the application of statistical information, is just as operative in the physical sciences, e.g., in engineering, so that no difference in principle is involved here.

even predominantly important, is typical of the inexact sciences, as is the uncertainty as to the evidential weight to be accorded various pieces of *prima facie* information in view of indirect evidence provided by underlying regularities. Hence the great importance which must be attached to experts and to expertise in these fields. For the expert has at his ready disposal a large store of (mostly inarticulated) background knowledge and a refined sensitivity to its relevance, through the intuitive application of which he is often able to produce trustworthy personal probabilities regarding hypotheses in his area of expertness.

The important place of expert judgment for predictions in the inexact sciences is further indicated by the prominence of quasi-laws among the explanatory instrumentalities of this domain. Since the conditions of applicability of such generalizations are neither fully nor even explicitly formulable, their use in specific circumstances presupposes the exercise of sound judgment as to their applicability to the case in hand. The informed expert, with his resources of background knowledge and his cultivated sense of the relevance and bearing of generalities in particular cases, is best able to carry out the application of quasi-laws necessary for reasoned prediction in this field.

The Problem of the Predictive Use of Evidence in an Inexact Context

In summary, the foregoing illustrations of the predictive use of evidence may be said to indicate that we are frequently confronted with what must be considered as a problematical, and far from ideal, epistemological situation. For the examples we have been considering show that in assessing the probability of an hypothesis H — typically a description of some future event — we are in many instances required to rely not merely upon some specific and explicit evidence E, but also on a vast body of potentially relevant background knowledge K, which is in general not only vague in its extent (and therefore indefinite in content) but also deficient in explicit articulation. In many practical applications, particularly in the inexact sciences, not even that part of K which is suitably relevant to H can be assumed to be explicitly articulated, or even articulable. One is unable to set down in sentential form everything that would have to be included in a full characterization of one's knowledge about a familiar room; and the same applies equally, if not more so, to a political expert's attempt to state all he knows that might be relevant to a question such as, for example, that of U. S. recognition of Communist China.

These considerations point up a deficiency for present purposes in the usual degree-of-confirmation concept quite apart from those already mentioned. For such an indefinite K, we cannot expect $dc(H, E \& K)$ to be determinable or even defined. This suggests, as a first step, the desirability of introducing a concept $dc_K(H, E)$ — the "degree of confirmation of H on E in view of K" — which is defined to be equal to $dc(H, E \& K)$ whenever it is possible to articulate K fully within the same language in which H and E are stated. But how is such a quantity to be determined when K is not fully formulated? Furthermore in addition to the difficulty involved in formulating it completely, K almost invariably contains probability statements (both of an objective, or *dc*-, type, and of the indirect form "So-and-so attaches to H the personal probability p"). To date, there is no hint of any suggestion as to how '$dc(H, X)$' might be formally defined when X contains statements of this kind.

Faced with this situation — which is surely not likely to be resolved in the near future — we must either for the present renounce all claims to systematized prediction in the inexact sciences, or, as indicated earlier, turn to unorthodox methods which are based upon judicious and systematic reliance on expert judgment. One such course, to which we previously alluded, may possibly help us out of the present perplexity. Let A be an expert and $K(A)$ his relevant background knowledge. Then A's personal probability, pp_A

(H, E), may be taken as an estimate on our part of $dc_{K(A)}(H, E)$. Thus the device of using the personal probabilities of experts, extracted by appropriately devised techniques of interrogation, can serve as a means of measuring quantities of the *dc*-type even in cases where there is no hope of application of the formal degree-of-confirmation concepts.

It might seem that in resorting to this device we conjure up a host of new problems, because — to all appearances — we are throwing objectivity to the winds. Of course, since we insist upon remaining within our own definition of scientific activity, we do not propose to forego objectivity. However, before attempting to analyze the possibility of salvaging objectivity in this situation, it may be well to look at a few examples illustrating the application of expertise in the sense just described.

The Intrinsic Use of Experts for Prediction

A source of characteristic examples of the predictive use of expert judgment is provided by the field of diagnostics, especially medical diagnostics.[12] A patient, let us assume, exhibits a pattern of symptoms such that it is virtually certain that he has either ailment A or ailment B, with respective probabilities of .4 and .6, where these probabilities derive from the statistical record of past cases. Thus the entire body of explicit symptomatic evidence is (by hypothesis) such as to indicate a margin in favor of the prediction that the patient suffers from disease B rather than A, and thus may respond positively to a corresponding course of treatment. But it is quite possible that an examining physician, taking into consideration not only the explicit indicators that constitute the "symptoms" (e.g., temperature, blood pressure, etc.) but also an entire host of otherwise inarticulated background knowledge with regard to this particular patient, the circumstances of the case, etc., may arrive at a diagnosis of disease A rather than B. Thus the use of background information, in a way that is not systematized but depends entirely on the exercise of informal expert judgment, may appropriately lead to predictive conclusions in the face of *prima facie* evidence which points in the opposite direction.

Quite similar in its conceptual structure to the foregoing medical example are various other cases of predictive expertise in the economic sphere. The advice of an expert investment counsellor, for example, may exhibit essentially the same subtle employment of non-articulate background knowledge that characterized the prediction of the diagnostician.

Again, in such essentially sociological predictions of public reactions as are involved in the advertising and marketing of commercial products, the same predictive role of expert judgment comes into play. When the production of a motion picture is completed, a decision must be made regarding the number of prints to be made. There are economic reasons for an accurate prediction of the need: if too few prints are ready to meet the immediate demand, film rental income will be lost; on the other hand, the prints are costly, and an over-supply leads to considerable excess expenditure. Here again, as in the medical or economic examples, certain limited predictions can be based wholly on the record of past statistics in analogous instances. The presence of certain actors in the cast, the topic, theme and setting of the film, perhaps even its reception by preview audiences, may suggest a probability distribution for its demand. However, the major studios involved in motion-picture production are not content to rely on these explicit indicators alone. Aware of the potential influence of a whole host of subtle intangibles (e.g., so-called "audience appeal," timeliness with respect to current events, existence of competitive offerings), all of which are susceptible of explicit statistical treatment only with the greatest difficulty if at all, they prudently rely on the forecasts of professional experts in the

[12] An extensive and useful discussion of medical prediction is contained in P. E. Meehl's book on *Clinical vs. Statistical Prediction*, Minneapolis, 1954.

field, who have exhibited a demonstrated ability to supplement the various explicit elements by appropriate use of their capacities for an intuitive appraisal of the many intangible factors which critically affect the final outcome.

Other examples drawn from the applied sciences, engineering, industry, politics, etc. will easily suggest themselves. What they have in common is the reliance, in part or wholly, on an expert, who here functions in an intrinsic rather than extrinsic role. By *extrinsic expertise* we mean the kind of inventiveness, based on factual knowledge and the perception of previously unnoticed relationships, that goes into the hypothesizing of new laws and the construction of new theories; it is, in other words, the successful activity of the scientist qua scientist. *Intrinsic expertise*, by contrast, is not invoked until after an hypothesis has been formulated and its probability, in the sense of degree of confirmation, is to be estimated. The expert, when performing intrinsically, thus functions within a theory rather than on the theory-constructing level.

The Role of Prediction as an Aid to Decision Making

The decisions which professional decision makers — governmental administrators, company presidents, military commanders, etc. — are called upon to make inevitably turn on the question of future developments, since their directives as to present actions are invariably conceived with a view to future results. Thus a reliance upon predictive ability is nowhere more overt and more pronounced than in the area of policy formation, and decision making in general.

For this reason, decision makers surround themselves by staffs of expert advisers, whose special knowledge and expertise must generally cover a wide field. Some advising experts may have a great store of factual knowledge, and can thus serve as walking reference books. Others may excel through their diagnostic or otherwise predictive abilities. Others may have a special analytical capacity to recognize the structure of the problems in hand, thus aiding in the proper utilization of the contributions of the other two types of experts (e.g., operations analysts, management consultants, etc.). The availability of such special expertise constitutes for the decision maker a promise of increased predictive ability essential to the more effective discharge of his own responsibilities. Thus the ultimate function of expert advice is almost always to make a predictive contribution.

While the dependence of the decision makers upon expert advisers is particularly pronounced in social-science contexts, for instance, in the formulation of economic and political policies, such dependence upon expertise ought by no means to be taken to contradistinguish the social from the physical sciences. In certain engineering applications, particularly of relatively underdeveloped branches of physics (such as the applied physics of extremes of temperature or velocity) the reliance upon "know-how" and expert judgment is just as pronounced as it is in the applications of political science to foreign-policy formation. The use of experts for prediction does *not* constitute a line of demarcation between the social and the physical sciences, but rather between the exact and the inexact sciences.

Although we have held that the primary functions of expert advisers to decision makers is to serve as "predictors", we by no means intend to suggest that they act as fortune tellers, trying to foresee specific occurrences for which the limited intellectual vision of the non-expert is insufficient. For the decision-supporting uses of predictive expertise, there is in general no necessity for an anticipation of particular future occurrences. It suffices that the expert be able to sketch out adequately the general directions of future developments, to anticipate — as we have already suggested — some of the major critical junctures ("branch points") on which the course of these developments will hinge, and to make contingency predictions with regard to the alternatives associated with them.

While the value of scientific prediction for sound decision making is beyond question, it can hardly be claimed that the inexact sciences have the situation regarding the use of predictive expertise well in hand. Quite to the contrary, it is our strong feeling that significant improvements are possible in the predictive instruments available to the decision maker. These improvements are contingent on the development of methods for the more effective predictive use of expert judgment. In the final section we shall give consideration to some of the problems involved in this highly important, but hitherto largely unexplored area.

Justification of the Intrinsic Use of Expertise

We come back to the problem of preserving objectivity in the face of reliance upon expertise. Can we accept the utilization of intrinsic expert judgment within the framework of an inductive procedure without laying ourselves open to the charge of abandoning objective scientific methods and substituting rank subjectivity?

To see that explicit use of expert judgment is not incompatible with scientific objectivity, let us look once more at the medical-diagnosis example of the preceding section. Consider the situation in which a diagnostician has advised that a patient be treated for ailment A (involving, say, a major surgical operation) rather than B (which might merely call for a special diet). Our willingness, in this case, to put our trust in the expert's judgment surely would not be condemned as an overly subjective attitude. The reasons why our reliance on the expert is objectively justified are not difficult to see. For one thing, the selection of appropriate experts is not a matter of mere personal preference but is a procedure governed by objective criteria (about which more will be said in the ensuing section). But most importantly, the past diagnostic performance record makes the diagnostician an objectively reliable indicator (of diseases), in the same sense as one of any two highly correlated physical characteristics is an indicator of the other. ("If most hot pieces of iron are red, and vice versa, and if this piece of iron is red then it is probably hot.")

Even if the expert's explicit record of past performance is unknown, reliance upon his predictions may be objectively justified on the basis of general background knowledge as to his reputation as an expert. The objective reliability of experts' pronouncements may also be strongly suggested by the fact that they often exhibit a high degree of agreement with one another, which — at least if we have reason to assume the pronouncements to be independent — precludes subjective whim.

Epistemologically speaking, the use of an expert as an objective indicator — as illustrated by the example of the diagnostician — amounts to considering the expert's predictive pronouncement as an integral, intrinsic part of the subject matter, and treating his reliability as a part of the theory about the subject matter. Our information about the expert is conjoined to our other knowledge about the field, and we proceed with the application of precisely the same inductive methods which we would apply in cases where no use of expertise is made. Our "data" are supplemented by the expert's personal probability valuations and by his judgments of relevance (which, by the way, could be derived from suitable personal probability statements), and our "theory" is supplemented by information regarding the performance of experts.

In this manner the incorporation of expert judgment into the structure of our investigation is made subject to the same safeguards which are used to assure objectivity in other scientific investigations. The use of expertise is therefore no retreat from objectivity or reversion to a reliance on subjective taste.

Criteria for the Selection of Predictive Experts

The first and most obvious criterion of expertise is of course knowledge. We resort to an "expert" precisely because we expect his information and the body of experience at his disposal to constitute an assurance that he will be able to select the needed items of background information, determine the character and extent of their relevance, and apply these insights to the formulation of the required personal probability judgments.

However, the expert's knowledge is not enough; he must be able to bring it to bear effectively on the predictive problem in hand, and this not every expert is able to do. It becomes necessary also to place some check upon his predictive efficacy and to take a critical look at his past record of predictive performance.

The simplest way in which to score an expert's performance is in terms of "reliability": his *degree of reliability* is the relative frequency of cases in which, when confronted with several alternative hypotheses, he ascribed to the eventually correct alternative among them a greater personal probability than to the others.

This measure, while useful, must yet be taken with a grain of salt, for there are circumstances where even a layman's degree of reliability, as defined above, can be very close to 1. For instance, in a region of very constant weather, a layman can prognosticate the weather quite successfully by always predicting the same weather for the next day as for the current one. Similarly, a quack who hands out bread pills and reassures his patients of recovery "in due time" may prove right more often than not and yet have no legitimate claim to being classified as a medical expert. Thus what matters is not so much an expert's absolute degree of reliability but his relative degree of reliability, that is, his reliability as compared to that of the average person. But even this may not be enough. In the case of the medical diagnostician discussed earlier, the layman may have no information that might give him a clue as to which of diseases A and B is the more probable, while anyone with a certain amount of rudimentary medical knowledge may know that disease A generally occurs much more frequently than disease B; yet his prediction of A rather than B on this basis alone would not qualify him as a reliable diagnostician. Thus a more subtle assessment of the qualifications of an expert may require his comparison with the average person having some degree of general background knowledge in his field of specialization. One method of scoring experts somewhat more subtly than just by their reliability is in terms of their "accuracy": the *degree of accuracy* of an expert's predictions is the correlation between his personal probabilities p and his correctness in the class of those hypotheses to which he ascribed the probability p. Thus of a highly accurate predictor we expect that of those hypotheses to which he ascribes, say a probability of 70%, approximately 70% will eventually turn out to be confirmed. Accuracy in this sense, by the way, does not guarantee reliability,[13] but accuracy in addition to reliability may be sufficient to distinguish the real expert from the specious one.

The Dependence of Predictive Performance on Subject Matter

Not only are some experts better predictors than others, but subject matter fields differ from one another in the extent to which they admit of expertise. This circumstance is of

[13] For instance, suppose experts A and B each gave 100 responses, assigning probabilities .2, .4, .6, .8 to what in fact were the correct alternatives among 100 choices of H and ~H, as follows:

p	A	B
.2	10	0
.4	20	0

p	A	B
.6	30	60
.8	40	40

Then A is perfectly *accurate* (e.g., exactly 60 percent, or 30, of the 20 + 30, or 50, cases to which he assigned .6 were correct), but he is only 70 percent *reliable;* B, on the other hand, is 100% reliable, but his accuracy is quite faulty (e.g., 100 percent, rather than 60 percent, of the 60 cases to which he assigned .6 were correct).

course in some instances due to the fact that the scientific theory of the field in question is relatively undeveloped. The geology of the moon or the meteorology of Mars is less amenable to prediction than their mundane counterparts, although no greater characteristic complexity is inherent in these fields. In other cases, however, predictive expertise is limited despite a high degree of cultivation of a field, because the significant phenomena hinge upon factors that are not particularly amenable to prediction.

In domains in which the flux of events is subject to gradual transitions and constant regularities (say, astronomy), a high degree of predictive expertise is possible. In those fields, however, in which the processes of transition admit of sharp jolts and discontinuities, which can in turn be the effects of so complex and intricate causal processes as to be "chance" occurrences for all practical purposes, predictive expertise is inherently less feasible. The assassination of a political leader can altogether change the policies of a nation, particularly when such a nation does not have a highly developed complex of institutions that ensure gradualness of its policy changes. Clearly no expert on a particular country can be expected to have the data requisite for a prediction of assassinations; that is, his relevant information is virtually certain not to include the precisely detailed knowledge of the state of mind of various key figures that might give him any basis whatsoever for assigning a numerical value as his personal probability to the event in question. This situation is quite analogous to that of predicting the outcome of a particular toss of a coin; only the precise dynamic details of the toss's initial conditions might provide a basis for computing a probability other than $\frac{1}{2}$ for the outcome, and these details again are almost certainly unavailable. We may here legitimately speak of "chance occurrences", in the sense that not even an expert, unless he has the most unusual information at his disposal, is in a better position than the layman to make a reliable prediction.

In the inexact sciences, particularly in the social sciences, the critical causal importance of such chance events makes predictive expertise in an absolute sense difficult and sometimes impossible, and it is this, rather than the qualify of his theoretical machinery, which puts the social scientist in a poor competitive position relative, say, to the astronomer.

However, when the expert is unable to make precise predictions, due to the influence of chance factors, we can expect him to indicate the major contingencies on which future developments will hinge. Even though the expert cannot predict the specific course of future events in an unstable country, he should be able to specify the major "branch points" of future contingencies, and to provide personal probabilities conditionally with respect to these. Thus, for example, while it would be unreasonable to expect an expert on the American economy to predict with precision the duration of a particular phase of an economic cycle (e.g., a recession), it is entirely plausible to ask him to specify the major potential "turning points" in the cycle (e.g., increased steel production at a certain juncture), and to indicate the probable courses of development ensuing upon each of the specified alternatives.

Such differences in predictability among diverse subject-matter fields lead to important consequences for the proper utilization of experts. One obvious implication is that it may clearly be more profitable to concentrate limited resources of predictive expertise on those portions of a broader domain which are inherently more amenable to prediction. For example in a study of long-range political developments in a particular geographic area, it might in some cases be preferable to focus on demographic developments rather than the evolution of programs and platforms of political parties.

However, the most important consideration is that even in subject-matter fields in which the possibility of prediction is very limited the exercise of expertise, instead of being applied to the determination of *absolute* personal probabilities with respect to certain hypotheses, ought rather more profitably be concentrated on the identification of the relevant branch-points and the associated problem of the *relative* personal probabilities for the hypothesis in question, i.e., relative with regard to the alternatives arising at these branch-points.

Even in predictively very "difficult" fields — such as the question of the future foreign policy of an "unstable" country — the major branch-points of future contingencies are frequently few enough for actual enumeration, and although outright prediction cannot be expected, relative predictions hinging upon these principal alternative contingencies can in many instances serve the same purposes for which absolute predictions are ordinarily employed. For example, it would be possible for a neighboring state, in formulating its own policy toward this country, to plan not for "the" (one and only) probable course of developments but to design several policies, one for each of the major contingencies, or perhaps even a single policy which could deal effectively with all the alternatives.

Predictive Consensus Techniques

The predictive use of an expert takes place within a rationale which, on the basis of our earlier discussion, can be characterized as follows: We wish to investigate the predictive hypothesis H; with the expert's assistance, we fix upon the major items of the body of explicit evidence E which is relevant to this hypothesis; we then use the expert's personal probability valuation $pp(H, E)$ as *our* estimate of the degree of confirmation of H on the basis of E, i.e., as our estimated value of $dc(H, E)$.

This straightforward procedure, however, is no longer adequate in those cases in which *several* experts are available. For here we have not the single value $pp(H, E)$ of only one expert, but an entire series of values, one for each of the experts: $pp_1(H, E)$, $pp_2(H, E)$, etc. The problem arises: How is the best joint use of these various expert valuations to be made?[14]

Many possible procedures for effecting a combination among such diverse probability estimates are available. One possibility, and no doubt the simplest, is to select one "favored" expert, and to accept his sole judgment. We might, for example, compare the past predictive performance of the various experts, and select that one whose record has been the most successful.

Another simple procedure is to pool the various expert valuations into an average of some sort, possibly the median, or a mean weighted so as to reflect past predictive success.

Again, the several experts might be made to act as a single group, pooling their knowledge in round-table discussion, if possible eliminating discrepancies in debate, and the group might then — on the basis of its corporate knowledge — be asked to arrive at one generally agreeable corporate "personal" probability as its consensus, which would now serve as our *dc*-estimate. (One weakness in this otherwise very plausible-sounding procedure is that the consensus valuation might unduly reflect the views of the most respected member of the group, or of the most persuasive.)

One variant of this consensus procedure is to require that the experts, after pooling their knowledge in discussion, and perhaps after debating the issues, set down their separate "second-guess" personal probabilities, revising their initial independent valuations in the light of the group work. These separate values are then combined by some sort of averaging process to provide our *dc*-estimate. The advantage of such a combination of independent values over the use of a single generally acceptable group value is that it tends to diminish the influence of the most vociferous or influential group member. Incidentally, in any consensus method of this kind in which separate expert valuations are combined, we can introduce the refinement of weighting an expert's judgment so as to reflect his past performance.

[14] Compare A. Kaplan, A. L. Skogstad, M. A. Girshick, "The Prediction of Social and Technological Events", *Public Opinion Quarterly*, Spring 1950.

Another consensus procedure, sometimes called the "Delphi Technique", eliminates committee activity altogether, thus further reducing the influence of certain psychological factors, such as specious persuasion, the unwillingness to abandon publicly expressed opinions, and the bandwagon effect of majority opinion. This technique replaces direct debate by a carefully designed program of sequential individual interrogations (best conducted by questionnaires) interspersed with information and opinion feedback derived by computed consensus from the earlier parts of the program. Some of the questions directed to the respondents may, for instance, inquire into the "reasons" for previously expressed opinions, and a collection of such reasons may then be presented to each respondent in the group, together with an invitation to reconsider and possibly revise his earlier estimates. Both the inquiry into the reasons and subsequent feedback of the reasons adduced by others may serve to stimulate the experts into taking into due account considerations they might through inadvertence have neglected, and to give due weight to factors they were inclined to dismiss as unimportant on first thought.

We have done no more here than to indicate some examples from the spectrum of alternative consensus methods. Clearly there can be no one universally "best" method. The efficacy of such methods is very obviously dependent upon the nature of the particular subject-matter, and may even hinge upon the idiosyncrasies and personalities of the specific experts (e.g., on their ability to work as a group, etc.). Indeed this question of the relative effectiveness of the various predictive consensus techniques is almost entirely an open problem for empirical research, and it is strongly to be hoped that more experimental investigation will be undertaken in this important field.

Simulation and Pseudo-Experimentation

We have thus far, in discussing the intrinsic use of experts or of groups of experts, described their function as being simply predict, in the light of their personal probabilities, the correctness or incorrectness o proposed hypotheses. This description, while apt both in principle and often in practice, may in some instances be overly simplified.

For one thing, in situations concerned with complicated practical problems, no clear-cut hypothesis to which probability values could be meaningfully attached may be immediately discernible. For another, several kinds of expertise, all interacting with one another, may have to be brought to bear simultaneously in anything but a straightforward manner. Examples of such cases are provided by such questions as: "How can tension in the Middle East be relieved?", "What legislation is needed to reduce juvenile delinquency?" "How can America's schools improve science instruction?" Here, before even a single predictive expert can be used intrinsically, some at least rudimentary theoretical framework must be constructed within which predictive hypotheses can be stated. This, of course, calls for expertise of the extrinsic kind. Generally, the process involved is about as follows. The situation at hand (say, current crime patterns) is analyzed, that is, it is stated in terms of certain specific and, it is hoped, well-defined concepts; this step usually involves a certain amount of abstraction, in that some aspects of the situation that are judged irrelevant are deliberately omitted from the description. Then either some specific action is proposed, and a hypothesis stated as to its consequences on the situation in question or, more typically, a law or quasi-law is formulated, stating that in situations of the kind at hand actions of a certain kind will have such and such consequences.

A variant of this is of considerable epistemological significance. Instead of describing the situation directly, a *model* of it is constructed, which may be either mathematical or physical, in which each element of the real situation is simulated by a mathematical or physical object, and its relevant properties and relations to other elements are mirrored by corresponding simulative properties and relations. For example, any geographical map may be considered a (physical) model of some sector of the world; the planetary system can be simulated mathematically by a set of mass-points moving according to Kepler's laws; a city's traffic system can be simulated by setting up a miniature model of its road net, traffic signals, and vehicles; etc.[15] Now, instead of formulating hypotheses and predictions directly about the real world, it is possible instead to do the same thing about the model. Any results obtained from an analysis of the model, to the extent that it truly simulates the real world, can then later be translated back into the corresponding statements about the latter. This injection of a model has the advantage that it admits of what may be called *pseudo-experimentation* ("pseudo", because the experiments are carried out in the model, not in reality). For example, in the case of the analysis of the traffic system, pseudo-experimentation may produce reliable predictions as to what changes in the time-sequence of traffic signals will ease the flow of traffic through the city.

Pseudo-experimentation is nothing but the systematic use of the classical idea of a hypothetical experiment; it is applied when true experimentation is too costly or physically or morally impossible[16] or — as we shall discuss next — when the real-world situation is too complex to permit the intrinsic use of experts. The application of simulation techniques is a promising approach, whose fruitfulness has only begun to be demonstrated in documented experiments.[17] It is particularly promising when it is desirable to employ intrinsically several experts with varying specialties in a context in which their forecasts cannot be entered independently but where they are likely to interact with one another. Here a model furnishes the experts with an artificial, simulated environment, within which they can jointly and simultaneously experiment, responding to the changes in the environment induced by their actions, and acquiring through feedback the insights necessary to make successful predictions within the model and thus indirectly about the real world.

This technique lends itself particularly to predictions regarding the behavior of human organizations, inasmuch as the latter can be simulated most effectively by having the experts play the roles of certain members of such organizations and act out what in their judgment would be the actions, in the situation simulated, of their real-life counterparts.[18] Generally it may be said that in many cases judicious pseudo-experimentation may effectively annul the oft-regretted infeasibility of carrying out experiments proper in the social sciences by providing an acceptable substitute which, moreover, has been tried

[15] On simulation in traffic research see W. H. Glanville, "Road Safety and Traffic Research in Great Britain", *Journal of the Operations Research Society of America*, vol. 3 (1955), pp. 283–299; reprinted in J. F. McCloskey and J. M. Coppinger, *Operations Research for Management*, vol. II (Baltimore, 1956), pp. 82–100.

[16] Classical examples of such pseudo-experimentation are found in atomic physics and in military analysis. Atomic physics deals with particles so small as to preclude experimentation requiring direct manipulation and observation; what has been done here is to construct a mathematical model of certain atomic and nuclear processes and then to use Monte Carlo sampling techniques to conduct, not real, but paper experiments, in which the paths of fictitious particles of the model are "observed" as the latter go through a series of random collisions, deflections, or what not; in this "experiment" the features supposedly not under the control of the "experimenter" are assumed to be subject to given probability distributions, so that the chance fluctuations which would naturally occur can be simulated in the model by the operation of an artificial chance device. Similarly, the military, in order to evaluate the effectiveness of alternative weapon-systems (which clearly cannot be fully tested directly), conduct pseudo-experiments on simulation models.

[17] See, for instance, J. L. Kennedy and R. L. Chapman, *The Background and Implications of the Systems Research Laboratory Studies*, Symposium on Air Force Human Engineering, Publication No. 455, Nat. Ac. of Sc., Nat. Res. Council, 1956; R. L. Chapman, *Simulation in RAND'S Systems Research Laboratory*, and W. W. Haythorn, *Simulation in RAND'S Logistics Systems Laboratory*, both in Report of Symposium on System Simulation, Waverly Press, 1958.

[18] See, for example, the American Management Association study of *Top Management Decision Simulation* (New York, 1957).

and proved in the applied physical sciences.

Operational Gaming

A particular case of simulation involving role-playing by the intrinsic experts is known as operational *gaming*, especially war gaming. A simulation model may properly be said to be gaming a real-life situation if the latter concerns decision-makers in a context involving conflicting interests. In operational gaming, the simulated environment is particularly effective in reminding the expert, in his role as a player, to take *all* the factors into account in making his predictions that are potentially relevant; for if he does not, and chooses a tactic or strategy which overlooks an essential factor, an astute "opponent" will soon enough teach him not to make such an omission again.

Aside from the obvious application of gaming to the analysis of military conflict, of which there are numerous examples, ranging from crude map exercises to sophisticated enterprises requiring the aid of high-speed computing equipment, gaming has been used to gain insights into the nature of political and economic conflict. In the political field, cold-war situations have been explored in this manner, and in the economic field inroads have been made into an analysis of bargaining and of industrial competition.[19]

We note in passing that operational games differ greatly in the completeness of their rules. These may be complete enough so that at each stage the strategic options at the players' disposal are wholly specified, and also that the consequences resulting from the joint exercise of these options are entirely determined; this would mean that the model represents a complete theory of the phenomena simulated in the game. On the other hand, neither of these factors may be completely determined by the rules, in which case it is up to an umpiring staff to allow or disallow proposed strategies and to assess their consequences. Clearly, umpiring in this sense represents yet another important device for the use of expertise intrinsically within the framework of a scientific theory (viz. the model in question).

Review of the Main Theses

Before proceeding to a consideration of certain recommendations, which seem to us to emerge as conclusions from the analysis which has been presented, it is appropriate to pause briefly for a review of the main points of the foregoing discussion. Our starting point has been the distinction between the "exact" and the "inexact" areas of science. It is our contention that this distinction is far more important and fundamental from the standpoint of a correct view of scientific method than is the case with superficially more pronounced distinctions based on subject-matter diversities, especially that between the social and the physical sciences. Some branches of the social sciences (e.g., certain parts of demography), which are usually characterized by the presence of a formalized mathematical theory, are methodologically analogous to the exact parts of physics. By contrast, the applied, inexact branches of physical science — for instance, certain areas of engineering under "extreme" conditions — are in many basic respects

[19] Cf. C. J. Thomas and W. L. Deemer, Jr., "The Role of Operational Gaming in Operations Research", *Journal of the Operations Research Society of America* (JORSA), vol. 5 (1957), pp. 1–27; A. M. Mood and R. D. Specht, "Gaming as a Technique of Analysis", RAND Corporation paper P-579, October 19, 1954; W. E. Cushen, "Operational Gaming in Industry" in J. F. McCloskey and J. M. Coppinger, *Operations Research for Management*, vol. II (Baltimore, 1956), pp. 358–375; R. Bellman et al., "On the Construction of a Multi-Stage, Multi-Person Business Game, JORSA, vol. 5 (1957), pp. 469–503; F. M. Ricciardi, "Business War Games for Executives: A New Concept in Management Training", *Management Review* (1957), pp. 45–56; J. C. Harsanyi, "Approaches to the Bargaining Problem before and after the Theory of Games", *Econometrica* 26 (1955). F. M. Ricciardi et al., "Top Management Decision Simulation", *American Management Association*, 1957; G. K. Kalisch et al, "Some Experimental *n*-Person Games", published in *Decision Processes*, ed. by Thrall, Coombs and Davis; John Wiley 1954.

markedly similar to the social sciences.

This applies both to methods of explanation and to methods of prediction. Partly because of the absence of mathematically formalized theories, explanations throughout the area of inexact sciences — within the physical and the social science settings alike — are apt to be given by means of the restricted generalizations we have called quasi-laws. The presence of such less-than-universal principles in the inexact sciences creates an asymmetry between the methods of explanation and those of prediction in these fields. This suggests the desirability of developing the specifically predictive instrumentalities of these fields, for once the common belief in the identity of predictive and explanatory scientific procedures is seen to be incorrect, it is clearly appropriate to consider the nature and potentialities of predictive procedures distinct from those used for explanation. As for predictions in the inexact sciences (physical as well as social), these can be pragmatically acceptable (that is, as a basis for actions) when based on methodologically even less sophisticated grounds than are explanations, such as expert judgment, for example.

These general considerations regarding the methodology of the inexact sciences hold particularly intriguing implications for the possibility of methodological innovation in the social sciences. Here the possible existence of methods which are unorthodox in the present state of social-science practices merits the closest examination. This is particularly true with respect to the pragmatic applications of the social sciences (e.g., in support of decision making), in which the predictive element is preponderant over the explanatory.

One consideration of this sort revolves about the general question of the utilization of expertise. We have stressed the importance in the social sciences of limited generalizations (quasi-laws), which cannot necessarily be used in a simple and mechanical way, but whose very application requires the exercise of expert judgment. And more generally, when interested in prediction in this field (especially for decision-making purposes), we are dependent upon the experts' personal probability valuations for our guidance. A systematic investigation of the effective use of experts represents a means by which new and powerful instruments for the investigation of social-science problems might be forged.

Further, the use in social-science contexts of a variety of techniques borrowed from other, applied, sciences which are also inexact (e.g., engineering applications, military and industrial operations research) deserves the most serious consideration. For there are numerous possibilities for deriving leads as to methods which are potentially useful in the social sciences also; in particular the use of simulation as a basis for conducting pseudo-experiments comes to mind. Finally, there is the important possibility of combining simulation with the intrinsic use of expertise, especially by means of the technique of operational gaming. This prospect constitutes a method whose potential for social-science research has hitherto gone virtually wholly unexplored, and it is our hope that this neglect will soon be remedied.

Some Tasks for Methodological Research

The thoughts which we have set down in this paper are intended to represent a challenge to those who would like to see the applied social sciences narrow the gap that has been created between them and the applied physical sciences by the explosive progress of technology in the first half of this century. A particularly promising prospect, it seems to us, is a pragmatic reorientation of social science methodology along some of the lines which have proved successful in their fellow inexact sciences in the applied physical field.

In order to achieve this, much work has yet to be done. Aside from the need for further conceptual analysis, especially with regard to the status of quasi-laws in theory construction and the expansion of the degree-of-confirmation concept to languages containing relations and functions, there are numerous empirical studies that are suggested by the approach which we are recommending.

The following is a list of areas of such research. It is intended to be suggestive, rather than exhaustive, of the type of effort required to implement this new approach.

(1) *Methodology of expertise:*

(a) Performance of the individual expert: e.g., selection and training of experts, aids to their performance, scoring systems for predictions.

(b) Performance of groups of experts: e.g., methods of consensus formation, "Delphi" techniques of interrogation with feedback, investigation of other multi-expert structures.

(c) Psychological problems in the use of expert groups: e.g., reduction of respondents' bias in conference situations and as game players, simulation of motivation in pseudo-experiments requiring role-playing, man-machine interaction.

(2) *Methodology of pseudo-experimentation:*

(Here our suggestions are, on the whole, only obliquely methodological, since — in our opinion — a firm methodology will evolve gradually from a process of prolonged trial and error.)

(a) Simulation techniques in the social sciences: e.g., simulation of industrial or business processes or of the operation of some sector of the national economy, or of some governmental activity.

(b) Gaming techniques in the social sciences: e.g. gaming of industrial competition, cold-war games, foreign-trade and investment gaming.

(c) Problems inherent in pseudo-experimentation: e.g., the question of "controlled" experiments, problems of scaling arising in the translation of results from a simulation model to the real world.

In all of these areas some preliminary studies have been carried out, which — while insufficient in themselves — lend great promise to more extensive efforts. Along such lines, it seems to us, there lie valuable and as yet only fragmentarily exploited hopes of augmenting the range of the methodological instrumentalities of the applied inexact and, in particular, the applied social sciences.

IV

LAWS, THEORIES, and EXPLANATION in the SOCIAL SCIENCES

Brought together below are three interlocking groups of selections. The first of these confronts the ambiguous and elusive issue of whether, and in what sense, social scientists can formulate and establish scientific laws. As against Gewirth and Turner, Brown and Merton contend that there are generalizations within the social sciences that fulfill the same criteria as physical laws. And they insist that this is true whether *law* is meant as "an isolated proposition summarizing observed uniformities" or as "a statement of invariance derivable from a theory."

Brown's discussion is especially instructive. He rebuts in detail some of the standard separatist arguments designed to show that laws are beyond the reach of social scientists, e.g., that universal propositions in the social sciences are "too vague for testing;" that such propositions, if true at all, are covert tautologies which can be established by conceptual reflection or by appealing to definitions (see selection 19); that social scientists cannot develop a system of theoretical concepts by which to organize and explain functional relations, e.g., those listed on pages 240 and 246, between types of human conduct. Yet there remains at least one source of doubt which even Brown's laborious efforts do not entirely dispel.

Let us concede that his arguments secure an incontestable place for laws and theories — in the strictest sense — within the social sciences. But from this it does not follow that every dimension of man's activity is governed by laws. One point common to Gewirth, Peters and Tajfel, Malcolm, and Winch seems to be that the descriptions which identify many human actions are *incompatible* "with the concepts central to the activity of scientific prediction." Suppose I stand up at a meeting of Jehovah's Witnesses and that this act is provisionally regarded as an attempt to gain the floor by employing one of Robert's Rules of Order. Suppose further that my performance is subsequently shown to be the effect of a lawful and thus, presumably, unavoidable connection between swallowing certain liquids, which disturb the body fluids, and standing up before large crowds. Can it now be sustained that I acted *so as to attain a consciously sought goal*? Did I *have* a goal in the sense of something I sought *because* I preferred it to other options? The covering law explanation appears to indicate that what I did was not up to me at all, not under my rational control, not an expression of choice or desire, but simply a physical response to physiological and environmental stimuli. This explanation implies, then, that appealing to my values and beliefs, e.g., pointing out that Jehovah's Witnesses never operate by Robert's Rules of Order, would have been utterly useless: no such appeal, given what I imbibed, could have prevented my body from taking an erect position, perpendicular to the floor, feet planted on the ground, etc. In short, that piece of behavior can no longer be described as manifesting any intention whatever, no more than if it resulted from a post-hypnotic suggestion, or from a blast of wind that swept me from my seat and stood me upright. And this being true, no law of the form "Whenever A, then people stand up in order to gain the floor by Robert's Rules of Order" is even conceivable. More generally, phrases referring to intentional conduct — to what Collingwood called the inner aspect of action, and what Peters and Tajfel term human activity as opposed to bodily movement — *cannot* serve as the consequent clauses of empirical laws.

In brief, Brown's defense of the social sciences may fail in much the same way as that of Helmer and Rescher: he demonstrates only that when it comes to establishing laws, there is no *strong* distinction between the social and the physical scientist. This leaves intact the separatist view that whereas there are types of conduct characteristic of human agents (and thus at the center of social science) which are conceptually recalcitrant to subsumption under general laws, no a priori restrictions on lawfulness can be levied on bio-chemical processes or astronomical events. The truth of this view, no doubt, would mark a weak rather than a strong distinction between physical and social science. But it would still constitute grounds for separatism and against Brown's conclusion that "There are no good reasons at all for this belief [that social scientists cannot do better with respect to establishing laws than they have done], only poor ones."

The second of our three subsections continues much of the work begun in the first. It isolates for study a single theoretical position in social science and supplies a classical exposition, a philosophical critique, and a computer-based reconstruction of this viewpoint. By thus concentrating on Stimulus-Response behaviorism, this sub-section should provide a kind of testing ground for philosophical claims concerning the roles of, and relations between, laws, theories, and explanations in the social sciences.

For Kenneth Spence, S-R theory can be characterized as seeking quantitative laws of the form R = f(S), where R is defined by "measurements of the behavior of organisms" and depends for its occurrence and intensity on stimulus-variables consisting of "physical and social environmental factors and conditions (present and past)" which the experimenter can manipulate. The behavioral psychologist, therefore, has a twofold objective in connection with any given type of response: "(1) to discover what the relevant S variables are, and (2) to ascertain the nature of the functional relations holding between the two groups of variables." His major theoretical problem arises when these objectives are temporarily frustrated by the discovery of behavioral responses that have no obvious relation to changes in environmental conditions. Such cases, e.g., when last year's date is written several times at the outset of autumn, or where, in the midst of continuing joy and productiveness, a man suddenly takes his own life, are not unusual. After discussing several ways out here, Spence finally plumbs for the Hull-Tolman solution: that to account for R-variables requires not only environmental conditions but "theoretical constructs" which denote nonmanipulable "intervening variables." (There seem to be difficulties in this solution which Spence overlooks. For he indicates explicitly that, for Hull and Tolman, such theoretical notions as "habit strength" are definable "in terms of the independent [i.e. environmental] variables." This, however, appears to destroy the distinction between manipulable and intervening variables; and if the former cannot account for certain behavioral responses, how, then, can the latter — given that for Spence, Hull, and Tolman, theoretical constructs are only shorthand devices for conveniently referring to environmental and manipulable factors?)

The Hullian behaviorism to which Spence pays tribute is firmly opposed by Peters and Tajfel, in a critique which parallels in scope Winch's rejection of nomothetic (law-seeking) forms of sociology. Hull's doctrine that "an ideally adequate theory even of so-called purposive behavior ought . . . to begin with colorless movement and mere receptor impulses as such, and from these build up step by step both adaptive and maladaptive behavior" is the primary target for Peters and Tajfel: they regard this doctrine as irredeemable, a mistake in principle. For man is a "rule-following" and "goal-directed" animal. To answer accurately the question "What is Bill doing (in the kitchen, on his vacation, etc.)?", we cannot appeal exclusively to the movements of his body. (Nor can we depend solely on what is *regularly produced* by those movements, a criterion suggested by selection 23's reliance on the Turing test; see here pages 293 to 296 below.) As Collingwood insisted, we can hope to identify Bill's action only by focusing on his intentions and beliefs and upon the surrounding social context of norms and attitudes. Consider Pascal's praying before and after conversion: perhaps the very same *physical movements* but utterly different *actions*. Or the exchange of slips of paper, which (depending on intentions and norms) is now the repayment of a loan, now submission to compulsory taxation, now the result of armed robbery, now the distribution of forged currency. But "if behavior cannot ever be described purely in terms of movements, how much less can it be *deduced* from a theory which is concerned only with 'colorless movement'."

That behaviorism is equal to this sort of challenge is precisely the thesis of Newell and Simon's "computer behaviorism." They argue that digital computers do not merely manipulate symbols, but "carry out complex patterns of processes that parallel exceedingly closely the processes observable in human subjects who are thinking." This being so, human actions expressing goals, beliefs, and standards, e.g., playing chess and constructing arguments, can be performed or approximated by machines the behavior of which is causally determined and falls entirely within the covering law model. Does this not redeem the Hobbes-Hull vision of "a deductive system in which statements about human behavior could be deduced from more general laws, e.g., of mechanics or physiology?" At the very least, it makes a valiant effort to bridge Peters and Tajfel's supposedly unpassable gulf between bodily movements and rule-governed purposive actions.

There are two key concepts on which the computer behaviorism advanced in selection 23 is constructed: (1) that of an "elementary information process" (such as testing whether two symbols are identical, transforming one symbol into another, or rearranging the components of a symbol) and (2) that of a "program" or "sequence of elementary information processes," the steps in which yield a certain complex result, e.g., the proof of a theorem in geometry, normally attained by human thought. Given these concepts, Newell and Simon declare that "if we are able to write a program that, realized on a computer, simulates human behavior closely, we can assert that we have discovered a set of mechanisms at least *sufficient* to account for the behavior." They then show that such programs have already been written.

This line of argument renders somewhat suspect Peters and Tajfel's critique of behaviorism — especially their supposition that "mechanical explanations can never be sufficient for actions falling under the concept of rule-following." To Peters and Tajfel's question, "In what sense can a physiological theory of the brain be said to *explain* a geometer's conclusion or a move at chess?", computer behaviorism has a ready answer. In reaching their goals, the geometer and chess-master exhibit complex patterns of behavior. These patterns can be simulated by a machine that stores and correlates information. But this entails that high-level human activity is comparable to, *and thus quite possibly explainable by*, programs composed of elementary information processes. And as for these latter processes, they "can be explained by showing how they can be reduced to known physiological processes in the central nervous system and its appendages."

The issues raised by Peters and Tajfel concerning explanation become paramount in our concluding subsection. "What does it mean to explain human conduct, where the agents involved are committed to certain goals and standards, have mastered certain social conventions, and are employing rational judgment (e.g., testing their beliefs by the hypothetical-deductive method) to guide their behavior?" — "What form do explanations of this sort take?"

Winch, Donagan, and Dray agree in finding the covering law model an inadequate answer to these questions, and they continue Scriven's efforts (in selections 9 and 10) to fashion alternative patterns for analyzing explanations of rational conduct. All three philosophers stand deeply and consciously in Collingwood's debt: it will be useful to view them as attempting to reconstruct his thesis that to explain human acts we must understand them, where by *understanding* is meant "penetrating to the inside of events and detecting the thought which they express." The standard objection to Collingwood that this "detection" relies on an intuitive process (imaginative reenactment, empathy, *verstehen*) wholly beyond the reach of evidence and argument, should be tested against these three reconstructions.[1]

There does not seem to be total consensus, however, among Dray, Donagan, and Winch. Their accounts of what Dray terms "rational explanation," for example, reveal surface differences. On Donagan's analysis, to give a rational explanation is to reason *towards* an assertion concerning the intended goal for which an action was performed. But for Dray, rational explanations *proceed from* such intentional assertions — take them as premisses — and attempt to warrant conclusions that describe concrete historical acts. Consider, in addition, the extent to which each philosopher rejects the covering law model. What appears to emerge is a continuum of repudiation. Donagan claims only that explanations in history or social science can sometimes succeed without any appeal to empirical laws. Dray concurs with this. But he also contends that given the aim of some historical explanations (to show that a man's action "made perfectly good sense from his own point of view"), the introduction of empirical laws is not only unnecessary but always irrelevant to the task of rendering the performed action intelligible. And Winch takes an even more radical position. Of the three, he seems closest to this passage from R. S. Peters' *The Concept of Motivation.*

> . . . if we are in fact confronted with a case of genuine action (i.e. an act of doing some hing as opposed to suffering something), then causal explanations are *ipso facto* inappropriate. Indeed they rule out rule-following purposive explanations. To ask what made Jones do something is to rule out that he had some reason for doing it. Similarly to ascribe a point to his action is *ipso facto* to deny that it can be *sufficiently explained* in terms of causes . . . If the question is "Why did Jones walk across the road?" a *sufficient* explanation can only be given in terms of the rule-following purposive model — if this is a case of an action rather than of something happening to him. Answers in terms of causal concepts like 'receptor impulses' and 'colourless movement', or quasi-causal concepts like 'drive' are either not explanations because they do not state sufficient conditions or they are ways of denying that what has to be explained is a human action.[2]

A good part of Winch's case is built upon the doctrine that human action is governed not by *empirical laws* but by *social rules*, for example, that in poker three deuces beat two kings, or that a quarter, in American currency, has the same value as five nickels. For is it not these rules, rather than any laws, theories, or concepts the social scientist might devise, which must be consulted to decide whether two human acts are or are

[1] *Verstehen* is afforded more detailed consideration by the introductions to parts V and VIII below.

[2] Peters, R. S. *The Concept of Motivation.* New York and London, 1958, pp. 12 and 15.

not of the *same* type? An oriental anthropologist would simply have to accept our practice of counting as *married* not only those who participate in traditional rites as prescribed by their faiths, but those who exchange unceremonious vows before a non-ecclesiastical state official, and those as well who have simply managed to live with one another for seven years. Furthermore, Winch asserts, social rules are open-ended; they neither determine nor dictate what is to be done in all contexts. If a batch of pennies came from the U. S. Mint with several misspelled words, the decision as to their value would *not* be derivable from any existing rule. On the contrary, so Winch might argue, our rules would here be mute. Those who now use the coins would simply be placed in the position of choosing between alternative ways of extending their present conventions to cover this unexpected situation. Given considerations such as these, Winch draws the weak separatist conclusion that for many social phenomena, the ideal of scientific explanation and prediction by covering law is self-contradictory. "When we speak of the possibility of scientific prediction of social developments of this sort, we literally do not understand what we are saying. We cannot understand it, because it has no sense." This conclusion may be accessible to Donagan and Dray, but their arguments are designed to substantiate more cautious contentions. Dray, for example, does not attempt to show that once we recognize Louis XIV's military decision of 1688 as rational, or "appropriate at least to the circumstances as they were envisaged," it becomes *self-contradictory* to devise a Hempelian covering law explanation for that decision.

Hempel and Goldstein offer two ways of defending the utility of the covering law model in the social sciences. With arguments which are carried further in selections 35, 37, 46, and 48 below, they maintain that a nomothetic social science *can* provide casual explanations for rational conduct. Hempel begins by advancing a "necessary condition of adequacy for explanations": their *explanans* must supply good evidence for believing their *explananda*. He then charges that proposition 8 of the covering law position applies to Dray's notion of rational explanation. Referring to an agent's beliefs and aspirations to explain his intentional conduct can satisfy this necessary condition, Hempel avows, only by being supplemented in two directions: first, by a description of the agent's circumstances and second, by citing a *lawful connection* between the tendency to be rational in those circumstances and the sort of conduct to be explained. Left unsupplemented, rational explanations can at best clarify or elucidate the action to be explained; they cannot show why this action, rather than any other, occurred at all or at the time and place in question.

Goldstein's review turns one of Winch's key principles of method against the central thesis of *The Idea of a Social Science*. As we have seen, Winch maintains that in accounting for human conduct, social scientists must remain faithful to the criteria and concepts employed within the practices they investigate. His own book, however, involves an investigation of those practices operative *within contemporary social science*. Thus, given Winch's methodological position, this investigation must accept as bedrock the actual intentions and standards of practicing social scientists. It is Goldstein's claim that Winch fails to meet this self-imposed prescription: for "some [sociologists] take it be entirely within their purview to seek [causal] explanations of social phenomena. In other words, they are concerned to discover . . . how it was that this or that institution came to be as it is or how institutions of determinate type develop and change."

Winch, then, binds himself to reflect, rather than evaluate or propose changes in, the rules by which social scientists operate with such concepts as 'law' and 'explanation'.

Whatever form these rules take, he cannot consistently oppose them or recommend their elimination. Yet are they not quite permissive towards the idea of a nomothetic social science? Witness the continued sufferance by social scientists of positions like those of Mill, Pareto, Skinner, and Hull. Winch is pledged to echo this tolerance and thus, it seems, must inconsistently accept the covering law model as a live option for explaining and predicting the entire range of human activity. (Goldstein's view that only "nomothetic social science" can account for institutional change and development appears again in Part VII and is examined critically on pages 587 to 602, below.)

This section concludes with Norman Malcolm's attempt to establish that a certain form of "mechanism" is unintelligible. The version of mechanism attacked by Malcolm contends (i) that there are general laws which "connect neurophysiological states or processes with movements [of human bodies]" and (ii) that these laws alone — without reference to any nonphysiological factors — suffice to permit the explanation and prediction of every instance of human behavior. (Or, rather, of all conduct which is *not* simply the product of "forces . . . applied externally to the body," forces like the impact of a fist, bullet, or car.)

The argument Malcolm uses against mechanism rests, in part, on a distinction to which Donagan appealed in selection 26. Both Donagan and Malcolm affirm that the general propositions involved in a "purposive (rational) explanation" should not be confused with the universals essential to covering law explanations. The latter describe contingent correlations which, at best, are found to hold uniformly in this world, but would break down entirely in other conceivable universes. But "purposive principles" state conceptual (nonexperimental) truths; they affirm necessary connections between a person's having such psychological states as intentions, desires, aims, objectives, etc., and his performance of actions he believes to be required or useful for realizing them. Such principles, e.g., that linking the intention to do X with the performance of X in the absence of interference or that connecting the desire for Y in those who believe Z is requisite for that goal with an effort to realize Z — such principles, Malcolm avows, "are a priori."

Donagan employs this distinction between types of universals to support his thesis that explanations of what men do can avoid any reliance on covering laws. Malcolm accepts this thesis but in addition maintains that (mechanistic) covering law explanations are incompatible with purposive explanations: no behavior for which a (mechanistic) covering law explanation is located can be explained teleologically (and vice versa).

If there is some neurophysiological explanation for Jones' picking up the newspaper then it cannot be true that he did so in order to work the crossword puzzle or because (for the sake of) any other goal or objective. For the mechanistic account entails that Jones would have picked up that newspaper even if he had had no knowledge of how to work a crossword puzzle or that one was there to be worked, or even if he was repelled by the idea of spending time trying to solve one. That is, the explanandum would have occurred even in the total absence of the — or any — proposed teleological explanans. And this indicates that for mechanism, aims, decisions, and the like cannot be thought of as *necessary conditions* for the occurrence of human behavior. But neither can a consistent mechanist permit such factors to count as *sufficient conditions* of the acts men perform. To do so, Malcolm alleges, would contradict (ii), the assumption of a closed, single-factor system capable of predicting and explaining every bit of actual or potential human activity without recourse to independent variables of a nonphysiological sort. Mechanism, then, implies a third claim: (iii) that the intentions and aims of human beings never play any role in generating or explaining their behavior.

What is central to Malcolm's case can now be arrived at by simply conjoining his dictum that purposive principles are a priori with this third mechanistic doctrine. To say that purposive principles are necessary truths is to say that *if* there are any intentions or objectives, *then* some human acts can be explained by the beliefs and aims of the agents who perform them — beliefs and aims which conceptually imply the performance of those acts. (See Malcolm's example on page 335 below.) Mechanism, given (iii), rejects the consequent of this conditional. It is therefore constrained to reject the antecedent; that is, *to deny that men ever have desires, ambitions, plans, hopes, etc.* Were a mechanist to allow this dimension of human behavior, he would have to concede that what men do can occasionally be explained by appealing to their aspirations and opinions and, thus, not by electrical-chemical changes in the human organism.

But this total, though implicit, denial of human intentionality surely reduces mechanism to absurdity. For the assertion of mechanism, like the assertion of any view, is a piece of mental activity which can be performed only by those who do have intentions, desires, etc. Thus, anyone who asserts mechanism implies *both* that there are human purposes and that there are no human purposes: his performance refutes what is affirmed by his words. (Much as writing 'No sentence can be written' refutes what is affirmed by that sentence.)

In short, then, if Malcolm's argument is sound, the doctrine of mechanism cannot be consistently asserted. (Nor for that matter can it be believed.) It *is* possible to conceive of a universe in which mechanism would be true. What cannot be conceived is that we ourselves are situated in such a universe and *have retained the power to form beliefs and advance assertions*. For if we possess those capacities, then we have intentions, and if there are human intentions then not all of our behavior can be explained by mechanistic covering laws. Mechanism can hold, if at all, only in a universe where no one is able to talk about it, to express it, to reflect upon its merits, or debate it. And this alone should give pause to both psychologists (like Newell and Simon) and covering law theorists for whom science requires a commitment to a mechanistically determinist viewpoint according to which desires, aims, etc. can never serve to explain human conduct. Indeed, the very possibility of scientific inquiry, theorizing, and experimentation — which all involve purposes and intentions — seems incompatible with mechanism.

These objections to the doctrine of mechanism appear to lend substantial weight to a more general conclusion. Malcolm's attack is restricted to a single form of the covering law position, that focused exclusively on neurophysiological laws governing human conduct. But his arguments seem equally applicable to other varieties of nomothetic social science, e.g., those expounded in selections 21 and 51, which allege that human behavior is completely predictable by reference to laws utilizing independent variables of an environmental or societal sort (or to such laws in combination with neurophysiological laws). For these positions, as much as mechanism, are committed to proposition (iii), i.e., to the wholesale rejection of rational or purposive explanations. Hence, given the a priori status of purposive principles, they too cannot escape implying that men never have aims, objectives, preferences, etc.; and this means, as we have seen, that these varieties of the covering law position cannot be intelligibly asserted, believed, entertained, etc. Thus, in undermining mechanism, Malcolm may well have provided a strong line of defense for Winch's thesis that the very idea of a nomothetic social science is unintelligible and self-defeating.

Two Types of Social Uniformities

17

from *Social Theory and Social Structure*

ROBERT K. MERTON

Empirical Generalizations in Sociology

Not infrequently it is said that the object of sociological theory is to arrive at statements of social uniformities. This is an elliptical assertion and hence requires clarification. For there are two types of statements of sociological uniformities which differ significantly in their bearing on theory. The first of these is the empirical generalization: an isolated proposition summarizing observed uniformities of relationships between two or more variables.[1] The sociological literature abounds with such generalizations which have not been assimilated to sociological theory. Thus, Engel's "laws" of consumption may be cited as examples. So, too, the Halbwachs finding that laborers spend more per adult unit for food than white-collar employees of the same income class.[2] Such generalizations may be of greater or less precision, but this does not affect their logical place in the structure of inquiry. The Groves-Ogburn finding, for a sample of American cities, that "cities with a larger percentage engaged in manufacturing also have, on the average, slightly larger percentages of young persons married" has been expressed in an equation indicating the degree of this relationship. Although propositions of this order are essential in empirical research, a miscellany of such propositions only provides the raw materials for sociology as a discipline. The theoretic task, and the orientation of empirical research toward theory, first begins when the bearing of such uniformities on a set of interrelated propositions is tentatively established. The notion of directed research implies that, in part,[3] empirical inquiry is so organized that if and when empirical uniformities are discovered, they have direct consequences for a theoretic system. In so far as the research is directed, the rationale of findings is set forth before the findings are obtained.

Reprinted with permission of The Macmillan Company, New York, from *Social Theory and Social Structure* by Robert K. Merton, pp. 95–99.

[1] This usage of the term "empirical" is common, as Dewey notes. In this context, "*empirical* means that the subject-matter of a given proposition which has existential inference, represents merely a set of uniform conjunctions of traits repeatedly observed to exist, without any understanding of *why* the conjunction occurs; without a theory which states its rationale." John Dewey, *Logic: The Theory of Inquiry* (New York: Henry Holt & Co., 1938), 305.

[2] See a considerable collection of such uniformities summarized by C. C. Zimmerman, *Consumption and Standards of Living* (New York: D. Van Nostrand Co., 1936), 51 ff.

[3] "In part," if only because it stultifies the possibilities of obtaining fertile new findings to confine researches *wholly* to the test of predetermined hypotheses. Hunches originating in the course of the inquiry which may not have immediately obvious implications for a broader theoretic system may eventuate in the discovery of empirical uniformities which can later be incorporated into a theory. For example, in the sociology of political behavior, it has been recently established that the larger the number of social cross-pressures to which voters are subjected, the less interest they exhibit in a presidential election (P. F. Lazarsfeld, Bernard Berelson, and Hazel Gaudet, *The People's Choice* [New York: Duell, Sloan & Pearce, 1944], 56–64). This finding, which was wholly unanticipated when the research was first formulated, may well initiate new lines of systematic inquiry into political behavior, even though it is not yet integrated into a generalized theory. Fruitful empirical research not only tests theoretically derived hypotheses; it also originates new hypotheses. This might be termed the "serendipity" component of research, i.e., the discovery, by chance or sagacity, of valid results which were not sought for.

The second type of sociological generalization, the so-called scientific law, differs from the foregoing in as much as it is a statement of invariance *derivable* from a theory. The paucity of such laws in the sociological field perhaps reflects the prevailing bifurcation of theory and empirical research. Despite the many volumes dealing with the history of sociological theory and despite the plethora of empirical investigations, sociologists (including the writer) may discuss the logical criteria of sociological laws without citing a single instance which fully satisfies these criteria.[4]

Approximations to these criteria are not entirely wanting. To exhibit the relations of empirical generalizations to theory and to set forth the functions of theory, it may be useful to examine a familiar case in which such generalizations were incorporated into a body of substantive theory. Thus, it has long been established as a statistical uniformity that in a variety of populations, Catholics have a lower suicide rate than Protestants.[5] In this form the uniformity posed a theoretical problem. It merely constituted an empirical regularity which would become significant for theory only if it could be derived from a set of other propositions, a task which Durkheim set himself. If we restate his theoretic assumptions in formal fashion, the paradigm of his theoretic analysis becomes clear:

1. Social cohesion provides psychic support to group members subjected to acute stresses and anxieties.

2. Suicide rates are functions of *unrelieved* anxieties and stresses to which persons are subjected.

3. Catholics have greater social cohesion than Protestants.

4. Therefore, lower suicide rates should be anticipated among Catholics than among Protestants.[6]

This case serves to locate the place of empirical generalizations in relation to theory and to illustrate the several functions of theory.

1. It indicates that theoretic pertinence is not inherently present or absent in empirical generalizations but appears when the generalization is conceptualized in abstractions of higher order (Catholicism — social cohesion — relieved anxieties — suicide rate) which are embodied in more general statements of relationships.[7] What was initially taken as an isolated uniformity is restated as a relation, not between religious affiliation and behavior, but between groups with certain conceptualized attributes (social cohesion) and the behavior. The *scope* of the original empirical finding is considerably extended, and several seemingly disparate uniformities are seen to be interrelated (thus differentials in suicide rates between married and single persons can be derived from the same theory).

2. Once having established the theoretic

[4] E.g., see the discussion by George A. Lundberg, "The concept of law in the social sciences," *Philosophy of Science*, 1938, 5, 189–203, which affirms the possibility of such laws without including any case in point. The book by K. D. Har, *Social Laws* (Chapel Hill: University of North Carolina Press, 1930), does not fulfil the promise implicit in the title. A panel of social scientists discussing the possibility of obtaining social laws finds it difficult to instance cases (Blumer, *op. cit.*, 142-50).

[5] It need hardly be said that this statement assumes that education, income, nationality, rural-urban residence, and other factors which might render this finding spurious have been held constant.

[6] We need not examine further aspects of this illustration, e.g., (1) the extent to which we have adequately stated the premises implicit in Durkheim's interpretation; (2) the supplementary theoretic analysis which would take these premises not as given but as problematic; (3) the grounds on which the potentially infinite regression of theoretic interpretations is halted at one rather than another point; (4) the problems involved in the introduction of such intervening variables as social cohesion which are not directly measured; (5) the extent to which the premises have been empirically confirmed; (6) the comparatively low order of abstraction represented by this illustration and (7) the fact that Durkheim derived several empirical generalizations from this same set of hypotheses.

[7] Thorstein Veblen has put this with typical cogency: "All this may seem like taking pains about trivialities. But the data with which any scientific inquiry has to do are trivialities in some other bearing than that one in which they are of account." *The Place of Science in Modern Civilization* (New York: Viking Press, 1932), 42.

pertinence of a uniformity by deriving it from a set of interrelated propositions, we provide for the *cumulation* both of theory and of research findings. The differentials-in-suicide-rate uniformities add confirmation to the set of propositions from which they — and other uniformities — have been derived. This is a major function of *systematic theory*.

3. Whereas the empirical uniformity did not lend itself to the drawing of diverse consequences, the reformulation gives rise to various consequences in fields of conduct quite remote from that of suicidal behavior. For example, inquiries into obsessive behavior, morbid preoccupations, and other maladaptive behavior have found these also to be related to inadequacies of group cohesion.[8] The conversion of empirical uniformities into theoretic statements thus increases the *fruitfulness* of research through the successive exploration of implications.

4. By providing a rationale, the theory introduces a *ground for prediction* which is more secure than mere empirical extrapolation from previously observed trends. Thus, should independent measures indicate a decrease of social cohesion among Catholics, the theorist would predict a tendency toward increased rates of suicide in this group. The atheoretic empiricist would have no alternative, however, but to predict on the basis of extrapolation.

5. The foregoing list of functions presupposes one further attribute of theory which is not altogether true of the Durkheim formulation and which gives rise to a general problem that has peculiarly beset sociological theory, at least, up to the present. If theory is to be productive, it must be sufficiently *precise* to be *determinate*. Precision is an integral element of the criterion of *testability*. The prevailing pressure toward the utilization of statistical data in sociology, whenever possible, to control and test theoretic inferences has a justifiable basis, when we consider the logical place of precision in disciplined inquiry.

The more precise the inferences (predictions) which can be drawn from a theory, the less the likelihood of *alternative* hypotheses which will be adequate to these predictions. In other words, precise predictions and data serve to reduce the *empirical* bearing upon research of the *logical* fallacy of affirming the consequent.[9] It is well known that verified predictions derived from a theory do not prove or demonstrate that theory; they merely supply a measure of confirmation, for it is always possible that alternative hypotheses drawn from different theoretic systems can also account for the predicted phenomena.[10] But those theories which admit of precise predictions confirmed by observation take on strategic importance since they provide an initial basis for choice between competing hypotheses. In other words, precision enhances the likelihood of approximating a "crucial" observation or experiment.

The internal coherence of a theory has much the same function, for if a variety of empirically confirmed consequences are drawn from one theoretic system, this reduces the likelihood that competing theories can adequately account for the same data. The integrated theory sustains a larger measure of confirmation than is the case with distinct and unrelated hypotheses, thus accumulating a greater weight of evidence.

[8] See, e.g., Elton Mayo, *Human Problems of an Industrial Civilization* (New York: Macmillan Co., 1933), 113 *et passim*. The theoretical framework utilized in the studies of industrial morale by Whitehead, Roethlisberger, and Dickson stemmed appreciably from the Durkheim formulations, as the authors testify.

[9] The paradigm of "proof through prediction" is, of course, logically fallacious:

If *A* (hypothesis), then *B* (prediction).

B is observed.

Therefore, *A* is true.

This is not overdisturbing for scientific research, in as much as other than formal criteria are involved.

[10] As a case in point, consider that different theorists had predicted war and internecine conflict on a large scale at midcentury. Sorokin and some Marxists, for example, set forth this prediction on the basis of quite distinct theoretic systems. The actual outbreak of large-scale conflicts does not in itself enable us to choose between these schemes of analysis, if only because the observed fact is consistent with both. Only if the predictions had been so *specified*, had been so precise, that the actual occurrences coincided with the one prediction and not with the other, would a determinate test have been instituted.

Voluntarism: Social Uniformities Depend on the Choices of Men 18

Can Men Change Laws of Social Science?

ALAN GEWIRTH

Some Preliminary Distinctions

The relation between the natural and the social sciences, as it bears on their respective subject-matters, methods, and propositions, has long been a source of problems for the philosophy of science. The title of this paper is intended to indicate one of the most basic of these problems. Before developing my point, however, I wish to guard against a possible misinterpretation. I am not questioning the accepted fact that as knowledge in any field advances men may come to recognize the incorrectness of what they had previously regarded as "laws" in that field, and may consequently "change" these laws to take account of such increased knowledge. Let me call this kind of change of laws *doctrinal change*. The kind of change about which I am asking is rather a change in the subject-matter itself insofar as it is subject to laws — i.e., a change in the causal relations among the facts, objects, properties, events, or whatever they may be called, with which the science deals. Let me call this kind of change of laws *factual change*. Now, without inquiring more fully at the moment into the nature of scientific laws as such, we may say that the history of science shows that men can and do effect doctrinal changes in the laws of any science, natural as well as social, and formal as well as empirical. And it is recognized also, with minor exceptions to be noted later, that men cannot effect factual changes in the laws of the natural sciences, since these are independent of human volition or decision. The question I am asking, then, is whether men can effect factual changes in the laws of the social sciences.

One further terminological point by way of preliminary. Since we have distinguished two kinds of changes in scientific laws, we may likewise distinguish two different kinds or aspects of the laws themselves. "Law" is obviously a double-barrelled word; entirely apart from the ambiguities introduced by treating scientific laws as if they were political laws (of which more later), the term "law" may refer either to the cause-effect relations which actually obtain in the world, or to men's attempted knowledge and formulation of such relations. Let us, in keeping with our previous distinction, call the former *factual laws* and the latter *doctrinal laws*. Now for the most part I shall be dealing in this paper with men's factual change of factual laws of social science; and in this sense I shall use the terms "natural laws" and "social laws" as abbreviations for "the laws of the natural and the social sciences," respectively. Nevertheless, I wish to retain the title of this paper in its present form, for at least two reasons: (*a*) one of my main aims is to compare the degree of necessity or probability attainable in the natural and the social sciences; (*b*) I shall be wanting to refer to both natural and social laws in terms of the kinds of selectivity or discrimination involved in the scientific formulation of laws. This aspect, it is to be noted, is different from the aspect involving increased knowledge which led us to distinguish doctrinal from factual changes in scientific laws.

From *Philosophy of Science*, 21:3 (July, 1954), pp. 229–241.

Social Laws and Men's Reactions on Them

Now the general position I wish to present is the following. In dealing with social phenomena, social science deals largely if not entirely with things which impinge directly on men's values — wealth, power, various kinds of interpersonal relations, and so on. The aim of social science may be said to be to attain knowledge of the laws of these matters — that is, of their cause-effect relations. Since, however, man as conscious voluntary agent is in large part both the knower and the subject-matter of these laws, his knowledge of their impact on his values may lead him to react on the laws reflexively in order to change them. Consequently, the laws of the social sciences cannot have the same fixity or permanence as the laws of the natural sciences.

This reflexive reaction of men on social laws has interesting logical as well as social consequences. One of its familiar aspects is found in such reflexive situations as the "self-destroying prophecy" (cf. 4, pp. 121–22, 197ff.);[1] for example, if there is wide acceptance of a prediction that because of its superior wealth a nation will win a war in which it is presently engaged, this may lead to a complacency which results in losing the war. Here men's knowledge of a social "law" — the correlation, other things being equal, between superior wealth and military success — leads to action which removes the effective operation of the law.[2] Similar to this is the "self-fulfilling prophecy"; for example, the Keynesian economists' predictions that if certain policies are followed there will be no depression have resulted in demands for various kinds of governmental regulation and direct governmental concern with the prevention of depression. Here men's knowledge of a prediction based on social knowledge leads to action aimed at fulfilling the prediction.[3] Both these kinds of prophecy may be viewed as forms of "pragmatic implication," but in a more dynamic sense than is usually found in discussions of the relation between linguistic expressions and the users of those expressions. These modes of the influence of knowledge of social laws or propositions on their empirical effectuation must be sharply differentiated from Heisenberg's principle of indeterminacy according to which the attempt to observe an electron changes the characteristics of the electron. For an electron, unlike a social group, does not change its characteristics because of its own knowledge of those characteristics as disclosed by the observation of it.

A further consequence of this social reflexivity is that while at any given stage we may distinguish the linguistic discourse of a social group from the discourse of the social scientists studying that group, calling the latter "metalinguistic" in relation to the former, this distinction collapses when the users of the primary discourse become aware of the meta-linguistic discourse and use it to change their own discourse. As a familiar case in point I may cite the fact that the discourse of sociologists and social psychologists concerning the effects of the use of pejorative expressions to refer to various ethnic groups

[1] Merton's interpretation of this concept and of the "self-fulfilling prophecy," however, is more restrictive than that which is presented here.

[2] The self-destroying prophecy may be symbolized in either of the following two ways:

(1) $(\exists x)(Px[A \rightarrow C]) \rightarrow \{(\exists y)(\approx Ay) \rightarrow (\exists z)(\approx Cz)\}$.

"If there is a prediction P that a certain kind of action A will result in a certain consequence C, then this prediction has the result that the contrary [symbolized by the two negations placed one under the other] of action A occurs and that it results in the occurrence of the contrary of consequence C."

(2) $(\exists x)(Px[A_1 \rightarrow C]) \rightarrow \{[(\exists y)(A_1 y) \cdot (\exists z)(A_2 z)] \rightarrow (\exists w)(\approx Cw)\}$.

"If there is a prediction P that a certain kind of action A_1 will result in a certain consequence C, then this prediction has the result that action A_1 and also other action A_2 occur, and that these actions have the result that the contrary of consequence C occurs."

[3] The self-fulfilling prophecy may be symbolized as follows:

$$(\exists x)(Px[A \rightarrow C]) \rightarrow \{(\exists y)(Ay) \rightarrow (\exists z)(Cz)\}.$$

"If there is a prediction P that a certain kind of action A will result in a certain consequence C, then this prediction has the result that action A does occur and that it does result in the occurrence of consequence C."

has led in many cases to the disuse of those expressions — i.e., to a change in the primary language about which the sociologists were talking.

This reflexive characteristic of social laws, and the consequent contrast which I have drawn between them and natural laws in respect of fixity or permanence, involve many complex problems. The situation is by no means so simple as my discussion of it so far may have suggested. To unravel some of its complexities, let us consider two basic arguments against the position here presented. I shall call them "the argument from the pervasiveness of laws" and "the argument from the social determination of knowledge and action."

The Argument from the Pervasiveness of Laws

Let us agree that every social law, like natural laws, aims to state a correlation of selected and discriminated kinds of entity, and that it states this correlation, moreover, with the implicit or explicit recognition of the conditions under which the correlation holds. On this view, social laws are different both from so-called laws of history concerning the developmental relations among whole civilizations or historical epochs, and from inductive generalizations stated without recognition of qualifying conditions. Let us take as an example the following simplified version of an anthropological "law": "All matrilineal and patrilocal societies tend to develop certain kinds of stresses within their family units," where "matrilineal" means that the wealth is inherited through the females and "patrilocal" means that the married offspring live in or near the home of the husband's parents. Let us call this *Law A*; and let us assume that the specific characteristics of the stresses which I have vaguely called "certain kinds of stresses" have been made explicit enough to be objectively measurable: they may include, for example, a certain rate of desertions by the fathers, a certain proportion of quarrels resulting in legal or some similar kind of action, and so on. But now suppose further that all or many of the members of such a society become aware of this law, and realize therefore the cause of the stresses in their society. Obviously they may react in many different ways. Let us assume that one way in which they react is to change from a matrilineal to a patrilineal system. Now this does not of course invalidate Law A, any more than the traditional laws of supply and demand are invalidated by a change from a competitive economy, in which those laws hold, to a monopolistic economy, in which they do not. Rather, what has happened is that the conditions of Law A no longer exist, and instead there is a new set of conditions. But this new set has its own law, such as, for example, that "A patrilineal and patrilocal society will not tend to develop stresses of the kind generated when the society is matrilineal." Let us call this *Law B*. The argument from the pervasiveness of laws, then, asserts that men cannot change social laws, but can only exchange the conditions of one law for those of another; and that for each set of conditions there are laws, i.e., relatively constant correlations, which exist among the different characteristics of men's social acts and institutions.

In addition to this exchange of conditions, there are two other ways in which the argument from the pervasiveness of laws asserts that men's intervention does not change social laws. One way is by specification, the other by generalization. Let us take Law A again, and let us suppose that the society reacts to its knowledge of this law not by changing from a matrilineal to a patrilineal society but rather by instituting special symbols of respect for the fathers. And let us assume that this experiment works: the society remains matrilineal and patrilocal, but the addition of the special symbols of respect is followed by a sharp diminution and ultimately a cessation of the kinds of stresses previously experienced. Has this development invalidated Law A? Obviously not;

instead we now have *Law C*: "A matrilineal and patrilocal society in which there are special symbols of respect for the father will not tend to develop stresses of the kind generated when there are not such symbols." Here, as in Law B, we have exchanged one set of conditions for another, but this new set is related to the old set not as contraries but rather as specific to general, since we have added a new determinant. But this in turn means that Law A must now be stated with a corresponding specifying condition: "A matrilineal and patrilocal society *in which there are no special symbols of respect for the father* will tend to develop stresses within its family units." In this way men's intervention through their knowledge of Law A does not change that law but rather leads to a knowledge of one of its specifying conditions.

The other way in which the argument from the pervasiveness of laws makes its point is by generalization. Suppose that, imbued with the cultural relativism of which anthropologists have made so much, we conduct sufficient empirical research to find some societies which are matrilineal and patrilocal and yet develop no stresses of the kinds asserted in Law A. Here, obviously, we would look for the conditions which differentiate the two kinds of society; let us assume that a social myth of maternal divinity is found among the societies which do not develop the kinds of stresses in question, and is not found among the societies that do. This, then, could lead to a specification of Law A, as above in Law C. But in addition it could lead us to look for the more general law or rule governing the occurrence of stresses in all societies, both matrilineal and patrilineal. Such a general law might be, for example, that "All societies in which authority and prestige are separated from responsibility tend to develop internal frictions." Let us call this *Law D*. Such a law would not be changed by human intervention, for both its conditions and its terms would be general enough to subsume the specific kinds of changes which men's intervention might bring about. This generalizing technique is similar to that used by proponents of "natural laws" and "natural rights" in the ethical and political senses when they wish to show that such laws and rights are not invalidated by apparent exceptions.

Nor is this all. For the argument from the pervasiveness of laws goes on to point out that all three ways of answering the assertion that men's intervention can change social laws apply to the laws of the natural as well as the social sciences. Of specification and generalization this is too obviously the case to require discussion. But it also applies to the first way, that of the exchange of conditions. An invention like the elevator or the airplane does not invalidate Galileo's law of falling bodies, but rather embodies the results of conditions different from the free fall in a perfect vacuum which is the condition of Galileo's law. And man can at least to some extent control these conditions, just as he can control the conditions which will determine whether one social law empirically obtains or another. Hence, just as inventions like the airplane involve not the disproof but rather the application of physical laws through men's intervention, so too with men's intervention in relation to social laws.

Another Statement of the Argument

The points which have been made so far may also be put in another way as follows. In the case of any factual law, natural or social, we may distinguish two different aspects, which may be called the *conditional* and the *existential*. The *conditional* aspect consists in the law viewed as a hypothetical correlation of variables, of the form: *if x, then y*; where '*x*' represents certain conditions and '*y*' represents what occurs when those conditions occur. As the discussion of counterfactual conditionals has made clear, such conditional laws may be true even when the antecedent is false, i.e., does not actually obtain; and the reason for such truth is different from that found in the comparatively trivial case of material implication.

Examples of such conditional antecedents are the unhindered operation of gravity in the natural sphere, and the operation of supply and demand in the social sphere. The *existential* aspect of factual laws, on the other hand, consists in the conditions and correlations which actually obtain at any given time. In their existential aspect, then, factual laws are true only when their antecedent conditions are true.[4] Now the argument from the pervasiveness of laws holds that natural and social laws, so far as their being changed by men is concerned, are similar in both their conditional and their existential aspects: in their conditional aspect neither kind of law can be factually changed by men, and in their existential aspect both kinds can be factually changed by men, since men can control the conditions which result in the actual occurrence or operation of one correlation as against another. For example, if we take Newton's law of gravitation and the economic laws of supply and demand in their conditional aspect, then these laws are eternally true in the sense that each sets forth a correlation of variables which remains true regardless of what men may do. And if we take these laws in their existential aspect, then each can be changed by men in that men can bring it about that the conditions which function as antecedents in these laws do not actually obtain (e.g., the airplane removes the free operation of gravity, and monopoly removes the free operation of the market). Moreover, this argument from the pervasiveness of laws goes on to hold that insofar as there is a difference at all between natural and social laws in respect of their being changed by men, this difference is at most one of degree only, not of kind, and is to be found only in the existential aspect of laws. For since men can effect fewer changes in their natural than in their social environment, it follows that among the laws which actually obtain natural ones reflect human operational changes to a lesser degree than do social laws. But this does not alter the fact that in principle both kinds of laws bear the same relation to human change.

Reply to the Argument

It is now time to see whether these considerations completely negate our initial assertion that man's knowledge of social laws may lead him to change these laws, and that consequently they cannot have the same fixity or permanence as natural laws. That our assertion requires many qualifications in the light of these considerations must certainly be admitted. But these with qualifications understood, it is still true and important.[5] The point which remains amid the objections we have considered may be put in this way. Let us consider three different relations which man may bear to scientific laws: namely, that he can *exchange* the laws, *apply* the laws, and *create* the laws. Man *exchanges* laws when he replaces the conditions under which one set of laws — i.e., one correlation of variables — obtains, for another set of conditions under which a different correlation obtains. Man *applies* laws when he uses a correlation which exists independently of his decisions to produce an effect which would not have occurred if he had not made that use of the correlation. Man *creates* laws, finally, when, by means of his free decision and consequent action, he causes a correlation to exist which did not exist before.

Now there have been many philosophies, like those of the Marxists, the operationalists,

[4] This distinction between the conditional and existential aspects of laws is not the same as Dewey's distinction between "universal" and "generic" propositions (2, pp. 264ff.). As here viewed, a law in its conditional aspect does not "present the analysis of a conception into its integral and exhaustive contents" (*ibid.*, p. 272).

[5] I shall not dwell on the far greater difficulties involved in applying experimental methods to confirm or disconfirm the correlations among the highly discriminated characteristics with which we said initially that social laws must deal. When one reads a book like (1) one becomes aware once more of how crude the attempts to isolate the relevant variables still are; and these difficulties are still found in the contemporary attempts to apply mathematical techniques to ascertain the relations among these variables.

and the pragmatists, which have tended to identify the relations which human action bears to natural laws, to social laws, and to technological inventions or artefacts. But all the analogies apart, the following important difference remains. Insofar as social laws follow from men's free decisions, men may create social laws. But men cannot create natural laws. In producing new artefacts, men apply natural laws which prëexist independently of human decisions to effect consequences which would not have occurred without human action.

The crucial issue on this question, of course, is whether men can create new social laws. Is it not rather, as was urged by the argument from the pervasiveness of laws, that men can only exchange the conditions under which one law holds for another set of conditions under which another law holds? The difficulty with this formulation, however, is that it seems to give to social laws the status of eternal correlations which exist apart from all creative activity on the part of men. Now I think that it is not too implausible to describe natural laws in this way, such that even the entities which emerge from operations of the kind typified by atom-smashing machines are nevertheless discovered in nature rather than being artefacts, just as the telescope may be said to find rather than make stars. But if man can to any extent make his own history, then his social laws cannot be characterized in the same way, for the very correlations in which such laws consist may be changed by men's decisions.

Let us analyze this point a little more closely in the following way. We may grant that, given precisely the same conditions, precisely the same effect will follow, so that if a different effect follows, there must have been different conditions. Consequently, if to change a law means to make a different effect follow from precisely the same conditions, then for men to change social laws is impossible. In this sense the argument from the pervasiveness of laws is unanswerable. Nevertheless, there are two interrelated considerations which mitigate this conclusion insofar as it is interpreted as applying against the possibility of men's creating new social laws. In the first place, human volitions or decisions may be among the conditions of social laws. Consequently, by changing the decisions one changes the effect, and therefore a new correlation is created. In this case one has indeed exchanged the conditions of one law for those of another, but the decisions in which those conditions partly consist are made by men, and consequently in this sense the new law or correlation is also made or created by men, and is not merely found by men in the sense in which they find the laws of natural objects which cannot be affected by human decision. It might be held, in accordance with the principle of generalization mentioned above, that all such laws are but applications of some more general and fundamental law which cannot be affected by human decision, just as technological inventions may be said to be applications of general physical laws which are independent of human volition. And it must indeed be admitted that there are rigidities as well as plasticities in the social sphere. To say that men can create new social laws is by no means to say that the possibilities of such creation are limitless. Entirely apart from the limitations imposed by the natural context of such laws, including man's physical environment and biological endowment, it may well be the case that there are limitations set by psychological and specifically social factors. However, the attempts of social scientists to find and state such overarching social laws or rigidities have not been promising. And even if they do exist, it seems safe to say, in view of the variety of human institutions, that the rigidities imposed by these psychological and social factors operate at a very high level of generality, within which there is a great deal of plasticity making possible the kinds of changes in social laws discussed above.

This brings me to my second consideration. As I have said, it is admitted that from precisely the same condition or cause the same effect always follows. But, as the debate over the plurality of causes has shown, all depends on what is meant by the "same cause" and the "same effect." In the social sphere, viewed as it actually exists, there never is exactly the same cause because man's history, including his learning from the past, makes a difference.[6] This does not, of course, mean, as it is sometimes taken to mean, that laws of social science are impossible; for such laws, like natural laws, abstract from these differences. But it does mean that man may create new laws of social science, because by setting up causes which are new in that they embody what he has learned from the past, he can control how these causes will operate — i.e., what effects they will produce. Hence we cannot say that he simply substitutes one prëexisting nexus of cause and effect for another, since what the nexus will be can itself be determined by man's knowledge and will.

Another Statement of the Reply

In terms of the distinction set forth above between the conditional and the existential aspects of laws, the considerations which have just been presented may be put as follows. (*a*) In their *conditional* aspect social laws can be changed by men in a sense in which natural ones cannot. This sense is that men can generate or create new correlations of social variables by making new decisions which function as antecedent conditions from which new consequences follow. In the natural sphere, on the other hand, men cannot generate such new antecedent conditions but can only exchange one set of conditions for another. Now it may be urged in reply that this difference is illusory, since in both the natural and the social sphere there are various possibilities, which ones are actualized being in both spheres partly dependent on human decision; and it may be urged further that such decision is itself the effect of antecedent conditions rather than a purely spontaneous act such as would differentiate it from the events which operate according to natural laws. The latter part of this objection will be dealt with below. Assuming for now that human decisions may occur in a way which is different from that which is operative in the natural sphere, it follows that social correlations may be changed by, just as they arise from, such decisions; while with natural correlations this is not the case. (*b*) In their *existential* aspect both natural and social laws can be changed by men, but in different senses. Men can exchange one set of conditions for another in both the natural and the social spheres, and can therefore determine which correlations will actually obtain. But in the natural sphere such correlations represent possibilities into which, as such, human decisions do not enter. For human decisions are external to the subject-matter of natural science; this is why we describe the substitution of the airplane for a free gravitational fall as a substitution of "art" for "nature," and not as a substitution of one natural correlation for another. This point is more than a merely terminological one precisely insofar as it serves to make a real differentiation, namely, between what does and what does not exist independently of human volition. But when men exchange one set of social conditions for another, and thereby change social laws in their existential aspect, human decisions are internal to such changes, because human decisions may be the antecedents of social correlations and not merely forces externally imposed on them as in the case of artificial changes in the natural sphere.

I may briefly sum up the point we have reached so far in another way as follows. It is recognized that the relations of implication which hold between antecedent and consequent in natural laws are different from

[6] Of course, there never is "exactly the same cause" in the natural sphere either. But the point of the contrast being drawn is that the spatio-temporal difference between what may otherwise be regarded as two instances of the "same" natural cause are not historical differences, since they do not involve learning from the past or other such forms of genetic relations.

those which hold in the case of purely logical relations like those of mathematics. My point then is that the relations of implication in social laws are different from both of these. For both within the antecedent and between the antecedent and the consequent in social laws, human decisions do or may enter. Therefore, even the kind or degree of eternal truth found in natural laws which may be said to hold only for our present cosmic epoch, is not found in social laws.

There still remain, however, some important difficulties in this conception. I turn to consider some of them now in connection with the second argument against the possibility of men's changing social laws.

The Argument from the Social Determination of Knowledge and Action

Our discussion of the first argument led us to emphasize the possibility of man's playing a creative role in effecting social laws through his knowledge of those laws. But it may well be argued that this way of differentiating social from natural laws is completely illusory.

In the first place, we must beware of overemphasizing the relation of conscious human purposiveness to social institutions. Those institutions are products of habit, custom, tradition, history, environment, far more than of deliberate human decision or contrivance. Consequently, man's conscious reaction on social laws in the light of his knowledge of them must be viewed as a possibility rather than as an actuality, although the stated purpose of much of social science research is to make such reaction possible.

In the second place, even where we can trace an explicit working of individual or collective decision, it is often possible to predict that decision by correlating it with causes which determine it to one object rather than another. The whole theory of the psychology of advertising rests on this principle, and so too do many of the attempts to predict how people will vote. Samuel Lubell in his book *The Future of American Politics* has shown how the will of the voter is determined by — or, if you prefer, correlated with — such factors as his economic, social, and religious background. Consequently, social knowledge and choice, so far from being independent causes of social change, are themselves rather the effects of social forces. The "sociology of knowledge," of course, is but a further development of this point.

In the third place, recent history has shown to what a large extent the sphere of indeterminacy which still remains in human choice may be cut down by political institutions. Orwell's book *1984* portrays how a dictatorship by building certain attitudes into its subjects could make their reactions to stimuli almost as predictable as the reactions of iron filings to a magnet. Something similar to this was suggested with approval a few years ago by Bertrand Russell when he wrote that what was needed was a science of mass psychology which would show how the people could be persuaded to follow the urgings of their leaders without question (5, p. 33). Russell conceived these leaders as completely benevolent social scientists, and their device of persuasion as a temporary one, but obviously its potentialities go far beyond such a context.

What such considerations suggest is that the factor of man's knowledge of social laws and his consequent creation of new laws can be used only in an extremely limited fashion, if at all, to differentiate social from natural laws. If man's very knowledge and intervention themselves follow social laws, then is it not illusory to hold than man through his knowledge can intervene to change social laws?

Three Questions Distinguished

This question involves at least three subordinate questions which must be carefully distinguished:

(*a*) Can men's knowledge lead to action which exerts a causal influence on the operation of social laws or which creates new social laws?

(*b*) Is that knowledge itself subject to causal laws?

(*c*) Are these latter laws always non-cognitive and non-rational, of the kinds mentioned above?

From confusing these three questions, and the respective answers to them, stem many of the perennial confusions of social philosophy and social science.

Let us take question (*b*) first; and let us assume an affirmative answer to it, in accordance with one interpretation of the principle of causality. Now even if men's actual knowledge is subject to causal laws, it does not follow that that knowledge cannot lead to changes in social laws or in the conditions under which those laws operate. All that follows is that one force or agency operating in society in accordance with its own causal laws acts on other forces having their own laws. Hence an affirmative answer to question (*b*) does not, as such, entail a negative answer to question (*a*). But what if the laws determining men's knowledge are themselves social laws? This of course brings us to question (*c*). If the operation of human knowledge is itself determined by social laws, then how can human knowledge react on those laws? In this case, would not social laws be all-inclusive and unchangeable by action based on knowledge, since that knowledge would have to step outside its causal framework in order to change the laws?

The error underlying this question is that of viewing social laws as so all-inclusive that from a small number of them there follow *en bloc* all social phenomena, including knowledge. But if we view social laws as specific correlations of distinct phenomena, then the causal laws determining men's knowledge may well be different from those determining other social phenomena, and thus there is no impossibility in knowledge leading to action which reacts on and changes the latter phenomena.

Up to this point we have been unduly patient with question (*c*). But actually there are important arguments against the causal determination of knowledge by social factors. I shall not go into the familiar ones revolving around the sociology of knowledge, but rather shall make a different though related point; one which brings out again in another way the contrast I have drawn between natural and social laws. For which social laws do in fact hold depends upon man's social institutions. Hence, the answers both to the question of whether man's knowledge can be an independent cause leading him to intervene in the social laws actually operating in his society, and to the question of what kinds of causes lead to that knowledge and intervention, depend upon the character of that society. In a totalitarian state the possibilities both of acquiring the relevant knowledge apart from determination by prevailing social forces, and of acting on that knowledge, are extremely limited if not non-existent for all but a very small group of men; and the tendency of such a state is to perpetuate a closed society in the sense that new knowledge and new forms of action have no means of acting on the social laws or correlations which actually prevail. On the other hand, many contemporary social scientists hold that the same thing is true of all societies, including democratic ones. For they assert that men's knowledge is itself relative to, because caused by, various non-rational factors of the kinds mentioned above, and consequently they strongly question whether men in democratic societies do or can act from knowledge as contrasted with various prejudices deriving from their economic, racial, religious backgrounds and so on. I wish to devote the remainder of this paper to pointing out four confusions which result from the way in which many contemporary scientists, taking off from the view just noted, interpret social scientific laws and their relation to social knowledge and social change.

Four Confusions

The first confusion is the assumption that for a social cause to be scientifically ascertainable is for it to be non-rational. This confusion results from the interpretation which many contemporary social scientists make of their aim of using methods and attaining laws like those of the natural sciences. This aim, as such, need not be criticized insofar as it stems from a praiseworthy desire for objectivity and rigor, for, if correctly interpreted, it is too general to account by itself for the confusion I am talking about. But many contemporary social scientists interpret this aim in such a way that only non-rational factors of the kind mentioned above are viewed as scientifically ascertainable causes of men's attitudes and actions, on the analogy of physical and biological forces whose causal operation is independent of man's knowledge or reason. This interpretation, however, is by no means a result solely of empirical observation of how men actually think and act. It is rather the result of confusing scientific determinism with the view that it is impossible for such factors as reason and knowledge to play an independent causal role in social action, and hence with the view that these factors, if admitted at all, are to be regarded as passive effects of non-rational and non-cognitive causes.

I might point out parenthetically that this consideration, while relevant to current meta-ethical issues of the relation of reason and knowledge to values and choice, does not presume any one answer on those issues if such answer is interpreted sufficiently broadly. In other words, the point I am making could be fitted into Hume's doctrine as well as Aristotle's or Kant's.

Closely related to this first confusion is a second — the confusion between the operation of social laws and the absence of conscious social action based on knowledge. This confusion usually takes the form of the plea that men not interfere through legislation or other means with the operation of social or economic laws. It is based on the view, derived variously from the natural-law, social-Darwinian, and other schools of social thought, that all social laws operate in some kind of automatic fashion akin to laws of physical or biological nature, so that all conscious attempts by men to effect changes in the operation of these laws are simply ill-conceived modes of interference with the inevitable. Now it is important not to deny one of the insights on which this view is based — the important influence of custom and tradition both in the shaping of social uniformities and, on the side of value, in the achievement of social stability. But to recognize this is not to deny that conscious human action based on knowledge of past social uniformities can effect different uniformities, so that such action involves not the substitution of non-law for law, but rather the substitution of one law for another, the latter being created by men's knowledge and consequent action.

This second confusion, however, leads directly to a third — the confusion of social scientific laws and the knowledge of such laws both with the absence of political freedom and with political laws. This confusion leads men to fear the acquisition of knowledge of social scientific laws because they fear that such knowledge will lead to political laws curtailing their freedom. Now I would certainly not want to deny this possibility. But it is only one of the possibilities; it is not logically entailed by the acquisition of social knowledge. On the contrary, to know the conditions and consequences of freedom is itself to know social scientific laws, in the sense of causal correlations between freedom and other variables. The contrast between a free political society and an enslaved one is quite different from the contrast between an ignorant and a knowing society; on the contrary, it may well be argued that the preservation of freedom in the modern world requires much knowledge of its conditions and consequences. As Dewey has said, the problem of democracy is in this sense an intellectual problem (3, p. 126). Whether such values as political freedom will or will not be better preserved if men attain knowledge of social scientific laws and use that knowledge to substitute one set of social uniformities for another, is obviously an empirical question. But this question is not to be answered by confusing social scientific laws and the knowledge of such laws with the absence of political freedom.

Finally, there is a fourth confusion to which one aspect of the two preceding confusions frequently leads — namely, the confusion between the need for social knowledge and the political hegemony of the social scientists. This confusion sometimes takes the form of the insistence that since the social scientists or "social psychiatrists" know social laws, including the conditions of the preservation and extension of democracy, they must therefore be the sole rulers, manipulating the masses for their own good. I shall not comment on the ancient problem of the relation between knowledge and virtue on which this confusion partly rests. But it is obviously illegitimate to conclude that because some men have most knowledge of the conditions of freedom, they must therefore have most political power to effectuate those conditions. On the contrary, one of the propositions which such knowledge might well be held to establish is that freedom requires individual responsibility and government responsible to the governed.

In summary, I have tried in this paper to present considerations upholding two main points. (1) Man through his awareness of the impact of the laws of social science on his values may intervene, in a way which is impossible in the natural sciences, to remove some of those laws from actual operation and to create new laws of social science. In this sense man can effect a factual change in the laws. (2) The knowledge from which this interventional activity emerges need not itself be uniquely or completely determined by social laws or uniformities insofar as these are viewed as non-rational or non-cognitive.

References

[1] Chapin, F. S., *Experimental Designs in Sociological Research.* New York, 1947.

[2] Dewey, John, *Logic, the Theory of Inquiry.* New York, 1938.

[3] Dewey, John, *The Public and Its Problems.* New York, 1927.

[4] Merton, R. K., *Social Theory and Social Structure.* Glencoe, Illinois, 1949.

[5] Russell, Bertrand. "The Science to Save Us from Science," *New York Times Magazine*, March 19, 1950.

Conventionalism: Social Uniformities Are Covert Definitions 19

The Quest for Universals in Sociological Research

RALPH H. TURNER

In a book which has maintained attention and perhaps increased in influence over two decades, Florian Znaniecki describes the method he names "analytic induction," and designates it as *the* method which should be adopted in all sociological research.[1] Analytic induction is merely a special name for one formulation of a basic philosophy that research must be directed toward generalizations of *universal* rather than *frequent* applicability.[2] But Znaniecki's statement is unusually unequivocal and is specifically oriented toward sociological research. Hence it makes an excellent point of departure for a study of contrasting methodologies.

Znaniecki's position has recently been challenged by W. S. Robinson, who depicts analytic induction as an imperfect form of the method Znaniecki calls enumerative induction.[3] Robinson's contentions are further discussed by Alfred Lindesmith and S. Kirson Weinberg in replies to his paper.[4] The three discussions extend our understanding of the method, but leave some questions unanswered.

Methodological advance requires more than the mere tolerance of alternative methods. Any *particular* methodology must be examined and assessed in the light of the total process of research and theory formulation.[5] Accordingly, the objective of the present paper is to offer a definition of the place of the search for universals in the total methodology for dealing with non-experimental data. The procedure will be to examine specific examples of empirical research employing the analytic induction (or similar) method, to note what they do and do not accomplish, to establish logically the reasons for their distinctive accomplishments and limitations, and on these grounds to designate the specific utility of the method in relation to probability methods.

From the *American Sociological Review*, 18:6 (December, 1953), pp. 604–611, with "Comment on Discussions of the Analytic Inductive Method" by Robert C. Angell and "Reply to Angell" by Turner from the *American Sociological Review*, 19:4 (August, 1954), pp. 476–478.

This paper has benefited from discussion with W. S. Robinson's seminar in methodology and from a critical reading by Donald R. Cressey.

[1] Florian Znaniecki, *The Method of Sociology*, New York: Farrar and Rinehart, 1934.

[2] This point is brought out by Alfred R. Lindesmith in his comments in the *American Sociological Review*, 17 (August, 1952), p. 492.

[3] W. S. Robinson, "The Logical Structure of Analytic Induction," *American Sociological Review*, 16 (December, 1951), pp. 812–18. Robinson's argument may not altogether escape a logical pitfall. He first makes a careful description of the analytic induction procedure, but does it by describing its elements within the framework of statistical method. Any such operation necessarily slights any aspects of the first framework which lack counterparts in the second. The conclusion that analytic induction is a special but imperfect form of statistical procedure would then be inherent in the operation itself rather than a legitimate finding.

[4] "Two Comments on W. S. Robinson's 'The Logical Structure of Analytic Induction,'" *American Sociological Review*, 17 (August, 1952), pp. 492–95.

[5] Lindesmith's statement that, "Statistical questions call for statistical answers and causal questions call for answers within the framework of the logic of causal analysis" (*ibid.*, p. 492), seems to be an evasion of the problems of *why* and *when* each type of question should be asked. "Methodological parallelism" is of dubious fruitfulness.

EMPIRICAL PREDICTION

Robinson's contention that actual studies employing the method of universals do not afford a basis for empirical prediction appears sound. However, it is only when the method is made to stand by itself that this limitation necessarily applies. Furthermore, the reason for the limitation is more intimately linked to the intrinsic logic of the method than the incidental fact that investigators using the method have tended to neglect the right-hand side of the four-fold table.[6] These statements may be substantiated and elaborated by an examination of selected studies.

Lindesmith's well-known study of opiate addiction will serve as a useful first case. The causal complex which is essential to the process of addiction involves several elements. The individual must use the drug, he must experience withdrawal distress, he must identify these symptoms or recognize what they are, he must recognize that more of the drug will relieve the symptoms, and he must take the drug and experience relief.[7]

From the standpoint of predicting whether any given individual will become an addict or not, the formulation has certain limitations. First, it does not tell who will take the drug in the first place, nor give any indication of the relative likelihood of different persons taking the drug.[8] Second, the thesis itself affords no cue to variability in intensity of withdrawal symptoms, nor any guide to instances in which the symptoms will be mild enough not to result in addiction. Third, the theory does not provide a basis for anticipating who will recognize the symptoms and the means of securing relief. Fourth, personal and social factors involved in taking or not taking the drug to relieve the identified distress are not indicated. We cannot predict in an empirical instance unless there is some way of anticipating which people, given exposure to the drug, will recognize the nature of the withdrawal symptoms, will identify the means of relief, and will take that means of relief.[9] Finally, Lindesmith's theory does not indicate to us what will be the pattern of the addict's behavior, since this is determined by the cultural definition and treatment of the drug and its addicts. In sum, Lindesmith provides us with a causal complex which is empirically verified *in retrospect*, but which does not in itself permit prediction that a specific person will become an addict nor that a specific situation will produce addiction.

Donald R. Cressey's statement regarding the violation of financial trust likewise is posited as a system of universal generalizations and is similar to Lindesmith's in format.[10] Three elements are essential to trust-violation. The person who will violate a financial trust has, first, a "non-sharable financial problem," a difficulty which he feels he cannot communicate to others. Second, he recognizes embezzlement as a way of meeting this problem. And third, he rationalizes the prospective embezzlement, justifying it to himself in some way.

First, the points at which Lindesmith's and Cressey's statement are parallel and

[6] W. S. Robinson, *op. cit.*, pp. 814–16. The writer doubts that this limitation inheres logically in the conception of analytic induction as described by Znaniecki.

[7] Alfred R. Lindesmith, *Opiate Addiction*, Bloomington: Principia Press, 1947, pp. 67–89, *et passim*.

[8] Some of Lindesmith's argument with current theories of drug addiction (*ibid.*, pp. 141–64) rest upon a difference of purpose. Some of the theories he criticizes can be defended if reworded in terms of likelihood of first taking the drug in other than a medical treatment situation, rather than in terms of the likelihood of becoming addicted.

[9] Lindesmith does not overlook these considerations in his descriptive treatment of the process. However, his treatment of them remains anecdotal and impressionistic rather than systematic and they are not integrated into the rigorous statement of his theory. The nearest he comes to a systematic statement concerning one of these variables is his observation that, "as long as a patient believes he is using the drug solely to relieve pain, and regards it as a 'medicine,' he does not become an addict." (*Ibid.*, p. 56). Weinberg suggests the use of measurement in some of these connections (*op. cit.*, p. 493).

[10] *Other People's Money*, Glencoe: The Free Press, 1953. A brief statement of the theory also appears as, "Criminal Violation of Financial Trust," *American Sociological Review*, 15 (December, 1950), pp. 738–43.

points at which they are not parallel may be noted. The withdrawal symptoms and the non-sharable problem can be equated as the conditions which require some relief which cannot be secured through conventional channels. There is also a parallel between recognition that the drug will relieve the distress and recognition of embezzlement as a possible solution to the none-sharable problem. On the other hand, because drug addiction ensues from but one type of problem, withdrawal distress, Lindesmith can specify the taking of an opiate as essential. Cressey can specify no specific "first step" because of the variety of problems which may come to be non-sharable. The rationalization stage is absent from Lindesmith's formulation though he discusses it as a *frequent* phenomenon.

It is difficult to find a logical reason why rationalization should be *essential* in the one instance and merely *frequent* in the other. Perhaps the explanation lies, not in the logic of the phenomena themselves, but in the conditions necessary for a sense of closure on the part of the investigators. Since Lindesmith is explaining the existence of a continuing psychological state, it is sufficient for his purposes that the prospective addict be carried from a particular state of recognition (the symptoms and role of the drug) to an overt act with specific psychological consequences (relief by taking the drug). Cressey, however, is explaining a single action and so he seeks to fill the gap more fully between the particular state of recognition (that embezzlement will solve a non-sharable problem) and the act of embezzling, which he does with the rationalization.[11]

In light of the parallels between the two schemes, it is not surprising that the same limitations with regard to empirical prediction apply to Cressey's statement as did to Lindesmith's. The theory does not indicate who will have non-sharable problems, what specific conditions will make a problem non-sharable and in what circumstances a problem may cease to be non-sharable. Nor do we have a guide to the circumstances surrounding recognition of embezzlement as a solution to the problem. And, finally, there are no systematic indicators of who will be able to rationalize and who will not.

There are perhaps two general reasons why the Lindesmith and Cressey studies do not produce empirical prediction, reasons which are applicable because of the very specifications of their method itself. One of these reasons has already been extensively illustrated, namely, that there is no basis for determining beforehand whether the conditions specified as necessary will exist in a particular instance.

The second general reason for lack of empirical prediction is that the alleged *preconditions* or essential causes of the phenomenon under examination cannot be fully specified apart from observation of the condition they are supposed to produce. In any situation in which variable "A" is said to cause variable "B", "A" is of no value as a predictor of "B" unless we establish the existence of "A" apart from the observation of "B". This limitation is in particular applicable to Cressey's study. Is it possible, for example, to assert that a problem is non-sharable *until* a person embezzles to get around it? If a man has not revealed his problem to others today, can we say that he will not share it tomorrow? The *operational* definition of a non-sharable problem is one that has not been shared up to the time of the embezzlement. Similarly, Cressey must be referring to some *quality* in the recognition of embezzlement as a solution which may not be identifiable apart from the fact that under appropriate conditions it eventuates in embezzlement. With embezzlement techniques and tales of successful embezzle-

[11] Perhaps there is an object lesson indicated by this comparison. If the perspective of the investigator can determine what will be necessary for inclusion as the *essential* elements, there may be no theoretical limit to the number of such perspectives and consequently to the variations in what is considered essential. Such an observation would make Znaniecki's dictum that the investigator can arrive at a point beyond which no new knowledge about a class can be added difficult to defend. (Cf. Znaniecki, *op. cit.*, p. 249).

ment a standard part of the folklore of banks, offices handling public and private payrolls, and the like, mere recognition of embezzlement as a solution to problems is probably a near-universal characteristic of persons in a position to be able to embezzle. Similarly, rationalizations of embezzlement are part of the folklore and their use is standard joking behavior among persons in such positions. Consequently both recognition of embezzlement as a potential solution and ability to rationalize the act only become discriminating conditions when some sort of qualitative or quantitative limitation is imposed upon them. But under the present formulation it is only possible to identify what is a sufficient recognition or a sufficient ability to rationalize by the fact that they eventuate in embezzlement.

Lindesmith's theory, though less subject to this limitation, reveals the same vulnerability. Since withdrawal distress varies in degree according to size of dose and the number of shots taken, and since several shots may precede the existence of addiction as Lindesmith defines it, definition of the point at which the individual is taking the drug *to relieve withdrawal distress* as distinct from the point at which he is simply taking another shot must be arbitrary in some cases. But the distinction is crucial to Lindesmith's theory, since before this point the individual is not addicted and presumably may interrupt the process, while after this point he is addicted and the process is complete. Hence, the identification of what constitutes an effective recognition of the relief the drug will bring can only ultimately be determined by the fact that addiction follows such recognition.[12]

As a final case, we shall refer to a study which is in important respects rather different, but which is couched in terms of a parallel logic. In Robert C. Angell's well-known study of fifty families that suffered a serious reduction in income during the Depression, he attempted to work out a set of categories which could be applied to a family before the Depression which would predict how it would respond to the drop in family income. On the basis of assessments of "integration" and "adaptability," Angell "predicts" the response to financial crisis in terms of a "vulnerability-invulnerability" continuum and a "firm-readjustive-yielding" continuum.[13] Through his designation of a presumably comprehensive pair of concepts for describing those characteristics of the family which are essential in predicting his post-crisis variables, Angell follows an analytic induction model, though his variables are not simple attributes as are those of Lindesmith and Cressey.

On the surface, Angell's formulation looks a good deal more like a device for empirical prediction since he provides categories which can be assessed before the process of responding to the Depression gets under way and without reference to the consequences. A careful examination of the nature and manner of assessment of the two essential variables will indicate whether the impression is justified.

The idea of integration seems to refer to the degree to which a family is a unit, which is a fact not observable in the same direct sense as the fact of taking a drug, for example. Integration conveys a meaning or feeling which is recognized by a number of symptoms, such as affection, common interests, and sense of economic interdependence. Integration in practice, then, is identified by an impressionistic assessment of several observable variables.[14] Of these vari-

[12] Lindesmith admits some vagueness on the matter of what genuinely constitutes knowledge that an opiate will relieve withdrawal distress, but regards the vagueness as a present limitation of his knowledge rather than an intrinsic limitation of his method. Cf. *op. cit.*, p. 77.

[13] Robert C. Angell, *The Family Encounters the Depression*, New York: Scribner's Sons, 1936.

[14] Not only is the weighting of the various data of observation impressionistic but these criteria are themselves impressionistic. The implicitly statistical nature of Angell's operation has been noted before and his documents subjected to a restudy under Social Science Research Council auspices. In the restudy, scales for the measurement of integration and adaptability were devised to objectify ratings and translate them into numerical values. Ruth Cavan, *The Restudy of the Documents Analyzed by Angell in "The Family Encounters the Depression."* Unpublished.

ables there is no single one by which alone integration can be identified, nor is there any single "symptom" which may not be lacking in families classified as highly integrated.

The prediction which is provided by this scheme is *theoretical* prediction according to an analytic induction model. But the theoretical prediction cannot be converted into empirical prediction unless integration can be assessed beforehand. The assessment is made by an implicitly statistical operation, a mental weighting of several items of observation. In order, then, to gain *empirical* prediction the investigator shifts over to an "enumerative induction" procedure.

The concept of adaptability is both more important[15] and more complex, combining two elements as Angell uses the term. First, if a family has been flexible in the face of minor crises or problems that have occurred in the past, it is said to be adaptable and the prediction that it will maintain its unity in the face of a larger crisis is consequently made. This, of course, is merely an application of the principle that there is a constancy in the response of a given system to situations of the same sort, and has no causal significance. The other aspect of adaptability consists of a number of criteria, such as commitment to material standards, concerning which the same comments apply as in the case of integration.

Thus in the three cases cited empirical prediction is not provided by statements of universally valid relationships taken alone. What, then, do such efforts accomplish?

ANALYTIC INDUCTION AS DEFINITION

What the method of universals most fundamentally does is to provide definitions. Not all definitions are of equal value for deriving scientific generalizations, and the definitions produced by the analytic induction procedure are intended to be characterized by causal homogeneity.

The effort at causal homogeneity is evident in the refinements of definition that accompany the method. In the process of attempting to generalize about addiction Lindesmith had to distinguish between those drugs that produce withdrawal distress and those that do not. Early in his work he concluded that it would be futile to seek a single theory to explain both types. Cressey points out that he could not study everyone who is legally defined as an embezzler. Unless he restricted his subjects, for example, to those who entered the situation in good faith, he could not form valid generalizations having universal applicability. Angell also rules out certain types of families. He recognized that some of his families were units merely in a formal sense, and that he could not observe uniform principles which would be applicable to the latter.

Saying that the principal accomplishment of the search for universals is to make definitions depends upon showing that the generalizations which it produces are deducible from the definitions. This is clearest in the case of Lindesmith's theory. In Lindesmith's presentation he has outlined the essential stages in becoming addicted by the time that he has arrived at his full definition of the phenomenon. The essential stages are implicit in the concept of addiction as he presents it.[16]

In place of the empirical attributes viewed essential by Lindesmith, Angell constructs two theoretical categories to which he ascribes the character of essentiality. But Angell is really getting the definition of his causal variables from the dependent or effect variables which he sets up. Adaptability seems to correspond to the firm-yielding dimension and integration to the vulnerability dimension. Adaptability and integration are the logically deducible counterparts to the dependent variables.

Cressey's formulation is less completely amenable to this interpretation. The recog-

[15] Reuben Hill, *Families Under Stress*, p. 132, citing Cavan, *op. cit.*

[16] W. S. Robinson has suggested this in his "Rejoinder to Comments on 'The Logical Structure of Analytic Induction,'" *American Sociological Review*, 17 (August, 1952), p. 494.

nition of embezzlement as a solution is a logically deducible component, since one cannot perform a purposive self-conscious act unless its possibility is recognized. By definition the subjects of Cressey's study possessed long standing conceptions of themselves as law-abiding individuals, and were socially recognized as such at the time of the offense. While perhaps not from the definition alone, at least from the body of established theory which is implicit in the definition, it follows that the individuals must at the time of the crime in some way reconcile their behavior with their law-abiding self-conception. Indeed, we cannot help wondering whether failure to report rationalization could be entirely independent from the criteria by which an investigator would exclude some subjects from his study on grounds of doubting the honesty of their initial intentions.

The non-sharable problem, however, is probably only partially deducible. Given the fact that all people have problems that might be solved by stealing, given the fact that these subjects were mature individuals, and recognizing that they must, by definition, have resisted situations in the past which could have been improved by stealing, then it would seem to follow that a very distinctive type of problem would be required for people to deviate from their established life-patterns. The non-sharability of the problem might be deducible as a *frequent* characteristic, but probably not as a universal characteristic.

Thus, with the exception of non-sharability, the theories that have been examined serve chiefly to delimit a causally homogeneous category of phenomena, the so-called essential causes of the phenomenon being deducible from the definition.

It is, of course, not accidental but the crux of the method that these generalizations should be deducible. It is through the causal examination of the phenomenon that its delimitation is effected. The operation in practice is one which alternates back and forth between tentative cause and tentative definition, each modifying the other, so that in a sense closure is achieved when a complete and integral relation between the two is established. Once the generalizations become self-evident from the definition of the phenomenon being explained, the task is complete.

THE INTRUSIVE FACTOR

The next step in our argument must be to ask why the search for universals does not carry us beyond formulating a definition and indicating its logical corollaries, and why it fails to provide empirical prediction. The answer may be that there are no universal, uniform relations to be found except those which constitute logical corollaries of conceptual definition. The positing of operationally independent causal variables, empirically assessible prior to the existence of the postulated effect, always seems to result in relationships of statistical probability rather than absolute determination.[17]

A minor reason for these limited findings is the fact of multiple determination, with which analytic induction is rather ill-equipped to cope. When such complex phenomena as family integration, rather than individual behavior, are examined, the method very rapidly shifts into the ideal-type technique, which is no longer subject to the sort of straight-forward empirical verification as analytic induction. As in Angell's study, the logic of the method is preserved but the empirical problems become quite different.

But as the central thesis of this paper we shall call attention to another explanation for the absence of universal, uniform relations which are not logical corollaries of

[17] These remarks and some of the subsequent observations must be qualified by noting that Cressey's "non-sharable problem" is an apparent exception. If the statements in this paragraph are correct we should expect further research to eventuate either in some modification of the concept, "violation of financial trust," or in the reevaluation of the non-sharable problem as a *frequent* rather than essential characteristic.

definitions. The "closed system," which is the core of Znaniecki's statement and whose isolation is the objective and accomplishment of the method, is a causally self-contained system. As such, it is not capable of activation from within, but only by factors coming from outside the system. While, by definition, uniform relations exist within closed causal systems, uniform relations do not exist *between* any causal system and the external factors which impinge on it. *External variables operating upon any closed system do not have a uniform effect because they have to be assimilated to the receiving system in order to become effective as causes.* The outside variable has to be translated, in a sense, into a cause relevant to the receiving system. Normally there will be alternate ways in which the same external variable may be translated depending upon the full context within which it is operative. The situation in which a man finds himself, for example, can only activate the closed system of the embezzlement process when it becomes translated into a non-sharable problem. Cressey finds no type of problem, phenomenologically speaking, which necessarily and uniformly becomes a non-sharable problem.

The external factor which activates a system may be referred to as an *intrusive* factor. This idea is taken from Frederick Teggart's discussion of what he calls an "event." "We may then define an event as an intrusion from any wider circle into any circle or condition which may be the object of present interest."[18] There are always intrusive factors which are accordingly not predictable in terms of the causal system under examination, but which serve to activate certain aspects of the system. The same idea may be thought of as levels of phenomena. There are no uniform relations between levels of phenomena, only within levels. *Empirical* prediction always concerns the way in which one closed system is activated by various intrusive factors. Hence empirical prediction always requires some statistical or probability statements, because there is some uncertainty or lack of uniformity in the *way* in which the intrusive factors will activate the causal system and even in *whether* they will activate the system.

UNIVERSALS AND STATISTICAL METHOD

The utility of defining universals within closed systems lies in the translation of *variables* into *concepts*. A variable is any category which can be measured or identified and correlated with something else. A concept is a variable which is part of a theoretical system, implying causal relations. That correlations among variables, of themselves, do not provide a basis for theory, or even for anticipating future correlations, is well known. Analytic induction fails to carry us beyond identifying a number of closed systems, and enumerative induction fails to go beyond the measurement of associations. The functions of the two methods are not only distinct; they are complementary. When the two methods are used together *in the right combination*,[19] they produce the type of findings which satisfies the canons of scientific method.

What the identification of closed systems does is to provide a basis for organizing and interpreting observed statistical associations. For example, valid research would probably reveal some correlation between liking-to-run-around-with-women and embezzlement. Cressey's findings do not discredit such an observation but afford a basis for interpreting it. In the light of certain American mores such a behavior pattern is likely, in some

[18] Frederick J. Teggart, *Theory of History*, New Haven: Yale University Press, 1925, p. 149. Quoted by Clarence Marsh Case, in "Leadership and Conjuncture: A Sociological Hypothesis," *Sociology and Social Research*, 17 (July, 1933), p. 513.

[19] In no sense can those research reports which devote a section to statistical findings and another section to case study findings be said to illustrate the thesis of this paper. In most cases such contrasting categories refer only to the method of data *collection*, the method of *analysis* being enumerative in both cases, but precise in the former and impressionistic in the latter.

circumstances, to create a problem which would be difficult to discuss with others. The crucial aspect of this behavior for the determination of embezzlement would be its creation of a non-sharable problem.

With the closed system described it is possible to take the various correlations and get order from them. Identification of the closed system also gives us guides to significant variables, correlations that would be worthy of test. At the present point it should be profitable to search for the kinds of situations which most often become non-sharable problems, the characteristics which are correlated with the ability to rationalize an activity which would normally be regarded as contrary to the mores of society, the personal and situational characteristics associated with taking opiates (other than by medical administration) sufficiently to experience withdrawal symptoms. A study of correlations between certain sex patterns and the acquisition of non-sharable problems would build cumulatively in a way that a study of correlation between the former and embezzlement would not do. Some quantitative measure of such correlation would in turn provide the basis for using the closed system formulation for empirical prediction.[20]

One useful indication of the way in which a statement of universals can function in the total research operation is afforded by Edwin Sutherland's "differential association" theory of criminality.[21] While this theory is not the product of a specific empirical research operation of the sort that Lindesmith or Cressey undertook, the form of Sutherland's proposition is that of the analytic induction model. He employs a felicitous term in stating his theory. Differential association, he says, is "the specific causal process" in the genesis of systematic criminal behavior. He does not say that differential association is *the* cause or the *only* one; poverty and the like may be in some sense causes. But differential association is the specific causal process through which these other factors, or more removed causes, must operate. Poverty and other correlated factors only facilitate criminal behavior because they affect the person's likelihood of learning a pattern of criminality from a model of criminality which is presented to him. The differential association theory identifies a hypothesized closed system, in terms of which the many correlated variables gain their meaning.

There are many theories already extant which have this same character, but which have not always been viewed as logical counterparts to the analytic induction method. Edwin Lemert's proposition that, "The onset of insanity coincides with the awareness of one's behavior as being invidiously different from that of all other people's," points to the same sort of *specific causal process* in the genesis of insanity, or "secondary psychotic deviation."[22] And Sorokin's interpretation of Durkheim's theory of suicide follows the same form.[23]

Statements of this sort are devices for placing in bold outline the meaningful components of the phenomenon under study. In order to achieve the form of a universally valid generalization the investigator either states his causes as inferential variables (Angell), or states empirically continuous variables as attributes (Lindesmith, Cressey). In the latter case, the dividing point between the two phases of the crucial attribute is identifiable only retrospectively on the basis that the specified sequence is or is

[20] Cressey proposes a study of such related conditions in much the same manner as is indicated here, but does not clarify whether this should be by a further extension of the method he has used or by the measurement of probabilities. Cf. *Other People's Money*, Chap. V.

[21] Edwin H. Sutherland, *Principles of Criminology*, Chicago: J. B. Lippincott Co., 1939, pp. 4–9. The third edition of Sutherland's work is cited here because he has modified the features of his theory most relevant to the argument of this paper in his fourth edition (1947).

[22] Edwin M. Lemert, *Social Pathology*, New York: McGraw-Hill, 1951, p. 428.

[23] Pitirim A. Sorokin, *Society, Culture and Personality*, New York: Harper, 1947, pp. 8–13.

not completed. But if the essential components of the causal complex are viewed as continuous variables, capable of measurement independently of completion of the hypothesized sequence, the *essential degree* of the components will vary from instance to instance. Hence, in the process of designating the essential causes in a manner susceptible to empirical identification prior to their expected effect, the investigator must recast his thesis in terms of probability rather than uniform and universal relations.

A danger of the search for universals lies in the inadequate utilization of much valuable data. Cressey has information on the types of backgrounds his subjects came from, but because these are not universals the information has been filed away, or handled impressionistically. Lindesmith likewise secured abundant information which he uses only to demonstrate that absolute uniformity does not exist. Angell describes the frequent characteristics of the integrated and the adaptable family, but he does not systematize this material because such aspects of it are not universals. In these cases the imposition of particular methodological restrictions has limited what can be found out about the phenomenon under examination.

Analytic induction or some logical counterpart of the method is an essential aspect of research directed toward accumulating an ordered body of generalizations. But, for the reasons developed in this paper, Znaniecki's statement that, "analytic induction ends where enumerative induction begins; and if well conducted, leaves no real and soluble problems for the latter,"[24] represents an untenable position. It is through conceiving the "essential" conditions in a closed system as the avenues through which correlated factors can operate as causes, that generalizations about closed systems can escape their self-containment and probability associations may be organized into meaningful patterns.

[24] Florian Znaniecki, *The Method of Sociology*, p. 250.

Comment on Discussions of the Analytic Induction Method

To the Editor:

I sat patiently on the sidelines when W. S. Robinson cast only inferential aspersions on my *The Family Encounters the Depression* in his discussion of analytic induction in the December, 1951, *Review*. But now that Ralph H. Turner has added insult to injury in his article, "The Quest for Universals," in the December, 1953, *Review*, I feel that I must enter the arena.

I have no real quarrel with Robinson. If analytic induction is what he interprets Znaniecki and Cressey to mean by that term, then I should not have said I was using it. For I did not first define a phenomenon to be explained and then look for causes of it. I first took an intrusive factor — the depression — and asked what previous characteristics of families would enable one to predict what aftereffects. The result is that I did not fail to look for situations with the same causes but different effects. The table on page 261 of my book shows in fact that in two causal sequences out of 24 I admit by the phrase "conflicting evidence" that a given original type and a given degree of depression pressure do not always produce the same result.

I had thought of analytic induction in somewhat broader terms: as that method in which the investigator does not accept ready-made conceptualization, but plays around with the relationships and the units of analysis until he hits upon a scheme that is very parsimonious in explanatory power. This at any rate is what I did.

My difference of view with Turner runs deeper. He states that I got the definition of my causal variables from the dependent or effect variables that I set up. I have pointed out to Dr. Turner in private correspondence that historically this was not the fact, that a reading of the Appendix will show that the way of categorizing the effect situations was the last step in the study. He now admits this may have been the case but argues that logically the causal variables are derivable from the effects. He thinks that what he calls the invulnerable-vulnerable dimension implies the integration continuum as cause, and the firm-readjustive dimension implies the adaptability continuum as cause. I would make two points in denying this.

First, the whole study is dealing with the effect of a depression, and the invulnerable-vulnerable dimension therefore implies adaptability as cause just as much as it does integration. Empirically, more than this was demonstrated, for the table on page 261 shows that the crucial differences for the invulnerable-vulnerable result are those in adaptability not in integration.

Second, the firm-readjustive dimension was only required because of changes on the ecological level for these families. This dimension has no logical counterpart in the original typology. This can be seen by inspecting the results at any level of depression pressure. "Firmly invalnerable" only occurs when ecological positions are the same; "readjustively invulnerable" only occurs when ecological positions are modified or changed.

The upshot of the matter as I see it is that not only did I not chronologically derive my independent variables from my dependent variables but that the original types show no one-to-one logical relation to the dependent variables. If Turner had argued that the depression-pressure variables were logically related to the firm-readjustive dimension, while the adaptability and integration were both related to the invulnerable-vulnerable dimension, he would have had a better case.

I think that both Robinson and Turner err in treating my work as in the same general category as that of Lindesmith on opiate addiction and Cressey on embezzlement. It does appear that it is very difficult for them to specify the last link in their causal chains — taking dope to relieve withdrawal symptoms, and a non-sharable problem — unless the effect — addiction or embezzlement — has already taken place. One cannot predict the outcome, because it has happened by the time the last cause is specified. Hence it is perhaps true that they are providing definitions rather than generalizations. This is not, I believe, true of my work. All the conditions — even the family changes on the ecological level — can be analyzed before the final changes on the socio-psychological level take place, and real predictions can be made.

I do not wish my argument with Turner to obscure the fact that I believe the main thesis of his article a most provocative one. He says: "Empirical prediction always requires some statistical or probability statements, because there is some uncertainty or lack of uniformity in the *way* in which the intrustive factors will activate the causal [closed] system and even in *whether* they will activate the system." There is support for this in my study. Given the intrustive factor, a severe loss of income, and given the type of family, I could not predict the result. I found that I had to know the changes on the ecological level in addition. But is not this worth while? Is it not valuable to know that, if a highly integrated, moderately adaptable family encounters a loss of income that entails the shift to another breadwinner, it will prove vulnerable?

Robert C. Angell

Reply to Angell

To the Editor:

I am happy to have the opportunity to correct three unintended impressions which may have come from faulty expression in my article and to expand another point which deserves more than the cursory treatment I gave it.

(1) To depreciate Professor Angell's work was the furthest thought from my mind. Indeed it is just because *The Family Encounters the Depression* constitutes a sort of milestone in research that I followed Robinson's lead in trying to reinterpret its methodology so that

later work might go beyond it in the manner of cumulative science.

(2) Having been well steeped in Angell's methodological appendix during graduate school days, I never supposed that Angell actually secured his dependent variables first and then sat down to deduce independent variables. An unfortunate carelessness in the use of language on page 608[25] may give this erroneous impression, though the general statement about the actual operation at the top of page 609[26] presents the more accurate picture as I see it. For the thesis of my paper it is irrelevant from which side of the closed system the operation commences; all that matters is that when the system is complete the independent variables are deducible from the definition of the phenomena being predicted.

(3) Any impression that I am repudiating the method of analytic induction is unfortunate. In contrast to analytic induction imperialists (the "only" method) and isolationists (you ask your kind of question and I'll ask mine), I contended that the vital importance of the method was best seen in its contribution to the total methodology of sociology.

(4) Since Angell's work was mentioned only cursorily to round out the documentation for my thesis, no real effort was made to substantiate my claim that his independent variables are deducible from his dependent variables. Consequently, I shall attempt to fill this gap with the following statement.

Angell's chief dependent variable consists of two kinds of change in the family: (a) reduction in degree of integration and (b) change in family patterns which *do not* involve change in degree of integration. For convenience we may call these (a) *vertical* and (b) *horizontal* change. By the very fact of making such a distinction, Angell is telling us that there have to be two kinds of families — those which can change without lessened integration and those which cannot change without lessened integration. Since the former is equivalent to his definition of the *adaptable* family and the latter to the *unadaptable*, it is immediately evident that his independent variable of adaptability is a simple restatement of his dependent variables and hence completely deducible from them.

As Angell has pointed out, relations of this sort can only be meaningful if a minimum (unspecified) of integration is initially present. In this way his other independent variable, *integration*, enters the picture. The special one-to-one combination of *yielding* as dependent category and *unintegrated* as the independent category takes care of this case. Above this minimum of integration, the *vulnerable* are by definition the *unadaptable* families and the *invulnerable* are by definition the *adaptable*.

Angell then tells us that horizontal change may be of two kinds: (b-1) involving no basic alteration in family role structure and (b-2) involving basic alterations. The adverbs *firmly* and *readjustively* are employed to designate this dichotomy as a dependent variable. The terms *similar positions* and *changed positions*, to refer to the poles of the independent variable, are simple counterparts to the foregoing dependent variable.

On page 261 of *The Family Encounters the Depression*, Angell summarizes the relations between his independent and dependent categories. Referring only to his polar types (i.e., omitting *moderately* integrated and adaptable combinations), and only to cases with the necessary minimum of integration, the foregoing observations may be summarized so as to relate to Angell's summary table. We infer that a family will (a) retain its pre-existing level of integration without shifting roles (firmly invulnerable) if it has some integration, is capable of change without loss of integration, and the crisis does not force role changes on it (Type I — integrated and adaptable, similar positions); but will (b) retain its pre-existing level of integration while shifting roles (readjustively invulnerable) if it has some integration, is capable of change without loss of integration, and the crisis forces role change on it (Type I —

[25] [*Page 232, this volume. Editor's note.*]
[26] [*ibid, page 233.*]

integrated and adaptable, changed positions). The family will (c) lose integration (vulnerable) if it is not capable of change without loss of integration (unadaptable, regardless of integration and changed position).

Finally, since b-1 is a small change and b-2 a large change, there are by definition some families which can adjust to a change of the former type and not to the latter. If the limits to the category, *moderate adaptability*, are appropriately set, it can be made to include only these families. This apparently is what Angell has done, since moderately adaptable families (Types II and V) become vulnerable only when forced to adjust to *changed positions*.

The foregoing logically self-contained system becomes worth while to the degree to which it can be supplemented by precise instructions for the empirical identification of all variables. In keeping with the thesis of my paper, Angell accomplishes this identification by an operation which is implicitly statistical.

Ralph H. Turner

20

The Accessibility of Genuine Social Laws and Theories

from *Explanation in Social Science*

ROBERT BROWN

Empirical Generalizations

It is often asserted that the social sciences have not established any genuine laws. But this assertion can be taken in two quite different ways. It may be understood as claiming that the universal hypotheses put forward have not been well tested. Clearly, it is only the social scientists who can decide whether this is so. For the critics' competence to do this is open to serious doubt, since the answer to the question 'What constitutes being well tested in this particular case?' does not depend merely on logical and methodological requirements common to all the sciences. The answer depends also on the body of knowledge that is relevant to the particular problem; and there is every reason for supposing that the social scientist has a better command of this body of knowledge than have his critics.

However, the charge that the social sciences have produced no genuine laws, i.e. ones that stand up to tests, need not be an attack on the quality of the evidence available. It may be interpreted as asserting the rather different view that no hypotheses of the appropriate kind — hypotheses which if they stood up to tests would be genuine laws — have in fact been advanced by social scientists. This view claims that the candidates put forward to not possess the necessary *logical* qualifications for being submitted to serious testing. Now this assertion may seem to be so obviously false as to be not worth making.

Consider a random list: (1) 'Magical belief and ritual fortify confidence and reduce anxiety', (2) 'The imposition of direct taxes produces a higher degree of satisfaction in the taxed than the imposition of the levy by excise taxes', (3) 'People who participate in high involvement relationships show high ability to empathize', (4) 'The higher the cohesiveness of a human group, the higher will be the correlation between popularity rank and perceived leadership rank', (5) 'Industrial workers strike for higher wages only if (*a*) they believe that they can maintain themselves during a period of unemployment (*b*) they believe that their employers are able to pay higher wages', (6) 'The strength of the drinking response varies directly with the level of anxiety in the society.'

Whether or not any one of these statements has been well tested, each of them, when given in its complete form, may seem to be open to proper testing. For each of them appears to have the structure represented by the formula 'All As are Bs' and to be testable by taking As and considering whether they are Bs. A more refined version of this is 'For any X, if X were to have the property A, then X would have the property B.' The same kind of formula will serve when more than two qualities or relations are associated. We can use the most complicated member of our list as an example. It becomes: 'For any human group, if such a group were to

From *Explanation in Social Science* by Robert Brown, Aldine Publishing Co., Chicago, 1963, and Routledge & Kegan Paul, Ltd., London, 1963, pp. 133–140, 145–154, and 171–190. Subtitles were supplied in part by the editor.

have the property of cohesiveness, the higher its cohesiveness, the higher the correlation between popularity rank and perceived leadership rank.'

Statements of universal hypotheses can be correctly phrased in a number of ways, and it does not much matter here into which of the various forms they are cast. We need only reiterate that universal hypotheses are assertions about relationships. They do not unconditionally assert the existence of the objects, states, or events which are said to be related. They assert that if certain kinds of things exist, then certain relations must exist among them; that if, for example, properties A and B are present, a given change in A will always be accompanied or followed by a given change in B; or they assert that if certain events occur, then so will certain others. Hence, to argue that none of the hypotheses proposed by social scientists are appropriate candidates for laws will be to argue that no claim to have discovered an invariable relationship has in fact been made by social scientists.

One familiar way of discussing invariable relations is in terms of necessary and sufficient conditions. We can remind ourselves that universal hypotheses are commonly thought to assert of two properties A and B, that (1) an instance of property A is a necessary condition for an instance of property B, (2) an instance of property A is a sufficient condition for an instance of B, or (3) an instance of property A is a necessary and sufficient condition for an instance of property B. It is important to emphasize that these are conditions of causal and not of logical connections. To say, for example, that A is both a necessary and sufficient condition of B is to claim that they are in fact *always* associated. On the view that, roughly speaking, causal connection amounts to invariable association, the relationship between A and B is a causal one. It is not a relationship of entailment: the existence of property B cannot be logically deduced from the existence of property A. The terms 'necessary condition' and 'sufficient condition' are, of course, often used in this logical sense. Mathematicians speak of a set of necessary and sufficient properties when they mean that the presence of other properties logically follows from the presence of the set. But we are concerned only with the former sense of the terms and not with this latter sense. The difference between the two senses parallels that between the logical sense of 'proof' (entailment) and the empirical sense of 'proof' (overwhelming evidence). Our question, then becomes: 'Are those statements which assert such empirical relations represented on our list? Would any social scientist be prepared to say that our examples provide sufficient conditions or necessary conditions, or both? If he would, then we should have to consider whether there was any logical or methodological reason for refusing to admit his candidates to examination. If he would not, we should have to answer the question 'Why not?'

Let us return to the examples on our list. If magical belief and ritual are sufficient to fortify confidence and reduce anxiety, then these effects *must* occur whenever the belief and ritual are present. If the striking of industrial workers for higher wages is a sufficient condition for the presence of their beliefs about self-maintenance and the ability of employers to pay, these beliefs have to occur when the strike occurs. Conversely, the fortifying of confidence and the reduction of anxiety will be necessary conditions for the occurrence of magical belief and ritual — conditions in whose absence the belief and ritual cannot occur. In the same fashion, the strikers' beliefs will be a necessary condition of their striking. This is so, we may recall, because A is a sufficient condition for B if and only if B is a necessary condition for A. One benefit, therefore, of picking out the necessary and sufficient conditions expressed in statements is that it immediately becomes obvious that expressions like 'depends on', 'varies with', and 'contingent upon' are too vague for scientific purposes. Each of them can be interpreted as stating that A is a sufficient condition for B, or that B is a sufficient condition for A, or that A is sufficient for B and B for A. The example which asserts that the strength of the drinking response varies directly with the level of anxiety in the society lends itself, in the absence of further information, to all these interpretations. The same ambiguity is displayed by the other generalizations that we listed: Is magical belief necessary to fortify confidence, or merely sufficient? Or both? Or do none of these apply? And we do not know whether it is being asserted that an increase in the cohesiveness of a human group is sufficient and necessary for an increase in the correlation between popularity rank and perceived leadership rank. Perhaps the first increase is only a sufficient condition of the second increase.

It seems, then, that if we maintain that universal hypotheses should provide us with either necessary or sufficient conditions or both, our examples of generalizations are open to reasonable criticism. We do not know whether any of them claims to provide us with sufficient or necessary conditions, whether any of them is to be taken as doing so only if amplified in certain ways, or whether any of them is to be understood as asserting neither sufficient nor necessary conditions. In brief, the view that no hypotheses of the appropriate form have been advanced by social scientists may not be so absurd as it seems at first sight.

There is still another point of attack on the ability of social scientists to produce laws. It is simply this: even if we assume that well tested hypotheses of the appropriate type do exist, it is nevertheless true that they are of the most elementary type. They are nothing more than crude empirical generalizations, empirical not in the sense in which it is contrasted with logical, but in the sense of not being theoretical. They resemble in origin and form the assertion that if anything were made of refined gold, then that gold object would be ductile. The account merely includes the case in question within a given class which has a certain property. Similarly, any person who participates in a 'high involvement relationship' is included within the class of people who 'show high ability to empathize'. Hypotheses of this type, it is said, merely generalize from known cases to all cases. They explain the behaviour of a thing only in the sense of classifying it with other things which behave in that way. But, the argument continues, genuine sciences begin where social science stops: physics and chemistry *begin* by explaining empirical generalizations in terms of theoretical laws and their associated theories, whereas the most that social scientists, except perhaps economists, can do is to derive empirical laws from more general ones of the same kind. It is doubtful whether this process of derivation can even be said to explain, since the very same question arises concerning the last generalization as arose concerning the first. If the original question was 'Why did those people show high ability to empathize?' the answer might be 'Because they were participating in high involvement relationships, and all people who do that show such ability'. Yet the same question reappears as 'Why do all people who participate in those relationships exhibit that ability?' Hence, the critics conclude, any such classifying hypothesis cannot be used as an explanation, since it does not dispel the original puzzle.

There are two different charges, then, with which we can deal here. The first is that none of the hypotheses advanced by social scientists is properly framed; and the second is that while some are properly framed they are no more than empirical, i.e. non-theoretical, generalizations. It will be economical to consider the two claims jointly. This really amounts to considering the second charge, because it contains the contradictory of the first. If we can discover a well-framed hypothetical generalization we shall falsify both charges at once.

Let us begin by reminding ourselves of the kinds of hypotheses which, according to their critics, social scientists ought to put forward. They ought to be concerned with either (1) the regular association of properties, whether these be in sequence or simultaneous, or (2) the relations between properties, measurable directly or indirectly, such that changes in some of the properties are mathematically expressible as functions of changes in other of the properties. This, in general, is said to be the form taken by laws in the physical sciences; and the social sciences — if they are sciences — ought to display generalizations with these features. Our problem now is to find out whether they do.

One difficulty is that the hypotheses are often not clearly stated. It is left to the reader to pick out the generalizations upon which the argument depends. Thus in a study[1] of fertility rates amongst different socio-economic classes in the United States, it was found that specific lines of work were not significantly correlated with fertility rates. If, however, larger classes of these occupational groups were formed a 'consistent rank order' emerged. The class consisting of the three occupational groups of professional workers, clerks, and proprietors, had the lowest rate of fertility in the sample drawn; service and craft workers had rates from 13 to 26 per cent higher than those of the first class; operatives and labourers had rates from 28 to 51 per cent higher; farm owners and farm labourers had, in general, rates from 43 to 72 per cent higher than the rates of the least fertile class. It was found, in addition, that within each class there was some variation over a period of time in the fertility rank of occupational groups. In 1910 and 1940, for example, the clerks in the North-east region had a slightly higher rate of fertility than the professional people in that same region. In 1940 this position was reversed for the Western region.

Suppose, then, we take this variation within such a narrow range to be a puzzle worth explaining. How can we do so? The suggestion is that the variation be taken as evidence that the class consists of groups 'having the same general values and modes of living, and thus the same level of fertility'.[2] The word 'thus' in the phrase is a sign of an attempted generalization; it asserts a connection between certain modes of living, with their associated attitudes, and certain levels of fertility. But do clerks belong in this class, then? They do not, after all, have the same economic or social status as proprietors or professional people. The answer to this is that clerks 'might be classed with other white-collar groups since they tend to imitate their patterns of living. It is possible for clerks to have the same general attitudes and the same general style of living as professionals and proprietors, although unable to express this style of living and its associated attitudes on the same social and economic plane as the people whom they imitate.'[3]

For our purposes it does not matter whether the generalization connecting modes of living with fertility levels was held before the occupational groups were formed into classes, or whether the differences amongst the four classes suggested the generalization. In either case, this generalization and the classifying of the four occupational groups affected each other, since the explanation given of the smallness of the variation found within the least fertile class was that its three groups share the same pattern of living. This could hardly be an explanation unless a generalization which related pattern of living and fertility rate were presupposed. Its soundness would provide, in turn, a reason for retaining the classification system: different fertility rates could be explained in terms of occupational class and the associated style of life.

Now the statement that clerks have the same 'mode of living' as professional persons and proprietors is a statement of one of the initial conditions. We have to produce evidence that members of these groups do in fact share the same pattern of living. In order to do this we have to define 'pattern of living' in such a way that we provide criteria for classifying occupational groups into their appropriate patterns. Only if

[1] R. Dinkel: 'Occupation and Fertility in the United States', *American Sociological Review*, Vol. 17, No. 2, April 1952.

[2] *Ibid.*, p. 183.

[3] *Ibid.*

we can give such criteria shall we be in a position to frame a generalization connecting the different patterns with different rates of fertility. An obvious criticism of the study, therefore, is that since no criteria of 'pattern of living' are specified, no testable generalization has been put forward. The result is that no scientific explanation of the change in relative position within one class has been offered. All that has really been advanced is a proposal to look at the association between mode of life and fertility rate. But this cannot be done until we substitute some testable properties for those vaguely referred to by the phrase 'mode of life'.

Thus the need for a generalization has arisen, but it has not been successfully met. It arose because an attempt was made to explain why clerks fell into the same fertility class as proprietors and professional people. The generalization failed because it was improperly framed. The upshot of our discussion of the present example, then, is simply this: there is in the social sciences a class of studies which to the casual reader appear to contain explanations in terms of law-like statements, whereas in fact, they do not. What they do contain are hints as to which properties or situations or events may be connected and, hence, ought to be investigated. Such studies are actually prolegomena to future generalizations.

Untestability is a defect not confined to any particular field of social science. For example, a similar vagueness is displayed by the following generalizations, the first of which is taken from political science, and the second from economics. (1) 'When the need for protection against external pressure is removed, the suppression of internal freedom produces (as in Poland) an unbalance, chemically explosive and impossible to be maintained except by direct force.'[4] (2) 'A substantial increase in the quantity of money within a relatively short period is accompanied by a substantial increase in prices.'[5] These two differ in an important respect, however. The economic generalization can be made more precise; the 'substantial increase' needed depends upon a number of factors which can be partially specified, e.g. the volume of the increase as compared to the total amount of money, and the counter-inflationary measures taken by the government, such as a rise in the bank rate. But it is difficult to see how this can be done for the other generalization. Is the first clause to be interpreted as referring to the beliefs of the general population about foreign enemies? Or the claims of the military establishment? And what is the relationship between the suppression of internal freedom and the resultant imbalance?

An hypothesis may be untestable for different reasons, not only because the properties it refers to are poorly defined. The untestability may result from the generalization being — to put it briefly but crudely — 'true by definition'. If it is, there can be no question, naturally, of submitting the hypothesis to tests. The social sciences are filled with instances of analytic statements (ones whose denials can be shown to be self-contradictory) that have been unwittingly treated as empirical assertions. This confusion arises in two familiar ways. Firstly, a particular expression may ordinarily be taken as true by definition and yet not be clearly marked as such. Thus it may be said that a rational entrepreneur tries to make marginal cost and marginal revenue equal. This doesn't look to be merely a definition, but a closer analysis reveals that in fact it is. We can put the generalization in this fashion: 'If: (1) An entrepreneur seeks maximum profits. (2) His marginal cost curve does not fall so fast as (or, rises more rapidly than) his marginal revenue curve. (3) These curves are continuous. *Then:* He operates at the output where marginal revenue equals marginal cost.'[6] Sentences (1), (2) and (3) jointly entail the conclusion. In brief, it logically

[4] G. Catlin: 'Political Theory: What Is It?', *Political Science Quarterly*, Vol. 72, No. 1, March 1957, pp. 14–5.

[5] M. Friedman: *Essays in Positive Economics*, 1953, p. 11.

[6] G. Stigler: *The Theory of Price*, 1947, p. 4.

follows from the definition of 'rational entrepreneur', taken together with such definitions as those of 'marginal cost' and 'marginal revenue', that a rational entrepreneur will seek to equate cost and revenue of this kind. Hence, no empirical assertion is being made by the assertion that he does so.

Secondly, confusion may arise from a statement being taken first as empirical and later as analytic. The commonest cause of this change is the desire to avoid the inconvenience of having a cherished hypothesis open to falsification. The fact that the change has taken place often goes unrecognized for a period of time. Two examples chosen from a large number of cases will serve to illustrate this claim.

There is in economics a well-known case of an hypothesis with this type of chequered career; sometimes the hypothesis has been taken as true by definition and sometimes it has been interpreted as an empirical claim. It is the hypothesis known as 'transitivity of preference' or 'maximization of utility'. The problem arises in this way. Assume that a person's preferences satisfy certain postulates, in particular, the postulate of transitivity. This says that if a person prefers a to b, and b to c, he must prefer a to c. It can be shown that if this postulate is satisfied, we can always define a self-consistent utility function which is always maximized by the person's choice, that is, the person will always choose the alternative with the higher utility for him. If this postulate is not met, we cannot define such a self-consistent utility function. Now suppose the person actually displays intransitive preference such that at one time he prefers a to b, and b to c, but at a later time prefers c to a. Then if we take the postulate to be an empirical one, this case is a counter-example. However, we can always escape this conclusion by saying that at the first time he would really have preferred a to c, but at the second time his taste had changed and so he preferred c to a. With this stipulation the postulate becomes analytically true. We can state the general point thus: if certain parameters are so defined as to make mathematical formulae true by definition, then the application of these formulae beyond the area of their definition will require an empirical assumption. This will be the assumption that the relevant parameters are stable over a period of time. But the question whether they are stable or not is clearly one of fact. If we wish to avoid the possible falsification of this assumption, we can always do so by asserting that the parameters have changed. Then, of course, we shall be interpreting the formulae as analytically true. Both these positions have been taken by economists in the past, and some of them did not realize that there were two positions between which they were oscillating as convenience dictated.

Another example of an expression which has given rise to problems of interpretation in the past is that produced by Keynes. He said that '$S \equiv I$' where S = savings and I = investment. But it was not immediately realized that savings and investment are equivalent in this expression by definition, and that this is the result of Keynes taking 'investment' to include involuntary investment, e.g. unsold stock, as well as planned investment in stocks and machinery. When involuntary investment is excluded, savings and investment are not equivalent; the relationship between them becomes a matter for empirical investigation. Economists are well aware of this, however, and have taken that interpretation — empirical or analytic — which best suits their purposes at a given time. No confusion has arisen from this policy because they now mark the difference by calling the Keynesian interpretation 'ex-post savings and investment' and the other 'ex-ante savings and investment'. . . .

There is no doubt that all the examples so far considered — the well formed and the ill-formed alike — are empirical generalizations, that is, they are all derived from or based upon *observations.* They contain no references to the existence of abstract or theoretical objects, processes, or states. For social scientists, it is said by their critics, have no *theories* with which to explain their empirical generalizations. Their efforts are spent upon producing more and more general forms of empirical hypotheses from observation and experiment, whereas in the more advanced sciences this is not so. In them, laws are obtained by deduction from theories, or by deduction combined with transliteration into the vocabulary of experimental work; it is by the latter method that empirical laws are obtained in physics and chemistry. Scientists in those fields are primarily interested in the theories which allow them to explain empirical laws, and not, in contrast to social scientists, in the production of such laws.

This is, in outline, what one common complaint about the use of empirical generalizations in the social sciences amount to. We shall argue against this complaint that in fact there are both well-framed hypotheses and theories in the social sciences. We shall argue, further, that the presence of abstract or theoretical objects is irrelevant to the question of whether there are such hypotheses and theories. We begin by listing some examples of well-formed hypotheses:

(1) 'Societies in which marriage is allowed or preferred with mother's brother's daughter but forbidden or disapproved with father's sister's daughter will be societies in which jural authority over ego male, before marriage, is vested in his father or father's lineage, and societies in which marriage is allowed or preferred with father's sister's daughter but forbidden or disapproved with mother's brother's daughter will be societies in which jural authority over ego male, before marriage, is vested in his mother's brother or mother's brother's lineage.'[7]

(2) 'For men, the length of sickness absence decreases directly with the length of employment service.'

(3) 'Labour turnover increases directly with the distance of worker's residence from work and inversely with the level of unemployment.'

(4) 'The trade cycle (rise and decline of employment, prices, profits, and income) is caused by the "alternating excess and deficiency of investment in relation to saving by the consuming public, and the amount spent by industrialists with the Government on new investment".'[8]

(5) 'A rise in the price of any one good will result in a fall of demand for that good provided all other prices and money income remain unchanged.'

(6) 'If the price of a good rises the supply of that good forthcoming will be increased — other things being equal.'

(7) 'If there is unemployment it can be decreased by decreasing taxation of the poor and increasing taxation of the rich.'

(8) 'A country can improve its deficit on the balance of payments by devaluing its currency.'

Do these generalizations meet the requirements of invariable association, universality, and testability? Does each assert that a property — or state or situation or process — is either a necessary or sufficient condition of some other, or a necessary and sufficient condition of another? Clearly, all the statements listed might in fact be false; none of them need have its truth determined merely by definition of its terms or by logical demonstration. At least, all of them can be so interpreted that they are not analytic statements. It may be thought that numbers (5) and (6) are suspicious; that, for example, the phrase 'other things being equal' in number (6) will allow so many qualifications to be made that the statement will become logically true and, hence, unassailable. This need not be the case, however, for while such conditions as the presence of a market — sellers, consumers, supplies, etc. — are assumed, once these are stated, it is still open to test whether under such circumstances a rise in the supply of a good is the result of a rise in its price. Similarly, a rise in the price of a good is claimed to result in a fall in the quantity bought — if all other prices and money income remain unchanged. These latter conditions do not logically ensure that a rise in price will result in a fall of expenditure, since consumers could, if they wished, devote a larger proportion of their income to the purchase of the good in question. What the hypothesis claims is that they do not.

[7] G. Homans and D. Schneider: *Marriage, Authority, and Final Causes*, 1955, p. 51.

[8] E. Durbin: *Problems of Economic Planning*, 1949, p. 165.

None of the statements on our list, we have said, need have its truth determined by definition of its terms or by logical demonstration. Nor will the truth of any of them be decided by direct observation. Each generalization refers to an unlimited number of cases, past, present, and future; that is, each is a universal hypothesis which refers to events or things of a certain kind and not to particular instances. It is asserted that any country can improve its deficit balance of payments, that any unemployment can be decreased, that for any group of men belonging to a class with certain properties, the length of sickness absence decreases with service. Naturally, qualifications may have to be made concerning the kinds of country, unemployment, and man, of whom these statements hold. But the statements will remain universal ones because no particular country or period of unemployment or set of men will be mentioned. The hypotheses will apply to any objects that fall into the appropriate category, and no finite set of direct observations will be sufficient to provide a test for every one of an infinite set of cases.

Again, it will not be correct to say that any of our generalizations is too vague for testing. Each is briefly stated, but each can be so expanded as to permit us to formulate the conditions which would test it. Thus no one believes that a rise in the price of one good ever occurs in isolation from a rise in all other prices. The influences which raise its price also raise the prices of other goods at the same time. Yet if such a single rise *were* to occur, then according to our hypotheses, the supply of the good would increase and the quantity bought decrease. Testability in principle is all that we can require of any scientific hypothesis. Otherwise we shall eliminate from the sciences a large array of important statements about such things as frictionless surfaces and ideal gas molecules. A claim like 'If two perfectly elastic bodies were to collide, the total kinetic energy of the system would be the same before and after the impact' is testable in principle though not directly testable in practice. In this respect it is exactly like our economic example. The other examples do not even raise this problem. They are straightforward cases which can be directly tested once certain assumptions are made clear. It would not be reasonable, for example, to interpret statement number (2) as asserting that the length of sickness absence decreases directly with the length of employment service even under conditions of forced labour or in concentration camps. But qualifications such as these hold of all scientific generalizations. In the natural sciences it is quite common to speak of these as qualifications forming a 'text' which accompanies all hypotheses. The 'text' includes a number of different kinds of qualification, some of which apply only to hypotheses framed as equations; others apply to the kind of statement found on our list. The first kind is illustrated by an example of Bridgman's:

> . . . if I set up the mathematical theory of a body falling under the action of gravity, I have the equation $\frac{dv}{dt} = g$, but I have to supplement this by a 'text', saying that v is a number describing a property of the moving body which can be obtained by a certain kind of measurement, which is specified, that t is the time obtained by another kind of measurement, etc. . . . it must also specify the connection between the different symbols in the equation . . . the text specifies that the s and the t are the distance and time obtained by *simultaneous* measurements. The equation itself has no mechanism for demanding that s and t be simultaneous, and in fact this demand cannot be described in the language of the equation.[9]

The second sort of qualification laid upon a scientific hypothesis by its 'text' includes the definition of its terms and an accurate statement of the limits within which it is supposed to hold. Neither of these need appear in the generalization itself, and however obvious each is, critics of the social sciences often speak as though hypotheses of the type that we have listed are deficient in not containing such qualifications on their face. It

[9] P. Bridgman: *The Nature of Physical Theory*, 1936, pp. 59–60.

vorth the time, therefore, to remind our-ves that the generalizations of the natural ...ences do not differ on these points from those of the social sciences. One instance — that of Galileo's laws of projectile motion — is referred to by Holton, and his remarks are sufficient to indicate how similar the 'texts' are in the two fields.

> We find in his work a thorough examination of the major limitations involved; for example, he points out that the trajectory will not be parabolic for extremely large ranges because then the acceleration of gravity, being directed toward the center of our round earth, will no longer be parallel for different parts of the paths assumed in our equations. Of course this failure applies, strictly speaking, even to small trajectories, but in such cases it is by theory and test permissible to neglect it for our purposes, just as we have already neglected the effect of air resistance, rotation of the earth, variation of the value of g over the whole path, etc. . . . if we were required to deal with actual motions in which these secondary factors are not negligible, we are confident that we would surely be able to discover the laws guiding those smaller effects, and add them to our calculations.[10]

The eight examples on our list differ amongst themselves in the extent to which their scope has been accurately determined. They also differ amongst themselves in the degree to which a given investigator might feel 'confident that we would be able to discover the laws guiding those smaller effects' — those effects which have been deliberately neglected in the statement of the hypothesis because they do not substantially alter the major effect, or else complicate the hypothesis unduly, or both. The situation in the social sciences is more often the second alternative than the first. In other words, if we are required to deal with the actual price movements of goods where secondary factors like the rise in other prices are not negligible, we find it very difficult to discover the laws guiding those effects and add them to our calculations. But neither of these differences amongst the members of our list is peculiar to the social sciences; a list of hypotheses drawn from the natural sciences would show a similar variation with respect to our knowledge of their scope and our confidence that laws governing the 'smaller effects' could be discovered.

If it is true, as we have been arguing, that all the generalizations on our list seem to meet the three requirements of universality, testability, and uniformity of connection, is it also true that all our hypotheses give either necessary or sufficient conditions, or both? The briefest answer to this is that the question is somewhat misapplied.

Suppose we ask the same question of generalizations in the natural sciences. Take the simplest possible case like that of Boyle's Law. It states that at a given temperature the volume and absolute pressure of a gas vary inversely. But when we first learn about it we also learn that there are conditions under which it does not hold. Similarly, there are conditions to which Snell's Law does not apply. In those conditions it is not true that if a light ray is incident at a surface separating two transparent media, then it is also bent so that the ratio of the sine of the angle of incidence to the sine of the angle of refraction is constant for those media.

If we simply look at the statements of these laws, as we did at our list of social hypotheses in the opening pages of this chapter, then we shall find it difficult to answer the popular questions: 'Necessary condition? Sufficient? Or both?' Under some circumstances not mentioned in its statement, Snell's Law gives the sufficient conditions of the bending of the light ray in the manner indicated. Under other conditions it does not. When we know only what is given in the form of its brief statement we cannot answer the questions about necessary and sufficient conditions. And the same is true of Boyle's Law: for one, the type of gas has to be specified before we can correctly assert that such and such are the sufficient conditions for the pressure and volume of an enclosed gas to vary inversely. Hence, it is not a fair criticism of an hypothesis to say, in the absence of its 'text', that we do

[10] G. Holton: *Introduction to Concepts and Theories in Physical Science*, 1952, p. 270.

not know whether it is to be interpreted as asserting necessary conditions or sufficient ones, or both. It may be that the hypotheses on our first list are defective in not providing us with such conditions, but we shall never be able to show this merely by examining them without their accompanying glosses.

The generalizations of the social and natural sciences are exactly similar in this respect. Boyle's Law, we may recall, is accurate only for gases of very low density. It assumes an ideal gas — one without internal friction since its molecules are supposed to have no extension and to exert no forces on one another. As the density of an actual gas increases the accuracy of the law decreases, for when the molecules are nearer to each other the forces of attraction amongst them are greater; and the result of this is that the pressure is reduced. Yet the law's range of accuracy, while available to the interested student, is not usually included in the statement of the law itself. Nor is the scope of the hypothesis 'The higher the cohesiveness of a human group, the higher will be the correlation between popularity rank and perceived leadership rank' included in its statement. The question whether the relevant information *could* be made available to the interested auditor is an important but different one. The charge that it could not be, if substantiated, would mark the distinction between a proto-hypothesis and a fully developed one. Our claim, then, is that whatever the status of the examples on our first list, those on our second are supported by 'texts' at least as respectable — considering the difference in subject matter — as those of generalizations in the natural sciences.

Now let us examine the credentials of several of our generalizations in more detail. We begin with some remarks about the one concerning popularity and leadership rank, for it is drawn from our first, and, apparently, weaker list. What exactly does it assume? It takes cohesiveness to be 'the total of individual members' identifications with the group' and to depend 'upon the degree of member attachment resulting from the satisfaction of self-needs they have experienced through membership'.[11] Under conditions of low identification with the group a person will be receiving little satisfaction from it. 'He may then be expected to like or dislike fellow members purely on the basis of personal preference. However, when he is deeply concerned about the welfare of the group, he may then be expected to like most those members whom he perceives as making the most valuable contributions to the group.[12] This is substantially what the hypothesis claims about members of small groups. Four such groups were tested for cohesiveness and ranked. The index numbers for the groups were these: group A = 82, group B = 52, group C = 63, group D = 41. The most cohesive group was A, the least cohesive was D. The index was constructed on the basis of direct answers to questions put to members about their enjoyment of meetings, their liking for each other, and their willingness to sacrifice for the group. Then members' responses to two questions about the other members' popularity and the value of their contributions to the group were scored and correlated.

One result was that group A had a linear correlation of ·94 between the perceived leadership of any member ('amount of valuable contributions') and his popularity; group B of — · 19; group C of ·66; group D of ·20. This is support for the view 'that through time leadership and popularity roles may either merge or differentiate, depending on whether cohesiveness is increasing or decreasing, with specialization of these roles a function of low cohesion'.[13] Obviously, the negative correlation of ·19 for group B is anomalous and requires explanation. Equally obvious is the fact that the generalization does not present us with a mathematical relationship — even though all three prop-

[11] G. Theodorson: 'The Relationship Between Leadership and Popularity Roles in Small Groups', *American Sociological Review*, Vol. 22, No. 1, February 1957, p. 59.

[12] *Ibid.*, p. 60.

[13] *Ibid.*, p. 67.

erties are measured. Nothing is said about the functional connection amongst these properties. We do not know how closely the correlation between popularity and leadership varies with cohesiveness. But it does seem to be claimed that the presence of a higher (or lower) cohesiveness in one group than in another group, or at different periods in the same group, is always *sufficient* for the presence of an increased (or decreased) correlation between the other two properties.

Clearly, no information is given about the change in cohesiveness as a *necessary* condition of the change in correlation between leadership and popularity. Does this distinguish the present example from the cases of Boyle's Law and Snell's Law? Do they, in conjunction with their glosses, provide us with necessary conditions as well as sufficient ones? For Boyle's Law the answer is 'Yes'. Roughly speaking, there are four conditions which are both sufficient and necessary for the volume and absolute pressure of a gas to vary inversely. These are: (*a*) the gas must be of low density, (*b*) the gas must be compressed at constant temperature, (*c*) the temperature of the gas must be well above its liquefaction point, (*d*) no chemical association or dissociation must take place in the gas. Given these conditions, Boyle's Law holds approximately. If greater accuracy is required, van der Waal's Law can be employed.

Thus it is a difference between Boyle's Law and the hypothesis about group cohesion that the first is expandable so as to supply necessary conditions while the second is not — at present. Is this difference also exhibited in the case of Snell's Law? A moment's consideration will show that it is. What we must take into account are the conditions which change the velocity of light, that is, change the electromagnetic properties of media. The chief conditions affecting these properties are the colour (or wave length) of the light; the temperature variation within the media, especially the temperature of gases; any elastic strain to which the media are subjected; and in the case of crystalline media such as quartz and feldspar, the orientation of the direction of incidence with respect to the planes of the crystal. All these conditions affect the operation of Snell's Law: it does not hold under certain states of temperature change and elastic strain, or for certain kinds of light rays or for transparent crystals. Taken jointly, then, these four types of factors are the ones from which we can draw both the necessary and sufficient conditions required for Snell's Law to hold.

The question which now confronts us is whether *any* of the texts of the generalizations on our second list supply us with similar sorts of conditions. In the case of the anthropological example the situation is as follows. The hypothesis claimed that: 'Societies in which marriage is allowed or preferred with mother's brother's daughter but forbidden or disapproved with father's sister's daughter will be societies in which jural authority over ego male, before marriage, is vested in his father or father's lineage, and societies in which marriage is allowed or preferred with father's sister's daughter but forbidden or disapproved with mother's brother's daughter will be societies in which jural authority over ego male, before marriage, is vested in his mother's brother or mother's brother's lineage.' The phrase 'jural authority' means 'legitimate or constituted authority, and a person holds jural authority over others when, according to the stated norms of his group, he has the right to give them orders and they have the duty to obey'.[14]

The authors go on to make it clear that the presence of jural authority in conjunction with cross-cousin marriage is to be taken as a roughly sufficient[15] condition for the existence of a particular form of marriage. 'From our general theory we argued that, if the locus of jural authority over ego, before marriage, is his father, then, provided unilateral cross-cousin marriage is allowed at all, the matrilateral form will be the rule, and if the locus of jural authority over ego, before marriage,

[14] Homans and Schneider: *op. cit.*, p. 21.

[15] 'Roughly sufficient' because the authors may be correct in believing that they have found a counter-example to their hypothesis. *Ibid.*, p. 57.

is his mother's brother, the patrilateral form will be the rule.'[16] The difficulty with taking this hypothesis as a statement of the *necessary* conditions for the matrilateral and patrilateral forms is simply that all anthropologists know of societies which have both forms of cross-cousin marriage and only one locus of jural authority. In these societies it is obvious that the two forms of marriage cannot have as their necessary conditions the two loci of authority required by the hypothesis.

We have on our list some well-known examples drawn from economics, and a brief consideration of them will tell us something of their status. One asserts that a rise in the price of a good will produce a fall in its consumption. But no economist believes that a price rise is always sufficient to produce this effect. For if the good in question cannot easily be dispensed with, the consumers — being poorer — may decrease their purchases of luxury goods and increase their purchases of the necessity. This substitution will result in a rise in demand rather than in a fall. This may occur even though 'all other prices and money income remain unchanged', as the hypothesis demands. A more common situation is a rise in consumption for a particular luxury good after its price has been raised; the rise in price may accompany an increase in the prestige of the good and so increase its consumption. Hence, a price rise is not sufficient for a decrease in consumption, and certainly not necessary for such a decrease, since sometimes a price decrease produces a fall in consumption. A luxury good may lose prestige by having its price lowered and thus lose part of its market.

The same general conclusion holds of some of our other economic generalizations. We cannot take the price rise of a good to be sufficient to increase its supply. Sometimes the price may increase but the supply decrease, as in the case of a labour force that stops work once a particular level of real income has been reached. Any price rise that adds to their income will merely decrease the amount of the good which they need to produce in order to reach their desired standard of living. Again, unemployment may not 'be decreased by decreasing taxation of the poor and increasing taxation of the rich'. If the rich are taxed their incentive for investment may diminish and nullify the effects on unemployment of increased consumption by the poor. Similarly, a country may not improve its deficit on balance of payments by devaluing its currency. A country which devalues its currency hopes to improve its deficit in two ways. It expects import prices to be higher and export prices to be lower. Hence, it expects the country's imports to drop and its exports to rise. Neither of these effects may take place, however. Economists have shown that under certain conditions of demand the increase of exports and the decrease of imports may not be sufficient to produce the desired result.

These three generalizations are alike, then, in not actually providing sufficient conditions, though they may be interpreted as attempting to do so. Nor does any of these hypotheses supply necessary conditions. In each case — that of increased supply of a good, change of taxation, devaluation of currency — the presumed result can take place in the absence of the specified condition. The supply of a good can increase through many other means than by an increase in its price. Decreased taxation of the poor and increased taxation of the rich does not wait upon unemployment for its stimulus. A country could conceivably decide to revalue its currency for other reasons than that of affecting its balance of payments.

Now it is not likely that any economist ever believed that necessary conditions are provided by the economic generalizations on our second list. In the past, some may have believed that sufficient conditions are supplied in these cases, but the present view, certainly, would be that the hypotheses as stated merely assert strong tendencies and not perfect correlations or constant conjunctions, although the actual statements of the hypotheses are universal in form.

One question which we have been trying

[16] *Ibid.*

to answer is whether relevant information about necessary and sufficient conditions could be drawn from the texts of our sample hypotheses. The answer is an equivocal 'Yes'. Some cases have a settled answer and some cases do not. To ask, for instance, what sort of conditions the hypothesis about jural authority gives us is to ask the question of someone who might employ it professionally — some anthropologist. In this particular case the authors' words seem to indicate that they take the hypothesis to supply a roughly sufficient condition. Our reason for believing that they do not take it as supplying a necessary condition as well, is simply that we credit them with knowing what some other anthropologists also know, that there are societies with the required types of marriage and without the required types of jural authority. But if it so happened that the authors were not familiar with these examples, then they might wish to treat the hypothesis as supplying a necessary condition of a certain kind of marriage. Since a different investigator might treat the statement as supplying neither necessary nor sufficient conditions, it is not enough in such a case to ask 'What does the generalization assert?' We have to ask 'What was the generalization used to assert on such-and-such occasions?'

However, in contrast to these, there are also hypotheses for which there is a settled interpretation. Boyle's Law is an instance of this type and so is Snell's Law. There is no need, therefore, to distinguish in such cases between the question "What does the generalization assert?' and 'What was asserted by it on that particular occasion?' The interpretation does not change from one occasion to another, at least not in the way that the interpretation of a new hypothesis can change. Of course both laws have undergone such changes in the past. Boyle knew nothing about the factors of gas density and Snell nothing of the effects of elastic strain. Their original statements gave only some of the necessary conditions and part of the sufficient conditions, e.g. in Boyle's case the compression of the gas at constant temperature. With further work additional conditions have been provided, that is, the scope of the hypotheses has been more accurately determined and agreement on them reached by physicists.

There are, on our lists, generalizations with a history and status similar in these respects to those of Boyle's Law and Snell's Law. Economists are generally agreed upon the scope of the Laws of Supply and Demand, and the criticisms that we have raised of the two on our second list (numbers 5 and 6) are familiar to every economics student. They are, in fact, criticisms without an edge, since they are usually taken by economists as limits to the scope of the laws. It would be quite possible to qualify the generalization about rising price and increased supply so as to take account of the diminished output from certain labour forces. This is not necessary for the same reason it is not necessary that Boyle's Law incorporate a provision about chemical action or Snell's Law a proviso concerning temperature changes in the media. It would be extremely cumbersome to write into the statements of these laws all the qualifications which are understood to apply to them. In the same way, the generalization about taxation to relieve unemployment and the one about devaluation of currency resemble generalizations in the natural sciences. In both the natural sciences and the social sciences there are generalizations whose texts are generally taken as providing well-known limits of range and accuracy. In both fields, there are hypotheses which lack such texts, either because not enough is known, as in the case of high involvement relationships and ability to empathize, or because there is no general agreement as to what is known. . . .

Are There Theories in Social Science?

There is, of course, another sense of the term 'theory' and it is the one to which we shall devote most of our attention from this point onward. The sense is that assumed by critics when they assert, disapprovingly, that none of the social sciences except economics contains any formal theories. But the phrase 'formal theory' is used rather loosely. Thus the title 'formal theory' is often applied to a set of empirical generalizations, a set which jointly entails some additional generalization. This kind of formal theory, whether put in words or mathematical symbols, is simply the explanation-schema that we referred to in Chapter Three of Part One and again in the previous chapter. If, for example, we take Charles' Law and Boyle's Law to be empirical generalizations, as they originally were, then we can deduce the generalization that the pressure of a gas, when its volume remains constant, is directly proportional to the absolute temperature. But this shop-worn example would never be called a 'physical theory'. All three of these empirical generalizations can be deduced from the conjunction of a particular theory and a particular law, however. The theory is that of the kinetic theory of gases, and it states that there are molecules of gases, that they have certain properties such as elasticity, and that they follow Newton's laws of motion. The law adds to this theory the information that the absolute temperature of a gas is proportional to the average molecular kinetic energy.

The point is that Charles' Law and Boyle's Law were originally put forward as statements of observable regularities, whereas the kinetic theory of gases and the law associated with it could not be. Newton's laws contain, for example, such theoretical terms as 'force' and 'mass'. Each of these two terms can be explicitly defined only with the aid of the other, and not simply in terms of some set of observable properties. The relations of pressure, volume, and temperature to each other in a gas are explained, then, by means of a theory about the existence, movements, and energy of unobservable gas molecules. And it is this kind of formal theory which has attracted the attention and excited the envy of social scientists. They have asked whether in the social sciences, as in the physical ones, there are or can be formal theories of this sort, ones from which empirical generalizations are deducible but which contain statements about unobservable entities and relations as well.

Let us turn to a scrutiny of an empirical generalization that was mentioned earlier. It is a generalization which has attracted wider comment than many in the social sciences.[17] It says that 'Societies in which marriage is allowed or preferred with mother's brother's daughter but forbidden or disapproved with father's sister's daughter will be societies in which jural authority over ego male, [i.e. any man] before marriage, is vested in his father or father's lineage. . . .'.[18] Assume this to be (*a*) well tested and confirmed, and (*b*) to assert that the presence of a *rule* of matrilateral marriage under the stated condition is sufficient for the presence of a rule to the effect that jural authority over ego male is to be held patrilineally, and that the presence of the latter rule is also sufficient for the presence of the former rule. Let us take this to be a social analogue of the gas laws, and hence, like them, to cry out for theoretical explanation. We now ask how it is in fact explained by the anthropologists who put it forward.

It is explained in the following way. In some societies the father has jural authority over the son: the former has the right to give orders and the latter has the duty to obey. The two are not closely related by ties of affection. But the relations between mother's brother and ego are close, for the maternal uncle provides help, advice, and goods. He is a 'male mother' to his nephew in a way that his nephew's father is not. In other societies the father has no jural authority over the son. This authority is vested in ego's maternal uncle. In these circumstances father and son have a close relationship while son and uncle have not. Thus in the first situation ego will be 'fond of mother's

[17] See, for example, D. Emmett: *Function, Purpose and Powers*, 1958, pp. 100–1.

[18] Homans and Schneider, *loc. cit.*

brother, and as mother's brother and his daughter in the patrilineal complex, the Oedipus Complex if you will, are themselves particularly close to one another, he will tend to get fond of the daughter. Their marriage will be sentimentally appropriate; it will cement the relationship. Or, if women are indeed scarce and valued goods, and ego is in doubt where he can get one, he will certainly be wise to ask his mother's brother, on whom he already has so strong a sentimental claim'.[19] On the other hand, in those societies in which jural authority is held by the mother's brother, ego will become fond of the daughter of his father's sister and marriage with her will be the preferred form.[20]

It turns out, therefore, that the association between the two sorts of prescribed behaviour is explained in terms of the sentiments and emotions of the actors. The explanation makes implicit use of generalizations such as these: (1) a relationship in which are stressed the right of some members to command and the duty of the other members to obey, produces sentiments that inhibit the development of feelings of affection between the members of the two groups, (2) if ego is fond of his mother's brother, and this person in turn, is fond of his own daughter, then ego will tend to be fond of the daughter, (3) if ego is not fond of his father, then he will not be fond of his father's sister nor of her daughter.

The attempt to make these generalizations explicit reveals, perhaps, their inadequacy. But this does not matter. What is important here is that the statement of an observable regularity — the association between jural authority and type of marriage — is explained by means of a set of empirical generalizations concerning the psychology of the people involved. The case at hand is not analogous to the kinetic theory and the gas laws; here one statement of an empirical regularity is simply taken to be derivable from a number of others. And this kind of 'theory', while present in the social sciences, is not what many social scientists are seeking, rightly or wrongly, when they demand theories analogous to those of the physical sciences. The question, then, is 'Can these demands be met?'

A clear answer to this question requires that we first recognize two different methods by which a formal theory can arise. The difference between them is that of whether or not the theory was developed as an interpretation of a calculus. The point to be emphasized can be made in the following fashion. A deductive system or theory in the *natural* sciences — a formal theory — is couched in words or other symbols, at least some of which describe or refer to a subject matter. The system consists of: (1) a set of axioms which have these properties: their truth is assumed; their truth can be tested only by the testing of some of their logical consequences; they cannot be deduced from other statements within the system; (2) those statements (theorems) that are entailed by the axioms or by the axioms in conjunction with theorems and definitions; such theorems may be either theoretical laws, and so open to testing only by means of certain of their logical consequences, or they may be empirical generalizations and thus open to direct testing; (3) a set of definitions of some of the descriptive (non-logical) terms that appear in the axioms; other definitions may be introduced in the course of proving the theorems, but these will be based upon the earlier ones.

In contrast to this, an uninterpreted calculus is a system of axioms, theorems, and definitions, couched entirely in logical and mathematical symbols which refer only to the arrangement and kinds of other such symbols. These are the subject matter of the system. The axioms and theorems are formulas rather than statements, so that questions of truth and falsity do not arise. It is this sort of formal system which is transformed into an interpreted calculus when rules of meaning are given for certain of its logical and mathematical symbols. These rules of interpretation convert the formulas into statements. Formal scientific theories are a sub-class of the class of interpreted calculi — of interpreted axiomatic systems.

[19] *Ibid.*, p. 23.

[20] *Ibid.*, pp. 26–7.

Thus a formal theory in the sciences may stem from an uninterpreted calculus. Or the theory may never have passed through such a stage in its history. It may not have been first developed as a logical skeleton, but have sprung forth at birth decently equipped with a subject matter. Since it was never anything other than an interpreted system, to call it an 'interpreted calculus' is merely to say that it has a logical structure which, if exposed, could be laid out in terms of definitions, axioms and theorems. It is not to assert that its order of development was from uninterpreted calculus to interpreted calculus. This difference in the possible history of a formal theory corresponds to the difference between two meanings of the question 'Are formal theories used in any social science except economics?'

One meaning of the question is whether social scientists do and should construct calculi which by a process of interpretation can become empirical theories. Another meaning of the question is: 'Are there — and should there be — theories whose logical structure, when displayed, would be that of an uninterpreted calculus?' It might be the case that while, at present, there were no theories fit for such examination, it was desirable, nevertheless, for social scientists to produce them; and one way of doing so would be for them to construct calculi susceptible of interpretation as empirical theories. Another way would be for social scientists to produce their theories first and worry later about exposing the logical skeletons of those theories.

Before taking up this difference, it will be useful for us to consider several other features of physical theories. These features can be introduced by our stressing this point: the interpreted *axioms* of physical theories are not statements of observed regularities. They are not mere empirical generalizations. This is important because there is a temptation on the part of some social scientists to believe that a set of empirical generalizations which are deductively related — an explanation schema — can be turned by the procedures of logic into the social analogue of a physical theory like the gas theory. They believe that making explicit the logical structure of such a set, laying it out in terms of definitions, axioms, and theorems, is tantamount to producing a formal scientific theory of the kind desired. That it is not is easily seen.

No matter how much effort of this sort is put into a set of empirical generalizations, the sense in which they form a theory is the same as that which applies in the case of the 'theory' about matrilateral marriage. This claim can be supported by our considering how Herbert Simon has rewritten[21] a set of generalizations put forward by Homans in his book entitled *The Human Group*. Some of Homans' generalizations are: (1) 'If the scheme of activities is changed, the scheme of interaction will, in general, change also, and vice versa.' (2) 'If the frequency of interaction between two or more persons increases, the degree of their liking for one another will increase, and vice versa.' (3) 'Persons who feel sentiments of liking for one another will express those sentiments in activities over and above the activities of the external system, and these activities may further strengthen the sentiments of liking.'[22]

The four terms 'interaction', 'friendliness', 'activity', and 'external system' are used by Simon to prepare a list of symbols whose definitions are as follows:

'I — the average rate of *interaction* per member'; 'F — the average *friendliness* between pairs of members'; 'A — the average amount of time spent per member per day in *activity* within the group'; 'E — the average amount of time that would be spent per member per day in activity within the group if members were motivated only by the *external system*'. All four of these letters are taken to represent variable quantities; and these variables are interpreted as functions of time (t). The expression $E(t)$ is held to represent an independent variable and $I(t)$,

[21] 'A Formal Theory of Interaction in Social Groups' in *American Sociological Review*, Vol. 17, No. 2, April 1952.

[22] Taken from pp. 102–18 of *The Human Group*, 1950.

$A(t)$, $F(t)$, dependent variables. Three axioms are then laid down. The first one will indicate their type: 'The intensity of interaction depends upon, and increases with, the level of friendliness and the amount of activity carried on within the group.' In symbols this is: $I(t) = a_1F(t) + a_2A(t)$. Thus Simon writes that 'a_1F may be regarded as the amount of interaction generated by the level, F, of friendliness in the absence of any group activity. That is, if $A = 0$, then $I = a_1F$'.[23] After the necessary and sufficient conditions for stability of equilibrium have been provided, the results of changes can be deduced. For example, we can deduce a generalization not given in Homans' original group. This generalization is the theorem that 'an increase in the activities required of the group by the external environment will increase (when equilibrium has been re-established) the amount of group activity, the amount of friendliness and the amount of interaction. As E decreases toward zero, A, F and I will decrease toward zero.' Or where 'd' represents 'derivative':

$$\frac{dIo}{dEo} = a_1 \frac{dFo}{dEo} + a_2 \frac{dAo}{dEo} > 0.$$ [24]

If we now compare this theorem with the axiom given previously — from which the theorem is in part derived — we see that the testability of one is as direct as that of the other. Either they are both generalizations of observable regularities, or neither is. They do not differ in the way in which a statement about the molecules of a gas differs from a statement about the volume and pressure of that gas. The molecules of the gas cannot be directly inspected whereas its volume and pressure can be. This important difference, which is thought to be of crucial importance by some critics, is not reflected in Homans' theory, and so, of course, not in Simon's rendering of it.

There are, in addition, some obvious difficulties. Simon points out that it has to be assumed that the four variables can be measured. He also points out that in the first axiom it is assumed that the level of interaction responds almost immediately to changes in the level of friendliness and the amount of intra-group activity. No help is given on these two points by the original generalizations. Moreover, some of these unqualified generalizations are probably not true, e.g. that frequency of interaction increases degree of liking. But most of these defects are repairable in principle. The absence of theoretical axioms is not — according to the view that the particle theories of physics are to be regarded as a useful pattern for the theories of social scientists.

Yet why should they be? Is the absence of theoretical axioms a genuine defect? The answer that we are considering is that it is, because only the assertion of the existence of indiscernible entities, states, events, and relations, can terminate an otherwise endless series of 'why' questions; for only an existence claim of this kind rules out any further scientific answer. Surely, however, this reply is simply mistaken, and with it the view about the need for theoretical axioms. The reply is the result of a compound of errors, errors which are also responsible for the charge that social scientists produce 'mere empirical generalizations'. Once it is realized that supporters of such complaints have confused a number of different issues, the plausibility of these criticisms launched against theories in the social sciences vanishes.

At the outset it should be noted that even if an existence claim of the required sort were necessary for the termination of a series of 'why' questions, this would still not be sufficient reason for restricting the title 'explanation' to theories incorporating such a claim. An explanation does not cease to be an explanation because it leaves another puzzle in its wake. We judge the soundness of a theory by various criteria, e.g. fertility of testable consequences, economy of means, and compatibility with other knowledge. None of these calls for an end to all future questions originating from the limits of the

[23] Simon: *op. cit.*, p. 204.

[24] *Ibid.*, p. 206.

theory's power to explain. If that were required the results would be unpalatable. First and foremost, no theories except those of atomic and sub-atomic physics could properly be said to explain. Newton's theory of gravitation, classical mechanics and thermodynamics, would fail this test. So would most theories in most other fields of science. But there is no need to elaborate, since the confusion within the argument being examined is sufficiently shown by the fact that it wavers between viewing theoretical laws as those which cannot be directly tested — by inspection of their instances — and as those which make existence claims for indiscernible objects or events or relations. For this reason it can rule out, on the one hand, Newtonian theories as non-explanatory — because they make no atomic claims — and, on the other hand, find that the theories are genuine explanations — because they are more than empirical generalizations, i.e. cannot be directly tested in the required fashion.

The second result of restricting the title 'explanation' in the proposed way would be to eliminate all methods of explaining except one, and to make every explanation of that one kind (theoretical laws) an ultimate explanation. Explanations which refer to intentions, dispositions, reasons, and functions, would no longer properly be called 'explanations'; for while some of them do, on occasion, make existence claims, these claims do not seem to refer to indiscernible entities of the required type. Or do they?

This question underlines the chief cause of the confusion in the argument concerning the nature of theoretical laws. The muddle is caused by a failure to distinguish between two sorts of indiscernible entities. One sort consists of *idealizations* and the other sort consists of *unobservables*. Frictionless surfaces, volumeless molecules, perfect gases and vacuums are imaginary conditions, limiting cases which are extrapolated from the existing values of the relevant variables. These states are imaginary (or ideal) because they assume what, given the present laws of nature, is physically impossible: the total absence of certain properties such as friction and volume. There is no question, then, of these being observable conditions. They are idealizations. In sharp contrast to these are the unobservable particles like mesons and protons, or the larger units like molecules. Claims for the existence of these objects do not assume the absence of certain properties, but the presence of indiscernible ones which are related in complex ways to measurable properties. It is physically impossible to observe the particles, but this is not because physicists assume them to be imaginary objects. Whatever their statuses, a molecule and a volumeless molecule are quite unlike each other.

Now, clearly, an existence claim that is capable of providing an ultimate explanation must be one which, according to the view under examination, asserts the existence of unobservable entities. It obviously cannot assert the existence of idealizations — that would be to assert that they are *not* imaginary, not idealizations. Yet the desired explanation can hardly refer, in the social sciences, to unobservable particles and their properties. It must, then, refer to unobservable entities like the unconscious group-mind or to unobservable social relations like corporate ownership. But since we already possess unobservables of this sort, and it is a matter of fact that they do not perform the desired job, there must be something wrong either with the kinds of social unobservables so far employed or with the demand itself — the demand for this type of ultimate explanation. Now it is a question of fact whether there are unobservable social entities and relations which could play the role required of them. The evidence is surely against there being anything in the social life of human beings that can be said to exist in some sense different from the sense in which the Id exists or love exists, and if these are examples of the sort of entity needed for ultimate explanations, the obvious answer is that we already have such explanations. Yet far from terminating a series of 'why' questions, an explanation in terms of the Id, for example, merely increases our curiosity. We wish to know a great deal about the origin and development of the Id. The same is true in the very different case of physical particles. The discovery of the proton and the meson certainly did not provide the kind of ultimate explanation envisaged by supporters of the present argument.

The truth is that the recurrent charge against the social sciences, the one with which we have been concerned, is the result of conflating three familiar questions. The first is whether there are any idealizations in the social sciences as there are in the physical sciences. The second is a question upon which we have already touched, namely, 'Are formal theories used in any of the social sciences except economics?' The third question we have just now been considering. It is whether there are in the social sciences the kind of explanations that terminate a series of 'why' questions — ultimate explanations. When these questions are run together it is quite natural to conclude that explanation by means of 'mere generalization' is deficient on all three counts: the generalization is directly testable; it is not an interpreted axiom or theorem in a formal theory; it is not part of a formal theory which provides an ultimate explanation by confronting the questioner with an assertion of the existence of a fundamental feature of nature. Let us, then, consider each of these three questions at more length.

The problem of whether social scientists have produced hypotheses that are not directly testable is of little interest in itself. The answer is obvious: 'Yes, they have.' The reasons why hypotheses are not directly testable vary, however. The objects referred to may be observable only indirectly, as in the case of sub-atomic particles, or two properties may be so combined that they are never found separately, and so a statement about the effects of one taken by itself may be testable only indirectly because of the masking effects of the other property. But the reason which has been of interest to social scientists is neither of these. It is that some hypotheses make use of idealizations. The success of these in the physical sciences has encouraged the belief that they ought to be employed in the social sciences as well. Hence, part of the pejorative force of the phrase 'mere empirical generalizations' derives from the feeling that a statement of an idealization should either be substituted in place of the generalization or be joined to it.

The point at issue is whether idealizations are present in the work of social scientists. No one doubts that social scientists sometimes refer to 'ideal types'. It is a question, then, how similar these are to the idealizations of the natural sciences. Here we must recognize the distinction commonly made between 'extreme types' and idealizations. The former are simply the end points of a series that is ordered by certain criteria; that is, any property or set of properties that admits of degree, such as reverence for tradition or social status, will have extremes that may or may not have actual instances. Pure folk societies, for example, do not in fact exist today, but they could exist in the sense that they are not physically impossible. Idealizations, on the other hand, are physically impossible. Perfectly elastic bodies and perfectly straight lines are like perfect folk societies in being the end points of a serial array. The first two, however, differ from the third in that they are known to be extrapolations to the limits of the variables that they represent. It is also known that they cannot exist under present physical laws. 'Extreme types', on the other hand, such as pure folk societies, may or may not exist. When they do not exist it is simply because certain conditions which might well have been met under known laws happen not to have been met.

Thus our answer to the question 'How similar are the ideal types of the social sciences to the idealizations of the natural sciences?' must begin by distinguishing extreme types from idealizations. *Some* of the so-called 'ideal types' advanced by social scientists are extreme types and not idealizations. 'The Dandy', 'The Protestant Sect', and 'Gemeinschaft' are terms which are often used to refer to extreme types, and the similarity of these to an ideal pendulum or to any other idealization is, as we have just indicated, rather slight.

The other and more interesting question concerns the presence of genuine idealizations in social science. Are such notions as a perfect market, a perfect monopoly, and an economically rational agent, instances of extreme types or of idealizations? It has been suggested by some writers that notions of this kind are not idealizations, that they belong to theories which deliberately omit certain variables because they are not relevant. These theories are said to differ from theories which extrapolate to the physically impossible limits of their variables. We are asked to 'consider that it is not disturbing to say that there are no perfect gases or dimensionless points. Nobody ever thought there were. But to say that economic man or the ideal type of capitalism does not exist is to say that certain theories are false, either because they neglect unspecified but relevant variables or because the laws among those specified do not hold.'[25]

The reply to this is clear enough: whoever thought that economic man or ideal capitalism existed? Certainly not Max Weber, the best-known advocate of the use of ideal types. He says that 'An ideal type is formed by the one-sided accentuation of one or more points of view and by the synthesis of a great many diffuse, discrete, more or less present and occasionally absent *concrete individual* phenomena, which are arranged according to those one-sidedly emphasized viewpoints into a unified *analytical* construct (*Gedankenbild*). In its conceptual purity, this mental construct (*Gedankenbild*) cannot be found anywhere in reality. It is a *utopia*.'[26] It is no more disturbing to say that ideal capitalism does not exist than to say that there are no perfect gases. Neither in the one case nor in the other does the falsity of 'certain theories' hang upon the existence of the subject. Naturally, all theories omit variables taken to be irrelevant and only some theories make use of idealizations. This distinction has nothing to do, however, with the problem of whether such notions as ideal capitalism and economic man are genuine idealizations. The only reason for thinking that this distinction is relevant arises from a neglect of the notion of extreme types. It thus becomes easy to believe that our employment of phrases like 'economic man' commits us to the assertion of his existence, since such phrases are thought to refer only to actual instances. Ideal types are treated neither as extreme types which may or may not have existing instances, nor as idealizations which cannot have them. Instead a phrase like 'economic man' is taken to resemble in use one like 'melancholic man' as it appears in the sentence 'There goes a melancholic man'. But while melancholic men walk the streets economic men do not. They exist only in the pages of certain books and journals, and in the professional conversation of economists. Failure to remember this is a result of thinking that economic man is not a physical impossibility, and that therefo : he must exist. Yet the very question to be answered is whether notions like that of economic man concern what is impossible in this sense.

It may be well to remind ourselves of the kinds of assumptions which economists have in fact made about economic men. Here are some laid down by Frank Knight in connection with his analysis of perfect competition: (1) All members of the society act with complete rationality, that is, 'all their acts take place in response to real, conscious, and stable and consistent motives, dispositions, or desires; nothing is capricious or experimental, everything deliberate. They are supposed to know absolutely the consequences of their acts when they are performed, and to perform them in the light of the consequences.' (2) Each member 'controls his own activities with a view to results which accrue to him individually. Every person is

[25] M. Brodbeck: 'Models, Meaning, and Theories' in *Symposium on Sociological Theory*, ed. by L. Gross, 1959, p. 382.

[26] *The Methodology of the Social Sciences*, 1949, p. 90.

the final and absolute judge of his own welfare and interests.' (3) 'There must be "perfect mobility" in all economic adjustments, no cost involved in movements or changes.' (4) 'There must be perfect, continuous, costless intercommunication between all individual members of the society.'[27]

It is obvious that each of these assumptions is unsatisfiable — is physically impossible — in our world. The first assumption demands that every person have perfect foresight. The second demands that there 'be no way of acquiring goods except through production and free exchange in the open market'. It also makes it necessary that every person 'be free from social wants, prejudices, preferences, or repulsions, or any values which are not completely manifested in market dealing. Exchange of finished goods is the only form of relation between individuals, or at least there is no other form which influences economic conduct.'[28] The third assumption requires that 'all the elements entering into economic calculations — effort, commodities, etc. — must be continuously variable, divisible without limit. Productive operations must not form habits, preferences, or aversions, or develop or reduce the capacity to perform them. In addition, the production process must be constantly and continuously complete; there is no time cycle of operations to be broken into or left incomplete by sudden readjustments. Each person continuously produces a complete commodity which is consumed as fast as produced. The exchange of commodities must be virtually instantaneous and costless.'[29]

Surely no one would argue, given what is known of individual human behaviour and of the conditions under which societies can be formed and maintained, that any one of these assumptions — much less all of them — can be met. And if they cannot be satisfied, then it is true to say of them that they represent idealizations. As Lionel Robbins put it when writing of the notion of economic man, 'The purpose of these assumptions is not to foster the belief that the world of reality corresponds to the constructions in which they figure, but rather to enable us to study, in isolation, tendencies which, in the world of reality, operate only in conjunction with many others, and then, by contrast as much as by comparison, to turn back to apply the knowledge thus gained to the explanations of more complicated situations. In this respect, at least, the procedure of pure economics has its counterpart in the procedure of all physical sciences which have gone beyond the stage of collection and classification.'[30]

Having echoed what every economist knows — that idealizations are used in economics — we ought to go on to state what most social scientists also realize: that the distinction between extreme types and idealizations is not generally made in the other fields of social science, for it is not needed. It is not needed because a great deal of what is called 'theorizing in terms of ideal types' is usually classifying by means of extreme types. As characteristic specimens we can take the following pairs: folk society and urban society; mechanical solidarity and organic solidarity; gemeinschaft and gesellschaft; status society and contract society. The use of them gives rise to generalizations about their properties, but the way in which this occurs is different from what happens when idealizations are used. The latter are terms which are defined by a set of hypotheses that relate certain properties to each other, namely, those properties represented in a shorthand manner by such idealizations as a perfect market. The working out of the relationships amongst these properties is a logical exercise in the drawing of consequences and results in a deductive system. This deductive system will not be usable in the explanation of *any* occurrence until the system is given application, until, that is, the hypotheses are supplemented in such a way that the hy-

[27] Taken from *Risk, Uncertainty and Profit*, 1921, pp. 77–8.

[28] *Ibid.*, p. 78.

[29] *Ibid.*, pp. 77–8.

[30] *An Essay on the Nature and Significance of Economic Science*, 2nd edition, 1935, p. 94.

potheses become empirical statements. It is a perennial criticism levelled at economists that they produce deductive systems or calculi without being able to apply them usefully. The employment of extreme types does not raise this problem. They are classificatory devices. An individual case is assigned a position in a serial array, is classified, for example, as being much more like a contract society than a status society, according to the extent to which the individual case displays the properties taken as defining one or other of the extreme types.

Now when an idealization is used the behaviour of an ordinary market is explained in terms of its deviation from the behaviour of a perfect market. This is done by comparing what is observed of the former with what is deduced from the criteria of the latter. And, similarly, the behaviour of an ordinary contract society can be explained in terms of its deviation from the behaviour of an ideal contract society. Thus we can compare actual behaviour with the generalizations which have been suggested as applying to the ideal, e.g. 'All pure contract societies have developed from pure status societies'. But one point of difference between an extreme type and an idealization is that a person can use the latter as a means of explaining the presence of the former. He would never have occasion, however, to use an extreme type in an attempt to explain the presence of an idealization. It is a set of hypotheses (or the conditions referred to by these hypotheses). Since these conditions cannot exist, they do not require an explanation of their presence or distribution as do the properties referred to by the names of extreme types. For while the latter need not exist, they sometimes do, and then an explanation of their presence may be required. Of course there is no deductive system present in connection with them, and, hence, no problem of making use of it as a system of empirical laws. This point can be made clearer if we consider the example of the folk society.

Robert Redfield characterized the folk society as an ideal type that has these features: 'small, isolated, non-literate, and homogeneous, with a strong sense of group solidarity. The ways of living are conventionalized into that coherent system which we call "a culture". Behaviour is traditional, spontaneous, uncritical, and personal; there is no legislation or habit of experiment and reflection for intellectual ends. Kinship, its relationships and institutions, are the type categories of experience and the familial group is the unit of action. The sacred prevails over the secular; the economy is one of status rather than of market.'[31] The communities of Yucatan were found to display these features much more than certain Guatemalan societies. In the latter the small, stable, homogeneous society was discovered to have impersonal relationships, formal institutions, weak family organization, secular life, and individuals acting from personal advantage.[32] Such differences between types of society have led investigators to examine the degree to which the properties of the ideal folk society are associated with each other in various actual societies — what causal relations there are amongst them.

Thus 'the ideal folk society' and 'the perfect market' are both phrases which refer to sets of properties. In the case of the perfect market these are imaginary properties, and the statements which assert them are arranged in a deductive system so that it may be seen what consequences logically follow from these assumptions. The relating and explaining of the behaviour of actual markets in terms of their divergence from the behaviour of the perfect market is similar, in principle, to the physicist's problem in relating Boyle's Law to the behaviour of actual gases. The divergence between the ideal case and the actual one is taken by economists, as by physicists, to indicate the need for alterations in the law statements employed. The classification of actual cases according to the degree of their divergence from the ideal case

[31] 'The Folk Society', *The American Journal of Sociology*, Vol. LII, No. 4, January 1947, p. 293.

[32] *Ibid.*, p. 308.

is of secondary interest. What the use of the idealization is supposed to do is to permit an explanation to be advanced; the classification procedure is subordinate to this.

Precisely the opposite is true with respect to the use of extreme types: they are used to classify in the hope that an explanation of the behaviour of actual cases will be suggested by the comparison of the ideal and actual cases. The explanation can only be *suggested* because the properties of the extreme type, as the example of the folk society reveals, are not related by the hypotheses of a deductive system. What, for instance, are the logical consequences of the assertion that a society is 'traditional, spontaneous, and uncritical'? Obviously the assertion has consequences, but it is so vague that there would be considerable difficulty in working them out. It would not be impossible, however. Redfield himself provides a number of suggestions, e.g. that in a folk society there is 'no disposition to reflect upon traditional acts and consider them objectively and critically'.[33] This in itself would require much refinement, of course, but it might be transformed into a hypothesis which, in conjunction with others similarly refined, could be applied in the explanation of actual social processes. Yet unless these hypotheses formed part of a deductive system they would be of secondary importance in the use of extreme types. For they would be isolated hypotheses, and there would still remain the major work of relating the hypotheses to each other so that the presence of some explained the presence of others. We should want to know, for example, why in a folk society there is 'no disposition to reflect upon traditional acts'; we should also want to ask how this generalization is related to such other generalizations as those about the isolation or the size of the folk society.

The problem which we have been discussing is part of the more general problem whether outside economics, deductive systems are in fact used — not merely produced — by social scientists. And this topic, like that of the explanatory power of idealizations, is one upon which we have already embarked. We exclude economics because no one doubts that in one sense of 'used' formal theories are used in it. What is often doubted is the success of their application to the world. But this is a somewhat different matter from the question with which we are faced, namely, whether other social scientists can and do employ formal theories to explain social behaviour, even when that behaviour is taken to be drastically simplified for the occasion. It may be true that economists have difficulty in applying their theories to actual situations, and in *this* sense they may not use formal theories as much as some kinds of physicists do. Nevertheless, economists constantly formulate and try to apply deductive systems. We wish to know whether in this sense of 'use' their use of formal theories differs from that of the other social scientists.

We said earlier that there are two interpretations of the phrase 'use of formal theories'. One refers to the construction of calculi which can be transformed into empirical theories. The other refers to empirical theories which are sufficiently developed to admit of formalization. The two procedures are, of course, intimately connected in practice, for calculi are usually constructed with a view to a specific kind of interpretation. At least this is the case when the authors are scientists rather than mathematicians. In the social sciences, if the development of economics can be taken as a guide, we should expect that both procedures would be tried and that the results of each procedure, with respect to a given problem, would affect the other. What has so far occurred is that the attempts to rewrite sets of empirical hypotheses in the form of deductive systems — as in the theory of group interaction put forward by Simon — have revealed the deficiencies of the original theories. In the case of the theory just referred to, these defects included the absence of a measuring procedure for the properties of interaction, friendliness, and activity. Two courses of

[33] *Ibid.*, p. 299.

action were then possible: a method of measurement might be found; or failing that, the original theory might be abandoned. If the latter course were chosen, anyone who was seeking a calculus suitable for interpretation as a theory of group interaction would be influenced in his search by the knowledge that one interpretation would be ruled out, namely, that in terms of the three unmeasurable properties. But the relation between the two procedures is even closer than this. The way in which calculi are actually used in the production of rigorous empirical theories is not, at the present stage of social science, that of calculus seeking. Nor is it that of simply revealing the logical skeleton of informal theories. The process is perhaps best illustrated by some additional features of the example already considered — that of Simon's treatment of the theory of group interaction.

Firstly, the rewriting of an informal theory is likely to display its omissions. Thus once the generalizations of Homans' theory were stated as axioms it became necessary to make some further assumptions: for example, that the amount of activity and the level of friendliness referred to in the first axiom as producing the intensity of interaction, have an almost instantaneous effect upon that intensity. Nothing was said about this in the original generalization.

Secondly, the equations serving as axioms may be generalized so as to obtain conclusions previously unobtainable. When the assumption that the variables, I, A, F and E have linear relations was removed, it became possible to derive such new results as these: when E ('amount of activity imposed on the group by the external environment') falls below a certain value, F ('the level of friendliness') will fall to zero; if E is at or below this value, then A ('amount of activity carried on by members within the group') will fall to zero. To say that F and A are at zero is to say that the group disintegrates. This point was not dealt with in the initial generalizations or in their initial rewriting.

Thirdly, the axiom-set may be further extended so as to permit a number of empirical interpretations, that is, used as the logical structure of different empirical theories. There are three equations used as axioms in the linear system. These are reduced to two in the non-linear system; and in one of them the time rate of change of A as a function of A and F, with E as an independent variable, is represented by $\frac{dA}{dt} = \psi(A,F;E)$ where ψ is a function with unspecified properties. In order to apply this equation as an axiom in another theory, a theory about clique formation, Simon alters it somewhat. I, A, F, and E are defined as specifying behaviour in a group G_1. Then I_2, A_2, F_2, and E_2 are defined as specifying behaviour in Group G_2, the latter group being a sub-group of the former one. The new equation gives the time rate of change of A as a function of A_1, F_1, and A_2. An additional equation supplies the time rate of change of A_2 as a function of A_2, F_2, and A_1. In other words, the activity carried on by members within the larger group is taken to influence the activity within the clique, and vice versa. Another suggested interpretation of the same variables has the four letters with subscript one referring to the intensity of a particular person's activity within a certain group, and the four letters with subscript two referring to the intensity of that person's behaviour within a second group. The full set of equations then provides a theory of groups competing for the membership of a given person.

What we shall take this example to show is this: in the social sciences that we have been considering, with the possible exception of economics, there is no clear-cut difference between the application of the two procedures of calculi interpretation and theory formalization. This distinction is only useful in sciences which are mathematically more developed than the ones under discussion. When, as in most of the social sciences, the use of calculi has merely begun, no calculus can be fully interpreted in a satisfactory manner. The defects of the informal theory must first be revealed by the attempt to state it rigorously; then the effort to repair or improve the theory may suggest new sets of equations whose application to fresh topics can be investigated.

Hence, the question whether 'deductive systems are in fact used — not merely produced — by social scientists' has as its answer: 'Yes, work has begun in certain fields.' There are, for example, earlier publications like Rashevsky's book on the *Mathematical Biology of Social Behavior* in which such theories as that of imitative behaviour and of the distribution of wealth are put forward; Anderson's paper on obtaining probability distributions of changes in attitude over time,[34] and the two essays by Simon and Guetzkow concerned with group mechanism for ensuring social uniformity and for dealing with deviant members.[35] In the last few years there has been a spate of theoretical and experimental work on the topics which were released for general academic consumption by the development of servo-mechanism theory, learning theory, mathematical theories of communication, and the theory of games. But the rise to popularity of topics like those of rational choice and decision-making under uncertainty, or optimal information networks in social groups, ought not to mislead us. The extension of the mathematical methods of modern economics to the other social sciences is devoted only in small part to explanatory theories. Definition, classification, measurement, observation, testing and design, still require the major share of the scientist's attention. We can hardly expect, therefore, to identify the present mathematical revolution in the social sciences with an immediate and revolutionary increase in the number of useful theories. The lag between the rate of increase in the application of mathematical procedures to social science and the rate of increase in the production of formal theories may be considerable. In claiming that deductive systems are already being used by social scientists in much the same way as by economists, we are not claiming that the number of these theories is large. There is every prospect, however, of the number increasing substantially, and with it — for reasons previously suggested — the number and importance of idealizations as compared to extreme types.

We have said that the complaints about the exclusive use of empirical generalizations in the social sciences are based upon a conflation of three questions. The first is whether there are idealizations in the social sciences. To this we answered 'Yes, particularly economics'. But we could also have supplied examples from such fields of interest as the theory of behaviour within small groups. The second question is that of the presence of formal theories, and with this we have just dealt. The remaining question is whether there are ultimate explanations in social science — ones that terminate a series of 'why' questions by asserting the existence of a fundamental feature of nature. It is this query which we must now take up briefly.

What the people who ask this question have in mind is not entirely clear. They may believe that explanations in social science are reducible, in some sense of the term, to another and more fundamental kind, perhaps psychological ones. Or they may simply hold that quite independently of the problem of reducibility there is a problem concerning the types of properties — variables — which are employed in social explanations. But to say that there is such a problem can only amount to saying that we must distinguish between two sorts of social explanations: those which explain in terms of social properties, e.g. cohesiveness, free exchange, jural authority — and those which explain in terms of non-social properties like soil fertility, length of snow season, distance from the sea, and the average height of adult males in a given population. The first type of explanation provides an account of social events or situations in terms of other social events; the second type supplies an explanation in terms of non-social events. A social

[34] 'Probability Models for Analyzing Time Changes in Attitudes' in *Mathematical Thinking in the Social Sciences*, ed. by P. Lazarsfeld, 1954.

[35] In Simon: *Models of Man*, 1957.

scientist is chiefly concerned with the first kind: with explaining, for instance, the presence of incest taboos in terms of avoidance of sexual competition within the family, and not by means of a reference to an innate disposition of people. Our efforts to discriminate between these two kinds of explanation are made more difficult by the fact that statements of social events can themselves take two forms. In one form they are statements about the properties of individuals who are members of classes or groups. In the other form they are statements about the properties of classes or groups of human beings. The difference is illustrated by the statements (*a*) 'Any person who participates in high involvement relationships will show high ability to empathize' and (*b*) 'The higher the cohesiveness of a human group, the higher will be the correlation between popularity rank and perceived leadership rank.' Whereas the former refers to the properties of an individual person, the latter refers to the properties of a group of people.

Now the phrase 'fundamental feature of nature' is both pretentious and vague. Hence, when we ask whether the social sciences contain ultimate explanations — ones that assert the existence of such fundamental features — our question is the poorer for its use of this phrase. A social explanation can be ultimate in the sense that the properties or variables upon which it relies are not social ones, that is, are neither social group (and class) properties nor properties of members of these sets *qua* members. But an explanation supplied in the social sciences can also be ultimate in a different sense, in the sense that it is the terminal explanation in a series of a certain kind. This series will consist of explanations which refer only to social properties, and the last element of the series will be that explanation whose variables require explaining in terms of non-social properties. In other words, the ultimate explanation will be the final member of a series of social explanations — final because it will not itself have a *social* explanation. We might, for example, say that Ann's continued absence from meetings of her club was due to the low cohesiveness of the group, and account for the low cohesion in terms of the small satisfaction Ann and the other members received from belonging to the group; the explanation of this, in turn, might be stated by means of a reference to the needs arising from their self-images; these accounted for by referring to child-rearing practices, and the origin or persistence of the practices explained as the outcome of innate drives. Which member of the series is to be taken as ultimate, as asserting a 'fundamental feature of nature'? There is no way of telling. It is only if we know what mystifies a questioner that we can know what answer will satisfy him on this point. Is the human need for sleep a feature of this kind? If not, what is? In commencing the series which begins with 'Why do they need sleep?' we may continue until we reach either a physical explanation or a confession of ignorance, whichever occurs first.

There is, of course, another interpretation to be given to the demand for ultimate explanations. It may be interpreted simply as a confused way of claiming that statements about group properties are 'reducible' to some other sort of statement. It may be the claim that the reduction proceeds from group properties to the properties of individuals as members, or from either of these to the properties of individuals who are not members of the relevant groups or classes. Yet whatever type of reduction relation is supposed to be present, and whatever this relation is thought to hold between — concepts or statements — the search for an ultimate explanation will be a pursuit of the irreducible. It does not matter which non-social explanation is fixed upon as an irreducible one. For it will be trivially true that the social sciences do not in this sense of 'ultimate' provide ultimate explanations. However, the point of our previous arguments has been to help remove any critical force to which this admission may seem to expose us.

We can add one brief remark here. It is this. No matter what kind of reduction relation may hold between the hypotheses of the social sciences and those of, e.g. psychology, it does not follow that genuinely useful laws cannot be found in the social sciences. It does not follow for this reason: social generalizations are either about group-members or about groups. The only way in which these statements can be entailed by psychological generalizations — those about individuals *not* organized into groups — is by the addition of co-ordinating laws, i.e. laws connecting the psychological properties of an individual person with his social properties, his behaviour as a member of a group. But these coordinating laws have as much right to be called 'social laws' as have the social generalizations which they are to be used to entail. Thus if the reduction relation does hold, some genuine social laws must be present in order to make it possible. Clearly, all that the present attack on social laws can establish is that generalizations about group-properties are not useful because they are entailed by the conjunction of psychological laws and co-ordinating laws; that is, group-traits are causally determined by other sorts of properties. Even if this were established, however, it would be no argument for excluding generalizations about group members from the social sciences. Hence, it would not show these sciences to be lacking in genuine laws.

We have argued that there are theoretical hypotheses in the social sciences and formal theories as well. But we also know that they can be present when ultimate explanations of the irreducible variety are not present. The complaint about empirical generalizations arose from the mistaken view that they do not provide satisfactory explanations because they are not assertions of the existence of fundamental properties. We have denied their unsatisfactoriness, claiming that the two favoured features — theoretical hypotheses and formal theories — whose absence from the social sciences was thought to be responsible for this condition, are in fact present in those sciences. We have gone on to say that the demand for ultimate explanations in the social sciences is by no means clear. In any case it is not important, since the lack of such explanations is not a defect having to do with a want of theoretical hypotheses and formal theories. The latter are present and the former (ultimate explanations) are not; at least they are not present if the word 'ultimate' is interpreted in certain ways. In the face of this, it is wrong to assert that the social sciences produce only empirical generalizations, and that for this reason genuine explanations, ultimate ones, are missing from these fields. There are, we have said, many genuine explanations which are not ultimate in the sense of being irreducible. Any continued pressing of the criticism that the explanations of the social sciences are unsatisfactory because they are reducible must be based on the vacuous complaint that social science is not physical science. Similarly, the case against the social sciences may be given another — but probably short — lease on life by altering the charge from that of inherent inability to that of lack of success. But this is merely to say that the social sciences are not as successful as the physical sciences, and this has never been in dispute. What has been in question is whether there are good grounds for believing that social scientists cannot do better in the future. And our answer has been 'There are no good grounds at all for this belief, only poor ones'.

The Classical Case for Behaviorist Theory

21

The Nature of Theory Construction in Contemporary Psychology[1]

KENNETH W. SPENCE

Introduction

The task of the scientist has been described as that of attempting to discover ever more generalized laws by which the observable events within his field of study may be brought into interrelation with one another. To this end he develops and refines (mainly in the direction of quantitative representation) his concepts or variables, arranges highly controlled (experimental) conditions of observation and introduces theoretical constructions. While it is not the primary purpose of this paper to attempt a methodological analysis of these components of scientific method, it is necessary to begin our discussion by calling attention to two somewhat different roles or functions that one of them, construction of theory, plays in different fields of science or in the same field at different stages of development.

In some areas of knowledge, for example present day physics, theories serve primarily to bring into functional connection with one another empirical laws which prior to their formulation had been isolated realms of knowledge. The physicist is able to isolate, experimentally, elementary situations, *i.e.*, situations in which there are a limited number of variables, and thus finds it possible to infer or discover descriptive, low-order laws. Theory comes into play for the physicist when he attempts to formulate more abstract principles which will bring these low-order laws into relationship with one another, Examples of such comprehensive theories are Newton's principle of gravitation and the kinetic theory of gases. The former provided a theoretical integration of such laws as Kepler's concerning planetary motions, Galileo's law of falling bodies, laws of the tides and so on. The kinetic theory has served to integrate the various laws relating certain properties of gases to other experimental variables.

In the less highly developed areas of knowledge, such as the behavior and social sciences, theory plays a somewhat different role. In these more complex fields the simplest experimental situation that can be arranged usually involves such a large number of variables that it is extremely difficult, if not impossible, to discover directly the empirical laws relating them. Theories are brought into play in such circumstances as a device to aid in the formulation of the laws. They consist primarily in the introduction or postulation of hypothetical constructs which help to bridge gaps between the experimental variables. Examples of such theoretical constructs are legion in psychology, *e.g.*, Tolman's 'demand,' Hull's 'excitatory potential,' Lewin's 'tension system,' and a host of other mentalistic and neurophysiologically-sounding concepts. It is the purpose of this paper to examine the attempts of psychologists to discover general laws of behavior, particularly the auxiliary theoretical devices they have employed in doing so.

From the *Psychological Review*. 51:1 (January, 1944), pp. 47–68.

[1] The writer is greatly indebted to Dr. Gustav Bergmann for reading the manuscript and making valuable suggestions.

Theoretical Constructs in Psychology

Like every other scientist, the psychologist is interested in establishing the interrelations within a set of experimental variables, *i.e.*, in discovering empirical laws. At the present stage of development the variables (measurements) studied by the psychologist and between which he is attempting to find functional relations appear to fall into two main groups:

(1) *R*-variables: measurements of the behavior of organisms; attributes of simple response patterns (actones), complex achievements (actions) and generalized response characteristics (traits, abilities, etc.). These are sometimes referred to as the dependent variables.

(2) *S*-variables: measurements of physical and social environmental factors and conditions (present and past) under which the responses of organisms occur. These are sometimes referred to as the independent, manipulable variables.

While not all laws are quantitative, science typically strives to quantify its constructs and to state their interrelations in terms of numerical laws. The numerical laws the psychologist seeks may be represented as follows:

$$R = f(S).$$

The problem here is two-fold: (1) to discover what the relevant *S* variables are, and (2) to ascertain the nature of the functional relations holding between the two groups of variables.

In general, two radically opposed positions have been taken by scientists, including psychologists, as to the best procedure to follow in solving this problem. On the one hand are those who propose the introduction of theoretical constructs as described above. On the other there are the more empirically minded persons who attempt to refrain from the use of such inferred constructs and try to confine themselves entirely to observable data. An excellent defense of this latter viewpoint, along with a constructive proposal as to how such an approach can hope to discover general quantitative laws in psychology, is contained in the recent presidential address of Woodrow to the American Psychological Association (23). We shall leave consideration of the method proposed by Woodrow until later; certain criticisms he offers of the theoretical approach provide an excellent introduction to this method of discovering laws.

Beginning with the conception, more or less the same as that expressed at the start of this paper, that explanation in science consists in nothing more than a statement of established relationships of dependency (for psychology in terms of laws between measurements of environment and behavior) Woodrow goes on to protest that most psychologists seem to have been entirely too interested in postulating intermediate events occurring within the organism to explain the obtained measurements. The difficulty with such speculative constructs, he thinks, is that they cannot be measured because it is not possible to observe the interior of organisms. The result is that their specification must be left to the imagination. And as he says:

> . . . our imaginations have not failed us. The things we have stuck within the organism in the hope thereby of explaining behavior are almost without limit in number and variety. They include mental sets and cortical sets, traces, residues, synaptic resistance, inhibitory and excitatory substances, inhibitory and excitatory tendencies, determining tendencies, mental attitudes, sentiments, wishes, tensions, field forces, valences, urges, abilities, instincts, and so on and on. Very popular indeed is the animistic type of explanation (23, p. 3).

While it must be admitted with Woodrow that many of the theoretical constructs employed by psychologists have never been too satisfactorily specified, one must protest the lumping together of all theoretical constructs in such a completely indiscriminate manner. As a matter of fact, Woodrow has included in his list certain conceptions which were never meant to be explanatory concepts. Thus such terms as set, attitude, sentiment, and in some instances drive, are what Carnap (3) has termed *dispositional predicates or concepts*, because they refer to the disposition of an object to a certain behavior under certain conditions. They usually serve as names for events which do not appear in observable experience but instead are introduced into the scientist's language in terms of conditions and results which can be described in terms that refer directly to observable experiences. Such concepts are prevalent in all fields of science and serve a useful purpose.

Then, again, Woodrow has failed to distinguish in his list between what turn out upon analysis to be very different kinds of theoretical constructs. While some of them are little better than the animistic notions of primitive man, others have qualified as quite satisfactory in the sense that they have led to the formulation of behavioral laws. We turn now to the consideration of the different kinds of theories (theoretical constructs) that have been proposed in psychology.

Four Types of Theoretical Constructs

Theoretical constructs are introduced, as we have said, in the form of guesses as to what variables other than the ones under control of the experimenter are determining the response. The relation of such inferred constructs (I_a) to the experimental variables, measurements of S and R, is shown in the following figure. Here we have assumed an over-simplified situation for purposes of exposition.

S-variables	I-variables	R-variables
X_1	I_a	R_1

FIG. 21-1 Intervening variables

If under environmental conditions X_1 the response measure R_1 is always the same (within the error of measurement) then we have no need of theory. Knowing that condition X_1 existed we could always predict the response. Likewise if, with systematic variation of the X variable, we find a simple functional relation holding between the X values and the corresponding R values we again would have no problem, for we could precisely state the law relating them. But unfortunately things are not usually so simple as this, particularly in psychology. On a second occasion of the presentation of condition X_1, the subject is very likely to exhibit a different magnitude of response, or in the second example there may be no simple curve discernible between the two sets of experimental values. It is at this point that hypothetical constructs are introduced and the response variable is said to be determined, in part by X_1, and in part by some additional factor, or factors, I_a, I_b . . . , *i.e.*, $R = f(X_1, I_a, I_b \ldots)$. The manner in which these theoretical constructs have been defined by different psychologists permits a grouping of them into four categories: (1) animistic-like theories in which the relations of the construct to the empirical variables are left entirely unspecified, (2) neurophysiological theories, (3) theories involving constructs defined primarily in terms of the R variables and (4) theories involving constructs intervening between the S and R variables.

ANIMISTIC CONCEPTIONS

Little need be said about such instances of psychological speculation. They are included here merely for the purpose of completing the record. The invoking of such general concepts as the 'soul,' 'mind,' 'élan vital,' 'entelechy,' 'idea,' 'libido,' not to mention many more specific instances (*e.g.*, insight, instinct[2]) in order to account for the apparent capriciousness of the behavior of organisms has been all too prevalent in psychology. When not safe from disproof by reason of the fact that their locus is usually specified to be in some region within the organism un-

[2] Such terms, of course, when used as dispositional predicates serve the useful function of providing a name for the phenomenon.

accessible to observation, these concepts are rendered invulnerable by failure to specify what relations they might have either to the *S* or *R* variables. While such vagueness renders them unverifiable, it does insure them a vigorous and long career among certain types of thinkers. Needless to say, such vague conceptions receive little attention today among scientific-minded psychologists.

Neurophysiological theories

The extent to which neurophysiological concepts, defined in terms of the operations and instruments of the neurophysiologist, are employed in psychological theorizing is not nearly so great as is sometimes thought. As a matter of fact, if we employ such variables to help us out in our formulation of behavior laws we are not, strictly speaking, theorizing for such concepts are not hypothetical, but are empirically defined. In such instances we have stated a law interrelating environmental, organic and behavioral variables. As yet we do not have very many such laws, except in the case of the simplest kinds of behavior (sensory responses, reflexes, etc.).

There are, of course, many theoretical constructs in psychology which are supposed to represent hypothetical neurophysiological processes, but whose properties are defined either in terms of the response variables (type 3 theory), in terms of environmental factors and the response variables (type 4 theory), or just assumed to be operating without making any specification of their relations to either the environmental or response variables (type 1 theory). Examples of these are Köhler's construct of brain field (12) to explain perceptual and memory phenomena (type 3), Pavlov's constructs (16) of excitatory and inhibitory states (type 4), and certain neural trace theories of learning (type 1).

It will be seen that this category really cuts across the other three. Further consideration of some of these theories will be given in our discussion of the final two classes of theory.

RESPONSE INFERRED THEORETICAL CONSTRUCTS

The fact that the behavior of organisms varies even though the objective environmental condition remains unchanged has led some psychologists to assert that the laws of such behavior cannot be formulated in terms of objective environmental variables even though additional hypothetical constructs are employed to bolster the effort. These writers have insisted that behavior must be accounted for in terms of the psychological situation. Thus Lewin (13) in his book *Dynamic theory of personality* refers to what he describes as the complete failure of such German writers as Loeb, Bethe and other objectivists to develop an adequate theoretical interpretation of behavior in terms of the objective situation, *i.e.*, the physical situation as described by the operations of measurement of the physicist and/or the objective social situation as described by the sociologist. It is always necessary, he insists, to describe the situation as the subject sees or perceives it, *i.e.*, in terms of what it means to him. Typical quotations from Lewin's writings indicate the positive tone taken by such writers:

> For the investigation of dynamic problems we are forced to start from the psychologically real environment of the child (13, p. 74). Of course, in the description of the child's psychological environment one may not take as a basis the immediately objective social forces and relations as the sociologist or jurist, for example, would list them. One must rather describe the social facts as they affect the particular individual concerned (13, p. 75).
>
> One of the basic characteristics of field theory in psychology, as I see it, is the demand that the field which influences an individual should be described not in 'objective physicalistic' terms, but in the way in which it exists for that person at that time (15, p. 217).

As Lewin implies in the last quoted excerpt it would seem that this type of 'psychological' approach to the theoretical constructs of psychology is characteristic of the self-styled field theorists or Gestalt psychologists. Thus Koffka (10) makes use of the construct of 'behavioral environment' and the more inclusive construct of 'psychophysical field' which includes the former and the physiological field, while Köhler (11, 12) refers to 'phenomenal field' and to 'brain field.' Koffka and Köhler differ slightly from Lewin in that they introduce a physiological terminology in the description of the properties of some of their behavior-determining fields whereas Lewin does not. The methods of determining the structure and properties of these fields whether 'brain field,' 'behavioral environment' or 'life space' are, however, essentially the same, and as we shall see later, involve extensive use of the phenomenological type of introspection.

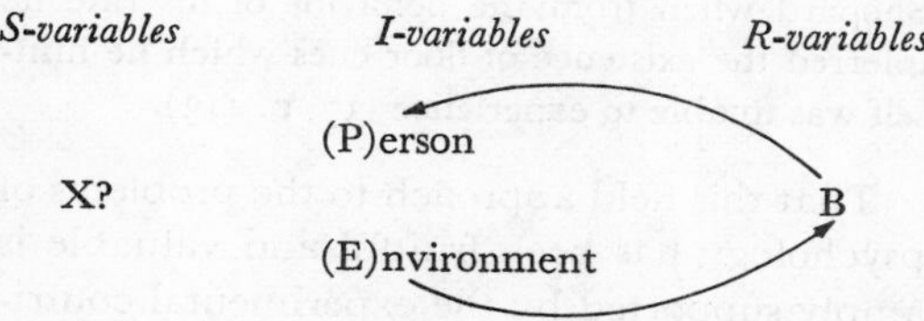

FIG. 21-2. Lewin's theoretical constructs

The nature of this type of theorizing may be made clearer by attempting to show how it fits into the schema we have already employed. Figure 21-2 makes use of the constructs of Lewin, who has been the most articulate of this group of writers so far as the exposition of the formal nature of his theorizing is concerned. Lewin employs the concept of life space to represent the totality of facts which determine the behavior (B) of an individual at a certain moment. The life space includes two groups of constructs, the person (P) and the psychological environment (E). Use is then made of certain concepts from geometry (topology and hodology) and dynamics to represent the existing relationships.[3] By means of what Lewin calls coordinating definitions these constructs are said to be related to empirical concepts.

Without going into detail, Figure 2 reveals an interesting fact. It is that little, if any, use is made of the *S*-variables in Lewin's theorizing.[4] The question immediately arises then as to what kinds of laws, if any, does Lewin arrive at. The functional relationship which frequently appears in his writings, $B = f(P, E)$, is obviously not a law of the type that psychologists were said to be interested in, *i.e.*, $R = f(S)$. But if it is not this kind of a law what kind is it? Some writers have implied that Lewin really does not attain any laws at all. They call attention to the fact that laws are statements of relations between *independently defined variables* and they ask what are the two sets of independent variables in Lewin's formula.

The answer to this question is not easy, and the writer is of the opinion that it has not been met in all instances of field theory. However, an examination of the methods employed by Lewin and his students in determining the structure and properties of their fields reveals that they depend heavily upon the phenomenological introspections of their subjects or themselves. If we now think

[3] There is considerable reason to doubt whether Lewin does much more than take over the terms of topology, making little if any use of the postulates (implicit definitions) of this formal system. Koch, after making a very thorough analysis of Lewin's formulations, states that Lewin "finds it expedient to abstract from the postulates (of topology) the properties with which they implicitly endow the constructs, instead of fully stating the postulates" (9, p. 148). In this sense, then, it may be said that Lewin employs very fragmentary parts or sub-systems of topology. As for the formal system of dynamics it remains thus far closeted, to use Koch's happy description, in Lewin's mind. Like so many of these field theorists, Lewin sets up a most attractive program for theory. Taken in conjunction with his interesting experiments the illusion is nicely created that there is some connection between them.

[4] Lewin states that the objective physical and social surroundings "have a relation to the life space similar to that which 'boundary conditions' have to a dynamic system" (15, p. 217). He believes that physicalistic behaviorism has made the mistake of treating such variables as if they were parts of the life space. Attention should be called here to the fact that Koffka concerned himself much more extensively with the objective environmental variables or the geographic environment as he called it. He discussed at some length the relations between the geographic and the behavioral environments — the traditional problem of perception (10).

of these as a kind of verbal response or 'perceptual' response, in which the subject tries to describe his own particular way of perceiving the objective situation, we see that Lewin's theory really does provide us with laws mediating between independent variables, *i.e.*, between two different responses of the subject, or as in some cases, between the experimenter's own perceptual responses and the subjects' subsequent response. Thus Lewin discovers what amount to laws of the following type: $R_1 = f(R_2)$.

Of course, such theorists do not always rely on such phenomenological introspections. Once certain laws of the above type have been formulated it is possible to formulate further laws between purely overt behavior items, neither of which are of this introspective, verbal type. There are also instances in which from the pattern of the observed response the theorist makes an inference as to the nature of the hypothetical field; and then by means of his postulates as to what happens in these fields he is able to make certain predictions as to subsequent behavior. An excellent example of the latter is Köhler's theoretical treatment (12) of perceptual problems involving reversible figures and the effects of prolonged inspection in certain types of simple perceptual situations. Thus in the light of perceptual behavior to reversible figures, he formulated the hypothesis that percept processes are associated with fields of electric currents in the nervous system. Then by means of postulates based on knowledge about electrolytical conduction he was able to predict other perceptual behavior.

By and large, however, the field theorist depends heavily upon phenomenological introspection in introducing his theoretical constructs. In order to understand the field of the subject he asks him to describe how he perceives the situation, or he infers it on the basis of his own introspections. With engaging frankness Snygg has made an appeal for the recognition of the important role that phenomenological introspection plays in these theories.[5] Thus he writes in connection with the problem of prediction:

> By postulate *B* the determining locus of action is the behaver's p.f. [phenomenological field]. This is not open to direct observation by an outside observer. The process of prediction therefore involves two steps: (1) the securing of an understanding of the subject's field by inference or reconstruction, (2) the projection of the future field.
>
> The first operation is of the common "Now why did he do that?" or "Under what circumstances would I have done that" character. Much of the topological work of Lewin is of this type and essentially the same procedure was used by Shepard when from the behavior of his rate he inferred the existence of floor cues which he himself was unable to experience (17, p. 413).

That this field approach to the problems of psychology has been fruitful and valuable is amply supported by the experimental contributions it has made, although in the writer's opinion, the theoretical superstructure has played a much less significant role than is sometimes credited to it. Furthermore, the phenomenological approach has its advantages, particularly in the complex field of social behavior of the human adult. It is obviously much easier to gain some notion as to the relevant variables determining such complex behavior by asking the individual to verbalize than it is to employ the procedure of trying to hypothesize them from knowledge of past history. Usually the latter is not available in sufficient completeness to make it even worthwhile to try to theorize as to the nature of such historical laws.[6]

A final point of no little importance is the failure of such field theories to provide us with laws which will enable us to control and manipulate the behavior-determining psychological field. Such laws are obviously a basic prerequisite to successful clinical therapy. While it may be true, as Snygg claims (17),

[5] Snygg also admits another obvious characteristic of such theoretical systems which some of its proponents have not always willingly acknowledged. Reference is made here to the fact that such systems are anthropomorphic.

[6] The situation in the case of animal behavior is somewhat different. Here one usually does have a pretty good record of the past history relevant to the present environmental situation.

that psychiatrists and teachers find the phenomenological approach most valuable in diagnosing behavior disorders, it is difficult to understand how the response-response laws it provides can be of much use in guiding therapeutic treatment. The latter requires a knowledge of what to do to the individual, what changes in his physical and social environment to arrange, in order to bring about the desired behavior changes. The laws telling us how to proceed in such matters are historical laws and involve as an important component of them objective variables representative of past and present factors in the physical and social environments. Psychiatrists and clinical psychologists who employed a purely phenomenological approach might or might not be successful at diagnosis; it is difficult to see how they could ever prescribe satisfactory reëducative procedures.[7,8]

THEORETICAL CONSTRUCTS AS INTERVENING VARIABLES BETWEEN S AND R VARIABLES

In sharp contrast to these response inferred theories with their emphasis upon the phenomenological approach is the point of view that theoretical constructs in psychology are to be regarded as 'intervening variables' which bring into relation with one another the dependent R variables on the one hand and the independent S variables on the other. As Bergmann and Spence (2) have previously pointed out, two psychologists in particular, Hull and Tolman, have advocated, each in his own individual way, this type of psychological theory. In a little known paper Tolman (22) has presented an excellent account of such a theoretical program, while in his new book *Principles of behavior* Hull (7) has demonstrated in actual practice how such intervening variables provide us with a formulation of the basic principles or laws governing simple learning behavior. The following discussion makes no attempt to give a systematic account of this theoretical procedure. Instead we shall merely outline very sketchily its main features and then single out one or two aspects of it for more detailed examination.

According to Hull and Tolman, theoretical constructs, or intervening variables have to be introduced into psychology either when we do not know all the important variables entering into a set of experimental events, or the precise nature of the interrelating function is not known. Consider, for example, the data obtained from conditioning experiments. These investigations have presented us with a wealth of data showing how the response variable changes or varies with the manipulation of certain other experimental variables. That is to say, various measurable aspects of response are studied as functions of the manipulable environmental variables and the data so obtained are plotted in the form of various curves.

The task of the psychologist here is to discover the precise nature of the interrelations holding within this set of variables. Instead of knowing merely that the response, R, is some function of the variables X_1, X_2, X_3, $\ldots X_n$, he desires to know the precise function. But in such a situation, involving as it does a large number of variables, the function relating the dependent and independent variables is so complicated that we are unable to conceive of it directly. It is necessary, say

[7] Bergmann has summed up this difficulty most succinctly in the form of the following questions: — "But even so, what is the predictive value of the suggestive metaphor 'psychological environment'? Is it not the business of science to ascertain which objective factors in the past and present states of the organism and its environment account for the difference in response, so that we can actually predict it instead of attributing it, merely descriptively and after it has happened, to a difference in the psychological environment?" (1).

[8] Mention should perhaps be made here of the fact that the theoretical constructs (factors) that Spearman (18), Thurstone (20), and other factor analysts arrive at are response derived and hence fall into this class. These men do not, of course, use the phenomenological method, but beginning with response intercorrelations (empirical $R - R$ relations) they arrive at hypothetical factors by various methods of mathematical analysis. Like the phenomenologists their theoretical factors have no tie-up with the S variables.

Hull and Tolman, to proceed by conceiving of it as broken down into successive sets of simpler component functions. These component functions begin by introducing new intervening constructs defined in terms of the independent variables. Further intervening variables are then introduced by stating them as functions of the first set of intervening constructs, until finally the dependent behavior variable is postulated to be a function of one or more of the intervening variables.

Thus Tolman, beginning with the empirical data that the response measure is some function (f_1) of two groups of independent variables (environmental variables and individual difference variables), writes:

In place of the original f_1 function, I have introduced a set of intervening variables, I_a, I_b, I_c, etc., few or many, according to the particular theory. And I have conceived a set of f_2 functions to connect these intervening variables severally to the independent variables on the one hand, and an f_3 function to combine them together and connect them to the final dependent variable on the other (21, p. 9).

It is characteristic of Tolman's theorizing, however, that it never gets beyond the programmatic stage. In his writings Tolman has merely shown how such a theoretical device as the 'intervening variable' can provide for the definition and proper utilization within psychology of such mentalistic terms as 'demands,' 'hypotheses,' 'traits,' 'discriminanda,' etc., but he never actually reaches the point of formulating a specific theory. In the present context this would, of course, require the precise specification of the various functions relating the intervening variables to the independent and dependent experimental variables. Instead of risking guesses on such matters, however, Tolman seems to prefer to ascertain them empirically by a series of what he calls 'standard experimental set-ups.' He believes the data from these studies will mirror the functions obtaining between the experimental (empirical) and intervening (theoretical) variables.[9]

Quite in contrast to such an approach, Hull has ventured to make guesses as to the precise nature of the functions introducing the intervening variables in his theoretical formulations. Thus he has attempted to formulate the basic laws of simple adaptive behavior (learning) by introducing a number of intervening variables.[10] Beginning with the experimental variables, he has introduced by means of specific mathematical functions such symbolic constructs as stimulus trace (s), habit strength ($_SH_R$), the limit of habit strength (M), excitatory potential ($_SE_R$), inhibitory potential (I_R), effective excitatory potential ($_S\bar{E}_R$), and so on. Ultimately the observable response variable, R, is stated to be some function of the final intervening variable (*e.g.*, $R = f(_S\bar{E}_R)$.) Despite the neurophysiological tone of some of the terms that Hull employs to designate these constructs, the mistake should not be made of interpreting them as physiological concepts. Their scientific meaning is given only by the equations introducing them, and in this respect they are strictly comparable to many similar, abstract, mathematical constructs employed by the physicist in his theorizing. The use of neurophysiological terms and such additional statements as Hull sometimes makes as to their possible locus in the nervous system merely serve the purpose of providing experimental hints to persons interested in such matters. It may or may not turn out that they represent actual neurophysiological states or conditions that

[9] Tolman has been accused (and he has usually made no denial) of employing the phenomenological method in his psychology, and, because he has worked with animals, of being guilty of anthropomorphism. The present writer's interpretation is that it is Tolman, the experimentalist, who uses phenomenological introspection; Tolman, the theorist, introduces his intervening variables in terms of objectively defined variables. The difference between Lewin and Tolman on this point is interesting. Lewin, as we have seen, employs the phenomenological method primarily in his theoretical efforts, whereas Tolman uses it chiefly in the formulation of experimental problems.

[10] Reference is made here to Hull's latest writings in which the 'intervening variable' technique is made more explicit. As Bergmann and Spence (2) have pointed out, Hull's earlier miniature systems (5, 8) really involved the definition of such mediating constructs.

will some day be measurable by independent neurophysiological procedures.

An example of the specific manner in which Hull introduces his theoretical constructs is shown by the equations which he employs to define the two constructs, habit strength ($_SH_R$) and the limit of habit strength (M). With all experimental variables except the number of reinforced trials (N) and the length of the delay of the goal reinforcement (L) constant, the two equations are:

$$_SH_R = M(1 - e^{-iN})$$
$$M = 100e^{-kL}$$

Grice (4) has recently shown how such precisely defined theoretical constructs may be tested. He employed several mazes of different absolute lengths involving a shorter and longer path to the goal and ran different groups of rats on each maze. On the basis of the above two equations the following rational equation was then derived mathematically to describe the rate of learning the mazes:

$$\left[N = b \log\left(\frac{e^{-kL} - e^{-kHL}}{e^{-kL} - e^{-kHL} - a}\right)\right].$$

Where N = number of pairs of trials on the two paths to learn the maze.
L = length of short path to goal.
H = ratio of long to short path length.
k, a, b = empirical constants.

This rational equation was then shown to fit the experimental data, whereas another equation

$$\left[N = b \log\left(\frac{\log H}{\log H - C}\right)\right]$$

derived from a logarithmic postulate[11] as to the relation of M to L was shown not to be in agreement with the experimental data.

Until constructs are introduced in some such precise fashion as Hull employs one really does not have a scientific theory, for it is only under such conditions that the possibility of verification or refutation exists. Unfortunately, much of what has passed for theory in psychology has been sadly lacking in this respect, a state of affairs which is largely responsible for many of the 'theoretical' controversies, and for the low regard in which theory is held in some quarters in psychology. That theory construction has not always been intelligently pursued, however, is no reason for doing without theory. Without the generalizations which theories aim to provide we should never be in a position to predict behavior, for knowledge of particular events does not provide us with a basis for prediction when the situation differs in the least degree. The higher the level of abstraction that can be obtained the greater will be both the understanding and actual control achieved.

[11] $M = 100 - K \log L$.

The Ultra-Positivistic Approach

All the methods of ascertaining the laws of psychology we have discussed so far have agreed, in principle at least, that it is necessary to introduce some type of symbolic construct. It is also apparent that agreement ceases as regards the extent to which the proponents of these different views have insisted on rigorous and objective specification. We turn now to a quite different approach to the same problem — that of the ultra-positivist or empiricist, who tries to eschew all types of theoretical constructs. Usually the writings of such persons are limited to negativistic, critical attacks on all theory. Recently, however, Woodrow has come forward with a constructive proposal as to how general mathematical laws of psychology may be discovered by a method which he believes avoids the necessity of introducing theoretical constructs.

Woodrow's method consists in an attempt to obtain by mathematical curve-fitting a general equation describing a wide variety of experimental facts. Thus, after plotting a series of experimental curves of such widely varying situations as learning to abstract, learning to associate numbers and letters, learning a maze, reaction time to different intensities of stimulation, the forgetting of monosyllabic words, brightness and pitch discrimination, the growth of intelligence, etc., Woodrow sought to fit these empirical curves by means of a single general equation. He found that such an equation could be found and that it took the following form:

$$Y = a + \sqrt{p^2 + k^2(1 - f^{X+d})^2}.$$

This equation states a law between two experimental variables, a dependent response variable Y, *e.g.*, errors, successes, latencies, etc., and an independent manipulable variable X, *e.g.*, number of practice periods, intensity of the stimulus, preparatory interval, etc. But it will be noticed further that the law includes more than these two variables. It also involves certain constants or unknowns, termed parameters, the a, p, k, f, and d in the equation. We cannot stop to discuss these parameters in too great detail here. Suffice it to say that the specific shapes of the different empirical curves determine what parameters it is necessary to assume. Two of them, a and d, have no particular psychological significance, they merely express the fact that either one or both variables may have been measured by scales with an arbitrary zero. The parameter, k, is introduced because all his curves exhibit a limit to improvement, no matter how favorable the status given the environmental variable. Another parameter, f, is determined by the rate of approach of the curve to this limit and p, finally, is introduced to take care of the fact that the lower part of the curve sometimes shows positive acceleration.

As Woodrow himself points out, these parameters may be thought of, if one so wishes, as representing hypothetical states or factors within the organism.[12] Woodrow prefers not to do so, for as he argues, it really makes little difference what the internal referents are since they cannot at present be independently measured anyway. From the point of view of finding a general equation or law that will fit the experimental data the important thing, Woodrow states, is to determine how many parameters are required and the mathematical function of each.

While in general sympathy with Woodrow's mathematical approach and his view that it is unnecessary to specify the factors or complexes of factors inside the organism which determine the values of the parameters, the writer is, nevertheless, of the opinion that such an equation as Woodrow obtains by his analysis is, on the whole, rather barren and sterile. Its defect is not that the factors *within* the subject are not specified, but rather that it fails to give any indication whatever of the conditions or variables even *outside* the subject which determine these parameters. In this respect Woodrow's approach is similar to the field theorists'. We shall have occasion later to point out other resemblances between these two approaches.

This criticism can be made clearer, perhaps, by contrasting the end result of Woodrow's empirical procedure with Hull's rational approach to the same problem. Woodrow's law specifies but a single experimental variable determining the response:

$$Y = f(X_1).$$

Hull's theorizing culminates in a much more comprehensive law. Thus in the case of his theoretical formulation of simple adaptive behavior (learning) his derivation involves the following series of steps:

$$(1)\quad \boxed{M} = f(T, G)$$
$$(2)\quad \boxed{H} = f(\boxed{M}, T', N)$$
$$(3)\quad \boxed{D} = f(T'')$$
$$(4)\quad \boxed{E} \doteq f(\boxed{D}, \boxed{H})$$
$$(5)\quad \boxed{I} = f(N, W, F)$$
$$(6)\quad \boxed{\bar{E}} = f(\boxed{E}, \boxed{I})$$
$$(7)\quad \boxed{R} = f(\boxed{\bar{E}}).$$

[12] Woodrow writes, "Now these parameters may refer to anything whatsoever, conscious, physiological, environmental, psychic, or purely imaginary. Here one is free to follow his predilections, whether for motives, excitatory and inhibitory substances, field forces, states of disequilibrium, inertia of the nervous system, abilities, or what not" (23, p. 4).

Here the squared symbols are intervening variables or hypothetical constructs. The other symbols represent the dependent response measure (R) and the various manipulable, environmental variables (T, G, T', etc.). By substituting in the successive equations, a single equation stating R as a function of seven environmental variables is obtained.[13]

$$R = f(T, G, T', N, T'', W, F)$$

The latter procedure thus comes much closer to achieving the goal of the scientist, that of discovering all of the experimental variables determining the response measure and the nature of the functional interrelations holding between them. If this is achieved, the parameters become known functions of these experimental variables and thus become experimentally manipulable. Woodrow's formulation, on the other hand, provides us with very little more information than we had when we started.

It is also interesting to note that a strong case can be made out for the position that Woodrow's method is really not a great deal different from those theoretical approaches which infer their constructs from the characteristics of the response. In introducing his parameters Woodrow is, in effect, assuming or postulating some kind of hypothetical factor. Thus, on noticing that some of his curves show an initial period of positive acceleration, Woodrow assumes a factor, p, "whose influence is greatest when the magnitude of the environmental variable is small" (23, p. 7). This factor is inferred, we see, from the characteristics of the response curve and is therefore in a certain sense akin to the hypothetical constructs of the field theorists which, as we have seen, are also inferred from the response characteristics. The important difference is that in arriving at these hypothetical factors Woodrow does not make use of the introspective report associated with a response but rather bases his constructs on the mathematical properties of a curve of successive response measures.

Conclusions

In summary, the present paper has stated the task of the psychologist to be that of discovering the general laws of behavior, and has attempted to present a brief and critical outline of five different methods of approaching this task. The conclusions that the writer believes may be drawn from this survey are:

1. That theory is still at a very primitive level in psychology, concerning itself primarily with the discovery of low-order laws rather than the integration of different realms of laws.

2. That there is a variety of different theoretical procedures possible in psychology.

3. That some psychologists substitute, often quite unconsciously, phenomenological introspection and anthropomorphic thinking for theorizing. There is, of course, nothing wrong with such introspection; it has often served as a means of formulating interesting and valuable experiments. In such instances, however, the credit should not be given to a theory.

4. That many theories in psychology have provided us with response-response (R-R) laws rather than stimulus-response (S-R) laws.

5. That the most promising theoretical technique, especially from the point of view of discovering the historical stimulus-response laws, is the so-called 'intervening variable' method proposed by Hull and Tolman.

[13] The reader may ask: Why have a series of equations that introduce intervening variables? Why not write the single equation from the beginning and avoid the hypothetical constructs? One obvious reason, of course, is that it is just not possible to conceive of such a complex function all at once. As Tolman says, one can arrive at it only by breaking it down into a series of simpler functions. The reader is referred to a recent article by Hull in which he gives other reasons for using intervening variables with multiple equations rather than a single equation (6).

References

[1] BERGMANN, G. Psychoanalysis and experimental psychology: A review from the standpoint of scientific empiricism. *Mind*, 1943, **52**, 122–140.

[2] ———, & SPENCE, K. W. Operationism and theory in psychology. PSYCHOL. REV., 1941, **48**, 1–14.

[3] CARNAP, R. Testability and meaning. *Philos. Sci.*, 1936, **3**, 419–471; 1937, **4**, 1–40.

[4] GRICE, G. R. An experimental study of the gradient of reinforcement in maze learning. *J. exp. Psychol.*, 1942, **30**, 475–489.

[5] HULL, C. L. Mind, mechanism and adaptive behavior. PSYCHOL. REV., 1937, **44**, 1–32.

[6] ———. The problem of intervening variables in molar behavior theory. PSYCHOL. REV., 1943, **50**, 273–291.

[7] ———. *Principles of behavior*. New York: D. Appleton-Century Co., 1943.

[8] ———, HOVLAND, C. I., ROSS, R. T., HALL, M., PERKINS, D. T., & FITCH, F. B. *Mathematico-deductive theory of rote learning*. New Haven: Yale University Press, 1940.

[9] KOCH, S. The logical character of the motivation concept. II. PSYCHOL. REV., 1941, **48**, 127–154.

[10] KOFFKA, K. *Principles of Gestalt psychology*. New York: Harcourt, Brace & Co., 1935.

[11] KÖHLER, W. *Gestalt psychology*. New York: Liveright Publishing Corp., 1929.

[12] ———. *Dynamics in psychology*. New York: Liveright Publishing Corp., 1940.

[13] LEWIN, K. *A dynamic theory of personality*. (Trans. by D. K. Adams and K. E. Zener) New York: McGraw-Hill Book Co., 1935.

[14] ———. *Principles of topological psychology*. (Trans. by Fritz and Grace Heider.) New York: McGraw-Hill Book Co., 1936.

[15] ———. Field theory and learning, pp. 215–242. In *Forty-First Yearbook National Society for the Study of Education*, Part II. Bloomington, Illinois. Public School Publishing Co., 1942.

[16] PAVLOV, I. P. *Conditioned reflexes: an investigation of the physiological activity of the cerebral cortex*. (Trans. and ed. by F. C. Anrep.) London: Oxford University Press, 1927.

[17] SNYGG, D. The need for a phenomenological system of psychology. PSYCHOL. REV., 1941, **48**, 404–424.

[18] SPEARMAN, C. *The abilities of man*. New York: Macmillan, 1927.

[19] SPENCE, K. W. Theoretical interpretations of learning. In *Comparative Psychology*, rev. ed. (F. A. Moss, ed.), New York: Prentice-Hall. 1942, Chap. 11.

[20] THURSTONE, L. L. *The vectors of mind*. Chicago: Univ. Chicago Press, 1935.

[21] TOLMAN, E. C. The determiners of behavior at a choice point. PSYCHOL. REV., 1938, **45**, 1–41.

[22] ———. Operational behaviorism and current trends in psychology. *Proc. 25th Anniv. Celebration Inaug. Grad. Stud.*, Los Angeles. The University of Southern California, 1936, pp. 89–103.

[23] WOODROW, H. The problem of general quantitative laws in psychology. *Psychol. Bull.*, 1942, **39**, 1–27.

That Behaviorism Cannot Account for Human Thinking

22

Hobbes and Hull—Metaphysicians of Behaviour

R. S. PETERS and H. TAJFEL

The Idea of a Universal System of Behaviour

It is sometimes instructive to compare modern systems of thought with those of the past not simply for the sake of pointing out what startling similarities can be found, but also because the past systems are usually less cluttered up with details and it is easier to see the logical difficulties they involve. This is particularly the case with mechanical systems for explaining human behavior; for in such systems there are certain crucial logical difficulties which can too easily be covered up by the intricacy and subtle devices of the latest machine.

There are many candidates to the title of 'the father of modern psychology'. But the claims of Thomas Hobbes can be pressed very strongly in that he was not only the first to suggest that human beings are machines, but also the first to attempt a systematic explanation of *all* human actions in terms of the same principles as were used to explain the behaviour of inanimate bodies. Descartes and others thought that animal behaviour and the *involuntary* actions of men could be mechanically explained, but not distinctly human actions, involving reason and will. Hobbes ruthlessly extended Galileo's assumptions into the innermost sanctuaries of human thought and decision. He claimed originality for his civil philosophy on this account. Indeed, he hoped that his name would be as famous in the history of psychology and social science as that of Harvey who extended the new science of motion to physiology.

Hobbes sketched a Grand Plan for the explanation of human behaviour — starting with simple motions in geometry and proceeding via mechanics, physics, and physiology and social science. A more limited version of this deductive dream is to be found in recent times in the work of C. L. Hull. The title of Hull's latest book is *A Behavior System*.[1] The aims of the enterprise are explicitly stated both in the latest book and in its predecessor, his *Principles of Behavior*,[2] published some ten years earlier. Thus, 'the objective of the present work is the elaboration of the basic molar behavioral laws underlying the "social sciences"'.[3] Elsewhere, it is said that:

> An ideally adequate theory even of so-called purposive behavior ought, therefore, to begin with colorless movement and mere receptor impulses as such, and from these build up step by step both adaptive behavior and maladaptive behavior. The present approach does not deny the molar reality of purposive acts (as opposed to movement), of intelligence, of insight, of goals, of intents, of strivings, or of value; on the contrary, we insist upon the genuineness of these forms of behavior. We hope ultimately to show the logical right to the use of such concepts by deducing them as secondary principles from more elementary objective primary principles.[4]

In the concluding pages of the *Principles of Behavior*, the Grand Plan is given an even more ambitious and more detailed expression. Through a 'systematization of the behavior sciences' based on the consistent use of certain

From the *British Journal for the Philosophy of Science*, 8:29 (May, 1957), pp. 30–44, Cambridge University Press.

[1] C. L. Hull, *A Behavior System*, New Haven, 1952.

[2] C. L. Hull, *Principles of Behavior*, New York, 1943.

[3] Hull, op. cit. p. 17.

[4] ibid., p. 25–26.

methodological rules, Hull hopes that ultimately treatises 'on the different aspects of the behavior sciences will appear'. These treatises will be based on systematic primary principles, and will present general or specific theories of individual and social behaviour, of 'communicational symbolism or language', of 'social or ritualistic symbolism', of economic, moral, and aesthetic valuation,

> of familial behavior; of individual adaptive efficiency (intelligence); of the formal educative processes; of psychogenic disorders; of social control and delinquency; of character and personality; of culture and acculturation; of magic and religious practices; of custom, law and jurisprudence; of politics and government; and of many other specialised fields of behavior.[5]

Now it would be very welcome to have a deductive system in which statements about human behaviour could be deduced from more general laws — e.g. of mechanics or physiology. But it may well be that this programme is a pipe-dream — especially if the model is based on mechanics. For the difficulties in developing such a system may not be empirical ones connected with the complexity of human behaviour, as is often thought, but *logical* ones connected with the categories of description appropriate to human action.

It used to be held that man was a rational animal and that his reason was of a different ontological status from the rest of his body — not subject to the laws of nature. As often, this metaphysical thesis may well have enshrined an important logical truth, namely that man is a rule-following animal and that adequate explanations in terms of efficient causes *alone* cannot be given for actions which are in accordance with rules, conventions, criteria, canons, and so on. The old time-honoured gulf between nature and convention may well have far more general application than is often realised.

It is our thesis that there are certain logical difficulties about *any* mechanical system of human behaviour. These exhibit themselves in a deductive system as gulfs

(*a*) between motions at a physiological level and human actions which are goal directed and usually conform to certain criteria or conventions,

(*b*) between motions of the body and consciousness — especially rational thought.

These gaps may well all be connected with man's peculiarity as a rule-following animal. Our hope in this paper is to exhibit the rather surprising similarity between the systems of Hobbes and Hull, and to substantiate, in places where the similarity between the systems is most apparent, the general thesis that mechanical explanations can never be *sufficient* for actions falling under the concept of rule-following.

Motions and Human Actions: The Similarity between the Theories of Hobbes and Hull

The basic presupposition of mechanistic explanation is that all causes are antecedent motions. As Hobbes put it, there can be no action at a distance, 'no cause of motion, except in a body contiguous and moved'.[6] Now a great many things happen for which there is presumably some cause, yet it is difficult to see any motion in a contiguous body which could have caused it. Recourse is therefore made to the notion of unobservable motions either within or between bodies. Hobbes exploited this move with considerable ingenuity. He managed to bridge the gap between the movements in external bodies, which were transmitted by means of a medium to the sense-organs, and the movements of the body in appetite and aversion by introducing the concept of 'endeavour' or 'conatus', which he defined as 'motion made in less space and time than can be given; that is motion made through the length of a point and in an instant or point of time'.[7] It was a term for *infinitely small* motions which he took

[5] ibid.

[6] T. Hobbes, *E.W.*, Vol. I, p. 124 (*E.W.* stands for *English Works* and is the standard way of referring to the Molesworth edition of Hobbes' Works. Similarly *L.W.* stands for *Latin Works*).

[7] T. Hobbes, *E.W.*, Vol. I, p. 206

over from the physical scientists and generalised to bridge the gap between physics, physiology, and psychology. It was a peculiarly subtle move; for although the term was used as a physical construct at the molecular level, it conveyed the suggestion of striving and direction which was so apt for the transition to psychological happenings at the molar level. So wherever there was a gap in observable motion — e.g. between the object and the sense-organ or between the stimulation of the sense-organ and the movements of the muscles in appetite and aversion, Hobbes postulated 'endeavours' which transmitted the motion.[8] For, according to his theory, motions from the external world not only move to the brain and produce images: they also affect the vital motions of the body which are manifest in the circulation of the blood, breathing, excretion, nutrition, and other such processes. When these incoming motions impede the vital motions, this is felt as pain and the parts of the body are acted on by the muscles 'which is done when the spirits are carried now into these, now into other nerves, till the pain, as far as possible, be quite taken away'[9]. Similarly in the case of pleasure, the spirits are guided by the help of the nerves to preserve and augment the motion. When this build-up of endeavours tends towards things known by experience to be pleasant, it is called an appetite; when it tends to the avoidance of what is painful, it is called an aversion. Appetite and aversion are thus 'the first endeavours of animal motion'. Even in the case of a few appetites and aversions which are born with men, such as those for food, excretion, etc., (which sound very much like the modern 'primary drives'), initiation of movement is from without.

Hull's system is surprisingly similar; he starts, as Hobbes did, from the simplest possible elements. An adequate theory of behaviour, he says, ought 'to begin with colorless movements and mere receptor impulses as such, and from these build up step by step both adaptive and maladaptive behavior'.[10] For Hobbes action was an outcome of an interplay between internal and external motions. Hull's analysis of the initiation of action is also based on an interplay of assumed minute motions within the 'neural structures'. Observable actions of the organism are for him, in most cases, the result of existing 'habit structures' slowly built up on the basis of previous experience, according to certain principles specified in his postulates. There is no direct cause-and-effect sequence, as in Hobbes, between the properties of the present stimulation and the consequent actions. But Hull's picture, made much more complex by the intervention of the past through learning, remains nevertheless an essentially mechanical picture. The extrapolation from minute occurrences to behaviour, while not based on a direct link between sensation and action, or external and internal motions following each other in a simple manner, is based on 'habit structures' built into the nervous system during the past, and active at the time of stimulation. The main difference here between Hobbes and Hull is not a difference of principle: it consists in the fact that Hull specifies the conditions of the past motions (learning) which led to the pattern of motions as it is observed in the present. The passing of the organism into action is the result of the preponderance of the 'strongest' of these motions. The concepts used by Hull at this stage of his analysis are stated in mechanical terms. A threshold is 'a quantum of resistance or inertia which must be overcome by an opposing force before the latter can pass over into action'.[11] The 'competition of reaction potentials' is basically a conflict of 'motions', the strongest of which 'wins', and thus determines action. The 'behavioral oscillation', a

[8] The concept of 'endeavour' also enabled Hobbes to give a substantial interpretation of dispositional terms. On his view, when we ascribe a 'power' or capacity to anything, we are making a statement about an actual build-up of minute motions. Even habits were explained as *actual motions* made more easy and more ready by perpetual endeavours.

[9] T. Hobbes, *E.W.*, Vol. I, p. 407.

[10] T. Hobbes, *E.W.*, Vol. I, p. 25.

[11] ibid. p. 323.

concept introduced in order to account theoretically for those unpredictable movements of the organism which could not be entirely explained by the momentary status quo between the competing 'reaction potentials', is conceived as an outcome of an infinite number of minute motions.

The basic principles concerning the inner workings of motives and incentives are very similar in both systems. Hobbes is concerned with a mechanical explanation of pain and pleasure. Hull is in need of simple assumptions, which would allow him to describe the 'mechanism' by which successful (i.e. rewarded) responses remain a part of the organism's habit equipment, while the unsuccessful ones are eliminated. Hobbes assumes an increase and decrease in vital motions. Hull's reductionism goes one step further. In his simplified scheme the nature of reinforcement consists essentially in a reduction in the internal stimulation (e.g. in hunger, thirst, fear) which follows the successful response. The locus of this reduction must, by necessity, remain vague. It is applied to primary drives by assuming, in each case, some specific internal pattern of stimulation to be reduced. More complex forms of motivation are reducible to the basic mechanism by a transition in which both the incentive nature of previously rewarded situations, and the intervention of some kind of stimulation to be reduced (e.g. anxiety) play their part.

The 'drive-reduction hypothesis' is the equivalent of Hobbes' decrease in vital motions. But Hobbes was content with the statement of the general principle, which then allowed him to go on talking about motivation in terms of efficient mechanical causes. Hull attempts to be more specific: the 'minute unobservable' finds its way into an explanation of 'secondary motivation'. The most explicit attempt at generalising the principle to various forms of human endeavour can be found in a recent paper by Brown,[12] in which anxiety reduction is made the basis of assigning to the 'reduction principle' the capacity of explaining a very wide range of human motivational phenomena.

As a matter of fact Hobbes did something rather similar in his theory of the passions, though at the molar level and without any pretence of relating his theory of 'passions' to his physiological theory; for all the 'passions' are represented as manifestations either of the desire for power or of the fear of death. Laughter, for instance, is explained as an expression of sudden glory when we light upon some respect in which we are superior to others; courage is aversion with hope of avoiding hurt by resistance; and pity is grief for the calamity of another rising from the imagination that a like calamity may befall ourselves. The reduction of all passions to the desire for power and the fear of death provided Hobbes with an exciting psychological analysis of politics and with great opportunities for coining epigrams; but it had a tenuous connection only with the physiological details of his theory of motivation. The Hullian reduction of complex behaviour, on the other hand, sketches a simplified 'picture' of our internal workings and transfers physiological description to behaviour at the molar level. And the use of 'avoidance behaviour' (such as behaviour due to anxiety) to redescribe other forms of motivation in terms of its negative forms is due, to a large extent, to the fact that 'avoidance behaviour' can be quite easily described in terms of reduction of internal stimulation. It can thus be linked with a vague physiological 'picture'; but, apart from this dubious advantage, its merits as an explanation are very questionable.[13]

The Illegitimacy of the Transition from Motions to Human Actions

The link with physiology, which we have described as 'a dubious advantage' is re-

[12] J. S. Brown, 'Problems Presented by the Concept of Acquired Drives', *Current Theory and Research in Motivation: A Symposium*, 1953.

[13] See, for instance, Harlow's comments on Brown's paper: Ibid., pp. 22–23.

garded by Hull as the chief strength of his theory. For he claims that eventually descriptions of actions at the molar level will be deducible from physiological postulates at the molecular level. But surely the link cannot be that of *deducibility*. Hamlyn[14] has recently discussed the confusion existing in some psychological theories, in which activities have been described in terms of movements, observable or unobservable. The distinctive features of activity, or behaviour, will be left out in such a description. For no fixed criterion can be laid down which will enable us to decide what series of movements constitutes a piece of behaviour — e.g. getting a treaty signed or winning a girl's affection. Descriptions of behaviour imply standards, which are loosely defined and which are interpretations at quite a different level from descriptions of movements. Of course behaviour involves movements; but it cannot be described simply in terms of movements. For similar pieces of behaviour can involve quite different movements.[15] *Some* movements in the body and brain, for instance, are necessary conditions for passing an examination, but it has yet to be shown that any *particular* movements are either necessary or sufficient. Now if behaviour cannot ever be *described* purely in terms of movements, how much less can it be *deduced* from a theory which is concerned only with 'colourless movement'.

By his analysis of motivation Hobbes hoped to substantiate his claim that: 'A final cause has no place but in such things as have sense and will; and this also I shall prove hereafter to be an efficient cause.'[16] And, of course, he was right in saying that human actions have efficient causes — external stimuli, movements of the sense-organs, internal motions, and so on. But this does not mean that a list of any such movements could ever be *sufficient* to explain actions. For actions are distinguished by the goals towards which movements are directed; the goal makes the movements part of an action of a certain sort. And since we cannot specify which movements *must* be involved in attaining the goal, so also we cannot specify *precisely* which antecedent movements are sufficient to initiate behaviour. This general logical difficulty holds against Hull's more complicated theory as well as against Hobbes' simpler one.

This kind of logical difficulty is even more glaring in Hobbes' theory of the passions. For most of our terms at this level of description are either like 'ambition' in assigning a certain kind of objective to an action or like 'honesty' in classifying an action as being in accordance with a certain rule or convention. It is most unplausible to suggest, as Hobbes did, either that such terms imply anything specific about the efficient causes which initiate behaviour of this kind,[17] or that such behaviour could be *deduced* from a theory concerned only with colourless movements. For a gross muddle of explanatory models is involved. Terms like 'ambition' and 'honesty' derive their meaning from a model of behaviour peculiar to goal-directed and rule-following activities, which is of quite a different logical type from that of mechanics. In this explanatory model an agent is assumed to have an objective (like being a professor, in the case of 'ambition'), and to have information about means which will lead to this objective in a manner which is both efficient and in accordance with certain conventions of appropriateness (as in the example of 'honesty'). This model forms a kind of explanatory ceiling in understanding human behaviour just as the mechanical model of bodies pushing other bodies formed an explanatory ceiling in the seventeenth-century understanding of nature. And all our psychological explanations are related to this model just as all explanations in classical economics presupposed the model of a rational man.

Now physiological descriptions can state

[14] D. W. Hamlyn, 'Behaviour', *Philosophy*, 1953, **28**, 132–145.

[15] A similar distinction between behaviour and physical movements was drawn in a different context by J. O. Wisdom, 'Mentality in Machines', *Proc. Arist. Soc.*, Sup. Vol. 26, 1952, 10–15.

[16] T. Hobbes, *E.W.*, Vol. I, p. 132.

[17] See R. Peters, *Hobbes*, Penguin Books, 1956, pp. 144–147.

necessary conditions for behaviour conforming to this model; for it is a truism to say that we cannot plan means to ends or be sensitive to social norms unless we have a brain. Similarly physiology, like psycho-analysis, can state conditions under which this type of behaviour breaks down. A man with a brain injury may well be insensitive to social pressures just as a man with an obsession may be incapable of taking the means necessary to bring about a desired objective. Obviously physiological theories are extremely *relevant* to explanations of action at the molar level of behaviour. But this does not mean that there is a *deductive* relation between them — that behaviour can be deduced from the physiological description *alone*. Our contention is that Hobbes and Hull were mistaken in assuming that the relation was of this sort.

But surely, it might be objected, Hull had much more rigorous standards of scientific method than Hobbes. Surely he must have introduced subsidiary hypotheses to bridge the gap between physiological and psychological descriptions. On the contrary, our case is that neither Hobbes nor Hull saw that these types of explanations were of logically different types. Hull's ultimate aim is a 'truly molecular theory of behaviour firmly based on physiology.'[18] As this is at present impossible because of the inadequacy of our knowledge, a molar approach based on the use of 'quasi-neurological principles' must serve for the time being. There are, however, 'degrees of the molar, depending on the coarseness of the ultimate causal segments or units dealt with. Other things equal, it would seem wisest to keep the causal segments small, to approach the molecular, the fine and exact substructural details, just as closely as the knowledge of that substructure renders possible.'[19]

This makes explicit Hull's assumption that the difference between physiology and psychology is only a difference in the 'coarseness of the ultimate causal segments or units'. There is no *logical* difference, on his view, between these explanations; it is merely a matter of the 'fineness' of the 'substructural details'. Yet as soon as he starts developing explanations instead of just making programmatic pronouncements, the logical gulf immediately appears. For instance, as Koch points out, 'stimulus' is conceptually defined by Hull either in terms of physical energy, or in terms of neural impulses. R is 'reaction or response in general (muscular, glandular, or electrical)'; but when Hull refers to stimuli or responses in his description of the behaviour of experimental rats, R comes to mean *actions* such as 'biting the floor bars', 'leaping the barrier', and so on.[20] Stimuli, to quote Koch again, 'are certainly not being specified in terms of independent physical energy criteria'. The symbols which previously referred to the 'substructural detail' are kept unchanged, but even at this low level of behavioural complexity, they acquire new meanings: they refer to *actions* classified in terms of their end-results.

This reference to the 'substructural detail' also occasions another query. What sort of description is appropriate to it? Is it in fact described in physiological terms? Or could it be that Hull, like Hobbes, makes a plausible transition from physiology to psychology by according the 'logically more primitive elements' a sort of twilight status? Hobbes found the elements on which he constructed his system in motions of particles of all sizes. When a jump into the unobservable became necessary, motions became shadowy 'endeavours' which belonged to minute particles of matter. The 'reality status' of minute motions in Hobbes' system was obvious and explicitly affirmed. Hull's position, however, is more ambiguous. The data for both sides of his formulae are stimuli and responses, or molar movements of the organism. Between these two classes of observables, a series of 'theoretical constructs' serves the attempt to express the infinite variation at both ends in some uniform, lawful, and communicable manner. The constructs are not meant to be

[18] Hull, op. cit., p. 20.
[19] ibid. p. 21.

[20] S. Koch, *Clark L. Hull in Modern Learning Theory*, New York, 1954, pp. 24–25.

observable, and are, or should be, unequivocally defined without reliance on 'substance'. Discussions about the doubtful status of these supposedly abstract links are a familiar feature of the recent psychological literature, and need not be invoked here in detail.[21] The main objection levelled against them is that they are not abstract, but have an implicit existential status. 'Habit strength' may well be an abstract quantifiable concept, but 'habit' or 'reaction potential' are for Hull not only theoretical constructs. They are also 'neural organisations', they form pseudo-physiological 'pictures' of what happens inside the organism. These events are described, as in Hobbes' system, in terms of minute motions. And just as Hobbes' 'endeavours' enabled him to slip unobtrusively from mechanical to psychological descriptions, so also Hull's language shuffles between that appropriate to a description of the physiology of the central nervous system and that which is used to describe observable molar events. But it is not definitely committed to either. A peculiar use of terms (e.g. 'reaction-potential') bridges the gap in both systems: language describing the 'primary elements' is still used in the description of behaviour, and the transition is achieved because its difficulties are ignored.

It is this which renders untestable an important aspect of Hull's theory. System-builders who aim at an 'explanation of human behaviour' and find their point of departure in any form of atomism must state clearly the steps which enable them to hope for such an achievement. It is true that many of Hull's hypotheses have been tested in a number of severely limited experimental situations. Indeed it is often said that testability is one of the main virtues of Hull's theory; for he was 'the first psychologist who could be proved to be wrong'.[22] But these tests only establish certain regularities of behaviour in extremely simple situations without showing how these regularities can be deduced from the underlying principles of internal motion. Neither do these tests in any way establish the applicability of such simple laws to forms of behaviour such as are outlined in his ambitious scheme which we have described above.

Consciousness and Rational Thought

If we can trust Hobbes' autobiography, his psychology was developed in part as an answer to a problem that haunted him for years. He had once been present at a gathering of learned doctors who were discussing problems connected with sensation. One of them asked what, after all, sensation was, and how it was caused. To Hobbes' astonishment not one of them was able to suggest an answer. Hobbes pondered over this for years until, after his meeting with Galileo, a solution suddenly occurred to him. He looked at the familiar process of sensation in the unfamiliar way he had learnt from Galileo

> . . . it occurred to him that if bodies and all their parts were to be at rest, or were always to be moved by the same motion, our discrimination of all things would be removed, and (consequently) all sensation with it; and therefore the cause of all things must be sought in the variety of motion.[23]

Sensation, which was but 'some internal motion in the sentient,' was a meeting place of motions. Deductions from a general mechanical theory were all that were required both to explain the peculiarities of sensation itself and the initiation of actions in response to external stimuli. These Hobbes proceeded to provide.

The selectivity of perception was explained by suggesting that while the organ retains

[21] See, for example, F. H. George, 'Logical Constructs and Psychological Theory', *Psychol. Rev.*, 1953, pp. 1–6; S. Koch, *Clark L. Hull in Modern Learning Theory*, New York, 1954; K. MacCorquodale and P. E. Meehl, 'On a Distinction between Hypothetical Constructs and Intervening Variables', *Psychol. Rev.*, 1948, **55**, 95–107. Koch's paper especially contains a very detailed discussion of the logical difficulties raised in Hull's system by the ambiguous, pseudo-physiological character of the 'theoretical constructs'.

[22] Derek Pugh, Review of *A Theory of Social Control*, *British Journal of Psychology*, 1955, **46**, 153.

[23] T. Hobbes, *L.W.*, Vol. I, p. 21.

motion from one object, it cannot react to another; similarly in attention the motion from the root of the nerves persists 'contumaciously', and makes the sense-organ impervious to the registering of other motions. The explanation of imagination is a straight deduction from the law of inertia:

When a body is once in motion, it moveth, unless something else hinder it eternally; and whatsoever hindreth it, cannot in an instant, but in time, and by degree, quite extinguish it; and as we see in the water, though the wind cease, the waves give not over rolling for a long time after; so also it happeneth in that motion, which is made in the internal parts of man, then, when he sees, dreams, etc. . . . Imagination therefore is nothing but decaying sense.[24]

The decay, of course, is not a decay in motion. For that would be contrary to the law of inertia. Rather it comes about because the sense-organs are moved by other objects. This explains the vividness of dreams. For in sleep there are no competing motions from the external world. When sense-impressions are constantly crowding in on us, the imagination of the past is obscured and 'made weak as the voice of a man in the noise of the day'. Thus the longer the time that elapses after sensing an object, the weaker our imagination.

There is something almost incredibly hard-headed and naive about Hobbes' gross materialism. To say that sensation and the conceptual processes are *nothing but* motions is rather like saying that kissing is simply a mutual movement of the lips or that work is moving lumps of matter about. Hobbes, too, is aided in this rather monstrous piece of metaphysics by using terms like 'agitation', 'celerity', 'disturbance', and 'tranquillity' to describe mental processes; for these terms have meaning as descriptions both of physical and psychological happenings. Hobbes could thus talk like a physiologist and preserve the common touch of everyday psychological description. But at any rate he did openly, not to say brazenly, make the transition from mechanics to psychology. He did not, however, seem to be sufficiently aware of the *sort* of gap that he is bridging. For just as he developed a *causal* theory of imagery and thought also that he was answering questions about the reference or *meaning* of images, so also he thought that differences between activities like perceiving, imagining, and remembering could be explained solely in terms of their efficient causes. But the distinction between sense and imagination is not *simply* that imagination is *decaying* sense any more than the distinction between imagination and memory is that the latter involves only the addition of a sense of pastness. For these activities have different names because they imply different logical criteria. Psychologically speaking perceiving may be the same as imagining in a given case. When we say, in spite of this that we did not *imagine* something, we are making a logical point, not a psychological one. Human actions imply criteria of distinction which are at quite a different logical level from that appropriate to stimuli, movements, and other such mechanical concepts.

Hobbes, then, leapt openly, if recklessly, from mechanics to psychology. Hull, who deals very little with sensation, either ignores the gap or bridges it by implied assumptions. He ignores problems connected with the status of consciousness and his assumptions about sensation are implicit in his development of a theory of learning rather than explicitly stated. Hobbes assumed that identical motions from the external world will lead to identical counter-motions in the organism; in other words, discrimination between various stimuli, and generalisation of responses to stimuli varying quantitatively and qualitatively will be a function of the degree of difference between the motions imposed on the organism from the outside. Hull, preoccupied with learning rather than with problems of perception, is interested only in the influence of past events on present perception. But again the conclusions reached in both systems are almost identical, as the common assumption is that, in the last analysis, it is the degree of identity of patterns

[24] T. Hobbes, *E.W.*, Vol. III, p. 4.

of minute motions which determines the degree of identity of perceptions. And no doubt there are such differences in minute movements. But it is questionable whether a knowledge of these alone would ever enable us to explain the differences in the descriptions of what we see. For such descriptions involve the use of conventions and standards of correctness which we impose on what we see. Man is a rule-following animal in perceiving as well as in moral behaviour, and it is this characteristic which makes all such causal theories unplausible as *sufficient* explanations of his activities.

Hobbes saw that it was man's capacity for using symbols in deductive reasoning and in descriptive languages which distinguishes him from animals, together with the theoretical curiosity that goes along with it. But he even suggested a mechanical explanation of language in his crude causal theory of signs. This was a grotesque failure because he never properly distinguished logical questions of the reference of signs from causal questions of their origin. Similarly he gave a mechanical explanation of choice. Will, he held, simply *is* the last desire in deliberating which emerges after an oscillation of impulses. Here again, in his writings on free-will, he never properly distinguished questions about the justification of actions (their reasons) from questions about their causes. Indeed, he seemed to think that *all* reasons for actions are rationalisations — a smoke-screen concealing the underlying thrust and recoil of a pleasure-pain calculating machine. But this is inadequate. For there is a manifest difference between compulsive and rational behaviour. A person who deliberates rationally about means to an end will be influenced by logically relevant considerations. For him there is a difference between good and bad reasons for a course of action. But for a compulsive there is no such similar distinction. No reasons will make any difference to what he does. Like a man under post-hypnotic suggestion he will only 'reason' to find excuses for what he is going to do anyway. Now any mechanical theory, even if it has recourse to minute motions, must face the glaring inappropriateness of giving causal explanations of transitions in terms of logical dependence. In what sense can a physiological theory of the brain be said to *explain* a geometer's conclusions or a move at a game of chess?

Hull suggests in his opening chapter that all sorts of formalised procedures like those of law, ritual, and government, can be explained by means of his mechanical theory. But, needless to say, he never gives an inkling of how this can be done. Is there much point in elaborating a system in such detail and making such far-reaching claims for the derivations which one day might be made from it, if the grave logical problems of applying such mechanical explanations to distinctively human behaviour are completely ignored? Hobbes saw the crucial gaps and audaciously, if unconvincingly, attempted to leap them. Could it not be said that the detail and alleged logical rigour of Hull's system, far from putting psychology on a truly scientific path, merely serve to conceal important logical difficulties in his system?

In his last book Hull wrote:

> It is clear from the foregoing discussion that natural-science methodology presumably will be able, ultimately, to deduce from its principles all kinds of behavior of organisms, whether generally characterised as good, bad, or indifferent. Moreover, since the passing of a moral judgement is itself a form of verbal behavior, either overt or covert, it is to be expected that natural-science theory will be able to deduce the making of moral judgements along with other forms of behavior.[25]

Now it is understandable that Hobbes should also have shared this methodological pipe-dream; for he lived before Hume and Kant had shown the logical impossibility of deducing statements about what ought to be from statements about what is the case. But any modern philosopher, who read this extract from Hull, would marvel at the naiveté of a man who thought that normative judgments could be deduced from a physiological theory. Our case, however, has not been a

[25] T. Hobbes, *E.W.*, Vol. III, p. 338.

laboured exposition of this obvious logical lapse. It has been, rather, to stress that the logical leap occurs in a much more interesting transition — in that from movements to actions. Misled by the obvious fact that physiological theories are extremely *relevant* to explanations of human actions, Hull, like Hobbes, thought that descriptions of human actions could be *deduced* from a physiological theory alone. This, in our view, is the basic logical mistake in mechanistic theories which both Hobbes and Hull commit in a surprisingly similar manner.

That "Computer Behaviorism" Can Account for Human Thinking 23

The Simulation of Human Thought

ALLEN NEWELL and HERBERT A. SIMON

Behaviorism and the acceptance of the norms of the natural sciences in psychology greatly restricted for a generation or more the range of behavioral phenomena with which the psychologist, as scientist, was willing to concern himself. Unless an aspect of behavior could be examined in the laboratory and could be recorded and measured in an entirely objective fashion, it was not, in the prevailing view, a proper subject of study.

There has been considerable relaxation of this austerity in the past decade, although not without misgiving and apology. A leading text on experimental psychology, for example, in introducing the topics of problem solving, insight, thinking, and language behavior, observes:

> These topics have often been omitted from textbooks in the past — perhaps because of some subtle aura of "mentalism." Historically, of course, thought and meaning were the central problems for psychology. The wide circle that American psychologists have been making through behaviorism seems to be bringing them back again to the same core of the science, but perhaps they are returning with more precise techniques and a more objective point of view than would otherwise have been attained. (15, p. 602).

There is no need to document in detail this resurgence in psychology of concern with the central topic of thinking. This subject had been kept alive during the heyday of behaviorism by a number of outstanding men — the names of Köhler, Tolman, Wertheimer, Bartlett, Duncker, and Maier, come at once to mind — who refused to allow fixed canons of rigor to bar them from studying the relevant and the significant. Their work provided, in turn, foundations on which the more recent investigators — Luchins, Heidbreder, Harlow, deGroot, Guetzkow, and Bruner, to mention some examples — have built.

Those who regard thinking as the core of psychological inquiry, and who urge a return to concern with it, do not want to turn the clock back. The behaviorists and operationalists are, of course, right in demanding objectivity, clarity, and rigor. Relatively few psychologists are satisfied with the vagueness of Gestalt language and with explanation at the level it permits. Few are satisfied with the eclectic language of James, and many find excessive vagueness and ambiguity in the "mediation" hypotheses of his middle-of-the-road descendants.

The task is not simply to restore thinking to the center of the psychological stage; it is to study thinking with as much methodological sophistication as we demand for simpler phenomena. Consequently, the increasing attention to thought processes does not merely reaffirm their importance; it reflects a growing belief that the techniques of psychological inquiry have become adequate, at least to some degree, to the subject matter. Whether the belief was fully justified a decade ago, when the resurgence began, is a moot question. The main thesis of this paper is that the belief is justified now — that the technological advances that are necessary to permit a theory of thinking to be formulated and tested have occurred.

From *Contemporary Trends in Psychological Theory*, The University of Pittsburgh Press, Pittsburgh, Pa., 1961, pp. 152–179.

The work reported here is part of a larger project in which the authors are engaged with their associate, J. C. Shaw. Many of the ideas reported here derive from that larger effort.

To understand complex phenomena we must have powerful tools of inquiry — tools for observing facts and tools for reasoning from complicated premises to their consequences. The invention of the telescope and of the calculus played crucial roles at one stage in the history of physics, and the invention of the cyclotron and of quantum mechanics at a later stage. New observing instruments made visible the previously invisible phenomena that had to be known if the theory was to advance. New analytic instruments made comprehensible the facts revealed by the telescope and cyclotron, which otherwise would have been inscrutable. A science of complex phenomena needs powerful machines for observing and powerful tools for reasoning.

The phenomena of human thinking are more complex than the phenomena that physics studies. In some respects the former are easier to observe than the latter — human verbal behavior is present and audible, neither submicroscopic nor as distant as the stars. (To be sure, we do not have instruments for observing cerebral events that are nearly as revealing as the instruments of physics.) But observable or not, human behavior has not been easy to interpret. We have had great difficulties in building successful theories to explain it.

Until a decade ago, the only instruments we had for building theories about human behavior were the tools we borrowed and adapted from the natural sciences: operationalism and classical mathematics. And so inadequate are these tools to the task that a highly respected psychologist offered in earnest the doctrine that we must build a science without a theory — surely a doctrine of desperation.

With the advent of the modern digital computer and the emergence of the concept of a *program* the situation is altered radically. The computer was invented as a machine to do arithmetic rapidly. But as matters turned out, a machine to do arithmetic was a machine that could manipulate symbols. It was natural to ask whether such a machine could perform some of the more general symbol-manipulating processes required for thinking and problem solving as well as the very specialized processes required for arithmetic. The answer, as we shall see, is "yes." There is now substantial evidence, which we shall review, that a digital computer, appropriately programmed, can carry out complex patterns of processes that parallel exceedingly closely the processes observable in human subjects who are thinking.

But the significance of the computer does not lie solely in its ability to exhibit humanoid behavior. It lies even more in the fact that we can specify with complete rigor the system of processes that make the computer exhibit this behavior — we can write a *program* that constitutes a theory of the computer's behavior in literally the same sense that the equations of Newtonian dynamics constitute a theory of the motions of the solar system. The genuinely new analytic instrument available for explaining human behavior is the program.

Thinking is to be explained by writing a program for a thinking process. If the program is complicated — as it usually is — so that it is hard to predict what behavior it will produce, we code the program for a computer. Then we compare the behavior of the computer so programmed with the behavior of a human subject performing the same tasks. Thus, the programming language provides a precise language for expressing theories of mental processes; the computer provides a powerful machine for grinding out the specific behavioral consequences of the theories, and for comparing these consequences in detail — sentence by sentence — with the verbal behavior of human subjects.

The methodology provides a powerful test of the sufficiency of the theories. For if a program is vague or incomplete, the computer will not operate — it will not do what we assert it will do. Conversely, if we are able to write a program that, realized on a computer, simulates human behavior closely, we can assert that we have discovered a set of mechanisms at least *sufficient* to account for the behavior. No dark corners are left in which vitalism or mysticism can lurk — nor even the vagueness of "mediational" hypotheses.

These are large claims. It is time to present the evidence for them. We can only do this, however, after stating a little more fully what we mean by an explanation of behavior and how a computer program can constitute an explanation of the processes of human thinking and problem solving.

What is an Explanation?

To *explain* a phenomenon means to show how it inevitably results from the actions and interactions of precisely specified mechanisms that are in some sense "simpler" than the phenomenon itself. Thus, a chemical reaction is explained by reducing it to the interactions of atoms having specified properties. A spinal reflex is explained by reducing it to a sequence of neural and synaptic processes.

For complex phenomena there may be, and usually are, several *levels* of explanation; we do not explain the phenomena at once in terms of the simplest mechanisms, but reduce them to these simplest mechanisms through several stages of explanation. We explain digestion by reducing it to chemical events; we explain the chemical reactions in terms of atomic processes; we explain the atomic processes in terms of the interactions of subatomic particles. Every flea has its little fleas, and the scientist's view accepts no level of explanation as "ultimate."

Programs explain behavior in terms of an intermediate level of mechanism, simpler than the behavior itself but more complex than neural events. The intermediate mechanisms provide a theory of the behavior, and provide also a starting point for the next stage of reduction — either to neural events or to still another level of mechanism above the neurological.

Concretely, human thinking is to be explained in terms of precisely specified simple mechanisms called *elementary information processes.* Elementary information processes are organized into complex processes — thinking, problem solving, verbal behavior — by *programs.* Programs are long, branching sequences of elementary processes. In the course of behavior, at each branch point a particular continuation is selected and followed conditionally on the outcome of a simple test (itself an elementary information process) of the identity or difference of a pair of *symbols.*

In summary, the study and explanation of complex human behavior is to proceed as follows:

1. Behavior is to be explained by specifying programs that will, in fact, produce the behavior. These programs consist of systems of elementary information processes.

2. Elementary information processes are to be explained by showing how they can be reduced to known physiological processes in the central nervous system and its appendages.

Since we are concerned here with only the first of these two tasks of explanation — the reduction of behavior to information processes — what guarantee exists against introducing vitalism by the back door? What is to prevent one of the elementary processes from harboring some kind of *elan vital*? Since explanation at the second level has not been carried out, we cannot guarantee directly that the human nervous system contains mechanisms capable of performing each of the elementary information processes. But we can insist that there exist *some* mechanism — a mechanism that can be explained completely at the level of physics — capable of performing all these processes. We can demand that the processes and the programs constructed of them be realized in a digital computer. If the computer executes the processes and, in executing them, simulates human thinking, then no vitalistic mystery can be hidden in the postulates.

We are not talking of a crude analogy between the nervous system and computer "hardware." The inside of a computer does not look like a brain any more than it looks like a missile when it is calculating its trajectory. There is every reason to suppose that simple information processes are performed by quite different mechanisms in computer and brain, and we shall sometime want to know what the brain mechanisms are as we now know the mechanisms of the computer. However, once we have devised mechanisms in a computer for performing elementary information processes that appear very similar to those performed by the brain (albeit by quite different mechanisms at the next lower level), we can construct an explanation of thinking in terms of these information processes that is equally valid for a computer so programmed and for the brain.

Programs as Explanations

We have described a program as a conditionally branching sequence of elementary information processes. To explain a behavior path by a program is quite analogous to explaining the path of a planetary system by a system of differential equations. The differential equations determine what will happen next (during the next "infinitesimal" interval of time) as a function of the exact state of the system at the beginning of the interval. The program determines what the mechanism will do next as a function of its exact state at the moment — this state being dependent, in turn, on the previous history of the system and its current environment.

How is the "right" program discovered — the one that explains the behavior? In the same way that the correct theory is found for any phenomena. One recipe is this: tape-record some human subjects who are thinking aloud while solving problems (make observations of the phenomena); try to write a computer program that you think will simulate the human protocols (formulate some differential equations); realize the program on a computer, and determine what behavior path it would follow when confronted with the same problems as the human subjects (integrate the equations numerically); compare the simulated with the actual behavior (compare the predictions with the data); modify the program on the basis of the discrepancies that are discovered (modify the equations). Repeat until you are satisfied with the fit.

A number of investigators have independently proposed this general path to the explanation of higher mental processes, and its origins can be traced back at least to Ach and the Wurzburg School. In recent times, perhaps the most explicit examples are to be found in deGroot's investigation of the thought processes of chess players (4) and in *A Study of Thinking* by Bruner and his associates (3). Bruner uses the term *strategy*, borrowed from the mathematical theory of games, for what we have called a "program." What the digital computer and the techniques of programming add is the machinery that gives us hope of following this path, not merely in principle and in general, but in fact and in detail.

Computer Simulation of a Program

The methodology outlined above requires that a computer simulate the sequence of verbal utterances of a human subject (or other symbolic behavior, such as button pushing). It is easy to understand how this can be done once we recognize that computers fundamentally have nothing to do with numbers. It is only by historical accident that we perceive computers as mechanisms for manipulating numerical symbols. They are, in fact, extremely general devices for manipulating symbols of any kind; and the elementary processes required to simulate human thinking could be performed by a computer that had no special capacity for rapid arithmetic — that could do no more than simple counting. The programs we shall describe make no essential use of the computer's arithmetic processes.

What processes can a general purpose computer perform? Some of the crucial ones are these:

1. It can *read* a symbol — transform a symbol presented to its input mechanisms into a different representation of that symbol in its internal storage (transform a pattern of holes on a punched card into a pattern of magnetism in core storage). The relation between the external and internal representation is quite flexible, almost arbitrary, and can be altered by the program.
2. It can *move* a symbol — reproduce in a storage location a symbol that is present in another storage location, with or without a change in the form of representation.
3. It can *generate* a symbol — create and store a pattern in one of its modes of internal representation.
4. It can *compare* two symbols, executing one program step if they are identical, but a different one if they are not.
5. It can *associate* two symbols, allowing access to one symbol (the associated symbol) when the other is given.

Programs can be written that combine these simple processes into processes that are slightly more complex. For example, a computer can be programmed to manipulate a series of symbols as a *list*, so that it can perform such operations as: "Put *this* symbol at the end of *that* list," or "Find a symbol on *this* list which is identical with *that* symbol." Such list structures, and the processes for operating on them, have many resemblances to human memory and association.

Finally, still more complex programs can be composed that enable a computer to respond to instructions like: "Solve the problems on the following list," "Print out the steps of the proof, giving the justification for each step," "Print out the processes used at each step of the problem-solving process: the methods, what is being noticed and attended to, what plans are formed, what sub-problems are created." When this last stage has been reached, the *trace* that the computer prints out while it is attempting to solve the problem can be compared, line by line, with the tape recording of the human thinking-aloud protocol. If the stream of words produced by the two processes is almost the same, then the computer program that produced the trace is an explanation of the thought process of the human subject in every significant sense of the word.

Testing Programs as Theories

The phrase "almost the same" glides over the whole problem of goodness of fit. Unfortunately, existing statistical theory offers no solution to the problem in the situation we have described, nor can we propose any simple answer. A rough and ready answer is that the evidence provided by five minutes of thinking aloud and the corresponding trace is so voluminous as to scarcely leave room for doubt whether a first approximation has been achieved or not. This is a subjective answer, and we should like to discuss a slightly more objective, though weaker one:

TURING'S TEST

No two human subjects solving the same problem will have the same program or produce the same protocol. Hence, any single program can only be a precise theory of the behavior of a single subject. There must be, however, close qualitative similarities among the programs and protocols of appropriately selected classes of subjects — if not, then it is meaningless to speak of a theory of human problem solving. Suppose that we mix ten traces of computer programs and ten human protocols in an urn. Suppose that a properly qualified human observer is unable to separate, with more than chance success, the protocols produced by the computer programs from those produced by the humans. Then we shall say that the programs which produced the computer traces pass *Turing's test*,[1] and provide a satisfactory explanation of the human protocols.

Turing's test can be applied in stronger or weaker forms. Comparison of the move chosen by a chess program with the moves chosen by human players in the same position would be a weak test. The program might have chosen its move by quite a different process from that used by the humans. For the task environment itself defines what are appropriate behaviors, and *any* mechanism capable of behaving adaptively in the environment might be expected to exhibit about the same external behavior. Similarity of function does not guarantee similarity of structure or of process.

If data are gathered, however, by the thinking-aloud technique or by other means, that indicate the processes used to select the behavior, it may, and usually will be possible to distinguish different ways of arriving at the result. If the program makes the same analysis as the humans, notices the same features of the board, overlooks the same traps, then we will infer, and properly, that down to some level of detail, the program provides an explanation of the human processes. The more minute and detailed the comparison between program and behavior, the greater will be the opportunities for detecting differences between the predicted and actual behaviors.

This method of theory building and testing meets the problem of induction no better and no worse than other methods. There never is, and can never be, a guarantee that some other theory will not explain the data equally well or better. As in other sciences, it will be time to face this problem when someone actually proposes an alternative theory that explains the data equally well and in comparable detail. Meanwhile, the validity of programs as theories can be tested in stronger and stronger form by pushing the level of detail of matching down toward the level of elementary information processes.

The Existing State of the Art

Several computer programs in existence at the present time can lay more or less claim to being theories of certain kinds of human problem-solving behavior — either by Turing's test or by more stringent criteria. A brief and partial inventory of such programs will give a better picture of where matters stand.

Not every computer program for performing complex tasks constitutes a theory of human problem solving. A program that solves large problems by relying substantially on the arithmetic speed and "brute force" of the computer in performing systematic routine calculations is certainly not a simulation of the program that humans use in solving similar problems. Most of the programs, for example, that have been written for solving operations research problems, and which incorporate such mathematical techniques as linear programming, solution of differential equations, etc., fall in this category. We will say nothing about these, for they were not constructed as simulations of human problem solving, and make no claims as theories of human thinking.

In general, computational routines of the kinds just mentioned tend to use systematic, arithmetic procedures (impracticable without the rapid "inhuman" arithmetic processes in modern computers), which are usually called *algorithms*. The programs that simulate human thinking tend to rely on less systematic, more selective search for paths to the solution. Their selectivity is based on relatively unsystematic rules of thumb, which seldom guarantee a solution to the problem, but which frequently yield solutions with

[1] A test of this sort was first proposed by A. M. Turing (17) in a discussion of whether a machine could think. Given two communication channels (say teletypes), one connected to a human, the other to a machine, a human interrogator was to identify which channel was the machine's. Active questioning was allowed, and the machine's problem was to fool the interrogator, despite the best efforts of the human on the other channel (who it was assumed would side with the interrogator) to reveal his identity.

relatively little processing. They make no use of the fast arithmetic processes available to the computer. We call such procedures *heuristics*. There is no hard-and-fast line between algorithms and heuristics, but it is easy to point to clear-cut examples of each.

We will comment briefly on some examples of types of problem-solving programs that are relevant for the simulation of thinking. The first three that are mentioned — programs for musical composition, for playing games, and for making business and engineering decisions — have generally been constructed with the goal of performing the task and without any special concern for human simulation. The same may be said, to a lesser extent, of the logic and geometry programs. However, many of these programs have a strong heuristic, rather than algorithmic, flavor, because it happens to be easier to solve the problems in question by imitating human tricks than by using the arithmetic speed of the computer.

The other two categories of programs: the General Problem Solver, and programs for "simple" processes, were written as direct attempts to simulate human processes. Most of our discussion will center on them.

1. *A program for musical composition.* In 1956, Hiller and Isaacson at the University of Illinois programmed the ILLIAC to compose music (6). The music has been judged tolerable by some modern ears, but could not pass Turing's test before an audience of musicians. Its interest lies in the fact that its rules of counterpoint approximate those of Palestrina.

2. *The Logic Theorist.* In 1956, J. C. Shaw and the authors programmed JOHNNIAC at THE RAND Corporation to discover proofs for theorems in the *Principia Mathematica* of Whitehead and Russell (9, 14). The program, in several variants, was able to prove about 70 per cent of the theorems in Chapter 2 of *Principia*. The program, distinctly heuristic in character, was derived largely from the introspections of its authors. Some learning programs were later incorporated in it that definitely modified its behavior, usually in an adaptive way. It could certainly not pass Turing's test if compared with thinking-aloud protocols, although many of its qualitative features match those of human problem-solvers (10).

3. *Game-playing Programs.* A program written by A. Samuel for checkers plays a strong game and incorporates some powerful learning programs, but cannot be considered a simulation of human checker-playing — it explores far too many continuations. Chess programs written by M. Wells and his associates at Los Alamos, and by A. Bernstein and his associates at IBM (1), can beat novices but not passable amateurs. These programs explore large numbers of continuations (800,000 per move in the Los Alamos program, and about 2,500 per move in the IBM program), although the latter also incorporates certain heuristics for finding plausible moves that resemble those used by human chess players.

A third chess player has been programmed by J. C. Shaw and the authors (11), incorporating about the same amount of selectivity as the program of a strong human player. The first aim has been to write a program that would play good chess, with simulation as a secondary objective. The program plays a game about as strong as the other two, with much more selectivity in its explorations, but could not yet pass Turing's test. (Parenthetically, the attraction of chess for these researches lies in the fact that it is a game of sufficient complexity and irregularity that a heuristic rather than an algorithmic approach is almost certainly required for strong play.)

4. *Business and Engineering Decisions.* Programs have been written, with purely pragmatic aims, for preparing payrolls, maintaining inventories and making purchases, designing electric motors and transformers, and the like, which incorporate many heuristic elements and which are probably not very dissimilar from the human processes they replace (2). None of these programs has been systematically investigated for the light it might throw on human processes;

probably none could pass Turing's test. Currently, an explicitly heuristic program is being written by F. Tonge (16) to handle an assembly line balancing problem that has proved too complex for existing algorithms.

5. *Geometry.* A theorem prover for geometry, developed by Gelernter and Rochester of IBM (5), produced its first complete proof in April, 1959. It probably will compete in skill with high school geometry students, and incorporates a number of heuristics used by humans — although fewer than are used by a skillful student. It will not, therefore, pass Turing's test.

6. *The General Problem Solver.* The Logic Theorist was superseded in 1957–58 by the General Problem Solver, which has been hand simulated but not yet fully tested on the computer. This new program will be described more fully in the next section. Its heuristics are based on general ideas for reasoning about problems in terms of means and ends, and are not specific to logic or any other subject matter. It was derived largely from analysis of human protocols, and probably can pass Turing's test for a limited range of tasks.

7. *"Simple" Human Behaviors.* The work on the Logic Theorist led to conjectures that certain "simple" psychological tasks, like responding in a partial reinforcement experiment or memorizing nonsense syllables, actually involve a great deal of problem-solving behavior. These conjectures are now being explored by J. Feldman, in a program for a binary choice experiment, and by E. Feigenbaum in an EPAM (Elementary Perceiver and Memorizer) program. These programs are being designed to simulate the behavior of subjects, in response to experimental instructions, over a range of standard psychological experiments. It is too early to evaluate them beyond saying that they show great promise of explaining the processes involved in recognizing patterns in sequences, distinguishing stimuli and responses of high and low similarity, serial and paired-associate memorizing, and the like. Both programs would have a good chance to pass Turing's test.

The General Problem Solver

To give substance to these generalities, we shall conclude by examining more closely what is perhaps the most advanced of these programs at the present time: The General Problem Solver (12, 13). The General Problem Solver was devised to simulate the behavior of some specific human subjects solving problems in symbolic logic in a task situation devised by O. K. Moore and Scarvia Anderson (8). Some thirty thinking-aloud protocols for these tasks have been recorded in the laboratory at Carnegie Tech. Comparison of these with data obtained for sixty-four subjects by Moore without requiring the subjects to think aloud indicates that there are no substantial differences in process under the two conditions.[2]

GPS, as we shall call the program, is called "general" because it is not limited to the task for which it was originally devised. Hand simulation indicates it can also solve the Whitehead and Russell logic problems, do trigonometric identities, perform formal integration and differentiation, and, with a small extension to the program, solve algebraic equations. As will be seen, there is reason to hope that it can be extended to an even wider range of tasks.

Before comparing GPS in detail with human behavior, we should like to observe that it does solve problems. Hence its program constitutes a system of mechanisms, constructed from elementary information processes, that is a sufficient system for performing certain tasks that humans perform. However much it may prove necessary to modify the details of the program for close human simulation, in its present form it constitutes an unequivocal demonstration that a

[2] Professor Moore kindly provided us with the full data on his subjects prior to publication.

mechanism can solve problems by functional reasoning.

In simplest terms, GPS is a program for reasoning about means and ends. It grew out of our observation that the protocols of laboratory subjects contained many statements of the following sorts: "So in all these now I have notes as to exactly *what I can do with them.*" (Paraphrase: "Here are some means at my disposal, what ends will they serve?") "I'm looking at the idea of reversing these two things now . . . *then I'd have* a similar group at the beginning." (Paraphrase: "If I use means X, I will achieve Y." "I'm *looking for a way*, now, to get rid of that symbol." ("What is the means to achieve this end?") "And now *I'd use* Rule 1." ("I'll apply means X.")

Closer scrutiny of the protocols reveals that the vast majority of the statements in them fall within this general framework. Simulating the behavior of these subjects requires a program that can handle problems in this kind of functional language. Further, the functional language makes no reference to the specific subject matter of the problem — in this instance symbolic logic. The program must be organized to separate its general problem-solving procedures from the application of these to a specific task. GPS is such a program.

The adjective "general" does not imply that GPS can reason about all or most kinds of problems; or that it will simulate all or most human problem-solving activity. It simply means that the program contains no reference to the task content, and hence is usable for tasks other than the one for which it was devised.

GPS operates on problems that can be formulated in terms of *objects* and *operators.* An operator is something that can be applied to certain objects to produce different objects (as a saw applied to logs produces boards). The objects can be described by the *features* they possess (boards have flat parallel sides), and by the *differences* between pairs of objects (a 2 x 4 is thicker than a 1 x 4). Operators may be restricted to apply to only certain kinds of objects (nails are used on wood, not steel); and there may be operators applied to several objects as inputs, producing one or more objects as output (joining four beams to produce a frame).

Various problems can be formulated in a task environment containing objects and operators: to find how to transform one object into another; to find an object with specified features; to modify an object so that a specified operator can be applied to it; and so on. In the task environment confronting our laboratory subjects, the objects were symbolic logic expressions (which the subjects were told were messages in code). The operators were

1. $AvB \Leftrightarrow BvA$
   $A \cdot B \Leftrightarrow B \cdot A$
2. $A \supset B \Leftrightarrow -B \supset -A$
3. $AvA \Leftrightarrow A$
   $A \cdot A \Leftrightarrow A$
4. $Av(BvC) \Leftrightarrow (AvB)vC$
   $A \cdot (B \cdot C) \Leftrightarrow (A \cdot B) \cdot C$
5. $AvB \Leftrightarrow -(-A \cdot -B)$
   $A \cdot B \Leftrightarrow -(-Av - B)$
6. $A \supset B \Leftrightarrow -AvB$
   $AvB \Leftrightarrow -A \supset B$
7. $Av(B \cdot C) \Leftrightarrow (AvB) \cdot (AvC)$
   $A \cdot (BvC) \Leftrightarrow (A \cdot B)v(A \cdot C)$
8. $A \cdot B \Rightarrow A$
   $A \cdot B \Rightarrow B$

FIG. 23-1. Rules for Transforming Logic Expressions.

twelve rules of logic for transforming one or two input expressions into an output expression. Figure 23-1 gives the first eight of these rules, enough for our illustrative purposes. For example, by Rule 1 an expression of the form $(A \cdot B)$ could be transformed into $(B \cdot A)$, thus reversing the order of the symbols. The problems given the subjects were to "recode," using the rules, one or more given logic expressions into a different logic expression. One problem, for example, was to transform $R \cdot (-P \supset Q)$ into $(QvP) \cdot R$.

A statement like: "I'm looking for a way, now, to get rid of that horseshoe" expresses a goal. The goal in this instance is to eliminate a difference (the "horseshoe" in the original expression versus the "wedge" in the desired expression) between one object and another. The goals that the subjects mention in their protocols take a variety of forms. We have incorporated three types of goals, which account for the vast majority

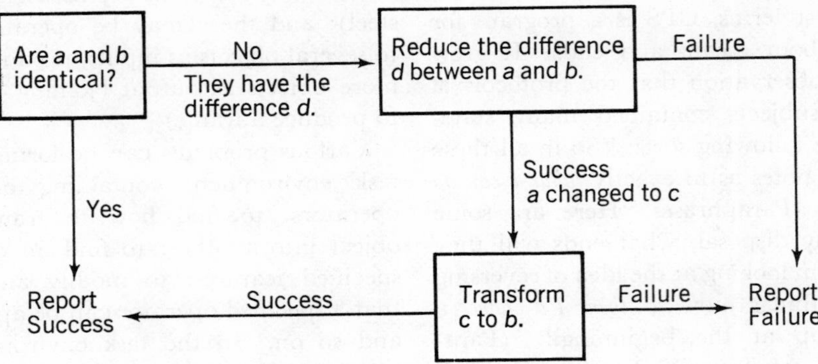

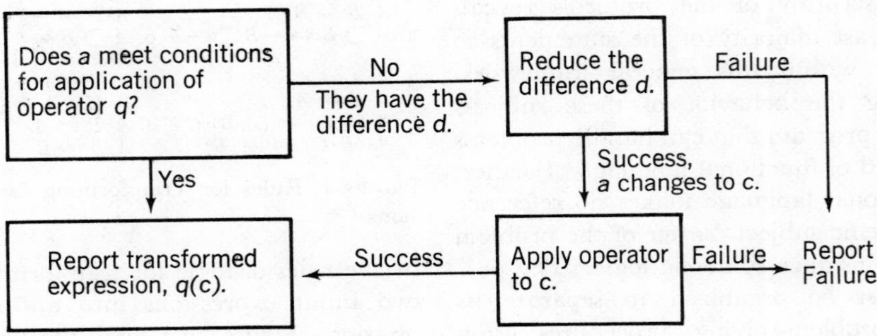

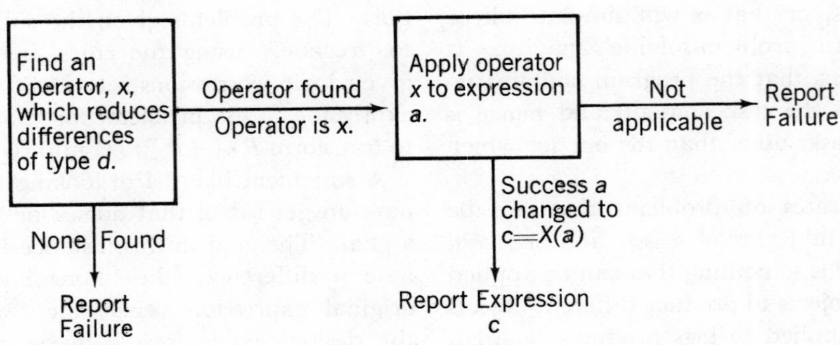

Fig. 23-2. Methods Associated with GPS Goals

of goal statements, in the present version of GPS. They are:

Goal Type No. 1: Find a way to *transform* object *a* into object *b* (i.e., a sequence of operators to accomplish the transformation).

Goal Type No. 2: *Apply* operator *q* to object *a* (or to an object obtained from *a* by transformations).

Goal Type No. 3: *Reduce* the difference, *d*, between object *a* and object *b* by modifying *a*.

The problems initially given the subjects established transform goals; "getting rid of the horseshoe" expresses a reduce goal; "And now I'd use Rule 1" states an apply goal.

To attain a goal, consideration of the goal must evoke in the problem-solver some idea of one or more means that might be relevant. The subject, for example, who says "I'm looking for a way, now, to get rid of that horseshoe," follows this statement with, "Ah . . . here it is, Rule 6. So I'd apply Rule 6 to the second part of what we have up there." Applying Rule 6 (see Figure 23-1) has been evoked as a method for getting rid of horseshoes.

Thus, the evoking process is represented in GPS by associating with each type of goal one or more methods for attaining a goal of that type. These are shown in Figure 23-2. Method No. 1, associated with Transform goals, consists in: (*a*) matching the objects *a* and *b* to find a difference, *d*, between them; (*b*) setting up the Type No. 3 subgoal of reducing *d*, which if successful produces a new transformed object, *c*; (*c*) setting up the Type No. 1 subgoal of transforming *c* into *b*. If this last goal is achieved, the original Transform goal is achieved. The match in step (*a*) tests for the more important differences (in terms of some priority list) first.

Method No. 2, for achieving an Apply goal, consists in: (*a*) determining if the operator can be applied by setting up a Type No. 1 goal for transforming *a* into the input form of the operator *q* [which we call $C(q)$]; (*b*) if successful, the output object is produced from the output form of $q[P(q)]$.

Method No. 3, for achieving a Reduce goal, consists in: (*a*) searching for an operator that is relevant to reducing the difference, *d*; (*b*) if one is found, setting up the Type No. 2 goal of applying the operator, which if attained produces the modified object.

To see how GPS goes about applying these goal types and methods to the solution of problems, consider a concrete example. We will use the problem mentioned earlier: to "recode" the expression, L_1, $R \cdot (-P \supset Q)$ into the expression L_0, $(QvP) \cdot R$. As we go along we will explain the recoding rules as far as is necessary to understand the example.

GPS begins by establishing the Type No. 1 goal of transforming L_1 into L_0. Among the information processes available to it — built up from the elementary processes, are a number of *tests* for the possible differences among pairs of expressions, for example:

1. A test whether the same or different *variables* (letters) appear in the two expressions;
2. A test whether each variable occurs the same or a different *number of times;*
3. A test whether a variable or group occurs in the same or in a different *position;*
4. A test whether a pair of connectives $(\cdot, v, \supset)$ is the same or different.

And so on. The tests may be applied to whole expressions or to corresponding parts of expressions (e.g., $(-P \supset Q)$ and (QvP)).

Method No. 1 applies these tests in order. It discovers a difference in position of the *R*'s in L_1 and L_0, and establishes the Type No. 3 goal of reducing this difference. For each difference, it has available a list of operators that are possibly relevant to removing a difference of that kind. (These lists can be constructed by GPS itself by examining the set of available operators.) In this case, it discovers that Rule 1, which transforms an expression of form $(A \cdot B)$ or (AvB) into an expression of form $(B \cdot A)$ or (BvA), respectively, affects differences in position. Consequently, it establishes the Type No. 2 subgoal of applying Rule 1 to L_1. This can be done by identifying *R* with *A* and $(-P \supset Q)$

with B in the rule, thus producing L_2, $(-P \supset Q) \cdot R$ as the output expression.

This done, the original goal now sets up the new subgoal of transforming L_2 into L_0. Repeating the cycle, a difference in connectives is found between the left-hand sides of L_2 and L_0, respectively; a rule, R_6, is found that changes connectives by transforming $(-A \supset B)$ into (AvB), hence transforms $(-P \supset Q) \cdot R$ into L_3, $(PvQ) \cdot R$.

A third repetition of the basic cycle discovers the difference in position between (PvQ) in L_3 and (QvP) in L_0, and applies R_1 to remove the difference. Finally, GPS discovers that the product of this transformation is identical with L_0, and declares the problem solved. We may summarize the steps as follows:

Step	Expression	Justification for Step
L_1	$R \cdot (-P \supset Q)$	Given
L_2	$(-P \supset Q) \cdot R$	Rule 1
L_3	$(PvQ) \cdot R$	Rule 6 inside parenthesis
L_0	$(QvP) \cdot R$	Rule 1 inside parenthesis

Comparison with Human Behavior

Granted that GPS can solve this problem, and many that are a good deal more difficult, why do we suppose that the processes of GPS resemble in any way the processes a human would use in solving the same problem? Let us compare GPS's processes, as just narrated, with the content of the protocol of a human subject solving the same problem. We shall let the reader judge whether the two processes are or are not closely similar. (Neither the particular problem nor the human protocol we shall examine was used in devising GPS.)

FIG. 23-3. Simulation No. 7 of Subject No. 9 on O. K. Moore Problem α 1.

Line	Simulation	Protocol
1	L_0: $(QvP) \cdot R$	(Expression to be obtained)*
2	L_1: $R \cdot (-P \supset Q)$	(Expression given at start)
3	Goal 0: *Transforms* L_1 and L_0	(Goal set by experimenter)
4	Match gives position difference (Δp)	I'm looking at the idea of reversing these two things now.
5	Goal 1: *Reduce* Δp between L_1 and L_0	(Thinking about reversing what?)
6	Search list of rules	The *R*'s . . .
7	Goal 2: *Apply* R_1 to L_1	
8	Match: R_1 applicable	
9	Test rule functions: reduces Δp	then I'd have a similar group at the beginning
10	no others	but that seems to be . . .
11	*Set to execute* R_1 when analysis complete	I could easily leave something like that 'til the end,
12	Goal 3: *Transform* right L_1 into left L_0	except then I'll . . .
13	Match gives position difference (Δp)	
14	Goal 4: *Reduce* Δp between right L_1 and left L_0	
15	Search list of rules	
16	Goal 5: *Apply* R_1 to right L_1	
17	Match: R_1 fails, right L_1 has $\supset$ (Δc)	(Applying what rule?)
18	Goal 6: *Apply* R_2 to right L_1	Applying, . . . for instance, 2.
19	Match: R_2 applicable	
20	Test rule functions: reduces Δp,	
21	but introduces unwanted $-(\Delta s)$	That would require a sign change. (Try to keep
22	Reject goal	talking, if you can)
23	Goal 7: *Apply* R_3 to right L_1	Well . . . then I look down at rule 3
24	Match: R_3 not applicable	and that doesn't look any too practical

* Statements in parentheses are experimenter's statements and explanatory comments. All other statements are the subject's.

25	Goal 8: *Apply* R_4 to L_1	Now 4 looks interesting.
26	Match: R_4 not applicable†	It's got three parts similar to that . . . and . . .
27		there are dots so the connective . . . seems to work easily enough,
28	Test rule functions: doesn't reduce Δp	but there's no switching of order.
29	Reject goal	
30	Goals 9 to 13: *Apply* R_5 to R_9 to L_1	
31	All goals fail on match	
32	or test of function.	
33	Search rules again, but don't reject without	I need that P and a Q changed so . . .
34	attacking subproblem	
35	Goal 14: *Apply* R_1 to right L_1	
36	Match: R_1 fails, right L_1 has $\supset$ (Δc).	I've got a horseshoe there. That doesn't seem
37	Test rule functions: reduces Δp, no others	practical any place through here.
38	*Set to execute* R_1, if applicable	
39	Goal 15: *Reduce* Δc between right L_1 and R_1	I'm looking for a way now, to get rid of that horseshoe.
40	Search list of rules, for rule with $\supset$ that	
41	reduces Δc.	
42	Goal 16: *Apply* R_6 to right L_1	Ah . . . here it is, Rule 6.
43	Match: R_6 applicable	
44	Test rule functions: reduces Δc	
45	reduces Δs	
46	*Set to execute* R_6 when analysis complete	
47	Goal 17: *Transform* right L_1, after reducing	
48	Δp, Δc, Δs, into left L_0	
49	Match: transformed right L_1 identical	
50	with left L_0	
51	Goal achieved, and analysis complete	
52	*Execute* R_6 on right L_1 (from line 46)	So I'd apply Rule 6 to the second part of what
53		we have up there.
54		(Want to do that?)
55		Yeah.
56	L_2: R$\cdot$(PvQ)	(OK, to line 1 you apply R_6. Line 2 is $R\cdot(PvQ)$
57	*Execute* R_1 on right L_2 (from line 38)	And now I'd use Rule 1.
58		(Rule 1 on what part? You can use it with the entire expression or with the right part.)
59		I'd use it in both places.
60		(Well, we'll do them one at a time . . . which do
61		you want first?)
62		Well, do it with P and Q.
63		
64	L_3: $R\cdot(QvP)$	($R\cdot(QvP)$. Now the entire expression?)
65	*Execute* R_1 on L_3 (from line 11)	Yeah.
66	L_4: $(QvP)\cdot R$	(On line 3, Rule 1 . . . you'd get $(QvP)\cdot R$)
67	Match: L_4 identical with L_0	And . . . that's it.
		(That's it all right, OK . . . that wasn't too hard.)

† But the subject mistakenly thinks R_4 is applicable; therefore tests its functions.

In the right-hand half of Figure 23-3 we reproduce, word for word, the human protocol, omitting only some introductory paragraphs. In the left-hand half we reproduce the trace (hand simulated) of a program that, we believe, approximates closely the processes of the subject's thinking. This program is not identical with the one we described for GPS, but incorporates some modifications to fit it to the empirical data. Basically, however, the objects, operators, differences, goal types, and methods that appear in this trace are those of GPS.

Scanning down the protocol, we see that the subject sets up the goal of transforming L_1 into L_0, notices the difference in order of terms in the two expressions, and considers reversing them (lines 4-9). Simultaneously, the program is establishing the same goal (Goal 0), noticing the same difference (line 4), discovering that Rule 1 reduces this difference (line 9), and fixating the idea of applying Rule 1 when the analysis is complete. (This distinction between overt and covert action is one of the modifications introduced.)

Next, the subject scans down the list of rules — there is explicit evidence that he looks at Rules 2, 3, and 4 — rejecting each because it doesn't apply (Rule 3), would introduce a new difference ("That would require a sign change"), or doesn't perform the function of switching the *P* and *Q* (Rule 4). Simultaneously, the program is establishing the goal of reducing the difference in order of *P* and *Q* (Goal 4), scanning the list of rules, and rejecting them for the same reasons.

Next, the subject observes that the horseshoe creates difficulty in changing the *P* and *Q* (lines 36 to 37), and erects the goal of eliminating the horseshoe, discovering that Rule 6 will do this (line 42). He applies Rule 6, then Rule 1 to the right-hand subexpression, then Rule 1 to the whole expression, and observes that he has solved the problem. Simultaneously, the program undertakes a second search for a rule that will reverse *P* and *Q* (lines 33-34), but now tackles as a subproblem getting an otherwise relevant rule to be applicable. Considering Rule 1, it establishes the subgoal (Goal 15) of changing the horseshoe to a wedge, finds Rule 6, checks whether this will solve the problem, then executes Rules 6, 1, and 1 (on the whole expression) in that order.

There are a number of interesting points of fine structure in the comparison of program with protocol that we cannot go into here. For example, the program searched all the rules the first time through, while the protocol of the subject gives evidence for only the first few. The cause of the discrepancy is not at all clear. The reader can use Figure 23-3 to discover and examine a number of such features.

In testing whether this program provides a good theory, or explanation, of the behavior of the human subject, we can raise two kinds of questions:

a) How much did we have to modify GPS to construct a program that would fit this subject's protocol?

b) How good is the fit of the modified program to the protocol?

In the next paragraphs we will discuss some of the methodological issues that are imbedded in these questions. We are, of course, considering a test of simulation that is much stronger than Turing's test, and perhaps the reader can be persuaded from the evidence thus far that GPS and its variants will pass Turing's test.

FITTING A GENERAL PROGRAM TO SPECIFIC BEHAVIOR

The form the theory takes is a program — in this case, GPS. But, as in the natural sciences, the theory is more appropriately expressed as a *class* of programs to be particularized and applied to concrete situations by specifying parameter values, initial conditions, and boundary conditions. For example, one subject may attach higher priorities to a difference in variables, another to a difference in connectives. GPS is fitted to these subjects' behavior by modifying the program to represent the difference in priorities — this is precisely what we did in constructing the example shown in Figure 23-3.

As in all fitting of theory to data, we must watch our degrees of freedom. If we are allowed to introduce a parameter change or a new mechanism for each bit of behavior to be explained, we will have explained nothing. The program must be a parsimonious description of the mechanisms generating the behavior. Let us point out — to be sure the reader understands — that the trace is the output of the program, and not modifiable at will. Any change in the program affects the trace in a number of places. A change to reduce one discrepancy — say the apparently more exhaustive initial search of the list of rules mentioned above — is likely to introduce new discrepancies. In the case in point, we were unable to find any simple change in the program that would remove this particular discrepancy, and yet leave the rest of the fit as good as it is.

COMPARING A TRACE WITH BEHAVIOR

The computer does not yet speak fluent idiomatic English, hence we cannot compare the trace with the subject's protocol literally word for word. The trace says: "Goal 1: Reduce Δp between L_1 and L_0." The subject says: "I'm looking at the idea of reversing these two things now." The trace says: "Goal 6: Apply R_3 to L_1." The subject says: ". . . then I look down at Rule 3." Instead of having the computer speak English, we could hope for a code (in the psychologist's sense of the word) that would reduce the human conversation to "problem-solving content." Again, techniques are currently lacking for doing this, but perhaps we can agree that a large amount of the content of the subject's remarks is captured in the computer's "phrases."

Further, the trace describes the information processes uniformly down to a specified level of detail, while the protocol fluctuates greatly in its explicitness — sometimes providing more detail, but usually much less. Thus in our search example, it is certainly possible that the subject scanned the entire set of rules, but simply failed to mention them after the first few. This kind of mismatch is probably inevitable, at least in the present state of our knowledge. The most we can aim for is a trace that avoids sins of omission and contradiction, although it may sometimes speak when the subject remains silent.

We do not mean that the level of detail in the protocol is arbitrary — in fact, we suspect that it is very much related to the mechanisms and functions of consciousness in problem-solving and learning. The distinction between conscious and unconscious does not appear in the present GPS mechanisms, and hence cannot be reflected in a non-arbitrary way in the trace.

The exhibit presented here provides a sample of the work that has been done in comparing GPS, and variants of it, with the problem-solving behavior of human subjects. The protocol shown here covers only four minutes of behavior. Relatively little simulation has been carried out to date — it is a painstaking activity. Our most intensive empirical study thus far has been the simulation of the behavior of a subject solving a considerably more difficult problem over a period of thirty minutes. We shall report on our findings in more detail elsewhere, but the following conclusions, from this intensive study, and from less detailed examination of about twenty other protocols seem reasonably certain:

1. Measured in terms of time and numbers of words, virtually all the behavior of subjects falls within the general framework of means-end analysis. The three goal types we have described account for at least three-fourths of the subjects' goals, and the additional goal types for which we find evidence are close relatives to those we have mentioned.

2. The three methods we have described represent the vast majority of the methods applied to these problems. One additional exceedingly important method — planning — has been incorporated in GPS (13), but limits on time prevent us from discussing it here. Planning appears in several different forms in the protocols, but in all of them it serves the function of temporarily omitting details in order to see if the main line of reasoning will yield a solution.

3. There are evidences that the programs of the subjects change — that they learn — in the course of problem solving. For example, initially they have to scan the rules, one by one, to find an applicable rule; later, once they create the goal of reducing a specified difference, they choose almost instantaneously a rule that is relevant to that particular difference. No clear distinction between learning and problem solving appears. Some of the learning takes place — and is used — in the course of attempting a single problem (one-half hour). In fact, the GPS network of goals and subgoals constitutes a "learning about the problem," so that on successive phases of the solution, the subject behaves very differently. Conversely, some of the learning occurs as the result of specific problem-solving activity devoted to learning.

Conclusion

In this paper we have described a method for the study of human problem-solving and other higher mental processes, have given an example of an application of the method, and have indicated the theory of human problem solving that emerges. We have drawn our examples largely from the work of ourselves and our associates, because it represents the only current undertaking with which we are familiar that includes detailed simulation of human protocols. There are, of course, other investigators who are exploring human problem solving, on the one hand, and simulation techniques, on the other.

The *method* consists in constructing a theory of central processes in the form of a program, or class of programs, demonstrating the sufficiency of the theory to produce problem-solving behavior by realizing it in a computer, and testing the theory against human processes by comparing the trace generated by the program with the protocol of a human subject.

The *application* consisted in constructing a general problem-solving program, capable of solving problems in logic and other domains, demonstrating that a computer so programmed could solve problems, and comparing its processes with those of human subjects in a problem situation designed by O. K. Moore.

The *theory* of human problem solving consists in a program, constructed of elementary information processes, for reasoning in terms of goals and methods for attaining those goals. Perhaps the most striking characteristic of this program is that it selects the paths it explores by first determining the functions that have to be performed, and then finding courses of action relevant to those functions. In this and other ways it reflects (and incorporates in determinate mechanisms) the "insightfulness" and "directedness" that has so often been observed as a salient characteristic of human problem solving. In terms of today's nomenclature in psychology, one could describe it as a "mediational" theory that encompasses "Gestalt" processes. Its novelty is that it is definite and that, at least in one problem area, it works.

It is easy to point to difficulties and unfinished tasks. Systematic methods for fitting programs to protocols and testing goodness of fit are nonexistent. The "General" Problem Solver is still highly specific compared with the humans it simulates. The construction and testing of learning programs has hardly begun. Only the most rudimentary programs for simulating "simple" human processes have been written, and these have not been tested. There is little information for selecting the correct set of elementary processes; and even less for connecting them with neural mechanisms.

In spite of this imposing agenda of unfinished business, we wish to record our conviction that it is no longer necessary to talk about the theory of higher mental processes in the future tense. There now exist tools sharp enough to cut into the tough skin of the problem, and these tools have already produced a rigorous, detailed explanation of a significant area of human symbolic behavior.

References

[1] BERNSTEIN, A., and ROBERTS, M. deV. Computer vs. chess player. *Scientific American*, June, 1958, 198: 6.

[2] BRENNER, W. C., SCHINZINGER, R., and SUAREZ, R. M. Application of high speed electronic computers to generator design problems. *AIEE Conference Paper*, 56–940, 1956.

[3] BRUNER, J. S., GOODNOW, J. J., and AUSTIN, C. A. *A Study in Thinking*. John Wiley & Sons, Inc., 1956.

[4] DEGROOT, A. D. *Het Denken van den Schaker*. Amsterdam, 1946.

[5] GELERNTER, H. L., and ROCHESTER, N. Intelligent behavior in problem-solving machines. *IBM Journal of Research and Development*, October, 1958, 2: 4.

[6] HILLER, L. A., Jr., and ISAACSON, L. M. *Experimental Music*. McGraw-Hill Book Co., 1959.

[7] KISTER, J., *et al.*, Experiments in chess. *J. Assoc. Computing Machinery*, April, 1957, 4: 2.

[8] MOORE, O. K., and ANDERSON, S. B. Modern logic and tasks for experiments on problem solving behavior. *J. Psychol.*, 1954, 38: 151–60.

[9] NEWELL, A., SHAW, J. C., and SIMON, H. A. Empirical explorations of the Logic Theory Machine. *Proceedings of the Western Joint Computer Conference*, IRE, February, 1957.

[10] NEWELL, A., SHAW, J. C., and SIMON, H. A. The elements of a theory of human problem solving. *Psych. Rev.*, March, 1958, p. 65.

[11] NEWELL, A., SHAW, J. C., and SIMON, H. A. Chess playing programs and the problem of complexity. *IBM Journal of Research and Development*, October, 1958, 2: 4.

[12] NEWELL, A., SHAW, J. C., and SIMON, H. A. The processes of creative thinking. P1320, The RAND Corporation, August, 1958.

[13] NEWELL, A., SHAW, J. C., and SIMON, H. A. Report on a general problem-solving program. *Proceedings of the International Conference on Information Processing, Paris, June 15–20, 1959*, 256–65. Butterworths, 1960.

[14] NEWELL, A., and SIMON, H. A. The logic theory machine. *Trans. on Information Theory*, Vol. IT-2, No. 3, September, 1956.

[15] OSGOOD, C. E. *Method and Theory in Experimental Psychology*. New York: Oxford University Press, Inc., 1953.

[16] TONGE, F. M. *Summary of a Heuristic Line Balancing Procedure Problem*. P1799, The RAND Corporation, September, 1959.

[17] TURING, A. M. Can a machine think? In, NEWMAN, J. R. *The World of Mathematics*. Vol. IV. New York: Simon and Schuster, Inc., 1956.

Rational Explanation Makes No Use of Empirical Laws 24

from *The Historical Explanation of Actions Reconsidered*

WILLIAM DRAY

. . . Let me try to sketch briefly what I take to be the conceptual foundation of most explanations of human actions in history. The function of an explanation is to resolve puzzlement of some kind. When an historian sets out to explain an historical action, his problem is usually that he does not know what reason the agent had for doing it. To achieve understanding, what he seeks is information about what the agent believed to be the facts of his situation, including the likely results of taking various courses of action considered open to him, and what he wanted to accomplish: his purposes, goals, or motives. Understanding is achieved when the historian can see the reasonableness of a man's doing what this agent did, given the beliefs and purposes referred to; his action can then be explained as having been an "appropriate" one. The point I want to emphasize is that what is brought out by such considerations is a conceptual connection between understanding a man's action and discerning its rationale. As Professor Hook once put it, there is a difference between showing an action to be peculiar and showing it to be confused.[1] There is similarly a difference between showing an action to be routine and showing it to have point.

Explanation which tries to establish a connection between beliefs, motives, and actions of the indicated sort I shall call "rational explanation." The following is a particularly clear example of it. (I hope I may therefore be pardoned for using an example I have used before for the same purpose.)

In trying to account for the success of the invasion of England by William of Orange, Trevelyan asks himself why Louis XIV withdrew military pressure from Holland in the summer of 1688 — this action being, he tells us, "the greatest mistake of his life."[2] His answer is: "Louis calculated that, even if William landed in England there would be a civil war and long troubles, as always in that factious island. Meantime he could conquer Europe at leisure." Furthermore, "he was glad to have the Dutch out of the way (in England) while he dealt a blow at the Emperor Leopold (in Germany)." He thought "it was impossible that the conflict between James and William should not yield him an opportunity." What makes Louis' action understandable here, according to Trevelyan, is our discovery of a "calculation" which was "not as absurd as it looks after the event." Indeed, the calculation shows us just how appropriate Louis' unfortunate action really was to the circumstances regarded as providing reasons for it. In fact, of course, the king, in a sense, miscalculated; and his action was, in a sense, not appropriate to the circumstances. Yet the whole purpose of Trevelyan's explanatory account is to show us that, for a man in Louis' position, with the aims and beliefs he had, the action was appropriate at least to the circumstances as they were envisaged.

For explanations of the kind just illustrated, I should argue, the establishment of a deductive logical connection between *explanans* and *explanandum*, based on the inclu-

From *Philosophy and History* edited by Sidney Hook, New York University Press, New York, 1963, pp. 108–110.

[1] "A Pragmatic Critique of the Historico-Genetic Method," in *Essays in Honor of John Dewey* (New York, 1929), pp. 163–71.

[2] *The English Revolution* (London, 1938), pp. 105–106.

sion of suitable empirical laws in the former, is neither a necessary nor a sufficient condition of explaining. It is not necessary because the aim of such explanations is not to show that the agent was the sort of man who does in fact always do the sort of thing he did in the sort of circumstances he thought he was in. What it aims to show is that the sort of thing he did made perfectly good sense from his own point of view. The establishment of such a connection, if it could be done, would not be a sufficient condition of such explanation either, since it would not itself represent the relation between the agent's beliefs and purposes and what he did as making the latter a reasonable thing to have done.

I might perhaps add — to avoid possible misunderstanding — that the issue between the appropriateness of applying the covering law and rational "models" to such cases has nothing to do with the question whether historical explanations are to be given in terms of people's "ideas" or in terms of "objective" conditions of their natural and social environment. For Professor Hempel, unlike certain materialist philosophers of history, would allow that the explanation of action is peculiar, at least in the sense of usually and properly making reference to the motives and beliefs of the agents concerned. He would admit, I think, that in offering explanations of the *doing* of actions, by contrast with, say, their success or failure, it is not *actual*, but *envisaged*, states of affairs to which we need to refer. Apart from this, however, explanations of action are, for Hempel, "not essentially different from the causal explanations of physics and chemistry."[3] For "the determining motives and beliefs," he says, ". . . have to be classified among the antecedent conditions of a motivational explanation, and there is no formal difference on this account between motivational and causal explanation." In view of what has been said about nondeducibility of the *explanandum*, it should be clear that my quarrel with this is that it does get the form, not the content, of rational explanations wrong.

[3] C. G. Hempel and P. Oppenheim, "The Logic of Explanation," reprinted in H. Feigl and M. Brodbek, *Readings in the Philosophy of Science* (New York, 1953), pp. 327–28.

Covering Laws Are Presupposed by Any Adequate Rational Explanation

25

from *Reasons and Covering Laws in Historical Explanation*

CARL G. HEMPEL

A Necessary Condition of Adequacy for Explanations

The two kinds of explanation by covering laws have this feature in common: they explain an event by showing that, in view of certain particular circumstances and general laws, its occurrence was to be expected (in a purely logical sense), either with deductive certainty or with inductive probability.[1] In virtue of this feature, the two modes of explanation clearly satisfy what is, I submit, a general *condition of adequacy* for any account that is to qualify as a rationally acceptable explanation of a given event. The condition is that any such explanation, i.e., any rationally acceptable answer to a question of the type 'Why did X occur?' must provide information which constitutes good grounds for the belief that X did in fact occur.[2] To state the point a little more fully: If the question 'Why did X occur?' is answered by 'Because Z is, or was, the case,' then the answer does not afford a rationally adequate explanation of X's occurrence unless the information that Z is, or was, the case constitutes good grounds for expecting or believing that X did occur: otherwise, the explanatory information would provide no adequate grounds for saying, as it were: "That explains it — that does show why X occurred!"

Two amplificatory remarks may be indicated. First: the condition of adequacy just stated is to be understood as a necessary condition for an adequate explanation, not as a sufficient one; certain kinds of information — such as the results of a scientific test — may provide excellent grounds for believing that X occurred without in the least explaining why.

Secondly, the covering law concepts of explanation, as schematically represented by the models, refer to the logic, not to the psychology, of explanation, just as metamathematical concepts of proof refer to the logic, not to the psychology, of proving mathematical theorems. Proofs and explanations that are adequate in the psychologic-pragmatic sense (which is of interest and impor-

From *Philosophy and History* edited by Sidney Hook, New York University Press, New York, 1963, pp. 146–149 and 152–158.

[1] For a fuller account of the deductive model see, for example, C. G. Hempel, "The Function of General Laws in History," *The Journal of Philosophy*, 39 (1942), 35–48. Reprinted in *Theories of History*, ed. P. Gardiner (Glencoe, Ill.: Free Press, 1959), pp. 344–56. See also C. G. Hempel and P. Oppenheim, "Studies in the Logic of Explanation," *Philosophy of Science*, 15 (1948), 135–75. Secs. 1–7 of this article are reprinted in *Readings in the Philosophy of Science*, eds. H. Feigl and M. Brodbeck (New York: Appleton-Century-Crofts, 1953), pp. 319–52. The former of these articles also deals with the relevance of covering law explanation to historical inquiry. A more detailed logical analysis of inductive-probabilistic explanation has been attempted in C. G. Hempel, "Deductive-Nomological vs. Statistical Explanation," in *Minnesota Studies in the Philosophy of Science*, eds. H. Feigl and G. Maxwell, III (Minneapolis: University of Minnesota Press, 1962), 98–169.

[2] The condition can readily be formulated so as to cover also explanations that are intended to account, not for an individual event or state of affairs, but for some general uniformity, such as that expressed by Kepler's second law, for example. But explanations of this latter kind — which are discussed, for example, in the second and third of the articles mentioned in n. 1 — need not be considered in this paper.

tance in its own right) of making someone "understand" whatever is being proved or explained may well be achieved — and are in fact often achieved — by procedures that do not meet the formal standards for the concepts of proof or explanation construed in a nonpragmatic, metatheoretical sense. For example, it may be sufficient to call to a person's attention just one particular fact or just some general principle he had overlooked or forgotten or not known at all: taken in combination with other items in his background knowledge, this may make the puzzling item, X, fall into place for him: he will "understand why" X is the case. . . .

The condition of adequacy here proposed conflicts with a claim that has been made particularly, but not exclusively, with respect to historical explanation, namely, that sometimes an event can be quite adequately explained by pointing out that such and such antecedent conditions which are necessary but not sufficient for its occurrence, were realized. As Mr. Dray mentions in his survey of various modifications that have been suggested for the covering law construal of explanation, this idea has been put forward by Frankel and by Gallie; it has also been strongly endorsed by Scriven, who offers this illustration in support of his view.[3] Paresis occurs only in persons who have previously suffered from syphilis; and the occurrence of paresis in a given patient can therefore be properly explained by antecedent syphilitic infection — and thus by reference to an antecedent which constitutes a necessary but far from sufficient condition: for in fact, only quite a small percentage of syphilitics develop paresis. This "explanation" clearly violates the condition of adequacy proposed above. Indeed, as Scriven is the first to point out, on the information that a person has had syphilis, "we must . . . predict that [paresis] will *not* occur."[4] But precisely because the statistical probability for syphilis to lead to paresis is so small, and because therefore on the given information we must rationally expect the given person *not* to have developed paresis, the information that the patient has had syphilis (and that only syphilitics can develop paresis) clearly no more explains the actual occurrence of paresis in this case than a man's winning the first prize in the Irish Sweepstakes is explained by the information that he had bought a ticket (and that only a person who has bought a ticket can win the first prize). . . .

Dray's construal. I now turn to some comments on the central topic of Mr. Dray's paper, the concept of rational explanation. Dray holds that the method, widely used by historians among others, of explaining human actions in terms of underlying reasons cannot be construed as conforming to the covering law pattern: to do so, he says, would be to give the wrong kind of reconstruction, it would get the form of such explanations wrong. In my opinion, Dray's arguments in support of this verdict, and his own alternative construal of such explanations, form a substantial contribution toward the formulation and clarification of the perplexing issues here at stake.

According to Dray, the object of explaining an action by reference to the reasons for which it was done is "to show that what was done was the thing to have done for the reasons given, rather than merely the thing that is done on such occasions, perhaps in accordance with certain laws."[5] The explanatory reasons will include the objectives the agent sought to attain and his beliefs concerning relevant empirical matters, such as the alternative courses of action open to him and their likely consequences. The explanation, according to Dray, then provides "a reconstruction of the agent's *calculation* of means to be adopted toward his chosen end in the light of the circumstances in which he found himself,"[6] and it shows that the agent's choice was appropriate, that it was the thing to do under the circumstances. The appraisal

[3] M. Scriven, "Explanation and Prediction in Evolutionary Theory," *Science*, 130 (1959), 480.

[4] *Ibid.* (Italics the author's.)

[5] W. Dray, *Laws and Explanation in History* (London: Oxford University Press, 1957), p. 124.

[6] Dray, *op. cit.*, p. 122. (Italics the author's.)

thus made of the appropriateness of what was done presupposes, not general laws, but instead what Dray calls a "principle of action," i.e., a normative or evaluative principle of the form 'When in a situation of type C, the thing to do is X.'[7]

The problem of criteria of rationality. Before considering the central question whether, or in what sense, principles of this kind can explain an action, I want to call attention to what seems to me a problematic assumption underlying Dray's concept of a principle of action. As is suggested by the phrase 'the thing to do,' Dray seems to assume (i) that, given a specification of the circumstances in which an agent finds himself (including, I take it, in particular his objectives and beliefs), there is a clear and unequivocal sense in which an action can be said to be appropriate, or reasonable, or rational under the circumstances; and (ii) that, at least in many cases, there is exactly one course of action that is appropriate in this sense. Indeed, Dray argues that on this score rational explanation is superior to statistical explanation because the question why an action had to be done often permits an answer that involves the rational ruling out of all possible alternatives — a result that cannot be achieved in a probabilistic explanation.

But the two assumptions just listed seem to be unwarranted or at least highly questionable. First of all, it is by no means clear by what criteria of rationality "the thing to do" in a given situation is to be characterized. While several recent writers assume that there is one clear notion of rationality in the sense here required,[8] they have proposed no explicit definitions; and doubts about the possibility of formulating adequate general criteria of rationality are enhanced by the mathematical theory of decisions, which shows that even for some rather simple types of decision-situation several different criteria of rational choice can be formulated, each of which is quite plausible and yet incompatible with its alternatives.[9] And if this is so in simple cases, then the notion of *the* thing to do under given circumstances must be regarded as even more problematic when applied to the kinds of decision and action the historian seeks to explain. I think, therefore, that the presuppositions underlying the idea of a principle of action require further elaboration and scrutiny.

However, in order not to complicate the remainder of my discussion, I will disregard this difficulty from here on and will assume, for the sake of the argument, that the intended meaning of the expression 'X is the appropriate, or rational, thing to do under circumstances of kind C' has been agreed upon and adequately specified by objective criteria.

The explanatory import of citing reasons for an action. The question we have to consider then is this: How can a principle of action serve in an explanatory capacity? Dray's account, both in his paper and in his book, would seem to suggest that a rational explanation of why agent A did X would take the following form:

> Agent A was in a situation of kind C.
> When in a situation of kind C, the thing to do is X.
> Therefore, agent A did X.

The first statement in the *explanans* specifies certain antecedent conditions; the second is a principle of action taking the place which, in a covering law explanation, is held by a set of general laws.

Thus conceived, the logic of rational explanation does indeed differ decisively from that of covering law explanation. But precisely because of the feature that makes the

[7] Dray, *Ibid.*, p. 132.

[8] For example, Q. Gibson, in his stimulating study, *The Logic of Social Enquiry* (London: Routledge and Kegan Paul; and New York: Humanities Press, 1960), asserts: "there may be various alternative ways of achieving an end. To act rationally . . . is to select what on the evidence is *the best* way of achieving it" (p. 160; italics the author's); and he refers to "an elementary logical point — namely, that, given certain evidence, there can only be one correct solution to the problem as to the best way of achieving a given end" (p. 162).

[9] For a clear account and comparative analysis of such criteria, see, for example, R. D. Luce and H. Raiffa, *Games and Decisions* (New York: John Wiley & Sons, 1957), ch. 13.

difference it cannot, I submit, explain why A did X. For by the general condition of adequacy considered earlier, an adequate *explanans* for A's having done X must afford good reasons for the belief or the assertion that A did in fact do X. But while the *explanans* just formulated affords good grounds for asserting that the appropriate thing for A to do under the circumstances was X, it does not provide good reasons for asserting or believing that A did in fact do X. To justify this latter assertion, the *explanans* would have to include a further assumption, to the effect that at the time in question A was a rational agent, and was thus disposed to do what was appropriate in the given situation. When modified accordingly, our *explanans* takes on a form which may be schematized as follows:

Agent A was in a situation of kind C.
A was a rational agent at the time
Any rational agent, when in a situation of kind C, will invariably (or: with high probability) do X,

and it will then logically imply (or confer a high inductive probability on) the *explanandum*:

A did X

Thus modified, the account will indeed provide an explanation of why A did in fact do X. But its adequacy for this purpose has been achieved by replacing Dray's evaluative principle of action by a descriptive principle stating what rational agents will do in situations of kind C. The result is a covering law explanation, which will be deductive or inductive according as the general statement about the behavior of rational agents is of strictly universal or of probabilistic-statistical form. This construal of an explanation by reasons is evidently akin to Ryle's conception of an explanation by reference to dispositions;[10] for it presents A's action, as it were, as a manifestation of his general disposition to act in characteristic ways — in ways that qualify as appropriate or rational — when in certain situations.

It might be objected[11] to the broadly dispositional analysis here proposed that the "covering law" allegedly expressed by the third statement in the *explanans* is not really an empirical law about how rational agents do in fact behave, but an analytic statement of a definitional character, which expresses part of what is *meant* by a rational agent — so that the given action is not actually explained by subsumption under a general law. However, this objection does not, I think, do justice to the logical character of concepts such as that of a rational agent. The reason, stated very briefly, is that such concepts are governed by large clusters of general statements — they might be called symptom statements — which assign to the dispositional characteristic in question various typical manifestations or symptoms; each symptom being a particular manner in which a person who has the dispositional characteristic will "respond to," or "act under" certain specific ("stimulus-") conditions. The third statement in our *explanans* is then just one of many symptom statements for the concept of rational agent. But the totality of the symptom statements for a given broadly dispositional concept will normally have empirical implications, so that they cannot all be qualified as definitional or analytic; and it would be arbitrary to attribute to some of them — e.g., the one invoked in our *explanans* — the analytic character of partial definitions and to construe only the remaining ones as having empirical import.[12]

In sum, then, I think that Dray's very

[10] G. Ryle, *The Concept of Mind* (London: Hutchinson's University Library, 1949). The construal here intended, which has been outlined only sketchily, differs, however, in certain respects from what I take to be Ryle's conception. To indicate this, I refer to the analysis here envisaged as "broadly dispositional." For a fuller account, see Hempel, "Rational Action," in *Proceedings and Addresses of the American Philosophical Association*, vol. XXXV (Yellow Springs, Ohio: Antioch Press, 1962); sec. 3.2 of that article, in particular, states and discusses the differences in question.

[11] An objection to this effect was in fact raised in the discussion by Professor R. Brandt.

[12] This idea is presented somewhat more fully in Hempel, "Explanation in Science and in History," in *Frontiers of Science and Philosophy*, ed. R. G. Colodny (Pittsburgh: University of Pittsburgh Press, 1962), sec. 6; also sec. 3.2 of Hempel, "Rational Action," *op. cit.*, has a direct bearing on this issue.

suggestively presented construal of explanations by reasons has a basic logical defect, which springs from the view that such explanations must be based on principles of action rather than on general laws. Dray explicitly makes a distinction between the two on the ground that the phrase 'the thing to do,' which characteristically occurs in a principle of action, "functions as a value-term," and that therefore there is a certain "element of *appraisal*" in a rational explanation, for it must tell us in what way an action "was *appropriate*."[13] But — and this seems to me the crux of the matter — to show that an action was the appropriate or rational thing to have done under the circumstances is not to explain why in fact it was done. Indeed, no normative or evaluative principle specifying what kind of action is appropriate in given circumstances can possibly serve to explain why a person acted in a particular way; and this is so no matter whether the action does or does not conform to the normative principle in question.

The basic point of the objection here raised has also been made by J. Passmore, who states it succinctly as follows: "... explanation by reference to a 'principle of action' or 'a good reason' is not, by itself, explanation at all. . . . For a reason may be a 'good reason' — in the sense of being a principle to which one *could* appeal in justification of one's action — without having in fact the slightest influence on us."[14]

It might perhaps be suspected that in arguing for a broadly dispositional analysis which presents explanations by reasons as having basically the logical structure of one or other of the covering law models, we are violating a maxim of which Mr. Dray rightly reminds us in his paper, namely, that a sound logical analysis must refrain from forcing historical explanation onto the Procrustean bed of some preconceived general schema, and that instead it must take careful account of the practice generally agreed to be acceptable within the discipline concerned; that it must show sensitivity to the concept of explanation historians normally employ. No doubt a historian who adduces an agent's presumptive reasons in order to explain his actions, may well conceive it to be his main task to show that in the light of those reasons, the action was the appropriate thing to have done. But in giving his account, the historian undoubtedly also intends to show why in fact the agent acted as he did — e.g., to take Dray's example, why Louis XIV in fact withdrew military pressure from Holland. And this question cannot be answered by showing that the action was a (or even "the") reasonable thing to do, given Louis' objectives and beliefs; for after all, many agents on many occasions do not actually do the rational thing. This observation seems akin to an objection raised by Strawson, to which Dray refers in his paper. Dray agrees there that human action can fall short of the ideal of rationality and he stresses that his claim is only that the criterion of rational appropriateness does function for actions that are not judged to be defective in various ways. But this seems to me the crucial point: If an explanation by reasons invokes standards of rationality then, to have the desired explanatory force, it must in addition make the empirical assumption that the action was not defective in relevant ways, i.e., that the agent was at the time disposed to act in accordance with the standards invoked, and that the external circumstances did not prevent him from doing so.

And it seems clear to me that a historian would simply see no point in displaying the appropriateness or rationality of an action if he did not assume that the agent, at the time in question, was disposed to act rationally (as he might not be under conditions of

[13] Dray, *op. cit.*, p. 124. (Italics the author's.)

[14] J. Passmore, "Review Article: Law and Explanation in History," *Australian Journal of Politics and History*, 4 (1958), 275. (Italics the author's.) Passmore then goes on to argue very briefly also that an explanation by reasons amounts to an explanation "by reference to a general statement," for to "take a 'reason' to be the actual explanation of anyone's conduct . . . is to assert, at least . . . the general statement: 'People of type X, in situation Y, act in such a way as to conserve the principle Z.' " (*Ibid.*)

extreme fatigue, under severe emotional strain, under the influence of drugs, and the like). And since, in an explanation by reasons, this essential presupposition will normally be taken for granted, it will not, as a rule, be explicitly mentioned; it is rather when departures from rationality are considered that the need is felt explicitly to specify disturbing circumstances. But while an elliptic formulation that forgoes explicit mention of the assumption of rationality may be quite satisfactory for practical purposes, i.e., in the pragmatic-psychological context of explanation, it obscures the logic of the explanatory argument; and surely, an analysis that makes explicit this essential assumption underlying the historian's account does not thereby force the method of explanation by reasons upon a Procrustean bed. . . .

Rational Explanation Rests on Analytic Truths

26

from *The Later Philosophy of Collingwood*

ALAN DONAGAN

Collingwood's exposition of the method of scientific history does not solve the philosophical problem with which he began. If the Baconian method is to be followed in history, it must be possible to deduce from a proposed answer to an historian's question that certain traces which survive from the past either are or are not of a certain kind. Unless such inferences were legitimate, no historian could connect an answer he has proposed with the evidence upon which he must decide either to reject or to persevere with it. Now in natural history, answers about the past are connected with evidence in the present by calculations according to laws of nature. Yet, Collingwood contended that an historian employs no laws: he 'need not and cannot (without ceasing to be an historian) emulate the [natural] scientist in searching for the . . . laws of events' (*IH*, 214). How can he, then, connect his hypotheses with his evidence?

Let us consider an example. In his *Autobiography* Collingwood described a specimen of the Baconian method in history which may be found in his own contribution to the *Oxford History of England*, vol. i, pp. 31-53. It is well known that Julius Caesar twice invaded Britain, and, after short campaigns, withdraw. What was the nature of these acts? This vague question must be replaced by a precise one. The fact that he did each time withdraw suggests the question: Was his withdrawal planned from the beginning? If it was, then his invasions would have been either punitive expeditions or demonstrations of force. Were they? The only evidence upon which these questions may be answered is contained in Caesar's *Commentaries*. If his invasions had been punitive expeditions, then it is a fair inference, first, that he would have said so in his *Commentaries*, and secondly, that the force he took would not have been greatly larger than he believed sufficient for that purpose. However, we find not only that he never did say in the *Commentaries* what he meant to effect by his invasions, but also that the force he took with him was comparable in size with the army later sent by Claudius, which sufficed to conquer the whole south of Britain. Both the answer that Caesar's invasions were merely punitive expeditions, and the answer that his early withdrawals were planned from the beginning, are therefore in conflict with the evidence.

Having disproved that Caesar's withdrawals were planned beforehand, Collingwood's next step was to ask what Caesar's intention had been if he had planned to remain. Presumably, it would have been completely to subdue at least a large part of the country. This answer is consistent with the evidence so far presented. Nor is there any evidence against it, except for those who think either that Caesar was too good a commander to fail in such an undertaking, or that, if he had failed, he was too candid an historian not to record it. However, there is ample evidence that Caesar was not invincible; and that he was scrupulous in avowing failure is not the impression left by his *Commentaries* as a whole: they plainly were designed to show him in as favourable a light as possible. Is there any other hypothesis that might be true? Collingwood at least could think of none. He therefore concluded that Caesar's invasion was a frustrated attempt completely to conquer at least part of Britain; and he

Alan Donagan, *The Later Philosophy of Collingwood* (1962), pp. 182–185, by permission of the Clarendon Press, Oxford.

claimed for this conclusion exactly what a natural scientist would claim for an hypothesis that satisfied all the experimental tests he could devise: '[F]uture historians will have to reckon with the question I have raised, and either accept my answer or produce a better one' (*A*, 131).[1] A better answer would be one that fits all the evidence which his fits, and also further evidence which his does not fit.

Do Collingwood's inferences, in this elaborate specimen of Baconian reasoning, rest on general laws? Although it is impossible here to examine each of its steps in detail, let us consider the first of them. Beginning with the question, 'Did Caesar intend only a punitive expedition or demonstration of force or did he intend something more?' Collingwood examined the first alternative, that Caesar intended no more than a punitive expedition, and reasoned that, if it were true, then Caesar would have stated that intention in his *Commentaries*, and that, since he did not state that intention, the first alternative must be false. Fundamentally, this argument is of a common logical form, the *modus tollendo tollens*, namely,

> It is true that if p then q, but false that q, so it is false that p.

It has, however, one complication. The protasis of the hypothetical premiss turns out, on analysis, to be a conjunction of three statements, only one of which is to be disproved. In full, therefore, the form of Collingwood's argument is:

> It is true that if p_1 and p_2 and p_3 then q, but false that q, so, since p_2 and p_3 are certainly true, it is false that p_1.

The argument itself, enunciated in full, runs:

> If Caesar's invasion had been a successful punitive expedition (p_1), and if he had written his *Commentaries* to advertise his successes (p_2) and had known that in order to advertise the success of his invasion (if it had been a success) it would have been necessary to make plain in his *Commentaries* what he had intended (p_3), then he would have made plain in his *Commentaries* what he had intended (q);
>
> But he did not make plain in his *Commentaries* what he had intended (q is false);
>
> So, since Caesar did write his *Commentaries* to advertise his successes (p_2), and did know that in order to advertise the success of his invasion it would have been necessary to make his intention plain (p_3), his invasion was not a successful punitive expedition (p_1 is false).

Collingwood contended that neither this argument, nor any of the others that compose his elaborate demonstration of what Caesar's intention was, presupposes any general law.

Only one part of Collingwood's argument can plausibly be supposed to be or to presuppose a general law, namely, its hypothetical premiss. Its categorical premiss, that Caesar did not make plain in his *Commentaries* what he had intended, is evidently not a general law. But it is equally evident that neither is the hypothetical premiss, as it stands, a general law; for it is about a single individual, Caesar. However, it may presuppose a general law. Does it? It is true that there could be no justification for asserting that if Caesar had succeeded in a certain enterprise, and had been writing a book to advertise his successes, and had known that to advertise his success in that enterprise he must make certain things plain in that book, then he would have made those things plain, unless the same assertion could be made of everybody. The hypothetical premiss about Caesar does presuppose a general hypothetical about anybody and everybody. Now, is that general hypothetical a law? A moment's reflection will show that it is not. A general law must admit of possible empirical falsification, but the general hypothetical presupposed by Collingwood's premiss does not. No conceivable empirical evidence would count against the proposition that if you hold

[1] I. A. Richmond, in *Roman Britain* (London: Penguin Books, 1955), p. 10, leaves the question open whether Caesar was trying to annex Britain or only to forestall British intervention in Gaul.

to your intention to bring something about, and believe that you must take certain steps to do so, then you will take those steps if you can. Any evidence which goes to show that you held that belief but did not take those steps, although you could have, also goes to show that you did not stick to your intention. Collingwood's hypothetical premiss therefore rests, not on a general law, but on an analytic truth which derives from the very concept of an intention. It follows that his argument neither contains nor presupposes any general law.

This analysis is at least a partial answer to the question with which we began, namely, How can an historian connect his conclusions with his evidence if he employs no general laws? One way in which he might do so would be by hypothetical premisses about what this or that individual would do in such and such circumstances. Our analysis also disposes of the common objection that all such hypothetical premisses about individuals rest on general laws. At least one such hypothetical does not, and it is quite plain that many others like it can be constructed.

Sociological Understanding and the Impossibility of Nomothetic Social Science

27

from *The Idea of a Social Science*
PETER WINCH

In the pages preceding this excerpt, Winch has been criticizing the accounts given J. S. Mill and T. M. Newcomb of motive-explanations. Though these accounts differ in many ways, they are agreed in "regarding explanations of actions in terms of the agent's motives as a species of causal explanation." And they also concur in construing causal explanations as those which conform to the canons of the covering law position. Winch now proceeds to draw on some ideas contained in Wittgenstein's *Philosophical Investigations* to present explanations which appeal to motives in another, and incompatible, light.

Motives, Dispositions and Reasons

Gilbert Ryle argues, against the kind of account advocated by Mill, that to speak of a person's motives is not to speak of any events at all, either mental or physical, but is to refer to his general dispositions to act in the ways in question. 'To explain an act as done from a certain motive is not analogous to saying that the glass broke, because a stone hit it, but to the quite different type of statement that the glass broke, when the stone hit it, because the glass was brittle.' (29: p. 87.) There are a number of objections to this. For one thing, there seems to be a danger of reducing motive explanations to the sort of vacuity feared by Newcomb. (An analogous point is made by Peter Geach; See 10: p. 5.) Again, Ryle's account runs into difficulties where we assign a motive to an act which is quite at variance with the agent's previously experienced behaviour. There is no contradiction in saying that someone who never before manifested any signs of a jealous disposition has, on a given occasion, acted from jealousy; indeed, it is precisely when someone acts unexpectedly that the need for a motive explanation is particularly apparent.

But for my present purposes it is more important to notice that though Ryle's account is different from Mill's in many respects, it is not nearly different enough. A dispositional, just as much as a causal, statement, is based on generalizations from what has been observed to happen. But a statement about an agent's motives is not like that: it is better understood as analogous to a setting out of the agent's *reasons* for acting thus. Suppose that *N*, a university lecturer, says that he is going to cancel his next week's lectures because he intends to travel to London: here we have a statement of intention for which a reason is given. Now *N* does not *infer* his intention of cancelling his lectures from his desire to go to London, as the imminent shattering of the glass might be inferred, either from the fact that someone had thrown a stone or from the brittleness of the glass. *N* does not offer his reason as *evidence* for the soundness of his prediction about his future behaviour. (Cf.

From *The Idea of a Social Science* by Peter Winch, Humanities Press, Inc., New York, and Routledge & Kegan Paul, Ltd., London, 1958, pp. 80–94, 108–116, 121–126, and 131–136.

Wittgenstein; 37: I, 629 ff.) Rather, he is *justifying* his intention. His statement is not of the form: 'Such and such causal factors are present, therefore this will result'; nor yet of the form: 'I have such and such a disposition, which will result in my doing this'; it is of the form: 'In view of such and such considerations this will be a reasonable thing to do'.

This takes me back to the argument of Chapter II, Section 2, which provides a way of correcting Ryle's account of motives. Ryle says that a statement about someone's motives is to be understood as a 'law-like proposition' describing the agent's propensity to act in certain kinds of way on certain kinds of occasion. (29: p. 89.) But the 'law-like proposition' in terms of which *N*'s reasons must be understood concerns not *N*'s dispositions but the accepted standards of reasonable behaviour current in his society.

The terms 'reason' and 'motive' are not synonymous. It would, for instance, be absurd to describe most imputations of motives as 'justifications': to impute a motive is more often to condemn than it is to justify. To say, for example, that *N* murdered his wife from jealousy is certainly not to say that he acted reasonably. But it is to say that his act was *intelligible* in terms of the modes of behaviour which are familiar in our society, and that it was governed by considerations appropriate to its context. These two aspects of the matter are interwoven: one can act 'from considerations' only where there are accepted standards of what is appropriate to appeal to. The behaviour of Chaucer's Troilus towards Cressida is intelligible only in the context of the conventions of courtly love. Understanding Troilus presupposes understanding those conventions, for it is from them that his acts derive their meaning.

I have noted how the relation between *N*'s intention and his reason for it differs from the relation between a prediction and the evidence offered in its support. But somebody who knows *N* and his circumstances well and who is familiar with the type of consideration which he is prone to regard as important, may on the basis of this knowledge predict how he is likely to behave. '*N* has a jealous temperament; if his emotions in that direction are aroused he is likely to become violent. I must be careful not to provoke him further.' Here I adduce *N*'s motives as part of the evidence for my prediction of his behaviour. But though this is possible, *given* that I already possess the concept of a motive, that concept is not in the first place learned as part of a technique for making predictions (unlike the concept of a cause). Learning what a motive is belongs to learning the standards governing life in the society in which one lives; and that again belongs to the process of learning to live as a social being.

The Investigation of Regularities

A follower of Mill might concede that explanations of human behaviour must appeal not to causal generalizations about the individual's reaction to his environment but to our knowledge of the institutions and ways of life which give his acts their meaning. But he might argue that this does not damage the fundamentals of Mill's thesis, since understanding social institutions is still a matter of grasping empirical generalizations which are logically on a footing with those of natural science. For an institution is, after all, a certain kind of uniformity, and a uniformity can only be grasped in a generalization. I shall now examine this argument.

A regularity or uniformity is the constant recurrence of the same kind of event on the same kind of occasion; hence statements of uniformities presuppose judgements of identity. But this takes us right back to the argument of Chapter I, Section 8, according to which criteria of identity are necessarily relative to some rule: with the corollary that two events which count as qualitatively similar from the point of view of one rule would count as different from the point of view of another. So to investigate the type of regularity studied in a given kind of enquiry is to examine the nature of the rule according to which judgements of identity are made in that enquiry. Such judgements are intelligible only relatively to a given mode of human behaviour, governed by its own rules.[1] In a physical science the relevant rules are those governing the procedures of investigators in the science in question. For instance, someone with no understanding of the problems and procedures of nuclear physics would gain nothing from being present at an experiment like the Cockcroft-Walton bombardment of lithium by hydrogen; indeed even the description of what he saw in those terms would be unintelligible to him, since the term 'bombardment' does not carry the sense in the context of the nuclear physicists' activities that it carries elsewhere. To understand what was going on in this experiment he would have to learn the nature of what nuclear physicists do; and this would include learning the criteria according to which they make judgements of identity.

Those rules, like all others, rest on a social context of common activity. So to understand the activities of an individual scientific investigator we must take account of two sets of relations: first, his relation to the phenomena which he investigates; second, his relation to his fellow-scientists. Both of these are essential to the sense of saying that he is 'detecting regularities' or 'discovering uniformities', but writers on scientific 'methodology' too often concentrate on the first and overlook the importance of the second. That they must belong to different types is evident from the following considerations. — The phenomena being investigated present themselves to the scientist as an *object* of study; he observes them and notices certain facts about them. But to say of a man that he does this presupposes that he already has a mode of communication in the use of which rules are already being observed. For to notice something is to identify relevant characteristics, which means that the noticer must have some *concept* of such characteristics; this is possible only if he is able to use some symbol according to a rule which makes it refer to those characteristics. So we come back to his relation to his fellow-scientists, in which context alone he can be spoken of as following such a rule. Hence the relation between *N* and his fellows, in virtue of which we say that *N* is following the same rule as they, cannot be simply a relation of observation: it cannot consist in the fact that *N* has noticed how his fellows behave and has decided to take that as a norm for his own behaviour. For this would presuppose that we could give some account of the notion of 'noticing how his fellows behave' *apart from* the relation between *N* and his fellows which we are trying to specify; and that, as has been shown, is untrue. To quote Rush Rhees: 'We see that we understand one another, without noticing whether our reactions tally or not. *Because* we agree in our reactions, it is possible for me to tell you something, and it is possible for you to teach me something'. (28.)

In the course of his investigation the scientist applies and develops the concepts germane to his particular field of study. This application and modification are 'influenced' both by the phenomena *to* which they are applied and also by the fellow-workers *in participation with* whom they are applied. But the two kinds of 'influence' are different. Whereas it is on the basis of his observation of the phenomena (in the course of his experiments) that he develops his concepts as he does, he is able to do this only in virtue of his participation in an established form of activity with his fellow-scientists. When I speak of 'participation' here I do not necessarily imply any direct physical conjunction or even any direct communication between fellow-participants. What is important is that they are all taking part in the same general kind of ac-

[1] Cf. Hume: *A Treatise of Human Nature*, Introduction — "'Tis evident, that all the sciences have a relation, greater or less, to human nature; and that however wide any of them may seem to run from it, they still return back by one passage or another." Hume's remark is a further reminder of the close relation between the subject of this monograph and one of the most persistent and dominant *motifs* in the history of modern philosophy.

tivity, which they have all *learned* in similar ways; that they are, therefore, *capable* of communicating with each other about what they are doing; that what any one of them is doing is in principle intelligible to the others.

Understanding Social Institutions

Mill's view' is that understanding a social institution consists in observing regularities in the behaviour of its participants and expressing these regularities in the form of generalizations. Now if the position of the sociological investigator (in a broad sense) can be regarded as comparable, in its main logical outlines, with that of the natural scientist, the following must be the case. The concepts and criteria according to which the sociologist judges that, in two situations, the same thing has happened, or the same action performed, must be understood *in relation to the rules governing sociological investigation.* But here we run against a difficulty; for whereas in the case of the natural scientist we have to deal with only one set of rules, namely those governing the scientist's investigation itself, here *what the sociologist is studying*, as well as his study of it, is a human activity and is therefore carried on according to rules. And it is these rules, rather than those which govern the sociologist's investigation, which specify what is to count as 'doing the same kind of thing' in relation to that kind of activity.

An example may make this clearer. Consider the parable of the Pharisee and the Publican (*Luke*, 18, 9). Was the Pharisee who said 'God, I thank Thee that I am not as other men are' doing the same kind of thing as the Publican who prayed 'God be merciful unto me a sinner'? To answer this one would have to start by considering what is involved in the idea of prayer; and that is a *religious* question. In other words, the appropriate criteria for deciding whether the actions of these two men were of the same kind or not belong to religion itself. Thus the sociologist of religion will be confronted with an answer to the question: Do these two acts belong to the same kind of activity?; and this answer is given according to criteria which are not taken from sociology, but from religion itself.

But if the judgements of identity — and hence the generalizatons — of the sociologist of religion rest on criteria taken from religion, then his relation to the performers of religious activity cannot be just that of observer to observed. It must rather be analogous to the participation of the natural scientist with his fellow-workers in the activities of scientific investigation. Putting the point generally, even if it is legitimate to speak of one's understanding of a mode of social activity as consisting in a knowledge of regularities, the nature of this knowledge must be very different from the nature of knowledge of physical regularities. So it is quite mistaken in principle to compare the activity of a student of a form of social behaviour with that of, say, an engineer studying the workings of a machine; and one does not advance matters by saying, with Mill, that the machine in question is of course immensely more complicated than any physical machine. If we are going to compare the social student to an engineer, we shall do better to compare him to an apprentice engineer who is studying what engineering — that is, the activity of engineering — is all about. His understanding of social phenomena is more like the engineer's understanding of his colleagues' activities than it is like the engineer's understanding of the mechanical systems which he studies.

This point is reflected in such commonsense considerations as the following: that a historian or sociologist of religion must himself have some religious feeling if he is to make sense of the religious movement he is studying and understand the considerations which govern the lives of its participants. A historian of art must have some aesthetic sense if he is to understand the problems confronting the artists of his period; and without this he will have left out of his account precisely what would have made it a history of *art*, as opposed to a rather puzzling external account of certain motions which certain people have been perceived to go through.

I do not wish to maintain that we must stop at the unreflective kind of understanding of which I gave as an instance the engineer's understanding of the activities of his colleagues. But I do want to say that any more reflective understanding must necessarily presuppose, if it is to count as genuine understanding at all, the participant's unreflective understanding. And this in itself makes it misleading to compare it with the natural scientist's understanding of his scientific data. Similarly, although the reflective student of society, or of a particular mode of social life, may find it necessary to use concepts which are not taken from the forms of activity which he is investigating, but which are taken rather from the context of his own investigation, still these technical concepts of his will imply a previous understanding of those other concepts which belong to the activities under investigation.

For example, liquidity preference is a technical concept of economics: it is not generally used by business men in the conduct of their affairs but by the economist who wishes to *explain* the nature and consequences of certain kinds of business behaviour. But it is logically tied to concepts which do enter into business activity, for its use by the economist presupposes his understanding of what it is to conduct a business, which in turn involves an understanding of such business concepts as money, profit, cost, risk, etc. It is only the relation between his account and these concepts which makes it an account of economic activity as opposed, say, to a piece of theology.

Again, a psychoanalyst may explain a patient's neurotic behavior in terms of factors unknown to the patient and of concepts which would be unintelligible to him. Let us suppose that the psychoanalyst's explanation refers to events in the patient's early childhood. Well, the description of those events will presuppose an understanding of the concepts in terms of which family life, for example, is carried on in our society; for these will have entered, however rudimentarily, into the relations between the child and his family. A psychoanalyst who wished to give an account of the aetiology of neuroses amongst, say, the Trobriand Islanders, could not just apply without further reflection the concepts developed by Freud for situations arising in our own society. He would have first to investigate such things as the idea of fatherhood amongst the islanders and take into account any relevant aspects in which their idea differed from that current in his own society. And it is almost inevitable that such an investigation would lead to some modification in the psychological theory appropriate for explaining neurotic behaviour in this new situation.

These considerations also provide some justification for the sort of historical scepticism which that underestimated philosopher, R.G. Collingwood, expresses in *The Idea of History*. (6: *passim.*) Although they need not be brought to the foreground where one is dealing with situations in one's own society or in societies with whose life one is reasonably familiar, the practical implications become pressing where the object of study is a society which is culturally remote from that of the investigator. This accounts for the weight which the Idealists attached to concepts like 'empathy' and 'historical imagination' (which is not to deny that these concepts give rise to difficulties of their own). It is also connected with another characteristic doctrine of theirs: that the understanding of a human society is closely connected with the activities of the philosopher. I led up to that doctrine in the first two chapters and shall return to it in the last two.

Prediction in the Social Studies

In my discussion of Oakeshott in the last chapter I noticed the importance of the fact that voluntary behaviour is behaviour to which there is an alternative. Since understanding something involves understanding its contradictory, someone who, with understanding, performs X must be capable of envisaging the possibility of doing not-X.

This is not an empirical statement but a remark about what is involved in the concept of doing something with understanding. Consider now an observer, *O*, of *N*'s behaviour. If *O* wants to predict how *N* is going to act he must familiarize himself with the concepts in terms of which *N* is viewing the situation; having done this he may, from his knowledge of *N*'s character, be able to predict with great confidence what decision *N* is going to take. But the notions which *O* uses to make his prediction are nonetheless compatible with *N*'s taking a different decision from that predicted for him. If this happens it does not necessarily follow that *O* has made a mistake in his calculations; for the whole point about a decision is that a given set of 'calculations' may lead to any one of a set of different outcomes. This is quite different from predictions in the natural sciences, where a falsified prediction always implies some sort of mistake on the part of the predictor: false or inadequate data, faulty calculation, or defective theory.

The following may make that clearer. To understand the nature of the decision confronting *N*, *O* must be aware of the rules which provide the criteria specifying for *N* the relevant features of his situation. If one knows the rule which someone is following one can, in a large number of cases, predict what he will do in given circumstances. For instance, if *O* knows that *N* is following the rule: 'Start with 0 and add 2 till you reach 1,000', he can predict that, having written down 104, *N* will next write 106. But sometimes even if *O* knows with certainty the rule which *N* is following, he cannot predict with any certainty what *N* will do: where, namely, the question arises of *what is involved* in following that rule, e.g. in circumstances markedly different from any in which it has previously been applied. The rule here does not specify any determinate outcome to the situation, though it does limit the range of possible alternatives; it is made determinate for the future by the choice of one of these alternatives and the rejection of the others — until such time as it again becomes necessary to interpret the rule in the light of yet new conditions.

This may throw some light on what is involved in the idea of a developing historical tradition. As I remarked earlier, Mill thought of historical trends as analogous to scientific laws and Popper wished to modify that conception by pointing out that the statement of a trend, unlike that of a true law, involves a reference to a set of specific initial conditions. I now want to make a further modification: even given a specific set of initial conditions, one will still not be able to predict any determinate outcome to a historical trend because the continuation or breaking off of that trend involves human decisions which are not determined by their antecedent conditions in the context of which the sense of calling them 'decisions' lies.

Two words of caution are necessary in connection with my last remark. I am not denying that it is sometimes possible to predict decisions; only that their relation to the evidence on which they are based is unlike that characteristic of scientific predictions. And I am not falling into the trap of saying that historical trends are consciously willed and intended by their participants; the point is that such trends are in part the *outcome* of intentions and decisions of their participants.

The development of a historical tradition may involve deliberation, argument, the canvassing of rival interpretations, followed perhaps by the adoption of some agreed compromise or the springing up of rival schools. Consider, for instance, the relation between the music of Haydn, Mozart and Beethoven; or the rival schools of political thought which all claim, with some show of reason, to be based on the Marxist tradition. Think of the interplay between orthodoxy and heresy in the development of religion; or of the way in which the game of football was revolutionized by the Rugby boy who picked up the ball and ran. It would certainly not have been possible to predict that revolution from knowledge of the preceding state of the game any more than it would have been possible to predict the philosophy of Hume from the philosophies of his predecessors. It may help here to recall Humphrey Lyttleton's rejoinder to someone who asked him where Jazz was going: 'If I knew where Jazz was going I'd be there already'.

Maurice Cranston makes essentially the same point when he notices that to predict the writing of a piece of poetry or the making of a new invention would involve writing the poem or making the invention oneself. And if one has already done this oneself then it is impossible to predict that someone else will make up that poem or discover that invention. 'He could not predict it because he could not say it was going to happen before it happened.' (8: p. 166.)

It would be a mistake, though tempting, to regard this as a piece of trivial logic-chopping. One appears to be attempting an impossible task of *a priori* legislation against a purely empirical possibility. What in fact one is showing, however, is that the central concepts which belong to our understanding of social life are incompatible with concepts central to the activity of scientific prediction. When we speak of the possibility of scientific prediction of social developments of this sort, we literally do not understand what we are saying. We cannot understand it, because it has no sense. . . .

Two things may be called 'the same' or 'different' only with reference to a set of criteria which lay down what is to be regarded as a relevant difference. When the 'things' in question are purely physical the criteria appealed to will of course be those of the observer. But when one is dealing with intellectual (or, indeed, any kind of social) 'things', that is not so. For their *being* intellectual or social, as opposed to physical, in character depends entirely on their belonging in a certain way to a system of ideas or mode of living. It is only by reference to the criteria governing that system of ideas or mode of life that they have any existence as intellectual or social events. It follows that if the sociological investigator wants to regard them *as* social events (as, *ex hypothesi*, he must), he has to take seriously the criteria which are applied for distinguishing 'different' kinds of actions and identifying the 'same' kinds of actions within the way of life he is studying. It is not open to him arbitrarily to impose his own standards from without. In so far as he does so, the events he is studying lose altogether their character as *social* events. A Christian would strenuously deny that the baptism rites of his faith were really the same in character as the acts of a pagan sprinkling lustral water or letting sacrificial blood. Pareto, in maintaining the contrary, is inadvertently removing from his subject-matter precisely that which gives them sociological interest: namely their internal connection with a way of living.

Miss G. E. M. Anscombe has remarked, in an unpublished paper, how there are certain activities — she mentions arithmetic as an example — which, unlike other activities, such as acrobatics, cannot be understood by an observer unless he himself possesses the ability to perform the activities in question. She notes that any description of activities like arithmetic which is not based on arithmetical (or whatever) capacities is bound to seem pointless and arbitrary, and also compulsive in the sense that the steps no longer appear as meaningful choices. This is precisely the impression of social activities which is given by Pareto's account of them as residues; but the impression is not a well-founded one, it is an optical illusion based on a conceptual misunderstanding.

This shows, I think, that the whole presupposition of Pareto's procedure is absurd: namely that it is possible to treat propositions and theories as 'experimental facts' on a par with any other kind of such fact. (See 23: Section 7.) It is a presupposition which is certainly not peculiar to him: it is contained, for instance, in Emile Durkheim's first rule of sociological method: 'to consider social facts as things'. Pareto's statement, and the others like it, are absurd because they involve a contradiction: in so far as a set of phenomena is being looked at 'from the outside', 'as experimental facts', it cannot at the same time be described as constituting a 'theory' or set of 'propositions'. In a sense Pareto has not carried his empiricism far enough. For what the sociological observer has presented *to his senses* is not at all people holding certain theories, believing in certain propositions, but people making certain movements and sounds. Indeed, even describing them as 'people' really goes too far, which may explain the popularity of the sociological and social psychological jargon word 'organism': but organisms, as opposed to people, do not believe propositions or embrace theories. To describe what is observed by the sociologist in terms of notions like 'proposition' and 'theory' is already to have taken the decision to apply a set of concepts incompatible with the 'external', 'experimental' point of view. To refuse to describe what is observed in such terms, on the other hand, involves not treating it as having *social* significance. It follows that the understanding of society cannot be observational and experimental in one widely accepted sense.

What I am saying needs qualification. I do not mean, of course, that it is impossible to take as a datum that a certain person, or group of people, holds a certain belief — say that the earth is flat — without subscribing to it oneself. And this is all Pareto thinks he is doing; but actually he is doing more than this. He is not just speaking of particular beliefs *within* a given mode of discourse, but of whole modes of discourse. What he misses is that a mode of discourse has to be *understood* before anyone can speak of theories and propositions within it which could constitute data for him. He does not really consider the fundamental problem of what it is to understand a mode of discourse. In so far as he thinks anything about it he regards it as simply a matter of establishing generalizations on the basis of observation; a view which was disposed of in Chapter III.

There is, unfortunately, no space available to discuss further examples of attempts, like Pareto's, to eliminate human ideas and intelligence from the sociologist's account of social life. But readers may find it instructive to re-read Durkheim's *Suicide* in the light of what I have been saying. It is particularly important to notice the connection between Durkheim's conclusion — that conscious deliberations may be treated as 'purely formal, with no object but confirmation of a resolve previously formed for reasons unknown to consciousness', and his initial decision to define the word 'suicide' for the purposes of his study in a sense different from that which it bore within the societies which he was studying. (9.)

Max Weber: Verstehen and Causal Explanation

It is Max Weber who has said most about the peculiar sense which the word 'understand' bears when applied to modes of social life. I have already referred to his account of meaningful behaviour and propose in the next two sections to say something about his conception of sociological understanding (*Verstehen*). (See 33: Chapter 1.) The first issue on which I mean to concentrate is Weber's account of the relation between acquiring an 'interpretative understanding' (*deutend verstehen*) of the meaning (*Sinn*) of a piece of behaviour and providing a causal explanation (*kausal erklären*) of what brought the behaviour in question about and what its consequences are.

Now Weber never gives a clear account of the *logical* character of interpretative understanding. He speaks of it much of the time as if it were simply a psychological technique: a matter of putting oneself in the other fellow's position. This has led many writers to allege that Weber confuses what is simply a technique for framing hypotheses with the logical character of the evidence for such hypotheses. Thus Popper argues that although we may use our knowledge of our own mental processes in order to frame hypotheses about the similar processes of other people, 'these hypotheses must be tested, they must be submitted to the method of selection by elimination. (By their intuition, some people are prevented from even imagining that anybody can possibly dislike chocolate).' (26: Section 29.)[2]

[2] [*Page 51, this volume. Editor's note.*]

Nevertheless, however applicable such criticisms may be to Weber's vulgarizers, they cannot justly be used against his own views, for he is very insistent that mere 'intuition' is not enough and must be tested by careful observation. However, what I think can be said against Weber is that he gives a wrong account of the process of checking the validity of suggested sociological interpretations. But the correction of Weber takes us farther away from, rather than closer to, the account which Popper, Ginsberg, and the many who think like them, would like to substitute.

Weber says:

> Every interpretation aims at self-evidence or immediate plausibility (*Evidenz*). But an interpretation which makes the meaning of a piece of behaviour as self-evidently obvious as you like cannot claim *just* on that account to be the causally *valid* interpretation as well. In itself it is nothing more than a particularly plausible hypothesis. (33: Chapter I.)

He goes on to say that the appropriate way to verify such an hypothesis is to establish statistical laws based on observation of what happens. In this way he arrives at the conception of a sociological law as 'a statistical regularity which corresponds to an intelligible intended meaning'.

Weber is clearly right in pointing out that the obvious interpretation need not be the right one. R. S. Lynd's interpretation of West Indian voodoo magic as 'a system of imputedly true and reliable causal sequences' is a case in point (15: p. 121); and there is a plethora of similar examples in Frazer's *The Golden Bough*. But I want to question Weber's implied suggestion that *Verstehen* is something which is logically incomplete and needs supplementing by a different method altogether, namely the collection of statistics. Against this, I want to insist that if a proffered interpretation is wrong, statistics, though they may suggest that that is so, are not the decisive and ultimate court of appeal for the validity of sociological interpretations in the way Weber suggests. What is then needed is a better interpretation, not something different in kind. The compatibility of an interpretation with the statistics does not prove its validity. Someone who interprets a tribe's magical rites as a form of misplaced scientific activity will not be corrected by statistics about what members of that tribe are likely to do on various kinds of occasion (though this might form *part* of the argument); what is ultimately required is a *philosophical* argument like, e.g., Collingwood's in *The Principles of Art*. (6: Book I, Chapter IV.) For a mistaken interpretation of a form of social activity is closely akin to the type of mistake dealt with in philosophy.

Wittgenstein says somewhere that when we get into philosophical difficulties over the use of some of the concepts of our language, we are like savages confronted with something from an alien culture. I am simply indicating a corollary of this: that sociologists who misinterpret an alien culture are like philosophers getting into difficulties over the use of their own concepts. There will be differences of course. The philosopher's difficulty is usually with something with which he is perfectly familiar but which he is for the moment failing to see in its proper perspective. The sociologist's difficulty will often be over something with which he is not at all familiar; he may have no suitable perspective to apply. This may sometimes make his task more difficult than the philosopher's, and it may also sometimes make it easier. But the analogy between their problems should be plain.

Some of Wittgenstein's procedures in his philosophical elucidations reinforce this point. He is prone to draw our attention to certain features of our own concepts by comparing them with those of an imaginary society, in which our own familiar ways of thinking are subtly distorted. For instance, he asks us to suppose that such a society sold wood in the following way: They 'piled the timber in heaps of arbitrary, varying height and then sold it at a price proportionate to the area covered by the piles. And what if they even justified this with the words: "Of course, if you buy more timber, you must pay more"?' (88: Chapter I, p. 142-151.) The important question for us is: in what circumstances could one say that one had *understood* this sort of behaviour? As I have indicated, Weber often speaks as if the ultimate test were our ability to formulate statistical laws which would enable us to *predict* with fair accuracy what people would be likely to do in given circumstances. In line with this is his attempt to define a 'social role' in terms of the probability (*Chance*) of actions of a certain sort being performed in given circumstances. But with Wittgenstein's example we might well be able to make predictions of great accuracy in this way and still not be able to claim any real understanding of what those people were doing. The difference is precisely analogous to that between being able to formulate statistical laws about the likely occurrences of words in a language and being able to understand what was being *said* by someone who spoke the language. The latter can never be reduced to the former; a man who understands Chinese is not a man who has a firm grasp of the statistical probabilities for the occurrence of the various words in the Chinese language. Indeed, he could have that without knowing that he was dealing with a language at all; and anyway, the knowledge that he was dealing with a language is not itself something that could be formulated statistically. 'Understanding', in situations like this, is grasping the *point* or *meaning* of what is being done or said. This is a notion far removed from the world of statistics and causal laws: it is closer to the realm of discourse and to the internal relations that link the parts of a realm of discourse. The notion of *meaning* should be carefully distinguished from that of *function*, in its quasi-causal sense, the use of which in social anthropology and sociology I shall not explore further here. . . .

The Internality of Social Relations

To illustrate what is meant by saying that the social relations between men and the ideas which men's actions embody are really the same thing considered from different points of view, I want now to consider the general nature of what happens when the ideas current in a society change: when new ideas come into the language and old ideas go out of it. In speaking of 'new ideas' I shall make a distinction. Imagine a biochemist making certain observations and experiments as a result of which he discovers a new germ which is responsible for a certain disease. In one sense we might say that the name he gives to this new germ expresses a new idea, but I prefer to say in this context that he has made a discovery within the existing framework of ideas. I am assuming that the germ theory of disease is already well established in the scientific language he speaks. Now compare with this discovery the impact made by the first formulation of that theory, the first introduction of the concept of a germ into the language of medicine. This was a much more radically new departure, involving not merely a new factual discovery within an existing way of looking at things, but a completely new way of looking at the whole problem of the causation of diseases, the adoption of new diagnostic techniques, the asking of new kinds of question about illnesses, and so on. In short it involved the adoption of new ways of doing things by people involved, in one way or another, in medical practice. An account of the way in which social relations in the medical profession had been influenced by this new concept would include an account of what that concept was. Conversely, the concept itself is unintelligible apart from its relation to medical practice. A doctor who (i) claimed to accept the germ theory of disease, (ii) claimed to aim at reducing the incidence of disease, and (iii) completely ignored the necessity for isolating infectious patients, would be behaving in a self-contradictory and unintelligible manner.

Again, imagine a society which has no concept of proper names, as we know them. People are known by general descriptive phrases, say, or by numbers. This would carry with it a great many other differences from our own social life as well. The whole structure of personal relationships would be affected. Consider the importance of numbers in prison or military life. Imagine how different it would be to fall in love with a girl known only by a number rather than by a name; and what the effect of that might be, for instance, on the poetry of love. The development of the use of proper names in such a society would certainly count as the introduction of a new idea, whereas the mere introduction of a *particular* new proper name, within the existing framework, would not.

I have wanted to show by these examples that a new way of talking sufficiently important to rank as a new idea implies a new set of social relationships. Similarly with the dying out of a way of speaking. Take the notion of friendship: we read, in Penelope Hall's book, *The Social Services of Modern England* (Routledge), that it is the duty of a social worker to establish a relationship of friendship with her clients; but that she must never forget that her first duty is to the policy of the agency by which she is employed. Now that is a debasement of the notion of friendship as it has been understood, which has excluded this sort of divided loyalty, not to say double-dealing. To the extent to which the old idea gives way to this new one social relationships are impoverished (or, if anyone objects to the interpolation of personal moral attitudes, at least they are *changed*). It will not do, either, to say that the mere change in the meaning of a word need not prevent people from having the relations to each other they want to have; for this is to overlook the fact that our language and our social relations are just two different sides of the same coin. To give an account of the meaning of a word is to describe how it is used; and to describe how it is used is to describe the social intercourse into which it enters.

If social relations between men exist only in and through their ideas, then, since the relations between ideas are internal relations, social relations must be a species of internal relation too. This brings me into conflict with a widely accepted principle of Hume's: 'There is no object, which implies the existence of any other if we consider these objects in themselves, and never look beyond the ideas which we form of them'. There is no doubt that Hume intended this to apply to human actions and social life as well as to the phenomena of nature. Now to start with, Hume's principle is not unqualifiedly true even of our knowledge of natural phenomena. If I hear a sound and recognize it as a clap of thunder, I already commit myself to believing in the occurrence of a number of other events — e.g. electrical discharges in the atmosphere — even in calling what I have heard 'thunder'. That is, from 'the idea which I have formed' of what I heard I *can* legitimately infer 'the existence of other objects'. If I subsequently find that there was no electrical storm in the vicinity at the time I heard the sound I shall have to retract my claim that what I heard was thunder. To use a phrase of Gilbert Ryle's, the word 'thunder' is theory-impregnated; statements affirming the occurrence of thunder have logical connections with statements affirming the occurrence of other events. To say this, of course, is not to reintroduce any mysterious causal nexus *in rebus*, of a sort to which Hume could legitimately object. It is simply to point out that Hume overlooked the fact that 'the idea we form of an object' does not just consist of elements drawn from our observation of that object in isolation, but includes the idea of connections between it and other objects. (And one could scarcely form a conception of a language in which this was not so.)

Consider now a very simple paradigm case of a relation between actions in a human society: that between an act of command and an act of obedience to that command. A sergeant calls 'Eyes right!' and his men all turn their eyes to the right. Now, in describing the men's act in terms of the notion of obedience to a command, one is of course committing oneself to saying that a command has been issued. So far the situation looks precisely parallel to the relation between thunder and electrical storms. But now one needs to draw a distinction. An event's character as an act of obedience is *intrinsic* to it in a way which is not true of an event's character as a clap of thunder; and this is in general true of human acts as opposed to natural events. In the case of the latter, although human beings can think of the occurrences in question only in terms of the concepts they do in fact have of them, yet the events themselves have an existence independent of those concepts. There existed electrical storms and thunder long before there were human beings to form concepts of them or establish that there was any connection between them. But it does not make sense to suppose that human beings might have been issuing commands and obeying them before they came to form the concept of command and obedience. For their performance of such acts is itself the chief manifestation of their possession of those concepts. An act of obedience itself contains, as an essential element, a recognition of what went before as an order. But it would of course be senseless to suppose that a clap of thunder contained any recognition of what went before as an electrical storm; it is our recognition of the sound, rather than the sound itself, which contains that recognition of what went before.

Part of the opposition one feels to the idea that men can be related to each other through their actions in at all the same kind of way as propositions can be related to each other is probably due to an inadequate conception of what logical relations between propositions themselves are. One is inclined to think of the laws of logic as forming a *given* rigid structure to which men try, with greater or less (but never complete) success, to make what they say in their actual linguistic and social intercourse conform. One thinks of propositions as something ethereal, which just because of their ethereal, non-physical nature, can fit together more tightly than can be conceived in the case of anything so grossly material as flesh-and-blood men and their actions. In a sense one is right in this; for to treat of logical relations in a formal systematic way is to think at a very high level of abstraction, at which all the anomalies, imperfections and crudities which characterize men's actual intercourse with each other in society have been removed. But, like any abstraction not recognized as such, this can be misleading. It may make one forget that it is only from their roots in this actual flesh-and-blood intercourse that those formal systems draw such life as they have; for the whole idea of a logical relation is only possible by virtue of the sort of agreement between men and their actions which is discussed by Wittgenstein in the *Philosophical Investigations*. Collingwood's remark on formal grammar is apposite: 'I likened the grammarian to a butcher; but if so, he is a butcher of a curious kind. Travellers say that certain African peoples will cut a steak from a living animal and cook it for dinner, the animal being not much the worse. This may serve to amend the original comparison'. (7: p. 259.) It will seem less strange that social relations should be like logical relations between propositions once it is seen that logical relations between propositions themselves depend on social relations between men. . . .

This view of the matter may make possible a new appreciation of Collingwood's conception of all human history as the history of thought. That is no doubt an exaggeration and the notion that the task of the historian is to re-think the thoughts of the historical participants is to some extent an intellectualistic distortion. But Collingwood is right if he is taken to mean that the way to understand events in human history, even those which cannot naturally be represented as conflicts between or developments of discursive ideas, is more closely analogous to the way in which we understand expressions of ideas than it is to the way we understand physical processes.

There is a certain respect, indeed, in which Collingwood pays insufficient attention to the manner in which a way of thinking and the historical situation to which it belongs form one indivisible whole. He says that the aim of the historian is to think the very same thoughts as were once thought, just as they were thought at the historical moment in question. (6: Part V.) But though extinct ways of thinking may, in a sense, be recaptured by the historian, the way in which the historian thinks them will be coloured by the fact that he has had to employ historiographical methods to recapture them. The medieval knight did not have to use those methods in order to view his lady in terms of the notions of courtly love: he just thought of her in those terms. Historical research may enable me to achieve some understanding of what was involved in this way of thinking, but that will not make it open to me to think of *my* lady in those terms. I should always be conscious that this was an anachronism, which means, of course, that I should not be thinking of her in just the same terms as did the knight of his lady. And naturally, it is even more impossible for me to think of *his* lady as he did.

Nevertheless, Collingwood's view is nearer the truth than is that most favoured in empiricist methodologies of the social sciences, which runs somewhat as follows — on the one side we have human history which is a kind of repository of data. The historian unearths these data and presents them to his more theoretically minded colleagues who then produce scientific generalizations and theories establishing connections between one kind of social situation and another. These theories can then be applied to history itself in order to enhance our understanding of the ways in which its episodes are mutually connected. I have tried to show, particularly in connection with Pareto, how this involves minimizing the importance of ideas in human history, since ideas and theories are constantly developing and changing, and since each system of ideas, its component elements being interrelated internally, has to be understood in and for itself; the combined result of which is to make systems of ideas a very unsuitable subject for broad generalizations. I have also tried to show that social relations really exist only in and through the ideas which are current in society; or alternatively, that social relations fall into the same logical category as do relations between ideas. It follows that social relations must be an equally unsuitable subject for generalizations and theories of the scientific sort to be formulated about them. Historical explanation is not the application of generalizations and theories to particular instances: it is the tracing of internal relations. It is like applying one's knowledge of a language in order to understand a conversation rather than like applying one's knowledge of the laws of mechanics to understand the workings of a watch. Non-linguistic behaviour, for example has an 'idiom' in the same kind of way as has a language. In the same kind of way as it can be difficult to recapture the idiom of Greek thought in a translation into modern English of a Platonic dialogue, so it can be misleading to think of the behaviour of people in remote societies in terms of the demeanour to which we are accustomed in our own society. Think of the uneasy feeling one often has about the authenticity of 'racy' historical evocations like those in some of Robert Graves's novels: this has nothing to do with doubts about a writer's accuracy in matters of external detail.

The relation between sociological theories and historical narrative is less like the relation between scientific laws and the reports of experiments or observations than it is like that between theories of logic and arguments in particular languages. Consider for instance the explanation of a chemical reaction in terms of a theory about molecular structure and valency: here the theory *establishes* a connection between what happened at one moment when the two chemicals were brought together and what happened at a subsequent moment. It is only *in terms of the theory* that one can speak of the events being thus 'connected' (as opposed to a simple spatio-temporal connection); the only way to grasp the connection is to learn the theory. But the application of a logical theory to a particular piece of reasoning is not like that. One does not have to know the theory in order to appreciate the connection between the steps of the argument; on the contrary, it is only in so far as one can already grasp logical connections between particular statements in particular languages that one is even in a position to understand what the logical theory is all about. (This is implied by the argument of Lewis Carroll, which I referred to earlier.) Whereas in natural science it is your theoretical knowledge which enables you to explain occurrences you have not previously met, a knowledge of logical theory on the other hand will not enable you to understand a piece of reasoning in an unknown language; you will have to learn that language, and that in itself *may* suffice to enable you to grasp the connections between the various parts of arguments in that language. George Simmel writes:

> The degeneration of a difference in convictions into hatred and fight occurs only when there were essential, original similarities between the parties. The (sociologically very significant) 'respect for the enemy' is usually absent where the hostility has arisen on the basis of previous solidarity. And where enough similarities continue to make confusions and blurred outlines possible, points of difference need an emphasis not justified by the issue but only by that danger of confusion. This was involved, for instance, in the case of Catholicism in Berne . . . . Roman Catholicism does not have to fear any threat to its identity from external contact with a church so different as the Reformed Church, but quite from something as closely akin as Old-Catholicism. (31:Chapter I.)

Here I want to say that it is not *through* Simmel's generalization that one understands the relationship he is pointing to between Roman and Old Catholicism: one understands that only to the extent that one understands the two religious systems themselves and their historical relations. The 'sociological law' may be helpful in calling one's attention to features of historical situations which one might otherwise have overlooked and in suggesting useful analogies. Here for instance one may be led to compare Simmel's example with the relations between the Russian Communist Party and, on the one hand, the British Labour Party and, on the other, the British Conservatives. But no historical situation can be understood simply by 'applying' such laws, as one applies laws to particular occurrences in natural science. Indeed, it is only in so far as one has an *independent* historical grasp of situations like this one that one is able to understand what the law amounts to at all. That is not like having to know the kind of experiment on which a scientific theory is based before one can understand the theory, for there it makes no sense to speak of understanding the connections between the parts of the experiment except in terms of the scientific theory. But one could understand very well the nature of the relations between Roman Catholicism and Old Catholicism without ever having heard of Simmel's theory, or anything like it.

Bibliography[3]

[1] ACTON, H. B. *The Illusion of the Epoch*, Cohen & West, 1955.

[2] ARON, Raymond, *German Sociology*, Heinemann, 1957.

[3] AYER, A. J. *The Problem of Knowledge*, Macmillan and Penguin Books, 1956.

[4] AYER, A. J. '*Can* There be a Private Language?', *Proceedings of the Aristotelian Society*, Supplementary Volume XXVIII.

[5] CARROLL, Lewis, 'What the Tortoise Said to Achilles', *Complete Works*, Nonesuch Press.

[6] COLLINGWOOD, R. G. *The Idea of History*, OUP, 1946.

[7] COLLINGWOOD, R. G. *The Principles of Art*, OUP, 1938.

[8] CRANSTON, Maurice, *Freedom: A New Analysis*, Longmans, 1953.

[9] DURKHEIM, Emile, *Suicide*, Routledge & Kegan Paul, 1952.

[10] GEACH, Peter, *Mental Acts*, Routledge & Kegan Paul, 1957.

[11] GINSBERG, Morris, *On the Diversity of Morals*, Heinemann, 1956.

[12] HUME, David, *Enquiry into Human Understanding*.

[13] LASLETT, Peter (Ed.), *Philosophy, Politics and Society*, Blackwell, 1956.

[14] LEVI, E. H. *An Introduction to Legal Reasoning*, University of Chicago, *c.* 1948.

[15] LYND, R. S., *Knowledge for What?*, Princeton, 1945.

[16] MALCOLM, Norman, Article in the *Philosophical Review*, Vol. LXIII, 1954, pp. 530–559.

[17] MANDELBAUM, Maurice, 'Societal Facts', *B. J. Sociol.*, VI, 4 (1955).

[18] MILL, J. S., *A System of Logic*.

[3] [*Some of the works cited here by Winch are not referred to in the segment of his book reprinted in this volume. Editor's note.*]

[19] NEWCOMB, T. M., *Social Psychology*, Tavistock Publications, 1952.

[20] OAKESHOTT, Michael, 'The Tower of Babel', *Cambridge Journal*, Vol. 2.

[21] OAKESHOTT, Michael, 'Rational Conduct', *Cambridge Journal*, Vol. 4.

[22] OAKESHOTT, Michael, *Political Education*, Bowes and Bowes, 1951.

[23] PARETO, Vilfredo, *The Mind and Society*, New York, Harcourt Brace, 1935.

[24] PARSONS, Talcott, *The Structure of Social Action*, Allen & Unwin, 1949.

[25] POPPER, Karl, *The Open Society and Its Enemies*, Routledge & Kegan Paul, 1945.

[26] POPPER, Karl, *The Poverty of Historicism*, Routledge & Kegan Paul, 1957.

[27] RENNER, Karl (with Introduction by O. KAHN-FREUND), *The Institutions of Private Law and their Social Function*, Routledge & Kegan Paul, 1949.

[28] RHEES, Rush, 'Can There be a Private Language?', *Proceedings of the Aristotelian Society*, Supplementary Volume XXVIII.

[29] RYLE, Gilbert, *The Concept of Mind*, Hutchinson, 1949.

[30] SHERIF, M. & SHERIF, C., *An Outline of Social Psychology*, New York, Harper, 1956.

[31] SIMMEL, GEORG, *Conflict*, Glencoe, Free Press, 1955.

[32] STRAWSON, P. F., Critical Notice in *Mind*, Vol. LXIII, No. 249, pp. 84ff.

[33] WEBER, Max, *Wirtschaft und Gesellschaft*, Tübingen, Mohr, 1956.

[34] WEBER, Max, *Gesammelte Aufsätze zur Wissenschaftslehre*, Tübingen, Mohr, 1922.

[35] WELDON, T. D., *The Vocabulary of Politcs*, Penguin Books, 1953.

[36] WITTGENSTEIN, Ludwig, *Tractatus Logico-Philosophicus*, Kegan Paul, 1923.

[37] WITTGENSTEIN, Ludwig, *Philosophical Investigations*, Blackwell, 1953.

[38] WITTGENSTEIN, Ludwig, *Remarks on the Foundations of Mathematics*, Blackwell, 1956.

To Explain Institutional Change Requires Nomothetic Social Science

28

Review of Winch's "The Idea of a Social Science"

LEON J. GOLDSTEIN

. . . The surprising theme of Mr. Winch's book — which is one of the *Studies in Philosophical Psychology* edited by R. F. Holland — is that the proper business of sociology is the elucidation of modes of discourse. One also learns, at least by implication, that one of the most important recent contributions, if not to sociology itself at least to the methodology of it, is Ludwig Wittgenstein's *Philosophical Investigations* (pp. 24ff.). But this is intended quite seriously, and nowhere in the book's Chapter 3, "The Social Studies as Science," which is the heart of the book — that part of it in which the author's views are given their most systematic exposition — is there the slightest indication that sociologists have some interest in the development of institutions. The only alternative to his view which is taken seriously enough to be discussed in this chapter is a sort of reductionist mechanism (pp. 75ff.). That social scientists may not be expected to predict the direction that jazz will take or the writing of a specific poem is taken to be reason enough to rule out nomothetic social science (p. 93f.). But while these might well be goals of a social science informed by principles such as those of Holbach or LaPlace, I must confess never to have seen this kind of thing given as the goals of social science as actually practiced today.

Winch argues that social science must comprehend the social situation it seeks to deal with in the way in which it is understood by the actors themselves (ch. 2). To be sure, this is not to be understood as meaning that social science merely records unthinkingly human acts which are performed unthinkingly. Implicit in every social act are rules which determine that this is the sort of thing that one does in the kind of situation confronting the actor. Usually, the actor acts without troubling to take account of the rules. But should he be challenged to defend his course, he might well be able to, and he would offer such defense as he could in terms of rules. The more sensitive he is to the rules which govern ordinary behavior in his society, the better the account will be that he offers. The sociologist is presumably one who takes the greatest pains with this sort of thing; he is one who is trained to elucidate the rules of the social game. This is on the analogy of the elucidation by linguistic philosophers of the rules of the various language games we are said to play. Sociology properly done, then, is just a special application of linguistic philosophy. (This view of sociology, it may be noted, is not to be mistaken for the perfectly sound view that some questions are to be answered by conceptual analysis and not empirical research — pp. 17f. — and one is at liberty to accept the latter without the former.)

How can the new conception of sociology that is offered in this book be justified? I think it must be admitted from the start that any argument which has as its conclusion "such and such is the nature of social science" and yet does not purport to be a description of what social scientists are doing must perforce be a *petitio principii*. This is the case for Winch's argument. He will argue against those who believe in the possibility of a nomothetic social science that social science can only be concerned with the elucidation of rules (not, of course, laws) governing social behavior. The conclusion is assured by the simple expedient of making sociology a

From *The Philosophical Review*, 69:4 (July, 1960), pp. 411–414.

discipline which does not seek to *explain* social phenomena but rather to *understand* the actions of human agents. As we have seen, it is concerned to elucidate the argument that a rational actor might give in defense of his course of action were he fully aware of the rules of social conduct in his society. Thus it is concluded that sociology is only what Winch will permit sociologists to do.

The fact of the matter is, however, that sociologists seem not to be aware of this restriction upon their activities and seek — with whatever success — to do other things. And some take it to be entirely within their purview to seek explanations of social phenomena. That is to say, they are concerned to discover, among other things, how it was that this or that institution came to be as it is or how institutions of determinate type develop and change. But the kinds of problems that these inquiries are called upon to solve cannot be solved through the elucidation of rules in Winch's sense.

The existence of a social rule presupposes the existence of an ongoing sociocultural system. (I use "existence" here only for ease of expression and not in order to give anyone metaphysical jitters.) It is possible, I suppose, to consider such a system as a system of rules (cf. p. 127f.). They suppose that human actors more or less know what sort of behavior to expect from normal fellow-men with whom they share their culture. But if I want to account for the existence of an institution, or if I want to explain the existence in this society of some particular rule, I cannot appeal to the rule to explain itself. Nor can I look for another rule of the same sort to explain my first rule. (At best, the rule can make intelligible the actions of an agent whose actions presuppose rules or institutions, though I suspect that the way Winch conceives of this it can only be done on the assumption that the agent is rational in all relevant respects.) To explain the presence of institutions, I must be able to specify the conditions which give them rise. Thus, even if we allow Winch's claim that what the sociologist studies is determined (not in the causal sense) by rules other than those of his investigation (p. 87), it is clear that if he is not permitted to go beyond the given rules he cannot explain them.

We have seen that Winch's argument is a *petitio*, but why should he wish to formulate an argument such as the one he does? That is, why does he wish to exclude nomothetic social science? The kinds of examples he uses in the course of his discussion suggest as one possible answer that he does not really appreciate that there can be diachronic studies of institutions. The problems he recognizes seem to be only those of individual actors, even though he takes social rules to be non-individualistic in character (p. 128), and it is clear that he makes no serious effort to distinguish between sociology and psychology. It seems suggested that a social science which was not merely the elucidation of rules would be a science which was concerned to uncover those causal factors which compel men to act as they do, and that this "idea of a social science" would be not only repugnant to our moral consciousness but would be at variance with our sense of not being compelled. It is worth repeating that the example that Winch offers of what is to be rejected in favor of his conception of social science is rather primitive mechanistic psychology (pp. 75ff.) which, however bad psychology it may be, is not sociology at all. Winch's point seems to be that men are not pushed about, either by inner forces or by the sort of external powers that J. W. N. Watkins has characterized as "holistic" (*British Journal for the Philosophy of Science*, VIII, 1957, 106f.). Rather he believes that they can, and often do, offer a fairly good account of themselves. But he fails to recognize that the account is always within a system of institutions which are taken for granted. Sociology is that discipline which, among other things, is supposed to account for such institutions. And it certainly cannot be claimed on the basis of anything that Winch has said that a nomothetic social science not having the repugnant features mentioned above is impossible.

Intentional Activity Cannot Be Explained by Contingent Causal Laws

29

The Conceivability of Mechanism

NORMAN MALCOLM

1. By "mechanism" I am going to understand a special application of physical determinism — namely, to all organisms with neurological systems, including human beings. The version of mechanism I wish to study assumes a neurophysiological theory which is adequate to explain and predict all movements of human bodies except those caused by outside forces. The human body is assumed to be as complete a causal system as is a gasoline engine. Neurological states and processes are conceived to be correlated by general laws with the mechanisms that produce movements. Chemical and electrical changes in the nervous tissue of the body are assumed to cause muscle contractions, which in turn cause movements such as blinking, breathing, and puckering of the lips, as well as movements of fingers, limbs, and head. Such movements are sometimes produced by forces (pushes and pulls) applied externally to the body. If someone forced my arm up over my head, the theory could not explain that movement of my arm. But it could explain any movement not due to an external push or pull. It could explain, and predict, the movements that occur when a person signals a taxi, plays chess, writes an essay, or walks to the store.[1]

It is assumed that the neurophysiological system of the human body is subject to various kinds of stimulation. Changes of temperature or pressure in the environment; sounds, odors; the ingestion of foods and liquids: all these will have an effect on the nerve pulses that turn on the movement-producing mechanisms of the body.

2. The neurophysiological theory we are envisaging would, as said, be rich enough to provide systematic causal explanations of all bodily movements not due to external physical causes. These explanations should be understood as stating *sufficient* conditions of movement and not merely necessary conditions. They would employ laws that connect neurophysiological states or processes with movements. The laws would be universal propositions of the following form: whenever an organism of structure S is in state q it will emit movement m. Having ascertained that a given organism is of structure S and is in state q, one could deduce the occurrence of movement m.

It should be emphasized that this theory makes no provision for desires, aims, goals, purposes, motives, or intentions. In explaining such an occurrence as a man's walking across a room, it will be a matter of indifference to the theory whether the man's purpose, intention, or desire was to open a window, or even whether his walking across the room was intentional. This aspect of the theory can be indicated by saying that it is a "nonpurposive" system of explanation.

The viewpoint of mechanism thus assumes a theory that would provide systematic, complete, nonpurposive, causal explanations of all human movements not produced by

From *The Philosophical Review*, LXXVII, No. 1 (Jan., 1968), pp. 45–72.

[1] If you said "Get up!" and I got up, the theory would explain my movements in terms of neurophysiological events produced by the impact of sound waves on my auditory organs.

external forces. Such a theory does not at present exist. But nowadays it is ever more widely held that in the not far distant future there will be such a theory — and that it will be true. I will raise the question of whether this is conceivable. The subject belongs to an age-old controversy. It would be unrealistic for me to hope to make any noteworthy contribution to its solution. But the problem itself is one of great human interest and worthy of repeated study.

3. To appreciate the significance of mechanism, one must be aware of the extent to which a comprehensive neurophysiological theory of human behavior would diverge from those everyday explanations of behavior with which all of us are familiar. These explanations refer to purposes, desires, goals, intentions. "He is running to catch the bus." "He is climbing the ladder in order to inspect the roof." "He is stopping at this store because he wants some cigars." Our daily discourse is filled with explanations of behavior in terms of the agent's purposes or intentions. The behavior is claimed to occur in order that some state of affairs should be brought about or avoided — that the bus should be caught, the roof inspected, cigars purchased. Let us say that these are "purposive" explanations.

We can note several differences between these common purposive explanations and the imagined neurophysiological explanations. First, the latter were conceived by us to be systematic — that is, to belong to a comprehensive theory — whereas the familiar purposive explanations are not organized into a theory. Second, the neurophysiological explanations do not employ the concept of purpose or intention. Third, the neurophysiological explanations embody contingent laws, but purposive explanations do not.

Let us dwell on this third point. A neurophysiological explanation of some behavior that has occurred is assumed to have the following form:

> Whenever an organism of structure *S* is in neurophysiological state *q* it will emit movement *m*.
>
> Organism *O* of structure *S* was in neurophysiological state *q*.
>
> Therefore, *O* emitted *m*.[2]

The general form of purposive explanation is the following:

> Whenever an organism *O* has goal *G* and believes that behavior *B* is required to bring about *G*, *O* will emit *B*.
>
> *O* had *G* and believed *B* was required of *G*.
>
> Therefore, *O* emitted *B*.

Let us compare the first premise of a neurophysiological explanation with the first premise of a purposive explanation. The first premise of a neurophysiological explanation is a contingent proposition, but the first premise of a purposive explanation is not a contingent proposition. This difference will appear more clearly if we consider how, in both cases, the first premise would have to be qualified in order to be actually true. In both cases a *ceteris paribus* clause must be added to the first premise. or at least be implicitly understood. (It will be more perspicuous to translate "*ceteris paribus*" as "provided there are no countervailing factors" rather than as "other things being equal.")

Let us consider what "*ceteris paribus*" will mean in concrete terms. Suppose a man climbed a ladder leading to a roof. An explanation is desired. The fact is that the wind blew his hat onto the roof and he wants it back. The explanation would be spelled out in detail as follows:

> If a man wants to retrieve his hat and believes this requires him to climb a ladder, he will do so provided there are no countervailing factors.
>
> This man wanted to retrieve his hat and

[2] A neurophysiological *prediction* would be of the same form, with these differences: the second premise would say that *O* is or will be in state *q* (instead of *was*), and the conclusion would say that *O will* emit *m* (instead of *emitted*).

believed that this required him to climb a ladder, and there were no countervailing factors.

Therefore, he climbed a ladder.

What sorts of things might be included under "countervailing factors" in such a case? The unavailability of a ladder, the fear of climbing one, the belief that someone would remove the ladder while he was on the roof, and so on. (The man's failure to climb a ladder would *not* be a countervailing factor.)

An important point emerging here is that the addition of the *ceteris paribus* clause to the first premise turns this premise into an a priori proposition. If there were no countervailing factors whatever (if the man knew a ladder was available, had no fear of ladders or high places, no belief that he might be marooned on the roof, and so on); if there were no hindrances or hazards, real or imagined, physical or psychological; then if the man did not climb a ladder it would not be true that he *wanted* his hat back, or *intended* to get it back.[3]

In his important recent book, *The Explanation of Behaviour*, Charles Taylor puts the point as follows:

> This is part of what we mean by "intending *X*," that, in the absence of interfering factors, it is followed by doing *X*. I could not be said to intend *X* if, even with no obstacles or other countervailing factors, I still didn't do it.[4]

This feature of the meaning of "intend" also holds true of "want," "purpose," and "goal."

Thus the universal premise of a purposive explanation is an a priori principle, not a contingent law. Some philosophers have made this a basis for saying that a purposive explanation is not a causal explanation.[5] But this is a stipulation (perhaps a useful one), rather than a description of how the word "cause" is actually used in ordinary language.

Let us consider the effect of adding a *ceteris paribus* clause to the universal premise of a neural explanation of behavior. Would a premise of this form be true a priori? Certainly not. Suppose it were believed that whenever a human being is in neural state *q* his right hand will move up above his head, provided there are no countervailing factors. What could be countervailing factors? That the subject's right arm is broken or that it is tied to his side, and so on. But the exclusion of such countervailing factors would have no tendency to make the premise true a priori. There is no connection of meaning, explicit or implicit, between the description of any neural state and the description of any movement of the hand. No matter how many countervailing factors are excluded, the proposition will not lose the character of a contingent law (unless, of course, we count the failure of the hand to move as itself a countervailing factor, in which case the premise becomes a tautology).

4. Making explicit the *ceteris paribus* conditions points up the different logical natures of the universal premises of the two kinds of explanation. Premises of the one sort express contingent correlations between neurological processes and behavior. Premises of the other sort express a priori connections between intentions (purposes, desires, goals) and behavior.

This difference is of the utmost importance. Some students of behavior have believed that purposive explanations of behavior will be found to be less basic than the explanations

[3] The correct diagnosis of such a failure will not be evident in all cases. Suppose a youth wants to be a trapeze performer in a circus, and he believes this requires daily exercise on the parallel bars. But he is lazy and frequently fails to exercise. Doesn't he really have the goal he professes to have: is it just talk? Or doesn't he really believe in the necessity of the daily exercise? Or is it that he has the goal and the belief and his laziness is a genuine countervailing factor? One might have to know him very well in order to give the right answer. In some cases there might be no definite right answer.

[4] Charles Taylor, *The Explanation of Behaviour* (New York, 1964), p. 33.

[5] E.g., Taylor says that the agent's intention is not a "causal antecedent" of his behavior, for intention and behavior "are not contingently connected in the normal way" (*ibid.*).

that will arise from a future neurophysiological theory. They think that the principles of purposive explanation will turn out to be dependent on the neurophysiological laws. On this view our ordinary explanations of behavior will often be true: but the neural explanations will also be true — and they will be *more fundamental*. Thus we could, theoretically, *by-pass* explanations of behavior in terms of purpose, and the day might come when they simply fall into disuse.

I wish to show that neurophysiological laws could not be more basic than purposive principles. I shall understand the statement that a Law L_2 is "more basic" than a law L_1 to mean that L_1 is dependent on L_2 but L_2 is not dependent on L_1. To give an example, let us suppose there is a uniform connection between food abstinence and hunger: that is, going without food for *n* hours always results in hunger. This is L_1. Another law L_2 is discovered — namely, a uniform connection between a certain chemical condition of body tissue (called "cell-starvation") and hunger. Whenever cell-starvation occurs, hunger results. It is also discovered that L_2 is more basic than L_1. This would amount to the following fact: food abstinence for *n* hours will not result in hunger *unless* cell-starvation occurs; and if the latter occurs, hunger will result *regardless of whether* food abstinence occurs. Thus the L_1 regularity is contingently dependent on the L_2 regularity, and the converse is not true. Our knowledge of this dependency would reveal to us the conditions under which the L_1 regularity would no longer hold.

Our comparison of the differing logical natures of purposive principles and neurophysiological laws enables us to see that the former cannot be dependent on the latter. The a priori connection between intention or purpose and behavior cannot fail to hold. It cannot be contingently dependent on any contingent regularity. The neurophysiological explanations of behavior could not, in the sense explained, turn out to be more basic than our everyday purposive explanations.[6]

5. There is a second important consequence of the logical difference between neurophysiological laws and purposive principles. Someone might suppose that although purposive explanations cannot be dependent on nonpurposive explanations, they would be refuted by the verification of a comprehensive neurophysiological theory of behavior. I think this view is correct: but it is necessary to understand what it *cannot* mean. It cannot mean that the principles (the universal premises) of purposive explanations would be proved false. They cannot be proved false. It could not fail to be true that if a person wanted *X* and believed *Y* was necessary for *X*, and there were absolutely no countervailing factors, he would do *Y*.[7] This purposive principle is true a priori, not because of its form but because of its meaning — that is, because of the connection of meaning between the words "He wanted *X* and he realized that *Y* was necessary for *X*" and the words "He did *Y*." The purposive principle is not a law of nature but a conceptual truth. It cannot be confirmed or refuted by experience. Since the verification of a neurophysiological theory could never *disprove* any purposive principles, the only possible outcome of such verification, logically speaking, would be to prove that the purposive principles have no application to the world. I shall return to this point later.

6. We must come to closer grips with the exact logical relationship between neural and purposive explanations of behavior. Can explanations of both types be true of the same

[6] Taylor puts the point as follows:
"Because explanation by intentions or purposes is like explanation by an "antecedent" which is non-contingently linked with its consequent, i.e., because the fact that the behaviour follows from the intention other things being equal is not a contingent fact, we cannot account for this fact by more basic laws. For to explain a fact by more basic laws is to give the regularities on which this fact causally depends. But not being contingent, the dependence of behaviour on intention is not contingent on anything, and hence not on any such regularities [*ibid.*, p. 44]."

[7] This is true if we use "wants *X*" to mean "is aiming at *X*." But sometimes we may mean no more than "would like to have *X*," which may represent a mere wish.

bit of behavior on one and the same occasion? Is there any rivalry between them? Some philosophers would say not. They would say that, for one thing, the two kinds of explanation explain different things. Purposive explanations explain actions. Neurophysiological explanations explain movements. Both explain behavior: but we can say this only because we use the latter word ambiguously to cover both actions and movements. For a second point, it may be held that the two kinds of explanation belong to different "bodies of discourse" or to different "language games." They employ different concepts and assumptions. One kind of explanation relates behavior to causal laws and to concepts of biochemistry and physiology, to nerve pulses and chemical reactions. The other kind of explanation relates behavior to the desires, intentions, goals, and reasons of persons. The two forms of explanation can co-exist, because they are irrelevant to one another.[8]

It is true that the two kinds of explanation employ different concepts and, in a sense, explain different things: but are they really independent of one another? Take the example of the man climbing a ladder in order to retrieve his hat from the roof. This explanation relates his climbing to his intention. A neurophysiological explanation of his climbing would say nothing about his intention but would connect his movements on the ladder with chemical changes in body tissue or with the firing of neurons. Do the two accounts interfere with one another?

7. I believe there *would* be a collision between the two accounts if they were offered as explanations of one and the same occurrence of a man's climbing a ladder. We will recall that the envisaged neurophysiological theory was supposed to provide *sufficient* causal explanations of behavior. Thus the movements of the man on the ladder would be *completely* accounted for in terms of electrical, chemical, and mechanical processes in his body. This would surely imply that his desire or intention to retrieve his hat had nothing to do with his movement up the ladder. It would imply that on this same occasion he would have moved up the ladder in exactly this way even if he had had no intention to retrieve his hat, or even no intention to climb the ladder. To mention his intention or purpose would be no explanation, nor even part of an explanation, of his movements on the ladder. Given the antecedent neurological states of his bodily system together with general laws correlating those states with the contractions of muscles and movements of limbs, he would have moved as he did regardless of his desire or intention. If every movement of his was completely accounted for by his antecedent neurophysiological states (his "programming"), then it was not true that those movements occurred *because* he wanted or intended to get his hat.

8. I will briefly consider three possible objections to my claim that if mechanism were true the man would have moved up the ladder as he did even if he had not had any intention to climb the ladder. The first objection comes from a philosopher who espouses the currently popular psychophysical identity thesis. He holds that there is a neural condition that causes the man's movements up the ladder, and he further holds that the man's intention to climb the ladder (or, possibly, his having the intention) is contingently identical with the neural condition that causes the movements. Thus, if the man had not intended to climb the ladder, the cause of his movements would not have ex-

[8] The following remarks by A. I. Melden present both of these points:
"Where we are concerned with causal explanations, with events of which the happenings in question are effects in accordance with some law of causality, to that extent we are not concerned with human actions at all but, at best, with bodily movements or happenings; and where we are concerned with explanations of human action, there causal factors and causal laws in the sense in which, for example, these terms are employed in the biological sciences are wholly irrelevant to the understanding we seek. The reason is simple, namely, the radically different logical characteristics of the two bodies of discourse we employ in these distinct cases — the different concepts which are applicable to these different orders of inquiry [A. I. Melden, *Free Action* (New York, 1961), p. 184]."

isted, and so those movements would not have occurred. My reply would be that the view that there may be a contingent identity (and not merely an extensional equivalence) between an intention (or the having of the intention) and a neural condition is not a meaningful hypothesis. One version of the identity thesis is that *A*'s intention to climb the ladder is contingently identical with some process in *A*'s brain. Verifying this identity would require the meaningless step of trying to discover whether *A*'s intention is located in his brain. One could give meaning to the notion of the location of *A*'s intention in his brain by stipulating that it has the same location as does the correlated neural process. But the identity that arose from this stipulation would not be contingent.[9] Another version of the identity thesis is that the event of Smith's having the intention *I* is identical with the event of Smith's being in neural condition *N*. This version avoids the above "location problem": but it must take on the task (which seems hopeless) of explaining how the property "having intention *I*" and the property "being in neural condition *N*" could be contingently identical and not merely co-extensive.[10]

The second objection comes from an epiphenomenalist. He holds that the neurophysiological condition that contingently causes the behavior on the ladder also contingently causes the intention to climb the ladder, but that the intention stands in no causal relation to the behavior. If the intention had not existed, the cause of it and of the behavior would not have existed, and so the behavior would not have occurred. A decisive objection to epiphenomenalism is that, according to it, the relation between intention and behavior would be purely contingent. It would be conceivable that the neurophysiological condition that always causes ladder-climbing movements should also always cause the intention to *not* climb up a ladder. Epiphenomenalism would permit it to be universally true that whenever any person intended to *not* do any action, he did it, and that whenever any person intended to do any action, he did not do it. This is a conceptual absurdity.

The third objection springs from a philosopher who combines mechanism with logical behaviorism. He holds that some condition of the neurophysiological system causes the preparatory movements, gestures, and utterances that are expressions of the man's intention to climb the ladder; and it also causes his movements up the ladder. The component of logical behaviorism in his over-all view is this: he holds that the man's having the intention to climb the ladder is simply a logical construction out of the occurrence of the expressions of intention and also the occurrence of the ladder-climbing movements. Having the intention is nothing other than the expressive behavior plus the subsequent climbing behavior. Having the intention is defined in terms of behavior-events that are contingently caused by a neurophysiological condition. The supposition that the man did not have the intention to climb the ladder would be identical with the supposition that either the expressive behavior or the climbing behavior, or both, did not occur. If either one did not occur, then neither occurred, since by hypothesis both of them have the same cause. Thus it would be false that the man would have moved up the ladder as he did even if he had not had an intention to climb the ladder.

I think that this third position gives an unsatisfactory account of the nature of intention. Actually climbing the ladder is not a necessary condition *simpliciter* for the existence of the intention to climb the ladder. It is a necessary condition *provided* there are no countervailing factors. But there is no definite number of countervailing factors, and so they cannot be exhaustively enumerated. In addition, some of them will themselves involve the concepts

[9] This point is argued in my "Scientific Materialism and The Identity Theory," *Dialogue*, 3 (1964); also in my forthcoming monograph, *Problems of Mind*, sec. 18, to be published in the Harper Guide to Philosophy, edited by Arthur Danto.

[10] For an exposition of this problem see Jaegwon Kim's "On the Psycho-Physical Identity Theory," *American Philosophical Quarterly*, 3 (1966)

of desire, belief, or purpose. For example: a man intends to climb the ladder, but also he does not want to look ridiculous; as he is just about to start climbing he is struck by the thought that he will look ridiculous; so he does not climb the ladder, although he had intended to. An adequate logical behaviorism would have to analyze away not only the initial reference to intention, but also the reference to desire, belief, purpose, and all other psychological concepts, that would occur in the listing of possible countervailing factors. There is no reason for thinking that such a program of analysis could be carried out.

Thus a mechanist can hope to avoid the consequence that the man would have moved up the ladder as he did even if he had not had the intention of climbing the ladder, by combining his mechanist doctrine with the psychophysical identity thesis, or with epiphenomenalism, or with logical behaviorism. But these supplementary positions are so objectionable or implausible that the mechanist is not really saved from the above consequence.

9. Let us remember that the postulated neurophysiological theory is comprehensive. It is assumed to provide complete causal explanations for all bodily movements that are not produced by external physical forces. It is a closed system in the sense that it does not admit, as antecedent conditions, anything other than neurophysiological states and processes. Desires and intentions have no place in it.

If the neurophysiological theory were true, then in no cases would desires, intentions, purposes be necessary conditions of any human movements. It would never be true that a man would *not* have moved as he did if he had *not* had such and such an intention. Nor would it ever be true that a certain movement of his was due to, or brought about by, or caused by his having a certain intention or purpose. Purposive explanations of human bodily movements would *never* be true. Desires and intentions would not be even potential causes of human movements in the actual world (as contrasted with some possible world in which the neurophysiological theory did not hold true).

It might be thought that there could be two different systems of causal explanations of human movements, a purposive system and a neurophysiological system. The antecedent conditions in the one system would be the desires and intentions of human beings; in the other they would be the neurophysiological states and processes of those same human beings. Each system would provide adequate causal explanations of the same movements.

Generally speaking, it is possible for there to be a plurality of simultaneous sufficient causal conditions of an event. But if we bear in mind the comprehensive aspect of the neurophysiological theory — that is, the fact that it provides sufficient causal conditions for all movements — we shall see that desires and intentions could not be causes of movements. It has often been noted that to say *B causes C* does not mean merely that whenever *B* occurs, *C* occurs. Causation also has subjunctive and counterfactual implications: if *B were to* occur, *C would* occur; and if *B* had *not* occurred, *C* would *not* have occurred. But the neurophysiological theory would provide sufficient causal conditions for every human movement, and so there would be no cases at all in which a certain movement would not have occurred if the person had not had this desire or intention. Since the counterfactual would be false in all cases, desires and intentions would not be causes of human movements. They would not ever be sufficient causal conditions nor would they ever be necessary causal conditions.

10. Let us tackle this immensely important point from a different angle. Many descriptions of behavior ascribe actions to persons: they say that someone *did* something — for example, "He signed the check," "You lifted the table," "She broke the vase." Two things are implied by an ascription of an "action" to a person[11]: first, that a certain state of affairs

[11] I am following Charles Taylor here: *op. cit.*, pp. 27–32.

came into existence (his signature's being present on the check, the table's being lifted, the vase's being broken); second, that the person intended that this state of affairs should occur. If subsequently we learn that not both conditions were satisfied, either we qualify the ascription of action or reject it entirely. If the mentioned state of affairs did not come into existence (for example, the vase was not broken), then the ascription of action ("She broke the vase") must be withdrawn. If it did come into existence but without the person's intention, then the ascription of action to the person must be diminished by some such qualification as "unintentionally" or "accidentally" or "by mistake" or "inadvertently," it being a matter of the circumstances which qualification is more appropriate. A qualified ascription of action still implies that the person played some part in bringing about the state of affairs — for example, her hand struck the vase. If she played no part at all, then it cannot rightly be said, even with qualification, that she broke the vase.

Suppose a man intends to open the door in front of him. He turns the knob and the door opens. Since turning the knob is what normally causes the door to open, we should think it right to say that *he* opened the door. Then we learn that there is an electric mechanism concealed in the door which caused the door to open at the moment he turned the knob, and furthermore that there is no causal connection between the turning of the knob and the operation of the mechanism. So his act of turning the knob had nothing to do with the opening of the door. We can no longer say that *he* opened the door: nothing he did had any causal influence on that result. We might put the matter in this way: because of the operation of the electric mechanism he had no opportunity to open the door.

The man of our example could say that at least he turned the knob. He would have to surrender this claim, however, if it came to light that still another electrical mechanism caused the knob to turn when it did, independently of the motion of his hand. The man could assert that, in any case, he moved his hand. But now the neurophysiological theory enters the scene, providing a complete causal explanation of the motion of his hand, without regard to his intention.

The problem of what to say becomes acute. Should we deny that he moved his hand? Should we admit that he moved his hand, but with some qualification? Or should we say, without qualification, that he moved his hand?

11. There is an important similarity between our three examples and an important difference. The similarity is that in all three cases a mechanism produced the intended states of affairs, and nothing the agent did had any influence on the operation of the mechanim. But there is a difference between the cases. In each of the first two, we can specify something the man did (an action) which would normally cause the intended result to occur, but which did not have that effect on this occasion. The action in the first case was turning the knob, and in the second it was gripping the knob and making a turning motion of the hand. In each of these cases there was an action, the causal efficacy of which was nullified by the operation of a mechanism. Consequently, we can rightly say that the man's action *failed* to make a contribution to the intended occurrence, and so we can deny that *he* opened the door or turned the knob.

In the third case is there something the man did which normally causes that movement of the hand? What was it? When I move my hand in the normal way is there something else *I do* that causes my hand to move? No. Various events take place in my body (for example, nerve pulses) but they cannot be said to be *actions* of mine. They are not things I do.

But in this third case the man *intended* to make a turning motion of his hand. Is this a basis for a similarity between the third case and the first two? Can we say that one's intention to move one's hand is normally a cause of the motion of one's hand, but that in our third case the causal efficacy of the intention was nullified by the operation of the neurophysiological mechanism?

On the question of whether intentions are causes of actions, Taylor says something that is both interesting and puzzling. He declares that to call something an action, in an unqualified sense "means not just that the man who displayed this behaviour had framed the relevant intention or had this purpose, but also that *his intending it brought it about*."[12] Now to say that *A* "brings about" *B* is to use the language of causation. "Brings about" is indeed a synonym for "causes."

12. Is there any sense at all in which a man's intention to do something can be a cause of his doing it? In dealing with this point I shall use the word "cause" in its widest sense, according to which anything that explains, or partly explains, the occurrence of some behavior is the cause, or part of the cause, of the behavior. To learn that a man intended to climb a ladder would not, in many cases, explain why he climbed it. It would not explain what he climbed it for, what his reason or purpose was in climbing it, whereas to say what his purpose was would, in our broad sense, give the cause or part of the cause of his climbing it.

In considering intention as a cause of behavior *X*, it is important to distinguish between the intention to do *X* (let us call this *simple intention*) and in the intention to do something else *Y* in or by doing *X* (let us call this *further intention*). To say that a man intended to climb a ladder would not usually give a cause of his climbing it; but stating his purpose in climbing it would usually be giving the (or a) cause of the action. It is a natural use of language to ask, "What caused you to climb the ladder?"; and it is an appropriate answer to say, "I wanted to get my hat." (*Question:* "Good heavens, what caused you to vote a straight Republican ticket?" *Answer:* "I wanted to restore the two-party system.") Our use of the language of causation is not restricted to the cases in which cause and effect are assumed to be contingently related.

13. Can the simple intention to do *X* ever be a cause of the doing of *X*? Can it ever be said that a person's intention to climb a ladder caused him to climb it, or brought about his action of climbing it? It is certainly true that whether a man does or does not intend to do *X* will make a difference in whether he will do *X*. This fact comes out strongly if we are concerned to predict whether he will do *X;* obviously, it would be important to find out whether he intends to do it. Does not this imply that his intention has "an effect on his behavior"?[13]

Commonly, we think of dispositions as causes of behavior. If with the same provocation one man loses his temper and another does not, this difference in their reactions might be explained by the fact that the one man, but not the other, is of an irritable disposition. If dispositions are causes, we can hardly deny the same role to intentions. Both are useful in predicting behavior. If I am trying to estimate the likelihood that this man is going to do so-and-so, the information that he has a disposition to do it in circumstances like these will be an affirmative consideration. I am entitled to give equal or possibly greater weight to the information that he intends to do it.

Not only do simple intentions have weight in predicting actions, but also they figure in the explanation of actions that have already occurred. If a man who has just been released from prison promptly climbs a flagpole, I may want an explanation of that occurrence. If I

[12] Taylor, *op. cit.*, p. 33 (my italics). Taylor says that an intention is *not* "a causal antecedent" of the intended behavior, for the reason that the intention and the behavior are not *contingently connected.* I think he may be fairly represented as holding that an intention does *cause* the intended behavior, although not in the sense of "cause" in which cause and effect are contingently correlated.

[13] Taylor's phrase, *op. cit.*, p. 34. In my review of Taylor's book ("Explaining Behavior," *Philosophical Review*, LXXVI [1967], 97–104), I say that Taylor is wrong in holding that a simple intention *brings about* the corresponding behavior. But now I am holding that he is partly right and partly wrong: right about previously formed simple intentions, wrong about merely concurrent simple intentions.

learn that he had previously made up his mind to do it, but had been prevented by his imprisonment, I have received a partial explanation of why he is climbing the flagpole, even if I do not yet know his further intention, if any, in climbing it. In general, if I am surprised at an action, it will help me to understand its occurrence if I find out that the agent had previously decided to do it but was prevented by an obstacle which has just been removed.

14. The simple intentions so far considered were formed in advance of the corresponding action. But many simple intentions are not formed in advance of the corresponding action. Driving a car, one suddenly (and intentionally) presses the brake pedal: but there was no time before this action occurred when one intended to do it. The intention existed only at the time of the action, or only *in* the action. Let us call this a merely concurrent simple intention. Can an intention of this kind be a causal factor in the corresponding action?

Here we have to remember that if the driver did not press the brake intentionally, his pressing of the brake was not unqualified action. The presence of simple intention in the action (that is, its being intentional) is an analytically necessary condition for its being unqualified action. This condition is not a cause but a defining condition of unqualified action. If this condition were not fulfilled, one would have to use some mitigating phrase — for example, that the driver pressed the brake by mistake. Thus, a simple intention that is merely concurrent cannot be a cause of the corresponding action.

15. Can we not avoid committing ourselves to the assumption that the pressing of the driver's foot on the brake was either intentional or not intentional? Can we not think of it, in a neutral way, as merely behavior? Yes, we can. But it *was* either intentional or not intentional. If the latter, then there was no simple intention to figure as a cause of the behavior. If the former, then the behavior was action, and the driver's merely concurrent simple intention was a defining condition and not a cause of the behavior. The "neutral way" of thinking about the behavior would be merely incomplete. It would be owing to ignorance and not to the existence of a third alternative. It is impossible, by the definition of "action," that the behavior of pressing the brake should be an action and yet not be intentional. Thus it is impossible that a merely concurrent simple intention should have caused the behavior of pressing the brake, whether the behavior was or was not action.

To summarize this discussion of intentions as causes: we need to distinguish between simple intentions and further intentions. If an agent does X with the further intention Y, then it is proper to speak of this further intention as the (or a) cause of the doing of X. Simple intentions may be divided into those that are formed prior to the corresponding actions, and those that are merely concurrent with the actions. By virtue of being previously formed, a simple intention can be a cause of action. But in so far as it is merely concurrent, a simple intention cannot be a cause of the corresponding action.

16. Let us try now to appraise Taylor's view as to the causal role of intention in behavior. He holds that it would not be true, without qualification, that one person stabbed another unless his intention to stab him "brought about" the stabbing (*ibid.*, p. 33). The example was meant to be of a previously formed intention — for Taylor speaks of the agent's *deciding* to stab someone. But a majority of actions do not embody intentions formed in advance. They embody merely concurrent intentions. The latter cannot be said to cause (bring about) the corresponding actions. Possibly because he has fixed his attention too narrowly on cases of decision, Taylor errs in holding that, in general, the concept of action requires that the agent's intention should have brought about the behavior. When the action is merely intentional (without previous intention) the agent's intention cannot be said to bring about his behavior. In such cases his intention gives his behavior the character of *action*, but it does

this by virtue of being a defining condition of action, not by virtue of being a cause of either behavior or action.

17. Our reflections on the relationship of intention to behavior arose from a consideration of three examples of supposed action — opening a door, turning a knob, making a turning motion of the hand. In the first two cases we imagined mechanisms that produced the intended results independently of the agent's intervention. Consequently, we had to deny that *he* opened the door or turned the knob. Then we imagined a neurophysiological cause of the motion of his hand, and we asked whether this would imply, in turn, that *he* did not move his hand.

Is the movement of his hand independent of his "intervention" by virtue of being independent of his intention? We saw previously (Section 8) that a comprehensive neurophysiological theory would leave no room for desires and intentions as causal factors. Consequently, neither the man's previously formed simple intention to move his hand nor his further intention (to open the door) could be causes of the movement of his hand.

18. We noticed before that it is true a priori that if a man wants Y, or has Y as a goal, and believes that X is required for Y, then in the absence of countervailing factors he will do X. It is also true a priori that if a man forms the intention (for example, decides) to do X, then in the absence of countervailing factors he will do X. These a priori principles of action are assumed in our everyday explanations of behavior.

We saw that mechanistic explanations could not be more basic than are explanations in terms of intentions or purposes.

We saw that the verification of mechanistic laws could not disprove the a priori principles of action.

Yet a mechanistic explanation of behavior rules out any explanation of it in terms of the agent's intentions. If a comprehensive neurophysiological theory is true, then people's intentions never are causal factors in behavior.

19. Thus if mechanism is true, the a priori principles of action do not apply to the world. This would have to mean one or the other of two alternatives. The first would be that people do not have intentions, purposes, or desires, or that they do not have beliefs as to what behavior is required for the fulfillment of their desires and purposes. The second alternative would be that although they have intentions, beliefs, and so forth, there always are countervailing factors — that is, factors that interfere with the operation of intentions, desires, and decisions.

The second alternative cannot be taken seriously. If a man wants to be on the opposite bank of a river and believes that swimming it is the only thing that will get him there, he will swim it unless there are countervailing factors, such as an inability to swim or a fear of drowning or a strong dislike of getting wet. In this sense it is not true that countervailing factors are present *whenever* someone has a goal. There are not *always* obstacles to the fulfillment of any purpose or desire.

It might be objected that mechanistic causation itself is a universal countervailing factor. Now if this were so it would imply that purposes, intentions, and desires never have any effect on behavior. But it is not a coherent position to hold that some creatures have purposes and so forth, yet that these have no effect on their behavior. Purposes and intentions are, in concept, so closely tied to behavioral effects that the total absence of behavioral effects would mean the total absence of purposes and intentions. Thus the only position open to the exponent of mechanism is the first alternative — namely, that people do not have intentions, purposes or beliefs.

What I have called "a principle of action" is a conditional proposition, having an antecedent and a consequent. The whole conditional is true a priori, and therefore if the antecedent holds in a particular case, the consequent must also hold in that case. To say that the antecedent holds in a particular case means that it is true of some person (or animal). It means that the person has some desire or intention, and also has the requisite belief. If this were so, and if there were no countervailing factors, it would follow that the person would act in an appropriate manner. His intention or desire would, in our broad sense, be a cause of his action — that is, it would be a factor in the explanation of the occurrence of the action.

But this is incompatible with mechanism. A mechanist must hold, therefore, that the principles of action have no application to reality, in the sense that no one has intentions or desires or beliefs.

Some philosophers would regard this result as an adequate refutation of mechanism. But others would not. They would say that the confirmation of a comprehensive neurophysiological theory of behavior is a logical possibility, and therefore it is logically possible that there are no desires, intentions, and so forth, and that to deny these logical possibilities is to be dogmatic and antiscientific. I will avoid adopting this "dogmatic" and "antiscientific" position, and will formulate a criticism of mechanism from a more "internal' point of view.

20. I wish to make a closer approach to the question of the conceivability of mechanism. We have seen that mechanism is incompatible with purposive behavior, but we have not yet established that it is incompatible with the existence of merely intentional behavior. A man can do something intentionally but with no further intention: his behavior is intentional but not purposive. One possibility is that this behavior should embody a merely concurrent simple intention. Since such intentions are not causes of the behavior to which they belong, their existence does not appear to conflict with mechanistic causation. Mechanism's incompatibility with purposive behavior has not yet shown it to be incompatible with intentional behavior as such.

But could it be true that sometimes people acted intentionally although it was never true that they acted for any purpose? Could they do things intentionally but never with any further intention?

If some intentional actions are purposeless, it does not follow that all of them could be purposeless. And I do not think this is really a possibility. I will not attempt to deal with every kind of action. But consider that subclass of actions that are activities. Any physical activity is analyzable into components. If a man is painting a wall, he is grasping a brush, dipping the brush into the paint, moving his arm back and forth. He does these things in painting. They are parts of his activity of painting. If someone is rocking in a chair, he is pushing against the floor with his feet, and pressing his back against the back of the chair. These are subordinate activities in the activity of rocking. If the one who is painting is asked why he is dipping the brush into the paint, he can answer, "I am painting this wall." This is an explanation of what he is doing in dipping the brush, and also of what he is dipping it *for*. It is a purposive explanation. A person can put paint on a wall, or rock in a chair, or pace back and forth, without having any purpose in doing so. Still these activities could be intentional, although not for any purpose.

Whether intentional or not, these activities would be analyzable into component parts. If the activity is intentional, then at least some of its components will be intentional. If none of them were, the whole to which they belong would not be intentional. A man could not be intentionally putting paint on a wall if he did not intentionally have hold of a brush. Now this is not strictly true since he might not be aware that he was holding a *brush*, rather than a roller or a cloth. But there will have to be *some* description of what he is holding according to which it is true that he is intentionally holding it and intentionally dipping it in the paint.

Thus an intentional activity must have intentional components. The components will be purposive in relation to the whole activity. If X is an intentional component of Y, one can say with equal truth that in X-ing one is Y-ing, or that one is X-ing in order to Y. In moving the pencil on the paper one is drawing a figure: but also one is moving the pencil in order to draw a figure.

I conclude that if there could be no purposive behavior, there could be no intentional activities. Strictly speaking, this does not prove that there could be no intentional action, since many actions are not activities (for example, catching a ball or winning a race, as contrasted with playing ball or running in a race). But many of the actions that are not activities are stages in, or terminations of, activities and could not exist if the activities did not. Although I do not know how to prove the point for all cases, it seems to me highly plausible that if there could be no intentional activities there could be no intentional behavior of any sort — so plausible that I will assume it to be so. A life that was totally devoid of activities certainly could not be a human life. My conclusion is that since mechanism is incompatible with purposive behavior, it is incompatible with intentional activities, and consequently is incompatible with *all* intentional behavior.

21. The long-deferred question of whether the man of our example moved his hand on the doorknob will be answered as follows. The action of moving his hand cannot be rightly ascribed to him. It should not even be ascribed to him with some qualification such as "unintentionally" or "accidentally," for the use of these qualifications implies that there are cases in which it is right to say of a man that he did something "intentionally" or "purposely." But mechanism rules this out. On the other hand, to say "He did not move his hand" would be misleading, not only for the reason just stated, but also for the further reason that this statement would normally carry the implication that his hand did not move — which is false. Neither the sentence "He moved his hand" nor the sentence "He did not move his hand" would be appropriate. We would, of course, say "He moved his hand" if we understood this as merely equivalent to "His hand moved." (It is interesting that we do use these two sentences interchangeably when we are observing someone whom we know to be asleep or unconscious: we are equally ready to say either "He moved his hand" or "His hand moved.") But if we came to believe in mechanism we should, in consistency, give up the ascribing of action, even in a qualified way.

22. We can now proceed directly to the question of whether mechanism is conceivable. Sometimes when philosophers ask whether a proposition is conceivable, they mean to be asking whether it is self-contradictory. Nothing in our examination has indicated that mechanism is a self-contradictory theory, and I am sure it is not. Logically speaking, the earth and the whole universe might have been inhabited solely by organisms of such a nature that all of their movements could have been completely explained in terms of the neurophysiological theory we have envisaged. We can conceive that the world might have been such that mechanism was true. In this sense mechanism is conceivable.

But there is a respect in which mechanism is not conceivable. This is a consequence of the fact that mechanism is incompatible with the existence of any intentional behavior. The speech of human beings is, for the most part, intentional behavior. In particular, stating, asserting, or saying that so-and-so is true requires the intentional uttering of some sentence. If mechanism is true, therefore, no one can state or assert anything. In a sense, no one can *say* anything. Specifically, no one can assert or state that mechanism is true. If anyone were to assert this, the occurrence of his intentional "speech act" would imply that mechanism is false.

Thus there is a logical absurdity in asserting that mechanism is true. It is not that the doctrine of mechanism is self-contradictory. The absurdity lies in the human act of asserting the doctrine. The occurrence of this act of assertion is inconsistent with the content of the assertion. The mere proposition that mechanism is true is not self-contradictory. But the conjunctive proposition, "Mechanism is true and someone asserts it to be true," *is* self-contradictory. Thus anyone's assertion that mechanism is true is necessarily false. The assertion implies its own falsity by virtue of providing a counterexample to what is asserted.

23. A proponent of mechanism might claim that since the absurdity we have been describing is a mere "pragmatic paradox" and not a self-contradiction in the doctrine of mechanism, it does not provide a sense in which mechanism is inconceivable. He may say that the paradox is similar to the paradox of a man's asserting that he himself is unconscious. There is an inconsistency between this man's act of stating he is unconscious and what he states. His act of stating it implies that what he states is false. But this paradox does not establish that a man cannot be unconscious, or that we cannot conceive that a man should be unconscious.

Now there is some similarity between the paradox of stating that oneself is unconscious and the paradox of stating that mechanism is true. But there is an important difference. *I* cannot state, without absurdity, that *I* am unconscious. But anyone else can, without absurdity, state that I am unconscious. There is only one person (myself) whose act of stating this proposition is inconsistent with the proposition. But an assertion of mechanism by any person whomsoever is inconsistent with mechanism. That I am unconscious is not (in consistency) statable by me. The unstatability is relative to only one person. But the unstatability of mechanism is absolute.

Furthermore, no one can consistently assert that although mechanism is unstatable it may be true. For this assertion, too, would require an intentional utterance (speech act) and so would be incompatible with mechanism.

We have elucidated a sense in which mechanism can properly be said to be inconceivable. The sense is that no one can consistently assert (or state, or say) that mechanism is, or may be, true.

If someone were to insist on asserting that mechanism is or may be true, his only recourse (if he were to be consistent) would be to adopt a form of solipsism. He could claim that mechanism is true for other organisms but not for himself. In this way he would free his assertion of inconsistency, but at the cost of accepting the embarrassments and logical difficulties of solipsism. He would also be repudiating the scientific respectability of mechanism by denying the universality of the envisaged neurophysiological laws.

24. Our criticism that mechanism is not a consistently statable doctrine is, of course, purely logical in nature. It consists in deducing a consequence of mechanism. Now one may feel that this consequence cannot refute mechanism or jeopardize its status as a scientific theory. It would seem to be up to science alone to determine whether or not there is a comprehensive neurophysiological theory to explain all bodily movements in accordance with universal laws. If scientific investigation should confirm such a theory, then so be it! To confirm it would be to confirm its consequences. If confirming the theory were to prove that people do not have desires, purposes, or goals, then this result would have to be swallowed, no matter how upsetting it would be not only to our ordinary beliefs but also to our ordinary concepts.

Almost anyone will feel some persuasiveness in this viewpoint. Determinism is a painful problem because it creates a severe tension between two viewpoints, each of which is strongly attractive: one is that the concepts of purpose, intention, and desire, of our ordinary language, cannot be rendered void by scientific advance; the other is that those concepts cannot prescribe limits to what it is possible for empirical science to achieve.

Let us see what would be the effect on our thinking of a scientific confirmation of mechanism. Suppose I am playing catch with a small boy. The ball escapes his grasp and he runs after it. Any observer would agree that the boy is running after the ball. This description implies that the purpose of the boy's running is to get the ball, or that he is running because he wants to capture the ball.

Now suppose a neurological technician

could explain and predict every movement of the boy's limbs without regard to the whereabouts of the ball, solely in terms of the changing states of the boy's neurophysiological system. Or, what is worse, suppose the technician could control the boy's movements by altering the states of his central nervous system at will — that is, by "programming." We can imagine that it should be impossible for us to tell in a given instance, by observation of the boy's outward behavior and circumstances, whether the boy's limbs were responding to programming or whether he was running in order to retrieve the ball. And suppose that in many instances when we thought the behavior was intentional, it was subsequently proved to us that exactly the same inner physiological processes occurred as on those occasions when the technician controlled the boy's movements. We can also suppose that the neurologist's predictions of behavior would be both more reliable and more accurate than are the predictions based on purposive assumptions.

If such demonstrations occurred on a massive scale, we should be learning that the principles of purposive explanation have a far narrower application than we had thought. On more and more occasions we (that is, each one of us) would be forced to regard other human beings as mechanisms. The ultimate outcome of this development would be that we should cease to think of the behavior of others as being influenced by desires and intentions.

25. Having become believers in mechanistic explanations of the behavior of others, could each of us also come to believe that mechanistic causation is the true doctrine for his own case? Not if we realized what this would imply, for each of us would see that he could not include himself within the scope of the doctrine. Saying or doing something *for a reason* (in the sense of grounds as well as in the sense of purpose) implies that the saying or doing is intentional. Since mechanism is incompatible with the intentionality of behavior, my acceptance of mechanism as true for myself would imply that I am incapable of saying or doing anything for a reason. There could be *a* reason (that is, a cause) but there could not be such a thing as *my* reason. There could not, for example, be such a thing as my reason for stating that mechanism is true. Thus my assertion of mechanism would involve a second paradox. Not only would the assertion be inconsistent, in the sense previously explained, but also it would imply that I am incapable of having rational grounds for asserting anything, including mechanism.

Once again we see that mechanism engenders a form of solipsism. In asserting mechanism I must deny its application to my own case: for otherwise my assertion would imply that I could not be asserting mechanism on rational grounds.

26. Some philosophers hold that if mechanism is true then a radical revision of our concepts is required. We need to junk all such terms as "intentionally," "unintentionally," "purposely," "by mistake," "deliberately," "accidentally," and so on. The classifying of utterances such as "asserting," "repeating," "quoting," "mimicking," "translating," and so forth, would have to be abandoned. We should need an entirely new repertoire of descriptions of a sort that would be compatible with the viewpoint of mechanism.

I think these philosophers have not grasped the full severity of the predicament. If mechanism is true, not only should we give up speaking of "asserting," but also of "describing" or even of "speaking." It would not even be right to say that a person *meant* something by the noise that came from him. No marks or sounds would mean anything. There could not be *language*.

A proponent of mechanism should not think that at present we are using the wrong concepts and that a revision is called for. If he is right, we do not use concepts at all. There is nothing to revise — and nothing to say. The motto of a mechanist ought to be: One cannot speak, therefore one must be silent.

27. To conclude: We have uncovered two respects in which mechanism is not a con-

ceivable doctrine. The first is that the occurrence of an act of asserting mechanism is inconsistent with mechanism's being true. The second is that the asserting of mechanism implies that the one who makes the assertion cannot be making it on rational grounds.

In order to avoid these paradoxes, one must deny that mechanism is universally true. One can hold that it is true for others but not for oneself. It is highly ironical that the affirmation of mechanism requires one to affirm its metaphysical and methodological opposite — solipsism.

The inconceivability of mechanism, in the two respects we have elucidated, does not establish that mechanism is false. It would seem, logically speaking, that a comprehensive neurophysiological theory of human behavior ought to be confirmable by scientific investigation. Yet the assertion that this confirmation had been achieved would involve the two paradoxes we have elucidated. Mechanism thus presents a harsh, and perhaps insoluble, antinomy to human thought.

Concluding unscientific postscript: I must confess that I am not entirely convinced of the correctness of the position I have taken in respect of the crux of this paper — namely, the problem of whether it is possible for there to be both a complete neurophysiological explanation and also a complete purposive explanation of one and the same sequence of movements. I do not believe I have really proved this to be impossible. On the other hand, it is true that for me (and for others, too) a sequence of sounds tends to lose the aspect of speech (language) when we conceive of those sounds as being caused neurophysiologically (especially if we imagine a technician to be controlling the production of the sounds). Likewise, a sequence of movements loses the aspect of action. Is this tendency due to some false picture or to some misleading analogy? Possibly so; but also possibly not. Perhaps the publication of the present paper will be justified if it provokes a truly convincing defense of the compatibility of the two forms of explanation.[14]

[14] A number of people have read various versions of this paper and I have profited from their criticisms. I am especially indebted to Elizabeth Anscombe, Keith Donnellan, Philippa Foot, G. H. von Wright, and Ann Wilbur. They are not responsible for the mistakes I have retained.

V

THE LANGUAGE of SOCIAL SCIENCE

The "language of social science" is not a topic for which the previous parts have left us unprepared. We have already witnessed several attempts to describe the relationship ("distance") between the concepts of the social scientist and those used by the persons on whom he performs experiments. We have seen the conclusion affirmed and attacked that statements of social uniformities are not empirically testable but, rather, bring together terms that are related "by definition," or by virtue of their assigned meanings. According to selection 19, in the "laws" of social science, "the alleged *preconditions* or essential causes of the phenomenon under examination cannot be fully specified apart from observation of the condition they are supposed to produce." Furthermore, consider this representative passage from B. F. Skinner's *Science and Human Behavior:*

> The unit of a predictive science is . . . not a response but a class of responses. The word "operant" will be used to describe this class. The term emphasizes the fact that the behavior *operates* upon the environment to generate consequences. *The consequences define the properties with respect to which responses are called similar.*[1] [final italics added]

Should we accept the stipulation that if the *upshot* of two acts, say, killing in self-defense and killing by lynching, is the same, then they are instances of the same type of behavior? To do so seems to eliminate all consideration of the beliefs and intentions of human agents and thus to prejudge the issue of whether men can perform actions which are not reducible to mere movements. And this in turn, given selections 27 and 29 and the argument presented on pages 207–208 above, prejudges the question of whether and to what extent a nomothetic social science is possible. So Skinner's separatist opponents are not alone in refusing to let future experimental results, or the "bare facts," determine whether there is an essential unity of method between the natural and the social sciences. What Skinner himself sets forth springs from an a priori (or at least nonempirical) limitation on the language of social science. He decides that he wants a nomological science of human behavior and then (on this basis alone?) proscribes exactly those ways of describing and classifying human activity which are most likely to conflict with that aim. Thus, Skinner's position, as much as Collingwood's or Winch's, rests on an analysis, or definition, of human action; in particular, on dictum D, that human actions consist solely of items of behavior that can be classified as "the same" or "different" without reference to the intentions and beliefs of those who perform them. What possible *observations* or *experiments* could justify D as more tenable than the contrary accounts of human activity advanced in selections 1, 13, 22, 27, and 29? Indeed, does not D serve as a rule restricting what can be introduced into Skinner's behavioral science as an acceptable or meaningful observation of human conduct?[2]

[1] Skinner, B. F. *Science and Human Behavior*, New York, 1953, p. 65.

[2] Skinner's upshot dictum has already appeared as an unargued presupposition of Turing's test, to which Newell and Simon appeal in selection 23. This dictum *may* also be implicit in the use of measurement and mathematical models for classifying and interpreting human behavior, see pages 483 to 496 below.

Proposition 9 of the covering law position places a similar restriction on permissible concepts in the social sciences. And by attacking this reductionist view, several of the preceding selections have hoped to bring down the entire edifice of covering law explanations, prediction-explanation symmetry, determinism, etc. Distinctions between the *language* of social and natural science, it has been urged, disrupt entirely the unity of method affirmed by proposition 2. Human actions, to use Miss Brodbeck's term, are irreducibly "mentalistic," and *for this reason* cannot be explained in conformity with nomothetic canons. Beginning with conceptual distinctions, e.g., between "behavior" (or "bodily movement") and "action," the "moral drawn is that the meaningful constituents of an action make it logically impossible to explain human actions causally, in the sense in which we can explain events like bodily movements." In this way, the case against proposition 9 is alleged to raise equally serious difficulties for propositions 2, 5, 7, and 8 of the covering law position.

In what follows, these issues, no longer peripheral, become the focus of systematic analysis and are used to generate fresh and deeper questions concerning "the language of social science." Rudolf Carnap's "Logical Foundations of the Unity of Science" is a classic and sophisticated statement of proposition 9, which it attempts to derive from the following three premisses: (1) a term Q^1 is reducible to a term Q^2 if finding out that Q^2 applies affords a "method of determination" for whether Q^1 applies; (2) "there is a behavioristic method of determination for any term of the psychological language"; and (3) any term for which there is a behavioristic reduction is itself reducible to the "physical thing-language," i.e., the "language that we use in speaking about the properties of the observable (inorganic) things surrounding us." Of these premisses, (3) seems most open to dispute. Some philosophers (perhaps Chisholm and Heidelberger among them) would concede that there are behavioral criteria for the application of mental concepts like 'is angry' or 'is deciding'. But they would insist that these criteria themselves either constitute *intentional actions* (in the sense introduced by selection 29 above) or must be identified by means of *psychological concepts* (in the sense under analysis in selections 33 and 34 below). In Wittgenstein's example in paragraph 444 of the *Philosophical Investigations*, activities such as setting a table for two, and repeatedly watching a clock and looking out a window are said to provide grounds for claiming that a certain man is *expecting* someone. These activities, though surely "behavioristic," seem no more physical than the state for which they supply evidence: like *expecting*, they also essentially involve intentions and beliefs (e.g., to determine the correct time; that people can arrive via the road beneath the window). Hence, while Carnap's (1) and (2) may well be true of *expecting* (or 'expecting'), the issue is less clear in regards to (3).

The article by F. Stuart Chapin, like that of Carnap, advocates a *monistic* account of permissible concepts for the social scientist. That is, both selections 30 and 31 assert that there is single kind of language (or type of term) which all social science discourse must employ on pain of being unintelligible or scientifically useless. Chapin contends that the only terms which can advance scientific research are those governed by definitions of a very special sort, i.e., operational definitions. "In the trend toward quantitative description or measurement in social psychology or sociology, we strive to define each concept in terms of the measurements upon it."

Operationism raises a number of fascinating problems. One of these is its apparent incompatibility with Ernest Nagel's pessimistic view concerning laws in the social sciences. In *The Structure of Science*, Nagel contends that "it is perhaps inevitable that the generalizations of present empirical social research should be statements of statistical rather than strictly invariant relations of dependence."[3] This contention he derives from the premise that "the terms employed in empirical social research frequently possess an indeterminate connotation."[4] More strongly, there is reason to doubt

> that the social sciences are likely to refine their current distinctions beyond a certain point — a point fixed by the general character of the problems they investigate and the level of analysis appropriate for dealing with those problems — unless indeed these disciplines as presently constituted are transformed almost beyond recognition.[5]

Nagel's position seems to conflict sharply with the implicit confidence of operationists that features such as "indeterminate connotation" can always be removed, without loss of meaning, from social and human action concepts so as to allow the rigorous formulation and testing of alleged behavioral uniformities.

Another difficulty for operationism attaches most plainly to its classical expression, i.e. the view criticized by Ennis under the heading "Giving a Set of Operations as the Meaning of the Concept." For operationists like Chapin, the meaning of a term such as 'courageous' is equated with a "series of acts performed by the investigator in the process of measurement." The question immediately arises as to how one decides whether the investigator's behavior provides an *accurate* way of measuring the characteristic it supposedly defines. Suppose that two distinct sets of operations are offered to define 'courageous'. What evidence can be used to defend one and reject the other? There seems, moreover, to be a dilemma here for operationists. Any given term either has or lacks meaning before an attempt is made to define it operationally. In the latter case, there is nothing for an operational definition to measure — either accurately or inaccurately. But in the former case, the term possesses meaning, has correct and incorrect uses, *prior* to acquiring operational criteria. And if this is so, how can we accept Chapin's proposal that the meaning of every "social concept depends upon the series of acts performed by the investigator?" (It is to meet this objection, and to show how one can choose between conflicting operational definitions, that Chapin discusses the tests of reliability and validity and applies them to his own definition of 'social status.')

The selections by Scriven, Chisholm, and Heidelberger raise serious criticisms of operational and reductionist programs. Scriven's essay, though primarily a broadside against B. F. Skinner's rejection of "the traditional fiction of a mental life," has clear applications to selections 30 and 31. It distinguishes four separate obstacles to *any* attempt to replace ordinary psychological terms by a "purified" language referring to either the operations of social scientists or the behavioral responses of their subjects. First, that the invented concepts always differ radically in meaning from those they displace; second, that the task of "itemizing the units of behavior" (or operations) with which any human action concept is to be equated is impossible to complete; third, that the protocol language shares with our ordinary concepts the very qualities — supposedly defects — that are offered as requiring an operationist or reductionist program, e.g., vagueness or "open-texture"; and last, that if operational or reductionist definitions in social science do *not* reflect what is ordinarily meant by their definienda (as seems to be the case with Skinner, Hempel, and Chapin), then the findings of social scientists will be irrelevant to questions of correlation and causality involving familiar types of human activity.

[3] Nagel, E. *The Structure of Science*, New York, 1961, page 506.
[4] Ibid, page 506.
[5] Ibid, page 507.

We can have our Taylor Scale on which we define a psychological concept of anxiety, but we can't avoid the question, "Does this give a good measure of anxiety as we ordinarily use the term?" Because if it doesn't we can't use it to find out whether students are made more anxious by subjective than objective examinations . . . [See page 395 below.]

Selections 33 and 34 analyze and extend the first, and possibly also the last, point in Scriven's case. They offer careful, albeit conflicting, accounts of the "psychological," and explain in fine detail how terms referring to Collingwood's inner aspect of human action can be distinguished from nonpsychological terms. Chisholm further argues that three prominent methods for eliminating psychological in favor of nonpsychological language are unsuccessful. Roughly, his claim is that these three approaches, parallels to which appear in selections 30, 31, and 35, either prohibit us from saying all that can be said intelligibly about beliefs and desires or illicitly introduce intentional presuppositions into their supposedly purified language.

Towards the end of his article, Chisholm expresses uncertainty as to the philosophical implications and significance of the thesis that psychological concepts are irreducible. Heidelberger is less restrained. He argues that the truth of this thesis (1) is incompatible with the type of reductionism advanced by "logical behaviorists" (see selection 30) and (2) cannot be used to refute the materialist doctrines that every particular mental event (my seeing the stadium lights go on at 8 P.M.) is identical with some physical event (a contraction of my pupillary muscles) and that persons are identical with their bodies. If Heidelberger is correct in maintaining (2), then the fact that psychological terms are irreducible, or that proposition 9 is false, may place no limits whatever on the ambitions of nomothetic social science. And this would entail, as selection 35 alleges, that the irreducibility thesis provides no evidence against what is essential to the covering law position.

On the other hand, this thesis may partially explain and justify the emphasis of separatist philosophers on such concepts ("faculties") as *verstehen*, understanding, and imaginative reenactment. Let us suppose that human action terms *are* irreducibly psychological in either Chisholm's or Heidelberger's sense and also, as seems plausible, that *sense-perception* allows one to recognize only such phenomena as are denoted by nonpsychological language, e.g., the terms in Carnap's "physical thing-language" (page 368 below). It would then follow that the evidence of sense-perception, by itself, can never establish whether any intentional concept applies in a specific case. Some other faculty — one exhibited in the mastery of psychological language — must be employed by those who come to know propositions about the beliefs, emotions, attitudes, and motives of their fellow men.

In other words, the irreducibility thesis permits a new interpretation of *verstehen:* as involving the ability to correctly use a set of concepts, e.g., *hoping*, *thinking*, *aspiring*, the application of which cannot be decided by the data of sense-perception. This interpretation should undercut a number of persistent misconceptions of, and objections to, *verstehen;* these, which include the following, are propounded sporadically in the writings of covering law theorists (see selections 5, 30, and 37 and Nagel's *The Structure of Science*, pages 480 to 485).

1. That there is a *feeling of verstehen* which can be defined as a "subjective experience of empathic identification," i.e. as the (quite possibly mistaken) feeling of resembling or being identical in some respect with another person.

2. That the *method of verstehen* consists in using the feeling of *verstehen* as a source of universal hypotheses. That is, to follow this method essentially involves inferring from what is true of oneself (whenever I throw a chair at X, I am angry with him) to a

lawlike proposition (anyone who throws chairs at other people is angry with them). The method of *verstehen*, in short, is a "mnemonic device": it generates hunches as to uniform behavioral regularities by concurrently appealing to (a) introspection of one's own experiences and (b) the *verstehen* feeling that one experiences life (or anger, etc.) in much the same way as others do.

3. That the universal hypotheses suggested by the method of *verstehen* cannot be verified either by that method itself or by the *verstehen* feeling. (Hempel: ". . . the subjective experience of empathic identification with a historical figure . . . constitutes no knowledge, no scientific understanding at all . . .") Such hypotheses must be tested and appraised by reference to the evidence of sense-perception and the findings of experimental procedures such as Mill's inductive methods. Theodore Abel puts this point by claiming that the operation of *verstehen* "is *not a method of verification* . . . In any given case the test of the actual probability [of the proposed correlation] calls for the application of objective methods of observation; e.g., experiments, comparative studies, statistical operations of mass data, etc."[6]

Now my contention is that, if we construe *verstehen* in terms of the mastery of irreducible psychological concepts, then propositions 1-3 above will neither truly describe it nor carry any weight against it. Those who possess this conceptual equipment do not necessarily, or on all occasions, feel an empathetic bond with the agents they are endeavoring to understand. If a man never experiences revenge, this need not prevent him from recognizing it in others or from discerning its conceptual connections to specific beliefs, intentions, and actions. What I have termed the feeling of *verstehen* is not, apparently, a necessary condition for successfully exercising the capacity to make true judgments containing psychological terms.

Separatist advocates of *verstehen*, moreover, have *not* been recommending a second-rate procedure for arriving at empirical or causal laws. On the contrary, they usually regard their operation as advancing judgments and arguments concerning the psychological characteristics of particular men on specific occasions. If universal propositions must be invoked, these should be analytic truths connecting sets of psychological concepts, such as those specified in selections 26, 29, and 39. (See here also pages 593 to 595 below.) In any case, inferring from one's own experience and behavior to what holds of all or most men seems no more indispensable for mastering psychological concepts than the inference from 'p seems necessary (possible) to me' to 'p is necessary (possible)' is for mastering modal notions. Do inferences from introspection and empathy play any role in the use of *verstehen* in selections 39 or 54?

As for proposition 3, our reconstruction of *verstehen* implies that the data of sense-perception can *never* suffice to establish any statement made on the basis of this capacity (any third-person psychological statement or any statement asserting an analytic connection between psychological concepts). On the other hand, if a claim of mine about one of your psychological features does require support, this can often be supplied by other propositions — so long as they too employ psychological concepts. In short, by linking *verstehen* to the irreducibility thesis, we may be able to represent it as a method for verifying (decisively supporting) conclusions as well as a source of hypotheses. And this is how *verstehen* is utilized in selections 26, 39, and 54, and in the introduction to part VII: in each of these cases, one *verstehen* judgment is said to be established by appealing to other statements which contain irreducible psychological notions.

[6] Abel, Theodore. "The Operation Called *Verstehen*," reprinted in Feigl, H. and May Brodbeck, *Readings in the Philosophy of Science*, New York, 1953, page 685.

Thus, though the truth value of what is asserted by employing *verstehen* cannot be determined by unaided sense-perception, this does not entail that such assertions are beyond all argument. The point to be stressed, rather, is that conclusions expressing *verstehen* (using irreducible psychological concepts) *can* be justified and falsified, but only by appealing to propositions *with the same logical feature.* To establish that it is revenge from which you are now acting, I must appeal not to nonintentional phenomena or regularities but to further descriptions of your objectives, expectations, hopes, etc. In this sense and this sense only are *verstehen* judgments "intuitive," "subjective," or "immediate." But being intuitive in this sense is no epistemological defect or calamity. It does not mark such judgments as arbitrary, untestable, or lacking in objectivity. It implies only that certain types of observations, i.e. those arising exclusively from sense-perception or framed entirely in nonintentional language, are irrelevant to the truth value of statements made on the basis of *verstehen.*

Interpreting *verstehen* as the ability to employ irreducible psychological concepts appears to have consequences besides that of rebutting the objections brought against this operation by covering law theorists. For one thing, it should help clarify why Dilthey and other separatists have maintained that the social sciences involve "the same kind of thinking as we use in the concerns of daily life." For *verstehen,* in the revised sense, is a capacity which to some extent everyone possesses who understands any portion of a language. Moreover, especially if one accepts Heidelberger's criterion,[7] psychological concepts have clear applications only to human agents. And this seems to lend support to the separatist view that there are essential contrasts between the methods of social and of natural science. *Verstehen,* as reconstructed, is an operation which both initiates and establishes hypotheses. It can thus be counted as a method of considerable importance to the social sciences, for these disciplines rely heavily on irreducible psychological concepts. Nonetheless, it is a method that natural scientists (none of whose concepts are irreducibly psychological) have neither any need nor the right to employ.

If the irreducibility thesis is true, proposition 9 must be rejected. What then of the standard separatist inference from the falsity of all reductionist views to the doctrine that there are a priori limits on the use of nomothetic explanations in the social sciences? As we have seen, selection 34 provides some warrant for questioning this line of argument, and in "Meaning and Action," May Brodbeck hopes to complete the task of exposing its fallaciousness. The separatist reasoning here appears to take at least two forms. One of these was advanced by Peters and Tajfel, who argued as follows: "No form of distinctively human or rational activity can be defined by appealing to behavioral or bodily responses; therefore, reference to such responses cannot serve to causally explain the (rational) conduct of human agents." A second was propounded by Peter Winch. Winch's conclusion, like that of Peters and Tajfel, affirms a weak separatism according to which the social sciences, but not the physical, must sometimes abandon empirical laws in order to explain their data. But his main premise is different: it is the claim that the terms denoting correlated phenomena in physical laws and theories are terms the meaning of which is entirely fixed by the natural scientist, whereas the terms used by social scientists (e.g., 'friend,' 'father,' 'revenge,' 'agreement,' 'worship') must remain governed by the practices and intentions of the persons under study. On Winch's view, whether two acts of kneeling are of the same type — say respect for superiors — depends not on what any social

[7] And, possibly, the criterion suggested by selection 29: that those (and only those?) concepts governed by *a priori* purposive principles are psychological.

scientist means by 'respect for superiors,' but on how this notion, as well as the action performed, is construed by those whose behavior he would understand.

Selections 22 and 27 base their weak separatist assertions on two different accounts of the language descriptive of human action. And though both of these accounts conflict with proposition 9, Miss Brodbeck — in contrast to Carnap and Chapin — is prepared to concede their truth. Her important thesis is that they offer no evidence whatever against the program of objectivism (or behaviorism), a program based on "the belief in physical determinism." Miss Brodbeck's counter-argument proceeds by distinguishing several different senses of the concepts 'meaning' and 'understanding.' With these distinctions, she provides an intricate but clear and sympathetic interpretation of a view implied by Scriven, analyzed and defended by Chisholm and Heidelberger, and hotly denied by most operationists and reductionists: that "since mentalistic terms do not referentially or intentionally mean the same as non-mentalistic terms, they cannot be replaced 'without residue' by such terms." She then employs these same distinctions to defend the covering law position. Her claim is that irreducible human actions, such as worshipping and saluting, can be "understood" not only by those who perform them or grasp their intention, but — in another sense — by anyone prepared to record their lawlike connections with environmental and physiological conditions. It would seem to follow that explaining one of my acts by subsuming it under causal laws is in no way incompatible with describing that act in terms which are irreducibly psychological. In short, those who uphold propositions 1–8 and the possibility of a complete nomothetic social science do not have any obligation to defend proposition 9 against its separatist critics. (The success of Miss Brodbeck's efforts will depend on whether she establishes that there are no human action concepts the application of which to Jones implies that he could have done otherwise, or that his behavior — attempting to gain the floor by Robert's Rules of Order — was *not* regulated by causal laws external to his control. But does she offer grounds for this view or simply assume its truth? See for example page 420, line 5. Alternatively, does her paper touch the main argument of selection 29: that since (1) men incontestably have intentions, desires, preferences, etc. and (2) these states are analytically linked to concrete behavior, it follows (3) that some human conduct can only be explained by a priori purposive principles and not by reference to contingent causal laws?)

If selection 35 recasts the covering law position, Robert Ennis' task in selection 36 is to construct a defensible form of the view that a term's meaning is intimately connected with the operations and instruments men use in deciding whether to apply it. His procedure is to identify, in order to avoid, certain difficulties in traditional operationist positions. And the view he arrives at, whatever its defects if any, seems to hold out definite advantages for the social sciences. For it purports to "enable (them) to connect their abstract terms to their instruments and procedures *without completely limiting the meaning of the terms to these instruments and procedures*" [italics added]. With the fulfillment of this ambition, both social science and operationism might come to age. Both could then be disassociated from extreme forms of behaviorism and reductionism, according to which consciousness is nothing but a complicated set of brain processes or conditioned responses. Social scientists could proceed with their inquiries without even tacitly taking sides on philosophical quandaries such as the Mind-Body problem or Free-Will vs. Determinism. So long as one's terms were operationally defined (in Ennis' tolerant sense), one could gather and explain uniformities (e.g., between the ability to master certain logical rules and the lack of musical talent) without assuming or denying (1) that every mental concept can be exhaustively defined in terms of physical or behavioral notions or (2) that human actions can be explained, predicted, and controlled by reference to empirical laws, and hence are involuntary. Ennis' revised operationism thus appears to allow one to either reject or remain neutral concerning every item in the covering law position, while accomplishing social science research consistent with the demands of objectivity, testability, and measurement.

The concluding articles by Hempel, Watkins, and Schutz are concerned with the use of "ideal types" in the social sciences. Their common topic may seem to carry us a long way from the merits and deficiencies of operationism and reductionism. But on some views, an ideal type (e.g. David Riesman's "inner-directed" man or the "perfect competition" economy) serves to articulate systematically the *definition* of a recurring trait of personality or form of institutional activity. This it may accomplish by citing the behavior, performance of which under specified circumstances is the criterion for establishing the possession of the trait or the existence of the institution being defined. But if ideal types embody definitions, then they must face the same problems that were raised against the operationist and reductionist programs; e.g., do they preserve the psychological or intentional aspects of human action concepts and by what tests can one decide between conflicting reconstructions of the same mode of individual conduct or type of social organization.

Furthermore, these articles extend a controversy opened by the preceding selections: is compatibility with the covering law position a requirement for acceptable concepts in the social sciences? The revised operationism formulated by Ennis, as we have seen, permits a negative answer here. But for Miss Brodbeck, the "only way a definition can be wrong is if it does not provide a significant term, that is, *one that figures in confirmable laws*" [italics added]. Hempel's "Typological Methods in the Social Sciences" appears to regard ideal types as sustaining Miss Brodbeck's analysis of definitional adequacy: on his view, such types essentially involve "behavioral regularities" and can only be understood as "theoretical systems embodying testable general hypotheses." Naturally enough, this account permits Hempel to deduce that ideal types fit remarkably well into the covering law position.

The fit, however, seems somewhat constricting. Is it not achieved at the cost of arbitrarily banning the utilization of ideal types where there is uncertainty concerning the specific behavioral regularities controlling a form of conduct, or where the social scientist prefers to remain open on the question of whether any such regularities can be located? If so, we seem again to be faced with the Skinnerian stipulation that the only terms acceptable for describing or interpreting the data of social science are those which comply with propositions 3, 5, and 8 of the covering law position. It is not clear, though, why anyone should accept this restriction on the conceptual resources of social scientists. For how many forms of human action could ideal types be devised, if we allowed ourselves to be limited by Hempel's conception of them? Can such types be constructed for, say, philosophical viewpoints or political ideologies? What are the "behavioral regularities" which control existentialists, or nominalists, or epistemological skeptics? For democratic socialists, regional anarchists, or Burkean conservatives? Moreover, psychological concepts (beliefs, objectives, values) are needed to identify and explicate any philosophical or political position. Would it not, therefore, violate the irreducibility thesis to locate those positions within ideal types that consist of *empirically* testable general hypotheses? For such hypotheses, it would seem, can be confirmed or verified by appealing solely to the evidence of sense perception, i.e. to judgments framed in *nonpsychological concepts*. Hempel's analysis of ideal types, along with Miss Brodbeck's notion of what makes a term significant, may thus mark the beginning of a retreat to reductionism.

Watkins is far less restrictive about ideal types. His view, which has affinities to Dray's notion of rational explanation, affirms that in certain cases "the premisses of a historical explanation must be the specific dispositions, beliefs, and relationships of actual people." Drawing a distinction between explanation in principle and explanation in detail, Watkins sees the latter as requiring ideal types that in no way involve uniformities of unlimited scope or "testable general hypotheses." On the contrary, they express "the dispositions which comprise a unique personality [and] apply to only one man over a limited period of time." Despite this narrow reference, such ideal types can serve to explain an individual's conduct as fully as dispositions (ideal types, behavioral regularities) which are predicated of all men. If Watkins is right here, social scientists who construct concepts (or "behavioral models") without attending to covering law canons do not thereby disable themselves from providing acceptable explanations of human action.

Selection 39 does not advance a third competing theory of ideal types and their role in social science explanations. Schutz's concern, rather, is to construct one such type and put it to sociological use. In doing so, he exploits the method of *verstehen*, at least in the sense introduced on page 356 above. For his model of the homecomer is a synthesis of concepts which are irreducibly psychological (shared system of relevances, pure we-relation, intimacy). This model, however, is not employed by Schutz to provide "explanations in detail," i.e., to render intelligible the behavior of this or that particular agent. Instead, we find *verstehen* directed towards analyzing the meaning of a recurrent form of human life. That is, selection 39 does not predicate 'homecomer' of given individuals so much as it formulates "second-order" statements descriptive of the sense carried by that notion. And this with the hope of uncovering its a priori connections (connections of meaning) with other similarly irreducible concepts.

This appears to turn the *verstehen* social scientist into a philosopher, bent on presenting or deducing logical consequences from self-evident propositions of trans-cultural scope; propositions which need no empirical testing since they follow from what is meant by their terms and cannot be consistently or sensibly denied.[8] Nonetheless, Schutz endeavors to derive (explain) certain contingent social facts (the large percentage of discharged World War II veterans who rejected both their old jobs and former communities) by appealing to his a priori-verstehen model, i.e., to the values, expectations, and attitudes he finds to be essential attributes of the homecomer. This explanatory effort places Schutz's ideal type in the category Watkins labels as "individualistic." Any such type, and they are common in economics, is guided by the principle of methodological individualism: that every large-scale social phenomenon, e.g., suicide rates, the Korean War — or, as with Schutz — a pattern of employment, is the intended or unintended consequence of "a particular configuration of individuals, their dispositions, situations, beliefs, and physical resources and environment." Both the principle of methodological individualism, and the idea that analytic truths can serve to explain social events or regularities, are elaborated and appraised in part VII below, the introduction to which relies in part on that idea to defend a revised formulation of Watkins' principle.

[8] In *The Idea of a Social Science*, Peter Winch defends a similar identification of philosophy and social science; e.g., pp. 40–50.

Psychological Terms Can All Be Reduced to "Observable Thing-Predicates" 30

Logical Foundations of the Unity of Science

RUDOLF CARNAP

What is Logical Analysis of Science?

The task of analyzing science may be approached from various angles. The analysis of the subject matter of the sciences is carried out by science itself. Biology, for example, analyzes organisms and processes in organisms, and in a similar way every branch of science analyzes its subject matter. Mostly, however, by 'analysis of science' or 'theory of science' is meant an investigation which differs from the branch of science to which it is applied. We may, for instance, think of an investigation of scientific *activity*. We may study the historical development of this activity. Or we may try to find out in which way scientific work depends upon the individual conditions of the men working in science, and upon the status of the society surrounding them. Or we may describe procedures and appliances used in scientific work. These investigations of scientific activity may be called history, psychology, sociology, and methodology of science. The subject matter of such studies is science as a body of actions carried out by certain persons under certain circumstances. Theory of science in this sense will be dealt with at various other places in this *Encyclopedia;* it is certainly an essential part of the foundation of science.

We come to a theory of science in another sense if we study not the actions of scientists but their results, namely, science as a body of ordered knowledge. Here, by 'results' we do not mean beliefs, images, etc., and the behavior influenced by them. That would lead us again to psychology of science. We mean by 'results' certain linguistic expressions, viz., the statements asserted by scientists. The task of the theory of science in this sense will be to analyze such statements, study their kinds and relations, and analyze terms as components of those statements and theories as ordered systems of those statements. A statement is a kind of sequence of spoken sounds, written marks, or the like, produced by human beings for specific purposes. But it is possible to abstract in an analysis of the statements of science from the persons asserting the statements and from the psychological and sociological conditions of such assertions. The analysis of the linguistic expressions of science under such an abstraction is *logic of science*.

Within the logic of science we may distinguish between two chief parts. The investigation may be restricted to the forms of the linguistic expressions involved, i.e., to the way in which they are constructed out of elementary parts (e.g., words) without referring to anything outside of language. Or the investigation goes beyond this boundary and studies linguistic expressions in their relation to objects outside of language. A study restricted in the first-mentioned way is called *formal;* the field of such formal studies is called formal logic or *logical syntax*.

Reprinted from the *International Encyclopedia of United Science* edited by Otto Neurath, pp. 42–62, by permission of The University of Chicago Press, Chicago.

Such a formal or syntactical analysis of the language of science as a whole or in its various branches will lead to results of the following kinds. A certain term (e.g., a word) is defined within a certain theory on the basis of certain other terms, or it is definable in such a way. A certain term, although not definable by certain other terms, is reducible to them (in a sense to be explained later). A certain statement is a logical consequence of (or logically deducible from) certain other statements; and a deduction of it, given within a certain theory, is, or is not, logically correct. A certain statement is incompatible with certain other statements, i.e., its negation is a logical consequence of them. A certain statement is independent of certain other statements, i.e., neither a logical consequence of them nor incompatible with them. A certain theory is inconsistent, i.e., some of its statements are incompatible with the other ones. The last sections of this essay will deal with the question of the unity of science from the logical point of view, studying the logical relations between the terms of the chief branches of science and between the laws stated in these branches; thus it will give an example of a syntactical analysis of the language of science.

In the second part of the logic of science, a given language and the expressions in it are analyzed in another way. Here also, as in logical syntax, abstraction is made from the psychological and sociological side of the language. This investigation, however, is not restricted to formal analysis but takes into consideration one important relation between linguistic expressions and other objects — that of designation. An investigation of this kind is called *semantics*. Results of a semantical analysis of the language of science may, for instance, have the following forms. A certain term designates a certain particular object (e.g., the sun), or a certain property of things (e.g., iron), or a certain relation between things (e.g., fatherhood), or a certain physical function (e.g., temperature); two terms in different branches of science (e.g., 'homo sapiens' in biology and 'person' in economics, or, in another way, 'man' in both cases) designate (or: do not designate) the same. What is designated by a certain expression may be called its *designatum*. Two expressions designating the same are called *synonymous*. The term 'true,' as it is used in science and in everyday life, can also be defined within semantics. We see that the chief subject matter of a semantical analysis of the language of science are such properties and relations of expressions, and especially of statements, as are based on the relation of designation. (Where we say 'the designatum of an expression,' the customary phrase is 'the meaning of an expression.' It seems, however, preferable to avoid the word 'meaning' wherever possible because of its ambiguity, i.e., the multiplicity of its designata. Above all, it is important to distinguish between the semantical and the psychological use of the word 'meaning.')

It is a question of terminological convention whether to use the term 'logic' in the wider sense, including the semantical analysis of the designata of expressions, or in the narrower sense of logical syntax, restricted to formal analysis, abstracting from designation. And accordingly we may distinguish between logic of science in the narrower sense, as the syntax of the language of science, and logic of science in the wider sense, comprehending both syntax and semantics.

The Main Branches of Science

We use the word 'science' here in its widest sense, including all theoretical knowledge, no matter whether in the field of natural sciences or in the field of the social sciences and the so-called humanities, and no matter whether it is knowledge found by the application of special scientific procedures, or knowledge based on common sense in everyday life. In the same way the term 'language of science' is meant here to refer to the language which contains all statements (i.e., theoretical sentences as distinguished from emotional expressions, commands, lyrics, etc.) used for scientific purposes or in everyday life. What usually is called science is merely a more systematic continuation of those activities which we carry out in everyday life in order to know something.

The first distinction which we have to make is that between *formal science* and *empirical science*. Formal science consists of the analytic statements established by logic and mathematics; empirical science consists of the synthetic statements established in the different fields of factual knowledge. The relation of formal to empirical science will be dealt with at another place; here we have to do with empirical science, its language, and the problem of its unity.

Let us take 'physics' as a common name for the nonbiological field of science, comprehending both systematic and historical investigations within this field, thus including chemistry, mineralogy, astronomy, geology (which is historical), meteorology, etc. How, then, are we to draw the boundary line between physics and biology? It is obvious that the distinction between these two branches has to be based on the distinction between two kinds of things which we find in nature: organisms and nonorganisms. Let us take this latter distinction as granted; it is the task of biologists to lay down a suitable definition for the term 'organism,' in other words, to tell us the features of a thing which we take as characteristic for its being an organism. How, then, are we to define 'biology' on the basis of 'organism'? We could perhaps think of trying to do it in this way: biology is the branch of science which investigates organisms and the processes occurring in organisms, and physics is the study of nonorganisms. But these definitions would not draw the distinction as it is usually intended. A law stated in physics is intended to be valid universally, without any restriction. For example, the law stating the electrostatic force as a function of electric charges and their distance, or the law determining the pressure of a gas as a function of temperature, or the law determining the angle of refraction as a function of the coefficients of refraction of the two media involved, are intended to apply to the processes in organisms no less than to those in inorganic nature. The biologist has to know these laws of physics in studying the processes in organisms. He needs them for the explanation of these processes. But since they do not suffice, he adds some other laws, not known by the physicist, viz., the specifically biological laws. Biology presupposes physics, but not vice versa.

These reflections lead us to the following definitions. Let us call those terms which we need — in addition to logico-mathematical terms — for the description of processes in inorganic nature *physical terms*, no matter whether, in a given instance, they are applied to such processes or to processes in organisms. That sublanguage of the language of science, which contains — besides logico-mathematical terms — all and only physical terms, may be called *physical language*. The system of those statements which are formulated in the physical language and are acknowledged by a certain group at a certain time is called the physics of that group at that time. Such of these statements as have a specific universal form are called *physical laws*. The physical laws are needed for the explanation of processes in inorganic nature; but, as mentioned before, they apply to processes in organisms also.

The whole of the rest of science may be called *biology* (*in the wider sense*). It seems desirable, at least for practical purposes, e.g., for the division of labor in research work, to subdivide this wide field. But it seems questionable whether any distinctions can be found here which, although not of a fundamental nature, are at least clear to about the same degree as the distinction between physics and biology. At present, it is scarcely possible to predict which subdivisions will be made in the future. The traditional distinction between bodily (or material) and mental (or psychical) processes had its origin in the old magical and later metaphysical mind-body dualism. The distinction as a practical device for the classification of branches of science still plays an important role, even for those scientists who reject that metaphysical dualism; and it will probably continue to do so for some time in the future. But when the aftereffect of such prescientific issues upon science becomes weaker and weaker, it may be that new boundary lines for subdivisions will turn out to be more satisfactory.

One possibility of dividing biology in the wider sense into two fields is such that the first corresponds roughly to what is usually called biology, and the second comprehends among other parts those which usually are called psychology and social science. The second field deals with the behavior of individual organisms and groups of organisms within their environment, with the dispositions to such behavior, with such features of processes in organisms as are relevant to the behavior, and with certain features of the environment which are characteristic of and relevant to the behavior, e.g., objects observed and work done by organisms.

The first of the two fields of biology in the wider sense may be called biology in the narrower sense, or, for the following discussions, simply *biology*. This use of the term 'biology' seems justified by the fact that, in terms of the customary classification, this part contains most of what is usually called biology, namely, general biology, botany, and the greater part of zoölogy. The terms which are used in this field in addition to logico-mathematical and physical terms may be called biological terms in the narrower sense, or simply *biological terms*. Since many statements of biology contain physical terms besides biological ones, the *biological language* cannot be restricted to biological terms; it contains the physical language as a sublanguage and, in addition, the biological terms. Statements and laws belonging to this language but not to physical language will be called *biological statements* and *biological laws*.

The distinction between the two fields of biology in the wider sense has been indicated only in a very vague way. At the present time it is not yet clear as to how the boundary line may best be drawn. Which processes in an organism are to be assigned to the second field? Perhaps the connection of a process with the processes in the nervous system might be taken as characteristic, or, to restrict it more, the connection with speaking activities, or, more generally, with activities involving signs. Another way of characterization might come from the other direction, from outside, namely, selecting the processes in an organism from the point of view of their relevance to achievements in the environment (see Brunswik and Ness). There is no name in common use for this second field. (The term 'mental sciences' suggests too narrow a field and is connected too closely with the metaphysical dualism mentioned before.) The term 'behavioristics' has been proposed. If it is used, it must be made clear that the word 'behavior' has here a greater extension than it had with the earlier behaviorists. Here it is intended to designate not only the overt behavior which can be observed from outside but also internal behavior (i.e., processes within the organism); further, dispositions to behavior which may not be manifest in a special case; and, finally, certain effects upon the environment. Within this second field we may distinguish roughly between two parts dealing with individual organisms and with groups of organisms. But it seems doubtful whether any sharp line can be drawn between these two parts. Compared with the customary classification of science, the first part would include chiefly psychology, but also some parts of physiology and the humanities. The second part would chiefly include social science and, further, the greater part of the humanities and history, but it has not only to deal with groups of human beings but also to deal with groups of other organisms. For the following discussion, the terms 'psychology' and 'social science' will be used as names of the two parts because of lack of better terms. It is clear that both the question of boundary lines and the question of suitable terms for the sections is still in need of much more discussion.

Reducibility

The question of the unity of science is meant here as a problem of the logic of science, not of ontology. We do not ask: "Is the world one?" "Are all events fundamentally of one kind?" "Are the so-called mental processes really physical processes or not?" "Are the so-called physical processes really spiritual or not?" It seems doubtful whether we can find any theoretical content in such philosophical questions as discussed by monism, dualism, and pluralism. In any case, when we ask whether there is a unity in science, we mean this as a question of logic, concerning the logical relationships between the terms and the laws of the various branches of science. Since it belongs to the logic of science, the question concerns scientists and logicians alike.

Let us first deal with the question of terms. (Instead of the word 'term' the word 'concept' could be taken, which is more frequently used by logicians. But the word 'term' is more clear, since it shows that we mean signs, e.g., words, expressions consisting of words, artificial symbols, etc., of course with the meaning they have in the language in question. We do not mean 'concept' in its psychological sense, i.e., images or thoughts somehow connected with a word; that would not belong to logic.) We know the meaning (designatum) of a term if we know under what conditions we are permitted to apply it in a concrete case and under what conditions not. Such a knowledge of the conditions of application can be of two different kinds. In some cases we may have a merely practical knowledge, i.e., we are able to use the term in question correctly without giving a theoretical account of the rules for its use. In other cases we may be able to give an explicit formulation of the conditions for the application of the term. If now a certain term x is such that the conditions for its application (as used in the language of science) can be formulated with the help of the terms y, z, etc., we call such a formulation a *reduction statement* for x in terms of y, z, etc., and we call x *reducible* to y, z, etc. There may be several sets of conditions for the application of x; hence x may be reducible to y, z, etc., and also to u, v, etc., and perhaps to other sets. There may even be cases of mutual reducibility, e.g., each term of the set x_1, x_2, etc., is reducible to y_1, y_2, etc.; and, on the other hand, each term of the set y_1, y_2, etc., is reducible to x_1, x_2, etc.

A *definition* is the simplest form of a reduction statement. For the formulation of examples, let us use '$\equiv$' (called the symbol of equivalence) as abbreviation for 'if and only if.' Example of a definition for 'ox': 'x is an *ox* $\equiv$ x is a quadruped and horned and cloven-footed and ruminant, etc.' This is also a reduction statement because it states the conditions for the application of the term 'ox,' saying that this term can be applied to a thing if and only if that thing is a quadruped and horned, etc. By that definition the term 'ox' is shown to be reducible to — moreover definable by — the set of terms 'quadruped,' 'horned,' etc.

A reduction statement sometimes cannot be formulated in the simple form of a definition, i.e., of an equivalence statement, '. . . . $\equiv$ . . . . ,' but only in the somewhat more complex form 'If . . . . , then: . . . . $\equiv$ . . . .' Thus a reduction statement is either a simple (i.e., explicit) definition or, so to speak, a conditional definition. (The term 'reduction statement' is generally used in the narrower sense, referring to the second, conditional form.) For instance, the following statement is a reduction statement for the term 'electric charge' (taken here for the sake of simplicity as a nonquantitative term), i.e., for the statement form 'the body x has an electric charge at the time t': 'If a light body y is placed near x at t, then: x has an electric charge at t $\equiv$ y is attracted by x at t.' A general way of procedure which enables us to find out whether or not a certain term can be applied in concrete cases may be called a *method of determination* for the term in question. The method of determination for a quantitative term (e.g., 'temperature') is the method of measurement for that term. Whenever we know an experimental method of determination for a term, we are in a position to formulate a reduction statement for it. To know an experimental method of determination for a term, say 'Q_3,' means to know two things. First, we must know an experimental situation which we have to create, say the state Q_1, e.g., the arrangement of measuring apparatuses and of suitable conditions for their use. Second, we must know the possible experimental result, say Q_2, which, if it occurs, will confirm the presence of the property Q_3. In the simplest case — let us leave aside the more complex cases — Q_2 is also such that its nonoccurrence shows that the thing in question does not have the property Q_3. Then a reduction statement for 'Q_3,' i.e., for the statement form 'the thing (or space-time-point) x is Q_3 (i.e., has the property Q_3) at the time t,' can be formulated in this way: 'If x is Q_1 (i.e., x and the surroundings of x are in the state Q_1) at time t, then: x is Q_3 at $t \equiv x$ is Q_2 at t.' On the basis of this reduction statement, the term 'Q_3' is reducible to 'Q_1,' 'Q_2,' and spatio-temporal terms. Whenever a term 'Q_3' expresses the disposition of a thing to behave in a certain way (Q_2) to certain conditions (Q_1), we have a reduction statement of the form given above. If there is a connection of such a kind between Q_1, Q_2, and Q_3, then in biology and psychology in certain cases the following terminology is applied: 'To the stimulus Q_1 we find the reaction Q_2 as a symptom for Q_3.' But the situation is not essentially different from the analogous one in physics, where we usually do not apply that terminology.

Sometimes we know several methods of determination for a certain term. For example, we can determine the presence of an electric current by observing either the heat produced in the conductor, or the deviation of a magnetic needle, or the quantity of a substance separated from an electrolyte, etc. Thus the term 'electric current' is reducible to each of many sets of other terms. Since not only can an electric current be measured by measuring a temperature but also, conversely, a temperature can be measured by measuring the electric current produced by a thermoelectric element, there is mutual reducibility between the terms of the theory of electricity, on the one hand, and those of the theory of heat, on the other. The same holds for the terms of the theory of electricity and those of the theory of magnetism.

Let us suppose that the persons of a certain group have a certain set of terms in common, either on account of a merely practical agreement about the conditions of their application or with an explicit stipulation of such conditions for a part of the terms. Then a reduction statement reducing a new term to the terms of that original set may be used as a way of introducing the new term into the language of the group. This way of introduction assures conformity as to the use of the new term. If a certain language (e.g., a sublanguage of the language of science, covering a certain branch of science) is such that every term of it is reducible to a certain set of terms, then this language can be constructed on the basis of that set by introducing one new term after the other by reduction statements. In this case we call the basic set of terms a *sufficient reduction basis* for that language.

The Unity of the Language of Science

Now we will analyze the logical relations among the terms of different parts of the language of science with respect to reducibility. We have indicated a division of the whole language of science into some parts. Now we may make another division cutting across the first, by distinguishing in a rough way, without any claims to exactness, between those terms which we use on a prescientific level in our everyday language, and for whose application no scientific procedure is necessary, and scientific terms in the narrower sense. That sublanguage which is the common part of this prescientific language and the physical language may be called physical thing-language or briefly *thing-language*. It is this language that we use in speaking about the properties of the observable (inorganic) things surrounding us. Terms like 'hot' and 'cold' may be regarded as belonging to the thing-language, but not 'temperature' because its determination requires the application of a technical instrument; further, 'heavy' and 'light' (but not 'weight'); 'red,' 'blue,' etc.; 'large,' 'small,' 'thick,' 'thin,' etc.

The terms so far mentioned designate what we may call observable properties, i.e., such as can be determined by a direct observation. We will call them *observable thing-predicates.* Besides such terms the thing-language contains other ones, e.g., those expressing the disposition of a thing to a certain behavior under certain conditions, e.g., 'elastic,' 'soluble,' 'flexible,' 'transparent,' 'fragile,' 'plastic,' etc. These terms — they might be called disposition-predicates — are reducible to observable thing-predicates because we can describe the experimental conditions and the reactions characteristic of such disposition-predicates in terms of observable thing-predicates. Example of a reduction statement for 'elastic': 'If the body x is stretched and then released at the time, t, then: x is elastic at the time $t \equiv x$ contracts at t,' where the terms 'stretched,' 'released,' and 'contracting' can be defined by observable thing-predicates. If these predicates are taken as a basis, we can moreover introduce, by iterated application of definition and (conditional) reduction, every other term of the *thing-language*, e.g., designations of substances, e.g., 'stone,' 'water,' 'sugar,' or of processes, e.g., 'rain,' 'fire,' etc. For every term of that language is such that we can apply it either on the basis of direct observation or with the help of an experiment for which we know the conditions and the possible result determining the application of the term in question.

Now we can easily see that every term of the *physical language* is reducible to those of the thing-language and hence finally to observable thing-predicates. On the scientific level, we have the quantitative coefficient of elasticity instead of the qualitative term 'elastic' of the thing-language; we have the quantitative term 'temperature' instead of the qualitative ones 'hot' and 'cold'; and we have all the terms by means of which physicists describe the temporary or permanent states of things or processes. For any such term the physicist knows at least one method of determination. Physicists would not admit into their language any term for which no method of determination by observations were given. The formulation of such a method, i.e., the description of the experimental arrangement to be carried out and of the possible result determining the application of the term in question, is a reduction statement for that term. Sometimes the term will not be directly reduced by the reduction statement to thing-predicates, but first to other scientific terms, and these by their reduction statements again to other scientific terms, etc.; but such a reduction chain must in any case finally lead to predicates of the thing-language and, moreover, to observable thing-predicates because otherwise there would be no way of determining whether or not the physical term in question can be applied in special cases, on the basis of given observation statements.

If we come to *biology* (this term now always understood in the narrower sense), we find again the same situation. For any biological term the biologist who introduces or uses it must know empirical criteria for its application. This applies, of course, only to biological terms in the sense explained before, including all terms used in scientific biology proper, but not to certain terms used sometimes in the philosophy of biology — 'a whole,' 'entelechy,' etc. It may happen that for the description of the criterion, i.e., the method of determination of a term, other biological terms are needed. In this case the term in question is first reducible to them. But at least indirectly it must be reducible to terms of the thing-language and finally to observable thing-predicates, because the determination of the term in question in a concrete case must finally be based upon observations of concrete things, i.e., upon observation statements formulated in the thing-language.

Let us take as an example the term 'muscle.' Certainly biologists know the conditions for a part of an organism to be a muscle; otherwise the term could not be used in concrete cases. The problem is: Which other terms are needed for the formulation of those conditions? It will be necessary to describe the functions within the organism which are characteristic of muscles, in other words, to formulate certain laws connecting the processes in muscles with those in their environment, or, again in still other words, to describe the reactions to certain stimuli characteristic of muscles. Both the processes in the environment and those in the muscle (in the customary terminology: stimuli and reactions) must be described in such a way that we can determine them by observations. Hence the term 'muscle,' although not definable in terms of the thing-language, is reducible to them. Similar considerations easily show the reducibility of any other biological term — whether it be a designation of a kind of organism, or of a kind of part of organisms, or of a kind of process in organisms.

The result found so far may be formulated in this way: The terms of the thing-language, and even the narrower class of the observable thing-predicates, supply a sufficient basis for the languages both of physics and of biology. (There are, by the way, many reduction bases for these languages, each of which is much more restricted than the classes mentioned.) Now the question may be raised whether a basis of the kind mentioned is sufficient even for the whole language of science. The affirmative answer to this question is sometimes called *physicalism* (because it was first formulated not with respect to the thing-language but to the wider physical language as a sufficient basis). If the thesis of physicalism is applied to biology only, it scarcely meets any serious objections. The situation is somewhat changed, however, when it is applied to psychology and social science (individual and social behavioristics). Since many of the objects raised against it are based on misinterpretations, it is necessary to make clear what the thesis is intended to assert and what not.

The question of the reducibility of the terms of psychology to those of the biological language and thereby to those of the thing-language is closely connected with the problem of the various methods used in psychology. As chief examples of methods used in this field in its present state, the physiological, the behavioristic, and the introspective methods may be considered. The *physiological approach* consists in an investigation of the functions of certain organs in the organism, above all, of the nervous system. Here, the terms used are either those of biology or those so closely related to them that there will scarcely be any doubt with respect to their reducibility to the terms of the biological language and the thing-language. For the *behavioristic approach* different ways are possible. The investigation may be restricted to the external behavior of an organism, i.e., to such movements, sounds, etc., as can be observed by other organisms in the neighborhood of the first. Or processes within the organism may also be taken into account so that this approach overlaps with the physiological one. Or, finally, objects in the environment of the organism, either observed or worked on or produced by it, may also be studied. Now it is easy to see that a term for whose determination a behavioristic method — of one of the kinds mentioned or of a related kind — is known, is reducible to the terms of the biological language, including the thing-language. As we have seen before, the formulation of the method of determination for a term is a reduction statement for that term, either in the form of a simple definition or in the conditional form. By that statement the term is shown to be reducible to the terms applied in describing the method, namely, the experimental arrangement and the characteristic result. Now, conditions and results consist in the behavioristic method either of physiological processes in the organism or of observable processes in the organism and in its environment. Hence they can be described in terms of the biological language. If we have to do with a behavioristic approach in its pure form, i.e., leaving aside physiological investigations, then the description of the conditions and results characteristic for a term can in most cases be given directly in terms of the thing-language. Hence the behavioristic reduction of psychological terms is often simpler than the physiological reduction of the same term.

Let us take as an example the term 'angry.' If for anger we knew a sufficient and necessary criterion to be found by a physiological analysis of the nervous system or other organs, then we could define 'angry' in terms of the biological language. The same holds if we knew such a criterion to be determined by the observation of the overt, external behavior. But a physiological criterion is not yet known. And the peripheral symptoms known are presumably not necessary criteria because it might be that a person of strong self-control is able to suppress these symptoms. If this is the case, the term 'angry' is, at least at the present time, not definable in terms of the biological language. But, nevertheless, it is reducible to such terms. It is sufficient for the formulation of a reduction sentence to know a behavioristic procedure which enables us — if not always, at least under suitable circumstances — to determine whether the organism in question is angry or not. And we know indeed such procedures; otherwise we should never be able to apply the term 'angry' to another person on the basis of our observations of his behavior, as we constantly do in everyday life and in scientific investigation. A reduction of the term 'angry' or similar terms by the formulation of such procedures is indeed less useful than a definition would be, because a definition supplies a complete (i.e., unconditional) criterion for the term in question, while a reduction statement of the conditional form gives only an incomplete one. But a criterion, conditional or not, is all we need for ascertaining reducibility. Thus the result is the following: If for any psychological term we know either a physiological or a behavioristic method of determination, then that term is reducible to those terms of the thing-language.

In psychology, as we find it today, there is, besides the physiological and the behavioristic approach, the so-called *introspective method.* The questions as to its validity, limits, and necessity are still more unclear and in need of further discussion than the analogous questions with respect to the two other methods. Much of what has been said about it, especially by philosophers, may be looked at with some suspicion. But the facts themselves to which the term 'introspection' is meant to refer will scarcely be denied by anybody, e.g., the fact that a person sometimes knows that he is angry without applying any of those procedures which another person would have to apply, i.e., without looking with the help of a physiological instrument at his nervous system or looking at the play of his facial muscles. The problems of the practical reliability and theoretical validity of the introspective method may here be left aside. For the discussion of reducibility an answer to these problems is not needed. It will suffice to show that in every case, no matter whether the introspective method is applicable or not, the behavioristic method can be applied at any rate. But we must be careful in the interpretation of this assertion. It is not meant as saying: 'Every psychological process can be ascertained by the behavioristic method.' Here we have to do not with the single processes themselves (e.g., Peter's anger yesterday morning) but with kinds of processes (e.g., anger). If Robinson Crusoe is angry and then dies before anybody comes to his island, nobody except himself ever knows of this single occurrence of anger. But anger of the same kind, occurring with other persons, may be studied and ascertained by a behavioristic method, if circumstances are favorable. (Analogy: if an electrically charged raindrop falls into the ocean without an observer or suitable recording instrument in the neighborhood, nobody will ever know of that charge. But a charge of the same kind can be found out under suitable circumstances by certain observations.) Further, in order to come to a correct formulation of the thesis, we have to apply it not to the kinds of processes (e.g., anger) but rather to the terms designating such kinds of processes (e.g., 'anger'). The difference might seem trivial but is, in fact, essential. We do not at all enter a discussion about the question whether or not there are kinds of events which can never have any behavioristic symptoms, and hence are knowable only by introspection. We have to do with psychological terms, not with kinds of events. For any such term, say, 'Q,' the psychological language contains a statement form applying that term, e.g., 'The person . . . is at the time . . . in the state Q.' Then the utterance by speaking or writing of the statement 'I am now (or: I was yesterday) in the state Q,' is (under suitable circumstances, e.g., as to reliability, etc.) an observable symptom for the state Q. Hence there cannot be a term in the psychological language, taken as an intersubjective language for mutual communication, which designates a kind of state or event without any behavioristic symptom. Therefore, there is a behavioristic method of determination for any term of the psychological language. Hence every such term is reducible to those of the thing-language.

The logical nature of the psychological terms becomes clear by an analogy with those physical terms which are introduced by reduction statements of the conditional form. Terms of both kinds designate a state characterized by the disposition to certain reactions. In both cases the state is not the same as those reactions. Anger is not the same as the movements by which an angry organism reacts to the conditions in his environment, just as the state of being electrically charged is not the same as the process of attracting other bodies. In both cases that state sometimes occurs without these events which are observable from outside; they are consequences of the state according to certain laws and may therefore under suitable circumstances be taken as symptoms for it; but they are not identical with it.

The last field to be dealt with is *social science* (in the wide sense indicated before; also called social behavioristics). Here we need no detailed analysis because it is easy to see that every term of this field is reducible to terms of the other fields. The result of any investigation of a group of men or other organisms can be described in terms of the members, their relations to one another and to their environment. Therefore, the conditions for the application of any term can be formulated in terms of psychology, biology, and physics, including the thing-language. Many terms can even be defined on that basis, and the rest is certainly reducible to it.

It is true that some terms which are used in psychology are such that they designate a certain behavior (or disposition to behavior) within a group of a certain kind or a certain attitude toward a group, e.g., 'desirous of ruling,' 'shy,' and others. It may be that for the definition or reduction of a term of this kind some terms of social science describing the group involved are needed. This shows that there is not a clear-cut line between psychology and social science and that in some cases it is not clear whether a term is better assigned to one or to the other field. But such terms are also certainly reducible to those of the thing-language because every term referring to a group of organisms is reducible to terms referring to individual organisms.

The result of our analysis is that the class of observable thing-predicates is a sufficient reduction basis for the whole of the language of science, including the cognitive part of the everyday language.

The Problem of the Unity of Laws

The relations between the terms of the various branches of science have been considered. There remains the task of analyzing the relations between the laws. According to our previous consideration, a biological law contains only terms which are reducible to physical terms. Hence there is a common language to which both the biological and the physical laws belong so that they can be logically compared and connected. We can ask whether or not a certain biological law is compatible with the system of physical laws, and whether or not it is derivable from them. But the answer to these questions cannot be inferred from the reducibility of the terms. At the present state of the development of science, it is certainly not possible to derive the biological laws from the physical ones. Some philosophers believe that such a derivation is forever impossible because of the very nature of the two fields. But the proofs attempted so far for this thesis are certainly insufficient. This question is, it seems, the scientific kernel of the problem of vitalism; some recent discussions of this problem are, however, entangled with rather questionable metaphysical issues. The question of derivability itself is, of course, a very serious scientific problem. But it will scarcely be possible to find a solution for it before many more results of experimental investigation are available than we have today. In the meantime the efforts toward derivation of more and more biological laws from physical laws — in the customary formulation: explanation of more and more processes in organisms with the help of physics and chemistry — will be, as it has been, a very fruitful tendency in biological research.

As we have seen before, the fields of psychology and social science are very closely connected with each other. A clear division of the laws of these fields is perhaps still less possible than a division of the terms. If the laws are classified in some way or other, it will be seen that sometimes a psychological law is derivable from those of social science, and sometimes a law of social science from those of psychology. (An example of the first kind is the explanation of the behavior of adults — e.g., in the theories of A. Adler and Freud — by their position within the family or a larger group during childhood; an example of the second kind is the obvious explanation of an increase of the price of a commodity by the reactions of buyers and sellers in the case of a diminished supply.) It is obvious that, at the present time, laws of psychology and social science cannot be derived from those of biology and physics. On the other hand, no scientific reason is known for the assumption that such a derivation should be in principle and forever impossible.

Thus there is at present *no unity of laws.* The construction of one homogeneous system of laws for the whole of science is an aim for the future development of science. This aim cannot be shown to be unattainable. But we do not, of course, know whether it will ever be reached.

On the other hand, there is a *unity of language* in science, viz., a common reduction basis for the terms of all branches of science, this basis consisting of a very narrow and homogeneous class of terms of the physical thing-language. This unity of terms is indeed less far-reaching and effective than the unity of laws would be, but it is a necessary preliminary condition for the unity of laws. We can endeavor to develop science more and more in the direction of a unified system of laws only because we have already at present a unified language. And, in addition, the fact that we have this unity of language is of the greatest practical importance. The practical use of laws consists in making predictions with their help. The important fact is that very often a prediction cannot be based on our knowledge of only one branch of science. For instance, the construction of automobiles will be influenced by a prediction of the presumable number of sales. This number depends upon the satisfaction of the buyers and the economic situation. Hence we have to combine knowledge about the function of the motor, the effect of gases and vibration on the human organism, the ability of persons to learn a certain technique, their willingness to spend so much money for so much service, the development of the general economic situation, etc. This knowledge concerns particular facts and general laws belonging to all the four branches, partly scientific and partly common-sense knowledge. For very many decisions, both in individual and in social life, we need such a prediction based upon a combined knowledge of concrete facts and general laws belonging to different branches of science. If now the terms of different branches had no logical connection between one another, such as is supplied by the homogeneous reduction basis, but were of fundamentally different character, as some philosophers believe, then it would not be possible to connect singular statements and laws of different fields in such a way as to derive predictions from them. Therefore, the unity of the language of science is the basis for the practical application of theoretical knowledge.

Selected Bibliography

LOGICAL ANALYSIS

CARNAP, R. *Philosophy and Logical Syntax*, London, 1935. (Elementary.)

———, *Logical Syntax of Language*, London, 1937. (Technical.)

REDUCIBILITY

CARNAP, R. "Testability and Meaning", *Philosophy of Science*, 3, 1936, and 4, 1937.

THE UNITY OF THE LANGUAGE OF SCIENCE; PHYSICALISM

Papers by NEURATH and CARNAP, *Erkenninis*, 2, 1932; *ibid.*, 3, 1933. Translation of one of these papers: CARNAP, *The Unity of Science*, London, 1934. Concerning psychology: papers by SCHLICK, HEMPEL, and CARNAP, *Revue de synthèse*, 10, 1935.

Operationism: "Measurement Is the Concept" 31

Definition of Definitions of Concepts

F. STUART CHAPIN

Applied sociology consists today more largely in the application of serviceable concepts and in tested techniques of social research, than in the application of laws or principles, which are few in verified number and usually too general in statement to solve some concrete problem.

Consequently it is to the serviceable sociological concept that we turn for some of the examples of fruitful applications of sociology. Social work and psychiatry are making increasing use of sociological concepts. This development is too apparent to be elaborated or even illustrated at this point. Disagreement among definitions of the same concept are frequent as Eubank[1] has shown, but, if the resulting arguments and discussions are not too protracted, they are probably indications of a healthy condition of normal growth of scientific vocabulary.

We come, therefore, to the question: What is a definition? It becomes necessary to try to define what we mean by the term definition as used in the description and differentiation of sociological concepts. In this brief paper we shall set down some criteria and distinctions that we have found helpful in our own thought, research, and writing.

If we begin with dictionary definitions, we find in *Oxford* that a definition is, "stating the precise nature of a thing or the meaning of a word." *Standard* states that a definition is, "the act or product of marking out, or delimiting, the outlines or characteristics of any conception or thing; determining the elements, attributes, or relations of one object so as to distinguish it, whether as an individual or one of a class, from other objects."

Concepts are general ideas and involve abstract thinking. Young[2] states the matter thus: "Abstract thinking constitutes the highest form of anticipatory response," and again, "Reasoning is a form of anticipatory response in which the behavior is foreseen in terms of images, ideas or concepts before it actually passes over into consummatory or overt conduct." Sapir[3] says, ". . . the speech element 'house' is a symbol, first and foremost, not of a single perception, or even of the notion of a particular object, but of a 'concept,' in other words, of a convenient capsule of thought that embraces thousands of distinct experiences and that is ready to take on thousands more." In Warren's *Dictionary of Psychology*, we find a concept defined as, "A mental state or process which refers (1) to more than one object or experience; (2) to one object in relation to others; when it represents a common aspect or attribute of the class it is an abstract idea." Recent experimental work in psychology has reported operational definitions of the term concept,[4] and finds that children showed in comparison with adults a smaller percentage of most common and generalized concepts; a larger percentage of personal, general and loose, and incorrect concepts; and a greater percentage of childish terms and phrases.

Concepts may go through such stages of development as: first, being implicit as

From *Social Forces*, 18:2 (December, 1939), The University of North Carolina Press, Chapel Hill, N.C., pp. 153–160.

[1] E. E. Eubank, *The Concepts of Sociology*, 1932.

[2] K. Young, *Social Psychology*, 1930, pp. 114–115.

[3] E. Sapir, *Language*, 1921, pp. 106–107.

[4] B. Johnson, "Development of Thought," pp. 1–7; F. T. Wilson, "Concepts of Children and College Students," pp. 63–67; *Child Development*, vol. 9, no. 1, March 1938; S. M. Mott, in vol. 10, no. 1, March 1939.

thought; second, becoming explicit in the wide use of a term; and third, attaining precise definition of this term, either verbally (in words), or heuristically (in diagrams or graphs), or operationally (in measurement and experiments). Since we are not here concerned with the developmental problem, it is the third stage that we shall consider.

Before we pass to a description of (1) verbal, (2) heuristic, and (3) operational definitions of sociological concepts, let us first consider some useful distinctions that aid in grouping the already large number of sociological concepts. To begin with, it helps to clarify our thought on this matter to make a rough dichotomy into (a) substantive or phenomenal concepts, which are descriptive of content, subject-matter and experience, and (b) methodological or procedural concepts, which are descriptive of the process of observation, analysis and study. The latter may be further grouped into general concepts drawn from the literature of logic and science, and more specific terms drawn from empirical sociology. The list of terms under the rubrics of this classification are not, of course, intended to be complete, but designed merely as examples.

Let us now take a term or concept frequently used in sociological research and often applied in social work and psychiatry and compare the verbal definition of this term with the operational definition of the same term. Take the term "morale," what does it mean? What is the concept of morale? Rundquist and Sletto[5] define it thus: ". . . the degree to which the individual feels competent to cope with the future and achieve his desired goals . . . feelings of insecurity and discouragement." No doubt there are those who would disagree with this statement and suggest another statement as a better definition. Argument and discussion would elaborate variations in terms of different sentences using different words. The definition just cited is a verbal definition. In its present form it consists of words about words. Since different individuals differ in the associations they have made with the same word, any conclusion of the controversy by adding more words is not likely to come from further discussion. What then needs to be done? Clearly we need to get the definition into some form that is susceptible of check, test or verification, in other words, we desire a more objective definition. This is exactly what Rundquist and Sletto did in their book, *Personality and the Depression*,[6] for here we find morale defined in terms of differences in score on a standardized attitude scale for employed and unemployed, men and women, students in day classes and in evening classes, etc., all giving the precise number of individuals concerned, tested under certain conditions, and in the year 1934. This is an operational definition of "morale." Its obvious superiority over a purely verbal definition is in its verifiability.

What is not so obvious is that an operational definition is extremely costly. To reach the operational definition of morale, Rundquist and Sletto spent thousands of dollars in several years of intensive and patient research. On the other hand, the verbal definition is inexpensive because words are cheap. This is not to depreciate verbal definitions to the degree to suggest that they be wholly eliminated from sociological science. Verbal definitions are now and will remain useful and necessary first steps; but they are only first steps. Advance in research that is sound should seek to replace verbal or word definitions of social concepts with operational definitions as rapidly as research permits. Of what practical use is a verbal definition of the physical concept "electricity"? Compared with this the ammeter reading and the voltmeter reading are definitions that are operational and practical as well as verifiable.

Operational definitions are not, of course, final or absolute. They are subject to correction and improvement with further research.

[5] E. A. Rundquist and R. F. Sletto, "Scoring Instructions for the Minnesota Scale for the Survey of Opinions," University of Minnesota Press, 1936.

[6] Published by the University of Minnesota Press, 1936.

SAMPLINGS OF SOCIOLOGICAL CONCEPTS

A. Substantive or Phenomenal, Descriptive of Content, Subject-Matter and Experience

accommodation
assimilation
attitude
attraction pattern
belief
competition
conflict
contact
convention
class structure
culture area
cultural change
culture complex
culture trait
custom
diffusion
emotion
feeling
folkway
friendship constellation
group
institution
invention
mobility
morale
mores
participation
pressure group
propaganda
public opinion
race prejudice
sentiment
social status
tradition

B. Methodological or Procedural, Descriptive of the Process of Observation, Analysis and Study

General

causation
deduction
induction
logic
proof
true*
verification
case method
control group
constants
field theory
hypothesis
index of interaction
intuition

Specific

personal history document
schedule
score card
social survey
sociometric scale
reliability
validity

Since Stevens,[7] for the field of psychology, and Lundberg,[8] for the field of sociology, have recently discussed operationalism in its implications for the sciences of human behavior, we shall dispense with further consideration of this subject except to analyze one very important problem of measurement in relation to the operational definition. The problem is this: since the operational definition of a social concept depends upon the series of acts performed by the investigator in the process of measurement, how can one be sure whether the scale of measurement used really does measure the subject or the objects to which it is applied? This is the problem of validity of the scale of measurement. But the operational definition that science holds up as a desired goal of objectivity states that the measurement *is* the concept.

Let us consider an illustration of this point. In the trend toward quantitative description or measurement in social psychology and sociology, we strive to define each concept in terms of the measurements upon it. Scales to measure public opinion are constructed and tested for validity. We say of a scale that has been standardized to measure public opinion, "Public opinion *is* what this scale measures." This is then the operational definition of the concept public opinion. Does this statement of operationalism make meaningless or false the basic question of validity, which is, "*Does* this scale measure that which it is designed to measure, namely, public opinion?" This apparent dilemma appears at first glance to be destructive of the very basis of operationalism, because the proposition appears to beg the question by assuming the conclusion

* It should be noted that the adjective "true" is converted into the noun "truth," thereby getting the social scientist into fruitless arguments of a metaphysical nature. The term "true" is meaningful.

[7] S. S. Stevens, "The Operational Basis of Psychology," *American Journal of Psychology*, vol. 47, April 1935, pp. 323–330, and "The Operational Definition of Psychological Concepts," *Psychological Review*, vol. 42, no. 6, Nov. 1935, pp. 517–527.

[8] G. A. Lundberg, "The Thoughtways of Contemporary Sociology," *American Sociological Review*, vol. 1, no. 5, Oct. 1936, pp. 703–723.

which is to be proved and making it part of the premises used to prove it. In reality, however, the dilemma is not a real one, because the assertion, "Public opinion *is* what this scale measures" is made only *after* the scale has been standardized. The process of standardization, if done thoroughly, disposes of the question of validity, so that the assertion of the operational form of the definition of public opinion does not beg the question.

Perhaps another illustration will clarify these points. In the process of developing the social status scale we first formulated (in 1926) a verbal definition of the concept social status as follows: "Socioeconomic status is the position that an individual or a family occupies with reference to the prevailing average standards of cultural possessions, effective income, material possessions, and participation in the group activities of the community."[9]

In the course of the next seven years, social status ratings obtained by checking a weighted list of articles in the living room of the family were secured on some 1500 homes in different parts of the United States. By 1933 the reliability of the scale was standardized by correlations of from + .90 to + .98 between scores on a first visit and scores on a second visit on the same homes, made by the same or by different visitors.[10] Meanwhile the validity of the scale was established by correlations of + .383 with income, and + .515 with occupational class on the standard norm group of 442 homes. Smaller and more homogeneous groups of homes selected from the 442, yielded higher coefficients such as, with income + .65, with occupation + .58, with social participation + .62, and with education + .54. Since the concept of the social status of any person or family represents a complicated group of factors in the community more likely to be grasped by adults than by children, it is evident that the definition of social status in terms of occupation, income, social participation and education, is superior to the use of only one term. The fact that the correlations of each of these four aspects of social status with the social status score is substantial (i.e. neither too small, which would suggest absence of relationship, nor too large, which would suggest spurious elements), we conclude that the social status score is a valid measure of the concept social status. When it is further shown that groups of families of different social classes such as relief or nonrelief, WPA and employed, unskilled working class families and professional men's families, have social status scores substantially different in magnitude on the average, the validity of this particular measure of social status seems well established for the time being at least.[11]

Data gathered in 1935 brought to a head another question related to the standardization of the social status scale. It was this: Should a correction in the final social status score be made for a family that *uses* its living room, *also* as a dining room, or bedroom, or kitchen? To secure an objective answer to this question, we set an arbitrary penalty for *each use* of the living room beyond its chief purpose as the main gathering place of the family, which would reduce the final score of the home by 6 points when the living room was used also as a dining room, by 9 points when used also as a kitchen, etc.[12] Next, the validity of this arbitrary system of penalty weights was tested by re-scoring and re-correlations of the original 442 standard norm homes, to see if the change in weights would affect the correlations. We found that the corrected scores showed an increase from +.383 to +.454 with income, and from +.515 to +.625 with occupational class. The multiple correlation coefficient, $R_{1.23}$ was similarly raised from .54 to .66. Higher coefficients were also obtained for the smaller and more homogeneous subgroups and a multiple correlation of $R_{1.2345} = .812$ was

[9] F. Stuart Chapin, *Contemporary American Institutions*, 1935, p. 374.

[10] *Ibid.*, pp. 386–390.

[11] *Ibid.*, and in other research results, both published and unpublished.

[12] See revised edition of 1936 "The Social Status Scale," paragraph #2, University of Minnesota Press.

obtained for social status score and the combined scores on income, occupation, social participation and education. This example of social status thus supplies concrete illustrations of the stages and problems the research worker encounters in an effort to reach an operational definition of a particular social concept. It also illustrates the justification for the statement that the process of standardization of a scale of measurement disposes of the question of validity *before* the scale measurements are used as an operational definition, thereby avoiding the dilemma that has seemed to confuse the meaning of operational definitions.

Let us now turn from examples of the operational definition of comparatively simple sociological concepts such as attitudes, morale, social status, etc., to the much more complex social concept "social institution." Can an operational definition of such a complicated concept be worked out? Will it always be necessary to use purely verbal definitions for entities in this area of sociological concepts? Cooley, Sumner and Allport, have all contributed useful verbal definitions. From these we constructed a verbal definition of a social institution to include the hypothesis of four type parts, common reciprocating attitudes, cultural objects of symbolic value, cultural objects possessing utilitarian value, and oral or written language symbols, all of which combine into a configuration possessing the properties of relative rigidity and relative persistence of form, and tending to function as a unit on a field of contemporary culture.[13] The hypothesis of four type parts was set up so that there might be portions of the configuration, each susceptible of description in some objective way. Since the various studies of this subject have been published, further elaboration of the reasons for this hypothesis and illustrating its use, will be found therein.[14] There remains, however, the problem of how to formulate a definition of social institution, which will express its configurational character in some unity of form. Here we find useful, as a transitional device, the heuristic definition. This type of definition uses diagrams, figures and graphic forms, to represent the concept as an entity. One of the merits of this form of definition is its visual appeal. It has been criticized, however, as running the risk of making the symbolic representation more complicated than the phenomena for which it stands.[15] Physical sciences have often used this heuristic form of definition to great advantage, as witness the system of graphic structural formulae of molecular and atomic structure used in physics and particularly in chemistry.[16] Its chief danger for use in sociology lies in the fact that such formulations once presented seem to the uncritical observer to attain an objectivity of genuine scientific validity, when their real purpose is to serve as devices of discovery for temporary and transitional use as so many bridges over the gap between verbal definitions and more useful operational definitions. Hence it is desirable wherever these visual devices are used to frankly state them as heuristic devices and not as more finished objective definitions.[17]

Figure 31-1 illustrates the use of the heuristic definition to represent the entity, "Baptist Church," as a social institution consisting of four type parts, religious attitudes as the central circle, from which there are bonds to the symbolic type part (cross, hymnal), to the utilitarian culture traits (church building), and the type part of descriptive language symbols (creed, doctrine, church rules). The field of culture against which this configuration appears is illustrated by the behavior segments of different individuals, A and B, who are also affili-

[13] F. Stuart Chapin, *Cultural Change*, 1928, pp. 44–52.

[14] *Contemporary American Institutions*, 1935, *op. cit.*, and p. 359.

[15] In reviews of my *Cultural Change*, W. F. Ogburn in *American Journal of Sociology*, vol. 35, no. 3, November 1929, and A. A. Goldenweiser in *Political Science Quarterly*, vol. 44, seem to present this criticism of my work.

[16] I. W. D. Hackh, "Development of Chemical Symbols" *Scientific Monthly*, March, 1935, pp. 199–217.

[17] See my review of Phelps' *The Laws and Principles of Sociology*, in *American Sociological Review*, vol. 2, no. 6, Dec. 1937, pp. 929–931.

ated with other institutional complexes, such as a bank, a lodge, politics, a club and a business enterprise. The church attitudes of these individuals are represented by the symbols a_1 and b_4, and their other institutional attitudes and habits similarly. Whether seem also to have found them useful. However, at this stage they are frankly heuristic and by no means scientific definitions.

The test of the degree to which such heuristic definitions of the concept "social institution" may serve as a bridge to pass

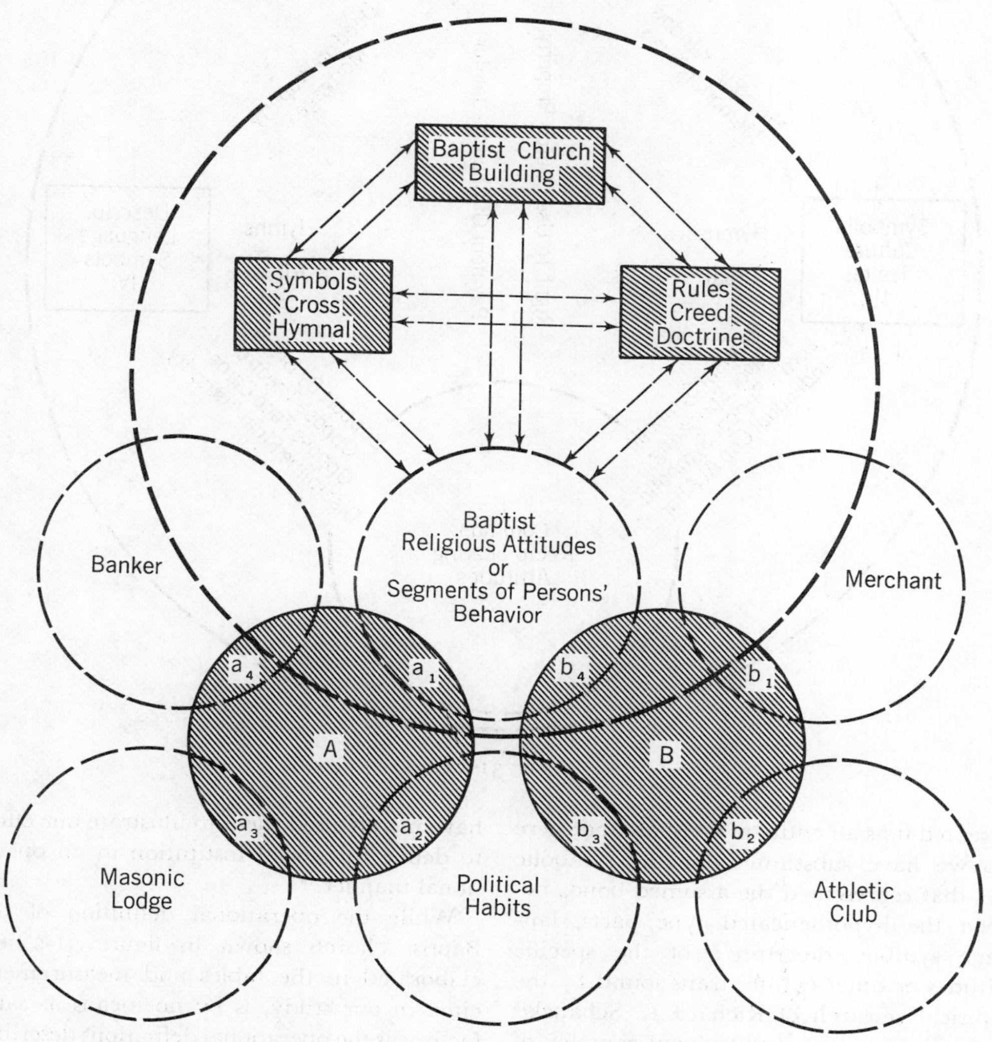

Fig. 31–1

these graphic devices are more or less complicated than the social phenomena they are used to represent, is for the reader and user to judge. They have been helpful in the clarification of my own thought, and students over the gap from purely verbal definition to operational definition is shown in figure 31-2. Here we have "lifted" the configuration of the four type-parts of the concept of "church" from its contemporary field of culture and

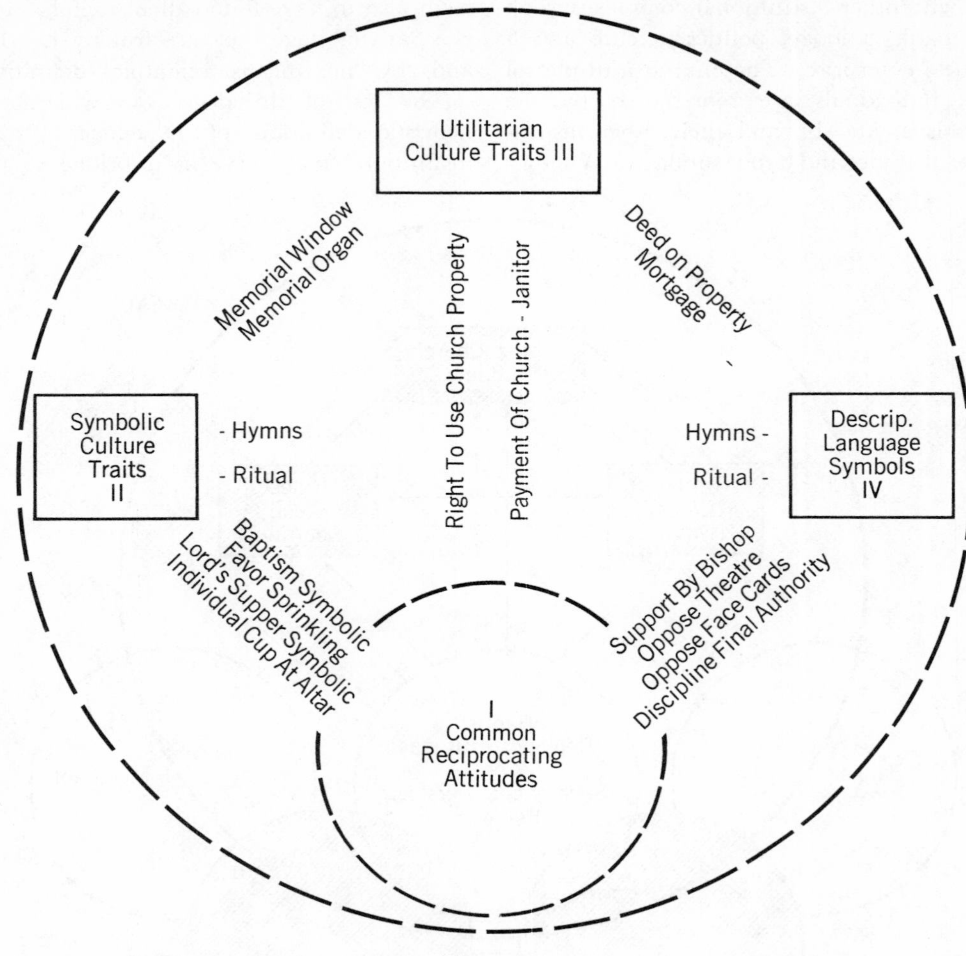

Fig. 31–2

presented it as an entity of a visual kind; here also we have substituted for the symbolic lines that represented the assumed bonds between the hypotheticated type parts, language symbols descriptive of the specific attitudes or other culture traits found by the empirical research of Richard L. Schanck[18] to be existing in the institutional complex of an actual small Baptist church in western New York State. Measured differences in the strength or conservatism of attitudes toward symbols, creed or property of the church, are presented in Schanck's monograph, and we have merely used them to illustrate our effort to define this social institution in an operational manner.[19]

While the operational definition of this Baptist church shown in figure 31-2 and elaborated in the tables and measurements cited in our study, is by no means as satisfactory as the operational definitions described for "morale" and for "social status," it represents a beginning at an operational definition of the social institution or concept "church," and does at least point the way toward scientific empiricism and away from meta-

[18] "A Study of a Community and Its Groups and Institutions Conceived of as Behaviors of Individuals", *Psychological Monographs*, vol. 43, no. 195, 1932.

[19] *Contemporary American Institutions*, 1935, pp. 211–217, 333–336, 367–371.

physical speculation in the area of complex sociological concepts. The "seeking to discover" attribute of the heuristic definition may clarify social concepts in three ways: (1) by breaking down the whole into parts that are individually susceptible of measurement, (2) by identifying the part-whole relationships, and (3) by helping to apprehend by visual means a pattern of component conceptual parts.

The recent work of Kurt Lewin[20] should be cited as an example of highly imaginative use of the heuristic definition of social concepts. The work of J. L. Moreno[21] is another example of the use of heuristic devices in exploring a promising borderline field of social concepts. Lundberg[22] has even more recently supplied a more realistic empirical base for this procedure, as has the work of Loomis.[23]

We may now conclude this sketchy discussion of definitions of sociological concepts by repeating the earlier suggestion, namely, that sociological concepts may be defined (1) verbally, (2) heuristically, and (3) operationally.

[20] "Field Theory and Experiment in Social Psychology; Concepts and Methods," *American Journal of Sociology*, vol. 44, no. 6, May 1939, pp. 868–896; and Ronald Lippitt, "Field Theory and Experiment in Social Psychology; Autocratic and Democratic Group Atmosphere," *American Journal of Sociology*, vol. 55, no. 1, July 1939, pp. 26–49.

[21] *Who Shall Survive?* 1934, and recent studies in *Sociometry*.

[22] "The Sociometry of Some Community Relations," *American Sociological Review*, vol. 2, no. 3, June 1937, pp. 318–335; and "Social Attraction-Patterns in a Village," *Sociometry*, vol. 1, no. 3 and 4, Jan. Apr., 1938, pp. 375–419.

[23] "Development of Planned Rural Communities," *Rural Sociology*, vol. 3, no. 4, Dec. 1938, pp. 383–409.

A Critique of Skinner's Operational Reduction of Mental Concepts

32

from *A Study of Radical Behaviorism*

MICHAEL SCRIVEN

. . . My specific contentions will be that [B. F.] Skinner, in general, underestimates (a) the empirical content and (b) the practical utility of propositions about 'mental states,' including unconscious ones, and that he over-estimates the commitments of psychoanalytic theory and hence the deleterious effects of Freud's influence.

Let us consider some of Skinner's proffered analyses of 'mental-state' ascriptions. At a very general level, he considers descriptions of purpose to be open to the same objections, and I shall begin by taking one such example.

> . . . we ask him what he is doing and he says, "I am looking for my glasses." This is not a further description of his behavior but of the variables of which his behavior is a function; it is equivalent to "I have lost my glasses," "I shall stop what I am doing when I find my glasses," or "When I have done this in the past, I have found my glasses." These translations may seem unnecessarily roundabout, but only because expressions involving goals and purposes are abbreviations (SHB, p. 90).[1]

Without agreeing or disagreeing with the thesis that "expressions involving goals and purposes are abbreviations," we may show that such expressions involve (i.e., are equivalent to, or imply) a great deal more than any one of Skinner's suggested "translations." If a man correctly describes himself or another as "looking for his glasses," then we can infer *all* of the following:

(1) He owns glasses or believes he does.

(2) He does not now know where they are.

(3) He is engaging in operant behavior of a type that has previously led him or others of whom he knows to find objects of this kind (Skinner's restriction to the man's *own* experience with *lost glasses* is clearly too narrow).

(4) The aspect of his behavior described under (3) will cease when he discovers his glasses.

There are certain 'mental-state' references in (1), (2), and (3). These, in turn, may be reduced to Skinnerian terminology (with or without loss — I am not now passing judgment on that aspect of the issue). To say that the man believes he owns glasses is necessary, since one could not correctly describe someone as "looking for *his* glasses" unless he believed that he possessed glasses. It is too strong a condition to require that he *actually* own glasses since they may, in fact, have fallen into the wastebasket and been long since consumed. But we do not have to imagine that beliefs are mysterious states of the man's forever unobservable mind; we can, in turn, reduce "X believes Y" to a series of statements, at least some of which are conditional and all of which involve probability of specified observable responses. We can, in fact, avoid the conditional element (again, perhaps, at some cost) by restricting the type of prediction we make. Without going to this extreme (the arguments for so doing are entirely philosophical, since the conditional has an ex-

From *Minnesota Studies in the Philosophy of Science*, Vol. I, edited by Herbert Feigl and Michael Scriven. The University of Minnesota Press, Minneapolis, Minn., pp. 105–130.

[1] [*Throughout his article, Scriven uses the following abbreviations to refer to Skinner's works: ATLN for "Are Theories of Learning Necessary?"; CPCT for "Critique of Psychoanalytic Concepts and Theories"; and SHB for Science and Human Behavior. Editor's note.*]

tremely respectable place in the logical vocabulary of science and mathematics), we can expect the analysis of "X believes Y" to involve a series of statements such as the following.

(a) If X is asked "Do you believe Y?" under standard conditions, he will reply "Yes" or "Indeed" or "Of course" with 80 per cent probability.

(b) If X is hypnotized or injected with specified amounts of sodium ethyl thiobarbiturate, he will respond as in (a) with 75 per cent probability.

In the same way, we can analyze statements (2) and (3), in which the word "know" occurs.

Two comments on these subsidiary analyses should be made. In the first place, each of the samples given contains arbitrary probability figures, presumably not based on research. How could one give a more precise analysis? Secondly, giving a *complete* list of the stimulus-response patterns that would be relevant is clearly a problem of equal difficulty. It is in the face of the peculiar intransigence of these problems that Skinner, amongst others, is led to abandon the entire vocabulary of 'mental-state' descriptions. Why not, he says, stick to the unambiguous observation language in view of the remarkable achievements possible within its boundaries (the moderate position) and the eventual necessity of returning to it, assuming that one could successfully complete the analysis of "believe," "know," etc. (the extreme position). The reply is that, if we are seeking to analyze any purpose, goal, desire, intention, or mentalistic language, we can succeed only by doing the analysis, not be considering another problem; it should be clear from the discussion above that Skinner's suggested "translations" are thoroughly inadequate.

This is not to deny that Skinner can do a great deal, much of it related to this problem, without actually solving the problem. One might ask whether the original problem is really worth troubling with, when we come to see the extreme vagueness of ordinary language. But the original problem and its relatives make up the problem of analyzing purposive behavior, i.e., *what we ordinarily call* purposive behavior (or mentalistic language of the other varieties mentioned); and we can't palm off an analysis of something that our intuition suggests is the "essential behavioral component" instead, because intuition isn't objective argument and people have widely varying intuitions on this matter. In fact, the subtleties involved in ordinary language are considerable and, as I shall later argue, highly functional. The arguments so far given are intended to support the thesis that Skinner's analysis is much too simple, and that a complete reduction to Skinnerian language ('operationally' definable terms in response probability statements) is extremely *difficult*. Now, before we conclude that some simplified reduction will *have* to be made if any scientific investigation is ever to be possible, let us examine some of Skinner's own "operationally definable" language and see whether it is really free of what we can call (after Waismann) the "open texture" of the ordinary language of intending, knowing, and believing, and a fortiori of unconscious attitudes. If it is not, we shall have to decide whether the gain involved in the "simplification" is actually sufficient to compensate for the confusion involved in changing the meaning of many familiar terms. After all, we could not get very far by defining "intelligence" as "the average rating on a 1–10 scale scored by three friends"; the proposed operational definition corresponds very poorly to our background notion of intelligence since it will not be at all constant for each individual — and it doesn't analyze the notion itself, merely referring it to others for analysis. Furthermore, it is spuriously operational since there is no one such rating, and it is a spurious improvement for all these reasons. Are Skinner's "reductions" substantially better than the original terms? He makes a poor start with "intelligent," of which he says it "appears to describe properties of behavior but in reality refers to its controlling relations" (SHB, p. 36).[2] The reality is that it describes a property of behavior, which does not at all prevent its analysis from

[2] [*Page 38, this volume. Editor's note.*]

involving reference to its controlling relations. Skinner's belief in the incompatibility of these alternatives presages an unsound analysis of the permissible and useful modes of definition.

Consider another example: in CPCT Skinner refers to

> . . . another pitfall into which Freud, in common with his contemporaries, fell. There are many words in the layman's vocabulary that suggest the activity of an organism yet are not descriptive of behavior in the narrower sense. Freud used many of these freely — for example, the individual is said to discriminate, remember, infer, repress, decide, and so on. Such terms do not refer to specific acts. We say that a man discriminates between two objects when he behaves differently with respect to them; but discriminating is not itself behavior. We say that he represses behavior which has been punished when he engages in other behavior *just because* it displaces the punished behavior; but repressing is not action. We say that he decides upon a course of conduct either when he enters upon one course to the exclusion of another, or when he alters some of the variables affecting his own behavior in order to bring this about; but there is no other "act of deciding" (p. 304).

Looking at this example of Skinnerian analysis, we can again ask (a) whether or how nearly the products of the analysis are equivalent to the original, and (b) whether they are really acceptable for Skinner's purpose, i.e., operationally pure. In this instance, I wish to concentrate attention on the second question. Skinner's analytic base here includes the following crucial terms: "behaves"; "behaves differently with respect to X and Y"; "behavior segment X displaces behavior segment Y"; "enters upon X to the exclusion of Y"; "alters variables affecting own behavior." Elsewhere in this paper, we find him *using* (not quoting from Freud) such terms as "reinforces," "verbally injures," "pattern of behavior," etc. Now, we all know pretty well what these terms mean. But it must be noted that to say an organism "behaves" is *not* to describe its behavior in Skinner's "narrower sense"; and to say that some of its behavior "displaces" other behavior is no more to describe behavior in Skinner's sense than to say that one course of action was decided on rather than another (unless one makes the erroneous assumption that the latter necessarily refers to some inaccessible inner activity, which Skinner would scarcely wish to do). It appears that one could reply to this complaint by giving a list of actions or activities of an organism such that the disjunction of them all is equivalent to "behaves." But, clearly, one could never complete such a list. Alternatively, then, could one not equate "behaves" to some concatenation of anatomically-physiologically defined movements? But this is a very awkward alternative, since there are clearly certain movements, like the patellar reflex, PGR, epileptic frenzies, paretic and aphasic behavior, which cannot be explained at all within molar psychology; and there are many 'motionless' states, ranging from the catatonic to the reflective, which Skinner thinks *are* susceptible to his type of explanation. It is significant that Skinner never attempts to define "behavior" in his book *Science and Human Behavior*. After all, the anatomical-physiological definition would be likely to create great difficulties in excluding physiological explanatory theories; and the alternative of a long list definition would, equally clearly, be interminable, especially since the progress of a science of behavior will itself bring about the extension of the list. Even more serious difficulties arise over the term "displaces"; deeply embedded as it is in a spatial analogy, it has in addition all the problems involved in defining its range of application, *viz.* segments of behavior.

Skinner constantly reiterates his complaints about *certain* metaphors and their awful effects ("When one uses terms which describe an activity, one feels it necessary to invent an actor . . ." [CPCT, p. 304]; qualified by "The point is not that metaphor or construct is objectionable but that particular metaphors and constructs have caused trouble and are continuing to do so" [CPCT, p. 301 — the rest of the paper makes it fairly clear that he doubts the utility of *any* metaphors or constructs in a science of *behavior*]). It is as well to remember that the whole language of reinforcement, displacement, satiation, etc. used by Skinner is loaded with metaphorical meaning, and meaning to which serious objections can be raised (especially if one takes the very tough line that Skinner does about metaphors — for example, he objects to "motivational interaction" on the grounds that it implies "arrangements or relationships among *things*, but what are the things so related or arranged?" [CPCT, p. 305]). I have discussed earlier in this paper the utility and legitimacy of using such concepts on a trial basis; their success and that of their subsequent partial redefinition is a matter for scientific appraisal. I want to stress the fact that, although Skinner raises the ghost of his extreme position in CPCT ("It would be difficult to prove or disprove . . . that metaphorical devices are inevitable in the early stages of any science" [p. 301] certainly suggests their superfluity in later stages), he could not possibly avoid these charges against his own system. For amongst "metaphorical devices" he includes the use of terms such as "force" and "essence," on which he says we "look with amusement [as part of the] science of yesterday" (CPCT, p. 301; he elsewhere, as previously mentioned, gives "vis viva" as an example [SHB, p. 27]). It is clear that these terms, which came into the scientific language with some metaphorical connotations, are now entirely respectable terms in mechanics, oleo-chemistry, and dynamics ("vis viva" = twice the kinetic energy) and *retain the greater part of their original connotations*. For example, Skinner says, "The motion of a rolling stone was once attributed to its vis viva" (SHB, p. 27); it still is. As far as I know, the ancients never imagined the stone was actually alive; they merely attached a name to the hypothesized property which would explain the motion — the property which turned out to be a multiple of the kinetic energy. They chose a word which would carry some connotation of "explanatory of motion" from the field which they best understood, where motion distinguished living things. They were saying, in effect, "Moving inanimate objects have some of the properties of living things; let us name the concept that explains this aspect of their behavior *their* type of 'life-force.'" It was exactly this line of thought which led to the introduction of the term "response"; there *may* have been, or still be, people so stupid as to feel it "necessary to invent an actor" who gives the response, but it seems unlikely.

Now, it may be the case that so many people have been misled by the use of terms such as "repress," "sublimate," "project," that the contribution of psychoanalytic theory has been neutralized; but at least the introduction of these terms was as legitimate as that of Skinner's terms. Certainly, at the level of criticism which Skinner introduces, he is no better off; for example, he says, "The notion of a conscious or unconscious 'force' may be a useful metaphor, but if this is analogous to force in physics, what is the analogous mass that is analogously accelerated?" (CPCT, p. 305). Analogies are defined as *incomplete* parallels: the "force" analogy comes not from mechanics, where the term has been partially redefined, but from the same place that mechanics got it, ordinary usage — and force is not defined as the product of mass and acceleration in ordinary usage but as "strength or energy; vigor" (Webster). Now, if no fundamental logical error is involved in using "metaphorical devices," as I have tried to show, then we should consider the possibility of redefining or reconstructing the theory rather than rejecting it. And, in fact, both Skinner in SHB and Ellis in this volume make serious attempts to do this.

Skinner's objections on this point — the use of "metaphorical devices" — are now, I think, boiled down to the claim that the ones he uses are less misleading than Freud's. And this ties in with his complaints about "Freud's explanatory scheme," to which I shall return in a moment. I hope to suggest that Skinner's explanatory scheme applied to psychoanalysis often provides an *interpretation* rather than an *alternative*.

The discussion of metaphor was introduced

in the course of analyzing Skinner's own terminology for conformity to Skinner's standards. I hope that I have shown its success in meeting these standards is different at most only in degree from that of the terms to which Skinner takes exception; his own terms still retain the property of open texture; i.e., there is the same type of difficulty about categorically defining "behavior" or "displacement" as there is about "purpose" or "belief."

Yet, there hangs above us the pall of smoke from the battle over introspection.[3] "How can one deny that 'purpose' and 'belief' are words with an inner reference, and sometimes with no external manifestations?" say the introspectionists, while the radical behaviorists fidget at this metaphysics ("the traditional fiction of a mental life" [CPCT, p. 302]). Here I wish only to argue that Skinner's analysis is unsound, even for a *behaviorist*, and does not achieve what he thinks it will achieve. It is not a special feature of *mentalistic concepts* that they cannot be given an explicit unambiguous definition in basic observation language ("the left hand was raised three inches, the head turned to the right about 45°, eye fixation remained constant, etc."); but it is a feature of *all useful scientific concepts*, including Skinner's own. This point is fundamental; and it is difficult to accept because the whole trend of thought since scientists really became self-conscious about their definitions, say with Mach, has been in the opposite direction. Indeed, it sounds reasonable and admissible to insist on terms that can be explicitly and unambiguously defined in terms of basic observations. It is, in fact, a valuable exercise to attempt this at any stage in the development of a science; but, if successful, one is merely taking a still photograph of a changing scene, and the motion, not the snapshot, shows progress. Both the philosopher and the scientist can learn from the snapshots, but they will not understand the changes without a great many snapshots and a good deal of inference. So it is with the changing meaning of scientific concepts: at any stage it is possible to give their cash value in terms of observations, but to understand them properly one must also know their role in the theory and have some idea of their future movements given certain contingencies. A term is fruitful only if it encourages changes in its own meaning; and, to some considerable extent, this is incompatible with operational definition. It is sometimes easier to learn how to use terms than to learn how to work out their cash value in a certain currency, and sometimes the reverse. We all know very well how to use terms such as "purpose" and "belief" and we can teach someone who doesn't speak the language how to use them (child or foreigner), but it's not easy to reduce them to Skinner's currency (and, some suspect, not possible). But Skinner won't pay in other currency, which he views with suspicion; and, if we want to collect the real value of our investment from him, we must compromise: collect a good deal from him on his terms and talk him around on the rest, perhaps by showing him some defects in his own coinage.

On Skinner's own terms, his analyses are not satisfactory; and, when we look at the currency itself, it seems to have the same weaknesses as the promissory notes that he won't negotiate.

There were two difficulties about our original analysis of "belief," which sprang from an attempt to improve Skinner's analysis of "looking for his glasses." The first, into which we have now gone at some length, stems from the impossibility of completely itemizing the units of behavior to which "belief" (in some way) refers, and is a difficulty which some of Skinner's basic terms share. The second was the difficulty of giving precise estimates of the

[3] Skinner's logical maneuvers in his skirmishes with introspection repay careful study. His case depends on a crucial misuse of perception language, e.g., a systematically ambiguous use of "see" (SHB, pp. 273–78). It is further weakened in CPCT by his argument that Freud's evidence for self-deception in introspection shows introspection not to be like observation. On the contrary, it shows how very much it is like observation (itself fallible), though it is not the observation of logically inaccessible inner states, but of states some of whose aspects are sometimes not externally displayed.

response-probability in *any* of the component statements. He would, I think, be the first to agree that the corresponding statements in his own system — i.e., dispositional statements involving response induction or stimulus discrimination and generalization — could not contain exact values except by arbitrary redefinition. Corresponding to "S believes p" would be "S discriminates red keys from green keys in a Skinner-box." We had difficulty in giving a cutting frequency for affirmative responses (to the question "Do you believe p?" put to S as a stimulus) which would differentiate a state of belief in p from one of uncertainty about p. Similarly, Skinner could not guarantee in advance the response-frequency or, indeed, the existence of discrimination, if we set up conditions different from those under which the S was trained — for example, there is the possibility of what he terms "emotional behavior."

A great deal more could be said about the comparison here with reference to the Behaviorist's philosophical thesis, but I wish to avoid direct engagements with this and instead bring the above points to bear on Skinner's account of Freud's "explanatory scheme." I would conclude this examination of Skinner's attack on purposive and mentalistic terminology by saying that the substitute he offers is not obviously required, is not as good as it could be, and, even if it were improved to its natural limits, would be insufficiently distinguishable from the original to justify the effort. Skinner is practically allergic to even the most harmless references to the 'mental life'; and I think this prevents him from seeing that, if his translations *were* really satisfactory, then there would be a 'mind' in his system, too. Consider, for example, this quotation: "One who readily engages in a given activity is not showing an interest, he is showing the effect of reinforcement" (SHB, p. 72). But a *very special type* of effect, one which it is *extremely important to distinguish* from the readiness to engage in a given activity springing from severe punishment for failure to do so. One can no more deny that Skinner has shown an interest in psychology during much of his academic life — i.e., the propriety of the phrase "showing an interest" in this case — than one can deny that this book has pages (i.e., since standard conditions obtain, the propriety of the phrase "books have pages") even if it does suggest ownership. We shall see how this hypersensitivity to one interpretation (quite possibly an unfortunate or unproductive one) leads him to underestimate the utility of psychoanalytic theory. It is by no means necessary to interpret these phrases in this way; and, in fact, we can improve Skinner's suggested behavioral analysis to the point where it provides a good scientific substitute for the original phrase. This could be described as 'translating the mind into behavioral terms'; or, equally well, it could be said to show that the reference to mind was not objectionable in the first place. To say that such phrases as "making up one's mind," "having an idea," etc. are "obvious" cases in which the mind and ideas are "being invented on the spot to provide spurious explanations" (SHB, p. 30) is to miss the point that these are genuine explanations but do not involve reference to some scientifically inaccessible realm. No one, without stretching an etymological point, reads into such phrases what Skinner objects to in them; they are invariably used as shorthand for a set of descriptive plus dispositional propositions, just as "believe," "behave," and "beta-particle" are.

Taking the bull by the horns, I shall argue that Skinner, partly because of errors of translation of the kind just discussed, underestimates the practical value and logical validity of explanations of behavior in terms of 'mental events.' Basic to all his arguments is the belief that any reference to inner states is an unnecessary complication, since eventually one has to explain *them* in terms of environmental variables. The counterargument that the egg comes before the chicken and that we must, therefore, get back inside the skin to the organism's inherited genetic composition in order to achieve a complete explanation would presumably cut no ice because, Skinner would say, we can't control the genes (or neurons). But we mustn't be misled by the combination of Skinner's use of the word "control" and Skinner's analyses of familiar processes. For example, he argues that "awareness of cause [of one's actions] has nothing to do with causal effectiveness" (CPCT, p. 305). But this is a verbal trick. He is not really denying (as he appears to) that the patient who attains insight into his aggressive remarks to his brother will often abandon them subsequently. He is (essentially) arguing that, since both insight and behavior improvement are due to changes in other environmental variables, it is wrong to say one of them *causes* the other, i.e., wrong to say that it is the awareness of the hostile impulses that reduces their effectiveness. He is not denying that the first might always be followed by the second or that the second might never occur without the first, i.e., that the process of bringing about the insight produces the remission of the symptoms. Now, analysts, including Freud, have long stressed the fact that mere enunciation of the relation between unconscious hostility and aggressive remarks will not bring to an end to the latter. Thus the analyst believes

(1) The hostile feelings (C_1) cause the aggressive behavior (E_1).

(2) Getting the patient to the stage where he volunteers the interpretation — i.e., getting-him-to-achieve-insight-in-this-respect (C_2) — causes the symptoms' disappearance (E_2).

Now, achieving insight is the standard psychoanalytic case of "awareness of cause," and it is followed by the termination of the causal relation (1); moreover, the process of achieving insight actually causes the improvement (as stated in (2)). It is, therefore, extremely misleading of Skinner to say "awareness of cause has nothing to do with causal effectiveness." It is trivially true that if A causes B under conditions C, and C does not contain a provision excluding an observer, then A will still cause B even if there is an observer. The analytic discovery was that, in certain cases of caused behavior, C *does* include such a prohibition and A no longer produces B in a patient P when P has learned about the connection (this schema oversimplifies in certain respects). It might appear that Skinner is making a more substantial point, that he is suggesting something empirically distinguishable from Freud. I am not clear that he is. The following quotation suggests there is no such tangible difference, but only a difference of emphasis: "Therapy consists, not in getting the patient to discover the solution to his problem, but in changing him in such a way that he is able to discover it" (SHB, p. 382). But on other occasions this is not clear: "The parallel between the excision of a tumor, for example, and the release of a repressed wish from the unconscious is quite compelling and must have affected Freud's thinking" (CPCT, p. 301) — and Skinner has made clear to me in conversation that he regards this as perhaps Freud's most serious error. Now, what is the pattern of explanation here? We have

1. The tumor (C_1) causes illness (E_1)
2. Removal-of-the-tumor (C_2) causes recovery (E_2)

and the analogy, which Skinner disputes, would be

1′. The repressed wish (C'_1) causes, say, stuttering (E'_1)

2′. Release-of-the-wish (C'_2) causes cure (E'_2).

If Freud thought that the "releasing of a suppressed wish from the unconscious" meant the mere uttering of the words, perhaps even parrotwise, after the analyst, and was in itself *curative*, then Skinner is disagreeing with Freud on empirical grounds. It seems clear enough that this was not Freud's view. But if Freud thought that the mere verbalization had little or no therapeutic value, whereas the 'spontaneous' *release* of a wish marked the penultimate stage of therapy for this symptom (culminated by the application of this insight), then I am not sure that Skinner would disagree, in view of the fact that he is presenting no new evidence. After all, discovering the wish makes it possible for P and the analyst to reorient P's behavior accordingly, and the fact that it has been voluntarily produced makes it likely the behavior will be successfully reoriented. If the reorientation is successful, could one not then say that producing the wish produced the cure *under these circumstances*? The hard work goes into achieving C'_2, but if we define cure as the actual vanishing of symptoms, then it *is* the release of the wish that produces it. Thus, we might agree with Skinner that *therapy* consists in changing the patient until he can achieve C'_2, but that the (proximate) cause of the *cure* is C'_2. And Freud would not, as far as I can see, disagree with this. I do not think this position justifies such strong statements as the following:

> Freud's contribution . . . [was] . . . not that the individual was often unable to describe important aspects of his own behavior, or identify important causal relationships but that his ability to describe them *was irrelevant* to the occurrence of the behavior or the effectiveness of the causes (CPCT, p. 304; my italics).

I have gone into this point in detail because I think it well illustrates the difficulty of dealing with Skinner's criticisms of Freud. An attempt to wholly disentangle his ideas about the formal status of psychoanalytic theory would be unrewarding, but I think it important to show that it rests on an erroneous dichotomy, which explains a great deal about the rest of his approach. He says, "No matter what logicians may eventually make of this mental apparatus, there is little doubt that Freud accepted it as real *rather than* as a scientific construct or theory" (CPCT, p. 301; my italics).

Skinner is here reaping the whirlwind of early positivism, and this eddy affects his position more seriously than his other philosophical inheritances from the same source.[4] The idea that scientific constructs are not "real" but are mere "explanatory fictions," as he goes on to describe them, is untenable; but, if one believes it, one will not be encouraged to invent many. It is a little misleading to insist that scientific constructs *are* real, although it is certainly better than the alternative (I have never heard anyone arguing whether theories are real: what would an unreal theory be like?). The issue is a spurious one; such constructs should always be said to be real in *such-and-such* a respect, but unreal — i.e., unlike such earthily real things as platypuses — in *such-and-such another* respect, etc., etc. Few are observable like animals but many have observable consequences, like the neutrino, and their existence is said to be confirmed when these consequences eventuate. Philosophy has outgrown such questions as "Do groups exist over and above their members?" "Do electrons really exist?" though it learned much from answering them. The answer must always be, "In a certain sense, yes, and in a certain sense, no." The important point is that a theory can and does proceed without having to distinguish each construct as "real" or "explanatory fiction"; there are other rules to be obeyed (those of factor-analysis in certain cases, for example) but not this rule. We may have grave reservations about the meaning, if any, of "libido," which we may awkwardly express by asking whether there really is a libido; but if a satisfactory answer can be given, it does not show that "libido" is *not* a scientific concept, that it is an observable: it would be a scientific construct, it would 'exist,' but it need not be actually observable as long as it has effects we can observe. The libido has to undergo the same examinations as Spearman's g, the concept of isostasy, and cultural lag. If they are satisfactory constructs, they may figure in explanations in a way we shall consider, although they are not observables and not all operationally difinable in terms of observables. But that does not make them "*fictions*"; indeed, "explanatory fiction" is a contradiction in terms: abbreviatory devices are not normally explanatory, and explanatory devices are never fictitious.

There is no obligation on the libido to be located in the brain, or to have spatial location at all; the rules are flexible, they require

[4] E.g., "Certain basic assumptions, essential to any scientific activity, are sometimes called theories. That nature is orderly rather than capricious is an example" (ATLN, p. 193).

only that we be able to make some objective distinction between cases in which the term can be properly applied and the rest. The same applies to Skinner's use of "reserve" (of responses — ATLN, p. 203) or the physicist's concept of entropy. But Skinner believes in the "observable-or-explanatory-fiction dichotomy," so he is at great pains in SHB to show that introspection is not a form of observation and, hence, that "conscious, as well as unconscious events [are] inferences from the facts" (CPCT, p. 302) — hence, are constructs and hence *unreal*. On one occasion, he puts it in this way: ". . . the act of self-observation [sic] can be represented within the framework of physical science. This involves questioning the reality of sensations, ideas, feelings, and other states of consciousness . . ." (CPCT, p. 304). The example which follows shows, as one might expect, that he is not going to question the *reality* of these things but the *reliability* of reports on them: the mystic's religious experience is not unreal but (according to Skinner's hypothesized psychoanalyst) incorrectly described as communion with a supernatural being. One can often show that someone's description of his sensations is inaccurate; it does not follow that he had none. Having arrived at the conclusion that mental events are unreal, Skinner feeds it back into the argument and attacks explanations in terms of mental states as circular and/or superfluous. Only in this way, as he sees it, can one get past the Scylla of explaining how the mind and body interact and the Charybdis of explaining how we can know the contents of another's mind. Union rules prevent me from divulging the secret of the problems which provide a guaranteed annual wage for philosophers; but it is not too difficult to show some very important ways in which mental states can figure in extremely respectable explanations, in whose company, indeed, no behaviorist should feel ashamed to be seen.

Suppose that we accept the behaviorist analysis of mental states that Skinner is anxious to sell us, making some modifications to the actual model he is vending, along the lines suggested in our account of "He's looking for his glasses" and "He's showing an interest in this activity." Ignore, for the moment, the twin difficulties of inexhaustibility and inaccuracy in specifying the exact propositions in behavior-language to which we reduce the mental state. Then, taking a simple case,

"X is in mental-state M."
= "If X is in circumstances Y, he will (with probability P) do Z."

Now, there will normally be many other circumstances (Y′, Y″, . . .) under which X will also do Z. For example, he will drink a glass of water (Z) not only when thirsty (M) — i.e., when he has been deprived of water for some time, etc. (Y) — but also when there is a gun at his back even if he is satiated (Y′), when he has been deprived of food and no food is now present (Y″), etc. Suppose that X is in an observation room, taking part in an experiment of whose purposes you are ignorant. You do not know whether he is being paid, deprived, or intellectually stimulated. At 3:00 P.M. he looks at the clock, takes up a glass of water, and drinks it. You ask, having these other possibilities in mind: Why did he drink? A perfectly proper and informative explanation is "Because he is thirsty." It is informative because you now know (always assuming the behaviorist analysis to be correct) that this means circumstances Y must obtain, as opposed to Y′, Y″, . . .

This type of request for an explanation is perhaps the most common of all. Skinner would describe it as a request for information about "the external variables of which behavior is a function" because he thinks that 'inner-state' language is really translatable into descriptions of external variables. But if it is, then explanations in terms of inner states are perfectly legitimate. And even if it is not, even if there is something more involved in reports on inner states, it is still true that they are *connected with* external variables, i.e., whatever "X is thirsty" may refer to, we *know* it is probabilistically connected with hours of deprivation, aversive preconditioning, etc., so that the *worst* charge that Skinner can lay is vagueness. Of course, he may not like the obscurity of the connection between a state of thirst and behavior; we can help him by accepting tentatively the identification of the two. Thus, one does not have to solve the mind-body problem in order to find out what independent variables are related to subjective reports of feelings of thirst, actual drinking without such reports, etc.; and even the decision that thirst is not *wholly* reducible to behavioral criteria does not imply that it is not a *good basis* for explanation, since it clearly has many behavioral consequences. It is not important to a public health officer in charge of mosquito control whether we *define* DDT in terms of its entomological effects or whether we define it chemically, as long as we don't *deny* its entomological effects; similarly, whether we say that thirst is or is not something more than a certain pattern of behavior is unimportant, as long as we agree that it is the psychologist who studies the *whole behavioral aspect*. The presence of vagueness not only affects his own more general concepts (notice the difficulties in distinguishing operant from response conditioning under certain circumstances) but also has certain virtues for a scientific concept in the field of behavior, a fact which will be further elaborated below.

The first point made, then, is that, on a radical behaviorist analysis of inner states, explanations in such terms are vital and legitimate. I did not say "on Skinner's analysis" because we have already made a number of improvements on that without abandoning radical behaviorism. To uncover some more of the very serious difficulties in Skinner's own analysis, I am going to examine one or two further instances of it, still on his own standards. Then I shall consider the results of our suggested changes in the radical behaviorist analysis of mental-state terminology, in an attempt to show that one can produce a fully scientific account that is much closer to being an analysis of the actual mental concepts we ordinarily employ, which Skinner views with such suspicion.

But what is Skinner's position?

> To what extent is it helpful to be told "He drinks because he is thirsty"? If to be thirsty means nothing more than to have a tendency to drink, this is mere redundancy. If it means that he drinks because of a state of thirst, an inner causal event is invoked. If this state is purely inferential — if no dimensions are assigned to it which would make direct observation possible — it cannot serve as an explanation (SHB, p. 33).[5]

All these conclusions are erroneous. Even if "to be thirsty means nothing more than to have a tendency to drink," it is by no means merely redundant to be told that *on this occasion* he drank because of that tendency *rather than* under compulsion or because of a tendency to eat or etc. To have a tendency is to have a certain disposition, and everyone has *some* disposition to drink, but it is not always that disposition which explains our drinking. When we are satiated, for example, we have a short-term disposition not to drink; and, in such a case, the statement that we drank because we were thirsty would not, even on Skinner's first analysis, be redundant; it would be false. It follows that Skinner does not see the importance of dispositions, nor does he see the nature of what I shall call "discrimination-explanations," i.e., explanations of event E as due to antecedents A *rather than* A′ or A″, all of which we realize are capable of producing E.

Of course, there *are* occasions on which pseudo explanations — looking rather similar to this one — are offered. If we explain someone's frequent sleepy appearance by saying he is a soporific type, we may well be deceiving ourselves. But to chastise the ordinary explanations of *individual events* by reference to dispositions, on the grounds that some explanations of *patterns of behavior* by reference to dispositions are redundant, is manifestly unfair. Skinner's failure to distinguish these is clearly shown in the following quotation:

> When we say that a man eats *because* he is hungry, smokes a great deal *because* he has the tobacco habit, fights *because* of the instinct of pugnacity,

[5] [*Page 37, this volume.*]

behaves brilliantly *because* of his intelligence, or plays the piano well *because* of his musical ability, we seem to be referring to causes. But on analysis these phrases prove to be merely redundant descriptions. A single set of facts is described by the two statements: "He eats" and "He is hungry." A single set of facts is described by the two statements: "He smokes a great deal" and "He has the smoking habit." . . . (SHB, p. 31).

This is guilt by association! Every one of these examples except the first is susceptible to Skinner's criticism; but the first is the vital one for his attack on mental states, partly because we don't introspect "having a smoking habit" whereas we do introspect "being hungry." It is a logical error, *even for a radical behaviorist*, to imagine that the same "set of facts" is described by "He eats" and "He is hungry" since, for a radical behaviorist, the second statement is equivalent to "He has a disposition to eat," i.e., "Under specifiable conditions it is P per cent probable that he will eat," which neither implies nor is implied by "He eats."

Skinner's third conclusion — that if thirst is a purely inferential state not susceptible to direct observation, it cannot serve as an explanation — is also in my view mistaken. I have argued above that it is only necessary for the hypotheses embodying scientific concepts to be susceptible to *confirmation*, not observation — or else temperature, inertial mass, and the spin of the electron would be illicit — and the argument applies here. Furthermore, it is possible to construct an example which will demonstrate this and, at the same time, answer any doubts that may have arisen in the reader's mind as to the propriety of explaining one observed drinking-event in terms of a disposition if the latter is interpreted as a construct out of drinking-events.

Suppose that we introduce the symbol Ω into psychological discourse in the following way: if an organism O is such that variable $v_1 > N_1$, while $v_2, v_3, \ldots v_n < N_2$, we shall say that O is in state $\Omega(\Omega(O))$. Further, if $v_1 \leq N_1$ while $v_2 + v_3$ or $v_2 + v_4$ or $v_3 + v_4$ or $\ldots > 2N_1$ and $v_1, v_2, v_3, \ldots v_n < N_2$, we shall also say that $\Omega(O)$. And if some one of $v_2, v_3, \ldots v_n \geq N_2$, we shall say that it is not the case that $\Omega(O)$. Notice that we have not said anything about the case $v_1, v_2, v_3, \ldots v_n \leq N_1$, except under certain conditions on the ratio N_1/N_2 between the constants. This example is a rough model of a personality or pathology category, interpreted operationally. Now, we have not in any sense assigned dimensions to Ω, any more than we do to schizophrenia. According to Skinner, then, "it cannot serve as an explanation" since no direct observation is possible. But it may provide a most useful means of classifying organisms, such that laws can be stated in simpler forms — i.e., it can be a step toward a sort of theory which Skinner approves of ("a formal representation of the data reduced to a minimal number of terms" [ATLN, p. 216]), and it can certainly figure in discrimination-explanations. What can Skinner say to resolve this contradiction? The necessary compromise seems obvious: Ω is satisfactory because it at least is *defined in terms of* observables. So it appears. And yet the word "state" occurs. Can we really infer from *any* formal considerations that O is in a certain state? Indeed not: one could not introduce a state defined by reference to the number of people within a one-mile circle with center fifty miles south of O without changing the present meaning of "state." "State" is a word that needs a great deal of unpacking; it is appropriate only when we are sure that a causal account of the phenomena that differentiate "states" can be given in terms of actual physical changes in the organism corresponding to changes of "state" in the proposed sense.

This simple fact makes the language of states at once more complex and more useful than Skinner allows, and it partially explains how the tie-in of psychoanalysis or psychology with neurology is so strong. As it stands, Ω can give us discrimination-explanations of the fact that certain variables have certain values (e.g., that X drinks or stutters or produces neologisms) insofar as it contains a reference to other variables which are causally related to those observed, and *it can only do that* by referring to a current state. Even the thirst case, which appears as the simplest possible example, where v_1 is the only variable on which Ω depends as well as being that which is explained, is less simple than it appears since, for the explanation to be valid, it must be the case that the earlier history of v_1 variation has causally effected the present state of O. It is immaterial that we cannot demonstrate this physiologically. As long as we have no direct evidence against it and it works as an explanation, then we have evidence for it, indirect evidence. But it must be true. Moreover, it is not incumbent on us to say how the matter could be tested by direct observation at all. We *may* believe that this will be possible, e.g., by identification with some neural and intestinal configuration; but we may also believe it will never be possible, as long as we are prepared to give (a) the conditions which will count as *confirming* evidence for and against the use of the construct, and (b) reasons for believing that some causal connection is possible between the independent environmental variables and the behavioral output variables. Thus, one could not, in the world as it now is, argue that an Ω defined by reference to the past population density of an area geographically distant from O could explain either the present drinking behavior or indeed almost any other behavior of O, since one can give no reasons for thinking that it could produce any present effects on O at all.

Now, it is this basic process in science — the process of ascribing states to substances and organisms — which forms the first level of theory-building; and it is one that Skinner cannot avoid himself, for example, when he describes an organism as "satiated." This term would have to be abandoned even if Skinner's data was still accepted, if we did not believe that the gratification had produced an effect on the organism that, in fact, persisted. Our reason for thinking this is true is the change in response frequency after unrestricted eating (for example) is allowed, when the reinforcement is food. This striking result, we would argue, shows clearly that an effect has persisted on the organism. Let us call this effect "satiation"; it is a state of the organism. Now, Skinner overlooks the theoretical element in this analysis and imagines he can define the word without any reference to state: he views it as a summary of past history. I have already shown that he gives a bad summary; now I am arguing that he is committed to more than a summary. The reason is that one cannot believe the past history to affect the present behavior except via a present state — and science *as a whole* (not molar psychology) must explain how this implicit hypothesis (supported by every success of molar psychology) is justified. It is a rare explanation which does not produce new discoveries — and one need give no further justification for neurologically-oriented behavior research. Skinner is misled by the argument that neural states are dispensable and inaccessible (for molar psychology) into behaving as though they are scientifically dispensable, which they are not, even if inaccessible, and into imagining that he does not use them. So, states may be "purely inferential" and *yet* "serve as an explanation." It is psychologically unfortunate if other people are really misled by talking about states — conscious or unconscious — into imagining that science should not be concerned with discovering the antecedents, but the sin is no worse than that of imagining states to be dispensable.

Skinner is seriously in error on this whole issue, and understandably so — for if he too often acknowledges this implicit and necessary belief in the state-differences brought about by various schedules, he would have to face the question, What sort of state-differences do you have in mind? The reply that he means no more by the state than "that which is produced by the past reinforcement schedule and which produces the future responses" would, of course, be open to his own objection that it is an "explanatory fiction," unless he can give directly observable properties to it. Certainly it is obvious that if the organism reacts differently, it is in a different state; but insofar as its reactions are physically determined by its neurology, so far it is obvious that neurology must provide the foundations for this basic assumption of molar psychology. Now it becomes clear why Skinner prefers to talk of functional dependency rather than causal dependency: because causal dependency is necessarily mediated by a state of the organism about which Skinner can say nothing. We cannot object to what Skinner does positively; but in his criticisms he implies that the supplementary activities are unnecessary and invalid, and in this he is surely wrong. Of repression and the other defense mechanisms, he says in CPCT that they should not be regarded "as activities of the individual or any subdivision thereof . . . but simply as ways of representing relationships among responses and controlling variables." But they *are* activities (successions of states) of the individual, the very ones necessary to link the controlling variables to the responses; and we can *still* agree that they are to be distinguished by study of the functional relationships they mediate. Skinner does not hold the only alternative position — that the childhood trauma itself directly causes (across space and time) the neurotic behavior — but at times he sounds very like it. The state of anxiety, he says, "is of no functional significance, either in a theoretical analysis or in the practical control of behavior" (SHB, p. 181). Well, it is an absolute necessity in the total scientific study of behavior to have such states, and the anxiety-reducing drugs show that this one has considerable functional significance in the control of behavior, somewhat contrary to the implications of this passage or of the even more dogmatic statement preceding it — "Any therapeutic attempt to reduce the 'effects of anxiety' must operate upon these [controlling] circumstances, not upon any intervening state."

I want now to suggest that the psychoanalytic or group dynamic or historical or sociological *approach* is an alternative (to molar psychology) of a most respectable kind for dealing with certain areas of behavior. From a certain point of view, these approaches are simply examples of molar approaches: they are molar approaches to molar behavior in certain areas — they are branches of molar behavior science. The psychoanalyst is taking a particular *pattern* of behavior as his unit — say the deprivation-desire-deed pattern in analyzing defences — which to the molar psychologist is quite a complex structure. I think that Skinner is in the position of a man who is asked for his suggestions at a research conference in the chemistry department, where they are tackling the problem of yeast assessment for bread-making. He says, "Find out all the physical properties of enzyme molecules and you'll have the answer." True, but only if old age is conquered in the meantime. Physics will some day perhaps be able to account for all chemical reactions, but today we have to evolve a selective approach via the chemical properties. It *may* not work, it may be necessary to get down to bedrock before a solid foundation can be laid; but it's well worth trying — and in chemistry it has paid off for a long time. Similarly in the social sciences, we can build up from the bricks of individual psychology or try to make a useful building with the large blocks of stones lying around with just a little chipping and perhaps a little more quarrying. And in psychology, we can work up from physiology or neurology, or tackle the issues more directly. Skinner is defending an approach to psychology which he rejects as an approach to psychopathology.

It is useless to complain that this is only a part of psychology; such an assumption is (a) extremely speculative and (b) even if true, no more effective than the argument that chemistry is only part of physics, which has hardly prevented chemists from discovering useful concepts at their own level. Skinner's extreme aversion to anything that looks like animistic talk leads him to miss the great wealth that can be mined from a logically sophisticated behavioristic analysis (*not* reduction — this is unnecessary and begs the philosophical question) of mental-state talk.

In particular, we can return to the two oversimplifications we made when beginning the discussion of "psychic states." A behavioristic analysis of "know" or "believe" has these two dimensions of flexibility (a better word than "vagueness," whose negative connotations spring from a failure to appreciate the necessity and utility of open texture in scientific language). How can this be useful in a science of behavior? How can it be anything but a drawback? The questions are immensely vain: for they presuppose that psychology is appropriate for or capable of answering such questions as What is knowledge? And, on the other hand, they are overly modest; for they presuppose that we have no idea how to shape the lists or estimate the probabilities.

Psychology should, of course, not be mainly concerned with epistemological questions, even though (a) its results may sometimes be relevant to them, and (b) the inspiration and description of research should not be independent of epistemological thought. Thus, psychologists concerned with "knowledge" characteristically ask such questions as these: What do seventh-grade math pupils know that sixth-graders do not? What does a man know about his childhood that he cannot immediately recall? Does a nondirective discussion result in the absorption of more knowledge than a lecture on the same topic? Does the teacher really know which of his pupils are the most intelligent? etc. There are endless experiments of this kind done, none of which fall into difficulties over the term "know"; though, of course, some others do, just as in physics some experiments are doomed from the beginning owing to faulty logical analysis. Only the crypto-philosophical psychologist inflates his experimental results into epistemological conclusions, and he is usually somewhat short on logical training. Even though some important questions are not properly answered by experiment — amongst them legal, literary, and logical ones — it is not necessary to reject as nonexperimental all problems involving mentalistic concepts, as Skinner does. For every man who can talk a language understands very well how to use these words, and can almost always tell a proper question from a nonsense-statement involving them. The fact that we can all use this language with great efficiency shows that one cannot judge the utility of a language by the test of whether it is reducible to a specific list of specific statements in the observation language. Nor even its scientific utility, for the language of many sciences has this feature. Thus for proper psychological questions, we shall, I suggest, no more frequently find ourselves in difficulty understanding or formulating a problem about knowledge or belief in ordinary language than if we invent some *vaguely related* and *still imprecise* (if still useful) language of our own. Inventing new terms is too frequently a substitute for analyzing the old ones and a move which only postpones the difficulties, for at some stage we try to relate the discoveries formulated in the new language to the problems formulated in the old. We can have our Taylor Scale on which we define a psychological concept of anxiety, but we can't avoid the question, "Does this give a good measure of anxiety as we ordinarily use the term?" Because if it doesn't, we can't use it to find out whether students are made more anxious by subjective than objective examinations, or patients less anxious by piped music in the waiting-room. The background concept and theory cannot be ignored, though they can nearly always be improved; they *have* to be studied. A similar study of scientific terms reveals, below that surface sheen of operationism, the same open texture or flexibility. The difference lies in the purpose, not the nature, of the definitions employed, or employable except for some variations of degree (which are not all in one direction).

The language of psychoanalysis, in particular, is very open-textured; it is a first approach. Being so, it runs the risk of becoming empirically meaningless, a ritual form of mental alchemy. But the *approach* is fully justifiable; and it is as wrong to suggest that Freud should have pinned his terms down to infant neurology (CPCT, p. 302) or, by the "simple expedient of an operational definition," to physical and biological science (CPCT, p. 305), as it would be to insist that the founders of radio astronomy should have early said whether a radio star was a solid body or a region of space. They introduced the term as a name for the hypothesized origin of short-wave electromagnetic radiation. It now appears they were justified in using a *name* (i.e., spatial location is well supported), but we cannot yet tell exactly what radio stars (physically speaking) are, what the name stands for. Freud introduced the concept of the ego-ideal or superego as the hypothesized repository of the learned censoring activities of the personality. It is less certain that he was justified in using a name and quite unclear what, if any, physical reference it will have. It certainly need have no observable or measurable referent ("... the most unfortunate effect of all" those due to Freud's use of a "mental apparatus" approach [CPCT, p. 305]) to be respectable, though the hypothesis of its existence or operation must have observable consequences that are reliably identifiable. It was obvious to Freud that these consequences will have their neural counterpart if they exist and that the superego will thus, at least indirectly, have a neural counterpart; no one knew more than that. But everyone knew, or thought they knew, a great deal about conscience, anxiety, and guilt; and Freud discovered a great deal more, just as a psychologist might discover a great deal more about knowledge by an extension of the experiments described above. And just as the psychologist might quite accurately sum up some of his discoveries by distinguishing two types of knowledge (say kinesthetic and verbal), so Freud could distinguish two stages in the development of the superego. Should we argue whether both types of knowledge *exist* or are *real*? We can, and we know how to do it in terms of correlation coefficients and chi^2 values — but it's an odd way to put the question. Does the superego exist? is it real? Well, we can deal with those questions, too, by pointing out certain undeniable features of behavior and arguing for their correlation and common subsumption under this heading. This doesn't show that the superego is observable, nor does it show that it is an explanatory fiction: Skinner's dichotomy is unsound. But — if it can be done — it justifies *talking about the superego*, which is as near as we can get to showing that it's real. It isn't real like a brain tumor, but it is real rather like an electric field; and it's certainly not unreal or a "fiction" or a "myth" like the aether — unless the arguments for it can be met, as those for the aether were met, on their own ground.

The other way of throwing over a theory, and a common one in the history of science, is to produce a better one. This Skinner would not be anxious to describe himself as doing. But his account of psychotherapy in SHB is an illuminating one, and it is theoretical. It is still far from being capable of dealing with the strange complexities of neurosis at an explanatory level, and it has no therapeutic success to support any claims for its practical efficiency. In fact, we have argued that while Skinner belabors Freud (somewhat unfairly, I think) for failing to give "an explicit treatment of behavior as a datum, of probability of response as the principal quantifiable property of behavior ..." (CPCT, p. 304), in short, for being too theoretical, Skinner is himself a little too upset by the idea of explanations involving mental states to do them justice, even in his own operational terms. It is sometimes these errors of emphasis, rather than of fact, that lead us to abandon an approach. In his discussion of early psychological theories, Skinner comments on the simple reflex approach with these words: "It is neither plausible nor expedient to conceive of the organism as a complicated jack-in-the-box with a long list of tricks, each of which may be evoked by pressing the proper button" (SHB, p. 49). Reading Skinner, one sometimes wonders whether it is any more plausible or expedient to conceive of the organism as a complicated (but transparent) marionette with a long list of tricks, each of which may be evoked by pulling the proper string.

References

[1] SKINNER, B. F. "Are Theories of Learning Necessary?" *Psychological Review*, 57: 193–216 (1950).

[2] SKINNER, B. F. *Science and Human Behavior*, New York: Macmillan, 1953.

[3] SKINNER, B. F. "Critique of Psychoanalytic Concepts and Theories," *Scientific Monthly*, 79: 300–5 (1954).

33 Irreducible Intentionality as the Mark of the Psychological

Sentences about Believing

RODERICK M. CHISHOLM

1. "I can look for him when he is not there, but not hang him when he is not there."[1] The first of these activities, Brentano would have said, is *intentional;* it may take as its object something which does not exist. But the second activity is "merely physical"; it cannot be performed unless its object is there to work with. "Intentionality," he thought, provides us with a mark of what is psychological.

I shall try to reformulate Brentano's suggestion by describing one of the ways in which we need to use language when we talk about certain psychological states and events. I shall refer to this use as the "intentional use" of language. It is a kind of use we can avoid when we talk about non-psychological states and events.

In the interests of a philosophy contrary to that of Brentano, many philosophers and psychologists have tried to show, in effect, how we can avoid intentional language when we wish to talk about psychology. I shall discuss some of these attempts in so far as they relate to the sorts of things we wish to be able to say about *believing*. I believe that these attempts have been so far unsuccessful. And I think that this fact may provide some reason for saying, with Brentano, that "intentionality" is a mark of what is psychological.

2. In order to formulate criteria by means of which we can identify the "intentional" use of language, let us classify sentences as simple and compound. For our purposes I think it will be enough to say that a compound sentence is one compounded from two or more sentences by means of propositional connectives, such as "and", "or", "if-then" "although", and "because". A simple sentence is one which is not compound. Examples of simple sentences are "He is thinking of the Dnieper Dam," "She is looking for a suitable husband for her daughter," "Their car lacks a spare wheel," and "He believes that it will rain." I shall formulate three criteria for saying that simple declarative sentences are intentional, or are used intentionally.

(a) A simple declarative sentence is intentional if it uses a substantival expression — a name or a description — in such a way that neither the sentence nor its contradictory implies either that there is or that there isn't anything to which the substantival expression truly applies. The first two examples above are intentional by this criterion. When we say that a man is thinking of the Dnieper Dam, we do not imply either that there is or that there isn't such a dam; similarly when we deny that he is thinking of it. When we say that a lady is looking for a suitable husband for her daughter, we do not commit ourselves to saying that her daughter will, or that she will not, have a suitable husband; and similarly when we deny that the lady is looking for one. But the next sentence in our list of examples — "Their car lacks a spare wheel" — is not intentional. It is true that, if we affirm this sentence, we do not commit ourselves to saying either that there are or that there are not any spare wheels. But if we deny the sentence, affirming "Their car does not lack a spare wheel," then we imply that there is a spare wheel somewhere.

From *Proceedings of the Aristotelian Society*, 56 (1955–1956), pp. 125–148, reprinted by courtesy of the Editor of the Aristotelian Society.

[1] L. Wittgenstein. *Philosophical Investigations*, p. 133e (London and New York: Macmillan, 1953).

(b) We may describe a second type of intentional use by reference to simple sentences the principal verb of which takes as its object a phrase containing a subordinate verb. The subordinate verb may follow immediately upon the principal verb, as in "He is contemplating killing himself"; it may occur in a complete clause, as in "He believes it will rain"; it may occur in an infinitive, as in "He wishes to speak"; or it may occur in participial form, as in "He accused John of stealing the money" and "He asked John's brother to testify against him." I shall say that such a simple declarative sentence is intentional if neither the sentence nor its contradictory implies either that the phrase following the principal verb is true or that it is false.[2] "He is contemplating killing himself" is intentional, according to this second criterion, because neither it nor its denial implies either that he does or that he doesn't kill himself; similarly with our other examples. But "He prevented John from stealing the money" is not intentional, because it implies that John did not steal the money. And "He knows how to swim" is not intentional, because its denial implies that he isn't swimming.

Sometimes people use substantival expressions in place of the kind of phrases I have just been talking about. Instead of saying, "I want the strike to be called off," they may say, "The strike's being called off is what I want." The latter sentence could be said to be intentional according to our first criterion, for neither the sentence nor its contradictory implies either that "there is such a thing as" the strike's being called off, or that there isn't — that is to say, neither implies that the strike will be, or that it will not be, called off.

Many intentional sentences of our first type may be rewritten in such a way that they become instances of our second type. Instead of saying "I would like a glass of water," one may say "I would like to have a glass of water." And instead of saying "He is looking for the Fountain of Youth," one may say "He is trying to find the Fountain of Youth." But some sentences of the first type seem to resist such transformation into the second type; for example, "I was thinking about you yesterday."

(c) If we make use of Frege's concept of "indirect reference," which is, of course, closely related to that of "intentionality," we can add another important class of sentence to our list of those which are intentional.[3] "Indirect reference" may be defined, without using the characteristic terms of Frege's theory of meaning, in the following way: a name (or description) of a certain thing has an indirect reference in a sentence if its replacement by a different name (or description) of that thing results in a sentence whose truth-value may differ from that of the original sentence.[4] It is useful to interpret this criterion in such a way that we can say of

[2] This criterion must be so interpreted that it will apply to sentences wherein the verb phrases following the principal verb are infinitive, prepositional, or participial phrases; hence it must make sense to speak of such phrases as being true or false. When I say of the phrase, following the main verb of "He accused John of stealing the money," that it is true, I mean, of course, that John stole the money. More generally, when I say of such a sentence that the phrase following the principal verb is true, or that it is false, my statement may be interpreted as applying to that new sentence which is like the phrase in question, except that the verb appearing in infinitive or participial form in the phrase is the principal verb of the new sentence. I should add a qualification about tenses, but I do not believe that my failure to do so is serious. It should be noted that, in English, when the subject of an infinitive or of a participle is the same as that of the principal verb, we do not repeat the subject; although we say "I want John to go," we do not say "I want me to go" or "John wants himself to go." When I say, then, that the last two words of "I want to go" are true, my statement should be interpreted as applying to "I shall go."

[3] By adopting Frege's theory of meaning — or his terminology — we could make this criterion do the work of our first two. But I have made use of the first two in order that no one will be tempted to confuse what I want to say with what Frege had to say about meaning. The three criteria overlap to a considerable extent.

[4] If E is a sentence obtained merely by putting the identity sign between two names or descriptions of the same thing, if A is a sentence using one of these names or descriptions, if B is like A except that where A uses the one name or description B uses the other, then the one name or description may be said to have an *indirect reference* in A provided that the conjunction of A and E does not imply B.

those names (or descriptions), such as "the Fountain of Youth" and "a building half again as tall as the Empire State", which don't apply to anything, that they are all names of the same thing. Let us add, then, that a simple declarative sentence is intentional if it contains a name (or description) which has an indirect reference in that sentence. We can now say of certain *cognitive* sentences — sentences which use words such as "know", "remember", "see", "perceive", in one familiar way — that they, too, are intentional. I may see that Albert is here and Albert may be the man who will win the prize; but I do not now *see that* the man who will win the prize is here. And we all remember that although George IV knew that Scott was the author of Marmion he did not know that Scott was the author of Waverley.

(d) With respect to the intentionality of compound sentences — sentences constructed by means of propositional connectives from two or more sentences — it is enough to say this: a compound declarative sentence is intentional if and only if one or more of its component sentences is intentional. "I will be gratified if I learn that Albert wins the prize" is intentional, because the if-clause is intentional. But "The career of Ponce de Leon would have been most remarkable if he had found the Fountain of Youth" is not intentional, because neither of its components is intentional. (In order that this final criterion be applicable to sentences in the subjunctive, we should, of course, interpret it to mean a compound declarative sentence is intentional if and only if one or more of the component sentences of its indicative version is intentional.)

3. We may now formulate a thesis resembling that of Brentano by referring to intentional language. Let us say (1) that we do not need to use intentional language when we describe non-psychological, or "physical," phenomena; we can express all that we know, or believe, about such phenomena in language which is not intentional.[5] And let us say (2) that, when we wish to describe certain psychological phenomena — in particular, when we wish to describe thinking, believing, perceiving, seeing, knowing, wanting, hoping, and the like — either (a) we must use language which is intentional or (b) we must use a vocabulary which we do not need to use when we describe non-psychological, or "physical," phenomena.

I shall discuss this linguistic version of Brentano's thesis with reference to sentences about believing. I do not pretend to be able to show that it is true in its application to believing. But I think that there are serious difficulties, underestimated by many philosophers, which stand in the way of showing that it is false.

I wish to emphasize that my question does not concern "subsistence" or "the being of objects which don't exist." Philosophers may ask whether it is possible to think about unicorns if there are no unicorns for us to think about. They may also ask whether you and I can believe "the same thing" if there is no proposition or objective toward which each of our beliefs is directed. But I am not raising these questions. Possibly the feeling that the intentional use of language commits us to the assumption that there are such entities is one motive for seeking to avoid such use. But I wish to ask only whether we *can* avoid such use and at the same time say all that we want to be able to say about believing.

4. The first part of our thesis states that we do not need to use intentional language when we describe non-psychological, or "physical," phenomena. I do not believe that this statement presents any serious difficulty. It is true that we do sometimes use intentional sentences in non-psychological contexts. The following sentences, for example, are all intentional, according to our criteria, but none of them describe anything we would want to call "psychological": "The patient will be immune from the effects of any new epi-

[5] Certain sentences describing relations of comparison (e.g. "Some lizards look like dragons") constitute exceptions to (1). Strictly speaking, then, (1) should read: "we do not need any intentional sentences, other than those describing relations of comparison, when we describe non-psychological phenomena."

demics" and "It is difficult to assemble a prefabricated house." But these sentences are not examples counter to our thesis. Anyone who understands the language can readily transform them into conditionals which are not intentional. (A compound sentence, it should be recalled, is intentional only if it has a component which is intentional.) Instead of using intentional sentences, we could have said, "If there should be any new epidemics, the patient would not be affected by them" and "If anyone were to assemble a prefabricated house, he would have difficulties." (Perhaps the last sentence should be rendered as "If anyone were to *try* to assemble a prefabricated house, he would have difficulties." In this version the sentence is intentional, once again, but since it contains the verb "to try" it can no longer be said to be non-psychological.)

I believe that any other ostensibly non-psychological sentence which is intentional can be transformed, in an equally obvious way, into a sentence conforming to our version of Brentano's thesis. That is to say, it will become a sentence of one of two possible types: either (a) it will be no longer intentional or (b) it will be explicitly psychological. Sentences about probability may be intentional, but, depending upon one's conception of probability, they may be transformed either into the first or into the second type. If I say "It is probable that there is life on Venus", neither my sentence nor its denial implies either that there is life on Venus or that there is not. According to one familiar interpretation of probability, my sentence can be transformed into a non-intentional sentence about frequencies — sentences telling about places where there is life and places where there isn't and comparing Venus with such places, etc. According to another interpretation, my sentence can be transformed into a psychological statement about believing — e.g., "It is reasonable for us to believe that there is life on Venus." Intentional sentences about tendencies and purposes in nature may be treated similarly. If we say, non-intentionally, "The purpose of the liver is to secrete bile," we may mean, psychologically, that the Creator made the liver so that it would secrete bile, or we may mean, non-intentionally, that in most live animals having livers the liver does do this work and that when it does not the animal is unhealthy.

There are people who like to ascribe beliefs, perceptions, plans, desires, and the like to robots and computing machinery. A computing machine might be said to believe, truly, that 7 and 5 are 12; when it is out of order, it may be said to make mistakes and possibly to believe, falsely, that 7 and 5 are 11. But such sentences, once again, are readily transformed into other sentences, usually conditionals, which are no longer intentional. If a man says that the machine believes 7 and 5 to be 11, he may mean merely that, if the keys marked "7" and "5" are pressed, the machine will produce a slip on which "11" is marked. Other intentional sentences about the attitudes of machines may be more complex, but I'm sure that, if they have been given any meaning by those who use them, they can be readily transformed into sentences which are not intentional. Indeed the ease with which robot sentences may be made either intentional or non-intentional may be one ground, or cause, for believing that sentences about the attitudes of human beings may readily be transformed in ways counter to our version of Brentano's thesis.

It should be noted, with respect to those universal sentences of physics which have no "existential import," that they are not intentional. It is true that the sentence, "All moving bodies not acted upon by external forces continue in a state of uniform motion in a straight line," does not imply either that there are, or that there are not, such bodies. But its contradictory implies that there are such bodies.

5. The second part of our version of Brentano's thesis states that, when we wish to describe anyone's believing, seeing, knowing, wanting, and the like, either (a) we must use language which is intentional or (b) we must use a vocabulary we don't need when we talk about non-psychological facts.

Perhaps the most instructive way of looking at our thesis is to contrast it with one which is slightly different. It has often been said, in recent years, that "the language of physical things" is adequate for the description of psychological phenomena — this language being any language whose vocabulary and rules are adequate for the description of non-psychological phenomena. If we do not need intentional language for describing physical things, then this counter-thesis — the thesis that the language of physical things is adequate for the description of psychological phenomena — would imply that we do not need intentional language for the description of psychological phenomena.

The easiest way to construct a non-intentional language for psychology is to telescope nouns and verbs. Finding a psychological verb, say "expects", and its grammatical object, say "food", we may manufacture a technical term by combining the two. We may say that the rat is "food-expectant" or that he "has a food-expectancy." Russell once proposed that, instead of saying "I perceive a cat," we say "I am cat-perceptive," and Professor Ryle has described a man seeing a thimble by saying that the man "is having a visual sensation in a thimble-seeing frame of mind."[6] Sentences about thinking, believing, desiring, and the like could readily be transformed in similar ways. But this way of avoiding intentional language has one serious limitation. If we wish to tell anyone what our technical terms mean, we must use intentional language again. Russell did not propose a definition of his technical term "cat-perceptive" in familiar non-intentional terms; he told us, in effect, that we should call a person "cat-perceptive" whenever the person *takes* something to be a cat. Our version of Brentano's thesis implies that, if we dispense with intentional language in talking about perceiving, believing, and expecting, we must use a vocabulary we don't need to use when we talk about non-psychological facts. The terms "food-expectancy", "thimble-seeing frame of mind", and "cat-perceptive" illustrate such a vocabulary.

I shall comment upon three general methods philosophers and psychologists have used in their attempts to provide "physical" translations of belief sentences. The first of these methods makes use of the concepts of "specific response" and "appropriate behavior"; references to these concepts appeared in the writings of the American "New Realists" and can still be found in the works of some psychologists. The second method refers to "verbal behavior"; its clearest statement is to be found in Professor Ayer's *Thinking and Meaning*. The third refers to a peculiar type of "fulfilment" or "satisfaction"; its classic statement is William James' so-called pragmatic theory of truth. I shall try to show that, if we interpret these various methods as attempts to show that our version of Brentano's thesis is false, then we can say that they are inadequate. I believe that the last of these methods — the one which refers to "fulfilment" or "satisfaction" — is the one which has the best chance of success.

6. When psychologists talk about the behavior of animals, they sometimes find it convenient to describe certain types of response in terms of the stimuli with which such responses are usually associated. A bird's "nesting responses" might be defined by reference to what the bird does in the presence of its nest and on no other occasions. A man's "rain responses," similarly, might be defined in terms of what he does when and only when he is in the rain. I believe we may say that some of the American "New Realists" assumed that, for every object of which a man can be said ever to be conscious, there is some response he makes when and only when he is in the presence of that object — some response which is *specific* to the object.[7] And they felt that the specific response vocabulary — "rain response", "fire response", "cat response" — provided a way of describing

[6] See Russell's *Inquiry into Meaning and Truth* (American edition), p. 142 (New York: Norton & Co., 1940) and Ryle's *Concept of Mind*, p. 230 (London: Hutchinson's Univ. Libr., 1949).

[7] See Chapter 9 of E. B. Holt, *The Concept of Consciousness* (London: G. Allen and Co., Ltd., 1914).

belief and the other types of phenomena Brentano would have called "intentional." This "specific response theory" is presupposed in some recent accounts of "sign behavior."

I think Brentano would have said that, if smoke is a *sign* to me of fire, then my perception of smoke causes me to *believe* that there is a fire. But if we have a specific response vocabulary available, we might say this: smoke is a sign to me of fire provided smoke calls up my *fire responses.* We might then say, more generally, that S is a sign of E for O provided only S calls up O's E-responses. But what would O's E-responses be?

What would a man's fire responses be? If smoke alone can call up his fire responses — as it may when it serves as a sign of fire — we can no longer say that his fire responses are the ways he behaves when and *only* when he is stimulated by fire. For we want to be able to say that he can make these responses in the presence of smoke and not of fire. Should we modify our conception of "fire response", then, and say that a man's fire responses are responses which are *like* those — which are *similar* to those — he makes when stimulated by fire? This would be saying too much, for in *some* respects *every* response he makes is like those he makes in the presence of fire. *All* of his responses, for example, are alike in being the result of neural and physiological events. But we don't want to say that all of the man's responses are fire responses. It is not enough, therefore, to say that a man's fire responses are *similar* to those he makes, or would make, in the presence of fire; we must also specify the *respect* in which they are similar. But no one, I believe, has been able to do this.

The problem isn't altered if we say that a man's fire responses constitute some *part* of those responses he makes in the presence of fire. More generally, the problem isn't altered if we introduce this definition: S is a sign of E provided only that S calls up *part* of the behavior that E calls up. It is not enough to say that the sign and the object call up *some* of the same behavior. The books in this room are not a sign to me of the books in that room, but the books in the two rooms call up some of the same behavior. And it is too much to say that S calls up *all* of the behavior that E calls up — that the sign evokes *all* of the responses that the subject makes to the object. The bell is a sign of food to the dog, but the dog, as we know, needn't eat the bell.

We might try to avoid our difficulties by introducing qualifications of another sort in our definition of *sign.* Charles E. Osgood proposes the following definition in the chapter entitled "Language Behavior," in *Method and Theory in Experimental Psychology* (New York: Oxford Univ. Press, 1953): "A pattern of stimulation which is not the object is a sign of the object if it evokes in an organism a mediating reaction, this (a) being some fractional part of the total behavior elicited by the object and (b) producing distinctive self-stimulation that mediates responses which would not occur without the previous association of nonobject and object patterns of stimulation" (p. 696). The second qualification in this definition — the requirement that there must have been a "previous association of nonobject and object" and hence that the thing signified must at least once have been experienced by the subject provides a restriction we haven't yet considered. But this restriction introduces a new set of difficulties. I have never seen a tornado, an igloo, or the Queen of England. According to the present definition, therefore, nothing can signify to me that a tornado is approaching, that there are igloos somewhere, or that the Queen of England is about to arrive. Hence the definition leaves one of the principal functions of signs and language unprovided for.

We may summarize the difficulties such definitions involve by reference to our attempt to define what a man's "fire responses" might be — those responses which, according to the present type of definition, are evoked by anything that serves as a sign of fire, and by reference to which we had hoped to define *beliefs* about fires. No matter how we formulate our definition of "fire responses", we find that our definition has one or another of these three defects: (1) a man's fire responses become responses that *only* fire can call up — in which case the presence of smoke alone will *not* call them up; (2) his fire responses become responses he sometimes makes when he *doesn't* take anything to be a sign of fire, when he *doesn't* believe that anything is on fire; or (3) our definitions will make use of intentional language.[8]

The "appropriate action" terminology is a variant of the "specific response" terminology. Psychologists sometimes say that, if the bell is a sign of food, then the bell calls up responses *appropriate* to food. And one might say, more generally, that a man *believes* a proposition *p* provided only he behaves, or is disposed to behave, in a way that is "appropriate to *p*," or "appropriate to *p*'s being true." But unless we can find a way of defining "appropriate", this way of talking is intentional by our criteria. When we affirm, or when we deny, "The knight is acting in a way that is appropriate to the presence of dragons," we do not imply either that there are, or that there are not, any dragons.[9]

7. In the second type of definition we refer to the "verbal behavior" which we would ordinarily take to be symptomatic of belief. This time we try to describe a man's belief — his believing — in terms of his actual uses of words or of his dispositions to use words in various ways.

Let us consider a man who believes that the Missouri River has its source in the northern part of Montana. In saying that he believes this, we do not mean to imply that he is actually doing anything; we mean to say that, if the occasion arose, he would do certain things which he would not do if he did not believe that the Missouri had its source in northern Montana. This fact may be put briefly by saying that when we ascribe a belief to a man we are ascribing a certain set of dispositions to him. What, then, are these dispositions? According to the present suggestion, the man is disposed to use language in ways in which he wouldn't use it if he didn't have the belief. In its simplest form, the suggestion is this: if someone were to ask the man "Where is the source of the Missouri River?" the man would reply by uttering the words, "In the Northern part of Montana"; if someone were to ask him to name the rivers having their sources in the northern part of Montana, he would utter, among other things, the word "Missouri"; if someone were to ask "Does the Missouri arise in northern Montana?" he would say "Yes"; and so on.

We should note that this type of definition, unlike the others, is not obviously applicable to the beliefs of animals. Sometimes we like to say such things as "The dog believes he's going to be punished" and "Now the rat thinks he's going to be fed." But if we accept the present type of definition, we cannot say these things (unless we are prepared to countenance such conditions as "If the rat could speak English, he'd now say 'I am about to be fed' "). I do not know whether this limitation — the fact that the definition does not seem to allow us to ascribe beliefs to animals — should be counted as an advantage, or as a disadvantage, of the "verbal behavior" definition. In any case, the definition involves a number of difficulties of detail and a general difficulty of principle.

The if-then sentences I have used as illustrations describe the ways in which our believer would answer certain questions. But

[8] If we say that smoke signifies fire to O provided only that, as a result of the smoke, "there is a fire in O's *behavioral environment*," or "there is a fire *for O*," and if we interpret the words in the quotations in the way in which psychologists have tended to interpret them, our language is intentional.

[9] R. B. Braithwaite, in "Belief and Action," (*Proceedings of the Aristotelian Society*, Supplementary vol. XX, p. 10), suggests that a man may be said to believe a proposition *p* provided this condition obtains: "If at a time when an occasion arises relevant to *p*, his springs of action are *s*, he will perform an action which is such that, if *p* is true, it will tend to fulfill *s*, and which is such that, if *p* is false, it will not tend to satisfy *s*." But the definition needs qualifications in order to exclude those people who, believing the true proposition *p* that there are people who can reach the summit of Mt. Everest, and having the desire *s* to reach the summit themselves, have yet acted in a way which has not tended to satisfy *s*. Moreover, if we are to use such a definition to show that Brentano was wrong, we must provide a non-intentional definition of the present use of "wish", "desire", or "spring of action".

surely we must qualify these sentences by adding that the believer has no desire to deceive the man who is questioning him. To the question "Where is the source of the Missouri?" he will reply by saying "In northern Montana" — provided he wants to tell the truth. But this proviso brings us back to statements which are intentional. If we say "The man wants to tell the truth" we do not imply, of course, either that he does or that he does not tell the truth; similarly, if we assert the contradictory. And when we say "He wants to *tell the truth*" — or, what comes to the same thing, "He doesn't want to *lie*" — we mean, I suppose, he doesn't want to say anything he *believes* to be false. Perhaps we should also add that he has no objection to his questioner *knowing* what it is that he believes about the Missouri.

We should also add that the man speaks English and that he does not misunderstand the questions that are put to him. This means, among other things, that he should not *take* the other man to be saying something other than what he is saying. If he took the other man to be saying "Where is the source of the *Mississippi*?" instead of "Where is the source of the Missouri?" he might reply by saying "In Minnesota" and not by saying "In Montana." It would seem essential to add, then, that he must not *believe* the other man to be asking anything other than "Where is the source of the Missouri?"

Again, if the man does not speak English, it may be that he will not reply by uttering any of the words discussed above. To accommodate this possibility, we might qualify our if-then statements in some such way as this: "If someone were to ask the man a question which, for him, had the same meaning as 'Where is the source of the Missouri?' has for us, then he would reply by uttering an expression which, for him, has the same meaning as 'In the northern part of Montana' has for us."[10] Or we might qualify our original if-then statements by adding this provision to the antecedents: "and if the man speaks English". When this qualification is spelled out, then, like the previous one, it will contain some reference to the meanings of words — some reference to the ways in which the man uses, applies, or interprets words and sentences. These references to the meanings of words and sentences — to their use, application, or interpretation — take us to the difficulty of principle involved in this linguistic interpretation of believing.

The sentences we use to describe the meanings and uses of words are ordinarily intentional. If I say, "The German word *Riese* means giant," I don't mean to imply, of course, either that there are giants or that there aren't any giants; similarly, if I deny the sentence. If we think of a word as a class of sounds or of designs, we may be tempted to say, at first consideration, that intentional sentences about the meanings and uses of words are examples which run counter to our general thesis about intentional sentences. For here we have sentences which seem to be concerned, not with anyone's thoughts, beliefs, or desires, but rather with the properties of certain patterns of marks and noises. But we must remind ourselves that such sentences are elliptical.

If I say, of the noises and marks constituting the German word *Riese*, that they mean giant, I mean something like this: "When people in Germany talk about giants, they use the word *Riese* to stand for giants, or to refer to giants." To avoid talking about things which don't exist, we might use the expression "gigantic" (interpreting it in its literal sense) and say: "People in Germany would call a thing *ein Riese* if and only if the thing were gigantic." And to make sure that the expression "to call a thing *ein Riese*" does not suggest anything mentalistic, we might replace it by a more complex expression about noises and marks. "To say 'A man calls a thing *ein Riese*' is to say that, in the presence of the thing, he would make the noise, or the mark, *ein Riese*."

Let us ignore all of the difficulties of detail listed above and let us assume, for simplicity, that our speakers have a childlike desire to call

[10] See Alonzo Church's "On Carnap's Analysis of Statements of Assertion and Belief," *Analysis*, Vol. 10 (1950).

things as frequently as possible by their conventional names. Let us even assume that everything having a name is at hand waiting to be called. Is it true that people in Germany would call a thing *ein Riese* — in the present sense of "to call" — if and only if the thing were gigantic?

If a German were in the presence of a giant and *took* it to be something else — say, a tower or a monument — he would not call it *ein Riese*. Hence we cannot say that, if a thing were a giant, he would call it *ein Riese*. If he were in the presence of a tower or a monument and *took* the thing to be a giant, then he would call the tower or the monument *ein Riese*. And therefore we cannot say he would call a thing *ein Riese* only if the thing were a giant.

Our sentence "The German word *Riese* means giant" does not mean merely that people in Germany — however we may qualify them with respect to their desires — would call a thing *ein Riese* if and only if the thing were gigantic. It means at least this much more — that they would call a thing by this name if and only if they *took* the thing to be gigantic or *believed* it to be gigantic or *knew* it to be gigantic. And, in general, when we use the intentional locution, "People use such and such a word to mean so-and-so," part of what we mean to say is that people use that word when they wish to express or convey something they *know* or *believe* — or *perceive* or *take* — with respect to so-and-so.

I think we can say, then, that, even if we can describe a man's believing in terms of language, his actual use of language or his dispositions to use language in certain ways, we cannot describe his use of language, or his dispositions to use language in those ways, unless we refer to what he believes, or knows, or perceives.

The "verbal behavior" approach, then, involves difficulties essentially like those we encountered with the "specific response" theory. In trying to define "fire response", it will be recalled, we had to choose among definitions having at least one of three possible defects. We now seem to find that, no matter how we try to define that behavior which is to constitute "using the word *Riese* to mean giant," our definition will have one of these three undesirable consequences: (1) we will be unable to say that German speaking people ever mistake anything for a giant and call something which is *not* a giant *ein Riese;* (2) we will be unable to say that German speaking people ever mistake a giant for something else and refuse to call a giant *ein Riese;* or (3) our definition will make use of intentional language.

The final approach I shall examine involves similar difficulties.

8. One of the basic points in the grammar of our talk about states of consciousness, as Professor Findlay has observed, is that such states always stand opposed to other states which will "carry them out" or "fulfil" them.[11] The final approach to belief sentences I would like to discuss is one based upon this conception of *fulfilment*. I believe that, if we are to succeed in showing that Brentano was wrong, our hope lies here.

Let us consider a lady who reaches for the teakettle, *expecting* to find it full. We can say of her that she has a "motor set" which would be *disrupted* or *frustrated* if the teakettle turns out to be empty and which would be *fulfilled* or *satisfied* if the teakettle turns out to be full. In saying that the empty teakettle would disrupt or frustrate a "motor set," I am thinking of the disequilibration which might result from her lifting it; at the very least, she would be startled or surprised. But in saying that her set would be fulfilled or satisfied if the teakettle turns out to be full, I am not thinking of a positive state which serves as the contrary of disruption or frustration. Russell has introduced the terms "yes-feeling" and "quite-so feeling" in this context and would say, I think, that if the teakettle were full the lady would have a quite-so feeling.[12] Perhaps she would have such a feeling if her expectation had just been challenged — if someone

[11] "The Logic of *Bewusstseinslagen*," *Philosophical Quarterly*, Vol. 5 (1955).

[12] See *Human Knowledge* (American edition), pp. 148, 125 (New York: Simon and Schuster, 1948); compare *The Analysis of Matter*, p. 184 (New York: Harcourt, Brace, 1927).

had said, just before she lifted the teakettle, "I think you're mistaken in thinking there's water in that thing." And perhaps expectation always involves a kind of tension, which is relieved, or consummated, by the presence of its object. But we will be on surer ground if we describe the requisite fulfilment or satisfaction, in negative terms. To say that a full teakettle would cause fulfilment, or satisfaction, is merely to say that, unlike an empty teakettle, it would not cause disruption or frustration. The kind of "satisfaction" we can attribute to successful expectation, then, is quite different from the kind we can attribute to successful strivings or "springs of action."

Our example suggests the possibility of this kind of definition: "S *expects* that E will occur within a certain period" means that S is in a bodily state which would be frustrated, or disrupted, if and only if E were not to occur within that period. Or, if we prefer the term "fulfil", we may say that S is in a bodily state which would be fulfilled if and only if E were to occur within that period. And then we could define "believes" in a similar way, or perhaps define "believes" in terms of "being-disposed-to-expect".

I would like to remark, in passing, that in this type of definition we have what I am sure are the essentials of William James' so-called pragmatic theory of truth — a conception which has been seriously misunderstood, both in Great Britain and in America. Although James used the terms "fulfil" and "fulfilment", he preferred "satisfy" and "satisfaction". In his terms, our suggested definition of "believing" would read: "S believes that E will occur within a certain period" means that S is in a bodily state which would be *satisfied* if and only if E were to occur within that period. If we say that S's belief is *true*, that he is correct in thinking that E will occur within that period, then we imply, as James well knew, that E is going to occur in that period — and hence that S's belief will be satisfied. If we say that S's belief is false, we imply that E is not going to occur — and hence that S's belief will not be satisfied. And all of this implies that the man's belief is true if and only if he is in a state which is going to be satisfied. But unfortunately James' readers interpreted "satisfy" in its more usual sense, in which it is applicable to strivings and desirings rather than to believings.

Our definitions, as they stand, are much too simple; they cannot be applied, in any plausible way, to those situations for which we ordinarily use the words "believe", "take", and "expect". Let us consider, briefly, the difficulties involved in applying our definition of "believe" to one of James' own examples.

How should we re-express the statement "James believes there are tigers in India"? Obviously it would not be enough to say merely, "James is in a state which would be satisfied if and only if there are tigers in India, or which would be disrupted if and only if there are no tigers in India." We should say at least this much more: "James is in a state such that, if he were to go to India, the state would be satisfied if and only if there are tigers there." What if James went to India with no thought of tigers and with no desire to look for any? If his visit were brief and he happened not to run across any tigers, then the satisfaction, or disruption, would not occur in the manner required by the definition. More important, what if he came upon tigers and took them to be lions? Or if he were to go to Africa, *believing* himself to be in India — or to India, *believing* himself to be in Africa?

I think it is apparent that the definition cannot be applied to the example unless we introduce a number of intentional qualifications into the definiens. Comparable difficulties seem to stand in the way of applying the terms of this type of definition in any of those cases we would ordinarily call instances of believing. Yet this type of definition may have an advantage the others do not have. It may be that there are simple situations, ordinarily described as "beliefs" or "expectations," which can be adequately described, non-intentionally, by reference to fulfilment, or satisfaction, and disruption, or surprise. Perhaps the entire meaning of such a statement as "The dog expects to be beaten" or "The baby expects to be fed" can be conveyed in this manner. And perhaps "satisfaction" or "surprise" can be so interpreted that our ordinary beliefs can be defined in terms of "being disposed to have" a kind of expectation which is definable by reference to "satisfaction" or "surprise". And if all of these suppositions are true then we may yet be able to interpret belief sentences in a way which is contrary to the present version of Brentano's thesis. But, I believe, we aren't able to do so now.

9. The philosophers and psychologists I have been talking about seem to have felt that they were trying to do something important — that it would be philosophically significant if they could show that belief sentences can be rewritten in an adequate language which is not intentional, or at least that it would be significant to show that Brentano was wrong. Let us suppose for a moment that we *cannot* rewrite belief sentences in a way which is contrary to our linguistic version of Brentano's thesis. What would be the significance of this fact? I feel that this question is itself philosophically significant, but I am not prepared to answer it. I do want to suggest, however, that the two answers which are most likely to suggest themselves are not satisfactory.

I think that, if our linguistic thesis about intentionality is true, then the followers of Brentano would have a right to take some comfort in this fact. But if someone were to say that this linguistic fact indicates that there is a ghost in the machine I would feel sure that his answer to our question is mistaken. (And it would be important to remind him that belief sentences, as well as other intentional sentences, seem to be applicable to animals.)

What if someone were to tell us, on the other hand, that intentional sentences about believing and the like don't really say anything and that, in consequence, the hypothetical fact we are considering may have no philosophical significance? He might say something like this to us: "The intentional sentences of ordinary language have many important tasks; we may use the ones about believing and the like to give vent to our feelings, to influence the behavior of other people, and to perform many other functions which psychiatrists can tell us about. But such sentences are not factual; they are not descriptive; they don't say things about the world in the way in which certain non-psychological sentences say things about the world." I do not feel that this answer, as it stands, would be very helpful. For we would not be able to evaluate it unless the man also (1) gave some meaning to his technical philosophical expressions, "factual", "descriptive", and "they don't say things about the world", and (2) had some way of showing that, although these expressions can be applied to the use of certain non-psychological sentences, they cannot be applied to the use of those psychological sentences which are intentional.

Or suppose something like this were suggested: "Intentional sentences do not say of the world what at first thought we tend to think they say of the world. They are, rather, to be grouped with such sentences as 'The average carpenter has 2.7 children,' 'Charity is an essential part of our obligations,' and 'Heaven forbid,' in that their uses, or performances, differ in very fundamental ways from other sentences having the same grammatical form. We need not assume, with respect to the words which make sentences intentional, such words as 'believe', 'desire', 'choose', 'mean', 'refer', and 'signify', that they stand for a peculiar kind of property, characteristic, or relation. For we need not assume that they stand for properties, characteristics, or relations at all." We could ask the philosopher taking such a stand to give us a positive account of the uses of these words which *would* be an adequate account and which would show us that Brentano was mistaken. But I do not believe that anyone has yet been able to provide such an account.

An Alternative Criterion for the Psychological

34

The Mental and the Physical

HERBERT HEIDELBERGER

In what has become a familiar passage Brentano wrote:

Every mental phenomenon is characterized by what the scholastics of the Middle Ages called the intentional (and also mental) inexistence (Inexistenz) of an object (Gegenstand), and what we could call, although in not entirely unambiguous terms, the reference to a content, a direction upon an object (by which we are not to understand a reality in this case), or an immanent objectivity. Each one includes something as object within itself, although not always in the same way. In presentation something is presented, in judgment something is affirmed or denied, in love (something is) loved, in hate (something) hated, in desire (something) desired, etc.

This intentional inexistence is exclusively characteristic of mental phenomena. No physical phenomenon manifests anything similar. Consequently, we can define mental phenomena by saying that they are such phenomena as include an object intentionally within themselves.

The passage is not altogether clear and has been misunderstood. Commenting on it, Anthony Kenny noted that not only in desiring do we desire something, but also in heating we heat something and in cutting cut something.[2] But Brentano's point is not that every mental phenomenon — or mental act — has an object, for physical acts also have objects, his point is rather than it is distinctive of mental acts that they may be related to inexistent objects, as opposed to physical acts which relate only to existing objects. So while I may love, hate, or desire something that does not exist, I cannot heat or cut something that does not exist. This thesis of Brentano's has been developed in recent years, most notably by Roderick Chisholm, into a linguistic thesis about psychological sentences and how they differ from non-psychological sentences.[3]

In the first section of this short paper I shall critically discuss this linguistic version of Brentano's thesis, in the second section I shall consider its significance for the mind-body problem, in the third section I shall offer an alternative conception of the psychological — one, incidentally, that Brentano also proposed — and finally in the fourth section I shall discuss the significance of this conception of the psychological.

1. In "Sentences About Believing" Chisholm sets forth three criteria for marking off intentional sentences. It is easy, however, to find sentences that meet these criteria and yet which are not psychological. For example, with respect to Chisholm's criterion (a), not only can I love, think of, and desire things that do not exist, I can also search for and hunt things that do not exist, as well as remark upon, write of, resemble, and be distinct from nonexistent things. (Although I cannot remember or gaze at nonexistent things.) With respect to (b), not only does "Harris believes that Socrates is mortal" and "Harris does not believe that Socrates is

[1] F. Brentano "The Distinction Between Mental and Physical Phenomena" (Translated from Brentano's *Psychologie vom Empirischen Standpunkt*) in R. M. Chisholm ed. *Realism and the Background of Phenomenology* (Glencoe, 1960), p. 50.

[2] *Action, Emotion and Will* (London, 1963) p. 195. Compare S. C. Brown "Intentionality Without Grammar" *Proceedings of the Aristotelian Society* (65, 1964–65).

[3] "Sentences About Believing" in this volume. See J. W. Cornman "Intentionality and Intensionality" *Philosophical Quarterly* (12, 1962) for a highly lucid, qualified defense of Chisholm.

mortal" imply nothing as to the truth value of "Socrates is mortal," but "It is contingent that Socrates is mortal" and its negation, "It ought to be the case that Socrates is mortal" and its negation, "That Socrates is both man and mortal implies that Socrates is mortal" and its negation, none of these either bears upon the truth value of "Socrates is mortal."[4] Finally, with respect to (c), we encounter indirect reference in propositional clauses attached to nonpsychological modal expressions such as "It is possible" and "It is necessary", as well as to the psychological expressions, "George knows" and "George sees". As George IV did not know that the author of Waverly authored Marmion, in spite of his knowledge that the author of Marmion authored Marmion; just so it is possible that the author of Waverly did not author Marmion, even if it is not possible that the author of Marmion did not author Marmion.

It is true that Chisholm makes only the modest claim that intentional language is not *needed* when we describe physical phenomena. In every instance he says, intentional sentences descriptive of physical phenomena can be transformed into nonintentional sentences, and he gives some examples. No doubt many of the sentences that I have cited can also be transformed into nonintentional sentences. For example, it may be urged that we don't need intentional language to express "It is contingent that p". A proposition is contingent when both it and its denial are possible, and 'possible', unlike 'contingent', is not intentional by criterion (b) (since the denial of "It is possible that p" implies that "p is false"). But, as we noted earlier, 'possible,' like 'contingent' *is* intentional by criterion (c). To accommodate "It is contingent," we may choose to put (c) aside and say that a sentence is intentional only if it satisfies either (a) or (b). This way of proceeding has the advantage of rendering "It is possible that" nonintentional, but it has the disadvantage of rendering as nonintentional sentences about knowing, perceiving, and seeing. And it has the more serious disadvantage of making it possible to transform belief sentences into language which is not intentional. A sentence of the form "S believes that p" may be rewritten as the disjunction, "S has the true belief that p or S has the false belief that p," that disjunction failing to be intentional by (d), since we have put (c) aside, and neither disjunct is intentional by (b). As it is likely that by making use of some artificial device of this sort we shall always be able to transform sentences that meet the criteria into sentences that do not, it would seem that intentional language is no more needed to express the psychological than it is to express the physical.[5]

2. More complex conceptions of intentionality, many of them quite ingenious, have been proposed by Chisholm and by others.[6] Rather than try to produce counter examples

[4] It should be observed that if we think of modal sentences as falling under Lewis' S5, then all of them will be necessarily true, if true and necessarily false, if false. In which case sentences of the form "it is contingent that p" and " — implies that p" will imply p if they are necessarily false and if they are necessarily true their negations will imply not-p; thus no sentences of these forms will be intentional by criterion (b). (I owe this point to Mr. J. Camp). But (i) it does seem very doubtful that Lewis' S5 *is* applicable to modal sentences as distinct from modal propositions and (ii) the sentence "The false sentence 'The Massachusetts city of Northampton has a population of more than 50,000' implies 'Some city in Massachusetts has a population of more than 50,000' " is true, though not necessarily true, and also intentional by criterion (b).

[5] Indeed there is a simple method for paraphrasing every sentence by an intentional sentence. If p is any sentence whatever it is equivalent to "(Smith has the true belief that p) or (not-Smith believes that p and p)"; and a simple method for paraphrasing every sentence by a nonintentional sentence: if p is any sentence whatever it is equivalent to "If (Smith has the true belief that p or Smith has the false belief that p) then Smith has the true belief that p." I am leaving out criterion (c) here and elsewhere, for there are ever so many nonpsychological sentences that satisfy (c) without satisfying either (a) or (b); cf. Cornman, op. cit.

[6] See, for example, R. M. Chisholm "On Some Psychological Concepts and the "Logic" of Intentionality" in H-N Castaneda ed. *Intentionality, Minds and Perception* (Detroit, 1967); R. Carnap *Meaning and Necessity* (Chicago, 1947) p. 53; R. C. Sleigh "Comments" in Castaneda. In his "Rejoinder" in Castaneda, Chisholm notes difficulties with the criteria suggested by Carnap and Sleigh and offers

to these let us ask ourselves what significance a criterion of the psychological of this kind would have.

In the 1930's Carnap, Hempel and others developed and defended logical behaviorism, the view that every psychological sentence may be transformed into — or is synonymous with — a sentence of what they called "the physicalistic language". Or to put the view in more platonistic terms: every proposition expressed by a psychological sentence is also expressed by a physicalistic sentence. Now let us suppose, as we might be led to suppose by some version of Brentano's thesis, that psychological sentences have a mark or characteristic that no physicalistic sentence has. Would it follow from this supposition that logical behaviorism is false? It would not. If this is not immediately evident it should become so if we consider a hypothetical language in which every psychological sentence begins with the letter 'A' and no physicalistic sentence begins with that letter; it obviously would not be correct to infer from this that no psychological sentence could be transformed into a physicalistic sentence or that psychological sentences express different propositions from those expressed by physicalistic sentences. For, of course, it might be that every sentence beginning with the letter 'A' is synonymous with a sentence beginning with another letter. The same point can be made about the linguistic mark of intentionality. We cannot rightly infer that logical behaviorism is false simply from the premise that psychological and only psychological sentences are intentional. We need the further premise that every sentence synonymous with an intentional sentence also is intentional. But this we do not know to be true; indeed, if, as I suggest, "S believes that p" is paraphraseable as "S truly believes that p or S falsely believes that p" then we know it to be false.

Suppose that in order to make sentences synonymous with or logically equivalent to intentional sentences themselves intentional, we say this: Any sentence synonymous with or logically equivalent to a compound sentence is intentional provided that one or more of the components of the compound are intentional by criteria (a) or (b); and not intentional if none of the components are intentional by those criteria. For example, we could say that all sentences of the form "S has the true belief that p" as well as "S has the false belief that p" are intentional because they are logically equivalent to compounds e.g. "S believes that p and p is true," one of whose components is intentional. And we could say further that sentences of the form, "It is contingent that p" and "q implies that p" are not intentional since they are equivalent to sentences neither of whose components are intentional — e.g. "It is contingent that p" is equivalent to "It is possible that p and it is possible that not-p." It should be noted, however, that we could adopt a different procedure and get opposite results. We could say that 'believes' is *not* intentional on the grounds that "S believes that p" is equivalent to "S has the true belief that p or S has the false belief that p" (We could also define 'true' so that it *would* be intentional, viz. "p is true" as "If anyone were to believe p then he would have a true belief that p"). And we could say further that sentences of the form, "It is possible that p" and "It is contingent that p" *are* intentional as they are equivalent to compounds both of whose components are intentional, viz. "It is possible that p" is equivalent to "q does not imply not-p and not-q does not imply not-p." Whether we adopt the first procedure and treat 'believes' as intentional and 'possible' as not intentional, or the second procedure and treat 'possible' as intentional and 'believes' as not inten-

one of his own, "A sentence prefix (e.g. Smith believes that) is intentional if, for every sentence q, the result of modifying q by M is logically contingent" (p. 54). This criterion is elaborated in Chisholm's article on "Intentionality" in P. Edwards ed. "Encyclopedia of Philosophy" (Glencoe, 1967) and the following seems to be a counter example to it: "the proposition which is a conjunction of a contradictory proposition and a true proposition implying the existence of unicorns implies that q."

tional, seems to be entirely a matter of convenience and familiarity and is without theoretical significance.

It may come as a surprise, but in Chisholm's own version of Brentano's thesis intentionality does not bear at all upon logical behaviorism. He summarizes his version of Brentano's thesis in these words.

> Let us say (1) that we do not need to use intentional language when we describe non-psychological, or "physical", phenomena; we can express all that we know, or believe, about such phenomena in language which is not intentional. And let us say (2) that, when we wish to describe certain psychological phenomena — in particular, when we wish to describe thinking, believing, perceiving, seeing, knowing, wanting, hoping and the like — either (a) we must use language which is intentional or (b) we must use a vocabulary which we do not need to use when we describe nonpsychological, or "physical", phenomena.

The first part of Chisholm's version of Brentano's thesis suggests, in effect, that we may, but need not, use intentional language in describing physical phenomena, and the second part suggests that we may, but need not, use intentional language in describing psychological phenomena. Indeed, in his paper, Chisholm cites examples of intentional as well as nonintentional sentences that describe physical phenomena, and he also cites examples of nonintentional sentences as well as intentional sentences that describe psychological phenomena. So far as intentionality is concerned then, psychological sentences differ in no important respect from physicalistic sentences.

But Chisholm says in clause (b) of (2) above that to describe certain psychological phenomena "we must use a vocabulary which we do not need to use when we describe nonpsychological, or 'physical' phenomena". What is that vocabulary? It is not the vocabulary of intentionality, for we do not need to use that vocabulary to describe psychological phenomena. The vocabulary he has in mind is our psychological vocabulary, the vocabulary that contains words like 'believes,' 'knows,' 'perceives' etc. Certain items of our psychological vocabulary, he is saying, cannot be replaced by, are not synonymous with, a physical vocabulary, the vocabulary we employ in describing physical phenomena. So Chisholm's version of Brentano's thesis comes simply to the claim that logical behaviorism is false; and that is not an empty claim on his part, for he goes on in the remainder of his paper to give reasons in support of it. But it is important to appreciate that this claim has nothing whatever to do with the linguistic marks of intentionality which he cites. What we have are two quite different theses, which we should be careful not to confuse. One is that no sentence, other than a psychological sentence, possesses certain marks of intentionality, (The Thesis of Intentionality). The second is that the vocabulary we employ in describing psychological phenomena cannot be replaced by a "physicalistic" vocabulary (Chisholm's version of Brentano's thesis). The truth of the second thesis does not follow from that of the first; the first, as it has been understood in this paper, is false; and the second, as we shall see, is true.

3. The criterion that I shall put forward is for psychological propositions, or more exactly for singular psychological propositions descriptive of psychological states, rather than for psychological sentences. To begin with, let us define a characteristic ψ, a characteristic which for the present we may regard as pertaining to every psychological proposition.

> A proposition p has the characteristic ψ provided that if p is known then p is known without independent evidence by exactly one person.

A necessary truth, such as the proposition that Red is a color, can perhaps be known without independent evidence, but if it can be known without independent evidence by one person it can be so known by more than one person. On the other hand, if I know a proposition about a physical thing then that is a proposition that must be supported by independent evidence; although given our present concerns it is not crucial that this be so. For even if such propositions could be known without independent evidence they, like necessary truths, could be known by more than one person without independent evidence; whereas, the proposition that I am in pain or the proposition that I believe that I am tall can be known to me without independent evidence, they cannot be known to anyone else without independent evidence.

The following two propositions, however, seem to be psychological, yet they do not satisfy the criterion: that the man in the corner desires a Lotus, and that stone does not desire a Lotus. The proposition that the man in the corner desires a Lotus does not satisfy the criterion for if, say, I am the man in the corner than I can know this only if I have some independent evidence that I am that man and therefore independent evidence is required in order for me to know that the man in the corner desires a Lotus. In the second example, we should assume that the stone knows nothing and that we know that it does not desire a Lotus, in which case either our knowledge requires independent evidence or if it does not it can be had by more than one person. To deal with these cases we must add a further clause to our definition.

A proposition p has the characteristic ψ provided that if p is a proposition formed from the function that x is F then there is some proposition formed from that function which is such that if it is known, it is known without independent evidence by exactly one person.

Again consider the proposition that the man in the corner desires a Lotus. It is formed from the function, that x desire(s) a Lotus, and there is some proposition formed from that function which, if known, is known without independent evidence by exactly one person. Such a proposition is: that I desire a Lotus. That that stone does not desire a Lotus may be accommodated in similar fashion.

Now let us say that a proposition is directly psychological when both it and its negation has ψ. Thus the proposition that I believe that I am tall is directly psychological, for both it and its negation can be known without independent evidence by exactly one person. A proposition may be said to be indirectly psychological provided (i) that it is neither inconsistent nor directly psychological and (ii) either it or its negation implies a proposition which is directly psychological. The proposition that I know that I am tall is indirectly psychological, for, although it cannot be known without independent evidence, it does imply the directly psychological proposition that I believe that I am tall. That I am delighted that you have finally come, implies that you have finally come; and that I have a sticking pain in my shoulder, implies that I have a shoulder, so that neither is directly psychological. But the first implies that I believe that you have finally come; and the second implies that I have a sticking pain; and as these latter propositions are both directly psychological, the propositions which imply them are indirectly psychological. The propositions, that Peter has an unconscious desire for a Lotus and that the man who desires a Lotus is a cellist, are also indirectly psychological, though perhaps not obviously so. The proposition that Peter has an unconscious desire for a Lotus implies that Peter desires a Lotus and, as we have seen, this proposition is formed from a function from which some directly psychological proposition e.g. I desire a Lotus, is formed. The proposition that the man who desires a Lotus is a cellist implies that the man who desires a Lotus desires a Lotus and this proposition too is formed from the now familiar function, that x desires a Lotus.

I suggest that no propositions other than psychological propositions are either directly or indirectly psychological, as I have explicated these terms; and every singular proposition descriptive of a psychological state is either directly or indirectly psychological. If this is correct then no sentence expressing a physicalistic proposition, or more generally a proposition lacking those features possessed by psychological propositions, no sentence of this kind could ever be a paraphrase of a sentence expressing a psychological proposition. For if there were such a paraphrase the paraphrased sentence would express a single proposition that both possessed and did not possess those features of psychological propositions. Since it is plainly impossible that such a proposition exist we can be sure that logical behaviorism is false.

4. Logical behaviorism, much discussed in the 1930's and 1940's, is now moribund if not entirely dead. In retrospect, it seems to have been a primitive doctrine and I do not consider its refutation to be an achievement of great importance. (The virtues, if any, of the proposed criterion of the psychological lie elsewhere). Far more difficult to deal with is materialism and I shall bring this short paper to a close with a brief discussion of it.

Logical behaviorism in effect, claimed an identity of psychological with physicalistic propositions; a kindred view, sometimes advanced, would identify psychological properties with physicalistic properties. But I take materialism to be a doctrine not about abstract entities — propositions or properties — but about particular phenomena — concrete events or things. Materialism, as I understand it, is the view that psychological particulars — every psychological event or entity — is identical with some physical particular. I want to show that materialism so understood has not been shown to be false by any of the considerations advanced previously in this paper.

Let us suppose with the materialist that a certain pain of mine, for example, the one I had yesterday at noon, is identical with a certain state of my brain at that time. Now if the criterion of the psychological proposed above is correct I can know without independent evidence that I am in pain, although I cannot know without independent evidence that I am in any particular brain state. There is nothing strange about that, however. I know without independent evidence, although many others know this without independent evidence as well, that if anything is identical with the evening star, it is identical with the evening star; but I do not know without independent evidence, and some people do not know at all, that if anything is identical with the evening star it is also identical with the morning star. Epistemic sentences, as noted earlier, involve indirect reference or failure of substitution. If someone knows — or knows without independent evidence — that a certain thing *a*, is *F*, it does not follow that he knows that *b* is *F*, even though *a* is identical with *b*.

So I do not think that we can use our criterion to show that mental events are not identical with physical events. Nor can we use it, or something similar to it, to show that we are not identical with our bodies.

According to Arnauld, Descartes had argued that he could not be identical with his own body, for,

> I am able to doubt whether I have a body, say, whether any body exists at all; yet I have no right to doubt whether I am or exist, so long as I doubt or think. Hence I who doubt and think am not a body; otherwise in entertaining doubt concerning body, I shall doubt myself.[7]

If Arnauld's interpretation is correct, as I believe it is, then Descartes was assuming that if a man doubts that a certain thing *a* exists and *a* is identical with *b*, that he thereby doubts or has a right to doubt — whether *b* exists. The assumption, I feel certain, is gratuitous. It is an historical fact that some of Vermeer's contemporaries doubted his existence though they did not doubt — and perhaps had no right to doubt — that there was a man who painted "The View of Delft", despite the fact that Vermeer was that man. Consequently, I suggest, that neither the criterion I have proposed for distinguishing psychological from nonpsychological propositions nor any other criterion formulated in terms of notions like that

[7] The Philosophical Works of Descartes ed. Haldane and Ross (Cambridge, 1934) p. 80.

of belief or knowledge insures the falsity of materialism; and, moreover, materialism, it seems to me, is a doctrine which may well be true.[8]

[8] I am indebted to Joseph Camp, Roderick Chisholm, Jaegwon Kim, and John Robison, and the editor of this volume for the considerable help they have given me with this paper.

The Covering Law Position Does Not Depend on Reductionist Assumptions

35

Meaning and Action

MAY BRODBECK

"What is left over if I subtract the fact that my arm goes up from the fact that I raise my arm?" ([9], p. 161, §621) One may interpret Wittgenstein's question to concern the nature of human action. Recently, that question has been given a certain answer from which a moral has been drawn regarding the nature of our knowledge and understanding of man. Briefly, the something "left over" that distinguishes a mere bodily movement from an action is, according to the answer, the *meaning* of that movement. The moral drawn is that the meaningful constituents of an action make it logically impossible to explain human actions causally, in the sense in which we can causally explain physical events like bodily movements. Though the answer itself requires considerable unpacking, it is, I believe, essentially correct. But once that necessary analysis is made, the moral drawn, I shall try to show, is a *non sequitur*.

An action, as I shall use that term, is any bit of behavior whose complete description, that is, an account of *what* is occurring, requires mention, in addition to manifest behavior, either of such things as the person's motives, intentions and thoughts or of such things as moral, legal, or conventional standards or rules. Strictly speaking, an explicit mention of standards is redundant, since they essentially involve thoughts or purposes. However, since these standards need not be in the mind of the person acting in accordance with a rule, as well as for other reasons that will appear as the argument unfolds, it may help to mention standards separately.

The discussions stimulated by Wittgenstein's question have revived one side of an old controversy embodied in the question, "Can there be a science of man and society?" The side now revived opposes the affirmative answer of those who stress an essential identity in method between the physical sciences and the study of man. The latter reason (in part) along the following lines. Other people's mental states, their thoughts, feelings, wishes, and hopes, are not directly accessible to public inspection. Nor can we test the everyday inferences we make to them, from what we do observe, in the same way that we can independently test, for instance, the inference from an observed change in color of a piece of litmus paper to a liquid's acidity. Though we frequently may be right in our everyday inferences to other people's mental states from their behavior, all we have to go on is what people choose to tell us or their observable behavior. Since there is no way of independently testing for the occurrence of these criteria and what they are criteria for, the proponents of a science of man eschew all talk about mental states. They maintain that nevertheless a complete description and causal explanation of human actions can be given *in principle* by means of terms that, like those of physical science, have reference only to objectively observable properties of material objects. The material objects of their concern are of course people's bodies, the characters, among

From *The Philosophy of Science*, 30:4 (October, 1963), pp. 309–324.

others, are the observable behaviors of these bodies under certain conditions and in certain environments. The mentalistic terms characterizing actions, like 'purpose' and 'thought', are, on this account, all eliminable by definitions using only nonmentalistic terms. On this view, the social scientist is a spectator of the human scene, noting its observable features and the connections among them. He seeks regularities in human behavior, just as the physicist looks for them in inanimate behavior. His assertions being based upon observation are also refutable by it. Like those of natural science, they are at best contingent, empirical truths. This view, within psychology, is of course known as behaviorism. For a broader notion to encompass all social areas, as well as to avoid certain connotations of that term, I shall call the doctrine "objectivism."

Revived now is the negative side of the controversy, namely, the insistence upon an intrinsic difference between the study of man and of things. The objectivist program is held to be hopelessly misguided, not merely because it is practically unfeasible but because it is radically mistaken. By the spectator methods, all that the objectivist can learn are, on this view, the external, overt features of actions. Their internal aspects, the motives, intentions, and reflections, by which overt behavior is understood as meaningful human action elude him entirely. To understand a human action is to know its motive. Motive explanations, however, are neither a species of causal explanations nor are they replaceable by such explanations. Social concepts, like money or voting, cannot be adequately described in "neutral" nonmentalistic terms or understood by objectivist methods. We observe only manifest behavior, like a hand going up or pulling a lever, not the internal meaning of an action, like hand-raising or voting. This meaning lies in the logical connections the action has with the complex of desires, intentions, choices, reasons, conventions and moral rules that are all inextricably involved together in social life. As participants in a community, we have learned to use these concepts. Understanding the language, we understand the meaning of other people's overt acts by analyzing the concepts appropriately applied to the situation, tracing their logical connections with the other mentalistic concepts. A matter of conceptual analysis, our understanding and knowledge of man is therefore *a priori* and necessary rather than, as with the natural sciences, *a posteriori* and contingent. The empirical science of man envisaged by the objectivist is thus *in principle*, that is, conceptually or logically, impossible.[1]

Since belief in the essential ineliminability of mentalistic terms is central to the current rejection of "objectivism," I shall call this position "mentalism." Possibly there is some incongruity in attributing "mentalism" to some among these critics who deny, or appear to deny, that terms ever have a reference to private mental states. But the mentalistic label seems to be justifiable not only historically, but also systematically, by the emphasis on the uneliminability of the mentalistic terms. The incongruity, if any, is, I suggest, not of my making.

First of all, I wish to explain some notions which, though now controversial, are nevertheless indispensable to clarity about the issues at stake.

The word 'concept' is ambiguous. In one usage, 'concept' is applied to those classes of words, either sounds or marks, that are used to refer to characters of things, either properties or relations. I shall call them terms. 'White' and '*bianco*' are two different words, but only one term. 'Concept' also has a mentalistic use, as applied to the content of a thought. I shall use 'concept' in this way for, generally, the content of any mental act, whether it be thinking, perceiving, believing, hoping, or intending. (A mental act is not, of course, an action, though they are intimately connected.) The *thought* of some-

[1] Extended statements of the position here outlined are to be found in [8] and [7]. I shall be concerned in this paper primarily, though not solely, with their formulations.

thing's being green, of a unicorn in the garden, or of rain tomorrow, are all, in this usage, concepts. Terms may be used to refer either to concepts, that is, to someone's thought of something, or to nonmentalistic things and their characters. When, in any context, we know the character or characters that a term is being used to refer to, the term has a reference or, as I shall call it, $meaning_1$. When, within natural science, the reference of a term, say, 'pressure', is known to be lawfully connected to other things, as the pressure of a gas is connected with its volume and temperature, then the term is also significant or "meaningful" or has what I shall call $meaning_2$. The $meaning_1$ of a term is a matter of convention; its $meaning_2$, if any, is a matter of fact. Only these two uses of 'meaning' are appropriately applied to scientific terms. They do not, however, exhaust the uses of 'meaning'.

Though concepts or mental states are the reference of some terms, they do not themselves refer to anything, any more than (nonlinguistic) physical states refer to anything. Yet, thoughts do "mean" other things, in a way in which nonmental or physical events do not "mean" anything. It is characteristic of mental acts generally, and of mental acts alone, that they "mean" or are directed toward something else. The thought or concept of a castle or of rain tomorrow is about a kind of material thing or event. What the thought "means" is, by a dead teleological metaphor, called its intention. Obviously, one need not adopt the metaphysics of an active Self to recognize that thoughts are about something. 'Meaning' is ambiguous even in this particular context. Sometimes the thought itself is called the "meaning," for it is that which means or intends. When used in this way, a "meaning" is what I am calling a concept. Sometimes, what the thought intends or means is called the "meaning". In this use, a meaning is often something nonmental, though, of course, we often also think about thoughts, our own and others'. I shall here use 'intentional meaning' so that intentional meaning or, briefly, $meaning_3$ is what a mental act intends, means, or is about. To have a thought or to think about something is one fact; what this thought intends or $means_3$ is a different, usually nonmental, fact.

Terms refer, concepts intend. The term 'green' $means_1$ the color green, because we have chosen to use the term in this way. $Meaning_1$ or reference is a complex natural or descriptive relation between language users, language, and the world. A set of marks or sounds does not intrinsically refer to anything. On the other hand, it is intrinsic to mental concepts that they mean or intend something else, either in the present, past, or future. Intentionality or $meaning_3$ is characteristic of thoughts, not something we bestow upon them. However, the $meaning_3$ relation between a thought and its intention is neither a natural relation, like taller or being to the left of, nor a causal relation. The reasons it is neither are fairly obvious. For there to be a descriptive relation, both terms of that relation must exist. But we can think what is false or imagine something that does not exist. Moreover, thinking about something does not, in any relevant sense, causally affect the thing thought about. $Meaning_3$, the relation between a thought and its intention, is, in a specificable sense, a logical relation.[2]

Still another difference between concepts and terms is crucial. Two terms may refer to or $mean_1$ the same thing. Two concepts never intend or $mean_3$ the same thing. The expressions 'the square of three' and 'the sum of 7 and 2' both may be used to refer to the same thing, namely, nine. But the concept or thought-of-three-square does not intentionally mean the same as the thought-of-the-sum-of-7-and-2. We may express thoughts in various ways, by action or by speech, but to describe them we need language. The linguistic expression describing the thought is the text of that thought. Two different linguistic events may express the same facts, but are the texts of two different thoughts. The sentence, S_1, "There are seven plus two buttons in the box"

[2] For details, see [1], [2], and [3].

referentially means the same as the sentence, S_2, "There are three-square buttons in the box," but they are the texts of two different thoughts, for the thought-that-S_1 does not intentionally mean the same as the thought-that-S_2, since one may firmly believe the former and doubt the latter. Though the *term* 'nine', means_1 the same as the *term* 'the square of three', the *concept* of nine does not intentionally mean, the same as the *concept* of the square of three. Even when two different expressions refer to the same thing, the concepts of which they are the texts do not have the same (intentional) meaning_3. Generally, in mental contexts, like Mary knows, believes, or remembers that-*S*, replacing the text of *S* with another expression having the same referential meaning need not preserve the truth of the whole statement. In fact, no two different concepts ever mean_3 the same, for they are different just because they have different intentional meanings. Intentional meaning of concepts is unique, while referential meaning of terms is not.

To think that it might snow tomorrow and to think about putting snowtires on the car are different thoughts, nor is either the same as actually performing that task or having a disposition to do so. Thinking about something, say, castles in Spain, is, like the dreary rain that may evoke the thought, a particular occurrence at a particular time. Generally such mental episodes are not *identical* with any behavior or dispositions to behave that, as we significantly say, manifest them. Moreover, bodily states manifest mental ones, not tautologically, as bending "manifests" flexibility, but contingently, as exploding manifests chemical composition. Our everyday statements about minds, our own and others, are categorical. The mentalistic terms they contain have reference to states of mind that, unlike bodily states, cannot be inspected publicly. Since mentalistic terms do not either referentially or intentionally mean the same as nonmentalistic terms, they cannot be replaced "without residue" by such terms. All this I take to be common sense, that is, something we all know from our own experience. I take it also to be a commonsensical core of the mentalistic thesis, whether or not its proponents would agree with my way of putting it.

Though we cannot observe another man's conscious states, we certainly often can tell what other people are thinking or feeling. We can do so because, whether voluntarily or involuntarily, we evince our mental states by overt physical features, including behavior, or by dispositions to exhibit such features under certain conditions. Privacy, in other words, does not entail ignorance about other people's mental states, merely that we know them differently from the way we know our own. Yet, though there are minds and bodies, there are no interacting minds. This is a piece of scientific common sense, that is, something scientists believe on the basis of their extended experience. This belief has two components. First, that there are no disembodied minds or, more precisely, whenever there is a mental state, there is always a corresponding bodily state, either neurological, physiological, behavioral, or some combination of these. The connection between mental states and such bodily states is correlational. That is how we can tell, by inference, what other people are thinking. Secondly, mental events parallel but do not interact with physical events. In other words, despite the correlation between mind and body, no mental state causally affects any material state and conversely. In a phrase, the view is that the physical world, including men's bodies, is causally closed with respect to minds. Unpacked, the phrase means that the laws used to explain and to predict physical phenomena need mention nothing nonphysical, in the broad sense of 'physical' which includes not only the terms of physics, but also overt behavior, utterances, physiological, and environmental characters that are describable in nonmentalistic terms. To deny that minds and bodies interact is to assert that the laws permitting us scientifically to explain human behavior need not mention anything mental. Parallelism and the belief in physical determinism form the basis for the objectivist belief that a *complete* account of human activities can be given in nonmentalistic terms.

Some philosophical problems arise because certain sets of facts, taken together, are perplexing. In the present instance, the common-sense fact, upon which the mentalists rightly insist, that mind and intelligence make a difference in the world seems to conflict with the denial of causal interaction between mind and body. Yet this denial is justified by what we know from the natural sciences. This is what makes it a piece of scientific common sense. To deny it outright is to tilt quixotically at wind mills. The contemporary mentalist does not deny it outright. Instead, he denies its relevance, by asserting that scientific, that is, causal explanation and descripton are "inappropriate" to the explanation and description of human activities. He accepts physical determinism for physical events, agrees and even insists that both cause and effect must be physical, but, denying that human actions can be completely described in physical terms, denies that causal attribution can legitimately be made to actions. Bodies and minds neither interact nor don't interact. Rather, there is a sort of parallelism between mind and body, reflected by two different realms of discourse or "conceptual systems," one for the mental, the other for the physical. Within each realm of discourse, different sorts of explanation are appropriate. We *understand* man by mentalistic explanation, for instance, by motives; we understand body by physical explanation, that is, by causes. The attempt to replace the former by the latter is a "conceptual" error, *a priori* doomed to failure.

Even granting such a "conceptual" parallelism, an action, like signalling or buying a house, is an event taking place at a particular time. Actions are as much facts in the world as earthquakes or any natural phenomenon in which mind does not play a role. A world with actions is different from one without them. Questions about actions, therefore, cannot *merely* be linguistic, for the conceptual systems in which action-terms occur, if they are to be of any relevance, must be about actual occurrences, in exactly the same sense as conceptual systems of physics are not speculative fancies but about physical occurrences. Two kinds of questions, in particular, that may be asked regarding any event cannot arbitrarily be ruled out on linguistic grounds alone. For one, one may ask whether action-events have causes, for there is nothing in the meaning of 'cause', as that term is normally used in science, to make this question in any sense "ungrammatical." The denial of interactionism does not follow from the meaning of 'cause', but from facts and laws of the kind I mentioned. It could be false, but it is not linguistic nonsense. Moreover, since actions are events, one may also legitimately ask how we know when statements about them are true or false. The answer given, as I mentioned earlier, is that all such statements are "conceptually," hence *a priori*, true. The *prima facie* rationalism of this answer to questions about matters of fact may, with some justice, lead one to suspect that something has gone radically wrong. Later, I shall try to locate what has gone wrong.

On the positive side, there is at least one sense in which the mentalists are certainly right in asserting that talk about actions or, for that matter, motives cannot have the same "meaning" as talk about behavior or, for that matter, causes. For such statements have, at the very least, different intentional meanings. The objectivist must show how, eschewing mentalistic terms, he can account for this difference in (intentional) meaning$_3$. And, since actions are events, he must also show how parallelism allows him to account adequately for the presence and efficacy of mind in the world. I shall first suggest how, within his framework, the objectivist can in principle accomplish this first goal and, then, by considering certain mentalistic objections, show how he can in principle also accomplish the second.

To every mental event there corresponds one or, more likely, several material events. What occurs when Jones sees a tree? There are the mental act of seeing, certain states of his body and, presumably, a tree in his immediate environment. When Jones says, "I see a tree," he describes directly his mental state. The objectivist scientist cannot do this, since the mentalistic term is not part of his vocabulary. This does not mean that Jones describes the situation for him. Jones' utterance is just part of the total situation that the scientist must describe in his own language. In his language, which is in principle different from that of his subject, he introduces an inseparable complex term 'seeing-a-tree', which contains neither 'seeing' nor, for that matter, 'tree'. This term is defined dispositionally by means of terms referring to those physical states of the person (including his verbal behavior if asked what he sees) that accompany Jones' state of consciousness when he sees a tree. Although *Jones'* term 'see' refers to a conscious state and the *scientist's* complex term 'sees-a-tree' refers to behavioral and environmental items, the latter term will be truly applicable to Jones if and only if Jones is in fact at that time seeing a tree. He knows this commonsensically, so to speak, not as a scientist. He knows it from self-examination when he applies the defined term to himself, or from what Jones tells him, though again, what Jones tells him is *data*, not description.

The investigator may of course make mistakes. But his mistakes will reveal themselves by failure of the predictions that he makes from his description. He will predict something different from Jones sees-a-tree, than from Jones sees-a-tiger. If Jones turns and runs, he may conclude that either he was wrong in applying his complex terms to Jones, or else he was wrong in defining 'seeing-a-tree' in the way he did. "Wrong" in the only way a definition can be wrong, namely, that it does not provide a significant term, that is, one that figures in confirmable laws. On the other hand, he might still be right. Jones might have a neurotic fear of trees. In that case, he has failed to take account of other operative factors. If he is right and, in principle, there is always a right physical description corresponding to the mental event, then we may speak of the former as an indirect reference to the latter. Analogously, the physicist indirectly refers to the perceptual color red when he speaks of "the color with the longest wave length." Seen in this way, objectivism is merely a way of talking about minds. By capturing its reflection in the material world, the behavior scientist can indirectly speak about mind. What then is the reflection of intentional meaning?

Meaning$_1$ (reference) and meaning$_2$ (significance) are applicable to the technical terms of science. Terms and expressions have meaning for persons. When the scientist investigates this "meaning," then 'meaning' becomes one of his technical terms, call it psychological meaning or meaning$_4$. Meaning$_4$ is thus a term within science, which must itself be given meaning$_1$[3]. Certain physical patterns have meaning$_4$ for an individual. Depending upon the circumstances and manner in which it is uttered, the sound 'fire' for instance may mean$_4$ to Jones either danger or warmth. Which it means$_4$, we determine by the bodily states, behavioral and physiological, that hearing the word elicits in Jones. Generally, 'meaning$_4$' refers to, or means$_1$, certain other things, verbal or nonverbal, that a person does upon hearing sounds or seeing certain marks. Jones' awareness of the referential use, if any, of the expression he hears is an essential part of the situation to which he reacts. But an expression need not have (referential) meaning$_1$, in order for it to have (psychological) meaning$_4$ for someone. 'The Lord is my shepherd' has no meaning$_1$, but it has meaning$_4$. People use it, utter it, and behave upon hearing or uttering it in certain ways. Similarly with many expressions of religion, poetry, exclamations, commands, and so forth. Being used on certain occasions, they have meaning$_4$.

As with 'seeing', so with 'meaning'. The psychologist's technical term occurs in a hyphenated expression, say, '*S*-means-*P*-to-Jones', defined in terms of a certain disposi-

[3] Meaning$_4$ and meaning$_2$ may both be called 'contextual meaning'; but meaning$_2$, like meaning$_1$, is *applicable to* scientific terms, including meaning$_4$.

tional relation holding between, first, the sounds S and Jones, he hears them, and, secondly, certain later states of Jones' body. Just as neither 'see' nor 'tree' occurs in 'seeing-a-tree', so neither 'S' nor 'means' occurs in 'S-means-P-to-Jones'. To put it differently, since S is a pattern of sounds and P a pattern of bodily states, verbal responses, and overt behavior, no substitution can occur in the hyphenated expression.[4] Therefore, from the fact that two expressions, two patterns of sounds, may both be used to refer to the same states of affairs, it does not follow that they both mean$_4$ the same to Jones. The intentional uniqueness of concepts is reflected by their having different linguistic texts. The observable responses to two different expressions may be different. (Psychological) meaning$_4$ depends, in other words, not only upon *what* is being asserted, but also upon the linguistic form in which it is asserted. This uniqueness of meaning$_4$, objectively defined, of linguistic expressions — experimentally established, by the way — reflects the uniqueness of (intentional) meaning$_3$ of thought or concepts. The shadow, if not the substance, of intentionality can thus be captured by the objectivist.

Before considering certain objections to this optimistic objectivist tale, it will be helpful to sort out some uses of 'understand'. I shall indicate the various uses by subscripts. The contexts in which these subscript-terms occur will explicate their uses.

I can understand$_1$ English but not Finnish. To understand a language is to know how to use certain classes of sounds or marks to express and to convey to others our thoughts, attitudes, queries, wishes, and, among other things, information about the world. To accomplish this, I must know the conditions for applying certain expressions and not others. What is involved in understanding$_1$ varies with the kind of expression. Some I understand$_1$ only in context when they are combined with other terms. Clearly, we could not use or understand$_1$ a language if all of its terms were understood only in context by means of other terms. Armed only with a wholly Finnish dictionary, I could not understand$_1$ Finnish. Some expressions, therefore, I understand$_1$ only if I know what conditions of myself, the world, or other people they are being used to express, that is, only if I know their (referential) meaning$_1$.

I do not understand$_2$ what it meant to have been a member of the Italian Resistance. Nor do I understand$_2$ what it means to lose an only son. This sense of 'understanding' has nothing to do with language, for of course I understand$_1$ what it is that I am said not to understand$_2$. I do not understand$_2$ these things because I have not had the special feelings, emotions, or attitudes that are aroused only by having undergone certain experiences or participated in certain kinds of events. Toward those who have my empathy is limited in a way it is not limited toward people with toothaches. For I understand$_2$ what it is to have a toothache. Understanding$_2$ is a mixture of knowing meaning$_1$ and meaning$_2$. I must know to what unique feelings, of pain or of grief, the terms are being used to refer, or, as in the case of being a member of the Italian Resistance, I must know what feelings were *associated with* those underground activities referred to by the term.

I do understand$_3$ what it meant to be a member of the Resistance, just as I understand$_3$ what a golden mountain would be like. The unique phenomenological experience that is the resultant of fear, patriotism, courage, hatred of tyranny, all acting jointly, I do not understand$_2$. But, because I understand$_1$ the meaning$_1$ of the phrase 'being a member of the Italian Resistance' and because I *also* understand$_2$ the meaning of fear, patriotism, and so on, I can understand$_3$ what it meant to be a member of the Resistance. In this sense too, since I have suffered the loss of loved ones, I can understand$_3$ what it means to have lost an only son, though I have never had a son. By understanding$_3$ one may empathize with the bereaved mother, though less completely than one who understands$_2$, that is, one who has also lost a son.

I understand$_4$ why Tom Jones left school; he wanted to make a lot of money quickly.

[4] See also Grossmann, [5].

If we know the motives and purposes of people's actions, then we understand$_4$ why people did what they did. Here we must distinguish between understanding$_1$ the action-term, that is, knowing to what the term is referring, and knowing the motive for the action. The purposes, duties, and so on, mentioned in the description of the action will, of course, be different from the purpose for which the action is performed. I shall return to this distinction presently. (Below, pp. 425–427). For the moment, let it stand that understanding$_4$ consists in knowing motives. This may mean knowing what an action itself is or in knowing motives for it.

I understand$_5$ that increased costs of production mean an increase in selling price. The pious man understands$_5$ that regular church attendance means salvation in after-life. The wife understood$_5$ that her husband's silence meant disapproval. The farmer understands$_5$ that a fiery red sunset means rain the next day. Generally, we understand$_5$ a kind of thing, event, or behavior when we know or believe that there are some *other* things, events, and so on, with which it is in some way associated. In other words, we understand$_5$ the meaning of something when it does not stand isolated, so to speak, before our minds. The "meaning" that we thus understand or attribute to events is what I called significance or meaning$_2$. If we do not know the meaning$_2$ of an event, then we do not understand$_5$ the phenomenon referred to by the term expressing the occurrence. Again, I can understand$_1$ what I do not understand$_5$. Obviously, this significance or meaning$_2$ need not reflect any true connections among things. Yet, true or false, imaginary or superstitious, all of these occurrences of 'understand$_5$' are the same use, for they imply that one kind of thing is believed to be connected with something else. Understanding$_5$ thus comprehends tested generalizations of science that give their terms significance, as well as the connections, whether from common experience or fancy, that people believe certain things have with others. When these associations of one thing with another actually do reflect empirical lawful connections, then understanding$_5$ coincides with scientific explanation. There are of course other uses of 'explain'.[5]

I turn now to criticisms of the objectivist program. The mentalist claims that "understanding of society cannot be observational and experimental" ([8], p. 110)[6] because, first of all, the investigator must understand the language of the people he studies. One learns a language by sharing a mode of life. The investigator, therefore, cannot stand in the observor-observed relation to his subject matter. Moreover, the natural scientist uses external criteria to decide when two events are of the same kind. But that two actions sharing no overt features are of the "same kind" must be decided by the participant, not the spectator. The method by which we understand others is accordingly subjective, not objective. Logically, therefore, there cannot be generalizations about man and society, as there are about stones and stars. What is involved in the idea, for instance, of prayer is a *religious* not a sociological question. An idea cannot be torn out of context, for it gets its meaning from the role it plays in the system. Men's actions are intelligible when we understand their motives and the rules in accordance with which they act. But appeals to standards and to motives "rule out" appeals to causes. Mechanical, causal explanations of human actions are therefore logically inappropriate.[7] Using the distinctions drawn among the various uses of 'meaning' and of 'understanding', I should like to examine these claims.

Does the fact that the investigator must understand$_1$ the language of the people he studies vitiate the objectivist thesis? By a fairly elaborate conditioning process, a child

[5] See also [4].

[6] [*Winch states this claim on page 324 of the present volume. Editor's note.*]

[7] Cf. [7], pp. 4, 12, *et pass.* and [8], pp. 78, 82, *et pass.* With respect to the ineliminability of mentalistic terms and the claim that motives cannot be causes, see also [6].

learns, say, to call a small, furry, meowing animal a cat, not a dog. He also learns to say "He was . . ." not "He were . . .". Pointing, obviously, is not the only method used in teaching a language. Nor can we teach the (referential) meaning$_1$ of mentalistic terms, like 'headache' and 'sorrow', by pointing. These are learned by means of their public accompaniments. It is truistic that learning a language is "rooted in a social context." Far from vitiating the objectivist thesis, the truism is a fundamental part of it. Yet undoubtedly there is a difficulty. An almost infinite number of sound patterns can be used to express the same terms. Moreover, only slight oral or typographical changes create huge differences in behavior. As the old "telegram-argument," frequently adduced by the idealists, insisted, there is an enormous difference between a telegram from a friend that says "Our son was killed" and one that reads "Your son was killed." The difference in (referential) meaning$_1$ and consequently in the reactions they arouse (meaning$_4$) is hugely disproportionate to the slight typographical differences between the marks on paper. A man presumably also reacts differently when he hears the words "I love you" than upon hearing "I love him." The considerable physical difference between 'you' and 'him' suggests how, *in principle*, the investigator could dispense with knowing a common language. And the argument on both sides is one of principle or "logic" only.

Still, the enormous difficulty of correlating slight differences in physical cues with huge differences in behavior are obvious. In *practice*, these difficulties may well be insuperable. In practice, therefore, except when he is actually studying (psychological) meaning$_4$, the investigator simply assumes that he and the subject understand$_1$ the same language. It is not hard to tell, in purely objective ways, whether or not a person understands$_1$ what is being said to him. People behave very differently if they understand$_1$ what is being said than if they do not. If two people understand$_1$ the same language, presumably because they have both learned it in the same social context, then they can communicate with each other. There is nothing inherently subjective about the success or failure of this communication. Once we know from a prior and different investigation that a language is understood$_1$, its users may be observed. The fact that the scientist *learns* the language as a participant in the social process does not imply that he can never, so to speak, stop being a participant. To think that it does is to fall victim to the genetic fallacy. The mentalist confuses how we come to understand$_1$ a statement of, say, a belief with using that understanding$_1$, once learned, to observe that an individual has a certain belief or, at least, says he has.

Most probably, in practice subject and scientist must, as we say, speak the same language. But our saying this leads to a second confusion, namely, between the scientist's language and that which he shares with the subject. For, as I mentioned earlier, in another sense they do not "speak the same language." The language that the scientist uses to *describe* what he learns about his subject is in principle not the same language that he may use to *communicate* with him. What Jones says (and what the investigator says to him in Jones' language) is part of what is going on, which the investigator describes in his own language. In other words, everything that Jones says occurs only within quotation marks in the investigator's language. The subject's use of, say, the term 'prayer' in certain ways and under specifiable conditions is an interesting and important, because meaningful$_2$ or lawfully significant, part of the investigator's *data*. If the latter *uses* that term to describe what is going on, its "meaning" in any and all senses of 'meaning' will not be the same as the subject's term.

The subject's *concept* of prayer will of course have an (intentional) meaning$_3$ for him that it will not have for a nonreligious person and need not have for the investigator. Only in this sense of 'meaning', is it even plausible to say that only the religious man can "make sense" of religion. The sociologist may understand$_4$ religion without also understanding$_2$ it.

For the participant, 'attending church services regularly' $means_{3,4}$ salvation in after-life. For the observor-scientist, the same behavior $means_2$ something quite different, namely, certain other actions of the person and perhaps certain effects upon the community. A sociologist may call two patterns of behavior in different cultures 'baptism', or two other patterns 'marriage', even though the Christian "would not agree" they were the same, ([8], p. 108),[8] not merely because they happen to have certain overt features in common, nor yet "arbitrarily," but because they are believed to be similarly connected to other aspects of behavior and society. To the economist, automobiles and human labor are both commodities, not because he is insensitive to human dignity, but because they have similar properties in relation to other things, such as supply and demand. In sum, the use of a common language for purposes of communication is not in itself "incompatible," as alleged, with the external observor-observed point of view.

To what are we referring when we use such terms as 'a smile,' 'a salute,' or 'money'? A salute, surely, had better be something observable. A smile is, according to Webster, a brightening of the eyes and upward curving of the corners of the mouth. Yet, a salute is more than a position of the hand. And to describe "writhing in pain" or "signing a contract" is indeed more than to give a description "in purely mechanical terms, using a set of space-time coordinates" ([8], p. 73 and [7], p. 13). "Money" is more than pieces of metal, paper, or beads. But is the "something more" of actions and artifacts only describable in nonphysical terms? *One* reason for thinking so is an invidious use of 'physical' in the narrow sense of that term. Such items as muscle-twitches, glandular secretions, shape and size are, on this usage, the only "physical" properties. But a pattern of overt behavior is also something physical, since it is certainly nonmental. A *second* reason for the belief that terms referring to actions and artifacts must $mean_1$ something "nonphysical" or "something more" than overt behavior is a mistaken notion of observable reference. On this usage, only manifest or "occurrent" characters are observable. But flexibility is no less observable than bent. Our everyday statements about actions are, as I mentioned before, mentalistic and categorical. But the scientific terms corresponding to these mentalistic ones, like 'seeing-green' or 'meaning-p' are all dispositional. Dispositional characters merely require more complex observations than do manifest ones; they are no less observable.

Actions, in one way or another, involve a reference to thought or purposes. An objectivist definition of 'purpose', corresponding to the mental state, can be constructed. The difference between just "walking down the street" and doing so "in order to mail a letter" is not in what is presently observed, but a way of speaking about something else which we expect to occur later bringing this action to a close. Or, as with 'looking for' something, it may be a way of speaking about some past event which led to the present behavior or, possibly, some combination of things in the past and future. All this makes 'purpose' a more complex term than 'tall', but not on that account "nonphysical." Generally, a *pattern* of behavior observed in the past or to be observed in the future toward things and other people is the "something more" than present or manifest characters that is $meant_1$ by defined terms referring to actions.

Social artifacts, like money, tools, and weapons, are defined by the behavior of people with respect to inanimate, material objects. In and of itself, a scarlet letter or a yellow arm-badge is no different in "meaning" from an iron cross or a purple heart. As material objects they are all equally "meaningless." What gives them (referential) $meaning_1$ as rewards or punishments is, of course, the behavior of people toward them. A cathedral is not just a pile of stones, not even just a pile of stones arranged in a certain pattern. 'Cathedral' (referentially) $means_1$ a physical structure of a certain kind *and* certain ways people behave towards it, like entering

[8] [*See page 323 of this volume. Editor's note.*]

it at certain intervals and performing certain activities, which *the people*, not the investigator, describe as worshipping. For the rest, the "meaning" of 'cathedral' is either the associations that people have to it, $meaning_4$ (reflecting intentional $meaning_3$), or else its $meaning_2$, that is, its connections with other aspects of the culture, such as the kind of economy or other behaviors, like being charitable. Such connections among kinds of behavior are observable. The investigator's own past experience, aided perhaps by a class of judges, may be drawn upon to determine tentatively the identifying characteristics of, say, "friendly" behavior. But this usable past is not part of the criteria by which he now identifies the action. The belief that it is and thus requires "participation," confuses the origins of a classification with what that category now refers to.

Not *all* of the past and future behaviors that are connected with, say, 'friendly', but not with 'hostile' actions, are part of the (referential) $meaning_1$ of the terms, only enough of them to distinguish friendly from hostile actions. How else could we assent to the proposition that a man may smile and smile, yet be a villain? It is true, even tautologically true, that "an idea gets its sense from the role it plays in a system" only if "meaning" is construed intentionally, as $meaning_3$ (reflected by the psychologist's $meaning_4$), or, for scientific terms, as significance or $meaning_2$. If I $understand_1$ another person's language, I don't necessarily also know all the "meaning" that his terms carry for him. From $understanding_1$ alone, we do not *ipso facto* learn everything that any user of that language might associate with terms. This must be discovered. Nor need I know everything about a system of religious beliefs in order to know the $meaning_1$ of 'baptism', any more than I need to know everything about an economic system in order to know the $meaning_1$ of 'money'. Neither to $understand_1$ a language nor to know the $meaning_1$ of its referential terms, need I know how everything is connected with everything else. I $understand_1$ the $meaning_1$ of 'sell' and of 'price', both terms with complex definitions, without also $understanding_5$ the connection between, say, selling price and cost price. Nor is the way they vary together merely a "conceptual" matter. Learning to use the word 'cost' does not entail learning all the laws of economics, any more than learning to use the word 'marriage' tells me all about marriage. Of course, to have "genuine understanding," if that means $understanding_2$, then one must *be* married. But "genuine understanding" may also mean knowing connections among things. And a bachelor sociologist's $understanding_5$ of this $meaning_2$, that is, the connections the institution of marriage has with, say, property-distribution, education, job-stability, and so on, may well exceed that of the most-often married person. Nor can he discover these things by analyzing the concept of marriage. The most one can thus discover, besides the legal definition of the term, is the (psychological) $meaning_4$ it has for certain people, the gratifications and responsibilities they associate with it. For the $meaning_2$ or significance of marriage he will have to grub among the facts.

A pervasive fusion of the various meanings of 'meaning' and of 'understanding', lends a specious plausibility to the insistence upon the "total context" in order to grasp "meaning" and have "genuine understanding." What a term is used to refer to ($meaning_1$) is confused, on the one hand, with the psychological associations ($meanings_{3,4}$) we have to it and, on the other, with the lawful connections ($meaning_2$) the object of reference has with other things. An uncritical use of 'concept', blurs the distinction between our thought of something, "our idea of it," and the characteristics referred to by a term which is the text of that thought. Thoughts or concepts are sometimes also called "meanings." By spinning out these "meanings," we are said to "understand" human and social concepts, man and society. If we unpack the various uses of 'meaning' and of 'understanding', it is clear that at best such "conceptual analysis" can tell us what things (some) people think go together, not how things are actually connected.

The difference between the action of raising my arm and the movement of my arm going up is that the former is done intentionally or for a purpose. The purpose need not be conscious; an action may be performed habitually, as reaching for a cigarette, or spontaneously, as jumping to dodge a car. In other words, there need not be any mental act present when performing an action. Automatic signalling for a left turn is also an action. However, a complete description of *what* was done, of the (referential) meaning$_1$ of 'signalling', requires mention of motives or purposes that are *part* of the action. Nor need these purposes be those of the person performing the action. Many of our actions require reference to a standard for complete description. To describe what is happening when a man tips his hat to a woman acquaintance requires a set of statements that mention, besides the regularity of his behavior, the presence in society of certain standards or norms. Norms don't exist by themselves; they ultimately involve mental acts. They may be explicated as, say, certain definite and durable expectations that people in a society have about each other's behavior. 'Expectation', in turn, can be defined by certain dispositions, such as the imposition of penalties if certain behavior does not occur. The new recruit's salute is not yet habitual, but may well become so. What makes it "rule-governed," while the habit of chain-smoking is not, is the recruit's membership in a hierarchically-structured institution in which such behavior is "expected." Regularity of behavior under certain circumstances characterizes both "rule-governed" and merely habitual behavior. The "something more" in the former is the different way in which these regularities were acquired.

The two expressions 'raising an arm' and 'arm going up' differ in "meaning" in all four senses of 'meaning', referentially, intentionally, psychologically, and in significance. In this sense, and so far as it goes, the mentalist's answer to Wittgenstein's question is correct. There is certainly difference in "meaning." The relevant differences, however, can be objectively construed without appealing to any vitiating participant "inside knowledge." In this respect, there is nothing about such terms marking them as "logically" different from those of natural science.

Behind the rejection of so-called "mechanical" explanation seems to lie the notion that any explanation that does not use mentalistic terms in their mentalistic sense is "mechanical," that is, is about movements in space, not about intelligent, purposive behavior. Partly, we have again the narrow use of 'physical', so that only the terms of physics and chemistry are physical or nonmental. But the definition of an action as a set of behavioral dispositions, bodily states, and environmental circumstances surely does not mention merely "movements." Nor, as I have suggested schematically in discussing 'purpose', is there any reason to believe that an objectivist account cannot be given of "intelligent" behavior, that is, the ability to vary behavior relative to a goal, under changing circumstances. Man of course "understands his situation," while a dog does not. This use of 'understanding' can be objectively construed by means of dispositional and occurrent factors present in and operating on the man but not the dog; for instance, his past learning of certain rules (standards and regularities) or his present awareness of them.

To be sure, explanation by causes is only one use of 'explain'. Citing a motive also explains, as does giving a detailed description, as when we explain, say, the structure of feudalism. These different uses of 'explain', among others, also have their corresponding senses of 'understand'. They are not mutually incompatible. Which is "appropriate" depends upon what the person wants to know. Sometimes motives are causes, sometimes not. Buying a house is an action whose complete description in "neutral" or nonmentalistic terms would be quite complicated, requiring mention among other things of certain legal statutes. But an answer to why Jones bought a house might well state a motive, namely, a desire for privacy. This motive is hardly part of the (referential) meaning$_1$ of 'buying a house'. It is, though, part of its meaning$_2$, that is, living in one's own house is a way of getting privacy. Here a motive is also a cause. Doubtless other (concurrent) causes are also operative. At other times, to cite a motive is not to give a cause but to tell *what* is happening, as when explaining what a signal or salute *is*. A reference to standards and motives will occur in the descriptions of these actions. But explaining *what* an action is and explaining *why* it occurred are two different things. Each may require mention of motives, though, of course, not *the same* ones. Jumping out a window is one action, of which the desire for death might be a cause. On the other hand, we would not say that a man committed suicide because he wanted to kill himself, since this wish is part of the (referential) meaning$_1$ of suicide.

Over-attention to cases of the latter kind perhaps is the source of a basic error that unfortunately pervades Melden's temperate and frequently illuminating book. He argues that a motive can never be a cause since, on good Humean principles, the cause must be logically distinct from the effect. He interprets this to imply that a description of the cause must not contain "any reference" to the effect. But 'wanting-to-do-X' mentions 'doing-X' and, generally, a description of a desire requires reference to the object desired. Hence, Melden concludes, they are not logically independent and motives cannot be causes for actions ([6], pp. 53, 114, 128). But there is no logical *implication* between wanting-to-do-X and actually doing X. The thought-of-snow-tomorrow means$_3$ or intends snow tomorrow, but it does not logically entail that it will snow tomorrow. No more does the thought-of-doing-X logically entail doing-X. An adequate analysis of the nature of mental acts and how they are related to their intentions is indispensable. Although the relation of meaning$_3$ between a thought and its intention is a logical one, the (occurrence of) thought itself no more entails its intention than, analogously, the logical relation 'or' permits the deduction of 'q' from 'p or q'. A thought, after all, can mean$_3$ what does not and never will exist. *The mental act of wanting-to-do-X is one fact. Doing X is quite another and distinct fact. The former might on some occasions cause the latter.*

In some contexts standards and motives are causes; in some other contexts, they describe the action. Those enchanted by "rule-governed" behavior now tell us again and again that unless something is done in accordance with a rule, it is not really an action. This restriction has the odd consequence that a man may act purposively and yet not be doing anything. A married man making advances to a choir boy is not really doing anything, but instead has something "happening" to him ([7], p. 10). I see no warrant either in common usage or in common sense for this restrictive use of 'action', based, at least in part, on a bad pun on "what is done" or "not done." Even granting the dubious doctrine that we only ask for a man's motives when he deviates from the "done" thing, we want the motives for his action, that is, for his purposive behavior, not for something, like a brick falling on his head, that merely happened to him. People are often punished for doing the "not done" thing, which is hardly reasonable if, like the brick, it just "happened" to them. Freud indeed taught us how narrow is the line between what a man does and what happens to him. But it was, alas, the sphere of the latter, not that of the former, which he restricted.

The distinction between the what and the why of actions is also relevant to the notion that causal explanations are only appropriate to our "deviations from norms" [7], p. 10) — (which, not quite incidentally, also may be instances of rational, purposive behavior). Partly, this view seems to stem from the fact that when we reply to a why-question by stating a norm, we often are explaining what is occurring, that being all the person wants to know. By definition, such an answer could not be given for "deviant" behavior. Even more fundamental is a pervasive equivocation between different uses of 'rule', once as a descriptive regularity and once as a prescriptive standard or norm. We do indeed consider that an insane man, incapable of judging between alternative courses of action, thus deviating from descriptively regular or normal human behavior, has things "happen" to him that a normal man "does." A man who deviates from a prescriptive norm, however, is not necessarily insane. He may be the only sane one among us.

On this possibly frivolous note, I conclude that the objectivist program emerges unscathed from the barrage of criticisms recently directed against it. Yet, some uneasiness about the objectivist thesis remains to be allayed. When all is said and done, is the objectivist talking about the "same facts" as we describe in everyday mentalistic language? *Can* talk about causes replace, without residue, talk about motives? Can the scientist's non-interactionist account be made to accord with our commonsense (and clinical) belief that mind and body do affect each other? As a final therapeutic step, it may pay to be explicit by distinguishing three uses of the phrase "same fact" that are relevant to this discussion.

1) Two statements may describe different states of affairs, yet be such that one of them is true (false) if and only if the other is also true (false). Such (synthetically) extensional equivalences may be said to express the $same_1$ fact. In particular, if to any given statement about a person's motives or other mental states, there is another containing only physiological, behavioral, and environmental terms that is extensionally equivalent to the first, then they express the $same_1$ fact. They do not mean the same either intentionally or referentially. The scientist's description, containing no terms referring to conscious states, thus "leaves out" minds. Talk about overt behavior and other physical items does not replace "without residue" talk about motives. On the other hand, since they express the $same_1$ fact, whenever the objectivist description is true of anyone, a corresponding mentalistic account will also be true.

2) We can strengthen, beyond mere extensional equivalence, the use of "same fact". The term 'red', for instance, directly refers to a color. Light waves cause but are not colors. However, the descriptive phrase 'the color with the longest wave length' is a way of indirectly referring to the color red. "The color of this book is red' and 'The color of this book is the color with the longest wave length' express the $same_2$ fact. Similarly, a mentalistic term, like 'thinking-about-$Italy_m$' directly describes a state of consciousness, while its objectivist parallel 'thinking-about-$Italy_0$' indirectly refers to this state. Generally, two different statements express the $same_2$ fact, if the terms in which they differ are related to each other as direct and indirect descriptions or ways of referring. Since corresponding mentalistic and objectivist statements in this twofold way express the $same_{1,2}$ facts, their "sameness" is stronger than the mere extensional equivalence of, say, 'Roses are red' and 'Sugar is sweet'.

We say that mental anguish, for instance, anxiety, causes ulcers or that a bodily wound causes pain. Our common language is interactionist through and through. Extensional equivalence and direct *versus* indirect reference permit us to fit scientific parallelism with this piece of interactionist commonsense. On the objectivist account, a mental state can affect the body only through its corresponding physical state. But the objectivist term '$anxiety_0$' is an indirect description of the mentalistic '$anxiety_m$'. They may thus each be used to express the $same_2$ fact. In particular, if it is true that $anxiety_0$ causes ulcers, we may also truly say that $anxiety_m$ causes ulcers. The two causal attributions, the everyday interactionist one and that of the objectivist, are extensionally equivalent and express the $same_1$ fact. Since they also express the $same_2$ fact, there is more than mere extensional equivalence. We can thus make sense both of our commonsense interactionism as well as of its scientific denial. This is as it should be for, as we know, philosophy leaves everything as it is.

3) The statement-form '*P* or *Q*' is logically equivalent to "not both not-*P* and not-*Q*'. By virtue of this tautology, 'Either Jones has a daughter or he has a son' expresses the

same$_3$ fact as 'It is not the case that Jones has neither a daughter nor a son'. Generally, two statements may be said to express the same$_3$ fact, if they are logically, that is, tautologically equivalent, or, to say the same thing differently, if the statement of their equivalence is analytic. Statements containing terms directly referring to mental states are not *tautologically* equivalent to statements containing their corresponding indirectly-referring objectivist terms. They do not therefore express the same$_3$ facts. However, most if not all action and other social terms must be explicated, that is, given "real definitions" of their (referential) meaning$_1$, whether in everyday speech or in science. Given such explications of usage, the terms, like 'owning property' or even 'behaving according to a standard', serve as abbreviatory expressions for the more complex ones. Statements containing the abbreviatory terms are then analytically equivalent to statements containing, in their place, the longer explicating expressions. They thus express the same$_3$ fact. But even in such cases, the two expressions, the short and the long ones, would not have the same (intentional or associational) meanings$_{3,4}$. Two expressions that are "logically" different in a use of 'logical' that encompasses and conflates several different ways that an expression can mean may yet be logically the same in a different and precise sense of 'logical'.

The crucial terms in this controversy are 'meaning' and 'understanding'. Often in philosophical controversy, once several uses of certain crucial terms have been distinguished, little remains to argue about. Doubtless this happy outcome is too much to hope for now, though I hope that some contribution has at least been made to clarity about the issues at stake. I hazard the diagnosis that a vast irresolution about the status of mind lies at the root of the revived attempt to resolve empirical matters of fact "logically" or "conceptually." Unwilling to grant ontological status to mind, what properly belongs to mind, our thoughts or concepts, is projected on to the world. This is the road, not trodden for the first time, that leads to anthropomorphic rationalism.

References

[1] Bergmann, Gustav, *Meaning and Existence* (Wisconsin, 1959), pp. 3–38, 106–14.

[2] Bergmann, Gustav, "Acts", *Indian Journal of Philosophy*, II (1960), pp. 1–30; 96–117.

[3] Bergmann, Gustav, "Purpose, Function, Scientific Explanation", *Acta Sociologica, 5* (1962), pp. 225–238.

[4] Brodbeck, May, "Explanation, Prediction, and 'Imperfect' Knowledge", *Minnesota Studies in the Philosophy of Science*, vol. III. H. Feigl & G. Maxwell, eds., Univer. of Minnesota Press (Minneapolis, 1962). Pp. 231–272.

[5] Grossmann, R., "Propositional Attitudes," *Philosophical Quarterly, 10* (1960), pp. 301–12.

[6] Melden, A. I., *Free Action* (London, 1961).

[7] Peters, R. S., *The Concept of Motivation* (London, 1958).

[8] Winch, P., *The Idea of a Social Science* (London, 1958).

[9] Wittgenstein, L. *Philosophical Investigations* (Oxford, 1953).

Operationism Can and Should Be Divorced from Covering Law Assumptions

36

Operational Definitions

ROBERT H. ENNIS

Introduction

On all sides we are warned that our results depend on the instruments and procedures used, and we are admonished to define our terms in a manner that takes account of these instruments and procedures (often this admonition specifies that the definition should be operational); yet we want to express our conclusions in terms that are not limited to the particular instruments and procedures. That sets my problem: How can we give operational definitions without unduly restricting the meaning of the terms in which we state our conclusions?

In this paper I shall examine various forms that operational definitions might take and shall develop and defend a set of guides for making these definitions. These guides will enable us to connect our abstract terms to our instruments and procedures without completely limiting the meaning of the terms to these instruments and procedures.

The Spirit of Operationism

An early expression of what has come to be called "operationism" is found in P. W. Bridgman's *The Logic of Modern Physics:* "The concept of length involves as much as and nothing more than the set of operations by which length is determined. In general, we mean by any concept nothing more than a set of operations; *the concept is synonymous with the corresponding set of operations*" (Bridgman, 1927; p. 5). Although Bridgman, who is regarded as the father of operationism, goes too far in this statement, the focus on instruments and procedures, which is the essence of operationism, comes through clearly. This focus may be viewed as one of the empiricist and pragmatic trends of recent years, as A. C. Benjamin has shown in his interesting summary and appraisal of Bridgman's ideas and their development under criticism (Benjamin, 1955).

As a thesis, the spirit of operationism can be loosely put as follows: *There is an important relationship between the meaning of a term and the instruments and procedures that one would use to see whether the term applies to a particular situation and, if so, how.*

Forms in Which This Spirit Has Been Expressed

In the literature on operationism one finds four basic approaches to operational definitions: 1) giving examples; 2) giving a set of operations as the meaning of a concept; 3) equating a phrase or sentence containing the

From the *American Educational Research Journal*, 1:3 (May, 1964), American Educational Research Association, Washington, D. C., pp. 183–198.

[1] The preparation of this paper was supported through the Cooperative Research Program of the Office of Education, United States Department of Health, Education, and Welfare. An earlier version was presented to the Philosophy of Education Society in San Francisco on April 8, 1963. I have profited from the criticisms of Professors H. Broudy, H. Burns, J. Canfield, D. B. Gowin, J. Millman, F. Neff, and N. Champlin, and a number of my students at Cornell University.

term in question with a phrase or sentence about a combination of operations and observations; and 4) providing implication relationships among operations, observations, and the concept in question. The proposed guides fit under the fourth approach, the description of which has been vague because of the several variations possible.

Since the defense of these guides rests heavily on showing the difficulties of the first three approaches, difficulties that are avoided if one follows the guides, we must look carefully at all four approaches.

GIVING EXAMPLES

Although Bridgman had something more rigorous in mind, the use of examples of abstract concepts sometimes indicates the instruments and procedures involved when using the concepts and, at an unsophisticated level, does provide an empirical interpretation. G. A. Lundberg, the sociologist, indicates endorsement of the example approach in the following statement: "The simplest form of an operational definition of a word is to point to its referent while enunciating the word. Thus we define the word 'cat' to a child by pointing to a certain kind of animal or a succession of animals denoted by the word in our language" (Lundberg, 1942a; p. 730).

Examples are very useful in clarifying terms because they connect them to the concrete world — concreteness is one of the virtues of operational definitions. But in giving an example, one does not necessarily specify a manipulation by an investigator, and thus exemplification misses some of the spirit of operationism. The "cat" example above does not specify a manipulation by an investigator; instead it specifies particular cats.

Nevertheless, it would not be a serious error to treat examples as operational definitions — provided that we have distinct names for what would then be two different kinds of operational definitions. Obvious, though rather wordy, names are "example-type operational definitions" and "manipulative operational definitions." For verbal economy I prefer to mark the distinction with the terms "example" and "operational definition," both of which have established usages. Accordingly, examples would not be operational definitions.

GIVING A SET OF OPERATIONS AS THE MEANING OF A CONCEPT (FORM: CONCEPT = OPERATIONS)

This approach is suggested by a strict interpretation of Bridgman's statement quoted earlier. According to this approach, *length* means a set of operations, such as putting down a ruler end over end and (presumably) counting the number of times this is done. *Length* means what you do; it is not a property of the thing you do it to. It does not mean what you find out; it means what you do when finding out.

If we apply this approach strictly to a concept often used in social-science research, *IQ* might mean administering and (presumably) scoring the *California Test of Mental Maturity*[2] (henceforth referred to as *CTMM*). An *IQ* would not then be a quality of a child; the child's IQ would mean what you had done to him.

Another feature of this approach is that it implies as many concepts of *length* (*IQ*, etc.) as there are ways of measuring it. According to Bridgman, the concept *length* in *length of a city lot* is different from the concept *length* in *length of a large piece of land* if measuring sticks alone are used for determining the first and measuring sticks plus triangulation for the second, because the sets of operations are different (Bridgman, 1927; p. 14). Similarly, there would be as many concepts of *IQ* as there are tests for IQ and ways of administering them. If meaning is identical with a set of operations, different operations imply different meanings. Bridgman says, "If we have more than one set of operations, we have more than one concept, and strictly there should be a separate name to correspond to each different set of operations" (Bridgman, 1927; p. 10).

[2] To simplify the presentation, I have not given the form, edition, or level of the tests discussed.

Thus, there are these two distinguishing features of this, the second, approach to operationism: (a) the meaning of a concept is limited to the operations, and (b) different operations imply different concepts. I shall criticize each feature.

(a) To treat the meaning of a concept (or term) as limited to set of operations seems odd, to say the least. When I say that the length of a bench is five feet, I intend to be talking about the bench — not about what I did. When I say that Johnny has a low IQ, I intend to be talking about Johnny — not about what I did. If one interprets Bridgman's original formula strictly, there seems no way to include the observations that one makes, observations that reveal the qualities measured. One cannot talk about the things measured; one can talk only about what the experimenter does — not about what he perceives.

It may be held that this reading of Bridgman's statements is unfair — that he did not mean them as I have presented them. Perhaps so. I do not see how anyone could really mean them that way although some sociologists and psychologists may appear to have so taken them.[3] An examination of *The Logic of Modern Physics* and the works of these social scientists reveals that it is hard to be sure just what they do mean. However, my purpose here is not to criticise them but to clarify the advantages and disadvantages of various expressions of the operationist spirit. Strictly interpreted, this, the second, approach to operationism neglects the results one gets after doing the operations.

(b) There is no doubt that people (including Bridgman in *The Logic of Modern Physics* and most social scientists that I have read on the subject) have taken seriously the second feature of the second approach to operationism (that different operations imply different concepts), and there has been considerable dispute on this point. I shall not go into it thoroughly here because to do so would require systematic treatment of the nature and content of scientific theories, about which there is a vast literature. I shall only comment on the serious difficulties of this view. These comments are carefully elaborated, however, because they contribute substantially to refuting the third (and most popular) approach to operationism.

The first point to clarify is how to tell if two operations are actually different. Is my administration of the *CTMM* at 9:00 a.m. on Monday, April 6, 1964, in Fall Creek School a different operation from my administration of the *CTMM* at 10:00 a.m. on Monday, April 6, 1964, in Belle Sherman School? The only differences are the time and place of administration. To my knowledge, no satisfactory criterion, operational or otherwise, has been provided by operationists of the concept *different operation.* This is a significant weakness of the thesis that different operations require different concepts. We do not know how different, or in what respects different, the operations have to be to require different concepts.

Let us, however, assume that different times and places do not require a judgment of different operations. But presumably the use of measuring sticks and that of measuring sticks plus triangulation would be different operations, as would the use of the *CTMM* and that of the *Lorge-Thorndike Intelligence Tests.* Similarly, using the mercury thermometer, the alcohol thermometer, and the resistance thermometer would be three different operations.

But why should there be two concepts of length, two concepts of IQ, and three concepts of temperature to correspond to the various operations mentioned in the previous paragraph? Why not one concept of length and two ways of measuring it? One concept of IQ and two ways of estimating it? One concept of temperature and three ways of determining it?

Let us consider the concept *temperature.* (Analogous things could be said about *length*, but these things would be considerably more difficult.) What would be the consequences of having three concepts of tempera-

[3] For examples, see Lundberg (1942b, p. 89), Stevens (1951, p. 28), and Marx (1951, p. 11).

ture, say *M-temperature* for the mercury thermometer, *A-temperature* for the alcohol thermometer, and *R-temperature* for the resistance thermometer? Since there are many more ways of measuring temperature, there would, of course, have to be many more concepts.

One difficulty is that people would misunderstand someone who held this view since people think of temperature as one quality, which is measured in various ways. But this is not an insuperable objection. One might stipulate three senses for the word "temperature" that represent qualities highly correlated with one another and hold that these senses should be distinguished for scientists and sloppily merged for laymen. This is a plausible answer; scientists are not bound by ordinary usage in their research.

A second difficulty, however, is that physics itself would become immensely more complicated. The law of thermal expansion would become three laws, one for each concept. (And since there are many more ways of measuring temperature, there would have to be many more laws, where previously we managed with only one.) Furthermore, the law based on *M-temperature* would extend over a different range from that of the law based on *R-temperature* since the two thermometers have different ranges. Not only convenience would be sacrificed, but also simplicity and elegance.

The attempt to explain differences in temperature would run into difficulty. The model provided by the kinetic theory of heat explains them by means of differences in the mean kinetic energy of molecules. There is just this *one* phenomenon, the mean kinetic energy of molecules, to explain differences in temperature. Minor aberrations and inconsistencies between instruments at extreme points have auxiliary explanations, but the fact remains that there is one underlying phenomenon associated with temperature in physical theory, which implies that temperature is just one thing. (This discussion assumes ordinary contexts; later on, we shall consider a special context with somewhat different results.)

Of course, we could conceivably elevate what I have called "auxiliary explanations" to the status of central explanations, in which case we could have a different central explanation for the phenomenon associated with each instrument, but to do so would be inconvenient. The simplest explanation, and the one that suffices in most cases, is the one that refers only to the mean kinetic energy of the molecules.

What about fruitfulness — the ability of theory to generate new predictions and to suggest new ways of looking at other fields? It is difficult to see how the complex structure that is implicit in the requirement that different operations imply different concepts could be a provoker of new ideas or an aid to seeing new applications; it would be so hard to see the structure as a whole, to see it intuitively.

While there is ordinarily only one concept of temperature functioning within our normal range of experience, the concept does become elusive in extreme situations. When we try to measure temperature at points successively farther from the earth's surface, different operations tend to call for different concepts *because different operations produce radically different readings at the same point* and because our interest in hotness and coldness out in space calls for great attention to sources of radiant heat. The reading on a thermometer depends on whether the thermometer is exposed to radiant heat and, if so, on the direction in which the thermometer is aimed. This is something like the dependence of a reading on whether a thermometer is in the sun or in the shade. There are needed, so to speak, a concept, *shade-temperature*, and a concept, *directional-radiant-temperature*. A thermometer suspended in a reflecting sphere would indicate shade-temperature (to the extent that the sphere successfully reflects radiant energy). A thermometer in a reflecting tube *open* at one end (thus admitting radiant energy from one direction) would indicate directional-radiant-temperature. Thus, under conditions that obtain as we leave the earth, it becomes convenient to have two concepts of temperature since different operations give answers that at times are radically different and since our fundamental concern, hotness and coldness, is radically affected by radiant heat.

In summary, once we are willing to bypass the difficulties attendant upon violating the conventions of everyday speech and ordinary technical language, the difficulty with having a different concept for each operation of temperature measurement is the inconvenience. But under certain conditions, given our interests, we have to accept this inconvenience because the results from two different methods of measurement disagree so greatly. The conclusion is that different operations do *not* by themselves imply different concepts although, under certain circumstances for certain purposes, they may call for different concepts.

Now, do the same considerations apply to *IQ*? In ordinary use (among teachers and others who use the concept but who are not scientists), IQ is held to be *one thing*, estimated with varying degrees of validity by the various intelligence tests. But this in itself is not sufficient reason for educational scientists to adopt a unitary concept. They might hold that the matter is not that simple — the measures we have differ so much that, although they contain common elements, they are not enough alike to warrant calling them measures of the same thing. At best, IQ tests correlate around .8. Thus they have much in common, but not *everything* in common, and we know from analyzing them that they emphasize different abilities, such as spatial reasoning, verbal facility, and numerical skill. Furthermore, there is not yet an explanatory theory for IQ comparable to the kinetic theory of heat. In view of these facts, it would be *safest* to develop a number of concepts of IQ, one for each test. (This, in effect, is part of what people are doing who say that "intelligence" means what is measured by a given intelligence test.)

But there still are the arguments for a unitary concept that depend on simplicity, intelligibility, and fruitfulness. In view of these considerations, I treat *IQ* as a single concept for research purposes in the Cornell Critical Thinking Project, with which I am associated. IQ in this sense is measured with some accuracy by the various tests and, in my experience, is well-enough related to the intellectual performance of people who are similarly motivated and whose backgrounds are roughly the same.

This is a matter about which reasonable men can differ. One may argue that the verbal score yielded by the *Lorge-Thorndike Intelligence Tests* emphasizes verbal ability more than does the score yielded by the *CTMM* and therefore we should treat these scores as connected to different concepts, perhaps *verbal IQ* and *general IQ*. If these scores correlate quite differently with the variable in which we are interested at this time — the ability to think critically, we have evidence for treating them as being connected to different concepts. The main point is that this is a question that must be settled by appealing to the circumstances and purposes involved. *Since it makes sense to argue about the question even after it is agreed that the operations are different, it follows that different operations do not by themselves imply different concepts of IQ.*

Again a difference in operations by itself does not imply different concepts, although different concepts are sometimes called for by different operations in conjunction with certain circumstances. In spite of the fact that the second approach to operational definitions is unsatisfactory on the basis of the first feature alone, detailed examination of the second feature was worth while because rejection of the claim that different operations imply different concepts is a central part of the argument against the third approach to operational definitions.

EQUATING A PHRASE OR SENTENCE CONTAINING THE TERM WITH A PHRASE OR SENTENCE ABOUT A COMBINATION OF OPERATIONS AND OBSERVATIONS

This appears to be the approach of the radical behaviorists; for example, B. F.

Skinner (1953, p. 585). It is May Brodbeck's approach in N. L. Gage's *Handbook of Research on Teaching* (Brodbeck, 1963; p. 50) and may be the approach actually intended by Bridgman in *The Logic of Modern Physics.* A first statement of this form follows:

> 3.1a. "*X* has the property *T*" means the same as "A given operation was performed and a given observation was made,"

where *T* is, or contains, the term being defined. Example 1 below is an operational definition of *IQ* according to Form 3.1a.

> Example 1: "*X* has an IQ of *n*" means the same as "*X* was given the *CTMM* and received a score of *n*."

Form 3.1a is limited to cases where *T* is in a *sentence* that is equated to another sentence. I should like to generalize the form so that *T* can appear in either a phrase *or* a sentence that is equated to another phrase or sentence:

> 3.1b. "*Tx*" means the same as "*OPx* and *OBSx*,"

where *Tx* is a phrase or sentence containing the term *T* to be defined; *OPx* is a phrase or sentence about the performance of operations; and *OBSx* is a phrase or sentence about observations. *OPx* and *OBSx* may be merged into one phrase or sentence. Example 1 fits Form 3.1b, as does example 2 below.

> Example 2: "A person's IQ" means the same as "a person's score resulting from the administration of the *CTMM*" (or, more simply, "a person's score on the *CTMM*").

The term (or concept) *IQ* is tied down to a particular intelligence test in this, the third, approach to operational definitions; but, in contrast to the second approach, an IQ is a characteristic of a person, not of the operations performed, though it is still dependent on those operations.

An immediate objection presents itself. In example 1, let us assume that *X* actually has an IQ of, say, 120. If this is not known because he has not yet taken the test, one is obliged to say that it is false that he has an IQ of 120 since the statement alleged to be identical in meaning is false; that is, it is false that *X* was given the *CTMM*, so it is false that he was given it and got a score of 120. Hence, by this interpretation, it must be false that he has an IQ of 120. This contradicts our assumption that he has an IQ of 120. No matter what IQ we assume *X* to have, a contradiction develops. Since he must have some IQ, the definition is faulty.

A similar problem exists for the phrase approach. According to example 2, a person who does not have a score on the *CTMM* does not have an IQ at all since "score on the *CTMM*" and *IQ* mean the same thing. If that were so, it would make no sense for a principal to ask his guidance counselor to obtain IQ's for new students who had never before been tested since, by this interpretation, they have no IQ's (because they have no scores on the *CTMM*).

A way out of this difficulty is to use between *OPx* and *OBSx* an implication relationship that is expressed conditionally and can be put in the subjunctive mood. The revised form is:

> 3.2. "*Tx*" means the same as "If *OPx*, then *OBSx*." Our sentence example becomes:
>
> Example 3: "*X* has an IQ of *n*" means the same as "If *X* is (were) given the *CTMM*, he will (would) get a score of *n*."
>
> Our phrase example becomes:
>
> Example 4: "A person's IQ" means the same as "the score he will (would) get if given the *CTMM*."

There are problems remaining, but the use of implications that can be put in the subjunctive[4] solves this first one. If a person has

[4] See Chisholm (1949), Goodman (1952), von Wright (1957), and Will (1947) for interesting discussions of counter-factual conditionals. This problem need not bother us here unless we try to reduce all logical relationships to conjunction and negation (or something similar) — an unwise course, in my opinion.

never taken the *CTMM* — even if he is never going to take it, he nevertheless has an IQ, perhaps never to be known. And if he has taken it and has a score, there still is no inconsistency, for that does not preclude his being given it again.

In future examples, reference to the subjunctive will be omitted for simplicity's sake. But it should be understood that each example is intended to be convertible to the subjunctive — if need be. Furthermore, phrase-type examples will no longer be given; with appropriate modifications, the general points to be made apply also to them.

Let us now consider another difficulty with the third approach. It limits the meaning of a concept to a particular set of operations (in the case discussed above, the administration of the *CTMM*) together with the results of this set of operations. Thus, like the second approach, it implies that different operations require different concepts. As indicated earlier, this view is generally false — although, under certain circumstances and purposes, different operations do require different concepts.

What is needed is a format that will not commit us to having different operations require different concepts in all cases but will permit some leeway. We must replace the relationship, *means the same as*, with one that does not limit the meaning to a particular set of operations. An implication relationship that does not claim equivalence of meaning will meet this requirement. This idea leads us to the fourth approach.

PROVIDING IMPLICATION RELATIONSHIPS AMONG OPERATIONS, OBSERVATIONS, AND THE CONCEPT

We can avoid the difficulty caused by the relationship, *means the same as*, by replacing it with the relationship, *if and only if*.[5] The amended form follows:

> 4.1. *Tx;* if and only if; if *OPx*, then *OBSx*.

The use of "if and only if" permits us to have two, or more, different kinds of operations to measure the same thing. The following examples can *both* be operational definitions of the same concept, *temperature:*

> Example 5: *X* has a temperature of *t;* if and only if; if a mercury thermometer is inserted in *X*, the thermometer will read *t*.

> Example 6: *X* has a temperature of *t;* if and only if; if an alcohol thermometer is inserted in *X*, the thermometer will read *t*.

If "means the same as" appeared in these definitions instead of "if and only if," we should be committed to saying that "mercury thermometer" means the same as "alcohol thermometer." In effect, the if-and-only-if formulation allows several accurate ways of measuring the same thing.

If we apply this approach to the measurement of *IQ*, another problem becomes prominent. There is much less agreement among IQ tests than there is among thermometers. Even the if-and-only-if formulation seems too rigid. Consider these two possible definitions of the concept *IQ*:

> Example 7: *X* has an IQ of *n;* if and only if; if the *CTMM* is administered to *X*, *X* will get a score of *n*.

> Example 8: *X* has an IQ of *n;* if and only if; if the *Lorge-Thorndike Intelligence Tests* are administered to *X*, *X* will get a score of *n*.

Together these definitions commit us to saying that a person will get the same score on the *CTMM* as on the *Lorge-Thorndike*. For at least two reasons we do not want to be fully committed to this.

[5] This approach is along the lines recommended by Carl Hempel (1952, 1961), who has applied Rudolph Carnap's (1953) notion of the *reduction sentence* to the formulation of operational definitions. My approach differs from theirs primarily in the interpretation of the if-then relationship, theirs being a truth-functional interpretation and mine being an ordinary-language interpretation. See P. F. Strawson's *Introduction to Logical Theory* (1952) for a discussion of the difference. If the reader who is unacquainted with this difference in approach simply interprets if-then sentences in the way to which he is accustomed, he will be interpreting these sentences as they are here intended.

First, the conditions of administration may not be standard for both tests in any given pair of situations. If one test is administered under standard conditions and the other is not, we can hardly expect the same scores. This difficulty can be handled by adding some such phrase as "under standard conditions." It is desirable that a list of standard conditions be available, perhaps in the test manual. Incidentally, this same qualification holds for thermometers when precision is necessary.

Second, each instrument has its idiosyncrasies, which inevitably interfere with measurement at some level of precision. If these are large enough to make a practical difference, some word like "approximately" should be added to the operational definition. Since the idiosyncracies of IQ tests do make a practical difference at the level of precision at which they are used, "approximately" should probably be added to operational definitions of *IQ*. I should not ordinarily add it to operational definitions of *temperature* since the idiosyncracies of thermometers do not make a significant difference in the contexts with which I am familiar. However, for certain purposes and situations, some qualifying word should be added for thermometers also.

To remind us of the qualifications, we can add "(WQ)," which stands for "with qualifications," to Form 4.1:

> 4.2. *Tx;* if and only if; if *OPx*, then *OBSx* (WQ).

An operational definition of *IQ* might look like this:

> Example 9: *X* has an IQ of approximately *n;* if and only if; if the *CTMM* is administered to *X* under standard conditions, *X* will get a score of *n*.

In this example, "approximately" was inserted in the clause containing the concept being defined, *IQ*. This is the proper place for the qualifier when we are trying to judge what someone's IQ is; the method of determination gives an approximation. On the other hand, when we are reasoning from an assumption about what someone's IQ is to a predicted score, "approximately" should appear in the clause about the score:

> Example 10: *X* has an IQ of *n*; if and only if; if the *CTMM* is administered to *X* under standard conditions, *X* will get a score of approximately *n*.

Thus, the location of the qualifiers, as well as the decision about whether to make them explicit, depends to some extent on the situation. Henceforth I shall use "(WQ)" in the examples, leaving placement of the qualifiers to be determined by the context.

People who are not adept at dealing with complicated if-then relationships tend to find Form 4.2 hard to understand. Some read into it the suggestion that a person who has not been given the test does not have an IQ. They also are puzzled by the three occurrences of the word "if" so close together. A more understandable formulation follows:

> 4.3. If *OPx;* then *Tx*, if and only if, *OBSx* (WQ).

> Example 11: If the *CTMM* is administered to *X* under standard conditions; then *X* has an IQ of *n*, if and only if, he gets a score of *n* (WQ).

Although this new formulation is easier to understand, it does not say quite the same thing as Form 4.2. To see this, consider the situation in which we are trying to make a judgment about an individual's IQ on the basis of his score on the *CTMM*. Using 4.3, we can conclude that *X* probably has an IQ of approximately *n*, where *n* is the score that we have. However, using 4.2, we cannot draw that conclusion without an auxiliary assumption: our conclusion that *X* has an IQ of approximately *n* depends on the *generalization* that *n* is the score he gets *whenever* he takes the test; it does not rest simply on his getting the score of *n* this time. To make this generalization, one would probably assume that the score we have is typical for him, an assumption we often make in dealing with test scores. Form 4.3 has this assumption built in, so we should not use 4.3 unless we are fairly confident that the scores on which we are basing our judgments are typical.

Neither formulation allows us to escape the problem of typicality. The problem is faced in applying 4.2 and in adopting 4.3. Since we shall want to adopt 4.3 without being completely committed to the belief that all the scores are typical, the word "probably" should be included among the qualifiers referred to by "(WQ)."

Forms 4.2 and 4.3 suffice for the majority of cases calling for an operational definition of a concept (or term). Why do they not suffice for all cases? The trouble is that they commit us to giving the same conditions as both necessary *and* sufficient for the use of the phrase containing the concept. For example, given the administration of the *CTMM* under standard conditions, a student's getting a score of *n* is roughly a necessary and sufficient condition for saying that probably his IQ is approximately *n*. That we sometimes want to avoid such a commitment can be seen in a situation that faced the staff of the Cornell Critical Thinking Project. The discussion will use 4.3 as a springboard, but with appropriate modifications I could say the same things starting from 4.2.

We built a test called *The Cornell Conditional Reasoning Test*, Form X. Among its seventy-two items are six that supposedly test for mastery of the principle that denial of the consequent implies denial of the antecedent; in other words, knowledge that the following form is valid:

p implies *q*	(*p* is the antecedent; *q* the consequent)
q is false	(denial of consequent)
therefore, *p* is false	(conclusion: denial of antecedent)

Here is one of the six items:

29. Suppose you know that

    If the bicycle in the garage is Bob's, then it is red.
    The bicycle in the garage is not red.

    Then would this be true?
    The bicycle in the garage is not Bob's.

A. YES	It must be true.
B. NO	It can't be true.
C. MAYBE	It may be true or it may not be true. You weren't told enough to be *certain* whether the answer is YES or NO.

The correct answer is YES.

The other five items embodying this principle vary in several ways: the valid conclusion is denied (making the answer NO); the content is abstract; the premises are reversed and the antecedent negated; the truth status of the conclusion is obviously different from the validity status of the argument. The six items are numbered 8, 16, 22, 29, 35, and 39.

Our problem, somewhat simplified, was how to give an operational definition of "mastery of the principle that denial of the consequent implies denial of the antecedent." One approach is to change the concept. As stated, it refers to a dichotomous variable, *mastery*, whereas we could shift to a continuous variable, *degree of mastery*, (IQ and *temperature* are continuous variables.) The revised question would be: "What is an operational definition of 'degree of mastery of the principle that denial of the consequent implies denial of the antecedent'?" We can answer that question with the following operational definition:

> Example 12: If *X* is given *The Cornell Conditional Reasoning Test*, Form X; then *X* has mastered to the degree *k* the principle that denial of the consequent implies denial of the antecedent, if and only if, he gets a score of *k* right on the following items: 8, 16, 22, 29, 35, and 39 (WQ).

Using this definition, we obtain a score that can vary from zero to six and that indicates *degree of mastery* of the principle. But this score has limitations. It means little to people who are not well acquainted with the test or with the scores of other individuals whose degree of mastery of this principle is known. Yet the audience for our results is likely to consist largely of such people.

Another drawback is that one of *our* interests is the determination of the per cent of students of a given description who have *mastered* the principle. This interest calls for the judgment that a particular student has or has not done so; it does not call for a judgment about his *degree* of knowledge. We need a definition that will fit our attempts to judge with some assurance whether a student has mastered this principle.

One might suppose that these difficulties could be handled by a definition that gave a certain minimum score as a necessary and sufficient condition for having mastered the principle. For example,

> Example 13: If *X* is given *The Cornell Conditional Reasoning Test*, Form X; then *X* has mastered the principle that denial of the consequent implies denial of the antecedent, if and only if, *X* answers correctly at least *four* of these items: 8, 16, 22, 29, 35, and 39 (WQ).

In this example, getting at least four items right is a rough necessary-and-sufficient condition for a person's knowing the principle (we assume that he takes the test). However, we do not want to be committed to any one minimum score as both necessary and sufficient; we do not want to draw that sharp a line between mastery and nonmastery. What we should like to say is something to the effect that getting at least *five* right is a probable sufficient condition and getting at least *four* right is a probable necessary condition. That is, we should like to say of a student who gets at least five right that he probably has mastered the principle and of a student who gets fewer than four right that he probably has not mastered it. About the students who get exactly four right, we are not sure what to say. They are borderline cases — and we should like a definition form that will allow us to leave them that way.

The following form permits us to present the sufficient condition:

> 4.4. If *OPx;* then, if *OBSx*, then *Tx* (WQ).[6]

The operational definition corresponding to this sufficient-condition form follows:

> Example 14: If *X* is given *The Cornell Conditional Reasoning Test*, Form X; then, if *X* answers correctly at least five of items 8, 16, 22, 29, 35, and 39, *X* has mastered the principle that denial of the consequent implies denial of the antecedent (WQ).

The following form permits us to present the necessary condition:

> 4.5. If *OPx;* then, *Tx*, only if *OBSx* (WQ).[7]

The operational definition corresponding to this necessary-condition form follows:

> Example 15: If *X* is given *The Cornell Conditional Reasoning Test*, Form X; then *X* has mastered the principle that denial of the consequent implies denial of the antecedent, *only* if *X* answers correctly at least four of these items: 8, 16, 22, 29, 35, and 39 (WQ).

To give an operational interpretation of the concept, *knowledge that denial of the consequent implies denial of the antecedent*, we supply both operational definitions, each of which provides a partial interpretation. Combined, they still do not provide a complete interpretation of the concept, but they give a basis on which to work and reason.

It is not necessary to agree with our *specific* decisions in the case above to see the need for Forms 4.4 and 4.5. That is, without contradicting my basic thesis, one can hold that answering correctly a minimum of *one* certain number of the items should be considered *both* necessary and sufficient, or one can hold that the number of items in the necessary condition should differ from that in the sufficient condition but that *four* and *five* are not the proper numbers. It is neces-

[6] The sufficient-condition form corresponding to 4.2 is: *Tx*; if; if *OPx*, then *OBSx* (WQ). This form, with the adjacent "if's," is harder to understand.

[7] The necessary-condition form corresponding to 4.2, which again is harder to understand, is: *Tx*; only if; if *OPx*, then *OBSx* (WQ).

sary only to see that these forms may sometimes be needed.

In summary, I recommend that operational definitions start with an if-clause that specifies an operation or a set of operations and that this clause be followed by an implication relationship between a phrase or sentence containing the concept (or term) to be defined and a phrase or sentence specifying an observation or a set of observations. Appropriate qualifications should be implicit or explicit.

Operational Interpretation Versus Operational Definition

Now that all these qualifications have been introduced, one may wonder if the result is a definition at all. It does not exhaust the meaning of a concept; it is loose; and a pair of operational definitions of the same concept sometimes implies an empirical fact. For example, the two definitions of *IQ* using the *CTMM* and the *Lorge-Thorndike* imply a high correlation between the tests; this is certainly an empirical matter. Some people regard the implication of empirical facts as a serious defect, for presumably definitions should give the meaning of concepts, not give facts.

Fortunately, the utility of the guides that I am proposing does not depend on the resolution of this difficult question. If one boggles at calling the examples I have given "operational definitions," call them "operational interpretations." In either case they help indicate the meaning of a concept, and they do so by focusing on concrete things, especially the manipulations of investigators. They help both to delimit and to fill in the meaning of a concept. What harm is there in calling them "definitions" so long as we remember that they differ from the classical type of definition, which provides expressions that are equivalent in meaning? Since their purpose and function is to indicate *meaning*, the most reasonable term for them, it seems to me, is "operational definitions." But I do not insist on this, for not much turns on the terminology.[8]

The Necessity for Deliberate Manipulation

Carl Hempel, among others, has suggested that a *deliberate manipulation* by an investigator is not really necessary for an operational definition — that all we need is some condition, whether it be a deliberate manipulation or not. He points out that although emphasis on deliberate operations "is of great interest for the practice of scientific research, . . . it is inessential in securing experimental import for the defined term" (Hempel, 1961; p. 59). It is true that a deliberate manipulation is not a necessary condition for experimental import, but there is an important distinction in discussions of the methodology of scientific research between those definitions that specify manipulations and those that specify other conditions.

If we were proceeding on the assumption that all terms must be operationally defined, Hempel's advice should be heeded because not all terms require manipulation by an experimenter as part of their interpretation (unless such activities as *looking* are regarded as manipulations, in which case operationism reduces to empiricism). Perhaps Hempel offered his advice in the context of an assumed recommendation that all terms be operationally definable. If one does not make that recommendation, one can preserve an independent meaning for the term "operationism," a meaning that emphasizes the manipulations of an investigator. In this case, a

[8] The philosopher would say that the sharp distinction between analytic and synthetic statements is blurred by using the term "definitions." The question is a difficult and subtle one, but I might note that the sharpness of this distinction in the area of empirical science has been questioned recently even in the writings of Carl Hempel, who says (1961, p. 66), "It . . . appears doubtful whether the distinction between analytic and synthetic sentences can be effectively maintained in a formal model of the language of empirical science." Keith Donnellan (1962) has provided a valuable discussion of this question.

recommendation that a term be defined operationally would imply that the definition should specify some bona fide manipulations by the research worker.

As with the case in which it was possible (but not preferable) to call examples "operational definitions," I recommend that we preserve the independent meaning of "operational definition" and that some other term, perhaps "conditional definition,"[9] be used to cover both operational definitions and definitions that are similar in form but contain a non-manipulative condition in the first if-clause. This approach will preserve the necessary distinctions without violating the original spirit of operationism as expressed by Bridgman and recognized for its value by many empirical scientists.

Summary

In this paper I have examined various forms for the operational definition of concepts, or terms, and have formulated the following set of guides:

A. Operational definitions should

1. start with an if-clause specifying the nature of the operation performable by the investigator.
2. contain an implication relationship that holds when a given operation has been performed. This relationship can be necessary (but not sufficient), sufficient (but not necessary), or both necessary and sufficient.
3. be convertible to the subjunctive mood if they are not already in the subjunctive.
4. not be taken to require a separate concept for each operational definition. Some concepts will have many operational definitions.
5. contain, either explicitly or implicitly, qualifying words or phrases like "approximately," "probably," and "under standard conditions."

B. Three useful forms for operational definitions follow:

Let: *Tx* represent a phrase or sentence containing the term (or concept) *T* being defined. For example, "*X* has an IQ of *n*," in which IQ is the concept.

OPx represent a phrase or sentence about the performance of an operation or a set of operations. For example, "*X* is (were) given the *CTMM*."

OBSx represent a phrase or sentence about an observation or a set of observations. For example, "*X*'s score is (will be, would be) *n*."

WQ indicate that certain qualifications like "approximately" and "probably" should be included in the definition.

Form 1. In which *OBSx* is a necessary and sufficient condition, given *OPx*:

If *OPx*; then *Tx*, if and only if, *OBSx* (WQ). (4.3)

Example: If *X* is given the *CTMM*; then *X* has an IQ of *n*, if and only if, *X*'s score is *n* (WQ).

Form 2. In which *OBSx* is a sufficient condition, given *OPx*: If *OPx*; then, if *OBSx*, then Tx (WQ). (4.4)

[9] Rudolph Carnap (1953) has suggested "reduction sentence," a term in widespread use among philosophers. Because this term is closely associated with truth-functional logic and suggests that abstract concepts are reduced to concrete terms without loss (this is not Carnap's intent), I prefer "conditional definition." This term is free from these connotations and indicates the conditional aspect of the definition.

Form 3. In which *OBSx* is a necessary condition, given *OPx*: If *OPx*; then *Tx*, only if *OBSx* (WQ). (4.5)

It was not claimed that all definitions in the empirical sciences should be operational. It was assumed that it is often a good idea to define concepts (or terms) operationally because the specific connections alleged between the concrete world and an abstract concept are important and because an especially important set of these connections involves the particular instruments and procedures used by the investigator.

References

BENJAMIN, A. Cornelius. *Operationism.* Springfield, Ill.: Charles C. Thomas, 1955, 154 pp.

BERGMANN, Gustav. "Sense and Nonsense in Operationism." *The Validation of Scientific Theories.* (Edited by Philipp G. Frank.) New York: Collier Books, 1961, pp. 46–56.

BERGMANN, Gustav, and SPENCE, Kenneth W. "Operationism and Theory Construction." *Psychological Theory.* (Edited by Melvin H. Marx.) New York: Macmillan Co., 1951, pp. 54–66.

BRIDGMAN, Percy W. *The Logic of Modern Physics.* New York: Macmillan Co., 1927. 228 pp.

BRIDGMAN, Percy W. "The Present State of Operationalism." *The Validation of Scientific Theories.* (Edited by Philipp G. Frank.) New York: Collier Books, 1961, pp. 75–80.

BRODBECK, May. "Logic and Scientific Method in Research on Teaching." *Handbook of Research on Teaching.* (Edited by Nathaniel L. Gage.) Chicago: Rand McNally and Co., 1963, pp. 44–93.

CARNAP, Rudolph. "Testability and Meaning." *Readings in the Philosophy of Science.* (Edited by Herbert Feigl and May Brodbeck.) New York: Appleton-Century-Crofts, 1953, pp. 47–92.

CHAPIN, F. Stuart. *Contemporary American Institutions.* New York: Harper and Brothers, 1935. 423 pp.

CHAPIN, F. Stuart. "Definition of Definitions of Concepts." *Social Forces* 18: 153–60; December 1939.

CHISHOLM, Roderick M. "The Contrary-to-Fact Conditional." *Readings in Philosophical Analysis.* (Edited by Herbert Feigl and Wilfrid Sellars.) New York: Appleton-Century-Crofts, 1949, pp. 482–97.

COOMBS, Clyde H. "Theory and Methods of Measurement." *Research Methods in the Behavioral Sciences.* (Edited by Leon Festinger and Daniel Katz.) New York: Dryden Press, 1953, pp. 471–535.

DODD, Stuart C. "Operational Definitions Operationally Defined." *American Journal of Sociology* 48: 482–89; January 1943.

DODD, Stuart C. "A System of Operationally Defined Concepts for Sociology." *American Sociological Review* 4: 619–34; October 1939.

DONNELLAN, Keith S. "Necessity and Criteria." *Journal of Philosophy* 59: 647–58; October 25, 1962.

FEIGL, Herbert. "Operationism and Scientific Method." *Readings in Philosophical Analysis.* (Edited by Herbert Feigl and Wilfrid Sellars.) New York: Appleton-Century-Crofts, 1949, pp. 498–509.

FRANK, Philipp G., editor. *The Validation of Scientific Theories.* New York: Collier Books, 1961. 220 pp.

GOODMAN, Nelson. "The Problem of Counterfactual Conditionals." *Semantics and the Philosophy of Language.* (Edited by Leonard Linsky.) Urbana, Ill.: University of Illinois Press, 1952, pp. 231–46.

GRÜNBAUM, Adolf. "Operationism and Relativity." *The Validation of Scientific Theories.* (Edited by Philipp G. Frank.) New York: Collier Books, 1961, pp. 83–92.

HEMPEL, Carl G. *Fundamentals of Concept Formation in Empirical Science.* International Encyclopedia of Unified Science, Vol. 2, No. 7. Chicago: University of Chicago Press, 1952. 93 pp.

HEMPEL, CARL G. "A Logical Appraisal of Operationism." *The Validation of Scientific Theories.* (Edited by Philipp G. Frank.) New York: Collier Books, 1961, pp. 56–69.

KOCH, Sigmund, editor. *Psychology: A Study of a Science*, Vol. 3. New York: McGraw-Hill Book Co., 1959. 837 pp.

LANGFELD, Herbert S., editor. "Symposium on Operationism." *Psychological Review* 52: 241–94; September 1945.

LAZARSFELD, Paul F. "Latent Structure Analysis." *Psychology: A Study of a Science*, Vol. 3. (Edited by Sigmund Koch.) New York: McGraw-Hill Book Co., 1959, pp. 476–543.

LUNDBERG, George A. "Operational Definitions in the Social Sciences." *American Journal of Sociology* 47: 727–43; March 1942a.

LUNDBERG, George A. *Social Research*. Second edition. London: Longmans, Green and Co., 1942b. 426 pp.

MARGENAU, Henry. "Interpretations and Misinterpretations of Operationalism." *The Validation of Scientific Theories*. (Edited by Philipp G. Frank.) New York: Collier Books, 1961, pp. 45–46.

MARX, Melvin H. "The General Nature of Theory Construction." *Psychological Theory*. (Edited by Melvin H. Marx.) New York: Macmillan Co., 1951, pp. 4–19.

SCHLESINGER, G. "P. W. Bridgman's Operational Analysis: The Differential Aspect." *British Journal for the Philosophy of Science* 9: 299–306; February 1959.

SJOBERG, Gideon. "Operationalism and Social Research." *Symposium on Sociological Theory*. (Edited by Llewellyn Gross.) Evanston, Ill.: Row Peterson and Co., 1959, pp. 603–27.

SKINNER, Burrhus F. "The Operational Analysis of Psychological Terms." *Readings in the Philosophy of Science*. (Edited by Herbert Feigl and May Brodbeck.) New York: Appleton-Century-Crofts, 1953, pp. 585–95.

STEVENS, S. Smith. "Psychology and the Science of Science." *Psychological Theory*. (Edited by Melvin H. Marx.) New York: Macmillan Co., 1951. pp. 21–54.

STRAWSON, Peter F. *Introduction to Logical Theory*. London: Methuen and Co., 1952. 266 pp.

VALOIS, A. John. *A Study of Operationism and Its Implications for Educational Psychology*. Washington, D. C.: Catholic University Press, 1960: 162 pp.

WILL, Frederick L. "The Contrary-to-Fact Conditional." *Mind* 56: 236–49; July 1947.

WRIGHT, George H. VON. *Logical Studies*. New York: Humanities Press, 1957. 195 pp.

Ideal Types in Social Science Comply with Covering Law Requirements 37

Typological Methods in the Social Sciences

CARL G. HEMPEL

Introduction

The concept of type has played a significant role in various phases of the development of empirical science. Many of its uses are by now of historical interest only; but some branches of research, especially psychology and the social sciences, have continued up to the present to employ typological concepts for descriptive and for theoretical purposes. In particular, various typologies of character and physique have been propounded as providing fruitful approaches to the study of personality; the investigation of "extreme" or "pure" types of physical and mental constitution has been advocated as a source of insight into the functioning of "normal" individuals; and as for social science, the use of ideal types has been declared one of the methodological characteristics which distinguish it essentially from natural science.

Considering these recent uses of typological concepts and the various claims concerning their peculiar significance, it appears to be a matter of some interest and importance to have a reasonably clear understanding of their logical status and their methodological function. Now, there exists a voluminous literature on the subject, but a large part of it suffers from a definite inadequacy of the logical apparatus used for the analysis of the issues at hand. In particular, many of the studies devoted to the logic of typological concepts use only the concepts and principles of classical logic, which is essentially a logic of properties or classes, and thus is incapable of dealing adequately with relations and with quantitative concepts. In a manner illustrative of this situation, Max Weber, who so impressively champions the method of ideal types in the social sciences, makes a clear negative statement about their logical status: they cannot be defined by *genus proximum* and *differentia specifica*, and concrete cases cannot be subsumed under them as instances[1] — i.e., they are not simply class, or property, concepts; but when it comes to a positive characterization, he resorts to much less precise, and often metaphorical, language. An ideal type, according to Weber, is a mental construct formed by the synthesis of many diffuse, more or less present and occasionally absent, concrete individual phenomena, which are arranged, according to certain one-sidedly accentuated points of view, into a unified analytical construct, which in its conceptual purity cannot be found in reality; it is a utopia, a limiting concept, with which concrete phenomena can only be compared for the purpose of explicating some of their significant components.[2] This characterization, and many similar accounts which Weber and others have given of the nature of ideal types, are certainly suggestive, but they lack clarity and rigor and thus call for further logical analysis.

From *Science, Language and Human Rights*, Vol. I, American Philosophical Association, Eastern Division, University of Pennsyvania Press, Philadelphia, 1952, pp. 65–86.

[1] M. Weber, " 'Objectivity' in Social Science and Social Policy," in this book, p. 399.*

[2] *Ibid.*, pp. 346–399.*

* [*Page references here are to Philosophy of the Social Sciences, edited by M. Natanson (New York: Random House, 1963). Editor's note.*]

In addition to the logical status of typological concepts, some of the methodological claims which have been made for them appear to me to warrant reëxamination.

The present paper, then, is an attempt to explicate in outline the logical and methodological character of typological concepts, and to appraise their potential significance for the purposes they are intended to serve. The proposed investigation will naturally have to use some of the concepts and principles of contemporary logic; but it will not employ any symbolic devices. Our explicatory efforts will repeatedly invite comparative glances at concept formation in the natural sciences. By thus undertaking a comparative examination of certain aspects of the methodology of natural and social science, I hope this study will justify its inclusion in the present symposium on the concept of theory in the social and the physical sciences.

It is a familiar fact that the term "type" has been used in several quite different senses. I propose to distinguish here three main kinds of type concepts, which for brief reference, and pending further clarification, will be called classificatory, extreme, and ideal types. These will now be considered in turn.

Classificatory Types

The classificatory use of type concepts is illustrated by Ernst Kretschmer's rather influential typological theory of character and physique,[3] in which types are construed as classes. In this case, the logic of typological procedure is the familiar logic of classification, which requires no discussion here. Methodologically, classificatory type formation, like any other kind of classification in empirical science, is subject to the requirement of systematic fruitfulness: The characteristics which serve to define the different types should not merely provide neat pigeonholes to accommodate all the individual cases in the domain of inquiry, but should lend themselves to sound generalization and thus offer a basis for prediction. Thus, e.g., constitutional typologies often aim at defining their types by reference to certain physical properties which are empirically associated with a variety of psychological traits, so that every type represents a cluster of concomitant characteristics. This objective is the methodological kernel of the search for "natural" as distinguished from "artificial" classes or types.

In connection with classificatory types, brief reference should be made to the use of the term "typical" in the sense of "average," for that usage evidently presupposes a classification. Thus, the statement that the typical American college undergraduate is, say, 18.9 years old, purports to state the average value of a certain magnitude for a specified class. But since there are different kinds of average, and since none of these provides much information without an added measure of dispersion, it is clear that for any serious scientific purpose this use of the term "typical" has to be supplanted by a more precise formulation in statistical terms.

Extreme Types

Attempts at typological classification in empirical science are often frustrated, however, by the realization that those characteristics of the subject matter which are to provide the defining basis of the classification cannot fruitfully be construed as simple property concepts determining, as their extensions, classes with neatly demarcated boundaries. Thus, e.g., if we try to formulate explicit and precise criteria for the distinction of extravert and introvert personalities it soon becomes clear that the adoption of classificatory criteria drawing a precise boundary

[3] E. Kretschmer, *Physique and Character*. On the theory and technique of classificatory type formation in contemporary social research, see P. F. Lazarsfeld and A. H. Barton, "Qualitative Measurement in the Social Sciences: Classification, Typologies, and Indices," in *The Policy Sciences*, ed. D. Lerner and H.D. Lasswell. [*Reprinted as selection 41 in this volume. Editor's note.*]

line between the two categories would prove an "artificial," theoretically sterile procedure: it appears much more natural, much more promising systematically, to construe the two concepts as capable of gradations, so that a given individual will not be qualified either as extravert or as introvert, but as exhibiting each of the two traits to a certain extent. The purely extravert and the purely introvert personalities thus come to be conceived as "extreme" or "pure" types, of which concrete instances are rarely if ever found, but which may serve as conceptual points of reference or "poles," between which all actual occurrences can be ordered in a serial array. This general conception underlies several of the recent and contemporary systems of psychological and physical types, such as, e.g., Sheldon's theory of physique and temperament.[4]

What is the logical form of these "extreme" or "pure" type concepts? Clearly, they cannot be construed as class concepts: individual cases cannot be subsumed under them as instances, but can only be characterized as to the extent to which they approximate them. In other words, if the term "*T*" represents an extreme type, an individual *a* cannot be said either to be *T* or to be non-*T*; rather, *a* may be, so to speak, "more or less *T*." But exactly how is this "more or less" to be objectively defined? A description, however vivid, of an extreme type with which concrete cases are to be compared does not by itself provide standards for such comparison; at best, it may suggest a program of research, focusing attention upon certain empirical phenomena and regularities and stimulating efforts toward the development of a precise conceptual apparatus suited for their description and theoretical interpretation. But if an extreme type is to function as a legitimate scientific concept in scientific statements with clear objective meaning, then explicit criteria for the "more or less" of comparison must be provided. These criteria may take a nonnumerical, "purely comparative" form, or they may be based on quantitative devices such as rating scales or measurement.

The formally simplest, purely comparative form of an extreme-type concept *T* can be specified by laying down criteria which determine, for any two individual cases *a*, *b* in the domain under investigation, whether (i) *a* is more *T* than *b*, or (ii) *b* is more *T* than *a*, or (iii) *a* is just as much *T* as is *b*. For the concept of pure introversion as an extreme type, for example, this would require objective criteria determining, for any two individuals *a*, *b* whether they are equally introverted and, if not, which of them is the more introverted. Thus, an extreme type *T* of the purely comparative or ordering kind is defined, not by *genus* and *differentia* in the manner of a class concept, but by specifying two dyadic relations, "more *T* than" and "as much *T* as." Now, if the criteria defining those relations are to yield an ordering of all particular cases in a linear array reflecting increasing *T*-ness, then they must meet certain formal requirements: "more *T* than" must be an asymmetrical and transitive relation, "as much *T* as" must be symmetrical and transitive, and the two together must satisfy a trichotomy law to the effect that any two particular cases *a*, *b* meet the defining conditions for exactly one of the three alternatives (i), (ii), (iii) mentioned above.[5]

The kind of ordering concept here characterized is well illustrated by the definition, in mineralogy, of a purely comparative concept of hardness by reference to the scratch test: A mineral *a* is said to be harder than another, *b*, if a sharp point of a sample of *a* will scratch the surface of a sample of *b*, but not conversely. If neither of the materials is harder than the other, they are said to be of the same hardness. The two relations thus defined might be said to determine a purely comparative extreme type of hardness; but this terminology would tend to obscure rather than clarify the logic of the procedure, and it is not actually used.

In psychology and the social sciences, it is

[4] W. H. Sheldon, *The Varieties of Human Physique;* and W. H. Sheldon, *The Varieties of Temperament.*

[5] For details, see: C. G. Hempel and P. Oppenheim, *Der Typusbegriff im Lichte der neuen Logik*, ch. 3.

difficult, to say the least, to find fruitful objective criteria, analogous to those based on the scratch test, which will determine a purely comparative typological order. We find therefore that proponents of extreme-type concepts, insofar as they provide precise criteria and not merely suggestive programmatic characterizations, either end by construing their types as classes after all or else specify their typological orders by reference to rating scales or measuring procedures, which define a numerical "degree of T-ness," as it were. The first course is illustrated by Kretschmer's typology of physique and character: it uses the parlance of pure types for an intuitive characterization of the material to be investigated, while for exact formulations, it construes each of the main types as a class and accommodates the intermediate cases in some additional classes, designated as "mixed types." The second course is exemplified by Sheldon's typology of physique, which assigns to each individual a specific position on each of three seven-point scales representing the basic type traits of the theory: endomorphy, mesomorphy, and ectomorphy.

But once suitable "operational" criteria of a strictly comparative or of a quantitative kind have been specified, the pure types lose their special importance: they simply represent extreme places in the ranges defined by the given criteria, and from a systematic point of view, the typological terminology is no more significant than it would be to say that the specific electric conductivity of a given material indicated how close it came to the extreme, or pure, type of a perfect conductor.

The use of extreme-type concepts of the kind here considered reflects an attempt to proceed from the classificatory, qualitative level of concept formation to the quantitative one; ordering concepts of the purely comparative kind representing an intermediate stage. As long as explicit criteria for their use are lacking, they have, as we noted, essentially a programmatic but no systematic status; and once suitable criteria have been specified, the parlance of extreme types becomes unnecessary, for there are no logical peculiarities which differentiate extreme-type concepts from the other comparative and quantitative concepts of empirical science; their logic is the logic of ordering relations and of measurement; henceforth, we will therefore refer to them also as ordering types.

Methodologically, ordering as well as classificatory typologies belong, as a rule, to an early stage in the growth of a scientific discipline, a stage which is concerned with the development of a largely "empirical" concept system and with its use for description and for low-grade generalization. Systematic fruitfulness, which is an essential requirement for all stages of concept formation, here consists, in the simplest case, in a high correlation between the criteria which "operationally define" a typological order (such as certain anthropometric indices, say) and a variety of other graded traits (such as further anatomical and physiological indices or psychological characteristics). For quantitative scales, such correlations may assume, in favorable cases, the form of a proportionality of several variables (analogous to the proportionality, at constant temperature, of the specific electric and thermic conductivities of metals), or they may consist in other invariant relationships expressible in terms of mathematical functions.[6]

Ideal Types and Explanation in the Social Sciences

As was mentioned in the first section, ideal types, too, are usually presented as the results of isolating and exaggerating certain aspects of concrete empirical phenomena, as limiting

[6] A fuller discussion of the logic and methodology of ordering and quantitative procedures may be found in C. G. Hempel, *Fundamentals of Concept Formation in Empirical Science*, especially Section 11.

On the use of such procedures in typological studies, cf. Lazarsfeld and Barton, *op. cit.*, Hempel and Oppenheim, *op. cit.*, and R. F. Winch, "Heuristic and Empirical Typologies: A Job for Factor Analysis," *American Sociological Review*, XII, 1947, 68–75.

concepts which are not fully exemplified but at best approximated in reality.[7] Despite the suggestion conveyed by this description, I think that an adequate logical reconstruction has to assign to ideal types a status different from that of the extreme or pure types discussed above. For ideal types — or, as Howard Becker aptly calls them, constructed types — are usually introduced without even an attempt at specifying appropriate criteria of order, and they are not used for the kind of generalization characteristic of ordering types; rather, they are invoked as a specific device for the explanation of social and historical phenomena. I shall try to argue now that this conception reflects an attempt to advance concept formation in sociology from the stage of description and "empirical generalization," which is exemplified by most classificatory and ordering types, to the construction of theoretical systems or models. In order to amplify and substantiate this view, it will be necessary to examine more closely the character and function of ideal types as conceived by its proponents.

According to Max Weber and some writers holding similar views, the use of ideal types makes it possible to explain concrete social or historical phenomena, such as the caste system in India or the development of modern capitalism, in their individuality and uniqueness. Such understanding is held to consist in grasping the particular causal relationships which interconnect the relevant elements of the total occurrence under examination. If such relationships are to afford a sociologically significant explanation they must be, according to this view, not only "causally adequate" but also meaningful, i.e., they must refer to aspects of human behavior which are intelligibly actuated by valuation or other motivating factors. Weber characterizes the principles expressing those connections as "general empirical rules" concerning the ways in which human beings are prone to react in given situations; the "nomological knowledge" conveyed by them is said to be derived from our own experience and from our knowledge of the conduct of others. Weber mentions Gresham's law as a generalization of this kind: it is empirically well substantiated by the pertinent information available, and it is "a rationally clear interpretation of human action under certain conditions and under the assumption that it will follow a purely rational course."[8]

As for specific ways of discovering meaningful explanatory principles, Weber mentions the method of empathic understanding but adds the reminder that it is neither universally applicable nor always dependable. And indeed, as is made clear by the fuller argument presented in Professor Nagel's paper,[9] the subjective experience of empathic identification with a historical figure, and of an immediate — almost self-evidently certain — insight into his motivations, constitutes no knowledge, no scientific understanding at all, though it may be a guide in the search for explicit general hypotheses of the kind required for a systematic explanation. In fact, the occurrence of an empathic state in the interpreter is neither a necessary nor a sufficient condition of sound interpretation or understanding in the scientific sense: not necessary, for, as Professor Nagel's illustration shows, an appropriate theory of psychopathic behavior may provide the his-

[7] For detailed exposition and critical discussion of the concept of ideal type as used in social science, see especially the following works, which have served as guides in the present attempt at analysis and reconstruction: M. Weber, *On the Methodology of the Social Sciences*. M. Weber, *The Theory of Social and Economic Organization*. A. von Schelting, *Max Weber's Wissenschaftslehre*. T. Parsons, *The Structure of Social Action*, ch. 16. H. Becker, *Through Values to Social Interpretation*.

Further stimulating critical discussions of the concept of ideal type may be found in: F. Kaufmann, *Methodenlehre der Sozialwissenschaften*, especially Section 6 of the second part. J. W. N. Watkins, "Ideal Types and Historical Explanation," *The British Journal for the Philosophy of Science*, III, 1952, 22–43. [*Watkins' article is reprinted as selection 38 in this volume. Editor's note.*]

[8] *The Theory of Social and Economic Organization*, p. 98; cf. also pp. 107–109.

[9] [*Hempel refers here to Ernest Nagel's essay "Problems of Concept and Theory Formation in the Social Sciences," which originally appeared in Science, Language, and Human Rights (American Philosophical Association, Eastern Division, Philadelphia: University of Pennsylvania Press, 1952, Vol. I, pp. 43–64). Editor's note.*]

torian with an explanation of some phases of Hitler's actions even in the absence of empathic identification; not sufficient, for the motivational hypotheses suggested by the empathic experience may be factually unsound.

Weber himself stresses that verification of subjective interpretation is always indispensable; he adds that in the absence of adequate experimental or observational data, "there is available only the dangerous and uncertain procedure of the 'imaginary experiment' which consists in thinking away certain elements of a chain of motivation and working out the course of action which would then probably ensue, thus arriving at a causal judgment."[10] By thus establishing what *would* have happened *if* certain specified constituents of the situation had been different, this method yields "judgments of objective possibility," which form the basis of causal imputation in the social sciences. Those judgments evidently have the form of contrary-to-fact conditionals, and students of the currently much discussed logic of counterfactuals might be interested in Weber's fascinating illustration of the proposed method by reference to interpretive problems of historiography, among them the question of the significance of the Persian Wars for the development of Western culture;[11] Weber's discussion of these topics shows how well he was aware of the close connection between contrary-to-fact conditionals and general laws.

An ideal type, then, is meant to serve as an interpretive or explanatory schema embodying a set of "general empirical rules" which establish "subjectively meaningful" connections between different aspects of some kind of phenomenon, such as purely rational economic behavior, a capitalistic society, a handicraft economy, a religious sect, or the like. But then, in intent at least, ideal types represent not concepts properly speaking, but rather theories; and the idea naturally suggests itself that if those theories are to serve their purpose, they must have a character quite similar to that of the theory of ideal gases, say.[12] To elaborate and substantiate this conception, I will first try to show that the alleged differences between the explanatory use of ideal types and the method of explanation in natural science are spurious; then (in section 5) I will attempt a brief comparative analysis of the status of "idealized" concepts, and the corresponding theories, in natural and social science.

In natural science, to explain a concrete event means to explain the occurrence of some repeatable characteristic (a rise in temperature, the presence of corrosion, a drop in blood pressure, etc.) in a particular, i.e., at a specified place or in a specified object at a given moment or during a certain period of time (the air in New Haven during the morning hours of September 5, 1952, the hull of a specified ship, patient John Doe at a given time). Explanation of a concrete event does not and cannot reasonably mean an account of *all* the repeatable characteristics of a given particular, say *b*. For the latter include the fact that in such and such directions and at such and such spatiotemporal distances from *b*, there are particulars having such and such repeatable properties; as a consequence, to explain *all* the repeatable aspects of *b* is tantamount to explaining every concrete fact in the universe — past, present, and future. Evidently this kind of explaining a concrete occurrence "in its uniqueness" is no more accessible to sociology than it is to physics; in fact, even its precise *meaning* is quite problematic. Thus, all that can be significantly sought is the explanation of the occurrence of some repeatable charac-

[10] *Ibid.*, p. 97.

[11] *The Methodology of the Social Sciences*, pp. 164–188. An illuminating amplification and examination of Weber's analysis may be found in von Schelting, *op. cit.*, pp. 269–281.

[12] Parallels between ideal types and certain idealizations in physics have often been drawn, of course (cf., e.g., Weber, *The Theory of Social and Economic Organization*, p. 110; Becker, *op. cit.*, p. 125). It seems important, however, to make explicit the similarities involved and to show that they do not accord with the claim of a status *sui generis* for ideal-type concepts in the social sciences.

teristic U (which may be quite complex, of course) in a given particular b. The task of explaining Western capitalism in its uniqueness, for example, has to be construed in this fashion if it is to be at all significant; and it is then strictly analogous to the problem of explaining the solar eclipse of March 18, 1950. In either case, there are certain characteristics — their combination is referred to as U above — for whose occurrence an explanation is sought (in the case of the eclipse, e.g., those characteristics might include the fact that the eclipse was annular, not visible in the United States, of a duration of 4 hours and 42 minutes, etc.), but there are innumerable other characteristics for which no account is intended (such as, say, the number of newspapers in which the event was described). It is worth noting here that the event thus to be explained, $U(b)$ for short, is still unique because the particular b is unrepeatable.

In natural science, to explain a unique concrete event, say $U(b)$, amounts to showing that it had to be expected in view of certain other concrete events which are prior to or contemporaneous with it, and by virtue of specifiable general laws or theories. Formally, such explanation consists in the deduction of "$U(b)$" from those general principles and from the "boundary conditions" describing the antecedent and contemporaneous concrete occurrences.

As Max Weber's writings clearly show, an adequate explanation of a concrete event in sociology or historiography has to be of essentially the same character. Reliance on empathic insight and subjective "understanding" provides no warrant of objective validity, no basis for the systematic prediction or postdiction of specific phenomena; the latter procedures have to be based on general empirical rules, on nomological knowledge. Weber's limitation of the explanatory principles of sociology to "meaningful" rules of intelligible behavior, on the other hand, is untenable: many, if not all, occurrences of interest to the social scientist require, for their explanation, reference to factors which are "devoid of subjective meaning," and accordingly also to "non-understandable uniformities," to use Weber's terminology. Weber acknowledges that the sociologist must accept such facts as causally significant data, but he insists that this does "not in the least alter the specific task of sociological analysis . . . , which is the interpretation of action in terms of its subjective meaning."[13] But this conception bars from the field of sociology any theory of behavior which foregoes the use of "subjectively meaningful" motivational concepts. This either means a capricious limitation of the concept of sociology — which, as a result, might eventually become inapplicable to any phase of scientific research — or else it amounts to an *a priori* judgment on the character of any set of concepts which can possibly yield explanatory sociological theories. Clearly, such an *a priori* verdict is indefensible, and indeed, the more recent development of psychological and social theory shows that it is possible to formulate explanatory principles for purposive action in purely behavioristic, non-introspective terms.

In discussing, next, the role of experiments-in-imagination, which are, of course, well known also in the natural sciences, it will be useful to distinguish *two kinds of imaginary experiment: the intuitive and the theoretical*. An intuitive experiment-in-imagination is aimed at anticipating the outcome of an experimental procedure which is just imagined, but which may well be capable of being actually performed. Prediction is guided here by past experience concerning particular phenomena and their regularities, and occasionally by belief in certain general principles which are accepted as if they were *a priori* truths; thus, e.g., in "explaining" the equidistribution of results obtained in rolling a regular die, or in anticipating similar results for a game with a regular homogeneous dodecahedron, certain rules of symmetry, such as the principle of insufficient reason, are often invoked; and similar principles

[13] *The Theory of Social and Economic Organization*, p. 94.

are sometimes adduced in imaginary experiments involving levers and other physical systems with certain symmetry features. Imaginary experiments of this kind are intuitive in the sense that the assumptions and data underlying the prediction are not made explicit and indeed may not even enter into the conscious process of anticipation at all: past experience and the — possibly unconscious — belief in certain general principles function here as suggestive guides for imaginative anticipation rather than as a theoretical basis for systematic prediction.

The theoretical kind of imaginary experiment, on the other hand, presupposes a set of explicitly stated general principles — such as laws of nature — and it anticipates the outcome of the experiment by strict deduction from those principles in combination with suitable boundary conditions representing the relevant aspects of the experimental situation. Sometimes, the latter is not actually realizable, as when the laws for an ideal mathematical pendulum or for perfectly elastic impact are deduced from more general principles of theoretical mechanics. The question what *would* happen *if*, say, the thread of a pendulum were infinitely thin and perfectly rigid and if the mass of the pendulum were concentrated in the free end point of the thread is answered here, not by "thinking away" those aspects of a physical pendulum that are at variance with this assumption and then trying to envisage the outcome, but by rigorous deduction from available theoretical principles. Imagination does not enter here; the experiment is imaginary only in the sense that the situation it refers to is not actually realized and may indeed be technically incapable of realization.

The two types of experiment-in-imagination here distinguished constitute extreme types, as it were, which are rarely realized in their pure form: in many cases, the empirical assumptions and the reasoning underlying an imaginary experiment are made highly, but not fully, explicit. Galileo's dialogues contain excellent examples of this procedure, which show how fruitful the method can be in suggesting general theoretical insights. But, of course, intuitive experiments-in-imagination are no substitute for the collection of empirical data by actual experimental or observational procedures. This is well illustrated by the numerous, intuitively quite plausible, imaginary experiments which have been adduced in an effort to refute the special theory of relativity; and as for imaginary experimentation in the social sciences, its customary reliance on empathy underscores its fallibility. Professor Nagel's example of an attempt to anticipate the behavior of a trader in grain provides a good illustration of this kind of mental experimentation. Thus, the results of intuitive experiments-in-imagination cannot strictly constitute evidence pertinent to the test of sociological hypotheses; rather, the method has an essentially heuristic function: it serves to *suggest* hypotheses, which must then be subjected, however, to appropriate objective testing procedures.

The imaginary experiments mentioned by such writers as Max Weber and Howard Becker as a method of sociological inquiry are obviously of the intuitive variety; their heuristic function is to aid in the discovery of regular connections between various constituents of some social structure or process. These connections can then be incorporated into an ideal type and thus provide the basis for the explanatory use of the latter.

Ideal Types and Theoretical Models

We have argued that since ideal types are intended to provide explanation, they must be construed as theoretical systems embodying testable general hypotheses. To what extent is this conception reconcilable with the frequent insistence, on the part of proponents of the method, that ideal types are not meant to be hypotheses to be verified by empirical evidence, that deviation from concrete fact is of their very essence? As a point of departure in dealing with this question, let us consider more closely how those who hold such views conceive of the application of ideal-type concepts to concrete phenomena. There are few precise statements on this subject; perhaps the most explicit formulation has been given by Howard Becker, in an effort to develop what he terms "a logical formula for typology." Becker suggests that ideal, or constructed, types function in hypotheses of the form "If *P* then *Q*," where *P* is the type invoked, and *Q* is some more or less complex characteristic.[14] Concerning the application of such hypotheses to empirical data, Becker says: "In the very nature of type construction, however, the consequent seldom if ever follows empirically, and the antecedent is then empirically 'false.' If *Q′* then *P′*."[15] By this deviation from empirical fact, by the occurrence of *Q′* rather than *Q*, a constructed type acquires what Becker calls "negative utility": it initiates a search for factors other than those embodied in *P* to account for the discrepancy.[16] In this manner, according to Becker, "constructive typology makes *planned* use of the priviso 'All other conditions being equal or irrelevant' for the purpose of determining the 'inequality' or 'relevance' of the 'other conditions.'"[17]

This view calls for closer analysis, for it suggests — perhaps unintentionally — the use of the *ceteris paribus* clause for a conventionalistic defense of typological hypotheses against any conceivable disconfirming evidence.[18] To illustrate this point, let us imagine, by way of analogy, a physicist propounding the hypothesis that under ideal conditions, namely in a vacuum near the surface of the Earth, a body falling freely for t seconds will cover a distance of exactly $16t^2$ feet. Suppose now that a careful experiment yields results differing from those required by the hypothesis. Then clearly the physicist cannot be content simply to infer that the requisite ideal conditions were not realized: in addition to this possibility, he has to allow for the alternative that the hypothesis under test is not correct. To state the point now in terms of Becker's general schema: we could infer that *P* is not realized only if, in addition to the observational finding *Q′*, we could take the truth of the hypothesis "If *P* then *Q*" for granted; but for this assumption, we surely have no warrant; in fact, it would make the entire test pointless. Thus, from the occurrence of *Q′*, we can infer only that either *P* was not realized or the hypothesis, "If *P* then *Q*," is false.

Now, it might seem that we may with assurance assert our typological hypothesis if only we qualify it by an appropriate *ceteris paribus* clause and thus give it the form: "All other factors being equal or irrelevant, *Q* will be realized whenever *P* is realized." Evidently, no empirical evidence can ever disconfirm a hypothesis of this form since an apparently unfavorable finding can always be attributed to a violation of the *ceteris paribus* clause by the interference of factors other than those specifically included in *P*. In other words, the qualified hypothesis can be made unexceptionable by the convention to plead violation of the *ceteris paribus* clause whenever an occurrence of *P* is not accompanied by an occurrence of *Q*. But the very convention that renders the hypothesis irrefutable also drains it of all empirical content and thus of explanatory power: since the protective clause does not specify *what* factors other than *P* have to be equal (i.e., constant)

[14] *Op. cit.*, pp. 259–264. Becker describes the connection between *P* and *Q* as one of "objective probability." But since he uses the expression "If *P* then *Q*" in an inference of the *modus tollens* form, which does not hold for probabilistic implication — i.e., for statements of the form, "If *P* then probably *Q*" — it seems more adequate to construe Becker's remark as meaning that "If *P* then *Q*" is a typological hypothesis expressing an empirical generalization in Weber's sense. Such a generalization, like any other empirical hypothesis, can of course be only probable, and never certain, relatively to any body of pertinent factual evidence.

[15] *Op. cit.*, p. 262.

[16] M. Weber has similarly pointed to the heuristic utility of ideal types; cf. e.g., "'Objectivity' in Social Science and Social Policy," in this book, pp. 396, 407–409,* *The Theory of Social and Economic Organization*, p. 111.

[17] H. Becker, *op. cit.*, p. 264.

[18] On the use of the *ceteris paribus* clause, see also the excellent discussion in F. Kaufmann, *Methodology of the Social Sciences*, pp. 84f, 213f.

* [See editor's note, page 445 above.]

or irrelevant if the prediction of *Q* is to be warranted, the hypothesis is not capable of predictive application to concrete phenomena. Similarly, the idea of testing the given hypothesis becomes pointless. It is significant to note here by contrast that in the formulation of physical hypotheses, the *ceteris paribus* clause is never used: all the factors considered relevant are explicitly stated (as in Newton's law of gravitation or in Maxwell's laws) or are clearly understood (as in the familiar formulation of Galileo's law, which is understood to refer to free fall in a vacuum near the surface of the Earth); all other factors are asserted, by implication, to be irrelevant. Empirical test is therefore significant, and the discovery of discordant evidence requires appropriate revisions either by modifying the presumed functional connections between the variables singled out as relevant, or by explicitly introducing new relevant variables. Ideal-type hypotheses will have to follow the same pattern if they are to afford a theoretical explanation of concrete historical and social phenomena rather than an empirically vacuous conceptual schematism.

But is it not true, after all, that in physics as well, there are theories, such as those of ideal gases, of perfectly elastic impact, of the mathematical pendulum, of the statistical aspects of a game played with perfect dice, etc., which are not held to be invalidated by the fact that they possess no precise exemplification in the empirical world? And could not ideal types claim the same status as the central concepts of those "idealized" theories? Those concepts refer to physical systems satisfying certain extreme conditions which cannot be fully, but only approximately, met by concrete empirical phenomena. Their scientific significance lies, I think, in the following points: (a) The laws governing the behavior of the ideal physical systems are deducible from more comprehensive theoretical principles, which are well confirmed by empirical evidence; the deduction usually takes the form of assigning certain extreme values to some of the parameters of the comprehensive theory. Thus, e.g., the laws for an ideal gas are obtainable from more inclusive principles of the kinetic theory of gases by "assuming" that the volumes of the gas molecules vanish and that there are no forces of attraction among the molecules — i.e., by setting the appropriate parameters equal to zero. (b) The extreme conditions characterizing the "ideal" case can at least be approximated empirically, and whenever this is the case in a concrete instance, the ideal laws in question are empirically confirmed. Thus, e.g., the Boyle-Charles law for ideal gases is rather closely satisfied by a large variety of gases within wide, specifiable ranges of pressure and temperature (for a fixed mass of gas), and it is for this reason that the law can be significantly invoked for explanatory purposes.

The preceding analysis suggests the following observations on the "ideal" and the empirical aspects of ideal-type concepts in the social sciences:

(i) "Ideal" constructs have the character not of concepts in the narrower sense, but of theoretical systems. The introduction of such a construct into a theoretical context requires, therefore, not definition by *genus* and *differentia*, but the specification of a set of characteristics (such as pressure, temperature, and volume in the case of an ideal gas) *and* of a set of general hypotheses connecting those characteristics.

(ii) An idealized concept *P* does *not*, therefore, function in hypotheses of the simple form "If *P* then *Q*." Thus, e.g., the hypothesis "If a substance is an ideal gas then it satisfies Boyle's law," which is of that form, is an analytic statement entailed by the definition of an ideal gas; it cannot serve explanatory purposes. Rather, the hypotheses characterizing the concept of ideal gas connect certain quantitative characteristics of a gas, and when they are applied to concrete physical systems, they make specific empirical predictions. Thus, to put the point in a somewhat oversimplified form, what enters into physical theory is not the concept of ideal gas at all, but rather the concepts representing the various characteristics dealt with in the theory of ideal gases; only they are mentioned in the principles of thermodynamics.

(iii) In the natural sciences at least, a set of hypotheses is considered as characterizing an ideal system only if they represent what might be called *theoretical*, rather than *intuitive*, idealizations; i.e., if they are obtainable, within the framework of a given theory, as special cases of more inclusive principles. Thus, e.g., the formula for the mathematical pendulum as empirically discovered by Galileo did not constitute a theoretical idealization until after the establishment of more comprehensive hypotheses which (a) have independent empirical confirmation, (b) entail the pendulum formula as a special case, (c) enable us to judge the degree of idealization involved in the latter by giving an account of additional factors which are relevant for the motion of a physical pendulum, but whose influence is fairly small in the case of those physical systems to which the formula is customarily applied.

No theory, of course, however inclusive, can claim to give a completely accurate account of any class of empirical phenomena; it is always possible that even a very comprehensive and well-confirmed theory may be improved in the future by the inclusion of further parameters and appropriate laws: the most comprehensive theory of today may be but a systematic idealization within the broader theoretical framework of tomorrow.

Among the ideal-type concepts of social theory, those used in analytical economics approximate most closely the status of idealizations in natural science: the concepts of perfectly free competition, of monopoly, of economically rational behavior on the part of an individual or a firm, etc., all represent schemata for the interpretation of certain aspects of human behavior and involve the idealizing assumption that noneconomic factors of the sort that do in fact influence human actions may be neglected for the purposes at hand. In the context of rigorous theory construction, those ideal constructs are given a precise meaning in the form of hypotheses which "postulate" specified mathematical connections between certain economic variables; frequently, such postulates characterize the ideal type of behavior as maximizing a given function of those variables (say, profit).

In two important respects, however, idealizations in economics seem to me to differ from those of the natural sciences: first of all, they are intuitive rather than theoretical idealizations in the sense that the corresponding "postulates" are not deduced, as special cases, from a broader theory which covers also the nonrational and noneconomic factors affecting human conduct. No suitable more general theory is available at present, and thus there is no theoretical basis for an appraisal of the idealization involved in applying the economic constructs to concrete situations. This takes us to the second point of difference: the class of concrete behavioral phenomena for which the "idealized" principles of economic theory are meant to constitute at least approximately correct generalizations is not always clearly specified. This of course hampers the significant explanatory use of those principles: an ideal theoretical system, as indeed any theoretical system at all, can assume the status of an explanatory and predictive apparatus only if its area of application has been specified; in other words, if its constituent concepts have been given an empirical interpretation which, directly or at least mediately, links them to observable phenomena. Thus, e.g., the area of application for the theory of ideal gases might be indicated, roughly speaking, by interpreting the theoretical parameters "P," "V," "T" in terms of the "operationally defined" magnitudes of pressure, volume, and temperature of gases at moderate or low pressures and at moderate or high temperatures. Similarly, the empirical applicability of the principles of an ideal economic system requires an interpretation in empirical terms which does not render those principles analytic; hence the interpretation must not amount to the statement that the propositions of the theory hold in all cases of economically rational behavior — that would be simply a tautology; rather, it has to characterize, by criteria logically independent of the theory, those kinds of individual or group behavior to which the theory is claimed to be applicable. In reference to these, it has then to attach a reasonably definite "operational meaning" to the theoretical parameters, such as "money," "price," "cost," "profit," "utility," etc. In this fashion, the propositions of the theory acquire empirical import: they become capable of test and thus susceptible to disconfirmation — and this is an essential characteristic of all potential explanatory systems.

The results of the preceding comparison between the ideal constructs of economics with those of physics should not be considered, however, as indicating an essential methodological difference between the two fields. For in regard to the first of our two points of comparison, it need only be remembered that much effort in sociological theorizing at present is directed toward the development of a comprehensive theory of social action, relatively to which the ideal constructs of economics, in so far as they permit of empirical application, might then have the status of theoretical rather than intuitive idealizations. And quite apart from the attainability of that ambitious goal, it is clear that an interpretation is required for any theoretical system which is to have empirical import — in the social no less than in the natural sciences.

The ideal types invoked in other fields of social science lack the clarity and precision of the constructions used in theoretical economics. The behavioral regularities which are meant to define a given ideal type are usually stated only in more or less intuitive terms, and the parameters they are meant to connect are not explicitly specified; finally, there is no clear indication of the area of empirical applicability and consequent testability claimed for the typological system. In fact, the demand for such testability is often rejected in a sweeping manner which, I think, the preceding discussion has shown to be inconsistent with the claim that ideal types provide an understanding of certain empirical phenomena.

If the analysis here outlined is essentially sound, then surely ideal types can serve their purpose only if they are introduced as interpreted theoretical systems, i.e., by (a) specifying a list of characteristics with which the theory is to deal, (b) formulating a set of hypotheses in terms of those characteristics, (c) giving those characteristics an empirical interpretation, which assigns to the theory a specific domain of application, and (d), as a long-range objective, incorporating the theoretical system, as a "special case," into a more comprehensive theory. To what extent these objectives can be attained cannot be decided by logical analysis; but it would be self-deception to believe that any conceptual procedure essentially lacking in the first three respects can give theoretical understanding in any field of scientific inquiry. And to the extent that the program here outlined can actually be carried through, the use of "ideal types" is at best an unimportant terminological aspect, rather than a distinctive methodological characteristic, of the social sciences: the method of ideal types becomes indistinguishable from the methods used by other scientific disciplines in the formation and application of explanatory concepts and theories.

Conclusion

In sum, then, the various uses of type concepts in psychology and the social sciences, when freed from certain misleading connotations, prove to be of exactly the same character as the methods of classification, ordering, measurement, empirical correlation, and finally theory formation used in the natural sciences. In leading to this result, the analysis of typological procedures exhibits, in a characteristic example, the methodological unity of empirical science.

Methodological Individualism and Non-Hempelian Ideal Types

38

Ideal Types and Historical Explanation

J. W. N. WATKINS

Introduction

In this paper I shall consider: first, what sort of creatures ideal types should be if they are to be used in the construction of social theories; and secondly, what we do when we try to explain historical events by applying such theories to them.[1]

Holistic and Individualistic Ideal Types

It is only decent to begin a discussion of ideal types by considering Weber's views; but he held two successive conceptions of what an ideal type should be and do, without, I think, realising what important differences lay between them.

His earlier version is set out in an article translated under the title ' "Objectivity" in Social Science and Social Policy.' [2] At this time (1904) Weber believed that the social scientist should not try to imitate the natural scientist's procedure of systematically subsuming observation-statements and low order theories under more comprehensive laws. The social scientist should first decide from what point of view to approach history. Having decided, say, to treat its economic aspect, he should then select from this some unique configuration of activities and institutions, such as 'the rise of capitalism.' Then he should pin down and describe its components. His final task is to draw in the causal lines between these components, imputing 'concrete effects to concrete causes.'[3]

Reprinted from Feigl and Brodbeck's (eds.) *Readings in the Philosophy of Science*, by permission of the author and publisher, Appleton-Century-Crofts, © 1953, pp. 723–743.

Revised and expanded version of a paper that originally appeared in *The British Journal for the Philosophy of Science*, 3, 1952. Reprinted by kind permission of the author and the editor.

[1] It has been established by Professor K. R. Popper that the formal structure of a prediction is the same as that of a full-fledged explanation. In both cases we have: (*a*) initial conditions; (*b*) universal statements; and (*c*) deductive consequences of (*a*) plus (*b*). We explain a given event (*c*) by detecting (*a*) and by postulating and applying (*b*); and we predict a future event (*c*) by inferring it from some given (*a*) and postulated (*b*). Nevertheless, I think that in social science explanation and prediction should be considered separately, for two reasons. First, as Professor C. G. Hempel has pointed out in a most illuminating discussion of this problem (see his 'The Function of General Laws in History' in *Readings in Philosophical Analysis*, ed. H. Feigl and W. Sellars, New York, 1949, pp. 462–5) in history we often have to be content (and in fact *are* content) with what he calls an explanation *sketch*, i.e., a somewhat vague and incomplete indication of (*a*) and (*b*) from which (*c*) is not *strictly* deducible. And if we go back to a time when (*a*) but not (*c*) has occurred, this partial sketch of (*a*) and (*b*) will not allow us to predict (*c*). For example, we may be satisfied by the explanation that Smith insulted Jones because Jones had angered him, although we should *not* be prepared to admit that if Jones angers Smith in the future, Smith will necessarily react by insulting Jones.

Secondly, even the social scientist who can provide a *full-fledged* explanation of a past event will run into difficulties if he tries to predict similar events, because they will occur in a system which is not isolated from the influence of factors which he cannot ascertain beforehand. The Astronomer Royal can prepare a Nautical Almanac for 1953 because he is predicting the movements of bodies in a system isolated from extraneous influences, but the Chancellor of the Exchequer cannot prepare an Economic Almanac for 1953 because, even if he possessed sufficient knowledge to explain completely the 1951 levels of prices, production, investment, exports, etc., his predictions of future levels would undoubtedly be upset by unforeseeable, world-wide disturbing factors, the effects of any of which might be cumulative.

Hence, the problem of social prediction raises questions not raised by the problem of historical explanation; and this paper is not concerned with the former.

[2] Max Weber, *The Methodology of the Social Sciences*, trans. and ed. E. A. Shils and H. A. Finch, Illinois, 1949, ch. 2.

[3] *Op. cit.*, p. 79.

This programme could never be carried out; 'in any actual economic system so many factors are at work simultaneously that the effect of a single factor by itself can never be known, for its traces are soon lost sight of.'[4] And separate facts cannot be linked together as causes and effects with no reference to general laws. However, I will not press these criticisms of a methodological position which Weber tacitly abandoned later.

To assist the social scientist in this task of explaining particular events by relating them to their particular antecedents, Weber proposed his first version of the ideal type. This was to be constructed by abstracting the outstanding features from some (more or less clearly demarcated) historical complex, and by organising these into a coherent word-picture. The ideality of such a type lies in its simplification and aloofness from detail: it will be free from the detailed complexity of the actuality to be analysed with its aid. As this kind of ideal type emphasises the 'essential' traits of a situation considered *as a whole*, I call it 'holistic,' in contrast with the 'individualistic' ideal type described by Weber in Part I of his posthumous *Wirtschaft und Gesellschaft*.[5]

In this work he held that the social scientist's first task was to build up a generally applicable theoretical system; and for arriving at this he proposed the use of ideal types similar to the models used in deductive economics. These are constructed, not by withdrawing from the detail of social life, but by formalising the results of a close analysis of some of its significant details considered in isolation. The holistic ideal type was supposed to give a bird's eye view of the broad characteristics of a whole social situation, whereas the individualistic ideal type is constructed by inspecting the situations of actual individuals, and by abstracting from these: (*a*) general schemes of personal preferences; (*b*) the different kinds of knowledge of his own situation which the individual may possess; and (*c*) various typical relationships between individuals and between the individual and his resources. An individualistic ideal type places hypothetical actors in some simplified situation. Its premisses are: the form (but not the specific content) of the actors' dispositions, the state of their information, and their relationships. And the deductive consequences of these premisses demonstrate some principle of social behaviour, e.g. oligopolistic behavior. The ideality of *this* kind of ideal type lies: (i) in the simplification of the initial situation and in its isolation from disturbing factors; (ii) in the abstract and formal, and yet explicit and precise character of the actors' schemes of preferences and states of information; and (iii) in the actors' rational behaviour in the light of (ii). It is not claimed that a principle of social behaviour demonstrated by an individualistic ideal type will often have an exact empirical counterpart (though the principle of perfect competition has been precisely manifested, for instance in commodity-markets). But economists do claim that there is a limited number of basic economic principles, and that any economic phenomenon is a particular configuration of some of these, occurring at a particular place and time, which can be explained by a synthesis of the relevant ideal types, and by specifying the content of their formal premisses.[6]

[4] Walter Eucken, *The Foundations of Economics*, trans. T. W. Hutchison, London, 1950, p. 39.

[5] Translated by A. R. Henderson and Talcott Parsons as *The Theory of Social and Economic Organisation*, introd. by Talcott Parsons, London, 1947.

[6] 'This morphological study of economic history reveals a *limited* number of pure forms out of which *all* economic systems past and present are made up.' Eucken, *op. cit.*, p. 10 (my italics). The 'de-idealisation' of the pure principles of economic theory which occurs when they are combined into a particular configuration which is applied to an empirical counterpart, is exactly paralleled in the natural sciences. For example, Galileo combined the Law of Inertia (which describes the motion of a body not acted upon by any force — a condition which can never be realised), and the Law of Gravity (which describes the motion of a body in a vacuum which the experimenter cannot obtain), and the principles of air resistance, into a theoretical configuration which allows complete prediction of the trajectories of e.g. cannonballs, if the initial conditions are known. 'All universal physical concepts and laws . . . are arrived at by idealisation. They thereby assume that simple . . . form which makes it possible to reconstruct any facts, however complicated, by synthetic combination of these concepts and laws, thus making it possible to understand them.' (Ernst Mach, quoted by F. Kaufmann, *Methodology of the Social Sciences*, New York, 1944, p. 87.)

Weber was no Platonist; he proposed both kinds of ideal type as heuristic aids which, by themselves, tell you nothing about the real world, but which throw into relief its deviations from themselves. The individualistic ideal type was to assist in the detection of disturbing factors, such as habit and tradition, which deflect actual individuals from a rational course of action — a proposal I shall examine later. Now I shall examine the assumptions underlying Weber's earlier proposal to use holistic ideal types.

One might improve one's appreciation of the shape of a roughly circular object by placing over it an accurate tracing of a circle. This analogy brings out Weber's conception of the purpose, and manner of employing, holistic ideal types in three respects. (i) By comparing an impure object with an ideal construction the deviations of the former from the latter are thrown into relief; and Weber did regard this kind of ideal type as a 'purely ideal *limiting* concept with which the real situation . . . is *compared* and surveyed for the explication of certain of its significant components.' [7] (ii) Both the object and the construct are considered *as a whole.* (iii) The analogy involves what is presupposed by the idea of comparison, namely, a simultaneous awareness of the characteristics of both things being compared. And in 1904 Weber did assume that the social scientist can place his knowledge of a real situation alongside his knowledge of an ideal type he has himself constructed, and compare the two.[8] It is the simultaneous knowability of the features of both which enables holistic ideal types to be 'used as conceptual instruments for *comparison* with and *measurement* of reality.[9]

At this point an awkward question arises: If the characteristics of a historical situation have already been charted *before* the ideal type is brought into play, why bother with ideal types? They are not hypotheses[10] which guide the social scientist in his search for facts, for they are not supposed to be realistic, or empirical. A holistic ideal type is not a guess about reality, but an *a priori* word-picture — in other words, a definition. What Weber's earlier proposal amounts to is that holistic ideal types should be used as explicit definitions of those 'hundreds of words in the historian's vocabulary [which] are ambiguous constructs created to meet the unconsciously felt need for adequate expression and the meaning of which is only concretely felt but not clearly thought out.' [11]

Thus the holistic ideal type transpires to be something of a mouse, a mere demand for definitions;[12] and I shudder when I imagine each of those 'hundreds of words' being replaced by lengthy verbal definitions, though such defining *may* be helpful in particular circumstances. For instance, to order and classify a collection of variegated instances it may be necessary to construct a scale with limiting ideal types at either end. The survey of the constitutions of 158 Greek states was probably tidier and more systematic than it would have been if Aristotle's 'Monarchy-Aristocracy-Polity' and 'Tyranny-Oligarchy-Democracy' scales, or some equivalent, had not been used.

But such scales are for classifying facts already analysed, not for analysing raw material; and the real weakness of Weber's earlier proposal lies in the method of historical analysis which was to accompany the use of holistic ideal types. With *individualistic* ideal types, it will be remembered, we *start* with individuals' dispositions, information and relationships, and work outwards to the unintended consequences of their interaction (deducing a price-level, for example, from demand and supply schedules). But with *holistic* ideal types the analysis is supposed to proceed in the opposite direction. Here, the historian is supposed to start with the broad

[7] *Methodology*, p. 93.

[8] Thus he speaks of 'the relationship between the logical structure of the conceptual system . . . and what is immediately given in empirical reality' (*op. cit.*, p. 96). The term 'immediately given' should not, I think, be taken too seriously. What this phrase does imply is that the social scientist's knowledge of ideal type and corresponding reality are on an equal footing.

[9] *Op. cit.*, p. 97.

[10] *Op. cit.*, p. 90.

[11] *Op. cit.*, pp. 92–3.

[12] For a criticism of such demands, see K. R. Popper, *The Open Society and Its Enemies*, London, 1945, vol. 2, ch. 11, sect. ii.

(or 'essential') characteristics of an entire historical situation, and then to *descend* to an ever closer definition of its deviations from the ideal type with which it is being compared. In principle this descent from overall traits to detailed ingredients might continue until, *at the end of the analysis*, the relevant dispositions, information, and relationships of the people concerned had been established.

The idea that we can apprehend the overall characteristics of a social situation *before* learning something of the individual situations of the actors in it *appears* to be borne out by a statement such as, 'The British economy in 1850 was competitive.' This statement apparently attributes an overall characteristic to a demarcated whole, while saying nothing about individuals (just as 'The lake's surface was calm' says nothing about water-particles). Now the unintended merit of the holistic ideal type is that its use forces us to recognise the falsity of this idea. If, in order to assess the competitiveness of the British economy in 1850, we try to establish an ideal type of 'perfect competition' we shall at once find that we can only define it in terms of the preferences, information and relationships of individuals — an assertion which can be confirmed by turning in any economics text-book. In other words, we shall have established an *individualistic* ideal type.[13] But if knowledge of the general characteristics of a social situation is always derivative knowledge, pieced together from what is known of individuals' situations, then it is not possible for historical analysis to proceed *from* overall characteristics *towards* individuals' situations. The former is logically derivative from the latter. Weber's earlier conception of an ideal type presupposed that one can detect the essential traits of some historic 'whole' while remaining aloof from the detail of personal behaviour; but this belief is shown to be false when we actually construct such a type. It was probably this experience which later led Weber tacitly to abandon holistic ideal types and the impossible method associated with them, in favour of individualistic ideal types and the method of reconstructing historical phenomena with their aid.[14]

The assertion that knowledge of social phenomena can only be derived from knowledge about individuals requires one qualification. For there are certain overt features [15] which can be established without knowledge of psychological facts, such as the level of prices, or the death-rate (but *not* the suicide-rate). And if we detect more or less regular changes in such overt features we have something eminently suitable for analysis. But some people, over-impressed by the quasi-regularity of, for example, a long-term 'wave' in economic life, have supposed that such a thing possesses a sort of internal dynamic, and obeys its own laws; and that while *it* must therefore be taken as a datum, many other phenomena (such as bursts of inventiveness, emigration movements, outbreaks of

[13] Similarly, if we try to construct an ideal type for 'feudalism,' say, we shall at once find ourselves speaking of people's obligations and privileges towards their superiors, inferiors, the land, and so on.

[14] What I call a 'holistic ideal type' roughly corresponds to what Eucken called a 'real type,' a name he used to denote the 'stages,' such as 'city economy,' 'early capitalism,' 'mature capitalism,' through which, according to the Historical School of economists, any economic system develops. He also rejected such types in favour of individualistic ideal types (which he simply called 'ideal types') and he criticised Weber for confusing the two, but from a somewhat different viewpoint to my own. His fascinating book, *The Foundations of Economics*, contains a sustained plea for the fertile marriage of abstract theory and concrete fact, and a powerful criticism of the Historical School for blurring the distinction between the two; whereas I am arguing against methodological holism, and for methodological individualism. Our arguments tend to coincide because 'historicism' is closely related to 'holism': the belief in laws of development presupposes a 'whole' which undergoes the development. (See K. R. Popper, "The Poverty of Historicism," *Economica*, XI, 1944, pp. 91–2.) For Eucken's discussion of real and ideal types, see especially pp. 347–9.

[15] By 'overt feature' I do not mean something which can necessarily be directly perceived — it may be a highly theoretical construct. But whether it be the price of a marked article in a shop-window, or the average level of prices in 1815, an overt feature is something which can be ascertained without referring to people's dispositions, etc. See R. Stone, *The Role of Measurement in Economics*, Cambridge, 1951, p. 9.

war) can be explained as consequences of it.[16]

This is a sort of blasphemy. The Israelites also imputed their fortunes and misfortunes to a superior entity immune from their own activities; but they rightly called this 'God.' But economic cycles do not possess a quasi-divine autonomy. They are mere human creations — not deliberate creations, of course, but the unintended product of the behaviour of interacting people.

For the last few paragraphs a basic methodological principle has been struggling to emerge and the time has come to bring it into the open in order to clarify its meaning and status.

The Principle of Methodological Individualism

This principle states that social processes and events should be explained by being deduced from (*a*) principles governing the behaviour of participating individuals and (*b*) descriptions of their situations.[17] The contrary principle of methodological holism states that the behaviour of individuals should be explained by being deduced from (*a*) macroscopic laws which are *sui generis* and which apply to the social system as a whole, and (*b*) descriptions of the positions (or functions) of the individuals within the whole.

There is clearly an important difference between these two principles. What are my grounds for accepting the individualistic, and rejecting the holistic, method?

(1) Whereas physical things can exist unperceived, social 'things' like laws, prices, prime ministers and ration-books, are created by personal attitudes. (Remove the attitudes of food officials, shop-keepers, housewives, etc., towards ration-books and they shrivel into bits of cardboard.) But if social objects are formed by individual attitudes, an explanation of their formation must be an individualistic explanation.

(2) The social scientist and the historian have no 'direct access' to the overall structure and behaviour of a system of interacting individuals (in the sense that a chemist does have 'direct access' to such overall properties of a gas as its volume and pressure and temperature, which he can measure and relate without any knowledge of gas-molecules). But the social scientist and the historian can often arrive at fairly reliable opinions about the dispositions and situations of individuals. These two facts suggest that a theoretical understanding of an abstract social structure should be derived from more empirical beliefs about concrete individuals.[18]

But neither (1) the truism that social ob-

[16] I have written the above with the Russian economist Kondratieff in mind. He asserts that the view that long waves 'are conditioned by casual, extra-economic circumstances and events, such as (1) changes in technique, (2) wars and revolutions, (3) the assimilation of new countries into the world economy, and (4) fluctuations in gold production . . . reverse[s] the causal connections and take[s] the consequence to be the cause.' (N. D. Kondratieff, 'The Long Waves in Economic Life,' *Readings in Business Cycle Theory*, Blakiston Series, London, 1950, ch. 2, p. 35.) In other words, the long wave is *the* fundamental datum, in terms of which even such a strictly individual and psychological matter as human inventiveness is to be explained.

[17] This principle does not apply to the study of purely physical, biological or behaviouristic properties of human groups. Professor Hayek has drawn a very useful distinction between the 'natural sciences of society', such as vital statistics and the study of contagious diseases, and the 'social sciences' proper. (*Individualism and Economic Order*, London, 1949, p. 57.) Typical problems of the social sciences are war, unemployment, political instability, the clash of cultures. Professor M. Ginsberg has asserted that principles of historical interpretation 'are not necessarily exclusively psychological or even teleological: there may well be social laws *sui generis* . . .' (*Aristotelian Society, Supplementary Volume* XXI, 1947, 'Symposium: The Character of a Historical Explanation,' p. 77). The only example he gives of something determined by such laws is phonetic change. But phonetic change is either an unconscious, behaviouristic process to be studied by a natural science of society, or a deliberate process, in which case it can be explained individualistically, e.g., in terms of a man's desire to raise his social status by acquiring a superior accent.

[18] 'The social sciences . . . do not deal with "given" wholes but their task is to *constitute* these wholes by constructing models from the familiar elements. . . .' 'The whole is never directly perceived but always reconstructed by an effort of our imagination.' F. A. Hayek, *The Counter-Revolution of Science: studies on the abuse of reason*, The Free Press, Glencoe, Illinois, 1952, p. 56 and p. 214.

jects are created by personal attitudes, nor (2) the 'invisibility' of social structures, *entail* methodological individualism; they only support it.

(1) The fact that prices, for instance, are charged and paid by people, the fact that they are human creations, does not, by itself, entail that the whole price-system may not be governed by some overall law which is underivable from propositions about individuals. (2) A holist who denied that 'the English State, for example, is a logical construction out of individual people',[19] and who asserted that it is an organism which develops, and responds to challenges, according to underivable holistic laws, might also admit that only its individual components were visible and that any operational definition of the laws it obeyed would be in terms of individual behaviour.

Moreover, an extremely unlikely circumstance is conceivable in which methodological individualism would have to be demoted from a rule to an aspiration; for it apparently suffers this humiliation in the study of certain non-human societies.

One can see what upsets methodological individualism by considering three different systems of interacting components: (*a*) the solar system as conceived by classical mechanics; (*b*) the economic system as conceived by classical economics; and (*c*) a bee-hive.

(*a*) Here, methodological individualism is altogether adequate. The behaviour of the whole system can be explained by applying the inverse square law and the law of inertia to the system's components, if their relative positions, masses and momenta are known. Indeed, methodological individualism in the social sciences is analogous to the method of resolution and re-composition which characterizes Galilean and Newtonian physics: the method, namely, of analysing a complex whole into its atomic constituents, and into the simplest principles which they obey, and of deductively reconstructing the behaviour of the whole from these.

(*b*) Adam Smith stated that the individual

> generally, indeed, neither intends to promote the public interest, nor knows how much he is promoting it . . . ; by directing [his] industry in such a manner as its produce may be of the greatest value, he intends only his own gain, and he is in this, as in many other cases, led by an invisible hand to promote an end which was no part of his intention. (*The Wealth of Nations*, Bk. 4, Ch. 2.)

But the invisible hand is, strictly, gratuitous and misleading. What Smith actually showed was that individuals in competitive economic situations are led by nothing but their *personal dispositions* to promote unintentionally the public interest. Here again, methodological individualism is altogether adequate.

(*c*) Mr. E. S. Russell, basing himself on experiments by Rösch, has reported the following strange fact[20] (strange, that is, to the methodological individualist). If young worker-bees (whose normal function is to feed the larvae from their salivary glands) are segregated into one half of a hive sealed off from the other half, in which have been segregated the older worker-bees (whose salivary glands have atrophied and whose normal function is to produce wax from their newly developed wax-glands, and later, to forage), then the following will occur: after two days' dislocation and near-starvation some of the young workers will start foraging and their salivary glands will atrophy prematurely; while the atrophied salivary glands of some of the older workers will revive and continue functioning long after the normal period, enabling them to feed the larvae in their half of the hive. The bees' functions will be increasingly differentiated until the division of labour in both halves approximates that of a whole hive. Here it really is as if individual bees were led by an invisible hand, not merely to promote the interest of the whole half-hive, but to adapt drastically their biological structure in order to do so. It seems extremely difficult to believe that the emergence of these two new systems of specialised functions could be explained in-

[19] A. J. Ayer, *Language, Truth and Logic*, 2nd. ed., London, 1948, p. 63.

[20] See *The British Journal for the Philosophy of Science*, 1950, I, pp. 113–14.

dividualistically, in terms of the situations and principles of behaviour of each bee, because all the bees in each half-hive were of a similar type and in approximately the same situation, yet only the requisite number adapted themselves to new functions. Thus each half of the bifurcated bee-hive appears to be an organism in the sense that its components' behaviour is determined by teleological principles which apply to the whole half-hive and which cannot be derived from a knowledge of individual bees — though one hopes that this appearance is misleading and that the re-emergence of specialization will eventually be explained individualistically.

The principle whose status I have been trying to elucidate is a methodological rule which presupposes the factual assertion that human social systems are not organisms in the above sense. There is no evidence to suggest that this presupposition is false; but one cannot assert *a priori* that it is true. What one *can* assert is that *if* any social system were such an organic entity then it would be something utterly different from anything so far imagined. For the only sorts of organism so far imagined are (*a*) physical or biological; (*b*) mental; and (*c*) social; and it will be shown that social systems are none of these.

(*a*) It is at any rate plausible to say that the personalities of a mating couple are sometimes submerged beneath the biological laws of their physical union. But it would be stretching terms to call this a 'social system'; and in the case of such social organizations as the Comintern or the International Red Cross, it is clear that what holds these bodies together is not physical ties but the ideals, loyalties, discipline and beliefs of their dispersed members.

(*b*) Is the behaviour of a number of individuals ever regulated by some super-individual *mental* entity? It is just possible that this is so in the case of a panicking crowd or of an ecstatic revivalist meeting. But in general, 'group-minds' are very rightly out of fashion; for to impute a big social phenomenon (such as war) to a big mental counterpart (such as a 'nation's aggressive spirit') is not to explain but to duplicate.[21] Moreover, social phenomena which nobody wants are precisely those whose occurrence most needs explaining; and it would obviously be absurd to impute mass unemployment, for instance, to some mental counterpart such as a 'nation's laziness'.

(*c*) When a sociologist proffers a holistic law the entity whose behaviour it is supposed to determine is usually thought of as a special sort of organism, neither physical nor biological nor mental, but *social*. Alleged social entities such as 'The State', 'Capitalism', etc., however, are only hypostatizations of sociological terms. As we have seen, whenever we try to make these terms precise we find ourselves speaking individualistically.

Hence society is not an organism in any existing sense of the term. The ontological basis of methodological individualism is the assumption that society is not some unimagined sort of organism, but really consists only of people who behave fairly intelligibly and who influence each other, directly and mediately, in fairly comprehensible ways.

This section was intended to clarify and justify methodological individualism. We can now revert to the construction and use of ideal types.

Concluding Remarks on Ideal Types

The argument of section 2 can be summarised thus: An understanding of a complex social situation is always derived from a knowledge of the dispositions, beliefs, and relationships of individuals. Its overt characteristics may be *established* empirically, but

[21] This criticism is parallel to Aristotle's chief criticism of Plato's theory of Forms, to the effect that instead of accounting for their perceptible likenesses the Forms merely divert attention to transcendent duplicates. *Met.* 992a27.

they are only *explained* by being shown to be the resultants of individual activities.[22]

All this was recognised by the later Weber. In *The Theory of Social and Economic Organisation* ideal type construction means (not detecting and abstracting the overall characteristics of a whole situation, and organising these into a coherent scheme, but) placing hypothetical, rational actors in some simplified situation, and in deducing the consequences of their interaction.

Such intellectual experimenting *may* be fruitful even if some of the premisses are very unrealistic. For instance, the concept of a static economy in equilibrium aids the analysis of the changes and disequilibria of actual economies. And gross exaggeration of one factor may show up an influence which would otherwise have been overlooked. This is particularly important in social science where the influence of different factors can seldom be accurately calculated. If E is the *sort* of effect produced by F_1, and if F_1 and E are both present, the social scientist tends to assume that F_1 is *the* cause of E, whereas F_1 may have caused only a *part* of E, and an undetected factor F_2 may have caused the rest of E. For example, the domestic economic policy of country A will be a major influence on its own economy; but this may also be influenced by the domestic economic policy of country B. In order to show up this secondary influence, we might assume provisionally that A exports *all* its production to, and imports *all* its consumption from, B, and then deduce the effect on A of a change of policy in B.[23]

But that would be a preliminary intellectual experiment. The premisses of a finished ideal type should be sufficiently realistic for it to be applicable to historical situations. I now turn to the problem of application.

Historical Explanation

I shall consider three levels of historical explanation: (I) colligation (where ideal types play no significant role); (II) explanation in principle (which is the field *par excellence* for ideal types); and (III) explanation in detail (where ideal types are mostly constructed *ad hoc*, and rendered increasingly realistic until they become empirical reconstructions).[24]

(I) *Colligation.* The term 'colligation' has been revived by Mr. Walsh[25] to denote a procedure which is important, not because it is methodologically powerful, but because most 'literary' historians do in fact use it when they write, for example, constitutional history. It means 'explaining an event by tracing its intrinsic relations to other events and locating it in its historical context.'[26] Thus we begin to understand why a bill was enacted in May 1640 condemning Strafford to death when we learn of such matters as: his autocratic power in Ireland; Parliament's fear of the Irish army and Pym's ruthlessness as a parliamentary leader; the King's dependence on Parliament to pay indemnities to the Scottish army in the north; and the angry anti-royalist mob which beset Westminster during the bill's passage. It may also be better understood by being colligated with *subsequent* events. Thus the Long Parliament's later treatment of Laud and Charles suggests that its treatment of Strafford was

[22] An explanation may be in terms of the *typical* dispositions of more or less anonymous individuals, or in terms of the peculiar dispositions of specific individuals. (This is the basis of my distinction between 'explanation in principle' and 'explanation in detail.' See p. 465.) Thus, you might try to explain an election result in terms of how 'the Lancashire shopkeeper' and 'the non-party professional man' etc., felt; or, if you had an unlikely amount of knowledge, in terms of the dispositions of each elector.

[23] I owe this example to Professor J. E. Meade.

[24] Professor F. A. Hayek also draws a distinction between explaining in principle and explaining in detail, but he wishes to distinguish an explanation of why, say, a price will rise under certain conditions, from a quantitative prediction of the amount by which it will rise (*The Counter-Revolution of Science*, pp. 42–3); whereas I wish to distinguish between explanations in terms of *typical* dispositions, etc., and explanations in terms of the characteristics and personal idiosyncrasies of the principal actors concerned.

[25] See W. H. Walsh, *An Introduction to Philosophy of History*, London, 1951, ch. 3, § 3.

[26] *Op. cit.*, p. 59.

not eccentric, but part of a campaign against extra-parliamentary power.

However, as Mr. Walsh admits, colligation yields only what he calls a 'significant narrative', which is more than a chronicle, but less than a full explanation, of the events colligated.

(II) *Explanation in Principle.* The principle of the automatic governor can be demonstrated in a simple model which shows that a fall in some temperature, voltage, speed, pressure, etc., below a certain level will move a lever which will increase the supply of heat, etc.; and *vice versa*. Understanding this, you can explain the constant temperature of your car's circulating water *in principle* if you know that an automatic governor controls it, although you do not understand its detailed operation.[27]

Analogous explanations are used in applied economics. Consider the bargaining process. The principle of this is demonstrated in the following ideal type. Two rational agents are postulated. Each possesses one homogeneous, divisible good, and each knows the schedule of those combinations of various portions of his own and the other's good which he would exchange indifferently for the whole of his present good. These premisses are highly precise, and also highly formal. Call them α and β. From these it is deduced that only the limits within which a bargain will be struck are determined, and that within those limits the outcome will be arbitrary. Call this consequence ω. Now consider post-war Anglo-Argentinian trade negotiations. Here, we can, I think, detect factors A, B, c, d, . . . Z where: A and B are the resources and policies of the trade delegations, and are concrete examples of α and β; c, d, . . . are minor factors whose small influences on Z may partly cancel out; and Z is the outcome of the negotiations, the actual instability of Anglo-Argentinian trade relations, which is a rough empirical counterpart of ω. The 'α, β, ω' ideal type explains in principle the 'A, B, c, d, . . . Z' situation.[28]

In this example I have assumed that only one main economic principle, demonstrable in a single ideal type, was at work in the historical situation. But the situation will usually be more complex. Consider a wage-bargain. Perhaps there is a closed shop and limited entry into the trade union. The firm, a centrally planned organisation, buys its raw materials, which are rationed, through a government agency, and its machinery at the best price it can get from oligopolistic suppliers. By law it must export a proportion of its produce, and the export market is highly competitive. Its home prices are fixed by a cartel agreement.[29] The general situation is inflationary.

Here, the outcome of the bargaining process will be shaped by a number of economic principles besides that illustrated in the previous example. And in order to understand the whole situation in principle it would be necessary to build up a complex model from the relevant simple ideal types. Here, an '(α, β), (λ, μ), (σ, τ), . . . ω' model would be used to explain in principle an 'A, B, c, . . . L, M, n, . . . S, T, u, . . . Z' situation (where c . . ., n . . ., u . . . represent comparatively uninfluential factors).

The social scientist's explanations in principle lack the quantitative precision of explanations in mathematical physics. But he may claim that his explanations are at any rate 'intelligible' and 'satisfying,' whereas those of the natural scientist are not. The most universal laws which the latter applies in his explanations and predictions contain terms (e.g. 'elementary quantum of action')

[27] It is the principle of an invention rather than its physical detail which is usually described in patents. See M. Polanyi, *The Logic of Liberty*, London, 1951, p. 21.

[28] I owe this example to Professor Lionel Robbins.

[29] The definitions of perfect competition, oligopoly and monopoly provide, incidentally, good illustrations of the principle of methodological individualism. An entrepreneur faces: (*a*) perfect competition if the price at which he sells is determined for him; (*b*) oligopoly, if he can alter his price, but if this alteration may lead to price changes by his competitors which may force him to make further, undesired alterations to his own price; and (*c*) monopoly, if he can alter his price without causing undesired repercussions. Competition, oligopoly and monopoly are nothing but the outcome of the behaviour of interacting individuals in certain relationships.

whose connotation the layman cannot 'picture' or 'grasp.' Moreover, the status of these most universal laws is probably only temporary: they will probably come to be subsumed under higher order laws.

But the ultimate premisses of social science are human dispositions, i.e. something familiar and understandable (though not introspectable since they are not mental events). They 'are so much the stuff of our everyday experience that they have only to be stated to be recognised as obvious.'[30] And while psychology may try to explain these dispositions, they do provide social science with a natural stopping-place in the search for explanations of overt social phenomena. The social scientist might claim more. The natural scientist cannot, strictly speaking, *verify* valid hypotheses; he can only *refute* false ones.[31] He can say, 'If H, then E. But not-E. Therefore not-H.' But if he says, 'If H, then E. Moreover E. Therefore H' he commits the fallacy of affirming the consequent.[32] But a social scientist might claim that a valid social theory *can* be verified because both its conclusions *and* its premisses can be confirmed—'you assent to the former because they correspond with recognised social facts; and you assent to the latter because they correspond with your ideas of how people behave.' An example of the belief that a social theory can be wholly verified by being confirmed at both ends is to be found in Keynes' *General Theory*. There he asserts 'the fundamental psychological law, upon which we are entitled to depend with great confidence . . . from our knowledge of human nature . . . , that men are disposed, as a rule and on the average, to increase their consumption as their income increases, but not by as much as the increase in their income'; and *vice versa*.[33] He then shows that the empirical fact that no depression has worsened until 'no one at all was employed' is a deductive consequence of this law.[34] The theory is thus doubly confirmed, and therefore verified: 'it is *certain* that experience would be extremely different from what it is if the law did not hold.'[35] No natural scientist could claim so much for *his* laws. His explanations are 'surprising' in the sense that he explains the familiar in terms of the unconfirmable unfamiliar. But the social scientist explains the familiar in terms of the familiar. The element of surprise in *his* explanations lies in the logical demonstration of connections which had not been seen before between facts which are *prima facie* discrete.

But a double caution must be entered against the idea of double confirmation in social science: (i) The same conclusion can, of course, be deduced from different sets of premisses, and we cannot be certain that our set of psychological assumptions is the correct set. (ii) Even if our psychological assumptions *are* correct, and even if we *do* find that their deductive consequences correspond to recognised facts, we may nevertheless be mistaken if we explain these facts as a consequence of those psychological factors. This is because we can seldom calculate the relative influence of different psychological factors.[36] Thus Keynes' belief that people are disposed to save a smaller proportion of their income if their income diminishes may well be correct; his demonstration that this general disposition would not allow depressions to worsen indefinitely is immaculate; and the fact that depressions do not worsen indefinitely is undoubted. It is nevertheless conceivable that *no* depression has been halted because of this disposition. One may have been halted by an outbreak

[30] Lionel Robbins, *The Nature and Significance of Economic Science*, London, 1935, p. 79.

[31] See K. R. Popper, *Logik der Forschung*, Vienna, 1935, *passim*.

[32] See F. S. C. Northrop, *The Logic of the Sciences and the Humanities*, New York, 1948, pp. 108–9; and e.g. H. W. B. Joseph, *An Introduction to Logic*, Oxford, 1916, pp. 522–3.

[33] *The General Theory of Employment, Interest and Money*, London, 1936, p. 96.

[34] *Op. cit.*, p. 252.

[35] *Op. cit.*, p. 251 (my italics).

[36] I was myself inclined to accept the idea of double confirmation until Professor Popper pointed out to me the relevance of this consideration.

of war, another by an upsurge of confidence, another by a public works policy, and so on. In explaining social phenomena we must not be content with the detection of one factor which, singly, would have produced, after an unstated period, an unstated amount of an effect which may, in any particular situation, have been caused mainly by quite different factors.

If I am right in supposing that social theories derive sociological conclusions from dispositional premisses, we should expect to find that major theoretical advances in social science consist in the perception of some typical feature of our mental make-up which had previously been disregarded, and in its formulation in a way which is more deductively fertile and which goes to explain a wider range of facts, than the psychological generalisations relied on hitherto. And this is precisely what we do find. I think that it would be generally conceded that economics is the most mature social science, and that the two most striking advances made in economics during the last century are: (i) the 'revolution' which occurred in the early 1870's when Jevons, Menger and Walras introduced the concept of marginal utility; and (ii) the Keynesian 'revolution.'

(i) The classical economists saw that the price of a good must be partly determined by the demand for it, and that that demand must reflect the buyers' estimates of the good's utility — and yet diamonds, whose utility is low, fetch a far higher price than water, whose utility is high. So they tried to escape from their dilemma by saying that the price of a good is determined by the cost of its production, though this would obviously be untrue of an unwanted good which had been expensively produced. This difficulty dissolved with the introduction of the idea of the utility, not of a whole good, but of its least important, or 'marginal,' unit. For — and this is the recognition of a psychological contour-line which had not been clearly mapped before — it is in terms of that unit that we tend to value a whole good; and the more we have of the same good, the more its marginal utility diminishes. Hence, if diamonds became abundant and water very scare, their subjectively determined values would be reversed. F. H. Knight has given a vivid description of the elegance and power of the concept of marginal utility:

> To its admirers it comes near to being the fulfilment of the eighteenth-century craving for a principle which would do for human conduct and society what Newton's mechanics had done for the solar system. It introduces simplicity and order, even to the extent of making it possible to state the problems in the form of mathematical functions dealt with by the methods of infinitesimal calculus.[37]

(ii) The reader who is unfamiliar with Keynes' contribution to the theory of employment must take its value on trust, for it is impossible to describe it briefly. But here again we find that what it rests on is the perception and precise formulation of certain human dispositions which Keynes regarded as 'ultimate independent variables,'[38] and from which he could deduce such dependent variables (or overt phenomena, as I have called them previously) as the amount of employment and the general level of prices. At the heart of his *General Theory* Keynes placed 'three fundamental psychological factors, namely, the psychological propensity to consume, the psychological attitude to liquidity and the psychological expectation of future yield from capital-assets.' [39]

(III) *Explanation in Detail.* The mark of an explanation in principle is its reliance on typical dispositions and its disregard of personal differences. But it is often impossible to disregard these, for instance, in diplomatic history. Here, the premisses of a historical explanation must be the specific dispositions,

[37] F. H. Knight, *The Ethics of Competition*, London, 1935, p. 158.

[38] *Op. cit.*, p. 246. Of course, the variables are only 'independent' from the social scientist's point of view. The psychologist would probably consider them 'dependent'.

[39] *Op. cit.*, pp. 246–7.

beliefs and relationships of actual people. This is what I call 'explanation in detail.'

So far, I have allowed two questions to lie dormant: (i) What is the status of these dispositions, and wherein lies their explanatory power? (ii) What assumptions concerning people's rationality are we obliged to make when we explain something in terms of their dispositions and beliefs? These questions were not acute so long as explanations in principle were being considered. An explanation requires a general statement as its major premiss; and when we postulate a typical disposition we assert that all men (with trivial exceptions and minor deviations, and, perhaps, within a limited historico-geographical area) are prone to behave in a certain kind of way; and this gives us the generality we require. And we explain in principle by combining types which are, after all, ideal, and which may therefore be expected to contain idealised simplifications of real life, such as the assumption of fully rational behaviour in the light of preferences and beliefs.

But when we turn to explanations in detail these two questions do become acute. For we are here concerned with the variegated dispositions of actual people, and these appear to lack the generality which the major premiss of an explanation needs. And actual people do not behave altogether rationally, which suggests that we cannot go on assuming that they do. I shall discuss the first question under the head of 'Personality', and the second under the head of 'Rationality and Purposefulness'.

(i) *Personality.* A series of occurrences constitutes a person's life, and a complex and evolving system of dispositions constitutes his personality.[40] Dispositions 'are not laws, for they mention particular things or persons. On the other hand they resemble laws in being partly "variable" or "open." '[41] The dispositions which comprise a unique personality are, so to speak, 'laws' which apply to only one man over a limited period of time. It is as if the laws of chemistry concerning, say, mercury, applied only to a period in the life of one solitary bottle of mercury which has come into existence, matured, and will dissolve, and whose twin, we may confidently assume, never has existed, and never will.

All this presupposes that men do have personalities, i.e. that their behaviour is fairly consistent over a period of time if their personalities are not subjected to dissolvent shocks. This assumption of the quasi-permanence of personalities corresponds roughly — very roughly — to the natural scientist's belief in the permanence of the natural order.

The generalisations of psychology fit into this scheme in the following ways: (*a*) Some attribute a certain disposition to all men. The theory of the association of ideas is an example. (*b*) Others attribute certain dispositions to a certain type of man, e.g. the 'introvert.' (*c*) Yet others attempt to describe the dynamics of personality-development, deriving later dispositions from prior determining conditions in the light of psychological theory. (It is this search for the primitive determining conditions which leads back to the 'formative years' of early childhood.) An example is the theory of the 'incest-complex,' which asserts that a man who idealised his sister as a child will be prone to hypoaesthesia on marriage.

A disposition attributed to one man is no weaker than the same disposition attributed

[40] I have adopted the terminology of Professor G. Ryle's *Concept of Mind* (London, 1949; see especially ch. 5), but not that book's famous denial that a man has 'privileged access' to his own mind. Sitting beside the driver of a car who turns white and wrenches the steering-wheel over, I may perceive instantaneously *that* he fears an accident, but I do not *feel* his fear. Moreover, the historian is usually in the position of the policeman who tries to reconstruct what happened from skid-marks and reports of witnesses; and for him the dualism between uninterpreted overt behaviour (e.g. Jan Masaryk's fall from a Prague window) and its interpretation in psychological terms is very real.

But the following characteristic remarks suggest that Professor Ryle has now modified his original anti-dualism: 'We have . . . a sort of (graduatedly) privileged access to such things as palpitations of the heart, cramps, and creaks in the joints.' 'I have elsewhere argued for the idea that a tickle just *is* a thwarted impulse to scratch. . . . But I do not think now that this will do.' ('Feelings,' *The Philosophical Quarterly*, April 1951, 1, 198–9).

[41] Ryle, *Concept of Mind*, p. 123.

to all men in explaining and predicting that one man's behaviour. 'X will accept office' can be deduced from the minor premiss, 'X believes that if he refuses the office he has been offered he will find himself in the wilderness' in conjunction with *either* (*a*) the major premiss, 'All men seek power,' *or* (*b*) the major premiss, 'X is a power-seeker'; but whereas (*b*) may be true, (*a*) is the sort of statement which is likely to be false because men are not uniform.[42]

Similarly, a detailed description of one man's chess-playing dispositions (his knowledge of the rules, evaluations of the different pieces, and ability to see a certain number of moves ahead) together with his present beliefs about his opponent's intentions and the positions of the pieces, imply his next move, which could not be deduced from propositions about chess-players in general in conjunction with a description of the present state of the game.

Thus the idea that the historian's interpretative principles are simply generalisations about human nature, into which he must have special insight, is inadequate.[43] His knowledge of human nature in general has to be supplemented by a knowledge of the peculiar personalities of the principal actors concerned in the situation he is trying to understand, whether his problem be X's behaviour, or the chess-player's next move, or the rise of Christianity, or the Congress of Vienna.

The dispositions which the historian attributes to a personality he is trying to reconstruct resemble scientific laws in two further ways.

(*a*) They are postulated hypotheses which correspond to nothing observable, although observable behaviour can be inferred from them in conjunction with factual minor premisses. Consequently, in judging their validity we want to know, not the mental process by which the historian arrived at them, but their degree of success in accounting for what is known of the man's behaviour. The hypothetical dispositions postulated by the historian who has 'sympathetically identified himself with his hero' may be richer than those of the historian who has not done so, but it is not this which gives them a certificate of reliability. Professor Hempel has put the matter very clearly:

> The method of empathy is, no doubt, frequently applied by laymen and by experts in history. But it does not in itself constitute an explanation; it is rather essentially a heuristic device; its function is to suggest certain psychological hypotheses which might serve as explanatory principles in the case under consideration.[44]

And the historian is no more precluded from reconstructing a strange and unsympathetic personality than is the scientist from reconstructing the behaviour of an atom which does things he would not dream of doing himself.[45]

[42] On law-like dispositions of very limited generality, see R. Peters, 'Cure, Cause and Motive,' *Analysis*, April 1950, 10, no. 5, p. 106.

[43] This idea underlies Mr. Walsh's contribution to the symposium on 'The Character of a Historical Explanation' (*Aristotelian Society, Supplementary Volume* XXI, 1947). From it he infers that, since 'men's notions of human nature change from age to age' we must recognise 'the subjective element which history undoubtedly contains' (p. 66). The point is, do historians' notions of, say, Napoleon's personality change from age to age (not because of the discovery of fresh evidence, etc., but) arbitrarily?

[44] *Op. cit.*, p. 467. Failure to realise this is, I think, the weakness of R. G. Collingwood's *The Idea of History* (ed. T. M. Knox, Oxford, 1946).

[45] Failure to recognise this vitiates, I think, some of the argument in Professor F. A. Hayek's 'Scientism and the Study of Society' (*The Counter-Revolution of Science*, Part One). There, despite all the work done in abnormal psychology, he asserts: 'When we speak of mind what we mean is that certain phenomena can be successfully interpreted on the analogy of our own mind. . . . To recognise mind cannot mean anything but to recognise something as operating in the same way as our own thinking.' From this false premiss he correctly infers the false conclusion that 'history can never carry us beyond the stage where we can understand the working of the minds of the acting people because they are similar to our own' (pp. 77–9). Only a war-like historian can tackle a Genghiz Khan or a Hitler! Moreover, if it were true that people, young and old, do not recognise as mind what they cannot interpret on the analogy of their own mind, they would never learn to speak. For children must unconsciously realise that adult noises differ importantly from their own gibberish in being meaningful before they can begin to understand adult talk.

I hasten to add that I owe much to other parts of Professor Hayek's argument.

(*b* The dispositions which constitute a personality also resemble scientific laws in that they form a hierarchical system; and this is of considerable methodological importance. It is, of course, essential that the dispositions which a historian attributes to a historical figure should not be mere *ad hoc* translations of known occurrences into dispositional terms. It is no explanation of Brutus' behaviour to say that he was disposed to assassinate Caesar, though it would be a ground for an explanation to say that Brutus was disposed to place his loyalty to the State above his loyalties to his friends, if independent evidence were found to support this hypothesis. Moreover — and it is here that the idea of a hierarchy of dispositions is important — the historian who can explain some aspect of a person's behaviour *up to a certain time* in terms of a certain disposition, although his *subsequent* behaviour conflicts with this disposition, must not merely say that at that time the earlier disposition gave way to another. He should find a *higher order* disposition which helps to explain both earlier and later lower order dispositions, and hence the whole range of the person's behaviour. For example: suppose that Russian foreign policy is controlled by a consistent, integrated personality. Before 1939 Russia was disposed to pursue an anti-fascist foreign policy. But in 1939 came the Russo-German Pact. In order to explain this aberration it is not enough for the historian to say that the anti-fascist disposition was replaced. He must find a higher order disposition (e.g. 'Russian foreign policy is determined by considerations of national expediency, not by ideological factors') from which, in conjunction with factual premisses, the change in policy is derivable. In doing this it is clear that the historian will *not* be translating an occurrence (the signing of the pact) into dispositional terms, but deriving both the occurrence and the change in lower order dispositions from a more permanent and fundamental disposition.

In conclusion it should be said that the personality of a man in society comprises dispositions both of a more private and temperamental kind, and of a more public and institutional kind. Only certain individuals are disposed to weep during the death-scene in *Othello*, but all policemen are disposed to blow their whistles under certain circumstances and any Speaker in the House of Commons is disposed to disallow parliamentary criticism of exercises of the Prerogative. And these more public and institutional dispositions, which may vary very little when one man undertakes another's role, can be abstracted from the total, variegated flux of dispositions, and so provide the social scientist with a fairly stable subject-matter.[46]

(ii) *Rationality and Purposefulness.* Before asking what assumptions the historian is obliged to make about the rationality of those whose behaviour he is trying to interpret, we must establish a satisfactory 'definition in use' of the term 'rational behaviour.' Weber defined it, very austerely, as the deliberate and logical choice of means to attain explicit goals, in the light of existing factual knowledge. This is unsatisfactory for two reasons. (*a*) Whitehead said somewhere that 'civilisation advances by extending the number of important operations we can perform without thinking about them.' This morning's tooth-brushing was not irrational because done from habit and not from deliberations on dental hygiene. Our pursuit of goals need not be conscious in order to be rational. (*b*) Behaviour often does not conform to the end-means pattern. I may tell the truth, or go fishing, simply from a desire to do so, with no further end in mind.[47]

We escape these difficulties by saying that a person has behaved rationally if he *would* have behaved in the same way if, with the same *factual* information, he had seen the full *logical* implications of his behaviour, whether he actually saw them or not. And if we define purposeful behaviour as trying (consciously

[46] See Hayek, *Counter-Revolution*, p. 34.

[47] We invest our capital reluctantly in the hope of getting dividends. . . . But the angler would not accept or understand an offer of the pleasures without the activities of angling. It is angling that he enjoys, not something that angling engenders.' Ryle, *op. cit.*, p. 132. See also H. A. Pritchard, *Moral Obligation*, Oxford, 1949, pp. 10–11.

or otherwise) to do or achieve something wanted, it follows that fully rational behaviour is a limiting case of purposeful behaviour.

The historian who tries to interpret overt behaviour must assume that it is purposeful but not necessarily fully rational.[48] Consider a *crime passionel* committed by an enraged husband. A judge who assumed that the husband had behaved purposelessly could reconstruct the event in a number of quite arbitrary ways — perhaps cramp caused his finger to contract round the trigger of a gun which happened to be pointing at his wife's lover. But while the judge must not assume purposelessness he need not assume full rationality. The husband would probably have confined himself to threats and remonstrances if he had paused to consider the less immediate consequences of a violent course of action.

The assumption of purposefulness is constantly made by those who attempt the most intensive analysis of human behaviour, i.e. practising psycho-analysts. It has often been pointed out that the psycho-analyst is on the side of rationality in that he tries to cure his patients. More interesting from our point of view is his assumption that the behaviour of an *uncured* patient is thoroughly purposeful. Suppose a patient forgets to wind his watch, and so arrives late at his father's funeral. Unlike the layman, the psycho-analyst will not attribute the stopped watch to accidental forgetfulness, to a purposeless psychic aberration. He will ask his patient *why* he *wanted* his watch to stop — maybe he felt guilty on having a death-wish fulfilled and so created an excuse for avoiding the funeral. This would certainly be purposeful behaviour, and might even be regarded as rational behaviour based on misinformation.[49]

(iii) *Conclusion.* Having considered the status of dispositions and the problem of rationality, we can now return to explanations in detail.

Weber advocated using individualistic ideal types, which depict rational behaviour, to show up the partial irrationality of actual behaviour. But this is unacceptable. Suppose that a historian wishes to interpret a general's behaviour during a battle. He has reconstructed, as best he can, both the dispositions which constitute that aspect of the general's personality with which he is concerned, and the general's information about the military situation. Suppose that, in conjunction, these dictate retreat as the rational course of action, but that the general is known to have given the signal to advance. Now the historian, like the psycho-analyst, will not want to leave puzzling overt behaviour uninterpreted; but according to Weber he should simply call this a deviation from the ideally rational course of action implied by the premisses of his theoretical reconstruction of the situation. But since an irrational aberration can be attributed to anything from boredom to panic, this procedure would result in thoroughly arbitrary reconstructions. Rather, the historian must discover the most satisfactory amendment to the premisses of his ideal type (constructed more or less *ad hoc* to depict the main features of the general's personality and situation) which will remove the discrepancy between what it implies and what happened. Perhaps there is independent evidence to suggest that the general was more lion-hearted than the historian had supposed; or perhaps he had underestimated the enemy's strength, or, in estimating the immediate consequences of an advance, he had overlooked a more distant undesirable repercussion. When *ad hoc* ideal types are used in detailed historical explanations, they have to be amended and amended until they cease being ideal constructs and become empirical reconstructions. The historian who claims to have interpreted a historical situation should be able to show: (*a*) that the behaviour of the actors in it flows from their personalities and situational beliefs; and (*b*)

[48] See Robbins, *op. cit.*, ch. 4, sect. 5.

[49] The mixture of rationality and misinformation due to childhood associations which psycho-analysis brings to the surface was pointed out to me by Professor Popper.

that significant events which no one intended are resultants of the behaviour of interacting individuals.

Summary

An individual's personality is a system of unobservable dispositions which, together with his factual beliefs, determine his observable behaviour. Society is a system of unobservable relationships between individuals whose interaction produces certain measurable sociological phenomena. We can apprehend an unobservable social system only by reconstructing it theoretically from what is known of individual dispositions, beliefs and relationships. Hence holistic ideal types, which would abstract essential traits from a social whole while ignoring individuals, are impossible: they always turn into individualistic ideal types. Individualistic ideal types of explanatory power are constructed by first discerning the form of typical, socially significant, dispositions, and then by demonstrating how, in various typical situations, these lead to certain principles of social behaviour.

If such a principle, or a number of such principles, is at work in a historical situation, the outcome of that situation can be explained anonymously, or in principle, by an application to it of the relevant ideal type, or combination of ideal types. If the idiosyncrasies of the actors concerned significantly influenced the outcome, it must be explained in terms of their peculiar dispositions and beliefs. In either case, the hypothetico-deductive method is used. The hypotheses consist of postulated dispositions, beliefs and relationships of (anonymous or specific) individuals; and their test lies in the correspondence or otherwise between their deductive consequences and what is known of the overt characteristics of the situation being reconstructed. How the historian establishes the overt characteristics of a vanished situation is another story.

An Ideal Type Based on Verstehen 39

The Homecomer

ALFRED SCHUTZ

The Phaeacian sailors deposited the sleeping Odysseus on the shore of Ithaca, his homeland, to reach which he had struggled for twenty years of unspeakable suffering. He stirred and woke from sleep in the land of his fathers, but he knew not his whereabouts. Ithaca showed to him an unaccustomed face; he did not recognize the pathways stretching far into the distance, the quiet bays, the crags and precipices. He rose to his feet and stood staring at what was his own land, crying mournfully: "Alas! and now where on earth am I? What do I here myself?" That he had been absent for so long was not the whole reason why he did not recognize his own country; in part it was because goddess Pallas Athene had thickened the air about him to keep him unknown "while she made him wise to things." Thus Homer tells the story of the most famous home-coming in the literature of the world.[1]

To the homecomer home shows — at least in the beginning — an unaccustomed face. He believes himself to be in a strange country, a stranger among strangers, until the goddess dissipates the veiling mist. But the homecomer's attitude differs from that of the stranger. The latter is about to join a group which is not and never has been his own. He knows that he will find himself in an unfamiliar world, differently organized than that from which he comes, full of pitfalls and hard to master.[2] The homecomer, however, expects to return to an environment of which he always had and — so he thinks — still has intimate knowledge and which he has just to take for granted in order to find his bearings within it. The approaching stranger has to anticipate in a more or less empty way what he will find; the homecomer has just to recur to the memories of his past. So he feels; and because he feels so, he will suffer the typical shock described by Homer.

These typical experiences of the homecomer will be analyzed in the following *in general terms* of social psychology. The returning veteran is, of course, an outstanding example of the situation under scrutiny. His special problems, however, have recently been widely discussed in many books and articles,[3] and it is not my aim to refer to them otherwise than as examples. We could refer also to the traveler who comes back from foreign countries, the emigrant who returns to his native land, the boy who "made good" abroad and now settles in his home town.[4] They all are instances of the "homecomer," defined as one who comes back for good to his home, — not as one returning for a

Reprinted from the *American Journal of Sociology*, 50 (1945), pp. 369–376, by permission of The University of Chicago Press, Chicago.

[1] The presentation follows the translation of Homer's *Odyssey* by T. E. Shaw ("Lawrence of Arabia") (New York: Oxford University Press, 1932).

[2] Cf. the present writer's paper "The Stranger," *American Journal of Sociology*, XLIX, No. 6 (May, 1944), 500–507.

[3] We mention, in the first place, Professor Willard Waller's *Veteran Comes Back* (New York: Dryden Press, 1944), an excellent sociological analysis of the civilian made into a professional soldier and of the soldier-turned-veteran who comes back to an alien homeland; also — Professor Dixon Wecter, *When Johnny Comes Marching Home* (Cambridge, Mass.: Houghton, Mifflin, 1944), with valuable documents relating to the American soldier returning from four wars and very helpful bibliographical references; finally, the discussion of the veteran problem in the *New York Herald Tribune*, "Annual Forum on Current Problems," October 22, 1944 (Sec. VIII), especially the contributions of Mrs. Anna Rosenberg, Lieutenant Charles G. Bolte, and Sergeant William J. Caldwell. See also the very interesting collection of servicemen's *Letters Home*, arranged and edited by Mina Curtiss (Boston: Little, Brown, 1944).

[4] Cf. the fine analysis of this situation in Thomas Wolfe's short story, "The Return of the Prodigal," in *The Hills Beyond* (New York: Harper & Bros., 1941).

temporary stay, such as the soldier on a thirty-day leave or the college boy spending the Christmas vacation with his family.

What, however, has to be understood by "home"? "Home is where one starts from," says the poet.[5] "The home is the place to which a man intends to return when he is away from it," says the jurist.[6] The home is starting-point as well as terminus. It is the null-point of the system of co-ordinates which we ascribe to the world in order to find our bearings in it. Geographically "home" means a certain spot on the surface of the earth. Where I happen to be is my "abode"; where I intend to stay is my "residence"; where I come from and whither I want to return is my "home." Yet home is not merely the homestead — my house, my room, my garden, my town — but everything it stands for. The symbolic character of the notion "home" is emotionally evocative and hard to describe. Home means different things to different people. It means, of course, father-house and mother-tongue, the family, the sweetheart, the friends; it means a beloved landscape, "songs my mother taught me," food prepared in a particular way, familiar things for daily use, folkways, and personal habits — briefly, a peculiar way of life composed of small and important elements, likewise cherished. *Chevron*, a Marine Corps newspaper, inquired what United States soldiers in the South Pacific miss most, outside of families and sweethearts. Here are some of the answers: " 'A fresh lettuce and tomato sandwich with ice-cold fresh milk to wash it down.' 'Fresh milk and the morning paper at the front door.' 'The smell of a drugstore.' 'A train and the engine whistle.' "[7] All these things, badly missed if not available, were probably not particularly appreciated so long as they were accessible at any time. They had just their humble place among the collective value "homely things." Thus, home means one thing to the man who never has left it, another thing to the man who dwells far from it, and still another to him who returns.

"To feel at home" is an expression of the highest degree of familiarity and intimacy. Life at home follows an organized pattern of routine; it has its well-determined goals and well-proved means to bring them about, consisting of a set of traditions, habits, institutions, timetables for activities of all kinds, etc. Most of the problems of daily life can be mastered by following this pattern. There is no need to define or redefine situations which have occurred so many times or to look for new solutions of old problems hitherto handled satisfactorily. The way of life at home governs as a scheme of expression and interpretation not only my own acts but also those of the other members of the in-group. I may trust that, using this scheme, I shall understand what the other means and make myself understandable to him. The system of relevances[8] adopted by the members of the in-group shows a high degree of conformity. I have always a fair chance — subjectively and objectively — to predict the other's action toward me as well as the other's reaction to my own social acts. We not only may forecast what will happen tomorrow, but we also have a fair chance to plan correctly the more distant future. Things will in substance continue to be what they have been so far. Of course, there are new situations, unexpected events. But at home, even deviations from the daily routine life are mastered in a way defined by the general style in which people at home deal with extraordinary situations. There is a way — a proved way — for meeting a crisis in business life, for settling family problems, for determining the attitude to adopt toward illness and even death. Paradoxically formulated, there is even a routine way for handling the novel.

In terms of social relationships, it could be said that life at home is, for the most part,

[5] T. S. Eliot, *Four Quartets* (New York: Harcourt, Brace, 1943), p. 17.

[6] Joseph H. Beale, *A Treatise on the Conflict of Laws* (New York: Baker, Voorhis, 1935), I, 126.

[7] Quoted from *Time*, June 5, 1944; other examples can be found in Wecter, *op. cit.*, pp. 495 ff.

[8] This term has been discussed in the afore-mentioned paper on "The Stranger," *loc. cit.*, pp. 500 ff.

actually or at least potentially life in so-called primary groups. This term was coined by Cooley[9] to designate intimate face-to-face relationship and has become a current, although contested,[10] feature of sociological textbooks. It will be helpful for our purpose to analyze some of the implications hidden in this highly equivocal term.

First of all, we have to distinguish between face-to-face relationships and intimate relationships. A face-to-face relationship presupposes that those who participate in it have space and time in common as long as the relation lasts. Community of space means, on the one hand, that for each partner the other's body, his facial expressions, his gestures, etc., are immediately observable as symptoms of his thought. The field of the other's expressions is wide open for possible interpretation, and the actor may control immediately and directly the effect of his own social acts by the reaction of his fellow. On the other hand, community of space means that a certain sector of the outer world is equally accessible to all the partners in the face-to-face relationship. The same things are within reach, within sight, within hearing, and so on. Within this common horizon there are objects of common interest and common relevance; things to work with or upon, actually or potentially. Community of time does not refer so much to the extent of outer (objective) time shared by the partners but to the fact that each of them participates in the onrolling inner life of the other. In the face-to-face relation I can grasp the other's thoughts in a vivid present as they develop and build themselves up, and so can he with reference to my stream of thought; and both of us know and take into account this possibility. The other is to me, and I am to the other, not an abstraction, not a mere instance of typical behavior, but, by the very reason of our sharing a common vivid present, this unique individual personality in this unique particular situation. These are, very roughly outlined, some of the features of the face-to-face relation which we prefer to call the "pure we-relation." It is, indeed, of outstanding importance in its own right because it can be shown that all other social relationships can, and for certain purposes have to be, interpreted as derived from the pure we-relation.

Yet it is important to understand that the pure we-relation refers merely to the formal structure of social relationships based upon community of space and time. It may be filled with a great variety of contents showing manifold degrees of intimacy and anonymity. To share the vivid present of a woman we love or of the neighbor in the subway are certainly different kinds of face-to-face relations. Cooley's concept of primary groups, however, presupposes a particular content of such a relationship — namely, intimacy.[11]. We have to forego here the analysis of this ill-defined term which could be made explicit only by embarking upon an investigation of the layers of personality involved, the schemes of expression and interpretation presupposed, and the common system of relevance referred to by the partners. It suffices that the category of intimacy is independent of that of the face-to-face relation.

However, the term "primary group," as generally used, implies a third notion, which itself is independent of either of the two mentioned above, namely, the recurrent character of certain social relationships. It is by no means restricted to pure we-relations and to intimate relations, although we are going to choose our examples from them. A

[9] Charles H. Cooley, *Social Organization* (New York: Scribners, 1909), chaps. iii-v.

[10] Cf. R. M. MacIver, *Society* (New York: Farrar & Rinehart, 1937), chapter on the "Primary Group and Large Scale Association" (esp. p. 236 n.); Edward C. Jandy, *Charles H. Cooley, His Life and Social Theory* (New York: Dryden Press, 1942); pp. 171–81; Ellsworth Faris, "Primary Group, Essence and Accident," *American Journal of Sociology*, XXX (July, 1932), 41–45; Frederick R. Clow, "Cooley's Doctrine of Primary Groups," *American Journal of Sociology*, XXV (November, 1919), 326–47.

[11] We disregard here entirely Cooley's untenable theory of "primary ideals," such as loyalty, truth, service, kindness, etc.

marriage, a friendship, a family group, a kindergarten, does not consist of a permanent, a strictly continuous, primary face-to-face relationship but rather of a series of merely intermittent face-to-face relationships. More precisely, the so-called "primary groups" are institutionalized situations which make it possible to re-establish the interrupted we-relation and to continue where it was broken off last time. There is, of course, no certainty, but just a mere chance, that such a re-establishment and continuation will succeed. But it is characteristic in the primary group as conceived by Cooley that the existence of such a chance is taken for granted by all its members.

After these parenthetical and all too casual explications, we may, for the present purpose, stick to our previous statement that life at home means, for the most part, life in actual or potential primary groups. The meaning of this statement has now become clear. It means to have in common with others a section of space and time, and therewith surrounding objects as possible ends and means, and interests based upon an underlying more or less homogeneous system of relevances; it means, furthermore, that the partners in a primary relationship experience one another as unique personalities in a vivid present, by following their unfolding thought as an ongoing occurrence and by sharing, therefore, their anticipations of the future as plans, as hopes or as anxieties; it means, finally, that each of them has the chance to re-establish the we-relation, if interrupted, and to continue it as if no intermittance had occurred. To each of the partners the other's life becomes, thus, a part of his own autobiography, an element of his personal history. What he is, what he grew to be, what he will become is codetermined by his taking part in the manifold actual or potential primary relationships which prevail within the homegroup.

This is the aspect of the social structure of the home world for the man who lives in it. The aspect changes entirely for the man who has left home. To him life at home is no longer accessible in immediacy. He has stepped, so to speak, into another social dimension not covered by the system of coordinates used as the scheme of reference for life at home. No longer does he experience as a participant in a vivid present the many we-relations which form the texture of the home group. His leaving home has replaced these vivid experiences with memories, and these memories preserve merely what home life meant up to the moment he left it behind. The ongoing development has come to a standstill. What has been so far a series of *unique* constellations, formed by individual persons, relations, and groups, receives the character of mere *types*; and this typification entails, by necessity, a deformation of the underlying structure of relevances. To a certain degree the same holds good for those left behind. By cutting off the community of space and time, for example, the field within which the other's expressions manifest themselves and are open to interpretation has been narrowed. The other's personality is no longer accessible as a unit; it has been broken down into pieces. There is no longer the total experience of the beloved person, his gestures, his way of walking and of speaking, of listening and of doing things; what remains are recollections, a photograph, some handwritten lines. This situation of the separated persons is, to a certain degree, that of those in bereavement; "partir, c'est mourir un peu."

To be sure, there still are means of communication, such as the letter. But the letter-writer addresses himself to the type of addressee as he knew him when they separated, and the addressee reads the letter as written by the person typically the same as the one he left behind.[12]. Presupposing such a typicality (and any typicality) means assuming that what has been proved to be typical in the past will have a good chance to be typical in the future, or, in other words, that life will continue to be what it has been so far: the

[12] Cf. Georg Simmel's excellent analysis of the sociology of the letter in his *Soziologie, Untersuchungen über die Formen der Vergesellschaftung* (Leipzig, 1922), pp. 379–82.

same things will remain relevant, the same degree of intimacy in personal relationships will prevail, etc. Yet by the mere change of surroundings, other things have become important for both, old experiences are re-evaluated; novel ones, inaccessible to the other, have emerged in each partner's life. Many a soldier in the combat line is astonished to find letters from home lacking any understanding of his situation, because they underscore the relevance of things which are of no importance to him in his actual situation, although they would be the subject of many deliberations if he were at home and had to handle them. This change of the system of relevance has its corollary in the changing degree of intimacy. The term "intimacy" designates *here* merely the degree of reliable knowledge we have of another person or of a social relationship, a group, a cultural pattern, or a thing. As far as a person is concerned, intimate knowledge enables us to interpret what he means and to forecast his actions and reactions. In the highest form of intimacy, we know, to quote Kipling, the other's "naked soul." But separation conceals the other behind a strange disguise, hard to remove. From the point of view of the absent one the longing for re-establishing the old intimacy — not only with persons but also with things — is the main feature of what is called "homesickness." Yet, the change in the system of relevance and in the degree of intimacy just described is differently experienced by the absent one and by the home group. The latter continues its daily life within the customary pattern. Certainly, this pattern, too, will have changed and even in a more or less abrupt way. But those at home, although aware of this change, lived together through this changing world, experienced it as changing in immediacy, adapted their interpretative system, and adjusted themselves to the change. In other words, the system may have changed entirely, but it changed as a system; it was never disrupted and broken down; even in its modification it is still an appropriate device for mastering life. The in-group has now other goals and other means for attaining them, but still it remains an in-group.

The absent one has the advantage of knowing the general style of this pattern. He may from previous experiences conclude what attitude mother will take to the task of running the household under the rationing system, how sister will feel in the war plant, what a Sunday means without pleasure driving[13]. Those left at home have no immediate experience of how the soldier lives at the front. There are reports in the newspapers and over the radio, recitals from homecomers, movies in technicolor, official and unofficial propaganda, all of which build up a stereotype of the soldier's life "somewhere in France" or "somewhere in the Pacific." For the most part, these stereotypes are not spontaneously formed but are directed, censored for military or political reasons, and designed to build up morale at the home front or to increase the efficiency of war production or the subscription of war bonds. There is no warrant whatsoever that what is described as typical by all these sources of information is also relevant to the absent member of the in-group. Any soldier knows that his style of living depends upon the military group to which he belongs, the job allotted to him within this group, the attitude of his officers and comrades. That is what counts, and not the bulletin "All quiet on the western front." But whatever occurs to him under these particular circumstances is his individual, personal, unique experience which he never will allow to be typified. When the soldier returns and starts to speak — if he starts to speak at all — he is bewildered to see that his listeners, even the sympathetic ones, do not understand the uniqueness of these individual experiences

[13] This, of course, does not hold in case of a violent destruction of the home by catastrophes or enemy action. Then, however, not only may the general style of the pattern of home life have changed entirely but even the home itself may have ceased to exist. The absent one is then "homeless" in the true sense and has no place to return to.

which have rendered him another man. They try to find familiar traits in what he reports by subsuming it under *their* preformed types of the soldier's life at the front. To them there are only small details in which his recital deviates from what every homecomer has told and what they have read in magazines and seen in the movies. So it may happen that many acts which seem to the people at home the highest expression of courage are to the soldier in battle merely the struggle for survival or the fulfilment of a duty, whereas many instances of real endurance, sacrifice, and heroism remain unnoticed or unappreciated by people at home.[14]

This discrepancy between the uniqueness and decisive importance that the absent one attributes to his experiences and their pseudo-typification by the people at home, who impute to them a pseudo-relevance, is one of the biggest obstacles to mutual reestablishment of the disrupted we-relations. Yet the success or failure of the homecoming will depend upon the chance of transforming these social relations into recurrent ones. But, even if such a discrepancy did not prevail, the complete solution of this problem would remain an unrealizable ideal.

What is here in question is nothing less than the irreversibility of inner time. It is the same problem which Heraclitus visualized with his statement that we cannot bathe twice in the same river; which Bergson analyzed in his philosophy of the *durée*; which Kierkegaard described as the problem of "repetition"; which Péguy had in mind in saying that the road which leads from Paris to Chartres has a different aspect from the road which leads from Chartres to Paris; and it is the same problem which, in a somewhat distorted fashion, occupies G. H. Mead's *Philosophy of the Present*. The mere fact that we grow older, that novel experiences emerge continuously within our stream of thought, that previous experiences are permanently receiving additional interpretative meanings in the light of these supervenient experiences, which have, more or less, changed our state of mind — all these basic features of our mental life bar a recurrence of the same. Being recurrent, the recurrent is not the same any more. Repetition might be aimed at and longed for: what belongs to the past can never be reinstated in another present exactly as it was. When it emerged, it carried along empty anticipations, horizons of future developments, references to chances and possibilities; now, in hindsight, these anticipations prove to have been or not to have been fulfilled; the perspectives have changed; what was merely in the horizon has shifted toward the center of attention or disappeared entirely; former chances have turned into realities or proved to be impossibilities — briefly, the former experience has now another meaning.

This is certainly not the place to embark upon an analysis of the highly complicated philosophical problems of time, memory, and meaning here involved. They are just mentioned for two reasons: First, in the present state of the social sciences it seems always to be useful to show that the analysis of a concrete sociological problem, if only driven far enough, necessarily leads to certain basic philosophical questions which social scientists cannot dodge by using unclarified terms such as "environment," "adjustment," "adaptation," "cultural pattern," and so on. Second, this set of problem determines decisively the form, if not the content, of the attitude of the homecomer even if he does not find that substantial changes have occurred in the life of the home group or in its relations to him. Even then, the home to which he returns is by no means the home he left or the home which he recalled and longed for during his absence. And, for the same reason, the homecomer is not the same man who left. He is neither the same for himself nor for those who await his return.

This statement holds good for any kind of home-coming. Even if we return home after a short vacation, we find that the old accustomed surroundings have received an

[14] "Without exception G.I.'s most dislike tin-horn war and home-front heroics" is the summary of a poll by *Time* correspondents: "What kind of movies do G.I.'s like?" (*Time*, August 14, 1944).

added meaning derived from and based upon our experiences during our absence. Whatever the accompanying evaluation may be, things and men will, at least in the beginning, have another face. It will need a certain effort to transform our activities again into routine work and to reactivate our recurrent relations with men and things. No wonder, since we intended our vacation to be an interruption of our daily routine.

Homer tells of the landing of Odysseus' comrades at the island of the lotus-eaters. The lotus-eaters devised not death for the intruders but gave them a dish of their lotus flowers; and as each tasted this honey-sweet plant, the wish to return grew faint in him: he preferred to dwell forever with the lotus-eating men, feeding upon lotus and letting fade from his mind all longing for home.

To a certain extent, each homecomer has tasted the magic fruit of strangeness, be it sweet or bitter. Even amid the overwhelming longing for home there remains the wish to transplant into the old pattern something of the novel goals, of the newly discovered means to realize them, of the skills and experiences acquired abroad. We cannot be astonished, therefore, that a United States War Department survey of June, 1944,[15] showed that 40 per cent of the discharged veterans being sent back to civilian life through eastern "separation centers" did not want their old jobs back and did not want even to return to their old communities. On the Pacific Coast the percentage of those men was even greater.

A small-town newspaper celebrated the home-coming of the local hero, giving a full account of his feats of extraordinary boldness, efficient leadership, steadfastness, and willingness to assume responsibility. The recital ends with the enumeration of the decorations justly awarded to him and with the statement that Lieutenant X. had always enjoyed the good will of his community, where he had served for years as cigar clerk in a prominent local store. This case seems to be a rather typical one. A young man lives for years in a small town, a regular fellow, liked by everybody, but in an occupation which, honorable as it is, does not give him any chance to prove his worth. Quite possibly, he himself was not aware of what he could perform. The war gives him such an opportunity; he makes good and receives the reward he deserves. Can we expect, can we wish, that such a man should come home not only to family and sweetheart but also to his place behind the cigar counter? Have we not to hope that Lieutenant X. will avail himself of the facilities provided by Congress in the "G.I. Bill of Rights" to obtain a position in civil life more appropriate to his gifts?

But — and here we touch upon a chief problem of the homecomer — it is unfortunately an unwarranted assumption that social functions which stood the test within one system of social life will continue to do so if transplanted into another system. This general proposition is especially applicable to the problem of the returning veteran. From the sociological point of view, army life shows a strange ambivalence. Considered as an in-group, the army is characterized by an exceptionally high degree of constraint, of discipline imposed authoritatively upon the behavior of the individual by a controlling normative structure. The sense of duty, comradeship, the feeling of solidarity, and subordination are the outstanding features developed in the individual — all this, however, within a frame of means and ends imposed by the group and not open to his own choice. These features prevail in times of peace as well as in times of war. However, in times of war they do not regulate the behavior of the members of the in-group in relation to members of the out-group — that is, the enemy. The combatant's attitude toward the enemy in battle is, and is supposed to be, rather the opposite of disciplined constraint. War is the archetype of that social structure which Durkheim calls the state of "*anomie*." The specific valor of the fighting warrior consists in his will and adroitness in overcoming the other in a desperate struggle of

[15] According to *Time*, June 12, 1944.

power, and it cannot be easily used within that pattern of civilian life which has prevailed in Western democracies. Moreover, the homecoming soldier returns to an in-group, the homeworld in the postwar period, which itself is marked by a certain degree of *anomie*, of lack of control and discipline. He finds, then, that *anomie* is no longer to be the basic structure of his relations with the out-group but is a feature of the in-group itself, toward the members of which he cannot apply the techniques permitted and required within the *anomie* situation of battle. In this civil world he will have to choose his own goals and the means to attain them and can no longer depend upon authority and guidance. He will feel, as Professor Waller puts it, like a "motherless child."

Another factor supervenes. In times of war the members of the armed forces have a privileged status within the community as a whole. "The best for our boys in the service" is more than a mere slogan. It is the expression of prestige deservedly accorded to those who might have to give their life for their country or at least to those who left family, studies, occupation, and the amenities of civil life for a highly valued interest of the community. The civilian looks at the man in uniform as an actual or future fighter; and so, indeed, the man in uniform looks at himself, even if he performs merely desk work in an army office somewhere in the United States. This humbler occupation does not matter; to him, too, the induction marked a turning-point in his life. But the discharged homecomer is deprived of his uniform and with it of his privileged status within the community. This does not mean that he will lose, by necessity, the prestige acquired as an actual or potential defender of the homeland, although history does not show that exaggerated longevity is accorded to the memory of glory. This is partly because of the disappointment at home that the returning veteran does not correspond to the pseudotype of the man whom they have been expecting.

This leads to a practical conclusion. Much has been done and still more will be done to prepare the homecoming veteran for the necessary process of adjustment. However, it seems to be equally indispensable to prepare the home group accordingly. They have to learn through the press, the radio, the movies, that the man whom they await will be another and not the one they imagined him to be. It will be a hard task to use the propaganda machine in the opposite direction, namely, to destroy the pseudotype of the combatant's life and the soldier's life in general and to replace it by the truth. But it is indispensable to undo the glorification of a questionable Hollywood-made heroism by bringing out the real picture of what these men endure, how they live, and what they think and feel — a picture no less meritorious and no less evocative.

In the beginning it is not only the homeland that shows to the homecomer an unaccustomed face. The homecomer appears equally strange to those who expect him, and the thick air about him will keep him unknown. Both the homecomer and the welcomer will need the help of a Mentor to "make them wise to things."

VI

MEASUREMENT and MATHEMATICS in the SOCIAL SCIENCES

At the very least, the problems of this section are continuous with those which arise from considering the language — concepts, definitions, etc. — employed by social scientists. For one thing, it may be held that compatibility with some form of measurement is the much pursued touchstone of acceptable concepts in the social sciences: is this not suggested by S. S. Stevens' claim that "measurement is the backbone of scientific method?" Secondly, as Lazarsfeld and Barton point out, nothing can be measured without what they call "indicators," the purpose of which is to "translate a concept into a set of instructions to the researcher, telling him what to look for as a basis of judgment in each case." This reliance on indicators, however, unleashes the same question that plagued operationists: are the indicators designed to measure and compare what is grouped together by antecedent principles? If so, how does one assess the accuracy of, or choose between, alternative indicators? Furthermore, Shapley and Shubik would certainly agree with Simon's view that "mathematics is a language" which provides precise definitions for such pivotal social science concepts as 'rational behavior,' 'power,' 'preference,' 'group identification,' etc. But any program which exchanges mathematical concepts for ordinary ones must be prepared to deal with Scriven's contention that "inventing new terms is too frequently a substitute for analyzing the old ones and a move which only postpones the difficulties, for at some stage we try to relate the discoveries formulated in the new language to the problems formulated in the old."

In selection 40, S. S. Stevens describes the methods and some of the findings of psycho-physics. Stevens conceives of this science as endeavoring to discover the "laws of sensation," that is, correlations between the energy of physical stimuli and the processes and activities involved in sense-perception. Given his analysis, perception is impossible without the occurrence of sensations ("bare messages") or unorganized bits of data impressed upon us by changes in "external energy that activate a sense-organ and its receptors." According to Stevens, these sensations, which include pain, warmth, brightness, and loudness, all have attributes which are subject to the most exact and quantitative modes of measurement. Such attributes, e.g., duration and intensity, are what Lazarsfeld and Barton refer to as "variables": like Centigrade temperature or velocity, they permit comparisons not merely in terms of whether given data possess (or possess more or less of), a certain attribute (it is *warm* today, Bill is *faster than* Tom), but in terms of percentage ratios (it is *three times as warm as* yesterday, he travels only *half as fast* on land). Alternatively, for every variable (fixed-interval) concept, there is a scale on which distinct pairs of points [(40°, 50°); (140°, 150°)] are separated by fixed and equal intervals.

The notion of sensation concepts as variables suggests an argument supporting B. F. Skinner's view of the science of human behavior. For if the behavior involved in sense-perception is open to the same sort of measurement as the speed or impact of moving bodies, what reason can there be for claiming that it is *impossible* to fulfill the psycho-physicist's quest for laws of sensation? And if *this* quest can succeed, it seems warranted that *no* limits of an a priori sort can be set on the covering law model: only future experiments can tell to what extent, if any, the methods of the physical sciences can be relied on to explain and predict human conduct. (But is it an empirical question whether concepts like *pain*, *loudness*, and *brightness* are *variables*?)

If Stevens' account of such sensations as perceived weight (see pages 505–506) is correct, then measurement cannot be wholly excluded from the social sciences. But is there *no* truth in the claim that what is characteristic of men and their institutions *does not allow of measurement*? In selection 41, Lazarsfeld and Barton attempt to salvage what is sound in this claim. Their efforts are based on avoiding two extreme positions which, they hold, make the same faulty assumption: *that phenomena allow of measurement only if they fall under variable concepts.* From this assumption, and a commitment to the necessity of measurement for scientific inquiry, it follows that social scientists should exorcise all concepts (including those which refer to beliefs and decisions) which resist translation into fixed-scale equivalents. The second position insists that a language restricted to variable notions is too sparse to capture what is distinctive in the activities and social forms which human beings initiate and organize. Since it also identifies measurable concepts with variables, this position arrives at the prescription that measurement should be scrapped in favor of "an entirely intuitive approach to the understanding of society" (in particular, to the classification and organization of data).

It is Lazarsfeld and Barton's contention that the social sciences need not reject *either* the demand for measurability or the demand to go beyond variable concepts. On their view, there is a family of activities involved in classifying, comparing, and interpreting data which are the present stock-in-trade of many social researchers. When these activities (which they subsume under "qualitative measurement") are systematically analyzed and codified, it will become clear that nonvariable (and intentional) concepts such as 'pessimism,' 'authority,' and 'pacifism' are not incompatible with measurement. Thus, claim Lazarsfeld and Barton, the social scientist who restricts himself to observing measurable phenomena does not thereby diminish his capacity to describe and explain the entire compass of human behavior.

Two processes of concept-formation are central to the middle ground advocated by Lazarsfeld and Barton: (1) the identification of indicators which provide operational instructions for applying a concept in any given case and (2) the segmentation of complicated or conflict-ridden concepts ("adjustment") into more restricted and less controversial dimensions ("appearance," "response to interviews"), each of which may in turn be subdivided in the interest of even greater "objectivity." When qualitative measurement relies on indicators or segmentation, it departs at several points from the ideal of quantitative measurement as S. S. Stevens sees it exemplified in psycho-physics. For one thing, the indicators employed, though "simpler" than the original concept, are often not variables; in Stevens' terms (page 504), they are measurable only by nominal or ordinal scales. Secondly, the application of these indicators is not always fixed by operational instructions which entirely eliminate reasoned disagreement. These instructions can carry one only part of the way, and must be supplemented by professional experience and seasoned judgment. Third, nonquantitative decisions will have to be made, on occasion, concerning the relative weight of data yielded by distinct, and possibly conflicting, segments or indicators. Our authors ask, for example, whether badly chewed fingernails and untied shoelaces are equally revealing signs of maladjustment. "It is useless," they assert, "to break down a classification into highly objective indicators if we have no reasonable way of deciding how to recombine them." But "reasonable" is probably not a precisely measurable notion. (What would be meant by claiming that one course of action is *three times as reasonable* as another?) And in any case, there may be several equally reasonable procedures for recombination.

But these departures from quantitative measurement, Lazarsfeld and Barton maintain, do not warrant the conclusion that the subject matter of the social sciences is beyond measurement or can be grasped only by some direct and untestable form of intuitive insight. It is possible to standardize the training of those who compile and compare data and this should enhance the reliability (consistency, repeatability) of their judgments and decrease their dependence on unstated assumptions. Furthermore, "as a rule, any degree of segmentation and specification of indicators makes classification more objective — more likely to be agreed upon and more easily communicable." In short, objective measurement (collecting, classifying, comparing, interpreting data) can proceed without resorting to any program of fixed-scale translation. By dropping the assumption that measurement requires variable concepts, we eliminate the need to choose between a social science stripped of everything except variables and a social science which relies wholly on uncheckable intuitions. There emerges a third option, a synthesis of the demand for objective measurement and the demand for nonvariable concepts.

Compromises on philosophical issues have a way of satisfying no one. We may expect both "objectivists" and "subjectivists" to find fault with Lazarsfeld and Barton's attempt to occupy the middle of the road. For one thing, do the qualitative methods they codify lend any "objectivity" to classification procedures within the social sciences? On page 538 below, two key problems in concept-formation are distinguished: "The one is *which criteria* [indicators] to choose; the other is *how to combine* several criteria into one index so that ranking becomes possible." Do Lazarsfeld and Barton provide "objective" procedures for resolving these two problems?

Consider concept A ("exercise of family authority"), the ordinary application of which (we may assume) is not governed by any devices of qualitative measurement. In this sense, the use of this term in prescientific contexts is guided solely by "unaided intuition". To remove this deficiency, the social scientist introduces the two indicators, *corporal punishment* and *interference by the parent in the child's affairs.* What gain in "objectivity" is yielded by this move? Must not intuition now be employed, and controversy break out, in answering *three* questions instead of just one: (1) in what circumstances is it correct to apply each of these indicators; (2) how are the two indicators to be weighed against, and recombined with, one another to yield a single judgment concerning the original attribute; (3) do the indicators really measure A, or some other property which is neither necessary nor sufficient for the presence of A? Lazarsfeld and Barton, of course, do not argue that complete objectivity can be attained — at present — in the ranking, classifying, etc. of phenomena studied by social scientists. But they do claim that the techniques of qualitative measurement augment the degree of objectivity which the social sciences can attain. Yet even this seems open to dispute, if questions (1) — (3) can always be asked after every specification of indicators or segmentation of dimensions. The most that qualitative measurement seems to accomplish is to shift the focus of intuition; to place a new (and larger) set of questions before the bar of intuitive judgment. The point has been deftly expressed by L. W. Beck:

However much the instruments of social science localize and control the subjective contribution to observations, the design, choice, and evaluation of instruments still depend upon the same kind of insight that social philosophers have always possessed or claimed; otherwise the results of instrumental observation may be very neat and elegant, but they have no noticeable relevance to the prescientific problems which led to the development of these, rather than other, instruments.

Hence the social scientist, equipped with the finest batteries of tests, is still in the position of the legendary people who wished to weigh a pig very accurately. They planed the board to which the pig was to be tied until it was of identical thickness, measured in "milli-micro-mulahs," throughout its length; they used as counterweights stones whose sphericity had been established within limits of one "milli-micro-mulah;" they carefully balanced the pig and board against the stones — then they asked the first stranger who came along to estimate the weight of the stones.[1]

There is thus some danger that qualitative measurement merely opens up new opportunities for, and does not decrease, the social scientist's reliance on "art and intuition." Moreover, sitting out in the middle of the road, Lazarsfeld and Barton seem equally open to certain criticisms raised in part V against crude operationists. The following passage seems pivotal to their concept of qualitative measurement:

As a general rule, the more we segment the judgment, the more concrete and objective the indicators become; hence, different classifiers are more likely to agree, and the judgment procedure can be communicated and duplicated by others. The ideal situation would be to reduce a complex concept to such clear and unambiguous indicators that the classification procedure would become mechanical; anyone with the same set of instructions could duplicate the observations and judgments of any other observer. [See page 525 below.)

What Lazarsfeld and Barton regard as the "ideal situation" seems to conflict with the view that psychological concepts are both irreducible and indispensable for any complete account of human conduct. Does "concrete" here carry much the same meaning as "physical" or "nonmental" as understood in selections 33 and 34 above? If so, this passage invokes social scientists to replace psychological by nonpsychological concepts, a proposal that would prevent them from recognizing and explaining a great many important and familiar kinds of human activity. The "objectivity" sought by Lazarsfeld and Barton may well presuppose the behaviorist and operationist elimination of the mental common to selections 30 and 31 and criticized by Scriven, Chisholm, and Heidelberger.

The supposed objectivity yielded by qualitative measurement may have additional costs. How much is gained and how much lost, for example, when the quest for a "simple and objective" indicator of child-readership leads us to assume that "any comic book is, roughly speaking, the equivalent of any other?" (From a child's point of view?) Or when it is stated that a combination of *conflicts with* and *confidence in* authority "can practically be disregarded" as far as constituting the "highest degree of acceptance" of authority? Or when it is stated that income is a variable concept, from which it follows that the distance from 0 to 1000 dollars is the *same* as that between 1,000,000 and 1,001,000 dollars? Is this not a substitution of mathematical equality (a nonpsychological concept) for, say, "means as much as" or "are seen as equally desirable" (psychological concepts)? The issue here seems to turn on what is to be meant by the "distance" between sums of money. Is it wholly a matter of the *mathematical properties* (twice as large as, etc.) of the sums (mathematical distance);

[1] Beck, L. W. "The 'Natural Science Ideal' in the Social Sciences," *The Scientific Monthly*, 68, 1949, page 389.

or does it involve how much one sum is *preferred* to another (psychological distance)? In asserting that income is a variable concept, are Lazarsfeld and Barton implying that mathematical distance is an (the best, the sole) index of psychological distance?

Further, Lazarsfeld and Barton believe that the objectivity introduced by qualitative measurement is the only alternative to "impressionistic judgment" and fixed-scale measurement. But their notion of an objective concept may be overly restrictive: is the application of every objective concept free from controversy, complexity, and other sources of uncertainty? To make a system of classification more *objective*, as they define this term, is to make its application "more likely to be agreed on." Is this objectivity, or its shadow? Routine duplication, habitual agreement, tidy consensus appear to have replaced the aim of examining phenomena from the widest possible variety of perspectives, allowing their identity and interrelations to become accessible through the conflict and fusion of these divergent frames of reference. Objectivity is not a transparent concept, but it may not be even roughly equatable with likelihood of agreement. And if such an equation should turn out to be correct, we would then need to be told why every concept in the social sciences should be "objective." [2]

Consider the two concepts "driving a car down Main Street on Sunday afternoon" and "conspicuous consumption." Should we refuse to permit the latter into the vocabulary of social science simply because it does not generate as much agreement as the former? Is "conspicuous consumption" less objective simply because less agreement can be obtained about its application in particular cases? Would we necessarily produce a gain in its objectivity by reducing it to operational indicators (or segments) on the order of "driving a car . . ."? To eliminate, through segmentation or simple-concrete indicators, the clash of discordant definitions and judgments, the various risks and uncertainties involved in weighing and applying criteria — such purgation might destroy the only sort of objectivity open to many forms of discourse concerning human agents. In the social sciences, objectivity might sometimes emerge only after genuine dialogue and dialectic between disputants had run its course, i.e., where there is no pre-decided and blanket ban against persistent controversy or irreconcilable disagreements.

Lazarsfeld and Barton, in brief, assume that there are just two types of objective concepts: those that allow of quantitative and those that allow of qualitative measurement. And their account of both types seems to confront us with notions that, in principle at least, can be equated with or reduced to indicators of a "concrete" or nonpsychological sort; indicators the use of which can be mastered by anyone whose perceptual senses are intact. We can say, therefore, that according to Lazarsfeld and Barton, a necessary condition for measurement is reducibility to nonpsychological indicators. But there may well be objective concepts that do not allow of any such reduction, e.g., Chisholm's intentional concepts, those H. L. A. Hart spoke of as "defeasible,"[3] those W. B. Gallie labelled "essentially contested,"[4] and those Frank Sibley grouped under the heading of "aesthetic."[5] If any of these apply to human

[2] One claim of selection 53 and the introduction to part VIII is that a concept can be objectively employed even though *only some* and not all men — i.e., those committed to certain values or principles — can master it or duplicate observations framed by its employment.

[3] Hart, H. L. A., "The Ascription of Responsibility and Rights," reprinted in Flew, A. G. N. (ed), *Logic and Language*, First Series, Oxford, 1960, pages 145–166.

[4] Gallie, W. B., "Essentially Contested Concepts," reprinted in Black, Max (ed), *The Importance of Language*, Englewood Cliffs, 1962, pages 121–146.

[5] Sibley, Frank, "Aesthetic Concepts," reprinted in Margolis, Joseph (ed), *Philosophy Looks at the Arts*, New York, 1962, pages 63–87.

agents, then some of man's activity is not measurable, at least given Lazarsfeld and Barton's analysis of measurement. There may be a point in social science where one must choose between the ideal of measurement and the ideal of accurate description. An unlimited commitment to the former may prevent one from identifying (and explaining) certain forms of human conduct, i.e., those falling under objective concepts that do not satisfy the reducibility condition of measurement.

It is oversimple then, as Lazarsfeld and Barton rightly insist, to contend that every judgment which does not contain a variable concept expresses nothing but an uncheckable intuition. But it may also be oversimple, though less so, to contend that social scientists who reject both quantitative and qualitative measurement (as construed in selection 41) must fall back on incorrigible personal impressions. There may be additional options: types of concepts which, though incompatible with a necessary condition for (any form of) measurement, nonetheless allow us to distinguish between better and worse applications, more and less reasonable judgments. Lazarsfeld and Barton appear to deny these additional possibilities. As a result, they may grant less than they should to the view that social scientists cannot always work with, or inquire into, phenomena that allow of measurement.

In selections 40 and 41, mathematics and measurement are linked in various ways. The former, for example, recommends the use of two- and three-dimensional graphs to sharpen differences between, and to allow ways of ranking, competing indices of the same concept (see pages 538–544). And it is S. S. Stevens' view that:

> None of the seven basic problems of psychophysics can be solved without the use of statistics. The reason for this is obvious. The behavior of living organisms is variable. Seldom does their behavior repeat itself exactly from moment to moment. Nor does the behavior of one individual always duplicate that of another. For this reason the answers to psychological questions are nearly always statistical answers. They are usually given in terms of averages and variabilities — the elementary but important concepts in what has lately become a highly developed branch of mathematics. [See page 507 below.]

Shapley and Shubik's "method for evaluating the distribution of power in a committee system" is yet another instance of the alliance between mathematics and measurement. Their definition of power in terms of the relative frequency of a voter being pivotal to "the success of a winning coalition" allows us to speak of one group as having 3/5 or 4 times the power of another, i.e., permits an equal interval scale of power. Moreover, it apparently yields a nonarbitrary zero point: "the charman of a board consisting of an even number of members (including himself) has no power," they assert, "if he is allowed to vote only to break ties." Finally, this definition is what might be termed "mathematically operational." That is, to measure the power of the United States Senate in relation to its House of Representatives or that of the veto-empowered members of the United Nations Security Council requires *no* operations beyond those of permutation, division, and addition. No "operations" on, or inquiries into, the lives of actual or projected members of the group under study need be carried out. Any and all observations of or empirical laws concerning the hopes, interests, culture, education, etc. of power-seekers and power-sufferers are besides the point. It is in this sense that Shapley and Shubik wish to present an entirely "a priori" method for measuring power: in their case, the solidarity of mathematics and measurement is particularly pronounced. It is not that mathematics is employed to clarify, rank, or otherwise compare already gathered data, as e.g., in the case of statistics. On the contrary, *the data is obtained by performing the requisite mathematical operations*. The alliance has virtually become an identity.

Shapley and Shubik's short paper is intended to serve only as a "first step" in the mathematical reduction of political power. But that step, regardless of size, has its dangers. For one thing, despite the authors' claim that "any scheme for imputing power among the members of a committee either yields the power index defined above or leads to a logical inconsistency," there do seem to be alternative mathematical options. Consider a government with three chambers, each operating by majority rule, each required for a bill to pass, and with relative sizes of 1, 3, and 5. Shapley and Shubik contend that in any such case "the division of power is in the proportions of 32:37:25." But is it self-contradictory to suppose that the chambers have equal amounts of power, a result reached by considering the cases in which each of the houses, *taken collectively*, is pivotal and ignoring the pivotal/nonpivotal status of individual members within the various chambers? (Roughly, the vote of one man or group is *pivotal* wherever it decides the fate of a given proposal.) Here Shapley and Shubik would certainly appeal to what their seventh footnote calls *additivity*. But the question still remains: is it self-contradictory to deny that power is additive?

Or take the case (page 553) of

> . . . a board with five members, one of whom casts two extra votes. If a simple majority (four out of seven votes) carries the day, then power is distributed 60% to the multivote member, 10% to each of the others. To see this, observe that there are five possible positions for the strong man, if we arrange the members in order at random. In three of these positions he is pivotal. Hence his index is equal to 3/5.

We suppose that Jones has the extra votes. Now a priori it is equally likely, in any given case, that each of the other men will vote with Jones as that they will vote against him. Hence, we shall stipulate that where the probability of Smith voting with Jones is ½, 1/n is to be added to the latter's votes, where n equals the number of voters besides Jones. In this way, a conflicting index of power is created. For our five-man board, everyone but the weighted member has two votes; he will have four. Thus, Jones can now be assigned a power index of 100%: from an a priori standpoint, he can always count on enough votes to swing a majority (4 out of 7). Alternatively, though, we could specify his power index as: 4:2:2:2:2; that is, 4/12 or 33 1/3%. None of these purely mathematical procedures seem "logically inconsistent." If they are self-consistent, then on mathematical or a priori grounds, they are all equally tenable, and thus, there is no mathematical way of disqualifying them in favor of the index proposed by Shapley and Shubik. Given this, can any of them claim to shed more light than the others on the ordinary concept of power, i.e., that employed within the domain studied by the political scientist and expressed in such statements as "The most *powerful* political faction in Italy favors nationalizing the spaghetti industry" or "The Senate has *far more power* than the House of Representatives"?

Shapley and Shubik recognize that their mathematical model cannot be expected "to catch all the subtle shades and nuances of custom and procedure that are to be found in most real decision-making bodies." Nonetheless, they believe it "may be useful in the setting up of norms or standards, the departure from which will serve as a measure of, for example, political solidarity, or regional or sociological factionalism, in an assembly." But how can departures be distinguished from nondepartures? Under what circumstances can it be correctly claimed that an instance conforming to the model actually occurred?

Let us concede that in groups which actually possess the formal structure of our five-man committee, the weighted member is found to be on the winning side in some specific percentage of the cases, say 3/5. (We can call this the *correlated percentage.*) It does not follow that wherever one member of a group wins in 3/5 of the cases, we have an instance of the formal structure. His winning may be the result of intimidation or bribery or arise from the widespread indifference of the other members to most issues. A power ratio of 3/5 for a given person, in short, may be due to factors that would have produced that percentage *regardless of the formal structure of the group.* It would appear then that actual and merely apparent instances of the model cannot be distinguished by any mathematical calculation of percentages. Even if we consider only those cases in which the correlated percentage appears, the tabulation and ordering of logical possibilities cannot decide when our formal structure has been an operative force and when the correlated percentage is the result of other variables. For to make such a decision, it is necessary to know certain counter-factuals, e.g., what would have happened if the members had been strangers instead of business associates, if more of them had been affected economically by the issues, etc.

Furthermore, the factors requiring control here would seem to include intentional phenomena such as beliefs, aims, interests, expectations, and principles. We must know, that is, that the correlated percentage did not arise merely because Jones, Smith, and Green *conspired* to vote together on certain issues or because most members *believed* Jones to be more competent than themselves on the issues requiring a vote. Would it be far wrong to suggest that a given group can be counted as exemplifying our formal structure only if the desire to maintain that structure explains the occurrence of the correlated percentage? If the model is satisfied only when there is a desire or decision to see it implemented, something of a paradox seems to arise. For the model reduces power to a clearly nonpsychological notion: the relative frequency of an individual occurring in a certain numerical position in an ordering of all those who can vote. Yet to apply this model to any group requires an inquiry into the beliefs, hopes, choices — the psychological features — of that group's members. We thus have a nonintentional model which can be satisfied only by intentional activities and interactions: perhaps this is only the semblance of paradox.

In brief then a mathematical index of power generates an indefinite number of "formal structures" in which power is differentially distributed among groups or individuals. But for the index to be of use to the social scientist, e.g., as defining an ideal or extreme type, it must be possible to determine when an actual institution or association deviates from, approaches, or exemplifies one of these a priori structures. How is this to be done? We cannot simply appeal to the correlated percentage, for this can be equally well exhibited by both deviations and exemplifications. Can it be done (as Shapley and Shubik appear to suggest in their next to last paragraph) without appealing to what particular men believe and desire, i.e., without frustrating the model's apparent aim of reducing a psychological concept to a nonpsychological one?

In "Some Strategic Considerations in the Construction of Social Science Models," Herbert A. Simon discusses several additional ways in which mathematics can prove useful to social scientists. One of these is the provision of a "common language" into which the motley findings of separate sciences can be translated and then derived from a minimal number of theories. For example, Simon claims that adaptive behavior, which he treats as one form of rationality, can be expressed by differential equations that also describe the activities of "servo-mechanisms" and physiological systems that operate by principles involving negative feedback. If this is true, mathematics may offer a way of developing the thesis of selection 23, i.e., that a theory of human problem-solving can be "constructed of elementary information processes" which are reducible to "physiological processes in the nervous system and its appendages." Similarly, we are told that the "Berlitz model" (page 565) is equally capable of predicting whether (1) an individual will master a certain skill or (2) different institutions or groups will perform a joint activity requiring coordination of their separate functions. At the very least, this model is designed to authorize predictions of failure — in both types of cases — given that the original rate of activity is "below a certain critical level."

But it is mathematical models of rational behavior on which Simon's paper concentrates most heavily. And though he does not explicitly analyze his sense of 'model,' it does not seem to depart very far from the notions of extreme and ideal types discussed by Carl Hempel in selection 37. Simon's mathematical models have difficulties parallel to those raised in connection with the techniques of qualitative measurement and the mathematical reduction of power. For one thing, rationality appears to be entirely detached from intentionality. In "optimizing" models (pages 557–564), to be rational comes to selecting "that course of action which leads to the set of consequences most preferred," i.e., in which the successful pursuit of a single best option is central. In models of adaptive rational behavior, rationality consists in "minimaxing," or in continually protecting oneself against substantial adversities, even where this does not yield total or maximum realization of one's desires. Both models, whatever their differences,[6] identify rationality with *attainment*. But men can succeed — obtain what they want most or avoid major disasters — without being rational; e.g., by good luck or through the benevolence or stupidity of others. And many of those who fail to optimize or minimax their desires are rational nonetheless. The runner who wishes to win or to improve his relative standing among milers, and is prevented from doing so by superior athletes, is not on that account irrational or less rational than his faster running competitors. (This assumption that rational behavior, problem-solving, thinking, etc. is a matter of *attainment* and not of *intention*, of what is done and not the motives and beliefs which explain and get expressed in what is done, is a key feature of the Turing test discussed in selection 23. Unless one accepts this reduction of intentional to nonintentional language, it is difficult to see how Turing's test could show that machines think, as opposed to merely indicating that the results produced — attained — by what they do closely resemble the results of activities performed by thinking agents.)

Closely linked with this "de-intentionalization" of rational activity is Simon's overall neglect of one of the major elements in the concept of rational action which emerges from selections 1, 13, 18, 22, 24, 29, and 33 above. It is Dray's view, for example, that a rational explanation "aims to show that the sort of thing (the agent) did make perfectly good sense *from his own point of view* [emphasis added]." This seems to imply that rationality is not a matter of choosing what will in fact, or according to publicly shared criteria, maximize or minimax the chances of goal-realization. It is manifested, rather, by actions which the agent *believes* will have desirable consequences. However, consideration of the agent's view of his circum-

[6] It seems at least arguable that to minimax is simply to adopt as one's *most preferred goal* that of decreasing the chances of suffering great loss, i.e., that minimaxing is a special case of optimizing. If this is so, Simon's claim (page 560) that minimaxing models can escape certain difficulties which attach to optimizing models may be on shaky ground.

stances and of his conception and evaluation of the results arising from various options, seems to be largely absent from Simon's models. Consider his account of the Berlitz model:

The figure [page 565 below] shows that whether our student eventually becomes discouraged and fails to complete his course, or whether he is successful in learning French depends on his starting point . . . The value of D_0 represents the difficulty of the language to him at the outset, and x_0 the amount of time he initially devotes to practice. If the point (x_0, D_0) lies above the dotted line, he will ultimately become discouraged and give up his lessons . . . [See page 565 below.]

Dray or Dilthey might prefer to rewrite this passage as follows:

The figure shows that whether our student eventually becomes discouraged and fails to complete his course, or whether he is successful in learning French depends on *what he regards as* his starting point. The value of D_0 represents how difficult the language *appeared to him* (i.e., how difficult he *thought* it would be for him to learn it) at the outset, and x_0 the amount of time he *viewed himself* devoting to practice initially. If he *believes* the point from which he starts lies above the dotted line (i.e., believes the language is too difficult for him or will require too much of an outlay of time), he will ultimately become discouraged and give up his lessons . . .

There is a passage in which Simon attempts to handle this question of tying rationality to the agent's perspective, rather than to any set of objective criteria concerning, e.g., the most effective strategies for attaining certain goals. On page 563, he asserts:

We can incorporate the individual's expectations into the behavior model. Then we require a theory of how he forms those expectations — a theory of his forecast model. His expectations may take the form of specific predictions, or of probability distributions of the predicted variable. If we take the latter alternative, then we may wish to define rational choice as the choice that maximizes the expected value (in the statistical sense) of the criterion variable. This approach adds nothing essentially new to our optimization model.

But is nothing new added? Collingwood and others would argue that what a man believes at T′ cannot be known except by imaginatively reconstructing the actions he goes on to perform *after* that time. Empirical regularities may allow us to easily predict whether Charley's desire to resist the draft will be more fully or permanently attained by requesting a student deferment or by pleading for CO status. But how can we tell whether Charley *believes* that one is a better strategy than the other without waiting to see what he actually selects in a situation where he has had, and believes he has had, ample opportunity to think them both through? A man's actions tomorrow often serve to identify the beliefs which he holds today. Hence, to predict tomorrow's actions by appealing to today's beliefs may be a circular and senseless procedure, one that appears comparable to predicting that Bill will pitch a shutout on the basis that the opposing team will score no runs against him. Or like predicting that two men, described as close friends, will not knowingly, willingly, and persistently injure one another.

Thus, if Simon makes room for the factor of belief in his models, the something "new" which may emerge is that those models lose a portion of their predictive power. The connection between a man's beliefs (predictive base) and his actions (projection) is not a contingent one like, say, the relation between his beliefs and whether he has right or left dominance. It is a conceptual or a priori connection, like that between the premisses and conclusion of a (deductively) valid argument, or between the claim that John is taller than Eric and the claim that Eric is shorter than John. To employ

Simon's belief-incorporating model, one must establish the agent's beliefs (expectations); but how is this to be done without appealing to the very actions the model is designed to predict? The conclusion or projection must be established before we can claim to know one of the key premisses in its derivation.

Thus, if Simon's models of rationality exclude the agent's perspective, then they falsely identify rational acts with those that *happen* to produce some desired set of consequences. On this interpretation, a man on a ship in the Antarctic Ocean who wished to return to his family in Denmark but believed he would never be able to and hence decided to commit suicide by jumping overboard, but was picked up, brought back to life, and returned to Denmark by a stray Danish vessel, would have to be described as having performed rationally. But considering the agent's perspective may defeat, at least in part, the predictive aims of the models. For in this case the predictum and the predictans appear analytically connected: rather than predicting, the model would offer at most an explication of what is *meant* by the alleged predictive base. It might serve as a definition of a particular kind of rational activity, but it would not offer any empirical (or empirically testable) regularities connecting actions of that kind with any other sort of even or phenomena. In sum, the belief component of rational activity may pose difficulties for Simon, whether or not he incorporates it in his models.

This "belief-dilemma" can be clarified by considering the graph on page 567 which relates "intensity of motivation" to "achievement level." On the basis of this graph, Simon alleges that "as the achievement level exceeds B, the drive toward improvement of skill disappears." If the antecedent here is read as referring to the actual and *not* to the believed level of achievement, then this claim is open to a number of objections. It appears to overlook, for example, individuals ignorant of standards of achievement, those who are self-hating, and those who raise their standards with each new success. More important, on this reading the graph implies that men who have exceeded B but *want* to keep on improving or *believe* they haven't yet reached their *desired* level of achievement, will cease their efforts to improve nonetheless. This though is descriptive not of rational (or purposive) activity but of compulsive behavior: the agent cuts off his endeavors *knowing that this will defeat rather than achieve his ends.* In short, on our first interpretation Simon's graph does not embody a model of rational conduct; on the contrary, it seems to be incompatible with such conduct.

But we may take this graph to assert: "As a man *thinks* he is approaching the level of attainment which he desires in a certain skill, he decreases his efforts to improve that skill." This provides a reference to the believed level of achievement, yet it seems little more than an instance of the tautology (or a priori purposive principle) that men cease to strive after that which they believe they have already obtained. As a conceptual truth, it is credible enough. The cessation of striving is a major part of what is meant by a person's believing that he is about to get what he is after, be it a certain level of achievement or anything else. But what predictions can be generated from this conceptual truth? It is compatible with every contingent proposition, and hence supports no specific prediction (or empirical generalization) more than any other. It gives no hint whatever as to when a person is likely to give up attempting to refine one of his skills. At most it declares that this will occur *when men think they have reached the level they want to attain.* But what is the criterion for this, if not their ceasing to improve the skill in question? Thus, on one interpretation (where actual achievement and not the agent's view of it is the antecedent condition), Simon's graph excludes and hence cannot predict *rational* action. But where reference *is* made to the agent's perspective, the graph appears to yield only a fairly empty, and certainly predictionless, tautology. (But perhaps there is some third interpretation which is not subject to either of these objections.)

Simon's models depart in another way from the ordinary and nonmathematical concept of rationality. For they are all "end-indifferent" in the sense that they provide no way to evaluate the rationality of alternative aims, as opposed to alternative strategies for achieving a given end. On page 558, it is affirmed that "the criterion (regarded as a "final end") is itself not an object of rational calculation, but a given. The model would be equally a model of rational behavior if the entrepreneur chose to maximize his losses, or his gross revenue instead of his profit." Surely though there are some ends which it is rational not to pursue, or which cannot be pursued for their own sakes, e.g., insanity, bodily injury, death, etc. Given our present notion of rationality, it is possible to speak of ends which are rational and others which are irrational, as well as rational procedures for realizing certain goals. But Simon's models seem to exclude this possibility, and for reasons which are not brought to light.

The three difficulties we have raised against Simon's treatment of rationality — de-intentionalization, the belief-dilemma, and end-indifference — suggest some serious questions. They render it problematic that his models can be used to understand or predict human conduct. Or, better, that they can be employed to predict or identify those types of rational activity (involving intentionality, geared to the agent's perspective, allowing evaluation of ends) in the absence of which there is no sense in speaking of man's history, his scientific inquiries, cultural and social institutions, etc. Simon alleges that if we are to predict a man's behavior, the "knowledge that he is rational is only a small part — almost an insignificant part — of the information we require." This may be true only if we adopt the truncated notion of rationality embedded in his models.

Further, the suspicion is hard to suppress that the price of introducing mathematics and measurement into the social sciences may *often* be too high. These tools, like the crude operationist programs criticized by Ennis, seem to require that we discard as "subjective," "untestable," "imprecise," "intuitive," "ambiguous," etc. exactly those concepts without which the first step towards describing human activity cannot be taken. To prescribe that observations and data be classified and ranked solely by means of terms, categories, typologies, scales, indices, and models which allow of qualitative measurement (in Lazarsfeld and Barton's sense), quantitative measurement, or translation into mathematical formulae may suit the behaviorist who wants both dependent and independent variables to be "described in terms of physical properties." It may help to make the social sciences into a sub-case of the natural sciences, or to render the two methodologically indistinguishable. But it may do so by forbidding the use of human action concepts, or concepts which are purposive (intentional) in the sense of selection 29, or concepts the mastery of which requires *verstehen*,[7] or which can be used objectively even though they cannot, in principle, be reduced to nonpsychological or operational indicators. Or, in other words, by divesting us of a science of *man*. The problems of the ethical theorist, e.g., is there an a priori connection between justice and human happiness, can there ever be a justification for punishment, cannot be resolved by advising him to observe and classify the various moral codes which human communities have adopted as binding.

[7] As interpreted on page 356 above and on page 700 below.

This advice may point out a clearer and less controversial subject matter, but at the cost of making the newfound inquiries irrelevant to the original set of issues in moral philosophy. Does the imposition of mathematics and measurement upon the data of social science represent a parallel increase of precision and loss of relevance?

This question becomes more insistent given the arguments advanced by Norman Malcolm against attempts to measure, by "physical techniques," when dreams occur and how long they last. Malcolm's analysis of dreaming is an application of a more general position in the philosophy of mind, a position which is illustrated in this passage from Part II of Wittgenstein's *Philosophical Investigations:*

> The criteria for the truth of the *confession* that I thought such and such are not the criteria for a true *description* of a process. And the importance of the true confession does not reside in its being a correct and certain report of a process. It resides rather in the special consequences which can be drawn from a confession whose truth is guaranteed by the special criteria of *truthfulness*.[8]

Let us suppose that Jones claims there is a cow in the parlor (C) and moreover that his statement is made sincerely. Does it follow that C is true? Of course not. The sincerity (truthfulness) of this claim does *not* guarantee its truth or ensure against a mistake. In general, beliefs and assertions about physical objects (descriptions of processes) are hardly incorrigible: anyone who affirmed C could be shown to be in error by what others produce as evidence, even if he refused to accept that evidence. But suppose now that Jones closes his eyes and says that he is imagining (or is expecting, hoping for, dreaming of, desiring) a cow in the parlor and suppose, again, that he is sincere in what he says. Will it not follow this time that Jones' report must be accepted? That he does have the "mental state" he reported? Malcolm and Wittgenstein maintain that this is the case, that (some) first-person psychological reports are immune to error, or incorrigible: "the descriptions people give of their private states provide a determination of what those states are and whether they are the same." According to these two philosophers, many of the concepts brought under analysis by selections 33 and 34 are concepts for which sincere first-person testimony is a decisive criterion. If a person who understands what it is to hope for something claims he is hoping to inherit a fortune, then though he can be lying or joking, he cannot be *mistaken*.

> . . . if someone tells a dream or says that he had one he is not making a 'subjective' report which may or may not agree with 'objective fact'. His waking impression is what establishes that he had a dream, and his account of his dream establishes what the content of his dream was. If he has a vague impression of his dream then it was a vague dream. If he is not certain whether he dreamt then there is an uncertainty in reality. His impression is the criterion of reality and therefore it cannot be characterized as 'subjective'. 'Subjective' and 'objective' are *one* in the case of dreams — which is to say that this distinction does not apply. [See page 579 below.]

This view of first-person psychological statements as incorrigible (their truth being guaranteed by their truthfulness) has important consequences for the issues in both this part and part V. It gives rise to an argument we can state as follows:

1. *Dreaming* (along with other psychological concepts) necessarily involve(s) first-person incorrigibility.
2. Measurement (operational definitions, reductions to physical or physiological terms, quantitative or qualitative indicators, mathematical indices and models)

[8] Wittgenstein, L. *Philosophical Investigations*, New York, 1953, page 222e.

necessarily involve(s) first-person corrigibility. (No one's sincerity ensures against his measuring incorrectly, even in his own case.)

3. Thus, *dreaming* (and other psychological concepts) is (are) incompatible with measurement: it is logically impossible to rely on techniques of measurement as the sole or decisive test for whether a dream occurred, how long it lasted, or what it was like.

If this argument goes through, then proposition 9 of the covering law position is false. Moreover, a weak separatism according to which there are a priori limits on exactness or measurement for the concepts of social science but no such limits for those of physical science seems justified: none of the terms employed by natural scientists appear to involve first-person incorrigibility. Furthermore, the ideal advocated by Lazarsfeld and Barton (and at least suggested by selections 30, 31, and 40) of devising objective indicators for all concepts of interest to the social scientist must be given up. There are features of human conduct ("He *had the same dream* three nights in succession," "He *is hoping* to go to the opera," "She *suddenly thought* how much John resembled his father") for which neither qualitative nor quantitative measurement is a possibility.

Psychophysics: The Application of Quantitative Measurement to Psychological Phenomena

40

Sensation and Psychological Measurement

S. S. STEVENS

The chief business of the living organism is adaptation to its ever-changing environment. The protozoan, swimming along near the muddy floor of a pond, turns aside from the sharp cold of a fresh current and moves toward a safer region. Man's problems and man's responses may be more complicated than the protozoan's, yet man, crossing the street in traffic, dodging taxicabs in the five-o'clock rush hour, solves similar problems of avoidance in similar ways. Both cases involve perception: the protozoan perceives cold and the man perceives the oncoming rush of steel and glass which is the taxicab. All organisms, from protozoan to man, preserve themselves in a careless universe by a knowledge of the external world which comes to them through their sensory mechanisms.

The preceding chapter has dealt with problems of perception. In perception the organism does all it can to get the best possible information about the external world. A piece of coal in the sunshine may reflect more light than a piece of notepaper in the shade; yet we see the coal as black and the paper as white. The constancy phenomenon has come into play here; it helps us to recognize these and other objects in a way which has most meaning for us. So too the organism gets the third visual dimension of space; it sees that a mountain or a trolley car has not only height and width but also solidity. As it 'interprets' the data from its two eyes, so also the organism 'interprets' the data from its two ears, not merely hearing a sound — the horn of the taxicab — but knowing also the direction from which it came. In short, in one way or another the organism musters all its resources to the end that it may get the most valuable information about its environment; and this process we call *perception.*

From *Foundations of Psychology*, edited by E. G. Boring, John Wiley & Sons, Inc., (New York, 1948), pp. 250–268.

SENSATION IS THE CORE OF PERCEPTION

The way from the external world to the brain is via the sense organs, and these remarkable organs, responding to light, sound, heat, cold, pressure, touch, etc., are the windows through which we look out at the world about us. The sense organs start the messages along the nerves, the highways to the brain. When these messages merge at the higher centers of the nervous system, when they organize themselves and modify one another through interactions and associations, we call the result perception. But the bare messages themselves, isolated and apart from their mutual influences, we call sensations.

We get at sensations by analysis, by paying attention to certain aspects of our perceptions. It is much like the artist painting his landscape. Where the casual observer sees a valley partly shadowed by a rocky hill, the artist sees a patch of purple jutting into a field of green and speckled by reddish brown dots. By selective attention he analyzes the organized scene into patches of color and he translates these sensations into pigments on canvas.

The student of sensation goes farther. He learns to attend not only to color as such but also to its several modes of variation, to its redness and whiteness and grayness. And the object of his analysis is an understanding of the behavior of sensory processes: How do sensations arise? what causes them to change? how many aspects of them can be separately distinguished and how can the aspects be measured? what takes place in the sense organ and in the sensory nerves? and how do these events depend upon the physical, chemical or mechanical happenings in the world outside? The answers to these questions are the laws of sensation, laws that are based upon careful experimental measurements.

Stimulus and Attributes

In order to understand the laws of sensation we must first know what is meant by a stimulus and by attributes of sensation such as quality and intensity.

STIMULUS

A stimulus is any change in external energy that activates a sense organ and its receptors. It is a stimulus only when it stimulates. Light is not a stimulus to a totally blind person. The radio waves that fill the air are not a direct stimulus to any organism that we know of. Many phenomena of nature affect no sense organs, and these phenomena come to our attention only indirectly by way of their effects or by way of the elaborate inferences of science. The important phenomena that can be classed as stimuli are mechanical, thermal, acoustic, chemical and photic.

Man himself reacts to many kinds of *mechanical* stimulation. He has the tactual sense of his skin, by which he appreciates the presence, size and shape of the objects with which he comes in contact. He can feel pain, which warns him of violent or dangerous contact. He perceives his own posture by means of the proprioceptive organs that lie in his muscles and joints. By their use and by vision he maintains his erect position. He perceives certain contractions of his stomach and calls them hunger. He perceives dryness in his mouth and throat and calls it thirst. These instances are samples of the wide variety of mechanical events which can act as stimuli in man.

Thermal stimulation is also effective for man. He must keep the temperature of his body constant. If it varies a little he may be ill; if it varies much he may die. Although his body is equipped with a remarkable system for automatic thermostatic control, he needs also to help out by conscious adaptive behavior. The thermal sense tells him when to put on heavier or lighter clothes, when to start the electric fan, when to turn on the radiator.

Acoustic stimulation affects most animals that live in the air and some that live in water. Hearing, which shares with vision the important function of giving information about distant stimuli, is a very important and highly developed sense. Persons suddenly made deaf, and deprived of speech and music, seem to suffer even more from their deficiency than the blind. These people say that they live in a "dead world." Sound, more than anything else, signifies that the world is alive and moving.

Taste and smell are *chemical* senses, the direct descendants of the chemical sense of fishes. Taste is a liquid sense; it is stimulated only by substances in solution. Smell is an air sense; it is activated by small particles of substance diffused in the air. Although a highly developed sense, smell is little used by man, who, with his erect posture, keeps his nose away from the ground where most of the smells lie. The dog, nose to ground, finds how extremely informative olfactory stimuli can be.

Vision is the *photic* sense, and light is man's most important stimulus, even though the other senses may, in the blind, become remarkably effective substitutes for vision. Whereas the lower animals sense only the intensity of light, man and some of the higher vertebrates can discriminate its wave length as well; that is to say, they can see hues as well as blacks, grays and whites. Probably this sensitivity to difference in the wave length of light is one of man's most recent sensory acquisitions, for the development of color vision is still incomplete in that an appreciable portion of the population is color blind. Most animals are also color blind, responding to differences in the energy, but not differences in the wave length, of light.

ATTRIBUTES OF SENSATION

Since there are many ways in which a sensation can change, an observer, experiencing a sensation, describes it completely only when he has specified its value with respect to every possible dimension of change. These possible dimensions constitute the attributes of sensation.

Suppose a congenitally blind man were suddenly given perfect vision and shown a red square. This single experience would not teach him anything about the attributes of visual sensation, but we could soon show him what some of them are. First, we could change the square in *quality* by altering its hue toward orange or purple or gray, telling the man that this sort of change is a change in the qualitative attribute of color. Then we could change the square in size to teach him about the attribute of *extension*. To change the time of its exposure would be to exhibit *duration* to him. Some psychologists think that hues also have an attribute of *intensity*, which they call *brightness*. A difficulty arises here, however, because *brightness* is *whiteness*, and white is a color quality. At any rate all the other sensations have an intensitive attribute. Tones can be loud, smells and tastes strong, pressures and pains intense.

It is conventional to classify the sensory attributes under four main heads: *quality*, *intensity*, *extension* and *duration*. There can be, however, many more than four sensory attributes, for there are just as many attributes as there are possible modes of variation of sensation. In his course in psychology the college student often discovers attributes that are new to him, for most people do not know, until they are taught, that colors vary in three dimensions in a system that is represented by a solid figure and that tones change in volume and density as well as in pitch and loudness. Perhaps there are some sensory attributes which the psychologist himself has not yet discovered.

The problem of attributes comes up for animals as well as persons. For instance, size is an attribute of visual experiences. Can a rat perceive *size*? Yes, because he can learn to choose, for a reward, the larger of two circles. Can a rat perceive *shape* as such, independently of all the other spatial properties of visual stimuli? Probably not. Figure 40-1 shows the stimuli of an experiment which was arranged to test the capacity of human and animal subjects to perceive triangularity as such. The subject was first trained to choose the triangle and avoid the square in the standard pair of stimuli, *S*. He was then tested to see whether he would choose the triangle instead of the other figure in each of the other seven pairs of stimuli, *A* to *G*. If he chose the triangle in preference to the square in *S* because it was a triangle, he should choose the triangle instead of the circle in *A* and the inverted triangle in *B*; he should choose the triangle instead of the rotated square, without regard to the rotation of the triangle, in *C* to *F*; and he should prefer the dark triangle to the dark square in *G*. Since each pair of figures is equated in total area and thus in total brightness, and since the triangle was shown as often on the right as on the left, it can be argued that shape — not brightness, angular position or size — must have been the basis for the original discrimination in *S*. The general problem has proved, however, too hard for the rat. A chimpanzee almost succeeded in it, and a child did succeed. Thus it is apparent that a human being is able to analyze a perception more specifically into its attributes than a rat or even a chimpanzee.

It is important to realize that a person has to learn about particular attributes before he can describe experience in terms of them. People learn readily enough to distinguish between size and brightness, but most animals do not. Color-blind persons do not easily discover the defects in their color sense because they are not especially trained to analyze their color experiences. Instead they are told that the grass is green and that the rose is red, although these two objects may be to them the same color. And faced with the task of making an impossible color analysis, they avoid giving attention to color attributes, and rely, when they can, upon their knowledge of the nature of objects. No roses, they remind themselves, are green, and grass is never red.

Fig. 40–1. *Discrimination of Shape* The subject was trained to choose the triangle in pair *S*. Then the experiment was arranged to discover whether he would choose, without further training, the triangle in each of the pairs *A* to *G*. The stimuli were large, and were presented with the triangle as often at the right as at the left. A child learned to discriminate 'pure triangularity' in this way; a chimpanzee almost, but not quite, succeeded; a rat failed. [From L. W. Gellerman, *J. genet. Psychol.*, 1933, **42,** 14.]

QUALITY

All the senses but hearing seem to be based upon a few *unique qualities*, which may unite in fusions to give other secondary qualities.

In *vision* the seven unique qualities are red, yellow, green, blue, white, gray and black. All other colors occur as blends of these unique colors. (See pp. 270–274.)[1] In *smell* the unique qualities are fragrant, ethereal, spicy, resinous, burned and putrid, and a huge number of intermediates that fit in among these six. (See p. 356.) In *taste* the unique qualities are sweet, saline, sour and bitter, and for these, too, there are intermediates. (See p. 353.) In *somesthesis*, the body sense, the unique qualities are pressure, pain, warmth and cold. There are also a great many complex patterns of these four qualities, like hunger, dizziness and itch. (See p. 360.) *Hearing* is the one sense that cannot be reduced to a few unique qualities. The tones form a continuous series of qualities from the lowest pitch to the highest. Instead of a mere four or seven unique qualities we have in hearing all the separate pitches the ear can hear, a thousand or more.

Why do we experience different qualities? Why is a sight so different in quality from a sound? How can the brain tell a smell from a pat on the hand? Actually, there is almost no satisfactory physiological theory of sensory quality. All we know about quality is that the fibers for each of the five senses lead to a particular part of the cerebral cortex. It seems probable that of the four unique qualities of the sense of touch each has its special nerve fibers; that, in hearing, although a given tone excites many fibers, its quality may be dependent upon the excitation of one particular fiber more than the others. In vision it seems likely that there are only three

[1] [*This and the following page references are to the book in which Stevens' essay first appeared,* Foundations of Psychology, *edited by E. G. Boring (New York: John Wiley & Sons, 1948). Editor's note.*]

kinds of nerve fibers in the optic nerve, and that the six or seven unique colors are not differentiated physiologically from the others until the excitation has reached the brain. There the mystery is complete. All we can say is that, when an organism is making a qualitative discrimination, it is distinguishing between the excitation of different systems of nerve fibers.

Quality indicates *what* neural system is functioning, which fibers are excited. Intensity, extension and duration merely tell *how* the system is functioning. That is why quality seems to be more fundamental than the other attributes, why we talk about the loudness of a pitch but not the pitch of a loudness, about the duration of a red but not the redness of a duration.

INTENSITY

Usually the intensity of a sensation increases when the energy of its stimulus is increased. A paperweight makes more noise if it drops from the desk to the floor than if it drops only a few inches. On the other hand, intensity of sensation also varies with the sensitivity of the sense organ. In hearing, for instance, sensitivity is greatest in the middle of the musical scale. A tone in this region, therefore, requires less energy than a low tone in order to sound equally loud.

Both vision and hearing are senses tuned to respond to certain limited ranges of a continuous stimulus. The electromagnetic waves, some of which we call light, extend through a long range (see Fig. 114, p. 275); yet the retina responds to only a limited range of these wave lengths. The long infrared waves and the short ultraviolet waves are invisible under most circumstances. For visible light the retina is least sensitive at the two extremes of the spectrum and most sensitive in the middle. (See Fig. 126, p. 291.) Similarly the ear responds to only a limited range of tonal frequencies, being completely deaf to very low and very high frequencies and most sensitive to the middle frequencies of the musical range. (See Fig. 154, p. 324.) Thus it is plain that, if we wish to predict the intensity of a sensation, we must know about the stimulus, its frequency and its energy, and we must know about sensitivity as well. The sensitivity of the organism to a given stimulus is just as important as the energy of the stimulus.

Psychophysics

The obvious fact about sensation is that it arises from an interaction. Some form of energy impinges upon a sensitive receptor in a living organism, and the organism reacts. The organism sees, hears, smells, tastes, feels. These reactions are psychological processes, set in motion by physical events. When we study sensation, therefore, what we discover is the relation between those two aspects of the universe commonly called the *mental* and the *physical*. We learn how experience depends upon stimulation. We learn what it takes by way of a cause to set off a response in a perceiving organism.

Psychophysics was christened by G. T. Fechner, a physicist and philosopher, who in 1860 gave us a treatise on a new science of the "relation between mind and matter" — meaning the relation between sensation and the stimulus that causes it. Fechner's basic notion was simple. He believed that, if he could measure both the strength of a stimulus and the magnitude of the sensation it arouses, he would have a formula relating physics and psychology. He asked, for example, how great is the loudness we experience when we listen to a sound wave of a given energy. Or how bright, subjectively, is a light of so many candle-power?

These are complicated questions, as later chapters will show. We no longer give them the same answers that Fechner gave, for psychophysics has moved ahead, and new methods of psychophysical investigation have been evolved. These methods are used nowadays to answer practical, everyday questions as well as to settle theoretical problems. They are essential to engineers and designers as well as to psychologists. All attempts to adapt machines and gadgets to the sensory capacities of human beings raise problems in psychophysics which can be solved by its methods.

The story of the telephone is a case in point. The earliest instruments were unreliable devices. You spoke your message and the listener asked, "What did you say?" You shouted into the mouthpiece and he still did not understand. Trial-and-error on the part of inventors brought improved clarity, but the last word in high-fidelity transmission was impossible until the psychophysics of hearing had been explored. In one of the world's largest research laboratories careful studies were made of the behavior of the ear: its sensitivity to different frequencies, its response to sounds of varying intensity, its ability to hear tones masked by noise. These researches established the performance requirements of the telephone: how it should transmit the sounds of speech in order for them to be correctly perceived. Knowing what they were aiming at, the designers could then proceed.

PSYCHOPHYSICAL PROBLEMS AND METHODS

The procedures used in psychophysical studies are as varied as ingenious researchers confronted by complex problems can make them. There are two useful ways, however, of classifying them: (1) by the type of judgment or reaction made by the subject in the experiment; (2) by the method of presenting, controlling and measuring the stimulus. Thus the problem has two facets: the psychological and the physical. There are several ways of getting at the psychological experience of the subject — ways of having him respond — and there are many procedures for manipulating the physical energies and forces to which he is exposed. In general, our choice of procedures is guided by the nature of the problem we set ourselves, but we often find it impossible to follow what might be the ideal method. We cannot, for example, change the intensity of a smell by known physical amounts in the way we can alter the intensity of a light. Many problems in psychophysics must wait on further developments in the other sciences.

It is the business of psychophysics to ask questions about the behavior of man and animals. And since the character of a science is revealed by the kind of questions it poses — and by the way it tracks down the answers — we do well to list the types of questions asked and answered by psychophysical procedures. Of course these are technical, scientific questions, designed to reveal the laws and principles of behavior. They are the kinds of questions that involve measurement and experimentation guarded by careful controls. Broken down into their principal categories, we find that these questions raise seven kinds of psychophysical problems.

(1) *Absolute thresholds.* What is the smallest stimulus that will set off a response on the part of an organism?

> *Example.* How faint is the faintest light a man can see? (*Answer.* Five to seven quanta of light energy falling on the retina may produce a visual response. A quantum is the smallest package of light energy possible in nature.)

(2) *Differential thresholds.* What is the smallest *change* in a stimulus that can be detected?

> *Example.* How many ounces must be added to a pound in order to make it feel heavier? (*Answer.* About half an ounce.)

(3) *Equality.* What values must two stimuli have in order to produce equality in a given attribute?

> *Example.* What intensity of red light appears as bright as a given intensity of green light? (*Answer.* The red light must have about eight times the physical intensity of the green light.)

(4) *Order.* Given a set of stimuli, what is their order of progression from least to greatest with respect to some attribute or quality?

Example. What is the relative merit of the music of these composers: Bach, Beethoven, Chopin, Grieg, Tschaikovsky, Wagner? (*Answer.* By 308 members of four leading symphony orchestras the music of these composers was preferred in the order: Beethoven, Wagner, Bach, Tschaikovsky, Chopin and Grieg.)

(5) *Equality of intervals.* When is the apparent difference between two experiences the same as the difference between two other experiences? Or, as a special case, when does one sensation appear to be equidistant between two other sensations?

Example. What note on the piano has a pitch that sounds equidistant between middle C and the C four octaves above it? (*Answer.* Not the C at the second octave above middle C, as you might suppose, but the note G above this C.)

(6) *Equality of ratios.* When is the apparent ratio between two experiences the same as the apparent ratio between two other experiences? Or what stimuli produce sensations having a given ratio with respect to each other?

Example. How many ounces *feel* half as heavy as a pound? (*Answer.* About eleven ounces. Eight ounces feel much less than half as heavy as a pound.)

(7) *Stimulus rating.* How accurately can a person name the correct physical value of a stimulus which he can sense but cannot measure directly?

Examples. Several of them, mostly unanswered questions: How accurately can aviators estimate their height in feet above the ground? How well can policemen estimate the speed of passing cars? How precisely can a farmer estimate the area of a field? In trying to answer these questions the experimenter would usually be interested, not only in the accuracy of the estimate itself but also in the factors which tend to increase or decrease the accuracy. Some of these factors would come under the heading of what we commonly call illusions.

To each of the types of problems listed above we can apply a variety of psychophysical procedures. In other words, we can present the stimuli in a variety of ways and we can ask the subject to indicate his response in several manners. These methods and their many variants have important uses in psychology in all its branches. Some of them permit the detailed scrutiny of the function of the sense organs themselves. Some of them enable us to measure sensation and tell how one sensory experience compares with another. Others have more practical uses. They make it possible to grade commodities like leather and perfumes and wines in terms of psychological scales set up by experienced judges. They even provide the basis of techniques that are used in the polling of public opinion and in the assessment of consumer attitudes.

Scales of Measurement

Measurement is the backbone of the scientific method. Primitive peoples usually speak of "a lot of" this or "a little of" that. Scientists, trying to get away from being primitive, like to pin numbers on things. They are not content with the mere statement that something is hot or cold. Instead, they ask what its temperature is in terms of degrees on a scale. Not many centuries ago there were no scales of temperature and no way of making hot and cold a quantitative matter. Methods of measuring temperature had to be devised. Someone in the middle of the seventeenth century had to invent a thermometer.

Psychology uses many of the scales employed in the other sciences, and it also invents scales of its own with which to measure in psychological dimensions. We have scales for measuring attitudes, intelligence, learning, sensation, etc. Some of the scales are rather crude affairs; some show considerable refinement. The accuracy and usefulness of any scale depend, of course, upon the care and ingenuity of its creator, but they also depend upon other things, particularly upon which of the four basic kinds of scale is being used. These four categories of scales are called by the names (1) *nominal scale*, (2) *ordinal scale*, (3) *interval scale* and (4) *ratio scale*.

(1) The *nominal scale* is the most primitive of the four. In fact it is not, in the ordinary sense, a scale of measurement at all. But for the sake of completeness we must include it here, because it is what we achieve when we pin numbers on objects or on classes of objects in order to keep track of them. For example, a coach numbers the football players on his team, or a manufacturer uses a model number to stand for a class of automobiles. There is actually more to this simple-minded procedure than meets the eye, for if the coach could not tell his players apart in the first place, he could not give each player a different number. And it is only because the automobile maker thinks all of a certain group of cars are equal in some respect that he gives them all the same model number.

We see, therefore, that the nominal scale is not entirely trivial. It has great practical importance, and, what is of more interest to us, its creation really depends upon our ability to determine (*a*) that something is present (so that we can give it a number) and (*b*) what other things are equal to it (so that we can give them the same number). In other words, we have to be able to answer the psychophysical problem of equality — problem 3 in our list above.

(2) The *ordinal scale* is more interesting. It is the kind of scale we can set up whenever we can determine the rank order of a set of items. Thus the composers listed on page 503 are arranged on an ordinal scale of merit, from greatest to least, in the opinion of other musicians. A scale of rank order cannot be set up unless we can solve problem 4 above: the determination of the direction of a difference.

On the ordinal scale of musical merit we find that Beethoven is better than Wagner, who is better than Bach. But this scale does not tell us how much better Beethoven is than Wagner; nor whether the difference between these two is the same as the difference between Wagner and Bach. In other words, the ordinal scale is not a quantitative scale in the layman's sense of the term quantitative. It is nevertheless a very useful device, as is shown by the fact that many such scales are in daily use. They are used to rate applicants for jobs, to scale personality traits, to measure intelligence and to grade examination papers. (See Fig. 40-2 for ordinal scales.)

When the instructor gives you A, B, C or D on a term paper he is using an ordinal scale. Of course he may give a numerical instead of a letter grade, but that does not change the situation. When you get 90 and your friend gets 70, it means that your paper is somewhat better than his (from the instructor's point of view), but you cannot say how much better it is. This is true simply because there is no way of knowing whether the *units* on the instructor's grading scale are equal from unit to unit. Is the difference between 70 and 80 the same as the difference between 80 and 90? Since neither you nor the instructor can answer that question, we are forced to conclude that he grades on an ordinal scale.

Actually, if you were to count up all the scales described in books on psychology, you would find that most of them are ordinal scales. It is far easier to arrange things in rank order than it is to devise scales for measuring them in terms of equal units. But rank ordering is not always easy. How, for example, would you scale the following traits in order of their importance for success in business: perseverence, courage, honesty, initiative, optimism, friendliness, intelligence, loyalty?

(3) The *interval scale* is one on which the units are equal but on which the zero point is arbitrarily chosen. The ordinary Fahrenheit temperature scale is a good example. The units (degrees) are equal, but the zero point is just an arbitrary temperature chosen by the German physicist, Fahrenheit, that of a freezing mixture of ice and salt. The

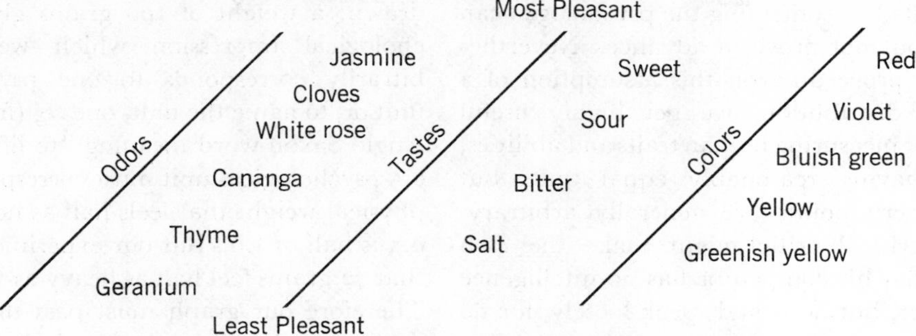

Fig. 40–2. *Some ordinal scales of pleasantness-unpleasantness* *Odors:* samples from a list of 14 olfactory stimuli ranked by 8 observers using the method of paired comparisons (each stimulus compared with each other stimulus). *Tastes:* average rank order obtained from 7 to 10 observers who rated each taste on a three-point scale. The concentrations used were 20 times the threshold concentration (the least concentration detectable as different from plain water). At other concentrations the rank order may be different. For example, at 10 times the threshold concentration salt is preferred to bitter. *Colors:* 18 squares of colored paper were ranked by 1279 college students using the method of paired comparisons. Many factors and causes may alter a person's preference for colors. [Data from J. G. Beebe-Center, *Pleasantness and unpleasantness*, Van Nostrand, 1932.]

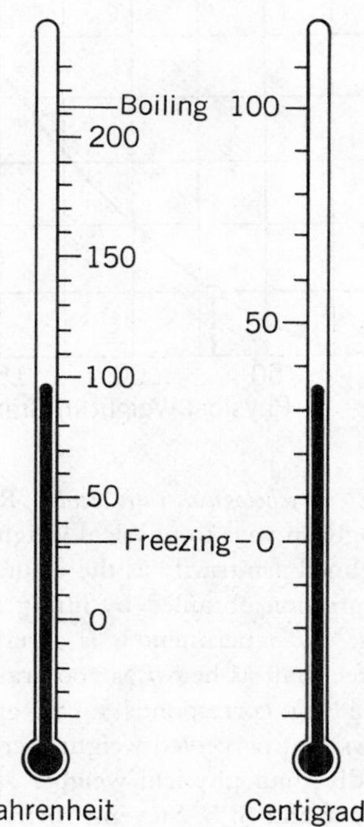

Fig. 40–3. *Interval scales* On each scale the units are of equal size, but the Fahrenheit units are five-ninths as large as the centigrade units. Each scale has a different zero point, and neither zero point on the scale represents a 'true' or 'absolute' zero in temperature.

centigrade scale is another example of an interval scale, and it has a different zero point, the temperature of ice water without salt (Fig. 40-3). On both these scales we know that the units are equal because we set up the units by marking off equal distances on a column of mercury or alcohol, which expands with increasing temperature. Then each rise of one degree in temperature lengthens the column by the same amount. By this procedure we solve for temperature scales the problem of equality of intervals, the same kind of problem we listed on page 503 as psychophysical problem 5.

When equal intervals can be determined for sensation, intelligence or some other psychological variable, scales having equal units can be established. The intelligence tester makes the units on his scale as equal as possible by adjusting (*a*) the difficulty of the items on his test and (*b*) the numerical credit given the testee for passing a given item. He then concludes that the units are equal if a large group of children, chosen at random, make scores that distribute themselves according to the normal curve (p. 507). His conclusion is correct, of course, only provided the intelligence of the children is really normally distributed — something the psychologist can *assume* but not prove in advance. Nevertheless, by proceeding on this assumption of a normal distribution, we get highly useful scales for measuring human traits and abilities, scales having reasonably equal units but whose zero points are generally arbitrary. An uncritical critic might make the rash claim that his competitor has no intelligence whatever, but he would speak loosely, for no one knows what zero intelligence is.

(4) True zero points are possible only on *ratio scales*. And in order to set up a ratio scale we must be able to determine not only equal intervals but equal ratios as well. Scales of length, weight and electrical resistance are examples of ratio scales. In fact so are most of the other scales used in physics. We can demonstrate that two inches is half of four inches and that four inches is half of eight inches. If we knew nothing about these ratios we should not know where to put the zero point on the scale, and *vice versa*.

The *stimuli* used in psychophysical experiments are nearly always measured on ratio scales. The *sensations* produced by these stimuli can also be measured on ratio scales whenever we can solve the psychophysical problem of sensed ratios (problem 6, p. 503). For example, if we can find out what weights feel half as heavy as what other weights, we can set up a ratio scale of perceived weight, as distinct from the physical weight which we measure in pounds and ounces. With the aid of the psychological scale of weight, we might then be able to tell the grocer how to package his dried beans so that a package of one size will feel fifty per cent heavier, say, than the next smaller size.

Figure 40-4 shows a ratio scale of perceived weight. This scale was obtained by the simple procedure of having a group of subjects select from among a graded series of weights the one that felt half as heavy as a given standard. Standards weighing different amounts were used, of course, and the complete data were employed to construct the curve in Fig. 40-4. The dotted lines illustrate the basis on which the curve was drawn; a weight of 100 grams gives a psychological impression which we say arbitrarily corresponds to one psychological unit or, to name the unit, one *veg* (from an old Anglo Saxon word meaning "to lift"). Then 0.5 psychological unit must correspond to the physical weight that feels half as heavy, since 0.5 is half of 1.0. But our experiment tells us that 72 grams feel half as heavy as 100 grams. Therefore our graph must pass through the cross and also through the circled point on the plot — the point indicated by the dotted lines connecting the value of 0.5 veg on the vertical scale with 72 grams on the horizontal scale.

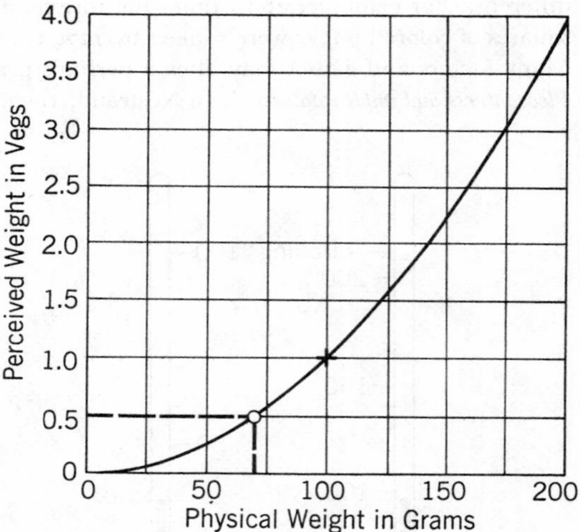

Fig. 40–4. *Psychological ratio scale* Relates perceived weight in vegs to physical weight in grams. A *veg* is defined arbitrarily as the value of the subjective impression obtained by lifting a weight of 100 grams. By experiment it is determined that 72 grams feel half as heavy as 100 grams. Therefore half a veg corresponds to 72 grams. The curve shows that perceived weight increases much more rapidly than physical weight. [Data from R. S. Harper and S. S. Stevens, *Amer. J. Psychol.*, 1948, 61.]

By extending this logic we obtain other points on the curve, and eventually we map out the entire graph relating perceived weight and physical weight.

Statistics and Measurement

None of the seven basic problems of psychophysics can be solved without the use of statistics. The reason for this is obvious. The behavior of living organisms is variable. Seldom does their behavior repeat itself exactly from moment to moment. Nor does the behavior of one individual always duplicate that of another. For this reason the answers to psychological questions are nearly always statistical answers. They are usually given in terms of averages and variabilities — the elementary but important concepts in what has lately become a highly developed branch of mathematics.

CENTRAL TENDENCY

The common everyday notion of an average — so familiar to baseball fans — is usually one of three measures of *central tendency.* The statistician's name for the average is the *mean.* And two other measures of central tendency are the *median* and the *mode.* We shall define these measures with the aid of an illustration.

Suppose we show a group of ten subjects a horizontal line twenty-four inches long and ask them to estimate its length. The ten estimates might give us the following distribution of guesses: 17, 18, 20, 20, 20, 22, 22, 24, 27, 30. What, then, is the mean or average estimate? In order to obtain the mean we add up all the individual estimates (scores) and divide by the number of scores. This gives twenty-two inches as the mean estimate of the group of ten subjects. We conclude that on the average they underestimated the length of the line.

We might also ask another question about these estimates: What value divides the scores into two groups such that the estimates of half the subjects are equal to or lower than this value and half are equal to or higher than this value? The answer gives us the *median* of the distribution. In our example the median would be the value midway between the scores for the fifth subject, who guessed 20, and the sixth subject, who guessed 22. The median then is 21 inches. Fifty per cent of the guesses lie above this point and 50 per cent lie below.

The *mode* is simply the value in the distribution that occurs with greatest frequency. Since 20 inches was guessed more often than any other value, we see at once that the mode is 20 inches.

Which of these three measures of central tendency should we use? The answer depends upon what we want to know, the kind of question we ask. Generally speaking, the mean is the most useful measure in the sense that it is the most stable. If we were to enlist

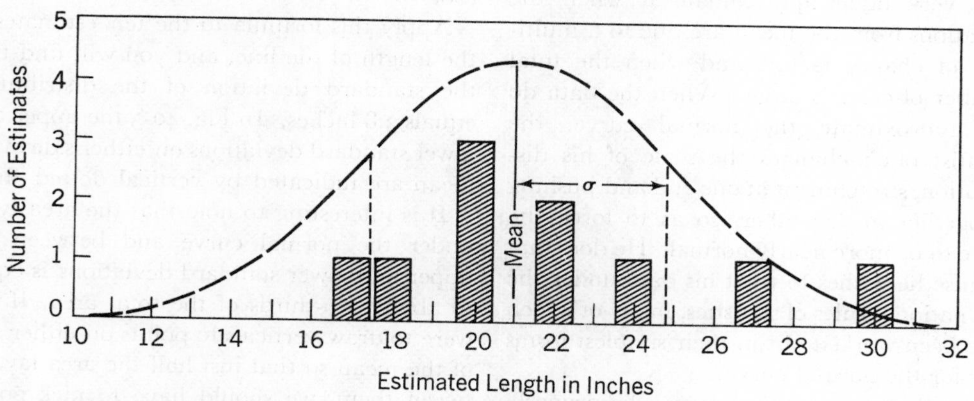

Fig. 40–5. *Distributions of data* The heights of the vertical bars show how many times each value on the horizontal scale was given as the estimated length of a line. The dotted curve shows the shape of a *normal distribution* (see text). The distance indicated by σ is the *standard deviation* of the distribution.

another 10 subjects for our experiment and get 10 more guesses, the mean of the second group would probably not be very different from that of the first — not so different, at any rate, as the median of the second group compared with the median of the first. And the mode would be the least stable of all. This fickleness on the part of the mode is unfortunate, because the mode is extremely simple to determine. Apparently what comes easiest in statistics is often not worth very much.

The data for 10 subjects, plotted as vertical bars in Fig. 40-5, show a roughly bell-shaped distribution: the judgments tend to cluster near the mean. They indicate that the line tends to be underestimated, but they also show that the judgments above the mean are spread out further than those below. In other words, the distribution tails off more gradually at the right than at the left. If we observed 1000 cases instead of 10, we should get rid of all the small irregularities in the curve, but these other two features might remain as the facts of the case, provided we still use this scale of inches for measuring them. More often than not we get underestimations, yet the overestimations, when they do occur, show larger departures from the average of the group.

The dotted curve of Fig. 40-5 is the so-called curve of *normal distribution*. Observed data very often approximate it when the deviations from the mean are due to a multitude of chance factors and when the total number of cases is large. When the data do not approximate the normal curve, the scientist often changes the scale of his distribution, stretching it at one end and pushing it together at the other, so as to force the curve to be more nearly normal. He does that because he wishes to treat his data under the conventional rules of statistics, many of which have been worked out in their simplest forms only for the normal curve.

It is clear that when data can be properly represented by the normal curve, their mean, median and mode all have the same value, for the normal distribution is symmetrical about its single mode. (On normal distribution, see also pp. 418 f.)

VARIABILITY

Measures of variability tell us how widely the data scatter about their mean. The important measures of variability are the *range*, the *standard deviation* and the *probable error*.

The *range* is simply the difference between the highest and the lowest score. As with the mode, we come by it easily but it tells us relatively little. The range of guesses for the length of the line in our experiment is $30 - 17 = 13$ inches. Common sense tells us that another group of ten subjects would probably not scatter its guesses over precisely this same range. So what is needed is a more stable measure of variability.

The *standard deviation* gives us this greater stability and is the most important measure of variability in the whole field of statistics. In technical language the standard deviation, designated by the Greek letter sigma (σ), is defined as the square root of the mean of the sum of the squares of the deviations from the mean. What this boils down to is simply that, in order to compute σ, we first find the mean, then we subtract the value of the mean from each score in turn. We then square each of the results, add them all up, divide by the number of scores and finally take the square root.

Apply this formula to the ten estimates of the length of the line, and you will find that the standard deviation of the distribution equals 3.8 inches. In Fig. 40-5 the upper and lower standard deviations on either side of the mean are indicated by vertical dotted lines.

It is interesting to note that the area lying under the normal curve and between the upper and lower standard deviations is equal to about two-thirds of the total area. If we were to draw verticals to points on either side of the mean so that just half the area lay between them, we should have to pick points nearer the mean. Those points, with half the area below the curve lying between them, are the values defining the *probable error* (P.E.).

In numerical terms it turns out that the probable error is equal to 0.6745σ. The probable error gets its name from this fact: If the scores that scatter about the mean are regarded as errors, the probability is 50-50 that a particular error will lie inside the limits set by the probable error.

Thresholds

All living organisms exhibit the phenomena known as *thresholds*. Some stimuli affect them; others do not. Some lights are too faint to be seen, some sounds too faint to be heard. But, as the intensity of a light or a sound is increased, there comes a point at which it is seen or heard. At any instant, it appears, this point at which a stimulus just crosses the threshold must be fixed, definite and precise. But, unfortunately, at two different instants the threshold point is not the same. The organism's properties do not stay put. Instead, its sensitivity bobs up and down from moment to moment. Consequently, when we want to determine the threshold we have to make repeated measurements and we have to apply statistical procedures to the resulting data. For this reason it is commonly said that *the threshold is a statistical concept.*

When we examined the seven basic problems of psychophysics, we saw that there are two kinds of threshold, *absolute* thresholds and *relative* or *differential* thresholds. The absolute threshold is the value of a stimulus which is (on the average) just noticeable or just detectable. The differential threshold is that difference between two stimuli which is (on the average) just noticeable. The measurement of both types of threshold has long been an important problem in psychology, and for their measurement elaborate procedures and precise statistical treatments have been devised. All these methods have one aim in common: They try to draw stable conclusions from measurements on variable organisms. These conclusions are important to science, and they are often of great practical importance as well. Some people earn their living measuring other people's thresholds.

Suppose, for example, a man is applying for a job as a radio operator. Obviously he must have normal hearing. That means that his absolute threshold for sound must not be significantly above normal. Since speech is the most important kind of sound he must hear, we might say that he must have a normal absolute threshold for speech.

Standardized threshold tests for speech were developed during the recent war as an aid in the rehabilitation of aural casualties. Carefully chosen words were recorded on phonograph records, and by means of special electrical circuits these words could be reproduced at the listener's ear in graded steps of intensity. The problem then is (1) to determine the faintest intensity at which the listener can hear the speech and (2) to compare this intensity with that at which a normal listener hears the words. How this is done can be illustrated with the aid of Fig. 40-6. We shall assume that our listener has a fairly large hearing loss, sufficient to cause his friends to raise their voices.

First let us consider the threshold of the normal listener. We find, of course, that at a given faint intensity he hears some of the words and not others, because his sensitivity varies. If we raise the intensity slightly, he hears a larger percentage of the words. Finally, if we make the speech loud enough, he hears all the words. If, therefore, we plot the percentage of the words he hears at each level of intensity, we obtain the curve in Fig. 40-7. This is usually a long S-shaped curve. It approximates, in fact, the *ogive* form of the normal distribution curve, the form which shows us, not the number of cases for each value of the stimulus, but the number of cases *up to and including* each value of the stimulus. It is a cumulative curve. It starts at zero per cent for the stimulus that is always ineffective and reaches 100 per cent at the stimulus that is always effective.

Having plotted the percentage of words which the listener hears at successive intensity levels, we are ready to decide what value we shall call the threshold for speech. Both common sense and convention tell us that the threshold ought to be defined as the intensity corresponding to the 50 per cent point on the curve. This is the speech intensity that will be heard correctly half the time. If we regard the listener's responses to the words as comprising a frequency distribution, this 50 per cent point is the *median* of the distribution.

For the hard-of-hearing listener we carry out precisely the same procedure. We plot a curve showing how his correct responses depend upon intensity and we pay attention to the 50 per cent point. Then, since we

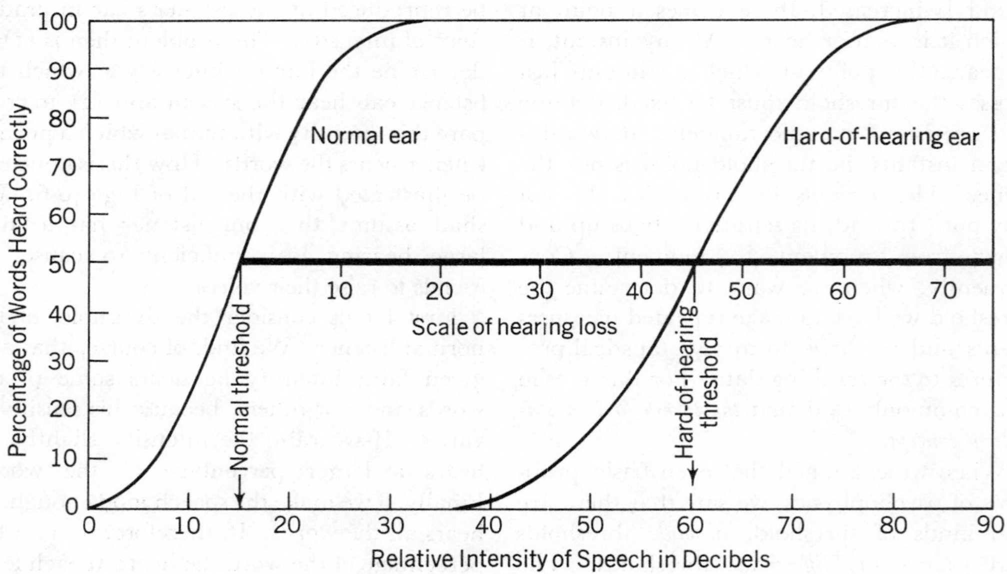

Fig. 40–6. *Psychometric functions for absolute thresholds* The two curves (psychometric functions) show how the percentage of words heard correctly increases as the intensity level of the speech (in decibels) is raised. The intensity at which half the words are heard correctly is defined as the absolute threshold. Amount of hearing loss is the difference between the threshold of the patient and the threshold of a normal ear.

measure hearing loss relative to the normal threshold, we simply take the spread between the two 50 per cent points as the quantitative measure of hearing loss. In the example before us this loss is 45 decibels, a large enough loss to call for a hearing aid. (For a fuller account of the intelligibility of speech, see pp. 345-349.)

The S-shaped curves in Fig. 40-6 are known as *psychometric functions.* Curves of this sort are obtained whenever we present carefully graded stimuli and record the frequencies with which a subject responds to them. The curves in Fig. 40-6 measure absolute thresholds, but similar functions are obtained when we measure relative thresholds by the same method.

Thus we can present pairs of stimuli graded as to the *difference* between them and ask the subject to respond by saying whether the second stimulus in each pair is *greater* or *less* than the first. We should then obtain two psychometric functions (one for judgments *greater*, one for judgments *less.*) The two functions would cross each other at their 50 per cent points. This crossing would usually fall near the value corresponding to *no* physical difference between the stimuli. On these two functions we should then have to decide the value of the differential threshold, obviously *not* the 50 per cent point. Here convention tells us we should choose the value of the physical difference which gives judgments of *greater* (or of *less*) 75 per cent of the second tone of each pair is higher or lower than the first tone. The percentages of correct judgments may then be tabulated and plotted as in Fig. 40-7. There we see plots for the average of the group of 95 students and plots for the average of the 11 best

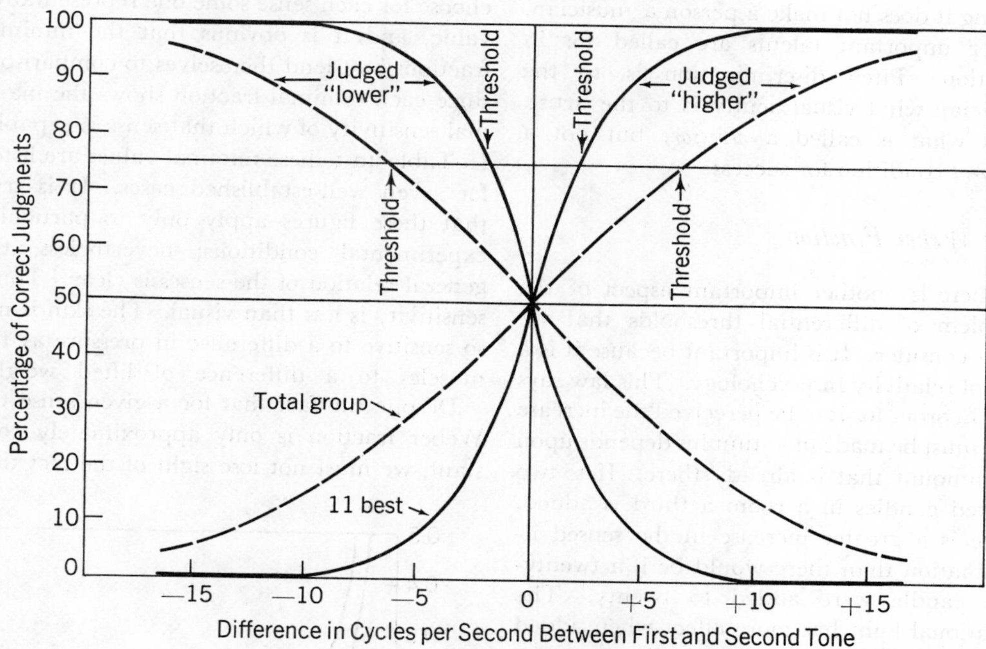

Fig. 40-7. *Psychometric functions for differential thresholds* Psychometric functions show how the correctness of pitch judgments depends upon the size of the stimulus difference. The dotted curves represent the composite scores made by 95 high school students who took the Seashore Test for Musical Talent. The solid curves are for the group of 11 students who scored highest on the test. The curves for the judgments *higher* and *lower* cross at the 50 per cent point, which coincides with zero difference between the two tones presented as stimuli. Thus, when there was no difference to be heard, the judgments followed the chance expectancy of 50–50.

time. This is reasonable enough if you think about it. The 75 per cent point is the midpoint of the distribution of judgments falling on *one side* of equality.

Figure 40-7 shows how all this works out in a practical situation. A group of 95 high school students was given one of the Seashore Tests designed to gauge musical ability. This test calls for the discrimination of small differences in pitch. Pairs of tones are sounded, and the listener tries to tell whether the students. These 11 listeners are clearly better at discriminating differences in pitch than the group as a whole. If we measure pitch discrimination as the difference in frequency (cycles of the tonal stimulus per second) correctly noticed 75 per cent of the time, we find that the group as a whole has an average differential threshold equal to 7 cycles per second. For the 11 best listeners the average is only 2 cycles per second. On the average these 11 people could tell the difference between a tone of 1000 cycles and a tone of 1002 cycles — which is very good discrimination indeed.

Pitch discrimination as good as this is a necessary asset to a musician. But a word of caution is in order here. Although good pitch discrimination is necessary, the fact of having it does not make a person a musician. Other important talents are called for in addition. Pitch discrimination is to the musician what visual acuity is to the artist. It is what is called a *necessary* but not a *sufficient* condition for success.

The Weber Fraction

There is another important aspect of the problem of differential thresholds that we must consider. It is important because it is a law of relativity in psychology. This law says that in order for it to be perceived the increase that must be made in a stimulus depends upon the amount that is already there. If to two lighted candles in a room a third is added, there is a greater increase in the sensed illumination than there would be if a twenty-first candle were added to twenty. The additional light has more effect when added to a lesser illumination. A cough counts for more in church than in the subway. In other words, the differential threshold for intensity gets larger as the intensity gets greater.

It is usual to measure relative sensitivity by taking the ratio of the differential threshold, which we may call ΔI, to the total intensity at which the threshold was obtained, which we may call I. This ratio $\Delta I/I$ is called the Weber ratio or the *Weber fraction*, because a century ago the physiologist, E. H. Weber, thought that it remained constant at different intensities. Modern research has corrected his view. Figure 40-8 shows the typical form of the *Weber function*, that is, the way $\Delta I/I$ changes with I. Although Weber held that such a function would be a horizontal straight line, actually the Weber function is, as the figure shows, a curve. The value of the Weber fraction first decreases rapidly as the intensity increases and then more slowly until it reaches a minimal value. Thereafter, it may remain constant, or occasionally it may again increase slightly.

In terms of the Weber fractions, it is possible to compare one sense with another with respect to differential sensitivity. Since the fraction varies within a single sense, we must choose for each sense some one representative value, and it is obvious that the minimal fractions best lend themselves to comparison, since each minimal fraction shows the maximal sensitivity of which that sense is capable. In Table 40-1 these minimal values are listed for seven well-established cases. It is true that these figures apply only to particular experimental conditions; nevertheless, the general relation of the senses is clear. Tonal sensitivity is less than visual. The skin is not so sensitive to a difference in pressure as the muscles to a difference of lifted weight.

Despite the fact that for a given sense the Weber fraction is only approximately constant, we must not lose sight of the fact that

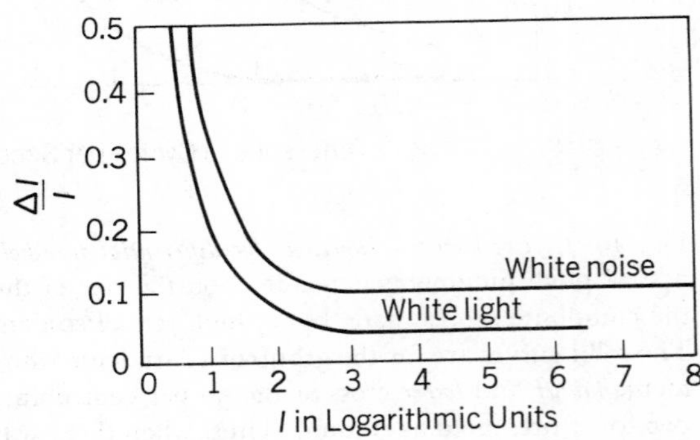

Fig. 40-8. *Typical Weber functions for vision and hearing.* The curves show the relation between the Weber fraction $\Delta I/I$, and the intensity of the stimulus, I. $I = 0$ is the absolute threshold. On the intensity scale each unit represents a tenfold increase in energy. White noise is a purely random mixture of all frequencies. It sounds like a sustained *Sh-h-h.* It is called *white* because, like white light, it is composed of all the perceptible frequencies acting simultaneously. [Data from G. A. Miller, *J. acoust. Soc. Amer.*, 1947, **19,** 609–619.] The measurements for white light were made with a small patch of light (visual angle = 28 minutes of arc) falling on the retinal fovea.

TABLE 40-1

Minimal Weber Fractions

For all cases below, except tones and smells, the Weber fraction has a minimal value in the middle range of intensities. The minimal values for tone and smell are for the maximal intensities after the Weber function has leveld off. Although each of the different values would be somewhat altered by a different choice of experimental conditions, the difference between 1/77 and 1/5 is so very great that there can be no doubt about the general fact that different sensory mechanisms differ significantly in sensitivity.

	Weber Ratio	*Weber Fraction*
Deep pressure, from skin and subcutaneous tissue, at about 400 grams	0.013	1/77
Visual brightness, at about 1000 photons	0.016	1/62
Lifted weights, at about 300 grams	0.019	1/53
Tone, for 1000 cycles per second, at about 100 db above the absolute threshold	0.088	1/11
Smell, for rubber, at about 200 olfacties	0.104	1/10
Cutaneous pressure, on an isolated spot, at about 5 grams per mm	0.136	1/7
Taste, for saline solution, at about 3 moles per liter concentration	0.200	1/5

the Weber function is a general statement that *relativity* is approximated in the world of sensory intensities. The principle of relativity signifies that a little thing means more to another little thing than it does to a big thing. A dollar means more in poverty than it does in wealth, whereas an error of an inch in the length of the equator matters less than an error of an inch in the fit of a shoe. Just so the Weber function means that differences that seem large at small intensities become quite unnoticeable at large intensities.

References

[1] Bartley, S. H. *Vision.* New York: Van Nostrand, 1941. Chap. 2.

A discussion of the principal facts of brightness discrimination with emphasis on the underlying physiological processes.

[2] Boring, E. G. *The physical dimensions of consciousness.* New York: Appleton-Century, 1933. Chaps. 2, 3 and 6.

A systematic discussion of the sensory attributes of intensity and quality in terms of a physical theory of mind.

[3] Boring, E. G. *Sensation and perception in the history of experimental psychology.* New York: Appleton-Century, 1942. Chap. 1.

Chapter 1 summarizes the work and thought on sensation and perception during the last three centuries.

[4] Guilford, J. P. *Psychometric methods.* New York: McGraw-Hill, 1936. Chaps. 2 to 6.

A comprehensive treatment of the classical psychophysical methods and their statistical bases.

[5] Stevens, S. S., and Davis, H. *Hearing: its psychology and physiology.* New York: Wiley, 1938. Chaps. 2 to 5.

A systematic analysis of the facts of auditory sensation with respect to pitch, loudness and the other tonal attributes.

[6] Troland, L. T. *The principles of psychophysiology.* New York: Van Nostrand, 1930. Vol. 2, especially sections 53, 54 and 61.

A systematic account of the psychophysical facts of all the senses with especial emphasis on vision.

41

Qualitative Measurement: A Codification of Techniques Unique to Social Science

Qualitative Measurement in the Social Sciences: Classification, Typologies, and Indices

PAUL F. LAZARSFELD and ALLEN H. BARTON

The idea that "social science must develop measurements" has sometimes led to misunderstandings. Some optimists want to start measuring social phenomena immediately with all the precision of the most advanced sectors of physical science; some pessimists deny that man and his works can ever be measured at all, and recommend an entirely intuitive approach to the understanding of society. The false assumption underlying both positions is that science can be carried on only with one particular kind of device — the quantitative scale with equal intervals and a zero point — and that aside from this device there is nothing but a chaos of guesswork and intuition.

It should be realized that systematic study can be carried on in the social sciences as elsewhere by many devices which are less precise than strict quantitative measurement but nonetheless far better than unaided individual judgment. It is the contention of this chapter that there is a direct line of logical continuity from qualitative classification to the most rigorous forms of measurement, by way of intermediate devices of systematic ratings, ranking scales, multidimensional classifications, typologies, and simple quantitative indices. In this wider sense of "measurement," social phenomena are being measured every day by both theoretically oriented and applied social researchers. One way to develop social science measurement is to *systematize these commonly performed research procedures*, by codifying exactly what successful researchers do in carrying out these simpler forms of measurement and exploring their logical implications.[1]

This chapter will point out a few of the significant problems along this continuum of measurement procedures. The first section deals with an operation which must precede any sort of actual measurement: the formation of the categories in terms of which the objects under study are to be classified or measured. The second section briefly notes some procedures for making the actual classification of items into given categories more systematic than pure personal judgment. The third considers the logic of multidimensional classifications and their relation to typologies. The final section discusses a few of the many problems raised when we try to combine various observations into quantitative indices.

The Formation of Qualitative Categories

Before we can investigate the presence or absence of some attribute in a person or a social situation, or before we can rank objects or measure them in terms of some variable, we must form the concept of that variable.

Reprinted from *The Policy Sciences*, edited by Daniel Lerner and Harold D. Lasswell with the permission of the publishers, Stanford University Press, Stanford, Calif., pp. 155–192.

[1] For a fuller discussion of codification, see the Introduction, by Paul F. Lazarsfeld, to Hans Zeisel's *Say It With Figures* (1947).

Looking at the material before us in all its richness of sense-data, we must decide what attributes of the concrete items we wish to observe and measure: do we want to study "this-ness" or "that-ness," or some other "-ness"? The precise origin of our notion of this-ness or that-ness may be extremely varied, but it usually seems to involve combining many particular experiences into a category which promises greater understanding and control of events.

In this way we put together a great many behavior items and come up with concepts such as adjustment, authoritarian leadership, prestige, or bureaucracy. When we have formed some such category, we may then break it down into component elements upon which to base research instruments — instructions to coders, ranking scales, indicators; these in turn may be recombined in multidimensional patterns, typologies, or over-all indices. These operations will be the subject of later sections of the chapter. At the moment we are concerned with the question: How does one go about forming such categories in the first place? Why pick out certain elements of the situation and not others? Why combine them in just these categories?

It can properly be argued that one cannot lay down a set of handy instructions for the categorization of social phenomena: such instructions would be nothing less than a general program for the development of social theory. One cannot write a handbook on "how to form fruitful theoretical concepts" in the same way that one writes handbooks on how to sample or how to construct questionnaires.

The purpose of this section is not that ambitious. It happens that research does not always begin with general theoretical categories and theoretically prescribed relations among them. At the present stage of the social sciences a great deal of research must be of an *exploratory* nature, aiming at qualitative answers to such questions as the following: What goes on in a certain situation? What do young people do when making up their minds about choosing a career? What kinds of reactions do people have to unemployment? What are the channels of information about public issues in an American community?

Where research contains exploratory elements, the researcher will be faced by an array of raw data for which ready-made theoretical categories will not exist. He must formulate categories before he can do anything else. Probably the best way to start is with fairly concrete categories — the sort of categories which experienced policy-makers or participants in the situation use, worked out in as clear and logical a form as possible. The job of figuring out what theoretical categories are applicable to the given field of behavior will be a long one, and will involve switching back and forth between concrete categories closely adapted to the data themselves and general categories able to tie in with other fields of experience, until both concrete applicability and generality are obtained. The immediate problem is to get the raw data classified in some reasonable preliminary way, so that it can be communicated, cross-tabulated, and thought about.[2]

We will therefore try to codify the procedure used by experienced researchers in forming such preliminary, concrete category systems for the raw materials turned up by exploratory research. Some of the rules are entirely general and formal, derived from textbooks of logic; others have grown out of practical experience. Most of the examples will be drawn from the classification of responses to open-ended questions, but it is hoped that the discussion will also be relevant to the analysis of communications content, of personal documents, and of systematic observations.

The requirements of a good classification system for free responses may be summed up in four points:

1. *Articulation:* The classification should proceed in steps from the general to the

[2] For a discussion of general versus concrete categories in content analysis, see Bernard Berelson, *The Analysis of Communication Content* (1951).

specific, so that the material can be examined either in terms of detailed categories or of broad groupings, whichever are more appropriate for a given purpose.

2. *Logical correctness:* In an articulated set of categories those on each step must be exhaustive and mutually exclusive. When an object is classified at the same time from more than one aspect, each aspect must have its own separate set of categories.

3. *Adaptation to the structure of the situation:* The classification should be based on a comprehensive outline of the situation as a whole — an outline containing the main elements and processes in the situation which it is important to distinguish for purposes of understanding, predicting, or policy-making.

4. *Adaptation to the respondent's frame of reference:* The classification should present as clearly as possible the respondent's own definition of the situation — his focus of attention, his categories of thought.

ARTICULATION

The basic purpose of classification is to simplify the handling of a great number of individual items by putting them into a smaller number of groups, each group consisting of items which act more or less alike in relation to the problem being studied. This raises the following problem: If the classification is kept very simple, with only a few broad groupings, it will combine many elements which are not very similar. Important distinctions of a more detailed sort will be lost completely. On the other hand, if the classification preserves all distinctions which may be of any significance, it will contain too many groups to be surveyed and handled conveniently.

The solution of this dilemma is to use an "articulate" classification: a classification with several steps, starting with a few broad categories and breaking them down into many more detailed categories. In this way one can eat one's cake and have it too: when a few broad categories are sufficient, only the simple first step need be used; when a more detailed study is required, the finer distinctions can be found preserved in the later, finer steps of the classification system.

An example will make clear the advantages of articulation. In a study of young people which was made in New Jersey during the 1930's, two thousand boys were asked the question, "What can the community do for its youth?" The replies were so numerous and diversified that a classification in several steps was needed for their analysis. The categories used, with their percentages of response, are shown in Table 41-1.

TABLE 41-1
(In Percentages)

Employment			24.5
More		18.7	
Better conditions		5.8	
Education			16.4
High school		3.9	
Free college		3.8	
Free vocational schools		2.0	
Free adult education		4.6	
Education in general		2.1	
Recreation			29.6
Community centers		9.8	
Outdoor activities		14.9	
Parks and playgrounds	6.2		
Swimming pools	5.3		
Other-outdoor facilities	3.4		
Clubs		4.9	
Other suggestions			5.4
No suggestions given			24.1
Total			100.0

Results presented in this form are much easier to read — they "make more sense" than a long list of detailed categories presented in a completely unstructured way. Furthermore they can be handled statistically in ways which would otherwise be impossible. If the sample were divided into small subgroups in terms of other variables, for instance age and income, the results for the many detailed categories might become statistically unreliable. However, the few broad categories of the first step could still be used with statistical confidence.

It is not always easy to fit detailed categories together to form an articulated system. Where, in the system given above, should one put the response, "better library facilities"? Is it "education" or "recreation"? The trouble here is that the concrete categories in which the data were gathered were not adapted to the final classification scheme. The scheme is set up in terms of "functions"; the answer, "library facilities," is in terms of a concrete institution with several functions. If the answers are to be classified in the present scheme, the right questions must be asked in the first place. When someone suggests a concrete institution with multiple functions, a further question must be asked to discover which of these functions the respondent had in mind.

It should also be kept clearly in mind that there are usually several alternate ways in which a classification can be formed. The responses to the youth survey might have been classified in terms of the distinction between activities aiming at economic advancement, at gratification of cultural wants, and at physical recreation. Some education activities would then fall into the "economic advancement" category, while the remainder, along with some of the recreation items, would fall into the "cultural gratification" category.

LOGICAL CORRECTNESS

A classification meets the requirements of logic if it provides exhaustive and mutually exclusive categories at each step of the classification.

An example of lack of exhaustiveness would be the classification of persons influencing voters as "family," "friends," "fellow workers," and "neighbors." This would leave no place for contacts with party workers or with casually encountered strangers. Of course, any classification can be made exhaustive by including an "other" category. This meets the purely logical requirement, but it defeats the purpose of the classification which is to distinguish elements which behave differently in terms of the problem under study.

Mutual exclusiveness means that there should be one and only one place to put an item within a given classification system. There are two sources of violations of this rule: (1) the use of categories on one step of the classification which are wholly included in others; and (2) the mixing of different aspects of objects in a single-dimensioned classification scheme.

An illustration of the first error would be the classification of sources of information as "mass media," "personal contacts," and "newspapers." Newspapers are obviously a subclass of mass media. We should either revise the first category to read, "mass media" (excluding newspapers), or else relegate "newspapers" to a second step in the classification under "mass media," perhaps along with "radio," "magazines," "television," and so on.

Lack of mutual exclusiveness due to mixing different aspects can be illustrated by the following classification of the output of a radio station: "musical programs," "dramatic programs," "serious programs," "recorded programs," etc. These categories belong to various dimensions and they must not be lumped together. If one is interested in classifying programs in terms of all these aspects simultaneously, a multidimensional classification must be set up. The categories of such a system are all possible combinations of the varieties on each dimension, for instance: "popular recorded music," "serious recorded music," "popular live music," and so on. Each program will then appear in only one category. If one is not really interested in combining the different aspects, each should be set up as a separate classification system.

ADAPTATION TO THE STRUCTURE OF THE SITUATION

The codification of practices that make for good classification has been easy so far, since it has dealt with matters of form. But now one comes to the heart of the matter: how to set up those particular categories which will be best adapted to the material and the problem being studied? The purpose of categories is to organize a great many concrete items into a small number of classes, so that the situation studied can be more easily understood. In the long run this must involve relating the categories used in any particular situation to more general systems of concepts which cover wide areas of human behavior, so that social theories can be developed which will make each particular situation easier to understand and control.

In many cases the researcher simply uses the customary terms of everyday life. Channels of political influence easily divide themselves into "mass media" and "personal contacts." "Mass media" again subdivide into "radio," "newspapers," "magazines," etc., on the basis of obvious physical and organizational distinctions. In other cases the researcher may take culturally given categories. For example, political values might be categorized as "liberty," "equality," and "fraternity," following the French Revolutionary slogan, and perhaps "security" would have to be added to adapt the system to current materials. Organizations are self-classified as "educational," "recreational," "religious," and so on.

In most exploratory research, however, the investigator will have to develop his own categories. It is naturally not possible to give completely general rules for forming categories which will be best adapted to *any* problem under study. But there is one frequently occurring type of situation for which fairly clear procedures can be laid down. This arises when one is trying to classify "reasons" for certain kinds of action: why people vote for a certain candidate, why soldiers stand up or break down under fire, why people migrate from place to place, or why pogroms, lynchings, or revolutions break out. This case, where the researcher must set up a classification of factors influencing a certain kind of action, will be discussed in detail here.

One starts with a collection of observations of people in those situations, reports about their behavior, or interview material in which the participants themselves are asked to explain their behavior. It is usually not possible to arrive at a satisfactory classification system simply by grouping items which seem similar in content. Rather it is necessary to build up a concrete picture or model of the whole situation to which the reports refer, and then locate the particular report within this "structural scheme." This involves an interacting process. First it is necessary to visualize the concrete processes and activities implied by the responses, through introspection and an imaginative qualitative analysis of the data, to get a preliminary scheme. Then one tries to apply this scheme systematically to the data, returns to the structural scheme for refinement, reapplies the revised scheme to the data, and so on. One may thereby end up with a classification rather different from that with which one started.

We will give two examples of this procedure of formulating a structural scheme for the classification of interview material; one is drawn from market research, the other from *The American Soldier*.[3]

Suppose we want to classify the reasons why women buy a certain kind of cosmetics. Women have a great many comments on their reasons which are hard to group if one takes them at face value. But visualize a woman buying and using cosmetics. She gets advice from people she knows, from advertising, and from articles in mass media; in addition she has her own past experiences to go on. She has her own motives and requirements: she uses cosmetics in order to achieve various appearance values so as to impress others — one might even find out whom — and perhaps to impress herself. The cosmetics have various technical qualities which relate to these desired results. She may also worry about possible bad effects on health or appearance. There are the

[3] Samuel A. Stouffer, *et. al.*, *The American Soldier* (*Studies in Social Psychology in World War II*, Vols. I and II [1949]).

problems of applying the cosmetics. And finally there is the expense. All of the women's comments might be related to the following scheme: "channels of information," "desired appearance values," "prospective 'audience'," "bad consequences," "technical qualities," "application problems," and "cost." The reason the comments would fit is that the scheme of classification matches the actual processes involved in buying and using cosmetics. These are the processes from which the respondent herself has derived her comments; the classification, so to speak, puts the comments back where they came from.

Suppose we are studying soldiers' behavior in combat. We ask certain general questions about their behavior, and get a great many responses which are hard to group. But let us, in the words of *The American Soldier*, "analyze the typical and general determinants of behavior in the immediate combat situation. A tired, cold, muddy rifleman goes forward with the bitter dryness of fear in his mouth into the mortar burst and machine-gun fire of a determined enemy."[4] What exactly is he up against? The authors list:[5]

1. Threats to life and limb and health
2. Physical discomfort
3. Deprivation of sexual and concomitant social satisfactions
4. Isolation from accustomed sources of affectional assurance
5. Loss of comrades, and sight and sound of wounded and dying men
6. Restriction of personal movement
7. Continual uncertainty, and lack of adequate cognitive orientation
8. Conflicts of values: *a*) Military duty vs. safety and comfort *b*) Military duty vs. family obligations *c*) Military duty vs. informal group loyalties
9. Being treated as a means rather than as an end in oneself
10. Lack of privacy
11. Long periods of enforced boredom, mingled with anxiety
12. Lack of terminal *individual* goals (short of end of war)

On the other hand there are factors which help to offset the stresses:[6]

1. Coercive formal authority
2. Leadership practices — example, encouragement
3. Informal group: *a*) Affectional support *b*) Code of behavior *c*) Provision of realistic security and power
4. Convictions about the war and the enemy
5. Desires to complete the job by winning war, to go home
6. Prayer and personal philosophies

With such an initial visualization of the situation, we can begin to classify free responses in interviews, statements in personal documents, in the mass media of communication, or reports by observers; and we can also reclassify the answers to a great many poll-type questions. Where the analyst has such intimate familiarity with the concrete material as well as the guidance of a certain amount of social theory, the set of categories which he creates is very likely to be useful for understanding the situation.

One brief example may be given of the role of social theory in improving the classification system. The authors of *The American Soldier* note that in many types of organization coercive formal sanctions are not as effective in themselves as they are through the informal group sanctions and the internal sanctions (guilt) which they call up.[7] It would therefore be advisable to get additional information from those respondents who mention formal sanctions as a factor in the combat situation, so that they can be further classified to show whether it is these sanctions *per se* or their effect *through informal and in-*

[4] *Ibid.*, II, 107. The chapter from which this and the following list were drawn was written by Robin M. Williams, Jr., and M. Brewster Smith.

[5] *Ibid.*, p. 77.

[6] *Ibid.* This list is adapted from p. 107.

[7] *Ibid.*, pp. 112–18.

ternal sanctions which are actually affecting the respondent's behavior.

Conversely the authors warn that the mentioning only of informal and internal sanctions by no means implies that formal sanctions play no role. The formal sanctions may play an important part in establishing the norms of the informal group and of the individual conscience, which thereafter will direct the individual's activities along lines laid down by the formal authority. Of course there will exist some informal group and individual norms which run contrary to those derived from the formal authority. A more complete structural scheme on which we might thus base a classification of men's behavior in combat (or of statements relating to it) is given in Table 41-2.

TABLE 41-2

How Norms Bear on Individual Behavior in Combat

Underlying Source of Norms	Channels
Norms of formal authorities	*Direct:*
	a) Formal sanctions
	b) Internal sanctions
	Via group norms:
	c) Informal group sanctions
	d) Internal sanctions
Norms of informal group	*e*) Informal group sanctions
	f) Internal sanctions
Individual norms	*g*) Internal sanctions

Examples of each of the categories in Table 41-2 would be:

a) I fight because I'll be punished if I quit.

b) I fight because it's my duty to my country, the Army, the government; it would be wrong for me to quit.

c) I fight because I'll lose the respect of my buddies if I quit.

d) I fight because it would be wrong to let my buddies down.

e) You have to look out for your buddies even if it means violating orders, or they won't look out for you.

f) You have to look out for your buddies even if it means violating orders because it would be wrong to leave them behind.

g) I am fighting because I believe in democracy and hate fascism.

One could go on to include other formal and informal groups outside the immediate army situation: churches, family, political groups, and so on, which are sources of norms important to behavior in battle.

To formulate once more the general procedure: the situation or process is visualized which serves as a frame of reference for the whole list of comments or behavior items to be classified, as required by the study. This situation or process is then divided into its different "natural parts" on the basis of experienced personal judgment or general theoretical directives. The thought moves in two directions, building up from the list of comments an organized model of the situation and concurrently dividing this whole into parts. Finally the two tendencies will have to meet. To put it another way: the line of progress is not directly from the single concrete piece of data to the group into which it might fit; it proceeds rather from the concrete answers to the overall structure which seems to be involved; from this structure the thought turns to the component parts, and here are found the adequate groups for the classification. In this process both intimate knowledge of the concrete situation and the guidance of social theory are needed, both to formulate the initial structural scheme and to refine it as one goes on trying to fit the concrete material into it.

Besides true theoretical models there are certain types of fairly standard structural schemes which have been developed in applied research for use in standard situations. These are discussed in some detail in Zeisel's *Say It With Figures* (1947). We shall only list them here:[8]

1. *The push-pull scheme,* used in studies of reasons for migration from place *A* to place

[8] This list is adapted from chapter i, "How to Tabulate Reasons."

B, or for shifting one's preference from any item *X* to any other item *Y*. The elements in this scheme are: the attributes of *X* and the attributes of *Y*.

2. *The attributes-motives-influences scheme*, used in classification of reasons for choosing a given item *X*. The elements of this scheme are: the attributes of *X*, the motives of the respondent, the channels of influences concerning his choice.

3. *The technical-properties-resulting-gratification scheme* for studying "what is it about *X*" that the respondent likes. The elements of this scheme are: technical properties of *X*, resulting gratifications from *X* to the respondent. (For instance: I like *X* beer because it's made with more malt, and more malt means better flavor; I like *X* because he is honest, and an honest mayor means lower taxes; I like the New Deal because it uses Keynesian economic techniques, and that eliminates mass unemployment.)

4. *The where-is-it, what-barrier-keeps-it-there, who-is-to-blame scheme* for studying respondent's explanation of shortages of anything. (For instance: sugar is short because it comes from Java, and Java is occupied by the Japanese — so it's the Japs' fault. Or: there's plenty of sugar in the country; the government is keeping it back to create a war psychology, so the government — or the enemy who makes such action necessary to the government — is to blame.)

5. *The underlying-reasons-precipitating-cause scheme*, used in classifying answers to the questions "why did you do so and so?" and "why did you do it *just then*?" This just adds one or several stages to *any* of the elements in the attributes-motives-influences scheme. (For instance: I wanted a car, and when they came out with such nice models I went out and bought one; or, I wanted a car, but when I met my girl friend I just had to have one so I bought one; or, I wanted a car, and when the salesman came around and talked to me about it I bought one.)

ADAPTATION TO THE RESPONDENT'S FRAME OF REFERENCE

One of the first things one notices in applying a structural scheme to the analysis of interview material is that the responses of any given individual may be seriously incomplete in terms of the whole scheme. If this is simply the result of poor interviewing — for instance, of failing to follow up "why" questions with proper detailed probes — the ultimate remedy is good interviewing. But if the incompleteness and vagueness are inherent in the respondent's definition of the situation, they cannot be eliminated and one may not want to eliminate them.

For example, a survey of the Norwegian public asked about their explanations for the bad postwar living conditions and their ideas of what should be done about them.[9] The whole array of answers could be classified only in terms of an outline of all major elements of the Norwegian economy. Most individual answers, however, covered only a small part of that structure. Some people wanted less taxes, but did not know what expenses should be cut; others wanted more imports without explaining where the foreign exchange would come from; some people had specific proposals about particular industries, while others had only general suggestions for "more freedom" or "fairer distribution." This was natural, since the respondents who had not followed professional discussions of the economic situation could hardly obtain from their own experience a coherent picture of the whole economic structure.

However, the object of the survey was not to study the Norwegian economy itself, but rather to find out what the public's perceptions and attitudes regarding the economic situation were, and how these related to the respondents' socioeconomic position and political behavior. Therefore, the economic structural scheme was used only as a basis for a much looser and more "psychological" set

[9] Unpublished research on "Psychological and Sociological Implications of Economic Planning," carried out by the Sociological Institute, University of Oslo, under the direction of Allen H. Barton.

of categories. Respondents were classified in terms of whether they focused on the production or the income-distribution side of the economy, what goals they seemed to look toward, and which policy measures they advocated. The result was not to find out what the respondent thought about all economic questions, but to find out what economic questions he thought about, and what his opinions were with regard to *those* questions. To classify the many respondents who gave partial or vague answers, special categories had to be introduced at each level of the classification scheme. A highly simplified version of the classification scheme is given in Table 41-3 to make clear what is involved in adapting a set of categories not only to the objective situation but also to the respondent's frame of reference.

This classification might not tell much about the state of the Norwegian economy, but it would tell a great deal about the state of mind of the Norwegian people. Of those giving relatively definite answers, we would know how many thought mainly of altering the income distribution and how many thought in terms of improving production. We would know how many desire change in each of various directions, and how many have unclear notions about what kind of change they want. We would know how many choose each of several major alternative policies as means to their goals, and we know how many have no idea how to achieve their desired goal. Among the remainder, Group III, we see the interesting phenomenon of those who have policies to suggest, but who cannot say exactly what they are supposed to accomplish.

It is not implied that the responses classified above should be taken at face value. If it turned out that most businessmen wanted lower taxes and less controls "in order to encourage production," while workers wanted higher wages and more participation in management, also "to encourage production," one might suspect that in many cases self-interest was being rationalized. It is an interesting fact that the actual results found many poor people demanding greater equality, but practically no rich people overtly demanding greater inequality. It might be possible by intensive interviewing to obtain material for a classification in terms of "deeper" feelings and beliefs. A trained psychologist handling intensive interviews or case histories might be able to classify respondents in terms of hidden or unconscious motives, using cues and indicators which he is specially trained to notice and interpret.

Something of this kind was done by Roethlisberger and Dickson in their study of workers' complaints in the Western Electric Plant. A complaint was considered "not only in relation to its alleged object, but also in relation to the personal situation of the complainant. Only in this way is the richer significance of the complaint realized. The significance of B's grouch about piece rates is better grasped in relation to the increase financial obligations incurred by his wife's illness; C's attitude toward his boss is greatly illuminated by the experience he relates in connection with his father; D's complaint about smoke and fumes is more readily understood in relation to his fear of contracting pneumonia."[10]

Another way in which classification was adapted to the respondent's frame of reference was to distinguish two types of items in the work situation: "(1) topics which in general the worker takes for granted unless something goes wrong; (2) topics which he does not take for granted even if they are favorable. . . . Subjects such as tools, machines, lockers, washrooms . . . are not talked about unless there is some complaint to be made. This is particularly true of most items relating to plant conditions; therefore, topics with a high index of dissatisfaction in this area do not necessarily indicate poor working conditions."

[10] This example and the following are taken from F. J. Roethlisberger and W. J. Dickson, *Management and the Worker: An Account of a Research Program Conducted by the Western Electric Company, Hawthorne Works, Chicago* (1939), pp. 248–68.

TABLE 41-3

Classification of Responses to Questions on What Should Be Done About Economic Situation

I. Answer in terms of changing the income distribution:

Goal	Means
1. More equality	*a*) Taxes and controls *b*) Social welfare services *c*) Measures against private capital *d*) No means specified
2. Less equality	*a*) Less taxes and controls *b*) Less welfare services
3. Vague: "Better," "Fairer," etc.	*a*) Vague or no answers

II. Answer in terms of improving production:

Goal	Means
1. Raise physical production	*a*) Raise wages *b*) Labor participation in management *c*) Less controls and taxes *d*) "Everyone work harder" *e*) No means specified
2. More rational production	*a*) Better central planning *b*) Less controls and taxes

III. Economic sector and goal not clearly specified:

a) More controls (purpose unspecified)
b) Less taxes and controls (reason unspecified)
c) Unspecified changes in tax system
d) "Continue government's policies" (unspecified)
e) Other suggestions of unspecified purpose

Still another such distinction was made when three categories of objects of complaint were distinguished: those referring to objectively ascertainable facts ("the doorknob is broken"); those referring to more subjective sense experiences ("the work is dirty" or "the room is hot"); and those referring to social facts ("ability doesn't count") or to social norms ("unfairness") which are not sensory elements at all.

It should be noted that the kind of classification scheme given in the Norwegian example above can also serve a quite different purpose: the tabulation of incomplete data resulting from unsatisfactory data-gathering techniques. This problem arises when one must analyze superficially carried out open-ended questions, unsystematically gathered case materials, or documents originally written for other purposes. The meaning of the categories is rather different in this case: the "vague" and "unspecified" categories do not necessarily constitute real categories of people; they may largely measure deficiencies in the data-gathering procedure. By separating out the incomplete answers, one may observe the distribution of the remaining complete answers. However, one should always realize that if the people with incomplete data could be properly classified, they might upset the proportions observed. The type of classification suggested clarifies the situation as much as possible, but it also indicates the margin of possible error involved in basing one's conclusions only on the portion of respondents about whom full data is available.

The Problem of Systematizing Qualitative Judgments

When we have formed a set of categories on the basis of inspection of the data, practical experience, and theoretical consideration, we must apply them. We must take the objects under study and decide in which category to place them. Where the categories are concrete the actual classifying process is no great problem. Such classifications as the rank of soldiers, the sex of respondents or story characters, the crimes with which the objects of news stories are officially charged, and the major branches of the mass communications industry simply make themselves.

But there are a great many concepts which are not so easy to apply. When is a news story sensational, a child maladjusted, a leader authoritarian? Is the army characterized by a caste system? Has union leadership become bureaucratized? Are the rank and file apathetic? Is the atmosphere of a group permissive, co-operative, competitive? Even seemingly obvious concepts turn out to be difficult in application — how, for example, do we draw the line between "front line troops" and "rear echelons"? How close to the enemy must the soldiers be, how often, under what conditions? How about artillerymen, supply truck drivers, regimental headquarters men, air crews?

It is sometimes argued that application of the most important concepts in social science must remain forever subjective and impressionistic. It is held that many phenomena are so complex and subtle that proper classification requires an insight and an unconscious ability to notice and combine enormous numbers of petty details — qualities which can come only to people of special gifts through long experience. The skilled politician or business leader, it is held, can assess the "group atmosphere" in a committee room in a way which no ordinary person, however equipped with devices and instructions, can possibly do. Social science must remain more of an art than a systematic, mechanical procedure.

That there is a large element of truth in this position cannot be denied. It would be too much to expect that any layman could be given brief instructions to make psychiatric diagnoses; however, it is to be hoped that people can be trained to do so systematically over a period of several years. Natural gifts may help, but such classification should not be entirely dependent on the availability of a few great artists of diagnosis. The same applies to social research. It should be possible to systematize the procedure for classification in terms of sociological concepts so that (1) researchers can be trained in a reasonably short time to perform classification with a high degree of agreement, (2) research procedures can be communicated to others, and (3) investigations can be duplicated and extended. In any given situation, the research worker using systematic procedures may be unable to compete with the innately gifted and long-experienced artist in the field; in the long run, however, the cumulation and refinement of research knowledge should carry us further than art and intuition.

The first advance beyond impressionistic judgment as a research instrument is the specification of the *indicators* upon which the classifier's decision is to be based. In this way we translate a concept into a set of instructions to the researcher, telling him what to look for as a basis of judgment in each case. There are various ways in which indicators can be used in classification. They may simply be used as the basis for an over-all judgment.

A more systematic procedure is to break the judgment down into separate segments. A number of broad areas of indicators may be specified, and a judgment made on each rather than making one over-all judgment. Of course, when a judgment is segmental, the segments must be recombined in some way, a process which leads to serious problems. The combination of segmental judgments may take the form of a *multidimensional classification*, such as a "profile" of ratings or a "response pattern" in which the whole pattern of segmental judgments is preserved; or it may take the form of adding them together in some way, to form an over-all *index*. Segmentation can be repeated on several levels, with each main area of judgment being subdivided into more specific indicators, and these further divided into as much detail as we care to go.

As a general rule, the more we segment the judgment, the more concrete and objective the indicators become; hence, different classifiers are more likely to agree, and the judgment procedure can be communicated and duplicated by others. The ideal situation would be to reduce a complex concept to such clear and unambiguous indicators that the classification procedure would become practically mechanical; anyone with the same set of instructions could duplicate the observations and judgments of any other observer. However, the more we segment, the larger looms the problem of recombining the segmental judgments. Also, as was suggested earlier, some concepts are so complex and the possible indicators so many and subtle that it will not be practical, for a long time at least, to reduce them to a set of entirely objective, concrete, easy-to-observe indicators.

This does not mean that nothing can be done to objectify such complex concepts. It is certainly possible to make human judgment *somewhat* objective by systematizing the training and instruction of classifiers as much as possible. As a rule, *any* degree of segmentation and specification of indicators makes classification more objective — more likely to be agreed upon and more easily communicable. A classic example of this rule is the procedure used in judging horses, as described by J. R. Commons:[11]

> The "general appearance" of the draft horse is now given a weight of 29 points, and this is subdivided into "weight," 5 points, "form," 4 points, "quality," 6 points, "action," 10 points, and "temperament," 3 points. "Head and neck" are given 8 points, subdivided into "head," "forehead," "eyes," "ears," "muzzle," "lower jaw," and "neck," with one or two points each. . . . The scorer goes over the horse, noticing in detail all the points specified, and he marks down opposite each his judgment of the degree to which the horse before him is deficient in that particular point.

The reader who is unfamiliar with draft-horse judging will be aware that these are hardly instructions which anyone could follow and come to the same judgments; the rules work only when there is a common body of understanding as to what is meant by the various terms and what represents good and bad characteristics. Nonetheless, the adoption of this segmentation results in agreement within one or two points between experienced raters using the full hundred-point scale.

Let us apply this procedure to the judgment of children's "adjustment." Even if we do no more than specify certain broad areas of data to which the raters are to pay attention — e.g., "appearance," "response to interviews," "attitude toward others," "attitude toward self" — we will increase reliability and make it somewhat easier for others to repeat our work. There is still required, however, a certain body of common training and experience, such as might be found among trained child psychologists, to make such a vague procedure work at all well. In addition we may specify more detailed indicators for each area (e.g., "appearance: excessively untidy hair and clothing, chewed fingernails; rigid facial expression; posture abnormally rigid or abnormally slack; etc."). By this means reliability will be still further enhanced and our reliance on an unstated body of common knowledge lessened. Such reliance is, of course, still far from eliminated — it is still up to the classifier to apply his own standards of what is "ex-

[11] J. R. Commons, "Standardization of Housing Investigations," *Quarterly Publications of the American Statistical Association* (later, *Journal of the American Statistical Association*), XI (1908), 319–26. The quotation, from pp. 320–21, is also quoted in Genevieve Knupfer, *Indices of Socio-economic Status* (Ph.D. dissertation, Columbia University, privately printed [1946]), pp. 54–55.

cessively" untidy or "abnormally" rigid. If, however, there is seldom any serious disagreement about an indicator, one can leave it without further definition. At some point one has to stop defining one's terms and rely on a common understanding of the language.

If segmentation of the judgment increases reliability, it also raises the difficult problem of how the segments are to be put together again. It is useless to break down a classification into highly objective indicators if we have no reasonable way of deciding how to recombine them. Let us suppose that we are studying the relation of comic-book reading to maladjustment in children.[12] In classifying children as to their readership we have a relatively simple problem. The basic indicator is whether the child read or did not read a comic book at some given time; upon this we can elaborate various classifications, such as the number of comic books read per week. The indicator is simple and objective; it is, moreover, additive on the basis of assuming that any comic book is, roughly speaking, the equivalent of any other.

But in classifying children's adjustment, when a great many indicators are specified in detail, we have the problem of combining very unlike pieces of behavior. Are badly chewed fingernails and untied shoelaces equally bad? Should each count one point on a maladjustment score? How much weight should be assigned to an extremely submissive attitude toward one's parents? What if the latter is combined with an extremely aggressive attitude toward one's schoolmates? In the actual study in which this problem presented itself, it was solved by a sort of qualitative-quantitative compromise. Children were rated into four classes, partly according to the number of behavior areas in which they showed "serious" symptoms of maladjustment (appearance, behavior during interview, reaction to questioning, attitude toward others, and attitude toward self); partly according to the number of areas of daily life (school, home, relations with other children, etc.) which were affected; and partly according to the classifier's judgment of the degree to which the maladjustment impaired the child's personality (for example, his judgment of whether the child had insufficient self-confidence to be self-reliant in any situation or whether the child had gone so far as to stop trying to cope with reality).

These same problems arise in case after case. We want to investigate sensationalism in news stories. What indicators are implied by our concept of sensationalism? Such things come to mind as the use of superlative forms, exclamatory sentences, or emotional terms; the description of lurid details; and so on. Or, perhaps, we want to investigate pessimism in Protestant sermons over the last half-century. We must specify the kind of subjects which indicate pessimism, and then go through the printed records classifying sermons as pessimistic or not according to whether the specified indicators appear. Or, we want to classify the relations between characters of minority and majority ethnic groups in magazine fiction, according to whether there is equality, subordination, or superordination of the minority characters. We must work out a list of the main types of indicators of subordination, equality, or superordination which are likely to appear in such material.[13]

Several examples of the qualitative use of indicators in classification are found in *The American Soldier*. It was desired to classify selectees and Regular Army men according to whether they identified themselves with their soldier roles or continued to think of themselves as civilians. The notion of "identifying with a group" suggests a complex phenomenon for which one might want various and complex indices. It turned out that, for a rough classification, it was enough to ask the men the following question: "Which do you prefer to wear on furlough, uniform or civilian clothes?" On this basis

[12] Katherine M. Wolf and Marjorie Fiske, "The Children Talk About Comics," in Paul F. Lazarsfeld and Frank N. Stanton, *Communications Research 1948–49* (1949). See especially Appendix A, pp. 299–300.

[13] Berelson, *op. cit.*

it could be said that less than a third of the selectees, as contrasted with almost two-thirds of the regulars, identified themselves with their Army role.[14] The absolute figures are to be used with caution, since they are based only on this single qualitative indicator; the group comparison, however, is so highly significant that for this purpose no other index seems necessary.

In other instances the indicator for a concept may be found by contrasting the answers given on two questions. Toward the end of the war, the Research Branch found that 81 percent of a sample of enlisted men believed that *civilians* would consider a private or a private first class "not good enough to get a rating," while only 25 percent felt that *other soldiers* would have this attitude.[15] This simple comparison of attitudes imputed to civilians and those imputed to other soldiers might be considered an indicator of a soldier's feelings of "in-group" versus "out-group" relations.

At another point in their analysis, Stouffer and his associates were looking for indicators of a "caste system" in Army life. Had this concern been a major one, the analysts might have proceeded in a number of different ways. First of all, they might have carried out a survey among officers and enlisted men, noting the numbers and kinds of contacts which took place between them. From such a survey, quantitative indices of caste structure might have been developed. Or, a second type, an "institutional analysis," might have been undertaken. Here the researchers would have examined all the formal regulations of the Army, studied lines of communication, and so on. From such an analysis they would have decided the extent to which the Army exhibited features typical in a caste structure. Neither type of data was immediately available, and since the point was of incidental rather than primary importance, no attempt was made to collect the data in precisely this form.

The indicator actually used by the Research Branch was the existence of a ritualistic tradition which would not have been maintained had the Army not had certain elements of a caste system. The authors note that while it was possible for enlisted men to become officers, there was no direct promotion: "Enlisted men selected for officer candidate school were first discharged from the Army and then readmitted in their new and very different status."[16] Just as it is impossible to move from one caste to another, in an ethnic caste situation, so an enlisted man about to become an officer must leave the Army system before re-entering in his new status. The indicator of caste features in the Army was a custom sanctioned and maintained by formal rules of Army procedure.[17]

Having discussed the more *qualitative* use of indicators, we may now turn to the ways in which such segmental judgments may be *systematically* combined to classify objects — first, by means of multidimensional classifications, and second, by the use of quantitative indices.

Multidimensional Classification and Typological Procedures

The concept of type is normally used to refer to special compounds of attributes. In speaking of the midwestern type of American, one may have in mind certain physical features, certain attitudes and habits, and certain affiliations and talents attributed to the inhabitants of this region. When one is speaking of books or types of governments, a special combination of attributes is thrown into relief. Sometimes not all the attributes entering into a typological combination can be enumerated. When a psychologist describes the extrovert type, he hopes that the initial formulation of the term will lead to further research which will find more and

[14] Stouffer, *op. cit.*, Vol. I, p. 64, Chart III.
[15] *Ibid.*, p. 231.
[16] *Ibid.*, p. 56 n. 2.
[17] A number of additional examples from *The American Soldier* are discussed in Patricia L. Kendall and Paul F. Lazarsfeld, "Problems of Survey Analysis," in R. K. Merton and P. F. Lazarsfeld, *Continuities in Social Research* (1950).

more attributes entering into this particular combination. There can and will be much discussion on how such a special combination of attributes is found, delineated, and justified. The very fact, however, that by a "type" one means a specific attribute compound will hardly be denied. Therefore a methodological discussion of the concept of type can begin with a survey of the different kinds of attributes which can enter into such a compound.

THREE KINDS OF CHARACTERISTICS

Three different kinds of attributes may be advantageously distinguished. Here we follow the discussion of Hempel and Oppenheim, who have explored this subject in great detail in their work *Der Typusbegriff im Lichte der Neuen Logik*.[18] The first may be called a *dichotomous attribute*, by which is meant an attribute which can be predicated only as belonging or not belonging to an object. Something can be either square or not square, all wood or not all wood, dead or alive. In many places people are either Protestant or Catholic, Democratic or Republican, Negro or white, middle class or working class. Thus, any attribute which permits only two mutually exclusive applications is called a dichotomous attribute, or simply a dichotomy.

Differing from the dichotomy is the *variable*, which is an attribute permitting any number of gradations and, in addition, implying the possibility of measurement in the most exact sense of the word. Size is a variable: an object can have any one of an infinite number of sizes, and its size can actually be measured in fixed units. These measuring units have the property that each interval is equal to each other such interval — one inch is as long as any other — so that it makes sense to compare distances between two sets of points. Moreover, there is an absolute zero point to size, so that we can say meaningfully that one object is so many times longer than another. With variables the zero point of which is arbitrary, such as centigrade temperature, we cannot make such ratios — it is meaningless to say that an object at 10° C. is "twice as hot" as one at 5° C. The variable is the attribute used generally in the natural sciences and the one presupposed in mathematics (from which the term is taken).

Between these two kinds of attributes a third broad variety of measurement can be distinguished: one in which objects only can be ranked in comparison with one another, either individually or in groups. It is distinguished from the dichotomy in that it permits more gradations — anything from three ranked groups up to a precise ranking for each of a multitude of objects. It is distinguished from the variable in that it does not permit actual measurement on a scale of equal-sized intervals and a zero point. Thus, it does not permit us to talk of the *distance* between two points or the *ratio* of two sizes.

An example of the more continuous form of this type of measure is furnished by mineralogy. Minerals can be arranged in order of their softness; of two minerals one is termed the softer when it can be scratched by the other. Thus, it is not possible to decide whether one mineral alone is "soft," but only which of two is the softer. Social and psychological research works extensively with such ranking scales. Intelligence is defined in such a way that with the help of tests it can be determined which of two individuals is more intelligent; attitudes are so defined that, with the help of expert "judges," one can state that one attitude is more favorable toward peace than another one. These attributes by which people can be ranked but not measured we call *serials*.[19]

There is an important practical relation

[18] Carl G. Hempel and P. Oppenheim, *Der Typusbegriff im Lichte der Neuen Logik* (Leiden, 1936), discussed in Paul F. Lazarsfeld, "Some Remarks on the Typological Procedures in Social Research," *Zeitschrift für Sozialforschung* (Leipzig), VI (1937), 119–37.

[19] These remarks are intended only to make such distinctions as are needed for the following discussion. For a fully systematic approach to the logic of measurement the reader is referred to the various publications of Professor Stevens of Harvard University.

between these three kinds of attributes: it is always possible to transform a variable into a serial and a serial into a dichotomy, but no transformation in the reverse direction is possible. We can use income in dollars to measure economic status; or we can transform this into a continuous serial ranking scale so that we can say who is higher than whom, or into a ranking scale for broad groups by taking the upper third, middle third, and lower third (or any other grouping) as our classes; or we can simply dichotomize into "above average" and "below average" (or above and below any other point we wish).

SERIAL OPERATIONS

The logical analysis of the serial is of special importance because it permits a better understanding of what shall be called serial operations. The best-known of these operations is the *standardization* of a serial rank order. After objects have been ranked in a continuous order in terms of a serial, it is often useful to simplify the ranking by cutting it up into a number of groups. For instance, a random sample of fifty political writers might be ranked by judges according to their pacifism. Then those fifty writers might be subdivided into ten groups, from the 10 percent who are most pacifistic to the 10 percent least pacifistic. These ten groups are called *quasi-intervals* because they correspond to some extent to the real intervals established by a variable. The difference, however, can be illustrated as follows: In regard to income, a variable, people can be grouped into real intervals, such as $0 through $999, $1,000 through $1,999, $2,000 through $2,999, and so on. The number of people who fall into these real intervals is a matter of empirical inspection, and a meaningful distribution curve is produced. Suppose, however, we convert income into a serial and divide people into groups ranging from the lowest 10 percent to the highest. The number of people in these quasi-intervals is given by definition, and the "length" of the interval is not established. The very idea of "length" does not make sense for quasi-intervals without the introduction of additional assumptions. The quasi-intervals produced by dividing a serial into arbitrary groups are also different from the "scale types" of a social-distance or Guttman scale. Such a scale also produces a set of ranked groups, but the divisions are based on particular patterns of response. To the extent that the scale items are independently meaningful, the ranked groups produced are not arbitrary, but "natural" and meaningful.

Once we have established a set of quasi-intervals in a particular sample, such as the ten grades of pacifism among authors, we may want to grade additional authors with respect to pacifism. This is made possible by the following procedure: For each of the ten grades of pacifism, one author can be selected and carefully described as characteristic of his particular grade of pacifism. These ten characteristic authors would be called *standards*. When a new author has to be classified, his grade of pacifism can be established according to the standard to which he is most akin. (The problem of borderline cases is omitted here as yielding no fundamentally new aspect.) This procedure has been most recently applied to simplify the measurement of prestige status of the inhabitants of small towns. For each of the several "social classes" certain "typical" families are named, and the families to be rated are compared to these standards.

The relation between a serial order and standards can be inverted. So far, it has been assumed that the serial order was established first and the standards were derived afterward. In many cases, the standards are established first and the serial order derived from them. For example, Zimmerman[20] grouped fifty towns in Massachusetts in a serial order for which one standard was the idea of a completely agricultural community and the other a completely industrialized one. Against this serial, Zimmer-

[20] Carle C. Zimmerman and Merle E. Frampton, *Family and Society* (1935).

man examined the success of efforts to get the unemployed to cultivate subsistence gardens. He found that the nearer a community was to the industrial standard, the less successful was the effort. In a study of mechanization by Charlotte Bühler,[21] two standards were established: In one, a man controls a complicated machine such as an automobile or a crane; in the other, the man is dominated by the machine, as is a worker who performs only one operation on a moving belt. It is possible to group the various procedures in a factory in serial order according to their similarity to one or the other standard.

The definition of the serial, in these examples just cited, is not given completely by the two standards. Two communities never differ only in one respect. They differ with regard to a number of variables: size, proportion of foreign-born, weather, and so on. Therefore, it is always necessary to indicate *in which respect* two concrete standards shall be used to establish a serial order — that is to say, in which respect other objects should be ranked between the two standards. To summarize, a serial operation consists either in deriving standards from a serial order, or in defining a serial order with the help of standards.

ATTRIBUTE SPACE AND ITS REDUCTION

Standards and their connection with serial operations throw light upon the logic of certain typological systems. It can be shown that many typologies only standardize serials or define a serial with the help of one or more standards. One talks of "polar types," "intermediate types," or "scale types." In such cases, the concept of type is practically identified with what has been introduced here as a standard. It is mainly a matter of definition if those standards should be called "types" or not. At the beginning of this paper a type was defined as an attribute compound. For the rest of these remarks, therefore, the word is used in this sense. Those "types" which are the result of serial operations on one attribute only might be called *quasi-types*.

It is now necessary to introduce the concept of attribute space. Suppose that for a number of objects, three attributes are taken into consideration: size (a variable), beauty (a serial), and the possession of a college degree (a dichotomy). It is possible to visualize something very similar to the frame of reference in analytic geometry. The *X* axis, for instance, may correspond to size; in this direction, the object can actually be measured in inches. The *Y* axis may correspond to beauty; in this direction, the objects can be arranged in a serial order so that each object gets a percentile rank number, percentile Number 1 being the most beautiful. The *Z* axis may correspond to the academic degree; here each object has or does not have a degree. Those two possibilities shall be designated by plus and minus, and shall be represented arbitrarily by two points on the *Z* axis on the two opposite sides of the center of the system. Each object is then represented by a certain point in this attribute space. If the objects to be grouped are the women in a certain sample, then a particular woman who is five and a half feet tall, who would rank rather low in a beauty contest, and who has a college degree, might be represented by the following symbol: 66″; 37%; plus. To each individual would correspond a certain point. (Because of the fact, however, that a dichotomy and a serial are included, not every point would correspond to an individual.) The reader is invited to familiarize himself by examples of his own with this very useful concept of attribute space; each space will, of course, have as many dimensions as there are attributes according to which the individuals of the group are classified.

In the frame of an attribute space, the operation of reduction can be defined and explained. In order to have a simple example, the following three dichotomous attributes will be discussed first: to have (+) or not to have (−) a college degree; to be of

[21] Charlotte Bühler, *Der menschliche Lebenslauf* (Leipzig, 1933).

white (+) or colored (−) race; and to be a native (+) or a foreign-born (−) American. Only the eight combinations, as shown in Table 41-4, are possible.

TABLE 41-4

Combination Number	College Degree	White	Native American
1	+	+	+
2	+	+	−
3	+	−	+
4	+	−	−
5	−	+	+
6	−	+	−
7	−	−	+
8	−	−	−

(Combination 6, for example, is the white foreign-born without a college degree.)

By reduction is understood any classification as a result of which different combinations fall into one class. Suppose that an effort is made to estimate roughly the social advantages which correspond to the eight combinations of college degree, race, and nativity. It is possible (no question of the actual facts shall be implied here) to argue in the following way: To be a Negro is such a disadvantage in this country that college degree and nativity make little difference. Therefore, the combinations numbered 3, 4, 7, and 8 fall into one class of greatest discrimination. For the whites, nativity is much more important than education because you can substitute for college by self-education, but you cannot amend foreign birth. Therefore, the combinations 2 and 6 form the next class — the foreign-born white — which is presumably less discriminated against than the Negroes. Among the native-born whites, education may be an important selective factor. Therefore, a special distinction is introduced between the combinations 1 and 5. Thus an order of social advantage is established: the native white with college degree, the native white without college degree, the foreign-born white irrespective of education, and the Negro irrespective of nativity and education.

There are at least three kinds of reduction which should be distinguished: (*a*) the functional, (*b*) the arbitrary numerical, and (*c*) the pragmatic.

a) In a functional reduction there must exist an actual relationship between two of the attributes which reduces the number of combinations. If, for instance, Negroes cannot acquire a college degree, or if tall girls are always judged more beautiful, certain combinations of variables will practically not occur and in this way the system of combinations is reduced. The elimination of certain combinations can either be a complete one, or these combinations may occur so infrequently that no special class need be established for them. The social distance scale is a case where just such a functional reduction leads not only to a typology but to a group-ranking serial.

b) The arbitrary numerical case of a reduction is best exemplified by index numbers. In the analysis of housing conditions, for instance, the following procedure is frequently used: Several items, such as plumbing, central heating, and refrigeration are selected as especially indicative, and each is given a certain weight. Central heating and a refrigerator in a house without plumbing might be equivalent to plumbing without the other two items, and therefore both cases get the same index numbers. Of course, the weights for such procedure can originate in different ways. Recently the technique of "latent structure analysis" has been developed, by which weights can be derived from a mathematical model "fitted" to the empirical data. This involved subject can only be mentioned here.[22]

c) In the case of functional reduction, certain combinations are eliminated in view of relationships existing between the variables themselves. In the case of pragmatic reduc-

[22] Those who wish a relatively simple introduction to latent structure analysis are referred to S. A. Stouffer, *et. al.*, *Measurement and Prediction* (*Studies in Social Psychology in World War II*, Vol. IV).

tion, certain groups of combinations are contracted to one class in view of the research purpose. The example of degree-race-nativity given above offers such a pragmatic reduction. In considering the concrete problem of discrimination, no distinction was made among the other qualifications of the Negroes, all of whom were regarded as one class. Here is another example from a study of leisure-time activities among young people. The question was raised: Are youngsters from less desirable homes more likely to stay at home than the more well-to-do young people who might more probably patronize the character-building organizations of the community? For the distinction between a desirable and an undesirable home, two data were available: the employment status of the father, and the existence or nonexistence of a living room in the house. It was decided to attribute a desirable home to those cases in which the father was employed and a separate living room was available. When the father was unemployed or no living room was available or both disadvantages applied, the home was called undesirable. Here, by pragmatic reduction, three of the four possible combinations were opposed as one class to the fourth combination as another class. In any pragmatic reduction, numerical factors will play a role. The desirable type of home, for instance, was twice as frequent as the undesirable, although this latter type included three combinations; such numerical differences are frequently a very good lead for pragmatic reductions.

A few added observations will clarify the operation of reduction discussed above. Reduction involves a grouping of attribute combinations. Suppose a great number of married couples are studied as to the attitude of the women to their husbands, and as to the economic success of the husband; *Y*, the attitude of the wife, is a serial, ranked from a very favorable to a very unfavorable attitude; *X*, the success of the husband, is also a serial, ranked from very great to very little success. It would be possible to carry through two independent standardizations, each along one axis: success and attitude might each be standardized to three grades — high, medium, and low. As a result there would be nine combinations, themselves standards of different attitude-success configurations.

Suppose we find through further analysis that if the wife's attitude toward the husband is highly favorable, then economic success makes little difference in marital relations; whereas if the wife has only a medium attitude toward him, he needs at least a medium success to make the marriage go well; and if the wife's attitude is low, only great economic success by the husband can save the marriage. We may now classify all these marriages into two groups: one for which the attitude-success combinations are favorable for good marital relations, and one for which the combinations are unfavorable. This involves a reduction which can be diagrammed as shown in Figure 41-1.

The reduction of a multidimensional attribute space can in some cases lead to a one-dimensional order which may be treated as a standardized serial. Take as an example of a rather complex serial the well-known extroversion-introversion distinction. One possible way to measure this is to describe vividly a person who corresponds to the idea of a complete extrovert, and to give a corresponding standard for the idea of an introvert. Then it is roughly possible to observe a great number of individuals and to rank them in an order according to the degree to which they resemble the standard extrovert or introvert. There is, however, another way to proceed. One could measure by certain tests an individual's sociability and similar traits, and then grade him according to the procedure described above, and even redefine him with the help of standards.

A very well-known case in which a functional reduction leads to a set of classes rankable along one dimension is the social-distance type of scale, lately developed in great detail by Guttman. This is a series of two or more questions which have the property of cumulation: if you are "positive" (exhibit a certain attribute) on one of the higher ques-

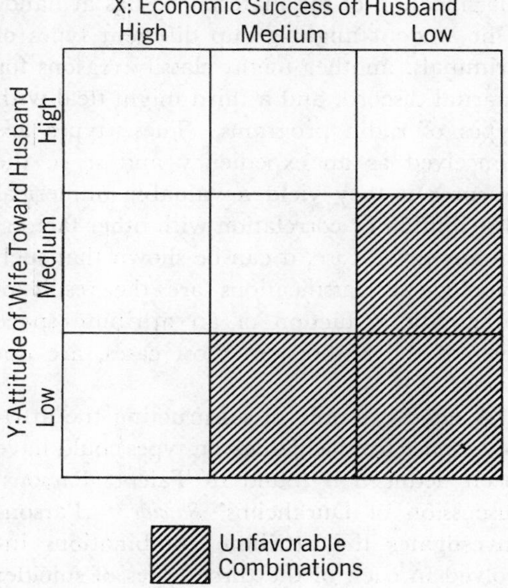

Fig. 41–1

tions on the scale, you must be positive on all the lower questions up to that point. Thus, we can classify people on their attitude toward any racial group according to their willingness to accept members of the group in the relationships given in Table 41-5.

If no other combinations of response appear, or if they appear very infrequently, we can unambiguously rank people in four groups: we will know that all the yes-yes-yes people are more favorable in attitude toward the group in question than any of the others, that the yes-yes-no group is more favorable than the yes-no-no group, and so on.

TABLE 41-5

Work in Same Plant	Have as Friend	Have Close Relative Marry
No	No	No
Yes	No	No
Yes	Yes	No
Yes	Yes	Yes

The first rank order achieved by a rather primitive definition of a serial and the second one gained by the systematic reduction of a high-dimensional attribute space might not show any difference. There is, however, a great likelihood that the second procedure leads, in its further application, to much more reliable and scientifically valuable results. It can safely be stated that most progress in measurement consists in taking this step: the substitution, for an impressionistic rank order, of a systematic process of reduction logically representing the definition of a serial.

SUBSTRUCTING THE ATTRIBUTE SPACE OF A TYPOLOGY

It is now the contention that these typological systems which are not the result of a serial operation are nothing but the result of a reduction of a more dimensional attribute space. This statement has to be understood in the right way. It is by no means alleged that typological systems ought to originate in such a combination procedure as has been exemplified so far. Quite the contrary—there is great variety in conceiving a system of types for different scientific purposes, and it would be very worth while to analyze the different means by which types have been established in different fields of research. That is, however, not the purpose of these remarks. The only claim made here is that once a system of types has been established by a research expert, it can always be proved that in its logical structure it could be the result of a reduction of an attribute space.

This procedure of finding, for a given system of types, the attribute space in which it belongs and the reduction which has been implicitly used is of such practical importance that it should have a special name. The term "substruction" is suggested.

When substructing to a given system of types the attribute space from which and the reduction through which it could be deduced, one never assumes that the creator of the types really had such a procedure in mind. One only claims that, no matter how he actually found the types, he could have found them logically by such a substruction. In the case of a functional reduction, this fact is quite evident. If, for instance, two racial types are established (as, for example, the white and the Negro), and the former is supposed to have all good qualities and the latter all bad ones, the logical procedure evidently is this: In a very high dimensional space with a great number of attributes introduced, one among them racial descent, the statement is made that there is a high correlation between racial affiliation and each of the other attributes. Therefore, most of the logically possible combinations (for instance, Negro race and high quality of character) should practically never occur, and in this way the two racial types would be established exactly according to the procedure of functional reduction described earlier. In cases where arbitrary numerical reduction is used, the creator of the types is usually aware of the procedure, as when cost-of-living indices or character "profiles" are suggested. Sometimes it may require more thought to bring the reduction used into clear relief. How about the old distinction between the visual, the acoustic, and the motor types? Evidently the procedure is that each individual is placed in an attribute space of three dimensions giving his visual, motor, and acoustic abilities. Then the following rule is used: The ability in which the individual is most outstanding gets the weight "1"; the other two get the weight "0." In other words, only the best-developed ability should be considered, and the other two disregarded in deciding to which of the three types a certain person belongs. Thus, each individual is attributed to one type. (If intermediate types or correlations with other qualities are suggested, the matter becomes more complicated, but no new logical element is introduced.) The same analysis is possible, for instance, with the six value types of Spranger.

It is the substruction corresponding to the pragmatic reduction which is of the greatest practical importance in empirical social research. The most common use of types is made when a writer gives an impressionistic classification of the material he has at hand. One student might group different types of criminals, another might classify reasons for marital discord, and a third might deal with types of radio programs. These types are conceived as an expediency and serve the purpose if they yield a valuable numerical distribution or correlation with other factors. In any given case, it can be shown that such typological classifications are the result of pragmatic reduction of an attribute space even if the authors, in most cases, are not aware of it.

A good example of substructing the attribute space from which given types could have been deduced is found in Talcott Parsons' discussion of Durkheims' *Suicide*.[23] Parsons investigates the attribute combinations involved in each of the three types of suicide: the altruistic, the egoistic, and the anomic. In altruistic suicide there are strong group norms emphasizing the subordination of the individual to the group and the small valuation of individual life. In egoistic suicide there are also strong group norms, but they emphasize the individual's freedom and his individual responsibility. Anomic suicide takes place under very different circumstances from the first two. It takes place when there are no group norms or when norms are weakened.

Two major dimensions can now be set up: the existence or nonexistence of group norms, and their content if present. The result is the attribute space set forth in Table 41-6.

TABLE 41-6

Attribute Space for Durkheim's Types of Suicide

Existence of Norms	Content of Norms	
	Individualism	*Collectivism*
Norms exist	(Egoistic suicide)	(Altruistic suicide)
Norms do not exist	(Anomic suicide)	

[23] Talcott Parsons, *The Structure of Social Action* (1949), pp. 328–37.

Such a formulation not only clarifies the theoretical meaning of Durkheim's distinction between the three types of suicide, but also leads naturally to further questions. What other kinds of behavior are alternatives to suicide in each situation? Do these categories exhaust the possible types of social norms? (What about introducing an intermediate or mixed category? Parsons suggests that Roman Catholics occupy an intermediate position between the extreme subordination of the individual of the Army or certain Oriental cultures, and the lack of group support which the Protestants experience. As a result, none of these types of suicide is very frequent among Catholics and their total rate is relatively low.)

Whenever a writer uses such a typological classification, he should substruct to it a corresponding attribute space and the reduction connected therewith, in order to be aware of what is logically implied in his enumeration of types. There would be many advantages in this discipline. The writer would see whether he has overlooked certain cases; he could make sure that some of his types are not overlapping; and he would probably make the classification more valuable for actual empirical research. This practical value of a substruction deserves special attention. If a student creates a typology of family discord, his contribution is valuable only if in any concrete case it is possible to say whether the given discord belongs to a certain type or not. For this purpose, criteria have to be worked out. These criteria, in general, point directly to the attribute space from which the type has been reduced. Therefore, the substruction of the adequate attribute combinations to a given system of types adapts them better to actual research purposes. As an example, there is reported here an adventure in substruction which summarizes once more all the points made so far.

For a study of the structure of authority in the family, conducted by the International Institute of Social Research, a questionnaire was devised pertaining to authoritarian relations between parents and children.[24] The director of the study, E. Fromm, suggested four types of authoritarian situations as a theoretical basis in outlining the study: complete authority, simple authority, lack of authority, and rebellion. The procedure of reduction and substruction made it possible to attain a thorough research procedure and at the same time to exhaust all possible significance of Fromm's types.

An authoritarian situation in a family is determined by the way the parents exercise their authority, by the way in which the children accept it, and by the interrelations between exercise and acceptance. Two main categories in the questionnaire covered the matter of exercise: Questions were asked to discover (I) whether parents used corporal punishment and (II) whether they interfered with such activities of their children as recreation and church attendance. Two groups of indices were used in regard to acceptance: The children were asked (III) whether conflicts in various fields of their activity were frequent, and (IV) whether they had confidence in their parents.

To study the exercise of authority, the indices of corporal punishment and interference were treated as dichotomies. (No new problem of principle would arise if they were treated as serials; as a matter of fact, interference was a serial since the number of interferences was used as an index.) By this means, the combinations shown in Table 41-7 were reached.

TABLE 41-7

	Combinations			
	X	–	Y	Z
I. Corporal punishment...	+	+	–	–
II. Interference..........	+	–	+	–

("Plus," in this scheme, meant that the attribute was present, and "minus" that it was absent.) It was then possible to reduce

[24] International Institute of Social Research, *Studien über Autorität und Familie* (Paris, 1936).

this scheme to a rough one-dimensional order of intensity of exercise. The combination *plus-plus* (corporal punishment is used and interference is frequent) was apparently the strongest form, and *minus-minus* the weakest. The type of exercise in which corporal punishment is used but no interference in the child's activities is attempted can be eliminated as practically contradictory. The combination *minus-plus* was therefore left as a median degree of exercise. The three combinations *plus-plus*, *minus-minus*, and *minus-plus* can then be reduced to the one-dimensional order *X*, *Y*, and *Z*, with *X* being the strongest degree.

The same procedure may be applied to the indices pertaining to acceptance of authority as shown in Table 41-8.

TABLE 41-8

	Combinations			
	A	B	–	C
III. Conflicts..............	–	–	+	+
IV. Confidence...........	+	–	+	–

The combination *minus-plus* (absence of conflicts and existence of confidence) is readily seen to be the highest degree of acceptance. *Plus-minus*, the inverse combination, is the weakest. The combination *plus-plus* can practically be disregarded. Confidence will hardly exist together with persistent conflicts. If a few such cases come up, they might first be either eliminated or be lumped together with the medium degree of acceptance. Later, they might be studied separately, as "deviant cases" are frequently the source of important refinements of the analysis.[25] The combination *minus-minus* (no conflicts and no confidence) is roughly a median grade. The three grades of acceptance are then labeled *A*, *B*, and *C*, grade *A* being the highest degree.

Here two separate reductions have been carried through: The two-dimensional space constituted of corporal punishment and interference has been reduced to the serial "exercise of authority." In the same way, conflict and confidence were reduced to "acceptance of authority."

A further step leads to the drawing of a chart (see Table 41-9) which constitutes the attribute space into which the four initial types of authority will have to be placed. It turns out that nine combinations are logically possible, while Fromm suggested only four types. By the procedure of substruction, the last scheme will have to be matched with Fromm's types (which were, of course, conceived in a wholly different way).

TABLE 41-9

		Acceptance *A*	*B*	*C*
Exercise...........	*X*	1	2	3
	Y	4	5	6
	Z	7	8	9

It may be assumed that Fromm's type of complete authority is covered by the combinations 1 and 2. Simple authority is covered by combinations 4 and 5. The lack of authority is represented by combination 8, and rebellion by 3 and 6. For greater clarity the substruction is repeated in another form in Table 41-10.

Combinations 7 and 9 are not covered. Apparently it was assumed that neither voluntary acceptance of nor rebellion against an authority which is scarcely exercised is possible. The substruction, however, may be used as a tool for discovery. It discloses the possibility that children might long for an authority which no one offers them. These discovered combinations suggest further research.

It may again be stressed strongly that this whole analysis does not limit the research man in the actual sequence of his work. It is by no means postulated that he should start by deciding what attributes he wants to use,

[25] Patricia L. Kendall and Katherine M. Wolf, "The Analysis of Deviant Cases in Communications Research," in Lazarsfeld and Stanton, *Communications Research* 1948–49 (1949).

TABLE 41-10

Combination	Type	Exercise	Acceptance
1 and 2	Complete authority	Strong (X)	Voluntarily accepted (A) or just accepted (B)
4 and 5	Simple authority	Medium (Y)	Voluntarily accepted (A) or just accepted (B)
8	Lack of authority	Weak (Z)	Just accepted (B)
3 and 6	Rebellion	Strong (X) or medium (Y)	Refused (C)

then proceed with the reduction, and so finally get his system of types. Often it might be much better for the student to become deeply acquainted with his material (especially if many attributes are involved), and then bring order into it by first blocking out a few main types on a completely impressionistic basis. After doing so, he can reconsider the matter and substruct to his own typological intuitions an adequate attribute space, thereby bringing into relief the reduction which he has used implicitly in constructing his impressionistic typology. The best results probably will be gained by using this combination of an initial general survey and a subsequent systematic analysis. The example just given provides a good illustration.

TRANSFORMATIONS

The problem comes up whether to every given system of types only one attribute space and the corresponding reduction can be substructed. The answer is probably "no." At least the typological classifications used in current social research are somewhat vague and therefore more than one logical substruction can usually be provided for them. The different attribute spaces originating in this way can, however, be transformed one into another. The procedure of transformation is very important because it is the logical background of what is generally understood as an interpretation of a statistical result. It could be shown that such an interpretation is often nothing else than transforming a system of types from one attribute space into another with different co-ordinates, and therewith changing simultaneously one reduction into another. We shall confine our discussion of this question to one example.

A few hundred pupils were grouped in a rough way according to their physical development and according to their scholastic achievements. (Both concepts, by the way, were introduced as serials.) Combinations of these two attributes yielded five rather distinct types. The physically underdeveloped children were either especially bright or especially unsuccessful. The same was true for well-developed children; most of them also appeared among the two scholastic extremes. The children of medium physical development were, on the whole, medium in their scholastic achievement as well. Relatively few children were of medium physical development and especially good or bad in their schoolwork; and relatively few children of unusually good or bad physical condition were medium in their ability in school.

The result was interpreted in about the following terms. Among the physically underdeveloped children there are two types: those who are too handicapped to be successful in school, and those who overcompensate for their physical weakness and do especially well in school. Every teacher knows those two types from his own experience. Among the especially well-developed children, one group is the all-round type, combining mental with physical maturity. The other group is the "hoodlum" type which on the basis of strength has such a good position in class that it does not consider it necessary to make an effort in schoolwork. If this interpretation is analyzed in the light of the previous considerations, it turns out that these types can be described in two completely different sets of dimensions. Instead of the original attributes of physical and mental developments, new terms are now used, such as overcompensation, which is or is not operative; parallelism between physical and mental activity; recognition by schoolmates, which is or is not present. Such an interpretation consists logically of substructing to a system of types an attribute space different from the one in which it was derived by reduction, and of looking for the reductions which would lead to the system of types in this new space. That is what transformation means.

Some Notes on the Use of Indices

We have seen that broad concepts must be broken down into segments to be systematically observed. Loyalty, cohesion, discrimination, size, shape, beauty, and so on, have to be spelled out in terms of more specific criteria or indicators. These indicators must fulfill two requirements. They should be rather easily ascertained: it should be easier to detect their presence or absence, in the case of dichotomous attributes, or to rank them, in the case of serials, than the original concept as a whole. Also, they should correspond reasonably well to the larger universe of characteristics which we have in mind when we use the original concept. Thus, if we start with the concept of "level of living," dollar income may be a very bad indicator for some people — for instance, farmers whose income consists to an important degree of their own produce. By a "bad indicator" we mean one that does not vary in a close enough correspondence to all the other things which we mean by the concept "level of living."

The moment we have a number of indicators for one concept, the problem arises of how they are to be combined.

Suppose *A* outranks *B* on criterion *x*, but *B* outranks *A* on criterion *y*. Then we are no better off than before, unless we can combine *x* and *y* into one index. The special advantage of an index is that it allows us to rank objects in terms of complex concepts, where we have many indicators to take into account, on a single one-dimensional scale. We have already mentioned the possibility of reducing a qualitative multidimensional classification to a set of rankable categories. The index performs the same function for indicators which are continuous variables. Instead of telling us that a series of cells in a multidimensional attribute space are the same as far as we are concerned, it tells us that all points on a certain line or surface in measurement space are equivalent, by giving them the same index number.

It is at this point that the distinction between *two problems* becomes quite obvious. The one is *which criteria* to choose; the other is *how to combine* several criteria into one index so that ranking becomes possible. The following remarks will deal exclusively with the second type of problem.

It is important to realize that we do not have to combine the criteria into one index. The personality profile, for instance, compares people by a set of criteria which are not combined. There are certain typological procedures (such as those discussed above) which combine criteria incompletely so that a simplified presentation but no ranking ensues. In physics, sets of variables are represented as vectors. The physicist uses these vectors without combining them into one index. At other times, he does form indices. The position of a point on a piece of paper is indicated by two pieces of information. Sometimes they are combined into the index of distance. Then all the points on the paper can be ranked according to their distance from, let us say, the left upper corner of the paper. Another index might lead to a different ranking, perhaps the distance from the left edge of the paper.

Indices can be classified usefully in a variety of ways. The most important distinction is, of course, the number of dimensions from which they were derived. A cost-of-living index is based on as many dimensions as there were items included in the original budget. If all expenses are divided into clothing, food, recreation, health, and "others," then the original material has five dimensions. Suppose, however, that these five types of expenses are given in percentages of the total expenses. Then one of the five expense items can always be computed when the other four are given; all five have to add up to 100 percent. In this case, we will say that the index has only four degrees of freedom. Because this conception is more general than the notion of dimension, we wish to talk exclusively about the former. By *degree of freedom of an index*, we mean the number of variables upon which an index is based and which can vary independently of one another.

It is always possible to state how many degrees of freedom an index has. But the same index can be interpreted as having different kinds of dimensions. We are free to shift from one set of variables to another, but the number of independent variables will always be the same as long as we deal with the same material.

A somewhat more difficult distinction to formulate is introduced by the following example: Some people have longish, haggard faces and other people round, friendly ones. In order to make this distinction more precise, the anthropologist introduces the notion of a cephalic index. He takes perhaps five different measures for each head and combines them by a specific formula. Here the head is the basic unit under observation and the five measures are the dimensions of the index.

There are also certain index procedures where a number of criteria are combined not into one but into several indices. The purpose of the indices then is to reduce the multiplicity of the original information into a smaller number of dimensions. Sometimes it even happens that the number of indices is the same as the number of criteria or variables. In this case the advantage of the indices does not lie in a simpler arrangement of objects. The mathematician would formulate this situation as follows: Observations can be described by a variety of systems of coordinates. Sometimes one and sometimes another is more useful. We can pass from one system to another by so-called transformations. Under certain conditions indices are nothing but formulas for such transformations.

The literature on indices contains a number of recurring observations. They will be listed now as a reminder to the reader; in the course of the subsequent sections we will come back to some of them. An effort will be made to give these intuitive observations a more clear-cut "operational" meaning.[26]

a) The simplest situation develops if there exists an outside criterion against which the two formulas can be compared. In this case we are in the well-investigated realm of prediction studies. By a variety of techniques we can decide why one index correlates better with the outside criterion than the other. We also know that two indices might have only a low correlation with each other and still have the same correlation with the outside criterion (interchangeability of indices). This whole type of problem has been so well discussed by many authors that it will not be touched upon further in this discussion.

b) Factor analysis and related practices are also a specific kind of index formation. They will not be discussed here. In a more complete presentation it would, however, be necessary to include them. Indices, as well as factor analysis, could be better understood if one were to see how much logical similarity actually exists between them. (Quite a number of indices which have been used in literature could be profitably compared with a factor analysis of the same material on which the indices are based, but because of the dif-

[26] Many of our examples are taken from Hans Zeisel, *Say It With Figures* (1947). The reader is referred to chap. vii, "Indices," for detailed descriptions of the indices.

ficulty of the subject matter, it is not feasible to include it within the confines of this chapter.)

c) Sometimes it is possible to see immediately that two indices, based on the same material but using different formulas, imply different ideas as to what is to be studied. Suppose that in a certain district the Democrats had 30 percent of the vote in the previous election and now have 40 percent of the vote. Two indices could be used to measure the success of the Democratic party in this district. One might be 10/30 and the other 10/70. In the first index the implied meaning of success is as follows: 'The Democrats were weak in this district, and the index shows that votes are hard to win there. Consequently, a 10 percent victory there is much more impressive than one in another district where the party already has 50 percent of the vote." The use of the second index implies: "In this district it was easy to gain 10 percent, since 70 percent had not yet been converted. It is much more difficult to gain 10 percent if only 50 percent are available for conversion."

d) In another group of cases we have the feeling that two index formulas "mean something quite different." In the Western Electric study,[27] workers were asked what they liked and disliked about different aspects of their jobs; they were also left free not to comment at all on any of the aspects. Two indices were formed. One was termed *urgency* — referring to the proportion of workers who made comments, irrespective of whether the comments were friendly or unfriendly. The second was termed *feeling tone* — referring to the ratio of favorable over unfavorable comments. No one feels confused if two such indices are used, because they seem to indicate different objects, although they are based on exactly the same material. A similar example is given by Zeisel when he discusses the reading indices which he has developed. It is not easy to say, however, why in these cases we feel that the indices are distinct but not contradictory. Presently an effort will be made to formulate somewhat more precisely the idea of indices which are based on the same material but "mean different things."

e) Another case which can be handled in a reasonably satisfactory way is that in which the notion of weight can be introduced. Suppose the material to be analyzed consists of the first and second choices among candidates made by a group of people. One gets different rankings for the popularity of the various candidates according to the weights which one gives to the first and the second choices. It seems that if two formulas express clearly different weighting systems, no one feels that a problem is involved. The indices are simply taken as measuring different notions of popularity or whatever it may be. Zeisel's discussion of baseball indices shows how changing the weights can change the meaning of an index: the batting average measures frequency of any sort of safe hit, while an index weighting each hit by the number of bases indicates the power of the hitter as well.

f) There are, however, some situations which are clearly difficult to handle. Such situations arise when two index formulas seem to express the same idea but still lead to contradictory results. The most drastic problem develops if one index ranks *A* above *B* and the other index turns the order around. This will be the first main point which we will discuss in detail.

THE "AREA OF AMBIGUITY"

If two indices describe the same situations, based on the same material, their performance can differ only because they use different formulas. Before the merits of two index formulas can be judged, they must be compared carefully. Such comparison is best done in a number of steps.

The most urgent aspect of the problem becomes clear if we take two items, *A* and *B*, for which the two indices contradict each other. One index ranks *A* above *B*, the other *B* above *A*. Take, for example, a study in which the women in a factory are asked what they like

[27] Roethlisberger and Dickson, *Management and the Worker* (1939), chap. xi.

and dislike about their jobs.[28] They mark a check list which contains, among other items, the topics "Supervision" and "Cafeteria"; each such topic can get a rating of favorable, unfavorable, or not mentioned. (See Table 41-11.)

There are three possible responses; but when expressed in percentages they must add up to 100 percent, so that once two of the percentages are given the third is also determined. Therefore we say that the material on each topic has two degrees of freedom. Now the question is raised: Which is better, the supervision or the cafeteria? Someone might say that the supervision is better, since it has 30 percent more likes than dislikes, while for the cafeteria this difference is only 24 percent. Someone else might feel that the cafeteria is better, since it has 2.2 likes for each dislike, while for the supervision this ratio is only 2 likes per dislike. In the first case the index *L*-minus-*D* was used; in the other case, the index L/D. The proportion of likes here is indicated by L and the proportion of dislikes by D.

TABLE 41-11
(In Percentages)

Topic	Liked	Disliked	Not Mentioned	Total
Supervision	60	30	10	100
Cafeteria . .	44	20	36	100

Thus we have two contradictory results: the supervision is rated as more or less popular than the cafeteria according to which index we use. Obviously the two indices express somewhat different things, but it is rather difficult to see what the difference is between L/D and *L*-minus-*D*. They both increase with L and decrease with D.

To approach this problem we must first establish certain concepts. Both of these indices have two degrees of freedom, that is, L and D can vary independently of one another. Therefore they can be graphed in a two-dimensional diagram. The data in Table 41-11 are presented in this form in Figure 41-2.

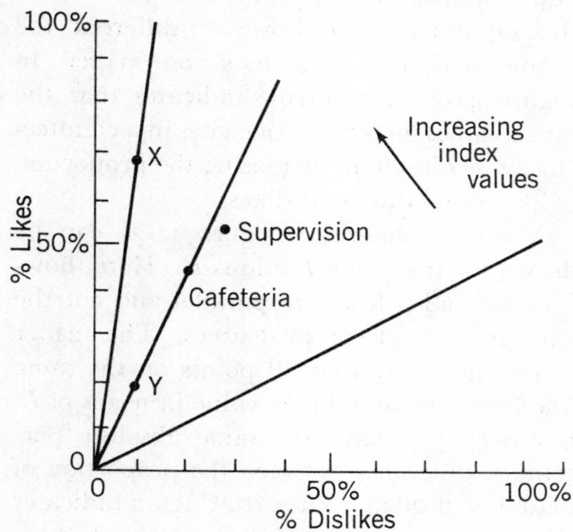

Fig. 41–2

In this diagram each topic is represented by a point, whose distance from the left side of the diagram indicates the proportion of dislikes, and whose distance above the bottom of the diagram indicates the proportion of likes. Besides the topics of supervision and cafeteria, we have shown two other possible distributions of answers. Topic *X* would be one where there are a great many more likes than dislikes. Topic *Y* has twice as many likes as dislikes, the same ratio as the cafeteria, but it has relatively few comments altogether.

How would the indices fit into such a diagram? The lines in Figure 41-2 give the answer L/D. A specific point corresponds to a "configuration," that is, the distribution of comments on a certain topic. The line through this point and the origin connects all the points or configurations which have the same index value L/D, i.e., the same ratio

[28] These examples are based on problems arising in studies by the General Motors Corporation.

of likes to dislikes. As we pointed out, topic Y has the same index value as the cafeteria. Any other line through the origin would be another such "index line" of constant index value on L/D. The "index distance" — i.e., the difference in index value — between Y and X and between *cafeteria* and X would be the same for L/D, however different the geometrical distances look on paper in Figure 41-2. The arrow indicates that the index values increase as one goes in a counter-clockwise direction, increasing the proportion of likes in relation to dislikes.

A similar diagram (Figure 41-3) can be drawn for the index L-minus-D. Here, however, all index lines are parallel and cut the axes at an angle of 45 degrees. The reader can easily verify that all points on the same line have the same index value in terms of L-minus-D, i.e., have the same absolute percentage difference between the proportion of likes and dislikes. The arrow again indicates the direction in which the index value increases, from the lower right to the upper left in the diagram.

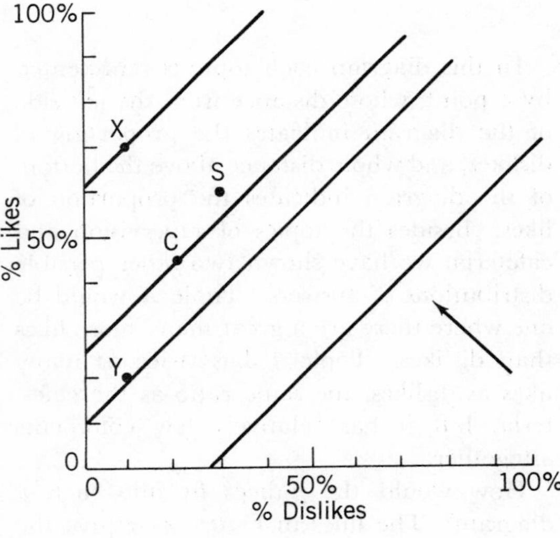

Fig. 41-3

Now let us combine the two pictures in a specific way (Figure 41-4). We choose one particular point or configuration, let us say

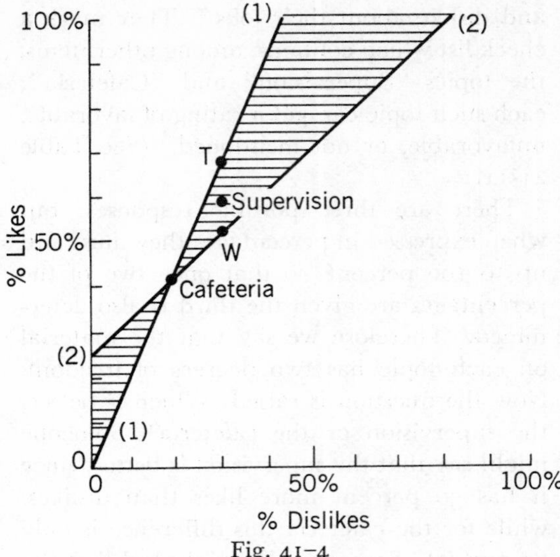

Fig. 41-4

the cafeteria topic, and draw from it two index lines. Line (1) contains all the configurations which have the same index value as *cafeteria* according to L/D. Line (2) similarly contains all the configurations which have the same index value as *cafeteria* according to the index L-minus-D.

We have also indicated the configurations of two other possible topics, T and W. While T is on the same level as *cafeteria* according to L/D, W is on the same level as *cafeteria* according to L-minus-D. Both T and W have the same percentage of dislikes, about 10 percent more than *cafeteria*, but while W has also 10 percent more likes, T has 22 percent more. In terms of index L-minus-D, only an equal increase in likes is required to compensate for a given increase in dislikes, so that on this index W manages to stay on the same level as *cafeteria*. But in terms of index L/D, to stay on the same level as *cafeteria* a topic must preserve the same *ratio* of likes to dislikes. Since *cafeteria* has 2.2 likes per dislike, a topic with 10 percent more dislikes than *cafeteria* needs 22 percent more likes to stay on the same L/D index level. Topic T has enough, but W has not and therefore falls below *cafeteria* on the L/D index.

The difference between the two indices might be verbalized as follows: the L-minus-

D index makes the same percentage increase in likes equally "visible" whatever the amount of dislikes. The *L/D* index, on the other hand, acts somewhat similarly to the perception phenomena which follow the Weber-Fechner law: A given absolute increase in the percentage of likes is more or less visible depending on the level of dislikes from which one starts. To stay on the same *L/D* index level, an item's likes must increase proportionately to compensate for a given increase is dislikes.

Thus far, the diagram in Figure 41-4 has only put into graphic form what we could have obtained by some good initial reasoning. But it also contains something new, the shaded area between the two index lines. This is the "area of ambiguity." For as we move from the point representing *cafeteria* into this area, something disquieting happens. The *L/D* index goes down and the *L*-minus-*D* index goes up. Each point in this area lies *below cafeteria* on *L/D*, but *above* it on *L*-minus-*D*. We immediately see that this is exactly what happens with the point representing *supervision*: it lies within the area of ambiguity of the two indices in relation to *cafeteria*. In the same way, if we drew the two index lines starting from *supervision*, we would find *cafeteria* within its area of ambiguity.

The main importance of this area of ambiguity between two indices can be brought out by pursuing this example one step further. We have found that in certain cases two indices seem to express equally well the concept we want to put into numerical terms. But there are specific cases where the two indices contradict each other. By comparing two configurations, *X* and *Y*, we find that, according to one index, *X* has more of the concept than *Y*, and, according to the other index, *X* has less than *Y*. In a more precise formulation, this means that *X* and *Y* are in each other's area of ambiguity as far as the two indices are concerned. But besides being an embarrassment, this also points to a precise next research step. For we can now compare *X* and *Y* according to a third criterion. Suppose, for example, we ask each worker to say which she dislikes more, the cafeteria or the supervision. Such a paired comparison is a psychological technique which has an old tradition and much to recommend it. *If* X *comes out better, then the index is better which puts* X *above* Y.

We want indices mainly to establish crude rank orders. Two indices are often equally useful as long as they establish the same rank order between the same objects. The only reason we might have to make a decision between them is that they have an area of ambiguity. Therefore, it is only in this area that they have to be tested. When a third criterion should be employed cannot, of course, be decided on a priori grounds, but one point is important: Only in the area of ambiguity can we get results merely by seeing which of the two configurations is higher on a third criterion. In all other sections of the diagram we would have to make many more comparisons, which would greatly complicate our reasoning. One can easily verify this point by working out a similar experiment in which two indices are tested against a third criterion but two configurations are used which lie outside the shaded area of Figure 41-4.[29]

We end this discussion of ambiguity with the following observation: Certain pairs of indices have a very broad area of ambiguity. As a result, their index lines divide the plane of points into two roughly equal areas — one in which they agree and one in which they disagree. One can easily verify that this is the case, for example, for the index pair *L*-plus-*D*

[29] The reader who would like to work out an example of the area of ambiguity can find one in Harold F. Gosnell's classic social experiment, *Getting Out the Vote* (1927), p. 115. Gosnell measures the effect of his stimulus by the index *E*-minus-*C*, where *E* is the percentage voting in the experimental group and *C* the percentage voting in the control group. Another index one might use is

$$\frac{E - C}{100 - C},$$

the "Effectiveness Index" described in Appendix A of Vol. III, "Experiments in Mass Communications," of *Studies in Social Psychology in World War II*. Using this index one gets a ranking of groups in terms of the effect of the stimulus quite different from the results Gosnell obtained with his index.

and L/D corresponding to *urgency* and *feeling tone*, mentioned earlier. It is also true for the two indices of election success mentioned earlier. These are indices about which we feel that they "mean something different." Inversely, indices seem to "mean about the same" when, in purely geometrical terms, their area of ambiguity is small.

In the case of indices with three degrees of freedom, the whole discussion could easily be repeated by applying it to a space rather than to a plane of points. The Zeisel-White indices of readership, for example, have three degrees of freedom. They are derived from readership surveys and their "material" gives for a sample of articles the proportions of respondents who have seen each article (x), started reading it (y), and finished reading it (z). For each article the following indices are formed:

$$I_1 = x \qquad I_3 = \frac{z}{y}$$

$$I_2 = \frac{y}{x} \qquad I_4 = z.$$

It can easily be verified that all these indices are planes in a three-dimensional space, where each axis corresponds to one of the variables just mentioned. These planes all have a large "volume of ambiguity." Consequently they are experienced as measuring different aspects of readership configurations.

THE RELATION OF PERSONAL AND UNIT INDICES

We have already pointed out some of the logical differences between various kinds of social research data. The *dichotomous attribute* has been distinguished from the *serial* and the *continuous variable.* The single datum or indicator has been distinguished from the *index*, which is a combination of several data characterizing an object. Another distinction which must now be discussed is the *level of aggregation* of the object of the datum or index. Personal data characterize individuals: whether or not a man has been promoted (a dichotomous attribute), military rank (a serial), or length of service (a variable). Unit data characterize some aggregation of people: the promotion rate in a unit, the average length of service, or the type of heavy equipment belonging to the unit. Of course, people can be aggregated in many different ways, some of which imply social interaction and others only categorization by the observer. A "unit" in our sense will be any aggregation — an Army company, a neighborhood, an occupational category, a political party. Within any system of aggregation there may be many levels — the soldier, squad, platoon, company, and so on, or the individual, neighborhood, district, city, and so on.

Our main interest here is directed toward the logical relationship between data applying to objects of different levels of aggregation. We will discuss the simplest instance of two levels only: personal data and data of one higher unit. In order to be as concrete as possible, we start with data (see Table 41-12) taken from Table 18, in Volume II, page 450, of *The American Soldier.*[30] Here

[30] Stouffer *et al., op. cit.*

TABLE 41-12

Anxiety Symptoms and Certain Related Factors Among Combat Infantrymen in Four Divisions in the South and Central Pacific Areas (March-April 1944)

	Division *A* S. Pacific	Division *B* S. Pacific	Division *C* Cen. Pacific	Division *D* Cen. Pacific
Percentages who have had malaria....	66	41	2	2
Percentages receiving critical scores on the Anxiety Symptoms Index......	79	63	56	44
Median number of days in combat....	55	31	19	3
Number of cases....................	1,420	1,388	1,298	643

four Army divisions, each a unit, are compared in a variety of ways. The first row shows the proportion of malaria cases in the four divisions and the second row the proportion of soldiers exhibiting a pre-established number of neurotic symptoms. A glance at the two rows shows that the greater the incidence of malaria the greater also the incidence of neurotic cases. Let us look at the character of the data in the first row. On an individual level, the only possible distinction is between those who have had malaria and those who have not. But a unit of soldiers (in this case, a division) can be characterized by the proportion of soldiers with malaria. The personal datum, *incidence* of malaria, is an attribute. The malaria *rate*, which is a continuous variable, corresponds to it as a unit datum. This correspondence will be called that of Type I. (The number of times a soldier has had malaria would be a summation over time, which is excluded from the present discussion.)

Now let us turn to the unit datum in the third row. Each individual soldier was obviously characterized first by a continuous measure — the length of time he had been in combat. The unit is characterized by an average formed over the personal data, in this case the median. If the personal datum is a variable and the corresponding unit datum an average of the same variable we shall talk of correspondences of Type II. For the sake of completeness we should also reflect a moment on the index used in the second row. It is based on an index of psychoneurotic symptoms developed by the Research Branch. This was originally a serial in which soldiers could vary over a wide range of scores. But, for a variety of reasons, this serial was reconverted on the individual level into a dichotomous attribute: soldiers were divided according to whether their score was above or below the critical level. Out of this dichotomy, then, a continuous rate was formed on the group level just as in the case of malaria. (This double conversion, however, is rare and will not be considered further.)

On a somewhat impressionistic level, the two types mentioned so far have something in common. The personal datum and the corresponding unit datum have what one might call psychological similarity. We use practically the same terms in talking of the malaria-beset soldier and the malaria-infected division or in talking of the veteran soldier and the veteran division. We shall see presently that the similarity does not need to be as great as the linguistic usage suggests.

If the personal datum is a variable, then there can be still another correspondence. It is entirely possible that two divisions will have the same "median number of days in combat" and still differ in an important respect. One division may be quite homogeneous in that most of its soldiers have had the same amount of combat experience. The other division may have received many replacements, so that some of its soldiers have much more than the median amount of combat experience while others have hardly any. It is quite obvious that this homogeneity of experience can apply only to a unit; by the logic of the way it is measured, homogeneity can only be a unit datum and never a personal datum. We shall speak of correspondence of Type III when the unit datum is a standard deviation, a measure of skewness, or any other parameter of a distribution derived from a personal-datum variable.

In the three types discussed so far, the personal data could be attributed to individuals without any reference to the unit. Number of days in combat, number of psychoneurotic symptoms, and incidence of malaria are typical examples of this kind. We may call these *primary characteristics* of the individual. There are, however, certain personal data which imply a reference to other members of the unit. The best examples to draw on here are so-called sociometric measures. Whether a person chooses as a friend a man in his own unit or in some other unit; whether a man is chosen as a friend by many people in his unit or by few — these would be typical examples of what one might call *relational characteristics* of individuals. They are predicated about individuals but refer to other individuals in their definition. The corresponding unit data can be of three kinds, repeating, as it were, the previous three types of correspondence. The structure of a unit, for instance, could be characterized by the even distribution of sociometric choices over all members of the unit, or by the concentration of choices on a few "leaders." The cohesion of the group might be characterized by the ratio of choices made within and outside the unit. We shall lump together as Type IV all those cases in which the personal datum is of a relational nature, and the corresponding unit datum is any kind of aggregate of the individual relational datum. (In a more systematic discussion this would not be justified, but in the present context Type IV is mentioned only for the sake of completeness, and will not be further discussed. The treatment of these sociometric data is a broad and important field in itself.)

Each of the types of unit datum discussed so far has some individual datum corresponding to it. Homogeneity of combat experience can be predicated only about a unit, but the index is formed on the basis of data characterizing individual members of the group. Such characteristics of a unit based on the distribution of data pertaining to its component elements may be called *analytic characteristics*. There is, however, one kind of unit datum which is distinguished by the fact that no individual datum can correspond to it. If we are trying to measure the amount of battle strain which a division has undergone, we can of course use all the analytic characteristics listed in Table 41-12 and discussed above. But we might also use, for instance, the condition of the heavy equipment of the division — the extent to which its artillery, trucks, or mess equipment are worn out. The state of the divisional heavy equipment is something which, even as a datum, pertains only to the division and not to its individual members. It is thus a *primary characteristic of the unit* in just the same sense as "having malaria" is a primary characteristic of the individual. We thus have five main correspondences between personal data and unit data, as listed in Table 41-13.

The personal data in Types I, II, and III are *primary characteristics* of individuals; in Type IV they are *relational characteristics*. The unit data corresponding to all of these are *analytic characteristics of the unit*. Finally in Type V we see that the unit itself can have *primary characteristics*.

It should be helpful to think of a variety of areas where these distinctions apply. A good example can be taken from ecology. A neighborhood can have analytic characteristics such as suicide rate, average income, or range of incomes, based on primary characteristics of individuals. It can also have analytic characteristics such as the proportion of shopping which people do within its borders, or the frequency of social contact between its residents, which are based on relational characteristics of individuals. Finally, it can have certain primary characteristics of its own: the playground areas to be found within it, or whether it provides a common meeting place for its residents. The speed law in this neighborhood is also a primary property, while the proportion of residents who get tickets for breaking the speed law is an analytical property. Unit characteristics of all these types can be combined into an index of "goodness of neighborhood"; Thorndike has done exactly this sort of thing in measuring the "goodness" of cities.

There is one more kind of characteristic which has not been mentioned, however. This arises when we characterize an individual not by his primary characteristics but by the characteristics of the unit to which he belongs. Race is a primary characteristic of an individual, but "living in a mixed area" is an individual characteristic derived from the type of unit to which he belongs. Boys may be classified as rich and poor, delinquent and nondelinquent, but also as coming from areas with a high delinquency rate, or coming from areas without playgrounds. These characteristics which can be predicated of a unit only by drawing upon data from higher levels of aggregation may be termed *contextual characteristics*. They can occur on any level: neighborhoods, for instance, may be characterized not only by primary and analytic characteristics but also by such contextual characteristics as belonging to a city where the suicide rate is high, where the majority votes Republican, or where the school system sets high standards.

These contextual properties are of special importance because they cover at least part of what writers sometimes loosely call "sociological variables." Let us analyze one concrete example, taken from a study done by Herta Herzog for Columbia University's Bureau of Applied Social Research.[31] The study dealt with the attitude toward venereal disease (VD) in a Middle Western city. A sample of about one thousand cases was interviewed, and each respondent was asked questions such as: whether he knew anyone who had VD, whether he had had any discussions of some recent literature on VD, whether he had ever thought of getting a VD checkup, and so on. From the answers to these questions a crude index of "proximity to syphilis" was constructed. The problem of aggregating various attributes of an individual has already been discussed in this chapter; suffice it to say here that by common-sense weighting of items, people could be classified on a ten-point "proximity score" indicating the extent to which they were acquainted and/or concerned with VD problems. From our present point of view, this is a primary characteristic of each individual.

At one point in the study the problem arose of getting some idea as to what accounts for variations in "proximity to VD." One obvious notion was that men would have a greater proximity than women, as measured by the proportion of people in each sex group who have a proximity score of six or higher. This was actually the case — high proximity is about twice as frequent among men as among women. This is typical of the sort of result obtained in sampling surveys: a cross tabulation of one primary personal characteristic against another. There would also be general agreement that the interpretation would lead into the sociologist's notion of "role": that women are expected to be more sheltered and to avoid all matters relating to

[31] Herta Herzog, unpublished study for Bureau of Applied Social Research, Columbia University.

TABLE 41-13

Nature of Personal Datum	Nature of Corresponding Unit Datum
Type I:	
An attribute pertaining to one person only	A rate
Type II:	
A variable pertaining to one person only	An average
Type III:	
As in Type II	A parameter of the distribution of the variable, e.g., standard deviation or measure of skewness
Type IV:	
A datum involving the relation of the individual to other individuals	Any of the statistical aggregates used in the previous types
Type V:	
No information about the individual member is involved	The unit datum is a primary characteristic of the unit, not based upon characteristics of individual members

sex (except childbearing). (Whether the notion of "role" corresponds to the type of relational characteristic mentioned in our preceding list under Type IV would be an interesting topic for discussion, but cannot be pursued further here.)

However, the same respondents could also be classified by a contextual property. For the districts in which each person lived, the number of reported syphilis cases was known. It was therefore possible to classify each person according to whether he lived in a district with a high or low rate of syphilis. If we were studying the districts of the city, this would be used as an analytic characteristic of the district, but by classifying individuals according to a characteristic of the district in which they live, we use the same datum as a contextual characteristic on the personal level.

All the respondents were divided into two groups according to whether in the preceding year their district had reported more or less than twenty-five cases of syphilis. (The districts were of about equal size and therefore the use of absolute figures was permissible.) It now became possible to study in more detail what accounts for variations in "proximity to VD." Is it the primary characteristic of sex (which here stands for something like a biographical summary of experiences), or is it the contextual characteristic of the individual, the type of district in which he or she lives? The answer, restricted to white respondents, is given in Table 41-14.

TABLE 41-14
Proportion with
"High Degree of Proximity"

	25 or More Cases of Syphilis Reported in District		Under 25 Cases of Syphilis Reported in District	
	Percent	*Base*	*Percent*	*Base*
Men. . . .	59	41	28	252
Women.	18	49	13	342

It can be seen that high proximity is very frequent indeed among men who live in exposed districts and quite low among women who live in sheltered districts. But among men in *sheltered* districts 28 percent have high proximity, while among women in *exposed* districts 18 percent have high proximity. It thus turns out that for this one study the sex role is more important than the residential context. Speaking colloquially, men in sheltered districts are more likely to get in touch with VD problems than women in exposed districts. Or, to put it in terms of the table, the differences between the first and second row are larger than the differences between the first and second column.

This type of joint use of primary and contextual indices is undoubtedly of great promise for social research. Other examples come readily to mind. Workers in England are more likely to vote for the Labour party than are white-collar people. But a worker in a white-collar district is less likely to vote Labour than a worker in a workingman's district. In the same way, the insanity rate among Negroes in all-Negro sections of a city seems to be lower than the insanity rate of Negroes in mixed areas.

As a side issue, another aspect of this kind of index formation might be mentioned. Sometimes personal indices and unit indices can be used interchangeably and sometimes they cannot. Prior to the existence of public opinion polls, for instance, most of our knowledge of voting behavior was based on election statistics collected by precincts. A typical ecological voting study would show that, at least in the twentieth century, in American cities districts with low average rent showed a higher proportion of Democrats than districts with high average rent. But this interchangeability need not always hold true. A general observation, for instance, would lead us to believe that the proportion of car owners will be lower the further down we go in the income levels. But some wealthy districts in New York City probably have a smaller proportion of car owners than poor districts in sparsely settled rural areas where car ownership is more necessary for making a living. *Within* districts the personal characteristics, "car ownership" and "income," will probably be positively related. But if the unit of analysis is the district, and the proportion of car owners and average income are used to characterize the districts, the relationship might conceivably be negative. Systematic analysis of this type of situation would probably lead to a clarification of some of the problems involved in the "structural approach."[32]

This section has been able to cover briefly only a few of the large number of problems connected with the use of indices, just as the chapter as a whole has dealt with only bits and pieces of the problems of measurement in the social sciences. We cannot even discuss here the complicated formal-mathematical approach to these problems which was mentioned earlier, that of "latent structure analysis."[33] Latent structure analysis was developed to do for qualitative data what factor analysis can do for quantitative data. Although only in its early stages of development, latent structure analysis holds out the hope of systematizing a number of the problems discussed here: the problem of combining observable items to form concepts and categories; the relation of one supposed indicator of a complex concept to others; the logic of dichotomies and serials in relation to measurements; and the problems of combining indicators in quantitative indices.[34]

[32] A discussion of a larger number of examples can be found in Patricia L. Kendall and Paul F. Lazarsfeld, "Problems of Survey Analysis," in Merton and Lazarsfeld, *op. cit.*

[33] Stouffer *et al.*, *Measurement and Prediction.*

[34] The writing of this article was facilitated by a grant from the Human Resources Research Institute of the Air University, Maxwell Air Force Base, to the Bureau of Applied Social Research, Columbia University. This article is Publication A-130 of the Bureau of Applied Social Research, Columbia University.

A Mathematical Reduction of Power

42

A Method for Evaluating the Distribution of Power in a Committee System

L. S. SHAPLEY and MARTIN SHUBIK

In the following paper we offer a method for the *a priori* evaluation of the division of power among the various bodies and members of a legislature or committee system. The method is based on a technique of the mathematical theory of games, applied to what are known there as "simple games" and "weighted majority games."[1] We apply it here to a number of illustrative cases, including the United States Congress, and discuss some of its formal properties.

The designing of the size and type of a legislative body is a process that may continue for many years, with frequent revisions and modifications aimed at reflecting changes in the social structure of the country; we may cite the role of the House of Lords in England as an example. The effect of a revision usually cannot be gauged in advance except in the roughest terms; it can easily happen that the mathematical structure of a voting system conceals a bias in power distribution unsuspected and unintended by the authors of the revision. How, for example, is one to predict the degree of protection which a proposed system affords to minority interests? Can a consistent criterion for "fair representation" be found?[2] It is difficult even to *describe* the net effect of a double representation system such as is found in the U. S. Congress (i.e., by states and by population), without attempting to deduce it *a priori*. The method of measuring "power" which we present in this paper is intended as a first step in the attack on these problems.

Our definition of the power of an individual member depends on the chance he has of being critical to the success of a winning coalition. It is easy to see, for example, that the chairman of a board consisting of an even number of members (including himself) has no power if he is allowed to vote only to break ties. Of course he may have prestige and moral influence and will even probably get to vote when someone is not present. However, in the narrow and abstract model of the board he is without power. If the board consists of an odd number of members, then he has exactly as much power as any ordinary member because his vote is "pivotal" — i.e., turns a possible defeat into a success — as often as the vote of any other member. Admittedly he may not cast his vote as often as the others, but much of the voting done by them is not necessary to ensure victory (though perhaps useful for publicity or other purposes). If a coalition has a majority, then extra votes do not change the outcome. For any vote, only a minimal winning coalition is necessary.

Put in crude economic terms, the above implies that if votes of senators were for sale, it might be worthwhile buying forty-nine of them, but the market value of the fiftieth (to the same customer) would be zero. It is possible to buy votes in most corporations by purchasing common stock. If their policies are entirely controlled by simple majority votes, then there is no more power to be

From *The American Political Science Review*, 48:3 (September, 1954), pp. 787–792.

[1] See J. von Neumann and O. Morgenstern, *Theory of Games and Economic Behavior* (Princeton, 1944, 1947, 1953), pp. 420 ff.

[2] See K. J. Arrow, *Social Choice and Individual Values* (New York, 1951), p. 7.

gained after one share more than 50% has been acquired.[3]

Let us consider the following scheme: There is a group of individuals all willing to vote for some bill. They vote in order. As soon as a majority[4] has voted for it, it is declared passed, and the member who voted last is given credit for having passed it. Let us choose the voting order of the members randomly. Then we may compute the frequency with which an individual belongs to the group whose votes are used and, of more importance, we may compute how often he is *pivotal*. This latter number serves to give us our index. It measures the number of times that the action of the individual actually changes the state of affairs. A simple consequence of this formal scheme is that where all voters have the same number of votes, they will each be credited with $1/n$th of the power, there being n participants. If they have different numbers of votes (as in the case of stockholders of a corporation), the result is more complicated; more votes mean more power, as measured by our index, but not in direct proportion (see below).

Of course, the actual balloting procedure used will in all probability be quite different from the above. The "voting" of the formal scheme might better be thought of as declarations of support for the bill, and the randomly chosen order of voting as an indication of the relative degrees of support by the different members, with the most enthusiastic members "voting" first, etc. The *pivot* is then the last member whose support is needed in order for passage of the bill to be assured.

Analyzing a committee chairman's tie-breaking function in this light, we see that in an *odd* committee he is pivotal as often as an ordinary member, but in an *even* committee he is never pivotal. However, when the number of members is large, it may sometimes be better to modify the strict interpretation of the formal system, and say that the number of members in attendance is about as likely to be even as odd. The chairman's index would then be just half that of an ordinary member. Thus, in the U. S. Senate the power index of the presiding officer is — strictly — equal to 1/97. Under the modified scheme it is 1/193. (But it is zero under either interpretation when we are considering decisions requiring a two-thirds majority, since ties cannot occur on such votes). Recent history shows that the "strict" model may sometimes be the more realistic: in the present Senate (1953–54) the tie-breaking power of the Vice President, stemming from the fact that 96 is an even number, has been a very significant factor. However, in the passage of ordinary legislation, where perfect attendance is unlikely even for important issues, the modified scheme is probably more appropriate.

For Congress as a whole we have to consider three separate bodies which influence the fate of legislation. It takes majorities of Senate and House, with the President, or two-thirds majorities of Senate and House without the President, to enact a bill. We take all the members of the three bodies and consider them voting[5] for the bill in every possible order. In each order we observe the relative positions of the straight-majority pivotal men in the House and Senate, the President, and also the 2/3-majority pivotal men in House and Senate. One of these five individuals will be the pivot for the whole vote, depending on the order in which they appear. For example, if the President comes after the two straight-majority pivots, but before one or both of the 2/3-majority pivots, then he gets the credit for the passage of the bill. The frequency of this case, if we consider all possible orders (of the 533 individuals involved), turns out to be very nearly 1/6. This is the President's power index. (The calculation of this value and the following is quite complicated, and we shall not give it here.) The values for the House as a whole

[3] For a brief discussion of some of the factors in stock voting see H. G. Gothman and H. E. Dougall, *Corporate Financial Policy* (New York, 1948), pp. 56–61.

[4] More generally, a minimal winning coalition.

[5] In the formal sense described above.

and for the Senate as a whole are both equal to 5/12, approximately. The individual members of each chamber share these amounts equally, with the exception of the presiding officers. Under our "modified" scheme they each get about 30% of the power of an ordinary member; under the "strict" scheme, about 60%. In brief, then, the power indices for the three bodies are in the proportion 5:5:2. The indices for a *single* congressman, a *single* senator, and the President are in the proportion 2:9:350.

In a multicameral system such as we have just investigated, it is obviously easier to defeat a measure than to pass it.[6] A coalition of senators, sufficiently numerous, can block passage of any bill. But they cannot push through a bill of their own without help from the other chamber. This suggests that our analysis so far has been incomplete — that we need an index of "blocking power" to supplement the index already defined. To this end, we could set up a formal scheme similar to the previous one, namely: arrange the individuals in all possible orders and imagine them casting *negative* votes. In each arrangement, determine the person whose vote finally defeats the measure and give him credit for the block. Then the "blocking power" index for each person would be the relative number of times that he was the "blocker."

Now it is a remarkable fact that the new index is exactly equal to the index of our original definition. We can even make a stronger assertion: *any scheme for imputing power among the members of a committee system either yields the power index defined above or leads to a logical inconsistency.* A proof, or even a precise formulation, of this assertion would involve us too deeply in mathematical symbolism for the purposes of the present paper.[7] But we can conclude that the scheme we have been using (arranging the individuals in all possible orders, etc.) is just a convenient conceptual device; the indices which emerge are not peculiar to that device but represent a basic element of the committee system itself.

We now summarize some of the general properties of the power index. In pure *bi*cameral systems using simple majority votes, each chamber gets 50% of the power (as it turns out), regardless of the relative sizes. With more than two chambers, power varies inversely with size: the smallest body is most powerful, etc. But no chamber is completely powerless, and no chamber holds more than 50% of the power. To illustrate, take Congress without the provision for overriding the President's veto by means of two-thirds majorities. This is now a pure tricameral system with chamber sizes of 1, 97, and 435. The values come out to be slightly under 50% for the President, and approximately 25% each for the Senate and House, with the House slightly less than the Senate. The exact calculation of this case is quite difficult because of the large numbers involved. An easier example is obtained by taking the chamber sizes as 1, 3, and 5. Then the division of power is in the proportions 32:27:25. The calculation is reproduced at the end of this paper.

The power division in a multicameral system also depends on the type of majority required to pass a bill. Raising the majority in *one* chamber (say from one-half to two-thirds) increases the relative power of that chamber.[8] Raising the required majority in all chambers simultaneously weakens the smaller house or houses at the expense of the larger. In the extreme case, where unanimity is required in every house, each individual in the whole legislature has what amounts to a veto, and is just as powerful as any other individual.

[6] This statement can be put into numerical form without difficulty, to give a quantitative description of the "efficiency" of a legislature.

[7] The mathematical formulation and proof are given in L. S. Shapley, "A Value for N-Person Games," *Annals of Mathematics Study No. 28* (Princeton, 1953), pp. 307–17. Briefly stated, any alternative imputation scheme would conflict with either *symmetry* (equal power indices for members in equal positions under the rules) or *additivity* (power distribution in a committee system composed of two strictly independent parts the same as the power distributions obtained by evaluating the parts separately).

[8] As a general rule, if one component of a committee system (in which approval of all components is required) is made less "efficient" — i.e., more susceptible to blocking maneuvers — then its share of the total power will increase.

The power index of each chamber is therefore directly proportional to its size.

We may examine this effect further by considering a system consisting of a governor and a council. Both the governor and some specified fraction of the council have to approve a bill before it can pass. Suppose first that council approval has to be unanimous. Then (as we saw above) the governor has no more power than the typical councilman. The bicameral power division is in the ratio 1:N, if we take N to be the number of councilmen. If a simple majority rule is adopted, then the ratio becomes 1:1 between governor and council. That is, the governor has N times the power of a councilman. Now suppose that the approval of only one member of the council is required. This means that an individual councilman has very little chance of being pivotal. In fact the power division turns out to be N:1 in favor of the governor.[9] If votes were for sale, we might now expect the governor's price to be N^2 times as high as the average councilman's.

Several other examples of power distribution may be given. The indices reveal the decisive nature of the veto power in the United Nations Security Council. The Council consists of eleven members, five of whom have vetoes. For a substantive resolution to pass, there must be seven affirmative votes and no vetoes. Our power evaluation gives 76/77 or 98.7% to the "Big Five" and 1/77 or 1.3% to the remaining six members. Individually, the members of the "Big Five" enjoy a better than 90 to 1 advantage over the others.

It is well known that usually only a small fraction of the stock is required to keep control of a corporation. The group in power is usually able to muster enough proxies to maintain its position. Even if this were not so, the power of stockholders is not directly proportional to their holding, but is usually biased in favor of a large interest. Consider one man holding 40% of a stock while the remaining 60% is scattered among 600 small shareholders, with 0.1% each. The power index of the large holder is 66.6%, whereas for the small holders it is less than 0.06% apiece. The 400:1 ratio in holdings produces a power advantage of better than 1000:1.[10]

The preceding was an example of a "weighted majority game." Another example is provided by a board with five members, one of whom casts two extra votes. If a simple majority (four out of seven votes) carries the day, then power is distributed 60% to the multivote member, 10% to each of the others. To see this, observe that there are five possible positions for the strong man, if we arrange the members in order at random. In three of these positions he is pivotal. Hence his index is equal to 3/5. (Similarly, in the preceding example, we may compute that the strong man is pivotal 400 times out of 601).

The values in the examples given above do not take into account any of the sociological or political superstructure that almost invariably exists in a legislature or policy board. They were not intended to be a representation of present day "reality." It would be foolish to expect to be able to catch all the subtle shades and nuances of custom and procedure that are to be found in most real decision-making bodies. Nevertheless, the power index computations may be useful in the setting up of norms or standards, the departure from which will serve as a measure of, for example, political solidarity, or regional or sociological factionalism, in an assembly. To do this we need an empirical power index, to compare with the theoretical. One possibility is as follows: The voting record of an individual is taken. He is given no credit for being on the losing side of a vote. If he is on the winning side, when *n* others voted with him, then he is awarded the probability of his having been

[9] In the general case the proportion is N − M + 1:M, where M stands for the number of councilmen required for passage.

[10] If there are two or more large interests, the power distribution depends in a fairly complicated way on the sizes of the large interests. Generally speaking, however, the small holders are better off than in the previous case. If there are two big interests, equal in size, then the small holders actually have an advantage over the large holders, on a power per share basis. This suggests that such a situation is highly unstable.

the pivot (or blocker, in the case of a defeated motion), which is $1/n + 1$. His probabilities are then averaged over all votes. It can be shown that this measure gives more weight than the norm does to uncommitted members who hold the "balance of power" between extreme factions. For example, in a nine-man committee which contains two four-man factions which always oppose each other, the lone uncommitted member will always be on the winning side, and will have an observed index of $1/5$, compared to the theoretical value of $1/9$.

A difficulty in the application of the above measure is the problem of finding the correct weights to attach to the different issues. Obviously it would not be proper to take a uniform average over all votes, since there is bound to be a wide disparity in the importance of issues brought to a vote. Again, in a multicameral legislature (or in any more complicated system), many important issues may be decided without every member having had an opportunity to go on record with his stand. There are many other practical difficulties in the way of direct applications of the type mentioned. Yet the power index appears to offer useful information concerning the basic design of legislative assemblies and policy-making boards.

Appendix

The evaluation of the power distribution for a tricameral legislature with houses of 1, 3, and 5 members is given below:

There are 504 arrangements of five X's, three O's, and one ϕ, all equally likely if the nine items are ordered at random. In the following tabulation, the numbers indicate the number of permutations of predecessors ( ) and successors [ ] of the final pivot, marked with an asterisk. The dots indicate the pivots of the three separate houses.

$O\ \dot{O}\ O\ X\ X\ \dot{\phi}\ \dot{X}\ X\ X$ — (60) $\dot{X}$* [1]
$O\ \dot{O}\ X\ X\ \dot{\phi}\ \dot{X}\ O\ X\ X$ — (30) $\dot{X}$* [3]
} 150 pivots for X

$O\ X\ \dot{X}\ \dot{X}\ X\ X\ \dot{\phi}\ \dot{O}\ O$ — (42) $\dot{O}$* [1]
$O\ X\ X\ \dot{X}\ X\ \dot{\phi}\ \dot{O}\ O\ X$ — (30) $\dot{O}$* [2]
$O\ X\ X\ \dot{X}\ \phi\ \dot{O}\ O\ X\ X$ — (20) $\dot{O}$* [3]
} 162 pivots for O

$O\ \dot{O}\ O\ X\ X\ \dot{X}\ X\ X\ \phi$ — (56) ϕ*
$O\ \dot{O}\ O\ X\ X\ \dot{X}\ X\ \dot{\phi}\ X$ — (35) $\dot{\phi}$* [1]
$O\ \dot{O}\ O\ X\ X\ \dot{X}\ \dot{\phi}\ X\ X$ — (20) $\dot{\phi}$* [1]
$O\ \dot{O}\ X\ X\ \dot{X}\ X\ X\ \dot{\phi}\ O$ — (21) $\dot{\phi}$* [1]
$O\ \dot{O}\ X\ X\ \dot{X}\ X\ \dot{\phi}\ O\ X$ — (15) $\dot{\phi}$* [2]
$O\ \dot{O}\ X\ X\ \dot{X}\ \dot{\phi}\ O\ X\ X$ — (12) $\dot{\phi}$* [3]
} 192 pivots for ϕ

Power indices for the houses are 192/504, 162/504, and 150/504, and hence are in the proportion 32:27:25, with the smallest house the strongest. Powers of the individual members are as 32:9:9:9:5:5:5:5:5.

The Mathematical Reduction of Rationality

43

Some Strategic Considerations in the Construction of Social Science Models[1]

HERBERT A. SIMON

SECTION I: MODELS OF OPTIMIZATION

It is my aim in this paper to discuss some problems of strategy in theory construction in the social sciences. To put the matter more modestly, I should like to set forth, illustrate, and discuss some of the basic strategic considerations that have guided my own work in the formulation of theories — and particularly mathematical theories — of various aspects of human behavior.

The undertaking requires some preface. First, I should like to rule out of bounds the question of whether mathematics has any business in the social sciences. I will simply assert, with J. Willard Gibbs, that mathematics is a language; it is a language that sometimes makes things clearer to me than do other languages, and that sometimes helps me discover things that I have been unable to discover with the use of other languages. What the contribution of mathematics will be to the social sciences can perhaps be more fruitfully evaluated some generations hence when that contribution — if any — has been made.

Second, we shall be concerned with *applied* mathematics, and hence we shall be as concerned with the field of application as with mathematics itself. The strategy of mathematical theorizing must come primarily from the field about which the theorizing is to be done. The aim of a language is to say something — and not merely to say something about the language itself. Mathematical social science is, first and foremost, social science. If it is bad social science (i.e., empirically false), the fact that it is good mathematics (i.e., logically consistent) should provide little comfort.

In the first section, I should like to comment, in a completely unmathematical fashion, upon certain current trends in social science research that have an important bearing upon the strategy of theory construction. In succeeding sections of this and the following chapter I shall attempt to draw out more specifically the implications of these basic trends, illustrating the discussion with a few of the relatively primitive mathematical social science models that are now in existence.[2]

The Reintegration of The Social Sciences

The social sciences — weakened by a half-century of schisms among economists, political scientists, sociologists, anthropologists, and social psychologists — are undergoing at present a very rapid process of reintegration. This development is so rapid, and so obvious from even a casual survey of the journals and

Reprinted with permission of The Macmillan Company, New York, from *Mathematical Thinking in the Social Sciences* edited by Paul Lazerfeld, pp. 388–406. Copyright 1954 by the Free Press, a Corporation.

[1] I am indebted to a number of colleagues and others for helpful comments on an earlier draft of this paper. Among these are Messrs. G. L. Bach, Read Bain, W. W. Cooper, R. M. Cyert, H. Guetzkow, P. Lazarsfeld and members of the University Seminar on Organization at Columbia University.

[2] Since I have taken as my central theme the canons of strategy that have guided my own work, I hope I may be pardoned for including a disproportionate number of footnote citations to others of my own publications where particular topics have been treated at greater length. More adequate references to predecessors, contemporaries, and collaborators will be found in these other publications.

new books in these fields, that it hardly requires documentation.[3] The common diplomatic language for the scientists participating in the process is the language of sociology and social psychology, and the common core of theory — the rules of international law, if you like — is theory drawn primarily from those two fields.

An important cause of this development is that, in attempting to understand and analyse the large events in the political and economic scene — the wars, elections, and depressions — the social scientist has been forced to a recognition that all such events are aggregated from the interrelated behavior of human beings. The theoretical models, and the predictions based on models, of the larger scene have required him to make assumptions (explicit or implicit) about the motives, understandings, and abilities of these human beings. Critical attention to these assumptions, and a desire to validate them in a scientifically respectable manner, has gradually and inexorably driven social science back to the molecular phenomena of human behavior in a social environment.

Of course, psychological postulates — generally contrived in the comfort of the armchair — have long been a part of social science theory. What is new in the present situation is that the student of aggregative phenomena is now confronted with a growing body of social psychological and sociological theory and empirical verification that places a check on his free imagination and requires him to reconcile his postulates with this theory and these data. To state the matter in a more constructive way, social psychology and sociology are, perhaps for the first time, reaching a stage of development where they can make a positive contribution toward the foundations on which the more aggregative theories are built.

MODELS OF EXISTING SOCIO-PSYCHOLOGICAL THEORY

It is from these important trends that I would derive a first canon of strategy. If mathematics is to play an important role in the development of social science theory, then a great deal of experience must be gained as to what kinds of mathematics are likely to be useful, and as to what are some of the promising ways of imbedding fundamental psychological and sociological concepts and phenomena in mathematical models. What form shall human motives take in such models, how shall the rational and the nonrational aspects of human behavior be represented, what kind of mathematical schemes will conveniently represent the interactions of human groups, and so on?

The starting point, if this strategy is adopted, is the task of translating into the language of mathematics some of the concepts and some of the propositions that appear promising and fundamental in the growing body of social-psychological theory. In one sense, such translations will not say anything that is not already known — they will merely say it in another language. In another sense it is improbable that any great amount of translation of verbal theories into mathematical language can take place without significant advances in the clarity of the concepts imbedded in the theory.

The few areas where any considerable amount of activity of this sort has already been undertaken will suggest what might be accomplished. The most important of these is economics, where, to cite one example from many, the attempt to construct mathematical models of utility theory has rubbed off a great deal of fuzziness from the concept of "rational behavior," and has laid bare some of the basic methodological problems in the operational definition and measurement of "utility."[4]

[3] The economist who is still practising intellectual isolationism can begin to reform himself by reading a book like George Katona, *Psychological Analysis of Economic Behavior* (McGraw-Hill, 1951); the political scientist can try David B. Truman, *The Governmental Process* (Knopf, 1951); the organization theorist, Herbert A. Simon, Donald W. Smithburg, and Victor A. Thompson, *Public Administration* (Knopf, 1950).

[4] Further elaboration of this point will be found in the section below on preference fields.

Perhaps these advances could have been made without mathematics, but the fact is that they weren't.

A widespread effort to translate into mathematical language the core of existing social science theories will make another, and very direct, contribution to the reintegration of the social sciences. By translating from the specialized languages of the several social sciences to the common language of mathematics, unsuspected relationships will be discovered among theories that have been developed independently in these several sciences. In later sections of this paper I shall cite some examples of this — notably an example of two closely related theories, one drawn from the economist's theory of the firm, the other from the notion of organizational equilibrium discussed by administrative theorists.

NEED FOR A PLURALITY OF MODELS

A second canon of strategy is suggested by the magnitude of the task proposed. In social psychology today — much less the other social sciences — we do not have a theory, but theories — disconcertingly many of them. *Realism would suggest that we attempt to construct, not a mathematical model, but a plurality of mathematical models.* Once we have learned to imbed particular pieces of social reality in particular pieces of theoretical models, the interconnections among these will begin to suggest themselves. This has been the path of development of even the most successful of the sciences.

In the succeeding sections of this paper I shall suggest a number of central concepts that, I believe, should receive the attention of model builders and I shall survey some of the approaches that have been employed already to incorporate these concepts in models.

Models of Rational Behavior

As far as economic and administrative theory are concerned, man has been conceived primarily as a rational animal. The concept of rationality has played a prominent, but much less central, role in the other social sciences. Since economics, of all the social sciences, has had by far the greatest assistance from mathematics, it is not surprising that models of rational behavior are far more advanced than mathematical models of other aspects of behavior.

The most advanced theories, both verbal and mathematical, of rational behavior are those that employ as their central concepts the notions of: (1) a set of alternative courses of action presented to the individual's choice; (2) knowledge and information that permit the individual to predict the consequences of choosing any alternative; and (3) a criterion for determining which set of consequences he prefers.[5] In these theories rationality consists in selecting that course of action which leads to the set of consequences most preferred. (At a later point of our discussion we will see that this definition of rationality is somewhat too restrictive, but we may accept it temporarily as a starting point for analysis.)

Practically the whole of classical economic theory is constructed within the framework of this model. As an example of a mathematical version of it, which will serve to indicate how a verbal theory can be mathematized, we may take a very simple model of the theory of the firm. In this simple example there is a single rational human being, an "entrepreneur" who is operating a firm that manufactures a single product from a single raw material. (1) The alternatives open to the entrepreneur are to employ more or less of the raw material. (2) The consequences of a given course of action are that he will incur a cost (determined by the price of the raw material, and the quantity used), and he will

[5] For an extended (verbal) discussion of this model, and a comparison with the less satisfactory "means-ends" model employed by Parsons, Tolman and others, see H. A. Simon, *Administrative Behavior* (Macmillan, 1947), ch. 4. *Cf.* Paul A. Samuelson, *Foundations of Economic Analysis* (Harvard U. Press, 1947), pp. 21–3, 97–8.

receive a revenue (determined by the price of the product, and the quantity produced with the given amount of raw material). We assume that he knows the price at which any specified amount of raw material can be bought, the price at which any specified amount of product can be sold, and the maximum amount of product that can be produced from a given amount of raw material. That is, he knows his "supply curve," his "demand curve," and his "production function." (In this model, the supplier and the consumer need not be regarded as rational human beings, their behavior being specified and known.) (3) The entrepreneur's criterion is that he wishes the largest possible profit — the largest attainable difference between total revenue and cost of production.

THE MATHEMATICAL TRANSLATION

In the language of mathematics, let y be the quantity of product made, and x the quantity of raw material bought. Let $p = p(y)$ be the price of the product, which is assumed to depend on the quantity sold; and $P = P(x)$ be the price of the raw material, assumed to depend on the quantity bought. Let the quantity of product obtainable from a given quantity of raw material be given by $y = f(x)$. Then the entrepreneur's alternatives are a range of values of x. The revenue, $yp(y) = f(x)p(f(x))$, and the cost $xP(x)$, are the consequences which can be calculated when x is known. The criterion is to maximize the profit, $\pi = yp(y) - xP(x)$, regarded as function of x. The rational behavior is given by the well-known "marginal" condition,

$$\frac{d\pi}{dx} = \frac{df}{dx} p[f(x)] + f(x) \frac{dp}{dy}\frac{df(x)}{dx} - P(x) - x\frac{dP}{dx} = 0 \qquad (1)$$

Translating this equation back into English, it says that the rational entrepreneur will fix his output at the point where marginal cost equals marginal revenue.

Several features of this model deserve notice, as generally characteristic of models of rational behavior. Certain variables — in this case x — are regarded as "strategic" variables, controllable by a rational being. Other variables — in this case π — are the criterion, and measure of the goal he is seeking. The limits of attainment are set by conditions outside his control — relationships he must accept — which determine the value of the criterion as a function of the strategic variable. The problem of rationality then becomes a problem in maximization — to find the greatest value of the criterion, regarded as a function of the strategic variables.

SIGNIFICANCE OF THE LIMITS OF RATIONALITY

If we regard this model as a description of the actual behavior of some entrepreneur, we see that if we are to predict his behavior, the knowledge that he is rational is only a small part — almost an insignificant part — of the information that we require. His intention to be rational leads to particular behavior only in the context of conditions in which his behavior takes place. These conditions include both (1) the limits expressed by the demand curve, the supply curve, and the production function — we might regard these as the limits of his "abilities" in the situation — and (2) the limits expressed by the criterion function. The criterion (regarded as a "final end") is itself not an object of rational calculation, but a given. The model would be equally a model of rational behavior if the entrepreneur chose to maximize his losses, or his gross revenue instead of his profit.

Indeed, our principal use for such models is in predicting how the entrepreneur's behavior will be affected by a change in the environment that conditions or "bounds" his rationality. For example, we may wish to predict how the price and output of the product will be altered, assuming the entrepreneur always to behave rationally, if there occurs a shift in the demand function. To do this, we can regard the price of the product, p, as depending both on the quantity sold, y, and upon a parameter (i.e., a coefficient regarded as constant in the short run, but as possibly varying in the long run), a, which may vary, for example, with changes in consumers' tastes: $p = p(y,a)$. Each change in a shifts the whole demand curve — relating p to y — to right or left. If we follow the maximizing procedure previously described for finding the optimal value of x, this value will now depend on a — that is, a will in general appear in equation (1). Hence, we can regard equation (1) as a statement of relationship between x and a — a statement of how production, under the assumption of the entrepreneur's rationality, will vary with shifts in demand.[6]

We may summarize our discussion to this point by saying: that a simple model of rational behavior leads quite naturally to maximizing procedures and, in mathematical translation, to the methods of the differential calculus; and that the specific features of interest in any particular model arise primarily from the particular conditions under which rationality is exercised. This second point perhaps deserves to be dignified as a third canon of strategy: *In mathematical models incorporating rational and nonrational aspects of behavior, the non-rational aspects can be imbedded in the model as the limiting conditions that "bound" the area of rational adjustment.*[7]

Qualifications on the Model of Rational Behavior

The previous paragraph registers my conviction that improvement in the model of rational behavior will come primarily through careful attention to the boundaries of the area of rationality. In the remaining sections of this paper, I shall try to make this recommendation more explicit. We can begin our examination of these boundaries by looking at some of the extensions and amendments to the rational model that economists have been led to by their attempts to extend that model to broader and broader classes of phenomena.

RATIONALITY OF MORE THAN ONE

The rationality of the classical maximizing procedures is essentially the rationality of Robinson Crusoe. For each rational individual in the model must take as fixed "givens" the patterns of behavior of the other individuals — he must regard these others not as rational beings, but as some kind of responsive or unresponsive mechanism. The classical theory found three paths that gave promise of leading out of this wilderness:

(1) *Perfect Competition.* In the theory of perfect competition, each participant assumes that what he does is such an insignificant part of the total picture that it will have no effect on the others. Hence, if he can predict the behavior of the others, and adjust his own behavior to the prediction, his adjustment will not have repercussions that would disturb the prediction.

(2) *Imperfect Competition.* If the participants will adjust their behavior to each other, but each participant can predict what the adjustments of the others to his behavior will be, then he can determine which of his own behavior alternatives will be optimal in the light of the prediction. This was our procedure in the simple model used in the previous section. The demand curve and the supply curve each constitutes a prediction of the price that the customer or supplier, respectively, will pay or require for the quantity of product or raw material the entrepreneur decides upon. The customer and supplier are supposed to regard the price as something given — as something they cannot influence.

[6] The method just illustrated is the method of comparative statics. See Samuelson, *op. cit.*, pp. 7–20 for a more complete discussion.

[7] This "canon of strategy" was first proposed by the author as a basic principle for the guidance of research in administrative theory. See *Administrative Behavior*, pp. 39–41, 240–4.

(3) *Cournot's Oligopoly Theory.* If the customer and the supplier in the previous case were just one whit cleverer, the solution there given would be untenable. If the entrepreneur assumes they are going to adjust to his behavior, and acts in anticipation of that adjustment, why do not they, in turn, assume that he is going to adjust to their behavior and act in anticipation of that adjustment? The imperfect competition model admits rationality of all participants, but does not permit the same level of cleverness in the customer or supplier as in the entrepreneur. The limits on his rationality, as it is postulated, are broader and less restricting than the limits on theirs — he tries to outguess them, but they do not try to outguess him.

Cournot sought a way out of this difficulty by permitting *each* participant, in a two-person model, to guess at the reaction of the other, and to behave accordingly. Equality of cleverness was restored, and if dynamic stability was present the actual behaviors would in fact conform to the predicted behavior. (At the equilibrium point, the participants would predict correctly on a wrong basis.) But the Cournot model, while consistent with the assumptions of rationality, is not a model of unlimited cleverness. For either participant, if he knew the other was following the Cournot procedure, could form some new, and more accurate, expectations of that other's reactions to his choices, and use this new prediction to better his position. This way lies madness, for it leads to an infinite regress of prediction in which A predicts what B will predict as to A's prediction of B's reaction to A's behavior — and so on, ad infinitum.[8]

The conclusion we reach from our examination of models of rationality involving the behavior of more than one person is that we must adopt one of two alternatives: (a) on the one hand, we can assume that not more than one participant is unlimitedly clever in predicting the reactions of the other participants to his behavior; (b) on the other hand, we can seek a new definition of rationality that does not identify rationality with a simple maximization process. The first approach — assumptions of rationality and maximization, but limited cleverness — is the one involved in all three paths described above: perfect competition, imperfect competition, and oligopoly theory. The second approach, abandonment of simple maximization, was adopted by von Neumann and Morgenstern in their pioneering work on the theory of games.[9] By replacing the maximum, in the definition of rationality, with a more sophisticated mathematical concept, the minimax, the difficulty is avoided[10] — at the expense of attributing to human beings a cleverness they have perhaps not often exhibited outside the more successful poker-playing circles.

No attempt will be made here to evaluate the respective merits of the two approaches to rationality. The von Neumann model may be the more useful approach to the question of optimal behavior — i.e., for a book on how to play successful poker. The model of limited cleverness may be more useful in the description of actual rational behavior — at least until such time as most people have learned to minimax rather than to maximize.

REACTION TIME — RATIONALITY AND DYNAMICS

The outguessing difficulty is only one of the problems that can be raised in connection with the classical model. Another is the question of speed of adjustment. In our simple model of the theory of the firm, the

[8] For a description of the Cournot model see R. G. D. Allen, *Mathematical Analysis for Economists* (Macmillan, 1938), pp. 200–204; 345–347. The Cournot model has an obvious affinity to sociological models, like those of Mead and Cooley, which involve "taking the role of the other." These models are discussed in Theodore M. Newcomb, *Social Psychology* (Dryden Press, 1950), ch. 9.

[9] J. von Neumann and O. Morgenstern, *The Theory of Games and Economic Behavior* (Princeton U. Press, 1944), pp. 8–15, 31–45. For a nontechnical introduction to the theory of games, see John McDonald, *Strategy in Poker, Business and War* (Norton, 1950), particularly the Introduction and Part 2.

[10] Von Neumann and Morgenstern, *op. cit.*, pp. 88–95.

entrepreneur is assumed to know not only the shape of the demand curve, but also its position at any given time — i.e., the value of the parameter a. For many situations a more realistic assumption would be that he does not have this detailed knowledge, but only discovers his optimal position by experimenting and learning on the basis of his experience and his mistakes. For example, he might have some information about marginal costs and marginal revenue, but only in the neighborhood of the position in which he is actually operating. He might then adopt the rule of behavior that he will continue to increase his output so long as his marginal revenue is in excess of marginal cost, and decrease it whenever he finds marginal cost in excess of marginal revenue. In equations, the assumption is:

$$\frac{dx}{dt} = b\left\{\frac{df}{dx}\,p\,[f(x)] + f(x)\,\frac{dp}{dy}\,\frac{df(x)}{dx} - P(x) - x\,\frac{dP}{dx}\right\}, \qquad (b > 0). \quad (2)$$

Now if "other conditions" like the parameter a remain reasonably steady, and if the system satisfies certain other stability requirements, it turns out that the optimal solution, in the sense of equation (1), is actually the stable equilibrium position of the time path described by equation (2)[11]. When this is true, equation (2) may be taken as a definition of rational behavior under the restrictions of information that have been assumed. *How* rational it is, will depend, of course, on the size of the coefficient b, which measures the adjustment rate, for if this coefficient is large the adjustment and the approach to the equilibrium will be rapid, while if b is small, the approach will be slow. If, now, a fluctuates moderately (there are shifts from time to time in demand), a large b will prevent the entrepreneur from ever departing very widely from the optimal output, while a small b may permit very wide departures, and consequent loss of profit.

[11] The specific requirements with respect to stability have been discussed in full by Samuelson, *op. cit.*, ch. 9, and do not need to be reviewed here.

The difference between the kind of rationality depicted in equation (1) and the kind depicted in equation (2) might be described as follows. Two popcorn men are vending their wares on a very large county fair ground. Their profits will depend on keeping their wagons in the part of the fair ground where as dense a crowd as possible has assembled. The crowd is in continual motion. The first popcorn man has radio equipment on his wagon on which he has arranged to receive from all parts of the fair ground frequent reports on the size of the crowd. As soon as he learns where it is densest, he speeds to that part of the ground. The second popcorn man has less modern equipment. He keeps his cart in motion in the direction of increasing density of the crowd, and away from the direction of decreasing density.

Amount of Information and Speed of Adjustment. Now if one is willing to include amount of information and speed of adjustment among the boundaries of rationality, a large number of interesting possibilities offer themselves. In the first place, while it seems to be almost always possible to construct a stable dynamic system whose equilibrium position corresponds to the maximum of a given static system, it is often possible to construct more than one such dynamic system. In terms of our "dynamic" definition of rationality, it would then occur that there would be more than one rational pattern of behavior in a given situation.

For example, in the usual dynamization of the theory of markets — leading to the well-known cobweb phenomena — it is assumed that when supply is out of balance with demand, a price adjustment will take place in the short-run to "clear the market," while in the long run, an adjustment in the quantity supplied will restore the suppliers to their position of profit maximization. An alternative dynamic mechanism can be constructed in which a lack of balance between supply and demand leads to an adjustment in the quantity supplied, while if the current price does not provide suppliers with a "reasonable" profit, a price adjustment takes place. With suitable assumptions, this second model has the same position of equilibrium, and virtually the same stability conditions as the first.

To predict an individual's behavior under these circumstances, we would have to know, not only that he was being rational, but also whether he was exhibiting rationality of species A (corresponding to one dynamic system) or rationality of species B (corresponding to another). In the long run — in equilibrium — it would not make any difference, but as Keynes has pointed out, in the long run we are all dead.

Optimizing versus Adaptive Behavior. As we move from the static model to the dynamic, our original definition of rationality (selection of that course of action which leads to the set of consequences most preferred) becomes somewhat too restrictive. On the one hand, we may build the concept of rationality, as in the earlier models, upon the ability of the individual to discover a "best" situation and to move toward it, either instantaneously (as in the static models) or gradually (as in the dynamic). On the other hand, we can base an alternative notion of rationality on the ability of the individual to distinguish "better" (or "preferred") from "worse" directions of change in his behavior and to adjust continually in the direction of the "better." A rational process in which the choice of a "best" is central we will call optimization; a rational process in which movement toward a "better" is central we will call adaptation. Clearly, as is shown by the models of dynamic adjustment toward an optimal equilibrium, the two species of rationality are not mutually exclusive. In spite of the overlap, however, we will find the distinction useful in progressing through the whole continuum of models of rational behavior from those, on the one extreme, incorporating instantaneous optimization to those, at the other extreme, requiring only that minimum of adaptation which may be essential for survival.

Now, taking the next step along the continuum, and freeing the dynamic model we have already discussed from its ties with the corresponding static system, we may view it as follows:

An individual has a certain criterion, by means of which he judges his situation. Call the criterion θ_s. He measures his actual situation, θ_0, and its departure, $(\theta_s - \theta_0)$, from the criterion. He then adjusts his behavior at a rate that is proportional to the difference between the actual and the criterion. In the model previously discussed, for example, the criterion is that the marginal revenue should equal the marginal cost; the actual situation is described by the difference between the (actual) marginal revenue and the (actual) marginal cost. He then adjusts his behavior — the variable x — at a rate assumed to be proportional to this difference. In equations, the system is:

$$\theta_s = 0 \qquad (3)$$

$$\theta_0 = \left\{\frac{df}{dx}\, p\,[f(x)] - f(x)\,\frac{dp}{dy}\,\frac{df(x)}{dx} - P(x) - x\,\frac{dP}{dx}\right\} \qquad (4)$$

$$\epsilon = \theta_s - \theta_0 = -\theta_0 \qquad (5)$$

$$\frac{dx}{dt} = b\epsilon \qquad (6)$$

An engineer looking at this model would recognize in it something he is accustomed to call a "servomechanism" or a "closed-loop control system." If we follow the engineer's terminology in calling the difference between the actual state of the system and the criterion an "error," then we may say that the system is an adaptive one in which the individual measures the error in his behavior, and adjusts the behavior seeking to eliminate the error. Norbert Wiener has argued persuasively that the servomechanism model may be a useful model for describing physiological, psychological, and sociological adaptive systems.[12]

[12] Norbert Wiener, *Cybernetics* (Wiley, 1948), particularly ch. 4. An introduction to servomechanisms will be found in H. Lauer, R. Lesnick, and L. E. Matson, *Servomechanism Fundamentals* (McGraw-Hill, 1947),

There is yet another sense in which the notion of an adaptive system is broader than the notion of optimizing behavior. Optimization carries at least the connotation of conscious deliberation, foresight, and intention. Adaptation, on the other hand, more generally connotes appropriateness for survival, movement toward equilibrium. Now the two notions of optimization and survival are combined in the classical economic theory of pure competition in an ingenious fashion. But there is no reason why we cannot consider systems that are adaptive, in the sense of possessing a stable equilibrium position toward which the system continually moves, without postulating an optimizing mechanism (in the conscious sense) that explains the adaptation. As a matter of fact, refusal to consider such systems would make all of biology hopelessly anthropomorphic. It may be argued that a similar refusal in the social sciences would make those sciences hopelessly economomorphic.

At any rate it would appear that there is a large number of possible dynamic models of social behavior that deserve to be examined quite apart from their possible linkage to models of static optimizing behavior, and quite apart from any insistence that the "criterion" in terms of which the system adjusts need be a conscious goal of rational action. In the next chapter we shall proceed to an examination of several such models, but before we do so, some concluding comments need to be added under the present heading of "Qualifications on the Model of Rational Behavior."

INCOMPLETE INFORMATION AND UNCERTAINTY

In the previous section, we examined one way in which the model of rational behavior can be altered to take account of limits on information and speed of adjustment. In that section we were concerned primarily with the individual's information about the behavior of other individuals. He may also, of course, have incomplete information about the nonhuman conditions that surround his activity. We may sketch briefly a number of schemes for handling the problem:

(1) We can incorporate the individual's expectations into the behavior model. Then we require a theory of how he forms those expectations — a theory of his forecast model. His expectations may take the form of specific predictions, or of probability distributions of the predicted variable. If we take the latter alternative, then we may wish to define rational choice as the choice that maximizes the expected value (in the statistical sense) of the criterion variable. This approach adds nothing essentially new to our optimization model. It is the approach that, in combination with the von Neumann game theory, dominates modern statistical theory — e.g., the Neyman-Pearson theories of testing hypotheses and the sequential analysis theories of Wald.[13]

(2) We can assume that the individual adjusts to his changing situation without forecasting. This leads again to dynamic models of the servo-mechanism type.[14]

(3) We can assume that the individual balances the costs of postponing decisions against the advantages of obtaining additional information before he makes them. Then we are led to the theory of the timing of decisions. J. Marschak has shown how such an approach can be used to explain certain aspects of liquidity preference — the preference for holding assets in relatively liquid form — and I have shown that the same approach can be used as a basis for explaining, on rational grounds, the authority relationship between employer and employee and the comparative

---

ch. I. The idea of biological and human feedback systems goes back to the physiologist Claude Bernard. See Alfred J. Lotka, *Elements of Physical Biology* (Williams and Wilkins, 1925), pp. 362–416.

[13] These theories are discussed by Jacob Marschak elsewhere in this volume.

[14] H. A. Simon, "On the Application of Servo-mechanism Theory in the Study of Production Control," *Econometrica*, Vol. 20, 1952, pp. 247–268.

advantages of an employment or a sales contract for accomplishing a particular task.[15]

PREFERENCE FIELDS

In our initial model of optimizing behavior, we assumed that a criterion function exists. In the case of the entrepreneur, the criterion function has traditionally been his profit, in the case of the consumer, his "utility." This has led to the question of whether such a function exists, and this question, in turn, to some very fruitful examinations of the whole subject of preference fields. In those cases where we are willing to admit that an unambiguous field exists — where at the very least, each possible outcome can be judged as "better," "the same," or "worse" than each other possible outcome — we are assuming again a very global kind of rationality. We are assuming that the individual possesses a very wide span of attention, and a single consistent system of values that he applies simultaneously to the whole range of action.

There has been only a little exploration into the possibilities of models that make less global assumptions about the consistency, comprehensiveness, and stability of the individual's preference field.[16] Yet these limits of rationality — limits on the consistency of choice — certainly have empirical importance in many areas of behavior. I can offer at the moment no concrete suggestions as to the way in which such limits can effectively be incorporated in a model, but simply call to the reader's attention this potentially significant area for theoretical work.

Conclusion

This completes our survey of the various directions that have been pursued in the construction of models of that species of rational behavior we have called optimization. We have seen that as soon as we begin to introduce limits upon the speed of adjustment and upon the range of alternatives over which choice is exercised, we begin to move from models of optimization to models of adaptation. The next section will be devoted to a further investigation of this latter class of models.

SECTION II: MODELS OF ADAPTIVE BEHAVIOR

Theory construction, largely the work of mathematical economists, in the area of rational human behavior has been developing, as we have just seen, in the direction of more and more explicit attention to the various limitations upon the capacity of human beings to behave in a "perfectly" rational fashion. Of the various amendments to the classical model, perhaps the most radical is the one — leading to dynamics — that shifts the focus from "optimal" behavior to "adaptive" behavior. In the present section I shall explore some of the implications of this shift. Rather than to speculate about the problem in the abstract, our procedure will be to exhibit several models that show how various kinds of behavior, viewed as an adaptive process, can be handled. We will begin with a model of individual behavior, and proceed to some models of behavior in groups.

Motivation and Learning

In psychological formulations of adaptive human behavior, the concepts of motivation and learning are central.[17] The notion of motivation is closely connected with the "criterion" in the models of optimization,

[15] Jacob Marschak, "Role of Liquidity under Complete and Incomplete Information," Papers and Proceedings, *American Economic Review*, vol. 39, May, 1949, pp. 182–195; H. A. Simon, "A Formal Theory of the Employment Relationship," *Econometrica*, July 1951, vol. 19, pp. 293–305.

[16] For an example of some recent work in this field, see Kenneth J. Arrow, *Social Choice and Individual Values* (Wiley, 1951), pp. 9–21.

[17] The contrast between the optimizing man of the economists and the adaptive man of the psychologists is discussed in Simon, *Administrative Behavior*, chapter 4 (previously referred to), and chapter 5.

while learning is connected with changes in such limitations on rationality as "state of information" and "technology." In the present model we shall not attempt any further exact translation from the previous concepts, but will start afresh.

THE "BERLITZ" MODEL

We suppose that there is an activity in which an individual engages from time to time, and that he can engage in varying amounts of it each day. As he engages in it, it becomes progressively easier for him (this is our "learning" assumption). To the extent that he finds it pleasant, he engages in it more frequently; to the extent he finds it unpleasant, he engages in it less frequently. Its pleasantness depends on how easy it is for him. (The latter two statements comprise our "motivation" assumption.)

As a concrete example, we may suppose that our individual has subscribed to a correspondence course to learn French by the Berlitz method. Each day he spends a certain amount of time in practice. As he practices, the language becomes easier; so long as the difficulty is greater than a certain level, he finds the work unpleasant, and tends to shorten his practice sessions. (We assume our student to be a kind of hedonist.) If he reaches a certain level of skill, however, the work becomes pleasant, and he will tend to practice for a longer period.[18]

Let x be the rate (say, in hours per day) at which the activity is performed. Let D be the level of difficulty, and let us assume (learning) that the difficulty decreases logarithmically with practice:

$$dD/dt = -aDx \qquad (7)$$

Let us assume that at any given level of difficulty, practice is pleasurable up to a certain point, and unpleasant beyond that point, and that $x = \bar{x}(D)$ is this satiation level of activity. We assume then (motivation) that:

$$dx/dt = -b(x - \bar{x}) \qquad (8)$$

The two equations for dD/dt and dx/dt permit us to predict the time paths of D and x if we know their initial values, D_0 and x_0 at time t_0. Several representative time paths are shown in Figure 43-1.

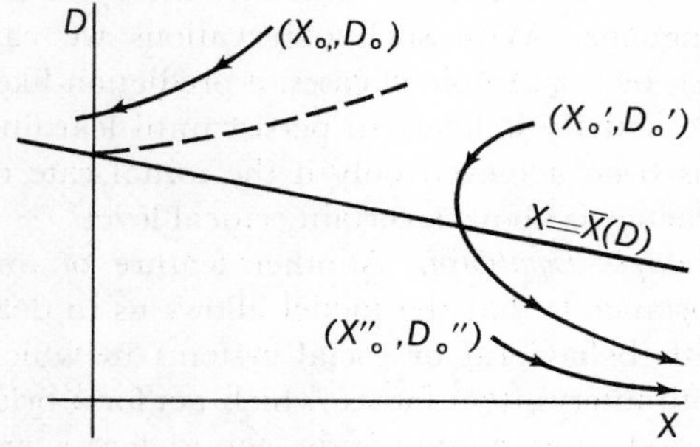

Fig. 43–1

The figure shows that whether our student eventually becomes discouraged and fails to complete his course, or whether he is successful in learning French depends on his starting point (and, of course, on the relative magnitudes of a and b and the shape of $\bar{x}(D)$). The value of D_0 represents the difficulty of the language to him at the outset, and x_0 the amount of time he initially devotes to practice. If the point (x_0, D_0) lies above the dotted line, he will ultimately become discouraged and give up his lessons; if, instead, he begins at (x_0', D_0'), between the dotted line and the line $x = \bar{x}(D)$, he will suffer some discouragement at the outset, but practice will ultimately become pleasant and he will learn the language. If he begins at (x_0'', D_0''), practice will be pleasant from the outset, and he will learn.

Clearly one would want to refine this model before trying to verify it from actual situations, but even in its highly simple form it exhibits some of the qualitative features we would expect to find in such situations, and illustrates in what a natural manner differential equations can be employed in a model of adaptive behavior.

[18] There are other less trivial situations that exhibit the characteristics of this model, as will be shown later, but this one is simple, and will serve to illustrate the point.

Prediction and Verification. One interesting feature of a model of this sort is that it permits qualitative predictions to be made that are very easy to test empirically. We do not need to trace out in detail the time path of the system, but merely to observe whether the activity terminates before learning was completed, or whether it ends in mastery of the language. With such observations we can test, over a sample of cases, a prediction like: the activity is likely to persist until learning has been achieved only if the initial rate of practice is above a certain critical level.

Multiple Equilibria. Another feature of importance is that the model allows us to deal with behavioral or social systems in which both intermittent forces, which act for a brief period, and continuously acting forces are at play. The intermittent force in this case would be the individual's decision to subscribe to the language course and devote a certain amount of time to practice (i.e., the determinants of the initial position). The continuous forces would be the process of learning and the varying motivation as the resolution was actually carried out (i.e., the forces determining the path from the initial position). A Spencer would say that the final outcome is determined by the continuous interplay of forces immanent in the behavioral interaction itself; a Bentham would say that the outcome is determined by the intermittent intervention — the determination of the initial conditions.[19] The two views are in fact not contradictory provided the system has more than one position of final equilibrium. In this case an intervention can "jar" the system from one position of equilibrium to another.

A possible application of this notion is to the theory of political and social "reform" movements. It is notorious that such movements are short-lived, at least in their active and influential phases. If they are effective, it must be through disturbance of a system of forces previously in equilibrium, and a sufficient shift in initial conditions to permit the system to move toward a new equilibrium with a different stable constellation of forces.

There would seem to be a wide class of social phenomena that could be studied in terms of a model embodying this feature of multiple equilibria. Gunnar Myrdal's theory of social change appears to be of this sort, as do most theories of revolution.[20] The relationship between "formal" organization (which operates in considerable part through intermittent pressures) and "informal" organization might also be expressed in these terms.[21]

A Social Interpretation of the "Berlitz" Model. It might appear that we are not justified in discussing the applicability to social systems of a model that represents, after all, the behavior of a single human being. In fact, however, the writer was originally led to construct this model in order to represent a social situation. In an organization where accountants were given the task of providing accounting information to operating executives, it was found that if understanding between accountants and operators was good, they tended to communicate frequently with each other; when it was bad, less frequently. Moreover, frequent communication, by helping them understand each other's languages, made communication easier. By renaming the variable x "frequency of communication between accountants and operators," and the variable D "difficulty of communication between accountants and operators," we

[19] See William Archibald Dunning, *A History of Political Theories: From Rousseau to Spencer* (Macmillan, 1920), pp. 211–24, 395–402. As Carl Becker puts it: "Whereas the 18th century held that man can by taking thought add a cubit to his stature, the 19th century held that a cubit would be added to his stature whether he took thought or not." (Article on "Progress" in *Encyclopedia of the Social Sciences*, vol. 12, p. 498.)

[20] See Gunnar Myrdal, *An American Dilemma* (Harper, 1944), Appendix 3. While Myrdal does not speak explicitly of multiple equilibria this seems to be an implicit element of his model. For a mathematical model, along these lines of revolutionary change see Nicolas Rashevsky, *Mathematical Biology of Social Behavior* (Chicago U. Press, 1951), chapter 13. I might add that I am greatly indebted to Professor Rashevsky's work, which he discusses elsewhere in this volume, for stimulating my thinking along the general lines of this and the following section.

[21] For definitions of "formal" and "informal" see Simon, Smithburg, and Thompson, *op. cit.*, pp. 85–90.

obtain in the model a clear representation of this social system.

FURTHER COMMENTS ON MOTIVATION

If we compare the notion of motivation in the present model with the notion of a preference field, discussed earlier, we find one important difference that has not been mentioned. In a preference field we can say that one alternative is preferable or "more pleasant" than another, but there is no natural zero-point for pleasantness: we can distinguish more or less of pleasantness, but cannot speak of pleasantness and unpleasantness in any absolute sense. In the "Berlitz" model, the function $\bar{x}(D)$ does define such a dividing line, or zero separating pleasantness from unpleasantness.

We can reconcile the present viewpoint with the earlier one by supposing that our student, if he does not study his language, can engage in some other activity which, when $x > \bar{x}$, is more pleasant than the work on his language. Then to say that an activity is "unpleasant" simply means that there is an alternative that is preferable. The zero-point of preference for an activity is defined by what the economist would call the "opportunity cost" of the activity.[22]

From the standpoint of psychological theory, however, it would appear that a "natural" zero-point can be defined with respect to motivation. This zero-point arises from two related psychological mechanisms. The first of these is the dependence of strength of motivation upon the relationship between the level of aspiration and the level of achievement.[23] The second of these is the qualitative change in motivation that takes place under conditions of frustration.[24]

We take as our independent variable the difference between the actual level of skill of an individual in performing a task and the level of skill to which he aspires. If achievement exceeds aspiration, this variable will be positive; if the two are equal, zero; if aspiration exceeds achievement, negative. Now the psychological evidence would appear to indicate that the strength of drive toward the activity is related to achievement in somewhat the fashion indicated in Figure 43-2.

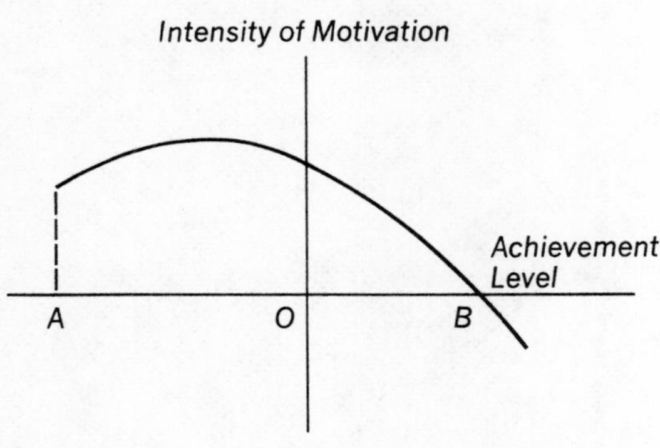

Fig. 43–2

As the achievement level exceeds B, the drive toward improvement of skill disappears. We may call this "satiation." On the other hand, as the achievement level falls below A, the drive changes its character. Instead of engaging in rational, adaptive behavior, the individual in his frustration engages in behavior best described as non-adaptive or "neurotic."

The evidence generally indicates that

[22] *Ibid.*, pp. 492–8.

[23] Norman R. F. Maier, *Psychology in Industry*, pp. 244–7.

[24] *Ibid.*, pp. 57–70.

frustration will not occur if there are alternative activities available that are regarded as desirable. In this case the aspiration level for the first activity will simply fall, until point B is reached. Frustration occurs when *all* alternatives are regarded by the individual as distinctly unpleasant — when he is faced with a dilemma rather than a choice. But this distinction between dilemma and choice suggests, again, a natural zero of motivation which is distinct from the zero of satiation. The latter would seem to correspond best with the notion of zero opportunity cost. . . .

The Incorrigibility of Dream-Reports Limits the Scope of Psychological Measurement

44

from *Dreaming*

NORMAN MALCOLM

The Concept of Dreaming

Where does the concept of dreaming come from? We are strongly inclined to think of dreaming as an inward state or process of the soul, and to suppose that each of us arrives at the concept of dreaming through taking note of the process in himself. But this idea gives rise to insoluble problems. For one thing, how could it be determined that the inner states of different people were the *same* and, therefore, that they meant the same thing by the word 'dreaming?' Even more serious, how could one know that the inner state one calls 'dreaming' is the same in oneself each time? Perhaps there is not enough regularity in one's application of the sound 'dreaming' for it to even qualify as a *word*! An appeal to one's own memory impression of its being the same state each time would be useless, because there would be no possibility of one's determining whether this impression was true or false. I am applying to dreaming the points made by Wittgenstein in his attack on the notion that one learns what thinking, remembering, mental images, sensations, and so on, are from 'one's own case'.[1]

One may think to overcome these difficulties by allowing that the *descriptions* that people give of their private states provide a determination of what those states are and whether they are the same. But if one takes this line (which is correct) one cannot then permit a question to be raised as to whether those descriptions are in error or not — for this would be to fall back into the original difficulty. One must treat the descriptions as the *criterion* of what the inner occurrences are. 'An "inner process" stands in need of outward criteria' (Wittgenstein, § 580).

What we must say, although it seems paradoxical, is that the concept of dreaming is derived, not from dreaming, but from descriptions of dreams, i.e., from the familiar phenomenon that we call 'telling a dream'. If after waking from sleep a child tells us that he saw and did and thought various things, none of which could be true, and if his relation of these incidents has spontaneity and no appearance of invention, then we may say to him 'It was a dream'. We do not question whether he really had a dream or if it merely seems to him that he did.

> People who on waking tell us certain incidents (that they have been in such-and-such places, etc.). Then we teach them the expression 'I dreamt', which precedes the narrative. Afterwards I sometimes ask them 'did you dream anything last night?' and am answered yes or no, sometimes with an account of a dream, sometimes not. That is the language-game . . .
> Now must I make some assumption about whether people are deceived by their memories or not; whether they really had these images while they slept, or whether it merely seems so to them on waking? And what meaning has this question? — And what interest? Do we ever ask ourselves this

From *Dreaming* by Norman Malcolm, Humanities Press, Inc., New York, and Routledge & Kegan Paul, Ltd., London, 1960, pp. 54–90.

[1] For an explanation of these points readers may care to refer to my review of the *Philosophical Investigations* (*Philosophical Review*, October, 1954) and to my article 'Knowledge of Other Minds' (*Journal of Philosophy*, November 6, 1958 Vol. LV, No. 23.)

when someone is telling us his dream? And if not — is it because we are sure his memory won't have deceived him? (And suppose it were a man with a quite specially bad memory? —) (Wittgenstein, p. 184).

That this question is not raised is not a mere matter of fact but is essential to our concept of dreaming. If someone questioned whether there really are dreams corresponding to peoples' reports of dreams presumably he would have some idea of what would settle the question. He would not be using the report of a dream as the criterion of what the dream was, and so he would have to mean something different by 'dreaming'.

Assuming that dreams can yield important information about the dreamer, what yielded the information would be truthful accounts of dreams. The question whether the dreamer's memory deceives him when he reports the dream after waking cannot arise, unless indeed we introduce a completely new criterion for the report's 'agreeing' with the dream, a criterion which gives us a concept of 'truth' as distinct from 'truthfulness' here (*Ibid.*, pp. 222–223).

We speak of 'remembering' dreams, and if we consider this expression it can appear to us to be a misuse of language. When we think philosophically about memory the following sort of paradigm comes most naturally to our minds: I spoke certain words to you yesterday. Today I am requested to give an account of what those words were. The account I give is right or wrong. This is determined by whether it agrees with your account and that of other witnesses, perhaps also by whether it is plausible in the light of what is known about you and me and the circumstances yesterday, and perhaps by still other things. But when I speak of 'remembering' a dream there is nothing outside of my account of the dream (provided that I understand the words that compose it) to determine that my account is right or wrong. I may amend it slightly on a second telling — but only slightly. If I changed it very much or many times it would no longer be said that I was 'telling a dream'. My verbal behaviour would be too unlike the behaviour on which the concept of dreaming is founded.[2] That something is implausible or impossible does not go to show that I did not dream it. In a dream I can do the impossible in every sense of the word. I can climb Everest without oxygen and I can square the circle.[3] Since nothing counts as determining that my memory of my dream is right or wrong, what sense can the word 'memory' have here?

But of course it is no misuse of language to speak of 'remembering a dream'. We are taught this expression. Only we must be mindful of its actual *use* and of how sharply this differs from the use of 'remembering' that appeared in our paradigm. Failure to observe this results in such an argument as the following:

Dreaming is a real experience. And since dreams can be remembered they must be conscious experiences. Just as it is correct to say that a dreamer really dreams and does not merely dream that he dreams, so it is correct to say that a dreamer is really aware of the contents of his dream and does not merely dream that he is aware of them (Yost & Kalish; see Chapter 1).

I do not understand what the first statement ('Dreaming is a real experience') could mean other than that people really do have dreams — which is undeniable. A philosopher has spoken of 'the theory that we don't dream, but only remember that we have dreamt' (Manser, pp. 226–227), but if there is this 'theory' it must result from confusion about the criterion of dreaming. The second statement in the argument above ('And since dreams can be remembered they must be conscious experiences') seems to embody the

[2] We are told that a patient under psychoanalysis may radically revise his first account of a dream, after six months of treatment. Because this reaction is so dissimilar to the normal phenomenon of telling dreams it is better, I think, to say that in psychoanalysis there is a different concept of dreaming than to say that in psychoanalysis one finds out what one really dreamt.

[3] What would be more senseless than to suppose that someone should not be able to distinguish propositions from tables? But Moore had a dream in which he could not do this. See J. M. Keynes, *Two Memoirs* (Hart-Davis, 1949), p. 94.

mistake of supposing that all uses of 'remembering' conform to the same paradigms. If I remember today how someone flapped his arms yesterday, then yesterday I must have been aware of the flapping arms. Does it follow that if I remember today a dream of last night, then last night I must have been aware of the dream or of its 'contents'? First, there is no warrant for thinking that 'remembering a dream' carries exactly the same implications as 'remembering a physical occurrence'. Next, considering the impossibility of establishing that someone was aware of anything at all while asleep and the possibility of establishing that he dreamt how can it *follow* from his remembering a dream that he was aware of the dream when he dreamt it? Finally and most importantly, what is the *meaning* of this pilosophical claim? (For it does not appear to be a mere decision to call dreams 'conscious experiences' because we speak of 'remembering' dreams). What would be one's criterion for saying that a sleeper is aware of his dream? I do not see what it could be other than his telling a dream on waking up. If that is what it is then the use of the philosopher's sentence, 'People are aware of their dreams', is the same as the use of the sentence, 'People have dreams'. Consequently the philosophical claim, 'When people dream they are aware of their dreams' (or: 'Dreams are conscious experiences'), says absolutely nothing.

I know one wishes to make this protest: 'To say that one dreamt is not just to say that, on waking, one has the impression of having dreamt. No: one means that, over and above the impression, a dream was really there!' One might add: 'The impression comes to one when awake but the dream occurred during sleep; therefore they cannot be the same.'

But I am not trying to maintain that a dream *is* the waking impression that one dreamt. This would be self-contradictory. Indeed I am not trying to say what dreaming *is*: I do not understand what it would mean to do that. I merely set forth the reminder that in our daily discourse about dreams what we take as determining beyond question that a man dreamt is that in sincerity he should tell a dream or say he had one.

It is not easy to understand the relation between dreams and waking convictions of having dreamt. The dream and the waking conviction are not one and the same thing, in the sense that the morning star and the evening star are one and the same. Are they *two* things, numerically different? Let us say so. Then the question is: How are these two things related? Can we say they are logically independent of each other in the sense that either could exist regardless of whether the other existed? Now it is possible to think of a case in which a man believes falsely that he did not dream: e.g. he woke up in the middle of the night and told a dream to someone, but on waking in the morning he has the impression of having had a dreamless sleep. The possibility of this case, however, does not prove the logical independence of dreams from waking impressions, because here we relied on his telling a dream in the night as establishing that he dreamt. If we try to suppose that mankind might have told dreams without ever having dreams, or might have had dreams without ever having told dreams, we are in an embarrassment as to what would establish the existence of a dream. We may say that dreams and waking impressions are two different things: but not — two logically independent things.

One cause of difficulty is a temptation to think that when one states the criterion for something one says what that something *is* — one *defines* it. But this is wrong. The criterion of someone's having a sore foot is what he does and says in certain circumstances: and *that* is not a sore foot. Considering this, one may be inclined to think that there cannot be a *criterion* (something that settles a question with certainty) of someone's having a sore foot or having dreamt, but merely various 'outer' phenomena that are empirically correlated with sore feet and dreams. This view, however, is self-contradictory: without criteria for the occurrence of these things the correlations could not be established. Without criteria the sentences 'His foot is sore', 'He had a dream', would have no use, either correct or incorrect. We must admit that there is a criterion for the use of 'He dreamt' and also admit that it does not tell us what a dream *is*, does not give the 'essence' of dreaming (whatever that might mean), but gives the conditions that determine whether the statement 'He dreamt' is true or false.

Our puzzlement over the criterion of dreaming is partly due to the fact that the sentence for which we want a criterion is in the *past* tense. How can a present occurrence, a person's telling a dream, be the criterion for something that happened previously, the dream? Well, why not? If we abandon the assumption that the criterion and the something of which it is the criterion must be identical, then why cannot a present occurrence be the criterion of a past occurrence? We feel a reluctance to admit that this can be so, and we incline towards the thought that the criterion of the occurrence of a dream is to be found in some behaviour, or in some physiological process, that is supposed to be simultaneous with the dream. This reluctance is largely due, I think, to the assumption just mentioned. But a contributing factor is a certain haziness that is present on the periphery of our ordinary discourse about dreams. I will explain this.

If a young man in love utters his sweetheart's name in his sleep and smiles and sighs, it would be natural for anyone to say 'He is dreaming about his sweetheart'. But how should we be using this sentence? I mean: should we be predicting that if he were awakened he would be able to relate a dream or at least say he had one? Is our criterion his testimony on waking or his present behaviour? We say of a dog, when he whines and twitches his feet in sleep, 'He must be having a dream': and here there is no question of what he will tell us when he wakes up. This use of language is not quite serious; one draws no practical consequences from the supposition that a dog is dreaming. But in the case of the young man who says 'Mabel' in his sleep we might draw important conclusions (e.g. that he should be introduced to some other girl). If on waking he does not recall a dream we may say 'You have forgotten it'. But how are we using *this* expression? Does it just mean 'So; you have no dream to tell?', or does it mean 'You had a dream all right but now it has slipped your mind?'

One might suppose that when we say 'He is dreaming', on the basis of his sighs and mutterings in sleep, that either we are using his behaviour as our *criterion* that he is dreaming or else as *evidence* that he will be able to relate a dream, the latter being our criterion. This would be so if our use of language was always clearly one thing or another, always had a definite purpose. I believe that here it is not so. When we say that someone is dreaming on the basis of his behaviour in sleep, our words do not fall definitely into either alternative, and indeed have no clear sense.

The case of nightmares is somewhat different. It is certain that there is *a* sense of 'nightmare' where the criterion is behaviour. When a man cries out, struggles, appears to be afraid, is difficult to arouse, and continues to exhibit traces of fear as he awakens, we call it a nightmare regardless of whether he can tell a dream. His state was, however, so unlike the paradigms of normal sleep that it is at least problematic whether it should be said that he was 'asleep' when those struggles were going on.

These odd phenomena and curious uncertainties in our use of language should not obscure the fact that our primary concept of dreaming has for its criterion, not the behaviour of a sleeping person but his subsequent testimony. If someone tells a dream we do not think of doubting its occurrence on the ground that his sleep was thoroughly quiet and relaxed. In this sense of 'dream' a dream has a *content* (a dog's dream has none) which is described when the dream is related. Dreaming in this primary sense is of great interest to people and also poses philosophical problems. Dreaming that has a purely behavioural criterion is of little interest.

Perhaps the greatest cause of perplexity about the telling of a dream as the criterion of the occurrence of a dream is the fact that one cannot apply this criterion to oneself. One does not find out that oneself had a dream by applying that criterion. One uses it only for 'He had a dream', not for 'I had a dream'. This asymmetry may lead one to deny that the third person sentence is governed by this criterion. 'I do not determine that *I* had a dream on the basis of my telling a dream. I use "I had a dream" and "He had a dream" in the *same* sense. Therefore, that another person tells a dream cannot be the thing that determines for me that he had a dream'. The trouble with this fallacious argument lies in the phrase 'the same sense'. One can rightly say that the two sentences are used in the same sense, as contrasted (for example) with the case in which the word 'dream' in one of them meant day-dream. But what *is* 'the same sense' here? To use the sentences of this asymmetrical pair in the same sense (in so far as they can be used in the same sense) is to use them in the normal way, where telling a dream serves as a criterion of verification for the one but not the other. To use the sentences 'I weigh 170 pounds' and 'He weighs 170 pounds' in the same sense, in contrast, is to use them in accordance with the same method of verification (same or similar methods of weighing). What it is to use the sentences of a first person third person pair 'in the same sense' depends on what their normal use is. One cannot deduce what their normal use is from the fact that they are used in the same sense.

From the fact that one does not use the above criterion for deciding that one dreamt does it follow that there is not such a thing as *knowing* one dreamt? No. One has grounds sometimes for concluding that one dreamt, and this is knowledge in a proper sense of the word. An example would be to wake up with the impression that one had just painted the bedroom walls blue, and then to note that the walls are still yesterday's yellow: 'So it was a dream'. To find out one dreamt the incident is to find out that the impression one had on waking is false. As one can know one dreamt, so can one be mistaken. You wake up, for example, with the impression that a policeman came into your room during the night; other people in the house *say* this did not occur; you conclude you dreamt it: but the event really happened and the others conspired to deceive you. Suppose you awoke with the impression that you had felt a pain in your leg during the night but you did not know whether this was dream or reality. Would it be impossible for this question to be settled? No, not impossible. Someone might have heard you cry out and seen you hold your leg at some time in the night. There is a temptation to think that with pain there is no difference between 'real' and 'dreamt'. But there is as much of a distinction here as between having quarrelled with someone and having dreamt that one quarrelled.

I am inclined to believe that statements of the form 'I dreamt so and so' are always inferential in nature. I do not mean that one always arrives at them by explicit processes of inference but rather that one might always defend them as conclusions from certain facts or supposed facts. If someone were to ask you how you knew that you dreamt so and so, you could always mention something that you supposed proved or made probable that the thing in question did not occur and that therefore you dreamt it.

What can have no justification and requires none is your statement that you have the *impression* that so and so occurred. (You may or may not believe that it did occur.) In this sense you cannot find out that you dreamt, although you can find out that someone else dreamt. What it does make sense to find out is whether your impression corresponds with reality, and to discover that it does not is to discover that you had a dream.

I said previously that in a dream anything is possible. We can see why this is so. If we know that it is impossible for a certain thing to have occurred then the waking impression that it occurred is false, and we know therefore that one dreamt the impossible thing. Where the choice is between dream and reality the impossibility, in any sense, of a thing places it in a dream.

My assertion that the question 'How do you know you dreamt so and so?' can have the sense just described may appear to conflict with the claim at the beginning of this chapter that it is part of our concept of dreaming that we do not question whether someone had a dream or whether it merely seems to him that he did. But there is no conflict. What was meant there was that when someone on awaking 'remembers' certain incidents, and we know they did not occur, then we say he *dreamt* them, i.e. they 'occurred in a dream'. There is not a *further* question of whether a dream or the events of a dream really took place during sleep. If a man wakes up with the impression of having seen and done various things, and if it is known that he did not see and do those things, then it is known that he dreamt them. No problem remains of whether a dream really existed during his sleep, of whether anything *corresponds* to his memory of a dream.

It is to be noted that when someone says he dreamt so and so, he does not imply that while he was sleeping he was aware of being asleep or was aware of dreaming. When he says 'I dreamt so and so' he implies, first, that it seemed to him on waking up as if the so and so had occurred and, second, that the so and so did not occur. There is simply no place here for an implication or assumption that he was aware of anything at all while asleep. His testimony that he had a dream does not involve that nonsensical consequence.

I have said that the statement 'I dreamt such and such' implies that the such and such did not occur. Let us consider Pharaoh's dream, recorded in *Genesis* XLI, 17–24: (Revised Standard Version).

Behold, in my dream I was standing on the banks of the Nile; and seven cows, fat and sleek, came up out of the Nile and fed in the reed grass; and seven other cows came up after them, poor and very gaunt and thin, such as I had never seen in all the land of Egypt. And the thin and gaunt cows ate up the first seven fat cows, but when they had eaten them no one would have known that they had eaten them, for they were still as gaunt as at the beginning. Then I awoke. I also saw in my dream seven ears growing on one stalk, full and good; and seven ears, withered, thin, and blighted by the east wind, sprouted after them, and the thin ears swallowed up the seven good ears.

It is plain enough that if Pharaoh had believed that during the night he had actually gone out and stood on the banks of the Nile and seen seven thin cows eat up seven fat ones, he would not have put into his narrative the phrase 'in my dream'. But suppose Pharaoh's tale had gone like this: 'Behold, in the night it seemed to me that I was standing on the banks of the Nile; and it seemed to me that seven cows, fat and sleek, came up out of the Nile and fed in the reed grass; . . . etc.'. Would his declaration that this was a dream have the force of implying that it did not *seem* to him that he stood on the banks of the Nile, and all the rest?[4] Yes. For suppose it was independently known that it had seemed to him, at some time during the night, that those things were occurring. Suppose that someone had observed him to sit up in bed and exclaim 'Behold, there is the Nile before me and, lo, here are seven cows, fat and sleek . . .' Let us suppose that he stared, gestured and pointed as a man might who was hallucinated. Then we should have corrected his morning's narrative, saying 'No, it was not a dream. You had an hallucination at about midnight last night, in which those things appeared to you'.[5]

There is a restriction that needs to be put on the principle that 'I dreamt that p' implies 'not-p'. Someone in California might dream one night that Westminster Abbey was destroyed by fire and discover the next

[4] Note Descartes' remark: '. . . in sleep we continually seem to feel or imagine innumerable things which have no existence' (Descartes (2), I, p. 220).

[5] I am denying that a dream *qua* dream is a seeming, appearance or 'semblance of reality'. In telling a dream, however, one can say 'It seemed . . .', when this means that there was a vagueness or uncertainty in the dream. Otherwise it would be wrong to use this locution.

day that this had really happened. In this sense a dream could be 'veridical'. But if his dream narrative contained statements like 'I *saw* it burning', 'I *heard* the walls crashing'; or 'It *seemed to me* that I could see it burning and hear the walls crashing' — those statements, which ostensibly report experiences he had while asleep, would all be false. If we try to consider the statements composing the description of a dream in the normal use that they have outside of dream-telling discourse, then those among them that ostensibly report experiences of the speaker, are *necessarily* false — for if they were not false they could not properly be said to belong to the description of a *dream*. (Thus the claim is mistaken that it is merely a *contingent* matter that the visual, auditory and tactual contents of dreams are 'non-veridical'. See page 8.) There is however another way in which all the statements in a dream report, both those ostensibly reporting experiences and those ostensibly reporting physical events, may be taken, and when taken in this way 'I dreamt that *p*' entails '*p*'. This will be explained in Chapter 15.

Temporal Location and Duration of Dreams

Since the notion of a dream as an occurrence that is logically independent of the sleeper's waking impression has no clear sense, it follows that the notions of the location and duration of a dream in physical time also have no clear sense. I mean that this is so if one keeps to the primary concept, where the sole criterion of the occurrence of a dream is the waking report. One may be easily tempted however to *give* a sense to these notions, as the following will illustrate.

A considerable amount of scientific work has had the aim of trying to establish correlations between dreaming and various physiological phenomena such as brain potentials, action currents, galvanic skin responses, and blood pressure. I will refer to one very recent study. The authors begin by saying:

> The study of dream activity and its relation to physiological variables during sleep necessitates a reliable method of determining with precision when dreaming occurs. This knowledge, in the final analysis, always depends upon the subjective report of the dreamer, but becomes relatively objective if such reports can be significantly related to some physiological phenomena which in turn can be measured by physical techniques (Dement & Kleitman, p. 339).

The physiological phenomenon studied in their experiments was rapid eye movements, recorded by sensitive instruments. The procedure was to waken the subjects from sleep during periods of rapid eye movements (abbreviated 'REM') and also during periods when there were no rapid eye movements (abbreviated 'NREM'), in order to find out whether they could recall dreams. With 9 subjects there were 191 awakenings during REM periods and 160 awakenings during NREM periods. The incidence of dream recall was high after the REM awakenings (152 out of 191) and low after the NREM awakenings (11 out of 160). It was observed that the duration of REM periods that were not terminated artificially by an awakening varied from 3 to 50 minutes with a mean of about 20 minutes. This was thought to suggest a measure of the duration of dreams. To test this the following experiment was performed: Subjects were awakened either 5 or 15 minutes after the beginning of REM's and 'were required on the basis of their recall of the dream to decide which was the correct duration' of the dream. In 51 of the 5 minute awakenings the subjects decided in favour of 5 minutes a total of 45 times; in 60 of the 15 minute awakenings they decided in favour of 15 minutes a total of 47 times. The authors' conclusion is that all subjects, with one exception, 'were able to choose the correct dream duration with high accuracy'. They say of the one exceptional 'inaccurate' subject that he 'made most of his incorrect choices by estimating 15 minutes to be 5 minutes'. They add:

> This is consistent with the interpretation that the dream was longer, but he was only able to recall

the latter fraction and thus thought it was shorter than it actually was (p. 343).

They also say:

In addition to depending on the amount of actual dreaming, the lengths of the dream narratives were undoubtedly influenced by many other factors as, for example, the loquacity or taciturnity of S [the subject] (*Ibid.*).

An ingenious attempt was made to correlate the REM's with dream content. Sometimes the REM's were mainly vertical, sometimes mainly horizontal, sometimes a mixture of both. 'It was hypothesized that the movements represented the visual imagery of the dream, that is, that they corresponded to where and at what the dreamer was looking'. Only three cases of purely vertical movements were observed.

After each of these the dream content involved a predominance of action in the vertical plane. One S dreamed of standing at the bottom of a tall cliff operating some sort of hoist and looking up at climbers at various levels and down at the hoist machinery. Another S dreamed of climbing up a series of ladders looking up and down as he climbed. In the third instance the dreamer was throwing basketballs at a net, first shooting and looking up at the net, and then looking down to pick another ball off the floor. Only one instance of pure horizontal movement was seen. In the associated dream S was watching two people throwing tomatoes at each other (p. 344).

Twenty-one awakenings occurred after a mixture of movements and always the subjects reported that in their dreams they were looking at things close to them. Finally, the eye movements of subjects who were awake and were observing either distant or nearby occurrences, were recorded by the same apparatus. 'The eye-movement potentials in all cases were comparable in both amplitude and pattern to those occurring during dreaming'.

The following are among the conclusions drawn by the authors: The experiments indicate that dreaming 'occurred periodically in discreet episodes during the course of a night's sleep', that is to say, in periods of rapid eye movements. The few examples of dream recall when there were no eye movements 'are best accounted for by assuming that the memory of the preceding dream persisted for an unusually long time. This is borne out by the fact that most of these instances occurred very close, within 8 minutes, after the end of REM periods' (p. 345). Some previous views about the duration and 'progress' of dreams appear to have evidence against them:

There was nothing in the experiments reported in this paper to indicate that the dreams occurred instantaneously, or with great rapidity, as some have supposed. Rather, they seemed to progress at a rate comparable to a real experience of the same sort. An increment in the length of REM periods was almost invariably associated with a proportional increase in the length of the dream (p. 346).

Finally:

It seems reasonable to conclude that an objective measurement of dreaming may be accomplished by recording REM's during sleep. This stands in marked contrast to the forgetting, distortion, and other factors that are involved in the reliance on the subjective recall of dreams. It thus becomes possible to objectively study the effect on dreaming of environmental changes, psychological stress, drug administration, and a variety of other factors and influences (*Ibid.*).

These experimental findings would incline many people to want to employ the phenomenon of rapid eye movements as the *criterion* of the occurrence, temporal location and duration of dreams. If one consciously decided to do this one would then say of a person awakened during a period of these movements, who could recall no dream, that he had *forgotten* the dream (which undoubtedly occurred). One could say even that he had not been *aware* of the dream (just as it is often said that people are not always aware of their sensations); for what would be the difference here between saying that he had been aware of the dream but forgot it, and saying that he had not been aware of it when it occurred? The temptation to take the latter step would be nearly irresistible if a person who was awakened during an REM period insisted that he had *not* been dreaming. If someone had a 'long' dream (as measured by the duration of the REM period) but could recall only a 'short' dream (as measured by the number of words in his dream narrative and also by his impression that it was a 'short' dream) then one would say that he remembered only a 'fraction' of the dream, as Dement and Kleitman actually suggest. If a person who was awakened during a period of no eye movements related a dream, one would say (as Dement and Kleitman 'assume') that his memory of the *preceding* dream had persisted.

I do not claim that Dement and Kleitman actually made the decision to use eye movements as their criterion of dreaming. If they had done so, deliberately and consciously, their conclusions would not be as tentative as they are. At the same time they are strongly drawn toward that decision, and this is understandable. They want to do *scientific* work on dreams and therefore they need 'a reliable method of determining with precision when dreaming occurs' and exactly how long it lasts. This need is not filled by the criterion of 'subjective reports' of dreams.

The interest in a physiological criterion of dreaming is due, I believe, to an error that philosophers, psychologists, physiologists and everyone who reflects on the nature of dreaming tends to commit, namely, of supposing that a dream *must* have a definite location and duration in physical time. (This is an excellent example of what Wittgenstein calls a 'prejudice' produced by 'grammatical illusions'). It might be replied that a dream is surely an *event* and that an event must have a definite date and duration in physical time. But this gets one nowhere, for what justifies the claim that a dream is an event in *that* sense? There can be only as much precision in the common concept of dreaming as is provided by the common criterion of dreaming. The testimony of the sleeper does sometimes determine *when* a dream occurred. A man may say that he was dreaming 'just before' he awakened, or that he woke up 'in the middle' of a dream, or that in his dream he jumped from a cliff 'and then awoke'. This testimony does not provide however a determination that would be satisfactory to physical science. One has no idea what 'just before' the sleeper awakened would amount to on the clock: it is not *that* sort of determination. It is something he is *inclined to say* on waking up. It is no part of the concept of dreams to provide a translation of this impression into physical time.

There is however a feature of dream-telling that does appear to yield a determination in physical time. People often make connections between their dreams and physical events: e.g. 'I dreamt it was thundering; the thunder grew louder and louder; finally I awoke and realized that it was the hammering of the radiator'. It would seem that the dream is simultaneous with the physical event and therefore an exact time of occurrence by the clock can be fixed for both. Here the connection with a physical event was made directly by the testimony of the awakened person. But it might be established in a different way. It might be proved (and indeed there is considerable evidence for it — e.g. Ramsey, pp. 441–442) that the contents of dreams can be causally influenced by external stimulation of the sleeper (e.g. if his blankets were removed he would dream of snow, icebergs, and freezing cold). Then would it not be certain that the dream occurred at the same time as (or after) the physical event that causally influenced the content of the dream?

It would certainly be overwhelmingly natural for us to adopt this *convention* — for that is what it would be. No one would have directly observed any causal or temporal relation between dreams and physical occurrences (nor would it make sense to do so), but only between *reports* of dreams and physical occurrences. Since our usual criterion of the occurrence of a dream is the report, the natural step to take in assigning a location in physical time to a dream would be to say that the dream was simultaneous with the physical occurrence during sleep, if there was one, that influenced the waking account of the dream. This would be a definition and not a discovery. One is not *required* to give any sense to the location of dreams in physical time.

It might be said that since dreams occur *in* or *during* sleep, and since sleep is a phenomenon in physical time, therefore dreams must occur in physical time. But here one is being carried away by spatial imagery. The locution that dreams occur 'in' sleep is used in this way: people declare on awaking that various incidents *took* place (past tense) which did not take place. We then say that these incidents were *dreamt* (past tense). This is merely how we label the above facts, which imply nothing about the occurrence of dreams in physical time.

The natural convention mentioned above would still have unsatisfactory features from the standpoint of physical science. It would still rely on the awakened person's report; it would provide no criterion for the temporal location of dreams whose content could not be connected with external stimulation during sleep; and it would provide no criterion of *duration*. Consider this last point. There is of course a familiar notion of the duration of dreams. In telling a dream one sometimes says it was a 'short' or a 'long' dream. This is one's waking impression. But this is not duration in physical time. Dream-telling cannot yield *that* concept. Here it becomes obvious how new convention — stipulation — must enter the scene if that concept is to be provided.

Dement and Kleitman speak of the 'length' of a dream without realizing, apparently, that it has no clear sense and must be given one. They say that an increase in the length of the period of rapid eye movements was 'almost invariably associated with a proportional increase in the length of the dream' (p. 346). But what is their criterion of the *length* of a dream? It should not be the duration of the associated REM period, for that would make nonsense of their assertion of a *proportional relation* between the two. Yet their article contains an indication that this *is* their criterion. In giving an account of their experiment with the 'dream-duration estimates' of their subjects (where the latter were awakened after either 5 or 15 minutes of rapid eye movements and 'required on the basis of their recall of the dream to decide which was the correct duration') they report that all subjects save one 'were able to choose the correct dream duration with high accuracy' (p. 343). How is it decided what the correct dream duration was? Nothing explicit is said on this point in the article. The most plausible conjecture is that their criterion of the duration of a dream is the duration of the associated REM period. But if the duration of the two is identical then it is truly nonsense to say that an increase in the duration of the REM periods was 'almost invariably associated with a proportional increase in the length of the dream' (p. 346).

These physiologists are in a muddle about the duration of dreams because, I think, they do not realize that in the familiar concept of dreaming there is no provision for the duration of dreams in physical time.[6] They assume that this provision is already *there*, only somewhat obscured and in need of being made more precise. The truth is that this notion does not belong to the common concept of dreaming at all. To see this is to realize that to bring it in is to create a new concept under an old label.

That Dement and Kleitman have an erroneous picture of the concept of dreaming comes out, I believe, in their choice of the phrase 'the subjective report of the dreamer' (p. 339), and in their concluding remark that rapid eye movements would seem to provide

[6] Empirical studies of dreaming have produced the most divergent estimates of the duration of dreams, some investigators holding that dreams rarely last more than 1 or 2 seconds: others believe that it is 1 to 10 minutes. Dement and Kleitman, as reported above, think that dreams last as long as 50 minutes and that the average length is 20 minutes. These different estimates arise solely from the employment of different criteria of measurement. For an interesting survey of experimental work on dreams see Ramsey's article.

'an objective measurement of dreaming' in contrast to the ordinary reliance on the 'subjective recall' of dreams (p. 346). They take for granted that the distinction 'subjective-objective' applies to dreams. This distinction is identical with the distinction of 'appearance and reality'. But if someone tells a dream or says he had one he is not making a 'subjective' report which may or may not agree with 'objective' fact. His waking impression is what establishes that he had a dream, and his account of his dream establishes what the content of his dream was. If he has a vague impression of his dream then it was a vague dream. If he is not certain whether he dreamt then there is an uncertainty in reality. His impression is the criterion of reality and therefore it cannot be characterized as 'subjective'. 'Subjective' and 'objective' are *one* in the case of dreams — which is to say that this distinction does not apply.

Without an adequate realization of what they are doing, Dement and Kleitman are proposing a new concept in which the notions of location and duration in physical time and the subjective-objective distinction will all have a place. We ought to consider the consequences of these stipulations and ask ourselves whether it is appropriate to call this creation a concept of *dreaming*. If rapid eye movements during sleep became the criterion of dreaming one consequence is that if someone were to tell a dream it could turn out that his impression that he dreamt was *mistaken* — and not in the sense that the incidents he related had really occurred and so his impression was not of a dream but of reality. The new concept would allow him to be mistaken in saying he had a dream even if his impression that he had seen and done various things was false. Another consequence is that it would be possible to discover that a man's assertion that he had slept a dreamless sleep was in error: and here one would have to choose between saying either that he forgot his dreams or that he had not been aware of them when he dreamt them. People would have to be *informed* on waking up that they had dreamt or not — instead of their informing us, as it now is. It could turn out that there was a tribe of people among whom the phenomenon of telling a dream was quite unknown — and yet physiological experiments proved that all of them dreamt every night.

Consider how differently the new concept would be *taught*. As things are, a certain kind of narrative produced in certain circumstances is what we call 'telling a dream', and we teach a child to preface such narratives with the word 'I dreamt'. If the physiological criterion were adopted, telling a dream would be only a more or less reliable indication of dreaming. It would not be, as now, a matter of definition that someone who told a dream had dreamt. We should not be justified in teaching him to begin those narratives with 'I dreamt'. To teach him the new concept of dreaming we should have to explain the physiological experiment that provides the new criterion. If mankind should cease to tell dreams the physiological criterion of dreaming could still be employed with possible affirmative results. Much information about the 'dreaming habits' of people might continue to be collected. But what were then called 'dreams' would no longer be of interest to poets, psychoanalysts, philosophers, and to all of us, children and adults, who like a strange tale.

Considering the radical conceptual changes that the adoption of a physiological criterion would entail, it is evident that a new concept would have been created that only remotely resembled the old one. To use the name 'dreaming' for the new concept would spring from confusion and result in confusion. All of this can be avoided by holding firmly to waking testimony as the sole criterion of dreaming. Physiological phenomena, such as rapid eye movements or muscular action currents, may be found to stand in interesting empirical correlations with dreaming, but the possibility of these discoveries presupposes that these phenomena are *not* used as the criterion of dreaming. The desire to know more about dreaming should not lead scientists into transforming the concept in such a way that their subsequent discoveries do not pertain to *dreaming*.

A Queer Phenomenon

I have stressed the senselessness, in the sense of impossibility of verification, of the notion of a dream as an occurrence 'in its own right', logically independent of the waking impression, and to which the latter may or may not 'correspond'. Prior to that I argued that dreams cannot contain, or be identical with, judging, reasoning, feeling, imagery, and so on, for the reason that with respect to any of these things the question, 'How can it be *known* that this took place while he was *asleep*?', cannot be successfully answered — whereas the question, 'How can it be known that his *dream* occurred while he was *asleep*?', cannot be sensibly asked because of the entailment between dreaming and sleep. It may appear that these points are in conflict. On the one hand I say that the occurrence of a dream during sleep is impossible of verification, *if* one tries to conceive of dreaming as logically independent of the waking impression. On the other hand I say that the occurrence of reasoning, feeling, imagery, etc., during sleep is impossible of verification. Therefore the mark of distinction, which I laboured to make out, between dreams and these other things, seems to have vanished.

This is the appearance, but nevertheless the distinction is preserved, as I will try to explain. The question about the 'real existence' of dreams, i.e. whether dreams take place in logical independence of waking impressions, and whether the latter correspond or not to the dreams, is a purely metaphysical question that does not arise in the ordinary commerce of life and language. If one knew that someone was telling a dream in all naturalness and sincerity, one would have to be in a philosophical humour to propound a doubt as to whether a dream had really occurred during his sleep or whether he was mistaken in thinking so. One cannot have this doubt without violating in one's thinking the common use of language. This is not at all the case with respect to someone's imagined claim that he reasoned, made a decision, remembered something, felt a sensation, etc., while he slept. 'How do you know this occurred while you *slept*?', would be a natural and legitimate question, with nothing metaphysical about it. It would betray no confusion about the common concepts of dreaming and sleep. Quite the contrary. This proper question would cry to be asked: but no respectable answer could be made out — which would show that something was wrong with the claim that gave rise to the question.

Suppose however that no one did ask this question, not because of neglect or dull-wittedness, but because the question was considered to be inappropriate. What I am supposing is that we might take someone's assertion that he reasoned or made a decision or had some experience, *while he slept*, in such a sense that the request for proof or grounds ('How do you know this happened while you slept?'), was irrelevant — not a part of 'the language-game'. If we did this we should be taking the assertion in the same sense as the report of a dream!

To be sure, if his whole statement was merely, say, that he had made such and such a decision while asleep, we should not call this a report of a dream, because a *dream* is supposed to involve a number of incidents connected in some fashion. Telling a dream is telling a kind of *story*. In the story there can occur several incidents like deciding to quit one's job or feeling angry. To relate merely a single thing of this sort is not to tell a dream. But this is not an important point here. What is important is that the relation of some single happening or act (feeling angry or solving a problem) as having occurred during sleep, would have the same conceptual status as the report of a dream, *if* a request for grounds was inappropriate.

We can imagine a tribe of people who do not have any locution equivalent to 'I dreamt'. Sometimes they wake up with the impression of having thought, done, decided and felt various things while asleep. Their reports of these occurrences are taken in the way just supposed, the question of verification not being for them a relevant question. It would be right for the anthropologists who observed them to say that their reports are reports of *dreams*, even though these people have no words equivalent to 'dream' or 'dreamt'.

In general the expression 'I dreamt', as we use it, serves as a sign that the ensuing narrative of incidents in sleep is to be taken in this special sense, namely, that it will be inappropriate to request grounds for the statements that compose it. One could say: we accept the narrative without proof, not because we *assume* it will be true, but because the concept of truth that applies here has nothing to do with proof. In this respect telling a dream is like imagining something ('You are the mama tiger and I am the baby tiger'). It is unlike in the important respect that in it there is no place for inventiveness, for changing one's mind, for having things as one will. One tells a dream under the influence of an impression — *as if* one was faithfully recalling events that one witnessed. Telling a dream is undoubtedly a queer phenomenon.

'This "queer phenomenon" requires an *explanation*', we are inclined to protest: 'The most likely explanation of our seeming to recall certain experiences from sleep is that we did *have* those experiences while we slept'. But an 'explanation' explains nothing if it involves an unintelligible hypothesis. Nothing can count for or against the truth of this hypothesis. We can say either that there were experiences during sleep or that there were not, as we like. Whichever assertion we care to make, it can play no part in our daily employment of the concept of dreaming. 'A wheel that can be turned though nothing else moves with it, is not part of the mechanism' (Wittgenstein, § 271).

The above protest may take different forms. One can be puzzled as to why dreams are related in the *past tense*, if we did not actually think and experience various things in our past sleep. Or one can be struck by the fact that in relating dreams we use the *same language* that we employ in describing our normal perceptions. 'The cloak you wore in my dream was this identical red' (pointing at a piece of cloth). 'How can we make such a comparison as this', one wonders, 'unless we were aware in our sleep of something, possibly an image, of that exact colour? Surely we employ the same words *because* we experience in sleep things that are qualitatively similar to the things we experience when awake' (Yost & Kalish, p. 119).

Such 'inferences' get us nowhere: they turn a wheel that moves nothing. 'Our mistake is to look for an explanation where we ought to look at what happens as a "proto-phenomenon". That is, where we ought to have said: *this language-game is played*' (Wittgenstein, § 654). In a lecture Wittgenstein once said that it is an important thing in philosophy to know when to *stop*. If we cease to ask *why* it is that sometimes when people wake up they relate stories in the past tense under the influence of an impression, then we will see dream-telling as it is — a remarkable human phenomenon, a part of the natural history of man, something *given*, the foundation for the concept of dreaming.

It may be thought wrong to call dream-telling a 'language-game'. Wittgenstein introduces this phrase in connection with such examples as giving orders, teaching names, and counting objects, where there are various related actions of fetching things, repeating words, pointing, etc. He says he will 'call the whole, consisting of language and the actions into which it is woven, the "language-game" ' (*Ibid.*, § 7). But with dream-telling there are no actions but only language! For another thing, a 'language-game' is supposed to be something that is *learned*, and does one *learn* to tell dreams? We do have to learn the language we employ in telling dreams but the teaching occurs elsewhere and not in a language-game of dream-telling. To be sure we are taught to use the noun and verb 'dream'. But this is not essential: dreams could be told without this locution.

What we must learn is to *take* an after-sleep narration in a certain way: trying to ascertain if it is an invention or if it proceeds from a genuine impression; distinguishing this impression from a true or false recollection of events that occurred before the person slept, or while he (ostensibly) slept; not questioning the accuracy of the impression but accepting the narrative on the speaker's say-so. Learning to take an awakened person's past tense narrative in this way is learning the concept of dreaming. The speaker too cannot be said to have the concept unless he knows that his narrative is to be taken like that. To the extent he was unclear about this, it would be doubtful whether he was telling a dream, or relating events he believed himself to have participated in the day before, or making up a story, or a number of other things.

I heard of a small boy who, on waking up one morning, excitedly told a story about being chased by a wolf. He had tried to run into the house and struggled frantically with the kitchen door as the beast rushed toward him. Finally he got the door open and escaped. His mother said, 'It was a dream'. The boy exclaimed angrily, 'Well the next time I have a dream you leave the kitchen door open!' His mother knew the boy was telling a dream but the boy did not. We see here an ambiguity in 'He told a dream'. In a sense the boy did not tell a dream — he did not intend that his sentences should be given that special sense described above. But his mother gave them that sense when she said, 'It was a dream'.

There is a particular mode of employing and taking sentences that must be mastered for it to be true that one is telling a dream or understanding someone else to be telling a dream. This is the 'game' one learns. What is it then that is *not* learned? It is the initial inclination to *say* things like 'I was in a strange house; I saw the walls begin to sway; I became frightened and then I woke up'. This is the 'raw material' of the concept. The corresponding raw material in the language-game of 'slab and beam' (Wittgenstein, § 2) is, I suppose, the pupil's tendency to *respond* to the instructor's commands and gestures, e.g. to *look* where the latter points.

This comparison may, however, make the difference appear too slight. One reason for reluctance to speak of a 'language-game' of dream-telling is that the idea of a teacher-pupil relationship seems unsuitable there. No words need be taught at all. 'You dreamt it' could be taught but does not have to be. A peculiar mode of employing indicative sentences must be 'picked up'. There is rarely, if ever, explicit teaching. But this seems to be only a matter of degree: for when people learn games (in the normal sense of 'game') they commonly pick up more than they are explicitly taught.

I have no particular interest in defending the application of the phrase 'language-game' to dream-telling. A language-game is 'a game with language'. In dream-telling sentences are used and taken in a special way. Those *same* sentences are also used in quite other ways. Here the analogy with games is natural and striking. It is as if one made moves in chess with chess pieces, but sometimes used those *same* pieces to make moves in checkers, a very different game! There is some analogical appropriateness in saying that in dream-telling we are employing language in a game that differs sharply from the game we play with those same pieces of language when we describe a recent adventure or make up a story. On the other hand, dream-telling is a long way from 'slab-beam'. There is no 'whole, consisting of language and the actions into which it is woven'; no new words need be introduced; no explicit teaching need occur. Furthermore, dream-telling presupposes a previous mastery of uses of language that are very different from its use in dream-telling. 'Slab-beam' does not presuppose any previous understanding of language: it could be 'a complete primitive language' (*Ibid.*). Dream-telling could not. Considering these differences, if you regard 'slab-beam' as a *paradigm* of 'language-games' (which is a mistake, for it is intended to be an illustration of only *one* use of language) you will think it wrong to call dream-telling a language-game. But nothing of importance turns on accepting or rejecting this term of art.

Bibliography

DEMENT, W. and N. KLEITMAN. 'The Relation of Eye Movements During Sleep to Dream Activity: An Objective Method for the Study of Dreaming,' *Journal of Experimental Psychology*, Vol. 53, (1957), pp. 339–346.

DESCARTES, R. *The Philosophical Works of Descartes*, E. HALDANE and G. ROSS, 2 vols. (Cambridge, 1934).

MANSER, A. R. and L. E. THOMAS, *Symposium:* 'Dreams', *Proceedings of the Aristotelian Society*, Suppl. Vol. 30 (1956).

RAMSEY, G. 'Studies of Dreaming', *Psychological Bulletin*, Vol. 50 (1953).

WITTGENSTEIN, L. *Philosophical Investigations*. Blackwell, Oxford; Macmillan, New York, 1953).

YOST, R. M. Jr. and D. KALISH, 'Miss MacDonald on Sleeping and Waking,' *Philosophical Quarterly*, April (1955), pp. 109–124.

VII

THE INDIVIDUAL: PRODUCT or MAKER of SOCIETY?

Selection 38 employed the principle of methodological individualism (MI) to underwrite an analysis of ideal types which is incompatible with proposition 5 of the covering law view. In what follows, this principle receives further elaboration, confronts a variety of philosophical objections, and is set against ongoing programs of social science inquiry which firmly reject it. The exchanges between J. W. N. Watkins and his two philosophical critics are likely to leave the reader somewhat dissatisfied. It is not so much that the arguments offered are inconclusive, or that they involve false or question-begging premises. The difficulty is that these exchanges never seem to develop any stable or well defined content for the principle under debate. Watkins first presented his principle, in selection 38, as a "methodological rule," but one which "presupposes the *factual assertion* that human social systems are not organisms [in which] teleological principles that apply to the whole" determine what acts are performed by individuals (emphasis added). This factual presupposition appears to render MI empirically testable; in principle, we could observe a human society which shaped the behavior of its members to the same extent as the bisected beehives discussed on page 462 above. Yet in "Historical Explanation in the Social Sciences," Watkins views MI as not only methodological but metaphysical: like mechanism, "it is untestable. No experiment could overthrow it . . . it is a *regulative*, non-vacuous metaphysical principle."

The ambiguities in MI are further compounded by a remark Watkins makes in distinguishing MI from mechanism. "No description," he claims,

> however complete, of the productive apparatus of a society, or of any other non-psychological factors, will enable you to deduce a single psychological conclusion from it, because psychological statements logically cannot be deduced from wholly non-psychological ones. Thus whereas the mechanistic idea that explanations in physics cannot go beyond the impenetrable particles is a prejudice . . . , the analagous idea that an explanation which begins by imputing some social phenomena to human factors cannot go on to explain those factors in terms of some inhuman determinant of them is a necessary truth. [See page 607 below.]

But if MI is a *necessary truth*, how can it be a "regulative principle," directing inquiry towards certain kinds of explanations or theories and away from others? How can it be parallel to mechanism, which Watkins describes as "incompatible with various conceivable physical *theories*?" Watkins, apparently, construes the logical status of MI in three different ways: (1) as a methodological principle incompatible with certain conceivable observations; (2) as a methodological principle which has no observable implications, but is incompatible with certain theories; (3) as a necessary truth, which (presumably) is compatible with any self-consistent statement, whether observational or theoretical.

Philosophical positions can sometimes be clarified by examining the doctrines they are concerned to deny. Watkins' first paper characterized the opposition in three distinct ways: as affirming "macroscopic laws" which apply to social systems as wholes;

as viewing human societies as organisms with overall needs which produce the activities carried out by their individual members; and as maintaining that social phenomena (institutions, large-scale historical events) are not definable in terms of the activities of individual agents. Moreover, in a footnote to selection 45 that has received less attention than it merits, Watkins presents his principle as opposing the idea "that an individual [can be] frustrated, manipulated or destroyed or borne along by irreducible sociological or historical *laws*." What is an irreducible sociological or historical law (ISL)? One candidate for this title would be the claim that suicides in democratic nations tend to occur after the age of sixty but accumulate between the ages of 25 and 35 in monarchies. This claim affirms a uniform connection between two classes of social events (which I shall sometimes call a "social-social regularity"[1]): democratic political institutions (antecedent) and a certain suicide pattern (consequent). But to be "irreducible" this connection must meet a further condition beyond that of holding in a regular or constant manner. The human agents involved must find it unavoidable; that is, the world must be such that given the antecedent condition no individual or collective action by those agents can prevent the consequent. Even if *all* the persons in some democratic nation become aware of our suicide law and want to abolish the stated pattern while retaining a democracy, they will be unable to do so.

The denial of ISLs is quite a bit broader than Watkins' earlier notion of MI as opposed to "macroscopic laws . . . which apply to the social system as a whole." ISLs can but need not be macroscopic. Some of them fall under the category referred to by Mandelbaum as "functional-abstractive" and distinguished by him from global or macroscopic laws (see pages 644 to 646 below). This would seem to be the case with the suicide regularities mentioned above, as well as the base-superstructure laws of Marxism. In any case, however, appealing to what on Watkins' view MI denies, does not suffice to provide that position with an unequivocal sense.

Those who reject MI have not done appreciably better in bringing the issue into precise focus. Goldstein, for example, considers at length a theory of "kinship nomenclature" which appeals to four "socio-cultural variables." But he never quite fixes his sense of this latter notion, and thus leaves it obscure why the occurrence of a socio-cultural phenomenon, or its causal efficacy, automatically provides a counter-example to MI. Does he mean here to refer to historical conditions that cannot be explained by deducing them from the beliefs and interests of the agents involved, i.e., events which could not have been prevented no matter what beliefs and desires (all of) those agents developed? If so, "socio-cultural" phenomena are in a clear enough sense "nonhuman": they most certainly "impose themselves" on human agents. But Goldstein's second contribution, "The Two Theses of Methodological Individualism," explicitly declaims the positing of any such suprahuman factors:

> If methodological individualism is the thesis that denies the existence of these non-human entities [ones that determine what happens to men], it is clear that neither Mandelbaum . . . nor I, in my earlier paper on this subject, may be said to have opposed it. [See page 626 below.]

In that earlier paper (selection 46), however, Goldstein argues for a view he calls methodological collectivism. According to this view, social events are to be explained by reference to "socio-cultural variables" and without any "reference to the personalities and psychological propensities of particular persons." He also speaks approvingly, in that paper, of "socio-historical or socio-cultural laws" and contends that

[1] I borrow this term from a lecture given by Professor John Rawls.

the "logic of explanation requires . . . the use of general laws." All of which makes it difficult to see how he escapes being committed to nonhuman entities, in the sense of phenomena ("variables") that produce consequences which no set of human desires, beliefs, or efforts can avoid.

In the light of this point, moreover, it becomes extremely dubious that selection 48 succeeds in locating two distinct MI theses. The two theses, supposedly, are *ontological* and *methodological*. The first "denies the existence of certain alleged entities"; the second, "claims that all explanations in social science must, in the end, be reduced to individual dispositions." But what type of entity is denied by Watkins' ontology? Presumably, one that is "superhuman" and "imposes itself" on human beings. In other words, Watkins' ontology contends that there are no entities which defy explanations of a certain sort, that is, explanations which appeal only to the beliefs and interests of individual persons and dispense with general (and a fortiori, irreducible social) laws. The "ontological thesis" thus appears as a disguised version of the "methodological thesis." The former affirms that there are no social events (entities, regularities) that cannot be explained in individualistic terms (*No S are non-E*); the latter insists that whatever exists in society can be explained individualistically (*All S are E*). Consider again Watkins' contention that "What the methodological individualist denies is that an individual is ever frustrated . . . destroyed or borne along by irreducible sociological or historical *laws*." This is not the ambiguous assertion of two distinct claims, one methodological and the other ontological. It advances a single proposition, which can be equally well (and synonymously) expressed ontologically or methodologically. Ontologically, Watkins denies the existence of irreducible (unavoidable) social regularities. And this denial, surely, is just another way of declaring that whatever occurs in society or history can be explained in a way which shows how human agents could have avoided it.

These considerations, hopefully, remove one of the ambiguities that tend to blur MI. Others, however, remain. It has yet to be determined whether Watkins' principle has empirically testable consequences and if so of what sort. Moreover, what are we to make of the disquieting fact that both MI and its critics claim to provide the only way of accounting for the operation of "cultural conditioning"? (See here pages 623 and 630 below.) Is the assertion that men's characters and dispositions, etc. are the product of "enculturation", or of what Skinner might refer to as social patterns of reinforcement, incompatible with MI? Unfortunately, no clear-cut answer is open to us as yet; to arrive at one, we must first uncover some additional ambiguities in Watkins' formulation of that principle.

Consider the two statements: (a) that there are no ISLs and (b) that "no social tendency exists which could not be altered *if* the individuals concerned both wanted to alter it and possessed the appropriate information" (page 605). These lookalikes are by no means equivalent. The second appears to be virtually vacuous, at least in one natural construction. Of course, if every single human being remotely or directly involved in World War I had desired to prevent it and had known of a method for doing just that, then World War I would not have occurred. (Let's presume, as Watkins apparently does, that there are no conflicting desires, or at least none that are stronger than the desire to prevent the world war.) This is much like saying that if a man has a goal, then he will pursue it, if he has an opportunity to do so. Only in the case of (b), both the antecedent and consequent clauses are modified in parallel ways: if he has a goal, *and* knows how to reach it, *and* there is no opposition, then he will (not merely pursue, but) attain it. However, from the claim that whatever is desired with this kind of knowledge, and against no opposition, will be realized, it does *not follow* that there are no ISLs.[2] Statement (b) asserts a conditional which is compatible with the existence of any social regularity you care to mention, e.g., that democracies (unavoidably) have their highest suicide rates among the elderly. This law-candidate would not be threatened by the truism that *if* there was a way of maintaining both democratic institutions and another pattern of suicide rates, and *if* this was known by those living in a democracy, then they could effect a change in the existing pattern, *if* they desired to. This truism — which is about all that can be generated from (b) — does *not* assert that there is a way of keeping democracy and altering the suicide pattern; it does not assert or imply that our law-candidate is false. On the contrary, it affirms merely that *if* it were false, and known to be false, and this knowledge wedded to (an unopposed) desire to contravene the alleged regularity in question, then that alleged regularity would be successfully opposed.

In brief, (b), which Watkins describes as the "central assumption of the individualistic position," is too weak to reject even a single ISL. Given its conditional reference to "appropriate information," this interpretation of MI seems to degenerate into the claim that if we know there are no ISLs, then no social regularity is unavoidable. *If* there is "appropriate information" indicating how one can bring together capitalist industry and indentured slavery, then of course there is no ISL of the form: "Wherever a capitalist level of technology is present, slavery is excluded or destroyed." But the truth of (b)'s hypothetical cannot render the supposed tendency of industrial capitalism to eliminate slavery in any way suspect or avoidable: perhaps there is no such information of the "appropriate" sort.

How does the distinction between (a) and (b) bear on the issue of whether MI is compatible with cultural conditioning? Perhaps the answer is that (a) — but not (b) — entails that human actions are never the product of cultural conditioning. In any case where there is enculturation of personality traits, e.g., of thrift in successive generations of Huguenots, we are provided with a fairly clear sample of an ISL. For is not the idea of cultural conditioning incompatible with there being an alternative open to, or within the grasp of, the conditioned group? At one point, Goldstein contends:

> It was, to be sure, individual Huguenots who successfully competed in the business world of the seventeenth century. But this was presumably because the Huguenot upbringing or enculturation produced people who were adept at this sort of thing. [See page 630 below.]

If the "because" here is read strictly, then given the enculturation (S^1), there was no way of preventing the pattern of attitudes (S^2) that was "produced" in successive generations. S^1 and S^2, however, are social phenomena; we are thus presented with a uniformity which must be understood as an (alleged) ISL. If there are no irreducible social-social regularities, as MI asserts, then one group's dispositions, etc. can never be the dependent variable of another group's customs, habits, etc. The claim that cultural conditioning provides the explanation of a given social event, if true, tacitly establishes an ISL and refutes formulation (a) of MI. On the other hand, even if every human act, as Goldstein suggests, is the product of cultural conditioning, interpretation (b) would remain intact.

For in the case of Huguenot enculturation, to stick with this example, (b) claims merely that *if* both first and second generation Huguenots had wanted to free the latter from the habit of ploughing back profits into business holdings and *if* they had

[2] This is recognized clearly by Goldstein: see page 626 below, fn. 5.

known of a way to accomplish this, and *if* they were unopposed by non-Huguenots, then the habits which did in fact develop would not have developed. In other words, if there is no uniform connection between Huguenot training and the development of Huguenot traits of thrift, then the latter can be absent despite the presence of the former. No cultural determinist, even the most doctrinaire, would care to deny this entirely hypothetical (and seemingly empty) statement. Interpretation (b), in any case, does not claim that there is a way to circumvent the effects of alleged conditioning. As in the case of ISLs, it merely stipulates what would or could obtain if a tactic for circumvention were known and its success universally desired.

My suggestion then is that Goldstein and others have focused on (a) and thereby correctly located a portion of Watkins' position that is incompatible with the cultural conditioning of social patterns. But they overlook (b), a view which may explain Watkins' insistence that MI is liberal enough to leave room for enculturation. In a way, therefore, both parties are correct; for (b) is compatible, while (a) is not, with cultural conditioning.

Consider further (c), that "every complex social situation, institution, or event is the result of a particular configuration of individuals, their dispositions, situations, beliefs, and physical resources and environment" (page 604). This is yet another formulation of MI presented by Watkins, and the one to which he appeals most regularly when arguing that his view is consistent with cultural conditioning. The trouble with (c) is much the same as the trouble with (b): both look equivalent to, but in fact are far weaker than, (a). Like (b), this third interpretation of MI seems to edge perilously close to vacuity.

We return to patterns of suicide. Let us imagine that, under controlled conditions, democratic nations are unable to prevent the extremely high rate of their elder members committing suicide. Such a situation, if it existed, would certainly provide grounds against MI, as conceived in line with (a). But would it conflict to any extent with (c)? Our ISL maintains that a certain suicide pattern (a complex social situation) is the (inescapable) result of democratic political institutions. But surely the causal factor or independent variable here can be fitted under the heading of a "particular configuration of individuals, their dispositions, situations, beliefs, . . ." To say that country A has a democratic government is to say that most of its citizens share certain dispositions and beliefs. Thus when the suicide pattern is explained as an unavoidable consequence of social-social causality, this in no way deviates from (c)'s requirements.

The disposition of a Catholic to believe suicide is a venal sin is certainly the disposition of an individual person. To appeal to the possession, by Catholics, of this disposition in order to explain why members of that faith display a relatively low suicide rate is to appeal to a social-social regularity, i.e., that Catholics tend to regard certain types of acts as sinful. Such an explanation, therefore, might well be incompatible with (a): it introduces one social phenomenon to explain another. Yet the explanation is perfectly harmonious with (c), for it appeals to the dispositions of human agents. Where does (c) go wrong? Apparently, in the following assumption: that if the existence of a social event or tendency is explained by citing dispositions that can only be ascribed to individual persons, then that event or tendency has been shown to be avoidable — and not the inescapable result of another social phenomenon. This assumption reaches the light in footnote 8 on page 610 and in the following passage:

. . . methodological individualism allows the formation, or 'cultural conditioning' of a widespread disposition to be explained only in terms of other human factors and not in terms of something *in*human such as an alleged historicist law which impels people willy-nilly along some predetermined course. [See page 607 below.]

But "other human factors" spreads a net wide enough to catch societal facts or large-scale social phenomena like moral codes, economic trends, etc. And the fact that "other *people*, their habits, inertia, loyalties, rivalries, etc." are the constituents of the social environment confronting Jones is compatible with there being a uniform connection between what other men do and the social activities in which Jones participates; and this uniformity, for all that its constituents are *people*, might be unavoidable. (Leslie White makes much this same point on pages 662–665 below.)

The ambiguity between (a) and (c), like that between (a) and (b), may shed further light on the relation between MI and cultural conditioning. As argued above, (a) denies that such conditioning ever takes place. But does (c)? Not in any univocal way. The crucial passages, once again, are those where the Huguenots are discussed; here (c) is at work in its least promising form. The explicandum is a social regularity: "Huguenot traders were relatively prosperous in 17th century France." To explain this uniformity in line with (c), the dispositions of individual Huguenots are introduced; in particular, the tendency to "plough back into their businesses a larger proportion of their profits than was customary among their Catholic competitors." Goldstein points out, however, that "ploughing back" is a social phenomenon. Further, the existence of what Watkins calls a "widespread disposition" is the existence of a social fact. Much the same analysis will hold for the disposition brought forth to explain "ploughing back," viz, the "general thriftiness which Calvinism is said to encourage." At each stage, one social tendency is introduced to explain another; we are assaulted with a series of social-social uniformities and neither they nor the original explicandum (relative prosperity of 17th century Huguenots) are argued, much less shown, to be *avoidable*.

(C) then is compatible with the falsity of (a): it sanctions, whereas (a) rejects, explanations that rely on ISLs. And this makes (c) compatible with cultural conditioning. As far as what this interpretation of MI asserts, "training in thrift" may be the sufficient condition for eliciting or producing typical Huguenot attitudes and beliefs. The explicans here falls plainly into the category of "other human factors." An explanation which referred to such training exclusively would not deviate at all from the dictum that "every complex social situation . . . is the result of a particular configuration of individuals, their dispositions, situations, beliefs, etc." The explicandum is explained by appealing to a certain pattern of enculturation which is *simultaneously* a "particular configuration of individuals, their dispositions, etc . . ." *and* a "large scale [social] phenomenon." All of which serves to exhibit the compatibility of (c) with cultural conditioning and its virtual emptiness, at least in comparison with (a).

Given its wholly hypothetical cast, (b) may be irretrievably vacuous. On the other hand, (c) can be salvaged if we consider an issue which Watkins mentions but does not discuss at length. That is, (c) — which can be viewed as articulating the positive dimension of MI — must be brought into conformity with (a), which identifies precisely what MI rejects. It is necessary, in short, to describe the distinction between those social science explanations which conform to MI and those which do not. We have just found that the criterion of "[deduction] from statements about the dispositions, beliefs, resources, and inter-relations of individuals" is simply too broad; at any rate, it is far more accommodating than (a). For this test allows explanations which appeal to social-social regularities, i.e., which conclude that their explicanda (be they events or uniformities) are the products of ISLs. Watkins raises this issue in section 5 of selection 45, but he does not provide much by way of explicit codification of the standards MI requires an explanation to satisfy.

There are two steps by which we can fill this gap and thereby bring (c) more in concord with (a). First, examples of explanations that do comply with MI must be constructed. Second, criteria must be abstracted which can help in judging when a given explanation does conform to MI and when it does not. And these criteria must be strong enough to rule out appeals to cultural conditioning and to prohibit the pseudo-MI explanation of Catholic suicide patterns discussed on page 591 above. The three following explanations seem to me to satisfy (c) without thereby violating (a): i.e., their explicans do not appear to affirm or presuppose social-social regularities.

I

1. Illiterates are persons who derive no pleasure from reading (studying, etc.) books and who can make little or no use of them.
2. Persons who do not desire and have little or no use for a given type of thing do not pursue (or purchase) it, unless compelled.
3. In country A, no one compels illiterates to purchase books.
4. In country A, illiterates can become literate and can purchase books; that is, no social or legal obstacles prevent them from so doing.

---

5. Hence, in country A illiterates purchase few or no books.

II

1. Supermarket owners desire to maximize *assurance* of profits (not amount) and believe that this goal can be achieved by accumulating vast stocks and selling at lower prices than one's competition.
2. Individuals with the desire and belief mentioned in premise 1 accumulate vast stocks and sell at lower prices than their competition, unless otherwise compelled.
3. In country B, no one compels (all) would-be supermarket owners to not accumulate vast stocks, etc.
4. In country B, there are no social or legal obstacles preventing supermarket owners from choosing other careers, or other aims and beliefs than those mentioned in premise 1 (e.g., they could become school teachers, or truck drivers, or lawyers; they could desire to maximize the *amount* of their profits).

---

5. Hence, in country B supermarkets regularly sell items at lower prices than non-supermarkets.

III

1. People committed to democracy want to keep the individuals who govern them under the control of the populace.
2. People committed to democracy believe that wherever the military is not controlled by elected representatives, citizen control over government diminishes or is subverted.
3. People with the desire and belief mentioned in premises 1 and 2 will keep their

military forces under the control of elected representatives, unless compelled otherwise.

4. In Sweden most people are committed to democracy; and they are not compelled to allow their military forces to escape control by elected representatives.
5. There are no social or legal obstacles preventing Swedish citizens from developing anti-democratic attitudes.

---

6. Hence, the Swedish nation has tended to keep its military forces under the control of elected government officials.

In each of these three cases, the explicandum is a social-social connection between two phenomena which we may refer to as S^1 and S^2 (or the explicandum is the tendency of a social group, e.g., Swedish citizens, regularly to act in certain ways, e.g., place controls on their military forces). The basic pattern here may be roughly described as follows. (i) S^1 (country A's illiterates, country B's supermarkets, Swedish nation) is characterized in terms of the possession or lack of certain beliefs, desires, attitudes, and so forth on the parts of the individuals involved in it (e.g., having no use or desire for books); (ii) these beliefs, etc. are then asserted to imply the performance or nonperformance of certain activities (not purchasing books) which constitute or are the criterion for S^2. (Or, better, this implication is said to hold in the absence of compulsion directed against such performance or nonperformance; and it is further asserted that compulsion of this sort was not operative.) It is finally alleged (iii) that no legal or social coercion was employed which prevented the individuals in question from adopting beliefs and desires other than those mentioned in (i); i.e., that other occupations, forms of life, capacities, were open to them.

Now given that (i) — (iii) are true in a particular case, it seems reasonable to argue that MI has been used to reduce or explain an alleged social-social regularity or ISL. For the explicandum will have been derived from *avoidable* beliefs and dispositions of individual agents. Our explicans will contain analytic statements of the *All As are Bs* form (e.g., premisses 1 and 2 in argument III). But no ISLs or *empirical* regularities of any sort will have been employed. In sum, a reduction of a social tendency (event, regularity) will be carried out which complies not only with (c) but with (a) as well.

Let us replace (c) then by a fourth formulation of MI. The former asserts merely that every social tendency is the result of the dispositions, beliefs, situations, resources, etc. of individuals. This fourth formulation, (d), will affirm that the occurrence of any social phenomenon or pattern can be explained by deducing it from true statements of four sorts: ascriptions of beliefs and desires to individuals; propositions asserting that little or no compulsion was introduced to prevent those individuals from acting on the beliefs and desires in question; conceptual analyses of those beliefs and desires and their combined implications; and claims to the effect that the beliefs and desires under analysis are (were) avoidable, in the sense that there are (were) no social or legal obstacles preventing the individual agents involved from developing alternative beliefs and/or desires. (To abbreviate this, we can say that according to (d), any social event or regularity is deducible from the avoidable dispositions of individual agents.)

A number of important consequences arise if we make this substitution of (d) for (c). In the first place, MI will now be construed as the conjunction of contentions (a) and (d), and this should dissipate some of the previously noted ambiguity in that doctrine. For example, MI is now univocal in its rejection of Goldstein's view that ". . . the kinds of dispositions to be found in people of any given type are socially induced dispositions." Cultural conditioning, as commonly understood, assumes that some social-social connections are neither avoidable nor purely conceptual, and hence it cannot be considered compatible with our reconstruction of Watkins' position. Secondly, since — as argued on page 590 — (b) is wholly consistent with cultural conditioning, it follows from the above that our revised MI can be sharply distinguished from this element of what Watkins maintains. It is important to make this distinction inasmuch as (b) can offer no objection even to Watkins' prime example of an anti-MI doctrine: dialectical materialism. "Marx," alleges Watkins, "professed to believe that feudal ideas and bourgeois ideas are more or less literally generated by the watermill and the steam engine." But even if Marx did hold some such view, he could still consistently affirm (b). For (b) claims only that if men desired to do so and knew how, they could avoid the connection between technology and superstructure. Marx could grant this, but insist that, in fact, men are never permitted by technology to desire anything but the corresponding superstructure. Or that there is no information truly describing a way to have feudal technology and avoid feudal ideology and hence nothing for men to know in this regard. (Of course, *if* such true information were accessible, it might well make a difference in what men were able to do.) Thus (b) is compatible with technological determinism and for this reason is useless to any methodological individualist who wishes to deny that there are ISLs. We do well, in short, to keep a clear separation between (b) and revised MI.

Finally, revised MI can be freed from the ambiguity on which selection 48 focuses. For reasons already noted, if MI consists of (a) and (d), then the "methodological" and "ontological" theses are simply two ways of expressing the same assertion. Ontologically, MI asserts that no irreducible social regularities or unavoidable social-social connections exist. Methodologically, the revised position contends that an explanation which conforms to the criteria involved in (d) — which uses only the four types of premisses mentioned on page 594 above — can always be found for any given social phenomenon or regularity. Both of these theses are equivalent to the claim that no social phenomena exist which defy explanations of a certain sort. That is, to assert the existence of "irreducible" or *sui generis* social events is to assert that there are social events for which no explanation conforming to (d) can be found (and vice versa). Some adherents of MI, for example, those who not only accept (a) and (d) but also reject the main contention of Mandelbaum's "Societal Facts," might be correctly charged with holding an ontological position distinct from their methodological one. But revised MI is not concerned to deny that there are social (or societal) facts over and above psychological ones. It is not concerned with defining this or that social custom or institution; it aims to exhibit how whatever occurs in society is not the direct result of some other social condition but is, in the sense already indicated, avoidable. Some or all social facts, like Mandelbaum's institution of banking, may be impossible to analyze thoroughly without bringing in a reference to other social phenomena. But this does *not* entail that those "irreducible social facts" are unavoidable or are not explainable by reference to the avoidable dispositions of particular human agents.

A second consequence of revised MI involves the attempt, by Mandelbaum and Goldstein, to construct middle-ground positions. In "Societal Laws" Mandelbaum writes:

> . . . it is widely and erroneously assumed that those who reject methodological individualism must accept a position which is termed "methodological holism." It is the primary purpose of

this paper to show that there are in fact several alternatives to methodological individualism, and that not all of them entail an acceptance of "holism." [See page 642 below.]

Similarly, Goldstein maintains in "The Inadequacies of Methodological Individualism" that ". . . there are problems confronting social science that require solutions not amenable to individualistic analysis and yet are not holistic or historistic." We have already seen that Watkins does not identify unambiguously the class of positions to which he is opposed. There are some passages in which he expressly rejects only a subset of ISLs: to wit, those that are holistic — "macroscopic laws which are *sui generis* and which apply to the social system as a whole." If it is assumed that these alone are the ISLs which MI denies, it becomes easy enough to formulate a third position which is neither individualistic nor holistic: i.e., one that plumbs for nonmacroscopic but nonetheless unavoidable social-social uniformities. This assumption, moreover, makes it possible to contend that methodological individualists tend to equate "a rejection of methodological individualism with the acceptance of methodological holism." Or that they overlook third possibilities, and derive their own view by combining the recognition of real defects in holism with the illusion that one must choose either holism or MI. "Mr. Watkins," Goldstein assures us, "views all non-individualistic theories as holistic."

But in selection 45, there are indications that Watkins does not regard holistic (and historicist[3]) laws as exhausting the set of possible ISLs. On the contrary, this set includes any and every social regularity which is irreducible or inescapable: witness his rejection of the base-superstructure uniformities of Marxism and footnote 8 on page 610. In any case, if MI is identified with the conjunction of (a) and (d), the resulting position denies a great deal more than holistic or historicist laws. Revised MI does not equate a rejection of its tenets with a commitment to global (or in Mandelbaum's sense, "global-directional") laws or with the notion that social systems are organic wholes the overall needs of which determine and explain the behavior of the individuals who compose them. Watkins may occasionally appear to operate with the simplistic dichotomy: "One is either an individualist or a holist." But revised MI can safely abandon that dichotomy in favor of another that is considerably more comprehensive: "One either holds that there are some ISLs or one holds that there are none."

In brief, though Watkins may ignore (not explicitly reject) alternatives to his view besides that of holism-historicism, there are no such alternatives ignored by revised MI. We either subscribe to (a)'s total rejection of social-social causality or we deny it, holding that there is at least one irreducible social uniformity. Whatever is true of selections 38 and 45, revised MI has no need to defend itself by focusing exclusively on the excesses of holism. On the contrary, it can attack what is common to *all* opponents of MI — holists, historicists, middle-grounders: namely, their affirmation of ISLs.

A third consequence of our restatement of MI is that it allows us to deal effectively with alleged ISLs. Goldstein, for example, views the following as social laws: (i) that Huguenot upbringing with its emphasis on thrift produced the Huguenot proclivity to plough profits back; and (ii) that a society's form of kinship nomenclature is determined by four "socio-cultural variables," i.e., "the rule of marriage, the form of the family, the rule of descent, and the rule of residence." Revised MI can handle (i) and (ii) in two different ways. These strategies, moreover, can be deployed against any alleged ISL and upon the success of either, contentions (a) and (d) will be left entirely intact.

[3] In the sense Watkins clarifies on page 605 below.

Watkins could point out, first of all, that neither of the uniformities affirmed by (i) and (ii) has been shown, or even argued by Goldstein, to be *unavoidable*. Perhaps they are merely statistical or accidental connections like (iii) that between taking the National Geographic and taking Newsweek or (iv) that between having exactly three male cousins and not getting a doctorate in geology. Neither (iii) nor (iv) is supported by empirical evidence, as far as I know. But let us imagine that we have found them to hold in a uniform manner. Would this by itself refute MI's denial of irreducible social regularities? I think not. More would have to be supplied to indicate that the individuals involved were somehow prevented from avoiding these social patterns. What would happen to a man who kept on receiving National Geographic but lost his desire for Newsweek: would he find himself constantly reordering the latter?

This first strategy can be extended. Thus far, we have used it only to insist that not all uniform social patterns are ISLs. Goldstein, in other words, does nothing to warrant that (i) and (ii) offer more of a challenge to MI than (iii) and (iv). But revised MI can take the present strategy further by providing an individualist reduction of the purported uniformities, a procedure we shall refer to as *individualization*. For example, one could endeavor to show that what Goldstein calls the socio-cultural variable (the alleged social cause) did not prevent young Huguenots from taking up other dispositions besides "ploughing back". Perhaps the Huguenots were alive to the choice of becoming, and were permitted to become, Catholics; they may also have been able to accept a degree of voluntary poverty within their own faith. It might be demonstrable that with initiative and resolution, the economic restrictions forbidding Huguenots to purchase land, titles, and political offices could have been revoked or disregarded; and with these no longer operative, the impetus to plough back would have significantly diminished. If any one of these possibilities actually obtained, the uniformity — in Watkins' words — has an "innocent" explanation, that is, one that shows how men could have escaped it. This being so, the uniformity is not irreducible and provides no grounds against MI. Abstractly, the tactic of individualizing an alleged ISL (which affirms an unavoidable connection between S^1 and S^2) involves establishing that the individuals exposed to the practices or patterns definitive of S^1 had alternatives open to them besides that of developing the dispositions characteristic of S^2, i.e., that no social or legal barriers — only their own indifference or weakness — prevented those individuals from selecting the alternative options in question. In this way, even if the regularity is conceded, its unavoidability is brought into question.

There is a second line of strategy open to revised MI. This consists in showing that indeed S^1 and S^2 are unavoidably connected, but only in the sense that there is a conceptual or analytic link (what selection 29 called a "connection of meaning") between them. More precisely, it aims at revealing that the activities constituting S^2 are part of what is meant by the dispositions and beliefs which constitute S^1. Thus we are not presented with two distinct phenomena but with only one, for which there are two different locutions. Where this can be established, the relation between S^1 and S^2 will be much the same as that between "(perceived) attainment level" and "intensity of motivation" in the uniformity advanced by Simon in selection 43 (see pages 492-494 above). Or consider the claim that if a man is an arsonist, then he must regularly attempt to start fires, if he has the opportunity. This necessary or "unavoidable" connection can hardly be counted as an obstacle or impediment. There is no alternative which its truth prevents our man from realizing; there is nothing he is blocked from making the object of choice. Given this "regularity," one cannot be both an arsonist and (to simplify) never start fires. But the "cannot" here is applicable to concepts and statements: it is *inconsistent* to describe a man as being an arsonist and then to deny that he regularly starts fires, though he has ample opportunity. That is, the words "arsonist who starts no fires . . ." have no literal sense. We do not have here two different properties held together by an irresistible bond, i.e., *being an arsonist* and *lighting fires regularly, if one has the chance*. There is only one, which in English can be referred to by two different expressions.

Now if the statement of an alleged ISL turns out to be a definition or to be conceptually true, then it too will register no obstacle to the performance of any action. Its truth will not reveal that there is a describable option (e.g., getting water to boil at 60°F., or seeing around a building, or synthesizing a salt not dissolvable in water) which men are unable to undertake or any state of affairs they are prevented from realizing. The alleged ISL will indicate only that anyone we describe as having a certain set Q of beliefs and dispositions we cannot *consistently* describe as lacking what necessarily follows from or is implied by Q. And what cannot be said without inconsistency may, of course, be said quite frequently.

But is this strategy (let us call it "de-empiricizing") really applicable to the uniformities introduced by Goldstein? It will be instructive here to consider Goldstein's second counter-example and to begin by examining two statements with some parallel features: (v) The present military ranking system in the U. S. Army determines that there are different terms for captains and majors (i.e., determines officer-nomenclature); (vi) Our present coin system determines that there are different terms for nickels and dimes (i.e., determines currency-nomenclature). Now it seems to me that (v) and (vi) are conceptually true and not the expression of unavoidable empirical laws. The present military ranking system includes or is manifested by the system of distinguishing ranks by titles like 'major' and 'captain' etc. What would it be like for us to have the present coin system and yet have no verbal equipment for distinguishing dimes and nickels? If our *language* does not recognize any distinction here — if say we reclassify all nickels as dimes, thinking the former have become useless — then we no longer have the present coin system. Suppose the word 'nickel' comes to acquire a new sense: 'coin worth three quarters'. If so, then once again we have a new coin system: indeed that the word had altered its sense could only be shown by (means) that people would now trade three quarters for some new coin on an equal basis. Thus, to speak of the nomenclature rule *is* to speak of a rule of conduct within the coin system. Can we imagine having the present military ranking system without being able to identify, distinguish between, and communicate about majors and captains, i.e., without having any verbal rules which distinguish between what is meant by 'major' and what is meant by 'captain'? The absence of such rules would mean that types of officers we now keep distinct are lumped together, say under the title of 'majtains': but then they are equals in authority, and this implies that we lack a part of our present ranking system.

In both of these cases, the verbal or nomenclature rules are not conceptually separable from the systems which are said to "determine" them. On the contrary, that such systems are operative presupposes a shared ability to make distinctions between, and express and understand judgments about, different types of phenomena. And to have this ability is to have mastered a set of verbal rules concerning the distinctions and the phenomena in question.

We have the impression that there are two sets of rules. In one only words are involved. The other concerns significant actions like buying, selling, saluting, giving and receiving orders, etc. But the separation is artificial. For what are the words supposed to mean? Surely what is meant by the terms 'nickel', 'quarter', 'major', and 'captain' is shown by, and cannot be cut loose from, what Americans do with and accept for the coins and how they treat and interact with majors as opposed to captains. To have a set of practices concerning the rights, duties, and privileges of different ranks (conduct rules) already implies the existence of a set of concepts distinguishing types of officers (nomenclature rules). It therefore makes sense to say that conduct rules determine verbal or nomenclature rules only if this "determination" is thought to arise from an analytic connection. Only if the statement "conduct rules determine verbal rules" is intended to assert that no set of conduct rules specifying differential treatment for types of phenomena in a given area A of human life (currency, military ranking) is conceivable for those who have no concepts with which they distinguish between and communicate about the phenomena within A. To "determine," in this context, is to logically imply: in the words of selection 19, "the alleged *preconditions* or essential causes [conduct rules] cannot be fully specified apart from . . . the condition [verbal rules] they are supposed to produce." And this sense of "determine," as we have seen, does not imply that any state of affairs is unattainable by human effort. It does not serve to express a lawful and unavoidable connection between logically distinct classes of events, but merely announces an explication of the meaning carried by the antecedent concept. As such, propositions expressing this sense of "determine" can pose no threat to MI.

The relevance of de-empiricizing, and of our discussion of (v) and (vi), to Goldstein's second counter-example should be plain. For is not the relation of "determination" that Goldstein asserts to hold between rules of marriage, etc. and kinship nomenclature much the same as that affirmed in our two parallel statements and analysed above? Would not a change in "kinship nomenclature" suffice to indicate that one or more of the antecedent rules had altered: how could we begin to establish that a change in the concepts referring to the family had really taken place, except by observing the "form of the family"? Can one tell whether the meaning of 'mother' has altered or just what the term 'cousin' means in a certain culture without examining the "sociocultural variables" introduced as the antecedent in (ii)? It would seem that verbal rules merely involve the labelling of distinctions that have already been made in the activities which conform to the conduct rules. Indeed, what distinctions are being labelled can only be made out by examining those latter activities. There are not two questions: (1) "Does group A have these verbal rules?" and (2) "Does group A have these conduct rules?" For to say that it has the verbal rules can only be true if it has the conduct rules. And if the group should adopt alternative verbal rules this would imply that it had adopted other conduct rules as well. In brief, there appears to be a conceptual and not an empirical connection betwen having conduct rules and having verbal rules (in the same specific area, e.g., the family, currency, etc.). If this is the case, (ii) would not be an ISL but, rather, an analytic truth; and Watkins could employ the tactic of de-empiricization to undermine this second purported counter-example to MI.

In summary, revised MI can rely on two different strategies to defeat claims of social-social causality. First, it can examine the situations in which the supposed regularity held and endeavor to establish that there were alternatives to S^2 which S^1 did not prevent, that is, that those involved in S^1 would have been allowed by statute and custom to escape S^2. Success in this type of venture will *individualize* the allegedly irreducible connection by providing it with an explanation in terms of beliefs and dispositions that were not socially required or unavoidable. Secondly, if the connection begins to look unavoidable, our reformed individualist can inquire whether it is logically impossible to have the beliefs, aims, and activities characteristic of S^1 without having those characteristic of S^2. If a logical or conceptual connection can be established between S^1 and S^2, then the purported ISL has been *de-empiricized* and this, in another way, destroys its force against revised MI.

Besides presenting specific counter-examples to Watkins' principle, Goldstein raises a more general objection, one he also raised against Peter Winch in selection 28. According to Goldstein, "... the assertion of the principle of methodological individualism implicitly rules out the possibility of diachronic social theory." And the task of such theory, he continues, is that of accounting for *changes* in social systems; it raises "the question of how the [social] situation came to be as it is." Now it strikes me as puzzling that anyone should charge MI (or for that matter the Winch-Dray-*et al* position) with being unable to explain social change. (But this puzzlement may only manifest too simple a notion of social change.)

Let us assume that the dominant pattern of protest and revolt among American Negroes between 1950 and 1960 has recently altered, and that a new pattern has emerged in its place. The shift has been from a mixture of nonviolent civil disobedience and legal appeals to the federal government and the mainstream of White America (S^1) to reliance on self-protection associations which accept violence in self-defense coupled with a separatist trend toward regional or community autonomy (S^2). Presumably, all of this can be properly counted as a change within a "socio-cultural system." Can MI account for this change without implicitly relying on social-social laws? It would seem so. On one hand, the individuals involved in both S^1 and S^2 have a constant goal: liberation from the obstacles of racial injustice and discrimination. But the beliefs held commonly by Negroes in 1958 are not — or are not entirely — those held by Negroes in 1968. In particular, their original belief that progress toward equality in job opportunities, better education, and protection against racism could be made by appealing to the white community's conscience and utilizing its courts and laws has now been shattered. In its place is the view that the exploited class must liberate itself by means of its own efforts and cannot rely on the federal government any more than the states, Democrats more than Republicans, northerners more than southerners. Given this change in belief (which seems rational enough in the light of more than a decade of accumulated evidence) and the constant goal (which the Negro could relinquish, since society would surely allow him to play a more submissive role), we have individualized from S^1 to S^2. Social change, at least in some cases, thus seems entirely compatible with MI: the model invoked by this principle attempts to show that of the beliefs and aspirations involved in S^1, some remained constant and others altered, that this alteration (and constancy) was not socially unavoidable, and that the new set of beliefs and aspirations entails or constitutes a new social fact S^2. MI, in short, can explain social change without appealing to ISLs; and its explanations in this area do not require the introduction of any new principle or assumption. The MI approach to social change seems nothing but a special case of its general approach to supposedly irreducible social regularities or patterns.

To sum up, revising MI so that it consists of (a) and (d) appears to strengthen it in at least five ways. First, this revision eliminates certain ambiguities attaching to earlier formulations of MI (i.e., does MI allow for the cultural conditioning of desires and beliefs; is MI opposed only to holistic positions; does MI assert both an ontological and a methodological thesis); second, it liberates MI from any connection with two contentions that appear vacuous and are fully compatible with social-social causality (i.e., doctrines (b) and (c)); third, it allows MI to reject the oversimple disjunction "individualism or holism" and replace it with the more inclusive "either there are ISLs or there are not"; fourth, this reconstruction provides two strategies by which individualists can rebut alleged instances of ISLs or social-social causality; i.e., individualization and de-empiricization; and last, it discloses a way in which MI can account for "social change" without falling back on empirical (covering)laws.

Naturally, even if all of these five points carry, it does not follow that MI is true. What does follow is (1) that certain weaknesses in that position can be removed, thus disarming the most common objections to it; and (2) that subsequent criticisms, to be cogent, will have to attack (a) and (d) of revised MI — together with the associated strategies of individualization and de-empiricization — instead of continuing to protest the acknowledged defects of (b) and (c).

Selections 51 and 52 merit some attention here for they implicitly question MI's utility for the actual inquiries being carried out by social scientists. Watkins himself seems most concerned to meet those objections which view MI as excluding prevalent forms of social science research. On page 624, he asserts: "Whatever attitude he may adopt to general criticisms a methodologist certainly ought to attend very seriously to a heartfelt protest that his methodology would stifle some live and kicking piece of research which is producing interesting results."

But can MI account for the sorts of theory propounded by White and Radcliffe-Brown? Given the positions of these front-rank social scientists, we may be forced to concur with Goldstein's judgment that "the principle [MI] is entirely too restrictive and would preclude social scientists asking what on the face of it seem like perfectly reasonable questions. And this, in turn, would radically limit the possibilities of social science theory formation." Emile Durkheim's methodology (of which White explicitly approves) is the direct contrary of MI:

> We must, then, seek the explanation of social life in the nature of society itself. It is quite evident that, since it infinitely surpasses the individual in time as well as in space, it is in a position to impose upon him ways of acting and thinking which it has consecrated with its prestige.[4]

Consider also Leslie White's account of the genius as "a person in whose organism a significant synthesis of cultural elements has occurred." Or Radcliffe-Brown's notion of joking behavior as cementing the sentiments on which social order depends. Do they not involve explanations that clearly conflict with MI, as revised above?

Our two social scientists would probably claim to have discovered, established, or utilized ISLs in providing explanations of social facts. However, the anti-MI views expressed in selections 51 and 52 may fare no better against the twin strategies of de-empiricization and individualization than the complaints lodged by Goldstein. For example, do White's arguments on pages 656 to 657 below manage to escape the charge that his "C⟶M" connections are disguised tautologies? What is the criterion for saying that a given "musical cultural tradition" (C^1) exists, if not the "musical behavior" (M^1) exhibited by individuals within C^1? Has White attempted to show that there is a law by which the actual changes in musical traditions, e.g., from Baroque to Romantic, from Tchaikovsky to Stravinsky, could have been foreseen? Or consider his "culturological explanation of slavery" (pages 651 to 652). The evolution of technological forces, we are told, accounts for both the origin and extinction of slave-

[4] Durkheim, Emile. *The Rules of Sociological Method.* New York, 1964, page 102.

holding as an institution. But does White supply grounds for the view that the technology of the southern states from 1607-1860 permitted no option besides slavery? (During the 17th and early 18th centuries the North and South were hardly separate in technological development, yet slavery never became a social pattern outside the latter.) Why cannot the productive instruments of capitalism be profitably combined with a social system in which slaves are retained, compelled to develop industrially useful skills, and forbidden to unionize? Many southern cities had factory-slaves by 1830: does White show that this trend could not have become dominant, that "cultural phenomena" prevented it from being more widely pursued? And what of societies with the same economic-technological development as the anti-bellum South: why were they not all slave-owning? Perhaps the level of technology does not have a uniform relation to slavery. Nonmechanized agrarian societies have often found it possible to exist without either serfdom or chattel slavery. In short, individualization may be the only way of accounting for the connections — should there be any — between (1) industrialization and the end of slavery in the U.S. and (2) slavery's origin and the ability of a family group "to produce considerably more than it requires for its continued existence."

Can individualization and de-empiricization account for, or rebut, all of the data, interpretations, and arguments presented in selections 51 and 52? I think they can, but no proof of this shall be attempted here. In any case, it is clear that these two strategies can play a very useful role in evaluating MI. Where either succeeds, MI comes off completely unstained. But should they both fail in any given case (any alleged ISL), this will provide evidence of a decisive sort against MI. For if a social regularity cannot be shown to be avoidable and is not a disguised conceptual truth, then the evidence for its existence is evidence that at least one social fact cannot be explained by reference to the four types of statements mentioned by formulation (d) of revised MI (page 594 above). Thus, regardless of whether individualization and de-empiricization are successful, appealing to them provides a crucial test for the adequacy of MI.

Social Phenomena Result from the Activities of Individual Agents

45

Historical Explanation in the Social Sciences

J. W. N. WATKINS

Introduction

The hope which originally inspired methodology was the hope of finding a method of enquiry which would be both necessary and sufficient to guide the scientist unerringly to truth. This hope has died a natural death. Today, methodology has the more modest task of establishing certain rules and requirements which are necessary to prohibit some wrong-headed moves but insufficient to guarantee success. These rules and requirements, which circumscribe scientific enquiries without steering them in any specific direction, are of the two main kinds, formal and material. So far as I can see, the formal rules of scientific method (which comprise both logical rules and certain realistic and fruitful stipulations) are equally applicable to all the empirical sciences. You cannot, for example, deduce a universal law from a finite number of observations whether you are a physicist, a biologist, or an anthropologist. Again, a single comprehensive explanation of a whole range of phenomena is preferable to isolated explanations of each of those phenomena, whatever your field of enquiry. I shall therefore confine myself to the more disputable (I had nearly said 'more disreputable') and metaphysically impregnated part of methodology which tries to establish the appropriate *material* requirements which the *contents* of the premisses of an explanatory theory in a particular field ought to satisfy. These requirements may be called regulative principles. Fundamental differences in the subject-matters of different sciences — differences to which formal methodological rules are impervious — ought, presumably, to be reflected in the regulative principles appropriate to each science. It is here that the student of the methods of the social sciences may be expected to have something distinctive to say.

An example of a regulative principle is mechanism, a metaphysical theory which governed thinking in the physical sciences from the seventeenth century until it was largely superseded by a wave or field world-view. According to mechanism, the ultimate constituents of the physical world are impenetrable particles which obey simple mechanical laws. The existence of these particles cannot be explained — at any rate by science. On the other hand, every complex physical thing or event is the result of a particular configuration of particles and can be explained in terms of the laws governing their behaviour in conjunction with a description of their relative positions, masses, momenta, etc. There may be what might be described as unfinished or half-way explanations of large-scale phenomena (say, the pressure inside a gas-container) in terms of other large-scale factors (the volume and temperature of the gas); but we shall not have arrived at rock-bottom explanations of such large-scale phenomena until we have deduced their behaviour from statements about the properties and relations of particles.

Reprinted from the *British Journal for the Philosophy of Science*, 8 (1957), pp. 104–117, Cambridge University Press.

This is a typically metaphysical idea (by which I intend nothing derogatory). True, it is confirmed, even massively confirmed, by the huge success of mechanical theories which conform to its requirements. On the other hand, it is untestable. No experiment could overthrow it. If certain phenomena — say, electromagnetic phenomena — seem refractory to this mechanistic sort of explanation, this refractoriness can always (and perhaps rightly) be attributed to our inability to find a successful mechanical model rather than to an error in our metaphysical intuition about the ultimate constitution of the physical world. But while mechanism is weak enough to be compatible with any *observation* whatever, while it is an untestable and unempirical principle, it is strong enough to be incompatible with various conceivable physical *theories*. It is this which makes it a *regulative*, non-vacuous metaphysical principle. If it were compatible with everything it would regulate nothing. Some people complain that regulative principles discourage research in certain directions, but that is a part of their purpose. You cannot encourage research in one direction without discouraging research in rival directions.

I am not an advocate of mechanism but I have mentioned it because I am an advocate of an analogous principle in social science, the principle of methodological individualism.[1] According to this principle, the ultimate constituents of the social world are individual people who act more or less appropriately in the light of their dispositions and understanding of their situation. Every complex social situation, institution, or event is the result of a particular configuration of individuals, their dispositions, situations, beliefs, and physical resources and environment. There may be unfinished or half-way explanations of large-scale social phenomena (say, inflation) in terms of other large-scale phenomena (say, full employment); but we shall not have arrived at rock-bottom explanations of such large-scale phenomena until we have deduced an account of them from statements about the dispositions, beliefs, resources, and inter-relations of individuals. (The individuals may remain anonymous and only typical dispositions, etc., may be attributed to them.) And just as mechanism is contrasted with the organicist idea of physical fields, so methodological individualism is contrasted with sociological holism or organicism. On this latter view, social systems constitute 'wholes' at least in the sense that some of their large-scale behaviour is governed by macro-laws which are essentially *sociological* in the sense that they are *sui generis* and not to be explained as mere regularities or tendencies resulting from the behaviour of interacting individuals. On the contrary, the behaviour of individuals should (according to sociological holism) be explained at least partly in terms of such laws (perhaps in conjunction with an account, first of individuals' roles within institutions and secondly of the functions of institutions within the whole social system). If methodological individualism means that human beings are supposed to be the only moving agents in history, and if sociological holism means that some superhuman agents or factors are supposed to be at work in history, then these two alternatives are exhaustive. An example of such a superhuman, sociological factor is the alleged long-term cyclical wave in economic life which is supposed to be self-propelling, uncontrollable, and inexplicable in terms of human activity, but in

[1] Both of these analogous principles go back at least to Epicurus. In recent times methodological individualism has been powerfully defended by Professor F. A. Hayek in his *Individualism and Economic Order* and *The Counter-Revolution of Science*, and by Professor K. R. Popper in his *The Open Society and its Enemies* and 'The Poverty of Historicism', *Economica*, 1944–45, **11-12.** Following in their footsteps I have also attempted to defend methodological individualism in 'Ideal Types and Historical Explanation' this *Journal*, 1952, **3,** 22, reprinted in *Readings in the Philosophy of Science*, ed. Feigl and Brodbeck, New York, 1953. This article has come in for a good deal of criticism, the chief items of which I shall try to rebut in what follows. [*Watkins' "Ideal Types and Historical Explanation" is reprinted as selection 38 in this volume. Editor's note.*]

terms of the fluctuations of which such large-scale phenomena as wars, revolutions, and mass emigration, and such psychological factors as scientific and technological inventiveness can, it is claimed, be explained and predicted.

I say 'and predicted' because the irreducible sociological laws postulated by holists are usually regarded by them as laws of social development, as laws governing the dynamics of a society. This makes holism well-nigh equivalent to historicism, to the idea that a society is impelled along a pre-determined route by historical laws which cannot be resisted but which can be discerned by the sociologist. The holist-historicist position has, in my view, been irretrievably damaged by Popper's attacks on it. I shall criticise this position only in so far as this will help me to elucidate and defend the individualistic alternative to it. The central assumption of the individualistic position — an assumption which is admittedly counter-factual and metaphysical — is that no social tendency exists which could not be altered *if* the individuals concerned both wanted to alter it and possessed the appropriate information. (They might want to alter the tendency but, through ignorance of the facts and/or failure to work out some of the implications of their action, fail to alter it, or perhaps even intensify it.) This assumption could also be expressed by saying that no social tendency is somehow imposed on human beings 'from above' (or 'from below') — social tendencies are the product (usually undesigned) of human characteristics and activities and situations, of people's ignorance and laziness as well as of their knowledge and ambition. (An example of a social tendency is the tendency of industrial units to grow larger. I do not call 'social' those tendencies which are determined by uncontrollable physical factors, such as the alleged tendency for more male babies to be born in times of disease or war)[2]

My procedure will be: first, to de-limit the sphere in which methodological individualism works in two directions; secondly, to clear methodological individualism of certain misunderstandings; thirdly, to indicate how fruitful and surprising individualistic explanations can be and how individualistic social theories can lead to sociological discoveries;

[2] The issue of holism *versus* individualism in social science has recently been presented as though it were a question of the existence or non-existence of irreducibly social *facts* rather than of irreducibly sociological *laws*. (See M. Mandelbaum, 'Societal Facts', *The British Journal of Sociology*, 1955, **6***, and E. A. Gellner, 'Explanations in History', *Aristotelian Society*, Supplementary Volume **30**, 1956.) This way of presenting the issue seems to me to empty it of most of its interest. If a new kind of beast is discovered, what we want to know is not so much whether it falls outside existing zoological categories, but how it behaves. People who insist on the existence of social facts but who do not say whether they are governed by sociological laws, are like people who claim to have discovered an unclassified kind of animal but who do not tell us whether it is tame or dangerous, whether it can be domesticated or is unmanageable. If an answer to the question of social facts could throw light on the serious and interesting question of sociological laws, then the question of social facts would also be serious and interesting. But this is not so. On the one hand, a holist may readily admit (as I pointed out in my 'Ideal Types' paper, which Gellner criticises) that all observable social facts *are* reducible to individual facts and yet hold that the latter are invisibly governed by irreducibly sociological laws. On the other hand, an individualist may readily admit (as Gellner himself says) that some large social facts are simply too complex for a full reduction of them to be feasible, and yet hold that individualistic explanations of them are in principle possible, just as a physicist may readily admit that some physical facts (for instance, the precise blast-effects of a bomb-explosion in a built-up area) are just too complex for accurate prediction or explanation of them to be feasible and yet hold that precise explanations and predictions of them in terms of existing scientific laws are in principle possible.

This revised way of presenting the holism *versus* individualism issue does not only divert attention from the important question. It also tends to turn the dispute into a purely verbal issue. Thus Mandelbaum is able to prove the existence of what he calls 'societal facts' because he defines psychological facts very narrowly as 'facts concerning the thoughts and actions of specific human beings' [in this volume, page 636.] Consequently, the *dispositions* of *anonymous* individuals which play such an important role in individualistic explanations in social science are 'societal facts' merely by definition.

* [*Mandelbaum's article is reprinted in this volume as selection 49. Editor's note.*]

and fourthly, to consider in somewhat more detail how, according to methodological individualism, we should frame explanations, first for social regularities or repeatable processes, and secondly for unique historical constellations of events.

Where Methodological Individualism Does Not Work

There are two areas in which methodological individualism does not work.

The first is a probability situation where accidental and unpredictable irregularities in human behaviour have a fairly regular and predictable overall result.[3] Suppose I successively place 1,000 individuals facing north in the centre of a symmetrical room with two exits, one east, the other west. If about 500 leave by one exit and about 500 by the other I would not try to explain this in terms of tiny undetectable west-inclining and east-inclining differences in the individuals, for the same reason that Popper would not try to explain the fact that about 500 balls will topple over to the west and about 500 to the east, if 1,000 balls are dropped from immediately above a north-south blade, in terms of tiny undetectable west-inclining and east-inclining differences in the balls. For in both cases such an 'explanation' would merely raise the further problem: why should these west-inclining and east-inclining differences be distributed approximately *equally* among the individuals and among the balls?

Those statistical regularities in social life which are inexplicable in individualistic terms for the sort of reason I have quoted here are, in a sense, inhuman, the outcome of a large number of sheer *accidents*. The outcome of a large number of decisions is usually much less regular and predictable because variable human factors (changes of taste, new ideas, swings from optimism to pessimism) which have little or no influence on accident-rates are influential here. Thus Stock Exchange prices fluctuate widely from year to year, whereas the number of road-accidents does not fluctuate widely. But the existence of these actuarial regularities does not, as has often been alleged, support the historicist idea that defenceless individuals like you and me are at the chance mercy of the inhuman and uncontrollable tendencies of our society. It does not support a secularised version of the Calvinist idea of an Almighty Providence who picks people at random to fill His fixed damnation-quota. For we can control these statistical regularities in so far as we can alter the conditions on which they depend. For example, we could obviously abolish road-accidents if we were prepared to prohibit motor-traffic.

The second kind of social phenomenon to which methodological individualism is inapplicable is where some kind of physical connection between people's nervous systems short-circuits their intelligent control and causes automatic, and perhaps in some sense appropriate, bodily responses. I think that a man may more or less literally smell danger and instinctively back away from unseen ambushers; and individuality seems to be temporarily submerged beneath a collective physical *rapport* at jive-sessions and revivalist meetings and among panicking crowds. But I do not think that these spasmodic mob-organisms lend much support to holism or constitute a very serious exception to methodological individualism. They have a fleeting existence which ends when their members put on their mufflers and catch the bus or otherwise disperse, whereas holists have conceived of a social whole as something which endures through generations of men; and whatever holds together typical long-lived institutions, like a bank or a legal system or a church, it certainly is not the physical proximity of their members.

[3] Failure to exclude probability-situations from the ambit of methodological individualism was an important defect of my 'Ideal Types' paper. Here, Gellner's criticism (op. cit. p. 163) does hit the nail on the head.

Misunderstandings of Methodological Individualism

I will now clear methodological individualism of two rather widespread misunderstandings.

It has been objected that in making individual dispositions and beliefs and situations the terminus of an explanation in social science, methodological individualism implies that a person's psychological make-up is, so to speak, God-given, whereas it is in fact conditioned by, and ought to be explained in terms of, his social inheritance and environment[4]. Now methodological individualism certainly does not prohibit attempts to explain the formation of psychological characteristics; it only requires that such explanations should in turn be *individualistic*, explaining the formation as the result of a series of conscious or unconscious responses by an individual to his changing situation. For example, I have heard Professor Paul Sweezey, the Harvard economist, explain that he became a Marxist because his father, a Wall Street broker, sent him in the 1930's to the London School of Economics to study under those staunch liberal economists, Professors Hayek and Robbins. This explanation is perfectly compatible with methodological individualism (though hardly compatible, I should have thought, with the Marxist idea that ideologies reflect class-positions) because it interprets his ideological development as a human response to his situation. It is, I suppose, psycho-analysts who have most systematically worked the idea of a thorough individualist and historical explanation of the formation of dispositions, unconscious fears and beliefs, and subsequent defence-mechanisms, in terms of responses to emotionally charged, and especially childhood, situations.

My point could be put by saying that methodological individualism encourages *innocent* explanations but forbids *sinister* explanations of the widespread existence of a disposition among the members of a social group. Let me illustrate this by quoting from a reply I made to Goldstein's criticisms.

> Suppose that it is established that Huguenot traders were relatively prosperous in 17th-century France and that this is explained in terms of a wide-spread disposition among them (a disposition for which there is independent evidence) to plough back into their businesses a larger proportion of their profits than was customary among their Catholic competitors. Now this explanatory disposition might very well be explained in its turn — perhaps in terms of the general thriftiness which Calvinism is said to encourage, and/or in terms of the fewer alternative outlets for the cash resources of people whose religious disabilities prevented them from buying landed estates or political offices. (I cannot vouch for the historical accuracy of this example.)
>
> I agree that methodological individualism allows the formation, or 'cultural conditioning', of a widespread disposition to be explained only in terms of other human factors and not in terms of something *in*human, such as an alleged historicist law which impels people willy-nilly along some pre-determined course. But this is just the anti-historicist point of methodological individualism.

Unfortunately, it is typically a part of the programme of Marxist and other historicist sociologies to try to account for the formation of ideologies and other psychological characteristics in strictly sociological and non-psychological terms. Marx, for instance, professed to believe that feudal ideas and *bourgeois* ideas are more or less literally generated by the water-mill and the steam-engine. But no description, however complete, of the productive apparatus of a society, or of any other non-psychological factors, will enable you to deduce a single

[4] Thus Gellner writes: 'The real oddity of the reductionist [i.e. the methodological individualist's] case is that it seems to preclude *a priori* the possibility of human dispositions being the dependent variable in an historical explanation — when in fact they often or always are' (op. cit. p. 165). And Mr. Leon J. Goldstein says that in making human dispositions methodologically primary I ignore their cultural conditioning. (*The Journal of Philosophy*, 1956, **53,** 807.) [*Goldstein's article is reprinted in this volume as selection 46; see in particular, page 616 below. Editor's note.*]

psychological conclusion from it, because psychological statements logically cannot be deduced from wholly non-psychological statements. Thus whereas the mechanistic idea that explanations in physics cannot go behind the impenetrable particles is a prejudice (though a very understandable prejudice), the analogous idea that an explanation which begins by imputing some social phenomenon to human factors cannot go on to explain those factors in terms of some inhuman determinant of them is a necessary truth. That the human mind develops under various influences the methodological individualist does not, of course, deny. He only insists that such development must be explained 'innocently' as a series of responses by the individual to situations and not 'sinisterly' and illogically as a direct causal outcome of non-psychological factors, whether these are neurological factors, or impersonal sociological factors alleged to be at work in history.

Another cause of complaint against methodological individualism is that it has been confused with a narrow species of itself (Popper calls it 'psychologism') and even, on occasion, with a still narrower sub-species of this (Popper calls it the 'Conspiracy Theory of Society')[5]. Psychologism says that all large-scale social characteristics are not merely the intended or unintended result of, but a *reflection* of, individual characteristics.[6] Thus Plato said that the character and make-up of a *polis* is a reflection of the character and make-up of the kind of soul predominant in it. The conspiracy theory says that all large-scale social phenomena (do not merely reflect individual characteristics but) are deliberately brought about by individuals or groups of individuals.

Now there are social phenomena, like mass unemployment, which it would not have been in anyone's interest deliberately to bring about and which do not appear to be large-scale social reflections or magnified duplicates of some individual characteristic. The practical or technological or therapeutic importance of social science largely consists in explaining, and thereby perhaps rendering politically manageable, the unintended and unfortunate consequences of the behaviour of interacting individuals. From this pragmatic point of view, psychologism and the conspiracy theory are unrewarding doctrines. Psychologism says that only a change of heart can put a stop to, for example, war (I think that this is Bertrand Russell's view). The conspiracy theory, faced with a big bad social event, leads to a hunt for scapegoats. But methodological individualism, by imputing unwanted social phenomena to individuals' responses to their situations, in the light of their dispositions and beliefs, suggests that we may be able to make the phenomena disappear, not by recruiting good men to

[5] See K. R. Popper, *The Open Society and its Enemies*, 2nd edn., 1952, ch. 14.

[6] I am at a loss to understand how Gellner came to make the following strange assertion: '. . . Popper refers to both "psychologism" which he condemns, and "methodological individualism", which he commends. When in the articles discussed [i.e., my "Ideal Types" paper] "methodological individualism" is worked out more fully than is the case in Popper's book, it seems to me to be indistinguishable from "Psychologism".' Finding no difference between methodological individualism and a caricature of methodological individualism, Gellner has no difficulty in poking fun at the whole idea: 'Certain tribes I know have what anthropologists call a segmentary patrilineal structure, which moreover maintains itself very well over time. I could "explain" this by saying that the tribesmen have, all or most of them, dispositions whose effect is to maintain the system. But, of course, not only have they never given the matter much thought, but it also might very well be impossible to isolate anything in the characters and conduct of the individual tribesmen which *explains* how they come to maintain the system' (op. cit. p. 176). Yet this example actually suggests the lines along which an individualistic explanation might be found. The very fact that the tribesmen *have never given the matter much thought*, the fact that they accept their inherited system uncritically, may constitute an important part of an explanation of its stability. The explanation might go on to pin-point certain rules — that is firm and widespread dispositions — about marriage, inheritance, etc., which help to regularise the tribesmen's behaviour towards their kinsmen. How they come to share these common dispositions could also be explained individualistically in the same sort of way that I can explain why my young children are already developing a typically English attitude towards policemen.

fill the posts hitherto occupied by bad men, nor by trying to destroy men's socially unfortunate dispositions while fostering their socially beneficial dispositions, but simply by altering the situations they confront. To give a current example, by confronting individuals with dearer money and reduced credit the Government may (I do not say will) succeed in halting inflation without requiring a new self-denying attitude on the part of consumers and without sending anyone to prison.

Factual Discoveries in Social Science

To explain the unintended but *beneficial* consequences of individual activities — by 'beneficial consequences' I mean social consequences which the individuals affected *would* endorse *if* they were called on to choose between their continuation or discontinuation — is usually a task of less practical urgency than the explanation of undesirable consequences. On the other hand, this task may be of greater theoretical interest. I say this because people who are painfully aware of the existence of unwanted social phenomena may be oblivious of the unintended but beneficial consequences of men's actions, rather as a man may be oblivious of the good health to which the smooth functioning of his digestion, nervous system, circulation, etc., give rise. Here, an explanatory social theory may surprise and enlighten us not only with regard to the connections between causes and effect but with regard to the existence of the effect itself. By showing that a certain economic system contains positive feed-back leading to increasingly violent oscillations and crises an economist may explain a range of well-advertised phenomena which have long been the subject of strenuous political agitation. But the economists who first showed that a certain kind of economic system contains negative feed-back which tends to iron out disturbances and restore equilibrium, not only explained, but also revealed the existence of, phenomena which had hardly been remarked upon before.[7]

I will speak of organic-like social behaviour where members of some social system (that is, a collection of people whose activities disturb and influence each other) mutually adjust themselves to the situations created by the others in a way which, without direction from above, conduces to the equilibrium or preservation or development of the system. (These are again evaluative notions, but they can also be given a 'would-be-endorsed-if' definition.) Now such far-flung organic-like behaviour, involving people widely separated in space and largely ignorant of each other, cannot be simply observed. It can only be theoretically reconstructed — by deducing the distant social consequences of the typical responses of a large number of interacting people to certain repetitive situations. This explains why individualistic-minded economists and anthropologists, who deny that societies really are organisms, have succeeded in piecing together a good deal of unsuspected organic-like social behaviour, from an examination of individual dispositions and situations, whereas sociological holists, who insist that societies really are organisms, have been noticeably unsuccessful in convincingly displaying any organic-like social behaviour — they cannot observe it and they do not try to reconstruct it individualistically.

There is a parallel between holism and psychologism which explains their common

[7] This sentence, as I have since learnt from Dr. A. W. Phillips, is unduly complacent, for it is very doubtful whether an economist can ever *show* that an economic system containing negative feed-back will be stable. For negative feed-back may produce either a tendency towards equilibrium, or increasing oscillations, according to the numerical values of the parameters of the system. But numerical values are just what economic measurements, which are usually ordinal rather than cardinal, seldom yield. The belief that a system which contains negative feed-back, but whose variables cannot be described quantitatively, is stable may be based on faith or experience, but it cannot be shown mathematically. See A. W. Phillips, 'Stabilisation Policy and the Time-Forms of Lagged Responses', *The Economic Journal*, 1957, 67.

failure to make surprising discoveries. A large-scale social characteristic should be explained, according to psychologism, as the manifestation of analogous small-scale psychological tendencies in individuals, and according to holism as the manifestation of a large-scale tendency in the social whole. In both cases, the *explicans* does little more than duplicate the *explicandum*. The methodological individualist, on the other hand, will try to explain the large-scale effect as the *indirect*, unexpected, complex product of individual factors none of which, singly, may bear any resemblance to it at all. To use hackneyed examples, he may show that a longing for peace led, in a certain international situation, to war, or that a government's desire to improve a bad economic situation by balancing its budget only worsened the situation. Since Mandeville's *Fable of the Bees* was published in 1714, individualistic social science, with its emphasis on unintended consequences, has largely been a sophisticated elaboration on the simple theme that, in certain situations, selfish private motives may have good social consequences and good political intentions bad social consequences.[8]

Holists draw comfort from the example of biology, but I think that the parallel is really between the biologist and the methodological individualist. The biologist does not, I take it, explain the large changes which occur during, say, pregnancy, in terms of corresponding large teleological tendencies in the organism, but physically, in terms of small chemical, cellular, neurological, etc., changes, none of which bears any resemblance to their joint and seemingly planful outcome.

How Social Explanations Should be Framed

I will now consider how regularities in social life, such as the trade cycle, should be explained according to methodological individualism. The explanation should be in terms of individuals and their situations; and since the process to be explained is repeatable, liable to recur at various times and in various parts of the world, it follows that only very general assumptions about human dispositions can be employed in its explanation. It is no use looking to abnormal psychology for an explanation of the structure of interest-rates — everyday experience must contain the raw material for the dispositional (as opposed to the situational) assumptions required by such an explanation. It may require a stroke of genius to detect, isolate, and formulate precisely the dispositional premisses of an explanation of a social regularity. These premisses may state what no one had noticed before, or give a sharp articulation to what had hitherto been loosely described. But once stated they will seem obvious enough. It took years of groping by brilliant minds before a precise formulation was found for the principle of diminishing marginal utility. But once stated, the principle — that the less, relatively, a man has of one divisible commodity the more compensation he will be disposed to require for foregoing a small fixed amount of it — is a principle to which pretty well everyone will give his consent. Yet this simple and almost platitudinous principle is the magic key to the economics of distribution and exchange.

The social scientist is, here, in a position analogous to that of the Cartesian mechanist.[9]

[8] A good deal of unmerited opposition to methodological individualism seems to spring from the recognition of the undoubted fact that individuals often run into social obstacles. Thus the conclusion at which Mandelbaum arrives is 'that there are societal facts which exercise external constraints over individuals' [in this volume, p. 641]. This conclusion is perfectly harmonious with the methodological individualist's insistence that plans often miscarry (and that even when they do succeed, they almost invariably have other important and unanticipated effects). The methodological individualist only insists that the social environment by which any particular individual is confronted and frustrated and sometimes manipulated and occasionally destroyed is, if we ignore its physical ingredients, made up of other *people*, their habits, inertia, loyalties, rivalries, and so on. What the methodological individualist denies is that an individual is ever frustrated, manipulated or destroyed or borne along by irreducible sociological or historical *laws*.

[9] I owe this analogy to Professor Popper.

The latter never set out to discover new and unheard-of physical principles because he believed that his own principle of action-by-contact was self-evidently ultimate. His problem was to discover the typical physical configurations, the mechanisms, which, operating according to this principle, produce the observed regularities of nature. His theories took the form of models which exhibited such regularities as the outcome of 'self-evident' physical principles operating in some hypothetical physical situation. Similarly, the social scientist does not make daring innovations in psychology but relies on familiar, almost 'self-evident' psychological material. His skill consists, first in spotting the relevant dispositions, and secondly in inventing a simple but realistic model which shows how, in a precise type of situation, those dispositions generate some typical regularity or process. (His model, by the way, will also show that in this situation certain things cannot happen. His negative predictions of the form, 'If you've got this you can't have that as well' may be of great practical importance.) The social scientist can now explain in principle historical examples of this regular process, provided his model does in fact fit the historical situation.

This view of the explanation of social regularities incidentally clears up the old question on which so much ink has been spilt about whether the so-called 'laws' of economics apply universally or only to a particular 'stage' of economic development. The simple answer is that the economic principles displayed by economists' models apply only to those situations which correspond with their models; but a single model may very well correspond with a very large number of historical situations widely separated in space and time.

In the explanation of regularities the same situational scheme or model is used to reconstruct a number of historical situations with a similar structure in a way which reveals how typical dispositions and beliefs of anonymous individuals generated, on each occasion, the same regularity.[10] In the explanation of a unique constellation of events the individualistic method is again to reconstruct the historical situation, or connected sequence of situations, in a way which reveals how (usually both named and anonymous) individuals, with their beliefs and dispositions (which may include peculiar personal dispositions as well as typical human dispositions), generated, in this particular situation, the joint product to be explained. I emphasise *dispositions*, which are open and law-like, as opposed to *decisions*, which are occurrences, for this reason. A person's set of dispositions ought, under varying conditions, to give rise to appropriately varying decisions. The subsequent occurrence of an appropriate decision will both confirm, and be explained by, the existence of the dispositions. Suppose that a historical explanation (of, say, the growth of the early Catholic Church) largely relies on a particular decision (say, the decision of Emperor Constantine to give Pope Silvester extensive temporal rights in Italy). The explanation is, so far, rather *ad hoc:* an apparently arbitrary *fiat* plays a key rôle in it. But if this decision can in turn be explained as the offspring of a marriage of a set of dispositions (for instance, the Emperor's disposition to subordinate all rival power to himself) to a set of circumstances (for instance, the Emperor's recognition that Christianity could not be crushed but could be tamed if it became the official religion of the Empire), and if the existence of these dispositions and circumstances is convincingly supported by independent evidence, then the area of the arbitrarily given, of sheer brute fact in history, although it can never be made to vanish, will have been significantly reduced.

[10] This should rebut Gellner's conclusion that methodological individualism would transform social scientists into 'biographers *en grande série*' (op. cit. p. 176).

The Explanation of Social Change Requires Irreducible Sociocultural Laws 46

The Inadequacy of the Principle of Methodological Individualism[1]

LEON J. GOLDSTEIN

Introduction

Not long ago, Mr. J. W. N. Watkins expressed himself in favor of "the principle of methodological individualism," a doctrine in the philosophical foundations of social science which demands that all of the concepts used in social science theory be exhaustively analyzable in terms of the interests, activities, volitions, and so forth of individual human beings.[2] It seems to me, however, that the principle is entirely too restrictive and would preclude social scientists asking what on the face of it seem like perfectly reasonable questions. And this, in turn, would radically limit the possibilities of social science theory formation. The purpose of the present paper is to make this clear.

Few would deny that Mr. Watkins' papers, together with the writings on the subject by Professors K. R. Popper[3] and F. A. Hayek,[4] are the most important attempts to provide an account of the principle. But while they do describe and even illustrate it, I fear that it cannot be said that they have attempted to provide a systematic argument in defense of it. A possible exception is Professor Hayek, who may wish his emphasis upon the subjective character of the data of social science to serve as such an argument.[5] But this emphasis either results from a confusion of the psychological and the phenomenological senses of "mind," in which the objective sociocultural *content* of thought and experience is treated exclusively from the subjective standpoint of the experiencing individual[6]; or it is an attempt to insist that no social systems are possible without people, as if to suggest that methodological collectivism[7] implies the opposite. But not even the

From *The Journal of Philosophy*, 53 (1956), pp. 801–813.

[1] The present paper is based upon a discussion first presented in my dissertation, *Form, Function and Structure: a Philosophical Study Concerning the Foundations of Theory in Anthropology* (unpublished manuscript in the Sterling Memorial Library, Yale University, 1954). Without imputing to him any responsibility for its content, I would like to thank my friend, Mr. Samuel E. Gluck, for his many helpful suggestions, without which this paper would be far less readable than it is.

[2] J. W. N. Watkins, "Ideal Types and Historical Explanation," *British Journal for the Philosophy of Science*, Vol. 3 (1952), pp. 22–43; "The Principle of Methodological Individualism" *ibid.*, pp. 186–189.*

* [*The first of these two papers is reprinted as selection 38 in this volume. Editor's note.*]

[3] Karl R. Popper, *The Open Society and Its Enemies*, Princeton, 1950 (1st English ed., 2 vols., London, 1945). References will be given to the Princeton edition, with references to the first English edition following in parentheses.

[4] F. A. Hayek, *The Counter-Revolution of Science*, Glencoe, Ill., 1952. This is a volume of papers that were first published elsewhere.

[5] See May Brodbeck, "On the Philosophy of the Social Sciences," *Philosophy of Science*, Vol. 21 (1954), pp. 140–156, pp. 142ff., for other comments on this subject.

[6] See my "Bidney's Humanistic Anthropology," *Review of Metaphysics*, Vol. 8 (1955), pp. 493–509, pp. 501f.

[7] I have retained the term "methodological collectivism" inasmuch as it is the term used in the literature of our subject, but I do feel it to be an awkward expression and even a misleading one. I would have preferred to use "sociologism," which would suggest that some concepts of social science theory are entirely sociocultural and not to be treated as individualistic or psychologistic.

stronger doctrine of ontological collectivism (e.g., Hegel) requires so absurd a thesis, and thus it appears that Professor Hayek's point offers no systematic support to the principle.

The present paper will attempt to point out that there are problems confronting social science that require solutions not amenable to individualistic analysis and yet are not holistic or historicistic. Methodological collectivism does not deny that there is much to be usefully learned from the study of the individualistic aspects of human action, but it does insist that merely because all human cultures are first discovered through the activities of their individual members it does not follow that there are no possible problems for which the particular individuals are irrelevant. In most of their activities people behave in culturally sanctioned ways, and this way of expressing it immediately suggests the feasibility of conceptually separating the man from his culture.[8] Unless this conceptual separation is possible, I cannot see how we can ever account theoretically for any *way* of behaving; all we can discuss are individual behavers. It is not irrelevant to point out that the references and citations in the writings of the aforementioned methodological individualists clearly suggest that they are very much interested both in history, which is largely concerned with the descriptive reconstruction of action within a given situation, and theoretical economics, which provides a highly abstract account of economic behavior within economic and social institutions the existence of which is already assumed. To the theoretical questions of institutional development and change, of major interest to sociologists and anthropologists, they seem to have paid little attention. And it is precisely upon the analysis of such questions that the principle of methodological individualism breaks down.

A Non-Individualistic Sociocultural Theory

To anthropological writers, kinship and the nomenclature of kinship have long been matters of interest. Few things may seem as trivial as the terms we use to designate the people to whom we are related; we call our aunts "aunt" and our cousins "cousin" and there the matter ends. Consequently a brief illustration of the anthropological view may well be in order. Were we to learn of a group that used one and the same kin-term to denote both the mother and the mother's younger sister but a separate and distinct term for the mother's older sister, our reaction would probably be one of amused indifference. To anthropologists, however, such information would suggest that the preferred choice for a second wife is the younger sister of the first wife but not her older sister. As a potential, or even actual, stepmother of the children of her sister, having to them a sociological relationship not unlike that of their own mother, she is called by the same term. Whether or not this is true for any given society would have to be determined by empirical field research. But our example does suggest that kinship nomenclature is affected by sociological factors, and further suggests the feasibility of constructing a systematic theory about the sociocultural determination of systems of such nomenclature.[9]

Although thinking along the above lines has been suggestive and useful, it must be admitted that no small amount of it has been

[8] *Cf.* Georg Simmel, *The Sociology of Georg Simmel*, tr. and ed. by Kurt H. Wolff, Glencoe, Ill., 1950, pp. 26ff.

[9] *Cf.* A. R. Radcliff-Brown: "There are some who would regard this kind of terminology as 'contrary to common sense,' but this means no more than that it is not in accordance with our modern European ideas of kinship and its terminology. . . . The Choctaw and Omaha terminologies do call for some explanation; but so does the English terminology, in which we use the word 'cousin' for all children of both brothers and sisters of both mother and father — a procedure which would probably seem to some non-Europeans to be contrary not only to common sense but also to morals. What I wish to attempt, therefore, is to show you that Choctaw and Omaha terminologies are just as reasonable and fitting in the social systems in which they occur as our terminology is in our social system." (*Structure and Function in Primitive Society*, London, 1952, pp. 55f.)

hit-or-miss, after-the-fact speculation attempting to rationalize seemingly strange terminologies.[10] It is, therefore, to the credit of Professor George Peter Murdock that he has attempted to bring some order into these studies through the development of a theory which attempts to show that the state or form of any given system of kinship nomenclature is determined by (or is a function of) the states or forms of certain specified sociocultural variables.[11] These are four in number: the rule of marriage, the form of the family, the rule of descent, and the rule of residence. For the purpose of the present paper we will have no need to discuss these, nor need we be concerned about the empirical adequacy of the particular theory introduced as our example.[12] My concern here is only with the kind of theory it is and the tenability of formulating such theories. For each of these variables Professor Murdock has determined the possible types — there being only a very small number of ways of reckoning descent, through either parent or through both, and similarly for the other variables — and one is thus able to determine the number of possible combinations that could be had. And this would be the number of possible types of social system, if it should prove to be theoretically advantageous to define the social system in terms of these variables. But regardless of any more widespread application of such social system types, it is clearly a *methodological* assumption of the given theory that we may talk about a system that is defined in terms of five variables, the four *relatively independent* variables mentioned and the system of kinship nomenclature.[13]

For any given empirical sociocultural system it is possible to determine which of the limited number of social system types it is. But it is also possible to talk meaningfully about system types that have never been discovered. One hypothetically, but perhaps not nomologically,[14] possible rule of residence, the "amitalocal" rule, could be characterized as a "cultural provision that unmarried females take up their residence with a paternal aunt and bring their husbands to their aunt's home when they marry."[15] Since no social system having this feature has ever been described any characterization of such a system would not be what Mr. Watkins calls an "individualistic ideal type," that is, a type constructed out of specifically observed social experience. On his view, until you have determined empirically that such a type exists — or, for the sake of those who tend to impute strange philosophical beliefs to every use of realistic language, that the type is a model for the social behavior in some empirical sociocultural system — it has no content and is theoretically superfluous. I fear that some thinkers have determined to insist that social science must labor under restrictions it would never occur to them to impose upon physical science. Were they more consistent they would forbid our talking about ideal gases and free swinging pendulums; we can only speculate upon what they might have said to Mendeleef about the then

[10] An example of this is discussed *ibid.*, pp. 56ff.

[11] George Peter Murdock, *Social Structure* (New York, 1949), Ch. 7, "The Determinants of Kinship Terminology."

[12] It might be worth while if some symbolic logician would attempt to re-state in formal language the theory as it is now, in order to learn both if the theorems are a self-consistent set and if it might not be possible to derive still more of them once the limitations of the English language are overcome.

[13] Of course, we may hope that similar theories may be constructed to account for change in each of the variables of the present theory. Professor Murdock seems to think that change in the rule of residence is most important for change in the kinship system, and seeks to show in Chapter 8 how the form of the rule is related to economic matters. Could we anticipate theoretically changes of a specific kind in the rule, then we would be able, further, to anticipate changes in the nomenclature of kinship. And while all such theories would define or postulate methodologically systems or types, there is no reason to think that their theoretical use implies reification, though Mr. Watkins asserts that he cannot allow the use of sociologistic concepts unless it can be shown that their reification would be justified (*loc. cit.*, p. 189). *Cf.* Marion J. Levy, Jr., *The Structure of Society*, Princeton, 1952, pp. 30f.

[14] Ward H. Goodenough, "Amitalocal Residence," *American Anthropologist*, N. S., Vol. 53 (1951), pp. 427–429.

[15] Murdock, *op. cit.*, p. 71.

existing gaps in his periodic table. But no physicist would recognize any obligation to accept such guidance and there is no reason for social scientists to do so either. Professor Murdock's theory makes it perfectly proper for us to talk about systems that have never been discovered. Indeed, there are some possible occasions that may require us to believe that some determinate type of system, for which we have no evidence of a factual or individualistic nature, did exist. We are informed that the evidence is overwhelming that avunculocal residence[16] "can never develop out of neolocal, bilocal, or patrilocal residence."[17] In consequence, a social system having an avunculocal rule of residence cannot have been preceded by any type other than one or another of those with a matrilocal rule. Also, it may be the case that the possibilities for change at any given time are restricted by the fact that not all of the forms that any given variable may have are compatible with all of the present forms of the others. If we know, on historical evidence, that a given people had at one time a social system type out of which its present type could not have developed, we would be required — assuming Murdock's theory or some modification of it — to conclude that some other social system type, for the existence of which we have no other evidence, did in fact exist. (Here too those who would feel better about it may translate my sentence into another one, replacing the idea of an existing social system with that of a model for social behavior. My own feeling is that the form of expression is of no consequence to my argument, but that realistic language is less complicated.)

Some Characteristics of the Theory

Relevant to the problem of the present paper are two characteristics of the theory of kinship nomenclature: (1) it is not amenable to analysis according to the prescription of methodological individualism and yet is not holistic or historicistic; and (2) it is not psychologistic inasmuch as all its concepts are entirely upon the sociocultural level, making no appeal to the psychological dispositions of individual people.[18]

To characterize a society in terms of the variables of the theory is to say nothing about the human individuals of whom it consists. To know that in such and such a society descent is reckoned in the female line or that residence is avunculocal provides no information about the aspirations and activities of particular persons. Finally, to discover that anticipated changes in the economy of the society will make the present rule of residence inconvenient or anachronistic, and that the present forms of other variables of the social system will make some specific form of change the most reasonable to expect, requires no reference to the personalities and psychological propensities of particular persons.[19]

But while the theory we have been con-

[16] Under an avunculocal rule of residence a young man would settle with his maternal uncle and bring his bride to live there; under a neolocal rule a married couple establishes an independent household; and under a bilocal rule such a couple has the option of settling with the family of either the husband or the wife.

[17] Murdock, *op. cit.*, p. 207.

[18] My own view is that methodological individualism cannot be separated from psychologism, but Professor Popper advocates an individualistic sociology which is autonomous (an incongruous position which Mr. Watkins, in his recognition of the psychologistic nature of his thesis, has been consistent enough to avoid, *op. cit.*, pp. 28f*.). Nevertheless, he is forced to admit some psychological laws but seeks to avoid the issue by calling them trivial.

* [*See pp.* 608*f*., *this volume. Editor's note.*]

[19] In a private communication, Dr. J. O. Wisdom wonders whether I perhaps "use the phrase 'methodological individualism' quite differently from Popper or Watkins." I suppose he has in mind the recent attempt by Mr. Watkins, in a rejoinder to Miss Brodbeck's paper ("Methodological Individualism: A Reply," *Philosophy of Science*, Vol. 22 (1955), pp. 58–62), to distinguish between a methodological individualism which allows the use of anonymous individual concepts and detailed individualistic explaining. He claims that he means to advocate the former (p. 62), and rereading his earlier paper I can see that there is an element of this present. But that Miss Brodbeck and I should both have misunderstood his intention suggests that there is a basis for the misunderstanding in the paper itself. And since the paper has achieved some degree of fame, as attested by its inclusion in an important anthology of *Readings*

sidering is not individualistic, it is also not holistic or historicistic. Professor Murdock has sought to specify the variables that bear upon the sociocultural phenomena he seeks to deal with. There is no appeal to the nature of the whole, no notion that what occurs in change is the actualization of inherent potentiality. Use of the term "methodological holism" where others speak of "methodological collectivism" indicates that Mr. Watkins views all non-individualistic theories as necessarily holistic. But this results from not paying sufficient attention to the kind of theory we are presently discussing. Professor Murdock claims no inevitable necessity for the kind of change he describes. But he does insist that whenever the theoretically necessary and sufficient conditions obtain for some determinate kind of kinship system, then we may reasonably expect that kind of system to appear.[20] The individual characteristics of the members of the society need not be taken into account.

I have said that the theory of kinship nomenclature is not psychologistic, but in view of Professor Murdock's own assertion to the effect that one "system of organized knowledge which has significantly influenced this volume is behavioristic psychology," [21] a remark or two on this point is necessary. I believe that we have here a confusion of two points: one concerning the enculturation of the individual and the other concerning sociocultural change. The former quite clearly requires that reference be made to psychology and in particular to the theory of learning. The other has no such requirement. The behavior of every member of the society may be treated from the vantage point of psychological theory, and if the phenomena dealt with by social theory had no effect upon the behavior of individuals we may be sure that there would be no resultant social change. But it is the experience of social science that the basic bio-psychological similarity of human beings in general makes it unnecessary to take account of the psychology of individuals when explaining sociocultural change[22]; it is enough to deal with variables that are entirely on the sociocultural level. As Miss Brodbeck well remarks, "Psychological laws may be ubiquitous, but social laws may be formulated without taking them into account." [23] While societies consist of human beings, the psychological basis of individual

---

in the Philosophy of Science (ed. by H. Feigl and M. Brodbeck, New York, 1953), to warn possible readers against what I deem to be a methodological inadequacy seems perfectly justified, quite apart from Mr. Watkins' clarification.

The clarification, it may be noted, does not result in any methodological improvement. Mr. Watkins would have social science rely heavily upon (general as well as individual) psychological dispositions in constructing its explanations, but he seems entirely to ignore the recent studies by anthropologists and psychologists of the cultural conditioning of such dispositions. And well he might, for I cannot see how he could ever deal with such matters while insisting upon a theory which makes psychological dispositions methodologically primary. Moreover, even where there may be dispositions that are universal among men, these could not be used in explaining how any given social institution of a specific people (or its particular disposition set) came to be as it is. Mr. Watkins' paper, then, while it does provide illustrations of what I discuss below as synchronic social studies, remains, even as clarified, methodologically inadequate, for it does not allow the possibility of formulating the kind of a diachronic sociocultural theory of which Murdock's is an example.

[20] Mr. James B. Watson ("Four Approaches to Cultural Change: A Systematic Assessment," *Social Forces*, Vol. 32 (1953), pp. 137–145) has attempted to treat Murdock's theory as historicistic or, in his term, "developmental." A careful reading of his paper, however, makes it clear that his error results from mistaking some theorems of the theory for the theory itself. He notes that given some antecedent state of the social system, Professor Murdock allows that only a small number of possible states may succeed it. (A really developmental theory would not permit a number of alternatives.) But he has failed to note that the reason for this is that given the forms of the variables in that antecedent state, only a limited number of the changes possible in any one of them would be compatible with the existing forms of the others taken together. Thus, we have not the paradoxical eventless change of historicistic theories, but the precise specification of the reasons for change.

[21] Murdock, *op. cit.*, p. xvi; see also p. 131.

[22] See, A. L. Kroeber, *The Nature of Culture*, Chicago, 1952, Part I; and Leslie A. White, *The Science of Culture*, New York, 1949. [*White's views here are expressed in selection 51 below; see for example, pp. 662 to 665. Editor's note.*]

[23] Brodbeck, *loc. cit.*, p. 53.

learning and behavior plays no *logical* role in the kind of explanation represented by the theory we have been considering. Stated in another way, while the comparatively stable bio-psychological nature of the human race may be a *necessary* condition for human sociocultural systems, it is not a *sufficient* condition for the specific forms of any of them.

Synchronic and Diachronic Social Studies

It was remarked earlier that the methodological individualists seemed to be interested in one kind of social study to the exclusion of any other kind. In terms more common, perhaps, among social scientists — at least among anthropologists — than philosophers, it may be said that they are more concerned with the development of synchronic social research and tend to ignore the possibilities for diachronic social theory. Logically, there is no opposition between the two, and it is not uncommon to find the same scholar concerned with both. But there are differences between the two approaches, and I raise the matter here because the assertion of the principle of methodological individualism implicitly rules out the possibility of diachronic social theory. It is concerned solely with the actions of individuals within a given sociocultural context and is incapable of recognizing as a *theoretical* problem the question of how the situation came to be as it is. To be sure, methodological individualists reiterate the so-called distinction between ideographic (historical) and nomothetic disciplines, and insist that the answer to diachronic questions must be given only by historical reconstruction. But it is clear that the logic of explanation requires, at least implicitly, the use of general laws,[24] and I cannot see that historical reconstruction is an exception to the rule. (Indeed, if the well-known selective character of historical research is not to give way to promiscuous subjectivity, the utilization of sociohistorical or sociocultural laws as providing criteria of relevance is certainly both required and implied.) Professor Popper tries to avoid this difficulty to his methodological individualism by insisting that the laws required for the rational justification of the results of historical inquiry are only trivial,[25] but he never troubles to specify just what are the logical properties of trivial laws that make them more acceptable than the more weighty members of the species. Nor does he show how the latter may be left out once the former have been admitted. I suspect that he may fear that there can be no serious socio-historical law that is not at the same time historicistic. But in this he is mistaken, as the example of Murdock's theory of kinship nomenclature clearly demonstrates.

I shall use the term "synchronic social now" to refer to that period of time within which the given sociocultural system[26] remains more or less stable. For most purposes, the persistence of the system may be assumed, and when an individual plans his day-to-day affairs he need not be concerned about social change. Governments, however, which plan for much longer periods, might well be so concerned, and it is certainly amazing how often they are unable to anticipate the results of their own plans. Which need not mean that they ought to give up necessary planning, but rather that they should

[24] Carl G. Hempel, "The Function of General Laws in History," *Journal of Philosophy*, Vol. 39 (1942), reprinted in H. Feigl and W. Sellars, eds., *Readings in Philosophical Analysis*, New York, 1949, pp. 459–471; Hempel and Paul Oppenheim, "Studies in the Logic of Explanation," *Philosophy of Science*, Vol. 15 (1948), pp. 135–175*; Popper, *op. cit.*, pp. 445ff. and 720ff. (II, pp. 248ff. and 342ff.); and R. B. Braithwaite, *Scientific Explanation*, Cambridge, 1953, p. 2.

[25] Popper, *op. cit.*, p. 448 (II, pp. 251f.).

[26] I do not necessarily mean by "sociocultural system" the sum of all the institutions available to the people of any group. Indeed, inasmuch as I doubt that we shall ever have theories about such a sum, there need be no fear that my term opens the way for holism. As indicated in note 13 and the text, I am satisfied to mean by the term nothing more than what is defined by the variables of a sociocultural theory.

* [*This article is reprinted as selection 5 in this volume. Editor's note.*]

recognize the value of diachronic social research. (Professor Hayek prefers that they give up planning and conveniently opts for a doctrine that makes diachronic theory impossible.) For it is obvious that social systems do change, and accounting for such change is the task of diachronic social studies. Such studies are intended to deal with how the synchronic social now develops from the previous synchronic social now[27] and the conditions for such change in general. And while the logic of explanation is the same for both, diachronic explanations do differ materially from synchronic ones.

Consider what is involved when the social behavior of some individual person is predicted or explained. What is required is knowledge about relevant institutions. I know that A will do such and such next week because I know that he will then be in a situation that requires that sort of behavior, even as was B some months before. In other words, I know what sort of behavior is expected or deemed rational under specified conditions during the synchronic social now. Thus, while my prediction of A's action, or my explanation of *B*'s, does involve future or past time, it does clearly presuppose the relative stability or persistence of certain institutions. My explanation takes the institutional framework for granted without attempting to explain it, and focuses upon the individual actor. And this is all that Professor Popper does when he talks about the logic of the situation. The "rational man" is able to act wisely only to the extent that his familiarity with the relevant institutions of the synchronic social now is adequate to that end. If confronted with sudden basic changes in these institutions, his knowledge of former expectations and possibilities would avail him little; nor would those who based their predictions of his behavior on that same knowledge fare any better.

Actually, on the basis of the knowledge referred to, specific explanations or predictions of individual social behavior are not yet possible. We require, as Professor Popper has himself said, both general statements or laws and statements of specific facts. Relative to the explanation of individual behavior, all we have so far is the latter, and even that only in part. The account of the synchronic now is only a descriptive statement. It tells how people in a given community tend to act, how they have come to behave in certain circumstances, what is deemed by them to be the best behavior when things are such and so. And while we may state these facts in a general way, giving the appearance of a social law of restricted scope, if our interest is in the behavior of some specific person this will not serve as a theoretical explanation. To be sure, if in society *s*, all men of *t* type in circumstance *c* do some specific thing, and if *A* is such a *t* in *c*, we may expect him to do the same thing. But it is almost never that we can say something significant about all men of any type, and what often happens is that social scientists, rather than find out what determines the exceptions, protect their generalizations with a strong *ceteris paribus*. But this seems to reduce the generalization to the trivial point that if *A* is the kind of person who behaves — at least in matters of the sort under discussion — in the socially accepted manner, then he will behave in the socially accepted manner.

Whether or not any individual behaves in the accepted or in the rational manner will depend upon his personal psychological make-up. To complete our explanation, then, we must add two additional factors. First we must have specific data concerning the person himself, data of the sort that psychological theory deems to be diagnostic of the kind of person he is. And, finally, we need some system of psychological theory. It then turns out that the sociocultural data only provided us with information concerning the ways in which the members of our subject's group behave, that is, they provided factual criteria of usual behavior. But the problem to be solved, a prediction or ex-

[27] It seems convenient to talk about past and future synchronic social nows instead of cluttering up our terminology with such phrases as "synchronic social then" or "synchronic historical then."

planation of a specific person's action, is one that is theoretically a psychological problem.[28]

While synchronic questions are concerned with behavior within a specific sociocultural context, which may often be amenable to individualistic analysis, diachronic questions are of another sort. They do not take the situation for granted but are rather concerned with how the situation came to be as it is. This involves, for any specific situation, an historical reconstruction. But it also requires, at least in principle, a theoretical justification for the reconstruction. And this can be provided only by a system of sociocultural laws. There is nothing absurd about the possibility of discovering such laws, and the fact that the principle of methodological individualism is not compatible with the search for them is hardly ground for the rejection of a perfectly tenable program. Such laws would be concerned with the kinds of conditions under which determinate change may be expected in sociocultural systems, and if the theoretically necessary and sufficient conditions for some determinate kind of change were to obtain, we may reasonably expect that the change would take place. Who the people are whose institutions are changing is not relevant to the problem. The view of the methodological individualist seems to be that social change results from conscious effort, though the results are often more than people bargained for. A return to our example will suffice to cast doubt upon this view. There is evidence enough that kinship systems do change, but it is absolutely untrue that every so often the people of a society get together to discuss the feasibility of bringing change about, especially inasmuch as people tend to think that their system reflects the order of things and the true morality. And in a sense, of course, this is true, for it reflects the order of things social within their own sociocultural system and defines for them the range of the application of incest prescriptions[29] as well as the limits of the moral obligations imposed by kinship.

A brief statement must be made about people. Methodological individualists like to caricature the views of their opponents by suggesting that the latter believe in peopleless systems of culture. This is not even true of ontological collectivism,[30] and is surely false when ascribed to the methodological view. What we know about social systems we have learned from observing the behavior and probing the thoughts of particular human beings. Furthermore, the only way to test the truth or falsity of any diachronic theory of sociocultural change would be to observe individual behavior. Noticing that certain changes were taking place, we might predict that after a while, say a generation, a certain type of kinship system will prevail in a given society. This means that under specifiable conditions of human intercourse specific behavior may be expected; people will be related to others in determinate social ways and will act in ways compatible with those relations. It is the task of the social scientist to work out the implications of these relationships in full, taking account of the fact that the specific content of social action will differ from culture to culture, even among cultures having the same type of kinship system.[31] The social scientists of the next

[28] Richard Brandt, in Part VI of his *Hopi Ethics, A Theoretical Analysis* (Chicago, 1954), deals with his subject in the manner of synchronic studies. While it often seems that he wishes to provide a sociocultural account of the Hopi value system, this system is actually assumed by him, and his main effort is to show how individual Hopi develop certain attitudes. Indeed, he calls his approach a "contemporary context theory of ethical norms," and his theoretical apparatus is quite explicitly psychological.

[29] *Cf. ibid.*, p. 207, for an example of this.

[30] Hegel, for example, begins his *Philosophy of Right* with an analysis of what he calls "abstract right," which is concerned with the individual's subjective experience of right and value.

[31] For example, the same kind of social system type, so-called Normal Eskimo, is to be found in the Andaman, Copper Eskimo, American, and Ruthenian societies, among others (Murdock, *op. cit.*, p. 228). Surely the interests, aspirations, activities, and conscious goals of people in these widely separated groups are sufficiently different to make doubtful the thesis that it is these that determine the persistence or change of social structure.

generation may then seek to discover how, indeed, the individual persons in the society do behave in the specified situations. And thus the prediction will be confirmed or not, depending on how individuals do act.

What methodological collectivism does not admit is that all the general concepts of social science may be exhaustively analyzed in terms of the actions, interests, and volitions of specific individuals. Such a view of our concepts would leave us with theories the entire contents of which were the facts that suggested them in the first place, having no further power of prediction or explanation.[32] Nor does it admit the truth of Mr. Watkin's claim that only concepts or types constructed out of observed social activity are admissible. No one has discovered a society with an amitalocal rule of residence, but, in light of Murdock's theory, it is surely not meaningless to talk about social systems having this feature. Finally, methodological collectivism insists that inasmuch as the problems of social science differ from those of psychology — the former being concerned, at least in part, with questions of sociocultural development, persistence, and change, the latter with individual behavior — the claim that all sociocultural concepts are, in the end, psychological is untenable. While the experience of each person is subjective, neither the content nor the occasion of the experience is. The individual subjectively experiences the norms of society and its accumulated knowledge and lore, but the social scientist deals with these contents in their objective or social character. I strongly suspect that no little amount of confusion on this point stems from the failure to distinguish between the psychological or subjective and the phenomenological or sociocultural[33] concepts of mind.[34]

[32] *Cf.* Braithwaite, *op. cit.*, pp. 67f.; and Lewis W. Beck, "Constructions and Inferred Entities," *Philosophy of Science*, Vol. 17 (1950), pp. 74–86.

[33] This notion is concerned with the content of experience, and is called phenomenological in epistemological discourse and sociocultural in social science discourse. I dare say that some idealistic phenomenologists would take issue with the idea that the status of such contents is sociocultural, but this cannot be discussed here.

[34] Mr. Watkins seems especially given to this confusion. In any event, he seems to treat the disposition of certain individuals to weep during the death scene in *Othello* (a psychological disposition) and the disposition of police officers or Speakers of the House of Commons to act in the manner prescribed for their offices (institutional or role behavior) as being essentially of the same sort [*see in this volume, p. 470*].

Methodological Individualism: A Reply to Criticism 47

The Alleged Inadequacy of Methodological Individualism

J. W. N. WATKINS

In a recent issue of this Journal Mr. Leon J. Goldstein attacked the principle of methodological individualism in social science[1] as formulated by me.[2] He says that he does not wish to defend the holist or historicist method against which I advanced an individualist method (though some of his remarks have, to my apprehensive ears, a somewhat historicist ring — for instance, he speaks on page *619** of the need to explain how a whole social situation came to be what it is by recourse to "a system of sociocultural laws"; but no doubt an innocent interpretation can be put on this unguarded remark). His thesis is that methodological individualism is intolerably restrictive since it prohibits not only historicist sociology to which he is opposed, but some perfectly legitimate and non-historicist kinds of description and explanation, particularly in anthropology. He also charges me with being unduly restrictive in two further ways and with intellectual confusion. Alas, it seems to me that his criticisms are baseless and that he has not undermined methodological individualism as I formulated it at all. To show this I am afraid that I shall have to indulge in an immodest amount of quotation of myself because most of his criticisms depend on misreadings of my views.

(1) Mr. Goldstein stresses again and again that many cultural phenomena cannot be explained in terms of the *personal* dispositions of *particular* individuals. He speaks of "problems for which the particular individuals are irrelevant" (p. *613*), of descriptions of kinship systems which make "no appeal to the psychological dispositions of individual people" (p. *615*), of sociological concepts which are not "analyzable in terms of the actions, interests, and volitions of specific individuals" (p. *620*), and more to the same effect. The unwary reader would certainly gain the impression that the methodological position he is attacking requires the explanation of any social situation, whether it be a unique situation, or a recurrent situation such as inflation, or a local situation which persists through long stretches of time such as some particular kinship system, to be in terms of the personal idiosyncrasies of separately identifiable individuals. This would certainly be an absurdly narrow requirement and it is one which I have explicitly and repeatedly disavowed. In the "Ideal Types" paper which Mr. Goldstein attacks, I said: "An explanation may be in terms of *typical* dispositions of more or less anonymous individuals" (*op. cit.*, p. *464*, italics in the original), and again: "The mark of an explanation in principle [the kind of explanation with which that paper was largely concerned] is its reliance on typical dispositions and its disregard of personal differences" (p. *467*). Moreover, I spent three pages of a five-page reply[3] (to which Mr.

From *The Journal of Philosophy*, 55 (1958), pp. 390–395.

[1] "The Inadequacy of the Principle of Methodological Individualism," this JOURNAL, Vol. LIII, No. 25 (December 6, 1956), pp. 801–813. [*Reprinted as selection 46 in this volume. Editor's note.*]

[2] "Ideal Types and Historical Explanation," in *Readings in the Philosophy of Science*, ed. by Feigl and Brodbeck. [*Reprinted as selection 38 in this volume. Editor's note.*]

* [*Page numbers in italics refer to this volume. Editor's note.*]

[3] "Methodological Individualism: A Reply," *Philosophy of Science*, Vol. 22, No. 1, January 1955.

Goldstein refers) to an earlier criticism insisting to the point of tedium "that an individualistic explanation of a social event need not refer to *specific* individuals," that it may be an "anonymous, shorthand individualistic explanation" which makes "only tacit references to anonymous individuals" (pp. 60–62, italics in the original).

Footnote 19 of Mr. Goldstein's article indicates that he became reluctantly aware, on reading that reply and re-reading my original article, that this is indeed my position. Unfortunately, he did not feel obliged to reconsider any of those criticisms which presuppose that I hold the absurdly narrow view which he attributes to me in the main body of his article. On the contrary. In footnote 34 he gives a *précis* of a further passage in my "Ideal Types" paper where I explicitly included not only the more personal or temperamental dispositions of people in their private capacity but also the more impersonal or institutionalized dispositions of people in their public capacity — dispositions "which may vary very little when one man undertakes another's role" (p. *470*) — and where I emphasized the special importance of the latter kind of disposition for social science; but instead of admitting that this is further evidence that I do not regard social science as a sort of multiple biography Mr. Goldstein complains that I have *confused* the latter kind of disposition with the former. First he knowingly puts a too narrow interpretation on my views; then he condemns statements of mine which conflict with that interpretation as evidence of my intellectual confusion!

(2) His article contains another very different line of criticism to the effect that "even where there may be dispositions that are universal among men, these could not be used in explaining how any given social institution of a specific people . . . came to be as it is" (p. *616*). On this criticism of myself I will make three comments. (a) It does at least have the merit of countering all his other criticisms which wrongly assume that I permit the use of only the peculiar dispositions of specific people. (b) However, when in my "Ideal Types" paper I was considering historical explanations of *unique* events, I said: "The idea that the historian's interpretative principles are simply generalisations about human nature . . . is inadequate. His knowledge of human nature in general has to be supplemented by a knowledge of the peculiar personalities of the principal actors concerned" (p. *469*). (I was speaking there of a detailed historical explanation of, say, some diplomatic manoeuvre, rather than of an explanation in principle of, say, some recurrent or persistent economic or anthropological situation.) (c) Even if Mr. Goldstein ignores (b) above, he cannot ignore the well-known logical fact that if you combine the same major premiss with different minor premisses you get different conclusions. The same typical disposition may, in slightly different circumstances, lead to widely different social results. For example, Professor Paul A. Samuelson has constructed an economic model where, given a *constant* marginal propensity to consume, "a single impulse of net investment will . . . send the system up to infinity at a compound interest rate of growth. On the other hand, a single infinitesimal unit of disinvestment will send the system ever downward at an increasing rate."[4]

(3) Mr. Goldstein says that my views are unjustifiably restrictive in a second way. He says that I hold that "until you have determined empirically that such a type [*i.e.*, a theoretical model] exists . . . it has no content and is theoretically superfluous" (p. *614*). He points out, quite rightly, that natural scientists use concepts like "ideal gas" and complains that I forbid social scientists to use an idealizing procedure which has proved so fruitful in physics. On this I have two comments. (a) I actually hold (though there was no occasion for me to mention this in my "Ideal Types" paper) that the empirical applicability of a theoretical concept *cannot* determine its meaning because one can

[4] "Interactions Between the Multiplier Analysis and the Principle of Acceleration," *Readings in Business Cycle Theory* (Blakiston Series, Vol. II), p. 268.

only discover whether it has any empirical application if one has *first* understood its meaning. (b) I cannot imagine why Mr. Goldstein supposes that I discourage the use of simplification and idealization in intellectual experiments in social science when I actually encouraged their use in my "Ideal Types" paper — my subject was, after all, *ideal* types. I wrote: "Such intellectual experimenting *may* be fruitful even if some of the premisses are very unrealistic. For instance, the concept of a static economy in equilibrium aids the analysis of the changes and disequilibria of actual economies. And gross exaggeration of one factor may show up an influence which would otherwise have been overlooked" (p. *464*). In footnote 6 I stressed the analogy between the use of idealized principles in economics and in natural science.

(4) I wonder what view Mr. Goldstein supposes he is rebutting when he solemnly announces: "It is absolutely untrue that every so often the people of a society get together to discuss the feasibility of bringing change about" (p. *619*). He is certainly not rebutting methodological individualism. I followed in the wake of Adam Smith (whose famous passage about the individual being led "to promote an end which was no part of his intention" I quoted) and Professors F. A. Hayek and K. R. Popper when I spoke of certain large social changes as "human creations — not deliberate creations, of course, but the unintended product of the behaviour of interacting people" (p. *461*). I said that part of the object of a historical reconstruction should be to show "that significant events which no one intended are resultants of the behaviour of interacting individuals" (p. *472*). In chapter 14 of *The Open Society and its Enemies* (a book to which Goldstein refers) Popper stressed the vast difference between methodological individualism proper and a naive conspiracy theory of society according to which all social changes are brought about deliberately. Hayek's *The Counter-Revolution of Science* (to which Goldstein also rightly refers as an authoritative statement of methodological individualism) is largely an examination of the important implications of the fact that neither the growth nor the working of most social institutions are the result of conscious design or control.

(5) Like some other critics of methodological individualism, Mr. Goldstein supposes that in making human dispositions methodologically primary I ignore their cultural conditioning (p. *616*). Thus my methodology is accused of being over-restrictive in a third way, in that it forbids attempts to explain the existence of a disposition which is widespread among the members of a particular social group. But this is not so, as an example will indicate. Suppose that it is established that Huguenot traders were relatively prosperous in 17th-century France and suppose that this is explained in terms of a widespread disposition among them (a disposition for which there is independent evidence) to plough back into their businesses a larger proportion of their profits than was customary among their Catholic competitors. Now this explanatory disposition might very well be explained in its turn — perhaps in terms of the general thriftiness which Calvinism is said to encourage, and/or in terms of the fewer alternative outlets for the cash resources of people whose religious disabilities prevented them from buying landed estates or political offices. (I cannot vouch for the historical accuracy of this example.)

I agree that methodological individualism allows the formation, or "cultural conditioning," of a widespread disposition to be explained only in terms of other human factors and not in terms of something *in*human, such as an alleged historicist law which forces people's dispositions into some predetermined mould. But this is just the anti-historicist point of methodological individualism to which Mr. Goldstein does not object.

(6) I turn, finally, to the particular counter-example which Mr. Goldstein cites against methodological individualism. I may say that I view this with much more sympathy than I view his other allegations. Whatever

attitude he may adopt to general criticisms a methodologist certainly ought to attend very seriously to a heartfelt protest that his methodology would stifle some live and kicking piece of research which is producing interesting results. Mr. Goldstein's counterexample concerns an anthropologist who has set himself the task of describing the structure and nomenclature of a certain kinship system. Of such a systematic description Mr. Goldstein says: "(1) It is not amenable to the prescription of methodological individualism and yet it is not holistic or historicistic; and (2) it is not psychologistic inasmuch as all its concepts are entirely upon the sociocultural level, making no appeal to the psychological dispositions of individual people" (p. *615*).

I readily agree that this piece of anthropological investigation does conflict with the narrow view of methodological individualism attributed to me by Mr. Goldstein: there is no doubt that you cannot explain the stability and peculiar characteristics of a kinship system in terms of the personal temperaments and private whims of the aunts and granddads who comprise it. The question is whether it could be explained in terms of certain widespread and anonymous dispositions and beliefs. I shall now show that it could.

In the first place, what creates kinship relations considered as social relationships is people's *attitudes* towards each other. True, these attitudes will be decisively influenced by their *beliefs* about the biological relationships between them. But, as Hayek has pointed out (*op. cit.*, p. 31), if *A* regards himself and is regarded by *B* and others as *B*'s father, then from a sociological point of view *A is B*'s "father" even if, as a matter of unknown biological fact, *B* is not the natural son of *A*.

Thus kinship relations are created by people's beliefs about, and consequent attitudes towards, each other. What gives a system of such relationships its stability and distinctive characteristics? Mr. Goldstein's answer, with which I agree, is: certain *rules* concerning marriage, inheritance, residence, etc., rules which help to regularize the behavior of a person towards each of his "relations" and their behavior towards him. Now a rule of this sort is simply a widespread disposition. To say, for example, that there is a system of primogeniture in a country is to say that widows, younger sons, daughters, their relations, friends, and the local authorities are all firmly disposed to acquiesce in the inheritance of a dead man's land by his eldest son. I conclude that there is no difficulty about the idea of an explanation of the stability and peculiar features of a certain kinship system in terms of certain widespread and persistent dispositions among its members. And I do not see any difficulty about the idea of a further explanation, also in individualistic terms, of how they came to share these dispositions. There is nothing mysterious about the way each of us acquires from example or precept certain habits of mind and behavior which are common in our society. My young children are already developing a typical English attitude towards policemen, and I do not need a "system of sociocultural laws" to explain this.

It is my belief that methodological individualism properly understood and methodological holism or historicism are exhaustive alternatives. I do not see how someone can abandon the idea that individuals (together with their material resources) are the only moving agents in history without introducing the idea that there are other, superhuman or subhuman, agencies at work in history. My resulting inclination to reject in advance the claim made by Mr. Goldstein and others that there is a legitimate position between an individualistic and an historicist methodology has not been weakened by a perusal of their arguments, all of which seem to me to collapse on examination. I therefore remain confident that methodological individualism excludes certain undesirable kinds of sociology without excluding anything desirable.

Methodological Individualism, Ontological Individualism, and the Enculturation of Psychological Dispositions

48

The Two Theses of Methodological Individualism

LEON J. GOLDSTEIN

The Ontological Thesis

It has become usual in the writings of methodological individualists to suggest that there is but one alternative to their methodological prescription in social science, and this they call 'holism'.[1] Maurice Mandelbaum has sought to counter this by offering a four part classification of types of sociological theories,[2] thus showing that the alternatives of the individualists is simply an instance of the fallacy of false disjunction. However, it is not at all likely that methodological individualists will find Mandelbaum's paper to the point; it does not deal with the problem that concerns them. I am not at all certain that Watkins, for example, would object to discourse about total societies — the usual meaning of 'holism' and the one with which Mandelbaum deals. He would only insist that such discourse must, at least in principle, be analysable into discourse about individuals and their dispositions, and he does refer approvingly to Ayer's statement that 'the English State . . . is a logical construction out of individual people'.[3] We need not be concerned with what Ayer here means by logical constructions, for I want only to show, since the English state is surely a social whole, that Watkins cannot be said to oppose a social whole. In this example, a holist is one who denies Ayer's assertion, not of necessity one who is interested in the English state.

According to Watkins, 'If methodological individualism means that human beings are the only moving agents in history, and if sociological holism means that some superhuman agents or factors are supposed to be at work in history, then these two alternatives are exhaustive'.[4] He further says, 'The central assumption of the individualistic position . . . is that no social tendency exists which could not be altered *if* the individuals concerned both wanted to alter it and possessed the appropriate information . . . This assumption could also be expressed by saying that no social tendency is somehow imposed on human beings "from above" (or "from

From the *British Journal for the Philosophy of Science*, 9 (1958), pp. 1–11, Cambridge University Press.

[1] Cf. J. W. N. Watkins, 'Historical Explanation in the Social Sciences', this *Journal*, 1957, **8**, 104–117.* In view of the many connotations of 'holism', I deem it regrettable that E. A. Gellner, in his otherwise admirable paper, 'Explanation in History', *Aristotelian Society Supplementary Volume XXX*, 1956, pp. 157–176, continues the practice of using 'holist' for everything non-indivualistic. I know of no really suitable term, but I much prefer the more cumbersome 'non-individualistic social science' to 'holism'. (And we shall see that they are by no means synonymous terms.)

* [*Reprinted as selection 45 in this volume. Editor's note.*]

[2] 'Societal Laws', this *Journal*, 1957, **8**, 211–224. [*Reprinted as selection 50 in this volume. Editor's note.*]

[3] *Language, Truth and Logic*, London, 2nd edn., 1950, p. 63; cited in Watkins, 'Ideal Types and Historical Explanation', in Feigl and Brodbeck, eds., *Readings in the Philosophy of Science*, New York, 1953, pp. 723–743; *462*; cf. p. *461* n. 18. [*Reprinted as selection 38 in this volume. Page numbers in italics refer to this volume. Editor's note.*]

[4] Op. cit., p. *605*.

below").'[5] Holists, it appears, are those who posit non-human entities which in some unexplained way are supposed to determine what happens to men. Human history, on this view, would, paradoxically, not be the history of men and their affairs, but rather of that entity or set of entities that impose themselves upon them. Holists may well be interested in entities that are total, that is, they may conceive their holistic entity to be a unitary sort of thing, and perhaps Hegel's *Weltgeist* is an instance of this. But it is not impossible that holists of more modest pretension could be concerned with entities of a less inclusive nature. Perhaps the 'basic patterns' of the anthropologist Kroeber are such lesser entities,[6] and it may be argued that their logic is rather like that of the *logoi spermatikoi* of Hellenistic thought.

If methodological individualism is the thesis that denies the existence of these non-human entities, it is clear that neither Mandelbaum, Gellner, in the paper cited above in a note, nor I, in my earlier paper on this subject,[7] may be said to have opposed it. Thus, one may wonder what the controversy is all about. The fact of the matter is, however, that under the rubric 'methodological individualism' Watkins has subsumed two positions. The one we have been dealing with is not a methodological position at all. This non-methodological — ontological — version of the principle of methodological individualism is that doctrine which denies the existence of certain alleged entities. The other, more truly methodological thesis is the one which claims that all explanation in social science must, in the end, be reduced to individual dispositions. I shall attempt to deal with what this means in the following section of the paper. For the present I wish to discuss further this ontological thesis. It is not enough, it seems to me, simply to separate the two individualisms and observe that it is quite likely that in the ontological version we discover a point of agreement for most of us who have been interested in this matter. For this, I have two reasons. The first is that the bulk of the rhetorical force of the arguments that are supposed to be in defence of the more methodological of the individualist theses comes from confusing its denial with denial of the ontological thesis, and the fact that for most of us the ontological holist thesis is untenable. The suggestion that non-individualistic social science has evil consequences for freedom and morality has never been made out. Instead, we are supposed to wonder just what can possibly be intended when we talk of freedom and morality in a social world exhaustively determined by non-human entities which impose its history upon man.

My second reason for being unwilling to end discussion of the ontological version is that we are often told that holism is inextricably bound up with another methodological evil, historicism,[8] and here, too, holism and non-individualistic social science are confused. The thesis of historicism is that nothing men do makes a difference; all that will happen happens of necessity given the nature of history, or society, or the dialectic, or the *Weltgeist*. But here 'history', 'society', 'the dialectic' or 'the *Weltgeist*' serve as possible names of a holistic entity, the existence of which both Watkins and I agree in denying. Historicism is, then, an appurtenance of holism, and neither has to do with the claim of some of us that social science must be non-individualistic. Methodological individualists have never shown that to deny the assertion that all explanation in social science must

[5] Ibid., *p. 605*, his italics. I agree with the main point of this statement and would add only that included in the 'appropriate information' may well be non-individualistic social laws. Dr. Israel Scheffler, of Harvard University, observes that what Watkins says about social tendencies is equally applicable to furniture and machines, any of which could be altered if the individuals concerned both wanted to and had suitable knowledge.

[6] A. L. Kroeber, *The Nature of Culture*, Chicago, 1952; cf. chs. 5, 9 and 23.

[7] 'The Inadequacy of the Principle of Methodological Individualism', *Journal of Philosophy*, 1956, **53**, 801–813. [*Reprinted as selection 46 in this volume. Editor's note.*]

[8] In Popper's sense of historicism, not Mannheim's. By 'historicism' Mannheim means the socio-historical determination of thought, which need not commit him to the view that in history we have the necessary actualisation of what was potential in earlier stages.

be in terms of individual dispositions entails historicism, and man's consequent helplessness, and I hope to suggest that this is not the case. If they think they have it is because they have not distinguished between their methodological and their non-methodological doctrines.

Whether or not one believes that non-individualism in social science can be defended without the risk of ontological error, it is surely the case that some social scientists have been aware of the distinctions that I have been trying to make above. Thus, Simmel says,

No matter whether we consider the group that exists irrespective of its individual members a fiction or a reality, in order to understand certain facts one must treat it as if it actually did have its own life, and laws, and other characteristics. And if one is to justify the sociological standpoint, it is precisely the difference between these characteristics and those of the individual existence that one must clarify.[9]

In the same way, Durkheim remarks,

So there is some superficiality about attacking our conception as scholastic and reproaching it for assigning to social phenomena a foundation in some vital principle or other of a new sort. We refuse to accept that these phenomena have as a substratum the conscience of the individual, we assign them another; that formed by all the individual consciences in union and combination. . . . Nothing is more reasonable, then, than this proposition at which such offense has been taken; that a belief or social practice may exist independently of its individual expressions. We clearly did not imply by this that society can exist without individuals, an obvious absurdity we might have been spared having attributed to us . . .[10]

In sum, there are any number of people who have given thought to this matter who would say with Professor Ginsberg, 'To assign characteristics to groups is by no means the same as to consider them as entities which exist independently of the individuals which compose them'.[11]

All of these passages show that their authors feel no need of the belief in hypostatic social entities, yet they insist that explanation in social science need not, and perhaps cannot be individualistic. If methodological individualists want to claim that this is not a consistent set of beliefs, they must show that the rejection of what I refer to as their methodological thesis entails or strongly supports the ontological position we have discovered that Watkins intends by the term 'holism'. But this has never been done, perhaps never even attempted. And I dare say it never will be so long as methodological individualists do not trouble to distinguish between the two kinds of individualism they support.

That the rejection of the methodological thesis does not entail or support holism[12] is suggested by Durkheim's referring to the community of consciousness or sentiment as a consequence of individuals living together. There are many such passages in his writings, and his failure to take pains in expressing himself on the point has led his critics to saddle him with belief in something called 'the group mind' or an actually existing collective. We have seen that he denies that this was his intention, but that apart, he is certainly not required to affirm it. It seems to me that a possible construction of Durkheim's words would have him advocating a point of view that may be named 'sociological emergence'. This would claim that, for whatever reasons, when human beings live together, share common experiences, and so forth, there emerge common sentiments and modes of representation [13] which would never have arisen apart from group life and which

[9] *The Sociology of Georg Simmel*, tr. and ed. by Kurt Wolff, Glencoe, Ill., 1950, p. 26.

[10] *Suicide*, tr. by Spaulding and Simpson, Glencoe, Ill., 1951, pp. 319 sq.

[11] *On the Diversity of Morals*, Melbourne, London, Toronto, 1956, p. 152.

[12] That is, the decision to reject the methodological thesis leaves one uncommitted so far as the ontological thesis is concerned, though it seems most reasonable that anyone who agrees with Watkins concerning the former ought to agree concerning the latter as well. Logically, this isn't necessary, for one, being so-minded, could develop a holism in which the holistic entity had about as much to do as a deistic god after the creation.

[13] Cf. his 'Individual and Collective Representations', in *Sociology and Philosophy*, London, 1953, pp. 1–34.

cannot be analysed into the bio-psychological characteristics of unsocialised individuals. A view such as this does not require the support of holism. Indeed, it is entirely incompatible with that doctrine as it has been characterised by Watkins. According to Durkheim collective sentiments emerge out of the social intercourse of human beings, but the holist view is that such sentiments are imposed upon us by non-human entities, the true source of human history. Furthermore, since on the view we are considering what men do does make a difference, there being no emergent sentiments unless there are human beings sharing common experiences, historicism is equally incompatible with it. Presumably, the kinds of sentiments, values, modes of representation, and so on, that emerge depend upon the sorts of experiences that are shared, and man is not treated as if he were caught in the grip of some strange and monstrous being whose necessary development determines the course of history.

Sociological emergence is not, to be sure, a sociological theory. It does not in any way explain how it is that social institutions emerge. Nor does it have any specifically testable consequences. But in these respects it is not unlike the methodological thesis of methodological individualism. This, too, explains nothing, nor does it purport to explain anything. No sociological theory need make explicit reference to sociological emergence; its usefulness is of another sort. When methodological individualists assail this or that theory as holistic, when in fact it simply uses concepts that are not reducible to individual dispositions, its defenders have always the possibility of pointing to methodological emergence or some variation of it. That is, since the nature of the criticism levelled against the theory is ontological rather than methodological, sociological emergence offers a way of meeting it. It affirms that social scientists may develop non-individualistic theories without being holists. And it has the further advantage of forcing the methodological individualists to defend their methodological thesis on methodological grounds. If non-individualistic social science does not commit untoward ontological sins, the methodological individualists are required to find better grounds for its rejection. The doctrine that all explanation in social science is ultimately in terms of individual dispositions is not established, indeed, in no way supported, by the untenability of holism.

Individual and Anonymous Dispositions

There is, as we have seen, a properly methodological thesis included under the rubric 'methodological individualism', namely, the claim that in social science all explanation is to be individualistic. This sometimes means that we are required to carry each explanation back, step by step, until we have transformed sociological explanations into psychological ones.[14] Very often in his writings Watkins talks about *individual dispositions*, and perhaps there is in this mode of speech a reference to the ontological matters discussed above. We are said to be interested in the dispositions of individual human beings and not those of societies or other holistic entities. But this apart, it will be interesting to discover what sorts of thing pass muster, in his view, as individual dispositions. Fortunately, he has himself provided us with a number of examples, and the following quotations may serve as an adequate sample.

> What Smith actually showed was that individuals in competitive economic situations are led by nothing but their *personal dispositions* to promote unintentionally the public interest . . .[15]

> Suppose that it is established that Huguenot traders were relatively prosperous in seventeenth-century France and that this is explained in terms

[14] 'From this truism I infer the methodological principle which underlies this paper, namely, that the social scientist can continue searching for explanations of a social phenomenon until he has reduced it to psychological terms' (Watkins, *British Journal for the Philosophy of Science*, *1952*, 3, 28 sq.)

[15] 'Ideal Types and Historical Explanation', p. *462*.

of a wide-spread disposition among them (a disposition for which there is independent evidence) to plough back into their businesses a larger proportion of their profits than was customary among their Catholic competitors. . . .[16]

Finally, in a letter to me and by way of attempted refutation of my claim[17] that the principle of methodological individualism is not adequate to deal with such social scientific work as the theory of kinship nomenclature in G. P. Murdock's *Social Structure*, Watkins writes,

What gives a kinship system its stability and distinctive characteristics is, as you say, certain *rules* about marriage, inheritance, residence, etc., which govern the behaviour of each member to his "relations". But a local rule of inheritance, say, is simply a disposition shared by pretty well everybody in the locality to deal with the property of dead persons in a determinate way. I conclude that there is no difficulty in the idea of an anthropological explanation of the characteristics of a kinship system in terms of disposition and beliefs.

It may be noted that Watkins's closing remarks in the material last quoted indicate that he has misconstrued the point of my paper. I did not there challenge the view that societies or parts of them could be characterised in individualistic terms, though I must confess that I have come more and more to doubt that even this is possible,[18] but rather the view that sociocultural theory must be individualistic. The problem to which Murdock addresses himself is that of accounting for how it is that systems of kinship develop and change. This is rather different from merely characterising or describing any given such system, and even if one believes that the characterisation may be done in individualistic terms, rather than in non-reducible institutional terms, the status of the sociological laws which govern the development and change of such systems may perhaps require separate determination.

But putting aside this distinction between characterising what I have called the 'synchronic social now', that is, the institution under study during that period of time within which it remains more or less stable,[19] and characterising the laws that govern it, we have to consider what can be meant by calling the dispositions cited in the above passages 'individual dispositions'. It has been made amply clear by Watkins that he wishes to include as individualistic not only the dispositions of specific people about whom we may have factual knowledge, but also the dispositions of anonymous people.[20] Detailed individualistic explaining may well be an ideal for which to strive, but in most instances it is not a realisable goal, and there seems to be no point in virtually ruling the social sciences out of business by insisting upon it. All of the examples quoted are instances of these so-called anonymous dispositions. They are not only the dispositions of specific individuals with whom the social scientist may be concerned, but if his explanation is adequate we should be able to discover in many other people, concerning whom factual evidence may yet become available, the same characteristics or dispositions described.

I do not doubt that it was individual Huguenots who ploughed back their profits into their respective businesses, but it is not at all obvious that ploughing back — or, for that matter, being a Huguenot — is anything but a social or sociocultural characteristic. Properly to understand this kind of behaviour I am required to know something about the economic conditions of seventeenth-century France, the kinds of business enterprises that flourished, which of them, if any, were especially noted for the concentration in them of Huguenots, and so forth. Presumably I would wish to know other things, not of an economic nature, which bear upon such matters; e.g. if the governments of European

16 Op. cit., p. *623*.

17 Goldstein, op. cit., pp. *613–617*.

18 Such characterisations would tend to blur the distinction between the rôles of individuals and the domains of institutions, to use the apt expression of Mr. Harold Weisberg. Cf. Mandelbaum, 'Societal Facts', *British Journal of Sociology*, 1955, **6**, 305–317. [*Mandelbaum's article is reprinted as selection 49 in this volume. Editor's note.*]

19 Op. cit., p. *617*.

20 Watkins, 'Methodological Individualism: a Reply', *Philosophy of Science*, 1955, **22**, 58–62, p. 62.

countries were wont to interfere in economic affairs, this could be an important bit of relevant information. And thus a more or less full picture of Huguenot economic activities could be developed. But in all this no mention is made of any individual; no concern is felt for the psychological characteristics of anybody. We do not, to be sure, deny, as Watkins thinks we must, that all the time individual human beings are making decisions to buy and sell, to manufacture in greater or lesser quantity, and to export or import this or that. But it is not obvious that we need be concerned with them in reconstructing the economic conditions of seventeenth-century France.

Similar observations may be made about the characterising of the social and kinship system of a people. Specific people are related in specific ways, but the rules governing the determination of these relations are expressed — by the ethnographer even when not fully understood by the people themselves — in ways that do not make reference to individuals or to psychological characteristics. For the most part, people are born into their kinship relationships, and it seems entirely a reversal of actual fact to say that such relations 'are the product of peoples *attitudes* to each other, though these are partly determined by their *beliefs* about their biological relations'.[21] It seems more reasonable to say that for the most part the proper attitudes towards one's various kin are cultivated during the enculturation process.

The point here is that the kinds of dispositions to be found in people of any given type are socially induced dispositions. It seems odd to talk about widely recurring dispositions among Huguenot entrepreneurs and not to wonder about the coincidence of the recurrence in just this group. It was, to be sure, individual Huguenots who successfully competed in the business world of the seventeenth century. But this was presumably because the Huguenot upbringing or enculturation produced people who were adept at this sort of thing. These were people who could operate effectively within the socioeconomic framework of the time.

It seems to me that methodological individualism makes sense only if it can demonstrate the relevance of psychological characteristics in explaining and describing social institutions, and hence I am unable to agree that anonymous dispositions are individualistic. Anonymous dispositions convey no information about anyone in particular, but individuals are individuals in particular. I am not, of course, saying that no individual is disposed to behave in such-and-such way, where 'such-and-such' refers to some anonymous disposition. Bank tellers, to use Mandelbaum's example, are disposed to behave in ways suitable to their occupation, but one cannot explain banking institutions in terms of such dispositions to behave. It is the institutional framework of banking which fixes the manner deemed suitable for tellers. And when some individual bank teller finally achieves his goal and is promoted to a junior vice presidency, his mode of behaviour changes. But it seems rather odd to say that he has now acquired a new set of personal dispositions and mean thereby that his psychological nature has undergone some change.[22] He has merely stepped into a new rôle and is now prepared to act in ways suitable to his new station in life.

In insisting upon the sociological character of the concepts with which we describe institutions and the social nature of so-called anonymous dispositions, it is not my intention to say that individual people make no difference. Likewise, such insistence need not lead to any undesirable ontological results. There are people and they do make a difference, and yet they are sufficiently similar — at least so we are told by many responsible students of social science[23] — that laws of social change may be

[21] From a letter from Watkins to me; it immediately precedes the long sentence quoted in the text above.

[22] Even if it were not odd it would not support the individualistic position inasmuch as it would suggest the dependence of personal dispositions upon nonpersonal institutional factors.

[23] This is implicit in a good deal of work that is done in the social sciences and has been explicitly insisted upon by a good many of those who work in those fields, especially by anthropologists. The well known comparative approach of anthropology would seem to make little sense if this were not believed.

formulated. Not, to be sure, historicistic laws of development, but laws in which the relevant variables are specified and the nature of the change made determinant without recourse to oracular pronouncements that obfuscate more than they clarify. I have suggested elsewhere [24] that Murdock's theory of kinship systems is an example of this sort of theorising. This theory proclaims no necessary successions; it requires — as does any theory — only that if it is accepted as true or approximately so, then given the theoretically necessary and sufficient conditions for the development of any kinship system of determinate type, then we may reasonably expect an instance of that type to develop.

Murdock himself actually thinks that behavioural psychology and psychoanalysis are relevant to his theory,[25] but in actual fact these play no logical role in the formulation of the theory or the derivation of its results.[26] I suspect that his interest in this may be part of a desire to avoid the reification of societies, holism as we now understand it. It is precisely this concern which leads us to sociological emergence, and it may well be that if one wanted to determine in specific detail the dynamics of emergence, so to speak, it would be necessary to make use of psychological theory. But I am not able to see that we are therefore required to reduce the social to the psychological any more than we do the psychological to other so-called levels of reality. Nor does it follow that because concern with the actual dynamics of emergence brings us to psychology, that psychological theory has any function at all in the formulation of sociological theories.

The notion that we can talk about the dispositions of anonymous people seems to me somewhat strange. I know what it means to characterise particular people in terms of their particular dispositions. If I am told that John is lazy, I understand that he is disposed to avoid work; if told that he is thrifty, I know him to be a careful man with a dollar (or a pound, as the case may be). These are personal dispositions, though the sort of behaviour characteristic of the expression of such dispositions seems to be cultural, not psychological. But it is one thing to attribute such tendencies to John, quite another to so-called anonymous individuals. I venture to suggest that wherever Watkins talks about anonymous dispositions or the dispositions of anonymous individuals he is simply attempting to talk about non-individual characteristics of societies or part of societies, or of socially induced ways of behaving, without being explicit about it. Anonymous individuals are referred to as a way of avoiding holism, but we have seen that this may be done in other ways. There are specific individuals and characteristics of social phenomena; each of these raises theoretical questions of its own, and it is the business of psychology and social science to deal respectively with them. But there is no science of the anonymous. What we have are not the characteristic dispositions of people we don't know, but the social behaviour of people in given situations quite apart from their personal dispositions.

[24] Op. cit., pp. *613–617*.
[25] *Social Structure*, New York, 1949, p. xvi.
[26] Goldstein, op. cit., pp. *616* sq.

That There Are Irreducible Social Facts

49

Societal Facts

MAURICE MANDELBAUM

Introduction

If one adopts Broad's distinction between critical and speculative philosophy, the following paper may be regarded as an attempt to deal with one of the major problems of a critical philosophy of the social sciences. Like all such attempts, this paper faces some difficulties which are not encountered in equally acute form by those who deal with the concepts and methods of the natural sciences. In the first place, the concepts and methods utilized in the natural sciences have been more sharply defined than have been those which social scientists employ. In the second place, there is less disagreement among natural scientists than among social scientists as to the purposes which actually do underlie, or which should underlie, their studies. In the third place, the relations among the various branches of natural science seem to be more easily definable and less subject to dispute than is the case among the social sciences. It is with one aspect of the relations among the various social sciences that this paper will be concerned.

There can scarcely be any doubt that there is at present a considerable measure of disagreement among social scientists concerning the relations which obtain among their various disciplines. For example, there is little agreement as to how the province of "social psychology" is related to general psychology on the one hand or to sociology on the other. There is perhaps even less agreement as to how sociology and history are related, or whether, in fact, history is itself a social science. Even the province of cultural anthropology which, in its earlier stages, seemed to be capable of clear definition, is now in a position in which its relations to the other fields of social science have become extremely fluid. This type of fluidity in the boundaries of the various social sciences, and the ease with which concepts employed in one discipline spread to other disciplines, has been quite generally regarded as a promising augury for the future of the social sciences. One notes the frequency with which "integration" is held up as an important programmatic goal for social scientists. But such pleas for integration are ambiguous. On the one hand, they may merely signify a recognition of the fact that attempts to understand some concrete problems call for co-operation between persons trained to use the concepts and methods of different social sciences, or that workers in one discipline should be aware of the methods and results of those who work in other fields. On the other hand, what some who plead for "integration" in social science seem to demand is that the various disciplines should merge into one larger whole. On such a view the goal of integration would be the achievement of a state in which all persons who work in the field of social science would operate with the same set of concepts and would utilize the same methods of inquiry. If I am not mistaken, it is sometimes assumed that the social sciences will have made their greatest advance when the individual social sciences which now exist will have lost their separate identities. In so far as this paper has

From *The British Journal of Sociology*, 6:4 (1955), pp. 305–317.

a practical purpose, its purpose is to indicate that "integration", taken in this sense, is a mistaken goal for sociologists and psychologists to pursue.[1]

In stating that I wish to argue against what some social scientists believe to be the most promising path which their sciences can follow, it is clear that this paper has what might be termed an injunctive character. I am attempting to rule in advance that certain modes of procedure should or should not be adopted by practising social scientists. To those trained in the critical philosophy of the natural sciences, such a procedure will doubtless seem both foolhardy and perverse. Yet, it is unavoidable. So long as there are fundamental differences among social scientists with respect to the types of concepts and types of method which they actually use, and so long as the criteria by means of which they measure the adequacy of these concepts and methods differ, every attempt to do more than compile a *corpus* of materials for comparison, will involve that the analyst of the social sciences should take his own stand with respect to the matters under debate. Where one can show reasons for the position adopted, the injunctive element in one's analyses cannot be claimed to be wholly arbitrary. It is in proportion to the strength of these reasons that any particular injunctive proposal is to be judged.

However, any proposal as to the relations which ought to obtain between two or more social sciences will presuppose a belief as to what the goal of the social sciences may be. Concerning this topic there is also a considerable amount of debate. However, I believe it possible to formulate a general statement which might be acceptable to all, leaving unprejudiced those specific issues which have divided social scientists into opposed camps. I submit that the following statement would be quite generally acceptable: it is the task of the social sciences to attain a body of knowledge on the basis of which the actions of human beings as members of a society can be understood. This definition of the aim of the social sciences does not rule out the possibility that an understanding of the actions of human beings as members of a society may be instrumental to some further aim, such as that of attaining the means of controlling human behaviour, or of promoting human welfare. (Nor, of course, does it affirm that this is the case.) Furthermore, it is to be noted that in this statement of the aims of the social sciences I have avoided prejudging this issue as to whether the body of knowledge which is sought can be formulated as a system of laws, and whether an understanding of human actions is equivalent to explaining these actions in the sense in which the term "explanation" is used in the natural sciences. Throughout this paper I wish to avoid raising these questions, and in so far as possible I shall confine my discussion to a neutral terminology which does not prejudge any of these issues. Wherever my language seems to suggest that I am using the model of explanation used in the natural sciences, my point could equally well be phrased in terms which are compatible with the view that the methods and concepts of the social sciences are utterly different from those employed in the natural sciences. And, conversely, where I use the language of "understanding", my discussion can equally well be rephrased in terms of the language of scientific "explanation".

Having now defined what I take to be the task of the social sciences, I can state the aim of this paper. My aim is to show that one cannot understand the actions of human beings as members of a society unless one assumes that there is a group of facts which I shall term "societal facts" which are as ultimate as are those facts which are "psychological" in character. In speaking of "societal facts" I refer to any facts concerning the forms of organization present in a society. In speaking of "psychological facts" I refer to any facts concerning the thoughts and the actions of specific human beings.

[1] In this paper I shall not be concerned with the other social sciences.

An Example of the Irreducibility of Societal Concepts

If it be the case, as I wish to claim, that societal facts are as ultimate as are psychological facts, then those concepts which are used to refer to the forms of organization of a society cannot be reduced without remainder to concepts which only refer to the thoughts and actions of specific individuals.[2] There are many reasons why the type of claim that I am putting forward has been doubted, and we shall note some of these reasons as we proceed. First, however, it will be well to lend some plausibility to the view by means of an example.

Suppose that I enter a bank, I then take a withdrawal slip and fill it out, I walk to a teller's window, I hand in my slip, he gives me money, I leave the bank and go on my way. Now suppose that you have been observing my actions and that you are accompanied by, let us say, a Trobriand Islander. If you wished to explain my behaviour, how would you proceed? You could explain the filling out of the withdrawal slip as a means which will lead to the teller's behaviour towards me, that is, as a means to his handing me some notes and coins; and you could explain the whole sequence of my action as directed towards this particular end. You could then explain the significance which I attached to the possession of these notes and coins by following me and noting how the possession of them led other persons, such as assistants in shops, to give me goods because I gave them the notes and coins which the bank teller had handed to me. Such would be an explanation of my observed behaviour in terms of the behaviour of other specific individuals towards me. And it might at first glance appear as if an explanation couched in terms of these interpersonal forms of behaviour would be adqeuate to cover all of the aspects of the case.

However, it would also be necessary for you to inform the stranger who accompanies you that it does not suffice for a person to fill out such a slip and hand it to just anyone he may happen to meet. It would also be only fair to inform him that before one can expect a bank teller to hand one money in exchange for a slip, one must have "deposited" money. In short, one must explain at least the rudiments of a banking system to him. In doing so one is, of course, using concepts which refer to one aspect of the institutional organization of our society, and this is precisely the point which I wish to make. (And the same point can be made with reference to how Malinowski has explained to *us* the Trobriand Islanders' system of ceremonial exchanges of gifts.) In all cases of this sort, the actual behaviour of specific individuals towards one another is unintelligible unless one views their behaviour in terms of their status and roles, and the concepts of status and role are devoid of meaning unless one interprets them in terms of the organization of the society to which the individuals belong.

To this it may be objected that any statement concerning the status of an individual is itself analysable in terms of how specific individuals behave towards other individuals, and how these in turn behave towards them. Thus it might be claimed that while the explanation of an individual's behaviour often demands the introduction of concepts referring to "societal status", such concepts are themselves reducible to further statements concerning actual or probable forms of behaviour. Thus, societal concepts might be held to be heuristic devices, summarizing repeated patterns of behaviour, but they would be nothing more: their real meaning would lie in a conjunction of statements concerning the behaviour of a number of individuals.

However, this view is open to serious objection. We have seen in the foregoing illustration that my own behaviour towards the bank teller is determined by his status. If the

[2] The term "ultimate" may, of course, have other meanings as well. In the present paper, however, I am taking the irreducibility of a set of concepts to be equivalent to the ultimacy of that set of facts to which these concepts refer.

attempt is now made to interpret his status in terms of the recurrent patterns of behaviour which others exemplify in dealing with him, then *their* behaviour is left unexplained: each of them — no less than I — will only behave in this way because each recognizes the teller of a bank to have a particular status. Similarly, it is impossible to resolve the bank teller's role into statements concerning his behaviour towards other individuals. If one wished to equate his societal role with his reactions towards those who behave in a particular way towards him, it would be unintelligible that he should hand us money when we present him with a withdrawal slip when he stands in his teller's cage, and yet that he would certainly refuse to do so if we were to present him with such a slip when we met him at a party. Bank tellers as well as depositors behave as they do because they assume certain societally defined roles under specific sets of circumstances. This being the case, it is impossible to escape the use of societal concepts in attempting to understand some aspects of individual behaviour: concepts involving the notions of status and role cannot themselves be reduced to a conjunction of statements in which these or other societal concepts do not appear.

[Precisely the same point may be made with respect to attempts to translate societal concepts into terms of the thoughts of individuals rather than into terms of their overt behaviour. If one should wish to say that I acted as I did towards the teller because I foresaw that through my actions he would be led to give me money, one would still have to admit that my anticipation of his response was based upon my recognition of the fact that he was a bank teller, and that the role of a bank teller demands that he should act as the bank's agent, and the function of a bank (so far as each depositor is concerned) is that of being a custodian of legal tender, etc. etc. Thus, in attempting to analyse societal facts by means of appealing to the thoughts which guide an individual's conduct, some of the thoughts will themselves have societal referents, and societal concepts will therefore not have been expunged from our analysis.]

Now I do not wish to claim that an individual's thoughts or his overt actions are wholly explicable in terms of status and roles. Not only does it seem to be the case that some actions may be explained without introducing these concepts, but it is also the case that two individuals, say two bank tellers, may behave differently towards me in spite of the identity in their roles. Thus, one may be friendly and the other hostile or aloof, and the nature of my own behaviour towards them will then differ. Thus it should be apparent that I am not seeking to explain all facets of individual behaviour by means of statements which only refer to societal facts. What I wish to contend is (*a*) that in understanding or explaining an individual's actions we must often refer to facts concerning the organization of the society in which he lives, and (*b*) that our statements concerning these societal facts are not reducible to a conjunction of statements concerning the actions of individuals. I take it that almost all social scientists and philosophers would grant the first of these contentions, but that many social scientists and most philosophers would reject the second, insisting that societal facts are reducible to a set of facts concerning individual behaviour.

The Criterion of "Irreducibility"

It is now necessary to state the criterion of irreducibility which the foregoing illustration has presupposed.

Let us assume that there is a language, *S*, in which sociological concepts such as "institutions", "mores", "ideologies", "status", "class", etc., appear. These concepts all refer to aspects of what we term "a society". That there is a language of this type is clear from the works of sociologists, anthropologists, and historians. It is also clear from the fact that we use such terms as "The President of the United States", or "the unmarried children of X". In order to define the meaning of the latter terms we must make reference to the Constitution of the United States, or to the laws which govern our marriage and kinship systems, and in these references we are employing societal concepts.

There is, of course, also another language, *P*, in which we refer to the thoughts and actions and capabilities of individual human beings. In making statements in this language (which, for want of a better name, I have called our "psychological language")[3] we are not using societal concepts. The differences between these two languages may be illustrated by the fact that the connotation of the term "The present President of the United States" carries implications which do not follow from the personal name "Dwight D. Eisenhower", and statements concerning the personality of Dwight D. Eisenhower carry no implications for our understanding of his societal role. This remains true even though we admit that in this case, as in most others, the status of an individual is often causally connected with the nature of his personality, and even though we also admit that an individual's personality is often connected with the fact that he occupies a particular status, or that he functions within this status as he does.

Put in these terms, my thesis that societal facts are irreducible to psychological facts may be reformulated as holding that sociological concepts cannot be translated into psychological concepts *without remainder*. What is signified by the stipulation "without remainder" must now be made clear.

It would seem to be the case that all statements in the sociological language, *S*, are translatable into statements concerning the behaviour of specific individuals, and thus would be translatable into the language *P*. For example, a statement such as "The institution of monogamous marriage supplanted the polygynous marriage system of the Mormons" could presumably be translated into statements concerning the actions of certain aggregates of individuals. However, it is by no means certain that such translations could be effected without using other concepts which appear in the sociological language. These concepts too might have their translations into *P*, but the translation of the concepts of *S* into *P* would not be complete if such translations still had to employ other concepts which appear in *S*. It is with respect to incomplete translations of this type that I speak of translations which cannot be effected "without remainder".

An analogue of this situation was pointed out by Chisholm in his criticism of C. I. Lewis's theory of knowledge.[4] According to Chisholm, thing-statements cannot be completely reduced to statements concerning sense-data because one must specify the conditions of the appearance of these sense-data, and in doing so one must again use thing-statements. And this is precisely the situation which we found to obtain in our illustration of the behaviour of a person withdrawing money from a bank.

Now, it might be argued (as it has sometimes been argued with respect to Chisholm's contention) that our inability to carry out such translations, without remainder, represents a practical and not a theoretical inability. According to those who take this view, the practical difficulty which is present arises from the indefinitely long conjunction of statements which we should have to make in carrying out our analyses, and to the fact that some of these statements would involve a foreknowledge of future events. But it is claimed that no theoretically important consequences follow from our inability to com-

[3] It will be noted that what I have termed our psychological language does not include terms such as "neural paths", "brain-traces", etc. My argument aims to show that societal facts are not reducible to facts concerning the thoughts and actions of specific individuals; the problem of whether both societal facts and facts concerning an individual's thoughts and actions are explicable in terms of (or, are in some sense "reducible" to) a set of physical or physiological correlates is not my present concern. It will readily be seen that this is not the point at issue. Those who seek to reduce societal facts to facts concerning individual behaviour are not attempting to speak in physical and physiological terms.

[4] Cf. Chisholm, "The Problem of Empiricism" in *Journal of Philosophy*, V, 45 (1948), pp. 512ff. (I am indebted to Roderick Firth for calling my attention to this analogue.)

plete a detailed analysis of a particular statement: such partial analyses as we can actually make may not have omitted any theoretically significant aspects of the statements which we wish to analyse. Such a rejoinder would be open to two objections, so far as our present discussion is concerned.

First, we are here concerned with the problem of the relations between two empirical disciplines. Therefore, if it be admitted that it is impossible in practice to reduce statements which contain societal terms to a conjunction of statements which only include terms referring to the thoughts and actions of specific individuals, the rejoinder in question might conceivably be significant from the point of view of a general ontology, but it would not affect my argument regarding the autonomy of the societal sciences.

Second, it is to be noted that whatever may be the case regarding Chisholm's argument concerning the relation of sense-data statements to thing-statements, the problem of reducing statements which include societal terms to statements which only concern specific individuals is not merely a question of how we may *analyse* action statements, but how we may *explain* certain facts. It has been my contention that if we are to explain an individual's behaviour when, say, he enters a bank, we must have recourse to societal concepts and cannot merely employ terms which refer to the fact that this individual makes marks on paper, approaches a specific point, hands the marked paper to another individual, etc. etc. He who knew all of this, and who also knew all of the other actions performed by the members of a society, would possess a series of protocol statements, or biographical "logs". Even though this set of logs included reference to all of the actions performed by all of the members of the society, no societal concepts would appear in it. However, this information would not make it possible for our omniscient collector of data to explain why the depositor fills out a slip in order to withdraw money, or why the teller will exchange notes and coins for such a slip. Such a transaction only becomes explicable when we employ the concept of "a bank", and what it means to speak of "a bank" will involve the use of concepts such as "legal tender", and "contract". Further, what it means to speak of "a contract" will involve reference to our legal system, and the legal system itself cannot be defined in terms of individual behaviour — even the legal realist must distinguish between the behaviour of judges and policemen and the behaviour of "just anyone". Thus, if we are to explain certain forms of individual behaviour we must use societal concepts, and these concepts are not (I have argued) translatable without remainder into terms which only refer to the behaviour of individuals.

Yet it is important to insist that even though societal concepts cannot be translated into psychological concepts without leaving this societal remainder, it is not only possible but is indeed necessary to make the *partial* translation. It is always necessary for us to translate terms such as "ideologies" or "banks" or "a monogamous marriage system" into the language of individual thought and action, for unless we do so we have no means of verifying any statements which we may make concerning these societal facts. Ideologies and banks and marriage systems do not exist unless there are aggregates of individuals who think and act in specific ways, and it is only by means of establishing the forms of their thoughts and their actions that we can apprehend the nature of the societal organization in which they live, or that we can corroborate or disallow statements concerning this organization. Yet, the necessity for this translation of specific sociological concepts into terms of individual behaviour in order that we may verify and refine our sociological statements does not alter the fact that the possibility of making such a translation always involves the necessity for using other societal concepts to define the conditions under which this behaviour takes place. Thus, the translation can never obviate the use of societal concepts and reduce the study of society to a branch of the study of the actions of individuals.

Objections

In the foregoing discussion I have been at pains to state my position in such a way as to avoid the most usual objections to the general type of view which I hold. However, it will be useful to comment on three objections which have frequently been raised against the view that societal facts are irreducible to psychological facts.[5]

The first of these objections may be termed the ontological objection. It consists in holding that societal facts cannot be said to have any status of their own since no such facts would exist if there were not individuals who thought and acted in specific ways. Now, to hold the view which I hold, one need not deny that the existence of a society presupposes the existence of individuals, and that these individuals must possess certain capacities for thought and for action if what we term a society is to exist. Yet, this admission does not entail the conclusion which is thought to follow from it: one need not hold that a society is an entity independent of all human beings in order to hold that societal facts are not reducible to the facts of individual behaviour. The warrant for the latter position is merely this: all human beings are born into a society, and much of their thought and their action is influenced by the nature of the societies in which they live; therefore, those facts which concern the nature of their societies must be regarded as being independent of them. To be sure, these facts are not independent of the existence of *other* individuals, and it will be from the forms of behaviour of these other individuals that any specific individual will have acquired his own societally oriented patterns of behaviour. But these individuals, too, were born into an already functioning societal organization which was independent of them. Thus, their societally oriented behaviour was also conditioned by an already existing set of societal facts, etc. etc.

To be sure, those who wish to press the ontological objection may insist that at some remote time in the history of the human race there were individuals who were not born into an already existing society, and that these individuals must have formed a societal organization by virtue of certain patterns of repeated interpersonal actions. Thus, they would seek to insist that all societal facts have their origins in individual behaviour, and that it is mistaken to argue, as I have argued, that societal facts are irreducible to the facts of individual behaviour. However, this rejoinder is clearly fallacious. Whatever may have been the origin of the first forms of societal organization (a question which no present knowledge puts us in a position to answer), the issue with which we are here concerned is one which involves the nature of societies as they exist at present. To argue that the nature of present societal facts is reducible to the facts of individual behaviour because the origins of a particular social system grew up out of certain repeated forms of behaviour is a clear example of the genetic fallacy. One might as well argue on the basis of our knowledge of the origins of the Greek drama and of the modern drama that every current Broadway play is really to be understood as a religious festival.

However, the above answer to the ontological type of objection is clearly not suffi-

[5] When we consider the type of "irreducibility" which has here been claimed to characterize societal facts, we must be prepared to allow that it may not be the only type of irreducibility to be found among "existential emergents". (On the meaning of this term, which has been borrowed from Lovejoy, cf. my "Note on Emergence", in *Freedom and Reason*, edited by Baron, Nagel, and Pinson; Free Press, Glencoe, Ill., 1951.) I am in fact inclined to believe that there is a stronger form of irreducibility than is here in question. This stronger form may be said to exist between, say, the colour "red" and brain events or light frequencies. In such cases it might be true that even a *partial* translation cannot be effected. All that I have wished to show is that while it is undeniable that we can and do make partial translations of societal concepts by using psychological concepts, these translations cannot be complete: we must always use further societal concepts to specify the conditions under which the observed forms of societally oriented behaviour take place.

cient.[6] It is, I hope, adequate to show that one usual form of countering my position is untenable; yet, the essential paradox remains. One can still legitimately ask what sort of ontological status societal facts can conceivably possess if it is affirmed that they depend for their existence on the activities of human beings and yet are claimed not to be identical with these activities. There are, it seems to me, two types of answer which might be given to this question. In the first type of answer one might contend that a whole is not equal to the sum of its parts, and a society is not equal to the sum of those individual activities which go to form it. This familiar holistic answer is not the one which I should be inclined to propose. In the first place, it is by no means certain that the principle of holism (as thus stated) is philosophically defensible. In the second place, such an answer assumes that what may be termed the "parts" of a society are to be taken to be individual human beings, and this is an assumption which I should be unwilling to make. All of the preceding argument entails the proposition that the "parts" of a society are specific societal facts, not individuals. If this were not the case, societal concepts could be translated into terms referring to individual behaviour if we had sufficient knowledge of all the interrelations among these individuals. Instead, we have found that an analysis of a statement which concerns a societal fact will involve us in using other societal concepts: for example, that what it means to be a depositor in a bank will involve statements concerning our legal system and our monetary economy. Similarly, what it means to be a college student cannot be defined without recourse to statements concerning our educational system, and such statements cannot be analysed without utilizing concepts which refer to statutory laws as well as to many other aspects of our societal organization. Thus, from the arguments which have been given, it follows that the "parts" of a society are not individual human beings, but are the specific institutions, and other forms of organization, which characterize that society. Once this is recognized, it remains an open question as to the extent to which any specific society (or all societies) are to be conceived holistically or pluralistically.

The second method of dealing with the ontological objection is the one which I should myself be inclined to adopt. It consists in holding that one set of facts may depend for its existence upon another set of facts and yet not be identical with the latter. An example of such a relationship would be that which a traditional epiphenomenalist would regard as existing between brain events and the contents of consciousness. Whatever objections one may raise against the epiphenomenalist view of the mind-body relationship, one would scarcely be justified in holding that the position must be false because the content of consciousness could not be different from the nature of brain-states and yet be dependent upon the latter. If one has reasons for holding that the content of consciousness *is* different from brain states, and if one also has reason for holding that it *does* depend upon the latter, one's ontology must be accommodated to these facts: the facts cannot be rejected because of a prior ontological commitment. And, without wishing to press my analogy farther than is warranted, I can point out that my statement concerning "the parts" of a society has its analogue in what those who hold to the epiphenomenalist position would say concerning the proper analysis of any statement referring to the content of an individual's field of consciousness. Just as I have claimed that the component parts of a society are the elements of its organization and are not the individuals without whom it would not exist, so the epiphenomenalist would (I assume) say that the parts of the individual's field of consciousness are to be found within the specific data of consciousness and not in the brain events upon which consciousness depends.

These remarks are, I hope, sufficient to

[6] In what follows I shall only be discussing human societies. The differences between "animal societies" and human societies are far more striking than are their similarities.

dispel the ontological objection to the position which I wish to defend. To be sure, I have not attempted to say what position should be assigned to societal facts when one is constructing a general ontology. To do so, I should have to say much more concerning the nature of societal facts, and I should of course also have to discuss the nature of other types of entity. Here it has only been my concern to suggest that what I have termed the ontological objection to my thesis is by no means as strong as it may at first glance appear to be: the admission that all societal facts depend upon the existence of human beings who possess certain capacities for thought and for action by no means precludes the contention that these facts are irreducible to facts concerning those individuals.

The second of the most usual objections to the thesis that societal facts cannot be reduced to psychological facts is an epistemological objection. This objection may take many forms, depending upon the theory of knowledge which is held by the objector. However, the common core of all such objections is the indubitable fact that societal concepts are not capable of being "pointed to", in the sense in which we can point to material objects, or to the qualities or activities of these objects. Whenever we wish to point to any fact concerning societal organization we can only point to a sequence of interpersonal actions. Therefore, any theory of knowledge which demands that all empirically meaningful concepts must ultimately be reducible to data which can be directly inspected will lead to the insistence that all societal concepts are reducible to the patterns of individual behaviour.

I shall not, of course, seek to disprove this general theory of knowledge. Yet it is possible to indicate in very brief compass that it is inadequate to deal with societal facts. Since those who would hold this theory of knowledge would presumably wish to show that we can be said to know something of the nature of human societies, and since they would also wish to hold that our means of gaining this knowledge is through the observation of the repeated patterns of activities of individuals, a proof that their theory of knowledge cannot account for our apprehension of the nature of individual action is, in the present context, a sufficient disproof of the epistemological type of objection.

In order to offer such a disproof, let us revert to our illustration of a depositor withdrawing money from a bank. In order to understand his overt actions in entering a bank, filling out a slip, handing it to a teller, receiving notes and coins, and leaving the bank, we must view this sequence of actions as one internally connected series. Yet what connects the elements within the series is the person's intention to withdraw money from his account, and this intention is not itself a directly observable element within the series. Thus, unless it be admitted that we can have knowledge of aspects of human behaviour which are not directly presented to the senses, we cannot understand his behaviour and therefore cannot understand that which we seek to understand; i.e., those societal facts which supposedly are the summations of instances of behaviour of this type. To this, it may of course be objected, that we have learned to attribute certain intentions to agents on the basis of our own experienced intentions, and when this introspective experience is combined with our observation of overt behaviour we learn to interpret human actions. Yet if this enlargement of our modes of knowing is allowed, there is no reason to stop with the facts of individual behaviour as the building-blocks of a knowledge of societal facts. Within our own experience we are no less directly aware of our own names, of our belonging to a particular family, of our status as youngsters or elders, etc., than we are of our own intentions. To be sure, our societal status must, originally, have been learned by us in a sense in which our intentions need not presumably have been learned. Yet, once again, we must avoid the genetic fallacy: the origin of our knowledge is not identical with that knowledge itself. Just as the concept of number has a meaning which need not be identical with the experiences through which it was learned, so the concept of a family, or of differentiated status due to age or sex, need not (even for a child) be identical with the experiences through which this concept was first made manifest. And to these remarks it should be added that once we have grasped the idea of status, or of family, or of authority, we can transfer this concept to situations which are initially alien to our own experience (e.g. to new forms of family organization) no less readily than we can apply a knowledge of our own intentions to the understanding of the intentions of those who act in ways which are initially strange to us. The problem of extending our knowledge from our own experience of others is not, I submit, more impossible in principle in the one case than in the other. And if this be so, there is no epistemological reason why we should seek to reduce societal facts to the facts of individual behaviour. Only if it were true that individual behaviour could itself be understood in terms of the supposedly "hard data" of direct sensory inspection would there be any saving in the reduction of societal facts to facts concerning this behavior. But, as I have indicated, this is not the case.

The third type of objection to the view which I have been espousing is the objection that such a view interprets individual men as the pawns of society, devoid of initiative, devoid even of a common and socially-unconditioned nature, conceiving of them as mere parts of a self-existing social organism.[7] However, such a view I have in fact already rejected. To hold, as I have held, that societal facts are not reducible without remainder to facts concerning the thoughts and actions of specific individuals, is not to deny that the latter class of facts also exists, and that the two classes may interact. Those who have in the past held to the irreducibility of societal facts have, to be sure, often gone to the extreme of denying that there are any facts concerning individual behaviour which are independent of societal facts. Such has not been my thesis. And it is perhaps worth suggesting that if we wish to understand many of the dilemmas by which individuals are faced, we can do no better than to hold to the view that there are societal facts which exercise external constraints over individuals no less than there are facts concerning individual volition which often come into conflict with these constraints.

[7] It is to be noted that some societally oriented behaviour is only intelligible when interpreted with respect to *both* a societal concept and an individual's intention (e.g. in our case of a person withdrawing money from a bank). However, other instances of societally oriented behaviour (e.g. customary observances of age and sex differences) do not involve a consideration of the agent's intentions.

That There Are, or May Be, Irreducible Social Laws

50

Societal Laws

MAURICE MANDELBAUM

In an earlier paper I argued that societal facts are not reducible, without remainder, to facts concerning individual behaviour.[1] In short, I argued against one of the basic theses of 'methodological individualism'. However, the issue of whether there are irreducible societal *facts* is not the main problem with which methodological individualism has been concerned. The main problem has been whether or not there are societal *laws* which are irreducible to laws concerning the behaviour of individuals. I would uphold the view that there are, and thus would reject a second thesis of methodological individualism.[2] However, before arguing this point it is necessary to disentangle the problem from some of the misleading issues which have become associated with it. In my opinion, these misleading issues have arisen because it is widely and erroneously assumed that those who reject methodological individualism must accept a position which is termed 'methodological holism'. It is the primary purpose of the present paper to show that there are in fact several alternatives to methodological individualism, and that not all of these alternatives entail an acceptance of 'holism'.[3]

I

Let us briefly review the issue between what has been designated as 'methodological individualism' and what has been designated as 'methodological holism'.[4]

The term 'methodological individualism' seems to have been derived from Schumpeter,[5] and two of its chief exponents are Popper and Hayek. As is well known, the writings in which both of the latter have discussed the methodology of the social sciences have been

From the *British Journal for the Philosophy of Science*, 8:3 (November, 1957), pp. 211–224, Cambridge University Press.

[1] 'Societal Facts', *British Journal of Sociology*, 1955, **6**, 305–317. [*Reprinted as selection 49 in this volume. Editor's note.*]

[2] It will be noted that my view is therefore more radical than that adopted by May Brodbeck in her attack on methodological individualism ('On the Philosophy of the Social Sciences', *Philosophy of Science*, 1954, **21**, 140–156). She rejects the view that there are irreducible societal laws (loc. cit. p. 155).

[3] In a further paper I hope to show how societal laws are to be distinguished from psychological laws, and to argue on the basis of that distinction for the irreducibility of societal laws.

[4] The most important recent formulations of methodological individualism probably are: the articles of Hayek which have been collected in his book *The Counter-Revolution of Science*, Glencoe, 1952; K. R. Popper, 'The Poverty of Historicism', *Economica*, N.S., 1944, **11**, 86–103 and 119–137; **12**, 69–89 (cf. especially p. 80 and p. 88) and his *Open Society and Its Enemies*, London, 1945, Vol. II, Chap. 14; J. W. N. Watkins, 'Ideal Types and Historical Explanation', *British Journal for the Philosophy of Science*, **3**, 22–43, and 'Methodological Individualism: A Reply', *Philosophy of Science*, **22**, 58–62. Also relevant is Isaiah Berlin, *Historical Inevitability*, Oxford, 1954.

Perhaps the most important recent attacks on the principle of methodological individualism are those of Brodbeck (as cited in note 2, above); M. Ginsberg, 'The Individual and Society', in his essays *On the Diversity of Morals*, London, 1957 and 'Factors in Social Change', in *Transactions of the Third World Congress of Sociology*, **1**, 10–19; E. A. Gellner, 'Explanations in History', *Aristotelian Society*, 1956, Suppl. Vol. 30, 157–176; L. J. Goldstein, 'The Inadequacy of the Principle of Methodological Individualism' *Journal of Philosophy*, 1956, **53**, 801–813.

[5] Cf. note 50 of Machlup, 'Schumpeter's Economic Methodology', *Review of Economics and Statistics*, 1951, **33**, 145–151.

works which have had a special polemical character: they were not merely discussions of methodology but were attacks on historicism, organicism, and social holism. For this reason, Popper and Hayek have tended to equate a rejection of methodological individualism with the acceptance of methodological holism. This over-simplified classification of alternative theories has now unfortunately become standard.

To illustrate the usual view of the dichotomy between methodological individualism and holism I shall quote a passage from J. W. N. Watkins' defence of methodological individualism:

> If social events like inflation, political revolution, 'the disappearance of the middle classes', etc., are brought about by people, then they must be explained in terms of people; in terms of the situations people confront and the ambitions, fears and ideas which activate them. In short, large-scale *social* phenomena must be accounted for by the situations, dispositions and beliefs of *individuals*. This I call methodological individualism.
>
> You may complain that this is commonsensical and hardly needed saying. The trouble is that some philosophers of history have made the opposite assumption . . . In the secularized version of [their] theory it is the social whole which so determines matters for the individual that he cannot avoid (or would be foolish to try to avoid: the determinism may be a little loose) fulfilling his function within the whole system. On this view, the social behavior of individuals should be explained in terms of the positions or functions of these individuals and of the laws which govern the system. These laws must be regarded as *sui generis*, applying to the whole as such and not derivable from individualistic principles. This I call methodological holism.[6]

In this passage it is to be noted that a denial of what is defined as methodological individualism is assumed to imply methodological holism. Further, methodological holism is identified with certain forms of the philosophy of history; it is not treated as a methodological principle which might be used by economists, political scientists, anthropologists, or empirical sociologists. Thus it is perhaps not unfair to say that in this passage there is a tendency to assume that the dichotomy between methodological individualism and methodological holism is equivalent to the dichotomy between an empirical explanation of social phenomena and the sort of philosophic interpretation which is characteristic of material philosophies of history.[7] What is more important, however, is that it is assumed that all so-called 'methodological holists' view a social system as an organic whole, the component parts of which are individual human beings. This is not necessarily the case. Some who reject methodological individualism would regard the component parts of a social system as being the institutions which comprise that system.[8] Therefore, *if* they hold that the whole determines the actions of the parts, they are not necessarily arguing that individual human beings are determined by the society as a whole — though they may of course also claim this. And, finally, this passage clearly involves the assumption that if one regards societal laws as being *sui generis* (i.e. as not being in principle reducible to laws concerning individual behaviour) then one must hold that such laws concern the society as a whole. In other words, a rejection of the principle defined as methodological individualism has been assumed to involve an acceptance of the thesis that, whatever societal laws there may be, these laws will concern the functioning of a society treated as an organic whole. It would therefore seem that anyone who wished to reject the *metaphysical* theses of holism in general (e.g. 'the whole is greater than the sum of its parts') would be committed to accepting the *methodological* principle which has been defined as 'methodological individualism'.

The root error in all this is, I believe, the

6 'Methodological Individualism', loc. cit. p. 58 sq.

7 This impression is strengthened by the passage omitted in the second paragraph of the above quotation, and by much of the argument used by Hayek. (For a discussion of the nature of material philosophies of history, cf. my article 'Some Neglected Philosophic Problems Regarding History', *Journal of Philosophy*, 1952, **49**, 317–329.)

8 This is also the view that I would hold. (Cf. 'Societal Facts', *this volume, pp. 639–640*.) [*Page numbers in italics refer to pages in this volume. Editor's note.*]

assumption that all who deny methodological individualism are committed to exactly the same positions as were those nineteenth-century philosophers who attacked the individualistic approach of the eighteenth century. More specifically, the tenets used to characterise 'methodological holism' are precisely those which were held in common by Comte, Hegel, and Marx. This is perhaps understandable in the light of the polemical purposes which we have noted in Popper and Hayek, but it is important to see that a rejection of methodological individualism does not entail an acceptance of an organismic or historicist view of society. This will become apparent in what follows.

I shall proceed by drawing two sets of distinctions concerning law-like statements. By combining these two sets of distinctions into a four-celled table it will be seen that those who accept the belief that there are (or may be) irreducible societal laws can be holding quite diverse views regarding these laws. Leaving aside those law-like statements which seek to reduce societal facts to facts concerning individual behaviour, a societal law could belong to any of the four classes which I shall distinguish. (At certain points it will become apparent that even these classes can be further divided into sub-classes.) It so happens, however, that the theories most frequently discussed by methodological individualists usually fall into only one of these classes. Thus it will be shown that the dichotomy which is usually drawn between methodological individualism and methodological holism is an over-simplified and misleading classification of types of social theory.

2

The first of the distinctions that I wish to draw is between 'a law of functional relation' and 'a law of directional change'. (I shall usually refer to these as 'functional' and as 'directional' laws.) The distinction between these two types of laws, which are sometimes referred to as synchronic and diachronic laws,[9] can perhaps most easily be illustrated through reference to the physical sciences. Boyle's law or Newton's inverse square law would be examples of *functional* laws, while the second law of thermodynamics would be the outstanding example of a *directional* law. In the field of history the distinction would be between what I have elsewhere called 'laws *concerning* history' and 'laws *of* history'.[10] Marx's theory of the relation between the economic organisation of a society and other institutions in that society (his doctrine of 'the superstructure') would be a functional law, i.e. a law *concerning* history. On the other hand, one may interpret his view of dialectical development as an attempt to formulate a law stating a necessary pattern of directional change in history, i.e. as a law *of* history.[11]

These two types of law are obviously differ-

[9] Cf. Goldstein's discussion, loc. cit. pp. 617 sqq. (It is to be noted that Goldstein does not deny the applicability of methodological individualism in synchronic studies, though I would do so.)

In an earlier article Edgar Zilsel referred to these as 'temporal laws' and 'simultaneity laws' and attempted to establish that both types are to be found in history (cf. 'Physics and the Problem of Historico-sociological Laws', *Philosophy of Science*, 1941, **8**, 567–579). It would seem that Zilsel's position with respect to methodological individualism is essentially similar to that held by Brodbeck.

In his *Philosophy of Science*, Madison, 1957, G. Bergmann draws a distinction between 'process laws' and 'laws of development' which, I believe, corresponds in many respects to the distinction which I have attempted to draw between functional and directional laws. (He also discriminates between these two types of law and two other types: 'cross-sectional laws' and 'historical laws'. The first of these is not relevant to our present problem; the second, as Bergmann shows, is in many cases reducible to a process law.)

[10] A Critique of Philosophies of History', *Journal of Philosophy*, 1948, **45**, 365–378.

[11] It appears to me that Marx failed to see the difference between these two types of explanation, and that the second type constitutes a survival of Hegelianism in his social theory. To be sure, there are passages in Marx which would make it appear that the pattern of directional change is merely the result of the forces which he attempts to analyse in terms of his economic theory and of his doctrine of 'the superstructure'. Nevertheless, it does seem equally plausible (at the very least) to maintain that he regarded the pattern which he traced in the history of mankind as having an inherent necessity in it, i.e. that it was 'inevitable', and was not merely the actual outcome of forces operating from moment to mo-

ent. While either would make prediction possible if we possessed adequate knowledge of the initial and boundary conditions of the state of affairs to which the law was to be applied, the first type of law (a functional law) would only enable us to predict immediately subsequent events, and each further prediction would have to rest upon knowledge of the initial and boundary conditions obtaining at that time. The second type of law (a directional law) would not demand a knowledge of subsequent initial conditions (though it would assume stability of boundary conditions), for if there were a law of directional change which could be discovered in any segment of history we could extrapolate to the past and to the future without needing to gather knowledge of the initial conditions obtaining at each successive point in the historical process.[12]

We now come to the second distinction which I wish to draw: a distinction between what I shall designate as '*abstractive* laws' and what I shall designate as '*global* laws.'

In an abstractive law the attempt is made to state a relation between specific aspects or components which are present in a state of affairs, and to state this relation in such a way that it will be applicable in all cases in which these particular aspects or components are present. In formulating such a law, the specific nature of the state of affairs in which these elements are to be found does not enter into the law itself, but is only considered with respect to the initial and boundary conditions which must be taken into account in applying the law.

On the other hand, it is possible to regard some entities in terms of their global properties, to consider them as unitary systems, or wholes. And it may be possible that when we so regard them we can formulate law-like statements concerning changes in their global properties, or concerning relationships between the nature of the system as a whole and the manner in which its component parts behave. In stating such a law we are considering the system as a system, and a reference to the properties of the system is included in the law which we formulate.

Now, in order to avoid an unnecessary misunderstanding, it must immediately be pointed out that the acceptance of a global law (or of the possibility that there are global laws) does not commit one to the position of 'emergence', or to any form of 'holism'. Such laws might be held to be derivative from laws concerning the component aspects of the system, and thus be reducible to abstractive laws. To be sure, one might not so regard them, and in that case one would in all likelihood be accepting the position usually designated as 'holism'. Yet even this is not necessary. For example, if one were to hold that there are laws concerning the relations between one component in a certain type of system, and the nature of any such system considered as a whole, and if one were also to hold that it is this component which determines the properties of the whole, then one would be formulating a law concerning the global properties of a system, and yet not be a 'holist' in the most usual sense of that term: it would be a part which determines the nature

---

ment. (Even on the latter interpretation of Marx, there are two possible alternative interpretations: (*a*) that the inevitability rests on the necessary pattern of development in the means of production, particularly the technology; (*b*) that the inevitability of the pattern is an expression of the ultimate dialectical process in all reality.)

A somewhat similar confusion between laws *of* history and laws *concerning* history is present in Toynbee. His concept of 'challenge and response' purports to throw light on the forces at work at each stage in the course of a civilisation's history, but the pattern of change which he traces seems to assume the shape of a quasi-inevitable directional tendency. In other words, the concept of 'challenge and response' performs the same sort of function as a law *concerning* history would perform in a scientifically oriented theory, while his construction of the histories of civilisation in terms of their stages is an attempt to show that there is an inherent tendency for the course of history to follow a definite pattern of development.

[12] Cf. the method of Henry Adams. It is to be noted that in those cases in which a directional law is derived from metaphysical principles (rather than being empirically derived), it is not even thought to be necessary to assume stability in the boundary conditions for a society.

of the whole, not the whole which determines the nature of its parts.

This last warning may help to elucidate the distinction which I have sought to draw between abstractive and global laws. The distinction is not one between non-holism and holism, but between laws which are formulated in terms of particular aspects or components which have been abstracted from a concrete state of affairs, and laws which are formulated in terms of the nature of particular types of system. In other words, there is a difference in what the laws are *about*. Abstractive laws are about the relationships between two aspects or components that occur in a variety of different concrete situations; the nature of the situations in which these aspects are embedded constitute the initial and boundary conditions which must be taken into account in applying the law. Global laws, on the other hand, are about the properties of systems, attempting to show how these systems change over time, or how the system as a whole is related to its component parts.

3

We have now drawn two distinctions: first, a distinction between laws concerning functional relations and laws concerning directional change; second, a distinction between abstractive laws and global laws. These distinctions engender four possibilities concerning law-like statements, and if we now examine the theories of those who have rejected the principle of methodological individualism we shall find that social theorists have attempted to formulate law-like statements of each of the four types. However, methodological individualism has been almost solely concerned with a criticism of the attempt to find *global laws of directional change*. It has in fact tended to identify the view that there are irreducible societal laws with a belief in laws of this type. If we now briefly examine each of the four types we shall be in a position to see to what extent, if at all, each may properly be regarded as holistic.

(i) Let us first examine the view that there are law-like statements which are both functional and global. Such laws would relate the global properties of a social system as a whole to one or more of its component parts, i.e. to its specific institutions or sanctioned usages.

As we have already noted, there are two main ways of proceeding in attempting to establish laws of this general type. On the one hand, we may regard the global properties as determinants of the properties possessed by component parts of the system. This is the case in Ruth Benedict's descriptive analysis of particular patterns of culture; it is also the case in Radcliffe-Brown's form of Functionalism in which the need for self-maintenance in a society considered as a whole determines specific usages, such as the punishment of criminals or funeral ceremonies.[13] Marx, on the other hand, would derive at least certain of the global properties of a social system (e.g. the defining characteristics of 'feudalism' or 'capitalism') from one specific component within that system, viz. the means of production. Others might seek to find a composition law by means of which, given the properties of two or more component parts of the system, the global properties of the system as a whole could be derived. All of these types of law would be instances of an attempt to state global laws of the functional type, i.e. laws which involve the relation of its components to the concrete nature of a system considered as a whole. I believe that it is obvious that not all of these attempts would be 'holistic' in the same sense.

[13] Cf. Radcliffe-Brown, 'On the Concept of Function in Social Science', *American Anthropoligist*, 1935, **37**, 394–402.* (The specific illustration used is to be found on p. 396.) Also, 'On Social Structure', *Journal of the Royal Anthropological Institute*, 1940, 70, 1–12.

It is to be noted that Radcliffe-Brown's form of Functionalism is to be distinguished from that held by Malinowski (after 1926). On this distinction, cf. Radcliffe-Brown, 'A Note on Functional Anthropology', *Man*, 1946, **46**, §30, and 'Functionalism: A Protest', *American Anthropologist*, 1949, **51**, 320–323.

* [*This article is reprinted as part of selection 52 in this volume. Editor's note.*]

(ii) It would also be possible to attempt to establish laws of directional change concerning global properties. Such laws would not be seeking to relate the properties of a system as a whole to the nature of one or more of its component parts, but would attempt to formulate a law-like statement concerning the successive states of a system. In other words, a law of this type would be a statement concerning a pattern of directional change in a social system considered as a whole, e.g., that there exists a specific sort of uni-directional development, or a cyclic flow, in the over-all aspects of a society. Such a law, of course, would not be intended to be merely a description of what has taken place in one social system during a restricted time interval, but would be held to be applicable at all times and with respect to all societies,[14] or with respect to all segments of one all-embracing historical process, viz. to the history of mankind as a whole.

A theory of history which is based on the belief in a law of this type would regard the over-all changes which took place as being 'inevitable'. Furthermore, such theories usually regard the directional law which they seek to establish as being an ultimate law, i.e. one not deducible from functional laws concerning the components of the systems. Where this is the case, we may legitimately speak of 'holism'. However, we must note that such a law might *not* be treated as ultimate. For example, it might not be wholly misleading[15] to rephrase Marx's doctrine concerning historical inevitability to make it appear that the law of directional change in history is a consequence of two other laws: a functional law asserting that the global properties of a social system are determined by the means of production, and a directional law concerning changes in this specific component. Such a position would still maintain the thesis that there is a law descriptive of the direction of social change in all social systems, and it would therefore espouse the doctrine of historical inevitability, but it would not be an example of 'holism'.

The above suggestion is not intended to be a contribution to the exegesis of Marx, but is included for two other reasons. First, it should serve to suggest that not all doctrines of historical inevitability are 'holistic', or (at least) equally 'holistic.'[16] Second, it serves to introduce the third general type of law with which we are concerned: the attempt to find a directional law which is abstractive in the sense that it is concerned with changes occurring in one component of a social system, and not with the social system considered as a whole.

(iii) Attempts to formulate laws of directional change concerning specific institutions, regardless of the societies in which they are embedded, have been very prevalent in anthropological and sociological theory. Among the many examples it is only necessary to call to mind theories of the necessary stages in religious development, or in marriage systems; attempts to formulate a law concerning the tendency of language to change from a more complex to a simpler structure, or of the arts to develop from the abstract-decorative toward the representational pole (or *vice versa*). There have, of course, also been attempts to trace cyclical changes (and to formulate laws concerning the sequence of such changes) in political forms or in styles of art. Whether these directional laws regarding specific institutions have been unidirectional or cyclic, those who have formulated them have not usually viewed them as derivative

[14] Of course, this may be limited to societies of a given type, e.g. to 'civilisations' but not to 'primitive societies'.

[15] Cf. note 11, p. *644*.

[16] It should also be noted that not all examples of holism in the philosophy of history accept the thesis of historical inevitability, if by 'inevitability' is meant that each stage in the development follows necessarily from the preceding stage. In Herder's philosophy of history, for example, the element of necessity is strongly stressed in each part of the process, but the process as a whole is not viewed as proceeding through an over-riding necessity. (For example, cf. *Ideen zur Philosophie der Geschichte der Menschheit*, 13th Book, 7th Chapter.)

from abstractive functional laws.[17] Rather, they have generally (but not always) regarded them as derivative from other laws of directional change. These more basic directional laws have usually been of either two kinds: laws concerning the direction of change in the total social system (i.e. directional laws of the global type) or laws concerning the changes in the nature of the human mind. By holding that there is a necessary direction of change in a society as a whole, and by holding that form of global law which states that the whole is so related to its parts that the parts are determined by the whole, a law of change concerning a specific institution follows. Or by holding that there is a particular pattern of growth in the capacities of the human mind, and by making the assumption that each institution will go through stages which reflect this growth, a law of change in a specific institution could be derived. These two alternative ways of deriving a law of directional change in a specific institution from some more ultimate law of change are not incompatible. They are not incompatible since it is possible to hold (and has often been held, e.g. by Comte and, in a sense, by Hegel) that the law of development which applies to the properties of society considered as one systematic whole, is a reflection of the development of the human mind or spirit. This should be recalled by those who tend to regard holist views of the structure of society as being primarily due to the tendency to regard societal facts as different from facts concerning human thought and action.

(iv) The fourth possible type of societal law which follows from our distinctions would consist in the attempt to state functional laws of the abstractive type. Among the examples of attempts to formulate such laws we may cite the following: statements concerning relationships between modes of production and marriage systems; between size of population and political organisation; between forms of economic organisation and political organisation; or, to cite a classic study of Tylor's[18] (which has been amplified and elaborated by Murdock in his *Social Structure*) between certain specific aspects of marriage systems, e.g. rules of residence and rules of descent.

It is to be noted that laws of this abstractive-functional type are different in aim from the laws of the other three types.[19] In being functional laws, they do not assume that there is any necessary direction of historical change, either within specific institutions or within a society considered as a whole. Furthermore, in being abstractive they seek to explain such changes as do occur in terms of the successive initial and boundary conditions which obtain at specific points in time, and do not assume that these conditions must be identical in all societies. In being abstractive they also remain uncommitted on the question of whether any particular society (or every society) can be regarded as a single organic whole; it becomes the task of empirical investigation to determine to what extent the various aspects of a given state of affairs *are* interrelated. Thus, those who hold that there are (or may be) abstractive-functional societal laws are neither committed to historicism nor to organicism, both of which have usually been held to be consequences of the rejection of methodological individualism.

4

Without entering into the empirical and methodological issues which are involved, I should like to state that I believe there are

[17] This is to be expected, since the attempt to formulate such a directional law of change with respect to a specific institution involves an isolation of that component from the other societal components which are contemporaneous with it.

[18] On a Method of Investigating the Development of Institutions; Applied to Laws of Marriage and Descent', *Journal of the Royal Anthropological Institute*, 1889, **18**, 245–269.

[19] To be sure, the purpose for which Tylor, as a social evolutionist, used his data concerning functional relations was primarily for the reconstruction of the evolution of marriage systems. It is also to be admitted that his explanations of *why* 'adhesions' took place were often couched in psychological terms. However, he does not appear to have believed that such psychological explanations were alone sufficient to account for the facts (cf. loc. cit. p. 248).

important reasons for doubting that we shall find irreducible societal laws of the first three types.[20] Therefore I venture the suggestion that *if* there are empirically derivable laws concerning social phenomena, and if these cannot all be reduced to laws concerning individual behaviour, those which cannot be so reduced will be abstractive laws concerning functional relations between specific types of societal facts. Whether such laws have been found, or whether we have reason to believe that they may be found, is not the question which I have proposed for this discussion. However, before closing, I should like briefly to indicate the various possible relationships which might obtain between psychological laws concerning the behaviour of individuals and laws which attempt to state functional relationships between specific aspects of social structures.

If one assumes that there are (or may be) laws which accurately express the functional relations between two or more specific types of fact in all societies (or in all societies of a specific type), it could be the case that these laws follow deductively from laws of individual behaviour when one takes into account the conditions obtaining in the societies in question. This is the view held by methodological individualism which rejects *irreducible* societal laws.

If, however, one believes that there are irreducible societal laws, two positions still remain open to one. One *might* hold that such laws are themselves sufficient (granted the initial and boundary conditions) to explain all that occurs in societies. To this position methodological individualists would doubtless be no less opposed than they are to a holistic view, since this view would also render human choice and human action nugatory in the realm of social affairs. On the other hand, one might hold that an adequate explanation of social phenomena would have to use *both* psychological laws and societal laws, and that neither of these types of law is reducible to the other.

There would, I submit, be nothing mysterious in such a claim.[21] When, for example, we wish to explain a concrete phenomenon of social history such as the failure of a particular soil conservation programme, we need to employ psychological generalisations concerning human behaviour, but we also need to employ generalisations drawn from the physical sciences concerning the effects of the conservation steps which were taken. In such cases of interaction between men and their physical environment no-one, I should suppose, would challenge the belief that an adequate explanation of the series of events would demand the use of laws belonging to different sciences, as well as demanding a knowledge of the initial conditions relevant to the application of each set of laws. Further, no-one, I should suppose, would argue that one set of these laws must be reducible to the other in order that we should be able to use both in explaining this concrete event. And I see no reason why an analogous situation could not obtain with respect to the explanation of social phenomena, i.e. that in such explanations we may need to employ both psychological and societal laws. A belief of this type would not entail the acceptance of historical inevitability, nor would it entail any form of holism. Finally we may note that such a view would not necessarily entail a rejection of the thesis that psychological laws are *always* relevant to the explanation of social phenomena. It could accept this thesis and yet hold that *in some cases*[22] a knowledge of the initial conditions under which individuals act, and a knowledge of the laws of individual behaviour, is not adequate to explain the outcome of their actions: for this one must also employ abstractive-functional generalisations concerning societal facts.

[20] Some reasons for doubting each of these three types are implicit in my earlier article, 'A Critique of Philosophies of History', *Journal of Philosophy*, 1948, **45**, 365–378. I shall discuss the issue in detail in a future article.

[21] I believe that Gellner is correct in thinking that many methodological individualists *would* think this 'mysterious'. (Cf. Gellner, loc. cit. pp. 167–168.)

[22] I should not myself be inclined to accept the more radical form of the doctrine here under consideration, viz. that in *all* cases this is true.

The purpose of this paper has been limited to pointing out that a rejection of methodological individualism is compatible with a number of diverse views concerning the nature of societal laws. Therefore the simple dichotomy of methodological individualism *or* methodological holism stands in need of drastic revision. It seems to me that the classification which I have offered may also help to point out frequently unnoticed similarities and diversities among social theorists, thus making an analysi of their tsheories somewhat more manageable. And if, as I believe, there are good empirical and methodological reasons to doubt the feasibility of establishing either abstractive or global laws of directional change, or global laws of a functional sort,[23] then the issue of whether there are irreducible societal laws can be confined to one set of claims: that there are (or are not) some irreducible laws governing the functional relationships of specific aspects or components in societal life. The establishment of such laws would not demand that we accept the thesis of historical inevitability, nor the political and moral implications of either historicism or organicism. Nor would it commit us to either the metaphysics, or the explanatory methods, of holism.

[23] I am here only referring to laws of this type which are claimed to be 'ultimate', i.e. not reducible to abstractive-functional laws.

Man Is Irrelevant to, but Determined by, the Culture Process

51

from *The Science of Culture*
LESLIE A. WHITE

Culturological vs. Psychological Explanations

The institution of slavery has often been interpreted as the outcome of man's inherent tendencies to commit aggressions upon others — of "man's inhumanity to man." An eminent psychologist, Wm. McDougall, once went so far as to postulate a high degree of an instinct of submission among African peoples to account for the prevalence of Negro chattel slavery. We know, however, that the institution of slavery has not been universal by any means. As a matter of fact, it did not make its appearance until relatively recent times — since the beginning of the Neolithic at least; the hundreds of thousands of years of human history that went before had no slavery. And many peoples of the modern world have had no slaves. Are we to assume that the instinct of aggression — or of submission — was not sufficiently developed during the early eras of human history, or among some of the peoples of recent times, to find overt expression in a traffic in human chattels?

If the origin of the institution of slavery has been interpreted psychologically, so has its extinction. A growing consciousness of human rights, an appreciation of the essential dignity of man (whatever that is), or the rising spirit of Christianity have all been invoked to explain the decline of this institution. One scholar, writing in the Encyclopedia of the Social Sciences, has asserted that "the movement against slavery . . . was largely the result of the rising spirit of democracy, etc."[1] By the same token, the institution came into being as a consequence of the rising spirit of slavery. Obviously, psychological and spiritual interpretations do not tell us very much actually. *Why* have aggressive — or submissive — tendencies resulted in a certain type of social institution among some peoples but not among others? Why has the spirit of democracy asserted itself at one time, the spirit of slavery at another?

A culturological explanation of slavery makes the institution readily intelligible. Slavery as an institution will exist and endure only when the master can derive profit and advantage by exploiting the slave. This is possible only when a family group is able to produce considerably more than it requires for its continued existence. The efficiency of production is of course determined by the degree of technological development. Slavery did not exist during the hundreds of thousands of years before Neolithic times because culture had not developed sufficiently to make it possible for a producer to be more than self-supporting. There certainly would be no point — even if it were possible — in one tribe of savages enslaving another if the latter required all that they were able to produce in order to subsist. Consequently, we find no slavery in early periods of human history, nor, in the modern world, among peoples on low levels of technological development. But when in the course of cultural evolution the

 Subtitles were supplied in part by the editor.

[1] Williams, p. 83.

productivity of human labor was sufficiently increased by technological progress so as to make exploitation profitable and advantageous, the institution of slavery came into being. Correspondingly, when culture — particularly the technological culture — had reached a certain point where it could no longer be operated efficiently by a human chattel, then the institution of slavery became extinct. Slavery died out, not because someone discovered the essential dignity of man, or because of a rising spirit of Christianity or Democracy, but because, as Lewis H. Morgan put it long ago, a freeman is a better "property-making machine" than a slave.[2] Modern industrial technologies could not be operated by ignorant, illiterate human chattels. Also, the slave owner suffered a handicap which does not affect the employer of free labor: the slave owner had to feed and care for his slaves whether he made money out of them or not; he had a substantial investment in them and he must safeguard this investment. The employer of free labor, however, is under no such obligation to his employees. If his profits diminish he can lay off some workers; if they cease, he can close up his establishment entirely without assuming responsibility for his employees; they can shift for themselves — go hungry, go on public relief, or resort to begging or to theft. Thus, at a certain stage of cultural development, slavery comes into being as a consequence of the resources and imperatives of the cultural system. At a subsequent and higher stage of cultural development, the institution becomes extinct because it is no longer compatible with the resources and exigencies of the socio-cultural system.

War is a tremendously impressive expression of human behavior that is often "explained" psychologically. In addition to the Great Men who make wars at their own sweet will, we find more generalized psychological explanations. According to *Time* Magazine (Aug. 23, 1948), a UN-sponsored International Congress on Mental Health, attended by "2,000 of the world's foremost psychiatrists and psychologists," gave forth such interpretations of the cause of war as the following: Wars are caused by a sense of guilt which causes you to do something violent, which in turn creates a sense of guilt. Thus the repetition of wars is explained as well as their origin. Another psychologist attributed wars to restraint upon sexual impulses which causes frustration which causes people to become aggressive. Still another thought that people have been made aggressive and violent by corporeal punishment during childhood.

Professor Gordon W. Allport, a psychologist at Harvard, quotes with approval a passage from the preamble of the charter of UNESCO: "Since wars begin in the minds of men it is in the minds of men that the defences of peace must be constructed."[3] Monsignor Fulton J. Sheen expresses the same view in only slightly different words: "World wars are nothing but projections of the conflicts waged inside our own souls, for nothing happens in the world that does not first happen inside a soul."[4] "A burst of military enthusiasm and a line of able rulers enabled Egypt to assume for several centuries an imperial position,"[5] according to an eminent orientalist, the late James H. Breasted. The common people were, however, "a naturally peaceful people," and consequently Egypt was not able to retain her position of preeminence. War has no "rational cause," said Franz Boas; it is due to a "mental attitude," the "emotional value of an idea."[6] Another anthropologist, Ralph Linton, finds that the Plains Indians did not fight for hunting grounds or other tangible advantages, but rather because they were "warlike."[7] To Ruth Benedict ". . . it is a commonplace that men like war . . . Over

[2] Morgan, p. 505.
[3] Allport, G. W., p. 22.
[4] Sheen, 1948.
[5] Breasted, 1909, pp. 516, 449.
[6] Boas, 1945, p. 101.
[7] "Superficially it might appear that the roving life of a Plains Indian tribe and the frequent contacts with other groups which this entailed would be likely to focus interest on war, but it need not have done so if the Plains Indians in general had not been warlike. After all, there was enough food and other natural resources in the Plains to take care of a much

and over men have proved that they prefer war with all its suffering."[8] William James tells us, in "The Moral Equivalent of War," that "modern man inherits all the innate pugnacity and all the love of glory of his ancestors . . . Our ancestors have bred pugnacity into our bone and marrow, and thousands of years of peace won't breed it out of us . . . The military instincts and ideals are as strong as ever." And the layman sums up his estimate of the future: "You can't do away with war; it's just human nature."

But *is* man by nature so pugnacious and militant? Compared with other animal orders, the Carnivores for example, the Primates are a rather timid lot. The "innate pugnacity" of which James speaks is often conspicuously lacking in the human species. Warfare is virtually non-existent among many primitive tribes. And in many instances where fighting does take place, the contestants do not meet each other face to face and slug it out man to man so that their "military instincts and ideals" can be exercised to the full. Instead, they resort to ambush, killing their victims before they have a chance to defend themselves. To slaughter helpless sleeping victims is quite sufficient to feed the "love of glory" of most peoples. And when free and open conflict does take place among primitive peoples, their pugnacity is often more vocal than military — as is usually the case among the lower primates. Often the fight ends when the first blood is drawn. And in modern nations pugnacity has been "bred so weakly in our bones and marrow" that every nation has to resort to conscription. And despite such stinging epithets as "draft dodger," the number of men who prefer the degradation of prison to the glory of war is considerable. Thus it would appear that the lust for fighting and killing is not over-riding in primates in general or in man in particular.

But even if it were, it would tell us very little about war, why it is fought and when, with whom and over what. To attempt to explain war by appeal to an innate pugnacity would be like explaining Egyptian, Gothic, and Mayan architecture by citing the physical properties of stone; or like explaining the industrial revolution by invoking an inventive tendency in the human mind. A culturological interpretation of war will, however, tell us something of significance. Wars are fought between societies, between sociocultural systems, between tribes and nations. It is the culture of any given situation that determines whether warfare shall be engaged in or not, and if so how, with whom and for what. In some cultural settings, warfare is non-existent; the mode of life as culturally defined has no place for it. In other situations there is only occasional skirmishing between tribes. Where rich hunting or fishing grounds are at stake, we can expect military contests. The same holds true for grazing lands and for fertile valleys when culture has reached the level of animal husbandry and agriculture. It may sound absurd and superfluous to say that peoples will not fight over grazing lands, fertile valleys, coal and iron deposits, foreign markets, oil reserves and uranium mines until culture has advanced to such levels of development as domestication of animals, cultivation of plants, steam and internal combustion engines, world trade, and uranium piles. But if one listens to those who talk about man's "innate pugnacity" he might easily get the impression that this was sufficient to account for everything.

Warfare is a struggle between social organisms, not individuals. Its explanation is therefore social or cultural, not psychological. We could never understand why the United States entered World War II — or any other war — by an inquiry into the psychological motives of men and women. One man wanted

larger population than the area supported, and these tribes were not driven into war by economic needs," *The Study of Man*, p. 461.

Professor Lowie, too, thinks that the Plains Indians fought "just for fun": the "Plains Indians fought not for territorial aggrandizement nor for the victor's spoils, but above all because fighting was a game worth while because of the social recognition it brought when played according to the rules," *Primitive Society*, p. 356.

[8] Benedict, 1942, p. 763.

to quit his distasteful job as bank clerk, another wanted adventure, a third sought release from an unbearable domestic situation, another wanted to see what the women of France, Samoa, or China are like, another wanted to wear a uniform, another fought for God, for Country, and the New Deal, and so on. Of course, most men went to war because they were obliged to — or accept the degradation of imprisonment or worse. To picture the multitudes of docile serfs and peasants of ancient Egypt, pre-Columbian Peru, China, or Czarist Russia going to war because of an "innate pugnacity and a love of glory" (James), or as Benedict says because "men *like* war" is grotesque. They were forced to go, driven to the slaughter like sheep. And if any were animated by "the love of glory" it came to them from propagandists, not from their innermost selves.

Again, supposing we grant merely for the sake of argument an innate pugnacity to men: Whom will they fight? If a poll had been taken among Americans in 1939 to discover the objects of their hostility, it is likely that England would have received more votes than any other nation with the possible exception of Russia. Yet we entered the war on the side of these two nations. When Russia was fighting "gallant little Finland" in 1939–40 our pugnacious instincts were leveled squarely at the Kremlin. The non-aggression pact between Russia and Germany in 1939 aroused our indignation and anger. But after the Germans invaded Russia in 1941, the orientation of our instincts changed. We then found in Soviet Russia a stout champion of democracy.

Psychological explanations are not only irrelevant here, they are pathetic. The psychological orientations were the result of the intercourse of nations, not the cause. The lust for blood and glory was at low ebb in the military camps in the United States in November, 1941. An international event at Pearl Harbor transformed a listless, disgruntled mass of conscripts into a spirited fighting force. It would make more sense to say that it is war that breeds the martial spirit than to argue that pugnacious instincts cause wars.

To be sure, there would be no wars if there were no people — human organisms with their hungers and fears, hopes and inertia — to fight them. But to explain warfare in terms of psychology is illusion. War is a cultural phenomenon, and we can not only explain it in cultural terms, but we can account for the presence or absence of the pugnacious "instinct," the love of glory, or the loathing of slaughter, in cultural terms also. World peace will come, if it ever does, not because we shall have bred out the pugnacious instinct, or sublimated it in mass athletic contests,[9] but because cultural development, social evolution, will have reached the ultimate conclusion of the age-old process of merging smaller social groups into larger ones, eventually forming a single political organization that will embrace the entire planet and the whole human race.

The phenomenon of race prejudice and inter-racial antagonisms is frequently regarded and explained as primarily a psychological phenomenon. Since the phenomenon is manifested in acts and attitudes of individual human organisms it is frequently taken for granted that the problem of race prejudice and inter-racial antagonisms is psychological from the standpoint of scientific explanation, and psychiatric from the point of view of therapy. Psychoanalysis has come forward with interpretations such as these: The Jew is identified with the law-giving, super-ego forming father, and also with the unrepentant parricide. The hated Jew is not really a person but a myth: he is "castrated" and feminine and yet exceedingly dangerous and over-sexed, a symbol at once of the id and of the super-ego. The Negro, according to one psychoanalytic interpretation, represents the nocturnal, sexual father,

[9] Even as recently as the summer of 1948, more than one psychologist solemnly suggested that international athletic contests, such as the Olympic games then in progress, might serve to prevent wars by working off aggressive tendencies in a peaceful manner.

whom the son wishes to castrate — hence the castrative aspects of lynching. Anti-Negro man-hunts resemble the hunting of animals in groups, both phenomena being derived from the banding together of the sons against the primal father.

These observations may or may not adequately characterize the experience of an individual psyche who is participating in the sociocultural process of racial antagonisms. But even if they do realistically describe the individual experience, they do not explain the social phenomenon at all. It is all too frequently assumed that a sociocultural phenomenon has been explained when one has isolated and defined the psychological experiences of an individual within that sociocultural context. Thus, it is said, men may identify the Negro with the father, their rival, and then proceed to give these inner feelings overt expression in acts and attitudes of hostility toward the Negro.

What these attempts at psychological interpretations fail to do, of course, is to explain why it is that the Negro represents the nocturnal father in some societies but not in others; why antagonisms are directed primarily toward one minority group rather than another; why racial antagonisms are lacking altogether in some situations. The fallacy of psychological interpretations of sociocultural phenomena consists in the assumption that the subjective psychological experience correlated with the institution has brought the institution into existence. It is as if one discovered — or came to believe — that riding in an airplane was the realization of sexually motivated dreams of flying; or that flying in airplanes gave one a sense of power and mastery, and concluded therefore that the *airplane*, as an element of culture, had been explained by citing sexual dreams and a will to power. We do not deny or minimize the subjective psychological experiences of the individual at all — although we would like to see some of the psychoanalytic interpretations supported with a little more verification. These experiences are of course real. But, we would argue, they are functions of sociocultural situations; not the causes of them. Individual psychological experience has been evoked *by* the social phenomenon of race antagonism just as the thrill of power and mastery is evoked by the airplane; it is not the subjective experience that produces the antagonism or the airplane.

There are non-psychoanalytic psychological interpretations of racial antagonisms, also. The "frustration-aggression" hypothesis has been called upon to explain inter-racial conflicts. A people is frustrated and becomes aggressive as a consequence, choosing perhaps a minority group upon which to vent the aggressive impulse. But here again, the great variety and range of inter-racial conflicts and antagonisms is not illuminated very much by merely pronouncing the magic couplet "frustration and aggression."

One of the weakest of psychological explanations of race prejudice with which we are acquainted is that given once by the late Franz Boas. The prejudice, he said, ". . . is founded essentially . . . on the tendency of the human mind to merge the individual in the class to which he belongs, and to ascribe to him all the characteristics of his class."[10] Just how the tendency of the human mind to identify an individual with "the class *to which he belongs*" produces racial prejudice and antagonism is not quite clear although Boas assures us that it "is not difficult to understand" in the light of this tendency of the human mind.

Psychological interpretations of race prejudice and inter-racial antagonisms are misleading and unsound because these problems are sociological and cultural rather than psychological. As we have pointed out, a description of subjective psychological experience correlated with an institution does not constitute an explanation of the institution. The experience of the ego is a function of the institution, not its cause. And, the institution must be explained culturologically.

We do not wish to undertake an exhaustive culturological interpretation of race preju-

[10] Boas, 1945, pp. 77–78.

dice at this point. We would suggest, however, that if investigation and analysis were carried out along the following lines one would come to a much deeper and more realistic explanation of this phenomenon than any amount of psychological or psychoanalytic inquiry can produce: Race prejudice and racial antagonisms are likely to appear in sociocultural situations in which (1) one group is competing with another for the possession of desirable lands (e.g., the American Indian frontier), for jobs or other economic advantages; (2) where a minority group endeavors to preserve its own integrity as a sociocultural group within a larger population; where it resists the effort of the larger society to assimilate it in an attempt to achieve a high degree of integration. Minority groups which attempt thus to maintain their own integrity, not only on the cultural plane but also by means of endogamy, are opposing the attempts of the larger society to achieve integration through assimilation, and are likely consequently to become the object of hostility and aggression from the larger society — which incidentally tends to reinforce the efforts of the minority group to maintain *its* integrity, and so on in a vicious circle. (3) Hostility toward a foreign power or toward a minority group within a society is often an effective means of unifying a nation. In times of national emergency or crisis, therefore, a nation may attempt to achieve inner unity and solidarity by fomenting hositility toward a foreign power — an old trick — or against a minority group within its gates — also an old trick.

We turn now from culturological problems that have been commonly attacked with psychological techniques to one that has seldom been so approached, namely, the question of matrilineal and patrilineal lineages or clans. Offhand, we cannot cite any attempts to explain these sociocultural phenomena in psychological terms, to say, for example, that one people had matrilineal clans because of identification with the mother imago, whereas another people were organized into exogamous patrilineal lineages because of narcissistic impulses or what not. Such psychological interpretations would however be no more misplaced than those we have just cited. *Why* would one people identify itself with the mother, another with the father? This is precisely the question at issue; the psychological interpretation merely raises the question, it does not answer it. The paucity or absence of psychological interpretations of unilateral organization is probably due however to lack of interest in clans rather than a realization of the irrelevance of psychological interpretation.

Our argument concerning the relationship of man the organism to his extra-somatic cultural environment may be summarized somewhat as follows: The musical behavior of peoples — the Viennese of 1798, the black folk of Harlem, 1940, the English before 1066, the Italians at the time of Palestrina, the Nigerians, Bantus, Chinese, Pueblo Indians, and Yakuts — varies. How are these variations to be explained? Certainly not in terms of biological differences. Everything that we know about comparative anatomy and physiology will lend no support whatever to a belief that Chinese music has one form and style because of certain biological characters of the Chinese whereas the peculiar biological traits of the Bantus, Indians, or Negroes produce their respective musical types. On the contrary, our knowledge of neuro-sensory-muscular systems supports the proposition that man may be considered a biological constant so far as his human (symbolic) behavior is concerned. We observe that musical styles vary within a society during the course of time without discovering any correlative biological variation whatever. And of course the musical style of one people may be adopted by another: *Swing Low, Sweet Chariot* did not originate in Dahomey or Cameroon. Thus we see that we cannot explain these variations of musical behavior, which we may represent by M_1, M_2, M_3, M_4 . . . M_n, in terms of the human organism, O. Variables cannot be explained in terms of a constant.

How then can these differences in musical

behavior be accounted for? They are to be explained in terms of different musical traditions or cultures, C_1, C_2, C_3, C_4 . . . C_n. Let us set forth our argument in a series of formulas.

$$O \times C_1 \longrightarrow M_1$$
$$O \times C_2 \longrightarrow M_2$$
$$O \times C_3 \longrightarrow M_3$$
$$O \times C_4 \longrightarrow M_4$$

O stands for the human organism; M_1, M_2, M_3, M_4 for different types of musical behavior, i.e., neuro-sensory-muscular reactions of the human organism; and C_1, C_2, C_3, C_4, for types of musical culture. The musical behavior in any particular instance is, of course, a compound made up of two distinct elements, the actions of nerves, glands, muscles, sense organs, etc., of man on the one hand (O), and the external, extra-somatic cultural tradition (C) on the other. Since, however, the human organism appears as a constant factor in all of our equations we may eliminate it entirely from a consideration of variations of behavior. Thus we strike out the O and re-write our equations thus:

$$C_1 \longrightarrow M_1$$
$$C_2 \longrightarrow M_2$$
$$C_3 \longrightarrow M_3$$
$$C_4 \longrightarrow M_4$$

As the musical cultural tradition varies, so will the musical behavior vary. The behavior is simply the response of the organism to a particular set of cultural stimuli. M is a function of C.

What is true of musical behavior is true also of linguistic behavior, or monetary, mathematical architectural, philosophic, religious — in short, of *any* kind of human behavior. We come then to the following formula: *human* behavior is the response of the organism *man* to a class of external, extra-somatic, symbolic stimuli which we call *culture*. Variations of human behavior are functions of a cultural variable, not of a biological constant. Human behavior as we find it amongst the various peoples of the world is to be explained therefore in terms of their respective cultures rather than by appeal to "human nature" or psychological tendencies.

If human behavior is to be explained in terms of culture, how are we to account for culture?

Culture is an organization of phenomena — acts (patterns of behavior), objects (tools; things made with tools), ideas (belief, knowledge), and sentiments (attitudes, "values") — that is dependent upon the use of symbols. Culture began when man as an articulate, symbol-using primate, began. Because of its symbolic character, which has its most important expression in articulate speech, culture is easily and readily transmitted from one human organism to another. Since its elements are readily transmitted culture becomes a continuum; it flows down through the ages from one generation to another and laterally from one people to another. The culture process is also cumulative; new elements enter the stream from time to time and swell the total. The culture process is progressive in the sense that it moves toward greater control over the forces of nature, toward greater security of life for man. Culture is, therefore, a symbolic, continuous, cumulative, and progressive process.

All of this means that culture has, in a very real sense, an extra-somatic character. Although made possible only by the organisms of human beings, once in existence and under way it has a life of its own. Its behavior is determined by its own laws, not by the laws of human organisms. The culture process is to be explained in terms of the science of culture, of culturology, not in terms of psychology. Let us illustrate these propositions with a simple example.

A symbolic language would, of course, have no existence were it not for human organisms. But once the linguistic process gets under way it proceeds along its own lines, in terms of its own principles and in accordance with its own laws. The linguistic process is composed of phonetic elements. These interact with one another forming various kinds of combinations and patterns — phonetic, syntactic, grammatical, lexical, etc. The language acquires form and structure and uniformities of behavior. In other words, it develops certain principles upon which it rests and in terms of which it functions.

Now this language has an extra-somatic, non-biological, non-psychological character. It had an existence prior to the birth of any individual speaking it; it comes to each person from the outside. It seizes upon the human organism at birth and equips it with specific linguistic patterns of behavior. Languages are transmitted from one generation or one people to another just as tools or ornaments are. The study of language is, therefore, *philology*, not biology or psychology. Although human organisms are prerequisite to the linguistic process they do not form a part of it *as such*, and are therefore irrelevant to the study and interpretation of it. We find no reference to nerves, glands, and sense organs in a manual on English grammar; no hopes, fears, desires, instincts or reflexes in a treatise on the Indo-European languages. Language may be treated as a closed system, as a process *sui generis*. Philology is a subdivision of culturology, not of biology or psychology.

What is true of language will hold for every other logically distinguishable portion of the culture process — technological, social, ideological — and for human culture as a whole. Culture is a continuum of interacting elements (traits), and this process of interaction has its own principles and its own laws. To introduce the human organism into a consideration of cultural variations is therefore not only irrelevant but wrong; it involves a premise that is false. Culture must be explained in terms of culture. Thus, paradoxical though it may seem, "the proper study of mankind" turns out to be not Man, after all, but Culture. The most realistic and scientifically adequate interpretation of culture is one that proceeds *as if* human beings did not exist.[11] . . .

Culture Controls and Is not Controlled by the Individual

One's conscience is often thought to be the most intimate, personal and private characteristic of one's ego. Here if anywhere one ought to find something that is wholly one's own, a private and unique possession. To an ordinary individual the conscience seems to be a mechanism, an inborn ability, to distinguish between right and wrong, just as he possesses a mechanism for distinguishing up from down, the vertical from the horizontal. Except, perhaps, that conscience seems deeper within one, a more intimate part of one's make-up, than semi-circular canals. After all, these canals are merely a mechanical device, whereas a conscience is an integral part of one's self, one's ego. Yet, for all the conviction that immediate experience carries, we can still be tricked by illusion. And this is exactly what has happened in the present instance. Our sense of balance, our distinction between up and down, is indeed a private faculty; it is built into our psychosomatic structure and has no origin or significance apart from it. But our conscience has a sociocultural origin; it is the operation of supraindividual cultural forces upon the individual organism. Conscience is merely our experience and our awareness of the operation of certain sociocultural forces upon us. Right and wrong are matters of sociocultural genesis; they are originated by social systems, not by individual biological organisms. Behavior that is injurious, or thought to be harmful, to the general welfare is *wrong*; behavior that promotes the general welfare is *good*. The desires inherent in an individual organism are exercised to serve its own interests. Society, in order to protect itself from the demands of the individual as well as to serve its own interests, must influence or control the behavior of its component members. It

[11] "Hence it is both possible and permissible to study the history of a folkway, or the evolution of culture in general, without reference to individuals or their organic and mental characteristics," (Geo. P. Murdock, "The Science of Culture," p. 206).

must encourage *good* behavior and discourage the *bad*. It does this by first defining the *good* and the *bad* specifically, and secondly, by identifying each *good* or *bad* with a powerful emotion, positive or negative, so that the individual is motivated to perform good deeds and to refrain from committing bad ones. So effective is this socio-psychologic mechanism that society not only succeeds in enlisting individuals in the cause of general welfare but actually causes them to work against their own interests — even to the point of sacrificing their own lives for others or for the general welfare. A part of the effectiveness of this social mechanism consists in the illusion that surrounds it: the individual is made to feel that it is *he* who is making the decision and taking the proper action, and, moreover, that he is perfectly "free" in making his decisions and in choosing courses of action. Actually, of course, this still small voice of conscience is but the voice of the tribe or group speaking to him from within. "What is called conscience," says Radcliffe-Brown, "is . . . the reflex in the individual of the sanctions of the society."[12] The human organism lives and moves within an ethical magnetic field, so to speak. Certain social forces, culturally defined, impinge upon the organism and move it this way and that, toward the good, away from the bad. The organism experiences these forces though he may mistake their source. He calls this experience conscience. His behavior is analogous to a pilotless aircraft controlled by radio. The plane is directed this way and that by impulses external to it. These impulses are received by a mechanism and are then transmitted to motors, rudders, etc. This receiving and behavior-controlling mechanism is analogous to conscience.

That conscience is a cultural variable rather than a psychosomatic constant is made apparent of course by a consideration of the great variation of definition of *rights* and *wrongs* among the various cultures of the world. What is right in one culture may be wrong in another. This follows from the fact that an act that will promote the general welfare in one set of circumstances may injure it in another. Thus we find great variety of ethical definition and conduct in the face of a common and uniform human organism, and must conclude therefore that the determination of right and wrong is social and cultural rather than individual and psychological. But the interpretation of *conscience*, rather than custom and mores, in terms of social and cultural forces serves to demonstrate once more that the individual is what his culture makes him. He is the utensil; the culture supplies the contents. Conscience is the instrument, the vehicle, of ethical conduct, not the cause. It is well, here as elsewhere, to distinguish cart from horse.

The *unconscious* also is a concept that may be defined culturologically as well as psychologically. Considered from a psychological point of view, "the unconscious" is the name given to a class of determinants of behavior inherent in the organism, or at least, having their locus in the organism as a consequence of the experiences it has undergone, of which the person is not aware or whose significance he does not appreciate. But there is also another class of determinants of human behavior of which the ordinary individual may be — and usually is — unaware, or at least has little or no appreciation of their significance. These are extrasomatic cultural determinants. In a general and broad sense, the whole realm of culture constitutes "an unconscious" for most laymen and for many social scientists as well. The concept of culture and an appreciation of its significance in the life of man lie beyond the ken of all but the most scientifically sophisticated. To those who believe that man makes his culture and controls its course of change, the field of cultural forces and determinants may be said to constitute an unconscious — an extrasomatic unconscious.

[12] Durkheim, 1938, pp. 1–2; Radcliffe-Brown, 1934, p. 531.

The unconscious character of the operation of culture in the lives of men can be demonstrated in many particular instances as well as in a general way. A moment ago we distinguished the unconscious factor in ethical behavior. The determinants of ethical behavior — why, for example, one should not play cards on Sunday — lie in the external cultural tradition. The individual, however, unaware of either the source or the purpose of the taboo, locates it in his inner self: his conscience is but the screen upon which the unconscious factors of society and culture project themselves.

Incest is defined and prohibited in order to effect exogamous unions so that mutual aid may be fostered and, consequently, life made more secure for the members of society. But of the existence and significance of these cultural factors all but a few are unconscious. To the individual, incest is simply a sin or crime that is inherently and absolutely wrong.

Or, take the rules of etiquette: A man in a certain society is not permitted to wear earrings or to use lipstick. The purpose of these restrictions is to define classes of individuals within society: a man, woman, priest, etc., is an individual who behaves positively in a certain manner and who must refrain from certain kinds of acts. By means of these definitions, prescriptions, and prohibitions, each individual is made to conform to his class and the classes are thereby kept intact. Thus, order is achieved in society, order both structurally and functionally. And, to conduct its life effectively a society must have order. But the individual seldom has any appreciation of the source and purpose of these rules; he is apt to regard them, if he thinks about them at all, as natural and right, or as capricious and irrational. Another example of the cultural unconscious.

The church is an organ of social control; it is a mechanism of integration and regulation. In this respect it has political functions just as does the State . . . .It operates to preserve the integrity of society against disintegration from within and against aggression from without. It is thus an important factor in a nation's war machine; it mobilizes the citizenry to fight against foreign foes. It must also strive to harmonize conflicting class interests at home. This it does frequently by telling the poor and the oppressed to be patient, to be satisfied with their lot, not to resort to violence, etc.[13] In these ways the Church like the State exercises political functions that are essential to the life of the society. Yet how many members of a congregation or of the clergy have any awareness of this aspect of the rituals, paraphernalia, theology, and dogma that occupy them?

The determinants of our form of the family lie so deep within our cultural unconscious that even social science has yet no adequate answer to the question why we prohibit polygamy (see p. 335). The Chinese, according to Kroeber, were long unaware that their language had tones. "This apparently simple and fundamental discovery," he says, "was not made until two thousand years after they possessed writing, and a thousand after they had scholars." [14] And they might not have made it even then had not "the learning of Sanskrit for religious purposes . . . made them phonetically self-conscious." Like the rustic who had been talking prose all his life without realizing it, the peoples of the Western world, too, have long been unconscious of much of the structure and processes of Indo-European languages.

Thus, in addition to the determinants of behavior that lie deep within the tissues of our own organisms, below the level of awareness, there is another class of determinants of which we are equally unconscious: forces and factors within the extra-somatic cultural tradition. The science of culture is endeavoring to discover, define and explain these unconscious cultural factors as psychoanalysis has undertaken to explore and make known

[13] "Religion teaches the laboring man and the artisan to carry out honestly and fairly all equitable agreements freely entered into; never to injure the property, nor to outrage the person, of an employer; never to resort to violence in defending their own cause, nor to engage in riot or disorder . . ." (Pope Leo XII's Encyclical on Condition of Labor, May 15, 1891, *The Official Catholic Year Book Anno Domini*, 1928), p. 540.

[14] Kroeber, 1944, p. 224.

the intra-organismal unconscious.[15] We may illustrate these two realms of the unconscious in the following diagram:

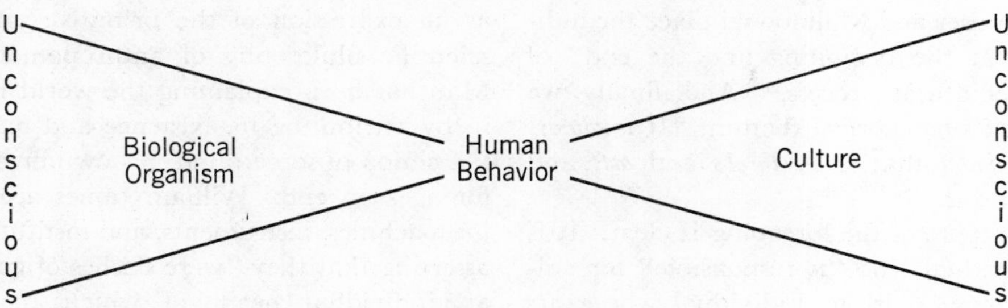

Fig. 51–1 Human behavior is a function of the biological organism on the one hand, and of the extra-somatic cultural tradition or process, on the other. The individual is more or less aware of some of the determinants of his behavior in each category, the cultural and the biological. But of others he is quite unaware, or has no adequate appreciation of the role they play as determinants of his behavior. These are the realms of the unconscious: the biological and the cultural.

The nature of the relationship between the mind of the individual human organism on the one hand and the external cultural tradition on the other may be illuminated by a critical examination of a certain thesis widely held in recent and current anthropological circles in the United States. Briefly stated, this thesis asserts that man has created culture, that culture is the accumulated product of the creative acts of countless individuals, that the individual is the *fons et origo* of all cultural elements, and, finally, that the culture process is to be explained in terms of the individual.

Thus Ralph Linton writes: "... the individual ... *lies at the foundation of all social and cultural phenomena*. Societies are organized groups of individuals, and *cultures* are, in the last analysis, *nothing more* than the organized and repetitive *responses* of a society's members. For this reason the *individual* is *the logical starting point* for *any investigation* of the *larger configuration*" [16] (emphasis ours). "If we had the knowledge and the patience to analyze a culture retrospectively," says Goldenweiser, "*every element* of it would be found to have had its beginning in the creative act of *an individual mind*. There is, of course, *no other source* for culture to come from ... An *analysis of culture*, if fully carried out, *leads back to the individual mind*" [17] (emphasis ours). Edward Sapir asserts that the "currency [of "any cultural element"] in a single community is ... an instance of diffusion that has radiated out, at last analysis, from a single individual." [18] Ruth Benedict declares that "no civilization has in it any element which in the last analysis is not the contribution of an individual. Where else could any trait come from except from the behavior of a man, woman or a child?" [19] Clark Wissler said that "the inventive process resides in individual organisms; so far as we know, it is a function of the individual organism." [20] Linton asserts that "it is the individual *who is responsible*, in the last

[15] Kroeber has a fine appreciation of the unconscious character of cultural determinants of human behavior as the section "Unconscious Factors in Language and Culture" in his *Anthropology* (1923) makes clear. But despite certain examples which he cites and which show quite clearly that the locus of the unconscious *is in the culture process*, he locates it "in the mind." Thus he says: "It is difficult to say where the creative and imitative impulses of fashion come from; which, inasmuch as the impulses obviously reside somewhere in human minds, means that they spring from the unconscious portions of the mind" (p. 127).

[16] Linton, 1945, p. 5.

[17] Goldenweiser, 1933, p. 59.

[18] Sapir, 1916, p. 43.

[19] Benedict, 1934, p. 253.

[20] Wissler, 1927, p. 87.

analysis, for *all additions to culture*" [21] (emphasis ours). Hallowell finds the conception of *cultural* influence unrealistic; "In the last analysis," he says, "it is *individuals* who respond to and influence one another." [22] Both Goldenweiser and Malinowski place the individual "at the beginning and the end" of the sociocultural process.[23] And, finally, we cite Sapir's categorical dictum: "It is *always* the *individual* that *really thinks* and *acts* and *dreams* and *revolts*."[24, 25]

The import of the foregoing is clear. It is the individual who "is responsible" for culture change; it is the individual who *really* does things; every cultural element has its beginning in the creative act of an individual mind, etc., etc. It would appear from our quotations that their authors feel that they are expressing a fundamental proposition and point of view. Nearly all of them use the phrase "in the last analysis" in setting forth their position. Their premises seem to appear to them so simple and so realistic as to be virtually axiomatic: "Every cultural element originates in the mind of an individual — of a man, woman, or child. Where else *could* it come from?" Culture is pictured as a great structure built by countless individuals, much as a coral reef is produced by myriads of marine organisms during the course of time. And, as the coral reef is explained in terms of the activities of marine organisms, so culture may be explained by citing the "creative acts of the individual human mind."

This view seems plausible enough: as a matter of fact, it appears to be virtually self-evident. Anyone can see for himself that it is man, human individuals, who chop down trees, build houses, pass laws, write sonnets, worship gods, etc. But we have become a bit wary of the self-evident and the obvious: anyone can see for himself that it is the sun, not the earth, that moves. But, thanks to Copernicus, we now know better.

Obvious and self-evident though the proposition that culture is made by individuals may appear to be, we must reject it as a means of explaining cultural processes or traditions. As a matter of fact, we regard it as an expression of the primitive and prescientific philosophy of anthropomorphism. Man has been explaining the world he lives in by attributing its existence and nature to the action of some mind, his own or a god's, for ages on end. William James accounted for machines, instruments, and institutions by asserting that they "were flashes of genius in an individual head, of which the outer environment showed no sign." [26] To Newton "this most beautiful cosmos could only proceed from the counsel and dominion of an intelligent and powerful Being."[27] To Plato, the material world was but the expression of "ideas in the mind of God." "Let there be light," said Yahweh, "and there was light." In the mythology of ancient Egypt, evreything came from the thinking and willing of the great artificer deity, Ptah.[28] Among our preliterate Keresan Pueblo Indians, Tsityostinako, or Thought-Woman, brought things to pass by acts of thought and will. And today, in line with this ancient and primitive philosophic tradition, we are told that culture has issued from the mind of man — of men, women, and children — and therefore if we are to understand culture and explain its content and course of change, we must do so in terms of the individual.

It is obvious, of course, that culture has emanated from the organisms of human beings: without the human species there would be no culture. We recognize also that a *generic* relationship obtains between culture as a whole and the human species in its, or their, entirety; the general character of culture is an expression of the biological properties of the human species. But, when it comes to an explanation of any particular

[21] Linton, 1938, p. 248.
[22] Hallowell, p. 174.
[23] Goldenweiser, 1935, p. 75; Malinowski, 1939, p. 964.
[24] We recall at this point Georg Simmel's emphatic assertion: "It is *certain* that *in the last analysis* only individuals exist," (emphasis ours); see p. 84.
[25] Sapir, 1917, p. 442.
[26] James, 1880.
[27] Newton, p. 544.
[28] Breasted, 1909, p. 357.

culture — and all the cultures of the world are particular, specific cultures — or to an explanation of the process of culture change in general, a consideration of the human organism, either in its collective or individual aspects, is irrelevant. The culture process is not explainable in terms of races, physical types, or of individual minds. It is to be explained in terms of culture itself. In short, the culture process is to be explained culturologically rather than biologically or psychologically.

Thus we do not account for differences between Chinese and Swedish culture by appeal to the physical, somatological, and innate psychological differences between the Chinese and the Swedish peoples. We know of no differences between cultural traditions, no specific feature of the culture process, that can be explained in terms of innate biological properties, physical or mental. On the other hand, we can explain the human behavior of Chinese and Swedish peoples as biological organisms in terms of their respective cultures.

The proposition just enunciated is generally accepted in the social sciences today. We no longer subscribe to racial explanations of culture. But the thesis that the sociocultural process is explainable in terms of individuals rests upon the same premise, namely, that biological factors are relevant to interpretations of the culture process. Thus, it is admitted that the biological factor is extraneous to an interpretation of the culture process when taken in its collective (i.e., racial) aspect, but, many scholars contend, it is not only relevant but fundamental when taken in its individual aspect. We regard this reasoning as unsound; a single individual organism is as irrelevant to an interpretation of the culture process as a group of individuals.

It might be well at this point to draw a distinction between two fundamentally different propositions. The individual himself is not irrelevant to the actual culture process. On the contrary, he is an integral and in one sense a fundamental part of it. Individuals do indeed enamel their fingernails, vote, and believe in capitalism as Lynd has observed. But *the individual is irrelevant to an explanation of the culture process.* We cannot explain the culture trait or process of enameling nails in terms of innate desire, will, or caprice. We can however explain the behavior of the individual in terms of the culture that embraces him. *The* individual, the average, typical individual of a group, may be regarded as a constant so far as *human*, symbolic behavior is concerned. The typical Crow Indian organism may be regarded as biologically equivalent to the typical English, Zulu, or Eskimo organism so far as his capacities and inclinations for human behavior are concerned. The alternative to this proposition is acceptance of a racial determinant of human behavior and culture. In the process of interaction between the human organism on the one hand and the extra-somatic cultural tradition on the other, the cultural factor is the variable, the biological factor the constant; it is the cultural factor that determines the variations in the resulting behavior. The human behavior of the individual organism is therefore a function of his culture. The individual becomes then the locus of the culture process and the vehicle of its expression. Thus we arrive at a culturological conception of individuality to add to those of anatomy, physiology, and psychology.

Since the earliest days of human history every member of the human species has been introduced at birth into a cultural environment of beliefs, customs, instruments, expressions of art, etc., as well as a natural habitat of climate, topography, flora and fauna. This cultural environment is a continuum, a tradition; it descends lineally from one generation to another, and it may diffuse laterally from one people to another. Culture is an elaborate mechanism whose function is to make life secure and continuous for *groups* of human beings. In order to perform these functions, culture must harness energy in one form or another and put it to work. Culture is, therefore, a thermodynamic system in a mechanical sense. Culture grows in all its aspects — ideological, sociological, and technological — when and as the amount of energy harnessed per capita per year is increased, and as the means of expending this energy are improved. Culture is thus a dynamic system capable of growth. A cultural tradition is a stream of interacting cultural elements — of instruments, beliefs, customs, etc. In this interactive process, each element impinges upon others and is in turn acted upon by them. The process is a competitive one; instruments, customs, and beliefs may become obsolete and be eliminated from the stream: stone axes give way to metal ones; science replaces myth and magic; tribe and clan become obsolete at a certain stage of social evolution and the state takes their place. New elements are incorporated into the cultural stream from time to time: metals, the wheel, beliefs consequent upon the use of the microscope, etc., enter the cultural tradition at certain stages of its development. New combinations and syntheses of cultural elements — i.e., inventions and discoveries — are continually being formed in this interactive process: the invention of the steam engine, the "discovery" of the Periodic System of the elements, the formulation of the laws of thermodynamics, etc., are new combinations or syntheses of cultural elements. A cultural tradition is therefore a dynamic system (powered by natural forces which it harnesses) that behaves and grows in terms of its own principles and laws. It may therefore be explained on its own level, in culturological terms rather than with the concepts of psychology, biology, chemistry or physics. It may be regarded as a system *sui generis*.

In relation to the process of culture change and growth the biological factor of man may be regarded as a constant and hence irrelevant to an explanation of the culture process. Relative to an explanation of the difference between the culture of the Swedes and that of the Chinese or Zulus, the biological factor — such things as skin, hair, or eye color, stature, innate abilities, etc. — may, as we have noted, be regarded as irrelevant. It is irrelevant also to an explanation of the differences between the culture of England in A.D. 1200 and that of A.D. 1900. We see, then, that to the problem of interpretation of the culture process, the biological factor of man is irrelevant. The culture process is explainable culturologically, not biologically or psychologically.

Let us now consider *the individual* in relation to the culture process. As we have noted, every individual is born into a culture that existed prior to his birth. This culture seizes upon him at birth and as he grows and matures equips him with language, customs, beliefs, instruments, etc. In short, it is culture that provides him with the *form* and *content* of his behavior as a human being. Thus, Crow Indian behavior is the response of the organism *Homo sapiens* to a particular organization of stimuli that we call "Crow culture." Similarly, American, Eskimo, and Zulu behaviors are the responses of the same kind of organism to other cultural traditions. *The individual* in each case is merely an organization of cultural forces and elements that have impinged upon him from the outside and which find their overt expression through him. So conceived, the individual is but the expression of a supra-biological cultural tradition in somatic form.

We turn now to the role of the individual in the process of culture growth, and specifically to the propositions that, "in the last analysis," it is the individual who "is responsible for all additions to culture"; that "every culture element is to be traced back to the creative act of an individual mind"; that it is *always* the *individual* who *really* thinks, acts, dreams, and revolts; and that the individual is "the logical starting point for *any* investigation of the larger configurations" such as society and culture.

To be sure culture is dependent upon the human species and could not exist without it. It is true also that the human species is composed of discrete physical entities that we call individuals. But the scholars that we have just quoted are doing more than to give utterance to these obvious and trite commonplaces. They are asserting that the individual is a prime mover, a determinant; that he is the cause, culture the effect; that it is the individual who "is responsible" for change in the culture process; and that, therefore, an explanation of "the larger configuration" of culture must lie in a consideration of *the individual*. And it is this proposition that we reject — and reverse: it is the individual who is explained in terms of his culture, not the other way around.

Let us consider inventions and discoveries, or any significant advance in the arts, science, or philosophy. To say that they are the achievements of certain individuals is merely to locate them, not to explain them. To say that the calculus was invented by Newton and Leibnitz is to identify these events historically or biographically but it does not explain them as events in a culture process. *Why* did these events take place when and where they did? We wish to know this too as well as what particular person made the invention or discovery. Merely to say "the individual" is no answer to this question. Nor is such a reply improved by limiting the individuals to persons of exceptional native ability. There were individuals of this category in the Middle Ages and in the Bronze Age and, in the time of Newton, they were sprinkled through the populations of Tibet, Bechuanaland, and the Andean Highlands. Why was not the calculus invented at other times and in other lands?

An invention, discovery, or other significant cultural advance is an event in a culture process. It is a new combination or synthesis of elements in the interactive stream of culture. It is the outcome of antecedent and concomitant cultural forces and elements. The Laws of Motion, formulated by Newton, were the synthesis of cultural elements historically identified with the persons of Kepler, Brahe, Galileo, and others. The occurrence of their formulation took place where and when it did because the circumstances of culture growth and history brought together the elements requisite to this synthesis at a particular time and place. We can trace the growth of these elements through time and place. Thus we explain the occurrence of this significant event culturologically. And, moreover, we explain the behavior of Newton by showing that the formulation of these laws was the response of his organism to certain cultural stimuli. We know virtually nothing about his nervous system directly; we make inferences concerning it on the basis of the effect of cultural stimuli upon him. In short, we know his mentality only through his culture. But Newton was also much concerned with theology and Biblical interpretation, which again is explained by the fact that he was born into a powerful theological "gravitational field" as well as a scientific one and that he felt the "pull" of the one as he did the other. In another age or culture, Newton would have devoted himself to such things as designing fish traps, hepatoscopy, or the elaboration of a theory of totemism. But when a certain concatenation of cultural forces and elements occurs at a given time and place they will become synthesized in the neuro-sensory-muscular-etc. system of one individual or another.

Nothing demonstrates more clearly the nature of the culture process and its expression in significant episodes of cultural advance, and at the same time the irrelevance of the individual to an explanation of this process, than the phenomena of multiple and simultaneous, but independent, inventions and discoveries. Time after time, in the history of science, mathematics and technology, an important invention or discovery has been made by anywhere from two to ten persons simultaneously and independently.[29]

[29] The following instances of multiple, simultaneous but independent inventions or discoveries are taken from the list compiled by Wm. F. Ogburn and published in his *Social Change*, pp. 90–102. Examples could be multiplied almost indefinitely.

Theory of planetary perturbations: Lagrange, 1808; Laplace, 1808.

Discovery of planet Neptune: Adams, 1845; Leverrier, 1845.

Discovery of sun spots: Galileo, 1611; Fabricus, 1611; Scheiner, 1611; and Harriott, 1611.

First measurement of parallax of star: Bessel, 1838; Struve, 1838; Henderson, 1838.

Introduction of decimal point: Bürgi, 1592; Pitiscus, 1608–12; Kepler, 1616; and Napier, 1616–17.

Discovery of oxygen: Scheele, 1774; Priestley, 1774.

The Periodic Law: De Chancourtois, 1864, Newlands, 1864; Lothar Meyer, 1864. Law of Periodicity:

To explain phenomena of this sort by invoking "coincidence," "fortuitous clusterings of genius," etc., as William James and others have done, is empty and sterile. A culturological interpretation, however, readily makes them intelligible: when growing and converging lines of cultural development reach a certain point, fusion and synthesis will take place. If culture is advancing on a wide front, these syntheses will find two or more independent and approximately simultaneous expressions. The invention or discovery is explained therefore in terms of a growing and interactive culture process; the individual inventors or discoverers are merely the loci and the vehicles of expression of this process.

To return now to Sapir's dictum that "it is always the individual who really thinks and acts and dreams and revolts." This statement does not merely distort the picture of human behavior; it inverts it. If he had said it is always the individual that *sleeps* and *yawns* and *hears* and *breathes*, we would offer no objection, for these activities *are* functions of individual organisms; there is no communal or group mechanism of yawning or breathing. But to say it is the individual who *does* such things as *human* thinking, feeling and acting is misleading to say the least; it implies a premise that is unwarranted. An individual can independently as an organism, yawn, sleep, and breathe.[30] But no one can think, act and feel as a human being as an independent, autonomous organism; he can do so only as a part of a sociocultural system. A question of technical terminology is involved here. It may be argued that the words *think*, *feel*, *dream*, etc., are properly applicable to neuro-sensory-muscular-etcetera systems only. If this ruling be accepted, then it is true of course that it is always the individual organism that thinks, feels, and acts. But it was not to set forth this tautology that Sapir took such pains and emphasis of expression. It was his purpose to present the individual as a prime mover, as an initiator and determinant of a process. And it is this proposition that we reject.

We may indeed say that thinking, feeling, and acting are functions of individual biological organisms. There is no communal nervous system, no group brain, of course. But, human thinking, feeling, and acting cannot be accounted for in terms of biological organisms, by saying that the individual *does* these things. Spitting, yawning, scratching, etc., are intelligible as functions of individual organisms. But believing in ghosts, dreaming of the Blessed Virgin, avoiding one's mother-in-law, scalping a vanquished foe, *as events* or *processes*, cannot be made intelligible merely by saying that it is the individual who does these things. In human thinking, feeling, and acting the individual is merely responding to stimuli, to cultural elements. But we cannot explain the form and content of the response merely by citing the biological organism that does the responding. Whether a person believes that a fever has been caused by bacteria or the violation of a taboo is a matter that is

---

L. Meyer, 1869, Mendeleeff, 1869.

Telescope: Lippershey, 1608; Della Porta, 1558; Digges, 1571; Johannides, Metius, 1608; Drebbel, Fontana, Janssen, 1608; and Galileo, 1609.

Law of Conservation of Energy: Mayer, 1843; Joule, 1847; Helmholz, 1847; Colding, 1847; and Thomson, 1847.

Telegraph: Henry, 1831; Morse, 1837; Cooke-Wheatstone, 1837; and Steinheil, 1837.

Cellular basis of both animal and vegetable tissue: claimed by Schwann, Henle, Turpin, Dumortier, Purkinje, Muller, and Valentin, all at about the same time: 1839.

Solution of the problem of respiration: by Priestley, Scheele, Lavoisier, Spallanzani, and Davy, all in 1777.

Sulphuric ether as an anaesthetic: Long, 1842; Robinson, 1846; Liston, 1846; Morton, 1846; and Jackson, 1846.

Self-exciting dynamo: claimed by Hjorth, 1866–67; Varley, 1866–67; Siemens, 1866–67; Wheatstone, 1866–67; Ladd, 1866; Wilde, 1863–67.

[30] Yawning, breathing, etc., although functions of an individual and autonomous organism, may be modified, of course, by cultural forces. It is interesting to note that Sapir, who has insisted so vehemently upon the autonomy of the individual in thinking, feeling and acting, should have taken pains, in another connection, to point out that *breathing* may function within and be modified by a sociocultural process ("The Unconscious Patterning of Behavior in Society," in *The Unconscious*, E. S. Dummer, ed., New York, 1927), pp. 117–18.

not made intelligible by invoking the individual organism who "always does" the believing. The organism is the same in both cases.

Thus we are left in the position where we have designated certain psycho-biological processes "thinking," "feeling," or "acting," but where we cannot explain these processes at all merely by considering them as individual phenomena. "It is always the individual who thinks, etc.," tells us, therefore, nothing of any significance. *What* does the individual think, and *why* does he think thus and so? This is what we want to know, and the conception of the individual as a prime mover, as an initiator or determinant of the culture process, as one who "is responsible" for all culture change, etc., will not give us the answer. On the contrary, it will effectively obscure or conceal it.

The events or processes that we technically designate "thinking, feeling, and acting" are, in so far as they are on the human, symbolic level, functions of sociocultural systems. They are, as a matter of fact, sociocultural processes. Note that we have said that these *events* and *processes* are functions of sociocultural systems. We have not said that "thinking," "feeling," and "acting" are sociocultural processes. An event is what it is — an event. When we label an event "thinking" we refer it to a neurologic context and to that kind of context only. But the very same *event* that is called "thinking" and thus referred to a neurologic context may also be referred to another context, a sociocultural context. Thus, believing in witches or bacteria as the cause of an illness is an event or process that can be referred to a psychologic context or to a culturologic context; it may be considered as a function of a nervous system or of a sociocultural system. But, although it is perfectly true that we can have no belief in witches apart from a nervous system, we learn virtually nothing about such a belief as an event, act, or process from a consideration of its neurologic aspect.

A belief in witches or bacteria as an event or process is to be explained in sociocultural terms rather than with neurologic concepts. The *believing* is the response of a human organism to a cultural stimulus. But *what* the organism believes is determined not by itself but by its culture. And the cultural element that serves as stimulus is not to be explained in terms of individual neurologic processes but in terms of other cultural elements and processes. Thus to say that believing in witches or bacteria is something that an individual *does* is either an empty tautology — "believing" being *by definition* an individual biological affair — or it implies a premise that is false, namely, that it is the individual who initiates and determines the belief. The individual had nothing to do with the origin of the belief; it was in the cultural tradition of his people before he was born. He did not originate it; it came to him from the outside. A belief in witches is the outgrowth of antecedent ideas and beliefs that we can trace back to the Old Stone Age. The belief in bacteria also is a synthesis of cultural elements, of concepts, microscopes, etc. Thus, the specific act or process of believing that witches or bacteria cause illness has been determined not by an individual organism at all but by a sociocultural system. The event is something that the culture has done to the individual rather than the other way around. If it be argued that some time, somewhere, there must have been a single individual who was the first person in history to believe that illness is caused by bacteria rather than by witches, it must be pointed out that this event, too, is merely a synthesis of cultural elements that have come to the individual from his circumambient cultural tradition.

To take this view of the relationship between the individual and the culture process is not to regard the former, as an organism, as a purely passive thing. The individual does not receive cultural material from the outside in a purely passive way, like a cup into which coffee is poured, nor does it reflect this material like a perfect mirror does an image. The human organism is a *dynamic* system. It not only receives cultural elements from the outside, it *acts* upon them. It is by virtue of the action of the neuro-sensory-glandular-etcetera system upon cultural elements that they are made to act and react upon one another, to form new combinations and syntheses. We do not therefore minimize the dynamic nature of the individual as an active as well as a reactive organism. We are merely saying that a consideration of the dynamic character of this organism does not help us to explain the form and content of its reactions and responses. The organism does the reacting, of course. But, in human behavior, the specific nature of its reactions is determined not by the organism but by cultural elements serving as stimuli.

Neither does our point of view regard all individuals as alike. On the contrary, we recognize that no two individuals are identical biologically. Since human organisms are the mediums of expression of the culture process, it follows that variations of cultural expression will be produced by variations of individual biological structure. But not all variations of expression of the culture process are due to individual biological variation by any means. The culture process is itself inherently variable. No two cultural elements — no two axes or fetiches, no two expressions of sentiment or attitude — are identically alike either. Some of the variation of expression of the culture process is due therefore to variation of cultural stimuli. Furthermore, it is a striking and significant fact that, within a fairly uniform cultural environment, the most diverse physical types — the tall and the short, fat and thin, lazy and energetic, endomorphs and ectomorphs, etc. — react in a highly uniform manner in such respects as language and dialect, attitudes, beliefs, food habits, rituals of social intercourse, and so on. Thus a consideration of individual biological variation only serves to make clearer and more emphatic the dominance of the cultural factor in the determination of human behavior. . . .

Bibliography

The following abbreviations are used for those serial publications, handbooks, and encyclopedias that are cited two or more times.

AA	American Anthropologist
AAA-M	American Anthropological Association, Memoirs
AJS	American Journal of Sociology
AM	Atlantic Monthly
AS	Annales du Service des Antiquités de Égypte
CE	Catholic Encyclopedia
EB	Encyclopedia Britannica, 14th ed.
ESS	Encyclopedia of the Social Sciences
JEA	Journal of Egyptian Archaeology
JRAI	Journal of the Royal Anthropological Institute
P-CAS	Proceedings, Congress of Arts and Sciences, St. Louis, 1904, Vol. 5, Boston, 1906.
P-MA	Papers of the Michigan Academy of Science, Arts, and Letters
S	Science
SF	Social Forces
SM	Scientific Monthly
SWJ	Southwestern Journal of Anthropology

ABEL, Th., 1929. "Is a Cultural Sociology Possible?" (AJS 35:739–52).

ALLPORT, F. H., 1924. Social Psychology. Boston.

ALLPORT, G. W., 1947. "Guide Lines for Research in International Cooperation," (Journal of Social Issues, 3:21–37).

ARGYLL, Duke of, 1972. Primeval Man. New York.

BAIKIE, James, 1926. The Amarna Age. London.

BAIN, Read, 1929. "Trends in American Sociological Theory," (in Trends in American Sociology, G. A. Lundberg, *et al.*, eds., New York). 1942. "A Definition of Culture," (Sociology and Social Research, 27: 87–94).

BALDWIN, J. M., 1906. "The History of Psychology," (P-CAS).

BASSETT, Raymond E., 1946. Letter to Editor, (S, 103:25–26).

BELL, E. T., 1931. The Queen of the Sciences. Baltimore. 1937. Men of Mathematics. New York.

BENEDICT, Ruth, 1934. Patterns of Culture. New York. 1939. "Edward Sapir," (AA 41:465–468). 1942. "Primitive Freedom," (AM, 169:756–763). 1943. "Franz Boas as an Ethnologist," (in Franz Boas, 1858–1942, by A. L. Kroeber *et al.*, AAA-M 61).

BERNARD, Jessie, 1929. "History and Prospects of Sociology." (in Trends in American Sociology. G. A. Lundberg *et al.*, eds. New York).

BERNARD, L. L., 1927a. "The Psychological Foundations of Society," (in An Introduction to

Sociology, J. Davis and H. E. Barnes, eds., Boston). 1927b. "Sociology and Psychology," (in The Social Sciences and their Interrelations, Wm. F. Ogburn and Alexander Goldenweiser, eds. New York). 1942. Introduction to Sociology. New York.

BIDNEY, David, 1944. "On the Concept of Culture and Some Cultural Fallacies," (AA 46:30–44). 1946. "The Concept of Cultural Crisis," (AA 48:534–552).

BOAS, Franz, 1908. "Anthropology." (in Columbia University Lectures in Science, Philosophy and Art. New York). 1928. Anthropology and Modern Life. New York. 1932. "Aims of Anthropological Research," (S, 76:605–613). 1936. "History and Science in Anthropology: a Reply," (AA 38:137–141). 1940. Race, Language and Culture. New York. 1945. Race and Democratic Society. New York.

BREASTED, J. H., 1909. A History of Egypt, revised edition. New York. 1912. The Development of Religion and Thought in Ancient Egypt. New York. 1929. "Ikhnaton," (EB). 1933. The Dawn of Conscience. New York.

BRETT, G. S., 1929. "History of Psychology," (EB).

BRIDGMAN, P. W., 1927. The Logic of Modern Physics. New York.

BUDGE, E. A. Wallis, 1923. Tutankhamen, Amenism, etc. London.

CARLSON, Anton J., 1926. "The Dynamics of Living Processes," (in The Nature of the World and Man, H. H. Newman, ed. Chicago).

CASE, E. C., 1934. "The Modern Biologist's Attitude Toward the Problem of Life," (The Michigan Alumnus Quarterly Review, 40:1–13).

CATTELL, J. McK., 1906. "Conceptions and Methods of Psychology," (P-CAS).

CHILDE, V. Gordon, 1936. Man Makes Himself. London. 1946. "Archeology and Anthropology," (SWJ 2:243–251).

CLARK, Grahame, 1946. From Savagery to Civilization. London.

CLODD, Edw., 1888. The Story of Creation. London.

COMPTON, A. H., 1940. "Science Shaping American Culture," (Proceedings, American Philosophical Society, 83:573–582).

COMTE, Auguste, no date. Positive Philosophy, translated by Harriet Martineau, one volume edition, Peter Eckler, publisher. New York.

COOLEY, C. H., 1897. "Genius, Fame, and the Comparison of Races," (Annals, American Academy of Political and Social Science, 9:317–358).

COOPER, John M., 1932. "Incest Prohibitions in Primitive Culture," (Primitive Man, 5:1–20).

DERRY, D. E., 1931. "Note on the Skeleton Hitherto Believed to be that of King Akhenaten," (AS, 31:115–119).

DESCARTES, R., 1901. Discourse on Method (in The Method, Meditations and Philosophy, translated and edited by John Veitch. New York).

DEWEY, John, 1920. Reconstruction in Philosophy. New York.

DOUGLASS, A. E., 1929. "The Secret of the Talkative Tree Rings," (National Geographic Magazine, 56:737–770).

DURKHEIM, Emile, 1897. Le Suicide. Paris. 1898. "La Prohibition de L'Inceste et ses Origines," (L'Annee Sociologique, 1:1–70). 1915. The Elementary Forms of the Religious Life, translated by J. W. Swain. London. 1933. The Division of Labor in Society, translated by George Simpson. New York. 1938. The Rules of Sociological Method, translated by S. A. Solvay and J. H. Mueller. Chicago.

EDGERTON, Wm. F., 1947. "The Government and the Governed in the Egyptian Empire," (Journal of Near Eastern Studies, 6:152–160).

EINSTEIN, A., 1929. "Space-Time," (EB). 1934. The World as I See It. New York. 1936. "Physics and Reality," (Journal of the Franklin Institute, 221: 349–382).

ELLWOOD, C. A., 1906. Remarks (P-CAS). 1944. "Culture and Human Society," (SF, 23:6–15).

ENGELBACH, R., 1931. "The So-Called Coffin of Akhenaten," (AS, 31:98–114).

FIELD, Stanley, 1943. "Fifty Years of Progress," (Field Museum News, Vol. 14).

FIRTH, Raymond, 1936. We, the Tikopia. New York.

FORTUNE, Reo, 1932. "Incest," (ESS).

FRANK, L. K., 1944. "What is Social Order?" (AJS, 49:470–477).

FRANKFORT, H., 1929. "The Affinities of the Mural Painting of El-Amarneh," (in The Mural Painting of El-Amarneh, H. Frankfort, ed., London).

FREUD, S. 1920. General Introduction to Psychoanalysis. New York. 1930. Civilization and its Discontents. New York. 1931. Totem and Taboo, New Republic ed. New York. 1938. The Basic Writings of Sigmund Freud, A. A. Brill, ed. (Modern Library ed. New York). 1939. Moses and Monotheism. New York.

GALTON, Francis, 1869. Hereditary Genius. London.

GARDINER, Alan H., 1917. "Philosophy, Egyptian," (Encyclopedia of Religion and Ethics, James Hastings, ed. Edinburgh and New York).

Gary, Dorothy, 1929. "The Developing Study of Culture," (in Trends in American Sociology, G. A. Lundberg *et al.*, eds. New York).

Gault, R. H. 1927. "Recent Developments in Psychology Contributory to Social Explanation," (in Recent Developments in the Social Sciences, E. C. Hayes, ed. Philadelphia).

Giddings, F. H., 1896. The Principles of Sociology (1921 printing. New York). 1906. "The Concepts and Methods of Sociology," (P-CAS). 1932. Civilization and Society. New York.

Gillin, John, 1936. The Barama River Caribs of British Guiana, (Papers, Peabody Museum, Vol. 14, No. 2. Cambridge). 1939. "Some Unfinished Business of Cultural Anthropology," (Ohio Archeological and Historical Quarterly, 48:44–52).

Glanville, S. R. K., 1929. "Amenophis and his Successors in the XVIIIth Dynasty," (in The Great Ones of Ancient Egypt, W. Brunton *et al.*, London).

Goldenweiser, A., 1917. "The Autonomy of the Social," (AA, 19:447–449). 1922. Early Civilization. New York. 1927. "Anthropology and Psychology," (in The Social Sciences and Their Interrelations, Wm. F. Ogburn and A. Goldenweiser, eds. New York). 1933. History, Psychology and Culture. New York. 1935. "Why I Am Not a Marxist," (Modern Monthly, 9:71–76). 1937. Anthropology. New York.

Goncourt, Journals, 1937. L. Galantière, ed. Garden City, New York.

Groves, E. R., 1928. Introduction to Sociology. New York.

Groves, E. R. and Moore, H. E., 1940. Introduction to Sociology. New York.

Gumplowicz, Ludwig, 1899. Outlines of Sociology. Translated by F. W. Moore. Philadelphia.

Hadamard, Jaques, 1945. The Psychology of Invention in the Mathematical Field. Princeton.

Hall, H. R., 1929. "Egypt, Religion," (EB).

Hallowell, A. Irving, 1945. "Sociopsychological Aspects of Acculturation," (in The Science of Man in the World Crisis, Ralph Linton, ed. New York).

Hankins, F. H., 1928. An Introduction to the Study of Society. New York.

Hardy, G. H., 1929. "Mathematical Proof," (Mind, 38:1–25). 1941. A Mathematician's Apology. Cambridge, England.

Harrington, H., 1929. "Roman Catholic Church" (in part; (EB).

Hart, C. W. M., 1938. "Social Evolution and Modern Anthropology" (in Essays in Political Economy, H. A. Innis, ed. Toronto).

Havens, R. D., 1944. "The Burden of Incertitude," (University of Rochester).

Hecht, Selig, 1947. Explaining the Atom. New York.

Herskovits, M. J., 1940. The Economic Life of Primitive Peoples. New York. 1945. "The Processes of Cultural Change," (in The Science of Man in the World Crisis, Ralph Linton, ed. New York).

Hewett, Edgar L., 1942. "From Culture to Civilization," (El Palacio, 49:133–142).

Hobhouse, L. T., 1924. Social Development. London.

Hooton, E. A., 1931. Up From the Ape. New York. 1937. Apes, Men and Morons. New York. 1939. Crime and the Man. Cambridge. 1943a. "Why We Study Apes and Monkeys," (Fauna, 5:2–6). 1943b. "Morons into What?" (Woman's Home Companion, 70:4, 96).

Huxley, T. H. 1870. The Physical Basis of Life. New Haven.

Hyvernat, Henry, 1909. "Egypt," (CE).

James, Wm. 1880. "Great Men, Great Thoughts and the Environment," (AM, 46:441–459). 1890. "The Importance of Individuals," (The Open Court, 4:2437–2440).

Jeans, James *et al.*, 1931a. "The Evolution of the Universe," (Appendix, Report of the Centenary Meeting, British Association for the Advancement of Science). 1931b. Essay in Living Philosophies. New York.

Kasner, Edw. and Newman, James, 1940. Mathematics and the Imagination. New York.

Keller, Helen, 1903. The Story of My Life. New York.

Kellogg, W. N. and L. A., 1933. The Ape and the Child. New York.

Kohler, W., 1926. The Mentality of Apes. New York and London.

Kroeber, A. L., 1917. "The Superorganic," (AA, 19:163–213). 1918. "The Possibility of a Social Psychology," (AJS, 23:633–650). 1919. "On the Principle of Order in Civilization as Exemplified by Changes in Fashion," (AA, 21:235–263). 1923. Anthropology. New York. 1928. "Sub-Human Cultural Beginnings," (Quarterly Review of Biology, 3:325–342). 1931. "The Culture-Area Concepts of Clark Wissler," (in Methods in Social Science, S. A.

Rice, ed. Chicago). 1936. "So-Called Social Science," (Journal of Social Philosophy, 1:317–340). 1944. Configurations of Culture Growth. Berkeley. 1948. "White's View of Culture," (AA, 50:405–415).

Kroeber, A. L. and Richardson, Jane, 1940. Three Centuries of Women's Dress Fashions; a Quantitative Analysis (Anthropological Records, Vol. 5, No. 2, University of California, Berkeley).

Leuba, J. H., 1925. The Psychology of Religious Mysticism. London.

Linton, Ralph, 1936. The Study of Man. New York. 1938. "The Present Status of Anthropology," (S, 87:241–248). 1941. "Potential Contributions of Cultural Anthropology to Teacher Education," (in Culture and Personality, American Council on Education. Washington, D. C.) 1945. The Cultural Background of Personality. New York.

Locke, John, 1894. An Essay Concerning the Human Understanding. London.

Lowie, R. H., 1917. Culture and Ethnology. New York. 1920. Primitive Society. New York. 1929. Are We Civilized? New York. 1933. "The Family as a Social Unit," (P-MA, 18:53–69). 1936. "Cultural Anthropology: a Science," (AJS, 42:301–320). 1940. Introduction to Cultural Anthropology, 2nd ed. New York.

Lynd, Robert S., 1939. Knowledge for What? Princeton.

MacCurdy, Geo. G., 1933. Human Origins, 2 vols. New York.

MacIver, R. M., 1930. "The Trend to Internationalism," (ESS, Vol. 1). 1934. "Sociology," (ESS). 1937. Society: A Textbook of Sociology. New York.

Mahaffy, J. P., 1915. "Cleopatra VI," (JEA, 2:1–4).

Malinowski, B., 1929a. The Sexual Life of Savages. London. 1929b. "Kinship," (EB). 1931. "Culture," (ESS). 1939. "The Group and Individual in Functional Analysis," (AJS, 44:938–964).

Mann, Thomas, 1942. "The Theme of the Joseph Novels." Washington.

Maxwell, J. Clerk, 1892. Matter and Motion. New York.

Mead, Margaret, 1943. Introduction to Is Germany Incurable? by R. M. Brickner. Philadelphia.

Meggers, Betty J., 1946. "Recent Trends in American Ethnology," (AA, 48:176–214).

Millikan, R. A., 1939. "Science and the World Tomorrow," (SM, 49:210–214).

Minkowski, H., 1923. "Space and Time," (in The Principles of Relativity, H. Lorentz et al. London).

Montagu, M. F. Ashley, 1937. "Physiological Paternity in Australia," (AA, 39:175–183).

Moret, Alexandre, 1912. Kings and Gods of Egypt. London and New York. 1927. The Nile and Egyptian Civilization. New York.

Morgan, L. H., 1877. Ancient Society. New York.

Murdock, Geo. P., 1932. "The Science of Culture," (AA, 34:200–215).

Myres, John L., 1948. Review of White, "The Expansion of the Scope of Science," (Man, 48:11).

Newberry, P. E., 1932. "King Ay, the Successor of Tutankhamun," (JEA, 18:50–52).

Newman, H. H., 1926. "The Nature and Origin of Life," (in The Nature of the World and Man, H. H. Newman, ed. Chicago).

Newton, Isaac, 1934. Principia Mathematica, F. Cajori, ed. Berkeley.

Novicoff, Alexander B., 1945. "The Concept of Integrative Levels and Biology," (S, 101:209–215).

Ogburn, Wm. F., 1922. Social Change. New York. 1933. "The Family," (in Recent Social Trends in the United States, one volume edition. New York).

Ogburn, Wm. F. and Nimkoff, Meyer F., 1940. Sociology. Boston.

Ogburn, Wm. F. and Thomas, Dorothy. 1922. "Are Inventions Inevitable?" (Political Science Quarterly, 37:83–98).

Ostwald, Wilhelm, 1907. "The Modern Theory of Energetics" (The Monist, 17:481–515). 1910. Natural Philosophy. New York. 1915a. "The System of the Sciences," translated by Thomas L. Blayney (The Rice Institute Pamphlet, 2:101-190. Houston, Texas). 1915b. "Principles of the Theory of Education," English translation (*ibid.*, 2:191-221).

Peet, T. E., 1926. "Contemporary Life and Thought in Egypt," (Cambridge Ancient History, Vol. 2. New York). No date. "Akhenaten, Ty, Nefertete, and Mutnezemt," (in Kings and Queens of Ancient Egypt, W. Brunton *et al.* New York).

Pendlebury, J. D. S. 1935. Tell el-Amarna. London.

Pohle, Joseph, 1911. "Priesthood," (CE).

Poincaré, H. 1913. The Foundations of Science.

New York.

RADCLIFFE-BROWN, A. R., 1923. "The Methods of Ethnology and Social Anthropology," (South African Journal of Science, 20:124–147). 1930–31. "The Social Organization of Australian Tribes," (Oceania, Vol. 1, Pts. 1 to 4). 1934. "Sanction, Social," (ESS). 1937. "The Nature of a Theoretical Natural Science of Society," (University of Chicago, mimeographed notes). 1940. "On Social Structure," (JRAI, 70:1–12).

RIVERS, W. H. R., 1916. "Sociology and Psychology," (The Sociological Review, 9:1–13).

ROOSEVELT, Franklin D., 1934. Public Addresses. Compiled by M. W. Hunt. Los Angeles.

ROSS, E. A. 1906. "The Present Problems of Social Psychology," (P-CAS).

RUFFER, Marc A., 1921. Studies in the Palaeopathology of Egypt. R. L. Woodie, ed. Chicago.

RUSSELL, H. N., 1939. "Stellar Evolution," (EB).

SALOMON, Gottfried, 1934. "Social Organism," (ESS).

SAPIR, E., 1916. Time Perspective in Aboriginal American Culture (Canada Dept. of Mines, Memoir 90. Ottawa). 1917. "Do We Need a Superorganic?" (AA, 19:441–447).

SCHARFF, Alexander, 1929. "Haremhab," (in The Great Ones of Ancient Egypt, W. Brunton *et al.* London).

SCHLESINGER, A. M., 1922. New Viewpoints in American History. New York.

SCHMIDT, W., 1934. "Primitive Man," (in European Civilization, Ed. Eyre, ed. London). 1939. The Culture Historical Method of Ethnology. New York.

SCHNIERLA, T. C., 1948. "Psychology, Comparative," (EB).

SCHRÖDINGER, Erwin, 1935. Science and the Human Temperament. New York.

SELIGMAN, B. Z., 1929. "Incest and Descent: Their Influence on Social Organization," (JRAI, 59:231–272).

SETHE, Kurt, 1921. "Beiträge zur Geschichte Amenophis IV," (Nachrichten von der Königlichen Gesellschaft der Wissenschaften zu Göttingen, Philologischhistorische Klasse aus dem Jahre 1921. Berlin).

SHAPLEY, Harlow. 1920. "Thermokinetics of *Liometopum apiculatum Mayr*," (Proceedings, National Academy of Sciences, 6:204–211). 1924. "Note on the Thermokinetics of Dolichoderine Ants," (*ibid.*, 10:436–439).

SHAPLEY, Harlow, ed. 1943. A Treasury of Science. New York.

SHEEN, Fulton J., 1948. "The Psychology of a Frustrated Soul," (The Catholic Hour, National Broadcasting Company, January 4).

SIMMEL, Georg, 1898. "The Persistence of Social Groups," (AJS, 3:662-698).

SLOCHOWER, Harry, 1938. Thomas Mann's Joseph Story.

SMALL, Albion W., 1905. General Sociology. Chicago.

SMITH, G. Elliot, 1912. The Royal Mummies. Cairo. 1923. Tutankhamen. London.

SOMERVILLE, Martha, ed. 1874. Personal Recollections of Mary Somerville. Boston.

SPENCER, Herbert. 1868. "On the Genesis of Science," (Essays: Scientific, Political and Speculative, Vol. 1. London). 1873. The Study of Sociology. New York.

SPYKMAN, N. J., 1925. The Social Theory of Georg Simmel. Chicago.

STEINDORFF, Geo. and SEELE, K. C., 1942. When Egypt Ruled the East. Chicago.

STERN, Bernhard J., 1929. "Concerning the Distinction between the Social and the Cultural," (SF, 8:264–271).

SWANTON, John R., 1943. Are Wars Inevitable? (Smithsonian War Background Studies, No. 12. Washington).

THOMAS, Wm. I., 1937. Primitive Behavior. New York.

TYLOR, E. B., 1871. Primitive Culture. Fifth edition, 1929 printing. London. 1881. Anthropology. London. 1888. "On a Method of Investigating the Development of Institutions; Applied to Laws of Marriage and Descent," (JRAI, 18:245–269).

WARD, Lester F., 1895. "The Place of Sociology among the Sciences," (AJS, 1:16–27). 1896. "The Filiation of the Sciences," (report by W. C. Winlock, S, 3:292–294). 1903. Pure Sociology. New York.

WASHBURN, Margaret F., 1946. "Social Psychology," (in Encyclopedia Americana).

WEIGALL, Arthur, 1923. The Life and Times of Akhnaton. London.

WESTERMARCK, Edw. 1921. The History of Human Marriage, 3 vols. London.

WESTGATE, Lewis G., 1943. "Man's Long Story," (SM, 57:155–165).

WHITE, A. D., 1896. A History of the Warfare of Science with Theology in Christendom, 2 vols., 1930 printing, New York.

WHITE, Leslie A., 1939. "A Problem in Kinship Terminology," (AA, 41:566–573). 1942. The

Pueblo of Santa Ana, New Mexico, AAA-M 60. 1943. "Keresan Indian Color Terms," (P-MA, 28:559–563). 1945. "History, Evolutionism and Functionalism: Three Types of Interpretation of Culture," (SWJ, 1:221–248).

WHITEHEAD, Alfred N., 1933. Science and the Modern World. Cambridge, England.

WILLEY, Malcolm M., 1929. "The Validity of the Culture Concept," (AJS, 35:204–219).

WILLEY, M. M. and HERSKOVITS, M. J., 1923. "The Cultural Approach to Sociology," (AJS, 29:188–199).

WILLIAMS, Mary W. 1934. "Slavery, Modern," (ESS).

WISSLER, Clark. 1923. Man and Culture. New York. 1927. "Recent Developments in Anthropology," (in Recent Developments in the Social Sciences, E. C. Hayes, ed. Philadelphia). 1929. An Introduction to Social Anthropology. New York.

YERKES, R. M. and A. W. 1929. The Great Apes. New Haven.

YOUNG, Kimball, 1934. An Introductory Sociology. New York. 1942. Sociology, a Study of Society and Culture. New York.

The Functional Unity of Social Systems: Is MI Incompatible With This Hypothesis?

52

On the Concept of Function in Social Science[1]

A. R. RADCLIFFE-BROWN

The concept of function applied to human societies is based on an analogy between social life and organic life. The recognition of the analogy and of some of its implications is not new. In the nineteenth century the analogy, the concept of function, and the word itself appear frequently in social philosophy and sociology. So far as I know the first systematic formulation of the concept as applying to the strictly scientific study of society was that of Emile Durkheim in 1895. (*Règles de la Méthode Sociologique.*)

Durkheim's definition is that the 'function' of a social institution is the correspondence between it and the needs (*besoins* in French) of the social organism. This definition requires some elaboration. In the first place, to avoid possible ambiguity and in particular the possibility of a teleological interpretation, I would like to substitute for the term 'needs' the term 'necessary conditions of existence', or, if the term 'need' is used, it is to be understood only in this sense. It may be here noted, as a point to be returned to, that any attempt to apply this concept of function in social science involves the assumption that there *are* necessary conditions of existence for human societies just as there are for animal organisms, and that they can be discovered by the proper kind of scientific enquiry.

For the further elucidation of the concept it is convenient to use the analogy between social life and organic life. Like all analogies it has to be used with care. An animal organism is an agglomeration of cells and interstitial fluids arranged in relation to one another not as an aggregate but as an integrated living whole. For the biochemist, it is a complexly integrated system of complex molecules. The system of relations by which these units are related is the organic structure. As the terms are here used the organism is *not* itself the structure; it is a collection of units (cells or molecules) arranged in a structure, i.e. in a set of relations; the organism *has* a structure. Two mature animals of the same species and sex consist of similar units combined in a similar structure. The structure is thus to be defined as a set of relations between entities. (The structure of a cell is in the same way a set of relations between complex molecules, and the structure of an atom is a set of relations between electrons and protons.) As long as it lives the organism preserves a certain continuity of structure although it does not preserve the complete identity of its constituent parts. It loses some of its constituent molecules by respiration or excretion; it takes in others by respiration and alimentary absorption. Over a period its constituent cells do not remain the same. But the structural arrangement of the con-

Reproduced by permission of the American Anthropological Association from the *American Anthropologist*, 37 (1935), pp. 397–402.

[1] This paper, which is based on comments that I made on a paper read by Dr. Lesser to the American Anthropological Association, is reprinted from the *American Anthropologist*, Vol. XXXVII, p. 3, 1935, where it accompanied Dr. Lesser's paper.

stituent units does remain similar. The process by which this structural continuity of the organism is maintained is called life. The life-process consists of the activities and interactions of the constituent units of the organism, the cells, and the organs into which the cells are united.

As the word function is here being used the life of an organism is conceived as the *functioning* of its structure. It is through and by the continuity of the functioning that the continuity of the structure is preserved. If we consider any recurrent part of the life-process, such as respiration, digestion, etc., its *function* is the part it plays in, the contribution it makes to, the life of the organism as a whole. As the terms are here being used a cell or an organ has an *activity* and that activity has a *function*. It is true that we commonly speak of the secretion of gastric fluid as a 'function' of the stomach. As the words are here used we should say that this is an 'activity' of the stomach, the 'function' of which is to change the proteins of food into a form in which these are absorbed and distributed by the blood to the tissues.[2] We may note that the function of a recurrent physiological process is thus a correspondence between it and the needs (i.e. necessary conditions of existence) of the organism.

If we set out upon a systematic investigation of the nature of organisms and organic life there are three sets of problems presented to us. (There are, in addition, certain other sets of problems concerning aspects or characteristics of organic life with which we are not here concerned.) One is that of morphology — what kinds of organic structures are there, what similarities and variations do they show, and how can they be classified? Second are the problems of physiology — how, in general, do organic structures function, what, therefore, is the nature of the life-process? Third are the problems of evolution or development — how do new types of organisms come into existence?

To turn from organic life to social life, if we examine such a community as an African or Australian tribe we can recognise the existence of a social structure. Individual human beings, the essential units in this instance, are connected by a definite set of social relations into an integrated whole. The continuity of the social structure, like that of an organic structure, is not destroyed by changes in the units. Individuals may leave the society, by death or otherwise; others may enter it. The continuity of structure is maintained by the process of social life, which consists of the activities and interactions of the individual human beings and of the organised groups into which they are united. The social life of the community is here defined as the *functioning* of the social structure. The *function* of any recurrent activity, such as the punishment of a crime, or a funeral ceremony, is the part it plays in the social life as a whole and therefore the contribution it makes to the maintenance of the structural continuity.

The concept of function as here defined thus involves the notion of a *structure* consisting of a *set of relations* amongst *unit entities*, the *continuity* of the structure being maintained by a *life-process* made up of the *activities* of the constituent units.

If, with these concepts in mind, we set out on a systematic investigation of the nature of human society and of social life, we find presented to us three sets of problems. First, the problems of social morphology — what kinds of social structures are there, what are their similarities and differences, how are they to be classified? Second, the problems of social physiology — how do social structures function? Third, the problems of development — how do new types of social structure come into existence?

Two important points where the analogy between organism and society breaks down must be noted. In an animal organism it is possible to observe the organic structure to some extent independently of its functioning.

[2] The insistence on this precise form of terminology is only for the sake of the analogy that is to be drawn. I have no objection to the use of the term function in physiology to denote both the activity of an organ and the results of that activity in maintaining life.

It is therefore possible to make a morphology which is independent of physiology. But in human society the social structure as a whole can only be *observed* in its functioning. Some of the features of social structure, such as the geographical distribution of individuals and groups can be directly observed, but most of the social relations which in their totality constitute the structure, such as relations of father and son, buyer and seller, ruler and subject, cannot be observed except in the social activities in which the relations are functioning. It follows that a social morphology cannot be established independently of a social physiology.

The second point is that an animal organism does not, in the course of its life, change its structural type. A pig does not become a hippopotamus. (The development of the animal from germination to maturity is not a change of type since the process in all its stages is typical for the species.) On the other hand a society in the course of its history can and does change its structural type without any breach of continuity.

By the definition here offered 'function' is the contribution which a partial activity makes to the total activity of which it is a part. The function of a particular social usage is the contribution it makes to the total social life as the functioning of the total social system. Such a view implies that a social system (the total social structure of a society together with the totality of social usages in which that structure appears and on which it depends for its continued existence) has a certain kind of unity, which we may speak of as a functional unity. We may define it as a condition in which all parts of the social system work together with a sufficient degree of harmony or internal consistency, i.e. without producing persistent conflicts which can neither be resolved nor regulated.[3]

This idea of the functional unity of a social system is, of course, a hypothesis. But it is one which, to the functionalist, it seems worth while to test by systematic examination of the facts.

There is another aspect of functional theory that should be briefly mentioned. To return to the analogy of social life and organic life, we recognise that an organism may function more or less efficiently and so we set up a special science of pathology to deal with all phenomena of disfunction. We distinguish in an organism what we call health and disease. The Greeks of the fifth century B.C. thought that one might apply the same notion to society, to the city-state, distinguishing conditions of *eunomia*, good order, social health, from *dysnomia*, disorder, social ill-health. In the nineteenth century Durkheim, in his application of the notion of function, sought to lay the basis for a scientific social pathology, based on a morphology and a physiology.[4] In his works, particularly those on suicide and the division of labour, he attempted to find objective criteria by which to judge whether a given society at a given time is normal or pathological, eunomic or dysnomic. For example, he tried to show that the increase of the rate of suicide in many countries during part of the nineteenth century is symptomatic of a dysnomic or, in his terminology, anomic, social condition. Probably there is no sociologist who would hold that Durkheim really succeeded in establishing an objective basis for a science of social pathology.[5]

In relation to organic structures we can find strictly objective criteria by which to distinguish disease from health, pathological from normal, for disease is that which either threatens the organism with death (the dissolution of its structure) or interferes with the activities which are characteristic of the organic type. Societies do not die in the same

[3] Opposition, i.e. organised and regulated antagonism, is, of course, an essential feature of every social system.

[4] For what is here called dysnomia Durkheim used the term anomia (*anomie* in French). This is to my mind inappropriate. Health and disease, eunomia and dysnomia, are essentially relative terms.

[5] I would personally agree in the main with the criticisms of Roger Lacombe (*La Méthode Sociologique de Durkheim*, 1926, ch. IV) on Durkheim's general theory of social pathology, and with the criticisms of Durkheim's treatment of suicide presented by Halbwachs, *Les Causes du Suicide*.

sense that animals die and therefore we cannot define dysnomia as that which leads, if unchecked, to the death of a society. Further, a society differs from an organism in that it can change its structural type, or can be absorbed as an integral part of a larger society. Therefore we cannot define dysnomia as a disturbance of the usual activities of a social type (as Durkheim tried to do).

Let us return for a moment to the Greeks. They conceived the health of an organism and the eunomia of a society as being in each instance a condition of the harmonious working together of its parts.[6] Now this, where society is concerned, is the same thing as what was considered above as the functional unity or inner consistency of a social system, and it is suggested that for the degree of functional unity of a particular society it may be possible to establish a purely objective criterion. Admittedly this cannot be done at present; but the science of human society is as yet in its extreme infancy. So that it may be that we should say that, while an organism that is attacked by a virulent disease will react thereto, and, if its reaction fails, will die, a society that is thrown into a condition of functional disunity or inconsistency (for this we now provisionally identify with dysnomia) will not die, except in such comparatively rare instances as an Australian tribe overwhelmed by the white man's destructive force, but will continue to struggle toward some sort of eunomia, some kind of social health, and may, in the course of this, change its structural type. This process, it seems, the 'functionalist' has ample opportunities of observing at the present day, in native peoples subjected to the domination of the civilised nations, and in those nations themselves.[7]

Space will not allow a discussion here of another aspect of functional theory, viz. the question whether change of social type is or is not dependent on function, i.e. on the laws of social physiology. My own view is that there is such a dependence and that its nature can be studied in the development of the legal and political institutions, the economic systems and the religions of Europe through the last twenty-five centuries. For the preliterate societies with which anthropology is concerned, it is not possible to study the details of long processes of change of type. The one kind of change which the anthropologist can observe is the disintegration of social structures. Yet even here we can observe and compare spontaneous movements towards reintegration. We have, for instance, in Africa, in Oceania, and in America the appearance of new religions which can be interpreted on a functional hypothesis as attempts to relieve a condition of social dysnomia produced by the rapid modification of the social life through contact with white civilisation.

The concept of function as defined above constitutes a 'working hypothesis' by which a number of problems are formulated for investigation. No scientific enquiry is possible without some such formulation of working hypotheses. Two remarks are necessary here. One is that the hypothesis does not require the dogmatic assertion that everything in the life of every community has a function. It only requires the assumption that it *may* have one, and that we are justified in seeking to discover it. The second is that what appears to be the same social usage in two societies may have different functions in the two. Thus the practice of celibacy in the Roman Catholic Church of today has very different functions from those of celibacy in the early Christian Church. In other words, in order to define a social usage, and therefore in order to make valid comparisons between the usages of different peoples or periods, it is necessary to

[6] See, for example, the Fourth Book of Plato's *Republic*.

[7] To avoid misunderstanding it is perhaps necessary to observe that this distinction of eunomic and dysnomic social conditions does not give us any evaluation of these societies as 'good' or 'bad'. A savage tribe practising polygamy, cannibalism, and sorcery can possibly show a higher degree of functional unity or consistency than the United States of 1935. This objective judgment, for such it must be if it is to be scientific, is something very different from any judgment as to which of the two social systems is the better, the more to be desired or approved.

consider not merely the form of the usage but also its function. On this basis, for example, belief in a Supreme Being in a simple society is something different from such a belief in a modern civilised community.

The acceptance of the functional hypothesis or point of view outlined above results in the recognition of a vast number of problems for the solution of which there are required wide comparative studies of societies of many diverse types and also intensive studies of as many single societies as possible. In field studies of the simpler peoples it leads, first of all, to a direct study of the social life of the community as the functioning of a social structure, and of this there are several examples in recent literature. Since the function of a social activity is to be found by examining its effects upon individuals, these are studied, either in the average individual or in both average and exceptional individuals. Further, the hypothesis leads to attempts to investigate directly the functional consistency or unity of a social system and to determine as far as possible in each instance the nature of that unity. Such field studies will obviously be different in many ways from studies carried out from other points of view, e.g. the ethnological point of view that lays emphasis on diffusion. We do not have to say that one point of view is better than another, but only that they are different, and any particular piece of work should be judged in reference to what it aims to do.

If the view here outlined is taken as one form of 'functionalism', a few remarks on Dr. Lesser's paper become permissible. He makes reference to a difference of 'content' in functional and non-functional anthropology. From the point of view here presented the 'content' or subject-matter of social anthropology is the whole social life of a people in all its aspects. For convenience of handling it is often necessary to devote special attention to some particular part or aspect of the social life, but if functionalism means anything at all it does mean the attempt to see the social life of a people as a whole, as a functional unity.

Dr. Lesser speaks of the functionalist as stressing 'the psychological aspects of culture', I presume that he here refers to the functionalist's recognition that the usages of a society work or 'function' only through their effects in the life, i.e. in the thoughts, sentiments and actions of individuals.

The 'functionalist' point of view here presented does therefore imply that we have to investigate as thoroughly as possible all aspects of social life, considering them in relation to one another, and that an essential part of the task is the investigation of the individual and of the way in which he is moulded by or adjusted to the social life.

Turning from content to method Dr. Lesser seems to find some conflict between the functional point of view and the historical. This is reminiscent of the attempts formerly made to see a conflict between sociology and history. There need be no conflict, but there is a difference.

There is not, and cannot be, any conflict between the functional hypothesis and the view that any culture, any social system, is the end-result of a unique series of historical accidents. The process of development of the race-horse from its five-toed ancestor was a unique series of historical accidents. This does not conflict with the view of the physiologist that the horse of today and all the antecedent forms conform or conformed to physiological laws, i.e. to the necessary conditions of organic existence. Palaeontology and physiology are not in conflict. One 'explanation' of the race-horse is to be found in its history — how it came to be just what it is and where it is. Another and entirely independent 'explanation' is to show how the horse is a special exemplification of physiological laws. Similarly one 'explanation' of a social system will be its history, where we know it — the detailed account of how it came to be what it is and where it is. Another 'explanation' of the same system is obtained by showing (as the functionalist attempts to do) that it is a special exemplification of laws of social physiology or social functioning. The two kinds of explanation do not conflict, but supplement one another.[8]

The functional hypothesis is in conflict with two views that are held by some ethnologists, and it is probably these, held as they often are without precise formulation, that are the cause of the antagonism to that approach. One is the 'shreds and patches' theory of culture, the designation being taken from a phrase of Professor Lowie[9] when he speaks of 'that planless hodge-podge, that thing of shreds and patches called civilisation'. The concentration of attention on what is called the diffusion of culture traits tends to produce a conception of culture as a collection of disparate entities (the so-called traits) brought together by pure historical accident and having only accidental relations to one another. The conception is rarely formulated and maintained with any precision, but as a half-unconscious point of view it does seem to control the thinking of many ethnologists. It is, of course, in direct conflict with the hypothesis of the functional unity of social systems.

The second view which is in direct conflict with the functional hypothesis is the view that there are no discoverable significant sociological laws such as the functionalist is seeking. I know that some two or three ethnologists say that they hold this view, but I have found it impossible to know what they mean, or on what sort of evidence (rational or empirical) they would base their contention. Generalisations about any sort of subject matter are of two kinds: the generalisations of common opinion, and generalisations that have been verified or demonstrated by a systematic examination of evidence afforded by precise observations systematically made. Generalisations of the latter kind are called scientific laws. Those who hold that there are no laws of human society cannot hold that there are no generalisations about human society because they themselves hold such generalisations and even make new ones of their own. They must therefore hold that in the field of social phenomena, in contradistinction to physical and biological phenomena, any attempt at the systematic testing of existing generalisations or towards the discovery and verification of new ones, is, for some unexplained reason, futile, or, as Dr. Radin puts it, 'crying for the moon'. Argument against such a contention is unprofitable or indeed impossible.

[8] I see no reason at all why the two kinds of study — the historical and the functional — should not be carried on side by side in perfect harmony. In fact, for fourteen years I have been teaching both the historical and geographical study of peoples under the name of ethnology in close association with archaeology, and the functional study of social systems under the name of social anthropology. I do think that there are many disadvantages in mixing the two subjects together and confusing them. See 'The Methods of Ethnology and Social Anthropology' (*South African Journal of Science*, 1923, pp. 124–47).

[9] *Primitive Society*, p. 441. A concise statement of this point of view is the following passage from Dr. Ruth Benedict's 'The Concept of the Guardian Spirit in North America' (*Memoirs*, American Anthropological Association, 29, 1923), p. 84: 'It is, so far as we can see, an ultimate fact of human nature that man builds up his culture out of disparate elements, combining and recombining them; and until we have abandoned the superstition that the result is an organism functionally interrelated, we shall be unable to see our cultural life objectively, or to control its manifestations.' I think that probably neither Professor Lowie nor Dr. Benedict would, at the present time, maintain this view of the nature of culture.

On Joking Relationships

A. R. RADCLIFFE-BROWN

The publication of Mr. F. J. Pedler's note[1] on what are called 'joking relationships', following on two other papers on the same subject by Professor Henri Labouret[2] and Mademoiselle Denise Paulme,[3] suggests that some general theoretical discussion of the nature of these relationships may be of interest to readers of *Africa*.[4]

What is meant by the term 'joking relationship' is a relation between two persons in which one is by custom permitted, and in some instances required, to tease or make fun of the other, who in turn is required to take no offence. It is important to distinguish two main varieties. In one the relation is symmetrical; each of the two persons teases or makes fun of the other. In the other variety the relation is asymmetrical; A jokes at the expense of B and B accepts the teasing good humouredly but without retaliating; or A teases B as much as he pleases and B in return teases A only a little. There are many varieties in the form of this relationship in different societies. In some instances the joking or teasing is only verbal, in others it includes horse-play; in some the joking includes elements of obscenity, in others not.

Standardised social relationships of this kind are extremely widespread, not only in Africa but also in Asia, Oceania and North America. To arrive at a scientific understanding of the phenomenon it is necessary to make a wide comparative study. Some material for this now exists in anthropological literature, though by no means all that could be desired, since it is unfortunately still only rarely that such relationships are observed and described as exactly as they might be.

The joking relationship is a peculiar combination of friendliness and antagonism. The behaviour is such that in any other social context it would express and arouse hostility; but it is not meant seriously and must not be taken seriously. There is a pretence of hostility and a real friendliness. To put it in another way, the relationship is one of permitted disrespect. Thus any complete theory of it must be part of, or consistent with, a theory of the place of respect in social relations and in social life generally. But this is a very wide and very important sociological problem; for it is evident that the whole maintenance of a social order depends upon the appropriate kind and degree of respect being shown towards certain persons, things and ideas or symbols.

Examples of joking relationships between relatives by marriage are very commonly found in Africa and in other parts of the world. Thus Mademoiselle Paulme[5] records that among the Dogon a man stands in a joking relationship to his wife's sisters and their daughters. Frequently the relationship holds between a man and both the brothers and sisters of his wife. But in some instances there is a distinction whereby a man is on joking terms with his wife's younger brothers and sisters but not with those who are older than she is. This joking with the wife's brothers and sisters is usually associated with a custom requiring extreme respect, often partial or complete avoidance, between a son-in-law and his wife's parents.[6]

The kind of structural situation in which the associated customs of joking and avoidance are found may be described as follows.

From *Africa* 13:3 (1940), pp. 195–210.

[1] 'Joking Relationships in East Africa', *Africa*, Vol. XIII, p. 170.

[2] 'La Parenté à Plaisanteries en Afrique Occidentale', *Africa*, Vol. II, p. 244.

[3] 'Parenté à Plaisanteries et Alliance par le Sang en Afrique Occidentale', *Africa*, Vol. XII, p. 433.

[4] Professor Marcel Mauss has published a brief theoretical discussion of the subject in the *Annuaire de l'École Pratique des Hautes Études, Section des Sciences religieuses*, 1927–8. It is also dealt with by Dr. F. Eggan in *Social Anthropology of North American Tribes*, 1937, pp. 75–81.

[5] *Africa*, Vol. XII, p. 438.

[6] Those who are not familiar with these widespread customs will find descriptions in Junod, *Life of a South African Tribe*, Neuchâtel, Vol. I, pp. 229–37, and in *Social Anthropology of North American Tribes*, edited by F. Eggan, Chicago, 1937, pp. 55–7.

A marriage involves a readjustment of the social structure whereby the woman's relations with her family are greatly modified and she enters into a new and very close relation with her husband. The latter is at the same time brought into a special relation with his wife's family, to which, however, he is an outsider. For the sake of brevity, though at the risk of over-simplification, we will consider only the husband's relation to his wife's family. The relation can be described as involving both attachment and separation, both social conjunction and social disjunction, if I may use the terms. The man has his own definite position in the social structure, determined for him by his birth into a certain family, lineage or clan. The great body of his rights and duties and the interests and activities that he shares with others are the result of his position. Before the marriage his wife's family are outsiders for him as he is an outsider for them. This constitutes a social disjunction which is not destroyed by the marriage. The social conjunction results from the continuance, though in altered form, of the wife's relation to her family, their continued interest in her and in her children. If the wife were really bought and paid for, as ignorant persons say that she is in Africa, there would be no place for any permanent close relation of a man with his wife's family. But though slaves can be bought, wives cannot.

Social disjunction implies divergence of interests and therefore the possibility of conflict and hostility, while conjunction requires the avoidance of strife. How can a relation which combines the two be given a stable, ordered form? There are two ways of doing this. One is to maintain between two persons so related an extreme mutual respect and a limitation of direct personal contact. This is exhibited in the very formal relations that are, in so many societies, characteristic of the behaviour of a son-in-law on the one side and his wife's father and mother on the other. In its most extreme form there is complete avoidance of any social contact between a man and his mother-in-law.

This avoidance must not be mistaken for a sign of hostility. One does, of course, if one is wise, avoid having too much to do with one's enemies, but that is quite a different matter. I once asked an Australian native why he had to avoid his mother-in-law, and his reply was, 'Because she is my best friend in the world; she has given me my wife'. The mutual respect between son-in-law and parents-in-law is a mode of friendship. It prevents conflict that might arise through divergence of interest.

The alternative to this relation of extreme mutual respect and restraint is the joking relationship, one, that is, of mutual disrespect and licence. Any serious hostility is prevented by the playful antagonism of teasing, and this in its regular repetition is a constant expression or reminder of that social disjunction which is one of the essential components of the relation, while the social conjunction is maintained by the friendliness that takes no offence at insult.

The discrimination within the wife's family between those who have to be treated with extreme respect and those with whom it is a duty to be disrespectful is made on the basis of generation and sometimes of seniority within the generation. The usual respected relatives are those of the first ascending generation, the wife's mother and her sisters, the wife's father and his brothers, sometimes the wife's mother's brother. The joking relatives are those of a person's own generation; but very frequently a distinction of seniority within the generation is made; a wife's older sister or brother may be respected while those younger will be teased.

In certain societies a man may be said to have relatives by marriage long before he marries and indeed as soon as he is born into the world. This is provided by the institution of the required or preferential marriage. We will, for the sake of brevity, consider only one kind of such organisations. In many societies it is regarded as preferable that a man should marry the daughter of his mother's brother; this is a form of the custom known as cross-cousin marriage. Thus his female cousins of this kind, or all those women whom by the classificatory system he classifies as such, are potential wives for him, and their brothers are his potential brothers-in-law. Among the Ojibwa Indians of North America, the Chiga of Uganda, and in Fiji and New Caledonia, as well as elsewhere, this form of marriage is found and is accompanied by a joking relationship between a man and the sons and daughters of his mother's brother. To quote one instance of these, the following is recorded for the Ojibwa. 'When cross-cousins meet they must try to embarrass one another. They "joke" one another, making the most vulgar allegations, by their standards as well as ours. But being "kind" relations, no one can take offence. Cross-cousins who do not joke in this way are considered boorish, as not playing the social game.'[7]

The joking relationship here is of fundamentally the same kind as that already discussed. It is established before marriage and is continued, after marriage, with the brothers- and sisters-in-law.

In some parts of Africa there are joking relationships that have nothing to do with marriage. Mr. Pedler's note, mentioned above, refers to a joking relationship between two distinct tribes, the Sukuma and the Zaramu, and in the evidence it was stated that there was a similar relation between the Sukuma and the Zigua and between the Ngoni and the Bemba. The woman's evidence suggests that this custom of rough teasing exists in the Sukuma tribe between persons related by marriage, as it does in so many other African tribes.[8]

While a joking relationship between two tribes is apparently rare, and certainly deserves, as Mr. Pedler suggests, to be carefully investigated, a similar relationship between clans has been observed in other parts of Africa. It is described by Professor Labouret and Mademoiselle Paulme in the articles previously mentioned, and amongst the Tallensi it has been studied by Dr. Fortes, who will deal with it in a forthcoming publication.[9]

The two clans are not, in these instances, specially connected by intermarriage. The relation between them is an alliance involving real friendliness and mutual aid combined with an appearance of hostility.

The general structural situation in these instances seems to be as follows. The individual is a member of a certain defined group, a clan, for example, within which his relations to others are defined by a complex set of rights and duties, referring to all the major aspects of social life, and supported by definite sanctions. There may be another group outside his own which is so linked with his as to be the field of extension of jural and moral relations of the same general kind. Thus, in East Africa, as we learn from Mr. Pedler's note, the Zigua and the Zaramu do not joke with one another because a yet closer bond exists between them since they are *ndugu* (brothers). But beyond the field within which social relations are thus defined there lie other groups with which, since they are outsiders to the individual's own group, the relation involves possible or actual hostility. In any fixed relations between the members of two such groups the separateness of the groups must be recognised. It is precisely this separateness which is not merely recognised but emphasised when a joking relationship is established. The show of hostility, the perpetual disrespect, is a continual expression of that social disjunction which is an essential

[7] Ruth Landes in Mead, *Co-operation and Competition among Primitive Peoples*, 1937, p. 103.

[8] Incidentally it may be said that it was hardly satisfactory for the magistrate to establish a precedent whereby the man, who was observing what was a permitted and may even have been an obligatory custom, was declared guilty of common assault, even with extenuating circumstances. It seems quite possible that the man may have committed a breach of etiquette in teasing the woman in the presence of her mother's brother, for in many parts of the world it is regarded as improper for two persons in a joking relationship to tease one another (particularly if any obscenity is involved) in the presence of certain relatives of either of them. But the breach of etiquette would still not make it an assault. A little knowledge of anthropology would have enabled the magistrate, by putting the appropriate questions to the witnesses, to have obtained a fuller understanding of the case and all that was involved in it.

[9] Fortes, M., *The Dynamics of Clanship among the Tallensi*. Oxford University Press, 1945.

part of the whole structural situation, but over which, without destroying or even weakening it, there is provided the social conjunction of friendliness and mutual aid.

The theory that is here put forward, therefore, is that both the joking relationship which constitutes an alliance between clans or tribes, and that between relatives by marriage, are modes of organising a definite and stable system of social behaviour in which conjunctive and disjunctive components, as I have called them, are maintained and combined.

To provide the full evidence for this theory by following out its implications and examining in detail its application to different instances would take a book rather than a short article. But some confirmation can perhaps be offered by a consideration of the way in which respect and disrespect appear in various kinship relations, even though nothing more can be attempted than a very brief indication of a few significant points.

In studying a kinship system it is possible to distinguish the different relatives by reference to the kind and degree of respect that is paid to them.[10] Although kinship systems vary very much in their details there are certain principles which are found to be very widespread. One of them is that by which a person is required to show a marked respect to relatives belonging to the generation immediately preceding his own. In a majority of societies the father is a relative to whom marked respect must be shown. This is so even in many so-called matrilineal societies, i.e. those which are organised into matrilineal clans or lineages. One can very frequently observe a tendency to extend this attitude of respect to all relatives of the first ascending generation and, further, to persons who are not relatives. Thus in those tribes of East Africa that are organised into age-sets a man is required to show special respect to all men of his father's age-set and to their wives.

The social function of this is obvious. The social tradition is handed down from one generation to the next. For the tradition to be maintained it must have authority behind it. The authority is therefore normally recognised as possessed by members of the preceding generation and it is they who exercise discipline. As a result of this the relation between persons of the two generations usually contains an element of inequality, the parents and those of their generation being in a position of superiority over the children who are subordinate to them. The unequal relation between a father and his son is maintained by requiring the latter to show respect to the former. The relation is asymmetrical.

When we turn to the relation of an individual to his grandparents and their brothers and sisters we find that in the majority of human societies relatives of the second ascending generation are treated with very much less respect than those of the first ascending generation, and instead of a marked inequality there is a tendency to approximate to a friendly equality.

Considerations of space forbid any full discussion of this feature of social structure, which is one of very great importance. There are many instances in which the grandparents and their grandchildren are grouped together in the social structure in opposition to their children and parents. An important clue to the understanding of the subject is the fact that in the flow of social life through time, in which men are born, become mature and die, the grandchildren replace their grandparents.

In many societies there is an actual joking relationship, usually of a relatively mild kind, between relatives of alternate generations. Grandchildren make fun of their grandparents and of those who are called grandfather and grandmother by the classificatory system of terminology, and these reply in kind.

Grandparents and grandchildren are united by kinship; they are separated by age and by the social difference that results from the fact that as the grandchildren are in process of

[10] See, for example, the kinship systems described in *Social Anthropology of North American Tribes*, edited by Fred Eggan, University of Chicago Press, 1937; and Margaret Mead, 'Kinship in the Admiralty Islands', *Anthropological Papers of the American Museum of Natural History*, Vol. XXXIV, pp. 243–56.

entering into full participation in the social life of the community the grandparents are gradually retiring from it. Important duties towards his relatives in his own and even more in his parents' generation impose upon an individual many restraints; but with those of the second ascending generation, his grandparents and collateral relatives, there can be, and usually is, established a relationship of simple friendliness relatively free from restraint. In this instance also, it is suggested, the joking relationship is a method of ordering a relation which combines social conjunction and disjunction.

This thesis could, I believe, be strongly supported if not demonstrated by considering the details of these relationships. There is space for only one illustrative point. A very common form of joke in this connection is for the grandchild to pretend that he wishes to marry the grandfather's wife, or that he intends to do so when his grandfather dies, or to treat her as already being his wife. Alternatively the grandfather may pretend that the wife of his grandchild is, or might be, his wife.[11] The point of the joke is the pretence at ignoring the difference of age between the grandparent and the grandchild.

In various parts of the world there are societies in which a sister's son teases and otherwise behaves disrespectfully towards his mother's brother. In these instances the joking relationship seems generally to be asymmetrical. For example the nephew may take his uncle's property but not vice versa; or, as amongst the Nama Hottentots, the nephew may take a fine beast from his uncle's herd and the uncle in return takes a wretched beast from that of the nephew.[12]

The kind of social structure in which this custom of privileged disrespect to the mother's brother occurs in its most marked forms, for example the Thonga of South-East Africa, Fiji and Tonga in the Pacific, and the Central Siouan tribes of North America, is characterised by emphasis on patrilineal lineage and a marked distinction between relatives through the father and relatives through the mother.

In a former publication[13] I offered an interpretation of this custom of privileged familiarity towards the mother's brother. Briefly it is as follows. For the continuance of a social system children require to be cared for and to be trained. Their care demands affectionate and unselfish devotion; their training requires that they shall be subjected to discipline. In the societies with which we are concerned there is something of a division of function between the parents and other relatives on the two sides. The control and discipline are exercised chiefly by the father and his brothers and generally also by his sisters; these are relatives who must be respected and obeyed. It is the mother who is primarily responsible for the affectionate care; the mother and her brothers and sisters are therefore relatives who can be looked to for assistance and indulgence. The mother's brother is called 'male mother' in Tonga and in some South African tribes.

I believe that this interpretation of the special position of the mother's brother in these societies has been confirmed by further field work since I wrote the article referred to. But I was quite aware at the time it was written that the discussion and interpretation needed to be supplemented so as to bring them into line with a general theory of the social functions of respect and disrespect.

The joking relationship with the mother's brother seems to fit well with the general theory of such relationships here outlined. A person's most important duties and rights attach him to his paternal relatives, living and dead. It is to his patrilineal lineage or clan that he belongs. For the members of his mother's lineage he is an outsider, though one in whom they have a very special and tender interest. Thus here again there is a

[11] For examples see Labouret, *Les Tribus du Rameau Lobi*, 1931, p. 248, and Sarat Chandra Roy, *The Oraons of Chota Nagpur*, Ranchi, 1915, pp. 352–4.

[12] A. Winifred Hoernlé, 'Social Organisation of the Nama Hottentot'; *American Anthropologist*, N.S., Vol. XXVII, 1925, pp. 1–24.

[13] 'The Mother's Brother in South Africa', *South African Journal of Science*, Vol. XXI, 1924.

relation in which there is both attachment, or conjunction, and separation, or disjunction, between the two persons concerned.

But let us remember that in this instance the relation is asymmetrical.[14] The nephew is disrespectful and the uncle accepts the disrespect. There is inequality and the nephew is the superior. This is recognized by the natives themselves. Thus in Tonga it is said that the sister's son is a 'chief' (*eiki*) to his mother's brother, and Junod[15] quotes a Thonga native as saying 'The uterine nephew is a chief! He takes any liberty he likes with his maternal uncle'. Thus the joking relationship with the uncle does not merely annul the usual relation between the two generations, it reverses it. But while the superiority of the father and the father's sister is exhibited in the respect that is shown to them, the nephew's superiority to his mother's brother takes the opposite form of permitted disrespect.

It has been mentioned that there is a widespread tendency to feel that a man should show respect towards, and treat as social superiors, his relatives in the generation preceding his own, and the custom of joking with, and at the expense of, the maternal uncle clearly conflicts with this tendency. This conflict between principles of behaviour helps us to understand what seems at first sight a very extraordinary feature of the kinship terminology of the Thonga tribe and the VaNdau tribe in South-East Africa. Amongst the Thonga, although there is a term *malume* (= male mother) for the mother's brother, this relative is also, and perhaps more frequently referred to as a grandfather (*kokwana*) and he refers to his sister's son as his grandchild (*ntukulu*). In the VaNdau tribe the mother's brother and also the mother's brother's son are called 'grandfather' (*tetekulu*, literally 'great father') and their wives are called 'grandmother' (*mbiya*), while the sister's son and the father's sister's son are called 'grandchild' (*muzukulu*).

This apparently fantastic way of classifying relatives can be interpreted as a sort of legal fiction whereby the male relatives of the mother's lineage are grouped together as all standing towards an individual in the same general relation. Since this relation is one of privileged familiarity on the one side, and solicitude and indulgence on the other, it is conceived as being basically the one appropriate for a grandchild and a grandfather. This is indeed in the majority of human societies the relationship in which this pattern of behaviour most frequently occurs. By this legal fiction the mother's brother ceases to belong to the first ascending generation, of which it is felt that the members ought to be respected.

It may be worth while to justify this interpretation by considering another of the legal fictions of the VaNdau terminology. In all these south-eastern Bantu tribes both the father's sister and the sister, particularly the elder sister, are persons who must be treated with great respect. They are also both of them members of a man's own patrilineal lineage. Amongst the VaNdau the father's sister is called 'female father' (*tetadji*) and so also is the sister.[16] Thus by the fiction of terminological classification the sister is placed in the father's generation, the one that appropriately includes persons to whom one must exhibit marked respect.

In the south-eastern Bantu tribes there is assimilation of two kinds of joking relatives, the grandfather and the mother's brother. It may help our understanding of this to consider an example in which the grandfather and the brother-in-law are similarly grouped together. The Cherokee Indians of North America, probably numbering at one time about 20,000, were divided into seven matri-

[14] There are some societies in which the relation between a mother's brother and a sister's son is approximately symmetrical, and therefore one of equality. This seems to be so in the Western Islands of Torres Straits, but we have no information as to any teasing or joking, though it is said that each of the two relatives may take the property of the other.

[15] *Life of a South African Tribe*, Vol. I, p. 255.

[16] For the kinship terminology of the VaNdau see Boas, 'Das Verwandtschafts-system der Vandau', in *Zeitschrift für Ethnologie*, 1922, pp. 41–51.

lineal clans.[17] A man could not marry a woman of his own clan or of his father's clan. Common membership of the same clan connects him with his brothers and his mother's brothers. Towards his father and all his relatives in his father's clan of his own or his father's generation he is required by custom to show a marked respect. He applies the kinship term for 'father' not only to his father's brothers but also to the sons of his father's sisters. Here is another example of the same kind of fiction as described above; the relatives of his own generation whom he is required to respect and who belong to his father's matrilineal lineage are spoken of as though they belonged to the generation of his parents. The body of his immediate kindred is included in these two clans, that of his mother and his father. To the other clans of the tribe he is in a sense an outsider. But with two of them he is connected, namely with the clans of his two grandfathers, his father's father and his mother's father. He speaks of all the members of these two clans, of whatever age, as 'grandfathers' and 'grandmothers'. He stands in a joking relationship with all of them. When a man marries he must respect his wife's parents but jokes with her brothers and sisters.

The interesting and critical feature is that it is regarded as particularly appropriate that a man should marry a woman whom he calls 'grandmother', i.e. a member of his father's father's clan or his mother's father's clan. If this happens his wife's brothers and sisters, whom he continues to tease, are amongst those whom he previously teased as his 'grandfathers' and 'grandmothers'. This is analogous to the widely spread organisation in which a man has a joking relationship with the children of his mother's brother and is expected to marry one of the daughters.

It ought perhaps to be mentioned that the Cherokee also have a one-sided joking relationship in which a man teases his father's sister's husband. The same custom is found in Mota of the Bank Islands. In both instances we have a society organised on a matrilineal basis in which the mother's brother is respected, the father's sister's son is called 'father' (so that the father's sister's husband is the father of a 'father'), and there is a special term for the father's sister's husband. Further observation of the societies in which this custom occurs is required before we can be sure of its interpretation. I do not remember that it has been reported from any part of Africa.

What has been attempted in this paper is to define in the most general and abstract terms the kind of structural situation in which we may expect to find well-marked joking relationships. We have been dealing with societies in which the basic social structure is provided by kinship. By reason of his birth or adoption into a certain position in the social structure an individual is connected with a large number of other persons. With some of them he finds himself in a definite and specific jural relation, i.e. one which can be defined in terms of rights and duties. Who these persons will be and what will be the rights and duties depend on the form taken by the social structure. As an example of such a specific jural relation we may take that which normally exists between a father and son, or an elder brother and a younger brother. Relations of the same general type may be extended over a considerable range to all the members of a lineage or a clan or an age-set. Besides these specific jural relations which are defined not only negatively but also positively, i.e. in terms of things that must be done as well as things that must not, there are general jural relations which are expressed almost entirely in terms of prohibitions and which extend throughout the whole political society. It is forbidden to kill or wound other persons or to take or destroy their property. Besides these two classes of social relations there is another, including many very diverse varieties, which can perhaps be

[17] For an account of the Cherokee see Gilbert, in *Social Anthropology of North American Tribes*, pp. 285–338.

called relations of alliance or consociation. For example, there is a form of alliance of very great importance in many societies, in which two persons or two groups are connected by an exchange of gifts or services.[18] Another example is provided by the institution of blood-brotherhood which is so widespread in Africa.

The argument of this paper has been intended to show that the joking relationship is one special form of alliance in this sense. An alliance by exchange of goods and services may be associated with a joking relationship, as in the instance recorded by Professor Labouret.[19] Or it may be combined with the custom of avoidance. Thus in the Andaman Islands the parents of a man and the parents of his wife avoid all contact with each other and do not speak; at the same time it is the custom that they should frequently exchange presents through the medium of the younger married couple. But the exchange of gifts may also exist without either joking or avoidance, as in Samoa, in the exchange of gifts between the family of a man and the family of the woman he marries or the very similar exchange between a chief and his 'talking chief'.

So also in an alliance by blood-brotherhood there may be a joking relationship as amongst the Zande;[20] and in the somewhat similar alliance formed by exchange of names there may also be mutual teasing. But in alliances of this kind there may be a relation of extreme respect and even of avoidance. Thus in the Yaralde and neighbouring tribes of South Australia two boys belonging to communities distant from one another, and therefore more or less hostile, are brought into an alliance by the exchange of their respective umbilical cords. The relationship thus established is a sacred one; the two boys may never speak to one another. But when they grow up they enter upon a regular exchange of gifts, which provides the machinery for a sort of commerce between the two groups to which they belong.

Thus the four modes of alliance or consociation, (1) through intermarriage, (2) by exchange of goods or services, (3) by blood-brotherhood or exchanges of names or sacra, and (4) by the joking relationship, may exist separately or combined in several different ways. The comparative study of these combinations presents a number of interesting but complex problems. The facts recorded from West Africa by Professor Labouret and Mademoiselle Paulme afford us valuable material. But a good deal more intensive field research is needed before these problems of social structure can be satisfactorily dealt with.

What I have called relations by alliance need to be compared with true contractual relations. The latter are specific jural relations entered into by two persons or two groups, in which either party has definite positive obligations towards the other, and failure to carry out the obligations is subject to a legal sanction. In an alliance by blood-brotherhood there are general obligations of mutual aid, and the sanction for the carrying out of these, as shown by Dr. Evans-Pritchard, is of a kind that can be called magical or ritual. In the alliance by exchange of gifts failure to fulfil the obligation to make an equivalent return for a gift received breaks the alliance and substitutes a state of hostility and may also cause a loss of prestige for the defaulting party. Professor Mauss[21] has argued that in this kind of alliance also there is a magical sanction, but it is very doubtful if such is always present, and even when it is it may often be of secondary importance.

The joking relationship is in some ways the exact opposite of a contractual relation. Instead of specific duties to be fulfilled there is privileged disrespect and freedom or even licence, and the only obligation is not to take offence at the disrespect so long as it is kept within certain bounds defined by custom, and not to go beyond those bounds. Any default in the relationship is like a breach of the rules

[18] See Mauss, 'Essai sur le Don', *Année Sociologique*, Nouvelle Série, tome I, pp. 30–186.

[19] *Africa*, Vol. II, p. 245.

[20] Evans-Pritchard, 'Zande Blood-brotherhood', *Africa*, Vol. VI, 1933, pp. 369–401.

[21] 'Essai sur le Don'.

of etiquette; the person concerned is regarded as not knowing how to behave himself.

In a true contractual relationship the two parties are conjoined by a definite common interest in reference to which each of them accepts specific obligations. It makes no difference that in other matters their interests may be divergent. In the joking relationship and in some avoidance relationships, such as that between a man and his wife's mother, one basic determinant is that the social structure separates them in such a way as to make many of their interests divergent, so that conflict or hostility might result. The alliance by extreme respect, by partial or complete avoidance, prevents such conflict but keeps the parties conjoined. The alliance by joking does the same thing in a different way.

All that has been, or could be, attempted in this paper is to show the place of the joking relationship in a general comparative study of social structure. What I have called, provisionally, relations of consociation or alliance are distinguished from the relations set up by common membership of a political society which are defined in terms of general obligations, of etiquette, or morals, or of law. They are distinguished also from true contractual relations, defined by some specific obligation for each contracting party, into which the individual enters of his own volition. They are further to be distinguished from the relations set up by common membership of a domestic group, a lineage or a clan, each of which has to be defined in terms of a whole set of socially recognised rights and duties. Relations of consociation can only exist between individuals or groups which are in some way socially separated.

This paper deals only with formalised or standardised joking relations. Teasing or making fun of other persons is of course a common mode of behaviour in any human society. It tends to occur in certain kinds of social situations. Thus I have observed in certain classes in English-speaking countries the occurrence of horse-play between young men and women as a preliminary to courtship, very similar to the way in which a Cherokee Indian jokes with his 'grandmothers'. Certainly these unformalised modes of behaviour need to be studied by the sociologist. For the purpose of this paper it is sufficient to note that teasing is always a compound of friendliness and antagonism.

The scientific explanation of the institution in the particular form in which it occurs in a given society can only be reached by an intensive study which enables us to see it as a particular example of a widespread phenomenon of a definite class. This means that the whole social structure has to be thoroughly examined in order that the particular form and incidence of joking relationships can be understood as part of a consistent system. If it be asked why that society has the structure that it does have, the only possible answer would lie in its history. When the history is unrecorded, as it is for the native societies of Africa, we can only indulge in conjecture, and conjecture gives us neither scientific nor historical knowledge.[22]

[22] The general theory outlined in this paper is one that I have presented in lectures at various universities since 1909 as part of the general study of the forms of social structure. In arriving at the present formulation of it I have been helped by discussions with Dr. Meyer Fortes.

VIII

OBJECTIVITY and VALUE JUDGMENTS in SOCIAL SCIENCE

It seems to be a tradition for social scientists, especially sociologists, to concede that their disciplines cannot achieve the sort of objectivity attained by the natural sciences. In many cases, as with Karl Mannheim, this concession has a double edge. Yes, there is a sense of "objective" in which to demand objectivity is to demand the cessation of social science; on the other hand, so it is often maintained, social scientists can satisfy standards of objectivity which would be out of place or nonsensical in the physical sciences. Consider the following passage, which is typical of those which assert that the social and natural sciences work with notions of objectivity.

In the language of the Anglo-Saxon world to be objective has meant to be impartial, to have no preferences, predilections or prejudices, no biases, no preconceived values or judgments in the presence of the facts. This view was an expression of the older conception of natural law in accord with which the contemplation of the facts of nature, instead of being coloured by the norms of conduct of the contemplator, automatically supplied those norms . . . .Necessary and wholesome as the emphasis on the distorting influence of cultural values and interests upon knowledge was . . . the positive and constructive significance of the evaluative elements in thought had to be recognized. If the earlier discussion of objectivity laid stress upon the elimination of personal and collective bias, the more modern approach calls attention to the positive cognitive importance of this bias. . . . Objectivity thus appears in a two-fold aspect: one, in which object and subject are discrete and separate entities, the other in which the interplay between them is emphasized. Whereas objectivity in the first sense refers to the reliability of our data and the validity of our conclusions, objectivity in the second sense is concerned with relevance to our interests.[1]

This thesis of contrasting species of objectivity (C) is easily recognized as an expression of the separatist contention that all talk of uniting the methods of physical and social science is vacuous or futile. It is more difficult to identify that of which there are alleged to be contrasting forms and to locate the grounds on which a case for C can be built.

Perhaps it will be suggested that selection 44 has already given evidence of a type of objectivity which, with respect to some of their concepts, is denied to social scientists. For in that selection, Norman Malcolm maintained that since dream-reports are incorrigible (what the dreamer reports sincerely must be true), it follows that " 'subjective' and 'objective' are *one* in the case of dreams — which is to say that this distinction does not apply." A consequence of Malcolm's position is that certain concepts descriptive of human agents ('He *dreamt* last night,' 'He now *has a mental image* of his mother.') are *incompatible* with operational definitions (or instruments of measurement) which are designed to outrank sincere first-person testimony. Now suppose that a philosopher or social scientist identifies objectivity with devices of measurement or operational indicators which replace or outweigh first-person

[1] Wirth, Louis. Preface to English edition of Karl Mannheim's *Ideology and Utopia*, pages xv and xvii.

testimony. With this stipulation, he would have invented a sense of "objective" which would be false of at least some concepts in the social sciences.

There is a second group of human action concepts which might also be said to lack objectivity. Consider the following set of statements: (i) "Hammett is a famous violinist," (ii) "That was a practice serve," (iii) "He's guilty of sedition," (iv) "Bill has just become a major in the Army," (v) "Your rights under law include making two phone calls, one to a lawyer". These statements are not incorrigible in the way that "I dreamt last night" is incorrigible. Hammett may sincerely think he is famous and yet be badly mistaken. But they are distinct nonetheless from statements like "The anti-missile missile is travelling at the speed of sound" and "The leaves have turned orange and yellow". The difference might be labelled by calling (i)–(v) "socially incorrigible": that is, if enough or the right persons believe or decide that they are true, then they are true[2]. If the Supreme Court declares a United States citizen to be a criminal, to be guilty of violating a certain law, then he is guilty of that violation. If a group of people are playing nontournament volleyball and a serve catches some of them offguard, when they unanimously call out "practice serve", a truth is thereby created. If all of his superior officers consider Bill to be a captain, then he is *not* a major. But the proposition that a car is travelling at 10 miles per hour does not logically follow from the claim that most or all people (or some set of authorities) believe or have decided that it is traveling at that speed. This notion of social incorrigibility may be explained as follows: a concept C is socially incorrigible if any statement of the form "a is C" follows from the claim that most or all people (or some set of officials) believe, or have decided, that a is C.

The same (artificial) sense of "objectivity" that is false of notions like dreaming is also false of socially incorrigible concepts. That is, both sets of concepts are incompatible with operational definitions and instruments of quantitative measurement. There can be no operations or scales which replace or overrule the concerted (or official) testimony of the individuals whose beliefs, desires, and decisions are the criterion for applying a socially incorrigible concept. When the jury declares that Jones is guilty of treason, and the system allows no higher or further appeal, then this declaration makes him guilty: nothing by way of the most exacting measurements or indicators can alter the social fact their decision has created. Perhaps the jury can reconvene, and proclaim a new verdict. But this only shows that the jury can change its mind, and not that there is an independent realm of facts conformity to which is the test of jury decisions. Men can and do change their dream-reports; does this imply that, to be true, these reports must correspond to the features of an antecedent reality, rather than simply being offered sincerely? To what features of a ball's flight, or of its relation to our actions, must the cry "Practice", conform, for a serve to count as merely practice?

There is a sense then in which objectivity cannot be attained at any point in the application of two important sets of human action concepts.[3] It has been mentioned, however, primarily to make sure we exclude it. For this notion of objectivity, which turns on being compatible with measurement or operational definitions, receives

[2] On page 624 above, J. W. N. Watkins appears to accept the idea that there are socially incorrigible concepts, and to incorporate it into his conception of MI.

[3] Nor, for either set, can this sense of objectivity be *desired*. For it is part of what they mean, or how they are used, that nothing can carry more weight than first-person (or concerted) testimony. To insist on objective indicators would not lend precision to a set of supposedly imprecise concepts, it would eliminate them entirely. One does not get a clearer form of Hindemith by insisting that his works be transcribed onto the eight-tone scale.

little or no stress in the thought of Mannheim, Weber, and Stark. More significant, it yields an *asymmetric* relation between the natural and social sciences. Certain concepts in the latter ('having a mental image,' 'practice serve,' 'major') are incompatible with a form of objectivity that is possessed by every concept in the physical sciences. This may provide evidence for weak separatism, but it does nothing to warrant belief in C. Let us try another route, one that begins with a generic account of objectivity which is then shown to be realized in contrasting ways by the natural and the social scientist.

When someone claims that a congressional investigation of government spending was conducted *objectively*, it is clear that he need not commit himself to the truth of the committee's conclusions. The investigators might have been tricked or they might have overlooked important evidence; perhaps they erroneously believed that deficit spending is a sign of wasted or precarious finances. The complexities of the topic might well escape or confuse even the most *objective* thinker. Thus, whatever objectivity comes to be, it is not a sufficient condition for attaining knowledge or warranted beliefs. A person who is objective in coming to believe P (or in investigating its truth value) may wind up in error nonetheless.

Is being objective, then, a *necessary* condition for acquiring knowledge and rejecting false beliefs? This view seems to be implicit in the passage quoted on page 691 above. But being alive and being conscious are also conditions without which it is logically impossible for a man to gain knowledge or reject error. Does being objective have a closer or more essential connection to knowledge than being alive? Such, I believe, would be the position of those social scientists who maintain C. Perhaps we can say that objectivity is a human attitude or trait which provides a *crucial* necessary condition for the acquisition of well-founded beliefs or knowledge. Its being crucial among necessary conditions might be argued for in two ways. First, the possession of objectivity seems to entail, but not be entailed by, the possession of most other necessary conditions of gaining knowledge (e.g., being alive, being conscious, understanding the propositions involved). Moreover, it is not also a necessary condition for misbegotten attempts to attain knowledge, e.g., those which issue in mistaken beliefs or arrive at no convictions whatever. That is, if one is not alive or not conscious during T, it follows that one could not gain knowledge or form warranted beliefs during T. *But it also follows* that one could not come to hold erroneous or inaccurate or confused beliefs during T. This means that being alive (being conscious) is a necessary condition not only for successful but for unsuccessful attempts to attain knowledge or reach justified opinions. But objectivity is necessary only for success; in its absence, it is entirely possible to be led to fallacious arguments, absurd conclusions, errors and omissions of all sorts.

My suggestion is that we understand objectivity as an attitude towards the truth value of propositions (that government spending has been wasteful; that Marxism demands armed revolution as a means to proletarian democracy). This attitude, while not sufficient, holds what might be termed a crucial status within the class of necessary conditions for acquiring propositional knowledge or warranted beliefs. And this for two reasons: first, there is a one-way entailment from being objective about a proposition P's truth value to most or all other necessary conditions for acquiring knowledge of P's truth value. And second, that unlike most other necessary conditions for attaining knowledge, objectivity is necessary only for cognitive success and not also for unsuccessful cognitive efforts.

With this brief account in mind, what can be said to distinguish objective attitudes in the social and natural sciences? How does objectivity differ in these two domains? The answer, according to Mannheim, Stark, and other sociologists of knowledge, lies in the fact that (part of) what is "crucially necessary" for arriving at knowledge or warranted beliefs in the social sciences is not only dispensable but a definite hindrance in the natural sciences (and vice versa). Let us use the term "value judgment" primarily to include any claim to the effect that something has aesthetic merit (is an aesthetic success or failure), is intrinsically desirable, is just, or is morally binding and, as well, the principles by which such claims are defended. It appears to be Mannheim's view that if a natural scientist permits his value judgments to play a role in determining the scientific hypotheses he accepts, the properties he ascribes to his data, or the derivations he finds demonstrable, this will betoken a failure of objectivity and, as such, prevent the acquisition of confirmed beliefs. It would be absurd to consider as relevant to the claim that a certain compound contains a benzene ring the value judgment that rings of that type are (or are not) desirable for human health. But just the opposite holds in the social sciences. Here if the inquirer casts aside his values, if he attempts, say, an ethically neutral investigation, he will fail to understand — he will distort or oversimplify — the phenomena he is studying. In brief, coming to know certain propositions about human conduct or institutional life, requires principles of value; but at no point is this the case in the physical sciences. And this, according at least to selection 53 below, is what distinguishes the objectivity of the social scientist from that of the natural scientist.

We have then defined objectivity generically as an attitude towards propositions which is a crucial necessary condition for acquiring knowledge. The claim now is that the precise nature of this attitude differs radically in the social and natural sciences. In the former, it involves (at least in some cases) a commitment to value judgments; in the latter, a commitment to the exclusion of such judgments. It deserves stress that this claim is decidedly *not* — is incompatible with — the view that the natural sciences have a greater claim to objectivity than the social sciences. On the contrary, it implies that there are two clashing sets of criteria for being objective and that neither the social nor the natural sciences can satisfy both.

This interpretation of C, which I shall abbreviate VC, can be challenged in two major ways.

Objection 1: Value-neutrality is no hindrance to objectivity in the social sciences; the social scientist can and should identify and explain his data without appealing to or presupposing any value judgments.

Objection 2: Value judgments are indeed indispensable in the social sciences, but this does not set them apart from the physical sciences. For "the scientist *qua* scientist makes value judgments," whether he be concerned with the physiology of vision, the half-life of mythologium, or the sociology of suicide.

Let us handle these objections separately. One way of countering objection 1 is to point out that the institutions and activities with which social scientists are concerned are what Max Weber termed "culturally significant;" that is, they typically represent themselves as conforming to, or establishing, norms and standards of every possible variety. Laws and governments declare themselves to be obligatory for their citizens, customs and practices are designed to maximize (alleged) values of equality and stability, and in general social phenomena ask to be thought of as more worth initiating or preserving than other available options.

Now it appears to be the shared view of Mannheim and Strauss that since most or all social phenomena strive to reach, or claim to reach, normative standards (moral, aesthetic, religious, epistemological, prudential), it follows that they cannot be understood without an appraisal of these normatively charged efforts. "Comprehension," Walter Kaufmann has written in a similar context, "without critical evaluation is impossible." One cannot critically evaluate the justice of Athenian democracy, however, if one lacks a concept of justice. Nor can one try the comparative merits of Baroque and Romantic chamber music or appraise the claim that the latter came into existence only when the former had exhausted its creative potential, without endorsing or presupposing aesthetic standards of one's own.

This line of argument may be assisted by Winch's position that

> . . . social relations fall into the same logical category as do relations between ideas. . . . If social relations between men exist only in and through their ideas, then, since the relations between ideas are internal relations, social relations must be a species of internal relation too. . . . It will seem less strange that social relations should be like logical relations between propositions once it is seen that logical relations between propositions themselves depend on social relations between men. (See pages 329, 327, and 328 above.)

The relevance of this position can be seen by reflecting on how we would test a person's understanding of, say, Hobbes' doctrine of the state of nature or Levi-Bruhl's theory of magic as low grade science. Or, for that matter, any doctrine in any domain. Surely the test involves determining whether our man could identify (i) the major objections to the doctrine, (ii) its leading competitors, and (iii) whether (and how) it could meet those objections and succeed where those competitors failed. Now if *social fact* is substituted for *doctrine* here, what results is the view that with social facts, no less than with ideas, "comprehension without critical evaluation is impossible." But is critical evaluation of normative claims consistent with the exclusion of all normative standards? If not, it would follow that a value-free social scientist could not understand his subject matter. For any social phenomena S, he could not determine the major objections to or failings in S, nor the alternatives to it, nor whether S could meet those objections, remedy its defects, or was preferable to the alternative options.

There is a second way of defending VC against objection 1. Let us imagine that we are studying the Hopi and are surprised one morning to find a normally placid Indian shouting angrily at his wife. The claim is then offered that he is voicing *indignation* over some aspect of her recent behavior, a view we eventually come to accept. How can such a claim be justified? Well, he believed she had done something blameworthy. This, as a minimum, would have to be shown. But how then to recognize that he has this belief, and did not erupt merely because some habit of his wife's had become annoying, or because she was (innocently but inconveniently) blocking him from something he desired? We have ascribed to our man a *moral* emotion. Moral emotions imply moral beliefs. But how do we pick out individuals with *moral beliefs*? Can we do so if we ourselves have none? If I have no concept of justice can I tell whether colonialized Asiatics felt themselves to be justly or unjustly treated by occidental powers: to be the losers in a series of fair fights or the victims of unwarranted aggression?

Consider: to know whether Jones believes he has been treated cruelly or kindly requires that I know what cruelty is — have some standards or paradigms to go by. But then to know whether Jones believes he has been treated unjustly requires that

I know what just treatment is, i.e. have some standards or paradigms to go by. But employing such standards is clearly an instance of making or being committed to certain value judgments. And the price of divesting oneself of such standards is that one cannot come to know, or acquire tenable beliefs about, the normative attitudes, beliefs, emotions, actions, etc. of human agents. Objectivity would thus seem to demand that the social scientist, qua social scientist, employ value judgments. In brief, a necessary condition for recognizing at least some of the attributes of persons and institutions is that one possess and employ moral concepts: a value-free social science, which is also wholly objective, is logically impossible. The sure consequence of ethical neutrality is misrepresentation and inaccuracy.

Now imagine a second case, in which we are confronted by an unfamiliar practice in which the infants of a community are separated at birth from their biological parents and enculturated by a constantly altering group of persons under 21. What sort of practice is this? One that fixes a sharp separation in status between child and adult or simply intends to afford leisure to the latter? One hypothesis might be that the practice is maintained because the community thinks it desirable for (in the best interests of) the children. How though can we tell if this *is* what they think? It is certainly relevant, and possibly conclusive, to learn that they believe that a person's mental health and stability are diminished if he is perpetually subjected to one and the same pair of authorities in childhood, and increased by experiencing an immense variety of patterns of control and care. The following inference, in other words, seems acceptable:

1 X believes A promotes the mental health of Y.
∴ 2 Hence, X believes A is good (desirable) for Y.

But can we accept this inference without also accepting the principle (P) that promoting the mental health of a person is desirable for that person? And this surely *looks like* a "principle of preference" or standard of value. Once again, it seems difficult to avoid the conclusion that principles of evaluation are tacitly involved in determining (fixing the nature of) of least some of the beliefs and activities of human agents. Without principles like P, it is doubtful whether any meaning could be assigned to statements of the form "X believes A to be desirable for Y", where A is an activity, goal, or practice and X and Y are human beings. The criteria for establishing belief ascriptions of this kind are themselves — or imply — normative criteria: *at this point, fact and value cease to be independent*. To recognize "the facts" in social science includes identifying the beliefs, attitudes, and feelings of specific human agents; and, contrary to objection 1, this seems impossible — in certain cases — for those without any commitment to value judgments.

It may clarify matters somewhat if the preceding remarks are applied to Ernest Nagel's attempt to show that there are "no compelling reasons for the claim that an ethically neutral social science is impossible." On page 745 below, Nagel considers a view very similar to VC; his arguments against this view rest on a distinction between

> two quite different senses of the term "value judgment": the sense in which a value judgment expresses *approval or disapproval* either of some moral (or social) ideal, or of some action (or institution) because of a commitment to such an ideal; and the sense in which a value judgment expresses an *estimate* of the degree to which some commonly recognized (and more or less clearly defined) type of action, object, or institution is embodied in a given instance. [Page 746 below.]

What relation holds between these two types of value judgments? According to Nagel, those which express approval and disapproval (appraising value judgments) are *not* entailed by, though they do imply, those which assert that a given characteristic is present to this or that degree (characterizing value judgments). It is clear, we are told, "that an investigator making a characterizing value judgment is not thereby logically bound to affirm or deny a corresponding appraising evaluation." Moreover, given this nonentailment, it follows, on Nagel's view, that there is nothing inherently impossible or self-defeating about the idea of a value-free social science.

Nagel's defense of objection 1 against VC can be criticized in two different ways. First of all, it ignores our first argument, according to which the social scientist must employ (appraising) value judgments because the phenomena he studies make normative claims; that is, represent themselves as desirable, binding, just, worth preserving, etc. One could admit that characterizing and appraising value judgments were logically distinct, and that the former do not entail any of the latter, but insist that both were needed within a *fully developed* social science. Given our first argument, it seems defensible that in the absence of *either* type of value judgment, one's understanding of social phenomena is impaired or incomplete; especially if appraisal value judgments can be defended in ways that make some of them more reasonable or worthy of belief than others. In brief, that there is a distinction between these two types of value judgments does not, in itself, appear to warrant claiming that the social sciences can dispense with either type. There is a one-way entailment between velocity judgments and direction judgments; this hardly leads us to believe that the former are scientifically superfluous. But there seems to be a close analogy here to the premise from which Nagel concludes that social scientists can proceed without advancing any appraising value judgments: for this premise merely asserts that these judgments entail, but are not entailed by, certain sorts of judgments essential to social science.

Secondly, Nagel's distinction itself is suspect. Perhaps it is true that the characterizing judgment "this animal is anemic" does not imply "it is undesirable for a given animal, or this animal, to continue being anemic." Or that from the description of certain religious attitudes as mercenary nothing can be inferred as to whether those attitudes are worthy of approval. But this hardly shows that there are *no* characterizing value judgments which constitute or imply appraising value judgments.

In fact, we have already seen cases (pages 695–696 above) which provide counterexamples to the universal dictum that "an investigator making a characterizing value judgment is not thereby logically bound to affirm or deny a corresponding appraising evaluation." To describe a man as believing that an act is wrong (just, honorable, obligatory) is to make a characterizing value judgment. To describe him as believing that someone is stout or is accelerating at the rate of 3 miles per second is also to advance a characterizing value judgment. But as the latter judgments can be made only by those who possess a concept of, or criteria for, "stoutness" or "accelerating. . .", so the former judgment is possible only if there are criteria for distinguishing right from wrong, just from unjust, etc. conduct. The difference is that in the stoutness case the criteria are not themselves appraising value judgments, whereas this is precisely their nature in any case where people are characterized as having moral (aesthetic, etc.) emotions, beliefs, attitudes, etc. To characterize a man as having a certain moral feeling may not indeed imply any appraisal value judgment of *him*, but it does imply general standards of appraisal; i.e., criteria for picking out what is desirable, obligatory, fair-minded, etc.

Nagel contends in a footnote that

> It is irrelevant to the present discussion what view is adopted concerning the ground upon which such judgments [appraising value judgments] supposedly rest — whether those grounds are simply arbitrary preferences, alleged intuitions of "objective" values, categorical moral imperatives, or anything else that has been proposed in the history of value theory. (See page 747 below.)

But is this really the case? Suppose that appraisal value judgments denote "objective" properties, as naturalists and intuitionists allege, and that they do so in addition to "expressing approval or disapproval." When I affirm that Jackson was unjust to his prisoners, I would then be attributing one of a certain cluster of properties to his behavior and (thereby) condemning it. (An analogy from aesthetics: one can both compliment and describe by pointing out the gracefulness of a dancer, or the tightly-knit structure of a novel.) The predicate 'is just' (and others) might well, in short, be used to characterize as well as to express or imply approval. The utilitarian formula that right is what maximizes the greatest happiness provides a clear example. If *this* specific "assumption about the foundations of appraising value judgments" is true, then the characterization of an act as maximizing happiness *entails* the appraising judgment that the act is binding or desirable. Nagel's claim that characterizing judgments never entail appraising judgments, I suggest, can only be accepted by those who regard evaluative (moral, aesthetic) language as noncognitive; those who adopt, in short, some version of the emotivist theory. Thus contrary to his footnoted disclaimer, Nagel does assume a (very controversial) position concerning "the ground upon which [appraising value judgments] supposedly rest."

There is some reason to suppose that the arguments just presented against objection 1 also cast considerable doubt on objection 2, an objection to VC which is implicit in the main thesis of selection 57 below. For the phenomena dealt with by the physical sciences cannot be said to (i) assume or advance normative claims or (ii) express normative attitudes, beliefs, or feelings. This being the case, the concepts used to identify and distinguish physical phenomena seem to be independent of value judgments: e.g., a moral idiot could be taught to recognize and measure instances of gravitational attraction, or the speed of sound in various media. The reasons given to show that social science requires values judgments (i.e., (i) and (ii) above) rely on features of conduct which seem incompatible with physical concepts.[4] It seems fair, therefore, to ask: what grounds can there be for the anti-separatist thesis of objection 2?

Rudner's answer here can be restated as follows:

1. Scientific inquiry cannot proceed without the activity of accepting (and rejecting) hypotheses which do not allow of complete verification, i.e., cannot be established with certainty.

2. This activity involves the making of decisions as to the strength of available evidence: is that evidence "strong enough" to warrant belief?

3. But any decision as to the strength of the evidence for an hypothesis of the type referred to in premise 1 will be "a function of the *importance*, in the typically ethical sense, of making a mistake in accepting or rejecting the hypothesis."

4. Thus, in accepting and rejecting hypotheses the scientist commits himself to ethical norms; and given premise 1, this entails that value judgments are intrinsic to scientific inquiry.

Consider, though, the following two situations. In the first I am to judge whether all

[4] Especially if a physical concept cannot also be a psychological concept, in the sense of selections 33 and 34.

of the pocket handkerchiefs which were and will be produced by a certain process are red. In the second, my task is to determine whether a certain type of man (latent homosexual) is responsible and sane and hence a good risk for jury duty. In both cases, I begin by examining 200 items out of the total population and I find them to be, respectively, red and responsible. But this piecemeal procedure is boring and so I ask myself whether the evidence thus far accumulated is sufficiently strong to warrant accepting H^1 (all of the handkerchiefs are red) or H^2 (all of the men are responsible and sane). Now plainly the importance of making a mistake in connection with H^2 is much greater than the importance of making an error in connection with H^1. On Rudner's view (premiss 3), we ought therefore to be willing to assert that the evidence for H^2 is substantially weaker than that gathered in support of H^1. This seems at the very least paradoxical. Given that we have no information about the size of either subject class (handkerchiefs produced in a certain way, latent homosexuals) and no other data on which to base a decision, there seems to be as much evidence for the humanly trivial hypothesis as for the humanly significant one. This being the case, decisions about the strength of evidence for hypothesis which are not completely verifiable do not always presuppose value judgments, and premise 3 is false.

This result can be reached in another way. Let us imagine two men with different moral beliefs. Mr. P., a pacifist, thinks that no duty is more sacred than that of preserving human life. General G., however, regards the individual as relatively insignificant. For him, the supreme good is the expansion and glorification of the fatherland — even if this involves some sacrifice of human life. If Rudner is correct, these conflicting value judgments require Mr. P. and General G. to make divergent decisions concerning the weight of evidence for given hypotheses. But that they are so required seems very dubious.

"Any human being will die if he imbibes a quart of arsenic at one sitting" is an hypothesis which both men, in principle, could agree had considerable confirmation. Does consistency with their notions of what is most desirable compel them to view the evidence differently? P will regard arsenic as dangerous and insist that it be carefully administered and utilized; G will think once but not twice about using it to liquidate those who refuse to submit to his country's manifest destiny. But these differences only underline their shared conviction as to the credibility of the arsenic hypothesis.

The hypothesis that birch rots more quickly in salt water than oak refers to a set of relationships that men found vastly more important prior to 1900 than they do today. Has this loss of importance influenced the extent of the evidence for our hypothesis? If not, how can a decision concerning the strength of that evidence be "a function of the *importance*, in the typically ethical sense, of making a mistake in accepting or rejecting the hypothesis?"

We can, however, set aside criticisms of premise 3; there is a more convincing and instructive way of defending VC against attacks based on Rudner's position. For that position can at most show that there is a certain *subclass* of value judgments which are essential to any "rational reconstruction" of both the natural and the social sciences; i.e., those entailed by any appraisal of the evidence for hypotheses which defy complete verification. Let us call the members of this subclass "E value judgments." VC, on the other hand, does *not* refer to E value judgments. It claims that what distinguishes the social scientist is that he makes what can be called identifying value judgments (I value judgments); i.e., those involved not in estimating evidence but — long before this — in identifying or classifying his data.

Suppose a social scientist is considering the hypothesis (H^3) that people who struggle against institutions they regard as unjust actually lend those institutions indirect support. On Rudner's view, a value judgment will be required when our scientist addresses the question; "Is the available evidence for H^3 sufficiently strong to warrant its acceptance?" In this way, supposedly, an E value judgment will enter into his scientific decision-making. But according to VC, any social scientist concerned with H^3 will have made a different type of value judgment prior to the point at which he estimates the evidence for and against this hypothesis. For in order to even begin gathering any such evidence, he must be able to recognize people who regard institutions as unjust, and to distinguish such people from those who are getting fewer benefits than they desire, but do not feel mistreated. And if the arguments on pages 694–696 above are sound, to make these identifications he must have a concept of justice, that is, he must know what makes actions just and unjust. Thus, before the social scientist who is investigating H^3 commits himself to any E value judgment, he has already committed himself to a I value judgment.

VC, in short, should be expressed as the claim that in the social sciences objectivity requires I value judgments, while in the natural sciences it requires the exclusion of I value judgments. And given this, Rudner's thesis — that E value judgments are essential to both forms of science — seems entirely compatible with VC.

My aim has been to clarify and develop a case for the separatist contention that objectivity takes distinct and clashing forms in the social and natural sciences. Along the way it was first argued that if an objective concept is defined as one for which quantitative indices or operational criteria can outweigh first-person, concerted, or official testimony, then many concepts descriptive of human actions and employed by social scientists lack objectivity. A second interpretation of objectivity (more faithful to its sense among social scientists like Mannheim, Weber, and Strauss) was then outlined. Here the trait of being objective was identified as a crucial necessary condition for acquiring knowledge of or evidence for given propositions. Moreover, the exact nature of this trait or disposition was held to be, in part, determined by the nature of the propositions being inquired into; more specifically, objectivity in the physical sciences was held to require the elimination of all value judgments from the process of classifying and identifying phenomena, whereas objectivity in the social sciences was claimed to involve the use of value judgments in the recognition and understanding of (certain) social and psychological phenomena.

If VC is true, the case for separatism cannot be easily dismissed. Moreover, VC may shed light on another issue central to the methodology of social science: the nature and justification of *verstehen*. Perhaps, in Mannheim's idiom, "it is no accident" that those social scientists who have spoken of distinct forms of objectivity have also emphasized "interpretative understanding" as a way of acquiring knowledge that is not available to the physical scientist. It was suggested on page 356 above that one aspect of *verstehen* is the ability to apply irreducible psychological concepts. VC might be thought of as registering a second aspect of this notion. That is, we could say that *verstehen* requires not only the mastery of intentional predicates but that form of objectivity, distinctive of *social* science, which involves the making of I value judgments as well. To understand the American party system by means of *verstehen*, then, would involve determining and critically appraising its normative features and claims; determining what that system views as just and unjust, what it sees as desirable for men, and whether such moral and evaluative beliefs are tenable. If this proposal is accepted, then wherever social science inquiry is carried on without any commitment to I value judgments, it will be false to claim that *verstehen* was employed; just as false as such a claim would be for inquiries where psychological predicates had been replaced by nonpsychological ones.

If *verstehen* is understood as involving value objectivity as well as the mastery of intentional language, it may be possible to give it additional support — beyond that extended on page 357 — against empiricist attacks like this one from Ernest Nagel's *The Structure of Science:*

> . . . it is by no means obvious that a social scientist cannot account for men's actions unless he has experienced in his own person the psychic states he imputes to them or unless he can successfully recreate such states in imagination. Must a psychiatrist be at least partially demented if he is to be competent for studying the mentally ill? . . . The factual evidence certainly lends no support to these and similar suppositions. Indeed, *discoursive* knowledge — i.e., knowledge statable in *propositional form* . . . is not a matter of *having* sensations, images, or feelings, whether vivid or faint; and it consists neither in identifying oneself in some ineffable manner with the objects of knowledge, nor in reproducing in some form of direct experience the subject matter of knowledge. On the other hand, discoursive knowledge . . . is the product of a process that deliberately aims at formulating relations between traits of a subject matter, so that one set of traits . . . can be taken as a reliable sign of other traits mentioned; and it involves as a necessary condition for its being warranted, the possibility of verifying these formulations through controlled sensory observation by anyone prepared to make the effort to verify them.[5]

There is too little space here to unravel all "the ambiguities in these pronouncements"; perhaps a few comments will spur someone else to complete the job. For one thing, the most serious proponents of *verstehen* (Dilthey, Weber, Mannheim) have been wary of reducing it to any indescribable unification of the knower and the known or to the mere having of certain images or feelings. Mannheim, at least in some passages, is clear enough on this point. It is clear, he tells us, that

> . . . every social science diagnosis is closely connected with the evaluations and unconscious orientations of the observer and that the critical self-clarification of the social sciences is intimately bound up with the critical self-clarification of our orientation in the everyday world. An observer who is not fundamentally interested in the social roots of the changing ethics of the period in which he himself lives, who does not think through the problems of social life in terms of the tensions between social strata, and who has not also discovered the fruitful aspect of resentment in his own experience, will never be in a position to see that phase of Christian ethics described above [the ethics of the earliest Christian communities . . . primarily intelligible, according to Mannheim, in terms of the resentment of oppressed strata] to say nothing of being able to understand it. It is precisely to the degree that he participates evaluationally (sympathetically or antagonistically) in the struggle for ascendancy of the lower strata . . . that he becomes aware of the dynamic significance of social tension and resentment. . . . In order to work in the social sciences one must participate in the social process, but this participation in collective-unconscious striving in no wise signifies that the persons participating in it falsify the facts or see them incorrectly. Indeed, on the contrary, participation in the living context of social life is a presupposition of the understanding of the inner nature of this living context. . . . The disregard of qualitative elements and the complete restraint of the will does not constitute objectivity but is instead the negation of the essential quality of the object. [Pages 708–709 below.]

For Mannheim, objectivity in social science — and hence *verstehen* — involves "participation in the social process." Does this view imply that only the insane

[5] Nagel, Ernest. *The Structure of Science*, New York, 1961, pages 483–484.

can understand the insane, or that a saint could not detect political ambition in his ecclesiastical comrades? The notion of value objectivity, which I have proposed we regard as an element of *verstehen*, affirms that social observers must have normative standards by which to comprehend and appraise the human activities they confront. This does not seem to demand that knower and known unite in an ineffable identity of emotions or attitudes. Indeed, on Mannheim's view, it may yield either "sympathetic" or "antagonistic" verdicts, condemnation and resistance as well as empathic identification.

Further, with VC as a basis, those who would defend *verstehen* can justifiably take issue with Nagel's fundamental presupposition concerning knowledge: viz, that nothing can be known except what can be verified through "controlled sensory observation." The arguments for VC purport to show that not all forms of objectivity (and hence knowledge) are open to anyone and everyone whose perceptual senses are intact. On the contrary, if those arguments go through, "controlled sensory observation" not only fails to be a necessary condition for acquiring certain kinds of knowledge about human agents, but effectively debars such knowledge. For in Nagel's hands, a restriction to controlled sensory observation, it seems fair to assume, would require the elimination of all I value judgments from classification and predication. Such a restriction is thus incompatible (given page 696 above) with the success of attempts to gain knowledge in many areas vital to the social scientist. Nagel's criticism of *verstehen*, in short, depends on a presumption that the arguments for VC render highly suspect: that what is necessary for objectivity and for coming to know is *the same in both the social and physical sciences*. If the proponents of *verstehen* link their method or approach to VC they can readily deny this presumption, thus leaving Nagel's objections at best inconclusive.

It seems to be characteristic of empiricists like Nagel to endeavor to persuade us that *verstehen* is methodologically superfluous. Interpretative understanding is said to be wholly a matter of the "origins" of an hypothesis and to be of no relevance to how it is tested or to how that hypothesis becomes certified as knowledge. If, however, *verstehen* involves the mastery of psychological concepts and the use of normative standards, and if psychological concepts are irreducible and the arguments for VC are sound, it begins to be implausible to view *verstehen* as superfluous. Such a view could be maintained only if those who lacked *verstehen* could nonetheless come to know whatever propositions were framed by virtue of interpretative understanding. As presently conceived, to lack *verstehen* is to lack the use (an understanding) of either (or both) intentional propositions or those which describe the normative attitudes, beliefs, and principles of human agents. One can hardly test or come to know a proposition one cannot understand. There are propositions, in short, which cannot be understood, much less evaluated or known, except by those who exercise *verstehen*. This being the case, for those propositions — and they form a large and important class within social science — interpretative understanding is methodologically indispensable. It is *not* merely a heuristic device for originating hypotheses (e.g., that a certain man felt indignation or that a tribal practice is preserved so as to benefit the children involved) that methods which do not involve *verstehen* can proceed to test and confirm or disconfirm. It cannot be set aside at any stage of the social scientist's inquiry into claims about the intentions or evaluative features of human acts and institutions.

The idea that *verstehen* is methodologically indispensable to social science is echoed in Erik Erikson's analysis of clinical (psychoanalytic) evidence: "there is no choice,"

Erikson contends, "but to put subjectivity into the center of an inquiry into evidence and inference in clinical work." His description of the steps involved in coming to accept a dream interpretation presents us with a classical instance of *verstehen*, in the sense just outlined: no operational or physicalistic indicators are introduced to replace intentional language; moreover, an effort is made to employ the analyst's own "emotional responses" and values as a source of evidence and understanding. It is this latter feature, Erikson asserts, which "highlights one methodological point truly unique to clinical work. . . . The evidence is not "all in" if [the analyst] does not succeed in using his own emotional responses during a clinical encounter . . . instead of putting them aside with a spurious claim to unassailable objectivity." Erikson's article, in short, emphasizes and supports the thesis that the social and natural sciences are built on conflicting forms of objectivity. What Erikson calls "disciplined subjectivity" (= *verstehen*?) is necessary for coming to know certain propositions about human agents but an obstacle when considering hypotheses concerning physical events or regularities.

"The Nature of Clinical Evidence" has a further merit. By providing a detailed specimen of interpretative understanding, this selection should permit close evaluation of the claims made both for and against *verstehen* throughout this anthology. The issues central to such an evaluation must certainly include the following:

1. Are *verstehen* judgments completely unarguable (intuitive, subjective, arbitrary) and beyond falsification; if not, how can conflicting interpretations be adjudicated?

2. Is *verstehen* methodologically superfluous, a process that can help in forming hypotheses but has no role in judging their truth or adequacy? Can the truth value of every *verstehen* judgment be established by those who lack *verstehen*?

3. In what ways, if any, do *verstehen* judgments differ from the empirical propositions which record the observations on which natural science is built? Are these judgments in any sense a priori; to what extent are they incompatible with the techniques of measurement and definition discussed in parts V and VI?

4. In what respects, if any, must A and B be alike (have the same experiences, attitudes, concepts, etc.) in order for A to come to know something about B by *verstehen*? If A seeks to understand B's activity by *verstehen*, how does the relation between A and B differ from that between a meteorologist and a storm he is studying?

Objectivity and Value Judgments in the Sociology of Knowledge

53

from *Ideology and Utopia*
KARL MANNHEIM

The Sociological Concept of Thought

This book is concerned with the problem of how men actually think. The aim of these studies is to investigate not how thinking appears in textbooks on logic, but how it really functions in public life and in politics as an instrument of collective action.

Philosophers have too long concerned themselves with their own thinking. When they wrote of thought, they had in mind primarily their own history, the history of philosophy, or quite special fields of knowledge such as mathematics or physics. This type of thinking is applicable only under quite special circumstances, and what can be learned by analysing it is not directly transferable to other spheres of life. Even when it is applicable, it refers only to a specific dimension of existence which does not suffice for living human beings who are seeking to comprehend and to mould their world.

Meanwhile, acting men have, for better or for worse, proceeded to develop a variety of methods for the experiential and intellectual penetration of the world in which they live, which have never been analysed with the same precision as the so-called exact modes of knowing. When, however, any human activity continues over a long period without being subjected to intellectual control or criticism, it tends to get out of hand.

Hence it is to be regarded as one of the anomalies of our time that those methods of thought by means of which we arrive at our most crucial decisions, and through which we seek to diagnose and guide our political and social destiny, have remained unrecognized and therefore inaccessible to intellectual control and self-criticism. This anomaly becomes all the more monstrous when we call to mind that in modern times much more depends on the correct thinking through of a situation than was the case in earlier societies. The significance of social knowledge grows proportionately with the increasing necessity of regulatory intervention in the social process. This so-called pre-scientific inexact mode of thought, however (which, paradoxically, the logicians and philosophers also use when they have to make practical decisions), is not to be understood solely by the use of logical analysis. It constitutes a complex which cannot be readily detached either from the psychological roots of the emotional and vital impulses which underlie it or from the situation in which it arises and which it seeks to solve.

It is the most essential task of this book to work out a suitable method for the description and analysis of this type of thought and its changes, and to formulate those problems connected with it which will both do justice to its unique character and prepare the way for its critical understanding. The method which we will seek to present is that of the sociology of knowledge.

The principal thesis of the sociology of knowledge is that there are modes of thought

From *Ideology and Utopia* by Karl Mannheim, 1936, pp. 1–5, 42–50, 265–258, and 281–285. Reprinted by permission of Harcourt, Brace & World, Inc., New York, and Routledge & Kegan Paul Ltd., London.

which cannot be adequately understood as long as their social origins are obscured. It is indeed true that only the individual is capable of thinking. There is no such metaphysical entity as a group mind which thinks over and above the heads of individuals, or whose ideas the individual merely reproduces. Nevertheless it would be false to deduce from this that all the ideas and sentiments which motivate an individual have their origin in him alone, and can be adequately explained solely on the basis of his own life-experience.

Just as it would be incorrect to attempt to derive a language merely from observing a single individual, who speaks not a language of his own but rather that of his contemporaries and predecessors who have prepared the path for him, so it is incorrect to explain the totality of an outlook only with reference to its genesis in the mind of the individual. Only in a quite limited sense does the single individual create out of himself the mode of speech and of thought we attribute to him. He speaks the language of his group; he thinks in the manner in which his group thinks. He finds at his disposal only certain words and their meanings. These not only determine to a large extent the avenues of approach to the surrounding world, but they also show at the same time from which angle and in which context of activity objects have hitherto been perceptible and accessible to the group or the individual.

The first point which we now have to emphasize is that the approach of the sociology of knowledge intentionally does not start with the single individual and his thinking in order then to proceed directly in the manner of the philosopher to the abstract heights of "thought as such." Rather, the sociology of knowledge seeks to comprehend thought in the concrete setting of an historical-social situation out of which individually differentiated thought only very gradually emerges. Thus, it is not men in general who think, or even isolated individuals who do the thinking, but men in certain groups who have developed a particular style of thought in an endless series of responses to certain typical situations characterizing their common position.

Strictly speaking it is incorrect to say that the single individual thinks. Rather it is more correct to insist that he participates in thinking further what other men have thought before him. He finds himself in an inherited situation with patterns of thought which are appropriate to this situation and attempts to elaborate further the inherited modes of response or to substitute others for them in order to deal more adequately with the new challenges which have arisen out of the shifts and changes in his situation. Every individual is therefore in a two-fold sense predetermined by the fact of growing up in a society: on the one hand he finds a ready-made situation and on the other he finds in that situation preformed patterns of thought and of conduct.

The second feature characterizing the method of the sociology of knowledge is that it does not sever the concretely existing modes of thought from the context of collective action through which we first discover the world in an intellectual sense. Men living in groups do not merely coexist physically as discrete individuals. They do not confront the objects of the world from the abstract levels of a contemplating mind as such, nor do they do so exclusively as solitary beings. On the contrary they act with and against one another in diversely organized groups, and while doing so they think with and against one another. These persons, bound together into groups, strive in accordance with the character and position of the groups to which they belong to change the surrounding world of nature and society or attempt to maintain it in a given condition. It is the direction of this will to change or to maintain, of this collective activity, which produces the guiding thread for the emergence of their problems, their concepts, and their forms of thought. In accord with the particular context of collective activity in which they participate, men always tend to see the world which surrounds them differently. Just as pure logical analysis has severed individual thought from its group situation, so it also separated thought from action. It did this on the tacit assumption that those inherent connections which always exist in reality between thought on the one hand, and group and activity on the other, are either insignificant for "correct" thinking or can be detached from these foundations without any resultant difficulties. But the fact that one ignores something by no means puts an end to its existence. Nor can anyone who has not first given himself whole-heartedly to the exact observation of the wealth of forms in which men really think decide *a priori* whether this severance from the social situation and context of activity is always realizable. Nor indeed can it be determined offhand that such a complete dichotomy is fully desirable precisely in the interest of objective factual knowledge.

It may be that, in certain spheres of knowledge, it is the impulse to act which first makes the objects of the world accessible to the acting subject, and it may be further that it is this factor which determines the selection of those elements of reality which enter into thought. And it is not inconceivable that if this volitional factor were entirely excluded (in so far as such a thing is possible), the concrete content would completely disappear from the concepts, and the organizing principle which first makes possible an intelligent statement of the problem would be lost.

But this is not to say that in those domains where attachment to the group and orientation towards action seem to be an essential element in the situation, every possibility of intellectual, critical self-control is futile. Perhaps it is precisely when the hitherto concealed dependence of thought on group existence and its rootedness in action becomes visible that it really becomes possible for the first time, through becoming aware of them, to attain a new mode of control over previously uncontrolled factors in thought.

This brings us to the central problem of the book. These remarks should make it clear that a preoccupation with these problems and their solution will furnish a foundation for the social sciences and answer the question as to the possibility of the scientific guidance of political life. It is, of course, true that in the social sciences, as elsewhere, the ultimate criterion of truth or falsity is to be found in the investigation of the object, and the sociology of knowledge is no substitute for this. But the examination of the object is not an isolated act; it takes place in a context which is coloured by values and collective-unconscious, volitional impulses. In the social sciences it is this intellectual interest, oriented in a matrix of collective activity, which provides not only the general questions, but the concrete hypotheses for research and the thought-models for the ordering of experience. Only as we succeed in bringing into the area of conscious and explicit observation the various points of departure and of approach to the facts which are current in scientific as well as popular discussion, can we hope, in the course of time, to control the unconscious motivations and presuppositions which, in the last analysis, have brought these modes of thought into existence. A new type of objectivity in the social sciences is attainable not through the exclusion of evaluations but through the critical awareness and control of them. . . .

In . . . earlier periods it was mostly a case of slow shifts in values and norms, of a gradual transformation of the frame of reference from which men's actions derived their ultimate orientation. But in modern times it is a much more profoundly disorganizing affair. The resort to the unconscious tended to dig up the soil out of which the varying points of views emerged. The roots from which human thought had hitherto derived its nourishment were exposed. Gradually it becomes clear to all of us that we cannot go on living in the same way once we know about our unconscious motives as we did when we were ignorant of them. What we now experience is more than a new idea, and the questions we raise constitute more than a new problem. What we are concerned with here is the elemental perplexity of our time, which can be epitomized in the symptomatic question "How is it possible for man to continue to think and live in a time when the problems of ideology and utopia are being radically raised and thought through in all their implications?"

It is possible, of course, to escape from this situation in which the plurality of thought-styles has become visible and the existence of collective-unconscious motivations recognized simply by hiding these processes from ourselves. One can take flight into a supra-temporal logic and assert that truth as such is unsullied and has neither a plurality of forms nor any connection with unconscious motivations. But in a world in which the problem is not just an interesting subject for discussion but rather an inner perplexity, someone will soon come forth who will insist against these views that "our problem is not truth as such; it is our thinking as we find it in its rootedness in action in the social situation, in unconscious motivations. Show us how we can advance from our concrete perceptions to your absolute definitions. Do not speak of truth as such but show us the way in which our statements, stemming from our social existence, can be translated into a sphere in which the partisanship, the fragmentariness of human vision, can be transcended, in which the social origin and the dominance of the unconscious in thinking will lead to controlled observations rather than to chaos." The absoluteness of thought is not attained by warranting, through a general principle, that one has it or by proceeding to label some particular limited viewpoint (usually one's own) as suprapartisan and authoritative.

Nor are we aided when we are directed to a few propositions in which the content is so formal and abstract (e.g. in mathematics, geometry, and pure economics) that in fact they seem to be completely detached from the thinking social individual. The battle is not about these propositions but about that greater wealth of factual determinations in which man concretely diagnoses his individual and social situation, in which concrete interdependences in life are perceived and in which happenings external to us are first correctly understood. The battle rages concerning those propositions in which every concept is meaningfully oriented from the first, in which we use words like conflict, breakdown, alienation, insurrection, resentment — words which do not reduce complex situations for the sake of an externalizing, formal description without ever being able to build them up again and which would lose their content if their orientation, their evaluative elements, were dropped out.

We have already shown elsewhere that the development of modern science led to the growth of a technique of thought by means of which all that was only meaningfully intelligible was excluded. Behaviourism has pushed to the foreground this tendency towards concentration on entirely externally perceivable reactions, and has sought to construct a world of facts in which there will exist only measurable data, only correlations between series of factors in which the degree of probability of modes of behaviour in certain situations will be predictable. It is possible, and even probable, that sociology must pass through this stage in which its contents will undergo a mechanistic dehumanization and formalization, just as psychology did, so that out of devotion to an ideal of narrow exactitude nothing will remain except statistical data, tests, surveys, etc., and in the end every significant formulation of a problem will be excluded. All that can be said here is that this reduction of everything to a measurable or inventory-like describability is significant as a serious attempt to determine what is unambiguously ascertainable and, further, to think through what becomes of our psychic and social world when it is restricted to purely externally measurable relationships. There can no longer be any doubt that no real penetration into social reality is possible through this approach. Let us take for example the relatively simple phenomenon denoted by the term "situation." What is left of it, or is it even at all intelligible when it is reduced to an external constellation of various reciprocally related but only externally visible patterns of behaviour? It is clear, on the other hand, that a human situation is characterizable only when one has also taken into account those conceptions which the participants have of it, how they experience their tensions in this situation and how they react to the tensions so conceived. Or, let us take some milieu; for instance, the milieu in which a certain family exists. Are not the norms which prevail in this family, and which are intelligible only through meaningful interpretation, at least as much a part of the milieu as the landscape or the furniture of the household? Still further, must not this same family, other things being equal, be considered as a completely different milieu (e.g. from the point of the training of the children) if its norms have changed? If we wish to comprehend such a concrete phenomenon as a situation or the normative content of a milieu, the purely mechanistic scheme of approach will never suffice and there must be introduced in addition concepts adequate for the understanding of meaningful and nonmensurative elements.

But it would be false to assume that the relations between these elements are less clear and less precisely perceivable than those that obtain between purely measurable phenomena. Quite on the contrary, the reciprocal interdependence of the elements making up an event is much more intimately comprehensible than that of strictly external formalized elements. Here that approach which, following Dilthey, I should like to designate as the understanding of the primary interdependence of experience (*das verstehende Erfassen des "ursprünglichen Lebenszusammenhanges"*[1]) comes into its own. In this approach, by use of the technique of understanding, the reciprocal functional interpenetration of psychic experiences and social situations becomes immediately intelligible. We are confronted here with a realm of existence in which the emergence of psychic reactions from within becomes evident of necessity and is not comprehensible merely as is an external causality, according to the degree of probability of its frequency.

Let us take certain of the observations which sociology has worked up by the use of the method of understanding and consider the nature of its scientific evidence. When one has stated concerning the ethics of the earliest Christian communities, that it was primarily intelligible in terms of the resentment of oppressed strata, and when others have added that this ethical outlook was entirely unpolitical because it corresponded to the mentality of that stratum which had as yet no real aspirations to rule ("Render unto Caesar the things that are Caesar's"), and when it has been said further that this ethic is not a tribal ethic but a world ethic, since it arose from the soil of the already disintegrated tribal structure of the Roman Empire, it is clear that these interconnections between social situations on the one hand and psychic-ethical modes of behaviour on the other are not, it is true, measurable but can none the less be much more intensively penetrated in their essential character than if coefficients of correlation were established between the various factors. The interconnections are evident because we have used an understanding approach to those primary interdependences of experience from which these norms arose.

It has become clear that the principal propositions of the social sciences are neither mechanistically external nor formal, nor do they represent purely quantitative correlations but rather situational diagnoses in which we use, by and large, the same concrete concepts and thought-models which were created for activistic purposes in real life. It is clear, furthermore, that every social science diagnosis is closely connected with the evaluations and unconscious orientations of the observer and that the critical self-clarification of the social sciences is intimately bound up with the critical self-clarification of our orientation in the everyday world. An observer who is not fundamentally interested in the social roots of the changing ethics of the period in which he himself lives, who does not think through the problems of social life in

[1] Here I use Dilthey's expression, leaving unsettled the question as to how his use of the term is different from that above.

terms of the tensions between social strata, and who has not also discovered the fruitful aspect of resentment in his own experience, will never be in a position to see that phase of Christian ethics described above, to say nothing of being able to understand it. It is precisely in the degree in which he participates evaluationally (sympathetically or antagonistically) in the struggle for ascendancy of the lower strata, in the degree that he evaluates resentment positively or negatively, that he becomes aware of the dynamic significance of social tension and resentment. "Lower class," "social ascendancy," "resentment" instead of being formal concepts are meaningfully oriented concepts. If they were to be formalized, and the evaluations they contain distilled out of them, the thought-model characteristic of the situation, in which it is precisely resentment which produced the good and novel fruitful norm, would be totally inconceivable. The more closely one examines the word "resentment" the more clear it becomes that this apparently non-evaluative descriptive term for an attitude is replete with evaluations. If these evaluations are left out, the idea loses its concreteness. Furthermore, if the thinker had no interest in reconstructing the feeling of resentment, the tension which permeated the above-described situation of early Christianity would be entirely inaccessible to him. Thus here, too, the purposefully oriented will is the source of the understanding of the situation.

In order to work in the social sciences one must participate in the social process, but this participation in collective-unconscious striving in no wise signifies that the persons participating in it falsify the facts or see them incorrectly. Indeed, on the contrary, participation in the living context of social life is a presupposition of the understanding of the inner nature of this living context. The type of participation which the thinker enjoys determines how he shall formulate his problems. The disregard of qualitative elements and the complete restraint of the will does not constitute objectivity but is instead the negation of the essential quality of the object.

But, at the same time, the reverse — the greater the bias, the greater the objectivity — is not true. In this sphere there obtains a peculiar inner dynamic of modes of behaviour in which, through the retention of the *élan politique*, this *élan* subjects itself to an intellectual control. There is a point at which the *élan politique* collides with something, whereupon it is thrown back upon itself and begins to subject itself to critical control. There is a point where the movement of life itself, especially in its greatest crisis, elevates itself above itself and becomes aware of its own limits. This is the point where the political problem-complex of ideology and utopia becomes the concern of the sociology of knowledge, and where the scepticism and relativism arising out of the mutual destruction and devaluation of divergent political aims becomes a means of salvation. For this relativism and scepticism compel self-criticism and self-control and lead to a new conception of objectivity.

What seems to be so unbearable in life itself, namely, to continue to live with the unconscious uncovered, is the historical prerequisite of scientific critical self-awareness. In personal life, too, self-control and self-correction develop only when in our originally blind vital forward drive we come upon an obstacle which throws us back upon ourselves. In the course of this collision with other possible forms of existence, the peculiarity of our own mode of life becomes apparent to us. Even in our personal life we become masters of ourselves only when the unconscious motivations which formerly existed behind our backs suddenly come into our field of vision and thereby become accessible to conscious control. Man attains objectivity and acquires a self with reference to his conception of his world not by giving up his will to action and holding his evaluations in abeyance but in confronting and examining himself. The criterion of such self-illumination is that not only the object but we ourselves fall squarely within our field of vision. We become visible to ourselves, not just vaguely as a knowing subject as such but in a certain role hitherto hidden from us, in a situation hitherto impenetrable to us, and with motivations of which we have not been aware. In such moments the inner connection between our role, our motivations, and our type and manner of experiencing the world suddenly dawns upon us. Hence the paradox underlying these experiences, namely the opportunity for relative emancipation from social determination, increases proportionately with insight into this determination. Those persons who talk most about human freedom are those who are actually most blindly subject to social determination, inasmuch as they do not in most cases suspect the profound degree to which their conduct is determined by their interests. In contrast with this, it should be noted that it is precisely those who insist on the unconscious influence of the social determinants in conduct, who strive to overcome these determinants as much as possible. They uncover unconscious motivations in order to make those forces which formerly ruled them more and more into objects of conscious rational decision.

This illustration of how the extension of our knowledge of the world is closely related to increasing personal self-knowledge and self-control of the knowing personality is neither accidental nor peripheral. The process of the self-extension of the individual represents a typical example of the unfolding of every kind of situationally determined knowledge, i.e. of every kind of knowledge which is not merely the simple objective accumulation of information about facts and their causal connections, but which is interested in the understanding of an inner interdependence in the life process. Inner interdependence can be grasped only by the understanding method of interpretation, and the stages of this understanding of the world are bound at every step to the process of individual self-clarification. This structure, in accordance with which self-clarification makes possible the extension of our knowledge of the world about us, obtains not only for individual self-knowledge but is also the criterion of group self-clarification. Although here, too, it should again be emphasized that only individuals are capable of self-clarification (there is no such thing as a "folk mind" and groups as wholes are as incapable of self-clarification as they are of thinking), it makes a powerful difference whether an individual becomes conscious of those quite special unconscious motivations which have characterized particularly his previous thinking and acting or whether he is made aware of those elements in his motivations and outlook which tie him to the members of a particular group.

It is a problem in itself as to whether the sequence which the stages of self-clarification follow is entirely a matter of chance. We are inclined to believe that individual self-clarification occupies a position in a stream of self-clarification, the social source of which is a situation common to the different individuals. But whether we are here concerned with the self-clarification of individuals or of groups, one thing is common to both, namely, their structure. The centrally important feature of this structure is that in so far as the world does become a problem it does not do so as an object detached from the subject but rather as it impinges upon the fabric of the subject's experiences. Reality is discovered in the way in which it appears to the subject in the course of his self-extension (in the course of extending his capacity for experience and his horizon).

What we have hitherto hidden from ourselves and not integrated into our epistemology is that knowledge in the political and social sciences is, from a certain point on, different from formal mechanistic knowledge; it is different from that point where it transcends the mere enumeration of facts and correlations, and approximates the model of situationally determined knowledge to which we shall refer many times in the present work.

Once the interrelationship between social science and situationally bound thinking, as it is for instance found in political orientation, becomes evident, we have reason to investigate the positive potentialities as well as the limits and dangers of this type of thinking. It is furthermore important that we take our point of departure in that state of crisis and uncertainty in which were disclosed the dangers of this sort of thinking as well as those new possibilities of self-criticism through which it was hoped that a solution could be found.

If the problem is attacked from this point of view, the uncertainty which had become an ever more unbearable grief in public life becomes the soil from which modern social science gains entirely new insights. These fall into three main tendencies: first, the tendency towards the self-criticism of collective-unconscious motivations, in so far as they determine modern social thinking; second, the tendency towards the establishment of a new type of intellectual history which is able to interpret changes in ideas in relation to social-historical changes; and, third, the tendency towards the revision of our epistemology which up to now has not taken the social nature of thought sufficiently into account. The sociology of knowledge is, in this sense, the *systematization* of the doubt which is to be found in social life as a vague insecurity and uncertainty. The aim of this book is on the one hand the clearer theoretical formulation of one and the same problem from different angles, and on the other the elaboration of a method which will enable us, on the basis of increasingly precise criteria, to distinguish and isolate diverse styles of thinking and to relate them to the groups from which they spring. . . .

THE SOCIOLOGY OF KNOWLEDGE AND THE THEORY OF IDEOLOGY

The sociology of knowledge is closely related to, but increasingly distinguishable from, the theory of ideology, which has also emerged and developed in our own time. The study of ideologies has made it its task to unmask the more or less conscious deceptions and disguises of human interest groups, particularly those of political parties. The sociology of knowledge is concerned not so much with distortions due to a deliberate effort to deceive as with the varying ways in which objects present themselves to the subject according to the differences in social settings. Thus, mental structures are inevitably differently formed in different social and historical settings.

In accordance with this distinction we will leave to the theory of ideology only the first forms of the "incorrect" and the untrue, while one-sidedness of observation, which is not due to more or less conscious intent, will be separated from the theory of ideology and treated as the proper subject-matter of the sociology of knowledge. In the older theory of ideology, no distinction was made between these two types of false observation and statement. Today, however, it is advisable to separate more sharply these two types, both of which were formerly described as ideologies. Hence we speak of a *particular* and of a *total* conception of ideology. Under the first we include all those utterances the "falsity" of which is due to an intentional or unintentional, conscious, semi-conscious, or unconscious, deluding of one's self or of others, taking place on a psychological level and structurally resembling lies.

We speak of this conception of ideology as *particular* because it always refers only to specific assertions which may be regarded as concealments, falsifications, or lies without attacking the integrity of the *total mental structure* of the asserting subject. The sociology of knowledge, on the other hand, takes as its problem precisely this mental structure *in its totality*, as it appears in different currents of thought and historical-social groups. The sociology of knowledge does not criticize thought on the level of the assertions themselves, which may involve deceptions and disguises, but examines them on the structural or noological level, which it views as not necessarily being the same for all men, but rather as allowing the same object to take on different forms and aspects in the course of social development. Since suspicion of falsification is not included in the total conception of ideology, the use of the term "ideology" in the sociology of knowledge has no moral or denunciatory intent. It points rather to a research interest which leads to the raising of the question when and where social structures come to express themselves in the structure of assertions, and in what sense the former concretely determine the latter. In the realm of the sociology of knowledge, we shall then, as far as possible, avoid the use of the term "ideology," because of its moral connotation, and shall instead speak of the "perspective" of a thinker. By this term we mean the subject's whole mode of conceiving things as determined by his historical and social setting.

The Two Divisions of the Sociology of Knowledge

THE THEORY OF THE SOCIAL DETERMINATION OF KNOWLEDGE

The sociology of knowledge is on the one hand a theory, and on the other hand an historical-sociological method of research. As theory it may take two forms. In the first place it is a purely empirical investigation through description and structural analysis of the ways in which social relationships, in fact, influence thought. This may pass, in the second place, into an epistemological inquiry concerned with the bearing of this interrelationship upon the problem of validity. It is important to notice that these two types of inquiry are not necessarily connected and one can accept the empirical results without drawing the epistemological conclusions.

The Purely Empirical Aspect of the Investigation of the Social Determination of Knowledge. In accord with this classification and disregarding the epistemological implications as far as possible, we will present the sociology of knowledge as a theory of the social or existential determination of actual thinking. It would be well to begin by explaining what is meant by the wider term "existential determination of knowledge" ("*Seinsverbundenheit*[2] *des Wissens*"). As a concrete fact, it may be best approached by means of an illustration. The existential determination of thought may be regarded as a demonstrated fact in those realms of thought in which we can show (*a*) that the process of knowing does not actually develop historically in accordance with immanent laws, that it does not follow only from the "nature of things" or from "pure logical possibilities," and that it is not driven by an "inner dialectic." On the contrary, the emergence and the crystallization of actual thought is influenced in many decisive points by extratheoretical factors of the most diverse sort. These may be called, in contradistinction to purely theoretical factors, existential factors. This existential determination of thought will also have to be regarded as a fact (*b*) if the influence of these existential factors on the concrete content of knowledge is of more than mere peripheral importance, if they are relevant not only to the genesis of ideas, but penetrate into their forms and content and if, furthermore, they decisively determine the scope and the intensity of our experience and observation, i.e. that which we formerly referred to as the "perspective" of the subject.

Social Processes Influencing the Process of Knowledge. Considering now the first set of criteria for determining the existential connections of knowledge, i.e. the role actually played by extra-theoretical factors in the history of thought, we find that the more recent investigations undertaken in the spirit of the sociologically oriented history of thought supply an increasing amount of corroborative evidence. For even to-day the fact seems to be perfectly clear that the older method of intellectual history, which was oriented towards the *a priori* conception that changes in ideas were to be understood on the level of ideas (immanent intellectual history), blocked recognition of the penetration of the social process into the intellectual sphere. With the growing evidence of the flaws in this *a priori* assumption, an increasing number of concrete cases makes it evident that (*a*)

[2] Here we do not mean by "determination" a mechanical cause-effect sequence: we leave the meaning of "determination" open, and only empirical investigation will show us how strict is the correlation between life-situation and thought-process, or what scope exists for variations in the correlation. [The German expression "*Seinsverbundenes Wissen*" conveys a meaning which leaves the exact nature of the determinism open.]

every formulation of a problem is made possible only by a previous actual human experience which involves such a problem; (*b*) in selection from the multiplicity of data there is involved an act of will on the part of the knower; and (*c*) forces arising out of living experience are significant in the direction which the treatment of the problem follows.

In connection with these investigations, it will become more and more clear that the living forces and actual attitudes which underlie the theoretical ones are by no means merely of an individual nature, i.e. they do not have their origin in the first place in the individual's becoming aware of his interests in the course of his thinking. Rather, they arise out of the collective purposes of a group which underlie the thought of the individual, and in the prescribed outlook of which he merely participates. In this connection, it becomes more clear that a large part of thinking and knowing cannot be correctly understood, as long as its connection with existence or with the social implications of human life are not taken into account.

It would be impossible to list all the manifold social processes which, in the above sense, condition and shape our theories, and we shall, therefore, confine ourselves to a few examples (and even in these cases, we shall have to leave the detailed proof to the instances cited in the index and bibliography).

We may regard competition as such a representative case in which extra-theoretical processes affect the emergence and the direction of the development of knowledge. Competition[3] controls not merely economic activity through the mechanism of the market, not merely the course of political and social events, but furnishes also the motor impulse behind diverse interpretations of the world which, when their social background is uncovered, reveal themselves as the intellectual expressions of conflicting groups struggling for power.

As we see these social backgrounds emerge and become recognizable as the invisible forces underlying knowledge, we realize that thoughts and ideas are not the result of the isolated inspiration of great geniuses. Underlying even the profound insight of the genius are the collective historical experiences of a group which the individual takes for granted, but which should under no conditions be hypostatized as "group mind." On closer inspection it is to be seen that there is not merely one complex of collective experience with one exclusive tendency, as the theory of the folk-spirit maintained. The world is known through many different orientations because there are many simultaneous and mutually contradictory trends of thought (by no means of equal value) struggling against one another with their different interpretations of "common" experience. The clue to this conflict, therefore, is not to be found in the "object in itself" (if it were, it would be impossible to understand why the object should appear in so many different refractions), but in the very different expectations, purposes, and impulses arising out of experience. If, then, for our explanation we are thrown back upon the play and counterplay of different impulses within the social sphere, a more exact analysis will show that the cause of this conflict between concrete impulses is not to be looked for in theory itself, but in these varied opposing impulses, which in turn are rooted in the whole matrix of collective interests. These seemingly "pure theoretical" cleavages may, in the light of a sociological analysis (which uncovers the hidden intermediate steps between the original impulses to observe and the purely theoretical conclusion), be reduced, for the most part, to more fundamental philosophical differences. But the latter, in turn, are invisibly guided by the antagonism and competition between concrete, conflicting groups.

To mention only one of the many other possible bases of collective existence, out of which different interpretations of the world

[3] For concrete examples cf. the author's paper "Die Bedeutung der Konkurrenz im Gebiete des Geistigen," *op. cit.*

and different forms of knowledge may arise, we may point to the role played by the relationship between differently situated generations. This factor influences in very many cases the principles of selection, organization, and polarization of theories and points of view prevailing in a given society at a given moment. (This is given more detailed attention in the author's essay entitled "Das Problem der Generationen."[4]) From the knowledge derived from our studies on competition and generations, we have concluded that what, from the point of view of immanent intellectual history, appears to be the "inner dialectic" in the development of ideas, becomes, from the standpoint of the sociology of knowledge, the rhythmic movement in the history of ideas as affected by competition and the succession of generations.

In considering the relationship between forms of thought and forms of society, we shall recall Max Weber's[5] observation that the interest in systematization is in large part attributable to a scholastic background, that the interest in "systematic" thought is the correlate of juristic and scientific schools of thought, and that the origin of this organizing form of thought lies in the continuity of pedagogical institutions. We should also mention at this point Max Scheler's[6] significant attempt to establish the relationship between various forms of thought and certain types of groups in which alone they can arise and be elaborated.

This must suffice to indicate what is meant by the correlation between types of knowledge and of ideas, on the one hand, and the social groups and processes of which they are characteristic.

The Essential Penetration of the Social Process into the "Perspective" of Thought. Are the existential factors in the social process merely of peripheral significance, are they to be regarded merely as conditioning the origin or factual development of ideas (i.e. are they of merely genetic relevance), or do they penetrate into the "perspective" of concrete particular assertions? This is the next question we shall try to answer. The historical and social genesis of an idea would only be irrelevant to its ultimate validity if the temporal and social conditions of its emergence had no effect on its content and form. If this were the case, any two periods in the history of human knowledge would only be distinguished from one another by the fact that in the earlier period certain things were still unknown and certain errors still existed which, through later knowledge were completely corrected. This simple relationship between an earlier incomplete and a later complete period of knowledge may to a large extent be appropriate for the exact sciences (although indeed to-day the notion of the stability of the categorical structure of the exact sciences is, compared with the logic of classical physics, considerably shaken). For the history of the cultural sciences, however, the earlier stages are not quite so simply superseded by the later stages, and it is not so easily demonstrable that early errors have subsequently been corrected. Every epoch has its fundamentally new approach and its characteristic point of view, and consequently sees the "same" object from a new perspective.

Hence the thesis that the historico-social process is of essential significance for most of the domains of knowledge receives support from the fact that we can see from most of the concrete assertions of human beings when and where they arose, when and where they were formulated. The history of art has fairly conclusively shown that art forms may be definitely dated according to their style, since each form is possible only under given historical conditions and reveals the characteristics of that epoch. What is true of art also holds *mutatis mutandis* good for knowledge. Just as in art we can date particular forms on the ground of their definite association with

[4] *Kölner Vierteljahrshefte für Soziologie* (1928), vol. viii.

[5] Cf. Max Weber, *Wirtschaft und Gesellschaft*, *op. cit.*, particularly the section on the sociology of law.

[6] Cf. especially his works, *Die Wissensformen und die Gesellschaft*, Leipzig, 1926, and *Die Formen des Wissens und der Bildung*, i, Bonn, 1925.

a particular period of history so in the case of knowledge we can detect with increasing exactness the perspective due to a particular historical setting. Further, by the use of pure analysis of thought-structure, we can determine when and where the world presented itself in such, and only in such a light to the subject that made the assertion, and the analysis may frequently be carried to the point where the more inclusive question may be answered, *why* the world presented itself in precisely such a manner.

Whereas the assertion (to cite the simplest case) that twice two equals four gives no clue as to when, where, and by whom it was formulated, it is always possible in the case of a work in the social sciences to say whether it was inspired by the "historical school," or "positivism," or "Marxism," and from what stage in the development of each of these it dates. In assertions of this sort, we may speak of an "infiltration of the social position" of the investigator into the results of his study and of the "situational-relativity" ("*Situationsgebundenheit*"), or the relationship of these assertions to the underlying reality.

"Perspective" in this sense signifies the manner in which one views an object, what one perceives in it, and how one construes it in his thinking. Perspective, therefore, is something more than a merely formal determination of thinking. It refers also to qualitative elements in the structure of thought, elements which must necessarily be overlooked by a purely formal logic. It is precisely these factors which are responsible for the fact that two persons, even if they apply the same formal-logical rules, e.g. the law of contradiction or the formula of the syllogism, in an identical manner, may judge the same object very differently.

Of the traits by which the perspective of an assertion may be characterized, and of the criteria which aid us to attribute it to a given epoch or situation, we will adduce only a few examples: analysis of the meaning of the concepts being used; the phenomenon of the counter-concept; the absence of certain concepts; the structure of the categorical apparatus; dominant models of thought; level of abstraction; and the ontology that is presupposed. In what follows, we intend to show, by means of a few examples, the applicability of these identifying traits and criteria in the analysis of perspective. At the same time, it will be shown how far the social position of the observer affects his outlook.

We will begin with the fact that the same word, or the same concept in most cases, means very different things when used by differently situated persons.

When, in the early years of the nineteenth century, an old-style German conservative spoke of "freedom" he meant thereby the right of each estate to live according to its privileges (liberties). If he belonged to the romantic-conservative and Protestant movement he understood by it "inner freedom," i.e. the right of each individual to live according to his own individual personality. Both of these groups thought in terms of the "*qualitative conception of freedom*" because they understood freedom to mean the right to maintain either their historical or their inner, individual distinctiveness.

When a liberal of the same period used the term "freedom," he was thinking of freedom *from* precisely those privileges which to the old-style conservative appeared to be the very basis of all freedom. The liberal conception was, then, an "*equalitarian conception of freedom*," in the case of which "being free" meant that all men have the same fundamental rights at their disposal. The liberal conception of freedom was that of a group which sought to overthrow the external, legal, non-equalitarian social order. The conservative idea of freedom, on the other hand, was that of a stratum which did not wish to see any changes in the external order of things, hoping that events would continue in their traditional uniqueness; in order to support things as they were, they also had to divert the issues concerning freedom from the external political realm to the inner non-political realm. That the liberal saw only one, and the conservative only another side of the concept and of the problem was clearly and demonstrably connected with their respective positions in the social and political structure.[7] In brief, even in the formulation of concepts, the angle of vision is guided by the observer's interests. Thought, namely, is directed in accordance with what a particular social group expects. Thus, out of the possible data of experience, every concept combines within itself only that which, in the light of the investigators' interests, it is essential to grasp and to incorporate. Hence, for example, the conservative concept of *Volksgeist* was most probably formulated as a counter-concept in opposition to the progressive concept of "the spirit of the age" (*Zeitgeist*). The analysis of the concepts in a given conceptual scheme itself provides the most direct approach to the perspective of distinctively situated strata.

The absence of certain concepts indicates very often not only the absence of certain points of view, but also the absence of a definite drive to come to grips with certain life-problems. Thus, for example, the relatively late appearance in history of the concept "social" is evidence for the fact that the questions implied in the concept "social" had never been posited before, and likewise that a definite mode of experience signified by the concept "social" did not exist before.

But not only do the concepts in their concrete contents diverge from one another in accordance with differing social positions, but the basic categories of thought may likewise differ.

So, for example, early nineteenth century German conservatism (we draw most of our illustrations from this epoch because it has been studied more thoroughly from a sociological point of view than any other), and contemporary conservatism too, for that matter, tend to use morphological categories which do not break up the concrete totality of the data of experience, but seek rather to preserve it in all its uniqueness. As opposed to the morphological approach, the analytical approach characteristic of the parties of the left, broke down every concrete totality in order to arrive at smaller, more general, units which might then be recombined through the category of causality or functional integration. Here it becomes our task not only to indicate the fact that people in different social positions think differently, but to make intelligible the causes for their different ordering of the material of experiences by different categories. The groups oriented to the left intend to make something new out of the world as it is given, and therefore they divert their glance from things as they are, they become abstract and atomize the given situation into its component elements in order to recombine them anew. Only that appears configuratively or morphologically which we are prepared to accept without further ado, and which, fundamentally, we do not wish to change. Still further, by means of the configurative conception, it is intended to stabilize precisely those elements which are still in flux, and at the same time to invoke sanction for what exists because it is as it is. All this makes it quite clear to what extent even abstract categories and principles of organization, which are seemingly far removed from the political struggle, have their origin in the meta-theoretical pragmatic nature of the human mind, and in the more profound depths of the psyche and of consciousness. Hence to speak here of conscious deception in the sense of creating ideologies is out of the question.

The next factor which may serve to characterize the perspective of thought is the so-called thought-model; i.e. the model that is implicitly in the mind of a person when he proceeds to reflect about an object.

It is well known, for instance, that once the typology of objects in the natural sciences was formulated, and the categories and methods of thought derived from these types became models, it was thenceforth hoped to solve all the problems in the other realms of existence, including the social, by that method. (This tendency is represented by

[7] Cf. the author's "Das konservative Denken," *Archiv für Sozialwissenschaft und Sozialpolitik*, vol. 57, pp. 90ff.

the mechanistic-atomistic conception of social phenomena.)

It is significant to observe that when this happened, as in all similar cases, not all the strata of society oriented themselves primarily to this single model of thought. The landed nobility, the displaced classes, and the peasantry were not heard from during this historical period. The new character of cultural development and the ascendant forms of orientation towards the world belonged to a mode of life other than their own. The forms of the ascendant world-perspective, modelled on the principles of natural science, came upon these classes as if from the outside. As the interplay of social forces brought other groups, representing the above-mentioned classes and expressing their life-situation, into the forefront of history, the opposing models of thought, as, for instance, the "*organismic*" and the "*personalistic*" were played off against the "functional-mechanistic" type of thought. Thus Stahl, for instance, who stood at the apex of this development, was already able to establish connections between thought-models and political currents.[8]

Behind every definite question and answer is implicitly or explicitly to be found a model of how fruitful thinking can be carried on. If one were to trace in detail, in each individual case, the origin and the radius of diffusion of a certain thought-model, one would discover the peculiar affinity it has to the social position of given groups and their manner of interpreting the world. By these groups we mean not merely classes, as a dogmatic type of Marxism would have it, but also generations, status groups, sects, occupational groups, schools, etc. Unless careful attention is paid to highly differentiated social groupings of this sort and to the corresponding differentiations in concepts, categories, and thought-models, i.e. unless the problem of the relation between super- and sub-structure is refined, it would be impossible to demonstrate that corresponding to the wealth of types of knowledge and perspectives which have appeared in the course of history there are similar differentiations in the substructure of society. Of course we do not intend to deny that of all the above-mentioned social groupings and units class stratification is the most significant, since in the final analysis all the other social groups arise from and are transformed as parts of the more basic conditions of production and domination. None the less the investigator who, in the face of the variety of types of thought, attempts to place them correctly can no longer be content with the undifferentiated class concept, but must reckon with the existing social units and factors that condition social position, aside from those of class.

Another characteristic of the perspective is to be found by investigating the level of abstraction, beyond which a given theory does not progress, or the degree to which it resists theoretical, systematic formulation.

It is never an accident when a certain theory, wholly or in part, fails to develop beyond a given stage of relative abstractness and offers resistance to further tendencies towards becoming more concrete, either by frowning upon this tendency towards concreteness or declaring it to be irrelevant. Here, too, the social position of the thinker is significant.

Precisely in the case of Marxism and the relation it bears to the findings of the sociology of knowledge can it be shown how an interrelationship can often be formulated only in that form of concreteness which is peculiar to that particular standpoint. It can be shown in the case of Marxism that an observer whose view is bound up with a given social position will by himself never succeed in singling out the more general and theoretical aspects which are implicit in the concrete observations that he makes. It might have been expected, for instance, that long ago Marxism would have formulated in a more theoretical way the fundamental findings of the sociology of knowledge concerning the relationship between human thought and the conditions of existence *in general*, especially

[8] The history of theories of the state, especially as viewed by F. Oppenheimer in his *System der Soziologie* (vol. ii, "Der Staat") is a treasure of illustrative material.

since its discovery of the theory of ideology also implied at least the beginnings of the sociology of knowledge. That this implication could never be brought out and theoretically elaborated, and at best only came partially into view, was due, however, to the fact that, in the concrete instance, this relationship was perceived only in the thought of the opponent. It was probably due, furthermore, to a subconscious reluctance to think out the implications of a concretely formulated insight to a point where the theoretical formulations latent in it would be clear enough to have a disquieting effect on one's own position. Thus we see how the narrowed focus which a given position imposes and the driving impulses which govern its insights tend to obstruct the general and theoretical formulation of these views and to restrict the capacity for abstraction. There is a tendency to abide by the particular view that is immediately obtainable, and to prevent the question from being raised as to whether the fact that knowledge is bound up with existence is not inherent in the human thought-structure as such. In addition to this, the tendency in Marxism to shy away from a general, sociological formulation may frequently be traced to a similar limitation which a given point of view imposes on a method of thinking. For instance, one is not even allowed to raise the question whether "impersonalization" (*Verdinglichung*), as elaborated by Marx and Lukács, is a more or less general phenomenon of consciousness, or whether capitalistic impersonalization is merely one particular form of it. Whereas this overemphasis on concreteness and historicism arises out of a particular social location, the opposite tendency, namely the immediate flight into the highest realms of abstraction and formalization, may, as Marxism has rightly emphasized, lead to an obscuring of the concrete situation and its unique character. This could be demonstrated once more in the case of "formal sociology."

We do not wish in any way to call into question the legitimacy of formal sociology as one possible type of sociology. When, however, in the face of the tendency to introduce further concreteness into the formulation of sociological problems, it sets itself up as the only sociology, it is unconsciously guided by motives similar to those which prevented its historical forerunner, the bourgeois-liberal mode of thought, from ever getting beyond an abstract and generalizing mode of observation in its theory. It shies away from dealing historically, concretely, and individually with the problems of society for fear that its own inner antagonisms, for instance the antagonisms of capitalism itself, might become visible. In this it resembles the crucial bourgeois discussion of the problem of freedom, in which the problem usually was and is posited only theoretically and abstractly. And even when it is so posited, the question of freedom is always one of political, rather than of social, rights, since, if the latter sphere were considered, the factors of property and class position in their relation to freedom and equality would inevitably come to light.

To summarize: the approach to a problem, the level on which the problem happens to be formulated, the stage of abstraction and the stage of concreteness that one hopes to attain, are all and in the same way bound up with social existence. . . .

The Acquisition of Perspective as a Pre-condition for the Sociology of Knowledge. For the son of a peasant who has grown up within the narrow confines of his village and spends his whole life in the place of his birth, the mode of thinking and speaking characteristic of that village is something that he takes entirely for granted. But for the country lad who goes to the city and adapts himself gradually to city life, the rural mode of living and thinking ceases to be something to be taken for granted. He has won a certain detachment from it, and he distinguishes now, perhaps quite consciously, between "rural" and "urban" modes of thought and ideas. In this distinction lie the first beginnings of that approach which the sociology of knowledge seeks to develop in full detail. That which within a given group is accepted as absolute appears to the outsider conditioned by the group situation and recognized as partial (in this case, as "rural"). This type of knowledge presupposes a more detached perspective.

This detached perspective can be gained in the following ways: (*a*) a member of a group leaves his social position (by ascending to a higher class, emigration, etc.); (*b*) the basis of existence of a whole group shifts in relation to its traditional norms and institutions;[9] (*c*) within the same society two or more socially determined modes of interpretation come into conflict and, in criticizing one another, render one another transparent and establish perspectives with reference to each other. As a result, a detached perspective, through which the outlines of the contrasting modes of thought are discovered, comes within the range of possibility for all the different positions, and later gets to be the recognized mode of thinking. We have already indicated that the social genesis of the sociology of knowledge rests primarily upon the last mentioned possibility.

Relationism. What has already been said should hardly leave any doubt as to what is meant when the procedure of the sociology of knowledge is designated as "relational." When the urbanized peasant boy, who characterizes certain political, philosophical, or social opinions to be found among his relatives as "rustic," he no longer discusses these opinions as a homogeneous participant, that is, by dealing directly with the specific content of what is said. Rather he relates them to a certain mode of interpreting the world which, in turn, is ultimately related to a certain social structure which constitutes its situation. This is an instance of the "relational" procedure. We shall deal later with the fact that when assertions are treated in this way it is not implied that they are false. The sociology of knowledge goes beyond what, in some such crude way as this, people frequently do to-day, only in so far as it consciously and systematically subjects all intellectual phenomena without exception, to the question: In connection with what social structure did they arise and are they valid? Relating individual ideas to the total structure of a given historico-social subject should not be confused with a philosophical relativism which denies the validity of any standards and of the existence of order in the world. Just as the fact that every measurement in space hinges upon the nature of light does not mean that our measurements are arbitrary, but merely that they are only valid in relation to the nature of light, so in the same way not relativism in the sense of arbitrariness but *relationism* applies to our discussions. Relationism does not signify that there are no criteria of rightness and wrongness in a discussion. It does insist, however, that it lies in the nature of certain assertions that they cannot be formulated absolutely, but only in terms of the perspective of a given situation.

Particularization. Having described the relational process, as conceived by the sociology of knowledge, the question will inevitably be raised: what can it tell us about the validity of an assertion that we would not know if we had not been able to relate it to the standpoint of the assertor? Have we said anything about the truth or falsity of a statement when we have shown that it is to be imputed to liberalism or to Marxism?

Three answers may be made to this question: —

(*a*) It may be said that the absolute validity of an assertion is denied when its structural relationship to a given social situation has been shown. In this sense there is indeed a current in the sociology of knowledge and in the theory of ideology which accepts the demonstration of this sort of relationship as a refutation of the opponents' assertion, and which would use this method as a device for annihilating the validity of all assertions.

(*b*) In opposition to this, there may be

[9] A good example is furnished by Karl Renner, in *Die Rechtsinstitute des Privatrechts* (J. C. B. Mohr, Tübingen, 1929).

another answer, namely that the imputations that the sociology of knowledge establishes between a statement and its assertor tells us nothing concerning the truth-value of the assertion, since the manner in which a statement originates does not affect its validity. Whether an assertion is liberal or conservative in and of itself gives no indication of its correctness.

(*c*) There is a third possible way of judging the value of the assertions that the sociologist of knowledge makes, which represents our own point of view. It differs from the first view in that it shows that the mere factual demonstration and identification of the social position of the assertor as yet tells us nothing about the truth-value of his assertion. It implies only the suspicion that this assertion might represent merely a partial view. As over against the second alternative, it maintains that it would be incorrect to regard the sociology of knowledge as giving no more than a description of the actual conditions under which an assertion arises (factual-genesis). Every complete and thorough sociological analysis of knowledge delimits, in content as well as structure, the view to be analysed. In other words, it attempts not merely to establish the existence of the relationship, but at the same time to particularize its scope and the extent of its validity. The implications of this will be set forth in greater detail.

What the sociology of knowledge intends to do by its analysis was fairly clearly brought out in the example we cited of the peasant boy. The discovery and identification of his earlier mode of thought as "rural," as contrasted with "urban," already involves the insight that the different perspectives are not merely particular in that they presuppose different ranges of vision and different sectors of the total reality, but also in that the interests and the powers of perception of the different perspectives are conditioned by the social situations in which they arose and to which they are relevant.

Already upon this level the relational process tends to become a particularizing process, for one does not merely relate the assertion to a standpoint but, in doing so, restricts its claim to validity which at first was absolute to a narrower scope.

A fully developed sociology of knowledge follows the same approach which we have illustrated above in the case of the peasant boy, except that it follows a deliberate method. With the aid of a consistently elaborated analysis of the perspective, particularization acquires a guiding instrument and a set of criteria for treating problems of imputation. The range and degree of comprehension of each of these several points of view becomes measurable and delimitable through their categorical apparatus and the variety of meanings which each presents. The orientation towards certain meanings and values which inheres in a given social position (the outlook and attitude conditioned by the collective purposes of a group), and the concrete reasons for the different perspectives which the same situation presents to the different positions in it thus become even more determinable, intelligible, and subject to methodical study through the perfection of the sociology of knowledge. . . .

Verstehen and the Method of "Disciplined Subjectivity"

54

The Nature of Clinical Evidence

ERIK H. ERIKSON

I

The letter of invitation to contribute to this Colloquium puts into the center of my assignment the question "*How does a . . . clinician really work?*" and gives to this task the necessary latitude by inquiring about the clinician's reliance on *intuition* ("or some other version of personal judgment") and about the use of *objectified tests*, ("relatively uniform among clinicians of different theoretical persuasions"). The letter concludes: "To the extent that intuition plays a role, in what way does the clinician seek to discipline its operation: by his conceptual framework? by long personal experience?" This emphasizes, within the inquiry of how a clinician works, the question of how he thinks.

Such an invitation is a hospitable one, encouraging the guest, as it were, to come as he is. It spares the clinician whatever temptation he might otherwise feel to claim inclusion in the social register of long established sciences by demonstrating that he, too, can behave the way they do. He can state from the outset that in one essay he can hardly offer more than phenomenological groundwork, perhaps necessarily of a markedly personal nature.

The invitation, in my case, is addressed to a psychotherapist of a particular "persuasion": my training is that of a Freudian psychoanalyst, and I train others — in the vast majority physicians — in this method. I shall make a sincere attempt to place vocation over persuasion and to formulate how the nature of clinical evidence is determined by a clinician's daily task. If I, nevertheless, seem to feel beholden to Freud's conceptual system — that is, a system originated around the turn of this century by a physician schooled in physicalist physiology — the reason is not narrowly partisan: few will deny that from such transfer of physicalistic concepts to psychology new modes of clinical thinking have developed in our time.

"Clinical," of course, is an old word. In the days when the church was the primary guardian of man's well-being, clinical referred to a priest's administrations at the deathbed — then the only gateway to true health, since all through life man owed a death. Later, the word was primarily applied to medical ministrations, as science and humanism joined forces in taking the short-range point of view that man owes himself a long and healthy life, or at any rate one free from disease. In our time and in the Western world, the word clinical is expanding rapidly to include not only medical but also social considerations, not only physical well-being but also mental health, not only matters of cure but also of prevention, not only therapy but also research. This means that clinical work is now allied with many brands of evidence and overlaps with many methodologies. Yet, I feel called upon to speak of the nature of evidence gathered in the individual clinical encounter itself.

Let me briefly review the elements making up the clinical core of medical work in general as the encounter of two people, one in need of help, the other in the possession of professional methods. Their *contract* is a therapeutic one:

Reprinted with permission of The Macmillan Company, New York, from *Evidence and Inference* edited by Daniel Lerner, pp. 73–95. © The Free Press 1959.

in exchange for a fee, and for information revealed in confidence, the physician promises to act for the benefit of the individual patient, within the ethos of the profession. There usually is a *complaint*, consisting of the description of more or less circumscribed pain or dysfunction, and there are *symptoms*, visible or otherwise localizable. There follows an attempt at an *anamnesis*, an etiological reconstruction of the disturbance, and an *examination*, carried out by means of the physician's naked senses or supported by instruments, which may include the laboratory methods. In evaluating the evidence and in arriving at diagnostic and prognostic inferences (which are really the clinical form of a *prediction*), the physician *thinks clinically* — that is, he scans in his mind different *models* in which different modes of knowledge have found condensation: the *anatomical* structure of the body, the *physiological* functioning of body parts, or the *pathological* processes underlying classified disease entities. A clinical prediction takes its clues from the complaint, the symptoms, and the anamnesis, and makes inferences based on a rapid and mostly preconscious cross-checking against each other of anatomical, physiological and pathological models. On this basis, a *preferred method of treatment* is selected. This is the simplest clinical encounter. In it the patient lends parts of himself to a laboratory procedure and as far as he possibly can, ceases to be a person, i.e., a creature which is more than the sum of its organs.

Any good doctor knows, however, that the patient's complaint is more extensive than his symptom, and the state of sickness more comprehensive than localized pain or dysfunction. As an old Jew put it (and old Jews have a way of speaking for the victims of all nations): "Doctor, my bowels are sluggish, my feet hurt, my heart jumps — and you know, Doctor, I myself don't feel so well either." The treatment, thus, is not limited to local adjustments; it must, and in the case of a "good" doctor automatically does, include a wider view of the complaint, and entail corresponding *interpretations* of the symptom to the patient, often making the "patient himself" an assistant observer and associate doctor. This is especially important, as subsequent appointments become part of a *developing case-history*, which step for step verifies or contradicts whatever predictions had been made and put to test earlier.

This, then, for better or for worse, is the traditional core of the clinical encounter, whether it deals with physical or with mental complaints. But in the special case of the *psychotherapeutic encounter*, a specimen of which I intend to present and to analyze presently, three items crowd out all the others, namely, *complaint*, *anamnesis*, and *interpretation*. What goes on in the therapist's mind between the verbal complaint addressed to him and the verbal interpretation given in return — this, I take it, is the question to be examined here. But this means: in what way can the psychological clinician make his own perception and thought reliable in the face of the patient's purely verbal and social expression, and in the absence of nonverbal supportive instruments? At this point I am no longer quite so sure that the invitation to "tell us how a . . . clinician really works" was very friendly, after all. For you must suspect that the psychotherapist, in many ways, uses the setting and the terminology of a medical and even a laboratory approach, claiming recourse to an anatomy, a physiology, and a pathology of the mind, without matching the traditional textbook clarity of medical science in any way. To put it briefly, the element of subjectivity, both in the patient's complaints and in the therapist's interpretations, may be vastly greater than in a strictly medical encounter, although this element is in principle not absent from any clinical approach.

Indeed, there is no choice but to put subjectivity into the center of an inquiry into evidence and inference in clinical work. The psychotherapist shares with any clinician the Hippocratic fact that hour by hour he must fulfill a *contract* with individuals who offer themselves to cure and study and who surrender much of their most personal inviolacy in exchange for the expectation that they will emerge from the encounter more whole and less fragmented than when they entered it.

The psychotherapist shares with all clinicians the further requirement that even while facing most intimate and emotional matters, he must maintain a constant inner traffic between his often dramatic observations and his conceptual models, however crude they may be. But more than any other clinician the psychotherapist must include in his field of observation a *specific self-awareness* in the very act of perceiving his patient's actions and reactions. I shall therefore not dwell on the various ways and means, widely invented and refined in our day, of objectifying the clinician's subjectivity through the introduction of essentially non-clinical checks into the clinical procedure. Rather, I shall claim that there is a core of *disciplined subjectivity* in clinical work which it is neither desirable nor possible altogether to replace with seemingly more objective methods — methods which originate, as it were, in the machine-tooling of other kinds of work.

II

As I proceed with the task of describing how the clinical method in psychotherapy "actually works," I find that I tentatively place myself next to the historian, although with no intention of crowding him. The words "history taking" and "case history" as used in the clinical field are more than mere figures of speech. They may serve us as a first step in making objective that element of subjectivity which in essence characterizes all the clinical arts and sciences.

R. G. Collingwood defines as an historical process one "in which the past, so far as it is historically known, survives in the present." Thus being "itself a process of thought . . . it exists only in so far as the minds which are parts of it know themselves for parts of it." And again: "History is the life of mind itself which is not mind except so far as it *both lives in historical process and knows itself as so living*."[1]

It is not my task to argue the philosophy of history. The analogy between the clinician and the historian as defined by Collingwood to me centers in the case-historian's highly "self-conscious" function in the act of history-taking, and thus in the process of the case. Beyond this the analogy breaks down; it could remain relevant for our work only if the historian were also a kind of clinical statesman, correcting events as he records them, and recording as he directs. Such a conscious clinician-historian-statesman may well emerge generations hence from our joint work, although by then he may not use our terms or be aware of our dilemmas. Some of you may already see him seeking a foothold in such crises as economic "recessions," as he alternately interprets what he observes as cyclic, pathological or beneficial, and makes history as he thus interprets it.

Let me restate the psychotherapeutic encounter, then, as an historical one. A person has declared an emergency and has surrendered his self-regulation to a treatment procedure. Besides having become a subjective *patient*, he has accepted the role of a formal *client*. To some degree, he has had to interrupt his autonomous life-history as lived in the unself-conscious balances of his private and his public life in order, for a while, to "favor" a part-aspect of himself and to observe it with the diagnostic help of a curative method: as he is "under observation," he becomes self-observant. As a patient he is inclined, and as a client encouraged, to historicize his own position by thinking back to the onset of the disturbance, and to ponder what world order (magic, scientific, ethical) was violated and must be restored before his "normal" place in history can be reassumed. He participates in becoming a *case*, a fact which he may live down socially, but which, nevertheless, may forever change his own opinion of himself.

The clinician, in turn, appointed to judge the bit of interrupted life put before him, and to introduce himself and his method into it, finds himself part of another man's most intimate life history. Luckily he also remains

[1] R. G. Collingwood, *The Idea of History* (New York: Oxford University Press, 1956), pp. 226–227.

the functionary of a healing profession with a systematic orientation, based on a coherent world image — be it the theory that man is surrounded by evil spirits, or under the temptation of the devil, or the victim of chemical poisons, or subject to inner conflicts, or the representative of destructive social forces. But in inviting his client to look at himself with the help of professional theories and techniques the clinician makes himself part of the client's life history, even as he asks the client to become a case history in the annals of healing.

In northern California I knew an old Shaman woman who laughed merrily at my conception of mental disease, and then sincerely — to the point of ceremonial tears — told me of her way of sucking the "pains" out of her patients. She was as convinced of her ability to cure and to understand as I was of mine. While occupying extreme opposites in the history of American psychiatry, we felt like colleagues. This feeling was based on some joint sense of the historical relativity of all psychotherapy: the relativity of the patient's outlook on his symptoms; of the role he assumes by dint of being a patient; of the kind of help which he seeks; and of the kinds of help he finds available. The old Shaman woman and I disagreed about the locus of emotional sickness, what it was, and what specific methods would cure it. Yet, when she related the origin of a child's illness to the familial tensions existing within her tribe, when she attributed the "pain" (which had gotten "under a child's skin") to his grandmother's sorcery (ambivalence) I knew she dealt with the same forces, and with the same kinds of conviction, as I did in my part of American culture and in my professional nook. This experience has been repeated in discussions with colleagues who, although not necessarily more "primitive," are oriented toward different psychiatric "persuasions."

To summarize: the disciplined psychotherapist today finds himself heir to medical methods and concepts, and allied with the procedures of the biological sciences. On the other hand, he recognizes his activities as a function of historical processes, and is forced to conclude that in some sense he is "making history" as he "takes" it.

III

It is in such apparent quicksand that we must seek the tracks of clinical evidence. No wonder that often the only clinical material which impresses some as being at all "scientific" is the evidence of the auxiliary methods of psychotherapy — neurological examination, chemical analysis, sociological study, psychological experiment, etc. — all of which derive their laws of evidence from a non-clinical field, and each of which, strictly speaking, puts the patient into nontherapeutic conditions of observation. Each of these methods may "objectify" *some* matters immensely, provide inestimable supportive evidence for *some* theories, and lead to independent methods of cure in *some* classes of patients. But it is not of the nature of the evidence provided in the psychotherapeutic encounter itself.

To introduce such evidence, I need a specimen. This will consist of my reporting to you what a patient *said* to me, how he *behaved* in doing so and what I, in turn, *thought* and *did* — a highly suspect method. And, indeed, we may well stand at the beginning of a period when consultation rooms (already airier and lighter than Freud's) will have, as it were, many more doors open in the direction of an enlightened community's resources, even as they now have research windows in the form of one-way screens, cameras, and recording equipment. For the kind of evidence to be highlighted here, however, it is still essential that, for longer periods or for shorter ones, these doors be closed, soundproof, and impenetrable.

I am not trying to ward off legitimate study of the setting from which our examples come. I know only too well that many of our interpretations seem to be of the variety of that given by one Jew to another in a Polish railroad station. "Where are you going?" asked the first. "To Minsk," said the other.

"To Minsk!" exclaimed the first. "You say you go to Minsk so that I should believe you go to Pinsk! You are going to Minsk anyway — so why do you lie?" There is a widespread prejudice that the psychotherapist, point for point, uncovers what he claims the patient "really," and often unconsciously, had in mind, and that he has sufficient Pinsk-Minsk reversals in his technical arsenal to come out with the flat assertion that the evidence is on the side of his claim. It is for this very reason that I will try to demonstrate what method there may be in clinical judgment. I will select as my specimen the most subjective of all data, a dream report.

A young man in his early twenties comes to his therapeutic hour and reports that he has had the most disturbing dream of his life. The dream, he says, vividly recalls his state of panic at the time of the "mental breakdown" which caused him to enter treatment half a year earlier. He cannot let go of the dream; it seemed painfully real on awakening; and even in the hour of reporting the dream-state seems still vivid enough to threaten the patient's sense of reality. He is afraid that this is the end of his sanity.

The dream: "*There was a big face sitting in a buggy of the horse-and-buggy days. The face was completely empty, and there was horrible, slimy, snaky hair all around it. I am not sure it wasn't my mother*." The dream report itself, given with wordy plaintiveness, is as usual followed by a variety of incidental reports, protestations and exclamations, which at one point give way to a rather coherent account of the patient's relationship with his deceased grandfather, a country parson. Here the patient's mood changes to a deeply moved and moving admission of desperate nostalgia for cultural and personal values once observed and received.

Everything said in this hour is linked, of course, with the material of previous appointments. It must be understood that whatever answer can come of one episode will owe its clarity to the fact that it responds to previous questions and complements previous half-answers. Such *evidential continuity* can be only roughly sketched here; even to account for this one hour would take many hours. Let me briefly state, then, that I listened to the patient, who faced me in an easy chair, with only occasional interruptions for clarification, and that I gave him a résumé of what sense his dream had made to me only at the conclusion of the appointment. It so happened that this interpretation proved convincing to us both and, in the long run, strategic for the whole treatment which, incidentally, ended well.

As I turn to the task of indicating what inferences helped me to formulate one of the most probable of the many possible meanings of this dream report I must ask you to join me in what Freud has called "free-floating attention," an attention which turns inward to the observer's ruminations while remaining turned outward to the field of observation, and which, far from focusing on any one item too intentionally, rather waits to be impressed by recurring themes. These will first faintly but ever more insistently signal the nature of the patient's distress and its location. To find the zone, the position, and the danger I must avoid for the moment all temptations to go off on *one* tangent in order to prove it alone as relevant. It is rather the gradual establishment of strategic intersections on a number of tangents that eventually makes it possible to locate in the observed phenomena that central core which comprises the "evidence."

IV

The patient's behavior and report confront me with a crisis, and it is my first task to perceive where the patient stands in the treatment procedure, and what I must do next. What a clinician must do first and last depends, of course, on the setting of his work. Mine is an open residential institution, working with severe neuroses, on the borderline of psychosis or psychopathy. In such a setting, our patients may display, in their most regressed moments, the milder forms of a disturbance in the sense of reality; in their daily behavior, they usually try to entertain, educate, and employ themselves in rational and useful ways; and in their best moments, they can be expected to be insightful and at times creative. The hospital thus can be said to take a number of risks, and to provide, on the other hand, special opportunities for the patient's abilities to work, to be active, and to share in social responsibilities. That a patient fits into this setting has been established in advance by several weeks of probationary evaluation. During this period the patient's history has been taken in psychiatric interviews with him and perhaps with members of his family; he has been given a physical examination by a physician and has been confronted with standardized tests by psychologists who perform their work "blindly," that is without knowledge of the patient's history; and finally, the results have been presented to the whole staff at a meeting, at the conclusion of which the patient is interviewed by the medical director, questioned by staff members, and assigned to "his therapist." Such preliminary screening has provided the therapist with an over-all diagnosis which defines a certain range of expectable mental states, indicating the patient's special danger points and his special prospects for improvement. Needless to say, not even the best preparation can quite predict what depths and heights may be reached once the therapeutic process gets under way.

A dream report of the kind just mentioned, in a setting of this kind, thus will first of all impress the clinical observer as a diagnostic sign. This is an "anxiety dream." An anxiety dream may happen to anybody, and a mild perseverance of the dream state into the day is not pathological as such. But this patient's dream appears to be only the visual center of a severe affective disturbance: no doubt if such a state were to persist it could precipitate him into a generalized panic such as brought him to our clinic in the first place. The original test report had put the liability of the patient's state into these words: "The tests indicate borderline psychotic features in an inhibited, obsessive-compulsive character. However, the patient seems to be able to take spontaneously adequate distance from these borderline tendencies. He seems, at present, to be struggling to strengthen a rather precarious control over aggressive impulses, and probably feels a good deal of anxiety." The course of the treatment has confirmed this and other test results. The report of this horrible dream which intrudes itself on the patient's waking life now takes its place beside the data of the tests, and the range and spectrum of the patient's moods and states as observed in the treatment, and shows him on the lowest level attained since admission, i.e. relatively closest to an *inability* "to take adequate distance from his borderline tendencies."

The first "prediction" to be made is whether this dream is the sign of an impending collapse, or, on the contrary, a potentially beneficial clinical crisis. The first would mean that the patient is slipping away from me and that I must think, as it were, of the emergency net; the second, that he is reaching out for me with an important message which I must try to understand and answer. I decided for the latter alternative. Although the patient acted as if he were close to a breakdown, I had the impression that, in fact, there was a challenge in all this, and a rather angry one. I can explain this only by presenting a number of inferences of a kind made very rapidly in a clinician's mind, but demonstrable only through an analysis of the patient's verbal and behavioral communications and of my own intellectual and affective reactions.

V

The experienced dream interpreter often finds himself "reading" a dream report as a practitioner of medicine scans an X-ray picture: especially in the cases of wordy or reticent patients or of lengthy case reports, a dream often lays bare the stark inner facts. At this point one may ask: But can *two* clinicians look at the same dream and see the same "stark inner facts"? This is a legitimate question, which I shall try to answer below.

Let us first pay attention to the dream images. The main item is a large face without identifying features. There are no spoken words, and there is no motion. There are no people in the dream. Most apparent then, are omissions. I say this on the basis of an inventory of dream configurations, which I published in a review of "the first dream subjected to exhaustive analysis" by Freud.[2] Such a methodological step is elementary, but clinical workers often fail to make explicit, even to themselves, what inventories of evidential signs they regularly but unwittingly scan. In my article I suggested a list of configurations against which the student can check the individual dream production for present and absent dream configurations. It must suffice here to indicate that the dream being discussed is characterized by a significant omission of important items present in most dreams: motion, action, people, spoken words. All we have instead is a motionless image of a faceless face, which may or may not represent the patient's mother.

The patient's precarious state and the urgency with which he looked at me when telling me his dream induced me to ignore for the moment the reference to his mother. His facial and tonal expression rather reminded me of a series of critical moments during his treatment when he was obviously not quite sure that I was "all there" and apprehensive that I might disapprove of him and disappear in anger. This focused my attention on a question which the clinician must sooner or later consider when faced with any of his patient's productions, namely, his own place in them.

While the psychotherapist should not force his way into his patient's dream images, sometimes he does well to raise discreetly the masks of the various dream persons to see whether he can find his own face or person or role represented. Here the mask is an empty face, with plenty of horrible hair. My often unruly white hair surrounding a reddish face easily enters my patients' imaginative productions, either as the feature of a benevolent Santa Claus or that of a threatening ogre. At that particular time, I had to consider another autobiographic item. In the third month of therapy, I had "abandoned" the patient to have an emergency operation (which he, to use clinical shorthand, had ascribed to his evil eye, that is to his as yet unverbalized anger). At the time of this dream report I still was on occasion mildly uncomfortable — a matter which can never be hidden from such patients. A sensitive patient will, of course, be in conflict between his sympathy, which makes him want me to take care of myself, and his rightful claim that I should take care of him — for he feels that only the therapist's total presence can provide him with sufficient identity to weather his crises. I concluded that the empty face had something to do with a certain tenuousness in our relation, and that one message of the dream might be something like this: "If I never know whether and when you think of yourself rather than attending to me, or when you will absent yourself, maybe die, how can I have or gain what I need most — a coherent personality, an identity, a face?"

Such an indirect message, however, even if understood as referring to the immediate present and to the therapeutic situation itself, always proves to be "overdetermined," that is, to consist of a condensed code transmitting a number of other messages, from other life situations, seemingly removed from the therapy. This we call "transference."

Among those who are acquainted with this kind of material, some would as a matter of course connect the patient's implied fear of "losing a face" with his remark that he was not sure the face was not his mother's — a double negation easily understood as an

[2] "The Dream Specimen of Psychoanalysis," *Journal of the American Psychoanalytic Association*, Volume II, Number 1, January, 1954.

affirmation. However, just because the inference of a "mother transference" is at present an almost stereotyped requirement, I should like to approach the whole matter by way of two methodological detours.

VI

Clinical work is always research in progress, and this patient's dream happened to fit especially well into my research at the time. I should say, in passing, that this can be a mixed blessing for the therapeutic contract. A research-minded clinician — and a literary one, as well — must always take care lest his patients become footnotes to his favorite thesis or topic. I was studying in Pittsburgh and in Stockbridge the "identity crises" of a number of young people, college as well as seminary students, workmen and artists. My work was to delineate further a syndrome called *Identity-Diffusion*, a term which describes the inability of young people in the late 'teens and early twenties to establish their station and vocation in life, and the tendency of some to develop apparently malignant symptoms and regressions. Such research must re-open rather than close questions of finalistic diagnosis. Perhaps there are certain stages in the life cycle when even seemingly malignant disturbances are more profitably treated as aggravated life crises rather than as diseases subject to routine psychiatric diagnosis. Here the clinician must be guided by the proposition that if he can hope to save only a small subgroup, or, indeed, only one patient, he must disregard existing statistical verdicts. For one new case, understood in new ways, will soon prove to be "typical" for a class of patients.

But any new diagnostic impression immediately calls for new psychosocial considerations. What we have described as a therapeutic need in one patient, namely, to gain identity by claiming the total presence of his therapist, is analogous with the need of young people anywhere for ideological affirmation. This need is aggravated in certain critical periods of history, when young people may try to find various forms of "confirmation" in groups that range from idealistic youth movements to criminal gangs.

The young man in question was one among a small group of our patients who came from theological seminaries. He had developed his symptoms when attending a Protestant seminary in the Middle West where he was training for missionary work in Asia. He had not found the expected transformation in prayer, a matter which both for reasons of honesty and of inner need, he had taken more seriously than many successful believers. To him the wish to gaze through the glass darkly and to come "face to face" was a desperate need not easily satisfied in some modern seminaries. I need not remind you of the many references in The Bible to God's "making his face to shine upon" man, or God's face being turned away or being distant. The therapeutic theme inferred from the patient's report of an anxiety dream in which a face was horribly unrecognizable thus also seemed to echo relevantly this patient's religious scruples at the time of the appearance of psychiatric symptoms — the common denominator being a wish to break through to a provider of identity.

This detour has led us from the immediate clinical situation to the vocational crisis immediately preceding the patient's breakdown. The "buggy" in the dream will lead us a step further back into the patient's adolescent identity crisis. The horse and buggy is, of course, an historical symbol of culture change. Depending on one's ideology, it is a derisive term connoting hopelessly old-fashioned ways, or it is a symbol of nostalgia for the good old days. Here we come to a trend in the family's history most decisive for the patient's identity crisis. They came from Minnesota where the mother's father had been a rural clergyman of character, strength, and communal esteem. Such grandfathers represent to many men of today a world as yet more homogeneous in its feudal values, masterly and cruel with a good conscience, self-restrained and pious without loss of self-esteem. When the patient's parents had moved from the north country to then still smog-covered Pittsburgh, his mother especially had found it impossible to overcome an intense nostalgia for the rural ways of her youth. She had, in fact, imbued the boy with this nostalgia for a rural existence and had demonstrated marked disappointment when the patient, at the beginning of his identity crisis (maybe in order to cut through the family's cultural conflict) had temporarily threatened to become a hot-rodder and a hep-cat — roles which were beneath the family's "class." The horse and buggy obviously is in greatest ideological as well as technological contrast to the modern means of locomotor acceleration, and, thus, a symbol of changing times, of identity diffusion, and of cultural regression. Here the horrible motionlessness of the dream may reveal itself as an important configurational item, meaning something like being stuck in a world of competitive change and motion. And even as I inferred in my thoughts that the face sitting in the buggy must *also* represent the deceased grandfather's, also framed by white hair, the patient spontaneously embarked on that above-mentioned series of memories concerning the past when his grandfather had taken him by the hand to acquaint him with the technology of an old farm in Minnesota. Here the patient's vocabulary became poetic, his description vivid, and he seemed to be breaking through to a genuinely positive emotional experience. Yet his tearfulness remained strangely perverse, almost strangled by anger, as if he were saying: "One must not promise a child such certainty, and then let him down."

I should point out here that as clinicians we consider a patient's "associations" our best leads to the meaning of an item brought up in a clinical encounter. By associated evidence we mean everything which comes to the patient's mind during a clinical session. Here, except in cases of stark disorganization of thought, we must assume that what we call the synthesizing function of the ego will, sometimes with but mostly without conscious knowledge, tend to associate what "belongs together" and condense seemingly separate items into strong images and affects, be the various items ever so remote in history, separate in space, and contradictory in logical terms. Once the therapist has convinced himself of a certain combination in the patient of character, intelligence, and a wish to get well, he can rely on the patient's capacity to produce during a series of therapeutic encounters a sequence of themes, thoughts, and affects which seek their own concordance and provide their own cross-references. It is, of course, this basic synthesizing trend in clinical material itself which permits the clinician to observe with free-floating attention, to refrain from undue interference, and to expect sooner or later a confluence of the patient's search for curative clarification and his own endeavor to recognize meaning and relevance. This expectation is in no way disproved by the fact that much of a clinician's work consists of the recognition and removal of the patient's inner and often unconscious resistances to his own wish to see clearly and to get well. We shall return to this point.

We add to our previous inferences the assumption that the face in the dream is a condensed representation of my face as that of his "doctor" who is not so well himself, and the face of his grandfather, who is now dead and whom as a rebellious youth the patient had defied — in fact, shortly before his death. The immediate clinical situation, then, and the patient's childhood history are found to have a common denominator in the idea that the patient wishes to base his future sanity on a man of wisdom and firm identity while, in both instances, the patient seems to fear that his anger may have destroyed, or may yet destroy, this resource. We have every reason to suspect that some of his insistence on finding security in prayer, and yet his failure to find it, belongs in the same context.

VII

The theme of the horse and buggy as a rural symbol served to establish a possible connection between the nostalgic mother and her dead father; and we now finally turn our attention to the fact that the patient, half-denying what he was half-suggesting, had said, "I am not sure it wasn't my mother." Here the most repetitious complaint of the whole course of therapy must be reviewed. While the grandfather's had been, all in all, the most consistently reassuring countenance in the patient's life, the mother's pretty, soft, and loving face had since earliest childhood been marred in the patient's memory and imagination by moments when she seemed absorbed and distorted by strong and painful emotions. The tests, given before any history-taking, had picked out the following theme: "The mother-figure appears in the Thematic Apperception Tests as one who seeks to control her son by her protectiveness of him, and by 'self-pity' and demonstrations of her frailty at any aggressive act on his part. She is, in the stories, 'frightened' at any show of rebelliousness, and content only when the son is passive and compliant. There appears to be considerable aggression, probably partly conscious, toward this figure." And indeed, it was with anger as well as with horror that the patient would repeatedly describe the mother of his memory as utterly exasperated, and this at those times when he had been too rough, too careless, too stubborn, or too persistent.

We are not concerned here with accusing this actual mother of having behaved this way; we can only be sure that she appeared this way in certain retrospective moods of the patient. Such memories are typical for a class of patients, and the question whether this is so because they have in common a type of mother or a typical reaction to their mothers, or both, occupies the thinking of clinicians. At any rate many of these patients are deeply, if often unconsciously, convinced that they have caused a basic disturbance in their mothers — a disturbance, which, of course, is one of the prime causes rather than an effect of the small child's anxiety and anger. No doubt, in our time, when corporal punishment and severe scolding have become less fashionable, parents resort to the seemingly less cruel means of presenting themselves as deeply hurt by the child's willfulness. The "violated" mother thus has become more prominent in the arsenal of guilt images, and in some cases proves to be a hindrance to the conclusion of adolescence — as if one had to go away back and away down to make an essential restitution before adulthood could be approached. It is in keeping with this trend that the patients under discussion here, young people who in late adolescence face a breakdown of "borderline" proportions, all prove partially regressed to the earliest task in life, namely, that of acquiring a sense of basic trust strong enough to balance that sense of basic mistrust to which newborn man, most dependent of all young animals, and endowed with fewer inborn instinctive regulations, is subject in his infancy. We all relive earlier and earliest stages of our existence in dreams, in artistic experience, and in religious devotion, only to emerge refreshed and invigorated. These patients, however, experience such "partial regression" in a lonely, sudden, and intense fashion, and most of all with a sense of irreversible doom. This, too, is in this dream.

Tracing one main theme of the dream retrospectively, we have recognized it in four periods of the patient's life: the present treatment — and the patient's fear that by some act of horrible anger (on his part or on mine or both) he might lose me and thus his chance to regain his identity through trust in me; his immediately preceding religious education — and his abortive attempt at finding through prayer that "presence" which would cure his inner void; his earlier youth — and his hope to gain strength, peace, and identity by identifying himself with his grandfather; and, finally, early childhood — and his desperate wish to keep alive in himself the charitable face of his mother in order to overcome fear, guilt, and anger over her emotions. Such redundancy points to a central theme which, once found, gives added meaning to all the associated material. The theme is: "Whenever I begin to have faith in somebody's strength and love, some angry and sickly emotions pervade the relationship, and I end up mistrusting, empty, and a victim of anger and despair."

You may be getting a bit tired of the clinician's habit of speaking for the patient, of putting into his mouth inferences which, so it would seem, he could get out of it, for the asking. Perhaps so, but the clinician has no right to test his reconstructions until his trial formulations have combined to a comprehensive interpretation which feels right, and which promises, when appropriately verbalized, to feel right to the patient. When this point is reached, the clinician usually finds himself compelled to speak.

We have not yet exhausted the categories of thought which must precede such intervention. I have not explicitly stated what my "persuasion," what specifically Freudian concepts of dream life would make me look for in this dream. If according to Freud a successful dream is an attempt at representing a wish as fulfilled, the attempted and miscarried fulfillment in this dream is that of finding a face with a lasting identity. If an anxiety dream startling the dreamer out of his sleep is a symptom of a derailed wish-fulfillment, the central theme just formulated indicates at least one inner disturbance which caused the miscarriage of trust. This becomes even clearer when we come to the mandatory question as to what was the remnant of the previous day which had upset the sleeping patient sufficiently to cause this dream. Why did the patient have this dream on the preceding night, of all nights?

You will not expect me to give an account of the previous day's appointment as well. Suffice it to say that the patient had confessed to increased well-being in work and in love and had expressed enhanced trust in, and even something akin to affection for me. This, paradoxically, his unconscious had not been able to tolerate. The paradox resolves itself if we consider that cure means the loss of the right to rely on therapy; for the cured patient, to speak with Saint Francis, would not so much seek to be loved as to love, and not so much to be consoled as to console, to the limit of his capacity. The dream shocks the patient out of his dangerous increase in self-confidence (and confidence in me) by reminding him of unwise trust and premature graduations in the past. The dream report communicates, protesting somewhat too loudly, that the patient is still sick. We must come to the conclusion that his dream was sicker than the patient was, although his treatment was by no means near conclusion.

A most comprehensive omission in all this material points to what is as yet to come: there is no father in these familial associations. The patient's father images became dominant in a later period of the treatment. You may also have missed a sexual interpretation of the dream. Did not Freud explain the Medusa, the angry face with snake-hair and an open mouth, as a symbol of the feminine void, and an expression of the masculine horror of femininity? It is true that some of the dream material which concerns the mother's emotions, could be easily traced to infantile observations and ruminations concerning "female trouble," pregnancy, and postpartum upsets. Facelessness, in this sense, can also mean inner void, and "castration." Does it, then, or does it not contradict Freudian symbolism, if I emphasize in this equally horrifying but entirely empty face, a representation of facelessness, of loss of face, of lack of identity? In the context of one interpretation, the dream image would be primarily symbolic of a sexual idea which is to be warded off, in the second a representation of a danger to the continuous existence of individual identity (and thus of the "ego"). Theoretical considerations would show that these interpretations can and must be systematically related to one another. In this case the controversy is superseded by the clinical consideration that a symbol is a symbol only when it can be demonstrated to be at work. Furthermore it would be futile to use sexual symbolism dogmatically when acute ego needs can be discerned as dominant in strongly concordant material. The sexual symbolism of this dream was taken up in due time, when it reappeared in another context, namely that of manhood and sexuality, and revealed the bisexual confusion inherent in all identity diffusion.

Controversies in regard to the therapeutic priority of particular interpretations can in principle be settled in discussions along the evidential lines sketched in this paper. However, since interpretation in this field must deal systematically with motivations which often are the more unconscious the more compelling they are, the whole area of evidential consensus is apt to be beclouded with age-old defensive attitudes of belief and disbelief. On the one hand, psychotherapists themselves are apt to solidify transient controversies in "schools" of thought which make dogmas out of theories and mark skepticism as resistance and unbelief, thus (unconsciously) using traditional methods of meeting the unknown where it is most personal. On the other hand, in the field of man's motivation, insights already firmly gained are forever subject to renewed repression and denial. It is in the very nature of man's intelligence that it can serve both the rational approaches to the facts of nature and also the rationalization and disguise of man's own nature. Therefore, in dealing with the *sense of evidence* in clinical matters, we must accept irrational belief as well as irrational disbelief as part of an inescapable dilemma which calls for a new kind of disciplined self-awareness.

VIII

So much for inferences concerning the meaning of the dream. It is not necessary in this presentation to insist that all of this and infinitely more can go through a clinician's head fast enough to make him react to the patient's behavior with whatever skillful determination is at his disposal. I may now confess that the initial invitation really requested me to tell you "how a *good* clinician works." I have replaced this embarrassing little word with dots until now when I can make it operational. It marks the good clinician that much can go on in him without clogging his communication at the moment of therapeutic intervention, when only the central theme may come to his awareness. On the other hand, he must also be able to call it all to explicit awareness when the circumstances permit the time to spell it out — for how else could such thinking be disciplined, shared and taught? Such sharing and teaching, however, if it is to transcend clinical impressionism, presupposes a communality of conceptual approaches. I cannot give you today more than a mere inkling that there is a systematic relationship between clinical observation on the one hand and, on the other, such conceptual points of view as Freud has introduced into psychiatry: a *structural* point of view denoting a kind of anatomy of the mind, a *dynamic* point of view denoting a kind of physiology of mental forces and of their transformations and, finally, a *genetic* point of view reconstructing the differentiation during distinct childhood stages of an inner organization and of certain energy transformations. But even as such propositions are tested on a wide front of inquiry (from the direct observation of children and perception experiments to "metapsychological" discussion), it stands to reason that clinical evidence is characterized by a human immediacy which transcends formulations ultimately derived from mechanistic patterns of thought.

To enlarge on this would lead me to the question of the collaboration of the clinician and the theoretician. Let me, instead, return to the problem of how, having perused all the above in his own mind, the clinician prepares for therapeutic intervention. For we have postulated that such intervention and the patient's reactions to it are an integral part of the evidence provided in the therapeutic encounter. Therapists of different persuasions differ as to what constitutes an interpretation: an impersonal and authoritative explanation, a warm and fatherly suggestion, an expansive sermon or a sparse encouragement to go on and see what comes up next. In each case, however, the tone of the interpretation will be influenced by the therapist's emotions, of which the patient is anxiously aware.

The preferred mode of interpretation (and this is the second prediction to be made in a clinical encounter) in our case necessarily included a relatively explicit statement of the therapist's emotional response to the dream report. Patients of the type of our young man, still smarting in his twenties under what he considered his mother's strange emotions in his infancy, can learn to delineate social reality and to tolerate emotional tension only if the therapist can juxtapose his own emotional reactions — hopefully more disciplined — to the patient's emotions. Therefore, as I reviewed with the patient in brief words most of what I have put before you, I was also able to tell him without anger, but not without some indignation, that my response to his account had included some feeling of anger. I explained that he had worried me, had made me feel pity, had touched me with his memories, and had burdened me with the proof, all at once, of the goodness of mothers, of the immortality of grandfathers, of my own perfection, and of God's grace. The demonstration that anger can be raised to the level of an educative and self-educative indignation is a not irrelevant by-product of many an interpretation.

The words used in an interpretation, however, are hard to remember and when reproduced often sound as arbitrary as any private language developed by two people in the course of an intimate association. Let me, therefore, state a generality instead. A good therapeutic interpretation, while often brief and simple in form, should be based on an implicit theme such as I have put before you, a theme common at the same time to a dominant trend in the patient's relation to the therapist, to a significant portion of his symptomatology, to an important period of his childhood, and to corresponding facets of his work and love-life. Although all of these trends may seem to be disparate enough further to bewilder the patient upon confrontation, clinical experience proves otherwise: they *are* (as I must repeat in conclusion) very closely related to each other in the patient's own struggling ego, for which the traumatic past is of course a present frontier, perceived as acute conflict. Such an interpretation, therefore, joins the patient's and the therapist's modes of problem-solving.

The intervention in this case, however, highlights one methodological point truly unique to clinical work, namely, the disposition of the clinician's "mixed" feelings, his emotions and opinions. The evidence is not "all in" if he does not succeed in using his own emotional responses during a clinical encounter as an evidential source and as a guide in intervention, instead of putting them aside with a spurious claim to unassailable objectivity. It is here that the requirement of the therapist's own psychoanalytic treatment as a didactic experience proves itself as essential, for the personal equation in the observer's emotional response is as important in psychotherapy as that of the senses in the laboratory. Repressed emotions easily hide themselves in the therapist's most stubborn blind spots.

What do we expect the patient to contribute to the closure of such evidence? What tells us that our interpretation was "right," and, therefore, made the evidence as conclusive as it can be in our kind of work? The simplest answer is that this particular patient was delighted when I told him of my thoughts and of my anger over his unnecessary attempts to burden me with a future which he could well learn to manage — a statement which was not meant to be a therapeutic "suggestion," a clinical slap on the back, but was based on what I knew of his inner resources as well as of the use he made of the opportunities offered in our clinical community. The patient left the hour — which he had begun with a sense of dire disaster — with a broad smile and obvious encouragement. In a most immediate way, this could be said to "clinch" the evidence; at least it shows that our predictions had not gone wildly astray.

I think I have outlined the rationale for my action and the patient's reaction. He had taken a chance with himself and with me, I thought. Under my protection and the hospital's he had hit bottom by chancing a repetition of his original breakdown. He had gone to the very border of unreality and had gleaned from it a highly condensed and seemingly anarchic image. I had shown him that the image, while experienced like a symptom, was in fact a kind of creation, or at any rate a condensed and highly meaningful communication and challenge, for which my particular clinical theory had made me receptive enough to be able to "talk back" without hesitation. A sense of mutuality and reality was thus restored, reinforced by the fact that while accepting his transferences as meaningful, I had refused to become drawn into them. I played neither mother, grandfather, nor God (this is the hardest), but had offered him my help as defined by my professional status in attempting to understand what was behind his helplessness. By relating the fact that his underlying anger aroused mine, and that I could say so without endangering either myself or him, I could show him that in his dream he had also confronted anger in the image of a Medusa — a Gorgon which, neither of us being a hero, we could yet slay together.

IX

This, then, is an example which ends on a convincing note, leaving both the patient and the practitioner with the feeling that they are a pretty clever pair. If it were always required to clinch a piece of clinical evidence in this manner, we should have few convincing examples. To demonstrate other kinds, however, would take other hours.

Undoubtedly some may be inclined to interpret what I have reported in a different way. Against such a contingency, I can only claim (and hope to have demonstrated) that there is enough method in our work systematically to force favorite assumptions to become probable inferences by cross-checking them diagnostically, genetically, structurally, and in a number of other ways, all sufficiently systematized to allow for orderly discussion. Furthermore, in the long run, clinical evidence consists of a series of such encounters as I have outlined here, the series being characterized by a concomitantly progressive or regressive shift in all the areas mentioned.

Clinical training essentially consists of the charting of such series. In each step, our auxiliary methods must help us to work with reasonable precision and with the courage to revise our assumptions and our techniques systematically, if and when the clinical evidence should show that we overestimated or underestimated the patient or ourselves, the chances waiting for him in his environment, or the usefulness of our particular discipline.

In order to counteract such subjectivity and selectivity as I have put before you today, whole treatments are now being sound-filmed so that qualified secondary observers can follow the procedure. This may be important in some lines of research, and advantageous in training; yet, it is obvious that this process only puts a second observer in the position to decide, on the basis of his reactions and selections, whether or not he agrees with the judgments made by the original observer on the basis of his unrecorded and unrecordable reactions and selections; all the while, between the recording and the analysis of the data, history will be found to have marched on.

Neither will the nature of clinical evidence change in such new developments as *group-psychotherapy*, where a therapist faces a group of patients and they face one another as well as him, permitting a number of combinations and variations of the basic elements of a clinical encounter. Clinical evidence, finally, will be much enhanced but not changed in nature by a sharpened awareness (such as now emanates from *sociological studies*) of the psychotherapist's as well as the patient's position in society and history.

It is in this historical connection that we may return to the fate of the world "clinical." The individualistic character of my specimen and of our conceptual framework will be found to have their most explicit opposite in the practices and theories in the Communist part of the world, where different views are held regarding neuroses (they are taken to be a matter of nerves, subject to neurological treatment); regarding psychiatry proper; and finally, regarding the asocial and, in a sense, amoral aspects of some emotional disturbance. In the Far East, the word "clinical" is again assuming an entirely different historical connotation, insofar as it concerns mind at all: in Communist China the "thought analyst" faces individuals considered to be in need of reform. He encourages sincere confessions and self-analyses in order to realign thoughts with "the people's will." It will be interesting to learn more by comparison about the ideological implications of concepts of mental sickness, of social deviancy, and of psychological cure.

The ideological relativity implicit in clinical work may, to some, militate against its scientific value. I could not indicate in this paper what can be gleaned from clinical theory and application. I could only try to give an introduction to the clinician's basic view which asserts that you may learn about the nature of things as you find out what you can do *with* them, but that the true nature of man reveals itself only in the attempt to do something *for* him.

The Social Sciences Cannot Be Value-Free

55

from *What is Political Philosophy?*
LEO STRAUSS

The rejection of political philosophy as unscientific is characteristic of present-day positivism. Positivism is no longer what it desired to be when Auguste Comte originated it. It still agrees with Comte by maintaining that modern science is the highest form of knowledge, precisely because it aims no longer, as theology and metaphysics did, at absolute knowledge of the Why, but only at relative knowledge of the How. But after having been modified by utilitarianism, evolutionism, and neo-Kantianism, it has abandoned completely Comte's hope that a social science modeled on modern natural science would be able to overcome the intellectual anarchy of modern society. In about the last decade of the 19th century, social science positivism reached its final form by realizing or decreeing that there is a fundamental difference between facts and values, and that only factual judgments are within the competence of science: scientific social science is incompetent to pronounce value judgments, and must avoid value judgments altogether. As for the meaning of the term "value" in statements of this kind, we can hardly say more than that "values" mean both things preferred and principles of preference.

A discussion of the tenets of social science positivism is today indispensable for explaining the meaning of political philosophy. We reconsider especially the practical consequences of this positivism. Positivistic social science is "value-free" or "ethically neutral": it is neutral in the conflict between good and evil, however good and evil may be understood. This means that the ground which is common to all social scientists, the ground on which they carry on their investigations and discussions, can only be reached through a process of emancipation from moral judgments, or of abstracting from moral judgments: moral obtuseness is the necessary condition for scientific analysis. For to the extent to which we are not yet completely insensitive to moral distinctions, we are forced to make value judgments. The habit of looking at social or human phenomena without making value judgments has a corroding influence on any preferences. The more serious we are as social scientists, the more completely we develop within ourselves a state of indifference to any goal, or of aimlessness and drifting, a state which may be called nihilism. The social scientist is not immune to preferences; his activity is a constant fight against the preferences he has as a human being and a citizen and which threaten to overcome his scientific detachment. He derives the power to counteract these dangerous influences by his dedication to one and only one value — to truth. But according to his principles, truth is not a value which it is necessary to choose: one may reject it as well as choose it. The scientist as scientist must indeed have chosen it. But neither scientists nor science are simply necessary. Social science cannot pronounce on the question of whether social science itself is good. It is then compelled to teach that society can with equal right and with equal reason favor social science as well as suppress it as disturbing, subversive, corrosive, nihilistic. But strangely enough we find social scientists very anxious to

Reprinted with permission of The Macmillan Company, New York, from *What Is Political Philosophy? and Other Studies* by Leo Strauss, pp. 18–26.

"sell" social science, i.e., to prove that social science is necessary. They will argue as follows. Regardless of what our preferences or ends may be, we wish to achieve our ends; to achieve our ends, we must know which means are conducive to our ends; but adequate knowledge of the means conducive to any social ends is the sole function of social science and only of social science; hence social science is necessary for any society or any social movement; social science is then simply necessary; it is a value from every point of view. But once we grant this we are seriously tempted to wonder if there are not a few other things which must be values from every point of view or for every thinking human being. To avoid this inconvenience the social scientist will scorn all considerations of public relations or of private advancement, and take refuge in the virtuous contention that he does not know, but merely believes that quest for truth is good: other men may believe with equal right that quest for truth is bad. But what does he mean by this contention? Either he makes a distinction between noble and ignoble objectives or he refuses to make such a distinction. If he makes a distinction between noble and ignoble objectives he will say there is a variety of noble objectives or of ideals, and that there is no ideal which is compatible with all other ideals: if one chooses truth as one's ideal, one necessarily rejects other ideals; this being the case, there cannot be a necessity, an evident necessity for noble men to choose truth in preference to other ideals. But as long as the social scientist speaks of ideals, and thus makes a distinction between noble and not noble objectives, or between idealistic integrity and petty egoism, he makes a value judgment which according to his fundamental contention is, as such, no longer necessary. He must then say that it is as legitimate to make the pursuit of safety, income, deference one's sole aim in life as it is to make the quest for truth one's chief aim. He thus lays himself open to the suspicion that his activity as a social scientist serves no other purpose than to increase his safety, his income, and his prestige, or that his competence as a social scientist is a skill which he is prepared to sell to the highest bidder. Honest citizens will begin to wonder whether such a man can be trusted, or whether he can be loyal, especially since he must maintain that it is as defensible to choose loyalty as one's value as it is to reject it. In a word, he will get entangled in the predicament which leads to the downfall of Thrasymachus and his taming by Socrates in the first book of Plato's *Republic*.

It goes without saying that while our social scientist may be confused, he is very far from being disloyal and from lacking integrity. His assertion that integrity and quest for truth are values which one can with equal right choose or reject is a mere movement of his lips and his tongue, to which nothing corresponds in his heart or mind. I have never met any scientific social scientist who apart from being dedicated to truth and integrity was not also wholeheartedly devoted to democracy. When he says that democracy is a value which is not evidently superior to the opposite value, he does not mean that he is impressed by the alternative which he rejects, or that his heart or his mind is torn between alternatives which in themselves are equally attractive. His "ethical neutrality" is so far from being nihilism or a road to nihilism that it is not more than an alibi for thoughtlessness and vulgarity: by saying that democracy and truth are values, he says in effect that one does not have to think about the reasons why these things are good, and that he may bow as well as anyone else to the values that are adopted and respected by his society. Social science positivism fosters not so much nihilism as conformism and philistinism.

It is not necessary to enter here and now into a discussion of the theoretical weaknesses of social science positivism. It suffices to allude to the considerations which speak decisively against this school. (1) It is impossible to study social phenomena, i.e., all important social phenomena, without making value judgments. A man who sees no reason for not despising people whose horizon is limited to their consumption of food and their digestion may be a tolerable econometrist; he cannot say anything relevant about the character of a human society. A man who refuses to distinguish between great statesmen, mediocrities, and insane imposters may be a good bibliographer; he cannot say anything relevant about politics and political history. A man who cannot distinguish between a profound religious thought and a languishing superstition may be a good statistician; he cannot say anything relevant about the sociology of religion. Generally speaking, it is impossible to understand thought or action or work without evaluating it. If we are unable to evaluate adequately, as we very frequently are, we have not yet succeeded in understanding adequately. The value judgments which are forbidden to enter through the front door of political science, sociology or economics, enter these disciplines through the back door; they come from that annex of present-day social science which is called psychopathology. Social scientists see themselves compelled to speak of unbalanced, neurotic, maladjusted people. But these value judgments are distinguished from those used by the great historians, not by greater clarity or certainty, but merely by their poverty: a slick operator is as well adjusted as, he may be better adjusted than, a good man or a good citizen. Finally, we must not overlook the invisible value judgments which are concealed from undiscerning eyes but nevertheless most powerfully present in allegedly purely descriptive concepts. For example, when social scientists distinguish between democratic and authoritarian habits or types of human beings, what they call "authoritarian" is in all cases known to me a caricature of everything of which they, as good democrats of a certain kind, disapprove. Or when they speak of three principles of legitimacy, rational, traditional, and charismatic, their very expression "routinization of charisma" betrays a Protestant or liberal preference which no conservative Jew and no Catholic would accept: in the light of the notion of "routinization of charisma," the genesis of the Halakah out of Biblical prophesy on the one hand, and the genesis of the Catholic Church out of the New Testament teaching, necessarily appear as cases of "routinization of charisma." If the objection should be made that value judgments are indeed inevitable in social science but have a merely conditional character, I would reply as follows: are the conditions in question not necessarily fulfilled when we are interested in social phenomena? must the social scientist not necessarily make the assumption that a healthy social life in this world is good, just as medicine necessarily makes the assumption that health and a healthy long life are good? And also are not all factual assertions based on conditions, or assumptions, which however do not become questionable as long as we deal with facts qua facts (e.g., that there are "facts," that events have causes)?

The impossibility of a "value-free" political science can be shown most simply as follows. Political science presupposes a distinction between political things and things which are not political; it presupposes therefore some answer to the question "what is political?" In order to be truly scientific, political science would have to raise this question and to answer it explicitly and adequately. But it is impossible to define the political, i.e., that which is related in a relevant way to the *polis*, the "country" or the "state," without answering the question of what constitutes this kind of society. Now, a society cannot be defined without reference to its purpose. The most well known attempt to define "the state" without regard to its purpose admittedly led to a definition which was derived from "the modern type of state" and which is fully applicable only to that type; it was an attempt to define the modern state without having first defined the state. But by defining the state, or rather civil society, with reference to its purpose, one admits a standard in the light of which one must judge political actions and institutions: the purpose of civil society necessarily functions as a standard for judging of civil societies.

(2) The rejection of value judgments is based on the assumption that the conflicts between different values or value-systems are essentially insoluble for human reason. But this assumption, while generally taken to be sufficiently established, has never been proven. Its proof would require an effort of the magnitude of that which went into the conception and elaboration of the *Critique of Pure Reason;* it would require a comprehensive critique of evaluating reason. What we find in fact are sketchy observations which pretend to prove that this or that specific value conflict is insoluble. It is prudent to grant that there are value conflicts which cannot in fact be settled by human reason. But if we cannot decide which of two mountains whose peaks are hidden by clouds is higher than the other, cannot we decide that a mountain is higher than a molehill? If we cannot decide, regarding a war between two neighboring nations which have been fighting each other for centuries, which nation's cause is more just, cannot we decide that Jezebel's action against Naboth was inexcusable? The greatest representative of social science positivism, Max Weber, has postulated the insolubility of all value conflicts, because his soul craved a universe in which failure, that bastard of forceful sinning accompanied by still more forceful faith, instead of felicity and serenity, was to be the mark of human nobility. The belief that value judgments are not subject, in the last analysis, to rational control, encourages the inclination to make irresponsible assertions regarding right and wrong or good and bad. One evades serious discussion of serious issues by the simple device of passing them off as value problems. One even creates the impression that all important human conflicts are value conflicts, whereas, to say the least, many of these conflicts arise out of men's very agreement regarding values.

(3) The belief that scientific knowledge, i.e., the kind of knowledge possessed or aspired to by modern science, is the highest form of human knowledge, implies a depreciation of pre-scientific knowledge. If one takes into consideration the contrast between scientific knowledge of the world and pre-scientific knowledge of the world, one realizes that positivism preserves in a scarcely disguised manner Descartes' universal doubt of pre-scientific knowledge and his radical break with it. It certainly distrusts pre-scientific knowledge, which it likes to compare to folklore. This superstition fosters all sorts of sterile investigations or complicated idiocies. Things which every ten-year-old child of normal intelligence knows are regarded as being in need of scientific proof in order to become acceptable as facts. And this scientific proof, which is not only not necessary, is not even possible. To illustrate this by the simplest example: all studies in social science presuppose that its devotees can tell human beings from other beings; this most fundamental knowledge was not acquired by them in classrooms; and this knowledge is not transformed by social science into scientific knowledge, but retains its initial status without any modification throughout. If this pre-scientific knowledge is not knowledge, all scientific studies, which stand or fall with it, lack the character of knowledge. The preoccupation with scientific proof of things which everyone knows well enough, and better, without scientific proof, leads to the neglect of that thinking, or that reflection, which must precede all scientific studies if these studies are to be relevant. The scientific study of politics is often presented as ascending from the ascertainment of political "facts," i.e., of what has happened hitherto in politics, to the formulation of "laws" whose knowledge would permit the prediction of future political events. This goal is taken as a matter of course without a previous investigation as to whether the subject matter with which political science deals admits of adequate understanding in terms of "laws" or whether the universals through which political things can be understood as what

they are must not be conceived of in entirely different terms. Scientific concern with political facts, relations of political facts, recurrent relations of political facts, or laws of political behavior, requires isolation of the phenomena which it is studying. But if this isolation is not to lead to irrelevant or misleading results, one must see the phenomena in question within the whole to which they belong, and one must clarify that whole, i.e., the whole political or politico-social order. One cannot arrive, e.g., at a kind of knowledge of "group politics" which deserves to be called scientific if one does not reflect on what genus of political orders is presupposed if there is to be "group politics" at all, and what kind of political order is presupposed by the specific "group politics" which one is studying. But one cannot clarify the character of a specific democracy, e.g., or of democracy in general, without having a clear understanding of the alternatives to democracy. Scientific political scientists are inclined to leave it at the distinction between democracy and authoritarianism, i.e., they absolutize the given political order by remaining within a horizon which is defined by the given political order and its opposite. The scientific approach tends to lead to the neglect of the primary or fundamental questions and therewith to thoughtless acceptance of received opinion. As regards these fundamental questions our friends of scientific exactness are strangely unexacting. To refer again to the most simple and at the same time decisive example, political science requires clarification of what distinguishes political things from things which are not political; it requires that the question be raised and answered "what is political?" This question cannot be dealt with scientifically but only dialectically. And dialectical treatment necessarily begins from pre-scientific knowledge and takes it most seriously. Pre-scientific knowledge, or "common sense" knowledge, is thought to be discredited by Copernicus and the succeeding natural science. But the fact that what we may call telescopic-microscopic knowledge is very fruitful in certain areas does not entitle one to deny that there are things which can only be seen as what they are if they are seen with the unarmed eye; or, more precisely, if they are seen in the perspective of the citizen, as distinguished from the perspective of the scientific observer. If one denies this, one will repeat the experience of Gulliver with the nurse in Brobdingnag and become entangled in the kind of research projects by which he was amazed in Laputa.

(4) Positivism necessarily transforms itself into historicism. By virtue of its orientation by the model of natural science, social science is in danger of mistaking peculiarities of, say, mid-twentieth century United States, or more generally of modern western society, for the essential character of human society. To avoid this danger, it is compelled to engage in "cross-cultural research," in the study of other cultures, both present and past. But in making this effort, it misses the meaning of those other cultures, because it interprets them through a conceptual scheme which originates in modern western society, which reflects that particular society, and which fits at best only that particular society. To avoid this danger, social science must attempt to understand those cultures as they understand or understood themselves: the understanding primarily required of the social scientist is historical understanding. Historical understanding becomes the basis of a truly empirical science of society. But if one considers the infinity of the task of historical understanding, one begins to wonder whether historical understanding does not take the place of the scientific study of society. Furthermore, social science is said to be a body of true propositions about social phenomena. The propositions are answers to questions. What valid answers, objectively valid answers, are, may be determined by the rules or principles of logic. But the questions depend on one's direction of interest, and hence on one's values, i.e., on subjective principles. Now it is the direction of interests, and not logic, which supplies the fundamental concepts. It is therefore not possible to

divorce from each other the subjective and objective elements of social science: the objective answers receive their meaning from the subjective questions. If one does not relapse into the decayed Platonism which is underlying the notion of timeless values, one must conceive of the values embodied in a given social science as dependent on the society to which the social science in question belongs, i.e., on history. Not only is social science superseded by historical studies; social science itself proves to be "historical." Reflection on social science as a historical phenomenon leads to the relativization of social science and ultimately of modern science generally. As a consequence, modern science comes to be viewed as one historically relative way of understanding things which is not in principle superior to alternative ways of understanding.

The Social Sciences Can Be Value-Free

56

from *The Structure of Science*

ERNEST NAGEL

The Value-Oriented Bias of Social Inquiry

We turn, finally, to the difficulties said to confront the social sciences because the social values to which students of social phenomena are committed not only color the contents of their findings but also control their assessment of the evidence on which they base their conclusions. Since social scientists generally differ in their value commitments, the "value neutrality" that seems to be so pervasive in the natural sciences is therefore often held to be impossible in social inquiry. In the judgment of many thinkers, it is accordingly absurd to expect the social sciences to exhibit the unanimity so common among natural scientists concerning what are the established facts and satisfactory explanations for them. Let us examine some of the reasons that have been advanced for these contentions. It will be convenient to distinguish four groups of such reasons, so that our discussion will deal in turn with the alleged role of value judgments in (1) the selection of problems, (2) the determination of the contents of conclusions, (3) the identification of fact, and (4) the assessment of evidence.

1. The reasons perhaps most frequently cited make much of the fact that the things a social scientist selects for study are determined by his conception of what are the socially important values. According to one influential view, for example, the student of human affairs deals only with materials to which he attributes "cultural significance," so that a "value orientation" is inherent in his choice of material for investigation. Thus, although Max Weber was a vigorous proponent of a "value-free" social science — i.e., he maintained that social scientists must appreciate (or "understand") the values involved in the actions or institutions they are discussing but that it is not their business as objective scientists to approve or disapprove either those values or those actions and institutions — he nevertheless argued that

> The concept of culture is a *value-concept*. Empirical reality becomes "culture" to us because and insofar as we relate it to value ideas. It includes those segments and only those segments of reality which have become significant to us because of this value-relevance. Only a small portion of existing concrete reality is colored by our value-conditioned interest and it alone is significant to us. It is significant because it reveals relationships which are important to us due to their connection with our values. Only because and to the extent that this is the case is it worthwhile for us to know it in its individual features. We cannot discover, however, what is meaningful to us by means of a "presuppositionless" investigation of empirical data. Rather perception of its meaningfulness to us is the presupposition of its becoming an *object* of investigation.[1]

It is well-nigh truistic to say that students of human affairs, like students in any other area of inquiry, do not investigate everything, but direct their attention to certain selected portions of the inexhaustible content of concrete reality. Moreover, let us accept the claim, if only for the sake of the argument, that a social scientist addresses himself exclusively to matters which he believes are important because of their assumed relevance to his cultural values.[2] It is not clear,

From *The Structure of Science* by Ernest Nagel, pp. 485–502, © 1961 by Harcourt, Brace and World, Inc., New York, and reprinted with their permission and that of Routledge & Kegan Paul Ltd., London.

[1] Max Weber, *The Methodology of the Social Sciences*, Glencoe, Ill., 1947, p. 76.

[2] This question receives some attention below in the discussion of the fourth difficulty.

however, why the fact that an investigator selects the materials he studies in the light of problems which interest him and which seem to him to bear on matters he regards as important, is of greater moment for the logic of social inquiry than it is for the logic of any other branch of inquiry. For example, a social scientist may believe that a free economic market embodies a cardinal human value, and he may produce evidence to show that certain kinds of human activities are indispensable to the perpetuation of a free market. If he is concerned with processes which maintain this type of economy rather than some other type, how is this fact more pertinent to the question whether he has adequately evaluated the evidence for his conclusion, than is the bearing upon the analogous question of the fact that a physiologist may be concerned with processes which maintain a constant internal temperature in the human body rather than with something else? The things a social scientist *selects for study* with a view to determining the conditions or consequences of their existence may indeed be dependent on the indisputable fact that he is a "cultural being." But similarly, were we not human beings though still capable of conducting scientific inquiry, we might conceivably have an interest neither in the conditions that maintain a free market, nor in the processes involved in the homeostasis of the internal temperature in human bodies, nor for that matter in the mechanisms that regulate the height of tides, the succession of seasons, or the motions of the planets.

In short, there is no difference between any of the sciences with respect to the fact that the interests of the scientist determine what he selects for investigation. But this fact, by itself, represents no obstacle to the successful pursuit of objectively controlled inquiry in any branch of study.

2. A more substantial reason commonly given for the value-oriented character of social inquiry is that, since the social scientist is himself affected by considerations of right and wrong, his own notions of what constitutes a satisfactory social order and his own standards of personal and social justice do enter, in point of fact, into his analyses of social phenomena. For example, according to one version of this argument, anthropologists must frequently judge whether the means adopted by some society achieves the intended aim (e.g., whether a religious ritual does produce the increased fertility for the sake of which the ritual is performed); and in many cases the adequacy of the means must be judged by admittedly "relative" standards, i.e., in terms of the ends sought or the standards employed by that society, rather than in terms of the anthropologist's own criteria. Nevertheless, so the argument proceeds, there are also situations in which

> we must apply absolute standards of adequacy, that is evaluate the end-results of behavior in terms of purposes we believe in or postulate. This occurs, first, when we speak of the satisfaction of psycho-physical 'needs' offered by any culture; secondly, when we assess the bearing of social facts upon survival; and thirdly, when we pronounce upon social integration and stability. In each case our statements imply judgments as to the worth-whileness of actions, as to 'good' or 'bad' cultural solutions of the problems of life, and as to 'normal' and 'abnormal' states of affairs. These are basic judgments which we cannot do without in social enquiry and which clearly do not express a purely personal philosophy of the enquirer or values arbitrarily assumed. Rather do they grow out of the history of human thought, from which the anthropologist can seclude himself as little as can anyone else. Yet as the history of human thought has led not to one philosophy but to several, so the value attitudes implicit in our ways of thinking will differ and sometimes conflict.[3]

[3] S. F. Nadel, *The Foundations of Social Anthropology*, Glencoe, Ill., 1951, pp. 53–54. The claim is sometimes also made that the exclusion of value judgments from social science is undesirable as well as impossible. "We cannot disregard all questions of what is socially desirable without missing the significance of many social facts; for since the relation of means to ends is a special form of that between parts and wholes, the contemplation of social ends enables us to see the relations of whole groups of facts to each other and to larger systems of which they are parts." — Morris R. Cohen, *Reason and Nature*, New York, 1931, p. 343.

It has often been noted, moreover, that the study of social phenomena receives much of its impetus from a strong moral and reforming zeal, so that many ostensibly "objective" analyses in the social sciences are in fact disguised recommendations of social policy. As one typical but moderately expressed statement of the point puts it, a social scientist

> cannot wholly detach the unifying social structure that, as a scientist's theory, guides his detailed investigations of human behavior, from the unifying structure which, as a citizen's ideal, he thinks ought to prevail in human affairs and hopes may sometimes be more fully realized. His social theory is thus essentially a program of action along two lines which are kept in some measure of harmony with each other by that theory — action in assimilating social facts for purposes of systematic understanding, and action aiming at progressively molding the social pattern, so far as he can influence it, into what he thinks it ought to be.[4]

It is surely beyond serious dispute that social scientists do in fact often import their own values into their analyses of social phenomena. It is also undoubtedly true that even thinkers who believe human affairs can be studied with the ethical neutrality characterizing modern inquiries into geometrical or physical relations, and who often pride themselves on the absence of value judgments from their own analyses of social phenomena, do in fact sometimes make such judgments in their social inquiries.[5] Nor is it less evident that students of human affairs often hold conflicting values; that their disagreements on value questions are often the source of disagreements concerning ostensibly factual issues; and that, even if value predications are assumed to be inherently capable of proof or disproof by objective evidence, at least some of the differences between social scientists involving value judgments are not in fact resolved by the procedures of controlled inquiry.

In any event, it is not easy in most areas of inquiry to prevent our likes, aversions, hopes, and fears from coloring our conclusions. It has taken centuries of effort to develop habits and techniques of investigation which help safeguard inquiries in the natural sciences against the intrusion of irrelevant personal factors; and even in these disciplines the protection those procedures give is neither infallible nor complete. The problem is undoubtedly more acute in the study of human affairs, and the difficulties it creates for achieving reliable knowledge in the social sciences must be admitted.

However, the problem is intelligible only on the assumption that there is a relatively clear distinction between factual and value judgments, and that however difficult it may sometimes be to decide whether a given statement has a purely factual content, it is in principle possible to do so. Thus, the claim that social scientists are pursuing the twofold program mentioned in the above quotation makes sense, only if it is possible to distinguish between, on the one hand, contributions to theoretical understanding (whose factual validity presumably does not depend on the social ideal to which a social scientist may subscribe), and on the other hand contributions to the dissemination or realization of some social ideal (which may not be accepted by all social scientists). Accordingly, the undeniable difficulties that stand in the way of obtaining reliable knowledge of human affairs because of the fact that social scientists differ in their value orientations are practical difficulties. The difficulties are not necessarily insuperable, for since by hypothesis it is not impossible to distinguish between fact and value, steps can be taken to identify a value bias when it occurs, and to minimize if not to eliminate completely its perturbing effects.

One such countermeasure frequently recommended is that social scientists abandon the pretense that they are free from all bias, and that instead they state their value assumptions as explicitly and fully as they

[4] Edwin A. Burtt, *Right Thinking*, New York, 1946, p. 522.

[5] For a documented account, see Gunnar Myrdal, *Value in Social Theory*, London, 1958, pp. 134–52.

can.[6] The recommendation does not assume that social scientists will come to agree on their social ideals once these ideals are explicitly postulated, or that disagreements over values can be settled by scientific inquiry. Its point is that the question of how a given ideal is to be realized, or the question whether a certain institutional arrangement is an effective way of achieving the ideal, is on the face of it not a value question, but a factual problem — to be resolved by the objective methods of scientific inquiry — concerning the adequacy of proposed means for attaining stipulated ends. Thus, economists may permanently disagree on the desirability of a society in which its members have a guaranteed security against economic want, since the disagreement may have its source in inarbitrable preferences for different social values. But when sufficient evidence is made available by economic inquiry, economists do presumably agree on the factual proposition that, *if* such a society is to be achieved, then a purely competitive economic system will not suffice.

Although the recommendation that social scientists make fully explicit their value commitments is undoubtedly salutary, and can produce excellent fruit, it verges on being a counsel of perfection. For the most part we are unaware of many assumptions that enter into our analyses and actions, so that despite resolute efforts to make our preconceptions explicit some decisive ones may not even occur to us. But in any event, the difficulties generated for scientific inquiry by unconscious bias and tacit value orientations are rarely overcome by devout resolutions to eliminate bias. They are usually overcome, often only gradually, through the self-corrective mechanisms of science as a social enterprise. For modern science encourages the invention, the mutual exchange, and the free but responsible criticisms of ideas; it welcomes competition in the quest for knowledge between independent investigators, even when their intellectual orientations are different; and it progressively diminishes the effects of bias by retaining only those proposed conclusions of its inquiries that survive critical examination by an indefinitely large community of students, whatever be their value preferences or doctrinal commitments. It would be absurd to claim that this institutionalized mechanism for sifting warranted beliefs has operated or is likely to operate in social inquiry as effectively as it has in the natural sciences. But it would be no less absurd to conclude that reliable knowledge of human affairs is unattainable merely because social inquiry is frequently value-oriented.

3. There is a more sophisticated argument for the view that the social sciences cannot be value-free. It maintains that the distinction between fact and value assumed in the preceding discussion is untenable when purposive human behavior is being analyzed, since in this context value judgments enter inextricably into what appear to be "purely descriptive" (or factual) statements. Accordingly, those who subscribe to this thesis claim that an ethically neutral social science is in principle impossible, and not simply that it is difficult to attain. For if fact and value are indeed so fused that they cannot even be distinguished, value judgments cannot be eliminated from the social sciences unless all predications are also eliminated from them, and therefore unless these sciences completely disappear.

For example, it has been argued that the student of human affairs must distinguish between valuable and undesirable forms of social activity, on pain of failing in his "plain duty" to present social phenomena truthfully and faithfully:

> Would one not laugh out of court a man who claimed to have written a sociology of art but who actually had written a sociology of trash? The sociologist of religion must distinguish between phenomena which have a religious character and phenomena which are a-religious. To be able to do this, he must understand what religion is. . . .

[6] See, e.g., S. F. Nadel, *op, cit.*, p. 54; also Gunnar Myrdal, *op. cit.*, p. 120, as well as his *Political Element in the Development of Economic Theory*, Cambridge, Mass., 1954, esp. Chap. 8.

Such understanding enables and forces him to distinguish between genuine and spurious religion, between higher and lower religions; these religions are higher in which the specifically religious motivations are effective to a higher degree. . . . The sociologist of religion cannot help noting the difference between those who try to gain it by a change of heart. Can he see this difference without seeing at the same time the difference between a mercenary and nonmercenary attitude? . . . The prohibition against value-judgments in social science would lead to the consequence that we are permitted to give a strictly factual description of the overt acts that can be observed in concentration camps, and perhaps an equally factual analysis of the motivations of the actors concerned: we would not be permitted to speak of cruelty. Every reader of such a description who is not completely stupid would, of course, see that the actions described are cruel. The factual description would, in truth, be a bitter satire. What claimed to be a straightforward report would be an unusually circumlocutory report. . . . Can one say anything relevant on public opinion polls . . . without realizing the fact that many answers to the questionnaires are given by unintelligent, uninformed, deceitful, and irrational people, and that not a few questions are formulated by people of the same caliber — can one say anything relevant about public opinion polls without committing one value-judgment after another?[7]

Moreover, the assumption implicit in the recommendation discussed above for achieving ethical neutrality is often rejected as hopelessly naive — this is the assumption, it will be recalled, that relations of means to ends can be established without commitment to these ends, so that the conclusions of social inquiry concerning such relations are objective statements which make *conditional* rather than categorical assertions about values. This assumption is said by its critics to rest on the supposition that men attach value only to the ends they seek, and not to the means for realizing their aims. However, the supposition is alleged to be grossly mistaken. For the character of the means one employs to secure some goal affects the nature of the total outcome; and the choice men make between alternative means for obtaining a given end depends on the values they ascribe to those alternatives. In consequence, commitments to specific valuations are said to be involved even in what appear to be purely factual statements about means-ends relations.[8]

We shall not attempt a detailed assessment of this complex argument, for a discussion of the numerous issues it raises would take us far afield. However, three claims made in the course of the argument will be admitted without further comment as indisputably correct: that a large number of characterizations sometimes assumed to be purely factual descriptions of social phenomena do indeed formulate a type of value judgment; that it is often difficult, and in any case usually inconvenient in practice, to distinguish between the purely factual and the "evaluative" contents of many terms employed in the social sciences; and that values are commonly attached to means and not only to ends. However, these admissions do not entail the conclusion that, in a manner unique to the study of purposive human behavior, fact and value are fused beyond the possibility of distinguishing between them. On the contrary, as we shall try to show, the claim that there is such a fusion and that a value-free social science is therefore inherently absurd, confounds two quite different senses of the term "value judgment": the sense in which a value judgment expresses *approval or disapproval* either of some moral (or social) ideal, or of some action (or institution) because of a commitment to such an ideal; and the sense in which a value judgment expresses *an estimate* of the degree to

[7] Leo Strauss, "The Social Science of Max Weber," *Measure*, Vol. 2 (1951), pp. 211–14. For a discussion of this issue as it bears upon problems in the philosophy of law, see Lon Fuller, "Human Purpose and Natural Law," *Natural Law Forum*, Vol. 3 (1958), pp. 68–76; Ernest Nagel, "On the Fusion of Fact and Value: A Reply to Professor Fuller," *op. cit.*, pp. 77–82; Lon L. Fuller, "A Rejoinder to Professor Nagel," *op. cit.*, pp. 83–104; Ernest Nagel, "Fact, Value, and Human Purpose," *Natural Law Forum*, Vol. 4 (1959), pp. 26–43.

[8] Cf. Gunnar Myrdal, *Value in Social Theory*, London, 1958, pp. xxii, 211–13.

which some commonly recognized (and more or less clearly defined) type of action, object, or institution is embodied in a given instance.

It will be helpful to illustrate these two senses of "value judgment" first with an example from biology. Animals with blood streams sometimes exhibit the condition known as "anemia." An anemic animal has a reduced number of red blood corpuscles, so that, among other things, it is less able to maintain a constant internal temperature than are members of its species with a "normal" supply of such blood cells. However, although the meaning of the term "anemia" can be made quite clear, it is not in fact defined with complete precision; for example, the notion of a "normal" number of red corpuscles that enters into the definition of the term is itself somewhat vague, since this number varies with the individual members of a species as well as with the state of a given individual at different times (such as its age or the altitude of its habitat). But in any case, to decide whether a given animal is anemic, an investigator must judge whether the available evidence *warrants* the conclusion that the specimen is anemic.[9] He may perhaps think of anemia as being of several distinct kinds (as is done in actual medical practice), or he may think of anemia as a condition that is realizable with greater or lesser completeness (just as certain plane curves are sometimes described as better or worse approximations to a circle as defined in geometry); and, depending on which of these conceptions he adopts, he may decide either that his specimen has a certain kind of anemia or that it is anemic only to a certain degree. When the investigator reaches a conclusion, he can therefore be said to be making a "value judgment," in the sense that he has in mind some standardized type of physiological condition designated as "anemia" and that he *assesses* what he knows about his specimen with the measure provided by this assumed standard. For the sake of easy reference, let us call such evaluations of the evidence, which conclude that a given characteristic is in some degree present (or absent) in a given instance, "characterizing value judgments."

On the other hand, the student may also make a quite different sort of value judgment, which asserts that, since an anemic animal has diminished powers of maintaining itself, anemia is an undesirable condition. Moreover, he may apply this general judgment to a particular case, and so come to deplore the fact that a given animal is anemic. Let us label such evaluations, which conclude that some envisaged or actual state of affairs is worthy of approval or disapproval, "appraising value judgments."[10] It is clear, however, that an investigator making a characterizing value judgment is not thereby logically bound to affirm or deny a corresponding appraising evaluation. It is no less evident that he cannot consistently make an appraising value judgment about a given instance (e.g., that it is undesirable for a given animal to continue being anemic), unless he can affirm a characterizing judgment about that instance independently of the appraising one (e.g., that the animal is anemic). Accordingly, although characterizing judgments are necessarily entailed by many appraising judgments, making appraising judgments is not a necessary condition for making characterizing ones.

Let us now apply these distinctions to some of the contentions advanced in the argument quoted above. Consider first the

[9] The evidence is usually a count of red cells in a sample from the animal's blood. However, it should be noted that "The red cell count gives only an estimate of the *number of cells per unit quantity of blood*," and does not indicate whether the body's total supply of red cells is increased or diminished. — Charles H. Best and Norman B. Taylor, *The Physiological Basis of Medical Practice*, 6th ed., Baltimore, 1955, pp. 11, 17.

[10] It is irrelevant to the present discussion what view is adopted concerning the ground upon which such judgments supposedly rest — whether those grounds are simply arbitrary preferences, alleged intuitions of "objective" values, categorical moral imperatives, or anything else that has been proposed in the history of value theory. For the distinction made in the text is independent of any particular assumption about the foundations of appraising value judgments, "ultimate" or otherwise.

claim that the sociologist of religion must recognize the difference between mercenary and nonmercenary attitudes, and that in consequence he is inevitably committing himself to certain values. It is certainly beyond dispute that these attitudes are commonly distinguished; and it can also be granted that a sociologist of religion needs to understand the difference between them. But the sociologist's obligation is in this respect quite like that of the student of animal physiology, who must also acquaint himself with certain distinctions — even though the physiologist's distinction between, say, anemic and nonanemic may be less familiar to the ordinary layman and is in any case much more precise than is the distinction between mercenary and nonmercenary attitudes. Indeed, because of the vagueness of these latter terms, the scrupulous sociologist may find it extremely difficult to decide whether or not the attitude of some community toward its acknowledged gods is to be characterized as mercenary; and if he should finally decide, he may base his conclusion on some inarticulated "total impression" of that community's manifest behavior, without being able to state exactly the detailed grounds for his decision. But however this may be, the sociologist who claims that a certain attitude manifested by a given religious group is mercenary, just as the physiologist who claims that a certain individual is anemic, is making what is primarily a characterizing value judgment. In making these judgments, neither the sociologist nor the physiologist is necessarily committing himself to any values other than the values of scientific probity; and in this respect, therefore, there appears to be no difference between social and biological (or for that matter, physical) inquiry.

On the other hand, it would be absurd to deny that in characterizing various actions as mercenary, cruel, or deceitful, sociologists are frequently (although perhaps not always wittingly) asserting appraising as well as characterizing value judgments. Terms like 'mercenary,' 'cruel,' or 'deceitful' as commonly used have a widely recognized pejorative overtone. Accordingly, anyone who employs such terms to characterize human behavior can normally be assumed to be stating his disapprobation of that behavior (or his approbation, should he use terms like 'nonmercenary,' 'kindly,' or 'truthful'), and not simply characterizing it.

However, although many (but certainly not all) ostensibly characterizing statements asserted by social scientists undoubtedly express commitments to various (not always compatible) values, a number of "purely descriptive" terms as used by natural scientists in certain contexts sometimes also have an unmistakably appraising value connotation. Thus, the claim that a social scientist is making appraising value judgments when he characterizes respondents to questionnaires as uninformed, deceitful, or irrational can be matched by the equally sound claim that a physicist is also making such judgments when he describes a particular chronometer as inaccurate, a pump as inefficient, or a supporting platform as unstable. Like the social scientist in this example, the physicist is characterizing certain objects in his field of research; but, also like the social scientist, he is in addition expressing his disapproval of the characteristics he is ascribing to those objects.

Nevertheless — and this is the main burden of the present discussion — there are no good reasons for thinking that it is inherently impossible to *distinguish* between the characterizing and the appraising judgments implicit in many statements, whether the statements are asserted by students of human affairs or by natural scientists. To be sure, it is not always easy to make the distinction formally explicit in the social sciences — in part because much of the language employed in them is very vague, in part because appraising judgments that may be implicit in a statement tend to be overlooked by us when they are judgments to which we are actually committed though without being aware of our commitments. Nor is it always useful or convenient to perform this task. For many statements implicitly containing both characterizing and appraising evaluations are sometimes sufficiently clear without being reformulated in the manner required by the task; and the reformulations would frequently be too unwieldy for effective communication between members of a large and unequally prepared group of students. But these are essentially practical rather than theoretical problems. The difficulties they raise provide no compelling reasons for the claim that an ethically neutral social science is inherently impossible.

Nor is there any force in the argument that, since values are commonly attached to means and not only to ends, statements about means-ends relations are not value-free. Let us test the argument with a simple example. Suppose that a man with an urgent need for a car but without sufficient funds to buy one can achieve his aim by borrowing a sum either from a commercial bank or from friends who waive payment of any interest. Suppose further that he dislikes becoming beholden to his friends for financial favors, and prefers the impersonality of a commercial loan. Accordingly, the comparative values this individual places upon the alternative means available to him for realizing his aim obviously control the choice he makes between them. Now the *total* outcome that would result from his adoption of one of the alternatives is admittedly different from the *total* outcome that would result from his adoption of the other alternative. Nevertheless, irrespective of the values he may attach to these alternative means, each of them would achieve a result — namely, his purchase of the needed car — that is common to both the total outcomes. In consequence, the validity of the statement that he could buy the car by borrowing money from a bank, as well as of the statement that he could realize this aim by borrowing from friends, is unaffected by the valuations placed upon the means, so that neither statement involves any special appraising evaluations. In short, the statements about means-ends relations are value-free.

4. There remains for consideration the claim that a value-free social science is impossible, because value commitments enter into the very *assessment of evidence* by social scientists, and not simply into the content of the conclusions they advance. This version of the claim itself has a large number of variant forms, but we shall examine only three of them.

The least radical form of the claim maintains that the conceptions held by a social scientist of what constitute cogent evidence or sound intellectual workmanship are the products of his education and his place in society, and are affected by the social values transmitted by this training and associated with this social position; accordingly, the values to which the social scientist is thereby committed determine which statements he *accepts* as well-grounded conclusions about human affairs. In this form, the claim is a *factual* thesis, and must be supported by detailed empirical evidence concerning the influences exerted by a man's moral and social values upon what he is ready to acknowledge as sound social analysis. In many instances such evidence is indeed available; and differences between social scientists in respect to what they accept as credible can sometimes be attributed to the influence of national, religious, economic, and other kinds of bias. However, this variant of the claim excludes neither the possibility of recognizing assessments of evidence that are prejudiced by special value commitments, nor the possibility of correcting for such prejudice. It therefore raises no issue that has not already been discussed when we examined the second reason for the alleged value-oriented character of social inquiry (pages 743–745 above).

Another but different form of the claim is based on recent work in theoretical statistics dealing with the assessment of evidence for so-called "statistical hypotheses" — hypotheses concerning the probabilities of random events, such as the hypothesis that the probability of a male human birth is one-half. The central idea relevant to the present question that underlies these developments can be sketched in terms of an example. Suppose that, before a fresh batch of medicine is put on sale, tests are performed on experimental animals for its possible toxic effects because of impurities that have not been eliminated in its manufacture, for example, by introducing small quantities of the drug into the diet of one hundred guinea pigs. If no more than a few of the animals show serious after-effects, the medicine is to be regarded as safe, and will be marketed; but if a contrary result is obtained the drug will be destroyed. Suppose now that three of the animals do in fact become gravely ill. Is this outcome significant (i.e., does it indicate that the drug has toxic effects), or is it perhaps an "accident" that happened because of some peculiarity in the affected animals? To answer the question, the experimenter must *decide* on the basis of the evidence between the hypothesis H_1: the drug is toxic, and the hypothesis H_2: the drug is not toxic. But how is he to decide, if he aims to be "reasonable" rather than arbitrary? Current statistical theory offers him a rule for making a reasonable decision, and bases the rule on the following analysis.

Whatever decision the experimenter may make, he runs the risk of committing either one of two types of errors: he may reject a hypothesis though in fact it is true (i.e., despite the fact that H_1 is actually true, he mistakenly decides against it in the light of the evidence available to him); or he may accept a hypothesis though in fact it is false. His decision would therefore be eminently reasonable, were it based on a rule guaranteeing that no decision ever made in accordance with the rule would commit either type of error. Unhappily, there are no rules of this sort. The next suggestion is to find a rule such that, when decisions are made in accordance with it, the relative frequency of each type of error is quite small. But unfortunately, the risks of committing each type of error are not independent; for example, it is in general logically impossible to find a rule so that decisions based on it will commit each type of error with a relative frequency not greater than one in a thousand. In consequence, before a reasonable rule can be proposed, the experimenter must compare the relative importance to himself of the two types of error, and state what risk he is willing to take of committing the type of error he judges to be the more important one. Thus, were he to reject H_1 though it is true (i.e., were he to commit an error of the first type), all the medicine under consideration would be put on sale, and the lives of those using it would be endangered; on the other hand, were he to commit an error of the second type with respect to H_1, the entire batch of medicine would be scrapped, and the manufacturer would incur a financial loss. However, the preservation of human life may be of greater moment to the experimenter than financial gain; and he may perhaps stipulate that he is unwilling to base his decision on a rule for which the risk of committing an error of the first type is greater than one such error in a hundred decisions. If this is assumed, statistical theory can specify a rule satisfying the experimenter's requirement, though how this is done, and how the risk of committing an error of the second type is calculated, are technical questions of no concern to us. The main point to be noted in this analysis is that the rule presupposes certain appraising judgments of value. In short, if this result is generalized, statistical theory appears to support the thesis that value commitments enter decisively into the rules for assessing evidence for statistical hypotheses.[11]

However, the theoretical analysis upon which this thesis rests does not entail the conclusion that the rules actually employed in every social inquiry for assessing evidence necessarily involve some *special* commitments, i.e., commitments such as those mentioned in the above example, as distinct from those generally implicit in science as an enterprise aiming to achieve reliable knowledge. Indeed, the above example illustrating the reasoning in current statistical theory can be misleading, insofar as it suggests that alternative decisions between statistical hypotheses must invariably lead to alternative actions having immediate practical consequences upon which different special values are

[11] The above example is borrowed from the discussion in J. Neymann, *First Course in Probability and Statistics*, New York, 1950, Chap. 5, where an elementary technical account of recent developments in statistical theory is presented. For a nontechnical account, see Irwin D. J. Bross, *Design for Decision*, New York, 1953, also R. B. Braithwaite, *Scientific Explanation*, Cambridge, Eng., 1953, Chap. 7.

placed. For example, a theoretical physicist may have to decide between two statistical hypotheses concerning the probability of certain energy exchanges in atoms; and a theoretical sociologist may similarly have to choose between two statistical hypotheses concerning the relative frequency of childless marriages under certain social arrangements. But neither of these men may have any *special values* at stake associated with the alternatives between which he must decide, other than the values, to which he is committed as a member of a scientific community, to conduct his inquiries with probity and responsibility. Accordingly, the question whether any special value commitments enter into assessments of evidence in either the natural or social sciences is not settled one way or the other by theoretical statistics; and the question can be answered only by examining actual inquiries in the various scientific disciplines.

Moreover, nothing in the reasoning of theoretical statistics depends on what particular subject matter is under discussion when a decision between alternative statistical hypotheses is to be made. For the reasoning is entirely general; and reference to some special subject matter becomes relevant only when a definite numerical value is to be assigned to the risk some investigator is prepared to take of making an erroneous decision concerning a given hypothesis. Accordingly, if current statistical theory is used to support the claim that value commitments enter into the assessment of evidence for statistical hypotheses in social inquiry, statistical theory can be used with equal justification to support analogous claims for all other inquiries as well. In short, the claim we have been discussing establishes no difficulty that supposedly occurs in the search for reliable knowledge in the study of human affairs which is not also encountered in the natural sciences.

A third form of this claim is the most radical of all. It differs from the first variant mentioned above in maintaining that there is a necessary *logical* connection, and not merely a contingent or causal one, between the "social perspective" of a student of human affairs and his standards of competent social inquiry, and in consequence the influence of the special values to which he is committed because of his own social involvements is not eliminable. This version of the claim is implicit in Hegel's account of the "dialectical" nature of human history and is integral to much Marxist as well as non-Marxist philosophy that stresses the "historically relative" character of social thought. In any event, it is commonly based on the assumption that, since social institutions and their cultural products are constantly changing, the intellectual apparatus required for understanding them must also change; and every idea employed for this purpose is therefore adequate only for some particular stage in the development of human affairs. Accordingly, neither the substantive concepts adopted for classifying and interpreting social phenomena, nor the logical canons used for estimating the worth of such concepts, have a "timeless validity"; there is no analysis of social phenomena which is not the expression of some special social standpoint, or which does not reflect the interests and values dominant in some sector of the human scene at a certain stage of its history. In consequence, although a sound distinction can be made in the natural sciences between the origin of a man's views and their factual validity, such a distinction allegedly cannot be made in social inquiry; and prominent exponents of "historical relativism" have therefore challenged the universal adequacy of the thesis that "the genesis of a proposition is under all circumstances irrelevant to its truth." As one influential proponent of this position puts the matter,

> The historical and social genesis of an idea would only be irrelevant to its ultimate validity if the temporal and social conditions of its emergence had no effect on its content and form. If this were the case, any two periods in the history of human knowledge would only be distinguished from one another by the fact that in the earlier period certain things were still unknown and certain errors still existed which, through later knowledge were completely corrected. This simple relationship between an earlier incomplete and a later complete

period of knowledge may to a large extent be appropriate for the exact sciences. . . . For the history of the cultural sciences, however, the earlier stages are not quite so simply superseded by the later stages, and it is not so easily demonstrable that early errors have subsequently been corrected. Every epoch has its fundamentally new approach and its characteristic point of view, and consequently sees the "same" object from a new perspective. . . . The very principles, in the light of which knowledge is to be criticized, are themselves found to be socially and historically conditioned. Hence their application appears to be limited to given historical periods and the particular types of knowledge then prevalent.[12]

Historical research into the influence of society upon the beliefs men hold is of undoubted importance for understanding the complex nature of the scientific enterprise; and the sociology of knowledge — as such investigations have come to be called — has produced many clarifying contributions to such an understanding. However, these admittedly valuable services of the sociology of knowledge do not establish the radical claim we have been stating. In the first place, there is no competent evidence to show that the principles employed in social inquiry for assessing the intellectual products are *necessarily* determined by the social perspective of the inquirer. On the contrary, the "facts" usually cited in support of this contention establish at best only a contingent causal relation between a man's social commitments and his canons of cognitive validity. For example, the once fashionable view that the "mentality" or logical operations of primitive societies differ from those typical in Western civilization — a discrepancy that was attributed to differences in the institutions of the societies under comparison — is now generally recognized to be erroneous, because it seriously misinterprets the intellectual processes of primitive peoples. Moreover, even extreme exponents of the sociology of knowledge admit that most conclusions asserted in mathematics and natural science are neutral to differences in social perspective of those asserting them, so that the genesis of these propositions is irrelevant to their validity. Why cannot propositions about human affairs exhibit a similar neutrality, at least in some cases? Sociologists of knowledge do not appear to doubt that the truth of the statement that two horses can in general pull a heavier load than can either horse alone, is logically independent of the social status of the individual who happens to affirm the statement. But they have not made clear just what are the inescapable considerations that allegedly make such independence inherently impossible for the analogous statement about human behavior, that two laborers can in general dig a ditch of given dimensions more quickly than can either laborer working alone.

In the second place, the claim faces a serious and frequently noted dialectical difficulty — a difficulty that proponents of the claim have succeeded in meeting only by abandoning the substance of the claim. For let us ask what is the cognitive status of the thesis that a social perspective enters essentially into the content as well as the validation of every assertion about human affairs. Is this thesis meaningful and valid only for those who maintain it and who thus subscribe to certain values because of their distinctive social commitments? If so, no one with a different social perspective can properly understand it; its acceptance as valid is strictly limited to those who can do so, and social scientists who subscribe to a different set of social values ought therefore dismiss it as empty talk. Or is the thesis singularly exempt from the class of assertions to which it applies, so that its meaning and truth are not inherently related to the social perspectives of those who assert it? If so, it is not evi-

[12] Karl Mannheim, *Ideology and Utopia*, New York, 1959, pp. 271, 288, 292*. The essay from which the above excerpts are quoted was first published in 1931, and Mannheim subsequently modified some of the views expressed in it. However, he reaffirmed the thesis stated in the quoted passages as late as 1946, the year before his death. See his letter to Kurt H. Wolff, dated April 15, 1946, quoted in the latter's "Sociology of Knowledge and Sociological Theory," in *Symposium on Sociological Theory* (ed. by Llewellyn Gross), Evanston, Ill., 1959, p. 571.

* [*Portions of this work have been reprinted as selection 53 of the present volume. Editor's note.*]

dent why the thesis is so exempt; but in any case, the thesis is then a conclusion of inquiry into human affairs that is presumably "objectively valid" in the usual sense of this phrase — and, if there is one such conclusion, it is not clear why there cannot be others as well.

To meet this difficulty, and to escape the self-defeating skeptical relativism to which the thesis is thus shown to lead, the thesis is sometimes interpreted to say that, though "absolutely objective" knowledge of human affairs is unattainable, a "relational" form of objectivity called "relationism" can nevertheless be achieved. On this interpretation, a social scientist can discover just what his social perspective is; and if he then formulates the conclusions of his inquiries "relationally," so as to indicate that his findings conform to the canons of validity implicit in his perspective, his conclusions will have achieved a "relational" objectivity. Social scientists sharing the same perspective can be expected to agree in their answers to a given problem when the canons of validity characteristic of their common perspective are correctly applied. On the other hand, students of social phenomena who operate within different but incongruous social perspectives can also achieve objectivity, if in no other way than by a "relational" formulation of what must otherwise be incompatible results obtained in their several inquiries. However, they can also achieve it in "a more roundabout fashion," by undertaking "to find a formula for translating the results of one into those of the other and to discover a common denominator for these varying perspectivistic insights."[13]

But it is difficult to see in what way "relational objectivity" differs from "objectivity" without the qualifying adjective and in the customary sense of the word. For example, a physicist who terminates an investigation with the conclusion that the velocity of light in water has a certain numerical value when measured in terms of a stated system of units, by a stated procedure, and under stated experimental conditions, is formulating his conclusion in a manner that is "relational" in the sense intended; and his conclusion is marked by "objectivity," presumably because it mentions the "relational" factors upon which the assigned numerical value of the velocity depends. However, it is fairly standard practice in the natural sciences to formulate certain types of conclusions in this fashion. Accordingly, the proposal that the social sciences formulate their findings in an analogous manner carries with it the admission that it is not in principle impossible for these disciplines to establish conclusions having the objectivity of conclusions reached in other domains of inquiry. Moreover, if the difficulty we are considering is to be resolved by the suggested translation formulas for rendering the "common denominators" of conclusions stemming from divergent social perspectives, those formulas cannot in turn be "situationally determined" in the sense of this phrase under discussion. For if those formulas were so determined, the same difficulty would crop up anew in connection with them. On the other hand, a search for such formulas is a phase in the search for invariant relations in a subject matter, so that formulations of these relations are valid irrespective of the particular perspective one may select from some class of perspectives on that subject matter. In consequence, in acknowledging that the search for such invariants in the social sciences is not inherently bound to fail, proponents of the claim we have been considering abandon what at the outset was its most radical thesis.

In brief, the various reasons we have been examining for the intrinsic impossibility of securing objective (i.e., value-free and unbiased) conclusions in the social sciences do not establish what they purport to establish, even though in some instances they direct attention to undoubtedly important practical difficulties frequently encountered in these disciplines.

[13] Karl Mannheim, *op. cit.*, pp. 300–01.

No Science Can Be Value-Free

57

The Scientist Qua Scientist Makes Value Judgments[1]

RICHARD RUDNER

The question of the relationship of the making of value judgments in a typically ethical sense to the methods and procedures of science has been discussed in the literature at least to that point which e. e. cummings somewhere refers to as "The Mystical Moment of Dullness." Nevertheless, albeit with some trepidation, I feel that something more may fruitfully be said on the subject.

In particular the problem has once more been raised in an interesting and poignant fashion by recently published discussions between Carnap (1) and Quine (3) on the question of the ontological commitments which one may make in the choosing of language systems.

I shall refer to this discussion in more detail in the sequel; for the present, however, let us briefly examine the current status of what is somewhat loosely called the "fact-value dichotomy."

I have not found the arguments which are usually offered, by those who believe that scientists do essentially make value judgments, satisfactory. On the other hand the rebuttals of some of those with opposing viewpoints seem to have had at least a *prima facie* cogency although they too may in the final analysis prove to have been subtly perverse.

Those who contend that scientists do essentially make value judgments generally support their contentions by either

A. pointing to the fact that our having a science at all somehow "involves" a value judgment, or

B. by pointing out that in order to select, say among alternative problems, the scientist must make a value judgment; or (perhaps most frequently)

C. by pointing to the fact that the scientist cannot escape his quite human self — he is a "mass of predilections" and these predilections must inevitably influence all of his activities not excepting his scientific ones.

To such arguments, a great many empirically oriented philosophers and scientists have responded that the value judgments involved in our decisions to have a science, or to select problem A for attention rather than problem B are, *of course*, extra-scientific. If (they say) it is necessary to make a decision to have a science before we can have one, then this decision is literally pre-scientific and the act has thereby certainly not been shown to be any part of the *procedures* of science. Similarly the decision to focus attention on one problem rather than another is extra-problematic and forms no part of the procedures involved in dealing with the problem *decided* upon. Since it is *these* procedures which constitute the method of science, value judgments, so they respond, have not been shown to be involved in the scientific method as such. Again, with respect to the inevitable presence of our predilections in the laboratory, most empirically oriented philosophers and scientists agree that this is "unfortunately" the case; but, they hasten to add, if science is to progress toward objectivity the influence of our personal feelings or biases on experimental results must be minimized. We must try not to let our personal idiosyncrasies affect our scientific work. The perfect scientist — the scientist

From *Philosophy of Science*, 20:1 (January, 1953), pp. 1–6.

[1] The opinions or assertions contained herein are the private ones of the writer and are not to be construed as official or reflecting the views of the Navy Department or the Naval Establishments at large.

qua scientist does not allow this kind of value judgment to influence his work. However much he may find doing so unavoidable *qua* father, *qua* lover, *qua* member of society, *qua* grouch, *when* he does so he is not behaving *qua* scientist.

As I indicated at the outset, the arguments of neither of the protagonists in this issue appear quite satisfactory to me. The empiricists' rebuttals, telling prima facie as they may against the specific arguments that evoke them, nonetheless do not appear ultimately to stand up, but perhaps even more importantly, *the original arguments* seem utterly too frail.

I believe that a much stronger case may be made for the contention that value judgments are essentially involved in the procedures of science. And what I now propose to show is that scientists as scientists *do* make value judgments.

Now I take it that no analysis of what constitutes the method of science would be satisfactory unless it comprised some assertion to the effect that the scientist as scientist accepts or rejects hypotheses.

But if this is so then clearly the scientist as scientist does make value judgments. For, since no scientific hypothesis is ever completely verified, in accepting a hypothesis the scientist must make the decision that the evidence is *sufficiently* strong or that the probability is *sufficiently* high to warrant the acceptance of the hypothesis. Obviously our decision regarding the evidence and respecting how strong is "strong enough", is going to be a function of the *importance*, in the typically ethical sense, of making a mistake in accepting or rejecting the hypothesis. Thus, to take a crude but easily manageable example, if the hypothesis under consideration were to the effect that a toxic ingredient of a drug was not present in lethal quantity, we would require a relatively high degree of confirmation or confidence before accepting the hypothesis — for the consequences of making a mistake here are exceedingly grave by our moral standards. On the other hand, if say, our hypothesis stated that, on the basis of a sample, a certain lot of machine stamped belt buckles was not defective, the degree of confidence we should require would be relatively not so high. *How sure we need to be before we accept a hypothesis will depend on how serious a mistake would be.*

The examples I have chosen are from scientific inferences in industrial quality control. But the point is clearly quite general in application. It would be interesting and instructive, for example, to know just how high a degree of probability the Manhattan Project scientists demanded for the hypothesis that no uncontrollable pervasive chain reaction would occur, before they proceeded with the first atomic bomb detonation or first activated the Chicago pile above a critical level. It would be equally interesting and instructive to know why they decided that *that* probability value (if one was decided upon) was high enough rather than one which was higher; and perhaps most interesting of all to learn whether the problem in this form was brought to consciousness at all.

In general then, before we can accept any hypothesis, the value decision must be made in the light of the seriousness of a mistake, that the probability is *high enough* or that, the evidence is *strong enough*, to warrant its acceptance.

Before going further, it will perhaps be well to clear up two points which might otherwise prove troublesome below. First I have obviously used the term "probability" up to this point in a quite loose and pre-analytic sense. But my point can be given a more rigorous formulation in terms of a description of the process of making statistical inference and of the acceptance or rejection of hypotheses in statistics. As is well known, the acceptance or rejection of such a hypothesis presupposes that a certain level of significance or level of confidence or critical region be selected.[2]

[2] "In practice three levels are commonly used: 1 per cent, 5 per cent and 0.3 of one per cent. There is nothing sacred about these three values; *they have become established in practice without any rigid theoretical justification.*" (my italics) (4:435). To establish significance at the 5 per cent level means that one is willing

It is with respect at least to the *necessary* selection of a confidence level or interval that the necessary value judgment in the inquiry occurs. For, "the size of the critical region (one selects) is related to *the risk one wants to accept* in testing a statistical hypothesis" (4: 435).

And clearly how great a risk one is willing to take of being wrong in accepting or rejecting the hypothesis will depend upon how seriously in the typically ethical sense one views the consequences of making a mistake.

I believe, of course, that an adequate rational reconstruction of the procedures of science would show that every scientific inference is properly construable as a statistical inference (i.e. as an inference from a set of characteristics of a sample of a population to a set of characteristics of the total population) and that such an inference would be scientifically in control only in so far as it is statistically in control. But it is not necessary to argue this point, for even if one believes that what is involved in some scientific inferences is not statistical probability but rather a concept like strength of evidence or degree of confirmation, one would still be concerned with making the decision that the evidence was *strong enough* or the degree of confirmation *high enough* to warrant acceptance of the hypothesis. Now, many empiricists who reflect on the foregoing considerations agree that acceptances or rejections of hypotheses do essentially involve value judgments, but they are nonetheless loathe to accept the conclusion. And one objection which has been raised against this line of argument by those of them who are suspicious of the intrusion of value questions into the "objective realm of science," is that actually the scientist's task is only to *determine* the degree of confirmation or the strength of the evidence which *exists* for an hypothesis. In short, they object that while it may be a function of the scientist *qua member of society* to decide whether a degree of probability associated with the hypothesis is high enough to warrant its acceptance, *still* the task of the scientist *qua* scientist is *just the determination* of the degree of probability or the strength of the evidence for a hypothesis and not the acceptance or rejection of that hypothesis.

But a little reflection will show that the plausibility of this objection is apparent merely. For the determination that the degree of confirmation is say, p, or that the strength of evidence is such and such, which is on this view being held to be the indispensable task of the scientist *qua* scientist, is clearly nothing more than *the acceptance by the scientist of the hypothesis that the degree of confidence is p or that the strength of the evidence is such and such;* and as these men have conceded, acceptance of hypotheses does require value decisions. The second point which it may be well to consider before finally turning our attention to the Quine-Carnap discussion, has to do with the nature of the suggestions which have thus far been made in this essay. In this connection, it is important to point out that the preceding remarks do *not* have as their import that an empirical description of every present day scientist ostensibly going about his business would include the statement that he made a value judgment at such and such a juncture. This is no doubt the case; but it is a hypothesis which can only be confirmed by a discipline which cannot be said to have gotten extremely far along as yet; namely, the Sociology and Psychology of Science, whether such an empirical description is warranted, cannot be settled from the armchair.

My remarks have, rather, amounted to this: any adequate analysis or (if I may use the term) rational reconstruction of the method of science must comprise the statement that the scientist *qua* scientist accepts or rejects hypotheses; and further that an analysis of that statement would reveal it to entail that the

---

to take the risk of accepting a hypothesis as true when one will be thus making a mistake, one time in twenty. Or in other words, that one will be wrong, (over the long run) once every twenty times if one employed an .05 level of significance. See also (2:ch. V) for such statements as "which of these two errors is most *important* to avoid (it being necessary to make such a decision in order to accept or reject the given hypothesis) is a *subjective matter* . . ." (p. 262) (my italics).

scientist *qua* scientist makes value judgments.

I think that it is in the light of the foregoing arguments, the substance of which has, in one form or another, been alluded to in past years by a number of inquirers (notably C. W. Churchman, R. L. Ackoff, and A. Wald) that the Quine-Carnap discussion takes on heightened interest. For, if I understand that discussion and its outcome correctly, although it apparently begins a good distance away from any consideration of the fact-value dichotomy, and although all the way through it both men touch on the matter in a way which indicates that they believe that questions concerning that dichotomy are, if anything, merely tangential to their main issue, yet it eventuates with Quine by an independent argument apparently in agreement with at least the conclusion here reached and also apparently having forced Carnap to that conclusion. (Carnap, however, is expected to reply to Quine's article and I may be too sanguine here.)

The issue of ontological commitment between Carnap and Quine has been one of relatively long standing. In this recent article (1), Carnap maintains that we are concerned with two kinds of questions of existence relative to a given language system. One is what *kinds* of entities it would be permissable to speak about as existing when that language system is used; i.e. what kind of *framework* for speaking of entities should our system comprise. This, according to Carnap, is an *external* question. It is the *practical* question of what sort of linguistic system we want to choose. Such questions as "are there abstract entities?," or "are there physical entities?" thus are held to belong to the category of external questions. On the other hand, having made the decision regarding which linguistic framework to adopt, we can then raise questions like "are there any black swans?" "What are the factors of 544?" etc. Such questions are *internal* questions.

For our present purposes, the important thing about all of this is that while for Carnap *internal* questions are theoretical ones, i.e., ones whose answers have cognitive content, external questions are not theoretical at all. They are *practical questions* — they concern our decisions to employ one language structure or another. They are of the kind that face us when for example we have to decide whether we ought to have a Democratic or a Republican administration for the next four years. In short, though neither Carnap nor Quine employ the epithet, they are *value questions*.

Now if this dichotomy of existence questions is accepted Carnap can still deny the essential involvement of the making of value judgments in the procedures of science by insisting that concern with *external* questions, admittedly necessary and admittedly axiological, is nevertheless in some sense a pre-scientific concern. But most interestingly, what Quine then proceeds to do is to show that the dichotomy, as Carnap holds it is untenable. This is not the appropriate place to repeat Quine's arguments which are brilliantly presented in the article referred to. They are in line with the views he has expressed in his "Two Dogmas of Empiricism" essay and especially with his introduction to his recent book, *Methods of Logic*. Nonetheless the final paragraph of the Quine article I'm presently considering sums up his conclusions neatly:

> Within natural science there is a continuum of gradations, from the statements which report observations to those which reflect basic features say of quantum theory or the theory of relativity. The view which I end up with, in the paper last cited, is that statements of ontology or even of mathematics and logic form a continuation of this continuum, a continuation which is perhaps yet more remote from observation than are the central principles of quantum theory or relativity. The differences here are in my view differences only in degree and not in kind. Science is a unified structure, and in principle it is the structure as a whole, and not its component statements one by one, that experience confirms or shows to be imperfect. Carnap maintains that ontological questions, and likewise questions of logical or mathematical principle, are questions not of fact but of choosing a convenient conceptual scheme or framework for science; and with this I agree only if the same be conceded for every scientific hypothesis. (3:71–72).

In the light of all of this I think that the statement that *Scientists qua Scientists* make value judgments, is also a consequence of Quine's position.

Now, if the major point I have here undertaken to establish is correct, then clearly we are confronted with a first order crisis in science & methodology. The positive horror which most scientists and philosophers of science have of the intrusion of value considerations into science is wholly understandable. Memories of the (now diminished but to a certain extent still continuing) conflict between science and, e.g., the dominant religions over the intrusion of religious value considerations into the domain of scientific inquiry, are strong in many reflective scientists. The traditional search for objectivity exemplifies science's pursuit of one of its most precious ideals. But for the scientist to close his eyes to the fact that scientific method *intrinsically* requires the making of value decisions, for him to push out of his consciousness the fact that he does make them, can in no way bring him closer to the ideal of objectivity. To refuse to pay attention to the value decisions which *must* be made, to make them intuitively, unconsciously, haphazardly, is to leave an essential aspect of scientific method scientifically out of control.

What seems called for (and here no more than the sketchiest indications of the problem can be given) is nothing less than a radical reworking of the ideal of scientific objectivity. The slightly juvenile conception of the cold-blooded, emotionless, impersonal, passive scientist mirroring the world perfectly in the highly polished lenses of his steel rimmed glasses, — this stereotype — is no longer, if it ever was, adequate.

What is being proposed here is that objectivity for science lies at least in becoming precise about what value judgments are being and might have been made in a given inquiry — and even, to put it in its most challenging form, what value decisions ought to be made; in short that a science of ethics is a necessary requirement if science's progress toward objectivity is to be continuous.

Of course the establishment of such a science of ethics is a task of stupendous magnitude and it will probably not even be well launched for many generations. But a first step is surely comprised of the reflective self awareness of the scientist in making the value judgments he must make.

References

[1] Carnap, R., "Empiricism, Semantics, and Ontology," *Revue Internationale de Philosophie*, XI, 1950, p. 20–40.

[2] Neyman, J., *First Course in Probability and Statistics*, New York: Henry Holt & Co., 1950.

[3] Quine, W. V., "On Carnap's Views on Ontology," *Philosophical Studies*, II, No. 5, 1951.

[4] Rosander, A. C., *Elementary Principles of Statistics*. New York: D. Van Nostrand Co., 1951.

Selected Bibliography

To assemble anything approaching an exhaustive bibliography of material in the philosophy of social science is out of the question. What does follow is a small but, I believe, valuable fragment of this burgeoning area. Items anthologized or discussed above are listed only where their claims to importance could not be overlooked. Asterisks have been placed by those works which include useful bibliographies of their own; roman numerals at the end of a listing indicate other parts in this anthology to which the enumerated item has relevance.

I. *Anthologies, Introductory Works, and General Perspectives*

ARGYLE, M., *The Scientific Study of Social Behavior.* London, Methuen & Co., Ltd., 1957. (VII)

ARON, R., *Main Currents in Sociological Thought.* New York, Basic Books, Inc., Publishers, 1965. (III, VI, VIII)

BECKER, H. and H. E. BARNES, eds., with the assistance of Emil Benoit-Smullyan and others, *Social Thought from Lore to Science*, 3rd. ed., 3 vols., New York, Dover Publications, Inc. 1961.

BRAYBROOKE, D., ed., *Philosophical Problems of the Social Sciences.* New York, The Macmillan Company, 1965. (IV, VIII)

BRODBECK, M., "On the Philosophy of the Social Sciences," *Philosophy of Science*, Vol. 21 (1954). (III, V)

*BRODBECK, M., *Readings in the Philosophy of Social Science.* New York, The Macmillan Company, 1968. (All sections)

CASSIRER, E., *An Essay on Man: An Introduction to a Philosophy of Human Culture.* New Haven, Conn., Yale University Press, 1945. (III, VII)

*CHAPPELL, V. C., ed., *The Philosophy of Mind.* Englewood Cliffs, N. J., Prentice-Hall, Inc., 1962. (IV, V)

COLLINGWOOD, R. C., *An Autobiography.* Oxford, Oxford University Press, 1962.

COWLING, M., *The Nature and Limits of Political Science.* London, Cambridge University Press, 1963. (III, IV)

DOHERTY, E. F., "Logic of the Social Sciences," *Sociological Review*, New Ser., Vol. 1 (1953). (III)

DOLLARD, J., and N. E. MILLER, *Personality and Psychotherapy.* New York, McGraw-Hill Publishing Company, Inc., 1950. (IV)

DRISCOLL, J. M. and C. S. HYNEMAN, "Methodology for Political Scientists: Perspectives for Study," *American Political Science Review*, Vol. 49 (1955).

EASTON, D., *The Political System.* New York, Alfred A. Knopf, Inc., 1953. (IV)

EASTON, D., ed., *Varieties of Political Theory.* Englewood Cliffs, N. J., Prentice-Hall, Inc. 1966.

FESTINGER, L. and D. KATZ, eds., *Research Methods in the Behavioral Sciences.* New York, The Dryden Press, Inc., 1953. (V, VI)

FURFEY, P. H., *The Scope and Method of Sociology: A Meta-Sociological Treatise.* New York, Harper & Brothers, 1953. (III, IV, VIII)

GEWIRTH, A., "Subjectivism and Objectivism in the Social Sciences," *Philosophy of Science*, Vol. 21 (1954). (III, IV)

GIBSON, Q., *The Logic of Social Inquiry.* New York, Humanities Press, 1960. (IV, V)

GROSS, L., ed., *Symposium on Sociological Theory.* Evanston, Ill., Row, Peterson and Company, 1959. (III–VIII)

GRÜNBAUM, A., "Causality and the Science of Human Behavior," *American Scientist*, Vol. 40 (1952). (III, IV)

*GUSTAFSON, D. F., ed., *Essays in Philosophical Psychology.* New York, Doubleday and Company, 1964. (IV, V)

HAMPSHIRE, S., "Can There Be a General Science of Man?", *Commentary*, Vol. 24 (1957).

HAMPSHIRE, S., ed., *Philosophy of Mind.* New York, Harper & Row Publishers, 1966. (IV, V)

HANDY, R., *Methodology of The Behavioral Sciences.* Springfield, Ill., Charles C Thomas, Publisher, 1964. (III)

HOSELITZ, B. F., ed., *A Reader's Guide to the Social Sciences.* Illinois, The Free Press of Glencoe, 1959.

KAPLAN, A., *The Conduct of Inquiry: Methodology for Behavioral Science.* San Francisco, Chandler, 1964. (All sections)

KAUFMANN, F., *Methodology of the Social Sciences.* New York, Oxford University Press, 1944. (III, IV, VIII)

LUNDBERG, G. A., *Foundations of Sociology.* New York, The Macmillan Company, 1939. (IV, V)

LUNDBERG, G. A., "Is Sociology Too Scientific?", *Sociologus,* Vol. 9 (1933).

MARTINDALE, D., *The Nature and Types of Sociological Theory.* Boston, Houghton Mifflin Company, 1960. (IV, VII)

MAYER, J., *Social Science Principles in the Light of Scientific Method.* Raleigh, N. C., The Duke University Press, 1941. (II-IV)

MILLS, C. W., *Images of Man: The Classical Tradition in Sociological Thinking.* New York, Oxford University Press, 1959. (III, VII, VIII)

MORGENBESSER, S., *Determinism and Human Behavior.* New York, Alfred A. Knopf, Inc., (announced).

NATANSON, M. ed., *Philosophy of the Social Sciences.* New York, Random House, Inc., 1963.

NEURATH, O., *Foundations of the Social Sciences,* Vol. II, No. 1 of the *International Encyclopedia of Unified Science.* Chicago, University of Chicago Press, 1941. (II-V)

PARETO, V., *The Mind and Society.* New York, Harcourt, Brace & Company, Inc., 1935.

PARSONS, T., and others, eds., *Theories of Society.* New York, The Free Press of Glencoe, 1961. (IV, VII, VIII)

RADCLIFFE-BROWN, A. R., *A Natural Science of Society.* Illinois, The Free Press of Glencoe, 1957. (II–IV)

REX, J., *Key Problems of Sociological Theory,* New York, Humanities Press, 1962. (IV)

RICE, S. A., ed., *Methods in Social Science: A Case Book.* Chicago, The University of Chicago Press, 1931.

ROBBINS, L., *An Essay on the Nature and Significance of Economic Science.* London, Macmillan & Co. Ltd., 1952. (IV, VII)

ROGERS, C. R. and B. F. SKINNER, "Some Issues Concerning the Control of Human Behavior," *Science,* Vol. 24 (1956). (III, IV)

*RUDNER, R., *Philosophy of Social Science.* Englewood Cliffs, N. J., Prentice-Hall, 1966. (III, IV, VII, VIII).

RUITENBECK, H. M., ed., *Varieties of Classic Social Theory* and *Varieties of Modern Social Theory.* New York, E. P. Dutton and Co., Inc., 1963.

RUNCIMAN, W. G., *Social Science and Political Theory.* London: Cambridge University Press, 1963.

SHAFFER, J., *Philosophy of Mind.* Englewood Cliffs, N. J., Prentice-Hall, 1968.

STRAUSS, A., ed., *Selected Papers by George Herbert Mead on Social Psychology.* Chicago, The University of Chicago Press, 1964. (III, V)

VAN DYKE, V., *Political Science: A Philosophical Analysis.* Stanford, Calif., Stanford University Press, 1960. (III, IV)

WATSON, J., *Behaviorism.* New York, W. W. Norton & Company, 1924. (IV)

WHITE, A. R., *The Philosophy of Mind.* New York, Random House, Inc., 1967. (IV, V)

WOOTON, B., *Testament for Social Science: An Essay in the Application of Scientific Method to Human Problems.* London, George Allen & Unwin, Ltd., 1950. (III, VIII)

ZNANIECKI, F., *The Method of Sociology.* New York, Farrar & Rinehart, Inc., 1934. (III, IV)

II. The Logic of Scientific Inquiry

*AYER, A. J. ed., *Logical Positivism,* Glencoe, Ill., The Free Press of Glencoe, 1959.

BARKER, S. F., *Induction and Hypothesis: A Study of the Logic of Confirmation.* Ithaca, N. Y., Cornell University Press, 1957.

BERGMANN, G., *Philosophy of Science.* Madison, Wis., The University of Wisconsin Press, 1957.

BLACK, M., "The Justification of Induction," in M. Black, *Language and Philosophy.* Ithaca, N. Y., Cornell University Press, 1949.

BRAITHWAITE, R. B., *Scientific Explanation.* London, Cambridge University Press, 1953. (IV)

BRIDGMAN, P. W., *The Logic of Modern Physics.* New York, The Macmillan Company, 1932. (V)

BUNGE, M., "Kinds and Criteria of Scientific Laws," *Philosophy of Science,* Vol. 28 (1961).

CAMPBELL, N. R., *What Is Science?* New York, Dover Publications, Inc., 1952.

COHEN, M. R., *Reason and Nature.* New York, The Free Press, 1953.

COLODNY, R. G., ed., *Beyond the Edge of Certainty.* Englewood Cliffs, N. J., Prentice-Hall, 1965.

DANTO, A. and S. MORGENBESSER, eds., *Philosophy of Science*. Cleveland, Meridian Books, World, 1960.

DUHEM, P., *The Aim and Structure of Physical Theory*. New York, Atheneum Publishers, 1962.

FAIN, H., "Some Problems of Causal Explanation," *Mind*, Vol. 72 (1963).

*FEIGL, H. and M. BRODBECK, eds., *Readings in the Philosophy of Science*. New York, Appleton-Century-Crofts, 1953. (III-IV)

FEIGL, H. and G. MAXWELL, eds., *Current Issues in the Philosophy of Science*. New York, Holt, Rinehart and Winston, Inc., 1961.

*FEIGL, H. and W. SELLARS, eds., *Readings in Philosophical Analysis*. New York, Appleton-Century-Crofts, 1949. (V)

FRANK, P., *Philosophy of Science*. Englewood Cliffs, N. J., Prentice-Hall, 1957.

GALLIE, W. B., "An Interpretation of Causal Laws," *Mind*, Vol. 48 (1939).

GOODMAN, N., *Fact, Fiction, and Forecast*. Cambridge, Mass., Harvard University Press, 1955.

GOROVITZ, S., "Causal Judgments and Causal Explanations, "*Journal of Philosophy*, Vol. 62 (1965).

GOUDGE, T. A., "Causal Explanation in Natural History," *British Journal for the Philosophy of Science*, Vol. 9 (1958).

HANSON, N. R., "On the Symmetry between Explanation and Prediction," *Philosophical Review*, Vol. 68 (1959).

HAWKINS, D., *The Language of Nature*. San Francisco, W. H. Freeman and Company, 1964.

HEMPEL, C. G., *Aspects of Scientific Explanation*. New York, The Free Press of Glencoe, 1965. (IV, V, VII)

HEMPEL, C. G., *Philosophy of Natural Science*. Englewood Cliffs, N. J., Prentice-Hall, 1966.

HESSE, M., "A New Look at Scientific Explanation," *Review of Metaphysics*, Vol. 17 (1963).

HOFSTADTER, A., "Universality, Explanation, and Scientific Law," *Journal of Philosophy*, Vol. 50 (1953).

HOSPERS, J., "On Explanation," *Journal of Philosophy*, Vol. 43 (1946).

JASPERS, K., "Truth and Science," *Philosophy Today*, Vol. 6 (1962).

KAHL, R., ed., *Studies in Explanation*, Englewood Cliffs, N. J., Prentice-Hall, 1963.

KATZ, J. J., *The Problem of Induction and Its Solution*. Chicago, The University of Chicago Press, 1962.

KEMENY, J. G., *A Philosopher Looks at Science*. Princeton, D. Van Nostrand Company, Inc., 1959.

KORNER, S., ed., *Observation and Interpretation*. London, Butterworth & Co. (Publishers), Ltd., 1957.

KUHN, T. S., *The Structure of Scientific Revolutions*, Chicago, The University of Chicago Press, 1963.

*MADDEN, E. H., ed., *The Structure of Scientific Thought*. Boston, Houghton Mifflin Company, 1960. (IV)

MARGENAU, H., *The Nature of Physical Reality*. New York, McGraw-Hill Publishing Company, Inc., 1950.

MEAD, G. H., "Scientific Method and the Individual Thinker," in J. Dewey's and others, *Creative Intelligence*. New York, Henry Holt and Company, Inc., 1917.

MEHLBERG, H., "The Range and Limits of the Scientific Method," *Journal of Philosophy*, Vol. 51 (1954).

MISCHEL, T., "Pragmatic Aspects of Explanation," *Philosophy of Science*, Vol. 33, (1966).

NAGEL, E., *The Structure of Science*. New York, Harcourt, Brace & World, Inc., 1961. (III–V, VII)

NAGEL, E., P. SUPPES, and A. TARSKI, eds., *Logic, Methodology, and Philosophy of Science*. Stanford, Calif., Stanford University Press, 1962.

NEWMAN, F., "Explanation Sketches," *Philosophy of Science*, Vol. 32 (1965).

NORTHROP, F. S. C., *The Logic of the Sciences and the Humanities*. New York, Meridian Books, Inc., 1959. (III)

PAP, A., *An Introduction to the Philosophy of Science*. New York, The Free Press of Glencoe, 1962.

POLANYI, M., *Science, Faith, and Society*. Oxford, Oxford University Press, 1946. (VIII)

POLANYI, M., "The Unaccountable Element in Science," *Philosophy*, Vol. 37 (1962).

POPPER, K. R., *The Logic of Scientific Discovery*. London, Hutchinson & Co. (Publishers), Ltd., 1959.

PUTNAM, H., *The Philosophy of Physics and Mathematics*. New York, Alfred A. Knopf, Inc. (announced).

RESCHER, N., "On Prediction and Explanation," *British Journal for the Philosophy of Science*, Vol. 8 (1958).

SCHEFFLER, I., *The Anatomy of Inquiry*. New York, Alfred A. Knopf, Inc., 1963.

SCRIVEN, M., "Discussion: Comments on Professor Grünbaum's Remarks at the Wesleyan Meeting," *Philosophy of Science*, Vol. 29 (1962).

SCRIVEN, M., "The Structure of Science," (review of Nagel's *The Structure of Science*) *Review of Metaphysics*, Vol. 17 (1963). (IV)

SKARSGARD, L. "Some Remarks on the Logic of Explanation," *Philosophy of Science*, Vol. 25, 1958.

SMART, J. J. C., "Theory Construction," *Philosophy and Phenomenological Research*, 1950–1951; Reprinted in A. FLEW, ed., *Logic and Language*. New York, Anchor Books, Doubleday & Company, Inc., 1965.

SUCHTING, W. A., "Deductive Explanation and Prediction Revisited," *Philosophy of Science*, Vol. 34 (1967).

SUPPES, P., *Axiomatic Method in the Empirical Sciences*. New York, Alfred A. Knopf, Inc. (announced).

TAYLOR, R., "Causation," *The Monist*, Vol. 47 (1963). (IV)

TOULMIN, S., *The Philosophy of Science*. London, Hutchinson & Co. (Publishers) Ltd., 1953.

USHENKO, A. P., A. HOFSTADTER, and A. GRÜNBAUM, "The Conception of Law in Science," a symposium, *Journal of Philosophy*, Vol. 50 (1953).

WIENER, P. ed., *Readings in the Philosophy of Science*. New York, Charles Scribner's Sons, 1953.

WILKIE, J. S., "Causation and Explanation in Theoretical Biology," *British Journal for the Philosophy of Science*, Vol. 1 (1950). (IV)

WOODGER, J. H., *Language and Biology*. Cambridge, Eng., Cambridge University Press, 1952. (V)

YOLTON, J. W., "Explanation," *British Journal for the Philosophy of Science*, Vol. 10 (1959).

III. Is Social Science Methodologically Distinct from Natural Science?

BEARD, C., *The Nature of the Social Sciences*. New York, Charles Scribner's Sons, 1934. (VII, VIII)

BECK, L. W., "The 'Natural Science Ideal' in the Social Sciences," *Scientific Monthly*, Vol. 68 (1949).

BECK, S. J., "The Science of Personality: Nomothetic or Idiographic?", *Psychological Review*, Vol. 60, (1953).

BIERSTEDT, R., "A Critique of Empiricism in Sociology," *American Sociological Review*, Vol. 14 (1949). (IV)

BIERSTEDT, R., "Sociology and Humane Learning," *American Sociological Review*, Vol. 25 (1960).

BUBER, M., *I and Thou*. New York, Charles Scribner's Sons, 1958. (IV)

BUBER, M., *The Knowledge of Man*, New York, Harper & Row, Publishers, 1965. (IV)

CASTELL, A., *The Self in Philosophy*. New York, The Macmillan Company, 1965.

CHAPIN, F. S., "The Experimental Method in the Study of Human Relations," *The Scientific Monthly*, Vol. 68 (1949).

COOK, T. I., "Science: Natural and Social," *Philosophy of Science*, Vol. 6 (1939).

CROCE, B., *Philosophy of the Practical*. London, Macmillan & Co., Ltd., 1913.

DIESING, P., "Objectivism vs. Subjectivism in the Social Sciences," *Philosophy of Science*, Vol. 33 (1966). (V, VIII)

DODD, S. C., "Scientific Methods in Human Relations," *American Journal of Economics and Sociology*, Vol. 10 (1951).

FEUER, L. S. and E. M. ALBERT, symposium on "Causality in the Social Sciences," *Journal of Philosophy*, Vol. 51 (1954). (IV)

GOLDBERG, A. S., "Political Science as Science," *Yale Political Science Research*, Library Publication No. 1. New Haven, Yale University Press.

GOLDENWEISER, A., "The Concept of Causality in the Physical and Social Sciences," *American Sociological Review*, Vol. 3 (1938). (IV)

GOLDENWEISER, A., "The Relation of the Natural Sciences to the Social Sciences," in *Contemporary Social Theory*, Harry Elmer Barnes, ed., New York, D. Appleton-Century Co., 1940.

GRÜNBAUM, A., "Historical Determinism, Social Activism, and Predictions in the Social Sciences," *British Journal for the Philosophy of Science*, Vol. 7 (1956).

GRÜNBERG, E., "Notes on the Verifiability of Economic Laws," *Philosophy of Science*, Vol. 24 (1957). (IV)

GRÜNBERG, E., and F. MODIGLIANI, "The Predictability of Social Events," *Journal of Political Economy*, Vol. 62 (1954).

GRÜNBERG, E., and F. MODIGLIANI, "Reflexive Predictions," *Philosophy of Science*, Vol. 32 (1965).

HALDANE, J. B. S., "The Argument from Animals to Men: An Examination of Its Validity to Anthropology," *Journal of the Royal Anthropological Institute of Great Britain and Ireland*, Vol. 86 (1956).

HANDY, R. and P. KURTZ, *A Current Appraisal of the Behavioral Sciences*. Great Barrington, Mass., Behavioral Research Council, 1964.

HART, C. W. M., "Some Obstacles to a Scientific Sociology," *Canadian Journal of Economics and Political Science*, Vol. 6 (1940). (VIII)

HODGES, H. A., *The Philosophy of Wilheim Dilthey*. London, Routledge & Kegan Paul, Ltd. 1952. (IV, V)

HUTTEN, E. H., "On Explanation in Psychology and Physics," *British Journal for the Philosophy of Science*, Vol. 7 (1956). (IV)

KLUBACK, W., *Wilheim Dilthey's Philosophy of History*. New York, Columbia University Press, 1956. (IV, V)

KNIGHT, F. H., "The Limitations of Scientific Method in Economics," in R. Tugwell, ed., *The Trend of Economics*, New York: Alfred A. Knopf, Inc., 1924.

LEVY, M. J. Jr., "Some Basic Methodological Difficulties in Social Science," *Philosophy of Science*, Vol. 17 (1950).

LEWIS, D. K. and J. S. RICHARDSON, "Scriven on Human Unpredictability," *Philosophical Studies*, Vol. 17 (1966). (IV)

LINDLEY, F., "The Control Factor in Social Experimentation," *Philosophy of Science*, Vol. 21 (1954).

LOUCH, A. R., "Science and Psychology," *British Journal for the Philosophy of Science*, Vol. 13 (1962). (IV)

LUNDBERG, G. A., "The Natural Science Trend in Sociology," *American Journal of Sociology*, Vol. 61 (1955).

MACFIE, A. L., "On the Break Between the Natural and the Social Sciences," *Philosophical Quarterly*, Vol. 1 (1951).

MACHLUP, F., "The Inferiority Complex of the Social Sciences," in M. Sennholz ed. *On Freedom and Free Enterprise: Essays in Honor of Ludwig von Mises*, Princeton, N. J., D. Van Nostrand Company, Inc., 1956.

MACHLUP, F., "The Problems of Verification in Economics," *Southern Economic Journal*, Vol. 22 (1955). (IV)

MACINTYRE, A., "A Mistake about Causality in Social Science," in P. Laslett and W. G. Runciman, eds., *Philosophy, Politics and Society*, 2nd ser., Oxford, Basil Blackwell & Mott, Ltd., 1962. (IV)

MACIVER, R. M., *Social Causation*. Boston, Ginn and Company, 1942. (IV)

MCKEON, R., "De Anima: Psychology and Science," *Journal of Philosophy*, Vol. 27 (1930).

MCLEOD, R. B., "The Phenomenological Approach to Social Psychology," in R. Tagiuri and L. Petrullo eds., *Person, Perception and Interpersonal Behavior*, Stanford, Calif., Stanford University Press, 1958. (IV, V)

OAKESHOTT, M., *Rationalism in Politics & Other Essays*. London, Methuen & Co., Ltd., 1962. (VII)

ORTEGA y GASSET, J., *Man and People*. New York, W. W. Norton & Company, Inc., 1957. (VII, VIII)

PFUETZE, P. E., *Self, Society, Existence: Human Nature and Dialogue in the Thought of George Herbert Mead and Martin Buber*. New York, Harper Torchbooks, 1961. (VII)

POLANYI, M., *The Study of Man*. London, Routledge & Kegan Paul, Ltd., 1959.

RICKMAN, H. P., ed., *Pattern and Meaning in History: Thoughts on History and Society of Wilheim Dilthey*. New York, Harper Torchbooks, 1961. (IV, V)

RICKMAN, H. P., "The Reaction Against Positivism and Dilthey's Concept of Understanding," *British Journal of Sociology*, Vol. 11 (1960). (IV)

ROSE, A. M., *Theory and Method in the Social Sciences*. Minneapolis, University of Minnesota Press, 1954. (IV)

ROSHWALD, M., "The Case for Indeterminism: A Reply to Grünbaum," *British Journal for the Philosophy of Science*, Vol. 7 (1956).

ROTWEIN, E., "On the Methodology of Positive Economics," *Quarterly Journal of Economics*, Vol. 73 (1959). (IV)

SABINE, G., "Logic and Social Studies," *Philosophical Review*, Vol. 48 (1939).

SCHELER, M., *Man's Place in Nature*. Boston, Beacon Press, 1961.

SCHUTZ, A., *Collected Papers*, M. Natanson, ed., 3 vol., The Hague, Martinus Nijhoff, 1962. (V)

SCRIVEN, M., "An Essential Unpredictability in Human Behavior," in B. B. Wolman and E. Nagel, eds., *Scientific Psychology: Principles and Approaches*. New York, Basic Books, Inc., Publishers, 1964. (IV)

SJOBERG, G., "The Comparative Method in the Social Sciences," with "Comments" by A. Rapoport, *Philosophy of Science*, Vol. 22 (1955).

SUPPES, P., "On an Example of Unpredictability in Human Behavior," *Philosophy of Science*, Vol. 31 (1964). (IV)

TIRYAKIAN, E. A., *Sociologism and Existentialism: Two Perspectives on the Individual and Society*. Englewood Cliffs, N. J., Prentice-Hall, 1962. (IV, VII)

VAN DE WALLE, W. E., "A Fundamental Difference Between the Natural and Social Sciences," *Journal of Philosophy*, Vol. 19 (1932).

VON MISES, L., *Human Action: A Treatise on Economics*, rev. ed. New Haven, Conn., Yale University Press, 1962. (IV)

WHITE, L. D., ed., *The State of the Social Sciences*. Chicago, The University of Chicago Press, 1956.

WILSON, C. B., "Methodology in the Natural and

Social Sciences," *American Journal of Sociology*, Vol. 45 (1940).

WOLFF, K. H., "The Unique and the General: Toward a Philosophy of Sociology," *Philosophy of Science*, Vol. 15 (1948). (IV)

ZANER, R. M., "An Approach to a Philosophical Anthropology," *Philosophy and Phenomenological Research*, Vol. 26 (1966). (V)

ZNANIECKI, F., *The Cultural Sciences, Their Origin and Development*. Urbana, Illinois, University of Illinois Press, 1952.

IV. Laws, Theories, and Explanation in the Social Sciences

ADAMS, E. M., "Mental Causality," *Mind*, Vol. 75 (1966).

ALBERT, E. M., "Causality in the Social Sciences," *Journal of Philosophy*, Vol. 51 (1954). (III)

ALEXANDER, P., "Rational Behaviour and Psychoanalytic Explanations," *Mind*, Vol. 71 (1962).

ALEXANDER, P. and A. MACINTYRE, "Symposium: Cause and Cure in Psychotherapy," *Proceedings of the Aristotelian Society*, Supplementary, Vol. 29 (1955).

ALSTON, W., "Wants, Actions, and Causal Explanation," (with comments by Keith Lehrer and rejoinder by Alston), in H. Castañada, ed., *Intentionality, Minds, and Perception*. Detroit, Wayne State University Press, 1967.

*ANDERSON, A. R., ed., *Minds and Machines*, Englewood Cliffs, N. J., Prentice-Hall, 1964.

ARGYLE, M., "Deductive Theories in Sociology," *Sociological Review*, new ser., Vol. 3, 1955.

AUSTIN, J. L., "A Plea for Excuses," and "Ifs and Cans," *Philosophical Papers*. London, Oxford University Press, 1961.

BARTLEY, W. W., 3d, "Achilles, the Tortoise, and Explanation in Science and History," *British Journal for the Philosophy of Science*, Vol. 13 (1962–1963).

BEATTIE, J. H. M., "Understanding and Explanation in Social Anthropology," *British Journal of Sociology*, Vol. 10 (1959). (V)

BENNETT, D., "Action, Reason, and Purpose," *Journal of Philosophy*, Vol. 62 (1965).

BENNETT, J., *Rationality*, London, Routledge & Kegan Paul, Ltd.; New York, Humanities Press, 1964.

BEROFSKY, B., "Determinism and the Concept of a Person," *Journal of Philosophy*, Vol. 61 (1964).

BEROFSKY, B., ed., *Free Will and Determinism*. New York, Harper & Row Publishers, 1966.

BRANDT, R. and KIM, J., "Wants as Explanations of Actions," *Journal of Philosophy*, Vol. 60 (1963).

BROAD, C. D., "Determinism, Indeterminism, and Libertarianism," in *Ethics and the History of Philosophy*. London, Routledge and Kegan Paul, Ltd., 1952.

BROAD, C. D., "Mechanical Explanation and Its Alternatives," *Aristotelian Society Proceedings*, (1918–1919).

BROAD, C. D., *The Mind and Its Place in Nature*, New York, Harcourt, Brace & World, Inc. 1929. (V)

BUCK, R. C. and W. SEEMAN, "Clinical Judges and Clinical Insight in Psychology," *Philosophy of Science*, Vol. 22 (1955). (VI)

CAMPBELL, C. A., "Is 'Free Will' a Pseudo-Problem?", *Mind*, Vol. 60 (1951).

CANFIELD, J., "Determinism, Free Will and the Ace Predictor," *Mind*, Vol. 70 (1961).

*CANFIELD, J., ed., *Purpose in Nature*. Englewood Cliffs, N. J., Prentice-Hall, 1966. (II)

CHISHOLM, R., ed., *Realism and the Background of Phenomenology*, Glencoe, Ill., The Free Press of Glencoe, 1962.

COHEN, J., "Teleological Explanation," *Proceedings of the Aristotelian Society*, (1950–1951).

DAHL, R. A., "Political Theory: Truth and Consequences," *World Politics*, Vol. 11 (1958).

DAHL, R. A., "The Behavioral Approach in Political Science," *American Political Science Review*, Vol. 55, (1961).

DANTO, A. C., *Analytical Philosophy of History*. New York, Cambridge University Press, 1965.

DANTO, A. C., A. DONAGAN, and J. W. MEILAND, "Symposium: Historical Understanding," *Journal of Philosophy*, Vol. 63 (1966).

DANTO, A. C., and S. MORGENBESSER, "Character and Free Will," *Journal of Philosophy*, Vol. 54 (1957).

DEUTSCH, K. W., "Mechanism, Teleology, and Mind," *Philosophy and Phenomenological Research*, Vol. 12 (1951).

DONAGAN, A., "Explanation in History," *Mind*, Vol. 66 (1957).

DRAY, W. H., *Laws and Explanation in History*. London, Oxford University Press, 1957.

*DRAY, W. H., ed., *Philosophical Analysis and History*, New York, Harper & Row Publishers, 1967.

DRAY, W. H., *Philosophy of History*. Englewood Cliffs, N. J., Prentice-Hall, 1964.

DUCASSE, C. J., "Explanation, Mechanism, and Teleology," in H. Feigl and W. Sellars, eds., *Readings in Philosophical Analysis*. New York, Appleton-Century-Crofts, 1949.

EMMET, D., *Function, Purpose, and Powers*. London, Macmillan & Co., Ltd., New York, St. Martin's Press, 1958.

ESTES, W. K., et al., *Modern Learning Theory*. New York, Appleton-Century-Crofts, 1954.

FAIN, H., "Prediction and Constraint," *Mind*, Vol. 67 (1958).

FARRELL, B. A., M. BRAITHWAITE, and C. D. MACE, "Causal Laws in Psychology," a symposium, *Aristotelian Society*, Supplementary Vol., 23 (1949).

FEINBERG, J., "Action and Responsibility," in Max Black, ed., *Philosophy in America*. Ithaca, N. Y., Cornell University Press, 1965.

FODOR, J., *Psychological Explanation*. New York, Random House, 1968.

FOOT, P., "Free Will as Involving Determinism," *The Philosophical Review*, Vol. 66 (1957).

FOOT, P., "Hart and Honoré: Causation in the Law," *Philosophical Review*, Vol. 72 (1963).

FOZZY, P. J., "Professor MacKay on Machines," *British Journal for the Philosophy of Science*, Vol. 14 (1963).

FRAZIER, E. F., "Theoretical Structure of Sociology and Sociological Research," *British Journal of Sociology*, Vol. 4 (1953).

FRIEDMAN, M., *Essays in Positive Economics*. Chicago, University of Chicago Press, 1953.

GALLIE, W. B., *Philosophy and the Historical Understanding*. London, Chatto & Windus, Ltd., 1964. (V)

GARDINER, P., *The Nature of Historical Explanation*. London, Oxford University Press, 1952.

GAULD, A., "Could a Machine Perceive?", *British Journal for the Philosophy of Science*, Vol. 17 (1966).

GEORGE, F. H., "Could Machines Be Made to Think?", *Philosophy*, Vol. 31 (1956).

GIEGER, T., "Human Society and Scientific Law," *Canadian Journal of Economics and Sociology*, Vol. 18 (1952).

GOLDSTEIN, L. J., "Evidence and Events in History," *Philosophy of Science*, Vol. 29 (1962).

GOLDSTEIN, L. J., "Theory in History," *Philosophy of Science*, Vol. 34 (1967).

GREGORY, R. L., "On Physical Model Explanations in Psychology," *British Journal for the Philosophy of Science*, Vol. 4 (1953). (III)

GRUNER, R., "Teleological and Functional Explanations," *Journal of Philosophy*, Vol. 75 (1966).

HAMLYN, D. W., *The Psychology of Perception*. New York, The Humanities Press, 1957.

HAMPSHIRE, S., *Freedom of the Individual*. New York, Harper & Row, Inc., 1965.

HANCOCK, R., "Interpersonal and Physical Causation," *Philosophical Review*, Vol. 71 (1962). (III)

HARRIS, E. E., "Teleology and Teleological Explanations," *Journal of Philosophy*, Vol. 56 (1959).

HARROD, R. F., "The Scope and Method of Economics," *Economic Journal*, Vol. 48 (1938).

HART, H. L. A., "The Ascription of Responsibility and Rights," *Proceedings of the Aristotelian Society*, (1948–1949); reprinted in A. Flew, ed., *Logic and Language*. New York, Anchor Books, Doubleday & Co., 1965.

HART, H. L. A. and A. M. HONORÉ, *Causation in the Law*. Oxford, Clarendon Press, 1956.

HARTNACK, J., "Free Will and Decision," *Mind*, Vol. 62 (1953).

HEMPEL, C. G., "Explanation in Science and in History," in R. G. Colodny, ed., *Frontiers of Science and Philosophy*. Pittsburgh, The University of Pittsburgh Press, 1962.

HEMPEL, C. G., "The Function of General Laws in History," *Journal of Philosophy*, Vol. 39 (1942).

HOBART, R. B., "Free Will as Involving Determinism and Inconceivable without It." *Mind*, Vol. 43 (1934).

HOSPERS, J., "Free-Will and Psychoanalysis," in W. Sellars and J. Hospers, eds., *Readings in Ethical Theory*. New York, Appleton-Century-Crofts, 1952.

HOVLAND, C. I. and E. B. HUNT, "Computer Simulation of Concept Attainment," *Behavioral Science*, Vol. 5 (1960). (V)

HUGHES, H. S., "The Historian and the Social Scientist," *American Historical Review*, Vol. 66 (1961). (VII)

HUGHES, H. S., *History as Art and Science*. New York, Harper & Row, Publishers, 1964. (VII)

HULL, C. L., "Knowledge and Purpose as Habit Mechanisms," *Psychological Review*, Vol. 37 (1930). (V)

HULL, C. L., "Mind, Mechanism, and Adaptive Behavior," *Psychological Review*, Vol. 44 (1937).

HUTCHINSON, T. W., *The Significance and Basic Postulates of Economic Theory*. London, Macmillan & Co., Ltd., 1938.

JARVIE, I. C., "Explanation in Social Science," *British Journal for the Philosophy of Science*, Vol. 15 (1964). (Review discussion of *Explanation in Social Science* by Robert Brown).

KAPLAN, O., "Prediction in the Social Sciences," *Philosophy of Science*, Vol. 7 (1940). (III)

KAUFMAN, F., "On the Postulates of Economic Theory," *Social Research*, Vol. 9 (1942).

KENNY, A., *Action, Emotion, and Will*. London, Routledge & Kegan Paul, Ltd., 1963. (V)

KING-FARLOW, J. and E. A. HALL, "Man, Beast, and Philosophical Psychology," *British Journal for the Philosophy of Science*, Vol. 16 (1965). (V)

KLUCKHOHN, C., "The Place of Theory in Anthropological Studies," *Philosophy of Science*, Vol. 6 (1939).

LAIRD, J., "Mechanized Mentality," *Philosophy*, Vol. 9 (1934).

LAVINE, T. Z., "Knowledge as Interpretation: An Historical Survey," *Philosophy and Phenomenological Research*, Vol. 10 (1950); Vol. 11 (1950).

LEACH, J., "Dray on Rational Explanation," *Philosophy of Science*, Vol. 33 (1966).

LEHRER, K., "Decisions and Causes," *Philosophical Review*, Vol. 72 (1963).

LEHRER, K., ed., *Freedom and Determinism*. New York, Random House, Inc. 1966.

LOGAN, F. A., et al., *Behavior Theory and Social Science*. New Haven, Conn., Yale University Press, 1955.

LOUCH, A. R., "The Very Idea of a Social Science," (review of P. F. Winch's *The Idea of a Social Science*), *Inquiry*, Vol. 6 (1963).

LYON, A., "The Prediction Paradox," *Mind*, Vol. 68 (1959).

MACINTYRE, A., "Determinism," *Mind*, Vol. 66 (1957).

MACINTYRE, A., *The Unconscious: A Conceptual Analysis*. London, Routledge & Kegan Paul, Ltd., 1962. (V)

MACINTYRE, A., and P. H. NOWELL-SMITH, "Symposium: Purpose and Intelligent Action," *Proceedings of the Aristotelian Society*, Supplementary Vol. 34 (1960). (V)

MACKAY, D. M., "Consciousness and Mechanism: A Reply to Miss Fozzy," *British Journal for the Philosophy of Science*, Vol. 14 (1963). (V)

MACKAY, D. M., "Mindlike Behavior in Artifacts," *British Journal for the Philosophy of Science*, Vol. 2 (1951). (V)

MACKAY, D. M., "On the Logical Indeterminacy of Free Choice," *Mind*, Vol. 69 (1960).

MACKAY, D. M., "The Use of Behavioural Language to Refer to Mechanical Processes," *British Journal for the Philosophy of Science*, Vol. 13 (1962). (V)

MADDELL, G., "Action and Causal Explanation," *Mind*, Vol. 76 (1967).

MADDEN, E. H., "Explanation in Psychoanalysis and History," *Philosophy of Science*, Vol. 33 (1966).

MANDELBAUM, M., "Historical Explanation: The Problem of 'Covering Laws'," *History and Theory*, Vol. 1 (1961). (II)

MARGOLIS, J., "Motives, Causes and Action," *Methodos*, Vol. 16 (1964).

MARTIN, A., "Empirical and A Priori in Economics," *British Journal for the Philosophy of Science*, Vol. 15 (1964).

MARTIN, A., "How Economic Theory May Mislead," *British Journal for the Philosophy of Science*, Vol. 8 (1957).

MARX, M., ed., *Theories in Contemporary Psychology*. New York, The Macmillan Company, 1963.

McDOUGALL, W., "Mechanism, Purpose, and the New Freedom," *Philosophy*, Vol. 9 (1934).

MELDEN, A. I., *Free Action*. New York, The Humanities Press, 1961.

MISCHEL, T., "Psychology and Explanations of Behavior," *Philosophy and Phenomenological Research*, Vol. 23 (1963).

MORGENBESSER, S. and J. WALSH, eds., *Free Will*. Englewood Cliffs, N. J., Prentice-Hall, 1962.

*MORRIS, H., ed., *Freedom and Responsibility* Stanford, Calif., Stanford University Press, 1961.

MUNZ, P., "Historical Understanding," *Philosophical Quarterly*, Vol. 3 (1953). (V)

O'CONNOR, D. J., "Determinism and Predictability," *British Journal for the Philosophy of Science*, Vol. 8 (1957).

OFSTAD, H., *An Inquiry into the Freedom of Decision*. Oslo, Oslo University Press, 1961.

PARSONS, T., *Essays in Sociological Theory*, 2nd. ed., Illinois, The Free Press of Glencoe, 1954.

PARSONS, T., R. F. BALES, and E. A. SHILS, *Working Papers in the Theory of Action*. Illinois, The Free Press of Glencoe, 1953.

PEARS, D. F., "Are Reasons for Actions Causes?", in A. Stroll, ed., *Epistemology: New Essays in the Theory of Knowledge*. New York, Harper & Row, Publishers, 1967.

PEARS, D. F., ed., *Freedom and the Will*. New York, St. Martin's Press, Inc., 1963.

PITT, J., "Generalizations in Historical Explanation," *Journal of Philosophy*, Vol. 56 (1959).

RAAB, F. V., "Free Will and the Ambiguity of 'Could'," *Philosophical Review*, Vol. 64 (1955).

SCRIVEN, M., *Determinism and Human Behavior*. New York, Alfred A. Knopf, Inc., (announced).

SKINNER, R. C., "Freedom of Choice," *Mind*, Vol. 72 (1963).

SMART, J. J. C., "Free Will, Praise, and Blame," *Mind*, Vol. 70 (1961).

SMITH, F. V., *The Explanation of Human Behavior*, 2nd. ed., London, Constable & Co., Ltd., 1960.

SPENCE, K. W., *Behavior Theory and Conditioning*, New Haven, Conn., Yale University Press, 1956.

STACY, R. W. and B. D. WAXMAN, eds., *Computers in Bio-Medical Research*, 2 vol., New York, Academic Press, 1965.

STONE, R., "The A Priori & the Empirical in Economics," *British Journal for the Philosophy of Science*, Vol. 15 (1964).

STOUT, G. F., "Mechanical and Teleological Causation," *Aristotelian Society Proceedings*, Supp. Vol. 14 (1935).

SWARTZ, M. J., "History and Science in Anthropology," *Philosophy of Science*, Vol. 25 (1958).

TAYLOR, C., *The Explanation of Behavior*. London, Routledge & Kegan Paul, Ltd., New York, Humanities Press, 1964. (III)

TAYLOR, J. G., "Towards a Science of Mind," *Mind*, Vol. 66 (1957).

TAYLOR, R. G., *Action and Purpose*, Englewood Cliffs, N. J., Prentice-Hall, 1966. (V)

TAYLOR, R. G., "Comments on a Mechanistic Conception of Purposefulness," *Philosophy of Science*, Vol. 17 (1950) (V)

THOMPSON, D., "Can a Machine Be Conscious?", *British Journal for the Philosophy of Science*, Vol. 16 (1965). (V)

TOLMAN, E. C., *Behavior and Psychological Man*. Berkeley, University of California Press, 1958.

TOLMAN, E. C., *Purposive Behavior in Animals and Men*. New York, Appleton-Century-Crofts, 1932.

*TURNER, M. B., *Philosophy and the Science of Behavior*. New York, Appleton-Century-Crofts, 1967.

WALSH, W. H., *An Introduction to the Philosophy of History*. New York, Harper Torchbooks, 1960.

WANN, T. W., ed., *Behaviorism and Phenomenology*. Chicago, The University of Chicago Press, 1964.

WHITE, M., *Foundations of Historical Knowledge*. New York, Harper & Row Publishers, 1965.

WIENER, N., *Cybernetics*. Cambridge, Mass., Massachusetts Institute of Technology Press, 1961.

WISDOM, J., *Philosophy and Psychoanalysis*. Oxford, Basil Blackwell & Mott, Ltd., 1953. (V)

WISDOM, J. O., "The Hypothesis of Cybernetics," *British Journal for the Philosophy of Science*, Vol. 2 (1951).

ZILSEL, E., "Physics and the Problem of Historico-Sociological Laws," *Philosophy of Science*, Vol. 18 (1941).

V. The Language of Social Science

ABEL, T. F., "The Operation Called *Verstehen*," *American Journal of Sociology*, Vol. 54 (1948); reprinted in Feigl and Brodbeck, *Readings in the Philosophy of Science*.

ABEL, T. F., *Systematic Sociology in Germany*. New York, Columbia University Press, 1929. (IV)

AGEE, J. and E. WALKER, *Let Us Now Praise Famous Men*. Boston, Houghton Mifflin Company, 1941. (IV)

ALPERT, H., "Operational Definitions in Sociology," *American Sociological Review*, Vol. 3 (1938.)

ANSCOMBE, G. E. M., *Intention*. Oxford, Basil Blackwell & Mott, Ltd., 1958. (IV)

ANSCOMBE, G. E. M., "Two Kinds of Error in Action," *Journal of Philosophy*, Vol. 60 (1963). (III)

BECHTOLDT, H. P., "Construct Validity: A Critique," *The American Psychologist*, Vol. 14 (1959).

BECKER, H., "Constructive Typology in the Social Sciences," *American Sociological Review*, Vol. 5 (1940). (III)

BECKER, H., "Interpretive Sociology and Constructive Typology," in *Twentieth Century Sociology*. New York, Philosophical Library, 1945. (III)

BENJAMIN, A. C., *Operationism*. Springfield, Ill., Charles C. Thomas, Publisher, 1955.

BERGMAN, G., "The Logic of Psychological Concepts," *Philosophy of Science*, Vol. 18 (1951).

BERGMAN, G., "Sense and Nonsense in Operationism," *Scientific Monthly*, Vol. 79 (1954).

BERGMAN, G. and K. W. SPENCE, "Operationism and Theory in Psychology," *Psychological Review*, Vol. 48 (1941); reprinted in M. H. Marx, ed., *Psychological Theory: Contemporary Readings*. New York, The Macmillan Company, 1951.

BLACK, M., "The Limitations of Behavioristic Semiotic," *Philosophical Review*, Vol. 56 (1947).

BLANSHARD, B. and B. F. SKINNER, "The Problem of Consciousness," a debate, *Philosophy and Phenomenological Research*, Vol. 26 (1967).

BLAU, P., "Operationalizing a Conceptual Scheme: the Universalism-Particularism Pattern Variable," *American Sociological Review*, Vol. 27 (1962).

Blumer, H., "The Problem of the Concept in Social Psychology," *American Journal of Sociology*, Vol. 45 (1940) (III)

Bridgman, P. W., "Operational Analysis," *Philosophy of Science*, Vol. 5 (1938) (with critique by A. F. Bentley entitled "Physicists and Fairies").

Chisholm, R. M., "The Descriptive Element in the Concept of Action," *Journal of Philosophy*, Vol. 61 (1964).

Chisholm, R. M., "Intentionality and the Theory of Signs," *Philosophical Studies*, Vol. 3 (1952).

Cornman, J. W., "Intentionality and Intensionality," *Philosophical Quarterly*, Vol. 12 (1962).

Cronbach, L. J. and P. E. Meehl, "Construct Validity in Psychological Tests," *Psychological Bulletin*, Vol. 53 (1955).

De Welhens, A., "The Phenomenological Concept of Intentionality," *Philosophy Today*, Vol. 6 (1962).

Feigl, H., "Operationalism and Scientific Method," *Psychological Review*, Vol. 52 (1945).

Fleming, B. N., "On Intention," *Philosophical Review*, Vol. 73 (1964).

Ginsberg, A., "Operational Definitions and Theories," *Journal of General Psychology*, Vol 52 (1955).

Gould, J., "The Vocabulary of Sociology," *British Journal of Sociology*, Vol. 14 (1963).

Hagen, E. E., "Analytical Models in the Study of Social Systems," *American Journal of Sociology*, Vol. 67 (1961).

Hampshire, S., *Thought and Action*. London, Chatto and Windus Ltd., 1959.

Hartung, F. E., "Operationalism: Idealism or Realism," *Philosophy of Science*, Vol. 9 (1942).

Hempel, C. G., *Fundamentals of Concept Formation in Empirical Science*, Vol. II, No. 7 of *International Encyclopedia of Unified Science*. Chicago, The University of Chicago Press, 1952.

Hempel, C. G., "The Logical Analysis of Psychology," *Revue de Synthese*, 1935 (reprinted in Feigl and Sellars, *Readings in Philosophical Analysis*). (III)

Hochberg, H., "Of Mind and Myth," *Methodos*, Vol. 11 (1959).

Hoffman, R., "Malcolm and Smart on Brain-Mind Identity," *Philosophy*, Vol. 52 (1967).

Israel, I. and B. Goldstein, "Operationism in Psychology," *Psychological Review*, Vol. 51 (1944).

Johnson, R. J., "Discussion: A Commentary on Radical Behaviorism," *Philosophy of Science*, Vol. 30 (1963).

Kluver, H., "Max Weber's 'Ideal Type' in Psychology," *Journal of Philosophy*, Vol. 23 (1926).

Lundberg, G. A., "Operational Definitions in Sociology," *American Journal of Sociology*, Vol. 47 (1942) (with rejoinder by H. Blumer).

Mandler, G. and W. Kessen, *The Language of Psychology*. New York, John Wiley & Sons, Inc., 1959. (VI)

McKinney, J. C., *Constructive Typology and Social Theory*. New York, Appleton-Century-Crofts, 1966.

Moore, A., "Chisholm on Intentionality," *Philosophy and Phenomenological Research*, Vol. 21 (1960).

Mundle, C. W. K., "'Private Language' and Wittgenstein's Kind of Behaviorism," *Philosophical Quarterly*, Vol. 16 (1966).

Nagel, T., "Physicalism," *Philosophical Review*, Vol. 74 (1965).

Ryle, G., *The Concept of Mind*. London, Hutchinson's University Library, 1949.

Salomon, A., "Max Weber's Methodology," *Sociological Review*, Vol. 1 (1934). (VIII)

Sellars, W., "Mind, Meaning, and Behavior," *Philosophical Studies*, Vol. 3 (1952).

Smart, J. J. C., "Sensations and Brain Processes," *Philosophical Review*, Vol. 68 (1959).

Stevenson, J. T., "Sensations and Brain Processes: A Reply to J. J. C. Smart," *Philosophical Review*, Vol. 59 (1960).

Weber, M., *The Theory of Social and Economic Organization*. New York, The Free Press of Glencoe, 1964. (VII, VIII)

Wisdom, J., *Other Minds*. New York, Philosophical Library, 1952.

VI. Measurement and Mathematics in the Social Sciences

Achinstein, P., "Models, Analogies, and Theories," *Philosophy of Science*, Vol. 31 (1965).

Achinstein, P., "Theoretical Models," *British Journal for the Philosophy of Science*, Vol. 16 (1965).

Ackoff, R. (with the collaboration of S. K. Gupta and J. S. Minas), *Scientific Method: Optimizing Applied Research Decisions*. New York, John Wiley & Sons, Inc., 1962.

Adams, E., "Elements of a Theory of Inexact Measurement," *Philosophy of Science*, Vol. 32 (1965).

APOSTEL, L., "Towards the Formal Study of Models in the Non-Formal Sciences," *Synthese*, Vol. 12 (1960).

ARGYLE, M., *The Scientific Study of Social Behavior*. London, Methuen & Co., Ltd., 1957.

ARROW, K., "Mathematical Models in the Social Sciences," in D. Lerner and H. Laswell, eds., *Recent Developments in the Policy Sciences*. Stanford, Calif., Stanford University Press, 1959.

ARROW, K., S. KARLIN, and P. SUPPES, eds., *Mathematical Methods in the Social Sciences*. Stanford, Calif., Stanford University Press, 1960. (V).

BAIN, R., "Measurement in Sociology," *American Journal of Sociology*, Vol. 40 (1935).

BENJAMIN, A. C., "The Logic of Measurement," *Journal of Philosophy*, Vol. 30 (1933).

BLACK, M., *Models and Metaphors*. Ithaca, N. Y., Cornell University Press, 1962.

BLALOCK, JR., H. M., "Theory, Measurement, and Replication in the Social Sciences," *American Journal of Sociology*, Vol. 66 (1961).

BRAITHWAITE, R. B., "Models in Empirical Studies," in E. Nagel, et al., eds., *Proceedings of the Congress of the International Union for the Logic, Methodology, and Philosophy of Science*. Stanford, Calif., Stanford University Press, 1960.

CHAPIN, F. S., "Measurement in Sociology," *American Journal of Sociology*, Vol. 40 (1935).

CHARLESWORTH, J. C., ed., *Mathematics and the Social Sciences*. Philadelphia, The American Academy of Political and Social Science, 1963.

CHURCHMAN, C. W., *Theory of Experimental Inference*. New York, The Macmillan Company, 1948.

CHURCHMAN, C. W. and P. RATOOSH, eds., *Measurement: Definition and Theories*. New York, John Wiley & Sons., 1959.

COHEN, M. R., and E. NAGEL, *An Introduction to Logic and Scientific Method*. New York, Harcourt, Brace & World, Inc. 1934. (II)

COLEMAN, J., *Introduction to Mathematical Sociology*. New York, The Free Press of Glencoe, 1964. (V)

DAVIDSON, D. and P. SUPPES, *Decision Making: An Experimental Approach*. Stanford, Calif., Stanford University Press, 1957. (V)

DEUTSCH, K., "Game Theory and Politics," *The Canadian Journal of Economics and Political Theory*, Vol. 20 (1954).

DINGLE, H., "A Theory of Measurement," *British Journal for the Philosophy of Science*, Vol. 1 (1950).

ESTES, W. K., "Of Models and Men," *American Psychologist*, Vol. 12 (1957). (V)

FREUDENTHAL, H., ed., *The Concept and the Role of the Model in Mathematics and Natural and Social Sciences*. The Netherlands, D. Reidel Publishing Co., 1962.

GUTTMAN, L., "A Basis for Scaling Qualitative Data," *American Sociological Review*, Vol. 9 (1944).

HESSE, M. B., *Models and Analogies in Science*. London, Sheed and Ward, Ltd., 1963; expanded edition, Indiana, University of Notre Dame Press, 1966.

HURWICZ., L., "The Theory of Economic Behavior," *American Economic Review*, Vol. 35 (1945); reprinted in James R. Newman, ed., *The World of Mathematics*. Vol. II, New York, Simon and Schuster, Inc., 1956.

JEFFREY, R. C., *The Logic of Decision*. New York, McGraw-Hill Book Company, Inc., 1965.

LAPIERE, R. T., "The Sociological Significance of Measurable Attitudes," *American Sociological Review*, Vol. 3 (1938).

LAZARSFELD, P. F., "Problems in Methodology," in R. K. Merton et al., eds., *Sociology Today*, Vol. I, New York, Basic Books, 1959; Harper Torchbook, 1965.

LAZARSFELD, P. F., and M. ROSENBERG, eds., *The Language of Social Research*. Glencoe, Ill., The Free Press of Glencoe, 1955.

LERNER, D., ed., *Evidence and Inference*. New York, The Free Press of Glencoe, 1959.

LERNER, D., ed., *Quantity and Quality*. Glencoe, Ill., The Free Press of Glencoe, 1961.

LUCE, R. D., R. R. BUSH, and E. GALANTER, eds., *Handbook of Mathematical Psychology*, 3 Vol., New York, John Wiley & Sons, Inc., 1963–1965. (IV)

LUCE, R. D. and H. RAIFFA, *Games and Decisions*. New York, John Wiley & Sons, Inc., 1957.

LUNDBERG, G. A., "Quantitative Methods in Social Psychology," *American Sociological Review*, Vol. 1 (1936).

MARCH, J. G., "An Introduction to the Theory and Measurement of Influence," *American Political Science Review*, Vol. 49 (1955).

MARCH, J. G., "Measurement Concepts in the Theory of Influence," *Journal of Politics*, Vol. 44 (1957).

MCNEMAR, Q., "Opinion-Attitude Methodology," *Psychological Bulletin*, Vol. 43 (1946). (V)

MEADOWS, P., "Models, System, and Science," *American Sociological Review*, Vol. 22 (1947).

MEEHL, P. E., *Clinical versus Statistical Prediction.*

Minneapolis, The University of Minnesota Press, 1954.

MICHEL, J. B., "The Measurement of Community Power on the Community Level," *American Journal of Economics and Sociology*, Vol. 23 (1964).

MORGENSTERN, O., "The Theory of Games," *Scientific American*, Vol. 180 (1949).

NAGEL, E., "Measurement," in A. Danto and S. Morgenbesser, eds., *Philosophy of Science*. New York, Meridian Books, 1960.

NAGEL, E., "Principles of the Theory of Probability," *International Encyclopedia of Unified Science*, Vol. I, Chicago, The University of Chicago Press, 1939.

NELSON, T. W. and S. H. BARTLEY, "Numerosity, Number, Arithmetization, Measurement, and Psychology," *Philosophy of Science*, Vol. 28 (1961).

NEUMANN, J. VON and O. MORGENSTERN, *Theory of Games and Economic Behavior*. Princeton, Princeton University Press, 1944.

PEARS, D. F., "Professor Norman Malcolm: Dreaming," *Mind*, Vol. 70 (1961).

PIKTER, A. G., "Utility Theories in Field Physics and Mathematical Economics," *British Journal for the Philosophy of Science*, Vol. 5 (1954).

REMMERS, H. H., *Introduction to Opinion and Attitude Measurement*. New York, Harper & Row Publishers, 1954. (V)

ROSENBLUETH, A. and N. WIENER, "The Role of Models in Science," *Philosophy of Science*, Vol. 12 (1945).

SCOTT, D. and P. SUPPES, "Foundation Aspects of Measurement," *Journal of Symbolic Logic*, Vol. 23 (1958).

*SHUBIK, M., ed., *Game Theory and Related Approaches to Social Behavior*. New York, John Wiley & Sons, Inc., 1964. (IV)

SHUBIK, M., ed., *Readings in Game Theory and Political Behavior*. New York, Doubleday & Company, Inc., 1954.

SIMON, H. A. (with A. ANDO, and F. M. FISHER), *Essays on the Structure of Social Science Models*. Cambridge, Mass., MIT Press, 1963.

SIMON, H. A., *Models of Man*. New York, John Wiley & Sons, Inc., 1957. (IV)

SIMON, H. A. and A. NEWELL, "Models: Their Uses and Limitations," in L. D. White, ed., *The State of the Social Sciences*. Chicago, The University of Chicago Press, 1956; reprinted in M. H. Marx, ed., *Theories in Contemporary Psychology*. New York, The Macmillan Company, 1963.

SNYDER, R. C., "Game Theory and the Analysis of Political Behavior," in *Research Frontiers in Politics and Government*. Brookings Lectures. Washington, D. C., The Brookings Institution, 1955.

SOLOMON, H., ed., *Mathematical Thinking in the Measurement of Behavior*. Glencoe, The Free Press of Glencoe, 1960.

SPECTOR, M., "Models and Theories," *British Journal for the Philosophy of Science*, Vol. 16 (1965).

STEVENS, S. S., "Mathematics, Measurement, and Psychophysics," in S. S. Stevens, ed., *Handbook of Experimental Psychology*. New York, John Wiley & Sons, Inc., 1951.

STEVENS, S. S., "On the Psychophysical Law," *Psychological Review*, Vol. 64 (1957).

STEVENS, S. S., "On the Theories of Scales of Measurement," *Science*, Vol. 3 (1946).

STEVENS, S. S., "The Surprising Simplicity of Sensory Metrics," *American Psychologist*, Vol. 17 (1962).

STONE, R., *Mathematics in the Social Sciences and Other Essays*. New York, M. I. T. Press, 1967. (IV, V)

STOUFFER, S. S., et al., *Measurement and Prediction*, Princeton, N. J., Princeton University Press, 1950.

STOUFFER, S. S., "Measurement in Sociology," *American Sociological Review*, Vol. 18 (1953).

SUPPES, P., "A Comparison of the Meaning and Uses of Models in Mathematics and the Empirical Sciences, *Synthese*, Vol. 12 (1960).

SUPPES, P. and A. TARSKI, eds., *The Axiomatic Method*, Amsterdam, North Holland Publishing Company, 1959.

SZANIAWSKI, K., "Some Remarks Concerning the Criterion of Rational Decision Making," *Studia Logica*, Vol. 9 (1960). (V)

THEOBALD, D. W., "Models and Method," *Philosophy*, Vol. 39 (1964).

TINTNER, G., "Scope and Method of Econometrics," *Journal of the Statistical and Social Inquiry Society of Ireland*. Cambridge, University of Cambridge Press, 1949.

WILKS, S. S., "Mathematics and the Social Sciences," in C. E. BOEWE and R. F. NICHOLS, eds., *Both Human and Humane*. Philadelphia, University of Pennsylvania Press, 1960. (V)

WILLIAMS, J. D., *The Compleat Strategyst, Being a Primer on the Theory of Games of Strategy*, rev. ed., New York, McGraw-Hill Publishing Company, 1966.

YEAGER, L. B., "Measurement as Scientific Method in Economics," *American Journal of Economics and Sociology*, Vol. 16 (1957).

VII. The Individual: Product or Maker of Society?

Aberle, D. (and others), "The Functional Prerequisites of a Society," *Ethics*, Vol. 60 (1950).

Acton, H. B., *The Illusion of an Epoch*. London, Cohen and West, 1955.

Agassi, J., "Methodological Individualism," *British Journal of Sociology*, Vol. 11 (1960).

Almond, G. A., "Introduction: A Functional Approach to Comparative Politics," in G. A. Almond and J. S. Coleman, eds., *The Politics of Developing Areas*. Princeton, N. J., Princeton University Press, 1960.

Bash, H. H., "Determinism and Avoidability in Sociohistorical Analysis," *Ethics*, Vol. 74 (1964).

Bergmann, G., "Holism, Historicism, and Emergence," *Philosophy of Science*, Vol. 11 (1944).

Berlin, I., *Historical Inevitability*. London, Oxford University Press, 1954.

Berlin, I., *Karl Marx*, 2nd. ed., London and New York, Oxford University Press, 1948.

Bidney, D., *Theoretical Anthropology*, New York, Columbia University Press, 1953. (III, IV)

Bierstedt, R., "The Meanings of Culture," *Philosophy of Science*, Vol. 5 (1938).

Black, M., ed., *The Social Theories of Talcott Parsons*. Englewood Cliffs, N. J., Prentice-Hall, 1961. (IV)

Brodbeck, M., "Methodological Individualism: Definition and Reduction," *Philosophy of Science*, Vol. 25 (1958).

Clark, S. D., "Sociology, History, and the Problem of Social Change," *Canadian Journal of Economics and Political Science*, Vol. 25, (1959).

Cohen, P. S., "The Aims and Interests of Sociology," *British Journal for the Philosophy of Science*, Vol. 14 (1963). (Review discussion of *The Poverty of Historicism* by K. R. Popper.)

Davis, K., "The Myth of Functional Analysis as a Special Method in Sociology and Anthropology," *American Sociological Review*, Vol. 24 (1959).

Deutsch, K. W., "Mechanism, Organism, and Society," *Philosophy of Science*, Vol. 18 (1951).

Durkheim, E., *The Rules of Sociological Method*. Glencoe, Ill., The Free Press of Glencoe, 1958. (III, IV)

Durkheim, E., *Suicide, A Study in Sociology*. Glencoe, Ill., The Free Press of Glencoe, 1951.

Evans-Pritchard, E. E., *Social Anthropology*. New York, The Free Press, 1954.

Firth, R. W., ed., *Man and Culture*, London, Routledge & Kegan Paul, Ltd., 1957.

Gellner, E. A., "Explanation in History," *Proceedings of the Aristotelian Society*, Supplementary Vol. 30, 1956. (IV)

Gellner, E. A., "Nature and Society in Social Anthropology," *Philosophy of Science*, Vol. 30 (1963).

Gellner, E. A., "Time and Theory in Social Anthropology," *Mind*, Vol. 67 (1958).

Ginsberg, M., "The Individual and Society," in his *Diversity of Morals*. London, William Heinemann, Ltd., 1956.

Ginsberg, M., *The Psychology of Society*. London, Methuen & Co., Ltd., 1921.

Goldstein, L. J., "The Logic of Explanation in Malinowskian Anthropology," *Philosophy of Science*, Vol. 24 (1957).

Gooch, G. P., "Some Conceptions of History," *Sociological Review*, Vol. 31 (1939).

Hayek, F. A., *The Counter-Revolution of Science*. Glencoe, Ill., The Free Press of Glencoe, 1952. (VIII)

Hayek, F. A., *Individualism and Economic Order*. Chicago, The University of Chicago Press, 1948. (VIII)

Hegel, G. W. F., *Reason in History*. New York, The Liberal Arts Press, Inc., 1953.

Hempel, C. G., "The Logic of Functional Analysis," in *Symposium on Sociological Theory*, L. Gross, ed., Evanston, Illinois, Row, Peterson & Company, 1959. (II, IV)

Henle, P., "The Status of Emergence," *Journal of Philosophy*, Vol. 39 (1942).

Hinshaw, Jr., V., "Can Philosophical Anthropology Be a Science? An Examination of Bidney's Philosophy of Culture," *The Ohio Journal of Science*, Vol. 51 (1951).

Hinshaw, Jr., V., and J. N. Spuhler, "On Some Fallacies Derived in David Bidney's Philosophy of Culture," *Central States Bulletin* (American Anthropological Association), Vol. 2 (1948).

Hobhouse, L. T., *Sociology and Philosophy, A Centenary Collection of Essays and Articles*. Cambridge, Mass., Harvard University Press, 1966.

Homans, G. C., *The Human Group*. New York, Harper & Row, Publishers, 1950.

Hook, S., *The Hero in History*. Boston, Beacon Press, 1955.

Jarvie, I. C., "Nadel on the Aims and Methods of Social Anthropology," *British Journal for the Philosophy of Science*, Vol. 12 (1961).

Jarvie, I. C., *The Revolution in Anthropology*, London, Routledge & Kegan Paul, Ltd., 1964.

Joynt, C. B. and N. Rescher, "The Problem of Uniqueness in History," *History and Theory*, I,

1961; reprinted in G. H. Nadel, ed., *Studies in the Philosophy of History*. New York, Harper Torchbooks, 1965. (III, IV)

Kluckhohn, C., "The Study of Culture," in D. Lerner, and H. D. Lasswell, eds., *The Policy Sciences*. Stanford, Calif., Stanford University Press, 1951.

Kluckhohn, C. and H. A. Murray, eds., *Personality in Nature, Society, and Culture*. New York, Alfred A. Knopf, Inc., 1950.

Krober, A. L., *The Nature of Culture*. Chicago, The University of Chicago Press, 1952.

Krober, A. L., "Structure, Function, and Pattern in Biology and Anthropology," *Scientific Monthly*, Vol. 56 (1943).

Krober, A. L. and T. Parsons, "The Concepts of Culture and of Social System," *American Sociological Review*, Vol. 23 (1958).

Leach, E. R., *Rethinking Anthropology*. London, University of London, Ltd., Athlone Press, 1962; New York, Humanities Press.

Lehman, H., "R. K. Merton's Concepts of Function and Functionalism," *Inquiry*, Vol. 9, 1966.

Lerner, D., ed., *Parts and Wholes*. New York, The Free Press of Glencoe, 1963.

Lesser, A., "Research Procedure and Laws of Culture," *Philosophy of Science*, Vol. 6 (1959).

Levy, M., Jr., *The Structure of Society*. Princeton, Princeton University Press, 1952.

Malinowski, B., *A Scientific Theory of Culture and Other Essays*. Chapel Hill, The University of North Carolina Press, 1944.

Malinowski, B., *Sex and Repression in Savage Society*. London, Routledge & Kegan Paul, Ltd., 1927.

Mandelbaum, M., "A Note on Emergence," in S. Baron, et al., eds., *Freedom and Reason*. New York, The Free Press of Glencoe, 1951.

Martindale, D., ed., *Functionalism in the Social Sciences*. Monograph No. 5 of the American Academy of Political and Social Science, Philadelphia, 1965.

Marx, K., *The Poverty of Philosophy*. New York, International Publishers Company, Inc., 1963.

Marx, K. and F. Engels, *The German Ideology, Parts I and II*. New York, International Publishers Company, Inc., 1947.

McCloskey, H. J., "The State as an Organism, as a Person, and as an End in Itself," *Philosophical Review*, Vol. 72 (1963).

Mead, G. H., *Mind, Self, and Society: From the Standpoint of a Social Behaviorist*, ed. with an introduction by Charles W. Morris, Chicago, The University of Chicago Press, 1934. (III–V)

Means, R. L., "Sociology and History: A New Look at Their Relationships," *American Journal of Economics and Sociology*, Vol. 21 (1962).

Meehl, P. E. and W. Sellars, "The Concept of Emergence," in H. Feigl and M. Scriven, eds., *Minnesota Studies in the Philosophy of Science*, Vol. I. Minneapolis, The University of Minnesota Press, 1956.

Moore, O. K., "Nominal Definitions of 'Culture'," *Philosophy of Science*, Vol. 19 (1952).

Nadel, S. F., *The Foundations of Social Anthropology*. Glencoe, Ill., The Free Press of Glencoe, 1951.

Nadel, S. F., *The Theory of Social Structure*. London, Cohen and West, Ltd., 1957.

Nagel, E., "A Formalization of Functionalism," in his *Logic Without Metaphysics*. New York, The Free Press of Glencoe, 1957.

Nagel, E., "Wholes, Sums, and Organic Unities," *Philosophical Studies*, Vol. 3 (1952).

Parsons, T., *The Social System*. Glencoe, Ill., The Free Press of Glencoe, 1951. (IV)

Parsons, T. and E. Shils, eds., *Toward a General Theory of Action*. Cambridge, Mass., Harvard University Press, 1951. (V)

Passmore, J., "History, the Individual, and Inevitability," *Philosophical Review*, Vol. 68 (1959).

Plekhanov, G., *The Materialist Conception of History*. New York, International Publishers Company, Inc., 1940.

Plekhanov, G., *The Role of the Individual in History*. New York, International Publishers Company, Inc., 1940.

Popper, K. R., *The Open Society and Its Enemies*. Princeton, N. J., Princeton University Press, 1950.

Radcliffe-Brown, A. R., *Method in Social Anthropology*. Chicago, The University of Chicago Press, 1958. (IV)

Rescher, N. and P. Oppenheim, "Logical Analysis of Gestalt Concepts," *British Journal for the Philosophy of Science*, Vol. 6 (1955).

Rhees, R., "Social Engineering," *Mind*, Vol. 56 (1947).

Scott, K. J., "Methodological and Epistemological Individualism," *British Journal for the Philosophy of Science*, Vol. 11 (1961).

Sears, R. R., "Social Behavior and Personality Development," in T. Parsons and E. A. Shils, eds., *Toward a General Theory of Action*. Cambridge, Mass., Harvard University Press, 1951.

Shils, E. A., "The Macrosociological Problem," in D. P. Ray, ed., *Trends in Social Science*. New York, Philosophical Library, Inc., 1961.

SIMMEL, G., *The Sociology of Georg Simmel.* Trans., ed. and with an intro. by Kurt H. Wolff, Glencoe, Ill., The Free Press of Glencoe, 1950.

SOROKIN, P. A. and R. K. MERTON, "Social Time: A Methodological and Functional Analysis," *American Journal of Sociology*, Vol. 42 (1937).

SPIRO, M. E., "Culture and Personality: The Natural History of a False Dichotomy," *Psychiatry*, Vol. 14 (1951).

TOLMAN, E. C., "Physiology, Psychology, and Sociology," in E. C. Tolman, *Behavior and Psychological Man.* Berkeley, The University of California Press, 1958.

WEISSHOPF, W. A., "Individualism and Economic Theory," *American Journal of Economics and Sociology*, Vol. 9 (1950).

WHITE, L. A., "The Concept of Culture," *American Anthropologist*, Vol. 61 (1959).

WHITE, L. A., *The Evolution of Culture.* New York, McGraw-Hill Publishing Co., Inc., 1959.

WHITE, L. A., "History, Evolutionism, and Func-, tionalism: Three Types of Interpretation of Culture," *Southwestern Journal of Anthropology*, Vol. 1 (1945).

*WHITE, L. A., *The Science of Culture.* New York, Farrar, Straus, & Cudahy, Inc., 1949.

VIII. Objectivity and Value Judgments in the Social Sciences

ALBERT, E. M., "Value Sentences and Empirical Research," *Philosophy and Phenomenological Research*, Vol. 17 (1956).

ALLEN, V. L., "Valuations and Historical Interpretation," *British Journal of Sociology*, Vol. 14 (1963). (IV)

ANGELL, R. C., "The Moral Dimension in Sociological Theory and Research," *Canadian Journal of Economics and Political Science*, Vol. 25 (1959).

ARROW, K. J., *Social Choice and Individual Values*, New York, John Wiley & Sons, Inc., 1951. (VII)

BAIN, R., "Natural Science and Value-Policy," *Philosophy of Science*, Vol. 16 (1949).

BECK, M., "Are Value Judgments Unscientific?", *Philosophical Review*, Vol. 54 (1945).

BECKER, H., "Supreme Values and the Sociologist," *American Sociological Review*, Vol. 6 (1941).

BECKER, H., *Through Values to Social Interpretation.* Durham, N. C., The Duke University Press, 1950. (V)

BECKER, H. and H. O. DAHLKE, "Max Scheler's Sociology of Knowledge," *Philosophy and Phenomenological Research*, Vol. 2 (1942). (V)

BENDIX, R., *Social Science and the Distrust of Reason.* Berkeley, The University of California Press, 1951. (III)

BENOIT-SMULLYAN, E., "Value Judgments and the Social Sciences," *Journal of Philosophy*, Vol. 42 (1945).

BERGMANN, G., "Ideology," *Ethics*, Vol. 61 (1951).

BISBEE, E., "Objectivity in the Social Sciences," *Philosophy of Science*, Vol. 4 (1937).

BLAKE, C., "Anthropology and Moral Philosophy," *Philosophical Quarterly*, Vol. 4 (1954). (III)

BLAKE, C., "Can History be Objective?", *Mind*, Vol. 64 (1955).

BOTTOMORE, T. B., "Some Reflections on the Sociology of Knowledge," *British Journal of Sociology*, Vol. 7 (1956).

BOWMAN, C. C., "Evaluations and Values Consistent with the Scientific Study of Society," *American Sociological Review*, Vol. 8 (1943).

BRAYBROOKE, D., "The Relevance of Norms to Political Description," *American Political Science Review*, Vol. 52 (1958). (III)

CHILD, A., "The Problem of Truth in the Sociology of Knowledge," *Ethics*, Vol. 58 (1947).

CLARK, J. A., "Ethics and the Social Sciences," *Philosophical Quarterly*, Vol. 6 (1956).

FEUER, L. S., *Psychoanalysis and Ethics.* Springfield, Ill., Charles C. Thomas, 1955.

FRIES, H. S., "On the Unity and Ethical Neutrality of Science," *Journal of Philosophy*, Vol. 39 (1942). (II)

GEIGER, G., "The Place of Values in Economics," *Journal of Philosophy*, Vol. 27 (1930).

GEWIRTH, A., "Psychoanalysis and Ethics: Mental or Moral Health," *The Christian Register*, Vol. 32 (1956).

GLUCK, S. E., "The Epistemology of Mannheim's Sociology of Knowledge," *Methodos*, Vol. 6 (1954). (V)

GOLIGHTLY, C. L., "Value as a Scientific Concept," *Journal of Philosophy*, Vol. 53 (1956).

GOODWIN, L., "The Historical-Philosophical Basis for Uniting Social Science with Social Problem Solving," *Philosophy of Science*, Vol. 29 (1962).

GORDON, R., "The Impact of the Social Sciences on Ethics," *Sociological Review*, new ser., Vol. 2, 1954.

GREENHUT, M. L., "Science, Art, and Norms in Economics," *Philosophy and Phenomenological Research*, Vol. 21 (1960). (III)

HART, H., "Value-Judgments in Sociology," *American Sociological Review*, Vol. 3 (1938).

HARTMAN, R. S., "Value, Fact, and Science," *Philosophy of Science*, Vol. 25 (1958).

HARTMANN, H., *Psychoanalysis and Moral Values*. New York, International Universities Press, Inc., 1960.

HILL, F. G., "Economic Theory, Value Judgments, and Economic Policy," *American Journal of Economics and Sociology*, Vol. 14 (1955).

HINSHAW, JR., V., "Epistemological Relativism and the Sociology of Knowledge," *Philosophy of Science*, Vol. 15 (1948).

HINSHAW, JR., V., "The Epistemological Relevance of Mannheim's Sociology of Knowledge," *Journal of Philosophy*, Vol. 40 (1943).

HINSHAW, JR., V., "The Objectivity of History," *Philosophy of Science*, Vol. 25 (1958).

HOROWITZ, I. L., *Philosophy, Science and the Sociology of Knowledge*, Springfield, Ill., Charles C Thomas, 1961.

HOROWITZ, I. L., "Social Science Objectivity and Value Neutrality: Historical Problems and Properties," *Diogenes*, Vol. 39 (1962).

HULL, C. L., "Value, Valuation, and Natural Science Methodology," *Philosophy of Science*, Vol. 11 (1944). (III)

HUTCHINSON, T. W., *Positive Economics and Policy Objectives*. Cambridge, Mass., Harvard University Press, 1964.

JEFFREY, R. C., "Valuations and Acceptance of Scientific Hypotheses," *Philosophy of Science*, Vol. 23 (1956), with "Discussion," by C. W. Churchman.

KELSEN, H., "Value Judgments in the Science of Law," *Journal of Social Philosophy and Jurisprudence*, 1942.

KLAPPHOLZ, K., "Value Judgments and Economics," *British Journal for the Philosophy of Science*, Vol. 15 (1964).

KNIGHT, F. H., "Fact and Value in the Social Science," in *Freedom and Reform: Essays in Economics and Social Philosophy*. New York, Harper & Row Publishers, 1947.

LAVINE, T. Z., "Karl Mannheim and Contemporary Functionalism," *Philosophy and Phenomenological Research*, Vol. 25 (1965). (VII)

LAVINE, T. Z., "Naturalism and the Sociological Analysis of Knowledge," in Y. H. Krikorian, ed., *Naturalism and the Human Spirit*. New York, Columbia University Press, 1944.

LEPLEY, R., "The Identity of Fact and Value," *Philosophy of Science*, Vol. 10 (1943).

LEVI, I., "Must the Scientist Make Value Judgments?", *Journal of Philosophy*, Vol. 57 (1960).

LICHTHEIM, G., "The Concept of Ideology," *History and Theory*, Vol. 4 (1965), reprinted in G. H. Nadel, ed., *Studies in the Philosophy of History*. New York, Harper Torchbooks, 1965.

LUNDBERG, G. A., "Science, Scientists, and Values," *Social Forces*, Vol. 30 (1952).

LYND, H. M., "The Nature of Historical Objectivity," *Journal of Philosophy*, Vol. 47 (1950).

MACKENZIE, P. T., "Fact and Value," *Mind*, Vol. 76 (1967).

MADDEN, E., *Philosophical Problems of Psychology*. New York, The Odyssey Press, Inc., 1962. (IV)

MANDELBAUM, M., *The Problem of Historical Knowledge: An Answer to Relativism*. New York, Liveright Publishing Corporation, 1938. (III, IV)

MANNHEIM, K., *Essays on Sociology and Social Psychology*. P. Kecskemeti, ed., London, Routledge & Kegan Paul, Ltd., 1956.

MANNHEIM, K., *Essays on the Sociology of Knowledge*. P. Kecskemeti, ed., London, Routledge & Kegan Paul, Ltd., 1952.

MANNHEIM, K., *Man and Society in an Age of Reconstruction*. London, Routledge & Kegan Paul, Ltd., 1940.

MARETT, R. R., "Fact and Value in Sociology," *Sociological Review*, Vol. 26 (1934).

MEEK, R. L., "Value-Judgments in Economics," *British Journal for the Philosophy of Science*, Vol. 15 (1964).

MEILAND, J. W., *Scepticism and Historical Knowledge*. New York, Random House, Inc., 1965. (IV, V)

MELDEN, A. I., "Judgments in the Social Sciences," in *Civilization*. Berkeley, The University of California Press, 1959.

MITCHELL, W. C., "Facts and Values in Economics," *Journal of Philosophy*, Vol. 41 (1944).

MOORE, A., "Psychoanalysis, Man, and Value," *Inquiry*, Vol. 4 (1961).

MYRDAL, G., *Value in Social Theory: A Selection of Essays on Methodology*. New York, Harper & Row Publishers, 1958.

NIEBYL, K. H., "The Need for a Concept of Value in Economics," *Quarterly Journal of Economics*, Vol. 54 (1940).

O'CONNOR, D. J., "Value Judgments and the Social Sciences," *Sociological Review*, new ser., Vol. 1 (1953).

PASSMORE, J. A., "Can the Social Sciences Be Value-Free?", in H. Feigl and M. Brodbeck, eds., *Readings in the Philosophy of Science*.

Passmore, J. A., "The Objectivity of History," *Philosophy*, Vol. 33 (1958).

Ratner, S., "Presupposition and Objectivity in History," *Philosophy of Science*, Vol. 7 (1940).

Rescher, N., "Values and the Explanation of Behavior," *Philosophical Quarterly*, Vol. 17 (1967). (IV)

Ries, R. E., "Social Science and Ideology," *Social Research*, Vol. 31 (1964).

Rose, A. M., "Sociology and the Study of Values," *British Journal of Sociology*, Vol. 7 (1956).

Roshwald, W., "Value-Judgments in the Social Sciences," *British Journal for the Philosophy of Science*, Vol. 6 (1955).

Rotenstreich, N., "The Value Aspect of Science," *Philosophy and Phenomenological Research*, Vol. 20 (1960).

Schmidt, P. F., "Ethical Norms in Scientific Method," *Journal of Philosophy*, Vol. 56 (1959).

Schumpeter, J. A., "Is the History of Economics a History of Ideologies?", in his *History of Economic Analysis*. New York, Oxford University Press, 1954.

Schumpeter, J. A., "Science and Ideology," *American Economic Review*, Vol. 39 (1949).

Shils, E. A., "Social Science and Social Policy," *Philosophy of Science*, Vol. 16 (1949).

Speier, H., "The Social Determination of Ideas," *Social Research*, Vol. 5 (1938).

Stark, W., *The Sociology of Knowledge*, Glencoe, Ill., The Free Press of Glencoe, 1958. (III, IV)

Streeton, P., "Economics and Value Judgments," *Quarterly Journal of Economics*, Vol. 64 (1950).

Taylor, P. W., "Social Science and Ethical Relativism," *Journal of Philosophy*, Vol. 55 (1958).

Urban, W. M., "Science and Values," *Ethics*, Vol. 51 (1941).

Voegelin, E., *The New Science of Politics: An Introduction*. Chicago, The University of Chicago Press, 1952. (I, III)

Warren, R. L., "Philosophy and Social Science in the Field of Values," *Journal of Philosophy*, Vol. 38 (1941).

Weber, M., *The Methodology of the Social Sciences*, Glencoe, Ill., The Free Press of Glencoe, 1949. (III–V):

Williams, E., "Sociologists and Knowledge," *Philosophy of Science*, Vol. 14 (1947).

Williams, M. J., "The Place of Value-Judgments in the Social Sciences," *American Journal of Economics and Sociology*, Vol. 4 (1945).

*Wolff, K. H., "The Sociology of Knowledge and Sociological Theory," in L. Gross, *Symposium on Sociological Theory*.

Index of Names

Index of Subjects